Praise for *Choosing the Right College*

"By far the best college guide in America . . . ***Choosing the Right College*** asks the right question: What is the right college for you, not what is the 'best' by some formula for ranking colleges and universities. In addition to a very thorough examination of the academic realities at these institutions, it goes into the social atmosphere, which can make or break the whole college experience."
　　—Thomas Sowell, nationally syndicated columnist

"*Choosing the Right College* is aimed at exposing the political biases of academe, the prevalence of permissive sex, and the lack of core curriculums to prospective students and their parents."
　　—*New York Times*

"American parents (and students) have long needed a reliable 'review' of our nation's universities so they can be sure they will not be supporting the systematic destruction of the values, faith, and worldview they have spent so many years building up. *Choosing the Right College* is the right book for them."
　　—Cal Thomas, nationally syndicated columnist

"If you're looking at the big-name schools, this [guide] will be of great value in helping you decide which one is for you."
　　—*New York Post*

"An excellent guide for students and parents—and probably the best available for a certain kind of student and parent."
　　—*National Review*

"An essential purchase for anyone seeking to make an informed choice concerning a college education."
　　—*First Things*

"If prospective students and their families want a critical look at what is taught at America's most powerful and celebrated schools, *Choosing the Right College* may be their only guide."
　　—*World*

"A valuable tool that asks more probing questions and provides far more significant answers than the typical college guide."
　　—Michael Medved, nationally syndicated radio host

"Perhaps the most refreshing feature of *Choosing the Right College* is that it looks beyond the 'usual suspects' to find great, unsung colleges."
　　—*Fresno Bee*

"This guide to colleges is by far the most factually based of any I have seen. . . . This review is in striking contrast to the subjective opinions recorded by *U.S. News & World Report*."
  —**John Silber**, former president of Boston University

"This guide is a must for parents who care more about their kids' integrity than about their credentials."
  —**Dr. Laura Schlessinger**, radio host

"A godsend for anyone who wants to know how to beat the academic establishment and actually get an education."
  —*National Catholic Register*

"Unmatched in laying out what parents and students have a right to expect from a good college—and which colleges fall short of providing it . . . Definitive and indispensable."
  —**Christina Hoff Sommers**, author of *The War Against Boys*

"Given the encyclopedic scope of this guide, one can only stand in awe of the consistency with which its editors have been able to grasp what makes each campus tick."
  —**Stephen H. Balch**, chairman of the National Association of Scholars

"An essential reference for prospective students and their parents."
  —*Homeschool Magazine*

"This is the book you need if you plan to attend an elite college without graduating as a politically correct zombie who knows nothing (at least nothing good) about his or her own civilization."
  —*Practical Homeschooling*

"To parents like me, this wise and informative book is a rich blessing."
  —**William Murchison**, syndicated columnist

"A godsend . . . Though brutal to certain 'hot' schools . . . it can be just as generous when it finds rigor and real respect for learning."
  —**Harry Stein**, from *How I Accidentally Joined the Vast Right-Wing Conspiracy*

"An indispensable guide for anyone who wants to make an informed and intelligent choice about one of the most important—and expensive—decisions most of us will ever make."
  —**Roger Kimball**, author of *Tenured Radicals: How Politics Has Corrupted Our Higher Education*

Choosing the Right College
2012–13

The Whole Truth About
America's Top Schools

Produced by the Intercollegiate Studies Institute

ISI BOOKS

Wilmington, Delaware

Choosing the Right College

Editor in Chief

John Zmirak

Senior Editors

Christian Tappe
Faye Ballard

Contributing Editors

Kathleen Blum, Jesse Brandow, Millie Dasher, William Herreid,
Rosie Herreid, Denis Kitzinger, Jonathan Leaf, Martin Lockerd,
Jessica Harvey, Paul Kniaz, Robert Spencer, Jane Schiano Wigutow

Editorial Interns

Eleanor LaPrade, Katherine Lloyd, John Martin

Core Curriculum Consultant

Mark C. Henrie

Get your FREE one-year subscription to www.CollegeGuide.org

Your purchase of *Choosing the Right College 2012–13* entitles you to a year's free subscription to the companion website **www.CollegeGuide.org**.

At **www.CollegeGuide.org** you get access not only to dozens of additional college profiles but also to special "top five" lists, expert tips on handling the admissions process, an "Ask the Editors" feature, and more. Your special subscription even gives you free digital access to the hugely popular Student Guides to the Major Disciplines—a $75 value. These reader-friendly introductions to the most important fields of knowledge in the liberal arts are invaluable guides to navigating the college experience.

To register for your one-year free subscription,
simply go to **free.collegeguide.org**.

Choosing the Right College 2012–13 was supported by grants from Mr. Gilbert I. Collins, Mr. and Mrs. Richard Gaby, the Grover Hermann Foundation, and the Sunmark Foundation. The Intercollegiate Studies Institute gratefully acknowledges this support.

This is the eighth edition of *Choosing the Right College.*

Library of Congress Cataloguing-in-Publication data is on file and available upon request.
ISBN: 9781610170055

Published by: ISI Books
Intercollegiate Studies Institute
3901 Centerville Road
Wilmington, DE 19807-1938
www.isibooks.org

Contents

Mid-Atlantic

South

Midwest

Contents

West

Asking the Right Questions:

Foreword

Walter E. Williams

This eighth edition of *Choosing the Right College* is a continuation of the Intercollegiate Studies Institute's vital mission to provide parents and prospective students with reliable information about colleges across our nation. For any parent, sending his seventeen- or eighteen-year-old son or daughter off to college can be a worrisome, fretful, possibly traumatic experience. Often it is the child's first extended stay away from home. Parents might worry whether their children will spend their money prudently, eat properly, conduct themselves in safe and healthy ways, and above all call home regularly. More often than not, leaving for college is also the first step toward leaving home permanently, save for those four or five years of holidays and summers, because when children graduate they are going to be young adults with jobs and out on their own.

On the pleasurable side of seeing one's children off to college is one's pride in their high school academic success. For many parents there is the nostalgia of their own college experiences—stimulating classes, debates, college sports, and the making of lifelong friends—and the hope that their children will enjoy the same. However, what parents recall of their own experiences might bear very little resemblance to the reality obtaining at many colleges today—even at a parent's alma mater. That is one of the reasons why *Choosing the Right College* is such an invaluable resource for parents and prospective college students. It provides unbiased, unwatered-down information about key academic, social, cultural, and safety issues at a broad range of American colleges—from confidential, "inside" sources.

Choosing the Right College's goal isn't ranking schools according to their ephemeral prestige or inherited reputations. Those factors too often mask the reality of a mediocre or deeply dysfunctional educational institution. Parents and students frequently get a false idea about the schools in which they're interested, in part from college admission personnel making high school recruitment visits to sell their college. Sometimes they boast of having this or that faculty member who has won the Nobel Prize or other mark of prestige. A parent's legitimate expectation is that his child will be exposed to and taught by these intellectual giants. The truth of the matter is often that these giants never set foot in a classroom—particularly an undergraduate freshman or sophomore class. It is all too common that a student spends much of his freshman and even his sophomore years in classes taught by graduate teaching assistants, some of whom have difficulty with the English language. This tactic, in the area of consumer fraud, is known as "bait and switch." In academia, it's called "emphasizing research." *Choosing the Right College* has compiled statistics (where schools are willing to release them) on the percentage of classes managed by graduate students instead of professors.

Many colleges place an undue emphasis on academic research that is for the most part useless, except for determining whether a professor gains tenure and promotion. Mark Bauerlein, author of *The Dumbest Generation*, has observed that between 1980 and 2006, there were 21,000 studies published on Shakespeare. What contribution will an additional study make to our knowledge? While additional research publications may add little to scholarship, they detract from the amount of time professors spend with their students. But teaching is what parents and students expect in return for the thousands of tuition dollars—in many cases $40,000 or more—they fork over to the college every year. The importance of student/professor contact becomes even more compelling when we consider the poor job that K–12 schools are doing—a job so bad that, as the Alliance for Excellent Education reports, "42 percent of community college freshmen and 20 percent of freshmen in four-year institutions enroll in at least one remedial course." That remedial education has a price tag of $3.7 billion.[1]

Many colleges, including those with top rankings, offer courses that have little or no academic content. Colleges such as UCLA have offered "Gay and Lesbian Perspectives in Pop Music" and the "History of Electronic Dance." Harvard University has offered "Hip Hop America: Power, Politics, and the Word" and "I Like Ike, but I Love Lucy: Women, Popular Culture, and the 1950s." At Bates College, students learned that all whites are racists in a course titled "White Redemption: Cinema and the Co-optation of African American History." Literature and history at some colleges consist of courses such as Antioch College's "Queer British Fiction," Wesleyan University's "Queering the American State: Politics and Sex After 1968," Bates College's "Black Lesbian and Gay Literatures," and University of Michigan's "How to Be Gay: Male Homosexuality and Initiation." Other courses that strain credulity have included "The Science of Harry Potter" at Frostburg State University, "Simpsons and Philosophy" at UC Berkeley, and UC Irvine's "The Science of Superheroes," where the professor taught the physics of flying and fluid dynamics with reference to Superman, and the strength of arachnid silk in terms of Spider-Man. It is a safe bet that college recruiters will not mention such classes, especially to tuition-paying parents.

A college graduate should be reasonably knowledgeable about world and U.S. history, great works of literature, philosophy, and science. However, many college graduates have less knowledge about our history, culture, and the world than high school graduates of fifty years ago. Moreover, their academic competence leaves much to be desired. According to the Department of Education's 2003 National Assessment of Adult Literacy, only 31 percent

---

1. "Paying Double: Inadequate High Schools and Community College Remediation," Alliance for Excellent Education, Issue Brief, August 2006, 1.

of college graduates were proficient in prose, only 25 percent in reading documents, and 31 percent in math.[2] No one should be surprised by these results; today's college curriculum is often long on fads and short on substance. The American Council of Trustees and Alumni produced a 2004 study titled "The Hollow Core: Failure of the General Education Curriculum," examining the curricula at fifty of the nation's leading universities. The study concluded that overall, college education today has declined steeply from past decades, when "students received a broad, general, and rigorous education that pushed their knowledge and thinking ability well past those who had only a high school education."[3] *Choosing the Right College* turns out to be a useful tool in finding out which colleges have a required liberal arts core curriculum mandating that every student master the basics of U.S. history, politics, Western religion, philosophy—and how, if you're a student at one of the schools that don't impose such requirements, you can put together your own "Do-It-Yourself" core curriculum from existing classes in the catalog.

Some guidance is surely in order, given that many college classes these days amount to little more than indoctrination in leftist propaganda. According to *Minding the Campus*, published by the Center for the American University at the Manhattan Institute for Policy Research, the sociology department at Arizona State University offered a course in "Collective Behavior and Social Movements," where the instructor gave students credit for participating in protests organized by local gay, feminist, and pro-illegal immigration groups. At the University of California at Santa Cruz, a course on "The Politics of the War on Terrorism" denied that al Qaeda carried out the terrorist attacks on the World Trade Center. ("How did Bush and Cheney build the fiction that al Qaeda was a participant in the 9/11 attacks?" the course description asked.)

Like the rest of us, professors are entitled to their own political views, but academic honesty demands that these views do not dominate and control their teaching. Most examples of ideological indoctrination currently involve professors on the political Left because the overwhelming majority of professors identify themselves as politically liberal.

According to an article written by Karl Zinsmeister, "The Shame of America's One-Party Campuses," political, and hence ideological, diversity is all but absent on campuses.[4] Zinsmeister sampled faculty political affiliation obtained from local voter registration records at several universities. He classified faculty who registered as members of the Democratic, Green, or Working Families Parties as leaning to the left. Those registered as Republicans or Libertarians were classified as leaning to the right.

The results were telling. The percentages of faculty found to be affiliated with the Right broke down as follows:

2. "A First Look at the Literacy of America's Adults in the 21st Century," National Assessment of Adult Literacy (NAAL), National Center for Education Statistics, U.S. Department of Education, 2006, available at nces.ed.gov/NAAL/PDF/2006470_1.PDF.
3. "The Hollow Core: Failure of the General Education Curriculum," American Council of Trustees and Alumni, April 2004, available at www.goacta.org/publications/downloads/TheHollowCore.pdf.
4. Karl Zinsmeister, "The Shame of America's One-Party Campuses," The *American Enterprise*, September 2002, 18–25.

- Brown University—5 percent.
- Cornell University—3 percent.
- Harvard University—4 percent.
- Penn State University—a whopping 17 percent.
- Stanford University—11 percent.
- UCLA—6 percent.
- UC Santa Barbara—1 percent.

Other universities in the survey followed the same pattern. In some departments, such as women's studies, African American studies, political science, sociology, history, and English, the entire faculty is leftist. Zinsmeister sarcastically concluded that one would find much greater political diversity at a grocery store or on a city bus.

In spring 2003, a broad, rigorous survey of American academics was conducted by the National Association of Scholars. It used academic association membership lists from six fields: anthropology, economics, history, philosophy (political and legal), political science, and sociology. It asked the question: "To which political party have the candidates you've voted for in the past ten years mostly belonged?" The question was answered by 96 percent of academic respondents. The results showed that anthropologists voted 30 to 1 in favor of Democrats, sociologists 28 to 1, political scientists 7 to 1, and economists 3 to 1. The average across all six fields was 15 to 1. Professor Dan Klein, one of the authors of the study, concluded that the social sciences and humanities are dominated by Democrats and there is little intellectual diversity.[5] According to a *Washington Post* article by Howard Kurtz, "72 percent of those teaching at American universities and colleges are liberal and 15 percent are conservative. . . . The imbalance is almost as striking in partisan terms, with 50 percent of the faculty members surveyed identifying themselves as Democrats and 11 percent as Republicans."[6] These patterns have shown no sign of changing in subsequent years.

Leftist domination of colleges often translates into a hostile political environment of officially sanctioned intolerance. According to the Foundation for Individual Rights in Education, at some colleges, students have been punished for expressing a religious objection to homosexuality or arguing that corporal punishment for children may be acceptable. Students in Illinois were told they could not hold a protest mocking affirmative action. Christian students in Florida were banned from showing *The Passion of the Christ*. A student in New Hampshire was expelled from the dorms after posting a flier that joked that female students could lose weight by taking the stairs.[7] Such incidents are rarely recounted to prospective students and their parents during recruitment sessions. You'll find them reported here, in the handy "green," "yellow," or "red" traffic lights awarded each school for its openness and fairness to conservative students and views.

5. "Surveys on Political Diversity in American Higher Education," National Association of Scholars, December 31, 2002, available at www.studentsforacademicfreedom.org/reports/Surveys.html.

6. "College Faculties a Most Liberal Lot, Study Finds," *Washington Post*, March 29, 2005.

7. The Foundation for Individual Rights in Education (thefire.org) has rich documentation of campus political abuses.

Many colleges have had speech codes that not only challenge credulity but clearly violate First Amendment guarantees. Under the ruse of ending harassment, Bowdoin College banned jokes and stories "experienced by others as harassing." Brown University banned "verbal behavior" that "produces feelings of impotence, anger or disenfranchisement" whether "unintentional or intentional." Colby College banned any speech that could lead to a loss of self-esteem. "Suggestive looks" have been banned at Bryn Mawr College and "unwelcomed flirtations" at Haverford College.

Even though many colleges are dominated by leftist ideology, a student still can get a good liberal arts education. *Choosing the Right College* has professors it recommends (not all of them political conservatives by any means) as well as courses in most important disciplines at every one of the colleges its reporters studied. A student who finds himself at a mostly intolerant campus should certainly seek out these teachers as allies, those courses as oases.

An important part of this guide is its appendix, "Asking the Right Questions in Choosing a College: What You Need to Know to Choose the Right College." It provides parents and students questions to ask that many administrators might like to avoid answering, such as: "On average, how many years does it take to graduate?" That question has considerable financial implications. Since many colleges have relieved their professors from full teaching obligations, required courses often fill up and become unavailable. That means a student might have to spend five, maybe six years to meet graduation requirements, and his family suffers the financial burden.

There are a number of college guides on the market. The one you're holding in your hands does a yeoman's job of informing parents and students about what many colleges would prefer to keep concealed.

Walter E. Williams is the John M. Olin Distinguished Professor of Economics at George Mason University. He is a syndicated columnist and the author of *Up from the Projects: An Autobiography.*

Foreword

Thomas E. Woods Jr.

Without realizing it, I have been doing *Choosing the Right College* an injustice. All these years I assumed that this book, now in its eighth edition, devoted the bulk of its space to chronicling the leftist bias to be found throughout university life in the United States. That can be useful information, I thought, but since that bias is everywhere, it can't necessarily help people choose among colleges. With few exceptions, no matter what college people choose there will be certain academic departments they will wish to avoid at all costs.

But what impressed me as I read this year's edition—the first one I've ever read—was how thorough and helpful it is. In the age of the Internet people sometimes assume that all the information they need can be found online if they look hard enough. And one can indeed find online information about various colleges. But a college website is going to tell you only what the administration wants you to hear, and I can't imagine that online college reviews by third parties could be as systematic as the book you hold in your hands. Practically every aspect of university life that a potential student would want to investigate can be found within these pages: academic life, core curricula (if any) in the Western tradition, sports, demographics, faculty, student life, housing, study-abroad opportunities, overall strengths and weaknesses, and interesting miscellanea.

Naturally, I couldn't help flipping ahead to the entry for Harvard, where I spent my own undergraduate years. Things have changed a bit since I was there, but I certainly recognize the institution this book describes. People have sometimes wondered how I could have spent four years at Harvard without winding up a sloganeering automaton, slavishly following chic opinion. My own experience as an undergraduate, which helps to answer that question, might be of some interest to students who wonder how they'll survive four years in a hostile milieu, and to parents who are justifiably concerned that eighteen years of raising decent and sensible children may go down the drain in just four.

I came from a relatively conservative, old Massachusetts town, one of the few in which the now-forgotten James Rappaport had defeated Senator John Kerry. I was not fully prepared for what I encountered in Cambridge.

On my way to the dining hall every night as a freshman I passed by people selling the *Workers' Vanguard*, a communist newspaper. I was genuinely stunned. I felt compelled to engage them in conversation. I actually thought I could make them abandon their position if I described to them what had actually happened in the wake of the Bolshevik Revolution, and challenged what Vladimir Brovkin, my professor for twentieth-century Russia, called the "good Lenin, bad Stalin" myth. I didn't make much headway, but the whole experience got me reading more and more history—which, to my surprise, eventually became my major. (You read that right: I owe my career to communism.)

In 1991, during my sophomore year, I even attended a meeting of the organization that published *Workers' Vanguard*, the Friends of the Spartacus Youth Club. The Soviet Union was falling apart by that time. The speaker passed around a hat asking for donations to keep the workers' paradise together. Where that $18.32 went is anyone's guess, but no one seemed to find this a peculiar request. The Bolshevik Revolution had ushered in "the freest society in the history of the world," the speaker told us, so it was urgent that we preserve those gains.

In my second semester one professor required that books for his course be purchased at a store called Revolution Books. Inside, portraits of some of history's greatest mass murderers adorned the walls. I decided I would find the books elsewhere.

I kept my sanity by joining student groups, including a student publication, where I could expect to find like-minded people around whom I didn't have to justify myself and with whom I could feel politically at ease. We were just preaching to the choir, some said. Maybe so. But the choir does need to be preached to from time to time, and in so doing we helped both ourselves and others—who, when they saw what we were writing and saying, realized they were not alone.

My experience is proof positive that with the proper formation and the help of a support network on campus, a nonleftist can not only survive but thrive even at a modern American university. The strange things I encountered in Cambridge did not cause me to abandon everything I held dear and promptly adopt the official line of fashionable opinion. To the contrary, it encouraged me to become all the more attached to and consistent in my views. Whatever these people were, I decided, I wanted to be pretty much the opposite.

Bizarre as some of my experiences surely were, it would be a mistake to suggest that those four years were a waste of time, or yielded me nothing but leftist propaganda. To be sure, in our day every educated person must to some extent be an autodidact. But even in our university system, shot through with problems though it is, determined students can still get a good education from scholars who have made genuine contributions to the sum total of human knowledge. Quality and standards can still be found, and good work is still rewarded. And that is one of the ways this book can help you: it pinpoints who the great scholars are, what the great programs are, which courses highlight an institution's strengths, what kinds of extracurricular enrichment you can pursue, and much else.

In my own days as a college professor I taught a good many adult students in my night classes. Nearly all of them were unusually industrious, and many told me they wished they had seized the opportunities before them the first time they tried making their way through college. You have the chance to do things right the first time, to understand the nature of the opportunity before you and to seize everything it has to offer. The book you hold in your hands can play a key role in one of life's critical decisions, and I am delighted to commend it to you.

Thomas E. Woods Jr., PhD, is a senior fellow at the Ludwig von Mises Institute in Auburn, Alabama. He is the author, most recently, of *Rollback: Repealing Big Government Before the Coming Fiscal Collapse* and the editor of *Back on the Road to Serfdom: The Resurgence of Statism*. His other books include the *New York Times* bestsellers *Meltdown* and *The Politically Incorrect Guide to American History*.

Finding and Following the Core

Mark C. Henrie

Faithfully following the strictures of the contemporary ideology of multicultural diversity, American university curricula today resemble a dazzling cafeteria indifferently presided over by an amiable and indulgent nutritionist. There are succulent offerings to suit every taste, and the intellectual gourmand can only regret that he has but four years to sample the fare. Never in history have there existed institutions providing such an array of fields of study—from Sanskrit to quantum mechanics, from neoclassical microeconomic theory to Jungian psychology, from the study of medieval folklore to the study of 1950s billboards. Everything which can repay study is studied, however small the dividend. The only constraint on the diversity of offerings is a financial one, which, given the truly astonishing wealth of American universities, is hardly a constraint at all.

But as every parent knows, children seldom choose to eat what's good for them. They seem irresistibly drawn to high-fat foods and sugary desserts. Or, sometimes, they develop a fixation upon one particular dish and will eat no others. Parents do what they can to ensure a balanced diet, and in years past, the university, standing in loco parentis, likewise made sure that the bill of fare, the courses required for graduation, were also "balanced." Various dimensions of intellectual virtue were each given their due: the basic cultural knowledge by which an educated man situates himself in history, a broad exposure to various methods of inquiry, the mastery and command that are the fruit of disciplinary specialization. Programmatically, this balance was achieved by a core curriculum in the literary, philosophical, and artistic monuments of Western civilization; a diverse set of requirements in general education; and a carefully structured course of studies in a major.

Things are rather different today, for we live in an era when the idea of a university—and therefore the university's institutional expression—has been transformed by the cultural currents that erupted in the 1960s. Commentators make much of the "tenured radicals" who have "destroyed" the traditional curriculum, and after reading so much about these depredations, we are apt to approach such views with skepticism: Can it really be that bad? How can we reconcile such doom-saying with the fact that American universities are the envy of the world, drawing the most talented students and faculty from around the globe? Are not American universities at the forefront of research in virtually every field? Are academia's critics perhaps pining nostalgically for a world that never was?

Such skepticism is not unwarranted, especially with regard to the most extreme claims of the critics: the American university is not on the point of collapse, and it is still possible to acquire a genuinely fine liberal arts education. Nonetheless, we can trace quite clearly the effect that the 1960s generation has had on the American university. That generation rebelled against their parents, and so, against the very idea of anyone or anything standing in loco parentis. Enthusiasts for various forms of Marxist and post-Marxist critique, they understood themselves not as inquirers standing on the shoulders of giants but rather as change-agents striving to overcome an inheritance of injustice. Like Thrasymachus in Plato's *Republic*, their sense of outraged injustice drove them to the moral relativism we now call postmodernism. But this very relativism led only to the dead end of self-contradiction, for it required them to deny that there could be any true standard of justice by which injustice could be admitted. Famously, they enjoined themselves to trust no one over thirty: obviously, the great works of the Western tradition, hundreds and thousands of years old, could not be trusted. They were instead to be deconstructed. Locked into an indiscriminate stance of questioning authority, they found themselves at length well over thirty and in the awkward position of being university authorities. What have been the effects on the curriculum?

The major

The system of majors still flourishes, reflecting the still high prestige of the disciplinary model of the natural sciences—reflecting, as well, the guild-like structure of the PhD system, which credentials faculty and serves as the basis for their institutional authority within the university. Yet outside the natural sciences, the structured sequencing of courses within the major—one course building upon another and probing to a deeper level—has been largely abandoned. For reasons associated with careerism, professors today are often more committed to their research than to their teaching obligations, and so they resist or reject a "rigid" curricular plan that would make frequent and irregular sabbaticals difficult. Moreover, faculty themselves have fundamental disagreements about the very nature of their disciplines and so find it impossible to reach a consensus about the "end" toward which a course of studies should be directed. The faculty's solution has been to avoid direction.

Students in a major are thus largely free to pick and choose as they please and as the current course offerings allow. Consequently, many students experience their major in a rather aimless way: the major does not "progress" or "culminate" in anything. Graduating students often do not understand themselves to have achieved even preliminary mastery of a discipline. Whereas "critical" methods of teaching and learning have been "pushed forward" to earlier and earlier years of study in the past generation, mastery of a discipline (in fields outside the natural sciences) has been "pushed back" to the MA years of graduate school.

General education and distribution requirements

A system of distribution and other general education requirements also persists. Commonly, students will find that they are required to reach a certain proficiency in a foreign language, that they will need to demonstrate command of written English, and that they will be required to take a prescribed number of courses in a range of fields of study. Sometimes these last, "distribution," requirements are vague: for example, they might prescribe twelve credits each from the sciences, humanities, and social sciences. Sometimes, the distribution requirements are more specific: e.g., two courses in math, one in the physical sciences and one in the life sciences, a course in history, a course in a non-Western subject, etc.

The theoretical justification for requirements in general education is broad exposure to various bodies of knowledge and approaches to understanding. There is an echo here of John Henry Newman's argument in his famous book *The Idea of a University* that a university is "a place of teaching universal knowledge," and that failure to take the measure of all areas of inquiry results in a kind of deformity of the intellect. Some students may grumble at these requirements, which take them away from pursuing their major subject with single-mindedness: in the university cafeteria, they want nothing but the lime Jell-o. Frequently, faculty members sympathize with such complaints. After all, the professors have themselves undertaken graduate studies in increasingly narrow fields; their liberal education is many years in the past, and their self-esteem depends on their standing in their particular disciplines, not on their reputation for the synthetic skills of the generalist. But Newman's argument about the humane value of broad learning remains compelling. Students should approach their general education requirements as a serious opportunity for intellectual growth.

Consider, for example, the requirement of mastery in a foreign language. Americans are notoriously bad at foreign languages; ambitious students may fear that their GPAs will suffer in language courses. But it really is true that some thoughts are better expressed in one language than another. Acquiring a foreign language can open up whole new worlds, and when kept up, a foreign language is a possession for life. Similarly, it is only through distribution requirements that the "two cultures" of science and the humanities are forced to engage each other in the modern university. Without this encounter, the student of the sciences risks falling into a value-free technological imperialism. Without this encounter, the student of the humanities risks falling into an antiquarian idyll, cut off from one of the major currents of the modern world.

There is also a simply practical advantage to distribution requirements. Today, about two-thirds of all students will change their major during their college career: many will change more than once. What students will "be" in life is almost certainly not what they thought they would "be" when they set off for college. Distribution requirements offer an opportunity to view the world from different intellectual perspectives. Who knows but that an unexpected horizon may prove to correspond to the heart's deepest desires?

The core curriculum

It is the core curriculum, a survey of the great works of Western civilization, which has fared the worst in the curricular reforms of the past generation. With few exceptions, the core curriculum has been simply eliminated from American higher education. Those of a suspecting cast of mind may speculate that this change has occurred for structural reasons. Following the model of the natural sciences, PhDs in the humanities are awarded for original "contributions to knowledge." But the great works of Western culture have been studied for centuries. What genuinely "new" insights can be gleaned there? Have aspiring PhD's perhaps turned, in desperation, to other subjects in which there is still something "original" to be said? If so, how can they be expected to teach the Great Books, which were not their subject of study? But then, the elimination of the core is also surely the result of a moral rejection: the generation of the 1960s, which admired the Viet Cong and cheered U.S. defeat in Southeast Asia, viewed their own civilizational tradition as a legacy not to be honored but to be overcome. The "privileging" of the great books of the West therefore had to end.

A more positive justification for the demise of the core is frequently given, however. In order to prepare students for the Multicultural World of Tomorrow, it is said, students must be exposed to the diversity of world cultures. A merely Western curriculum would be parochial, a failure of liberal learning. Moreover, since our modern or postmodern technological civilization is characterized by rapid change, it is more important to be exposed to "approaches to knowledge," to "learn how to learn," than it is to acquire any particular body of knowledge. Education then becomes nothing but the cultivation of abstract instrumental rationality, divorced from any content and divorced from any end. Consistent with these arguments, many universities now call their distribution requirements a "core curriculum." They claim to have undergone curricular development rather than curricular demise.

As a practical matter, this multicultural transformation of the curriculum can have two curious results. In the worst cases, what passes for a multicultural curriculum is nothing but a peculiar kind of Western echo chamber. Students are given over to studying Marxist critics in contemporary Algeria and neo-Marxist critics in contemporary Brazil and post-Marxist critics in contemporary France. All that is really learned are variations on the "critique of ideologies"—a legacy of one great Western mind, that of Karl Marx. In other cases, however, students really are exposed to the high cultures and great works of non-Western societies; but their encounter with Western high culture remains slight. We thus are presented with the spectacle of many students today who habitually associate high ideals, profound insight, and wisdom with every culture but their own.

What, then, is the abiding justification for the traditional core curriculum in Western civilization? Why is it a major premise of this guide that a university lacking a core curriculum is educationally deficient—even as we stand at the dawn of the Multicultural World of Tomorrow? The purpose of the core is not to inculcate any kind of Western chauvinism, certainly not any ethnocentrism that would prevent a student from exploring and learning from non-Western cultures. Indeed, one expects that it will be precisely those who have delved most thoughtfully into the wisdom of the Occident who will then be in a position to learn the most from the wisdom of the Orient—rather like Matteo Ricci and the other Jesuits who encountered Chinese civilization with such sympathetic results in the sixteenth century. Lacking a foundation in the depths of our own civilization, a student can approach another as little more than a tourist.

There are really two arguments for the traditional core. They concern the importance of high culture and the importance of history.

High culture

A not uncommon sight on a university campus during freshman week is a group of students sitting on the grass in the evening, one with a guitar, singing together the theme songs of vintage television sitcoms. In a society as diverse as America at the dawn of the twenty-first century, this is to be expected: television is one of the few things that young people from all walks of life have in common. But what are we to think when the same scene is repeated at senior week, four years later? Has higher education done its job when the only common references of those with a baccalaureate degree remain those of merely popular culture?

The core curriculum is the place in university studies where one encounters what Matthew Arnold called "the best that has been thought and said." Such a view of education is hierarchical, discriminating, judgmental: it reflects the fact that the high can be distinguished from the low, and the further understanding that the high can comprehend the low whereas the low can never take the measure of the high. By spending time with the best, with the highest expressions and reflections of a culture, the mind of the student is equipped for its own ascent. Without such an effort, the student remains trapped in the unreflective everyday presumptions of the current culture: the student remains trapped in clichés. The high culture of the traditional core curriculum is therefore liberating, as befits the liberal arts.

Throughout history there have been countless thinkers, poets, writers, and artists; the vast majority of all their labor has been lost, and most of them have been entirely forgotten. What survives are the truly great works that have been held in consistently high esteem through the changing circumstances of time and place. Thus, the traditional canon of Great Books—the common possession of educated men and women across the centuries of Western history—is not an arbitrary list, nor does the canon reflect relations of "power"; rather, as Louise Cowan has observed, the classics of a civilization "select themselves" by virtue of their superior insight. The presumptions and presuppositions of our lives, which lie so deep in us that we can scarcely recognize them, are in the great works made available for inspection and inquiry. High culture is a matter not of snobbish refinement but of superior understanding.

It is here that the core curriculum is indispensable. For every student brings to college a preliminary "enculturation"—we have all by the age of eighteen absorbed certain perspectives, insights, narratives, stereotypes, and values that communicate themselves to us in the prevailing popular culture. This enculturation is the common possession of a generation, whatever the diversity of their family backgrounds by class or ethnicity. But the artifacts of popular culture are always mere reflections of the possibilities glimpsed and made possible by works of high culture. The traditional core curriculum provides a student with access to that high culture; its higher "enculturation" provides a student with a vantage point from which he can grasp the meaning and implications of his everyday cultural presumptions. And he begins to hold something in common with the educated men and women of past ages; they become his peers.

One of the peculiar presumptions of our time is that novelty is good: social and technological transformations have given us a prejudice against tradition and in favor of "originality." But it is the great works of the traditional canon that constitute the record of true originality: that is why they have survived. Only by becoming familiar with them are we enabled to recognize just how derivative is much of that which now passes as original insight. A university that does not orient its students to high culture effectively commits itself to a project of deculturation, and thereby traps its students in a kind of permanent adolescence.

History

George Santayana famously asserted that those who do not remember the past are condemned to repeat it. Centuries earlier, Cicero observed that to know nothing of the world before one's birth is to remain always a child. These cautionary aphorisms are perfectly and pointedly true, and in the first instance they constitute one justification for the historical studies undertaken in a core curriculum. Practically speaking, there is wisdom to be found in experience. This wisdom is never more fully appreciated than when we experience the consequences of our actions at firsthand. But because human affairs exhibit certain recurring patterns, knowledge of history provides a stock of experiences at second-hand from which more general "lessons" may be drawn as well—at least, by those with ears to hear and eyes to see.

Nevertheless, these admonitions of Santayana and Cicero do not constitute the truly decisive historical reason for embarking on the traditional core curriculum. After all, insofar as human affairs exhibit patterns, and insofar as we approach history merely in search of the generally applicable "laws" or "rules" of human interaction, one may as well find one's stock of lessons in any given civilization as in any other. Anyone's history would be as good as anyone else's. It is because the contemporary academic mind views the matter in just this social-scientific way that it is necessarily driven to understand the traditional core curriculum's Western focus as nothing but the result of chauvinism or laziness.

But the core curriculum's particular emphasis on Western history is not the result either of ethnocentrism or of sloth. There is something far deeper going on here. Indeed, when history is approached merely as the raw material of social science, historical study in itself loses any intrinsic value; all that really matters in such a scheme are the "laws" that are abstracted from the pool of historical "examples." The core curriculum, however, does mean to value history in itself. How so?

All of us are born into a natural world governed by laws not of our making. Some of these laws are the laws of human nature and of human interaction, laws that apply in every time and place. But all of us are also born into the historical world at a particular time, and there is a certain unrepeatable (and unpredictable) quality to each historical moment, the result of free human choices. What is more, the historical moment we inhabit now is the outcome, in part, of the contingent history of our particular community, both recently and more remotely. In order to answer the first question of every true inquirer—What is going on here?—it is necessary to uncover the historical narrative of the present: that is, it is necessary to answer the question, What is going on now? To answer this question in any profound sense, it is necessary to understand the historical narrative of one's own civilization—to understand, as well, what was going on then. Consequently, the traditional core curriculum is not simply the study of the great books of the Western world isolated from their historical contexts; rather, that study proceeds side-by-side with an inquiry that locates those works in history. While the great works articulate the great human possibilities, not all human possibilities are equally available to us today. In effect, to understand the meaning of that relative availability (and unavailability) is to understand one's place in the stream of history, and this is the second argument for undertaking a core curriculum.

Typically, when a core curriculum has been poorly constructed, it reads history in a Whiggish way, or "progressively." In the Whig narrative, Western history tells the simple tale of how the world has progressed ever upward until it reaches its highpoint, the present (and in particular, me). Moreover, such a facile historical sense anticipates a future that is a straight-line extrapolation of the present. When the core is structured well, however, it leaves open the question of whether the present is the outcome of progress or decline. (The truth, it has been said, is that things are always getting both better and worse, at the same time.) A student who has learned the deep historical lessons of a core curriculum is as alert to the possibilities of historical transformation just ahead as he is to the possibility of continuity.

Today, it is extremely common for a college student to reach the end of four years of study with all requirements met but with a profound sense of disorientation and confusion, even disappointment. What's it all about? Usually, there will have been no sense of progression in the student's plan of study, no sense of mastery, no perspective touching deeply upon many connected subjects that might serve as the basis for ever-deeper inquiry with the passing of the years. There will have been no ascent to a truly higher culture, and no cultivation of historical consciousness.

What a lost opportunity!

The bad news is that it is most unlikely that we will see a return of the core curriculum in the next generation, and certainly not in time to benefit most of the readers of this guide. The good news is that much of the substance of the old core is still available, scattered across various courses in the departments. The eight courses that may constitute a "core of one's own" are here listed for each of the universities covered in this guide (excepting only those schools which still offer a true core); the rationale for these eight courses—what each contributes to the comprehensive perspective of the core—is given in my monograph, *A Student's Guide to the Core Curriculum* (ISI Books, 2000). Thanks to the elective system, the benefits of the core are not entirely beyond reach. The very best dishes are still available in the contemporary university-cafeteria: you simply have to choose them. Alas, that may entail occasionally passing on the chocolate cheesecake.

A curriculum is a "course"—like the course that is run by a river. A curriculum should take you somewhere. After four years of college, a graduating senior should be a different and better person than his former self, the matriculating freshman. Instead, most students today find themselves merely lost at sea, swamped by the roiling waters of various intellectual enthusiasms. Undertaking the discipline of a "voluntary" core curriculum today offers a student the prospect for the most profound of transformations—and the most delightful of journeys.

Mark C. Henrie holds degrees from Dartmouth, Cambridge, and Harvard. He is editor of the *Intercollegiate Review* and executive editor of *Modern Age*, both published by ISI. He is the author of *A Student's Guide to the Core Curriculum* (ISI Books) and editor of *Arguing Conservatism: Four Decades of the* Intercollegiate Review (ISI Books).

Why This Guide Exists and How to Use It

John Zmirak

I'd like to introduce this guide to major American colleges by talking about an enormous Spanish church. Begun in 1883 by the visionary architect Antonio Gaudi, the Shrine of the Holy Family in Barcelona is widely lauded as one of the greatest buildings in the Western world, even though it isn't even finished. (Work on the shrine is expected to continue until at least 2026.) Like most of the great cathedrals of Europe, it was planned on a scale that outstretched the life of its creator. That is, it was meant to remain the task of generations not yet born. Unlike monstrous monuments to dictators, or skyscrapers named for the state-subsidized moguls who financed them, the Shrine of the Holy Family was designed to point to truths that outlast the individual, to evoke not the ephemeral whirrings of a publicity or propaganda machine, but rather those eternal realities that underpin the lives of all men, everywhere, in every age. In its slow emergence from the Spanish stone, the shrine mimics the growth of civilization in the womb of time, the organic emergence of institutions like representative government and ideas like the dignity of the person and the sanctity of human life. Built in a boldly modern style, the shrine nevertheless pays homage to medieval and Renaissance influences. Designed by a solitary genius, it is now the work of a community.

One can find few better examples than this church of the healthy exercise of "tradition," as defined by the great modernist poet T. S. Eliot in his essay "Tradition and the Individual Talent." In that lastingly influential piece, Eliot describes tradition as something far different from a heritage passively accepted or a dead past preserved in amber. Instead, Eliot says:

> If the only form of tradition, of handing down, consisted in following the ways of the immediate generation before us in a blind or timid adherence to its successes, "tradition" should positively be discouraged. We have seen many such simple currents soon lost in the sand; and novelty is better than repetition. Tradition is a matter of much wider significance. It cannot be inherited, and if you want it you must

obtain it by great labour. It involves, in the first place, the historical sense, which we may call nearly indispensable to anyone who would continue to be a poet beyond his twenty-fifth year; and the historical sense involves a perception, not only of the pastness of the past, but of its presence; the historical sense compels a man to write not merely with his own generation in his bones, but with a feeling that the whole of the literature of Europe from Homer and within it the whole of the literature of his own country has a simultaneous existence and composes a simultaneous order.

It is this conception of tradition which infuses a real liberal arts education, of the sort we attempt to unearth at a wide variety of schools in this hefty volume. We find it is all too rarely offered. At many of these colleges, the heritage of our civilization, that slow accretion of truths of faith and reason which made possible the first stirrings of human liberty anywhere on earth, is tossed aside because of its inevitable imperfections—for instance, because our ancestors were too slow fully to extend that civilization's benefits to every individual of every race or either sex. In the place of a rich historical (and critical) understanding of the values that make the West, one finds in too many classrooms an angry, adolescent rejection of the institutions and influences that planted the seeds of our liberty and prosperity.

Like spoiled heirs who despise the family business that funds their leisure, contemporary professors indulge in Oedipal ideologies that focus on killing, over and over and over again, our fathers. The temptation of such tenured radicals is to take for granted the hard-won advances of Western millennia, to sneer at the staggering quantity of intellectual and humanitarian work undertaken by monks and humanists, Puritans and patriots, pedagogues and philanthropists in creating and nurturing that fragile, almost fancifully impractical institution we call a college—and its flower, freedom.

At many schools, the only alternative available to this brand of callow leftism comes in the form of hard-headed "realism," or the natural disdain felt by the practical-minded for abstruse pursuits. Undergraduates who might have developed an interest in the arts and humanities turn aside when they are taught to view the novels of Jane Austen through a jaundiced feminist lens, or the paintings of Renaissance masters as examples of aesthetic racism. Such students learn the false and poisonous lesson that the liberal arts are for "liberals"—and not the old-fashioned (nineteenth-century) lovers of liberty but rather the modern sort who combine certain features of both totalitarianism and libertinism. Students who might have (like Wallace Stevens) practiced poetry while making a living selling insurance are turned by necessity into philistines. And the arts are left to their enemies. The results are easy to see: grim, megalithic cities of soulless towers constructed by "practical" men whose only oases of art are narrow galleries full of protest works created by bitter Bohemians.

Which brings us back to Barcelona. Even as the great Shrine slowly grows toward its completion, its foundations are being undermined by the forces of bureaucracy and "progress"—specifically, a rail tunnel being dug by the city's government. The proximity of the tunnel—a mere seven feet—to the Shrine's deep roots in the stone, and the rumbling of incessant rail traffic, pose a mortal threat to the building, according to architects and structural engineers. These experts lodged a belated protest against the tunnel, but local businessmen sided with the diggers. In October 2010, just a few weeks before Pope Benedict XVI consecrated the Shrine as a basilica, the boring mechanism for the tunnel reached the site of the church, and began to dig under its foundations. Only time will tell if this work of modernity undermines the sacred in a grimly literal sense.

Such a casual willingness to endanger a timeless work of art for the sake of expediency recalls the successful attack waged by leftist reformers (and their pragmatist enablers) on the curricula of hundreds of U.S. colleges and universities in the 1960s and '70s. In the wake of Harvard University's decision to dismantle its core curriculum, nearly every institution of higher education in America eliminated the survey courses in history, art, literature, and other humanities which once had provided students of every ethnic and social background with the intellectual and cultural capital of centuries. The very mission of an American liberal arts college—to make available to the many the cultural riches once confined to the few—was abandoned. In the place of core curricula, we find vague, broad "distribution requirements," which require students not to master particular facts about, and questions posed by, the civilization that formed them, but rather to explore different "modes of analysis" and "ways of knowing." The implicit relativism of this endeavor is checked only by the occasional insistence of educators hostile to the West that students take politicized courses to broaden their cultural "diversity." (Ironically, many of these schools at the same time have watered down their requirements for the study of foreign languages—one element of genuine diversity which students should have to master.)

While at some schools distribution requirements can be fulfilled through admirable classes on the achievements of Oriental, pre-Columbian, or African civilizations, at others most of the classes that allow students to check off their "diversity" box are fixated on unreconstructed Marxist or radical feminist analyses. Ironically, while the deconstruction of curricula was promoted most fervently by ideologues of the Left, in many places it has been abetted by the complacence of administrators, trustees, and even professors unconcerned about the content of what they regard as distractions from the real business of universities: churning out employees, investors, and consumers.

The results of dismantling American education are undeniable: thoughtless decisions have produced ignorant students, a reality that has now been documented by the Intercollegiate Studies Institute (ISI), the organization that publishes this guide. According to ISI's studies, seniors at many elite schools know no more about American history, civics, and economics than do freshmen. Many know even less.

These results should trouble even those pragmatic parents whose primary concern is to advance their children's economic interests. In the ongoing worldwide economic contraction, traditional careers have become less stable. Previously successful adults are finding that they must change jobs and sometimes even professions. Instead of a dogged mastery of a particular trade, what people require today is the mental flexibility and cultural literacy that are the fruit of a genuine liberal arts education. This assertion is supported by research: Canadian economist Robert C. Allen of the University of British Columbia has found, for example, that a "background in social sciences and humanities appears to have a major impact on earning power. From their twenties to their fifties, men who graduate in humanities see their income rise, on average, by 78 percent. Graduates in social sciences see their income rise 106 percent over the same period. That compares favorably to a 47 percent increase in income for community college graduates and an average 76 percent increase for university graduates across all fields."

In other words, even on a nakedly economic analysis, pragmatism is impractical. It is folly to allow students to narrow their educations prematurely based on their unexamined preferences at age eighteen. Like those city fathers of Barcelona who are willing to risk the destruction of their city's most distinctive and attractive landmark, administrators who neglect the humane education of undergraduates are mistaken about both culture and economics. Like imprudent farmers, they are eating their seed corn. Indeed, they are microwaving it to serve with melted butter. It is our task in this book to help students outwit the educrats who have tried to pander to them, inflame them with ideology, or constrain their horizons while they are still young and eager to explore.

In this guide you will find colleges that survived the philistine outrages of the 1960s and '70s and have retained (or regained) their mission of humanistic education. You'll find others founded in response to the educational crisis of that time, schools that are consciously countercultural in their emphasis on the Great Books and great ideas. Mostly, however, you'll encounter profiles of highly selective public and private schools, including practical suggestions on how to obtain a serious education at these schools by carefully choosing courses and professors while avoiding the ideological traps that await the unwary.

Colleges can form your character—or twist it. They can challenge, enrich, and deepen your treasured beliefs—or trash them and leave you with nothing. They can help you develop lifelong friendships, professional contacts, and intellectual mentors—or drop you in the world with not much more than a degree and a load of debt. Success depends on choosing prudently.

Reading through these essays, you'll find comments by current students, professors, and graduates, quotations from research studies and investigative articles, analyses of curricula, fond reminiscences, and horror stories. Each profile has been compiled by a team of reporters who consulted a wide range of sources to give you the most candid, comprehensive, and up-to-date description of what life is really like on each campus. You'll read about elite Ivies where world-famous scholars deliver lectures to hundreds of ambitious pupils, tiny religious colleges that study the great books and the Bible, workaday state universities with a few excellent programs—and just about everything in between. You'll also learn which colleges have strong sports cultures, faith-filled chaplaincies, and good systems for providing academic advice. And which ones have coed bathrooms. Or dorm rooms.

Unlike some other guides, we are independently researched, written, and funded. (Believe it or not, some college guides make schools pay in order to be included.) Others let schools write their own profiles. How helpful is that? If you want to know what a school says about itself, go check its website. Or call its public relations department. (They sometimes call us, complaining about our candor.)

We're also up front about our point of view. We have a perspective, and it's laid out right here in these introductory pages—our view of what constitutes a good education. There are many different views out there on this topic, and most of them are partial or just plain wrong. Is a "good education" one that gives students the best chance to land a high-paying job? One that gives them entrée to the circles of cultural power? One that drenches them in diversity, introduces them mainly to foreign and marginalized cultures, and teaches them to undermine the "status quo"? And how should such an education be structured—like a Shoney's breakfast buffet, or like a healthy, balanced meal?

While it may seem un-American to say it, we don't believe in the absolute virtue of choice. Not every high school kid comes into college knowing what he needs to learn or how to learn it. What is more, U.S. secondary education does not compare to what is offered in Europe or Japan. The egalitarian ideology that pervades our secondary schools has dumbed most of us down. To expect American teenagers to take responsibility for planning every detail of their education is to guarantee that most of them will fail. They will emerge with a few specialties, a grab bag of information, and a pile of fashionable prejudices. This is what happens when we treat the fragile, multifarious fruit of thousands of years of human culture as a pile of consumer goods to be handled, sniffed, and accepted or rejected according to whim. We agree with what John Henry Newman wrote in 1852 when he described a university as

> an assemblage of learned men, zealous for their own sciences, and rivals of each other, . . . brought, by familiar intercourse and for the sake of intellectual peace, to adjust together the claims and relations of their respective subjects of investigation. They learn to respect, to consult, to aid each other. Thus is created a pure and clear atmosphere of thought, which the student also breathes, though in his own case he only pursues a few sciences out of the multitude. He profits by an intellectual tradition, which is independent of particular teachers, which guides him in his choice of subjects, and duly interprets for him those which he chooses. He apprehends the great outline of knowledge, the principles on which it rests, the scale of its parts, its lights and its shades, its great points and its little, as he otherwise cannot apprehend them. Hence it is that this education is called "Liberal."

One good test of a college is whether it teaches all its graduates—not just its English or philosophy majors—how to read and comprehend such a paragraph.

Another is whether its curriculum partakes in this broadly traditional vision of the mission of education as something that forms the self, trains the mind, disciplines the habits, and connects the student as one more link in a chain of civilized liberty that ties us to the ancient citizens of Athens, the prophets of Israel, the doctors of the church, the humanists and philosophers of the Renaissance, and the scientists of the Enlightenment.

The place that colleges still hold in our culture tells us that we remember, albeit dimly, that they are meant to form the free citizen, prepare the future parent, and fortify each man's soul. Universities train us to think and argue for ourselves, but also to listen to older and wiser authorities, to question but also to take seriously the wisdom of other periods and peoples, to learn from our contemporaries and then serve as mentors to the young. Most of us carry memories of one or two faculty members who stand as models of how to teach, how to counsel, how to correct—memories that guide us when we have children or students of our own. Schools also ought to teach us how to spend our time wisely, how to choose among the myriad political, cultural, and social options that a free society offers. (That—and not keeping the kids entertained—is the secret purpose of a university's extra-curricular activities.) The workload imposed should be sufficient to engage the bright and awaken the lazy. A university must challenge us to succeed, but also to get up again when we fail. It is by these criteria that this book judges a college.

Needless to say, we are often disappointed.

But after one recovers from the shock of seeing how far many schools have fallen, it is possible to seek out signs of hope. Let's admit that the great edifice of traditional education has crumbled, that the Roman aqueducts and Gothic arches are broken, and let us look (in Browning's words) for "love among the ruins." Few schools still fully embody a vision of liberal education that Newman would recognize. But at many of them, there are still significant remnants, or recent growths, of excellence—brilliant scholars, committed but fair-minded teachers, extraordinary libraries and museums, and intellectually motivated students. Some places have clung to their traditions (see Wabash College, Providence College, and the University of Chicago); some have begun to remember why they were founded (see Fordham, Baylor, and Gonzaga); and still others have sprung up to fill the academic void (see New St. Andrews, Patrick Henry, Thomas Aquinas, and Thomas More). And even on campuses where none of this is true, one can usually piece together a first-rate education by choosing carefully among professors and programs.

In selecting schools for this guide, we have included the top forty most selective national universities and the top forty most selective liberal arts colleges, according to the objective selectivity rankings also used by *U.S. News & World Report*. We have then chosen more schools from different regions of the country that have special emphases, unique virtues, or distinctive missions. This edition also includes three of the U.S. service academies (Army, Navy, and Air Force), which offer excellent educational opportunities for those willing to risk life and limb in defense of our country.

We couldn't fit every worthwhile school in a single book and hope to do any one of them justice. But for the first time we are providing buyers of this book complete, free access to our companion website, www.CollegeGuide.org, where dozens more schools are profiled, and additional resources are on offer, including an "Ask the Editors" feature, original essays dealing with issues in higher education, electronic editions of ISI's acclaimed *Student Guides to the Major Disciplines*, tips for navigating the admissions process, videos featuring students and alumni offering their take on their colleges, and more.

Inside this book, each institutional profile is divided into two sections: "Academic Life" and "Student Life." In the Academic Life section, our team of researchers gathered information pertaining to the following questions: What is the school's academic reputation? Is a genuine core curriculum in place? If not, how well do the general education requirements ensure that students receive a broad liberal arts education and take foundational courses? Who are the best professors and which are the best departments or programs? Which departments are the weakest or most politicized? What kind of academic advising do students receive? How strong are the relationships between faculty and students? What percentage of classes are small, intimate seminars? To what extent are graduate students relied on for teaching and grading? How bad is grade inflation?

A word is in order here about what we are attempting to do when we recommend professors. When we list an institution's "top professors," we are certainly not pretending to present an exhaustive list, nor are we applying a political test. Some of these professors are known to be conservatives, others radicals, but in most cases we have no idea where they stand politically. Instead, we commend professors named by their colleagues and students as being fair, nonpoliticized, and talented teachers.

Given these tough economic times, a couple of features in our profiles should prove especially useful. First, we report data not only on tuition and room and board but also such crucial factors as the extent of need-based financial aid a school provides and the average student-debt load of graduates. Our profiles take note of institutions that place an especially large financial burden on students (and their parents) and also those that provide relatively good values. Second, and perhaps even more important, is our "do-it-yourself" core curriculum. A student who enrolls in one of the many state-sponsored institutions covered here in order to take advantage of the in-state tuition his parents' taxes have long been underwriting will look in vain for an ordered, serious core curriculum that guides his studies to ensure he receives a real liberal arts education. That doesn't mean he can't get one at the school; the necessary courses are probably offered, but it will take some digging to find them. We have done the spadework ourselves. Just look at the suggested core curriculum box in any profile for a list of current, worthy courses that can be taken to obtain an introduction to the fundamentals of educated citizenship and lifelong learning.

In this "Suggested Core" box we highlight eight specific courses that cover the areas that together make up a traditional integrated core. These areas are:

1. Classical literature (in translation)
2. Ancient philosophy
3. The Bible
4. Christian thought before 1500
5. Modern political theory
6. Shakespeare
7. U.S. history before 1865
8. Nineteenth-century European intellectual history

The rationale behind this vision of the core curriculum is explained in detail in Mark C. Henrie's *A Student's Guide to the Core Curriculum* (available from ISI Books and on www. CollegeGuide.org). This grouping of courses reflects the input of dozens of distinguished professors from a wide variety of disciplines as to what a brief but genuine core curriculum ought to cover. If taught well—and especially if taught using primary texts—these courses will help students obtain a broad and sophisticated understanding of the narratives, beliefs, events, thinkers, and institutions that have shaped not only the world around them but also the core insights encoded in our culture and Constitution. If students take the eight courses we recommend, and especially if they can contrive to take them from professors we suggest, they should graduate with the basics of a true liberal arts education. That means they will have minds which are free to go on learning all through life from a vast variety of sources, supported by hard-won skills and guided by a sure intellectual compass.

The Student Life section tries to give readers an idea of what it's like to go to each school. Here is where we go into detail about each institution's residential life: Are all dorms coed? If so, are there coed rooms? Coed bathrooms? Does the school guarantee housing for all four years? Would you want to live in the dorms in any case? (Some are Gothic wonderlands, others Stalinist monoliths.) In this section we also try to give some idea of how students spend their time outside the classroom. Is this a service-oriented school? Do the kids party five nights a week or are they a studious, intellectual bunch? In addition, we discuss whether campus crime is a problem, the extent to which intercollegiate sports shape the campus atmosphere, and whether school traditions create a spirit of cohesion. There is much else in this section besides, depending on the character of the institution—including everything from quaint customs and school songs to curious but telling facts. (Did you know, for instance, that in the chapel of Washington and Lee, General Robert E. Lee is actually buried under the main altar? That Louisiana State University keeps a live tiger on campus? That Caltech freshmen are encouraged to try to vandalize the dorm rooms of seniors—who fortify them like bunkers to weather the siege?)

We also include short, representative incidents and evaluations of the state of political discourse, intellectual freedom, and free speech at the colleges we cover. These "red," "yellow" and "green" lights serve as shorthand for the state of civic liberty at a school. They are drawn from reports by students and faculty and journalistic accounts of the sometimes disturbing degree to which administrators and faculty members employ their institutional power to promote their own private ideological agendas or to contravene their schools' stated missions. For instance, we report in the current edition on the University of Illinois's decision to terminate an adjunct professor who taught a class on Catholic doctrine—for accurately reporting to students the Church's rejection of same-sex "marriage." These sidebars should help students and parents select which colleges are appropriate for them.

Finally, we provide some "vital stats" that we believe help bring into focus the character of each institution. These statistics reflect the best and most up-to-date information available as we went to press. Beware: the costs of tuition and room and board often increase between press time and the following school year. Also note that the precise metrics provided by schools for some statistical categories are not always the same, especially when it comes to schools' average standardized test scores.

As Mark Twain once quipped, "There are three kinds of lies: lies, damned lies, and statistics." We agree. Statistics can be spun like sugar into almost any shape. Take the "courses taught by graduate students" question, for example. While this number (which the majority of schools are not willing to give) provides a rough idea of how much teaching assistants are being used, it is almost always deceptively low. Typically, it does not include the discussion sections attached to large lecture courses, which are usually taught by graduate teaching assistants (TAs). Nor does it accurately reflect the percentage of students taught by TAs over the course of a semester, a statistic that we have never seen reported. Not that all TAs are necessarily bad teachers. But it's important to realize that you will probably spend a lot more of your time at some schools talking to harried graduate students than to the Nobel Prize winners featured in the college viewbook.

As always, we hope that *Choosing the Right College 2012–13* will do a better job than ever of informing students, parents, grandparents, teachers, and guidance counselors about the state of higher education. We offer it with our sincere belief that it is the most incisive and compelling college guide available.

John Zmirak took his doctorate in English literature from Louisiana State University and his BA from Yale. He has worked as a journalist for twenty years at periodicals ranging from *Investor's Business Daily* to the *National Catholic Register*, and he has taught writing at LSU and Tulane University. Currently writer in residence and assistant professor of literature at the Thomas More College of Liberal Arts, Zmirak is the author of *Wilhelm Röpke: Swiss Localist, Global Economist* and, most recently, *The Bad Catholic's Guide to the Seven Deadly Sins*.

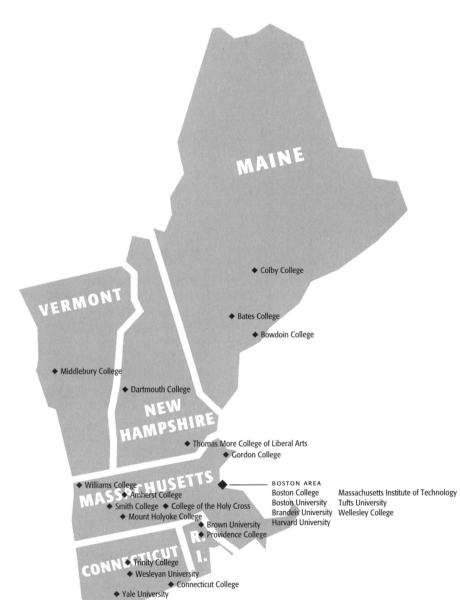

MAINE

◆ Colby College

◆ Bates College

◆ Bowdoin College

VERMONT

◆ Middlebury College

◆ Dartmouth College

NEW HAMPSHIRE

◆ Thomas More College of Liberal Arts
◆ Gordon College

◆ Williams College
MASSACHUSETTS
◆ Amherst College
◆ Smith College ◆ College of the Holy Cross
◆ Mount Holyoke College
◆ Brown University
◆ Providence College

R. I.

CONNECTICUT
◆ Trinity College
◆ Wesleyan University
◆ Connecticut College
◆ Yale University

BOSTON AREA
Boston College   Massachusetts Institute of Technology
Boston University   Tufts University
Brandeis University   Wellesley College
Harvard University

New England

Amherst College • Bates College • Boston College •
Boston University • Bowdoin College • Brandeis University •
Brown University • Colby College • Connecticut College •
Dartmouth College • Gordon College • Harvard University •
College of the Holy Cross • Massachusetts Institute of Technology •
Middlebury College • Mount Holyoke College • Providence College •
Smith College • Thomas More College of Liberal Arts •
Trinity College • Tufts University • Wellesley College •
Wesleyan University • Williams College • Yale University

Amherst College

Amherst, Massachusetts • www.amherst.edu

Self-directed studies

Founded in 1821 as a school for New England's elite, Amherst College is still one of the most prestigious liberal arts colleges in America. It is also one of the most univocally liberal. A traditional method for building men and women of character has been the discipline of a liberal arts education—including the requirement that they master core areas of knowledge essential to their own civilization, even in subject matters which lay outside their own private interests or academic strengths. This was the main purpose of the old-fashioned core curriculum, which once served as a gravitational center for education at liberal arts colleges, including Amherst.

No more. The college no longer maintains a core curriculum or even distribution requirements. Here Amherst insists that less is more: "In my view, the open curriculum is one of the strongest points because it allows students maximum freedom to explore their own interests. If somebody is interested in Western civilization, he will actually have more time to study it with the open curriculum because of the lack of core requirements in, for example, math or science," says one professor. We are not convinced. As another professor says, "The most impressive part of Amherst is the intellectual caliber of the faculty and student body. The most disappointing things about Amherst are its cultural degeneration (as shown by its 'Orgasm Workshops'), arrogance, elitism, and stifling political correctness."

Academic Life: Could I but ride indefinite

Amherst's good name was largely built on the school's onetime "New Curriculum," which required two years of basic coursework in the sciences, history, and English. But that curriculum was abolished in 1967 in favor of the current laissez-faire approach. The administration claims that its current laxity "ensures that each student in every classroom is there by choice."

Each faculty member advises only five students, meaning that students who need time and attention will get it. By sophomore year, the student selects a major area of study and an advisor within that field. This system, however, does increase the risk that a student will be "made in his liberal advisor's image," one undergrad warns. Recently, the college has made an effort to revamp pre-major advising because of many complaints. The institution has

VITAL STATISTICS

Religious affiliation: *none*

Total enrollment: *1,744*

Total undergraduates: *1,744*

SAT/ACT midranges: CR: *660–760*, M: *650–780*; ACT: *30–34*

Applicants: *7,679*

Applicants accepted: *16%*

Applicants accepted who enrolled: *38%*

Tuition and fees and room and board: *$50,820*

Freshman retention rate: *98%*

Graduation rate: *85% (4 yrs.), 94% (6 yrs.)*

Courses with fewer than 20 students: *70%*

Student-faculty ratio: *8:1*

Courses taught by graduate students: *none*

Most popular majors: *biology, economics, English*

Students living on campus: *98%*

Guaranteed housing for 4 years? *yes*

Students in fraternities or sororities: *none*

also turned toward an emphasis on writing and quantitative reasoning; absent core requirements, students had been passing through the college without sharpening such skills.

The only academic regulation that dictates a student's curriculum is within his major field of study. Most programs at Amherst require eight courses, usually built around the fundamental topics of the discipline. Yet the various majors can have acutely different requirements.

Economics majors must complete nine courses; in addition, students must pass a comprehensive examination before they can receive their degrees. Students must take three core theory classes, with a "suggested" order. At least one of the nine required courses must be an upper-level course.

English majors complete ten courses for the major, but students are completely free to choose which. Level I and II courses are primarily focused on writing. Level III and IV courses expand into film, cultural studies, literature, theoretical issues, and extensive writing. Students may also apply for a senior tutorial, an independent study program spanning one or two semesters within the major. In other words, the English department requires no coursework in the history of the language, Shakespeare, or even British or American literature. Students may instead opt for courses in film studies, creative writing, cultural studies, or gender studies. There are no senior honors courses, as there are in some other majors.

The history department requires nine courses and a concentration of four classes in either a particular geographical area, in a particular historic topic—such as colonialism or nationalism—or a comparative study of two areas. All majors are required to take a seminar involving a major research paper. Students must take a course in three of the six listed geographical regions: the U.S., Europe, Asia, Africa and Diaspora, Latin America and the Caribbean, and the Middle East. Further, students must take two courses in either pre-1800 history or pre-1800 history and comparative history. This means a history major could emerge without having studied the American founding or the Civil War.

The department of political science requires two introductory courses, distribution requirements, and a core concentration with four classes centered around a certain theme. Requirements include one course in three of the following areas: American government and politics; comparative politics; gender and politics; politics, law, and public policy; and political theory. Courses in this department are sometimes infused with teachers' personal views. "One professor referred to *Forrest Gump* as a work of Reaganite propaganda," a student reports.

Students seem to work hard at Amherst, especially if they are in the sciences. One physics major says that he and his classmates spend between four to six hours per night studying: "Although the workload is demanding, it is not usually burdensome. Most of the work is engaging and interesting."

Faculty are thick on the ground; the school enjoys an outstanding student-teacher ratio of 8 to 1, and the average Amherst class has only sixteen students. In such an environment, teacher-student interaction is, happily, inevitable.

Says one student: "The political science department is one of Amherst's best. Most of the professors in the department are both experts in their fields and very accessible. Also, for a small school, it has a wide range of courses. The philosophy department is also excellent. The professors I've had are remarkably intelligent and the small class sizes are helpful. The classics department has even smaller class sizes than philosophy and the community of students and faculty is very close-knit. I've only had one science class, but I've heard biology, chemistry, neuroscience and physics are all excellent as well."

One outstanding professor at Amherst is Hadley Arkes. "He is a great antidote to the political correctness on campus; his Colloquium for the American Founding series brings speakers to campus that would otherwise be marginalized," says a student. Other highly recommended teachers include Javier Corrales, Pavel Machala, Uday Mehta, and William Taubman in political science; Jonathan Vogel in philosophy; David Hansen in chemistry; Walter Nicholson, Frank Westhoff, and Geoffrey Woglom in economics; Allen Guttmann, William Pritchard, and David Sofield in English; Andreola Rossi and Rebecca Sinos in classics, and N. Gordon Levin in American studies and history. One student says of Levin, "He resists revisionist histories for reading and assigns noted scholars like Kissinger and Beschloss."

"About 40 percent of the school studies abroad . . . there are plenty of opportunities," a student reports. The school hosts an annual event that brings many of the overseas programs to campus so students can easily compare them. The website lists approved programs in China, Turkey, Egypt, France, Russia, Greece, India, Germany, Japan, Mali, Brazil, Spain, Italy, Tanzania, and Costa Rica, among others.

Amherst offers a limited range of language majors: Chinese and Japanese, Ancient Greek and Latin, French, German, Russian and Spanish. It does offer classes in Arabic, and many more foreign languages may be studied at Holyoke, Smith, and UMass or through the combined Five College Center for the study of World Languages. While Amherst has an

---

SUGGESTED CORE

1. European Studies 21, Readings in the European Tradition I or Classical Studies 23, Greek Civilization
2. Philosophy 17, Ancient Philosophy
3. Religion 21/22, Ancient Israel/Christian Scriptures
4. Religion 45, History of Christianity—The Early Years
5. Political Science 28, Modern Classics in Political Philosophy
6. English 35/36, Shakespeare
7. History 38, Era of the American Revolution
8. European Studies 22, The Invention of the Modern Self or Religion 49, Christianity, Philosophy, and History in the Nineteenth Century

undergraduate Italian club, Amherst College itself offers no courses in the language. Nor (despite the school's high Jewish population) does it offer classes in Hebrew.

Student Life: Industrious angels

The Amherst campus spreads over 1,000 acres. Campus facilities include the Robert Frost Library (with more than 900,000 volumes), and students have access to more than eight million books through the Five College Consortium, which combines the resources of Amherst, Hampshire College, Holyoke, Smith, and UMass. The renovated Mead Art Museum houses more than 15,000 works.

Amherst, Massachusetts, a town of 35,000 people, lies in the central part of the state, some ninety minutes west of Boston and three hours north of New York City. The town of Amherst "has a historic downtown that is well-lit, well-kept, and has a good collection of shops and restaurants," says one student. "There is not that much to do in the town, but for people interested in going to college in the country, yet who do not want to be cut off from the world, Amherst is a pretty good compromise." A bus system provides regular free transportation among the surrounding towns.

The tree-lined Freshman Quad, dominated on one end by Johnson Chapel and including several dormitories, forms the heart of the campus, which is pervaded by a peaceful college atmosphere. Stearns Church, built in 1873, once served as the campus chapel, but it was torn down in 1948 to "make room" for a modern arts building and was replaced with the college's present chapel. Today only the steeple of Stearns Church survives, and it dominates the school's skyline.

Some 98 percent of Amherst students live in the thirty-seven dorms on campus; the administration strongly discourages off-campus living, which requires special permission. All freshmen must live on campus, and are housed together. Housing is decided by a lottery system, using class-based rankings, and is guaranteed for four years. Three dorms have been dubbed "quiet, studying" dorms, and one dorm has been dubbed the "thesis-writing" dorm. Dorms are all coed and bathrooms are usually shared by floor, unless one has a suite.

Amherst offers students a choice of thirty-seven residential housing options. While all buildings are coed, some dorms do offer single-sex floors. On coed floors with only one bathroom, students vote on whether the bathroom will also be coed (most vote in favor). Out of deference to radical mores, members of opposite sexes are allowed to share rooms at

ACADEMIC REQUIREMENTS

According to Amherst's "Open" (i.e., empty) Curriculum, the First-Year Seminar is the only requirement students must satisfy outside the mandates of their majors. For the First-Year Seminar, students may choose from a wide variety of topics, including "Growing Up in America," "Reading Gender," and "Eros and Insight." A writing requirement is likely to be added but it may be incorporated into this seminar.

Amherst. Some space is also allocated for "theme housing" in which like-minded students live together to explore a foreign language, black culture, or health and wellness.

Students do not have the option of living in a fraternity or sorority house, since the college prohibits the Greek system on campus. This policy, however, has not discouraged students from exploring their inner Bacchus. Amherst's students are hardly shy when it comes to partying. "Dorm life can be summarized as follows: drinking, drinking, and more drinking. Residential counselors are pretty inactive. The only real function they serve in non-freshman dorms is to bill students for dorm damage," says one student. Theme parties—such as one called "Pimps and Hos"—are well known for sexual abandon. These parties, which one student describes as "meat markets," are organized by the student-run Social Committee. Amherst College also sponsors a weekly alcohol-free shindig called The Amherst Party (TAP for short), which is usually well attended.

There are some 140 student organizations on campus, the largest are the *Amherst Student* (the weekly student newspaper), Amherst Student Government, Amherst College Outing Club, Amherst College Diversity Coalition, and numerous musical groups. "I'd lived in a musical wasteland for eighteen years. The popularity of *a cappella* singing, guitar, and music in general at Amherst had a direct influence on me. I picked up the guitar my first year of college and began to take music theory classes," says one enthusiastic student. The school also has a radio station, WAMH. The college hosts the Breakdance Club, Asian Students Association, Much Ado About Knitting, Ping Pong Club, Political Union, Relay for Life, Cricket Club, Dance Club, English Traditions Club, and Students for a Free Tibet, to name a few. Not surprisingly, the ACLU, Feminist Alliance, Pride and Color for GLBTQREM (Gay, Lesbian, Bisexual, Transgendered, Queer, Racial and Ethnic Minorities), and the Amherst College Democrats are thriving, but there is not a single Republican group or politically conservative organization on campus.

As a whole, the students at Amherst are not very politically active. While there are speakers, lectures, and debates, students at Amherst have a reputation for placing their interests elsewhere. Still, the culture on campus is very liberal, and, as with everywhere else, the LBGTQ group is trying very hard to make the college a welcoming place for peoples with varying "sexual orientations."

The school boasts the oldest collegiate athletic program in the nation. In the first intercollegiate baseball game in history (1859), Amherst defeated Williams. Amherst offers twenty-seven Division III sports programs. Amherst came first in the 2010 National Collegiate Scouting Association Power Rankings for academic and athletic performance. The college is a member of the New England Small College Athletic Conference with ten other schools, including Bowdoin College and Tufts University. Some 32 percent of Amherst students participate in varsity sports and more than 80 percent take part in club and intramural sports. Named after Lord Jeffrey Amherst, the teams' mascot is "Lord Jeff," and Amherst teams are called the Jeffs. Since the Sears Cup—a measure of overall athletic success—has been keeping track of Division III programs, Amherst has never finished lower than twelfth in the nation. The Amherst-Williams football game is one of the college's most valued and long-standing traditions.

About 40 percent of the students in the Amherst class of 2013 identify themselves as "students of color." Currently, Amherst is evenly divided between male and female stu-

RED LIGHT

The dominant political ideology at Amherst is evident in the classroom and in every department, although bias varies by class and professor. Reports one student: "Many courses in English and history are hotbeds of postcolonialism, feminism, cultural relativism, revisionist history and other postmodern fads, though there are certain gem courses that can be found in each department. My worst experience at Amherst was with an American studies professor. In the course of a semester-long freshman seminar, rather than reading Plato and Locke to discuss eternal questions as addressed in legendary works, we learned about 'growing up in America.' Over these three months, we discussed racial identity (after which the professor concluded that Clarence Thomas was 'denying his blackness'), heard that guns were destroying America, and read a book titled *Ain't No Makin' It in a Low Income Neighborhood*. The thesis of the book is that hard work is futile for low-income minorities."

Amherst has a thriving and highly visible Democratic club but the school's Republican population is miniscule. At one point there was an alternative, conservative newspaper, the *Spectator*, but it has since gone defunct. The school sponsors an annual production of *The Vagina Monologues* and has eleven "activism" clubs such as the Feminist Alliance and the (gay) Pride Alliance. If there are any conservative groups or publications on campus, they must be operating in secret, since none of our sources were aware of them.

dents—no mean feat these days, when men are becoming ever scarcer on college campuses. Students in the class of 2013 hail from thirty-nine states, plus D.C., Puerto Rico, Guam, and twenty-three foreign countries.

A large part of the student body is Jewish and the campus has an active (and activist) Hillel group. "Each Friday, we hold our weekly Shabbat evening, which features a prayer service and home-cooked Kosher dinner," says a student. A Newman Club and a Christian Fellowship exist on campus; the latter is a chapter of InterVarsity Fellowship and holds weekly meetings. Down the street at UMASS–Amherst is a large and lively Newman Center for Catholic students.

The crime figures for Amherst are unremarkable. The most common form of crime on campus is burglary—specifically the theft of college property, a typical problem for college dorms. There were seven forcible sex offenses, four aggravated assaults, one count of arson and twenty-one burglaries on campus in 2009. All Amherst residential halls are secured with digital combination locks. One student says that although overall the campus is safe, certain areas of Amherst are "not completely desirable." For instance, the University of Massachusetts' Frat Row, right down the street from the college, is not a safe place for walking alone at night.

Amherst is pricey; during the 2010–11 school year, it estimated a comprehensive fee (including room and board) of $50,820. However, the school practices need-blind admissions, and provides aid to 53 percent of students, meeting the need of most admitted students. Recently, because of the financial aid, the school says that students are graduating with *less* debt than in the past—although it does not provide the numbers to prove this.

Bates College

Lewiston, Maine • www.bates.edu

Educating liberals

Bates College sits on 109 acres, thirty-five miles north of Portland, Maine. The first racially integrated, coeducational institution in the East, Bates College was founded by abolitionists just before the Civil War. While it carries on a tradition of academic excellence and is known for a tolerant atmosphere, the school has also adopted the lax curriculum and pervasive leftist politics that characterize most other colleges in the Northeast. However, thanks to intense student-faculty interaction and classmates who truly enjoy learning, a Bates student can receive a sound liberal education—if he knows where to look. Given the school's location, he'll also have the chance to ski, snowboard, hike, and commune with nature in a beautiful, bucolic region, at a school with a close-knit, supportive community. The typical Bates student seems more concerned with acquiring a thorough education than with life after school. As one student says, "Most people enjoy college now and think about a career later."

Academic Life: Short term and long term

Above all else, Bates prides itself on its academics and the quality of its professors. With a student body of around 1,700, Bates has all the advantages of a small, teaching-centered institution. The college has only ten students for every faculty member, and the average class size is a comfortable fourteen students. Even the largest lecture halls are intimate enough to encourage questions from students. With no graduate programs, there are no teaching assistants leading undergraduate courses. Professors devote almost all of their attention to teaching and most are quite accessible to their students. Even faculty members in the sciences put students as their highest priority; the research they conduct complements coursework and is rarely at the expense of students.

Like most other liberal arts colleges, Bates has long since given up on requiring its students to acquire "core" knowledge by taking a closely defined series of courses in Western culture, literature, and history. The general education requirements imposed by the school are lax. Nevertheless, most of the classes offered at Bates are academically solid, and students are known for an intellectual curiosity that drives many of them to study widely in fields outside their majors. Students have a vast array of courses from which to choose;

indeed, both students and administrators are proud of the curriculum's "flexibility." But Bates students can graduate without ever having taken a course in philosophy, English, history, or a foreign language—and that's more freedom than anybody needs.

A recently added feature of the Bates curriculum requires that students choose two four-course concentrations in addition to their majors. A "concentration" can be in a particular topic that spans various academic disciplines, or it can simply be four courses chosen from one academic department.

Currently, one of the features of Bates academic life is a short term in May. During this term, most students take one intense course, four days a week, for five weeks. This short term is quite popular, and offers a wide variety of offbeat, worthy courses. According to the school, "Recent off-campus Short Term units have focused on the study of Shakespearean drama and Renaissance culture in England; landscape painting and art history in Italy; [and] anthropological study in Bali." The short term also gives students the chance for internships in museums, hospitals, schools, newspapers, or state and federal government.

Bates is particularly strong in the sciences, and even the brightest students majoring in math, chemistry, biology, or physics feel challenged. A chemistry major says that when she tells people her course of study, their "first reaction is to cringe." The Bates science program has distinguished itself from those at other small liberal arts colleges in New England, and brings in millions of dollars in research grants.

Unfortunately, these monies have not been enough to keep the college out of financial difficulties. For a variety of historical reasons, Bates's endowment is far smaller than those of comparable institutions in the region. In 2006, Bates completed a major fundraising campaign that raised $121 million for the school, bringing it more in line with peer institutions. However, its endowment fell substantially after the stock market collapse of 2008, and as of September 2010 it stood at just $183 million, which is much lower than Middlebury's $815 million, Bowdoin's $753 million, and Colby's $500 million.

One of the virtues that Bates hopes will attract generous donors is its fine reputation for teaching. Strong departments include English, history, political science, psychology, and those in the hard sciences. Students praise Sanford Freedman for his Shakespeare class: "He requires students to read fast but carefully, really scrutinizing the texts," says one.

New England

The philosophy course includes a goodly number of serious offerings, including "Contemporary Moral Disputes," "Philosophy of Law," and "Moral Philosophy" with David Cummiskey. Says a student, "Students pore over Supreme Court writings and philosophical commentary to work their way through the principles of law. They read Aristotle, Locke, Mill, Hobbes, and Hume."

Students also praise courses in history, politics, and economics. Medievalist Michael Jones is called "an amazing lecturer," while historian John Cole "is good-humored and very tolerant." Bill Corlett is a political science teacher of the Marxist persuasion, whom students recommend as an open-minded teacher who enjoys intellectual interchange with conservatives. Students also laud math professor Pallavi Jayawant, who reportedly "finds a way to make every student 'get it.' She is always willing to help, and easy to reach." Another beloved professor is Mark Okrent, a veteran of the philosophy department, known for "enthusiasm and teaching classes very clearly." John Corrie, known as "the most enthusiastic professor on campus," delights in teaching music and conducting the choir. Heidi Chirayath, professor of sociology, wins praise for being open-minded to many points of view, and shows that she "will stick up for students whose ideas put them in the minority."

Other excellent professors include Jen Koviach-Cóté in chemistry; Amy Bradfield Douglass and Todd Kahan in psychology; Stephanie Richards in biology; Dolores O'Higgins in classical and medieval studies; Stephanie Kelley-Romano in rhetoric; and Paul Kuritz in theater.

Some "fluff" classes can be found in the disciplines of religion and women and gender studies—such as "The Decorated Body," a course that focuses "attention to the body as gendered and raced . . . [and] the ways that the body has been adorned and manipulated as an artistic medium through practices including painting, scarification, surgical manipulation, tattooing, piercing, branding, and hair adornment." The anthropology department is said to be quite hostile toward conservative viewpoints.

Bates requires of students a senior thesis. Seniors spend their final semester, and sometimes an entire year, working on the thesis, either conducting new research or preparing for a performance. As one student told the school newspaper, "It gave my major a real meaning. It was a nice finale to my Bates education." For many students, completing such an impressive academic project as undergraduates makes the prospect of graduate school less intimidating.

SUGGESTED CORE

1. History 106/108, Greek Civilization/Roman Civilization
2. Classical and Medieval Studies 271, Ancient Greek Philosophy
3. Religious Studies 235/236, Ancient Israel: History, Religion, and Literature/Introduction to the New Testament
4. Religious Studies 242, History of Christian Thought II: The Emergence of Modernity
5. Politics 191, Western Political Theory or Philosophy 272, Philosophy from Descartes to Kant
6. English 213/214, Shakespeare
7. History 140/141, Origins of the New Nation, 1500-1820/America in the Age of Civil War
8. Philosophy 273, Philosophy in the Nineteenth Century

New England

The English department requires its majors to take eleven courses in the subject with at least three covering literature composed before 1800. However many of the department's offerings sound depressingly recondite—such as "Constructing Sexuality in the Enlightenment," which warns that it relies "largely on the work of Michel Foucault." Similarly, "Sexuality in Victorian Literature" also cites "Michel Foucault [who] argued that the Victorians were far from silent on the topic of sexuality. . . ." Another class, "Shakespeare: Race and Gender," looks at how the author sought "to both question the status quo and to racialize existing power structures." Simply put, a Bates English grad need not read Shakespeare, Chaucer, or Milton, but if he does, it will likely be through a jaundiced lens.

The history major requires nine courses offered by the department. All majors must first take a "short course" in historical methods, two classes in the history of East Asia or Latin America, one introductory survey class, five classes in a "concentration area," and a senior thesis. The possible concentration areas are: East Asia, Latin America, Europe, the United States and premodern history. So a Bates history major could graduate without taking a single class on U.S. or European history. In the politics major, a student must take eleven courses, including five in a concentration area. He must also complete a senior essay. There is no course required on the American political system or Constitution.

Professors are well-integrated into the Bates community, and it is not uncommon for a student to have dinner with a professor or to become a personal friend of his family. "I was on a first-name basis with all my professors and got to know them well," a foreign language major says. Students report that advisors are helpful; one student says hers "provided not only academic advice, but also advice on my future decisions and other interests in my life that weren't necessarily academic." Independent study courses are quite popular, and students often work closely with professors either to explore a subject not offered in a traditional course or to perform new research.

ACADEMIC REQUIREMENTS

On top of the demands of a major, Bates students must meet the following quite lax, general-education requirements:

- One first-year seminar. Topics for 2010–11 included "Genealogy and the Art of Inquiry" and "Addictions, Obsessions, Manias."
- Two four-course concentrations, each focusing on a particular issue or topic. Choices include "The Ancient World," "Considering Africa," "Identity, Race, and Ethnicity," or "Water and Society," or any grouping of four courses in an academic department like philosophy or chemistry.
- Three classes listed as "writing-attentive." Examples include "Love and Friendship in the Classical World," and *The Lord of the Rings* in Context."
- Three courses requiring scientific reasoning, lab experience, or quantitative literacy. Choices include "The Milky Way Galaxy," "Great Ideas in Mathematics," and "Organismal Biology."

Bates offers programs for those studying Chinese, French, German, Ancient Greek, Latin, Japanese, Russian, and Spanish. Study abroad is extraordinarily popular: 70 percent of the student body goes abroad, usually during the junior year. The college sponsors a fall semester program in St. Petersburg, Russia, but Bates students travel all over the world for off-campus study, since the college allows students to avail themselves of a host of other international options sponsored by other colleges.

Student Life: Outing club

Bates College is the lone intellectual hotspot in the working class New England mill town of Lewiston, Maine. The campus is the undisputed center of student life. The college guarantees housing for all four years and requires students to live on campus, except by special permission.

Bates's dining halls are known for good food; students enjoy "Adventures in Dining," where the friendly staff get dressed up for events like "Sushi Night." This was buttressed in 2008 by a gift of $2.5 million to establish an endowment that would help "buy and serve more local, organic, and natural food," according to the *Chronicle of Higher Education*. That means that in the Bates cafeteria you'll find bagels with organic spelt flour from a Maine bakery and grass-fed ground beef from a Maine ranch—which is all to the good. Attractive new residence halls opened in September 2007 and look like hotels compared to the older dorms, which still have old-fashioned faucets—separate for hot and cold—in the bathrooms. "The dorms are so old and quaint—it's like going back in time," marvels one resident.

Outside of the classroom, most students participate in club and varsity sports; many engage in performing arts; and almost all take part in one of more than 110 student-run clubs or organizations. About 40 percent of students take on career internships, and more than two-thirds of recent graduates enroll in graduate study within ten years of graduation. The Bates Museum of Art specializes in Maine artists, but in April and May, studio art majors showcase their works there. The annual Gala is a college-wide formal featuring a live orchestra or band. Bates brings in a number of lecturers each year, although, one student complains, these aren't often conservative speakers.

Most of the dormitories are coed, but some have single-sex floors. Bates does not offer coed dorm rooms, but in some coed suites, students of opposite sexes might share a common bathroom. Students have to ask for suites, so no student will be forced to use a coed bathroom. Students also have an alcohol-free living option, and designated quiet houses and halls. Freshmen all live together in doubles, triples, or quads, with every fifteen or so students matched with a junior advisor. Some of these advisors are now complaining about their jobs. Says one, "I serve as a residence life staff member, and I am paid to ensure that students are safe and most importantly (from the college's perspective) politically correct. [We] go through hours of training in dealing with the many situations that arise in dorm life, but most training focuses on dealing with racist/biased speech and messages that may make different people uncomfortable for any reason."

Everything at Bates emphasizes the school's close-knit community atmosphere. Says a student: "The best aspect of Bates is that there are lots of different kinds of intelligent people.

YELLOW LIGHT

The Bates Republican Club is much more active on campus than it used to be, sponsoring conferences and speakers like former Pennsylvania Senator Rick Santorum, who was invited in March 2011 to speak on the threat of radical Islam. Back in 2005, the club helped to pass an Academic Bill of Rights, which declared that political and religious beliefs should not be singled out for ridicule, that students should not be forced to express a certain point of view in assignments, and that university funds should not be used for one-sided conferences. Contrarily, Bates incorporated a "Pledge of Social Responsibility" into its 2010 graduation ceremony, in which all soon-to-be graduates stand up and recite, "I, [student's name], pledge to explore and take into account the social and environmental consequences of any job I consider and will try to improve these aspects of any organizations for which I work."

Bates students of all political persuasions agree that the campus leans decidedly to the left. As one student says, "Bates is definitely left-leaning, and that is putting it mildly. But most teachers conduct classes with a fairly high level of political balance." Faculty have even been known to inject political opinions into seemingly harmless classes like "Cellular and Molecular Biology" and to have anti-Republican posters on office doors. On issues of religion, a student says, "Very few professors openly talk about their faith, but many are glad to talk about their lack of it."

They really expanded my beliefs." Life at Bates is said to revolve around the residences, the site of most cerebration and celebration alike. The close college community becomes even closer on typical weekend nights, when many students resort to tippling. Says one dorm resident, "Security is very lax about drinking beer, though a recent effort has been made to eliminate all hard alcohol from the premises." The school is applying increasing pressure to diminish alcohol consumption; one tactic tried was to have a "guilty by association" policy, whereby students in the same room with anyone possessing hard alcohol were subject to the same penalties as their host.

Opportunities for students to express their political views are available in the Democrat and Republican clubs. Both groups like to liven things up by bringing provocative speakers to the school, although recent activity has focused on the heated 2010 midterm elections rather than on philosophical debates. Other popular clubs include the Indigenous Student Network, which pushes radical social reforms. Overall, students are tolerant of differing views, and vocally biased professors are in the minority. One conservative student insists, "If you can back your view up with empirical evidence, it will be accepted." Elaine Tuttle Hansen, the college president, is known by students as "a decent and thoughtful person, without the agenda the college leftists might have hoped she would have."

Of course, you'd be a fool to spend four years in Maine and neglect the great outdoors. The Bates Outing Club is the most popular extracurricular organization; in fact, students are automatically registered as members when they arrive on campus. The club allows students to borrow backpacks, bikes, and tents at no cost, and it sponsors outings to the beach, mountains, and Maine ski resorts several times each semester. The shooting club is also a favorite, along with a sailing club. Both men's and women's hockey are very popular, attracting many fans while enjoying success in their respective divisions. The annual Lobster Bake is a huge feast at the beach, with all-you-can-eat lobster and clams. Student organizations sometimes sponsor trips to Portland and Freeport, the latter town a bargain shopper's paradise.

Bates is a very athletic campus, with around 60 percent of the student body participating in intramural sports. One-third of Bates students are varsity members of one of the Bobcats' thirty intercollegiate teams, which compete in the New England Small College Athletic Conference (NESCAC) against teams such as Amherst, Bowdoin, Colby and Tufts. Bates has excellent athletic facilities for a school of its size, including an indoor track and an ice arena.

Religion isn't a major priority for Bates students—most would prefer to study or ski. But as one student says, "For people willing to search, there are many opportunities to express one's faith." Despite this, many students choose to attend services off campus. The school's head chaplain, William Blaine-Wallace, who impresses students with his "enthusiasm and friendly spirit," was one of the first Episcopalian clergy to officiate in same-sex marriages in Boston. Bates Christian Fellowship holds Bible studies and prayer services each week. The school also hosts Hillel and a Catholic Student Community Center. Traditionally oriented Catholic students might wish to check out the Latin Mass offered at Lewiston's gorgeous Basilica of Saints Peter and Paul.

Lewiston is a tough town for the college. At one point, Bates College was surrounded by razor wire to keep out undesirable Lewistonians. The school's previous president tore down the fences to promote better college-community interaction. This may or may not have worked; excessive student drinking causes friction with unfriendly townfolk, and in May 2010, a call to the police for aid to a drunken student resulted in a fight between students and the police, in which an officer's leg was broken. Still, violence inflicted by or upon students is very rare; in 2009, Bates reported fourteen burglaries but no other crimes on campus.

Thanks in part to its small endowment, Bates has been forced to raise its fees each year. Bates does not list a separate cost for tuition, room, and board, but its comprehensive fee in 2010–11 came to a whopping $53,300. One student reports that "financial aid at Bates is very fair. It was my reason for attending the college, and the aid they gave is almost entirely composed of grants." Forty-five percent of students receive need-based aid, and the average student-loan debt of a recent graduate is a moderate $17,945.

Boston College

Chestnut Hill, Massachusetts • www.bc.edu

Jesuit brahmin

Boston College, founded by the Jesuits in 1863, has seen its profile rise in the last decade. *Newsweek* placed the school first in its list of "Twenty-Five New Ivies." Boston College's mission has "evolved beyond the local and regional—it has even moved past the national," claims college president William Leahy, S.J. During the past decade, under Rev. Leahy's leadership, the school has focused on the fundamentals of liberal education; slowly but steadily rededicated itself to the school's Catholic identity; added endowed chairs and professorships; made its admissions much more selective; built a top athletics program; increased the emphasis on research; and acquired large new parcels of desirable real estate. For ambitious students eager to attend an elite college with an ongoing faith tradition in a historic American city, BC might be the answer to their prayers.

Academic Life: Four years BC

Boston College is widely known for fostering first-rate classroom discussions, and close relationships between teachers and students. "Professors here have teaching as their prime motivating factor," a student says. "Very few are here for just research and publishing. Faculty members jump at the chance to interact with students."

For an institution of its size, BC does a decent job of ensuring that every undergraduate receives some exposure to the great texts of our culture. One professor points to the Jesuits on campus as the reason for this emphasis. He tells us, "The Jesuit presence on the campus, while smaller than in the past, continues to influence the way in which the 'great questions' are introduced and discussed, and there is clearly a sense that the purpose of a university is to shape the character of students by encouraging the discussion of serious things by serious people." Trendy or ideological courses are far outnumbered by solid, traditional classes. Opportunities for an excellent undergraduate experience abound at BC for the student who knows where to look.

Perhaps the worthiest academic option at BC is its Honors Program, which invites no more than 140 students to participate each year. Freshmen and sophomores in the program take a six-credit course titled "The Western Cultural Tradition." Reading only primary texts, students in this course begin with ancient Greek literature and philosophy, continue through the works of the Roman Empire, early Christianity, the Middle Ages, and the Renaissance, and end with major cultural, historical, and philosophical works of modernity. As juniors, students take an advanced seminar called "The Twentieth Century and the Tradition." The first semester of this course explores modernism, and the second semester covers postmodernism. Here students work their way through "Marxism, psychoanalysis, comparative anthropology, structuralism, poststructuralism, feminism, and the third-world critique of Eurocentric culture," according to the course description. Seniors in the Honors program end their BC years by writing a senior thesis or by participating in an integrative seminar, in which they study more deeply the texts they have encountered earlier in their college years.

The College of Arts and Sciences offers the Perspectives program, a four-year, interdisciplinary program "grounded in the great texts of Western Culture that seeks to integrate the humanities and natural sciences." All four Perspectives courses are year-long, double credit, with an evening class component, and each fulfills certain core requirements: "Perspectives on Western Culture," "Modernism and the Arts," "Horizon of the New Social Sciences," and "New Scientific Visions." In "New Scientific Visions," students explore major developments in the fields of mathematics, biology, physics, chemistry, and the earth and space sciences from ancient Greece "up through quantum mechanics, and contemporary cosmologies." Students in "Perspectives on Western Culture" will be introduced to the "Judeo-Biblical texts and to the writings of such foundational thinkers as Plato, Aristotle, Augustine, Aquinas, Luther, Bacon, Descartes, Hobbes, Locke, Kant, Hegel, and Kierkegaard." The first semester "considers the birth of the self-critical Greek philosophic spirit, the story of the people of Israel, the emergence of Christianity and Islam, and concludes with a consideration of medieval exploration of the relationship between faith and reason. This program also pays attention to non-Western philosophical and theological sources." One faculty member says the Perspectives program is a popular way for students to fulfill their core requirements.

The Boston College Core also includes a two-term survey of modern history, a two-course sequence in theology, and a math course. Moreover, undergraduates must also demonstrate proficiency in a foreign language.

PULSE, a program run by the philosophy department, operates in a similar manner to Perspectives, using some of the same texts, but it focuses more on ethics and politics.

VITAL STATISTICS

Religious affiliation: *Roman Catholic*

Total enrollment: *14,720*

Total undergraduates: *9,100*

SAT/ACT midranges: CR: *610–700*, M: *640–730*; ACT: *29–32*

Applicants: *29,932*

Applicants accepted: *31%*

Applicants accepted who enrolled: *25%*

Tuition and fees: *$40,542*

Room and Board: *$12,082*

Freshman retention rate: *93%*

Graduation rate: *88% (4 yrs.), 91% (6 yrs.)*

Courses with fewer than 20 students: *48%*

Student-faculty ratio: *13:1*

Courses taught by graduate students: *not provided*

Most popular majors: *finance, communications, economics*

Students living on campus: *80%*

Guaranteed housing for 4 years? *no*

Students in fraternities or sororities: *none*

This service-oriented program, established in 1969, represents a serious effort to combine philosophical learning with social service or advocacy. Some courses offered here include "Values in Social Service and Health Care," "Boston: An Urban Analysis," "Writing for the Cause of Justice," and "Philosophy of Community" I and II. Along with the course work, students in the program are placed with a service organization within the Boston community, where they work throughout the year.

Some of the strongest departments at BC are in the traditional liberal arts disciplines, such as philosophy. That department offers a broad selection of courses in Western thought, along with several courses covering topics such as ancient Chinese philosophy—an academically worthy way to satisfy the school's cultural diversity requirement. The university's Catholic heritage is central in the philosophy program, perhaps even more so than in the theology department. "Philosophy takes its Catholic character seriously," says one professor, "and this informs its hiring and its course offerings," such as courses in Catholic apologetics. Noteworthy faculty members include Richard Cobb-Stevens, Joseph Flanagan S.J., Jorge Garcia, Gary Gurtler S.J., Richard Kearney, Peter Kreeft, and Ronald Tacelli S.J.

Another outstanding department at BC is political science, where, according to one professor, students will find "a seriousness about the study of politics in its broader theoretical and historical context, and a very strong commitment to undergraduate and graduate teaching." The departments requirements are solid, including courses in American politics, comparative politics, international politics, and political theory. The department is proud of its heavy work load and emphasizes the importance of good writing. Distinguished teachers here include Nasser Behnegar, Christopher Bruell, Robert Faulkner, Christopher Kelly, Marc Landy, R. Shep Melnick, Susan Shell, Peter Skerry, and widely read liberal commentator Alan Wolfe. In 2008, the Gloria and Charles Clough Center for the Study of Constitutional Democracy, began sponsoring speakers, colloquia, and an undergraduate journal (among other projects), dedicated to the study of the principles and practice of constitutional democracy in the U.S. and abroad.

The English department has broad, detailed requirements. The department's requirements for its majors include a freshmen writing course, a class in poetry, one course in pre-1700 English literature, one in pre-1900 literature, and twelve courses total. However, it is possible that one might get through this program with only a passing acquaintance with Chaucer and Shakespeare.

The history department wisely requires of its majors a two-term survey course in American history, plus one four-credit class in historiography and seven more elective courses of which two must be in non-Western history and four in upper-division classes.

Students report that BC's theology department is disappointing, in part because "it has placed a lot of emphasis on interreligious dialogue," says a former student familiar with the program. Expect plenty of courses like "Liberation Christology" and "Women and the Church." As part of the BC curriculum, all undergraduates are required to complete a two-semester sequence in the theology department. The six sequences students can choose from

New England

are "Biblical Heritage," "Introduction to Christian Theology," "Exploring Catholicism: Tradition and Transformation," and "Religious Quest: Comparative Perspectives," "Person and Social Responsibility," and "Perspectives on Western Culture." Class sizes for these courses are small because they are usually taught by PhD students in their final year of study. Students have expressed disapproval of the direction some course sections have taken. One student in the "Biblical Heritage" sequence said the lecturer tried to shake his faith; however, as a conservative graduate student put it, "Many first year students haven't ever been exposed to biblical scholarship and they don't quite know what to do with it yet." One bonus for theology students is BC's membership in the Boston Theological Institute, which allows advanced students to take classes at Harvard Divinity School, the Weston Jesuit School of Theology, the Holy Cross Greek Orthodox School of Theology, and other schools. BC merged with Weston beginning with the 2008–9 academic year, pooling resources and making the library one of the best theological resources in the country. Students taking theology at BC should seek out Stephen F. Brown, David Hollenbach S.J., Frederick Lawrence, John J. Paris S.J., Margaret A. Schatkin, and Thomas E. Wangler, our sources report.

Other highly recommended faculty across the college include Michael J. Connolly in Slavic and Eastern languages, Thomas Epstein in the honors program, Thomas C. Chiles in biology, Michael Barry in finance, and Avner Ash, Gerard E. Keough (Emeritus), and Mark Reeder in mathematics.

ACADEMIC REQUIREMENTS

Every student enrolled in one of the five BC colleges serving undergraduates must complete what is called the University Core, which is really a set of distribution requirements:

- One course in the arts from the fine arts, music, or theater departments; both "Art and Myth in Ancient Greece" and "Dramatic Structure and Theatrical Process" count.
- Two courses in philosophy. Students select one of two tracks: Philosophy of the Person or Philosophy of Human Existence.
- A two-course sequence in theology.
- One course in literature, chosen from the classics, English, German studies, Romance languages, or Slavic and Eastern language departments. Options range from the English course, "Love, Sexuality & Gender" to the classics course "Heroic Verse: Homer, Virgil, and Beyond."
- "Modern History" I and II.
- One course in cultural diversity, with choices ranging from "Race, Class & Gender" to music course "Native North American Song."
- One course in mathematics.
- Two courses in natural science (biology, chemistry, geology-geophysics, or physics).
- Two courses in social science, chosen from the economics, political science, psychology, psychology in education, or sociology departments. A course like "Microeconomics" qualifies, as does "Love, Intimacy, and Human Sexuality."
- One course in writing.

New England

Overall, besides philosophy and political science, the school's strongest disciplines are economics, biology, chemistry, physics, and history. One professor says the English department is generally solid, but with "significant weaknesses." The finance department also has a fine reputation; the associate dean of the school of management told the *Boston College Chronicle* that the rising number of finance majors "is the fruit of a 'virtuous circle' of renowned faculty raising the stature of a department from which employers want to pluck talented graduates." The natural science departments have grown stronger in recent years, and the university offers plenty of opportunities to do real and worthy research in laboratory environments.

Weaker departments, students report, include education and sociology. The latter, says one student, "is at the center of leftist activism on campus, and should be avoided." The description for one sociology course, "Gender and Society," promises to "examine gender primarily as a social and structural construct." Another student describes courses on "child development, gender, et cetera" at the education school as "watered-down and liberal."

As for politics in the classroom, apart from the cultural diversity requirement, BC offers some interdisciplinary minors such as "faith, peace, and justice," African and African diaspora studies, and women's studies. History students are also free to waste their time in courses like "Introduction to Feminisms."

"Professors are quite approachable," says a student. The school's collegiality and good student-teacher ratio of 13 to 1 make possible close student-faculty relationships. The advising program has recently been improved, encouraging this close interaction even more. Before entering Boston College each student is paired with a faculty member who advises him, then once he declares a major, he gets a professor within the chosen department.

Over the past decade or two, Boston College has grown to become a serious research university, and as one faculty member tells us, "This has placed inevitable strains on the perennial conflict between research and teaching." He explains, "Excellence in teaching is expected. Nonetheless, hiring and promotion decisions continue to emphasize the publication of books, or the equivalent, and faculty are always aware of the competing demands on their time."

Among the languages offered at BC are Arabic, Bulgarian, Chinese, French, German, Ancient Greek, Hebrew, Italian, Japanese, Latin, Spanish, Polish, Portuguese, Russian, and Turkish. Students can elect majors in French, German, classics, Italian, Spanish, and Russian. Around 40 percent of BC undergraduates travel abroad in one of the sixty-six academic partnerships in any of twenty-seven countries. In 2010, fourteen Fulbright fellowships were awarded to students and to recent graduates of Boston College for a year of postgraduate study abroad.

Student Life: View from the Heights

As one of the most culturally rich cities in the nation, Boston offers splendid opportunities for the thousands of students attending more than eighty colleges in the area. From the 117-acre main Boston College campus in the affluent suburb of Chestnut Hill, it is a thirty-minute trolley ride to downtown Boston. The Chestnut Hill main campus, with its large Gothic-style buildings, is described as "very Cambridge-like." The Lower Campus has the theater, some residence halls for upperclassmen, the football stadium, athletic buildings, and a dining hall. The Middle Campus, the current academic heart of BC, includes the main library, most classroom buildings, and the student union. Upper Campus has most of the underclassmen residence halls.

At BC, there are living arrangements to accommodate the needs of nearly every undergraduate and to guarantee at least three years of on-campus housing. The school offers thirty-one dormitories, with freshmen housed on the school's Newton Campus (a one-and-a-half-mile bus ride from the main campus) or the Upper Campus. Eighty percent of undergraduates live in university housing. Opportunities for special-interest housing in 2010–11 included the 66 Honors House and the Gabelli Honors House, as well as the Healthy Alternatives Lifestyle floor, and the Romance Language floor. Residence halls separate men and women by floor. There are no single-sex dorms available, and while the housing office says that members of the opposite sex cannot stay in residence halls overnight, that rule is not strictly enforced.

The college's proximity to many other Boston-area colleges makes student-oriented activities readily available to BC undergrads. Popular are parties held by juniors and seniors at off-campus apartments and gatherings at Boston bars. Strong drink is readily available and joyously consumed at BC, but the administration has been cracking down on alcohol abuse, making it harder for underage students to obtain alcohol. For the most part, BC undergrads "are intellectually focused and serious about their studies," says one student. "At the same time, studies do not dominate their lives; they know how to let loose and have an active social life."

Among about 225 registered undergraduate student organizations at BC, students should have no trouble finding clubs to fit their interests. Besides multicultural groups, there are the typical political organizations, sports clubs, and professional societies, including the Economics Association and the Bellarmine Pre-Law Council. BC has no social fraternities or sororities. Student news publications include the twice-weekly *Heights* and the biweekly *Observer,* which defends Catholic orthodoxy and conservative principles on campus. BC has a vibrant music and arts scene, featuring jazz, classical, *a cappella*, folk, gospel, and swing on campus. The school's annual spring arts festival has become a showcase for hundreds of BC community musicians, writers, and visual and performing artists.

In 2010, as in years past, the student government promoted on-campus events for National Coming Out Week. The campus gay, lesbian, and bisexual group is not sanctioned by the administration—unlike Allies, a campus "gay-straight alliance." Allies claims to be a "support and education" group, not an advocacy group. BC's student guide was recently revised to state that any event featuring a speaker opposed to Catholic doctrine must be balanced by a speaker advocating such a doctrine. The changes came after uncertainties in the previous policy contributed to controversies—particularly the sponsorship of events by the Women's Health Initiative, an unrecognized new student group that advocates abortion on demand. "What we're trying to do is have clear guidelines and reminders that this is a Catholic and Jesuit University," the dean for student development told the *Heights.*

Major speakers chosen by the administration to address the campus have run the gamut politically. Boston College is not as uniformly liberal as most big-name colleges are

GREEN LIGHT

Boston College is one of the Jesuit colleges that has long been vexed by secularizers and heretics, but unlike most of its peer institutions, it is moving in the right direction—slowly but inexorably, with the clear support of the current administration. For instance, BC returned crucifixes and other Catholic images to its classrooms after decades of their absence. (They were taken down under the excuse that federal aid to the college demanded it. Which was, of course, a lie.) This return of Jesus to Jesuit classrooms came by direct request of President Rev. William P. Leahy, S.J., according to the *Boston College Observer*. "Bravo for Boston College!" says Patrick J. Reilly, president of the Cardinal Newman Society, a Catholic campus watchdog organization. "For Catholics, outward signs, symbols and practices of our faith are an important part of relating to God in a material world."

Unsurprisingly, a number of faculty responded with outrage. "I can hardly imagine a more effective way to denigrate the faculty of an educational institution. If that has been the purpose of the administration of Boston College, I congratulate them, as they have succeeded brilliantly," sniffed the chairman of the chemistry department, reports the *Observer*. At least one professor, the paper said, is "refusing to teach in classrooms adorned by a crucifix even if he should have to move his class to a different room at his own expense." But the days when Boston College employed radical feminist Mary Daly—who refused to teach male students in her women's studies classes—are long over. Daly left BC in 1999, and this mortal coil in 2010.

these days, says a professor. "There is a definite conservative voice on the campus that university officials make no effort to discourage," he says. "The level of debate is therefore superior to what it is on many campuses, and during the [last] presidential campaign the arguments for both candidates received respectful hearings, in forums that were spirited but civil." One notable exception occurred just a few days before a campus production of the *Vagina Monologues*, when the university held a campus-wide debate over the merits and shortcomings of the play—which in one scene celebrates the statutory rape of a young girl by an older woman. According to *The Observer*, the debate was heavily slanted in favor of the play: The five panelists included three tenured professors plus the executive director of the play. The lone voice opposing the play was a sophomore student. In their defense, the organizers of the debate claimed they could not find any faculty members who would speak against holding the *Monologues* on campus. If true, this speaks rather poorly for the school.

About 60 percent of Boston College students are Catholic, but their degree of involvement in religious activities varies. Opportunities abound for student participation, including daily liturgies, small faith-sharing communities (CURA and Salt & Light), and student clubs. "I have been impressed by the readiness of a small but (I think) increasing number of students to think and talk with one another about their Catholic faith and its implications," says a Jesuit instructor. The Campus Ministry office offers ecumenical and Catholic worship services. It sponsors service programs such as 4Boston, whose volunteers work at shelters, lunch kitchens, schools, youth centers, hospitals, and live-in facilities. Catholic students who adhere to official church teaching should seek out the St. Thomas More Society, an orthodox Catholic student group, while those attached to traditional liturgies should attend the weekly Latin Mass offered at Boston's Cathedral of the Holy Cross.

The school's sports programs are strong and getting stronger. The university fields twelve Division I varsity teams for men and fifteen for women. The Boston College Eagles are particularly strong in basketball, football, and hockey. The university consistently ranks among the best in the nation in terms of Division I student-athlete graduation rates; its football team has one of the highest graduation rates of any Division I-A program in the country. The $27 million, 72,000-square-foot Yawkey Athletics Center opened in spring 2005, and the Newton Campus Field Hockey Complex was completed that fall. The Newton Campus Soccer and Lacrosse Complex was completely renovated and updated in 2008.

Boston College's proximity to a major city makes it an occasional target for criminals. In 2009, the university reported eleven forcible sex offenses, five aggravated assaults, six burglaries, and three stolen cars. The Boston College Police are a police-academy-trained force with the power of arrest, and has a squad of detectives who conduct investigations into any on-campus crime. The university offers crime prevention workshops and sponsors a van and walking safety/escort service at night.

Boston College is an elite experience—a fact which is reflected in its price. Tuition in 2010–11 was $40,542. That makes Boston College the priciest school in town, more expensive than Harvard ($38,416), Boston University ($39,864), and MIT ($39,212). Room and board in 2010–11 added up to $12,082. Some 42 percent of the student body receives need-based financial aid, while the university pledges to meet 100 percent of a student's financial need. Still, more than half of the student body borrows money to pay for college, and the average student in the 2009 graduating class had $19,514 in student-loan debt.

Boston University

Boston, Massachusetts • www.bu.edu

Keeping faith

With about 18,500 undergraduates and 13,500 graduate students, Boston University is the nation's fourth-largest private university. Although it is overshadowed by neighbors like Harvard and MIT, BU has earned national respect and attracts top-tier students and faculty. Many BU students comment that they experience a heavier workload than their counterparts across town, in courses with equally distinguished professors. Its School of Theology is the oldest theological seminary of American Methodism and the founding school of Boston University.

Thanks to the efforts of former president John Silber (whose policies seem largely intact for now) Boston University offers a true core curriculum, providing students who seek it with the foundations of a liberal arts education. The core at BU, which participating students complete in their first two years, is designed for those who want to enjoy the traditional liberal arts experience within a larger university. Sadly, the core is not mandatory, but serious students will choose to take the core's small, faculty-led seminars that explore the best works of literature, art and music, and social, religious, scientific, and philosophical thought of the Western tradition—in combination with profound non-Western works.

Academic Life: Methodical ex-Methodists

Boston University offers more than 250 majors and minors from seventeen schools and colleges, including arts and sciences, fine arts, education, management, communication, general studies, health and rehabilitation sciences, hospitality administration, and engineering. One student says that "selecting a major can be a bit overwhelming if you are undecided."

Serious students will find the opportunity to flex their academic muscles, although it may take some digging. The college has a student-faculty ratio of 13 to 1, but professors are still praised for being readily available.

Particularly serious freshman and sophomores may apply to participate in an honors program in the College of Arts and Sciences of BU, which consists of four special classes, one per semester, on liberal arts subjects with the college's best faculty. Students enjoy special activities and trips, especially concerning the fine arts, and an annual lecture conducted by notable speakers. Honors classes may count toward fulfillment of core curriculum requirements.

With many colleges in Boston University, each section has its own academic advisors. Each full-time student has an advisor with whom to construct a particular program, and with a choice of major, receives advising in collaboration with that department. Students must consult with their advisors before registering for the next semester's courses, but for many students the program ends there. The advising program "is not very good unless you put effort into it," one student says.

The English department requires eleven courses, including literary analysis; two surveys in British literature; an introduction to ancient and medieval literature; and advanced-level courses in early American literature and literary criticism. Sadly, the department does not require a Shakespeare class. But most of the department's courses focus on important writers and their works, not on ideology.

The history department offers a general major, along with specialty tracks, such as the U.S.A./Canada, European, world/regional history, and intellectual/cultural history. There are also three intradisciplinary tracks: history and religion, history and art history, and history and international relations. Students in the general history program are required to take one course each in American, European, and world/regional history. In addition, one of the four courses must focus on premodern history. The major also calls for a methods/historiography course and two colloquia.

Political science majors must take eleven courses, including a choice of three at the introductory-level from a selection of five offerings in American politics, public policy, comparative politics, international relations, and political theory. They are then asked to choose from among those courses one area of specialty, which they declare as their subfield of study.

As a large university thinking small, Boston University makes sure that 56 percent of classes have fewer than twenty students. Only about 10 percent of courses have more than fifty students. "One of the legacies of John Silber is the awarding of substantial prizes for excellence in teaching, awarded with much fanfare at commencement," says a professor. One English major says that "most professors that I've encountered are really willing to help you. Every professor has office hours and if you make an effort, they'll take an interest in you." Graduate students teach some introductory courses each year, and lead almost all

VITAL STATISTICS

Religious affiliation: *none*
Total enrollment: *31,960*
Total undergraduates: *18,283*
SAT/ACT midranges: CR: *570–660*, M: *600–690*; ACT: *26–30*
Applicants: *37,795*
Applicants accepted: *58%*
Applicants accepted who enrolled: *11%*
Tuition and fees: *$39,314*
Room and Board: *$12,260*
Freshman retention rate: *90%*
Graduation rate: *77% (4 yrs.), 82% (6 yrs.)*
Courses with fewer than 20 students: *56%*
Student-faculty ratio: *13:1*
Courses taught by graduate students: *not provided*
Most popular majors: *business/marketing, psychology, journalism*
Students living on campus: *75%*
Guaranteed housing for 4 years? *no*
Students in fraternities: *5%* in sororities: *3%*

discussion and laboratory sections. One student warns, "Science TAs are often foreign and barely speak English." But "by your junior year, nearly all interaction is with professors," says another student.

Boston University has an impressive array of well-known scholars and writers, some of them serving in the interdisciplinary University Professors Program as well as members of individual departments. Students and faculty alike recommend noted conservative commentator Andrew Bacevich in international relations; William R. Keylor, Igor Lukes, and Nina Silber in history; Charles Glenn in education; Roye Wates in music; Christopher Ricks, Robert Wexelblatt, and (*Night* author) Elie Wiesel in humanities; Robert Pinsky, Charles Rzepka, Christopher Martin, and Rosanna Warren in English; Charles Griswold, Krzysztof Michalski, and David Roochnik in philosophy; James J. Collins in engineering; Dorothy S. Clark and Michael Elasmar in communications; Sheldon Glashow in physics; Walter Clemens, Walter D. Connor, and Sofía Pérez in political science; and David Eckel in religion.

Students and professors say that overall, the best departments are economics, biomedical engineering, philosophy, earth sciences, mathematics, and English. International relations, with a top-notch faculty, is one of the fastest growing majors. Reportedly, the most politicized departments are psychology and sociology, women's studies, and African American studies—in each of which some professors fail to equate scholarship with activism.

Faculty members who teach courses in the core curriculum program are known for being fair and even-handed in their approach to controversial topics. One student characterizes them as "scholarly, academic, and not biased at all." Another who participated in the core says the program is "pretty even-handed. 'Intro to Philosophy' is divided into Western and Eastern traditions so you get appropriate exposure to the classics." A professor adds that the core "is generally respectful of Western heritage and institutions, much more so than similar courses in other selective colleges." The Core Curriculum office publishes the *Journal of the Core Curriculum*, which promises to help the reader "navigate across a vast sea of intellectual inquiry and literary creativity."

In education, BU has "a solid commitment to forming teachers with solid liberal arts formations," says one professor. The School of Education has forged mutually beneficial links with inner-city schools in Boston and public schools in neighboring Chelsea. Boston University is one of five colleges that are in charge of public schools, of which it manages two in Boston.

The College of Communication hosts a number of learning laboratories. Among them are PRLab, AdLab, and HotHouse productions, "student-run production facilities that manage real-world public relations, advertising, and television campaigns," says the BU catalog. Under the leadership of former dean John Schulz, this college placed a strong emphasis on a broad liberal arts education combined with rigorous coursework and writing instruction.

Each year, almost 2,000 students participate in study-abroad programs of BU in locations in thirty cities, throughout twenty-five countries, on six continents. Says a student, "BU has a phenomenal study-abroad program. I did two semesters in London and got to work in Parliament as a science advisor. Everyone should find a chance to go abroad." BU also has an auxiliary campus in Washington, D.C., for students interested in government internships, and an auxiliary campus in Los Angeles focused on film and TV apprenticeships.

BU offers a large array of foreign languages, including Arabic, Chinese, French, Italian, Spanish, German, Ancient Greek, Hindi-Urdu, Japanese, Korean, Latin, Russian, Turkish, and a number of African languages.

Student Life: Heart of the city

Boston is not so much a college town as a town full of colleges. To study and live in a city so rich in American history and culture is an education in itself. BU's Charles River main campus, located in the Fenway-Kenmore neighborhood, consists of seventy-one acres extending from historic Back Bay westward along the south bank of the Charles. Architectural styles on campus include historic brownstone residences, towering modernist

---

ACADEMIC REQUIREMENTS

Boston University's liberal arts division imposes serious and worthy requirements for graduation. Students must:

- Take a two-course sequence focused on writing, reading, speaking, and research skills.
- Show proficiency in a foreign language at the advanced level, either through placement tests or coursework.
- Show competency in math, either through test scores or class work.

On top of these skill requirements, BU has general education requirements, which can be met by completing one of two programs:

a) The Core Curriculum, which includes eight integrated courses in humanities and natural and social sciences. Students in the program take two prescribed courses each semester during their first two years. Covering the history and Great Books of the West, from the ancient world through the Renaissance and into modernity, the Core provides students with a thorough and broad understanding of the intellectual tradition to which they are the heirs.

b) The Divisional Studies Program, a weaker alternative requiring two courses in each of the academic areas outside the student's area of concentration. There are four academic areas:

- Humanities. Choices include "Politics and Philosophy" and "Readings in World Literature."
- Mathematics and computer science. Options range from "Calculus" I to "Introduction to Computers."
- Natural sciences. Choices include "The Solar System" and "Earthquakes, Volcanoes, and Other Natural Disasters."
- Social sciences. Options here range from "Introduction to Archaeology" to "Physiological Psychology."

New England

structures, and recently constructed brick and brownstone buildings such as the Photonics Center. The Castle, a Tudor revival mansion, is located on tree-lined Bay State Road along with more university-owned historic mansions and ivy-covered brownstones. Once a private residence, today the Castle houses a bar, The Pub, and even hosts wedding receptions. Marsh Chapel, with stones in its foundation from Oxford's Jesus and St. John's colleges, according to one professor, "is not only the geographical, but in many ways, the intellectual/moral center of the university." The plaza in front of the chapel features a memorial to BU alumnus Martin Luther King Jr. and is a popular site for BU events.

Freshmen are required to live on campus, and Boston University guarantees four years of on-campus housing to students, unless they surrender their rooms. According to one student, "For a school of this size, the housing is impressive; an eclectic mix of remodeled brownstone walk-ups on Bay State Road and modern high rise towers on West Campus." Most freshmen live in large dormitories and can choose to live on single-sex floors or wings, single-sex dormitories, single-occupancy dorm rooms, specialty floors organized around academic interests, or apartment-style residences The dorms at BU are all coed, but men and women are usually in separate sections with their own bathrooms. There are ten dorms on campus.

Upperclassmen may opt for smaller residences, including one of more than one hundred brownstones, some of which overlook the Charles River. Many of these residences are used as specialty houses where students with common academic or social interests—a foreign language, philosophy, engineering, writing, music, community service, or hospitality administration, for example—can live together. Students in the Wellness House, for instance, agree to forgo drugs, alcohol, and smoking.

Boston's large metropolitan area offers students plenty of housing options off campus. But Boston is often rated one of the most expensive cities, with far more demand for housing than it has supply. As a consequence, in recent years, record numbers of Boston University students have sought on-campus housing, making competition for the most popular residences even fiercer. The university has been working to expand dorm space: the ten-acre Student Village, which features three residence halls opened in 2005. A twenty-six-story, 960-bed apartment and suite-style residence opened in fall 2009.

Students living on campus can swipe into any on-campus dormitory between the hours of 7:00 AM and 2:00 AM using their ID cards. Student residents can also sign in guests with photo identification at any time, day or night. Overnight visitors of the opposite sex are no longer (as they once were) required to seek a same-sex "co-host." This policy is not in force during finals weeks, however, when overnight guests are *verboten*.

There are some 500 student clubs and organizations at BU, such as the Alianza Latina, Amnesty International, Boston Scholars Club, Film Society, French Cultural Society, Hillel Students Organization, International Students Consortium, Outing Club, Photography Club, Ski & Snowboard Club, Students in Free Enterprise, Campus Ministries, Choral Group, Dance, Jazz, Opera, Film Society,and Zen Society. The school is pretty balanced with political clubs, hosting both College Democrats and College Republicans, as well as ACLU and Right to Life chapters. There are also twenty-six religious clubs running the gamut from Campus Crusade for Christ to Wiccan Student Alliance.

New England

Each year the student activities office hosts a month long World Fair complete with cultural shows, music performances, lectures, an outdoor Culturefest, and an International Student Ball. (Some 13 percent of BU undergrads are international students.) The annual Oxford-style Great Debate pits students against each other on issues of moment, and invites members of the audience to vote on the winners. The student-run *Daily Free Press* boasts the fourth-largest print run of Boston's daily newspapers; in addition to campus news, it reports on city, state, and national news. BU is a major force in the local arts scene. Notable arts organizations at BU include the Huntington Theatre Company, a professional theater in residence that is regarded as Boston's best. Derek Walcott, Nobel laureate and retired BU faculty member, founded BU Boston Playwrights' Theatre in the graduate creative writing department, dedicated to creating and producing new plays.

The university is one of only a handful of schools nationwide offering its students ROTC programs in all three services: Army, Navy, and Air Force.

The college sports a College Republican club of about a hundred or so members, but as a whole the student body does not seem to be overly politically active. Uniquely, at BU people complain that the administration is more conservative than the students.

Marsh Chapel houses some dozen chaplains of various faiths and multiple weekly religious services. The recently opened Florence and Chafetz Hillel House is ranked the number one Hillel facility in the world. Having four floors and a basement, it includes lounges, study rooms, and a kosher dining hall. The Newman House ministers to BU's Catholic community with many spiritual, social, and service activities including retreats and daily Masses.

The campus is close to Fenway Park, home of the Red Sox, and Boston's many musical, artistic, and cultural events keep students occupied. Anyone living in Boston should make sure to visit the palatial Isabella Stewart Gardner Museum and the Museum of Fine Arts. With easy access to Boston's rail-based mass transit system, "the T," the entire city is available for exploration.

The university fields twenty-one NCAA Division I varsity sports, most of which compete in the Colonial Athletic Conference, although there is no varsity baseball team. The Terrier's men's ice hockey team is almost always in the running for the NCAA title and

GREEN LIGHT

Politics are not entirely absent from BU's classrooms. But things could be much, much worse. One conservative student says that liberal professors usually present both sides equally and fairly, and welcome debate in class—even though some show their political prejudices by presenting the opposing viewpoint "so terribly that it looks pathetic." Says a professor, "One of the things I like about BU is that this is an institution that is always trying to get better. We are not afraid of self-criticism. There is no such thing as a 'political line' that dominates. My sense is that the BU faculty contains a healthy range of viewpoints."

In general, the students at BU seem more interested than the faculty in political activism and protest. One faculty member says that the student body is "less politicized and less politically active than seems to be the case elsewhere," and another says "much more of their energy goes into community service projects than into politics."

frequently wins the two-night Beanpot tournament held every February in Boston Garden—an annual competition among BU, Boston College, Harvard, and Northeastern. BU takes pride in its eighteen grads now playing in the NHL, the most of any college. Students choose from fifty intramural and club sports, ranging from sailing to the ever-popular ice broomball. In 2005, BU opened a $90 million Fitness and Recreation Center, right beside the school's new sports arena. According to one student, "The new athletic center is state of the art and includes a climbing wall, lazy river and ice rink that doubles as one of the largest concert venues in the city." The Boathouse, one of the country's best rowing centers, is located along the banks of the Charles River, site of the international Head of the Charles regatta each fall.

While a no-drinking policy is strictly kept in the dorms, there is a party scene at BU, most of it off campus. There are frat parties, with 3 percent of men enrolled in a fraternity and 5 percent of women in a sorority. However, with BU's curriculum, parties do not seem to overwhelm schoolwork.

According to one student, "The crime rate is often secondary to student carelessness. There were a series of assaults late at night on students returning to campus from bars/parties. In response, the university has significantly improved late-night transportation options." BU employs sixty trained police officers and a residential security staff of nearly seventy guards. The campus also features emergency call boxes and a student escort service. Burglaries are the most common type of on-campus crime: there were sixty-five in 2009. That year, the school also reported two forcible sex offenses, ten robberies, seven aggravated assaults, one arson, and two car thefts.

Tuition for BU in 2010–11 was $39,314, plus $12,260 (minimum) for room and board. Admissions are need blind, though the school does not guarantee it will cover the full financial need for all applicants. Some half of students receive need-based financial aid. The average recent graduate who borrowed emerged with a daunting $30,998 in student debt.

Bowdoin College

Brunswick, Maine • www.bowdoin.edu

Cold comforts

This fabled New England liberal arts college founded in 1794—whose legendary classics professor, Joshua Chamberlain, probably ensured a Union victory at the Battle of Gettysburg—does a decent job of living up to its reputation. At Bowdoin, students really do discuss ideas with their professors and classmates. The campus is indeed gorgeous in any season, although "it's *really* cold in winter!" shivers one student. Bowdoin's literature says that "the great mission of the college is to instill in students the love, the ways, and the habit of learning," but it offers them precious little guidance along these paths, instead insisting that "Bowdoin students must design an education in the context of their own developing goals and aspirations." We think students deserve more direction than that from the academic experts to whom their parents are writing enormous annual checks. Campus election polls continue to reveal a left-wing dominance, but outside the classroom, the college has seen an emergence of a more balanced debate on campus. Still, academic life is the highest priority at Bowdoin, whose students by and large graduate as well-informed and well-read citizens of the republic. And that's saying a lot.

Academic Life: Remembering Maine

In lieu of a core curriculum, Bowdoin students complete a series of broad distribution requirements in the following fields: mathematical, computational, or statistical reasoning; inquiry in the natural sciences; international perspectives; visual and performing arts; and the diversity category called exploring social differences. The choice of eligible courses in each field is broad and rather lax, allowing students to pursue either foundational subjects or idiosyncratic curiosity.

As a freshman, each student is assigned an advisor with similar academic interests; once he declares a major, the student may switch to a faculty member in his department. Thanks to these advisors, students who seek help get it. And seek it they should, because the curriculum itself provides little guidance. Students could theoretically graduate by taking courses such as "Music of the Caribbean" and "Lawn Boy Meets Valley Girl: Gender and the Suburbs," and nearly skipping American or Western history, art, and literature altogether.

Bowdoin's most salient virtue is its commitment to teaching over research and publishing, which other schools lean on to attract funding and publicity. Bowdoin prefers to

VITAL STATISTICS

Religious affiliation: *none*
Total enrollment: *1,777*
Total undergraduates: *1,777*
SAT/ACT midranges: CR:
   660–750, M: *650–750*; ACT:
   30–33
Applicants: *5,940*
Applicants accepted: *19%*
Accepted applicants who
   enrolled: *43%*
Tuition and fees: *$41,565*
Room and board: *$11,315*
Freshman retention rate:
   96%
Graduation rate: *89% (4 yrs.),
   94% (6 yrs.)*
Courses with fewer than 20
   students: *70%*
Student-faculty ratio: *9:1*
Courses taught by graduate
   students: *none*
Most popular majors:
   *economics, government,
   foreign languages and
   literatures*
Students living on campus:
   94%
Guaranteed housing for 4
   years? *no*
Students in fraternities or
   sororities: *none*

focus first on the close interaction between professors and students. Bowdoin encourages its faculty members to spend a majority of their time in the classroom, and students report that faculty are extraordinarily accessible and sincerely concerned with their education. Says one student, "The best aspect of Bowdoin is the professors and how they interact with the students. They are friends as well as mentors, and students have dinner and go bowling with them." If a student is having trouble in class, odds are that the Bowdoin professor will invite him to office hours. To give faculty time for teaching and advising, Bowdoin limits professors' loads to just two courses per semester and maintains the student-faculty ratio at an excellent nine to one, which allows for very intimate classroom settings. For the past decade, Bowdoin's median class size has hovered around sixteen.

Many courses are presented in cozy seminars. Over 60 percent of students participate in at least one independent study course, working closely with a professor. Freshman seminars, meant to help newcomers hone their academic skills, are required; students may choose from topics such as "The Korean War," a philosophy course on "Love," or the classics course "The Heroic Age: Ancient Supermen and Wonder Women." Less attractive options include the gender and women's studies department's "Anthropology of Science, Sex, and Reproduction" and the rather specialized "Black Women in Atlantic New Orleans." There are no graduate students at Bowdoin, and hence, no graduate teaching assistants. In foreign language classes, upperclassmen—mostly native speakers—sometimes lead discussion classes and run the language lab.

On the whole, courses at Bowdoin are rigorous, and students report that earning good grades demands a genuine commitment to learning. However, there are some notoriously easy courses that some students take only to fulfill distribution requirements, and in some departments grades are inflated. Good grades in social science courses are much easier to come by than in the quantitative sciences. The best departments at Bowdoin are government, economics, and some of the hard sciences.

In the government department, all majors must take classes in four fields: American government, comparative politics, political theory, and international relations. Classes on the United States Constitution and American political philosophy are required, and students can find worthy courses such as "Classical Political Philosophy" and "Religion and Politics" as well.

History majors do not have to take a single Western civilization class, but must take at least two courses in either African, East Asian, Latin American, or South Asian history.

One would expect a strong English department at a college that graduated Nathaniel Hawthorne and Henry Wadsworth Longfellow—and here Bowdoin does not disappoint. While its English faculty offers some fashionable courses in feminist and ethnic literature, it also serves up more traditional fare. English majors must take ten courses in their major, at least three of which must focus on pre-1800 British or Irish literature and one on "literature of the Americas." Bowdoin does not offer English composition courses, but the college does make an effort—a successful one, most students say—to continue its strong rhetorical tradition with the Bowdoin Writing Project, a peer tutoring program that links qualified students with those who would like to improve their writing.

Faculty most often lauded by Bowdoin students are Paul N. Franco, Jean M. Yarbrough, Richard E. Morgan, Christian P. Potholm II, and Allen L. Springer in government; Thomas Baumgarte and Stephen Naculich in physics; Gregory P. DeCoster, Guillermo Herrera, and B. Zorina Khan in economics; John C. Holt in religion; Steven R. Cerf in German; Robert K. Greenlee in music; William C. VanderWolk in French; Sarah F. McMahon and Patrick J. Rael in history; and Lance Guo in Asian studies. One student calls Greenlee a "genius," while Franco and Yarbrough are mentioned again and again as excellent government theory professors. Bowdoin students also highly praise Richard Morgan, some calling him "awesome" and "very learned, a great lecturer with a wealth of knowledge." Greg DeCoster is "so engaged and enthusiastic about his topic [economics], you could listen to him for hours."

The faculty at Bowdoin are predominantly leftist. One alumnus—otherwise a huge fan of the college, who "hated to leave"—admits that "the worst aspect of the college is that it's like 90 percent liberal. Instead of the rather superficial diversity they try to achieve merely culturally, I wish Bowdoin cultivated more diversity of opinion." The college has also garnered criticism for its encroachment on free speech in the form of a vaguely worded ban on jokes and stories "experienced by others as harassing." Another student agreed, "There is an overall intolerance of difference of opinion; Bowdoin is very politically correct." Indeed, he says that the religion department "has an open disrespect for traditional Catholic faith," as evidenced by such courses as "Sex and the Church" taught by militant feminist Elizabeth

---

SUGGESTED CORE

1. Classics 011: Shame, Honor, and Responsibility in Ancient Greece and Rome (or Classics 102, Introduction to Ancient Greek Culture)
2. Philosophy 111, Ancient Philosophy
3. Religion 215/216, The Hebrew Bible/New Testament in Its World
4. History 110, Medieval, Renaissance, and Reformation Europe (closest match)
5. Government and Legal Studies 241, Modern Political Philosophy or Philosophy 112, Modern Philosophy
6. English 210/211/212, Shakespeare's Comedies and Romances/Tragedies and Roman Plays/History Plays
7. History 233, American Society in the New Nation, 1763–1840 (closest match)
8. Government and Legal Studies 244, Liberalism and its Critics

Pritchard, whose academic research focuses on "the theological commitments of Marxist philosopher Theodor Adorno." She also teaches the basic "Christianity" course, described as "an introduction to the diversity and contentiousness of Christian thought and practice."

Bowdoin is host to the extremely radical Gay and Lesbian Studies and Women and Gender Studies departments, and according to students we consulted, some faculty in the anthropology, sociology, and African studies departments are also known to inject politics into the classroom. On the other hand, students report that the college's president, Barry Mills, is known as fair-minded toward people of diverse opinions. However, a recent push to diversify Bowdoin's professor base was focused entirely on hiring more professors of different ethnic backgrounds—rather than intellectual or political viewpoints.

Bowdoin's study-abroad programs are solid and quite popular; more than half of the student body chooses to study off campus. "It's pretty expensive but *so* worth it," one participant reports. "I appreciated having the easier classes so we could enjoy our surroundings." Bowdoin offers study-abroad programs all over the globe, including Botswana, Egypt, Cameroon, Kenya, Madagascar, Morocco, Senegal, Tanzania, China, Japan, India, Nepal, Sri Lanka, Korea, Thailand, Austria, Germany, France, Italy, Spain, Denmark, Czech Republic, Greece, Hungary, Ireland, Russia, Sweden, England, Israel, Jordan, Australia, New Zealand, Argentina, Chile, Costa Rica, Equador, Dominican Republic, Mexico, Panama, and Peru. The foreign language programs at Bowdoin are praiseworthy, offering solid instruction in nine languages: Chinese, French, German, Ancient Greek, Italian, Latin, Japanese, Russian, and Spanish.

ACADEMIC REQUIREMENTS

While it has no core curriculum, Bowdoin does impose some flimsy distribution requirements. To graduate, students must complete the following:

- One first-year seminar. Topics offered in 2010–11 range from "Shakespeare's Afterlives" to "Racism."
- One course in the natural sciences, which (curiously) could be a psychology class. Choices include anything from "Investigating Earth" to "Social Behavior."
- One math class. Qualifying courses include some from the economics, environmental studies, psychology, mathematics, and computer science departments. Options range from "Multivariate Calculus" to "Environmental Economics and Policy."
- One course in visual and performing arts. Options include "Introduction to Classical Music" and "Cultural Choreographies."
- One multicultural and diversity course, with choices ranging from "Ancient Greek Theater" to "Gay and Lesbian Studies."
- One course in International Perspectives, with options such as "The Courtly Society of Heian Japan" and "Global Sexualities, Local Desires."

Student Life: Outward bound

Compared with many small liberal arts colleges these days, Bowdoin should have nothing to complain about when it comes to finances; the college's endowment stands at $688 million. The school successfully completed a fundraising campaign goal of $275 million, a third of which is going to academic projects, a third to financial aid, a tenth to building projects, and the rest to student affairs and annual giving. Overall, the grand scheme is a fine one, with very little money earmarked for frivolity.

Although not all Bowdoin buildings are of the same architectural style, many have stood for over 200 years, and even those that are relatively new are considered attractive. The ever-popular Bowdoin Outing Club got a new building in 2003—the $1.25 million, 5,500-square-foot Schwartz Outdoor Leadership Center, which is environmentally friendly, with day lighting, radiant floor heating, and natural ventilation. Among the building projects that came out of the recent fundraising campaign are a new auditorium, a music recital hall, and renovation of the internationally recognized Bowdoin College Museum of Art.

Over 90 percent of the student body chooses to live in one of the college's residential spaces, which include singles, doubles, and suites in houses and dormitories. First-year students live together in separate dorms with upperclassmen residential advisors on each floor. Bowdoin offers no single-sex dormitories, and many students may find that members of the opposite sex live right next door; however in the freshman "bricks" four out of the six floors are single sex. There are no coed rooms, but bathrooms can be coed, if so ordered by house vote. Freshmen normally live in triples, whereas upperclassman may live in apartments or off campus. "Bowdoin has the best first-year housing of any college I've ever seen, with plenty of room for privacy and space," says one alumna. Some dorms that hadn't been updated since 1911 were recently renovated. There are also several substance-free dormitories available on campus, where even alcohol is prohibited. "The dorms are awesome; they provide unique living options," says a student. "One dorm, Cole Tower, is the second-tallest building in Maine. It has sixteen stories; you can see the ocean!"

Bowdoin ranks as one of the top colleges in the nation for student satisfaction in dining. The school also does a good job of placating its resident vegans, and has been lauded by the likes of PETA for furnishing abundant tofu and gluten. Bowdoin buys its produce from local farmers, and fish from local vendors, helping to support the waning agricultural sector in the region. There's even a Bowdoin organic farm. One can see why 97 percent of the off-campus students participate in the college meal plan. "The quality of food is awesome," raves one student.

Many students told us how "friendly" the typical Bowdoin student is. "I have met so many great people here: bright and very accepting," reports one. However, others complain about the lack of ethnic diversity. "This is one of the whitest campuses in America," groans one student. Somehow, Bowdoin students muddle through. No doubt it helps that, as one student says, "Everyone is accepted and made to feel welcome. There is no climate of snobbery at all."

A decade ago, most of the weekend activities on campus revolved around fraternities. But in 2000, the Bowdoin administration abolished fraternities and replaced them with a "college house" system. Some students complained about this, and the college was actually faced with litigation. However, this storm of contention blew over, and no one but alumni is said to miss the frats. Currently, the college assigns each freshman to a college house, each with its own set of residence halls, parties, and other social events. There is no structured socialization beyond the freshman year.

With more than half of partygoers under twenty-one, the administration has chosen to shift legal risks onto students themselves, requiring that a student "host" sign for every keg at a party; if any alcohol-related injuries occur, the student is held responsible. Social clubs have also been opened in free-standing houses, where the college attempts to teach students how to hold responsible parties. This has been moderately successful, changing the focus away from "beer blasts."

Bowdoin is a small college in a tight-knit New England community. Nevertheless, of the three elite Maine liberal arts colleges (Bates and Colby are the others), Bowdoin probably has the most social options available. Many activities center on sports teams. Most students at the school are involved in sports, varsity or intramural. "I came here for the hockey!" exclaims one. "I love how athletics and academics coexist here." The Bowdoin Polar Bears are Division III and highly competitive in twelve men's and fourteen women's sports teams.

Bowdoin hosts both College Republicans and College Democrats, the latter being more entrenched on this predominantly liberal campus. But the College Republicans have been very active in making their views heard on campus in recent years. "One important role that we can play is engaging the prevalent liberal sentiment and philosophy intellectually. We are going to do our best to bring conservative ideas into the Bowdoin community," explained 2010–11 CR president Steven Robinson to the *Bowdoin Orient*. He added that "it's troublesome that you can count the number of conservative professors here on one hand. The College Republicans would like to see an increase of intellectual diversity and more honest discussion of social and political issues." They are certainly doing their part in hosting conservative speakers, conferences, and meetings on campus and in growing their membership in recent years.

The Bowdoin chapel, a beautiful old Congregational-style church, underwent a four-year renovation and is now in magnificent, pristine condition. But one student says, "Spirituality is practically nonexistent at Bowdoin." Another admits, "Students here are generally proud of their aspirituality." Brunswick is home to churches of most major denominations, but students are said to attend mostly on major holidays. Student religious groups include the Catholic Student Union, the Bowdoin Christian Fellowship, and a strong Hillel club. The good news, however, is that Bowdoin students do, as a whole, seem to love their neighbors—or at least they serve them through various local community organizations. The Joseph McKeen Center for the Common Good provides Bowdoin students with plenty of opportunities to help both near and far, and often helps them participate in research projects and join community-based courses that will help them in future service.

Students report that the college does an excellent job of providing intellectual and artistic stimuli on campus, hosting frequent lectures, many political speakers, and a number of cultural events. Memorial Hall (built in the 1880s and completely renovated in 2000) and the more modern Pickard Theater are frequent venues. The Walker Art Building includes one of the top college art museums in the country, housing original portraits of Thomas Jefferson and James Madison. Extracurricular clubs occupy a good chunk of students' time, and options abound in theater, dance, politics, culture, and sports. By far the most popular organization is the Outing Club, which gives students the chance to explore the bucolic regions of Maine and northern New England. From mountain biking trips to sea kayaking on Casco Bay, there's something for every adventurous Bowdoin student. Says one wistful alumnus, "I loved the Bowdoin lifestyle. It is such a beautiful location on the coast of Maine, with a marvelous natural landscape. The atmosphere is studious but relaxed; sometimes the college is called 'Camp Bowdoin.' It felt like it."

In Brunswick, home to 21,000, Bowdoin has a true college town. A short walk from campus on Maine Street are coffeehouses, a local movie theater, a performing arts theater, about forty restaurants, bookstores, a local theater, and plenty of shops. The most popular off-campus hangouts are Jack Magee's Pub, Joshua's, and the Sea Dog. On Thursday nights, students go bowling in town. The Big Top is a favorite weekend breakfast locale. But despite Bowdoin's ideal location, students are dutiful enough that they usually sacrifice at least one weekend day to study, write papers, or read for class.

Bowdoin's rural location provides, not surprisingly, for a very safe environment. Says an insider, "The town is full of old folks and tenured professors. I'm safe." Statistics show that violent crime on or around campus is rare; substance abuse is certainly present, although incidents have diminished in recent years. In 2009, the school reported five forcible sex offenses and ten counts of burglary on campus.

Bowdoin's tuition in 2010–11 was $41,565, and room and board added up to $11,315. Forty-three percent of all students received need-based aid and the average indebtedness of recent graduates was a modest $18,382.

YELLOW LIGHT

Outside of the classroom, perhaps the most obvious political manifestations on campus arise from the Women's Resource Center. The center offers exclusively feminist fare, including information on student internships with the abortion provider Planned Parenthood. Other groups include environmental organizations, the College Democrats, and the Bowdoin Queer-Straight Alliance, which sponsors events like the annual Drag Ball.

An informal survey exploring the party affiliations of Bowdoin teachers and administrators showed that Democrats outnumber Republicans by twenty-three to one. However, student views are more intellectually diverse. The Bowdoin College Republicans are exceptionally active and visible, and has sought to ensure that conservative students have a voice on campus. The *Chronicle of Higher Education* reported that "the Bowdoin College Republicans spearheaded a successful effort to . . . officially endorse a version of the Academic Bill of Rights. The legislation . . . states that the College should be a place of learning and pursuit of excellence, rather than a forum for ideological indoctrination." For the most part, students of various political stripes feel secure enough to voice their opinions. Says one undergraduate, "Though a student may possess a minority opinion, anyone can find a support system here."

Brandeis University

Waltham, Massachusetts • www.brandeis.edu

New and improved

Brandeis is a relatively new university, founded in 1948 on what was formerly the property of Middlesex College, but it has accomplished a great deal in just over a half century. Not only are its 3,360 undergraduates exposed to excellent teaching in the humanities, sciences, and liberal arts in general, but the university is well regarded as a research institution serving both undergraduates and graduate students. A $620 million endowment (which represents a substantial increase since 2009, when the financial crisis peaked at the university) supports the enterprise. Though originally sponsored by the American Jewish community in the wake of World War II, Brandeis began as and remains a nonsectarian institution. Students on campus describe it as an open community enriched by its diverse population rather than one obsessed with the ideology of diversity.

Brandeis is named for Louis Dembitz Brandeis (1856–1941), the first Jewish Supreme Court justice. Before seeking out Justice Brandeis, the university's original backers approached Albert Einstein to ask if they might name the school after him. Conflicts with Einstein over the backers' fundraising endeavors and over partisan politics led him to dissociate himself from the school.

Academic Life: The right to be left alone

Like most schools these days, Brandeis eschews a real core curriculum, and merely asks its students to select a few courses from broad categories. According to the university, "Courses can double for the core curriculum, distribution, and concentration requirements. This allows for at least one-third of all courses taken to be elective courses." The setup also gives students ample opportunity to pursue multiple majors or minors. Brandeis's distribution requirements should be tighter. "If someone really wants to avoid a subject, it's far from impossible," says a student. Another says, "Brandeis will not tell you what you should think. And it will most definitely not choose your courses for you." One professor insists, "The curriculum here is well structured so that students take a good mixture of courses that are necessary fundamentals and fun electives, as well as being exposed to new ideas in their fields of study." The university in this regard subscribes to its namesake's famous formulation of the "right to be left alone."

New England

38

Each freshman is assigned an advisor (a faculty member or administrator) upon arrival and must consult with him before registering. The student gets a new faculty advisor when he selects a major, but isn't required to meet with him. "Most people I know honestly saw no need for their advisors," one student says. Twenty-year-olds who think they're above accepting counsel from famous scholars really are in need of advice.

The university consistently offers an overly-broad variety of courses to fulfill its requirements. A host of courses count as "intensive writing," ranging from "Reformation Europe" and "Mozart" to "Bollywood: Popular Film, Genre, and Society."

Quantitative reasoning courses range from "Introduction to Economics" to "Household and Family in Late Medieval and Early Modern Europe." Perhaps Albert Einstein was right to back away from the university; students report that there are ways to slide by without even brushing against laboratory science or math. If you intend to study science, one student warns that the department is "overly focused on premed students."

However, says one student: "The classes here are challenging in any discipline you study. The tests will ask you to think, not simply list facts. And you will get to know the library pretty well."

Though Brandeis doesn't require a course in Western history, it does require one in "non-Western and comparative studies." Most choices sound politicized, apart from a few solid offerings such as "Buddhist Art," "Introduction to the Qur'an," and "Third World Ideologies." Those who do love the West should explore Brandeis' excellent interdisciplinary major in European cultural studies (ECS). The major requires study of European literature along with "fine arts, history, music, philosophy, politics, sociology, and theater arts" and is intended "for those students who feel intellectually adventurous." The program requires an introductory seminar in ECS, followed by "The Western Canon," one comparative literature seminar, three classes in European literature, and three courses in related disciplines. Clearly, for the Brandeis student seeking the best liberal arts education available on campus, ECS is an excellent choice.

The English department seems fairly rigorous, requiring an introductory course, two classes in pre-1800 English literature, two classes in post-1800 English literature, and a course each in two of the following three categories: literary theory, media/film, and multicultural literature/world Anglophone, plus three electives. Although the major fails

VITAL STATISTICS

Religious affiliation: *none*
Total enrollment: *5,598*
Total undergraduates: *3,360*
SAT/ACT midranges: CR: *620–730*, M: *640–730*; ACT: *27–31*
Applicants: *6,815*
Applicants accepted: *40%*
Accepted applicants who enrolled: *28%*
Tuition and fees: *$38,994*
Room and board: *$11,214*
Freshman retention rate: *94%*
Graduation rate: *83% (4 yrs.), 87% (6 yrs.)*
Courses with fewer than 20 students: *61%*
Student-faculty ratio: 9:1
Courses taught by graduate students: *not provided*
Most popular majors: *social sciences, biological/life sciences, area and ethnic studies*
Students living on campus: *83%*
Guaranteed housing for 4 years? *no*
Students in fraternities or sororities: *none*

1. Humanities 10a, The Western Canon
2. Philosophy 161a or 162b, Plato/Aristotle
3. Near Eastern and Judaic Studies 111a/130a, The Hebrew Bible/New Testament
4. Near Eastern and Judaic Studies 128a, Introduction to Christianity (closest match)
5. Politics 182a, Liberal Political Thought
6. English 33a, Shakespeare
7. History 51a, History of the United States: 1607-1865
8. History 132b, European Thought and Culture since Darwin

to require students to study major Western authors, it certainly enables them to do so: "Shakespeare," "Spenser and Milton," and "Renaissance Poetry" fulfill the pre-1800 requirement. Post-1800 classes are less rigorous: "Literature and Medicine," "Queer Readings," and "Adolescent Literature from Grimm to Voldemort" are typical qualifying classes.

Brandeis's history requirements are vague: majors must complete nine courses in history, including one pre-1800, one post-1800, one U.S., one European, and one non-Western. One of the classes "must require a substantial research paper." Hence, a student could easily dabble in several subjects without mastering any.

Slightly more structured is the politics major, which calls for nine classes with at least one each in political theory, American politics, comparative politics, and international politics. Sadly, classes like "Social Movements in American Politics" or "Race, Inequality, and Social Policy" can fulfill the American politics requirements.

One undergrad notes that professors' personal politics "intrude in the classroom, to no end in—you would never guess—the politics department. I've also heard some in the economics and classical studies departments. . . . One conservative told me that whenever he raised his hand, the professor would address him as 'Republican.'"

How does this atmosphere influence individual students? Says one undergrad, "I've found Brandeis to have both altered and reinforced the viewpoints I had when I entered. . . . My conservative ideology is now [even more] firmly rooted in the concept of the free market—and I have realized the necessity of granting spheres of privacy in individual life."

In all, Brandeis offers forty-four majors (some interdisciplinary), along with forty-seven minors. Students list as among the strongest at Brandeis these departments: Near Eastern and Judaic studies (said by some to be the best in the country); English and American literature; classical studies; the sciences (including five emeritus professors, the faculty boasts eleven members of the National Academy of Sciences); history; and politics.

Among the best professors at Brandeis, students single out the following: Thomas Pochapsky in chemistry; Mary Campbell, Billy Flesch, Michael "Timo" Gilmore, and Caren Irr in English and American literature; Leonard Muellner in classics; Susan Dibble, Marya Lowry, and Janet Morrison in theater; Jerry Cohen in American studies; Gordie Fellman in sociology; Ray Jackendoff in linguistics and cognitive science; Graham Campbell and Susan Lichtman in fine arts; and Robert J. Art in international relations. In history, students laud David Hackett Fischer (a Pulitzer Prize–winning author) as "an amazing lecturer, truly dedicated to teaching," and call teacher John Schrecker "accessible and eloquent." Students also praise Mike Coiner as "everyone's favorite economics professor, more adept at distilling economic theory to hundreds of students than anyone else at Brandeis."

Brandeis's library system includes more than a million volumes and many other resources including microforms, and 35,000 video and audio titles. The archives of Soviet dissident Andrei Sakharov and his wife, Yelena Bonner, are held in a special collection.

Brandeis has an enviable student-faculty ratio of 9 to 1. Students report no problems with registering for classes or with their access to teachers. "Professors are very accessible," says one. In larger courses, professors deliver lectures, leaving teaching assistants to conduct discussion sections occasionally. One faculty member says, "Students are very highly motivated and curious. They often come by to discuss their ideas." Another professor says, "My classes have a high percentage of students engaged intellectually. I am never bored by the seminars I teach." And with more than twenty National Merit Scholars entering as freshmen each year, one would expect no less. "The number one priority at Brandeis is academics," says one student matter-of-factly.

Brandeis has done a good job of keeping politics out of most classrooms and promoting solid teaching along with research, but some departments and courses are weaker than others. A new program called Social Justice and Social Policy (SJSP), which offers a minor, is "basically a bunch of really liberal sociology classes and the like," a student says. The foundation course in the program is called "Crisis of the Welfare State." Brandeis's sociology and politics departments are also noteworthy for their politicization.

Outside the course catalog, one professor we spoke with also strongly recommended the university's study-abroad programs, observing: "The kids come back glowing." The university offers 250 such programs in seventy countries worldwide, and nearly half of juniors study abroad during the school year (even more do so in the summer). The program website claims that Brandeis students enjoy "a huge diversity of experiences . . . including studying neuroscience at Oxford University, conducting ethnographic research on sacred figures in Mongolia, and interning in special education classrooms in Sydney, Australia." Any student receiving need-based financial aid is eligible to apply for a Brandeis Scholarship for Study Abroad, and the university guides students towards dozens more study-abroad scholarships.

Brandeis requires students to show intermediate skills in a foreign language. Tongues taught include French, German, Hebrew, Italian, Spanish, Arabic, Chinese, Ancient Greek, Latin, Japanese, Russian, and (a rare option) Yiddish.

Student Life: World religions

Waltham, Massachusetts, home of Brandeis University, is nine miles west of cultural metropolis Boston. But suburban Waltham, a city of 60,000 on the Charles River, also has a variety of restaurants, interesting old buildings, and independent theaters. "It's definitely not a party school," says one student. "Don't be fooled by the school's proximity to Boston," says another. "Most students spend nights and weekends studying. If you do get out, it will probably be only as far as the highly suburbanized Harvard Square." But a third student says, "Brandeis is what you make of it. The school pours money into hundreds of student clubs and organizations that are constantly organizing events, dances, concerts, et cetera. I guarantee you that there is not a single weekend during the school year when the event

New England

calendar is completely empty." Students who do find time to get off campus can take the free school shuttle from Waltham to Boston.

A professor says, "At Brandeis there's a special tradition of concern which people are mindful of. You're always supposed to ask yourself, 'Are we serving social justice? In our courses? In our treatment of each other?'"

Yet, in the end, according to a student, "Brandeis is essentially a breeding ground for lawyers and doctors," and, ultimately, "The coolest thing about the place is getting an awesome job after college."

Those awesome (and high-paying) jobs are also good for Brandeis's fundraising campaigns. The Campaign for Brandeis aims to nearly double the school's endowment to $1.2 billion, improve academic programs, and contribute to capital projects like an impressive $154 million science center. After years of financial strain and controversy, things seem to be on the upswing at Brandeis.

Recent speakers have addressed political topics from a number of different viewpoints in recent years: Noam Chomsky, Dinesh D'Souza, Christopher Hitchens, congressman Barney Frank, and former senator Bill Bradley, among others.

University higher-ups occasionally discuss "diversifying" the campus, meaning in most cases that they would like to hire more professors "of color."

But the real push on campus for multiculturalism comes from students. One student

ACADEMIC REQUIREMENTS

While Brandeis has nothing like a traditional core, the basic curriculum in its College of Arts and Sciences imposes some distribution requirements. Students must take one among selected introductory courses from each of the four schools of the College:

- Humanities. For instance, "Roman History to 455 CE," "Mysticism and the Moral Life," or "Gender in Iranian Cinema."
- Social Science. Choices include "Economics of Third World Hunger," "History of the United States: 1607–1865," and "Feminist Critiques of Sexuality and Work in America."
- Science, such as "Introduction to Physics" or "Analyzing the American Jewish Community."
- Creative Arts, with classes such as "The Beatles: From 'Yesterday' to 'Tomorrow Never Knows,'" "Dialects for the Stage," and "Introduction to Drawing."

Students must also pass:

- Three writing-intensive courses (or two writing-intensive courses and an oral communication course). Options vary widely from "Conceptions of the Good Life" or "The Concept of Time" to "U.S. Foreign Economic Policy" or "Environment, Social Justice, and the Role of Women."
- One class in quantitative reasoning.
- One course in non-Western or comparative studies.
- Two semesters of physical education.
- Courses or tests to demonstrate third-semester proficiency in a foreign language.

admits that his peers "lack a certain open-mindedness" to opposing viewpoints. Besides groups representing ethnic minorities—many of which are primarily social networks—there are a number of leftist student political groups, including Students for a Just Society, Brandeis Humanists, Brandeis Labor Coalition, and the Feminist Majority Leadership Alliance. There are no conservative groups of similar size or stature; the College Republicans are essentially a social organization, although the 2010 elections did spur the development of a Brandeis Tea Party Chapter.

The student newspaper, the *Justice*, is a generally well-written publication that recognizes the separation between the news page and the editorial page. *Her Campus Brandeis* women's online magazine provides "a collegiette's guide to life," while the *Blowfish* and *Gravity Magazine* offer humorous takes on university and world news. *Chalav U'Dvash* is a journal of "Zionist Thought," published alongside several academic journals, like *Laurel Moon* literary journal, *Brandeis Law Journal, Philosophically Speaking*, and *Brandeis Economics and Finance Review*. The school sponsors BTV:65–Brandeis Television and WBRS 100.1 FM.

All told, more than 250 student-led groups on campus are funded by the Student Union, said by many to be left-leaning. Beyond media and political groups, the school sponsors ethnic groups like the African Students Organization, the Mixed Heritage Club, Chinese Cultural Connection, and the Russian Club. Students will also find hobby groups for potters, cheese-lovers, ballroom dancers, and natural living advocates, as well as performance groups like Colorguard, Jewish Fella Acapella, Voices of Praise gospel choir, and Tympanium Euphorium, as well as wacky clubs like the Ninja Band, which "appears at various unannounced locations across campus, plays loud and exciting music, and vanishes," and the not-so-subtly named Vagina Club, a feminist group.

Brandeis also hosts a variety of intramural and club sports for both men and women (including basketball, equestrian sport, gymnastics, aikido, fencing, volleyball, and tennis) to fill in the gaps in Brandeis's intercollegiate athletic program, which includes nine varsity teams for men and ten for women. Athletic facilities for all students include a pool, racket sports courts, a gymnasium, and a track.

The Judges, as the school's teams are known, compete in blue and white at the NCAA Division III. The school's mascot, Ollie the Owl, is named for Justice Oliver Wendell Holmes Jr., and provides a clear illustration of the brainy approach Brandeis students take toward athletics. While sports are certainly a part of the school, most students tend to choose academics over athletics. "Athletes in general are considered a minority and sometimes feel marginalized," says one student. "Most kids simply don't have the time to invest in sports. They read books and write papers."

Students generally comment on the remarkable religious tolerance that prevails at the school. Religious groups include Orthodox, Conservative, and Reform organizations for Jews, as well as Chabad and Hillel. Two Buddhist clubs, an umbrella group for Hindus, Jains, and Sikhs, a Muslim Students Association and the Brandeis Interfaith Group round out Baptist, Orthodox, and Catholic organizations. Students come from forty-six states and more than one hundred countries. International students make up 9.5 percent of the undergraduate student body (and 30 percent of the graduate student population), and 56

YELLOW LIGHT

Brandeis has found itself at the center of controversy in recent years. In 2009, plagued by a $10 million budgetary shortfall and a 25 percent drop in the school's endowment, then-president Jehuda Reinharz announced that Brandeis would be closing its Rose Art Museum and selling its $350 million, 6,000-object collection. The national media took notice, and Brandeis informed its student-employees who were working on fundraising campaigns that commenting on the school's decision would cause them to be put on probation. Restricting students' speech in this manner, of course, only added to the controversy.

Community (including donor) outcry led the school later to rescind its announcement. President Reinharz resigned almost immediately thereafter.

Before the national media was reporting on the art museum, it had focused on a professor who told his Latin American politics class that "wetbacks" was a discriminatory term used against Mexican immigrants. A student took offense at the use of the word and anonymously reported the Professor Hindley for using "inappropriate, racial" language. Hindley, a well-known liberal and professor of almost fifty years, was not granted a hearing, allowed to be defended by the rest of his students (who understood that he used the term educationally), or even formally notified of the charges against him. Rather, he was threatened with termination, informed that a monitor would be present in his classes for the rest of the term, and ordered to attend sensitivity training. He refused, and Brandeis did its best to ignore the media fallout, but kept the "sensitivity" monitor in Hindley's classes and has still failed to clear his name, simply declaring the matter "closed."

percent of all students are female. The school's brainy, egalitarian gestalt may be indicated by the administration's prohibition on fraternities and sororities. A few non-recognized fraternities and sororities do exist, but students, by and large, praise the absence of Greek life on campus.

Freshmen and sophomores are guaranteed spots in campus dorms, which are said to be adequate but not luxurious. The university is building more dormitories to solve a housing shortage that has forced some upperclassmen off campus. Brandeis's dorms are all coed, but some floors are single sex. The school currently hosts three Common Cause Communities—a philanthropic Alternative Spring Break floor for sophomores; a Substance Awareness for Everyday (SAFE) floor for juniors; and the Balanced Living House for seniors, who focus on healthy living and sponsor programs encouraging good health.

One female student observes, "Dorm life is amusing and enjoyable. After freshman year you can live in suites. There are no female or male dorms. The freshman dorms are usually single-sex by floor, though some are coed. Bathrooms are typically single sex, although when someone is drunk it doesn't matter." Sophomores or upperclassmen living on mixed-gender floors may opt for sex-neutral housing, where students may choose a roommate regardless of either person's sex. The school does discourage couples from living together.

All but two dorms are officially dry, and students say resident advisors will intervene to stop excessive noise. The school's alcohol policy is quite lenient, and the "wet" dorms allow alcohol for people of drinking age. At the school's Stein Restaurant, beer is on the menu alongside burgers and pasta. Although Brandeis's food is often criticized by students, it does, naturally, provide more kosher options than the typical school. Architecturally, the school is modern and run-of-the-mill. While the campus grounds themselves are quite nice, "the buildings are a bit of a mix and match," says one student. "Some are weird. Some are very ugly."

Brandeis's campus is quite safe: in 2009, the school reported one forcible sex offense, two aggravated assaults, eight burglaries, and one incident of arson on campus. Students report that they feel secure at the school. "Waltham is not a crime-ridden city, and there's always a late-night bus service. Safety is hardly your major concern," says one student.

Brandeis is pricey but generous. Tuition for 2010–11 was $38,994, and room and board $11,214. However, Brandeis's admissions decisions are need blind. Some 51 percent of students receive need-based aid, and Brandeis meets 81 percent of their demonstrated need. The average Brandeis student graduates with $26,000 in debt.

Brown University

Providence, Rhode Island • www.brown.edu

Amateur architects

Founded in 1764, Brown University was the third college in New England and the seventh in America. Brown boasts many strong departments, fine teachers, and bright, intellectually curious students. What it lacks is a curriculum. Not only is there no core; there are no distribution, language, math, or science requirements. Students need only prove their competency in writing and pass a minimum of thirty courses—taking, if they wish, all of them pass/fail—to gain a diploma. By placing a premium on choice and diversity at the cost of structure and direction, Brown provides a fascinating, tempting environment which "may be daunting for students who need more structure," according to one undergrad. Brown students, says the school's literature, are "architects of their own educational experience." Call us old fogies, but we prefer to rely on builders with a little more expertise.

Brown's small academic departments offer fewer course choices than one finds at other schools. Course enrollments are strictly limited and the university rarely opens up new sections. Thus, a student might not be able to get into the most popular classes until his senior year, if then. Brown's libraries are also small for an Ivy League school, partly due to the school's relatively modest endowment—which has, however, grown recently thanks to the energetic efforts of the administration and the generosity of alumni. Under current president Ruth Simmons, Brown launched the "Campaign for Academic Enrichment" to raise $1.4 billion for the endowment, new and improved facilities, academic programs, research, biology and medicine, financial aid, and expansion of faculty and staff. In June 2009, the school announced it had met its goal—nineteen months ahead of schedule.

The social and political atmosphere on Brown's campus are at the "progressive" cutting edge even of the Ivy League, which more reserved or traditional students should keep in mind before applying. (See the "SexPowerGod" dance and the "Naked Donut Run" on page 51.)

Academic Life: You get to put it together

Brown is proud of its laissez-faire approach, and the students who choose the school seem to like it. As one says, "Brown has a diverse and unique liberal arts education to offer. If you're not up for the task of crafting your own educational curriculum, advising is available."

New England

46

Another student lauds Brown's approach: "Students are free to attend graduate-level courses. There is a level of respect between the faculty and students. . . . Even as freshmen, students have the opportunity to work on graduate-level research projects with renowned faculty." Another agrees, "Brown is great because it has no general ed requirements. It means you can pursue what you love and dally in your curiosities."

This could be precisely the problem. The role of general education has traditionally been to pressure eighteen-year-olds to reach beyond their preconceived interests to embrace a holistic vision of knowledge. Brown leaves that up to chance.

A recent task force at the school, charged with re-examining its open curriculum admitted: "A modern liberal arts education is still defined in terms of a core curriculum comprised of several areas of knowledge. At Brown, rather than specifying these areas, we challenge you to develop your own core."

Students can take or avoid any class. Theoretically, they can even take all of their courses on a pass/fail basis (though few take this option). Parents should know—as prospective employers certainly do—that students can graduate from Brown without ever having taken American or world history, a foreign language, English, economics, philosophy, or a single science course. One student admits that there are some who feel at sea. However, "Brown has actively worked to improve academic advising and has made significant strides with the Meiklejohn Advising Program, which pairs up freshmen with upperclassmen mentors," this student says. "In short, if you're lost at Brown, there are plenty of resources to guide you." More than 1,000 students have applied for help since online applications to the Meiklejohn program were made available in 2008. As freshmen, Brown students are assigned an "advising partner," usually a faculty member, who guides the student through first-year courses and pre-major choices. The university says it expects students to "be prepared to articulate the reasons for [their] academic choices, and remain open to suggestions and new ideas." Once students have declared a concentration, they work with faculty advisors in their departments.

What academic structure there is at Brown is provided by the departments and concentrations, which often require students to take a core of fundamental courses. For instance, a student majoring in classics (a strong department at Brown) completes eight courses, including one in Ancient Greek or Latin language, two semesters of ancient his-

VITAL STATISTICS

Religious affiliation: *none*
Total enrollment: *8,233*
Total undergraduates: *6,244*
SAT/ACT midranges: CR: *650–760*, M: *670–780*; ACT: *28–33*
Applicants: *24,988*
Applicants accepted: *11%*
Accepted applicants who enrolled: *54%*
Tuition and fees: *$40,820*
Room and board: *$10,540*
Freshman retention rate: *97%*
Graduation rate: *86% (4 yrs.)*, *95% (6 yrs.)*
Courses with fewer than 20 students: *70%*
Student-faculty ratio: *9:1*
Courses taught by graduate students: *2%*
Most popular majors: *biology, economics, international affairs*
Students living on campus: *80%*
Guaranteed housing for 4 years? *yes*
Students in fraternities: *12%* in sororities: *4%*

SUGGESTED CORE

1. Comparative Literature 1410S, Classical Tragedy
2. Philosophy 350, Ancient Philosophy
3. Judaic Studies 470, The Hebrew Bible and the History of Ancient Israel and Religious Studies 400, New Testament and the Beginnings of Christianity
4. Religious Studies 110, Christianity
5. Political Science 110, Introduction to Political Thought
6. English 400, Introduction to Shakespeare or Comparative Literature 1410P, Shakespeare
7. History 510, American History to 1877
8. History 170, Great Modern European Thinkers or History 1220, European Intellectual and Cultural History: Exploring the Modern, 1880–1914

tory, and five other electives. Those merely concentrating in classics can choose from five different tracks: classics, Ancient Greek, Latin, a combined Ancient Greek and Latin program, or classics and Sanskrit. Comparative literature and geology get strong marks for teaching, as do applied math and international relations. The philosophy department bucks the trend toward deconstructionist nihilism, taking a sober, earnest approach to Continental philosophy. The hard sciences are serious and highly regarded by those who choose to study them.

English majors are required to take classes in literary theory and literary criticism, but not a Shakespeare course, although one is offered as an elective. The history department includes broad survey introductory courses, including American and world history, in its major requirements; however, a basic Western civilization class is not even available. The political science department is the fifth largest in undergraduate enrollment, and the program is excellent, requiring all majors to take courses in American politics, political theory, and international and comparative politics.

Brown students are effusive about their favorite teachers, such as the popular Stephen T. McGarvey in anthropology, who teaches the acclaimed course, "The Burden of Disease in Developing Countries." Brian Hayden in psychology is "phenomenal," according to a student, while another says that Susan Ashbrook Harvey's lectures in religious studies "feel like story time. She really cares about her students." Political science professor John Tomasi "is doing an outstanding job with the Political Theory Project, which exposes students to classical political philosophy; it's very popular," says an undergrad. Others offer praise for Matthew Zimmt in chemistry and Barrett Hazeltine in engineering (emeritus).

The weakest and most politicized departments are the usual suspects. Africana studies, the gender and sexuality department, the race and ethnicity program in American studies, and the urban studies program should be actively avoided, sources say.

From the president on down, Brown professors are accessible, students report. "My favorite aspect of Brown is the overall sense that administrators care about undergraduates and their experiences," says one. "At Brown's peer schools, such as Harvard or Yale, I don't think that's the case." Another student points to the helpful attitude of teachers: "If you enjoy learning and want to continue to do so, Brown is the place for you. You will be encouraged to achieve more through inspiration and individual passion."

Overwhelmingly, students seem to love Brown for one reason or another. It has been rated as the "second-happiest" school in the nation and the "happiest" Ivy League school.

The "pick and choose" atmosphere from the classroom to the dorm also makes it an open-minded place where anyone can find a niche. Says one alumnus, "I don't mean to be an unabashed Brown cheerleader, but it is really always improving. . . . Which is sad now that I've graduated." A current student says, "Overall, Brown's freedom allows you to seek the type of education you want. Conservative complaints about Brown are largely exaggerated. It is very easy to get a solid education at Brown, join religious groups, and take part in conservative activity if you seek it out. As a conservative at Brown, I am very happy with the overall experience."

Grade inflation is an issue at Brown, as at most schools these days. Much of the blame can be placed on the university's sloppy grading system, which does not include pluses or minuses. This means that students who really deserve a B+ will often get an A, to distinguish them from those who really deserve a C+, and so on. While this has been a topic of much discussion in recent years, Brown has no plans to change this system.

Brown University was singled out by Pulitzer Prize-winning *Wall Street Journal* reporter Daniel Golden, in his book, *The Price of Admission: How America's Ruling Class Buys Its Way into Elite Colleges—And Who Gets Left Outside the Gate.* According to Golden, Brown shows admission preference to children of the rich and famous, despite their sometimes inferior academic records, saying that "no university in the country has practiced celebrity admissions more assiduously or successfully."

Brown offers students a wide selection of foreign languages to study, including Latin, Ancient Greek, German, French, Spanish, Italian, Portuguese, Russian, Chinese, Japanese, Korean, Hebrew, Arabic, Hindi-Urdu, Persian/Farsi, Akkadian, and Czech. The university also sponsors many excellent study-abroad programs as well, to places such as the Czech Republic, Russia, Germany, Italy, England, Portugal, Spain, Greece, Brazil, Cuba, France, India, and Japan. Over 500 Brown undergraduates study outside the United States each year.

Student Life: Diverse dorms, sizzling social life

The attractions of Providence, Rhode Island (pop. 172,500) are within walking distance of campus. Brown is an urban school, and students can be seen milling up and down Thayer Street, visiting shops and restaurants. Providence has one of America's largest concentrations of original eighteenth and nineteenth-century homes and public buildings, many of them right by College Hill. It also offers virtually nowhere to park. Students walk, bike, or take buses and trams up the cobbled paths and through historic archways.

Brown sits at a high elevation with an excellent view of the city, which has retained most of its traditional charms and attractions. New buildings are going up on the campus with astounding speed. Completed construction projects include the 169,000-square-foot,

---

ACADEMIC REQUIREMENTS

Apart from those dictated by a student's major, none.

$95 million Sydney E. Frank Hall for Life Sciences; the relocation and renovation of the Peter Green House for the history department; the conversion of Pembroke Hall to house the humanities department and the new Pembroke Center for Teaching and Research on Women; construction of The Walk through five city blocks from Lincoln Field to the Pembroke Campus; and construction of the 35,000-square-foot, $40 million Perry and Marty Granoff Center for the Creative Arts. Many more renovations and new buildings are scheduled for completion in 2012.

Students find themselves caught up in a lovely city of manageable proportions and can meet a variety of people, if they take the time. No one should miss Water Fire on Saturday evenings in late summer and early fall, when a hundred floating bonfires are lit along the Providence River while gondolas stream by and eclectic music plays. The town offers plenty of interesting food spots, including a plethora of ethnic restaurants. The area surrounding the campus caters to students and their eccentricities, and there are all manner of trendy shops available. As the school's website boasts, Brown's "mosaic of campus life" consists of "closely connected neighborhoods" situated around the central College Green. Indeed, Brown offers a more "arm's length" experience of city life than fellow urban Ivies such as Harvard, Yale, Penn, or Columbia.

The campus is divided into five main areas. The largest is East Campus, but Pembroke Quad—once the home of Pembroke College, a women's college that merged with Brown in 1971—houses the most students. Residence halls are located no more than a six- or seven-minute walk from classes. The university does offer at least one hall exclusively for women each year. The Greek organizations are also single sex and occupy dormitory space.

The university has set a goal of having 90 percent of undergraduates live on campus, and offers virtually every type of living option, including suites and apartments, theme houses, and traditional dormitories, with plans for additional housing in the works. There are several coed bathrooms on campus, but a housing official says this is a mere "practicality." Brown also sets aside one dormitory for coed suites, where students can elect to live with a member of the opposite sex, although the university never randomly assigns men to room with women, or vice versa. There are now "gender-neutral" bathrooms on campus for the confused.

Currently, 80 percent of students live on campus, where, according to one undergrad, they are "lightly supervised by Resident Counselors as freshmen and Community Assistants thereafter. Neither of these positions comes with any power to enforce rules, they merely sell condoms and ask politely that we pay for them."

Brown is reputed to be more of a party school than the other Ivies. Indeed, Brown students enjoy the standard college drinking scene, found mainly at private parties rather than fraternities. Students discuss politics in the cafeteria and read the main student newspaper, the *Brown Daily Herald*—a decent paper for news coverage. The *Brown Noser,* founded in 2006, claims to be "Brown University's oldest satirical newspaper" where "most of what you read is false."

Its protean curriculum is just one reason that Brown enjoys a reputation as the most "progressive" of the Ivies. Another is its political atmosphere, which might well be described as a cloud of patchouli. Protests, which crop up frequently and for almost any reason, also prop up the school's reputation for leftism and rampant political correctness. Two students once asked the Registrar's office to change their official race and gender which, they argued, are nothing more than social constructs. The registrar, admirably, refused. A student reporter says, "If I hear gibberish being screamed from the Main Green, I grab my video camera, and I run as quickly as I can to see what sort of inane cause we are fighting for today." The student comments that such protests happen mainly during the warmer months. "The same people are involved in every single protest. For these students, it seems that protesting has become a pastime." Says one student, "Lots of people are liberal, yes. They are not raging liberals, they engage in peaceful protest and start initiatives in the hope of changing their community. As for conservative students, they are completely welcome. They are far less active on campus, which is no one's fault but their own."

That may not be entirely the case for some conservative students. An article in the *Brown Spectator* reported that at a campus College Republicans meeting, a rogue student asked the members of the organization, "Why would all of you come to Brown if you were conservative and you knew it was a liberal place?" Occasionally, the more liberal students at the university do impose this sense of ownership.

Brown's Queer Alliance hosts an annual "SexPowerGod" dance which gives students a chance to explore their sexual proclivities in a "sober, sane, safe and consensual environment," say event planners. So safe, in fact, that one year thirty students required medical attention after the event. None of the university's Department of Public Safety officers are allowed in; instead, attendees rely on student monitors who look out for any non-consensual activity. Students are not allowed to be intoxicated when they arrive and no alcohol is sold at the event, but the event boasts other attractions: a "booty box," free lubricant, consensual-sex patrols, and "sex techno." One year, the dance had a surprise guest: an undercover Fox News reporter, Jesse Watters, who described the event as "pure debauchery," witnessing same-sex kissing and hearing people having sex in the bathrooms. According to the *Brown Alumni Magazine,* "the annual dance has widespread appeal among students, many of whom use it as an opportunity to drink too much and wear almost nothing." Indeed.

In the same vein, every fall the Brown Association for Cooperative Housing throws the invitation-only "Naked Party" where all guests must remove their clothes upon entry, ostensibly to create a welcoming place where people of all body types can celebrate the naked human body. Then there's the "Naked Donut Run" at the end of each semester wherein various student groups walk naked through the libraries to offer donuts to students studying for exams.

Ironically, Brown was founded in 1764 as a Baptist alternative to then-Puritan Harvard and Yale. Rhode Island itself was set up originally as a haven of religious freedom for those persecuted for their beliefs, and there are still solidly religious organizations at Brown today. Since Rhode Island is statistically the most Roman Catholic state in the union, Brown is very close to dozens of old Catholic churches and one large Catholic college, Providence. The Brown-RISD Catholic community holds popular events and hosts outreach programs and solid lecturers. There is a variety of other faith groups on campus—from Imani to Quakers—and "all are welcoming," says a student. There is only one actual chapel on campus, Manning, which is on the second floor above the anthropology museum. The Memorial Room is known to be "a nice meeting room for informal religious gatherings."

YELLOW LIGHT

As at most New England colleges, conservatives are in the minority, and for that reason can garner a reputation for being silent and sullen. As one student complains, "I believe that, in response to the question, 'Why don't you participate in voter registration initiatives?' the College Republicans replied, 'We would only be registering Democrats, so why bother?'" Another self-described "mildly liberal" student opines that conservatives are actually too quiet on campus; they shouldn't be so shy, he thinks: "I feel that most of the Brown students I know are willing and interested to hear other intelligent viewpoints."

But change is in the air. As FrontPage Magazine reports, "A new generation of students has resurrected the Right. This nascent conservative community even publishes its own monthly magazine, the *Brown Spectator*." The paper is funded by The Foundation for Intellectual Diversity at Brown, founded by five recent alumni. The foundation also publishes *Closing Remarks*, a Christian literary and arts magazine. Several right-of-center groups, such as Students for Liberty and the College Republicans, have taken their place in Brown's marketplace of ideas.

Groups coordinate events and invite speakers open to all Brownies. There is also an "Interfaith House," where people of different faiths or none at all live together in "an open, communicative, learning environment," and an "Open House" for Jewish-Muslim dialog.

Stereotypically, sports at Brown take a back seat compared to the other Ivies, especially basketball-friendly Princeton and Penn. In fact, Brown's teams have improved markedly in recent years. The women's crew team has been particularly strong in recent years, winning six national championship titles between 1997 and 2009. Brown fields thirty-seven varsity teams, and the university also has some twenty club sports and an intramural program featuring flag football, Ultimate Frisbee, tennis, ice hockey, and other pursuits.

The arts play a larger part than do sports in student life at Brown. The school is a short drive from the Rhode Island School of Design (RISD, pronounced "ris-dee"), where students can register for art classes and receive course credit. Musical groups emerge at night like earthworms after a storm, and the campus dance groups perform frequently.

The breadth of campus groups spans from a juggling club to rugby, and there are many artistic and cultural groups among the over 300 student organizations, including student theater, a popular student-run radio station, and a wide variety of community and social outreach programs. Some of these outreaches include the new group Colleges Against Cancer which runs a Relay for Life event on campus to raise money for the American Cancer Society, and engages in cancer education, advocacy, and survivorship activities. Says one exhausted student, "There is so much to do at Brown . . . students complain that there is not enough time in the day to attend all the student-run activities they would like to." There are new clubs starting all the time. An insider says, "Due to the student-led nature of the campus, there is a large emphasis on innovation and planning new events. The Brown social scene is very much alive and vibrant."

Crime on campus is not bad for an urban school: In 2009, there were sixty-seven burglaries, one aggravated assault, one robbery, and ten forcible sex offenses (and one non-forcible) on campus. Brown's Department of Public Safety is an accredited law enforcement agency with more than eighty employees. It sponsors escort and safety van services as well as crime prevention workshops. A student says, "I feel very safe here, although we do get reports of crime maybe twice or three times a semester. It's not something that's constantly on your mind."

Like the other Ivies, Brown is astronomically expensive, with 2010–11 tuition at $40,820, and $10,540 for room and board. Brown reverted (after a budget-induced hiatus) to need-blind admissions in 2007, but it does not (unlike most other Ivies) guarantee to meet a candidate's full demonstrated need. Considering the cost, recent graduates' average indebtedness of $21,850 is quite moderate.

Colby College

Waterville, Maine • www.colby.edu

Some assembly required

Founded in 1813, Colby was first called the Maine Literary and Theological Institution, making it one of the oldest colleges in America. Since then, it has risen in prominence to become a well-respected liberal arts college. There are two other such top-tier colleges in Maine—Bowdoin and Bates—and even admissions officers at the three schools have trouble making their own schools stand out from the others. One Colby faculty member took a stab at it though: "Bates is too liberal, and Bowdoin is too snotty." Well, that settles that.

Like its peers, Colby offers small classes, close faculty-student interaction, strong study-abroad programs, a mostly considerate community atmosphere, and the surrounding beauty of Maine. Like most other elite schools in the Northeast, Colby has watered down its curriculum. So if a student does graduate with an integrated liberal arts education, it's because he really wanted one, and put it together himself. But with courage, drive, and intellectual focus, a Colby student can receive an excellent education. As one professor comments, "There are a lot of good and useful courses. It's just a matter of choosing." Perhaps the best thing about Colby is the intense commitment to teaching of its professors, with whom students have the opportunity to forge lasting intellectual relationships. Says another insider, "The faculty are truly committed to teaching; they take time to get to know the students."

Academic Life: See you at the buffet

The college's requirements for a liberal arts education, grandly titled the Colby Plan, don't amount to much. A campus tour guide's advice is to "take courses you're interested in, and you'll have no problem fulfilling the requirements." Indeed, Colby's distribution requirements are "so broadly defined that they hardly have much meaning," laments a professor. An incurious student could well emerge from Colby with little or no understanding of American history, philosophy, or literature—having instead knocked off his literature requirement (for instance) with courses like "Race and Gender in Shakespeare."

The required courses within some important departments remain solid, faculty members report. For instance, English majors still have to take three courses in pre-1800 English literature—which will usually include Shakespeare, although some students describe the

English department as rather ideological, with "an inordinate emphasis on gender and sexuality in the course topics." History majors take two courses each in North American and European history, as well as two in non-Western history, meaning they're likely to learn about the American founding. A student reports, "The government department is outstanding: academically rigorous, professional, and grounded in the classics of political science." While government majors don't face (as they should) a specific requirement in the study of the American political system, course options are very strong; a recent catalog showed choices such as "Roots of Modern Conservatism," "Federalism in American Constitutional Law," and "Totalitarianism in Literature." A student says of this discipline, "There is a general spirit of cooperation among [people of] various ideologies, and in recent years the chair of the department has passed back and forth between conservatives and liberals."

Other intellectually rigorous departments include economics, chemistry, mathematics, classics, and history. The geology department is said to have "a very strong record of graduating successful geologists." The math department has a strong menu of courses, particularly "Mathematical Modeling," and the "Topics" courses for senior math majors, such as "Topics in Real Analysis" and "Topics in Abstract Algebra."

Freshmen are assigned faculty advisors to help them plan their courses for the first couple of semesters. Students are required to get approval from their advisors before making any academic choices—such as choosing courses, adding a minor, or switching majors. However, complains one faculty member, "This 'approval' often involves simply pressing a button on a webpage. Some advisors will do it for all their advisees at once without talking to them. Others, like me, are more hard-nosed and try to use the process as a chance to offer some actual advising. But in the end, it once again depends on the student."

Students wax effusive about professors' dedication, asserting that faculty members put their time and thought into teaching, rather than publishing. One economics major says that she chose Colby precisely because of the close relationships that exist between professors and students. "When I visited Colby as a prospective student, an economics professor gave me her name and e-mail address," she says. "Now I'm majoring in economics, and I know every faculty member in the department. I come to office hours frequently, have dinner with them, and even babysit their kids." Another student says that professors

---

VITAL STATISTICS

Religious affiliation: *none*
Total enrollment: *1,838*
Total undergraduates: *1,838*
SAT/ACT midranges: CR: *630–720*, M: *640–720*; ACT: *28–31*
Applicants: *4,520*
Applicants accepted: *34%*
Accepted applicants who enrolled: *31%*
Tuition and fees and room and board: *$51,990*
Freshman retention rate: *94%*
Graduation rate: *82% (4 yrs.), 88% (6 yrs.)*
Courses with fewer than 20 students: *64%*
Student-faculty ratio: *10:1*
Courses taught by graduate students: *none*
Most popular majors: *social sciences, area and ethnic studies, biological and life sciences*
Students living on campus: *94%*
Guaranteed housing for 4 years? *yes*
Students in fraternities or sororities: *none*

SUGGESTED CORE

1. Classics 138, Heroes of the World
2. Philosophy 231, History of Ancient Greek Philosophy
3. Religion 143/144, Introduction to the Hebrew Bible/ New Testament
4. Philosophy 373, History of Medieval Philosophy
5. Government 272, Modern Political Theory
6. English 411, Shakespeare
7. History 131, Survey of U.S. History to 1865
8. Philosophy 359, Nineteenth-Century Philosophy

often share books with their students, attend campus events, and "are very willing to use their contacts and knowledge to steer you into programs." A faculty member says, "Colby obsessively emphasizes good teaching, so one could quite easily have only great professors."

Academically, says one student, "Colby is fantastic. Professors are top-notch, and most classes are small and well run." Another reports that "students who can take the pressure love their courses." For instance, Larissa Taylor's "Church History and Theology in Medieval Europe," is said to "give good insight into both the Church's development and medieval society." Joseph Reisert in government is said to have a "strong grounding in the classic works of political thought." Guilain Denoeux, a State Department consultant, gives students "an in-depth understanding of international relations. His 'Politics of the Middle East' course is not to be missed." Tony Corrado is a "campaign-finance guru who is well connected in Washington" and teaches students the practical aspects of American politics in courses such as "Interest-Group Politics."

Two classics professors, Joseph and Hanna Roisman, "teach all aspects of classical civilization from Greek tragedy to Roman battle tactics with enthusiasm and in-depth expertise." Professor Elizabeth Leonard is lauded as an expert on the Civil War. In geology, Robert E. Nelson ("Dr. Bob") makes a student "want to be a geology major. He's very, very inspiring!" Jeff Anderson in anthropology brings to bear "lots of first hand knowledge, having lived with the Apache and Navajo." Government teachers are "strong, open-minded, and fun to argue with," says a student. "They appreciate a different point of view." The history department is also "getting stronger," as is biology. Other recommended professors include Otto Bretscher, Fernando Q. Gouvea, Leo Livshits, and George Welch in mathematics; Whitney King in chemistry; Liam O'Brien in statistics; and David Findlay in economics.

Some students, however, are dissatisfied with humanities courses at Colby. One alumna reported: "There were two classes in four years in which I felt legitimately challenged and exposed to new material and perspectives. I wrote more papers about how literature made me 'feel' rather than . . . any sort of objective, quality/standard-based analysis."

Other students insist that most of their courses are rigorous. Says one: "Colby really pushes you to think. It's like a mini Ivy." Another complains, "It's really, really intense, too much so. Plenty of students find it difficult to satisfy the requirements." Colby has its tough courses, as one student relates: "It can be hard to come from a high school where you may have been at the top to a college where you are average. You learn to challenge yourself."

Colby attracts bright overachievers who are mostly cooperative rather than competitive. The Farnham Writers' Center is staffed by students eager to help classmates with papers. During exam time, the center is open twenty-four hours a day for those pulling the inevitable all-nighter. Calculus After Hours assists students with math, and is "dynamic, effective, and fun," say insiders.

Some programs are weaker than others. The religious studies department is largely staffed by feminists. Says one insider, "None of the faculty members in that department have any respect for tradition." The program lists few courses focusing on Christianity, if you can count courses like "*Jesus Christ Superstar*: The Bible in Film"—and even those are offered rarely. Other courses focus on women and feminism, film, non-Western religions, and more sociological studies of religion. One class is "Was God Married? Exploring the Goddess in the Ancient Near East," and another, "Contemporary Wicca: Formalists, Feminists, and Free Spirits." Sounds like an exorcism might be in order.

The anthropology department is limited, as such departments tend to be at small liberal arts schools, and offers a number of narrow or partisan courses. The interdisciplinary programs tend to be the most politicized: American studies; indigenous peoples of the Americas (a minor in the anthropology department); African and African American studies; and women's, gender, and sexuality studies. The philosophy and education departments have also been described as "given to trendy topics, such as issues related to gender and 'social justice.'"

A studio art major calls his department "pretty minimal," while another gripes that Colby is a "bad place to be an artist, musician, or just creative in general," but reports that he is grateful to the Musicians' Alliance and the Student Art Committee for their support.

In 1962, Colby became the first school in the nation to institute a 4-1-4 calendar (two four-month semesters separated by a January term), giving students the opportunity to take shorter courses during the January winter term, known as "Jan Plan." These courses are falling out of favor with professors, who claim Jan Plan has become ineffectual: "It is not possible to cram a semester's worth of work into a month." The college offers some fifty courses on campus during January, such as blacksmithing, photography, and pottery.

For students who need a break from New England, the school sponsors programs in Salamanca, Dijon, and St. Petersburg. The study-abroad program jointly sponsored by Bowdoin and Bates closed down in 2005, but students have dozens of other international opportunities—although one professor complains that "for some students it can become just a long vacation. It is up to the student to choose something worth doing." Language options on campus include Chinese, French, German, Ancient Greek, Latin, Hebrew, Italian, Japanese, Russian, and Spanish.

Student Life: Green day

While the 714-acre Colby campus is surrounded by lush scenery, the faculty and students are what makes the campus "green." Colby has recently committed to becoming 100 percent "eco-friendly." Says one insider, "Everyone is very pro-environment here, as befits rural Maine. Dr. Thomas Tietenberg has done much to strengthen the environmental studies program here; it's a lot more than just singing songs and holding hands." The school seeks "green" certification for new and renovated buildings, and regularly is recognized for its compliance with high environmental standards.

New England

The campus, though not historic, is quaint and charming, with red-brick buildings separated by lush, verdant lawns. Colby Green, a section of campus based on the style of a New England village green, is now finished, with newer buildings surrounding it, including the recently finished social science building. Downtown Waterville, Colby's hometown, is a fifteen-minute walk away, and boasts several good restaurants, a bowling alley, a movie theater, and other attractions. Some students, however, complain that outside of the usual fare of food and movies, the town offers very little. Sniffs one student, "Waterville is poor, white, and kind of stand-offish to Colby students."

However, on the campus, "Colby has pretty much everything one could reasonably ask for," says a student. "There are three well-run dining halls with a variety of meal choices." Colby is in the midst of a building boom, and has completed several attractive new classroom and departmental buildings—and remodeled its famously "postmodern" Cotter student union.

The administration pays much lip service to "diversity." Yawns one student, "The administration is constantly pushing diversity, with activities like mandatory supper seminars designed to sensitize students. A lot of us nap in the back." Incessantly, the lead "news" article in the *Colby Echo* will spotlight some instance or breach of multicultural dogma, and at least one editorial will plead for bringing more minorities to campus. The Colby Outdoor Orientation Trip (COOT) for freshmen now includes a diversity workshop, which explores topics including "the reasons people feel marginalized, [and] the ways in which people characterize gender," reports the *Echo*. Starting in 2001, Colby began publishing its annual "Diversity Reports." These reports, mandatory for all academic departments, are self-assessments that address issues of race, gender, and sexual orientation. Each department is responsible for updating progress on a yearly basis, but the college no longer offers this report to the general public. Some real diversity does exist on campus, thanks to scholarships that have substantially increased the number of international students. Reports one grateful professor, "These kids are really smart. Their presence has really improved the classroom, as their goal is to actually learn."

Political and religious diversity are dicier propositions, students report. Says one Orthodox Jewish student, "It is close to impossible to be kosher at Colby, and is also incredibly difficult for Muslim students." She complained that several professors violated university regulations by assigning midterms on Yom Kippur, while the kosher food options consist of "a small table with matzoh, soup, and boiled eggs. Sometimes bagels."

Says one student, "There aren't very many of us conservatives on campus, and we do feel lonely in some sense, but not beleaguered or under pressure." Mostly, in fact, students seem "apathetic." The largest political group on campus is the League of Progressive Voters, whose goal, as the college website explains, is to get students to vote. They are also "the most well-informed" says a student, "though they in general tend to showcase Democrats." One student sums up the atmosphere on campus: "Most students are preppy New Englanders, with a few hippies thrown in." Other groups include the Colby Democrats, Colby Republicans, Colby Chapter of the Roosevelt Institution, Colby Amnesty International, and the Environmental Coalition.

Non political groups proliferate, including the Arabic Language and Culture Club; Colby Ballroom Dance Club; Colby Cares About Kids; Colby Chess Club; Colby Cricket

Club; Colby Gymnastics Club; Colby Hipnotik (Dance Team); Colby Mountaineering Club; Colby Quidditch; Cycling Team; Equestrian Team; Gentlemen of Quality; iBike; Juggling Club; Maineliners (Figure Skating); Medieval Reading Society; Quilting Club; Society Organized Against Racism; Surf Club; Tuesday Night Film Club; and Women's Rugby.

In general, the college is not eager to promote spirituality. One professor comments, "The chapel is not at all central to the mainstream way of life here. In fact, few of my students know who Job is when I make the reference." Says a student, "Spiritual life here is mediocre all the way." The Colby Christian Fellowship is fairly vibrant, however; with some fifty active members, it hosts prayer and Bible discussion groups. The Catholic Newman Council offers a variety of activities in addition to weekly services, such as scripture studies and retreats. A Hillel group and several other smaller religious organizations serve those of other faiths.

Colby's housing and social life are focused on three traditional commons, each of which consists of several dorms—many of them renovated—its own dining hall, and meet-

---

ACADEMIC REQUIREMENTS

Colby imposes no core curriculum, but rather a loose set of distribution and other requirements. All students must complete:

- English 115, a freshman writing-intensive class.
- A modern language course.
- Two courses in the natural sciences, with at least one lab. This could include "Biology of Women" or "Chemistry for Citizens."
- One class in the arts (history, theory, or practice). Selections range from "The Dance Experience" to "Survey of Western Art."
- One course in historical studies. Choices include "Survey of United States History to 1865" and "Science, Race, and Gender."
- One class in literature. This could be "Tolkien's Sources" or "Women in Myth and Fairytale."
- One course in quantitative reasoning, which could be satisfied by "Single-Variable Calculus" or "Mathematics as a Liberal Art."
- One class in the social sciences. "Individuality and World-Traveling" and "Introduction to Psychology" are options here.
- Two courses dealing with "diversity issues," one dealing with the United States, and one with a foreign country. These could be "Schools and Society" or "Queer Identities and Politics."
- Three January programs. Choices include "Fresco Painting," "Blacksmithing," and "Montage, Sound, and Meaning in Film."
- Four out of seven wellness lectures in "mental, emotional, social, physical, and spiritual fitness." Recent offerings include: "What Happy Faces are Hiding: Talking About Depression," "The J-Spot, A Sex Educator Tells All," "Four Stages of Drinking," "HIV Positive Life," and "Life Without Ed," a seminar on eating disorders.
- The web-based anti-drinking program AlcoholEdu.

YELLOW LIGHT

One professor says of Colby, "There are occasional reports of faculty making light of conservative student opinions or of treating them as nondiscussable, though it is unclear how pervasive this actually is." In fairness to the school, the professor says, "There are reports of at least one tenure denial having been motivated by this kind of behavior in class." Most Colby students are said to be fair-minded. One student gave a presentation on the abortion issue in a politics and religion class; he says that students were at first shocked by his pro-life stance, but when he "demonstrated that I could do the work and make the presentation go well, it defused some of the tension."

But other conservative students complain of the atmosphere in the Colby classroom. One reports, "The school encourages a social and political environment that demands absolute conformity to the status quo, to political correctness." Complaints have also been raised about the "first-year book" that is carefully discussed at student orientation; it is now always about "diversity" issues. One professor says that "the first-year 'wellness seminars' tend to focus on the usual liberal shibboleths." As for the faculty as a whole, it is said there is "a lot of liberal bias, some of it unconscious, that molds the actions of the administration, particularly when it comes to student affairs."

ing spaces. The campus acquired an old convent that is now the Colby Garden dormitory. Students are free to move from one common to another each year, so they end up meeting a wide variety of students. Each weekend, one of the commons is responsible for a major social event, usually a dance or party of some sort. However, students admit that these events are not well attended.

Some 94 percent of the student body lives on campus in residences mixing freshmen with upperclassmen. Most campus residences are centrally located dormitories, except for one apartment complex in which about a hundred seniors live. Since the mid-1990s the campus has seen a multi-million dollar renovation in which dormitories were completely renovated. Colby offers no single-sex dormitories (or even single-sex floors) and students are bound to find themselves living next door to a member of the opposite sex. However, there are no coed dorm rooms or coed bathrooms in the residence halls. Men and women are permitted to share apartments as seniors. One living option is a quiet dorm, where residents and visitors must adhere to a twenty-one-hour-a-day quiet rule. All dorms on campus are nonsmoking, and there are also alcohol-free and substance-free residences available, as well as a Spanish language house.

Colby has its own on-campus pub, which serves alcohol, and many students spend weekends drinking together in dorm rooms. The college attempts to provide alternatives to alcohol; at least 50 percent of all social programming money must go into funding "dry" events. (In addition, a hard liquor ban was implemented in the 2010–11 school year.) Popular events include movie nights, and performances by hypnotists, comedians, and musicians. The student-run Coffeehouse brings in small-name bands every few weeks, and math professors lead a folk music night each week. Many students occupy their free time with activities in small niche clubs such as pottery or photography, politically oriented groups, or sports.

New England

Colby is a very athletic campus, with some 60 percent of students involved in some sport. Colby fields thirty-two varsity teams in the New England Small College Athletic Conference, and has eight club sports and numerous intramural sports. Colby's athletic center, rebuilt a decade ago, includes training facilities, competition courts in almost every sport, saunas, a climbing wall, and a swimming pool. The college's central Maine location encourages students to explore the outdoors. The Outing Club is the most active group on campus, organizing hiking, boating, skiing, and camping trips.

After the 2003 highly publicized death of a student at the hands of a Waterville local on parole, the school has focused keenly on student safety, fixing lights and cameras everywhere, rearranging the parking lot's access and controlling traffic. At this point, says an insider, "The greatest danger to Colby students is, quite honestly, themselves." The college is fairly secluded from the town of Waterville, and Colby has a security force that patrols the campus regularly, with a campus escort service and a safety shuttle. The only crimes reported on campus in 2009 were eight burglaries.

Colby doesn't come cheap; for 2010–11, tuition, room, and board (it's a package deal) cost $51,990. Beginning in 2008–9, Colby replaced all "packaged" loans (usually in the form of Perkins or Colby loans) with grants, meaning that students from now on can potentially graduate debt-free. Admissions are not need blind, but 38 percent of students receive need-based aid. The average student-loan debt of a recent graduate was $21,697.

Connecticut College

New London, Connecticut • www.conncoll.edu

New Athenians?

In 1910, Wesleyan University changed its charter to admit only men, leaving Connecticut women no place to earn a Bachelor of Arts degree. The next year, a group of Wesleyan alumnae founded Connecticut College for Women. Connecticut College's first students were exposed, tirelessly, to the intellectual foundations of Western civilization. Indeed, in 1922 the school itself adopted as its "Honor Code" a version of the Athenian Oath, to which the young of the ancient polis committed themselves at age seventeen.

This code, which also provides for a student-run judicial system and self-proctored exams, maximizes student flexibility and reduces end-of-term stress. Students take the code seriously: "Some even go to the point of ratting on classmates," one junior says.

However, the administration seems to grant much more weight to its "Diversity Statement," which pledges special treatment to "historically disadvantaged groups such as: African Americans, Hispanics, Asians, Native Americans, women, gay, lesbian, bisexual, and transgender people, and the differently-abled." Trying to reconcile ideals such as "intellectual diversity" with this kind of political correctness provokes a head-splitting predicament.

For those willing to traverse such thickets of scruple, Connecticut College is not a stifling environment. If CC students are no longer required to learn the best of the West, at least they are not forbidden to. The faculty are committed to teaching and students are intent on learning. Both conservative and liberal students say they feel comfortable speaking their minds in class, and those who call the gorgeous hilltop campus home enjoy its small-college atmosphere and quirky traditions—such as the college's unique camel mascot, and the "Camelympics," where dorms compete in games and activities.

Academic Life: Black and white and gray all over

The college's general education requirements are a little stricter than those of many liberal arts colleges, where administrators are abandoning core and even distributional requirements in order to give students more "flexibility." Nevertheless, CC students are free to fulfill key distributional requirements with courses such as "Introduction to Gender and Women's Studies: A Transnational Feminist Approach." They are equally free to avoid such courses and design a curriculum composed of foundational courses, such as "His-

New England

tory of Ancient Philosophy," "Introduction to European History," and "Chaucer, Shakespeare, Milton, and Company."

Students report that faculty members at CC are teachers first, researchers a distant second. One student says, "The professors take a genuine interest in us." A faculty member says, "This isn't a college for academics who are just looking to move on to the next big job who spend all their time applying for research grants or talking to their grad students. With a few exceptions, the professors are serious teachers." Classes are generally small, and are taught by the professors themselves. (There are few graduate students and no teaching assistants at Connecticut College.) Most students, says a sophomore, form tight relationships with their instructors, often eating dinner together, minding their children, and discussing ideas outside of class. But closeness with professors depends on the student. "Generally, you still have to make an effort if you want to get to know a professor outside class," a student says.

The best instructors, according to students, are William Frasure in government; Donald Peppard in economics; Robert E. Proctor in Italian; Catherine Spencer in French; Perry Susskind in mathematics; and John S. Gordon in English.

Students say Connecticut College is strongest in the arts, especially music, theater, and dance. Palmer Auditorium performance hall can seat most of the student body. Cummings Arts Center, which houses the art, art history, and music departments, holds three art galleries, studios, practice rooms, and a music library.

The government, philosophy, and economics departments are also described as solid. Government majors are required to take at least one course in each of four areas: political theory, comparative politics, United States politics, and international politics. The botany and biology departments are also reported to be strong; professors and students take advantage of the school's lush surroundings for research. Many of the school's most substantive classes can be found in the philosophy department, such as "History of Ancient Philosophy."

Most academic majors offer the opportunity for a solid liberal arts education. English majors are required to take courses in British, U.S., and world literature and from the medieval/Renaissance, Renaissance/Eighteenth Century/Romantic, and Modern periods. While some offerings seem dubious ("Constructing the Human," and "Literature and Race Criticism"), CC offers a number of traditional classes: the names Milton, Chaucer, Shake-

VITAL STATISTICS

Religious affiliation: *none*
Total enrollment: *1,911*
Total undergraduates: *1,906*
SAT/ACT midranges: CR: *610–700*, M: *610–690*; ACT: *25–30*
Applicants: *4,733*
Applicants accepted: *37%*
Accepted applicants who enrolled: *29%*
Tuition and fees and room and board: *$53,110*
Freshman retention rate: *90%*
Graduation rate: *83% (4 yrs.), 85% (6 yrs.)*
Courses with fewer than 20 students: *64%*
Student-faculty ratio: *9:1*
Courses taught by graduate students: *none*
Most popular majors: *social sciences, visual and performing arts, biological, life sciences*
Students living on campus: *98%*
Guaranteed housing for 4 years? *yes*
Students in fraternities or sororities: *none*

SUGGESTED CORE

1. Classics 203, Classical Epic
2. Philosophy 201, History of Ancient Philosophy
3. Religious Studies 113/114, Judaism's Bible/The New Testament
4. Philosophy 216, Medieval Philosophy
5. Government 214, Modern Political Thought
6. English 209/210, Shakespeare in the 1590s/After 1600
7. History 105, An Introduction to the History of the U.S.
8. Philosophy 202, History of Modern Philosophy or German Studies 425, Freedom and Revolution: The German Enlightenment into Romanticism

speare, Hemingway, and Joyce appear frequently. The net of the English department is cast broadly enough that most students will at least brush up against good literature.

History majors face an abundance of choices. They must take ten courses in the major, including one in four out of the five main geographical areas treated by the department (Africa, Asia, Europe, Latin America/Caribbean, and U.S.). That means the American founding and Civil War are simply optional topics among many.

The school's advising program is quite successful. Upon entry, every student is assigned a faculty and a student advisor. After a student declares a major, he is assigned (or chooses) a faculty advisor within his major. Students who need help navigating the school's required writing-intensive courses can visit the Roth Writing Center, where student tutors look over essays at any stage of revision.

Connecticut has its share of trendy and politicized programs. In general, however, "political bias creeps into the classroom most obviously through pedagogical decisions made by the administration," says one history major. "The college is willing to embrace alternative approaches to the liberal arts, sometimes selecting courses with controversial themes like homosexuality." There are gender and women's studies classes offered by nearly all the liberal arts departments, including French, Slavic Studies, and East Asian departments. There is even a class called "Introduction to Feminist Economics," and a course on gender issues in the Andes.

But in the classroom, a conservative student reports, many professors are fair and tolerant. "In the government department, for example, you'll find professors who are flamingly liberal but you couldn't tell in class," a student says. "Others are only moderately liberal, but they let everybody know it. The good thing though, is that you'd never be graded down for your views; professors are respectful. Outside of the obvious places—gender and women's studies and anthropology—it usually isn't too bad." It is true that one professor quoted in the alumni magazine *CC* proclaimed that her primary educational mission was to "emancipate from the *status quo*" and fight "systems of privilege, sexism, racism, heterosexism, classism," yadda yadda. But another progressive professor says, "I don't want to make my students think like me, but I want to give them the skills and tools to understand other perspectives. If they are liberals, conservatives or radicals, my job is to demonstrate the historical origin and impact of each position on American society."

A red flag hangs outside the history department, however. In 2008, its then-chair, Professor Catherine McNicol Stock, made a name for herself with an op-ed in the *Philadelphia Enquirer*, where she criticized candidate Sarah Palin for hailing from the Pacific North-

64

west—home, Stock said, of racists and "ultra-Christians" like (Oklahoma City bomber) Terry Nichols and (Unabomber) Ted Kaczynski.

Connecticut College has only about 1,990 students, but the school offers forty-one single-discipline majors and five interdisciplinary majors: Africana studies, American studies, behavioral neuroscience, environmental studies, film studies, as well as the option of interdisciplinary majors. Four interdisciplinary centers help students connect learning and life. The most unusual of the four is the Toor Cummings Center for International Studies and the Liberal Arts (CISLA), where students can learn a language, intern in a foreign country, and then produce an original project that pulls all their learning together. Additional programs include the Ammerman Center for Arts and Technology, the Goodwin-Niering Center for the Environment, and the Holleran Center for Community Action and Public Policy.

In 2005, professor David Kyuman Kim began directing the school's new Center for the Comparative Study of Race and Ethnicity. Professor Kim's stated goal is to build an entirely new educational structure dedicated to the "examination of power, structural inequality, and social justice" throughout the curriculum. Avoid it.

More than half the student body spends at least one semester in a foreign country. The college's Study Away/Teach Away program sends a group of ten to twenty students abroad to take courses with Connecticut College professors and local faculty. Recent programs have been held in India, Vietnam, Italy, South Africa, and the Czech Republic. CC is affiliated with many other universities, so students can study virtually anywhere in the world.

Connecticut College offers majors in classics, French, German, Italian, Japanese, Mandarin Chinese, Russian, and Spanish, plus courses in Arabic and Hebrew, among other tongues.

Student Life: No reason to walk

Add Connecticut College to the long list of gorgeous New England schools. The relatively new campus (the oldest building dates to 1915) of gray granite hearkens back to the country clubs that hosted the elite which built the school. From the Blaustein Humanities Center in Palmer Library, one can see the town of New London, Long Island Sound, and—on clear days—Long Island itself. The campus is designated as an arboretum, and it claims 223 species of trees from around the world along with countless varieties of flowering plants. In the spring, the campus's undulating grounds are exceptionally lovely with plentiful space to study, research, and enjoy the outdoors.

Connecticut College guarantees housing for all four years, and 98 percent of students live on campus. One student says that the result is "a genuine feeling that you're part of a college, a place where people really do know you." Some might find it a little too close-knit—all dormitories are coed, and all the bathrooms on coed floors are likewise used by ladies and gents. Sophomores and upperclassmen have the option to select a roommate of the opposite sex, including a boyfriend or girlfriend (although the school discourages couples from cohabiting, doing so is permissible). These "gender-neutral" rooms are scattered throughout all coed floors. For those who prefer privacy, there are a few single-sex floors available.

Before moving onto campus, freshmen go through a rigorous roommate selection process, and as a result, students tend to become close to their roommates throughout the remaining three years. Connecticut has a high percentage of single rooms, which most upperclassmen inhabit, so if a student misses the mad scramble to make friends during his freshman year, he may find himself happily or unhappily alone for the rest of his time at CC. A few areas are designated as specialty residences: students can live with students of like interests in the Earth House; and those living in the Language House can practice their skills by immersing themselves in a foreign language at dinner and in dorm activities. Recent student-chosen theme houses include Contemporary Religious Values, Studio Arts in the Community, and a house dedicated to Alternative Transportation. The campus also offers a quiet house, apartments, co-op living, and substance-free options. Students are free to eat at the campus' five dining halls (Freeman even offers vegetarian and vegan meals and Shabbat dinner on Friday nights), snack shop, or pub.

ACADEMIC REQUIREMENTS

In addition to the requirements for a major, students must take one "foundation course" in each of seven areas:

- Physical and biological sciences. Choices range from a standard introductory physics or biology course to less quantitative classes such as "Geophysics: Introduction to Physical Geology."
- Mathematics and formal reasoning. Options include advanced calculus and "Mathematics from a Cultural Perspective."
- Social sciences. Most of the classes offered here are solid, including survey courses in the basics of psychology and anthropology.
- Critical studies in literature and the arts. Most freshman English classes seem politicized—for instance, "Them and Us: Revisiting The American Dream," which promises to explode "the myth of the melting pot through its presentation of issues of race, class, gender and ethnicity." Solid options include surveys of American and British literature.
- Creative arts. Options to fulfill this requirement range from "The Art of Theater" to first-year classes offered by the dance in Pilates and yoga. The school's respected theater department is said to be less politicized than its English department.
- Philosophical and religious studies. Choices range from basic classes in logic, ethics, or the history of ancient philosophy to "Religious Expressions of Everyday Life," which also counts as a dance class credit.
- Historical studies. Choices range far too widely, from surveys of European or American history, to "Introduction to Indian Civilization."

Students also must take:

- A foreign language, to the intermediate level.
- Two courses designated as "writing intensive" or "writing enriched." (One is usually a freshman seminar.)

Because Connecticut College has no fraternities or sororities, many activities center on dorm life. Each hall adopts a faculty or staff member to participate in events with residents. For instance, "Dessert and Dialogue" allows students to discuss topics like "Representation of American Culture and the Super Bowl" with an invited faculty or staff member. Despite the college's small size, students should have no trouble finding clubs that interest them, whether academic, service, or issue-driven. There are eight singing groups at CC, including a gospel choir and Slavic Chorus and Russian Choir, several dance clubs, a comedy club, an organic gardening club, and many more clubs, groups, and troupes. Around 90 percent of the student body participates in some form of organized sport. The Camels compete on twenty-three teams at the NCAA Division III level in the New England Small College Athletic Conference against schools like Bowdoin, Middlebury, and Williams.

Harkness Chapel is a quaint New England-style church that seems to be used just as often for secular activities as for services. The college has on staff a Catholic priest, a Protestant minister, a Unitarian minister, and a rabbi for services and counseling. There are a few religious organizations like Hillel, Catholic, Protestant, and Unitarian Universalist ministries, and the InterVarsity Christian Fellowship, but these do not play a prominent role in campus life.

The school hosts college Democrats, Republicans, and "CC Left," but none of the groups are very active. Most of the school's "Issue Oriented" organizations are environmentalist or lean left: Feminist Majority, Renewable Energy Club, and so forth. CC does offer several language and culture clubs, as well as a Habitat for Humanity group, gaming club, and wilderness and cycling organizations. The six *a cappella* groups are the most popular campus clubs, with rumored hazing, tough competition, and political hierarchies.

Running a close second in campus activities are Thursday and Saturday night parties, which are largely centered around drinking. Students report that while they are not pressured to drink, doing so makes fitting in a lot easier. Drugs are less common at CC, and hard drugs nearly nonexistent. Although many students embrace the party lifestyle, they do

YELLOW LIGHT

If there is an established creed at CC, it is "diversity." "Diverse" sexual practices are celebrated, and the Lesbian, Gay, Bisexual, Transgendered, Queer, and Questioning (LGBTQ) Resource Center was established in 2007. It is one of the campus' most active institutions, providing mentoring programs workshops, and lectures. If a club or class is built around an issue, it is nearly always a leftist one, most commonly feminist or environmentalist. More alarming is the Center for the Comparative Study of Race and Ethnicity's goal to incorporate racial and ethnic studies into more traditional courses, making it ever more difficult for students to attain a classical liberal arts education. The average CC student probably won't mind much, though: most students report that their classmates are very liberal, white and wealthy. Although Republican groups maintain a small presence, no real conservative activity has taken root at CC.

The school received a "red light" label from the Foundation for Individual Rights in Education for maintaining secretive speech codes and bias incident policies—which no longer appear in its student handbook.

New England

67

spend much of the rest of their time studying. The school has a strict policy against underage drinking, but students say it's rarely enforced unless students seem unsafe or disruptive. Substance-free and quiet houses provide a haven for nonpartiers.

New London doesn't add much to the college—the large town is too far away for students to walk there, and they wouldn't find much anyway, save for beaches, a few restaurants, and one bar, the Oasis. Almost all evening and weekend activities occur on campus, including performances, lectures, and drinking. New London lies halfway between New York and Boston, and the Amtrak station is just a few minutes from the college. Students occasionally take the train to visit friends over weekends, but claim the trip can be costly. A student shuttle service, the Camel Van, will take students as far as Mystic, Connecticut, which students say is a little more exciting than New London.

Connecticut College is secluded enough that crime is minimal—although in 2009, the school reported four forcible sex offenses, one vehicle theft, and twenty-six burglaries on campus. Students need a PIN to enter residence halls, and although a safety walk service is offered, it is rarely used; students say they feel safe walking on campus, even late at night. Most students leave their dorm rooms unlocked and many leave their doors open when they are out. Campus Safety employs seventeen officers and dispatchers, and offers security phones, special lighting, officer and student patrols, as well as vehicle and bike registration.

The school is consistently ranked in the top ten most expensive colleges nationwide: tuition, room, and board (the school computes them all together) for 2010–11 is $53,110. Admission is not entirely need blind, but the college meets the full need of each student who does get in, through loans, grants, or work-study programs. Just under half of students receive need-based financial aid; 85 percent of financial aid is given in grants and scholarships averaging $29,902. One third of graduates carry debt, averaging $22,038.

Dartmouth College

Hanover, New Hampshire • www.dartmouth.edu

Traditions run deep

Dartmouth College was founded by the Reverend Eleazar Wheelock in 1755 as More's Charity School. Its original undertaking aimed to educate Connecticut's Native American youth who were preparing for missionary work. After a number of setbacks and royal interventions, Dartmouth College was established in 1769 as a school primarily for whites.

Traditions run deep at Dartmouth, and those who study here leave with a strong attachment to them. This leads many alumni to assist conservative undergraduates who resent the administration's efforts to reshape Dartmouth—for instance, by persecuting fraternities while supporting women's studies and gay programs, and de-emphasizing the football program.

In 2009, the college selected South Korean-born Dr. Jim Yong Kim as its president. A physician and anthropologist, Dr. Kim founded the philanthropic Partners in Health organization and has directed the World Health Organization's HIV/AIDS department. He announced as his goal to "train an army of leaders to engage with the problems of the world."

Dartmouth remains an institution beloved by its students and alumni, known for its rowdy Greek social life and close interaction between world-class faculty and students. In 2009, the school completed the seven-year, $1.3 billion "Campaign for the Dartmouth Experience," to which 70 percent of alumni donated. "What most impresses me about Dartmouth is the genuine love for the school shared by the student body," said a student. "[T]he Dartmouth spirit is powerful and enduring."

Academic Life: Parental guidance suggested

In lieu of a real core curriculum, Dartmouth imposes extensive but vague distributive requirements, which leave students a great deal of flexibility, and many of them know how to use. According to one junior, some students "manipulate their course selections to boost GPAs. Many majors are not tremendously time-intensive, so students are able to take a wide range of classes." Recently Dartmouth modified its requirements to include a "Culture and Identity" component. As a result, one student states, "one often has to bite the bullet and take a class on feminism, African-American heritage, or any of a number of similar courses,

VITAL STATISTICS

Religious affiliation: *none*
Total enrollment: *5,987*
Total undergraduates: *4,196*
SAT/ACT midranges: CR: *660–770*, M: *680–780*; ACT: *30–34*
Applicants: *18,132*
Applicants accepted: *13%*
Accepted applicants who enrolled: *48%*
Tuition and fees: *$40,437*
Room and board: *$11,838*
Freshman retention rate: *98%*
Graduation rate: *84% (4 yrs.), 94% (6 yrs.)*
Courses with fewer than 20 students: *64%*
Student-faculty ratio: *8:1*
Courses taught by graduate students: *none*
Most popular majors: *economics, government, psychology*
Students living on campus: *87%*
Guaranteed housing for 4 years? *no*
Students in fraternities: *47%* in sororities: *42%*

which vary in tone from liberal to ridiculously liberal." But more traditional subject matters are still taught at Dartmouth—and taught very well by distinguished scholars. A student just has to search them out.

The college offers over fifty majors, including interdisciplinary majors in African and African American studies, environmental studies, Native American studies, and women's studies. Students may also choose to work toward a double major or to create their own fields of study. "The economics major is exceptionally strong and popular at Dartmouth," says an undergrad. "It gives students access to a superb faculty and a broad range of classes. But since the major is popular, lower and mid-level classes can be large and/or difficult to get into. The number of economics majors has doubled in the last ten years, resulting in long waiting lists and crowded classrooms."

Not all courses are graded rigorously. Dartmouth, one of the elite schools suffering from grade inflation, has seen its average GPA go from 2.46 in 1958 to 3.42 in 2007, with 57 percent of course median grades in the A/A- range. In the Spring of 2010, nearly half of classes had an A- average grade, and only three classes (one biology, one economics, and one Spanish) recorded an average grade of B-. Dartmouth transcripts now also include such information as the size of the class and the median grade earned in the class—two numbers that could tell a more complete story of a student's grade.

Students aren't absolutely required to seek guidance in choosing courses, even though the flexible requirements would seem to make it a necessity. The college does assign advisors to freshmen, and students may choose new major-specific professors to advise them later. "Many students seek informal advising from various professors and peers," one student explains. Another student asserts that "the interaction between accomplished professors and undergraduates at Dartmouth is unmatched by any of its peer institutions."

Many students also use the Student Assembly's online Professor/Course Review to help select courses. More help comes from the conservative *Dartmouth Review,* which offers candid, sometimes biting assessments. (Most of the 4,000 students read the paper and more than 10,000 alumni subscribe.) The *Review* publishes and distributes a Freshman Issue that includes articles on "worst and best professors" and "courses of note." Professors' accessibility is uniformly and enthusiastically praised by students. With the popular Take Your Professor to Lunch program, students and professors use vouchers to enjoy a free lunch together

New England

at a local inn. Student-professor communication is also carried on through e-mail, especially in large classes.

Professors, not teaching assistants, teach all courses. This is a major benefit that should not be taken for granted, and isn't offered at every Ivy.

The most traditional and rigorous departments at Dartmouth according to students and professors are classics, economics, history, and religion. Among the many excellent professors at Dartmouth are Jeffrey Hart (emeritus) and Barbara Will in English; Paul Christesen in classics; John Rassias in French (all foreign language classes at Dartmouth use the now-famous Rassias method); Allen Koop and David Lagomarsino in history; Lucas Swaine in government; Colin Calloway in history and Native American studies and Ehud Benor in religion.

According to one student, "The usual suspects for liberal departments are anthropology, geography, women and gender studies, and English. History fits into this category, because the professors teach history from a social perspective and ram the importance of social movements down your throat. The government department is surprisingly fair." Other students cited Latin American studies as a politicized discipline.

The curricula of particular departments can be distorted by the anti-Western ideology of multiculturalism, deformed by dogmatic theory, or cut off by contemporary biases from the traditional content and form of liberal arts education. For instance, Dartmouth English majors can graduate without reading any Shakespeare or Milton—although they must complete two classes on literature from before the mid-seventeenth century, two from the mid-seventeenth to the nineteenth century, and one class on twentieth century literature, as well as a criticism and theory class.

History majors must take classes in geographical areas (U.S. and Canada, Europe, non-Western, and interregional) and five classes that form a concentration like "The Black Radical Tradition in America" or "Modern Europe: The Twentieth Century."

Government majors, unfortunately, face even less-stringent requirements: they must simply take two courses at the introductory level, six classes that form a concentration, and a senior seminar.

Beginning with the 2008–9 year, Dartmouth added the Daniel Webster Project, created by Professor James Murphy. The program strives to bring "ancient and modern perspectives to bear on issues of permanent moral and political importance." By offering lectures, conferences, and symposia on the Dartmouth campus, the Daniel Webster Project adds both new and forgotten voices to the intellectual life at Dartmouth. In November 2010, the program presented its third conference: "Personal Autonomy, Political Philoso-

---

SUGGESTED CORE

1. Classics 5, The Heroic Vision: Epics of Greece and Rome
2. Philosophy 11, Ancient Philosophy
3. Religion 4/5, Religion of Israel: The Hebrew Bible/ Early Christianity: The New Testament
4. History 43, European Intellectual and Cultural History, 400–1300
5. Government 64, Modern Political Thought
6. English 24, Shakespeare I
7. History 1, The United States, 1763–1877 or History 20, American Thought and Culture to 1865
8. History 51, Modern European Intellectual History, the Eighteenth and Nineteenth Centuries

New England

phy, and Democracy," which, like the previous two conferences, attracted scholars from all over the country to Dartmouth for a weekend. Students entering Dartmouth should seek out the program and its leaders.

The Ernest Martin Hopkins Institute, an official alumni organization, seeks to preserve traditional study at Dartmouth and functions as a watchdog reporting on the often intrusive attempts of the school to regiment student life. It provides some scholarships and works with like-minded student organizations to bring moderate and conservative speakers to campus. "Dartmouth students are no longer required to read Shakespeare, Dante, Plato, or even to know the basic facts of American history," says one alumnus associated with the group, "the school isn't easily influenced by outside groups, but our speakers program has been very successful."

Dartmouth's unique academic calendar consists of four ten-week terms, during which students can either schedule classes on campus, take vacation, perform research, take internships, or study at other institutions or abroad. Some 61 percent of Dartmouth undergraduates study abroad during their time at the college, making it number one among Ivy League schools in this category. Dartmouth students study off campus as close as Amherst or Vassar and in places as distant as Tokyo, the Cayman Islands, or Denmark.

Back on campus, three semesters of a foreign language are required; the school offers French, German, Japanese, Swahili, Ancient Greek, Latin, Arabic, Chinese, Spanish, Hebrew, Italian, or Russian.

Student Life: Sheepskin vs. pigskin

Dartmouth lies in the New Hampshire town of Hanover, located in the upper valley of the Connecticut River. The 200-acre campus, surrounded by woodland and mountains, offers students a beautiful setting for study. Concord, New Hampshire, is about an hour away by car, and Boston is a two-hour drive.

Dartmouth has male, female, and coed leagues for thirty-two clubs and twenty-two intramural sports. Dartmouth also fields thirty-one NCAA Division I intercollegiate teams. Dartmouth won the 2007 NCAA skiing title, the school's first championship in thirty-one years. About 80 percent of students participate in athletics at Dartmouth. Dartmouth has no official mascot and is known as "Big Green," but teams were called the Indians for a half-century, until the Trustees deemed the nickname incompatible with the school's original mission to further Native American education. The *Dartmouth Review* continues to refer to the school's teams as the Indians.

Other opportunities for outdoor recreation, especially of the winter variety, abound near campus. The Moosilauke Ravine Lodge offers accommodations and more than thirty miles of trails for hiking, biking, snowboarding, or skiing, as well as places to climb, paddle, and fish. The Dartmouth Skiway and the Silver Fox Ski Touring Center host skating and skiing, the Hanover Country Club has excellent golf facilities, and students can ride horses at the Morton Farm Riding Center. The Dartmouth Programs Office makes canoeing, riding, skiing, and gardening available to students, and the venerable Outing Club also has several affiliated organizations and clubs, including the Ledyard Canoe Club, Bait & Bullet, Boots

New England

& Saddles, Cabin & Trail, Mountaineering Club, Women in the Wilderness, and Ski Patrol. A 16,000-square-foot fitness center gives students access to sixty pieces of cardio equipment (half of which have their own TVs), forty weight machines, and ample free weights.

The college is often referred to as "Camp Dartmouth" and the "conservative party school," according to *TheDartmouth.com*. The long-flourishing Greek scene attracts about 60 percent of the eligible population—freshmen are not permitted to pledge—to join one

---

ACADEMIC REQUIREMENTS

Dartmouth has no core curriculum. Students must satisfy a set of general education requirements. Students must complete:

- An English composition course in freshman year called "Writing 5" and one of more than seventy first-year writing seminars offered by various departments. Choices here range from "Pompeii in Antiquity and in the Modern Imagination" to "Latin American Masculinities."
- A first-year seminar "structured around independent research, small group discussion, and intensive writing." Offerings include "Seven Wonders of the Ancient World," and "Environmental Justice."
- One course each on Western culture, Non-Western culture, and Culture and Identity. Choices include traditional fare, as well as "Introduction to Gay, Lesbian, and Transgender Studies," "Black Theater, U.S.A.," and "Beyond God the Father: An Introduction to Gender and Religion."
- Three semesters of a foreign language, or tests to show proficiency.
- One course in art (creation, performance, history or criticism). Classes range from "Byzantine Art" to "Gender and the Media."
- One course in literature. Options include "Anglo-Saxon and Scandinavian Epic and Saga," and "Queer Poetries."
- One class in systems and traditions of thought, meaning, and value. This could be fulfilled with courses ranging from "America's Founders and the World They Made" to "Indian Buddhism."
- One course in international or comparative study. Options include "Patterns of Religious Experience" and "The Arab-Israeli Conflict in Middle Eastern Literature and Film."
- Two classes in social analysis. Choices include "International Politics" and "Deviance and Social Control."
- One course in quantitative and deductive sciences. Options include "Calculus with Algebra" and "Discrete Probability."
- Two classes in the natural and physical sciences. Choices include "New England Landscapes and Environments" and "Dinosaurs."
- One course in technology or applied science. Options range from "Computer Architecture" to "Electronics: Introduction to Linear and Digital Circuits."
- One of the courses in the natural science, physical science or technology categories must have a laboratory, field, or experimental component.

of twenty-eight fraternity, sorority, and coed houses—despite the best efforts of the school to "henpeck them into submission through regulation," according to the *Review*. The newspaper writes that one of the main goals of freshman orientation is to turn students off from the school's infamous Greek life. (*National Lampoon's Animal House* was based on the stories of three Dartmouth fraternity members.) Under the auspices of Dartmouth president James Wright's power-grabbing Student Life Initiative, Greek houses were essentially annexed by the administration—which enables the school to subject them to its diversity requirements, and to keep a tight rein on all alcohol-related activity. Despite this pressure, the groups sometimes come out on top. Beta Theta Pi fraternity, which was de-recognized by the college in 1996 as part of a disciplinary action, returned to campus as Beta Alpha Omega in the fall of 2008.

Traditional residence halls and smaller social houses make up the nine residential communities that are home to around 87 percent of undergraduates. Students who dwell off campus usually live close enough that they share the same experiences as their on-campus friends. Nearly a third of the rooms are singles (most of which are assigned to upperclassmen), and many of the rooms have private or semi-private bathrooms. There are a few single-sex floors but no single-sex dorms. Substance-free residences are available to students, as are "academic affinity programs," which include the offices of ethnic clubs and societies as well as theme houses in language, eco-consciousness, cooperative living, and religion. "Gender neutral" housing is also available in several dorms and a new pilot program offered by the Office of Residential Life will focus on gender identity. Students interested in the program must complete an application that asks, "What is your biological sex? (Male/Female/Intersex)," and "What is your personal gender identity? (Man/Woman/Additional Gender Identity)." Although the buildings' architecture is generally lovely, fraternity houses are rumored to be in terrible condition and the *Dartmouth Review* reports that some students have complained of ants and rats infesting their rooms.

A review of the student newspapers reveals a litany of complaints about the school's attempts to turn the campus into a politically correct playpen. The traditional fall Bonfire event has not been completely eliminated, but it's now "bring your own binoculars" since the students aren't allowed anywhere near the fire. Students note that the school tries to compete with the Greek parties by throwing lavish-but-dry parties—which few attend.

Vocal conservatives have had some success in publicizing the gradual encroachment of political correctness into the college's academic and student life. The *Review,* with its constant calls for free speech, plays a large part in bringing unsavory issues to light, and the school administration does not always appreciate the favor. Two former editors illustrated the history of the paper in their book, *The Dartmouth Review Pleads Innocent.* William F. Buckley praised the book for exposing and challenging "the regnant but brittle liberalism" of the university system. For its part, the paper has occasionally published juvenile, genuinely offensive pieces. Still, the *Review* has had a positive impact on the campus as a strident conservative voice and appears to be resurgent after a short period of decline. Other student-operated papers include the far-left *Dartmouth Free Press* and the *Dartmouth* (the official school newspaper).

Students and alumni bemoan the fact that age-old traditions are given very little respect, although one student enjoys the fact that "every night at 6:00 PM, the Baker Tower bells play the Alma Mater. Many sing along."

Dartmouth sustains a lively political debate. The Young Democrats and the College Republicans are both active, and the Libertarian Party has recently become strong as well. New Hampshire's first-in-the-nation primary status gives Dartmouth students unprecedented access to aspiring presidential nominees. The 2008 election cycle brought senators John McCain and Barack Obama, and on behalf of Senator Hillary Clinton, former President Bill Clinton and other hopefuls to speak and meet with students on campus. In a partnership with MSNBC, the Democratic National Committee, the New Hampshire Democratic Party, and New England Cable News, Dartmouth played host to a Democratic presidential candidates debate.

Two hundred student organizations round out campus life: the AfriCaSo (the African and Caribbean Students Organization), the Gender, Sexuality, XYZ (GSX Club), and La Alianza Latina, among many others. Some, such as the Dartmouth Coalition for Life and the Dartmouth Animal Welfare Group, are only sporadically active. But Dartmouth offers something for everyone, with numerous singing and music groups, various dance troupes (from Ceili Irish Dancers to the Step Team), and twenty-two publications (the Asian-American *Main Street* and irreverent *Jack O'Lantern* round out a list of academic journals) and media outlets. Academic groups include the Italian Club, Chemistry Society, Societies of Black and Women Engineers, Architecture Club, Mock Trial Society, Parliamentary Debate Team, Latino Business Society, and Mathematical Society, among many others.

Performing arts and debate groups are particularly strong. Radio fans, too, find much to engage them at Dartmouth: WDCR and its sister station, WFRD, are the only completely student-run commercial broadcast stations in

GREEN LIGHT

In 2008, an infamous case arose: in a required freshman Writing 5 class, a professor (who has since moved on to Northwestern University) attempted to teach expository writing from a postmodern scientific perspective. In a nutshell, the professor wanted "to 'problematize' technology and the life sciences" by promoting the notion "that scientific knowledge is, in essence, a fraud perpetrated by the white male hierarchy." When challenged by her students, the professor accused her students of "fascist demagoguery" and cancelled classes for a week to consult her physician about "intellectual distress." She proceeded to e-mail her students to alert them that they were "being named in a potential class action suit that is being brought against Dartmouth College, which is being accused of violating federal antidiscrimination laws." The students were warned not to reply to the message "because it will be potentially used against you in a court of law." Although the professor had a hard time expressing just how Dartmouth had discriminated against her, she thought "maybe it has something to do with my ethnicity or my gender."

Such conflicts seem commonplace at Dartmouth: bright, conservative, and yes, possibly overconfident students and alumni challenge an administration determined to push a politically correct agenda. However, Dartmouth remains more ideologically open-minded than the typical university, having no speech codes and affirming a commitment to free expression, and even the most hardline leftist professors seem to appreciate healthy debate and worthy study, regardless of the political approach. Most of Dartmouth's controversy is lively and often good-natured, appropriate to a thriving university.

the United States. More than a hundred students carry out their operation, and the stations feature both rock music and political debate and discourse from across the spectrum.

More than 20 percent of Dartmouth students volunteer through the Tucker Foundation for community service. The organization was founded in 1951 to preserve and promote the spiritual and moral elements of campus life at Dartmouth. The foundation has shifted its focus away into more secular areas: community-based learning, "economic justice," and other philanthropic activities, like Habitat for Humanity and Alternative Spring Break, around town and around the world.

Also under the Tucker umbrella, religious groups abound; more than twenty-five are represented in the directory. The Aquinas House offers a daily Mass, the Orthodox Christian Fellowship offers a weekly vespers service with discussion following, the Muslim prayer room in Rollins holds daily prayers, and various Jewish groups sponsor services. There is an active evangelical Alpha Omega student group, as well as Mormon and Buddhist gatherings. The Society of Friends has weekly meetings and monthly speakers. Pastor Dean Crocker, a Presbyterian Church (U.S.A.) minister, is the College Chaplain, and he leads the weekly ecumenical Christian Rollins Chapel service.

The Collis Center is a popular hangout for food, beverages, and billiards. Both the Programming Board and the Hopkins Center bring live entertainment to campus. But when students free themselves from course work they usually socialize in the dorms or social houses. One student claims that "beer pong is the most popular social activity on campus."

Crime reports from 2009 reveal ten forcible sex offenses, five burglaries, two cases of arson, and one stolen car. The campus includes thirty-one emergency phones, patrol by security officers, safety escorts, transportation help for sick and injured students, and security guards for social events.

Dartmouth is expensive but generous. Tuition for 2010–11 came in at $40,437, and $11,838 for room and board. Students are also required to own computers. Admissions are need blind, and the college guarantees to meet the full need of accepted students. Some 58 percent of students receive need-based assistance in the form of scholarships, grants, work-study programs, or loans. For a brief time, Dartmouth, like its Ivy peers, eliminated tuition loans for students who came from families with annual incomes below $75,000 and offered need-blind admissions for international students. However, with a $100 million "structural deficit," Dartmouth is now offering small tuition loan packages ($2,500–$5,500) to families with less than $100,000 in annual income. Many students still take out loans to pay for room, board, books, and incidentals, and the average student-loan debt of a recent graduate was $19,081.

Gordon College

Wenham, Massachusetts • www.gordon.edu

Missionaries to New England

Gordon College was founded in Boston in 1889 as a missionary training institute, named for its founder, the Rev. Dr. A. J. Gordon, a famous Boston preacher. In 1955, Gordon moved to its Wenham, Massachusetts campus, and in 1985 merged with Barrington College. Today's Gordon College describes itself as New England's only traditional, nondenominational, Christian, liberal arts college. Gordon aspires to teach the latest in science, philosophy, literature and so forth, while working with the student's faith in Christ, not against it. (Believe it or not, such was the origin of almost all the Ivy League schools.) The school maintains a rigorous scholastic atmosphere, small classes, and a moderately strong core curriculum, guaranteeing students a broad-based, faith-infused education. Its merits have been recognized by the John Templeton Foundation's *The Templeton Guide: Colleges That Encourage Character Development.* For intellectually serious Evangelical Christian students who wish to study in the snowy northeast, Gordon is the first place to apply.

Academic Life: Freedom within a framework

The school's admissions committee says it is more interested in an integrated person than a rigorous academic profile. A faculty member reports, "The faculty, as well as the students, must articulate a basic Christian orthodoxy *and* a commitment to a vibrant intellectual life as Christians. What Harry Blamires [formerly of Wheaton] called the 'Christian mind' is overtly encouraged in both students and faculty." He continues, "Our best students match up with anyone, something we've discovered from our years of experience sending people to Oxford. Our students tend to be serious, earnest, and diligent without a lot of flash and dash. It may not attract headlines, but it's very satisfying in a classroom setting."

On top of a respectable core curriculum the school offers the interdisciplinary honors program called the Jerusalem and Athens Forum—principally a Great Books course in the history of Christian thought and literature. The forum is something any prospective Gordon student should seriously consider. The readings consist of authors such as Aristotle, St. Benedict, Adam Smith, and Aldous Huxley. (They even read ISI's *A Student's Guide to Liberal Learning,* we're proud to note.) According to Gordon, "The two-semester program is founded on the premise that the present and future suffer when the wisdom of the past

VITAL STATISTICS

Religious affiliation: *Christian (nondenominational)*
Total enrollment: *1,565*
Total undergraduates: *1,500*
SAT/ACT midranges: CR: *530–650*, M: *520–620*; ACT: *24–28*
Applicants: *1,701*
Applicants accepted: *71%*
Accepted applicants who enrolled: *39%*
Tuition and fees: *$29,458*
Room and board: *$8,100*
Freshman retention rate: *84%*
Graduation rate: *61% (4 yrs.)*, *72% (6 yrs.)*
Courses with fewer than 20 students: *65%*
Student-faculty ratio: *14:1*
Courses taught by graduate students: *none*
Most popular majors: *psychology, English, communication arts*
Students living on campus: *88%*
Guaranteed housing for 4 years? *yes*
Students in fraternities or sororities: *none*

is neglected." The program strives to help students reflect on the relationship between faith and intellect, deepen their own sense of vocation, and awaken their capacities for intellectual and moral leadership. All costs are covered by the program, which also gives students a stipend to help them subscribe to a scholarly periodical and pursue vocational exploration and career development. As one professor says, "The Jerusalem-Athens Forum is excellent and is our best on-campus program."

Gordon offers thirty-six majors across its five academic divisions: education, fine arts, humanities, natural sciences, and social sciences. The most popular majors are English, psychology, economics/business, bible/youth ministry, and education. The school confers three separate undergraduate degrees: the bachelor of science, bachelor of arts, and bachelor of music. While completing their academic programs, students have access to academic advisors who can guide them and will approve their course selections.

Teaching at Gordon is said to be strong. One student says of his teachers, "Every professor I have had is willing to spend time talking with students after classes as well as during regular office hours. Many professors have lunch with students in the cafeteria, getting to know them personally as well as academically."

However, some departments such as English rely heavily on part-time faculty. This must limit the accessibility of some professors to their students. The English and the communications departments are said to be a bit weak, due to aging teachers and the school's inability to hire full-time faculty. The chemistry department lacks equipment due to inadequate funding.

Quite a number of teachers come highly recommended. Gordon sources speak highly of Thomas Howard (director of the Jerusalem program) and Steve Alter in history; Timothy Sherratt, David Lumsdaine and Paul Brink in political studies; Bert Hodges in psychology; Steve Smith and Bruce Webb in economics and business; Bruce Herman in art; Dorothy Boorse in biology; Thomas Brooks and David Rox in music; and Jennifer Hevelone-Harper, chair of the history department. English majors take four courses in British and American literature (with at least one course in each), two in comparative literature, and three in rhetoric, theory and/or composition. It would be possible for a student to graduate without studying Shakespeare, but that student would still have studied a variety of foundational authors, such as Milton, Keats, Yeats, Eliot, and Faulkner. The English department offers a few politically charged courses like "Women's Literature," but most

New England

of the courses are good offerings of classic literature, from "Shakespeare" to "The Great American Novel."

The history and political studies majors are solid. History majors are required to take courses in ancient, medieval and modern European history, United States history, and also one course in the history of Asia, Africa, the Middle East, and Latin America. Within these requirements, there is freedom to choose specific courses, but most students would be exposed to essential topics of study, such as the American founding and the Civil War. Political Studies majors must take a class that focuses on the American Constitution, along with courses in American politics, comparative and international politics, and political theory. They are also encouraged to intern in public and private governmental settings. Gordon's music program is outstanding. At this relatively small school one can earn a bachelor's degree in music, in performance, in music education, or a master's degree in music education. The school also hosts a nonprofit organization, Christians in the Visual Arts, dedicated to supporting and educating painters of faith.

By working with the Council of Christian Colleges and Universities, Gordon offers some impressive off-campus opportunities, including semester-long programs in the Holy Land, Uganda, New Zealand, Russia, the Middle East, and China. The Gordon in Oxford program is available to select juniors and seniors. French majors can study in Aix, while art students have access to the Gordon in Orvieto program, for an interdisciplinary course in the cultural history of the Renaissance and two classes in studio, history, or theory. According to one undergrad, "All students are encouraged to study abroad for a semester during their time at Gordon. While not required, a good amount of students do study abroad, in places like Israel, Italy, India, and others." For students who are not busy earning next semester's tuition, the school also offers international seminars over breaks. Another program offers an integrated look at the Christian music industry, giving students a chance to spend a semester in Nashville, Tennessee. As part of the program, students use a recording studio, research song writing, develop a marketing plan, design a performance, and bring it all together with a capstone event—all in Music City U.S.A.

Gordon offers majors in French, German, Spanish, and a minor in Mandarin Chinese. There are also classes offered in Italian, Latin, Ancient Greek, and Hebrew.

SUGGESTED CORE

1. English 262: Classical Literature
2. Philosophy 202: History of Philosophy I: Ancient through Medieval
3. Biblical Studies 101/103: Old Testament History, Literature, and Theology/ New Testament History, Literature, and Theology
4. Biblical Studies 305: Development of Christian Thought
5. Political Studies 223: Theories of Politics (closest match)
6. English 372: Shakespeare
7. History 232: America 1492–1846
8. Philosophy: History of Philosophy II/III: Early Modern Philosophy/Late Modern Philosophy (closest match)

Student Life: Birdwatching and the Bible

Gordon's location in Wenham, Massachusetts, is a fine compromise between urban and rural. One student says, "The school is surrounded by woods and lakes, and the campus itself is by far the most beautifully groomed campus I have ever seen." There is enough countryside for students who like to hike, but Boston's Museum of Fine Art is less than an hour away. The school buildings, thirteen of which are residential, are located on several hundred acres of woodlands.

The campus is only three miles away from the Atlantic seashore and many affluent beach communities. Just down the road is Gloucester, Massachusetts, while north of campus is Plum Island, home to the Parker River National Wildlife Refuge, a 4,662-acre site. In the colder weather, students can head up to the major New England ski areas, which are only a few hours away. The nearest major city is Boston, which is accessible by train from the nearby city of Manchester-by-the-Sea. For direct access right from Gordon, students can take the weekend shuttle bus to the Boston T's Orange line.

Of the 1,500 undergraduate students, most live in one of thirteen dormitories. Students are required to live on campus unless they are married, live nearby, or are over twenty-three. Apartment-style buildings are reserved for upperclassmen, while the traditional dorms, usually triples, are for underclassmen. Not all dorms are segregated by sex, but male and female quarters are separated by a common area. During intervisitation, the school handbook warns, "doors must remain fully open and lights left on . . . and excessive or offensive displays of affection will not be acceptable." Resident assistants are expected

ACADEMIC REQUIREMENTS

Gordon's admirable core curriculum consists of the following:

- One course each in the Old and New Testaments, covering history, literature and theology.
- "The Great Conversation: Foundations in Thinking, Reading and Writing." Through both books and film, students explore the themes of love, suffering, community, and the good life. Authors studied range from Dante to Shusako Endo, and films from the works of Steven Speilberg to *Hotel Rwanda*.
- "The Examined Life," an introduction to philosophy.
- "The Scientific Enterprise," a course focusing on the relevance of natural science to a Christian worldview and contemporary issues (four credits).
- "Historical Perspectives on Culture, Belief and Civilization."
- An introduction to Christian Theology.
- Five thematic course requirements: The Natural World, which includes classes such as "Calculus," and "Brains, Minds and Persons"; The Human Person, with options ranging from "Christian Formation in Cultural Contexts" to "Women's Literature"; Aesthetic Sensibilities and Practices, featuring "Cave Art to Medieval" and "A Survey of Musical Masterworks"; Civic Responsibility, which includes "Justice" and "Forensic Science"; and Global Understanding, which can be satisfied through study abroad or through Gordon courses such as "Politics of Developing World" and "Britain, US and the Middle East."
- Two semesters in a foreign language. (Students may test out.)
- One noncredit wellness/physical education class.

to monitor interactions to avoid violations. The campus-wide visitation hours are Monday through Thursday 5:00 PM to 10:00 PM, Friday 5:00 PM to midnight, Saturday 1:00 PM to midnight, and Sunday 1:00 PM to 10:00 PM. Restrictions also apply to alcohol, dancing, and tobacco. In addition, the student handbook admonishes that pranks are to be respectful and courteous. (Are there any other kind?) There are no fraternities or sororities.

The school places a healthy emphasis on sport. Its athletes, known as the "Fighting Scots," compete in basketball, baseball, track and field, cross-country, lacrosse, softball, field hockey, tennis, swimming, volleyball, and soccer. The athletic facilities also include the Bennett Recreational Center, a 72,000-square-foot teaching and sporting venue with an outdoor rock gym and an indoor pool. The Brigham Athletic Complex is an artificial turf field for lacrosse and field hockey that is surrounded by an NCAA (Division III) caliber all-weather track. Intramural sports are encouraged. Sports camps for school-age boys and girls run all summer long on campus.

GREEN LIGHT

All students at Gordon are required to adhere to the school's statement of faith, which asserts the essentials of Protestant orthodoxy. However, the statement is basic enough that Catholic or Eastern Orthodox students might feel comfortable with it as well. Gordon College states that it bases its beliefs and philosophy on the Bible, but is not a "Bible college." One of its mottoes is "freedom within a framework." According to one faculty member, "Christian colleges come in all shapes and sizes. Please don't confuse us with places that are rather deliberately constructed to escape the challenges and responsibilities of contemporary life." The school says that its goal is not indoctrination, but education based in doctrine. The school is described by one professor as "generally respectful of Western/Christian history, but trying to globalize the curriculum a good bit."

While reason dominates in the classroom, formation in faith is the ribbon that weaves throughout the texture of life at Gordon. All students are required to earn thirty Christian Life and Worship credits each semester, regardless of work schedule. (Married students, parents, and commuters have fewer requirements.) Credits, also called sessions, are earned by attending Chapel services, the various convocations held each week, the annual college symposium, or the provost's film festival. The school proclaims that its goal is to "agree on the basics and show charity on the peripherals." Despite this irenicist attitude, students from a more liturgical church, such as Catholic or Orthodox, may find it difficult to fulfill both their own and the school's Sunday obligations. For those willing to travel, nearby Boston offers every kind of worship service imaginable.

Students at Gordon can participate in a variety of clubs, including some that focus on specific academic areas like biology, physics, German, and social work. Other clubs include: Cross-Country Ski Team, Ultimate Frisbee, Model United Nations, Gordon Film Society, Civil War Society, Karate Club, and a theater club called "Exit Ariel." The school hosts the College Republicans, but not the Democrats, and Gordon's Human Rights Club focuses on the rights of the unborn, not homosexuals and illegal aliens. Interested students can take part in the student-run publications, which include an art and poetry journal *Idiom; VOX*, a newsletter of student voices; and a student newspaper, the *Tartan*.

The Student Ministry Office has a vast array of opportunities for students to put their faith to work. The community outreach programs include Homeless Ministry, Adult ESL, Soup Kitchen, and Dance Outreach Ministry. The office's discipleship opportunities allow for students to engage in prayer, Bible study, discussion, and fellowship. Some of those ministries include Companions for the Journey (a mentoring program), and Orthodox Christian Fellowship. The Worship Cabinet Ministries leads and contributes to worship services on campus through music, drama, and the arts. Of course, all of these practices lead up to the missions the school runs during the school breaks, such as the spring-break trip to the Dominican Republic or the winter-break trip to Latin America.

Gordon is a very safe school. In 2009, the only crime reported on campus was a single case of arson.

The school reports that the cost of discipleship in 2010–11 was $29,458, with room and board at $8,100. Several scholarship programs are available, but most of the students take some form of government loans. Some 67 percent of students receive need-based financial aid, and the average student-loan debt of a recent graduating class was $32,405.

Harvard University

Cambridge, Massachusetts • www.harvard.edu

First

Harvard University was founded by Protestant divines in 1636, and it is the oldest university in the United States. Harvard has gone through many permutations, and its evolution continues. The last "golden age" for Harvard was the tenure of President Nathan Marsh Pusey during the years 1953–71. He raised the curricular standards, increased the number of undergraduates, tripled the size of the faculty, and accepted excellent students from public schools. As Brian Domitrovic has noted in the journal *Modern Age,* "Pusey's Harvard was the school's first real era of meritocracy."

Subsequent administrations set about dismantling some of Pusey's achievement—beginning with Harvard's impressive core curriculum—and molding Harvard into the quintessential modern research university with its attendant specialization, premature professionalism, and political correctness. Indeed, it was Harvard's abandonment of broad-based liberal education that set the trend followed by almost every major university in the country.

Nevertheless, Harvard is currently thriving: annexing whole neighborhoods to expand its campus and leading the cannibalistic rush to experiment on human embryos in search of stem cells. With a $24.7 billion endowment (the largest in the world), unmatched library facilities, a faculty that consists of the cream skimmed off the best universities in the world, and students who have survived a highly selective admissions process, Harvard will remain a powerhouse of intellectual life for the foreseeable future—despite its destructive love affair with leftist politics, curricular laxity, and the anti-Western cult of "diversity."

Academic Life: Genius observed

One Harvard professor says, wryly: "Of course we have a core curriculum. It contains over 350 courses!" Actually, Harvard's core is a modest set of distribution requirements, directing students to mostly excellent courses—many of which, however, are rather narrow and specialized. As a result, "Students can, if they want to and are persistent, get a very good traditional education; it's also possible to waste a lot of time."

Harvard changed its general education requirements in September 2009 for the first time since the late 1970s, but the new curriculum doesn't amount to much. Students must take one course each in aesthetic and interpretive understanding; culture and belief;

VITAL STATISTICS

Religious affiliation: *none*
Total enrollment: *21,006*
Total undergraduates: *6,655*
SAT/ACT midranges: CR:
   690–780, M: *690–790*;
   ACT: *31–34*
Applicants: *29,114*
Applicants accepted: *7%*
Accepted applicants who
   enrolled: *76%*
Tuition and fees: *$38,416*
Room and board: *$12,308*
Freshman retention rate:
   98%
Graduation rate: *88% (4 yrs.),*
   98% (6 yrs.)
Courses with fewer than 20
   students: *80%*
Student-faculty ratio: *7:1*
Courses taught by graduate
   students: *1%*
Most popular majors: *eco-
   nomics, political science,
   psychology*
Students living on campus:
   96%
Guaranteed housing for
   four years? *yes*
Students in fraternities or
   sororities: *none*

empirical reasoning; ethical reasoning; science of living systems; science of the physical universe; societies of the world; and the U.S. in the world. This won't require Harvard students to master particular bodies of knowledge (such as American history or the plays of Shakespeare), but will at least force students to take classes outside of their private, idiosyncratic interests.

Despite the shaky nature of its curriculum, Harvard offers the self-directed student an opportunity for a first-rate education. The Harvard catalog "is an astonishing document," says one graduate. "I don't know if any university in the world offers such an amazing array of courses on everything under the sun, most of them taught by serious, often outstanding scholars."

According to one professor, "Most Harvard students are very good at getting into Harvard. That requires a lot of skill and dedication—but not much curiosity. I'd characterize them, intellectually, as highly competitive but not very imaginative." One student says, "Most students at Harvard, while quite accomplished, are uninteresting—lacking intellectual curiosity, conversational skills, or in the worst cases general decency. The thing that separates them from other students is a pathological desire to succeed and to work as hard as they need to in order to do so. There are obviously many exceptions to this broad characterization, but I think it generally holds true."

Upon entering Harvard, each student is assigned a freshman-year advisor—a faculty member, university administrator, or graduate student—who helps the student choose courses and eventually declare a concentration. Later on, the student is assigned a concentration advisor (a faculty member or graduate student). "Advising is as varied as the advisors," says one student. "Most undergrads find that graduate student advisors know more than the faculty advisors, but it's very dependent on the person." One student says, "Although professors are required to hold one-hour long office hours each week, their accessibility depends on how busy they are. However, many faculty also choose to participate as freshmen advisors, and thesis advisors to seniors, as well as advise students informally."

Graduate "teaching fellows" interact with undergraduates more than many faculty do. As a history major says, "Professors here must publish to keep their jobs." Students don't seem to mind the emphasis on research. As one observed, "How else would most of the major disciplines be taught by the leading scholars in their fields?" TAs usually lead the weekly discussion sections that supplement lecture courses. "In some intro classes, graduate students do most of the teaching," another student says. In the opinion of one professor, "it has gotten to be conventional to split the professor's job into 'teaching' and 'research,' but for most of my colleagues these are external manifestations of a single underlying social process: we are trying to move the world of knowledge along, and to bring our colleagues and students with us as we go."

A few years ago the university appointed a nine-member committee, the Task Force on Teaching and Career Development, which issued an eighty-six-page report criticizing the school's "institutional priorities" that reward research over teaching. The report quotes one faculty member as saying, "In my department, teaching is de-emphasized to an extreme. . . . There is no training or guidance . . . and there's a silent understanding that you should put as little time into it as possible." Another says, "One of the biggest disappointments of my academic career has been hearing speeches from university presidents about how important teaching is, and on the other side see hiring decisions be made almost solely on publications and grant records. . . . I see how in my own career I earn high praise (and more money) for every paper or academic achievement, while every teaching achievement earns a warning about how I should not wander off research." The committee recommended eighteen strategies to "motivate and empower committed teachers as well as distinguished researchers, and actively encourage intelligent pedagogy as well as path-breaking research." One critic of the report complains that the recommendations simply ask professors to spend more time on teaching, without relieving their burden of research and publication. It still remains to be seen whether the university will implement institutional practices that actually support teaching and pedagogical improvement.

The leftward tilt of Harvard's faculty is partly balanced by the presence of several stellar thinkers in the center or on the right, who help "sober the academic discourse and attitudes on campus," in the words of a student. Of course, dozens more Harvard professors are stars in their fields, and for that reason are worth seeking out—although some are better teachers than others. Harvard undergrads are eager to praise certain challenging courses and professors, including Lino Pertile in romance languages and literature; Robert Levin in music; Daniel Donoghue, Louis Menand, Daniel Albright, and Robert Kiely in English; James McCarthy in earth and planetary sciences; Thomas Scanlon in philosophy; Jon Levenson of the Divinity School; Peter Hall, Harvey Mansfield, Michael Sandel, and Stephen Rosen in government; Robert J. Barro and Martin S. Feldstein in economics; and

SUGGESTED CORE

1. Culture and Belief 22, The Heroic and the Anti-Heroic in Classical Greek Civilization (closest match)
2. History 1300, Western Intellectual History: Greco-Roman Antiquity
3. Ancient Near East 120, Introduction to the Hebrew Scriptures and Religion 42, The Christian Bible and Its Interpretation
4. Religion 1450, History of Christian Thought: The Medieval West
5. Government 1061, The History of Modern Political Philosophy
6. English 71, Shakespeares: Talking Back to Shakespeare or English 124d, Shakespearean Tragedy
7. History 2400, Readings in Colonial and Revolutionary America - Proseminar
8. History 1304, Modern European Intellectual History Subject and Structure, Nietzsche to Postmodernism

New England

Ann Blair, James Hankins, and Mark Kishlansky in history. The loss of Samuel Huntington, a political scientist and noted author who died in 2008, was keenly felt on campus. Ernest May, a well-loved history teacher, also passed away in 2009.

The closest thing Harvard gets to great books are the courses Government 1060 and 1061, which cover ancient and modern political philosophy and are typically taught by the eminent Harvey Mansfield. One student referred to him as, "the only direct advocate of conservative principles at Harvard." Another student adds, "even if you don't want to become a political theorist, it's the type of curriculum that could change your intellectual outlook for life." He also recommended the "Government Sophomore Tutorial" as "an excellent survey class on American political thought."

The classics department draws mixed reviews. But a recent graduate says it is possible to avoid the politicized classes that apply "structuralism to Herodotus and Thucydides" in favor of the more rigorous composition courses. She notes that one professor teaches in the great Germanic tradition of philology, demanding of his students not just correct grammar but Ciceronian style. The department also offers courses in ecclesiastical Latin and medieval/Byzantine Greek. Another student adds, "I could not study Latin at a better place, including a seminary."

The English department promises that "whether engaged with literary giants such as Chaucer, Shakespeare, Milton, Dickinson, Keats, Woolf or in exploration of less famous authors, students in the English program have a rare opportunity to combine aesthetic pleasure, intellectual stimulation, and ethical deliberation in their plan of study." The first two terms of a student's English studies are spent in four "Common Ground" courses: "Arrivals"(earliest centuries of English literature), "Poets," "Diffusions" (American literature), and "Shakespeares." [sic] After these courses, students may make it up as they go, choosing electives. English honor students must take at least one foreign language literature course taught and read in the original language.

History majors may skip over fundamental American and European history courses, but must take classes in historical analysis, Western history, non-Western history, and pre-modern history, in addition to one reading seminar and one research seminar.

In like fashion, the government department offers "a very flexible concentration," yet thankfully requires sophomores to take a half course in each of four subfields: political theory, comparative government, American government, and international relations. One student says the program "offers a wide range of courses from a variety of political and methodological perspectives. For undergraduates, political theory and international relations are the highlights. Courses in these fields tend to bring up real issues of political conflict and are least likely to get bogged down in technical disputes." Junior government majors participate in a research seminar and seniors take a tutorial in which they have the option of writing a thesis.

The multicultural studies departments (e.g., African studies, women's studies), as well as the religion, social studies and language departments, are said to be heavily infused with a postmodern ideology. According to one student, "In courses in social studies, sociology, Af-Am, or WGS (women, gender, and sexuality), where the premise is a progressive notion of 'social justice,' politics cannot but help intrude into discussion, lecture, and ultimately grading. Religious students would do well to avoid the religion department, which is essentially taught by the Divinity School faculty, known for their lack of rigor and religion." Luckily, for a student with his ear to the ground such programs are easy to avoid.

Former Harvard president Lawrence Summers admitted that school is afflicted in certain departments by grade inflation. This phenomenon is especially rampant in the humanities and social sciences—as opposed to "disciplines like economics and physics [which] are places where the professoriate still believes in the value of concepts like 'truth,' and so are more likely to apply strict standards," a student says. As a result, one professor tells us, "Science students regularly do better in nonscience courses than nonscience students do in science courses." That same professor adds, "Surely a teacher wants to mark the few best students with a grade that distinguishes them from all the rest in the top quarter, but at Harvard that's not possible." One teacher counters: "In the five years I've taught here, I've never had someone breathing down my neck about a low grade I've assigned a student. I honestly haven't encountered this problem in my work here."

Harvard has a rigorous honors program for each of its majors. To enter the honors program, a student must have a high GPA and be willing to write an extensive senior thesis. For the English major, for instance, students must have a GPA of 3.40 or higher. In junior year they

---

ACADEMIC REQUIREMENTS

To fulfill Harvard's distribution requirements, students must take one class from each of the following eight categories:

- Aesthetic and interpretive understanding. Course options include "Literature in Revolution: Great Books in Moments of Cultural Transformation" and "Gender and Performance."
- Culture and belief. Possible class choices include "Human Being and the Sacred History of the West" and "Pathways Through the Andes: Culture, History, and Beliefs in Andean South America."
- Empirical reasoning. Students may choose from classes such as "Deductive Logic" and "Making Sense: Language, Logic, and Communication."
- Ethical reasoning. Course options include "Self, Freedom, and Existence" and "Classical Chinese Ethical and Political Theory."
- Science of living systems. Possible choices include "Molecules of Life" and "Human Evolution and the Human Body."
- Science of the physical universe. Class options include "The Energetic Universe" and "From Haute Cuisine to Soft Matter Science."
- Societies of the world. Students may choose from courses such as "Medieval Europe" and "Health, Culture, and Community: Case Studies in Global Health."
- The United States in the world. Class choices include "Is the American Racial Order Being Transformed?" and "Sex and the Citizen: Race, Gender, and Belonging in the United States."
- Students must also demonstrate, through coursework or test scores, competency in a foreign language equivalent to that attained by one year's study.

New England

will write a twenty page essay on a literary topic (there is also a creative writing option), and by the end of senior year they will have completed a researched thesis of at least 20,000 words.

Harvard's music, history, physics, mathematics, earth and planetary sciences, and other science departments are among the world's finest. Virtually all students agree that Harvard's research facilities and other resources are second to none, and that the university's biological science programs are as rigorous as any in the world. According to one student, "just like almost everything else, the sciences are taught by the leading scholars in their fields." Furthermore, "Undergraduates have numerous opportunities to do cutting-edge research in the labs on both the medical campus and the School of Public Health campus," says a former biology instructor. "You can't take short cuts around research." Unfortunately, one of those areas of research now involves embryonic stem cells. In a widely publicized move, Harvard decided to lavishly fund an institute devoted entirely to finding "therapeutic" uses for embryonic humans—whom researchers at Harvard and elsewhere hope to clone for use as spare parts in treating various diseases.

Opportunities for study abroad abound at Harvard, which sends students to thirteen countries in Africa, sixteen in Latin America and the Caribbean, fourteen in Asia, seventeen in Europe, twenty-one in the United Kingdoms, and five in the Middle East, as well as Australia and New Zealand. One of the programs allows students to attend the University of Edinburgh and work with the Scottish Parliament.

Harvard offers a stunning array of foreign languages on campus: Amharic, Bamanakan, Cape Verdean Creole, Chichewa, Dinka, Egyptian Hieroglyphs, Haitian Creole, Hausa, Igbo, Kinyarwanda, Luganda, Oromo, Somali, Tigrinya, Wolof, Xhosa, Zulu, Gikuyu; Swahili, Twi, Yoruba; classical Nahuatl; Modern and Old Irish, Modern, Middle and Old Welsh, Scottish Gaelic; Latin, Ancient Greek, modern Greek; Chinese, Japanese, Korean, Manchu, Mongolian, Uygher, Vietnamese; Old and Middle English; German, Swedish, Danish, Finnish, Norwegian, Old Norse; Indo-European, Hittite, Old Church Slavonic; Armenian, Akkadian, Sumerian, Arabic, Aramaic (Syriac, Turoyo), Hebrew, Iranian, Persian, Turkish, Yiddish; Catalan, French, Italian, Portuguese, Spanish; Sanskrit, Urdu-Hindi, Tibetan, Thai, Pali, Nepali, Tamil, Bengali; Russian, Ukrainian, Polish, and Czech.

Student Life: Parking in Harvard yard

Campus life is centered around Harvard Yard during freshman year, and a series of residential houses thereafter. Those houses serve as administrative units of the college as well as dormitories. Each house is presided over by a Master—a senior faculty member who is responsible for guiding the social life and community of the House—and a Resident Dean, who oversees students in the House. Though students reside in same-sex suites, house floors (but not bathrooms) can be coed.

Harvard students do not have a reputation for bacchanalian excess, but alcohol and drug use is far from unknown, in the houses and elsewhere. Most Harvard students, however, are too ambitious to jeopardize their future with reckless carousing. Some, for instance, take to prayer. "A lot of students seem to become more religious at Harvard," one student says. "The Catholic Students Association runs a tight ship." Students attend St. Paul's parish, next to campus. The church is also the home of the Boston Boy Choir School, the official choir for the Archdiocese of Boston. The choir sings each Sunday at the 11:00 AM Mass and is often joined by the adult choir. Lovers of more traditional fare may attend polyphonic Latin liturgies at Mary Immaculate of Lourdes Parish in nearby Newton, Mass.

Groups and support services exist for members of many creeds. The long serving chaplain Peter Gomes, who died in spring 2011, was openly gay, as is one of the other chaplains at Harvard's semi-official Memorial Church. Indeed, alumnus (and *New York Times* columnist) Ross Douthat complained back when he wrote for the *Harvard Salient* that the appointment of homosexual clergy at Harvard's chapel "was intended to establish Memorial Church as a place where those with orthodox religious views would not be welcomed. . . . Tolerance for gays, it is now clear, means intolerance for others, namely those who cling to what the administration obviously regards as outdated nonsense—the idea that not all sexual behavior is morally equivalent."

There are no fraternities or sororities on campus, but there are over 400 official student organizations that meet at the 50,000-square-foot Student Organization Center. In fact, Harvard caters to nearly as many extracurricular as intellectual interests—and does so with a distinctive style. As one student says, "Harvard's diversity is not always a bad thing. Everyone can find [his] flavor here." Harvard University athletics, intramurals, newspapers, and literary societies offer an unmatched variety of creative outlets and comfortable niches for students seeking a release from their studies. The most prestigious of these organizations are the *Harvard Crimson*, the justly

YELLOW LIGHT

Harvard undergraduates face a gamut of university mandated gender-neutral language requirements, sexual harassment policies, humorless affirmative action and sex tutorials, and sensitivity training sessions. The Freshman Dean's Office proudly announced that "in collaboration with the specialty Proctors, the academic year 2010–11 features programming addressing different areas of students' identities and wellbeing." The first featured event was "Bisexual, Gay, Lesbian, Transgender, and Queerness" in October, followed by the always popular "Sexual Assault/Sexual Harassment" tutorial.

RAs organize meetings between incoming freshmen and "peer contraceptive counselors," who distribute condoms and dental dams (don't ask), A student group, True Love Revolution (TLR), was founded in opposition to what former student co-president Justin S. Murray ('07) called Harvard's "hook-up culture." The non-sectarian group is dedicated to the promotion of premarital sexual abstinence and promotes chastity by distributing flyers and hosting seminars.

Conservative students do report that they have benefited greatly from having to defend their beliefs in class—and none have reported classroom harassment or punitive grading. As one graduate says, Harvard "retains a largeness of outlook that eclipses the more parochial liberalism of some people." On the other hand, many students find it difficult to communicate with certain segments of the student body because they consider Harvard's affirmative action policies downright divisive. "It creates a definite tension," says one source. "If you're a designated 'minority,' you spend your years as an undergraduate trying to prove to everyone else that you were one of the kids who got in based on merit."

famous *Harvard Lampoon*, Harvard's world-famous men's Glee Club, and the Hasty Pudding Club. "I sing madrigals, play sports, spend long hours in the dining hall," says one student. Other charming customs include fall foliage-viewing and apple-picking tours in the gorgeous New England countryside. There is also a Harvard Republican Club and a Harvard Right to Life group, among many other conservative political and religious organizations, although they are greatly outnumbered by liberal groups.

Harvard's football team hasn't won a national championship since 1919, but it and other varsity sports still attract the attention of the student body. The school fields thirty-eight varsity teams, giving it the largest Division I program, according to the university. Harvard has excellent facilities for tennis, squash, and other recreational sports. There are numerous intramural teams, most of which are formed around the residential houses. The university's literature says that about two-thirds of the student body participates, at some level, in athletic activities.

Cambridge offers many entertainment and dining options, from pizza to excellent restaurants, and some fine booksellers—although bookstores have been closing under the pressure of high local rent. Harvard Square is a quirky, pseudo-bohemian hangout for all manner of people and activity, including almost continual chess matches, and Boston is one of the nation's last truly livable large cities, with a vibrant downtown including numerous historical sites and countless stores and shops.

In January 2007, Harvard announced a multibillion-dollar plan to annex territory on the other side of the Charles River "to transform more than 200 acres into a second, more modern, Harvard Square, with retail space, academic buildings, athletic and cultural facilities, and student housing," according to the *New York Times*. This extension will take up a significant portion of the neighborhood known as Allston, which is already home to Harvard's Business School and its football stadium, said the *Times*. The project will take at least fifty years to complete. Like the Vatican, Harvard thinks in centuries.

Although Harvard's Cambridge campus is moderately safe, students should not forget that they live in a large city. According to one student, "The Harvard University Police Department is well-staffed, friendly, and very helpful to students." In 2009, the school reported one murder, seventeen forcible sex offenses, four aggravated assaults, three robberies, four car thefts, and twenty-four burglaries. Bicycles, wallets, and electronics—especially laptop computers—are the articles most frequently stolen.

Harvard's costs match its reputation. Tuition for 2010–11 was $38,416, with room and board at $12,308. Admission is need blind, and needy students are guaranteed all the aid they require. Harvard's financial aid policy reduces the contributions of families with incomes between $60,000 and $80,000 (those earning less than $60,000 are not required to contribute at all). Harvard's website reports that "Over the past decade we have increased our scholarship aid by 163% and this year [2010–11] we are awarding a record breaking $158 million in need based scholarship assistance to almost 60% of our students." Some 70 percent of student received need-based financial aid, and the average student-loan debt for recent graduates was a quite modest $8,100. Recently Harvard has decided to eliminate loans from its financial packages and replace them with grants.

College of the Holy Cross

Worcester, Massachusetts • www.holycross.edu

Give us Barabbas

Founded in 1843, the College of the Holy Cross is the oldest Catholic college in New England. Originally all-male, Holy Cross submitted to popular trends and went coed in the 1970s. The college is committed to undergraduate teaching and has resisted the profitable temptation to spawn graduate and professional schools. However, Holy Cross has succumbed to other snares—mainly at the expense of its religious heritage. In his *Ex Corde Ecclesiae*, Pope John Paul II wrote that a Catholic university is a "primary and privileged place for a fruitful dialogue between the Gospel and culture." Unfortunately, Holy Cross has followed those academic fashions that have secularized and standardized so many religious schools—and it has gone so far that sources on campus fear it has past the point of no return. The college places a heavy emphasis on "diversity," which it extends to sexual orientation, sponsoring a wide array of gay-themed programs.

Academic Life: The traditional and the trendy

Not long ago, Jesuit colleges required all their undergraduates, regardless of major, to obtain a minor in philosophy. Sadly, the academic program at Holy Cross requires very little mandatory liberal arts coursework—especially in philosophy, language, and religion, the very courses that once distinguished a Jesuit education. Rules about moral behavior have gone the way of the required courses in Latin, and the prevailing ethos is about what you would find at any blue state school in an age of soft-porn advertising.

Instead of a core curriculum, each student chooses from a number of courses to fulfill distribution requirements. For instance, he can satisfy his historical studies requirement by taking a course such as "Radicalism in America"—and nothing else. But one professor insists, "Students who seek such a grounding can get it if they seek out professors for advice early in their HC career—ideally, e-mailing some of those recommended in this guide during the summer before their freshman year." Holy Cross's distribution requirements include none that would necessarily acquaint students with the Jesuit tradition, Catholicism, or even Christianity. Instead, they may choose to study Islam, Buddhism, Hinduism, Confucianism, or Taoism.

In 2008–9, Holy Cross introduced a new program for all freshmen called Montserrat. Each student is assigned to one of five thematic "clusters": The Natural World, The

Divine, The Self, Global Society, or Core Human Questions. Then students take a small-group seminar that falls under the theme. "The Divine" cluster, for instance, offers seminars on "Hearing the Divine," "Jesuit Spirituality," and "Science and Religion," among others. Students live in residence halls with other members of their clusters and go on field trips and work together on community service projects. Students in "The Self" cluster, for instance, visited Boston's Museum of Fine Arts to "see how the Romans expressed the self in art." Students studying "The Natural World" made an inventory of invasive plant species at a local park, according to the program website.

These freshman seminars are limited to fifteen students, offering an intensive introductory academic experience. But few of them focus on fundamental issues and or great texts, while some are devoted to narrow topics (e.g., "Images of the Latino in American Cinema") that hardly offer a proper foundation for liberal arts education. One faculty member says that the program offers "year-long seminars with fancy titles, where the professors just do what they've always done."

The Honors Program is a bright spot. In this intellectually serious program, students explore themes in small classes of six to twelve. Sophomores begin by taking a team-taught course on "human nature." Throughout the semester, a number of professors explore that theme in the sciences, social sciences, humanities, and the arts. As juniors, students select another honors-level seminar (past topics have included "Music and Literature," "Reason and Faith," and "The Berlin Wall"). Every senior writes a thesis, and the results of the research are published in-house and presented in a conference at the end of the year. Admission to this program is selective.

The college's list of degree programs includes a mix of the trendy and the traditional. The Center for Interdisciplinary and Special Studies offers students "concentrations" in such fields as women's and gender studies, peace and conflict studies, environmental studies, and Africana studies. Courses include "Structures of Social Inequality," "Theology of Homosexuality," "Women, Spirituality, and Aging," and "Queer Theory."

Students say that classes in many departments are taught with a political bent, usually from the left. However, says one, "My professors respect my views so long as I back them up." During the academic year, faculty panels, and sometimes faculty-student panels, address contemporary issues from a variety of political perspectives. While the most

New England

politicized department is sociology, the history, religious studies, and English departments also trend sharply left. Of the English department, a professor says that "while it has a few very strong faculty, it has unfortunately tended to replace teachers who were devoted to literary classics with others who are interested in race/class/gender." The religious studies department offers such courses as "Feminist Perspectives in Theology," and "North American Theologies of Liberation," in which, according to the catalog, there will be "special attention given to black, U.S. Hispanic, and gay/lesbian theological works."

Academic advising is available at Holy Cross especially to students who take the initiative. The Academic Services and Learning Center offers, but does not require, academic advising.

Holy Cross prides itself on not having any classes taught by students in a graduate program.

Departments vary in the rigor their requirements for majors. English majors must take at least ten courses, four of them chosen from seven possible periods: medieval, Renaissance, eighteenth-century, nineteenth-century, or twentieth century British, or nineteenth-century or twentieth-century American. A student, however, cannot take more than three courses studying periods after the 1800s. Hence it would be hard for an English major to miss studying Shakespeare. The department also offers education and creative writing options.

History majors take at least ten courses, including "The Historian's Craft," two courses in U.S. history (any period), and two courses in Middle Eastern, Asian, Latin American, or African history. Four courses on Europe and two on premodern/preindustrial history are also required. A senior thesis is also required.

Holy Cross has one the largest, strongest undergraduate classics programs in the country. One professor reports, "Students fall in love with the classics." A major calls the department "first-rate." Another student says, "Two professors in particular I would mention are professors Ellen E. Perry and Blaise J. Nagy. They not only go above and beyond the call of helping students to grow in Latin, Ancient Greek, and ancient history, but also take students on trips to Italy on spring break so that they can learn firsthand about the glory of the past." Other recommended professors in the department include John D. B. Hamilton and Thomas R. Martin. The classics department hosts a chariot race on campus each year for local high school students.

Over the years, the political science department has distinguished itself as one of the finest in the country, taking a serious, historical, institutional, and philosophical approach to the discipline. Majors must take introductory courses in the following areas: American government, political philosophy, comparative politics, and international relations, in addition to at least six upper-division courses, some of which must be chosen from the

SUGGESTED CORE

1. Classics 103, Greek and Roman Epic
2. Philosophy 225, Ancient Philosophy
3. Religious Studies 118/126 Introduction to the New Testament/Introduction to the Old Testament
4. Religious Studies 117, History of Christianity I
5. Political Studies 228, Modern Political Philosophy
6. English 329, Shakespeare
7. History 202, Age of the American Revolution 1763–1815
8. Philosophy 241, Modern Philosophy (closest match)

New England

93

various subfields. Outstanding faculty include Donald R. Brand, Loren R. Cass, Caren G. Dubnoff, Daniel Klinghard, Vickie Langlohr, B. Jeffrey Reno, David L. Schaefer, Denise Schaeffer, and Ward J. Thomas.

In 2009, the college built a four story building costing $30 million to provide more chemistry classrooms and labs. Science and math studies seem strong at the school. On the college website, Holy Cross claims "an excellent record in preparing students for entrance to medical, dental, veterinary, and other professional schools." The mathematics and computer science department is also rigorous and respected.

One student says, "The professors are the best part of Holy Cross. Their doors are always open, they answer e-mails quickly, and they really want to get to know their students outside of the classroom. I've taught a professor to dance for his daughter's wedding, I've had a traditional Hungarian meal at a professor's house, and I've debated with my professors about all manner of things: Milton, Verdi's *Requiem*, Catholicism, the Geneva Convention."

In departments besides those listed above, students and faculty name the following as excellent teachers: Frederick J. Murphy in religious studies; Jeffrey Bernstein, Lawrence E. Cahoone, Christopher A. Dustin, and Joseph P. Lawrence in philosophy; Robert K. Cording, James M. Kee, Jonathan D. Mulrooney, Lee Oser, and Helen M. Whall in English; Nicholas Sanchez and David Schap in economics; Noel Cary in history; Jessica Waldoff and Sarah Grunstein in music; Virginia Raguin in visual arts; Robert H. Garvey in physics; John F. Axelson, Mark Freeman, Charles M. Locurto, and Amy Wolfson in psychology; Robert Bertin and Mary Lee Ledbetter in biology; Edward Isser and Steve Vineberg in theater; and Susan Sullivan and Victoria L. Swigert in sociology.

The College offers very strong premedical, prelaw, and accounting programs. Opportunities available to prelaw students include Mock Trial and Moot Court teams, and the chance to serve on the editorial board of a student-published law review, the *Holy Cross Journal of Law and Public Policy*, containing articles written by practicing lawyers and law professors.

Should students wish to take a break from regular campus life, foreign study beckons. The College currently offers study-abroad programs in England, Scotland, Australia, and elsewhere. In addition, there is a Washington Semester program in which students hold internship positions at various government, nonprofit, and media organizations while also completing an extensive research project on some area of public policy under the guidance of the regular faculty. One faculty member observes that college takes care to ensure that the internships are substantive (i.e., not secretarial in nature), and faculty work hard to ensure that the theses are based on serious research. At the end of the semester students return to campus for an oral examination on their theses as well as their overall Washington experience."

Beside Latin and Ancient Greek, Holy Cross also offers majors in Chinese, Italian, French, German, Spanish, and Russian.

Student Life: The exorcism room

Worcester, Massachusetts, is a college town with more than fifteen schools, including Assumption College, Clark University, and Worcester Polytechnic Institute. Holy Cross belongs to the Colleges of Worcester Consortium, an intercollegiate organization that allows students to take classes at member schools. With more than 36,000 college students in the area, Worcester is an appealing city. Students report that they generally enjoy the area because it offers plenty of cultural activities not always found in cities of its size. And if Worcester isn't happening enough, Boston is less than an hour away; New York City is a three-hour drive.

Holy Cross is located on a 174-acre wooded hill overlooking the city. The campus is divided into several quads with paths, manicured lawns, and walkways connecting the various groups of classical and modern buildings; there is a historic Jesuit cemetery and an arboretum. Students say the campus is pleasant and generally peaceful. About 88 percent of the approximately 2,900-member student body lives in the college's ten residence halls, where space is guaranteed for four years. Though the sexes are separated by floor, all dormitories are coed. Each room offers a high-speed Internet connection. Some rooms offer a view of the Fenwick clock tower, home of the Exorcism Room, where (according to legend) a long-ago exorcism ended in death. Other student traditions include leaving "a note to tomorrow" in the western tower of Fenwick Hall and the entire freshman class going sledding at the sight of the first snow.

A professor observes about the students at the school, "Like most schools at its level, Holy Cross has a mix of some students genuinely motivated by intellectual curiosity and others just here for the fun and the degree. Certainly we have a significant number of intel-

---

ACADEMIC REQUIREMENTS

While Holy Cross has no core curriculum, students do face certain distribution requirements. Students must take:

- One course in the arts. Options range from "Survey of Art: Renaissance to Modern Art" to "The History of Rock."
- One literature class, including everything from "Composition" to "Studies in World Literature."
- One religion course, where choices range from "Reformation and Counter Reformation" to "Feminist Perspectives in Theology."
- One philosophy class, such as "Medieval Philosophy" and "Religions: China and Japan."
- One history course. Any place or period will do, ranging from "The Rise of the Christian West to A.D. 1000" to "Latino History."
- One cross-cultural or "diversity" class. Options range from "East Asian Development" to "Queer Theory."
- Two social science courses. Choices include "Economic History of the United States" and "Drugs of Abuse."
- Two natural science and mathematics classes. Options here include "Atoms and Molecules" and "General Physics in Daily Life."
- Two foreign language courses.

New England

RED LIGHT

Campus speakers have included some who show a callous disregard of Catholic teachings on central moral issues. Since 2002, Holy Cross and its Women's Forum have hosted yearly performances of *The Vagina Monologues*, a play that, among other disturbing features, celebrates the lesbian statutory rape of a teenage girl. One student says, "[College president] McFarland himself defended the play by turning to moral relativism and emotivism, despite other attempts to appeal to Catholic moral teachings and objective truth."

Although there are both College Republicans and College Democrats on campus, neither seems to be highly active at present. Of political life at the college, one professor tells us, "There is a highly pronounced leftist bias, though a small minority of conservatives is tolerated if it behaves." Indeed, programming organized by the administration has exhibited a decidedly partisan, left-wing tilt, students complain. As one contact puts it, "To a remarkable degree for a Catholic institution, the college features a considerable amount of gay/lesbian programming."

lectually serious, motivated students. But there is a large party crowd as well."

Holy Cross undergrads can choose from more than a hundred student organizations, ranging from a ballroom dancing society to academic clubs like the Biology Society—and activist groups like the ABiGaLe and Allies, a homosexual and bisexual advocacy association that operates with college approval. Student Programs for Urban Development (SPUD), sponsored by the Chaplain's Office, is the largest student organization and serves more than twenty-five agencies in Worcester. Approximately 450 students (mostly female) volunteer annually. The Chaplain's Office also operates as the working arm of the administration's diversity efforts.

Says one student, "while from the top down things do not look good for the college's Catholic identity, there is a small group of committed Catholic students who are determined to spread the faith by witnessing to their peers." Traditional Catholic groups on campus include the Students for Life and Compass, a club for faithful Catholics. The *Fenwick Review*, a conservative student newspaper, publishes four or five issues each year. The administration met with protests five years ago, when it tried to close down the newspaper for satirizing the notion of "gay marriage." The school has since relented and the *Review* now flourishes.

While a mix of viewpoints can be found in the articles and editorials on the pages of the student weekly, the *Crusader*, readers should be prepared to also find faculty dismissing the teachings of the Catholic Church. In response to an article by a student defending traditional marriage, a religious studies professor wrote a letter condoning same-sex unions and criticizing "our society" and "many churches" that "still try to silence gay people."

Daily Mass is available at the St. Joseph Memorial Chapel and two other chapels. To accommodate students of other religions, the college also has Protestant and nondenominational services each Sunday and provides a Muslim prayer room. More traditional Catholic students should look into the weekly Latin Mass at St. Joseph's Parish in Fitchburg—a 20–30 minute drive away.

New England

The majority of students are involved in some type of organized athletic activity; one-quarter compete as varsity athletes. The college's athletic programs are housed in the expansive Hart Recreation Center, which boasts a fitness center in addition to a 3,600-seat basketball arena, an ice rink, and an Olympic-size swimming pool. On top of thirteen clubs and eight intramural sports, Holy Cross supports fifteen teams for men and twelve teams for women in its intercollegiate athletic program. The Crusaders compete in the Patriot League in twenty-four sports. Holy Cross has one of the highest student-athlete graduation rates of any NCAA Division I school. Among other athletic facilities, the college now offers a new set of ten first-rate outdoor tennis courts, and a minor-league baseball stadium on campus that is used by the college's own team during the school year and by the Worcester Tornadoes the rest of the time.

Like many colleges, Holy Cross has had trouble with student drinking. But the college has instituted a tough, zero-tolerance policy that it strictly enforces. On the whole, the campus is perceived as very safe. In 2009, Holy Cross reported one forcible sex offense, one aggravated assault, nine burglaries, and one motor vehicle theft. The college's public safety department supports several programs that promote campus security: a student escort service that helps late-night study bugs and partiers back to their dormitories, crime prevention workshops, and twenty-four-hour patrols. The Colleges of Worcester Consortium also sponsors a van service that transports students from campus to campus.

In 2010–11, Holy Cross tuition was $39,330, and room and board $10,940. About 55 percent of the student body receives need-based financial aid. Admissions are need blind, and the school promises to meet 100 percent of a student's financial need. The average recent graduate of Holy Cross bears a student-loan debt of $23,785.

Massachusetts Institute of Technology

Cambridge, Massachusetts • www.mit.edu

Whiz kids

The Massachusetts Institute of Technology was founded with fifteen students in 1865. From the start, the school stressed the importance of research; we've probably all benefited from something discovered or invented by an MIT scientist. Certainly, MIT excels in the sciences, especially engineering. However, even for those students who seek an education in the natural sciences MIT requires enough coursework in the humanities to also permit a decent introduction to the liberal arts. At the same time, liberal arts majors will find themselves in as much a rigorous program but must be aware of the science requirements, which, when mastered, make for a balanced and excellent education. Of the top schools in this guide, perhaps no other school can boast students who are so driven to accomplish things. "You won't find a cutthroat atmosphere here," says a student. "It's incredibly difficult, but your classmates are on your side."

Academic Life: Precision bearings

MIT comprises the following schools: Science; Engineering; Architecture and Planning; Humanities, Arts, and Social Sciences; the Sloan School of Management; and the Whitaker College of Health Sciences and Technology. Each except the last accepts undergraduates. MIT is home to about 4,000 undergrads and 6,000 graduate students. The Engineering School awards the most undergraduate degrees (40 percent of those conferred) and houses the most popular fields of study: computer science and engineering, electrical engineering and computer science, and mechanical engineering. The School of Science is the next largest, graduating about half as many students (mostly in biology and mathematics) as the Engineering School. The School of Humanities, Arts, and Social Sciences graduates fewer than a hundred students each year, with economics by far its most popular concentration, although the school offers twenty majors. Indeed, as one student told us, "The great secret of MIT is that it is a *great* place to study history, literature, music, and other liberal arts." Often, students will double major or minor in a humanities or social science program, combining with a science major. The School of Architecture and Planning awards roughly twenty-five degrees to undergraduates each year.

MIT structures the better part of each freshman's schedule. Seventeen "Subjects" or courses make up the "General Institute Requirements" (GIR): six core courses from calculus, physics, chemistry, and biology to be completed in the first year as well as one lab requirement (LAB); two Restrictive Electives in Science and Technology (REST); and eight humanities, arts, or social sciences courses ("HASS" requirements) as well as two communications requirements.

Students usually complete all "general institute requirements" by the end of their second year, the year during which they begin pursuing their majors. Majors are confusingly called "Courses" at MIT. Each under-graduate—even those in the humanities—is awarded an SB (really a Bachelor of Science) degree. Students have but little choice within the science requirements, unless one considers "Calculus with Theory" to be much of an alternative to "Calculus with Applications" or just plain "Calculus." But whichever course a student picks, it can be assumed, according to those on campus, that it is solid and essential to future studies at MIT.

MIT offers a number of freshman programs including five "learning communities" as an alterna-tive to mainstream classes: Concourse (highly recom-mended), Experimental Study Group, Media Arts and Sciences, Seminar XL, and Terrascope. According to the university, in these programs, "Students make progress comparable to other freshmen, but the manner in which individual institute requirements are met varies from program to program and among students within each program."

In addition to these freshman programs, students may participate in the Independent Activities Period (IAP), a four-week period in January, the one month in MIT's 4-1-4 academic calendar scheme, where they may pursue their own interests and programs. MIT is also one of the few remaining campuses that offer ROTC programs in three branches of the military: Army, Navy/Marine Corps, and Air Force.

For help in navigating the curriculum, MIT assigns a faculty or staff advisor to each freshman. Students meet their advisors weekly in certain freshman seminars. When a stu-dent selects a major, an upperclassman in that department becomes his mentor. Students say that faculty are busy, but willing to talk if you can find them at the right time. Persis-tence pays off.

Students attending MIT will surely have other helpers available, apart from their pro-fessors. Peer assistance here is incredibly strong. Says a student. "We're very collaborative here. We share. Basically, we have to work together if we're going to make it to graduation."

VITAL STATISTICS

Religious affiliation: *none*
Total enrollment: *10,384*
Total undergraduates: *4,232*
SAT/ACT midranges: CR: *650–760*, M: *720–800*; ACT: *32–35*
Applicants: *15,663*
Applicants accepted: *11%*
Accepted applicants who enrolled: *64%*
Tuition and fees: *$38,940*
Room and board: *$11,234*
Freshman retention rate: *97%*
Graduation rate: *83% (4 yrs.), 91% (6 yrs.)*
Courses with fewer than 20 students: *65%*
Student-faculty ratio: *7:1*
Courses taught by graduate students: *not provided*
Most popular majors: *engineering, computer and information sciences, physical sciences*
Students living on campus: *92%*
Guaranteed housing for 4 years? *yes*
Students in fraternities: *50%* in sororities: *35%*

New England

SUGGESTED CORE

1. Literature 21L.001, Foundations of Western Culture: Homer to Dante
2. Philosophy 24.01, Classics of Western Philosophy
3. Literature 21L.458, The Bible
4. History 21H.411, History of Western Thought, 500–1300
5. Political Science 17.03, Introduction to Political Thought
6. Literature 21L.009, Shakespeare
7. History 21H.101, American History to 1865
8. Literature 21L.002, Foundations of Western Culture: The Making of the Modern World

A normal MIT class is twelve units: three hours of class time, two hours in a discussion session, and seven hours of studying. How long students actually spend outside of class varies, of course. "I know of several student geniuses here who basically just show up for the exam at the end of the semester," says a student. "I, however, spend fifty to sixty hours studying per week," she qualifies. The university places no limits on students' course loads. While a typical course load is around forty-eight to sixty units, one mechanical engineering major says, "120 units is not unheard of."

MIT is a work-intensive, challenging environment, especially for freshmen. Wisely, MIT gives first-semester freshmen only pass/fail grades. During the second semester, freshmen earn As, Bs, or Cs; if they get a D or F, it will not appear on their transcripts. Even so, very little grade inflation is reported at MIT.

As students move into their Courses, grading becomes normal and the options for research open up even further. MIT's Undergraduate Research Opportunities Program (UROP) is used by approximately 85 percent of undergrads at some point in their careers; it offers hundreds of varied opportunities for students to assist with ongoing faculty research projects. Participants spend six to ten hours a week working for credit, for pay, or as volunteers—but the experience is priceless. MIT conducted more than $718.2 million of sponsored research in 2009 (involving both graduate and undergraduate students). "This school is filled with opportunities. Even as a freshman, you can plunge right in to internships and research opportunities. My friends at Harvard couldn't believe it when I told them," says a student.

MIT has about 1,025 faculty members, supplemented by some 800 graduate students employed as teachers and teaching assistants. Students are likely to be taught by a graduate student in some introductory courses. MIT puts its student to full-time professor ratio at an exceptionally low seven to one and claims that most faculty do teach undergraduates. As one professor says, "Unlike many Ivies or state schools, MIT offers an opportunity for any first-year student to take a class with a full professor." Sixty-five percent of the classes do not exceed twenty students. But MIT's lecture classes enroll hundreds of students. One sophomore told us, "My biology class (a required class) had more than 700 students. We couldn't even fit into the largest room on campus, so some of my classmates watched over a live-streaming video."

Conservative students sometimes complain of unfair grading, especially when their views differ from their professors' on hot-button "social issues." Still the overall atmosphere at MIT is said to be open-minded, if sometimes narrowly utilitarian.

MIT has nine Nobel Prize winners on the faculty; in the institution's history, "seventy-six present and former members of the MIT community have won the Nobel Prize," most recently (2010) Professor Peter A. Diamond in economics. The current faculty also includes twenty-three MacArthur Fellows, seventy-eight Guggenheim Fellows, and six Fulbright Scholars. Three former faculty members were winners of the Kyoto Prize. MIT does not mean you'll be invited for tea at the home of a Nobel laureate. You won't. But you might contribute to one of their research projects and start to make a name in your field.

A short list of professors recommended by students include Daniel Kleitman (emeritus) in mathematics; Wolfgang Ketterle in physics; Patrick H. Winston in computer science, Alan V. Oppenheim, Harold Abelson, and Gerald Jay Sussman in electrical engineering and computer science; Richard R. Schrock in chemistry; Joseph M. Sussman in civil and environmental engineering; Diana Henderson in literature; Pauline Maier, Jeffrey Ravel, and William Broadhead in history; and Sheila Widnall in aeronautics and astronautics.

To fulfill the degree requirements towards a major in literature, students must take at least ten subjects in literature of which no more than three may be introductory courses and at least three must be seminars. Students pursue courses either by historical periods or thematic complexes. Historical students choose among ancient and medieval; Renaissance and Restoration; Eighteenth Century and Enlightenment; Romanticism and nineteenth century; and twentieth century and contemporary culture. Thematic students pick courses from categories of historical period; genre and mode; film, media, and popular culture; gender and ethnic studies; or author study. Shakespeare would be possible, though hard, to miss.

History majors must take four required courses: one topical seminar, a seminar in historical methods, complete a thesis tutorial and a course in which students complete their thesis (final year of study). Additionally, the history major chooses six restricted electives. These must include "subjects drawn from two geographical areas, as well as one premodern (before 1700) and one modern subject." American history is not required.

The political science major must take both "Political Science Scope and Method" and a "Political Science Laboratory," and must select one class from each of four fields: political philosophy or theory, United States politics, public policy, and international/comparative politics. They also complete three political science electives and a senior thesis (including a preparatory seminar). Study of the U.S. Constitution would seem hard to avoid.

In recent years, fewer than 20 percent of the MIT student body studies abroad. That is low compared to liberal arts colleges, but high for engineering schools, where students tend to extend more effort in laboratories in this country. But the university does offer some excellent programs, such as the Cambridge-MIT exchange, and MIT-Madrid. Additional programs provide research and study opportunities to MIT students in China (including Taiwan and Singapore), France, Germany, India, Italy, Japan, Mexico, and Spain. MIT offers seven language majors: Chinese, French, German, Italian, Japanese, Portuguese, and Spanish.

Student Life: Particles accelerating

MIT students who can find the time to raise their nose from their books and beakers have the fascinating city of Boston to explore, featuring sporting events, concerts, museums, historical sites, restaurants, and bars of every kind. It is questionable how many of these treasures they can sample, given the academic load they all face. Students live in the cityscape of Cambridge, which stretches along the Charles River. There is nothing quaint about MIT's campus. Most of the buildings are called not by the name of a donor, professor, or famous

ACADEMIC REQUIREMENTS

MIT imposes a core curriculum, but it has very little to do with the liberal arts. All students must complete

Six science requirements:

- Two courses in calculus, for example "Calculus," "Calculus with Theory," or "Calculus with Applications."
- Two classes in physics, usually "Physics" I and "Physics" II.
- One chemistry course, for example "Principles of Chemical Science" or "Introduction to Solid-State Chemistry."
- One biology class, usually "Introductory Biology."
- One lab course (twelve units), such as "Robotics: Science and System" or "Environmental Chemistry and Biology Laboratory."
- Two science electives like "Circuits and Electronics," "Ecology I," or "Thermodynamics of Materials."

Eight courses in the Humanities, Arts, and Social Sciences division, coming from at least three of five areas:

- Literary and textual studies. Options here range from "Shakespeare" to "Introduction to Contemporary Hispanic Literature and Film."
- Language, thought, and value. Choices include "Classics of Western Philosophy" and "Darwin and Design."
- Visual and performing arts. Opportunities include "Introduction to Western Music" and "Traditions in American Concert Dance."
- Cultural and social studies. Choices range from "The Human Past: Introduction to Archaeology" to "Women and Global Activism in Art, Media, and Politics."
- Historical studies. Options here range widely, including everything from "The Ancient World: Greece" to "Technology in American History."

Students must compile three or four courses among these electives to form a "concentration." Concentrations can be as straightforward as economics or philosophy, or as interdisciplinary as black studies, labor in industrial society, or urban studies.

Students also take communications courses, one in each of four years; the first course is based on the student's level of ability, while the final two usually fall within the student's major. Students must also satisfy an additional writing-skills requirement (two-thirds of which can be completed before the student even starts coursework).

Students also need eight points of physical education credit and must pass a swimming test by the end of sophomore year.

MIT inventor, but instead are known by number. (Lobby 7, for instance, looks out onto busy Massachusetts Avenue.) This almost creepy custom, along with the concrete smorgasbord of buildings, gives MIT its distinctive, *Gattaca* atmosphere. Killian Court is among the oldest sections of campus, but the more striking architecture is provided by the modernist designs of I. M. Pei, Euro Saarinen, and Alva Aalto's Baker House dormitory. The Stata Building, designed by famed architect Frank Gehry and completed in 2004, is one of the most unusual buildings on campus, with its uneven walls and strange angles. "The vectors that come together to make a working building are supposed to represent all the ideas and diversity that come together to make MIT," a student tour guide explained. In 2007, however, MIT sued Gehry's architectural firm, citing negligence in its design. Already the $300 million building has faced cracks in the outdoor amphitheater, snow and ice falling from poorly designed window boxes, and leaks throughout the building.

Winters are hard in Boston, but thanks to an intricate tunneling system (second in the U.S. only to the Pentagon), MIT students rarely have to leave the warm indoors. "Once you figure it out, it can save you lots of chapped lips," says a student. Another interesting feature of the campus design is the Infinite Corridor, the "longest corridor in the nation," according to MIT sources.

Recent building projects included the extension of Fumihiko Maki's Media Lab in 2009 and the Sloan School of Management in 2010, and the completion of the new Ashdown House residence hall in 2008 and the PDSI Physics building in 2007. Alumnus David H. Koch gave $100 million to fund a cancer research center which opened in October 2010.

An abundance of extracurricular activities thrive at MIT: the school hosts an enormous number of exhibits, performances, and concerts each year, in addition to its own performing groups. According to one professor, "much current student energy is dedicated to public service, international issues, and fun academic pursuits such as robotics." The university is home to twenty-two religious student organizations, with a majority of evangelical Christian groups from Baptist, American Baptist to the United Church of Christ. The chaplaincy website also lists Muslim, Buddhist and Hindu organizations as well as a Roman Catholic group, underlining the school's multicultural and multiethnic identity. according to the *Boston Globe*, which quotes a senior as saying, "When I came to MIT, I was expecting it to be full of nerds—people who don't really put together science and religion. I was really surprised—and still am—by the volume of Christian fellowship here." The Fellowship of Catholic University Students (FOCUS) and the Catholic chaplaincy are described as vibrant and faithful.

Among the many other student organizations are College Republicans and College Democrats, a pro-life group, the Alpine Ski Club, Women's Water Polo and Volleyball, WMBR Radio (MIT's radio station), a Strategic Games Society and "Stammtisch," MIT's German conversation group. There is not much political activism on campus; most students are way too busy to engage in anything else besides their studies.

Institute housing, as the dorms are called, is coed (except for the all-female McCormick Hall), though most dorms have "single-gender living areas," according to the school. There are no freshman dorms at MIT; to discourage age segregation, dorms are mixed so that freshmen can potentially live right next door to seniors. MIT has an interesting way

GREEN LIGHT

When asked about the state of free speech and political fairness at MIT, one professor noted that the students are argumentative, and "love exploring every side of an issue." This teacher described the faculty's political views, as "located across the spectrum from left to right," noting that "MIT sports one of the most contrarian of opponents of the global warming hypothesis, and a recently tenured molecular biologist who opposes embryonic stem cell research; it also sports the renowned Noam Chomsky, a former CIA director (and chemist), and a former (woman) secretary of the Air Force."

MIT does not boast many political activists among its students. Students seem to hold a wide disparity of political ideas, but they don't spend time promoting them, rallying others to the cause, or demonstrating for them. They have too much work to do. One student tells us, "Instead of political activism, many students participate in social justice causes, fighting especially against poverty, hunger, and disabilities. MIT students tend to put their activism to work rather than to rallies."

of placing incoming freshmen into residence halls, with a program called Residence Exploration (Rex). The summer before matriculating at MIT, students are sent a video detailing each of the twelve residence halls. Students rank their top choices, and MIT assigns them to a dorm based on their selections. Then, when they arrive for freshman orientation in the fall, students have a week to test out their dwellings, and they can switch or rearrange if necessary. "It's a high stress environment here, so it helps to have a great living arrangement," says a student. One of the most coveted places to live is Baker Residence Hall, where 80 percent of the rooms face the Charles River, and where students can enjoy a relatively short walk to the center of campus.

After their freshman year, students may live in fraternities or sororities (MIT has thirty-three combined) or in cooperative housing. Fraternity and sorority housing is located just on the other side of the Charles River, a short walk from campus. Living off campus is an option, but rent in and around Boston is prohibitively high; MIT says only about 8 percent of undergraduates elect to live off campus each year.

About 20 percent of MIT undergrads participate in intercollegiate athletics, while nearly 75 percent of students participate in intramurals (there are eighteen sports) and informal recreation. Intramural offerings include bowling, dodgeball, and water polo. The school has thirty-three varsity teams and "provides the second most intercollegiate offerings among Division III institutions in America," according to the school. Except for one varsity team, MIT competes as part of the National Collegiate Athletic Association (NCAA) in Division III, and has produced 164 Academic All-Americans. MIT's top programs are men's track and field, women's track and field, men's swimming and diving, men's tennis, women's volleyball, men's volleyball, and women's swimming and diving.

Students who are interested in intramural or unstructured athletics can avail themselves of the stunning Zesiger Sports and Fitness Center, complete with an indoor track, ice arena, two pools, fitness floors, and more. "There's really something for everybody here," says a student. "You can choose rock climbing, ballroom dancing, archery, martial arts.

New England

You shouldn't have a problem finding something that interests you here." Every MIT student must also pass a hundred-yard swimming test, because, as one student conjectures, "We live next to the Charles River, and the wind could blow you in."

The school boasts a very active Greek life. Some 50 percent of the male student body are members of the twenty-seven fraternities, while 35 percent of women belong to one of six sororities.

With the workload students face, more than a few turn to liquor as a sedative. The Campus Alcohol Advisory Board promotes responsible drinking on and off campus. MIT is trying to develop a policy that meets the state's drinking laws but still allows students to get anonymous medical help. MIT's policy lets first offenders avoid an MIT alcohol citation, but fraternities can still face problems with the Cambridge Licensing Commission, which can suspend residence permits for underage drinking.

The campus is fairly safe. Larceny is the most common offense at MIT (126 reports in 2009), as at most other schools, and laptop computers are a common target. In 2009, MIT reported two motor vehicle thefts, one aggravated assault, three forcible sex offenses, and one arson on campus.

Tuition for 2010–11 was $38,940, and approximately $11,234 for room and board. Admissions are need blind, however, and the school guarantees that it will cover all demonstrated financial need. Approximately 90 percent of undergraduates receive some kind of financial aid, and the average student-loan debt of a recent graduating class was a modest $15,228.

Middlebury College

Middlebury, Vermont • www.middlebury.edu

Strong language

Any college blessed with the gorgeous campus and small-town charm of Middlebury College will surely attract some of the nation's best students. With its Old Stone Row and Old Chapel, Middlebury has been called, with just cause, New England's most beautiful campus. The quaint village of Middlebury is the ideal small college town, and from its "college on the hill" one has a view of Vermont's Green Mountains to the east and New York's Adirondack Mountains to the west.

One faculty member sums up the school this way: "The best aspect of Middlebury is the very high quality of teaching; from student evaluations, the students of Middlebury have great enthusiasm and respect for their teachers. The least favorable point is the miniscule representation of the conservative point of view amongst Middlebury faculty and the college as a whole." A student who holds alternative viewpoints must have courage and a strong backbone to flourish.

Academic Life: Bread Loaf and Arab nationalism

When Middlebury College was founded in 1800, students were expected "to read, translate, and parse Tully, Virgil, and the Greek Testament, and to write true Latin in prose, and [to] have also learned the rules of Vulgar Arithmetic," according to the college catalog. Needless to say, there are no such expectations today.

Middlebury may teach the liberal arts, but students are at liberty to choose which arts, as the college makes no stipulations as to which texts or ideas students should engage. Middlebury gives its students a great deal of flexibility in designing their curricula and consequently cannot guarantee that students will have a decent handle on the Western tradition before graduating—though they certainly are offered the resources to learn that tradition, if they choose. Middlebury does offer a sampling of obscure and trivial courses which can fulfill requirements. However, while gaps in students' educations are certainly possible, they are not the norm. "A student who was extremely adept and savvy could probably avoid most of the 'fundamental' courses, but my experience is that they do not try to do that," says one teacher. Over the decades, Middlebury students have shown themselves inclined to take solid classes.

For the most part, the college steers clear of the emphasis on professional preparation that one finds at larger colleges or research universities; Middlebury offers only the Bachelor of Arts degree, even for science majors. One professor reports, "This school is academically intense. Even those who major in the performing arts tend to do joint or double majors in order to cover a more traditional subject in depth. . . . We may not require that all of our students read the Western canon, but we teach much of it and we take it very seriously."

Insiders laud the close and frequent faculty-student interaction at Middlebury. "I know my teachers very well," a senior told us, "With very few exceptions, there are such great interactions and the profs are completely approachable. Sometimes you'll even get 'call me at home' on a syllabus—so long as you don't call at eleven when they're putting their two year old to bed." Middlebury is the kind of school where students and faculty form intellectual relationships that last for years.

From the beginning, Middlebury students are encouraged to foster academic relationships with their professors. Freshmen are required to take one of several first-year seminars, which are intimate, interdisciplinary, discussion-oriented courses with an intensive writing component. Some recent seminar course offerings have been "Love and Friendship in Literature and Philosophy," "The Blues and American Culture," and "The Game of Go." Seminar instructors also serve as advisors for students until they declare majors. After completing the first-year seminar, each student completes a college writing course, which can be chosen from among a number of academic fields.

Many Middlebury professors do conduct research, but teaching is by far the highest priority among faculty. Most faculty research is centered around senior thesis projects, and conversely, these projects tend to be informed by faculty interests. Professors—not teaching assistants—teach every course. Highly recommended professors at Middlebury include Hang Du of the Chinese department, a native speaker known to present his courses "with clarity and understanding; he makes us feel at home." Frank Winkler of the physics department has taught at Middlebury for decades, and engages students in his class with lively discussion topics. Jon Isham of the economics department, according to one admirer, "presents his class in a clear, impartial manner, stressing the facts of the market and the realities of the business rather than the abstract theories that some professors prefer to teach." Other highly praised teachers include John Bertolini, John Elder (emeritus),

VITAL STATISTICS

Religious affiliation: *none*
Total enrollment: *2,482*
Total undergraduates: *2,482*
SAT/ACT midranges: CR: *638–740*, M: *650–740*; ACT: *30–33*
Applicants: *7,904*
Applicants accepted: *18%*
Applicants accepted who enrolled: *43%*
Tuition and fees and room and board: *$52,500*
Freshman retention rate: *95%*
Graduation rate: *83% (4 yrs.), 92% (6 yrs.)*
Courses with fewer than 20 students: *75%*
Student-faculty ratio: *9:1*
Courses taught by graduate students: *none*
Most popular majors: *political science, economics, English*
Students living on campus: *97%*
Guaranteed housing for 4 years? *yes*
Students in fraternities or sororities: *none*

New England

107

SUGGESTED CORE

1. Classics and Classical Studies 150, Greek and Roman Epic Poetry
2. Philosophy 201, Ancient Greek Philosophy
3. Religion 280, Studies in Hebrew Bible
4. Religion 130, The Christian Tradition (closest match)
5. Political Science 318, Modern Political Philosophy
6. English 332, Shakespeare's Tragedies and Histories
7. History 203, U.S. History 1492-1861
8. Philosophy 225, Nineteenth-Century European Philosophy

Jay Parini, and David Price in English; Gregg Humphrey in teacher education; Richard Wolfson in physics; Charles Nunley and Nancy O'Connor (emerita) in French; and Paul Nelson and Allison Stanger in political science.

Middlebury is internationally known for its total-immersion foreign language programs, which bring in hundreds of students each summer. Middlebury offers majors in Arabic, Chinese, classics, French, German, Italian, Japanese, Portuguese, Russian, and Spanish, and the school provides a number of courses in foreign literature in translation. The international studies major allows students to specialize in the language and culture of Africa, East Asia, South Asia, Europe, Latin America, Russia and Eastern Europe, or the Middle East. The department sponsors lectures and symposiums frequently. Sixty percent of each Middlebury junior class studies abroad each year, in more than forty countries at more than ninety different programs and universities; the C. V. Starr–Middlebury Schools Abroad are in Argentina, Brazil, Chile, China, Egypt, France, Germany, Italy, Japan, Mexico, Russia, Spain, and Uruguay.

Though the language program is an important part of Middlebury College, "there are excellent programs across the curriculum" insists one professor. These include an esteemed classics department, and an academically diversified political science department. Another respected Middlebury program is the Bread Loaf School of English in nearby Ripton, Vermont, which offers courses in literature and writing. The school holds its famous Bread Loaf Writers' Conference each August, when some of the nation's most distinguished writers gather for seminars and workshops. Middlebury's environmental studies program is also well known in its field.

It should come as no surprise that this small northeastern liberal arts college in a notably liberal state leans to the left. A faculty member insists that "faculty and students support the discussion of controversial topics." But one student disagrees: "Any expression of conservative ideology on this campus draws either jeers or sneers, and I have many times felt very uncomfortable when four or five people at a time lambaste me for expressing even my most moderate positions. Though this is a racially and ethnically diverse school, there is only one accepted ideology." Another student reports, "This is a campus that swings far left. Liberal bias does creep into classrooms, particularly in the economics department." College Republicans complain that they were not invited to a question-and-answer luncheon for Chief Justice John Roberts when he came to address the school; they only heard about it through gossip, they claim, and wangled their way in at the last moment. The sole school newspaper, the *Middlebury Campus*, has a decidedly liberal slant.

The course offerings at the school reflect a certain bias. Middlebury offers more courses in women's and gender studies than in economics. Because the women's studies department is interdisciplinary, many of these courses can, regrettably, fulfill several of the distribution requirements—including literature, social sciences, art, and history, as well as "cultures and civilizations." Fortunately, Middlebury's English faculty have largely resisted the ideological fashions that have ruined once-proud departments elsewhere. It is one of the few English programs that still requires that its majors, who constitute some 10 percent of the student body, take a course in Shakespeare. A National Association of Scholars study of liberal arts colleges' English departments concluded that "Middlebury offers a relatively well-structured major containing a high proportion of foundational courses" and that "it has largely resisted the postmodernist tide, changing less in many respects than the other majors we examined."

Middlebury's strong tradition in English has been seriously weakened, however. In February 2004, both the English department and the American literature and civilizations department voted to merge into the "English and American literature" department and major. The department currently offers nine courses that claim to highlight the "problems" of sexuality and gender in literature, and some of even more questionable academic value, such as "Fictional Worlds," in which works to be studied include *The Matrix*, *Star Trek*, and *Dante's Inferno* (the videogame, not the poem). In addition to a vigorous "politically-correct" agenda in courses, one professor says the new combined major eliminated the four-course sequence in American literature that English majors were previously required to take. All discouraging news.

History majors are required to take one course in European, and one in American history, but once these are taken care of, they could only take courses in the Middle East or Asia, or choose among courses that include "Listening to Brazilian Popular Music," "History of Mexican Food," and "American Empire."

Political science majors must complete three introductory courses chosen from four subcategories: political theory, American politics, comparative politics, and international relations. These could either cover classic political texts or "basic problems in American politics, such as race, gender, foreign policy, and education." Once these have been completed, the student may choose seven additional courses from a menu that includes "Local Green Politics," "Same Sex Marriage and the Law," and "Jihad vs. McWorld."

Apart from the courses that cover such things as "Topics in Reproductive Medicine" and "Sexual Selection" in the Biology department, and "Ethnomathematics" in the Math department, Middlebury's math and science courses seem to be fairly straightforward.

Student Life: Uncommon commons

Upon entering the college, each "Mid" student is assigned to one of five commons, which will serve as the center of the student's academic, social, and residential life. Every commons has its own faculty head, dean, coordinator, and residential advisors. Though housing is relatively inexpensive in Middlebury, the college is overwhelmingly residential: 97 percent of students live on campus. First-year students can choose to live on either a single-sex or a coed floor, but floors for upperclassmen are all coed. (There are no coed dorm rooms or bathrooms, however.) The college also has substance-free floors available for those who request them. One resident admits, "Dorm visitation rules have always been relatively lax."

Within the commons system, students have additional choices regarding living arrangements. Academic-interest houses encourage learning outside the libraries and classrooms. These include total immersion language houses in Chinese, German, Italian, Spanish, Russian, Japanese, and French; the latter house's residents live in Le Château, a grand hall modeled on the Pavilion Henri IV of the Chateau de Fontainebleau. Other academic houses include the Environmental House, Queer Studies House, and the Pan-African–

ACADEMIC REQUIREMENTS

Middlebury students must complete two sets of distribution requirements: academic and cultural. The academic categories include a first-year seminar (a writing-intensive course taken in the first semester). A second writing-intensive course is to be completed by the end of sophomore year. Recent examples have included "Smart Girls: Intelligence and History," "Russia: Euro-Asian Nation," "Euripides and Athens," and "The Writing Workshop" I and II.

Students must also complete at least one course in seven of the following areas:

- Literature. A Shakespeare course would count. So would "Sexing the Canon."
- The arts. One could choose "Advanced Composition" or "Found Object Sculpture."
- Philosophical and religious studies. Choices range from "Ancient Greek Philosophy" to "Food in East Asian Religions."
- Historical studies. These courses range from "United States History: 1492–1861" to "Women and Gender in Africa."
- Physical and life sciences. Choices include "Physics in the Universe" and "Global Change Biology."
- Deductive reasoning and analytical processes. This lets students choose either mathematics classes such as "Non-Euclidean Geometry" or "Chinese Philosophy."
- Social analysis. Courses range across many departments, and include "American Economic History since 1900," "Sociology of Freakishness," and "Indian Cinema."
- Foreign languages. Options include Arabic, Chinese, classics, French, German, Italian, Japanese, Portuguese, Russian, and Spanish.
- Physical education. This requires two noncredit courses, which could include dance, exercise classes, or sports.

The culture and civilizations requirement entails one course on each of the following subjects:

- The civilizations of Africa, Asia, Latin America, and the Caribbean. These include "Politics in Israel," "Moral Economy," and "Drumming and Dance in Ghana."
- Comparative culture studies. "European and Asian Operas" and "Human Ecology" would fulfill this one.
- European civilization. Included are "The Rise and Fall of the Roman Republic," "The Historical Novel," and "United Kingdom Popular Culture."
- The cultures of the United States or Canada. These could include "The American Presidency," "Performing Culture: America's Dancing Bodies" or "Introduction to Disability Studies."

New England

Latino–Asian–Native American (PALANA) Center, a residence hall and cultural center for minority students. Such houses "are fairly popular and also sponsor events," one student says. "If the Spanish house sponsors a party, there'll be sangria, awesome music, and people will come in hordes." As for dining, Middlebury operates its own food service, and buys much of its food from local farmers and dairies.

Recent construction includes the much needed Davis Family Library which caters to the needs of students and professors. (While this building is state-of-the-art, one student says it looks like the Roman Colosseum, another that it looks like a spaceship.) The college has recently renovated the Hillcrest Environmental Center, the central location for the environmental studies program and the office of Environmental Affairs. Middlebury has recently purchased the Addison House, a nineteenth century house once owned by the college, but sold in 1910. Once renovated, the building will be used by College Communications. It is reported that other buildings, such as the freshman residence Battell Hall, are still in need of renovations.

To replace college fraternities, which were suppressed in 1990 for being "cliquish" and "exclusionary," the college offers six coed "social houses," which host parties, concerts, and other events. Binge drinking continues to be a problem. Students report that alcohol found its way even into the substance-free dorms. The Vermont liquor inspector has since cracked down on alcohol on campus. "Now," relates an insider, "there are no more alcoholic parties without a guest list. This leaves the freshmen to binge drink alone in their rooms."

Religious student groups, Bible discussions, and prayer meetings are available for students who want them, although few do. While admitting that religion is not very popular on campus, one insider allows, "Middlebury does cater to the religious student body relatively well." The Christian nondenominational group is very active but also, strangely, "very cliquey" says one student. "The Catholic group is more accepting, and they go to church together."

There are signs that things may be looking up for the conservative minority at Middlebury. As one professor says, "There is a good Republican Party on campus, a lively organization consisting of a small number of smart kids. However, I'd say about 95 percent of the faculty are leftist liberals, as is about 80 percent of the student body." Still, Middlebury is not as tolerant as campus literature claims. In March 2004, the student constitution committee denied a new pro-life student organization official college recognition.

Many Middlebury students are involved in leftist activist groups and their various protests. Particularly active are the pro-abortion and feminist organizations. Says one student, "There is no dialogue at all about the pro-choice issue. . . . Particularly disdained as well is the Christian viewpoint toward homosexuality. Those with conservative viewpoints are a silent minority who in general don't speak up for fear of losing friends."

Around half the student body participates in sports—varsity, club, or intramural. The Middlebury Panthers compete on thirty-one varsity teams in the NCAA Division III; since 1995, thirty of these have been championship teams. Recently the men's tennis team won the NCAA championship. The college encourages fitness through a physical education requirement. The college's location in western Vermont gives students other athletic outlets as well; skiing is as popular in the winter as hiking, biking, and camping are in the other seasons. Water sports are also popular; Otter Creek runs right through town. The

RED LIGHT

The most rampantly politicized program at Middlebury is its Arabic Summer School. According to an August 2006 report on the web-based news site Real Clear Politics, administrators and teachers in this program adhere to a rigid Arab nationalism. For example, in their maps, textbooks, lectures, and teaching materials, Israel doesn't exist, and the term "Arabi"—Arab fatherland—is used instead of "Middle East." (This would surprise the millions of Berbers, Copts, Turks, Kurds, Armenians, and Jews living in the region.) The Persian Gulf is referred to as the "Arabian Gulf," Syria's borders are marked "provisional," and Lebanon is designated as a province of a yet-to-be Arab super-state. These difficulties do not end with the classroom: alcohol is banned in the program (as it is not in other language departments). Halal dietary restrictions are enforced, "implying that all Arabic speakers are Muslims, and that all Muslims are observant; yet less than 20 percent of the Arabic school community was Muslim. No such accommodations [in dining] were made for Jewish students who kept kosher, even though they outnumbered the Muslims," as Real Clear Politics reported. Alone among the other programs, the Arabic school program ignored the Fourth of July. It is said those who did not share these views "were made to feel like dhimmis—the non-Muslim citizens of some Muslim-ruled lands whose rights were restricted because of their religious beliefs."

Rikert Ski Touring Center, the Middlebury College Snow Bowl, and the Ralph Myhre Golf Course are all operated by the college. According to students, the college's January term provides ample opportunities for skiing and other sports. Besides providing winter sports, this one-month semester gives students the opportunity to focus on one course or take an internship.

There are other popular groups on campus besides athletic ones: the Middlebury Radio Theater of Thrills and Suspense, for instance, presents new and vintage radio dramas on Saturday nights through the campus radio station and is syndicated by other college radio stations around the country. Other student organizations include, among many others: Amnesty International, The Bunker (a student-run bar and night club), The Christian Orthodox Association, College Democrats, College Republicans, Feminist Action at Middlebury, Hillel (Jewish), Hindu Student Association, InterVarsity Christian Fellowship, Islamic Society, Midd East Action, Middlebury Musician's Guild, Middlebury Open Queer Alliance, Middlebury Student Quakers, Newman Club, Prajna Meditation Club, Prayz (Nondenominational Christian), Roosevelt Campus Network, Unitarian Universalists of Middlebury, Voices of Indigenous People, and organizations for the various languages.

The town of Middlebury is only a five-minute walk from campus. Students enjoy an abundance of restaurants and shops—many more than one would expect in a town of only about 8,000. Along with Middlebury's natural surroundings and the plentiful campus events, the presence of the town means that students rarely if ever have good reason to be bored.

Middlebury lays claim to one of the great advantages of small-town New England: safety. Students can live and study on campus without worrying too much about how to get home from the library or a friend's dorm room. The Midd Ride Program and Safety Escorts transport students to and from various on-campus locations, and red emergency phones around campus can be used to contact police immediately. Says one student, "I feel completely safe and secure on campus." A faculty member remarks, "Overall, the campus is pretty safe; there are some scattered incidents of a bike being stolen or a room broken into. The dorms have recently been locked, with entrance only possible through the use of a student card." In 2009, the school reported five forcible sexual assaults and seven burglaries on campus.

Middlebury is a connoisseur's college, at a premium price. The "comprehensive" fee (including tuition, room and board, health and other fees) for 2010–11 was $52,500. Some 41 percent of students receive need-based aid. But the school admits students regardless of need and guarantees that it will meet every student's demonstrated financial requirements, and the average amount borrowed for the 2009–10 school year was $21,458.

Mount Holyoke College

South Hadley, Massachusetts • www.mtholyoke.edu

Designing women

Mount Holyoke is a small, highly selective, nondenominational college for women enrolling approximately 2,300 students who hail from forty-eight states and seventy countries. Founded in 1837 by progressive educator and chemist Mary Lyon, Mount Holyoke boasts that it graduates "independent critical thinkers who speak and write powerfully," while being "technologically savvy, and . . . distinguished by their ability to lead in a complex, pluralistic world."

In 2009, the board of trustees elected Lynn Pasquerella, a 1980 graduate of the college, the eighteenth president of Mount Holyoke. Students and faculty are very happy with the board's choice and believe she "represents the ideal of a Mount Holyoke education."

The school offers plenty of solid course offerings—among a host of less promising ones—and faculty members who genuinely care about their students' academic progress. Students choosing Mount Holyoke would do well to avoid courses that the college calls "innovative" and "experimental," since they are likely to be steeped in leftist politics.

Academic Life: Girls who wear glasses

Mount Holyoke is widely recognized for, in its own words, a "rigorous and innovative academic program, its global community, its legacy of women leaders, and its commitment to connecting the work of the academy to the concerns of the world." These are not idle claims: The college's academics are indeed rigorous and certainly innovative, its focus is strenuously global, and its graduates often go on to do great things. Famous alumnae include Emily Dickinson, playwrights Suzan-Lori Parks and Wendy Wasserstein, Frances Perkins (first female cabinet member in U.S. history), and Julia Phillips, the first female movie producer to win an Academy Award.

It is unfortunate that the school imposes no rigorous core curriculum, to ensure that every graduate has encountered the classics of Western literature, history of the United States, or canonical artworks and other achievements which traditionally have made up a liberal arts education. Instead, students are free to choose from an overly wide range of courses in a series of loosely defined intellectual categories. The school's foundational goals—a comprehensive knowledge of Western history, music, and arts—have suffered here (as elsewhere) under the assault of trendy academic theories and practices.

However, many students seem happy with the school's curriculum. One student says, "Our distribution requirements are enough, I think, to make sure every student intellectually expands herself 'out of the comfort zone.'" Another says, "We are very international, we have a macro, global focus, we are socially active, we have causes, and we want to do something with our careers which will make a difference."

The 287 faculty members of Mount Holyoke are impressive teachers dedicated to their students. They have also proven themselves to be busy scholars, research scientists, and artists. Well over half the faculty are women, and over 90 percent have doctorates. Students speak very highly of the school's teaching, one-on-one support from professors, and the fairness in grading. Six months after graduation, 86 percent of the class of 2008 were working or in advanced study. Of those students, 17 percent were attending graduate/professional schools. Typically, over 75 percent enroll in graduate or professional schools within ten years. Alumnae attend graduate school at places like Harvard, Yale, Stanford, and Georgetown, and the college has among its ranks Fulbright fellows and other award-winning scholars.

Students at Holyoke choose from among forty-eight departmental and interdisciplinary majors, or design their own programs. In addition to the standard programs such as physics and French, newer fields of study include interdisciplinary offerings like African American and African studies, Asian studies, Latin American studies, and gender studies—many of which are, predictably, politicized.

VITAL STATISTICS

Religious affiliation: *none*
Total enrollment: *2,304*
Total undergraduates: *2,288*
SAT/ACT midranges: CR: *610–730*, M: *600–720*; ACT: *27–31*
Applicants: *3,061*
Applicants accepted: *58%*
Applicants accepted who enrolled: *32%*
Tuition and fees: *$40,256*
Room and board: *$11,780*
Freshman retention rate: *90%*
Graduation rate: *78% (4 yrs.), 83% (6 yrs.)*
Courses with fewer than 20 students: *64%*
Student-faculty ratio: *9:1*
Courses taught by graduate students: *none*
Most popular majors: *biology, English, international relations*
Students living on campus: *93%*
Guaranteed housing for 4 years? *yes*
Students in fraternities or sororities: *none*

Students are assigned faculty advisors in their first year and may later change advisors when they settle on majors. Faculty keep long office hours and are reportedly very accessible. Many students speak warmly of teachers who welcome students seeking direction, intellectual answers, or "just to chat about life." Other Mount Holyoke women report that they visit their teacher's homes, meet their families, and eat with them in student dining halls. One student says, "I have formed at least ten to twelve substantive relationships with professors who I would/could/do go to for anything."

Mount Holyoke has long prided itself on its small classes; its student-faculty ratio is a strong 9 to 1. Professors teach all courses, although assistants sometimes lead laboratory sections. Students do, however, report frustration with frequent changes on the faculty, and

SUGGESTED CORE

1. Classics 212, Greek Tragedy and Film
2. Philosophy 201, Philosophical Foundations of Western Thought: The Greek Period
3. Religion 203/204, Introduction to the Hebrew Bible/Introduction to the New Testament
4. History 121, The Middle Ages: 300–1300
5. Politics 212, Modern Political Thought
6. English 211, Shakespeare
7. History 170, American History, Precolonial Through the Civil War
8. Critical Social Thought 250f, Classics in Nineteenth-Century Critical Social Thought

the number who are off on leave. "There is a lot of professor turnover, and a lot of sabbaticals happen at odd, overlapping times," one student says, "This means that it is tricky for students of smaller majors to fulfill course requirements, and for students to find willing or knowledgeable thesis advisors."

While many students report working extremely hard for their grades, one student remarks, "You don't have to lock yourself away in the library tower, stoking your internal fires with caffeine and hard labor to be a success here. You really just have to have an open mind, a willing heart, and a disciplined manner."

The politics of Mount Holyoke are decidedly leftist, and some students report that dogmatic professors are known to preach their views in the classroom. Although some students find the situation overbearing, one says that she avoids such classes through word-of-mouth, and by carefully reading course descriptions. Other students point to a genuine commitment on the part of the faculty to encourage opposing discussion and debate. One student says, "Conservative students may feel that they are a *minority* in some departments, but they won't feel unwelcome."

Some of the disciplines taught on campus where students of a traditional bent might feel left out include critical social thought, politics, international relations, and gender studies. Others which enjoy a more neutral reputation include economics, humanities, mathematics, and the science departments. One student describes her major as having "more Marxist, proto-feminist [and] leftist . . . professors than not. While they don't force their views on the students, the slant is immediately apparent," she says.

Professors at Mount Holyoke noted for their teaching include Kavita Khory in international relations; Joan Cocks, Penny Gill, Vinny Ferraro, and Chris Pyle in politics; Don Cotter in chemistry; Jonathan Lipman in history/Asian studies; Stephen Jones in Russian; and Bill Quillian in English. Jim Hartley in economics is also lauded for his introductory class, "The Great Books of Western Civilization." "It was the perfect balance of criticism and justification/explanation," says one student. The school is also home to Joseph Ellis, author of the popular history *Founding Brothers*.

During Mount Holyoke's January term, students participate in some form of internship or self-study, designed to help them explore their interests and plan their careers. Students have the liberty to take academically lightweight courses, prepare for the LSATs, MCATs, and GREs, or take time to work on a thesis. Some students opt to study abroad, taking a class trip for the month. Recent examples include a trip to the country of Georgia to study a "new democracy in the making," and another to South Africa to explore its

New England

education system. Some courses are noncredit and offered mostly for fun, such as "Intro to Watercolor Painting," or "Yummy Chinese Food (A Cooking Class)." "It's more fun than serious," one student says. "The formal academic aspect of it has faded," says a professor, who adds that because most faculty are preoccupied with administrative duties (hiring, for example) during that time of year, "they don't have time to teach January term." The dean of faculty has recently made the decision to "save the college $50,000 to $100,000" by not paying J-term faculty.

Holyoke made SATs optional for prospective students in 2001, and has found no difference in the success rates of students who choose to furnish scores and those who do not. At the same time, the policy has opened the college gates to many exceptional students for whom standardized tests are a significant roadblock, the school asserts.

Because Mount Holyoke belongs to the Five College consortium, its students are welcome to attend classes and events at Amherst, Hampshire, and Smith colleges, and the University of Massachusetts—offering them a much wider choice of courses (some 5,300 in all), and access to all the schools' libraries. They are linked by a high speed fiber optic network, and a free bus travels among the schools, which lie within a twelve-mile radius.

English majors are required to take an introductory course, two courses in literature written before 1700—which are generally straightforward, apart from some cross-listed gender studies classes—one in literature written between 1700 and 1900, and four chosen from a number of 300-level courses that include "Jane Austen: Fiction and Film," "Queer Kinship in Asian North American Literature and Film" and "Re-imagining Los Angeles: Multiethnic Fictions of Tomorrowland." A course covering Shakespeare in particular is not required, though students are likely to encounter him in the pre-1700 classes.

History majors are required to take courses covering three of the following regions: Africa, Asia, Europe, Latin America, and North America. They must also take five 300-level courses, a research seminar and one course that studies history before 1750. It is quite possible to fulfill these requirements without taking a single course on European or American history.

Politics majors must take one course each in American politics (which could be filled by "Environmental Politics in America"), comparative politics (such as "Chinese Politics"), international politics, and political theory (which could be filled by "Invitation to Feminist Theory"). Majors must also take three additional 300 level courses. No course in the U.S. Constitution is required.

Despite the school's small size, Mount Holyoke students have many worthy academic programs available, on campus and elsewhere. Among these are its Junior Year Abroad; Community-Based Learning programs; the Speaking, Arguing, and Writing Program; the Miller Worley Center for the Environment's programs; study abroad through the McCulloch Center for Global Initiatives in countries like Costa Rica, Chile, France, Germany, Hong Kong, Japan, South Korea, Spain, and the United Kingdom; and a variety of internships. Students can also take part in various exchange programs: the Twelve College Exchange, which allows students to spend a semester or two at another northeastern school such as Bowdoin, Wellesley, or the Thayer School of Engineering at Dartmouth College; and dual-degree engineering programs with the University of Massachusetts, Dartmouth College, and the California Institute of Technology.

New England

117

Language departments offer degrees in Ancient Greek, Chinese, French, German, Italian, Japanese, Latin, Russian, and Spanish, and further courses are offered as part of degrees like African, Asian, Jewish, Latin American, and Middle Eastern studies.

Student Life: South Hadley country club

The school is situated in the center of South Hadley, Massachusetts, a small town with a population of 17,300. With its red-brick, ivy-covered buildings, large oak and maple trees, and peaceful surroundings, Mount Holyoke is generally regarded as one of the loveliest campuses in the country. About 93 percent of students live on campus, in eighteen residence halls built in several different styles, from Victorian to Tudor to "Modern Institutional Ugly." Almost all residence halls house freshmen through seniors, nicely mixing the classes and encouraging mentor relationships.

Each hall has a living room area with a piano and grandfather clock, as well as a dining room with a kitchenette or full kitchen where students have the option of preparing their own meals. Each room has Internet access, and a phone line and cable-ready out-

---

ACADEMIC REQUIREMENTS

While Mount Holyoke falls far short of imposing a core curriculum, it does maintain some general education requirements. A student must complete courses in seven different categories, distributed among the following three curricular divisions:

- Three courses in the humanities: One must be in arts, language, and literature with choices such as "Seminar in Medieval Art: Chartres Cathedral," "Sophomore Seminar: War: What Is It Good For?," and "Film Theory: Feminist and Queer Theory through Film." Another course must come from history/philosophy religion, with options like: "Ancient Greece" or "Women and Gender in the Study of History; African Women: Food and Power." The third course can be from either of these broad groups.
- Two courses from two different disciplines, out of three subcategories, in science and mathematics—including at least one laboratory course in a natural or physical science. Choices include "Computer System and Assembly Language" and "Understanding Climate Change."
- Two courses from two different disciplines in the social sciences. The options here range from "United States Economic History" to "Anthropology of Reproduction."

Students must complete one course in "multicultural perspectives" devoted primarily to the study of "Africa, Asia, Latin America, the Middle East, or the nonwhite peoples of North America." Options include "New Face/s of Germany: Migration and Representations of Immigrants in Film and Text," "Spirituals and the Blues," and a host of courses in gender studies.

Students also must demonstrate intermediate proficiency in a foreign language through coursework.

let. The college also offers kosher/halal dining facilities. Milk and crackers (affectionately known as "M and Cs") are traditionally served in each residence hall during the evenings on Sunday through Thursday. Most bathrooms are single-sex, but each hall does have at least one coed bathroom for guests, who are allowed overnight stays. Ham Hall, Mount Holyoke's language hall, hosts Chinese, French, German, Italian, and Spanish language fellows, exchange students who help teach their own language in exchange for a stipend and a year in America. Each language has its own table in the dining hall, and occasionally holds private banquets.

Students may choose from over 150 active student organizations including the ACLU, Amherst Koinonia Church (Christian), Amnesty International, Coalition for Gender Awareness, Classics Society, College Democrats and Republicans, Entrepreneurship Club, Environmental Action Coalition, Feminist Collective, Jewish Student Union/Hillel, M&M (Mitzvahs & Mysticism), Model United Nations, Newman Association (Catholic), Pagan Wiccan Collective, Protestant Council of Deacons, Sisters of Hinduism Reaching Inwards, Student Coalition For Action, UMMA (Muslim), Youth Action International, and a number of study groups and sports clubs. The College Republicans have a beautiful logo and website, but apparently very little more. An attempt was made to start a pro-life group, but it never got off the ground, sources tell us.

The college recently named what had simply been called "New Residence Hall." It was finished in 2008 and the board of trustees hopes that the hall's 175 additional beds will free other residence halls for ongoing renovations. The hall was named Joanne V. Creighton Hall, after the recent college president.

MHC places great emphasis on global diversity. The college believes that its diversity "reflects the increasing globalization taking place in the world" and is a "valuable educational asset." One in three students is foreign or is African American, Asian American, Hispanic, Native American, or multiracial. In spite of its ethnic mix, students report that women from different countries usually stick together. However, an undergrad reports that "once people grow intellectually, they branch out and the cliques go away."

One attribute of MHC which deserves comment is its growing reputation as being a "lesbian school." One student says that campus lesbians are a vocal minority. "For some, being a lesbian is cool," she says. "Some girls think that it's the thing to do for support on a single-sex campus." Another student says that "a homophobic student will not survive on the MHC campus, where alternative sexual lifestyles are very visible and their proponents outspoken." Other students point out several coed opportunities at some of the campus events, including dances with men from neighboring colleges.

The college holds religious services on campus; on a given weekend, one might celebrate Sunday, Sabbath, or Shabbat. Catholic and Protestant services take place weekly in the Abbey Chapel, while Shabbat services are held at the "Elliot House," a campus spiritual center. The Elliot House also has daily call to prayer for Muslims, space for weekly gatherings, and a Japanese meditation tea house. The Abbey Interfaith Sanctuary, a renovated Christian chapel, holds sacred objects and texts from the various faith groups represented on campus. Five chaplains work on campus: Muslim, Protestant, Jewish, Catholic, and a Japanese tea-mistress. Together they call for "an inclusive community working towards

RED LIGHT

One might wish that political, philosophical, and intellectual diversity were valued as highly at Mount Holyoke (and elsewhere) as crude, demographic differences among elite students and scholars. The political imbalance at the college comes across from the embattled tone of the rhetoric on the school's College Republicans' website: "The Mount Holyoke College Republicans (MHCR) are the lone conservative voice on a campus of 2,200 students. The MHCR don't back down, inside the classroom or outside. MHCR strive to present conservative viewpoints on campus, no matter how strong the opposition, in order to accomplish a truly well-rounded education for all Mount Holyoke students." That website hasn't been updated in several years, so we can't tell if the group is still active.

A conservative student told the Clare Booth Luce Institute (a national group for conservative women) about her experience at Mt. Holyoke: "[I]t wasn't until college, when I was surrounded with extreme liberalism from my classmates and professors, that I really became concrete in my conservative beliefs and was able to stand up and articulate my conservative position to my peers, professors, and friends. Every day I am challenged and tested in my conservative beliefs . . . whether it's a professor making an unfair generalization about conservatives, classmates professing untruths about conservatives to the class, or friends making jabs."

spiritual depth, moral development, and social justice," while seeking to broaden the interfaith community, the school's website reports. Students who find campus religious activities to be too liberal should look into congregations in local towns that might offer more orthodox fare.

Time outside the classroom is rarely spent idly. Flyers and posters for forthcoming activities, including concerts and parties, are posted around campus by different clubs. Across the street from campus stands the college-owned Village Commons, which includes a small movie theater, restaurants, and shops. A popular coffee shop, the Thirsty Mind, sometimes hosts live acoustic music. About twenty minutes away, Northampton is popular for shopping and dining, while Amherst, twenty minutes in the other direction, is the choice for bars and pubs. Others look to the Five College network for their parties. One student says, "You can party and have a crazy, youthful, coed time at another of the five colleges, but then come home to sweet, peaceful MHC without worrying that you'll wake up to a mess in your own hallways."

Mount Holyoke students have enviable choices when it comes to extracurricular activities, many of which have a distinctly country-club character. The college maintains one of the finest equestrian centers available for students, which includes more than sixty boarding stalls, a large outdoor all-weather footing show arena, a permanent dressage arena, two indoor arenas, and a cross-country course through 120 acres of woods, fields, and streams. The college manages "The Orchards," an eighteen-hole championship golf course designed by Donald Ross. Within walking distance of the golf course is the state-of-the-art athletic and dance complex, which houses a twenty-five-meter, eight-lane pool, indoor track, numerous tennis, racquetball, volleyball, basketball, and squash courts, and weight training and cardiovascular fitness areas. The Mount Holyoke Lyons boast NCAA Division III teams in basketball, crew, cross-country running, field hockey, golf, lacrosse, riding, soccer, squash, swimming and diving, tennis, indoor and outdoor track and field, and volleyball. Participation in extracurricular arts such as dancing and singing are equally popular.

Mount Holyoke seems particularly concerned about security. The Department of Public Safety patrols the campus twenty-four hours a day. The campus is well lit and campus phones are always nearby. In 2009, there were twelve burglaries and two forcible sex offenses on campus. Students report feeling very safe, and benefit from safety training such as free RAD (Rape Aggression Defense) courses.

If Mount Holyoke is an oasis of learning, its prices mirror those of a resort. Tuition in 2010–11 was $40,256, with room and board at $11,780. However, 68 percent of undergraduates receive need-based financial aid, while other students get merit scholarships. The average debt of a recent graduate who borrowed was only $15,551.

Providence College

Providence, Rhode Island • www.providence.edu

Trusting in Providence

The onetime factory city of Providence, Rhode Island, has been revitalized over the past decade, to the point where it has fairly been dubbed the "Renaissance City." The college which bears its name has undergone its own renascence in recent years. The country's leading college run by Dominican friars—St. Thomas Aquinas's order—Providence College had been known for decades as a quality, solidly Catholic school. In the 1990s the school hit some hard times, and was accused of compromising on core principles of Catholic education. However, the college's president, Rev. Brian Shanley, O.P., an alumnus and former professor, was recently reelected for a second five-year term to continue on the path forged at his spring 2006 inauguration to steer the school back to its founding mission. His leadership has attracted a cadre of talented faithfully Catholic faculty and brought a new sense of vitality to the school—just in 2009 and 2010 alone, Providence College made 49 new tenure-track hires. The school's rediscovered focus on faith-filled liberal education is drawing better students and teachers, and attracting more national attention.

With its emphasis on the liberal arts and its substantial core curriculum, especially the Development of Western Civilization Program which takes the student through the intellectual history of the West, Providence College is a highly attractive choice.

Academic Life: Hounds of heaven

When most of America's colleges and universities were pitching those pesky core humanities requirements, PC was initiating its Development of Western Civilization program—referred to as just DWC by students and faculty. Since 1971, all students have been required to enroll in the twenty-credit sequence of courses in the Development of Western Civilization. Team-taught by four faculty drawn from the history, literature, philosophy, and theology, the DWC program guides students through a chronological and interdisciplinary examination of the major developments that have shaped Western civilization. Students entering Providence begin their study with Israel, Greece, and the Roman Republic, and end their year with the rise of Europe and the Middle Ages, Renaissance, and Reformation. The next course takes students through the Enlightenment and ends with closing of the nineteenth century. The final semester of the DWC program finishes at the end of the twentieth century, focusing on the fall of Communism and the papacy of John Paul II.

The program does have its critics. A DWC professor says, "The way Civ works now, the light never goes on. [The students] like certain aspects of the program but it's too much every day. It's like the Bataan Death March—for me and for them." Students seem to enjoy, or at least make the most of, the camaraderie that results from working through the program together. As one former student put it with a satirical grin, "PC pumps out great Jeopardy players." Another student, a math major, noted that, "if it weren't for Civ, I would have never taken any religion or philosophy, and I am very glad I did." Many students can identify with each other by their Civ "team." The "Civ Scream" is a tradition that has grown up around the program; the night before the DWC exams, freshman and sophomores gather on the quad area between Aquinas, Meagher, and McDermott Halls to let off steam after hours of studying. Sophomores design and print up T-shirts to mark the occasion.

Still absent from the PC's core curriculum is any required writing course. Outside of what is offered through the DWC Program, students can avoid writing-intensive courses throughout their four years at Providence.

Ambitious students should enroll in the Liberal Arts Honors program, which entails taking honors sections of six core requirement classes. Honors classes are slightly smaller in size, require more reading and writing—students are required to read the texts from the DWC program in their entirety—and are often conducted in a seminar style. Select freshmen—approximately 500 per year—are invited, and 125 typically enroll. Others may apply for the program after one or two semesters of superior work.

Most classes at Providence are quite small, thanks to a student-teacher ratio of 12 to 1. More importantly, the teachers are actually professors and not graduate assistants. Professors at PC are quite available to students, as one student says: "I feel like my professors not only know who I am, but care about who I am—they want me to succeed." Adds another student, "All teachers have office hours, and many allow you to come visit anytime; their doors are always open." Before choosing a major, students have faculty advisors appointed to them. They may choose new ones after selecting a major.

Most disciplines are solid, serious, and traditional. The most popular majors at Providence are biology, marketing, management, political science, English, education,

VITAL STATISTICS

Religious affiliation: *Roman Catholic*
Total enrollment: *4,673*
Total undergraduates: *3,938*
SAT/ACT midranges: CR: *520–640*, M: *540–650*; ACT: *23–28*
Applicants: *8,844*
Applicants accepted: *45%*
Applicants accepted who enrolled: *25%*
Tuition and fees: *$38,610*
Room and board: *$11,690*
Freshman retention rate: *92%*
Graduation rate: *84% (4 yrs.), 86% (6 yrs.)*
Courses with fewer than 20 students: *50%*
Student-faculty ratio: *12:1*
Courses taught by graduate students: *none*
Most popular majors: *biology, marketing, management*
Students living on campus: *76%*
Guaranteed housing for 4 years? *no*
Students in fraternities or sororities: *none*

and finance. Departmental requirements are—for most majors—impressive.

The English department requires ten courses: "Introduction to Literature," four courses in literature before 1800, four in literature after 1800, and one elective from either of these two fields. Options are solid, like "Shakespeare: Tragedies and Romances," "The Victorian Age," and "American Literature to 1865." The absence of the esoteric, and the emphasis on canonical authors, is noteworthy in the English department.

The same can be said for the history major, which has similarly rigorous requirements. Students are required to take multiple courses in both American and European history, like "History of the United States: From the Beginnings to 1815," and so on. Refreshingly, the history department professes to train students in "doing the work of history with the greatest possible objectivity, resisting personal and social prejudice and ideology."

Political science majors must take eleven courses, including "Politics" and "Introduction to Empirical Analysis"; and one course in each of these four fields: comparative government and politics, international relations, political theory, and American politics; a capstone senior seminar; and four electives, chosen from solid options.

Both the philosophy and theology departments are quite strong. One student says of them, "The philosophy faculty has undergone a transition from Dominican friars to predominantly lay professors over the past fifteen years," but nevertheless has become "more committed to the school's Catholic mission. Perhaps because of this, the department enjoys a very strong relationship with its upstairs neighbor, the theology department. Students and faculty from the two disciplines compete in a friendly but competitive softball game every semester." Providence requires its theology department members to obtain the *Mandatum* from the local bishop, after swearing an oath of fidelity to Church doctrine—a Vatican mandate which most Catholic colleges in the U.S. have chosen to defy.

According to students and faculty, business, marketing, and management are among the weaker programs at the college—which is unfortunate, since marketing and management are among the most popular majors. The school's library is somewhat small, but students have access to resources from other Rhode Island schools (such as Brown) and an extensive national inter-library loan system. One recent alumnus says that the college did a "great job in providing resources" any time they were needed.

Top teachers, students say, include Steven Lynch and Anthony Esolen in English. Says one student, "English has some great faculty. On my 'Development of Western Civilization' team, Dr. Robert Reeder is the English professor; he's young, energetic, and really loves to teach. I also have Dr. Brian Barbour for a Shakespeare course, and he is excellent! He is incredibly knowledgeable about what he teaches and he really has a passion for it." Also recommended are Michael O'Neill, and Patrick Macfarlane in philosophy; Mario DiNunzio (emeritus), Fred Drogula, and Patrick Breen in history; and Liam Donohoe in mathematics and computer science.

Providence compensates for its lack of preprofessional degrees by offering students a number of interesting special programs. Students interested in pursuing engineering can

New England

participate in the 3+2 program, moving after three years of engineering at Providence to spend two years studying an engineering concentration of their choice at either Columbia University or Washington University of St. Louis. Providence has a comparable 3+4 Optometry Program with the New England College of Optometry and a 4+1 BS/BA/MBA.

The college partners with a great number of study-abroad programs and foreign institutions of higher education. This grants the student the choice from more than fourteen countries in Europe, seventeen in the Middle East and Africa, five in Asia, Australia and New Zealand, and ten in Central and South America. The school requires no foreign language courses—although it does offer majors in classics, French, Italian, and Spanish and a minor in German.

Student Life: Red-brick Dominican

Nearly 70 percent of students come from New England and about 90 percent hail from the Northeast. One student recalled that "when I first came here it seemed like everyone came from New England and a lot of them already knew each other." This is to a degree true. The vast majority of students are white Roman Catholics from the region. So far, the college hasn't felt the need to twist itself into a pretzel to change its student body—which makes PC sound rather un-P.C.

The vast majority of PC students live on the 105-acre campus, which sits on a hill in the Northwest of the city. The college started with one red-brick building in 1919 and as the campus expanded, new buildings rarely deviated from that material. Notable among the buildings on campus are Harkins Hall—the original campus building—and St. Dominic Chapel, built in 2001. Recently completing a ten-year master plan begun in 2001, PC has greatly expanded and improved its campus. Additions have included the Concannon Fitness Center (2007), Jazzman's Café (2006), and a remodeled student union: the Slavin Center (2009). This state-of-the-art, 23,000-square-foot facility has a three-level glass façade, and contains top exercise equipment. Currently, the renovation of Phillips Memorial Library continues through 2013, with modifications on all three levels to include twenty-five group study rooms, the expansion of the book collection to half a million, and an increase in seats for students from 667 to 865.

Providence has fifteen dormitory and apartment buildings. Of these, nine are traditional dorms (four all women, four all men, and one coed by wing), five are apartments that are single sex by apartment, and one building of suites—aptly named Suites Hall—that is coed by floor. Underclassmen generally live in traditional dormitories with suites and apartments reserved for juniors and seniors. Housing is not guaranteed for all four years.

According to the student handbook, dorm residents "are expected to adhere to the norms and values associated with Catholic teaching." The mission statement from the Office of Residence Life insists that it "is strongly committed to upholding the Judaeo-Christian heritage of Providence College and the traditions of the Dominican Order that celebrate the dignity and sacredness of the individual." To help students comply with these ideals, the college limits visiting hours for guests of the opposite sex in rooms. Visitation hours for guests of the opposite sex begin at 10:00 AM and end at midnight on Sundays through Thursdays;

on Fridays and Saturdays, visitation hours begin at 10:00 AM and end at 2:00 AM. Violations of this policy are punishable by the school—although enforcement is up to the resident assistant in each dorm. Rules are interpreted more strictly in the all-female dorms.

Almost every dormitory on campus is home to at least one Dominican. "It's good for students," says one RA, "They think twice before stepping out of line in front of a member of the order that perpetrated the Spanish Inquisition." More than fifty Dominican friars and sisters who live on campus, serving as professors and advisors to students. The friars are a major fixture at PC; you can't miss the guys wearing the white habits and the black *cappas* striding across campus. "Pasta with the Padres" an annual event at the start of the school year, gives students an opportunity to meet and interact with the friars.

The campus ministry offers a number of opportunities for students, including Theology on Tap at McPhails and a number of service opportunities in Boston. Some students

ACADEMIC REQUIREMENTS

Providence College maintains a solid core curriculum and some other exemplary requirements:

- Twenty semester hours (equivalent to six or seven courses) in the "Development of Western Civilization." Team-taught by members of the departments of art, English, languages, history, philosophy, and theology, it deals "with major developments in the making of Western civilization from the classical period to the present." Participants are required to read primary works from the Western tradition—although only honors students must read the works in their entirety.
- One 200- and one 300-level course in theology. Choices are very solid—for example "Biblical Theology," "Foundations of Theology," or "Theology of St Thomas Aquinas" for the 200-level and "The Prophets," "The Synoptic Gospels," or "The Letters of St Paul" for the 300-level course.
- Two classes in philosophy, one of which must be in ethics, such as courses in business or biomedical ethics. The other course can be anything from "The Wisdom of Aquinas" to "Environmental Philosophy."
- Two classes in natural science; at least one course must have a "hands-on" component. This can be fulfilled by either a two-semester sequence in general biology, or chemistry or the like, or by two separate, approved courses which could include "How Things Work" and "Ethnobotany." (Those who have not taken a high school physics course will be required to take a physics-based natural science core course.)
- Two classes in social science. Choices range very widely between the fields of anthropology, economics, history, linguistics, political science, psychology, sociology, black studies, and women's studies.
- One class in mathematics, for example "Geometry" or "Introduction to Statistics."
- One course in fine arts, like "Basic Concepts of Music" or "Theater Appreciation."
- Three elective classes outside the student's major.
- Coursework or test scores to demonstrate English proficiency.

complain that campus ministry is preoccupied with social justice and weak on spiritual development, referring to it as "Catholic Lite." The school offers students daily Mass four times a day during the week and has five Sunday liturgies (including the Saturday Vigil). The Center for Catholic and Dominican Studies, which was founded in 2006, is meant to maintain, enhance, and promote the distinctive Catholic and Dominican mission of Providence College. The center offers multiple lectures each semester.

The events with the largest draw at PC are certainly the men's basketball games. Like the most of the other nineteen men and women's varsity sports programs at the college (including men's ice hockey, swimming and diving, and soccer as well as women's ice hockey, tennis, and volleyball), the men's basketball team are division I and play in the Big East Athletic Conference—a tough conference for such a little school. Friars basketball has long history as the "little team that could," appearing in the NCAA tournament on multiple occasions and going as far as the Final Four back in 1997. For home games, students watch the men's team play at the Dunkin Donuts Center—just "The Dunk" to students—in downtown Providence. Men's hockey, which plays in the elite conference Hockey East, also draws large crowds of students to their games against some of the best teams in the country. Other varsity sports include men and women's lacrosse, soccer, and cross-country. For students looking for something a little more recreational, PC has a number of intramural sports that play year round. Those include flag football, Ultimate Frisbee, Wiffle ball, and dodgeball.

Providence has over a hundred active student groups or organizations. Notable among these are the *Cowl*, the student newspaper, and the famous Blackfriars Theater group. Educational groups include a large number of Honors societies, plus groups like

GREEN LIGHT

Although there have been some vocally leftist professors on campus, their influence and numbers are said to be dwindling. With Fr. Shanley in office as president, the school has made great strides in returning the school to its Dominican Catholic roots. Libertarians and Republicans as well as Democrats are represented on campus. However, College Republicans dwarf the struggling College Democrats, reflecting the politics of the student body overall. All three groups host speakers and get involved in local and national politics but have difficulty galvanizing their fellow students to political action. "Students here are pretty apathetic," says one student.

Troublingly, when the Youth for Western Civilization chapter at Providence (not acknowledged by the university) invited its honorary chairman, former Colorado U.S. Representative Tom Tancredo, to speak in April 2009, the college blocked his appearance because of his stance on illegal immigration. (He considers it ... illegal.) The college stated that Tancredo's position "directly contrasts" with that of Providence Bishop Thomas Tobin—also a member of the school's Board of Trustees. It is ironic that the school took a firm stand against a non-Catholic politician who differed with the bishop's personal reading of an issue open to prudential argument among faithful Catholics—just a semester after inviting Rhode Island Senator Sheldon Whitehouse, one of the most pro-choice politicians in the U.S. Senate, to speak at the school. PC's actions sound to us less like standing up for Church teaching than catering to a member of its board.

the Law Society, the Debate Team, the American Council of Healthcare, and the Future Friars Executives. Active political groups on campus include College Democrats, College Republicans, and Libertarians. Those students who share an interest in the arts and music will also find a number of student groups, including an Irish Dance Club, an Orchestra and a Liturgical Choir. Colleges against Cancer and Urban Action are two example of PC Service Clubs. The Providence College Sailing team has some of the best sailing waters in the country in Narragansett Bay. Students can be part of the competitive traveling sailing team or sail for fun on weekends.

The city of Providence boasts five other colleges and universities, giving it the highest per capita concentration of college students in the country. Students can shop at the city's downtown mall Providence Place, or on Thayer Street, which boasts vintage clothing shops, bookstores, music, and restaurants. Providence's Federal Hill—the city's Little Italy—is another popular student destination, with over twenty restaurants in a quarter mile radius. (The nearby culinary school of Johnson and Wales University has allowed the city to retain top chefs.) Many students like to go to Rhode Island School of Design's Art Museum. Students can get around Providence through the use of the city's bus service, free to students with a PC ID. A student bus runs a dedicated loop throughout the neighborhood surrounding PC during the later hours of the day and into the evening. These transportation options are especially important to underclassmen, as PC students are not allowed to have cars on campus until their junior year. The beach and Boston are also both within an hour's drive and New York City is only four hours to the south.

And then there's the drinking. For years the college has struggled with a sobriety problem. Some shocking statistics of alcohol violations and student hospital admissions for drinking in the 2007–08 academic year led the school to crack down, hard. All hard liquor is banned from residence halls and apartment complexes, with the exception of McPhail's, the on-campus bar. The efficacy of these measures—which are highly unpopular with the majority of students—remains to be seen. There is plenty to do in Providence besides the off-campus party and, according to students, many students choose alternative activities on weekends.

Students report feeling safe at PC. The campus is largely pedestrian, with a perimeter fence and 24-hour guards staffing all campus entrances. Apart from underage drinking, crime is fairly infrequent. In 2009 there were sixteen burglaries, one sex offense, and one motor vehicle theft on campus. Campus police have responded well to a recent uptick in crime, bolstering their presence on campus and in the surrounding community, and working with the Providence Police Department.

Tuition for the 2010–11 academic year was $38,610, with room and board averaging $11,690. Admission is need blind, but the school is unable to guarantee full funding to students. The school does offer various need- and merit-based assistance. Some 52 percent of students receive need-based financial aid, and the average student-loan debt of a recent graduate is $33,297.

New England

Smith College

Northampton, Massachusetts • www.smith.edu

Amazons.com

Founded in 1871, Smith College is the largest private women's college in the United States and perhaps the most famous. It is also rated as one of the country's top liberal arts schools. The college is named after Sophia Smith, who provided funding for the school's land and first buildings. The college is famous for producing independent and ambitious women competent in their chosen professions. However, a conservative or religious student might find her independence tested by the school's thoroughgoing commitment to radical feminism, which pervades both classroom and campus.

Academic Life: Fill in the blank

Liberal arts have been a priority at Smith since its founding, but today the college places more of an emphasis on technology and the sciences, as well as majors such as education. Indeed, the traditional liberal arts curriculum no longer prevails at Smith—which, since 1970, has had no distribution requirements for graduation. None. (The only mandatory course is a writing-intensive class for first-time students.) This blank space, to be filled with the personal preferences of teenagers, has replaced Smith's once impressive curriculum.

Thus, Smith students must carefully structure their own programs if they wish to obtain an authentic liberal education. The bulletin *advises* students to select from among seven fields of knowledge: literature, historical studies, social science, natural science, the arts, foreign language, and mathematics and analytical philosophy. Impressively, a majority of the students complete six of the seven distribution suggestions. This is a lucky thing, because Smith does nothing to require that students graduating from this elite school have learned a thing about Greek philosophy, English literature, or American history.

Nevertheless, academics at Smith are described as "competitive," and students actively participate in class discussions. "They are an ambitious lot," says one faculty member. Currently, the most popular majors include psychology, government, art, economics, and English. A student may also design her own major, subject to approval.

Requirements for the majors provide some structure. English majors, for instance, are required to take two courses out of four "gateway" options: "Methods of Literary Study," part I or II of a British literature survey, or "American Literature before 1865"; two courses on literature before 1832; a seminar; courses on two of three major literary figures (Chaucer, Shakespeare, or Milton); two upper-level literature seminars (one taken in the senior year; and four additional courses within the department. One can take classes as traditional as "What Jane Austen Read: The Eighteenth-Century Novel" or as trendy as "Victorian Sexualities."

History majors must take five courses in their field of concentration and achieve "geographical breadth" by taking courses in three of the following areas: Africa, East Asia and Central Asia, Europe, Latin America, the Middle East and South Asia, and North America. Thus, a history major can graduate without ever learning anything about ancient or medieval history, the American Revolution, or the Civil War. Smith saw a sad departure with the recent retiring of two historians whose fields were British history and Renaissance and Reformation history. Instead of refilling these positions, the college hired historians in trendier fields (Africa and Asia).

The government department requires majors to take courses in American government, comparative government, political theory, and international relations. This is one of the more leftist and politicized departments as evidenced by courses such as "Colloquium: The Bush Years," which is essentially a semester-long diatribe against former President George W. Bush, the Republican Party, and conservative political theory. Similarly, the "Seminar in Political Theory: Religion and Democracy" is a hysterical denunciation of the "Religious Right" in America. The class draws consistent parallels between conservative Christians in America, intolerant Muslims in the Middle East, and Hindu nationalists in South Asia.

A rigorous interdepartmental major and minor in medieval studies are also offered at Smith. This may be the option at Smith that comes the closest to a traditional liberal arts education. All students enrolled in the major are required to achieve a working knowledge of Latin and to gain in-depth knowledge of the history, religion, and art of European civilization. A major in classical studies is also offered.

In May 2004, Smith became the first women's college to award diplomas in engineering. One professor states, however, that Smith's plan to incorporate engineering into the liberal arts has not been successful. There are so many requirements within the major itself that there is little wiggle room for adding humanities courses. The school recently added a BA in engineering arts. The degree, which is not accepted by the Engineering Accredita-

New England

tion Commission, is meant to be paired with "landscape studies, education, energy policy, ethics, [or] global development."

Smith does have a strong advising program. Each freshman is assigned a faculty advisor who helps direct her path until she declares a major, usually during her sophomore year. Then she chooses her own advisor within her department.

The student-faculty ratio at Smith is an excellent nine to one, and student-faculty relationships are reportedly strong. Classes are usually small—two-thirds of them have less than twenty students—and, although there is a small population of graduate students on campus, professors teach all the classes and grade all exams. Students rate the accessibility of Smith's faculty as one of the school's finest points.

Smith's extensive internship program, "Praxis: The Liberal Arts at Work," gives every student the opportunity to take part in a summer internship funded by the school. Many students take advantage of the program, obtaining positions at the White House, medical research facilities, or legal-aid programs. As one professor states, "With little financial investment, students have fabulous resources and opportunities at Smith; the internships they complete make for great experiences and 'get ahead' résumés."

Recommended faculty at Smith include Gregory White, Donald C. Baumer, J. Patrick Coby, and Marc Lendler in government; James Miller, Roisin O'Sullivan, Randy Bartlett, Roger Kaufman and Mahnaz Mahdavi in economics; Marnie Anderson, Ernest Benz, and Richard Lim in history; Craig Davis, Bill Oram, Jefferson Hunter, Dean Flower and Douglas Lane Patey in English; Dana Leibsohn in art history; Kevin Shea and Shizuka Hsieh in chemistry; John Brady in geology; Borjana Mikic and Glenn Ellis in engineering; Jocelyne Kolb in German; Justin Cammy in Jewish studies; and Andy Rotman, Suleiman Ali Mourad, and C. S. Lewis specialist Carol G. Zaleski in religion and biblical literature. Notable Smith graduates include neurobiologist and Olympian Victoria Chan Palay; authors Madeline L'Engle, Sylvia Plath, Gloria Steinem, and Betty Friedan; world-famous television chef (and former OSS operative) Julia Child; feminist legal scholar Catharine MacKinnon; columnist Molly Ivins; former first ladies Nancy Reagan and Barbara Bush; and Mary Josephine Rogers, foundress of the Maryknoll Sisters.

The school's president since 2002, Carol Christ, said recently that one of her main focuses is diversity and that she intends to explore how the campus can be even further "diversified" via admissions. And she seems to be getting her wish; the current student body is 11 percent Asian, 6 percent black, 7 percent Hispanic, and 15 percent "other/unknown." Christ also wants even more community-wide discussions and debates on issues of race, class, gender, and sexual identification.

SUGGESTED CORE

1. English 202, Western Classics in Translation, from Homer to Dante
2. Philosophy 124, History of Ancient and Medieval Western Philosophy
3. Religion 210/215, Introduction to the Bible I/II
4. Religion 231, The Making of Christianity (closest match)
5. Government 262, Early Modern Political Theory 1500–1800
6. English 256, Shakespeare
7. No suitable course.
8. Government 263: Political Theory of the Nineteenth Century or History 250: Europe in the 19th Century

With an endowment of over $1 billion, Smith has plenty of resources. The Career Development Office helps students decide what occupations to pursue and helps locate job opportunities. The Jacobson Center provides students with writing assistance, tutoring, and various skills workshops. The Clark Science Center maintains laboratories with state-of-the-art equipment, including a nuclear magnetic resonance spectrometer. The $50 million Ford Hall, built for engineering, computer science, chemistry, biochemistry, and molecular biology was completed in 2009. Smith's Center for Foreign Languages and Cultures houses a computer-based multimedia facility that uses interactive digital video and audio at individual workstations, allowing students to study at their own pace. One professor praises the abundance of library resources: "Smith's Rare Book Collection is the finest of any college in the country, containing materials from cuneiform tables through incunabula to contemporary small press-work. Many classes make use of these materials, and the Curator of Rare Books, a member of the art department, teaches a range of courses on the art and history of the book." Smith's library is stocked with more than 1.4 million volumes, and students also have access to the libraries of the other schools in the Five College consortium.

Almost 50 percent of students participate in a study-abroad program during their time at Smith. Smith is well known for its junior-year-abroad program, with choices including Florence, Hamburg, Geneva, and Paris. The college maintains a formal affiliation with programs in Japan, Mexico, Spain, and southern India. If those options aren't enough, more than a hundred other study-abroad programs have been preapproved by the school. Although a foreign language is not required at Smith, it is a distribution "suggestion," and the college offers a number of languages: Ancient Greek, Latin, Chinese, Japanese, Korean, French, German, Italian, Arabic, Russian, Portuguese, and Spanish.

Student Life: LUGs on the Mill

Smith's location in Northampton, Massachusetts—a college town with a population of about 30,000—provides students with a small-town environment that offers the cultural benefits of a metropolitan center. Indeed, Northampton received the top ranking in the book *The 100 Best Small Art Towns in America*. Students can visit a farmers' market, then browse at Thornes Marketplace, a thirty-store indoor shopping center. Northampton also has used bookstores, coffee shops, a variety of craftsy stores, and two art-house theaters.

Northampton is located right outside Smith's gates, but the school's semirural setting means students are only a five-minute walk from the countryside. Near campus, the Mill River flows, where students go for picnics and relaxation. Boston is only two hours away; New York is less than three. Normally, however, students prefer to stay on campus or on the campuses of nearby colleges, because academic and extracurricular life occupies most of their time. Most students ride bikes or walk to get around the area.

Culturally, Smith is a curious place—definitely not your grandmother's Smith. In one telling incident, in April 2003, by a campus-wide vote, Smith students decided to eliminate the words "she" and "her" from their student government's constitution, according to the *Chronicle of Higher Education*. Er, why? To avoid offending those Smith students who *don't*

New England

identify as women. Apparently, a small contingent of students consider themselves "transgender," and this all-female school feels constrained to placate them. In response to similar initiatives, Smith administrators have hired a part-time gender specialist "to provide counseling services and consultation to the college to support transgender students." Smith's Campus Diversity board works closely with the administration's Office of Institutional Diversity and the diversity committees associated with each campus residence.

Smith has an active lesbian community that is loud and proud. The group runs its own student organization, not to mention special committees for lesbians of color, bisexuals, and transgendered folks. Smith also offers health insurance benefits to domestic partners. Some students claim that a number of Smithies are merely "LUGs"—lesbians until graduation.

While the school does support the most radical sorts of lifestyle experimentation, it also affirms those who pursue more traditional endeavors, such as reproducing the species. Faculty members praise the college for providing employees with a semester of paid parental leave and high-quality childcare.

Smith has more than a hundred student clubs of all types. Arts and performing arts clubs include Celebrations (a multicultural dance company), Crapapella, Handbell Choir, the Wailing Banshees, and a *Vagina Monologues* group. German, Italian, Russian, astronomy and anthropology clubs exist, along with the Minority Association of Prehealth Students and the Union of Underrepresented Students in the Sciences. Asian, black, Chinese, South Asian, Indigenous, Korean, Latina, African and Caribbean, and Vietnamese students all have their own associations.

Most numerous are Smith's social and political action groups, which range from Amnesty International, College Republicans, and AWARE (Activist Women Advocating Rape Education) to Prism: Queer Students of Color, Size Matters (an "anti-sizeism" organization), Transcending Gender, and the Global AIDS Campaign. Students also have a weekly paper, the *Sophian*, and a campus radio station. A $23 million, 60,000-square-foot campus center was dedicated in 2003.

ACADEMIC REQUIREMENTS

One intensive writing course is required for each student during her first or second semester at Smith. Recent courses that meet the requirements range from "Approaches to Visual Representation," "Western Classics in Translation," "Introduction to Political Thinking," "Lions: Science and Science Fiction," "Rebellious Women," and "Geology in the Field," to "Writing Roundtable: Poverty."

Apart from that, no specific courses are required for a Bachelor of Arts degree, and no distribution requirements are in place. The college does require that students complete a major and take at least half of their courses outside the department of their major. One course (usually four credits) in each of seven major fields is required for students who want to earn Latin Honors at graduation.

Several religious groups are represented at Smith, like the Association of Smith Pagans, Al-Iman, Hillel, Newman Association, Unitarian Universalists, and the Radical Catholic Feminist Organization at Smith. Students call Smith Christian Fellowship "very strong," but in 2010, Smith laid off its three chaplains (one Protestant, one Catholic, and one Jewish). The dean of religious life, Jennifer Walters, said that the decision was a financial one, as fewer "than a hundred students were actually participating in regular religious services provided by the college. Maybe close to fifty total, to be honest."

Most Smithies live in one of thirty-nine self-governing houses; these accommodate between ten and a hundred students, drawn from all four classes. A limited number of seniors are allowed to live off campus with their families, but just 6 percent do so. Each campus house has its own unique traditions and style. Smithies should have no complaints regarding home accoutrements, which often include complete kitchens, dining rooms, pianos, and sometimes an in-house cook. Each bedroom has high-speed Internet access. Special-interest housing includes a French house, a senior house, and the Ada Comstock house for "non-traditional aged students." Family-style meals are served in some houses on Thursday nights, and students may invite faculty or staff to join them at dinner. Smoking is banned in every building at Smith; those wishing to light up must stand at least twenty feet away from any Smith facility.

Freshmen are well cared for. Before a student arrives on campus, one of the "heads of new students" contacts her to explain various campus details. Once at Smith, she helps the student during orientation. A Big Sister/Little Sister program puts new students in contact with seniors within the same "house" who leave gifts and clues about themselves for a week. The activity culminates in a tea where the first year students guess the identity of their big sisters; it promotes house bonding and a mentor relationship. First-year students are also offered a variety of seminars that emphasize writing, public speaking, group work, and library and quantitative skills.

Sports are a big part of life at Smith, and the Pioneers play in blue and white or blue and yellow uniforms (Smith doesn't have official colors). The school even offers an exercise and sports studies major. Smith's fourteen varsity teams compete in the NCAA Division III in basketball, crew, cross-country, equestrian sports, field hockey, lacrosse, skiing, soccer, softball, squash, swimming and diving, tennis, track and field, and volleyball. Intercollegiate club sports include fencing, rugby, kung fu, tae kwon do, ice hockey, synchronized swimming, golf, and Ultimate Frisbee. Intramurals and individual instruction are offered in more than thirty activities. The college opened a three-level, $4 million fitness center in January 2004. Outdoor recreational facilities include twenty-five acres of playing fields; a 400-meter, eight-lane, all-weather track; 5,000-meter cross-country course; crew facilities and boat houses; lighted tennis courts; indoor and outdoor riding rings, a five-acre hunt course, and turnout paddocks and horse trails. The athletic department also runs the Get Fit Smith program, which is a fun, free, hour-long workout session and requires no sign-up, as well as the Outdoor Adventure program, which offers trips throughout the year like hikes, canoeing, and caving expeditions.

The quality of social life at Smith is varied. Though there aren't any sororities, keg parties still find a place on campus. Plenty of young men from nearby colleges stay the weekend at Smith, and a bus system that runs until 2:30 AM gives easy access to coeducational colleges in the area. Smith has a large counseling department to help students deal with such issues as depression and eating disorders. According to the school's website, about 25 percent of the student body avails itself of these services each year.

Smith has one of the finest art museums in the country, with a permanent collection of more than 25,000 items that includes works by Eakins, Rodin, Copley, Picasso, Degas, and Matisse. Art, dance, music, and theater are all majors offered by the college and there are several theatrical, writing, and performance groups of various types. Noon concerts are held weekly in the Sage Hall for Performing Arts. Smith's Botanic Garden has more than 5,000 labeled and mapped plants and a Japanese tea house.

The college holds a formal convocation ceremony each year with an opening address by the school president and a performance by the Glee Club. Each fall, the president surprises the campus by declaring "Mountain Day," canceling all classes on short notice and providing food, activities, and the opportunity for students to enjoy the outdoors. On the day before commencement, alumnae escort graduating seniors, who parade around campus wearing white dresses and then plant ivy to symbolize the connection between the school and its graduates. That night the entire campus is lit with colored paper lanterns, providing a soft glow to the grounds that is perfect for reminiscing about bygone days and long-lost LUGs.

Smith is relatively safe compared to other schools; 2009 crime statistics listed four forcible sex offenses, three motor vehicle thefts, and ten burglaries. The school maintains a twenty-four-hour campus security force and forty emergency telephones throughout the

YELLOW LIGHT

Smith has leaned heavily to the left for a very long time. In February 2006, the *Chronicle of Higher Education* noted a sizeable student reaction when the ubiquitous *Vagina Monologues* made its annual appearance on campus. College Republicans posted flyers reading "Use your brain, the other sex organ," to protest the performance of the play—which celebrates, among other things, the seduction of a young teenage girl by a lesbian adult. This Republican club is one of a small handful of conservative groups on campus. (The once-active campus pro-life group is long defunct.) In general, both faculty and students admit that "going to Smith as a conservative is difficult."

Back in 2002, professor James Miller was denied tenure because, in part, he wrote for National Review Online. The conservative establishment, many alumnae, and the general public criticized Smith, and Miller was finally granted tenure in 2004. A few years later, protesters stormed the room where Ryan Sorba, chairman of the Young Americans for Freedom, had been invited to speak at a College Republican event. Sorba was offering a speech on "The Born Gay Hoax," which did not sit well with some Smith students, who forced Sorba out of the event. Still, students assert that there is a certain liberality toward minority opinions. In response to the Sorba event, Smith's administration held forums on free speech, and some of the protesters even apologized. Apart from a vocal minority determined to bring meaning to their college years through supposed political action, most Smith women know how to get along. As one professor states, "People treat each other well, and the college takes academic freedom very seriously."

campus, but emphasizes personal responsibility when it comes to safety. When asked, the majority of students declared they felt "extremely safe" on campus.

All these privileges come at a hefty price. Tuition for 2010–11 was a steep $38,640, and room and board $13,000; however, Smith assures prospective students that "Smith meets the full documented need, as determined by college policy, of all admitted students who apply for aid by the published deadlines." And most of the student body takes the college up on that offer. As college president Carol Christ states, "Smith outshines its peers in the economic diversity of its students." Sixty-three percent of Smith's student body receives financial aid averaging $34,526 from the college, but the average student load debt of a graduate was a heavy $21,753.

Thomas More College
of Liberal Arts

Merrimack, New Hampshire • www.thomasmorecollege.edu

Tradition takes work

A recent issue of *Communitas*, the magazine of Thomas More College, quotes T. S. Eliot: "Tradition . . . cannot be inherited, and if you want it you must obtain it by great labour." It was for that labor—the recovery and preservation of Western theological and cultural traditions, with all their attendant tributaries—that Roman Catholic laymen founded the college in 1978.

In recent years Thomas More College has sharpened this focus, revising its curriculum in accord with new educational injunctions from Popes John Paul II and Benedict XVI. The college did away with majors, believing that these needlessly stratified the tiny student body (each year fewer than one hundred students are enrolled). Now the school offers a general liberal arts degree.

The curricular changes began in 2008 and continued under the leadership of William Fahey, who in 2009 rose from the position of provost to become president. Fahey is only the third president in the college's thirty-plus-year history. Founding president Peter Sampo served for most of the school's life, stepping down in 2006. His successor, Jeffrey O. Nelson, launched a number of new programs, and the overhaul of the curriculum. The changes he implemented were not without controversy, splitting alumni, faculty, and to some extent students. Nelson resigned in April 2009, succeeded by Fahey, a classics scholar by training who had spent most of his teaching career at Christendom College. (Nelson now serves as executive vice president of programs at the Intercollegiate Studies Institute, which publishes this guide.)

The controversies that arose within the Thomas More community seem to have died down. The president explains that he would like to see the college become two things: in the minds of people in the academy, a scholarly equal to other Great Books programs, with a very intense intellectual program; and, in the minds of New Englanders, a vehicle for cultural renewal and vibrant Catholicism.

Above all, Thomas More College dedicates itself to forming well-rounded individuals whose spiritual, intellectual, and professional lives are consistent and integrated. "We want to be an institution that has a unity of vision," one professor explains. "We explore the unity of wisdom: human and divine. That makes us different from other schools." The school's website sums up the college's objective by noting, "The common good at which liberal education aims is nothing less than the whole truth about man and God."

VITAL STATISTICS

Religious affiliation: *Roman Catholic*
Total enrollment: *87*
Total undergraduates: *87*
SAT/ACT midranges: CR: *610–680*, M: *520–600*; ACT: *25–28*
Applicants: *95*
Applicants accepted: *60%*
Applicants accepted who enrolled: *52%*
Tuition and fees: *$16,100*
Room and board: *$9,100*
Freshman retention rate: *92%*
Graduation rate: *79% (4 yrs.)*
Courses with fewer than 20 students: *75%*
Student-faculty ratio: *10:1*
Courses taught by graduate students: *none*
Most popular majors: *not applicable*
Students living on campus: *95%*
Guaranteed housing for 4 years? *yes*
Students in fraternities or sororities: *none*

To bring that whole truth to students, Thomas More College offers a strong Great Books program, featuring lectures and discussion seminars that enable students to situate the books they're reading within the larger picture of the arc of Western civilization—particularly the seeds, growth, development, and decline of the great Catholic civilization of Europe.

Academic Life: Great Books and good conversations

Thomas More College is openly and proudly Catholic. But the college welcomes students of all faiths; it reports that 20 percent of its student body is not Catholic. Non-Catholics who value the classical approach and rigorous educational standards may consider the education Thomas More provides. One non-Catholic student observes that the school's commitment to orthodoxy does not lead to intellectual rigidity. "They're very open to debate," he says.

With its classical approach, Thomas More College is one of the few schools that offers a real core curriculum. "This is not a vocational school," explains a professor. "This isn't a place where you can learn a specialty and become a police officer or a machinist. Instead, it gives you a more solid outlook, equipping you for whatever focus you may have in life."

The revamped curriculum gives students a full introduction to the liberal arts. Central to this program is the Humanities Sequence, a full eight-semester set of courses that proceeds chronologically, beginning with the ancient Greeks and running up to the modern age. The Humanities Sequence encompasses literature, philosophy, history, political science, and more. Thomas More College avoids drawing artificial distinctions between these disciplines, aiming to allow students to grasp the full flavor of the intellectual ferment and development of a particular time. "The main thing we learn," one student explains, "is how to think. All the classes relate to one another in the service of that."

Study of literature, for example, is integrated into the Humanities course, not separated from the study of history and philosophy. The curriculum centers on great books—from Homer, Herodotus, Plato, Virgil, and Shakespeare to Flannery O'Connor, Walker Percy, T. S. Eliot, and Solzhenitsyn. The Thomas More curriculum is entirely free of the multiculturalist, feminist, and "queer" theory preoccupations that mar the curricula of mainstream colleges and universities today.

New England

History is likewise integrated into the Humanities Sequence, with the eight-semester course ranging through Greece, Rome, medieval Europe, the Renaissance and Reformation, the Enlightenment, American studies, and the modern age. Students study U.S. constitutional theory (reading, among other things, the *Federalist Papers* and Tocqueville) as part of a larger exploration of how the American character formed. Political theory ranges from Aristotle, Augustine, and Aquinas to John Stuart Mill, Lenin, the *Communist Manifesto*, and *Rerum Novarum*.

SUGGESTED CORE

The college's required Humanities sequence suffices.

Another key element of the curriculum is a two-semester sequence entitled "The Way of Beauty," taught by artist-in-residence David Clayton. All first-year students take this sequence. "The course," Clayton explains, "is directed towards the creation of beauty as well as its appreciation." It "weaves together geometry, musical harmony, and theology—as the great artists, writers, and thinkers of the Middle Ages always tried to do."

Thomas More College also requires students to study Latin or Ancient Greek, poetics, rhetoric, art and architecture, natural science, Euclidean geometry, logic, metaphysics, and theology. In addition, students take a three-semester writing course that focuses on emulating ancient, medieval, and great modern writers. One student explains: "The course shows you how to move people. This is what has appealed to people in the last two thousand years and more. Let's imitate it."

While all students take the same core courses in their first two years, juniors and seniors take one tutorial each semester, which allows them to pursue particular interests within the overall humanities framework.

With a student-faculty ratio of just 10 to 1, professors are extremely accessible to the students; academic advising takes place on both a formal and informal basis. Students say that the level of intellectual curiosity and seriousness is high. "Academically," one remarks, "there is no comparison with other schools. In other schools, you can get away with not learning. Not here." Another adds: "You develop good study habits here."

Such habits would appear to be essential, for "the academic level is pretty good," a student says. "People who come here are serious about study." On the downside: "Sometimes I feel as if my eyes are bleeding from the amount of reading that we have to do here." Another student sums up the challenges and rewards of the college's rigorous approach: "Some days I'm bombarded with work and I think, why did I come here? But I am so much better off intellectually and spiritually." The environment is intellectually charged: "In state schools, you leave class and you're out of school. Here, the discussion continues. Your classes don't end in the classroom." A professor agrees: "The students upon arrival here are very serious. The college's success in keeping the focus high is not top-down."

One negative on which many students agree involves the poor quality and limited utility of the college's science and math courses. One student says flatly, "If you're looking for a strong math and science school, Thomas More College is not for you." Another quips: "This is a school you would go to if you wanted to avoid all that." One calls it "the most terrible program for science in the history of all colleges." For natural history, students learn to identify various trees and birds, leading one to scoff that the course "would be better for Cub Scouts and Boy Scouts than for a college."

Math courses include the philosophy of logic and Euclidean geometry. "Euclid is great," says a student, "because it teaches you why these mathematical principles work; but it is necessary for modern life to know not just why they work, but how they work as well."

Theology and religion courses are required of all students throughout their time at Thomas More College, in accord with the school's firm commitment to Catholic orthodoxy. These are as wide-ranging as the rest of the curriculum, introducing students not only to the Bible, St. Augustine, St. Thomas Aquinas, John Henry Newman, and Popes John Paul II and Benedict XVI but also to writers such as Sophocles, Plato, Lucretius, Cicero, David Hume, Ludwig Feuerbach, William James, and François Mauriac. Students examine how Christian theology was influenced by the Stoics, Platonists, and Aristotelians. Ethics, politics, and economics are studied within the context of philosophy and theology.

Another fundamental element of the Thomas More experience is the Rome term: all students spend a semester in Rome during their sophomore year, living in a Maronite Catholic monastery. Villa Serenella, as it is known, is just five miles away from St. Peter's Basilica. While in Rome, students take classes focusing on pivotal figures of Roman, Italian, and European history and culture, including Livy, St. Peter, Marcus Aurelius, St. Francis of Assisi, Dante, Boccaccio, Shakespeare, Belloc, Ezra Pound, and more. The classes also introduce students to Roman art and architecture, leaving them ample time to explore the delights of the Eternal City. Moreover, Thomas More College maintains the Vatican Studies Center, which it describes as introducing students "to the work of the Holy See and the Catholic Church through tours of Vatican City State, Rome, and other sites in Italy of cultural and religious importance in the history of Christianity." The Vatican Studies Center allows the college to help arrange internships for its students as well.

Thomas More students similarly benefit from the college's Center for Faith and Culture in Oxford, England. Some students attend the college's two-week Oxford Studies Program, which explores the thought of G. K. Chesterton, John Henry Newman, Gerard Manley Hopkins, Hilaire Belloc, J. R. R. Tolkien, and others.

Students return to the main campus for their junior and senior years. Juniors must complete a major project consisting of an hour-long oral presentation, during which they field questions from a professor. Seniors complete, and have to be prepared to defend, a twenty- to twenty-five-page thesis; all students listen to a version condensed for oral presentation.

The only foreign languages offered are Ancient Greek and Latin; students take four semesters of one or the other.

Aside from the criticisms of the math and science courses, Thomas More students largely value the education they receive and admire their professors. No professor comes in for criticism on the basis of the quality of his or her work in general. Fortunately for students, the college does not lock faculty into the "publish or perish" mentality. On the contrary, the school expects professors to engage with students and to view full mastery of the material at hand as their primary responsibility. The website explains: "At Thomas More College, the academic life is founded upon the principle expressed by St. Thomas Aquinas that 'the vision of the teacher is the beginning of teaching,' that is, that the source or principle of the transmission of knowledge and wisdom is the teacher's own contemplative life." The teachers generally appear to live up to this challenge.

ACADEMIC REQUIREMENTS

Thomas More College offers one of the most comprehensive classical curricula available anywhere. The course of studies for all students is as follows:

Freshman Year:

- Language: Latin grammar or Ancient Greek grammar.
- Poetry/Fine Arts/Rhetoric: Sacred music and sacred geometry.
- Humanities: major Ancient Greek and Roman authors.
- Natural science: Natural history.
- Mathematics: Euclid's geometry.
- Theology: Bible, Augustine, Anselm, Aquinas, notable modern writers.

Sophomore Year:

- Language: Intermediate Latin, intermediate Ancient Greek.
- Poetry/Fine Arts/Rhetoric: Aristotle's *Poetics*, Isocrates, Roman orators.
- Humanities: major medieval authors and modern authors on Rome.
- Philosophy: Logic.
- Mathematics: Euclid's *Geometry*.
- Theology: Psalms, Church Fathers, St. Paul, Aquinas.

Junior Year:

- Tutorials: Topics of special interest of students and professors in small groups; student project.
- Rhetoric/writing: Johnson, Boswell, Orwell, writing practicum.
- Humanities: Renaissance, Reformation, Enlightenment writers, Vatican I.
- Natural science: Pre-Socratics, Aristotle's *Physics*, Galileo, Descartes, Newton, Aristotle's *On the Soul*.
- Ethics/Politics/Economics: Aristotle's *Nicomachean Ethics*, Augustine, Aquinas, John Paul II, Aristotle's *Politics*, Catholic social theorists

Senior Year:

- Tutorials: Topics of special interest of students and professors in small groups; student project.
- Thesis: Thesis research, writing and defense.
- Humanities: Aristotle's *Metaphysics*, Hume, Kant, Heidegger, texts from non-Christian religions.
- Philosophy: Aristotle's *Physics* and *Metaphysics*, Aquinas's *On Being and Essence*.
- Theology: Augustine, Aquinas's *Summa Theologiae*.

Numerous students give special praise to Humanities professors William Fahey (also the college president), Walter J. Thompson, and Christopher Olaf Blum; literature professors John Zmirak, Patrick Powers, and Amy Fahey; and Western civilization lecturer Sara Kitzinger.

"[William] Fahey, Thompson, and Blum," says one student, "present information in such a way, and can play devil's advocate in such a way, that they force you to examine all sides of the issue." A student who transferred into Thomas More College says of Fahey: "Having attended other universities, I'd be hard-pressed to find a better teacher."

Blum is "excellent at explaining things," one student remarks, while another adds, "He makes everything that you learn applicable to how you live your life."

One student marvels at Thompson's fluent command of the material at hand: "I don't know that I've ever met another person who can quote citations and explain things as effectively as he does without even opening a book."

Zmirak, who is writer in residence as well as assistant professor of literature, is "brilliantly witty, and good for understanding prose," a student comments. (Zmirak also serves as editor in chief of this guide.) Powers wins praise for his deft balancing of lecturing and discussion, while Amy Fahey and Sara Kitzinger are recognized for the consistent quality of their presentations.

In general, a student says, "professors are more than willing to engage you outside the classroom as well as inside the classroom. . . . All of the professors are amazing. I hadn't expected to love many of the professors, much less all of them."

Student Life: Competitive smoking

Thomas More College is located on fourteen acres in Merrimack, New Hampshire, a modest town of 27,000 near Nashua (population 87,000). The small campus, which has only five buildings, is "a bit isolated," by the account of both faculty and students. Most students, a professor says, "don't have cars, and can't get to Boston," which is about an hour south of the campus. "It is also a long walk to any city environment."

In March 2011 President Fahey announced that the school had put a down payment on a property in Groton, Massachusetts, about twenty miles to the south. Thomas More College said that it aims to move its undergraduate program to the new campus by 2014. The college purchased the Massachusetts property with an eye toward growth: the new location will be able to accommodate up to three hundred students. The New Hampshire campus, Fahey reported, will be retained for future graduate programs. The success of the move to Groton will depend on extensive fund-raising which will be required to construct new classroom buildings, dormitories, a library, and physically move an unused Catholic parish from several miles away to serve as the college's chapel.

As the school seeks the money to make the move, Merrimack remains the center of Thomas More life. While one student complains that "there's nothing to do besides school," others point to a variety of extracurricular options. Students stage a play in the fall (a recent performance was *The Importance of Being Earnest*), participate in a choral group, and engage in various other activities, including sailing and debate. One recent debate was

New England

set in the spring of 1776; students disputed the merits of the American colonies' declaring independence from England. A new series of medieval-style Catholic guilds give students the opportunity to gain hands-on experience with carpentry and woodworking, sacred art, music, and even raising chickens.

Students become more invested in their school than they might at larger institutions, as everyone is pressed into service as part of cleanup crews and kitchen crews. Work-study details are responsible for the upkeep and maintenance of the campus. This practical focus is born of necessity, given the college's small size, but it is in keeping with the school's philosophy of not separating the intellectual life from the whole of human existence and experience.

The small size of the student body prevents students from losing sight of why they are there. "We're a big family," says one. "We do everything together. We're very involved in each other's schoolwork and lives." That carries over after hours: "Dorm life is wonderful," according to one student. "It's like you're going to school with your extended family. We're forming bonds I was not expecting ever to form in college." Still another student enthuses: "You meet the best people here. The student body is a small concentration of people who are attracted to an intellectual and moral lifestyle." On the other hand, another student sees a downside: "The community is a double-edged sword. If you miss class one day,

> ## GREEN LIGHT
>
> Thomas More College fosters an environment of genuine academic exploration, free of the shallow propagandizing and political sloganeering that occurs at all too many schools, including those with an ostensibly Christian orientation. To be sure, students who are on the political Left may have a tough time at the college, given the strong pro-family and pro-life positions that characterize much of the student body. But professors generally do not import political content into the classroom unnecessarily, and students feel free to voice their views. Moreover, an ongoing series of student debates encourages an intellectual rigor that requires understanding the opposition's point of view and presenting it fairly.
>
> The focus at this Great Books college is traditionally far from contemporary partisan politics. That distance will likely become even greater if, as planned, Thomas More College relocates its undergraduate campus to Groton, Massachusetts, by 2014. In the past, students have gotten an up-close look at the realities of political campaigning when presidential candidates descend on the state for the critical New Hampshire primary. As such candidates as Ron Paul, Mitt Romney, and Pat Buchanan have addressed Thomas More students.

you may get glares. But it does make you more responsible and aware of your behavior." To be sure, the dynamics of such a tiny community will not appeal to every student.

Students are guaranteed housing all four years, and most choose to live on campus. The student body is small enough that there are only two dorms: one for men and one for women. The dorms do not allow visitation from the opposite sex. This is in keeping with the atmosphere of Catholic piety that pervades the college. Students can be disciplined for behavior that is taken for granted and even celebrated at most other schools, though they generally do not complain about the rules governing alcohol, intervisitation, and the like. In fact, many express gratitude for the school's forthright and encompassing Catholic per-

New England

spective. Most agree that there is not a big problem with drinking, drugs, or promiscuity. A senior does report that "there were problems with people drinking in the woods during my freshman and sophomore years, but last year and this year things are much better." Campus crime is virtually unheard of at Thomas More College.

As may be expected, the college features a healthy religious life. Mass is offered daily in the campus chapel, as is confession. The Byzantine Melkite Greek Catholic Divine Liturgy is also celebrated regularly in the campus chapel. The school's faithful Catholic emphasis permeates the entire life of the college. "I came here," notes a student, "and felt that Christ was actually breathing here."

Perhaps not surprisingly, Thomas More students tend to be much more conservative than students in larger colleges and universities. "Everybody's orthodox here," says a student, exaggerating only a little. Students participate in pro-life marches, as well as volunteer at a local soup kitchen. Still, a student's conservatism is not a given, and classes introduce students to a wide variety of perspectives.

Thomas More College offers no organized sports program, but students get free memberships at the YMCA across the street and have established a student-run soccer tournament.

Tuition for both in-state and out-of-state students costs $16,100 per year. Room and board are $9,100. Seventy-five percent of students receive need-based financial aid. The average student-loan debt of the class of 2009 was a significant $21,333. Sixty percent of graduates have gone on to obtain a graduate degree or a professional degree.

New England

144

Trinity College

Hartford, Connecticut • www.trincoll.edu

Free to be you and me

One of the oldest colleges in the country (and the second oldest in Connecticut), Trinity was founded in 1823 as Washington College and renamed in 1845. Though it was founded by the Episcopal church and retains an evocative name, Trinity is entirely secular today. The college is widely known and highly ranked for its formidable faculty and students; if only the school had a curriculum to match them. Although Trinity calls itself a liberal arts college, the college imposes nothing like a core program of studies. Instead, students face a set of weak distribution requirements. Says one professor: "Trinity is not truly a liberal arts school. I am surprised at some of the classes that fulfill the distribution requirements."

Academic Life: Pro-choice

Freshmen are required to participate in Trinity's First Year Program, which is intended to introduce freshmen to academic and community life through small seminars. However, most of the topics covered in seminars are better suited to leftist political consciousness-raising sessions than class work. Examples include: "Social Class/Social Clash: The Denial and Embrace of Classism in America," "Color and Money: Race and Class at Trinity and Beyond," "Hunting Heresy in the Fourth and Seventeenth Centuries," and (more promisingly) "God & Satan in Literature."

A student's seminar instructor serves as his academic advisor until he declares a major (typically in the fourth semester). Upperclassmen serve as mentors in the dormitories, strengthening and reinforcing academic engagement outside of the classroom.

Trinity offers thirty-eight majors, including engineering and environmental science, as well as interdisciplinary offerings, and nearly 900 courses from which to choose. Trinity invests a lot in its 2,300 undergraduates. The graduate school is tiny, with only about a hundred students, none of whom teach any classes. Only professors teach and Trinity's student-faculty ratio is a strong 11 to 1, but a student reports that "lots of intro classes are huge. My biggest class had sixty students." Some of the more popular majors at Trinity include economics, political science, history, English, and psychology. Trinity is one of relatively few liberal arts colleges to offer engineering. According to one student, "That is why I chose Trinity."

Special options at Trinity include the Guided Studies, Interdisciplinary Science, InterArts, Cities, and Human Rights programs. Other curricular options include Trinity/La MaMa Urban Arts Semester in New York City, domestic study programs, internships, independent study, and self-designed interdisciplinary majors.

The best option for any liberal arts student at Trinity is the Guided Studies Program, which offers twenty-five slots per year to outstanding entering students. The course work spans the first four semesters, but may be spread through five or six semesters. Classes offered have included: "The Biblical Tradition," "Philosophical Themes in Western Culture," "The Classical Tradition," "Major Religious Thinkers of the West," "Historical Patterns of European Development" and "Literary Patterns in European Development." According to one professor, "This program is great, but it was created as a reaction to the destruction of Trinity's curriculum." Another professor added that, "Some people at Trinity do not like the program. They think that it focuses on Western works, readings, and philosophy too much. They believe that other works from other cultures should be read alongside Western works." This multiculturalist anxiety has even crept into how the college describes the program. The course catalogue says, defensively, that "the program does not celebrate Western civilization to the detriment of other cultures. Rather, by furnishing students with greater knowledge of the West's leading cultural traditions it tries to nurture the educated self-awareness and habits of critical inquiry that make possible the comprehension of other traditions." Apology accepted.

For the English student, Trinity offers majors in literature and creative writing. Literature majors are required to take an introduction to literary studies, a class in literary theory, two classes in "cultural context," three advanced level classes in pre-1800 literature, two advanced-level classes in post-1800 literature, and two electives. Hence Shakespeare could slip through the cracks.

History majors must complete a survey course each in pre-1700 and post-1700 English or European history; an introductory class in U.S. history; three introductory classes in East or South Asian, African, Middle Eastern, Latin American, or Caribbean history; a course in historiography; a junior seminar; a senior seminar or year-long thesis project; and three elective classes.

Political science majors must fulfill a methods or language requirement and choose a concentration within the department: American government and politics, comparative politics, international relations, or political theory. Students must take the introductory class for their concentration as well as for other concentrations, two advanced-level classes within and outside of their concentrations, an elective in their concentration, a senior seminar, and a general elective. They could easily miss any courses on the American Constitution and political system.

Trinity does possess some great teachers. Student favorites include Edward Cabot in public policy and law; Judy Dworin and Michelle Hendrick in theater and dance; Donna-Dale Marcano and Erik Vogt in philosophy; Joan Morrison in biology; Vijay Prashad in international studies; and Francis Egan in economics.

College president James Jones is popular with both professors and students. Jones launched the Cornerstone Project, a comprehensive college-wide planning effort that reaffirmed Trinity's commitment to its students and to "global engagement." His efforts immediately elicited a college-record 56 percent participation in donations from alumni. Despite his busy schedule, President Jones still manages to teach at least one course each year. He lives in a house on campus and is frequently seen on campus walking his three Irish setters, Atticus, Colleen, and Ashlyn. According to one student, "I do not know how he does it, but he knows so many students by name. He is not what I think of when I think of a college president. He is so real and genuinely interested in all of his students."

Study abroad is by far the most popular special program at Trinity; an impressive 40 percent of students venture to foreign lands, some of them for three semesters. The college maintains its own program in Rome (the most popular), and many sites across the globe where Trinity has one or two professors teaching—such as the University of Vienna. If those locations do not satisfy a student, there are numerous more preapproved programs through other institutions from which a student may choose, from Greece to New Zealand to Vietnam. According to one student, "study abroad is amazing here. I went to South Africa and it changed my life."

Languages offered at the school are Arabic, Chinese, French, German, Ancient Greek, Hebrew, Italian, Japanese, Latin, Russian, and Spanish.

Student Life: Diversity for diversity's sake

Trinity is located in Hartford, Connecticut, the insurance capitol of the world—and home to the nation's oldest public art museum (Wadsworth Atheneum), the oldest public park (Bushnell Park), the oldest continuously published newspaper (the *Hartford Courant*), the second-oldest secondary school (Hartford Public), and the sixth-oldest opera company in

> **SUGGESTED CORE**
>
> 1. Classics 219, The Classical Tradition; or Classics 291, Ancient Greek Literature
> 2. Philosophy 281, Ancient Greek Philosophy
> 3. Religious Studies Religion 211/212, Introduction to the Hebrew Bible/New Testament
> 4. Religion 223, Major Religious Thinkers of the West I: Heresy and Orthodoxy in Conflict
> 5. Political Science 220, History of Political Thought II
> 6. English 351, Shakespeare
> 7. History 201, The United States from the Colonial Period through the Civil War
> 8. Philosophy 284, Late Modern Philosophy

the nation (the Connecticut Opera). As part of tuition, students receive public transportation passes (U-passes) for the city of Hartford to visit such institutions. Although these attractions exist, they are on the other side of the city. Students refer to the area surrounding Trinity as "blighted" or (in candid moments) "a ghetto."

All freshmen live in the same hall with other members of their First-Year Seminars. Trinity offers a number of residence halls, which range from 60 to 120 students. All of the freshman dorms are coed, although some floors in Elton are single sex. All bathrooms are single sex. Most students are pleased with campus housing, which is a good thing: Trinity has a residence requirement for the first two years and expects upperclassmen to live on-campus. Juniors and seniors may request to live off campus, but only 5 percent of them actually do so.

The heavy emphasis the school places on ethnic (rather than intellectual) diversity makes its mark. According to one student, "Trinity's push for diversity, especially among the dorms and student organizations, does nothing except help to segregate students even more. The Asians hang out with the Asians, the blacks with the blacks."

Trinity tries to spice up dorm life by offering a variety of living options, including theme houses. Praxis is a community service-themed dorm which requires a minimum of three hours of good works a week; the Fred Pfeil Community Project centers on organizing social life on campus; Summit Suites houses groups of four students who must come up with projects to better the Hartford community. One student says, "Summit Suites is very competitive to get into. The best project that I can remember was one in which students trained a seeing eye dog for a semester and then gave it to a blind resident of Hartford."

Trinity has numerous traditions. President Teddy Roosevelt was once awarded an honorary degree, which is commemorated with a plaque on the long walk; tradition holds that if a student steps on it, he will not graduate. According to one student, "most students keep this tradition. You always see students parting when they reach the long walk."

The Trinity College Chapel was built in the 1930s and is a beautiful space. Different denominations are represented in different parts of the building; for instance, there's a Catholic and an ecumenical section. According to Trinity, "the chaplaincy—in its many forms—is much more than just bricks and mortar . . . it is about encouragement, it is about dialogue, it is about listening." No surprise, then, that a student says, "I have never been in the chapel—wait, I was in there once for matriculation. A few students use it, but not many." Another student says of the chapel, "They will never tear it down because it is a landmark. It is the highest point in Hartford." Devout students should probably seek out local congregations that don't share space with incompatible faiths.

The campus is quite beautiful. The Main Quad, an area of grass that sits outside the Long Walk, is a favorite haunt for students when it is warm outside. The Long Walk consists of two halls, Seabury and Jarvis, and the Northern Towers—the earliest instances of Collegiate Gothic architecture in the United States, the school boasts. In 2008, the Long Walk was restored in a $32.9 million project. The Quad makes an impression, with trees planted in a "T" for "Trinity" shape and two Civil War cannons featured. Recent renovations included the improvement of Trinity Commons and Seabury Hall, and the school completed a $35-million renovation and expansion of the Raether Library and Information Technology Center.

Intercollegiate sports are popular at Trinity. The Trinity Bantams compete on fourteen men's and thirteen women's teams, including rowing, ice hockey, football, lacrosse, swimming and diving, and soccer. Forty-one percent of students participate in one or more during their career at Trinity. All sports are Division III, except for squash—which is Division I. (This *is* New England.) Trinity has held the world squash championships for ten years straight, beginning in 1998. The baseball team won the NCAA Division III World Series in 2008. Club sports at Trinity include equestrian, lacrosse, an outing club, which offers camping, kayaking, hiking, and climbing trips, as well as karate, a ski team, and a sailing club, among others. Activity can also be found through intramural sports like Ultimate Frisbee, zumba dance classes, broomball, Wiffle ball, and even a tug-of-war league.

Besides sports teams, there are more than one hundred student organizations at Trinity. In the words of one Trinity kid, "There are lots of students involved in everything." Especially if you have left-wing proclivities, it seems. Groups include an ACLU chapter, Women & Gender Resource Action Center, Feminists United, EROS (Encouraging Respect

ACADEMIC REQUIREMENTS

Students at Trinity do not face a traditional core curriculum, but a set of distributional requirements:

- Writing: The college's writing center evaluates the writing proficiency of all entering students. On the basis of this evaluation, some students may be required to take English 101. All students must also take two writing-intensive classes, one of which will likely be their first-year seminar and the other of which must be in their major field.
- Quantitative Literacy: All entering students must take a Quantitative Literacy examination administered by the Mathematics Center. Students who fail must take courses to reach a level of proficiency in all areas.
- Students must complete a year of a foreign language or demonstrate the requisite knowledge on a placement exam.
- First-Year Seminar: Entering freshmen must complete a themed seminar or the first semester of any one of the following programs: Guided Studies, Cities, Interdisciplinary Science, or InterArts.
- One course in the arts. Choices abound, from "Introduction to Classical Art and Archeology" to "History of Photography."
- One class in the humanities. Options range very widely, from "Classical Civilization" to "Architectural Design."
- One course in the natural sciences.
- One class in numeric and symbolic reasoning. (Math or logic classes will fulfill this.)
- One course in social sciences. Introductory courses in American studies or education will do.
- A class in "global engagement," which covers international issues, regions, or broad topics like global warming. Courses taken during study abroad suffice, as do classes in nearly every other department.

YELLOW LIGHT

No doubt about it, Trinity is a liberal campus. According to one professor, "there are some departments that religious conservatives should avoid, such as women's studies and human rights." One student says, "A religious conservative would fit in but he must learn quickly how to defend himself." However, another student insists, "Politics do not intrude in the classroom. All points are open for debate."

In 2008, an intense focus on race issues began at Trinity, according to the news site The Volokh Conspiracy. On TrinTalk, a web site unaffiliated with the college, an anonymous commenter posted a remark that was considered racially insensitive. The comment claimed that the admission of more minority students had led to a drop in the college's rankings. The campus Left came out in force in response to this isolated comment on a website and held protests on campus, demanding a searching "dialogue" on race issues. The controversy took a new twist when the author of the racist remarks was revealed—Lynda Ikejimba, who had emigrated to the United States from Nigeria when she was six. Ikejimba scurried to explain her actions, claiming that she made them in order to "test" the real racial feelings on campus. Since her original comments were deleted by the web admin shortly after she posted them, it would seem that the school passed the "test." However, students who were offended by the remarks disseminated them as widely as possible—prompting a campus furor. A professor told us that the provocateur "received no punishment whatsoever. That would not have happened had it been a white person."

of Sexualities), the Gay/Straight Alliance, *La Voz Latina*, the Asian American Student Association, Trinity College Black Women's Association, Men of Color Alliance, Arab American Association, a (Muslim) House of Peace, Temple of Hip Hop, and Imani, which is "dedicated to the advancement of black awareness on campus." Religious groups include an Interfaith Council, Hillel (Jewish), the (Catholic) Newman Club, and the Muslim Students Association. Several *a cappella* groups, such as After Dark, The Accidentals and The Trinitones, perform regularly on campus. Media outlets include a campus radio station (WRTC-FM), as well as the *Trinity Tripod*, the college's newspaper, the *Other Voice* (leftist), and Trinity Television. There are no conservative publications or media outlets on campus, although there is a Trinity College Republican club, whose goal is to "provide its members with an opportunity to get involved with the Republican party on a local, state, and national level," according to its website, but their membership is just a fraction of the Trinity College Democrats. Every year, the college's campus movie theater is proud to host a gay film festival.

Eighteen percent of students join fraternities or sororities. All Greek organizations at Trinity are required to be coed, and most students do not live in Greek housing. Trinity's small size does have one good effect: According to one student, "The hook-up culture here is tame. Random hook-ups here are not that random." Students tell us there is a major drinking scene on campus, especially on the weekends. In fact, there is a student group, T-Cert (Trinity College Emergency Response Team), comprised of EMT (Emergency Medical Technician) certified volunteers who keep quite busy on the weekends administering to student alcohol overdoses.

Beyond sports, clubs, and organizations, the school hosts the Quest Leadership Program, which takes freshmen on a week-long Appalachian Trail expedition prior to orientation. The school provides a second wilderness option to students—a two week jaunt through Killarney Provincial Park in Ontario, Canada.

Due to a parking shortage, freshmen are not permitted to bring cars. However, students have access to the Zipcar program, which provides "green" cars for hourly or daily rental. As at other schools, the Zipcar program is very popular on campus and in the surrounding community.

Trinity's location is a problem. Its hundred-acre campus is quite urban, and homeless men can occasionally be seen lounging in the common areas. One student says, "Crime is pretty bad because this section of Hartford is bad." The school reported six forcible sex offenses on campus , three cases of aggravated assault and one arson, as well as two robberies, twelve motor vehicle thefts, and sixteen burglaries in 2009. Bicycles, wallets, and electronics—especially laptop computers—are the articles most frequently stolen. According to one student, "Campus safety is okay. There is a shuttle if you do not want to walk around campus. There are also call boxes near each of the dorms and the campus is blue lighted." Another student tells us, "Security has improved tremendously in the three years that I have been here. There are lots of crime patrols and many students walking on campus. That used to never happen. You would have never seen people walking around at one in the morning."

Trinity's price outstrips its reputation. For 2010–11, tuition, room, and board amounted to an Ivy-level $53,380. Admission is need blind, and Trinity will meet all of a student's demonstrated need. At the request of professors, Trinity has started to offer a few merit-based scholarships. (Traditionally, all financial aid at Trinity was need-based.) According to one professor, "offering merit-based scholarships is a step in the right direction in terms of attracting the best and the brightest to Trinity. We are not Yale or Harvard. The only way to get that kind of academic talent is to attract the brightest kids to Trinity with scholarships." Some 44 percent of students receive need-based financial aid averaging $38,262. The 39 percent of students who borrow graduate with nearly $22,000 in debt.

Tufts University

Medford, Massachusetts • www.tufts.edu

Acting globally

Over the last 150 years, Tufts has grown from a small Universalist college into a flourishing research university. Today, the science and engineering departments, along with numerous preprofessional programs, are Tufts's particular strengths. The school's location near Boston is also an asset for urban-minded students.

Tufts has a global focus, laying heavy emphasis on foreign language and study-abroad programs, with many on-campus cultural events. Alas, Tufts's globalism goes beyond cosmopolitanism into the anti-Western ideology of multiculturalism, while affirmative action directs hiring and admissions decisions. But somewhere in the midst of the political correctness hides an opportunity for the discerning to find a genuine liberal arts education. Students will just have to seek it out.

Academic Life: Tuft enough

Tufts has no core curriculum, but instead maintains a set of distribution requirements. Many of the courses that fulfill them are foundational introductory classes. But a student could fulfill a number of these requirements with less serious choices, such as "America and the National Pastime" (a course about baseball) or "The Inclusive Classroom" for social sciences. "Undoubtedly, students can get away with it," one senior says. "With primary majors in women's studies, American studies, peace and justice studies, and the like, the arts and sciences curriculum can be easily manipulated so that a student might never take anything more difficult than introductory math and 'Women in Native American Culture.'" Happily, as another insider reports, "This is a good school with lots of smart students" who know better than to cheat themselves out of a good education.

Students can still study the foundations of Western civilization at Tufts in classes like "Western Political Thought" I and II, which cover the great books, and "The Meaning of America," which teaches the *Federalist Papers* and the writings of Lincoln. We're happy that such classes are offered—and wish they were required.

Students must meet further requirements within their majors, and certain majors are quite demanding. The international relations major comes with an eight-semester language requirement and twelve other courses, including an introduction to international relations,

"Principles of Economics," a course in international economics, a course focusing on "the historical dimension," and another on "theories of society and culture." They also take seven additional courses in a specific thematic cluster, such as "Regional and Comparative Analysis" or "Global Health, Nutrition, and the Environment."

Unfortunately, Tufts offers little guidance to its English majors. While encouraging them "to explore the full historical range of offerings" and "to include exposure to . . . women's studies, literary theory, historical materialism, and cultural studies," the department makes no significant requirements of its students. They must take one survey course, two pre-1860 and two post-1860, non-survey courses in British, American, or Anglophone literature, and five electives. Students could easily skip Shakespeare and Milton in favor of "Un-American Activities," "Postmodernism & Film," "The Politics of Reading," and "Nonwestern Women Writers."

History majors must complete a foundation seminar, a pre- or early-modern class, one course each in U.S., European, and non-Western history, and a "concentration core" of four related courses. Students may determine their own concentrations along thematic or geographic lines.

Political science majors must take two "foundational" courses in American politics, comparative politics, political theory, or international relations, as well as another class in each of those fields. Finally, a "methodology" class like "Political Behavior of Young People" is required, as is one upper-level seminar.

Despite the looseness of its curriculum, Tufts puts a high priority on teaching. Professors, not teaching assistants, teach nearly all classes. However, the mandatory freshman writing courses are taught by graduate students from various departments. Graduate students also lead most of the weekly discussion groups in large lecture courses.

With most classes small, students do get the opportunity to form relationships with professors, whom students consider "accessible." Professors in the sciences often use student assistants on research projects.

Students have a number of options when they need course advice. Freshmen can enroll in small-group seminars in which their professors will serve as their advisors. One student says, "This program was worthwhile because I met people in an academic setting, so I was guaranteed to get to know them better through the class." Another student says, "It was fun but the advising wasn't helpful at all." Freshmen who don't use these seminars

VITAL STATISTICS

Religious affiliation: *none*
Total enrollment: *10,252*
Total undergraduates: *4,800*
SAT/ACT midranges: CR: *680–750*, M: *680–790*; ACT: *30–33*
Applicants: *15,042*
Applicants accepted: *27%*
Applicants accepted who enrolled: *33%*
Tuition and fees: *$40,664*
Room and board: *$11,268*
Freshman retention rate: *96%*
Graduation rate: *85% (4 yrs.), 91% (6 yrs.)*
Courses with fewer than 20 students: *75%*
Student-faculty ratio: *9:1*
Courses taught by graduate students: *not provided*
Most popular majors: *international relations, economics, art*
Students living on campus: *98%*
Guaranteed housing for 4 years? *yes*
Students in fraternities: *13%* in sororities: *13%*

SUGGESTED CORE

1. Classics 31, Classics of Greece
2. Philosophy 151, Ancient Philosophy
3. Religion 21/22, Introduction to the Hebrew Bible/New Testament
4. Religion 35, Introduction to Christianity (closest match)
5. Political Science 42, Western Political Thought II
6. English 50/51, Shakespeare I/II
7. History 24/25, Revolutionary America, 1763–1815/Antebellum and Civil War America, 1815–1877
8. Philosophy 55, The Making of the Modern Mind

are appointed a faculty advisor and two upperclassmen as peer advisors, any of which they are free to change.

One student reports that some freshman English classes are politicized wastes of time, for instance, "Films about Love, Sex, and Society," a seminar which in the past has assigned students to watch a porn movie. The more politicized departments are the interdisciplinary programs, such as Latin American studies, Africa and the New World, and urban studies. The courses that fulfill the world civilizations requirement are also notoriously ideological. Some students also complain of a partisan slant in political science classes.

At Tufts, professors' political views are often obvious; many post political cartoons and slogans on their office doors. Their opinions often permeate classroom discussion as well. One philosophy and political science major says, "They do more than seep into the discussion—they *are* the discussion." This is not universally true, however. One student praises a philosophy professor who "takes a vote on what students think on a certain issue in class. One time, a student asked him what his thoughts were on the issue. He says, 'Wait to ask me until after the semester.'"

The nearly 800-student College of Engineering is held in high esteem on campus, and its website points out that the school has an attrition rate of zero, "while the average American engineering school loses about a third of its class." A student says of engineering majors, "I'm living with two engineers and they are always working; they have to work so hard, but when they come out they have so many job opportunities—they're set, they are ready for anything." Tufts recently finished renovating two engineering buildings—Anderson and Pearson halls.

Students say the best departments at Tufts are international relations, history, biology, child development, English, political science, economics, and philosophy. Outstanding professors at Tufts include Robert Devigne and Vickie Sullivan in political science; Judith Haber, Nan Levinson, Neil Miller, and Christina Sharpe in English; Peggy Hutaff and Joseph Walser in comparative religion; David Denby in philosophy; and Eric Todd Quinto in mathematics. In child development, students praise Donald Wertlieb and Calvin (Chip) Gidney, who is known as being "incredibly well spoken and knowledgeable." One student praised Gregory Carleton's Russian literature courses as "fascinating. He always sat down with his students to go over their writing."

Tufts strongly encourages students to study abroad, and around 45 percent of all undergraduates do. Options are many, including London, Madrid, Paris, sites in Japan, Chile, China, Ghana, or a semester spent on a ship at sea. Tufts also offers a summer study-abroad option in Talloires, France, that is highly praised by students who have participated. One student calls this program in the French Alps "a jewel."

Tufts offers studies in Chinese, French, Italian, German, Hebrew, Japanese, Ancient Greek, Spanish, Arabic, and Latin.

Student Life: The elephant in the ashtray

Nearly all Tufts students live in university residence halls, and Tufts offers an abundance of options. Special-interest houses allow students to base their residential life on a particular theme, including Africana, Asian American, Jewish, or Muslim culture, arts, and foreign languages. The Rainbow House is a "gay-friendly" residence hall that sponsors regular social and political events on related themes.

Freshmen can choose to live in one of three all-freshman dorms that feature live-in faculty members and upperclassman tutors in addition to the regular resident assistants. Tufts offers several single-sex options for women, but fraternities are the only single-sex option for men. Most dorms have young men and women living as next-door neighbors, although some separate the sexes by floor. A few halls have coed bathrooms, but they are single-use with lockable doors. Dormitories usually offer substance-free and "healthy living" floors, though alcohol can certainly be found in plenty at other dorms and at the fraternities. Dorms range in age from brand new to vintage 1957. Haskell and Wren Halls were built in the 1970s as "riot-proof" dorms. Says one resident, "It's terrible for meeting people."

The food on campus (once terrible) is on the upswing; locally grown foods are now available in the dining hall. Tufts has established contracts with some local restaurants, where students can use their meal cards as payment—even on take-out. Some fraternities have their own chefs.

The Tufts campus is located in the Boston suburbs of Somerville and Medford, neither of which can be described as a college town. For that sort of environment, students must take the "T" (subway) to Cambridge. Davis Square, a shopping and cultural center with small stores and a movie theater, is a short walk from campus.

Weekend social life for Tufts students revolves around Boston and its many colleges rather than around the campus. Tufts's Greek system is under great pressure from the administration, and just over a tenth of Tufts students pledge. Overall, the Tufts campus has become much less raucous, mostly due to more stringent drug and alcohol rules. According to one student, "They used to knock on your door if they smelled pot and ask you to stop. Now they call the police." Once allowed to use their discretion in reporting student infractions, RAs are now required to report everything.

Town-gown relations are reportedly very strained. Tufts students who live off campus have complained that residents resent the college kids who live in apartments in their communities. One student says, "A lot of neighbors are really obnoxious to the students. There was a noise complaint because students were merely talking in their apartment. The community loves going after Tufts students."

Several years ago, Tufts appropriated $500,000 per year for diversity programming. This has meant increased funding for the university's "Group of Six" culture centers: the Asian American Center; the Africana Center; the International Center; the Latino Center; the Lesbian, Gay, Bisexual, and Transgender (LGBT) Center; and the Women's Center.

Students say, "There is a great diversity here, with people from all over the world." Tufts is at least consistent and comprehensive in its definition of diversity; the "economically disadvantaged" are listed as a separate minority group. Tufts students have been heard to complain that there are too many "rich kids" on campus.

Alongside left-leaning student groups stand the Tufts Republicans and the *Primary Source*, "the journal of conservative and libertarian thought at Tufts University." The publication prides itself on publishing "honest criticisms regardless of political ideology." Both this newspaper and the Republican group are very active—which is a good thing for students. Says an undergraduate, "It is difficult to be a conservative on campus, but we get enough respect that it's not that bad." However, others assert, "Groups with right-wing opinions are small and shunned; no one cares what they think. It's very liberal here."

The Granoff Family Hillel Center is reportedly one of the most welcoming buildings on campus. The student body is around 20 percent Jewish, which makes Hillel "a huge presence." A rainbow of faiths are represented at Tufts, including Buddhist, Hindu, Baha'i, and Muslim. The Tufts Christian Fellowship, Protestant Student Fellowship, Unitarian Universalist, Eastern Orthodox, and Catholic Community at Tufts serve students of their respective churches.

Tufts also hosts hundreds of student clubs and organizations, from the Tufts Dance Collective, Wind Ensemble, Speech Team, or Students for Justice in Palestine to the Strategic Gaming Society, Freethought Society, Economics Society, Mock Trial, or Hellenic Society. Pen, Paint & Pretzels serves as an "umbrella organization for student-run performing

---

ACADEMIC REQUIREMENTS

In lieu of a core curriculum, Tufts imposes some distribution requirements. Students must take the following:

- Two courses in humanities, such as "Gender, Travel, and Imperialism," "Hemingway, Fitzgerald, Faulkner," or "Ancient Philosophy."
- Two classes in the arts, such as "Greek and Roman Tragedy," "Makeup Design and Application," or "North Indian Dance: Kathak."
- Two courses in the social sciences, with choices such as "Europe from the French Revolution," "Race and Class in American Politics," and "Anthropology and Feminism."
- Two natural sciences classes, chosen from options like "Radio Astronomy," "Human Physique," and "Biology and the American Social Contract."
- Two courses in mathematics, such as "Calculus," "Microbrewery Engineering," and "The Mathematics of Social Choice."
- One world civilizations class; two of the dozens of choices are "Introduction to the Qur'an" and "Childhood Across Culture."
- Two freshman-year writing courses (students can test out).
- Six courses in foreign language/foreign culture. These could include "Elementary German" or "Culture and Intimacy in South Asia."

arts groups," while the Red Watch Band works to end alcohol overdose deaths and the Tufts Mountain Club provides outdoor activities like cross-country skiing, biking, and rock climbing to its 225 members.

One popular campus event is the Naked Quad Run, which takes place on the first night of reading period in the fall semester, wherein students run around the Residential Quad in the buff (and often in the bitter cold). The administration has frowned on this Run in recent years due to the alcohol poisoning, injuries, and the "unsolicited" gropings involved.

Tufts boasts some more venerable traditions. It seems that the famous circus owner P. T. Barnum donated $50,000 to Tufts in the late 1800s and threw in the stuffed hide of his most famous elephant, Jumbo, as a bonus. The animal was destroyed in a fire in 1975, but some of his ashes are kept in a jar, which Tufts athletes rub before games for luck. The appropriately named Tufts Jumbos compete on thirty varsity teams in NCAA Divisions I (squash and sailing) and III (basketball, cross-country, lacrosse, and so forth), as well as in the New England Small College Athletic Conference.

A number of club and intramural teams are also available and popular. Says one student, "There's plenty of room to be who you are, and plenty of groups to join." A second enthusiast states, "There are an incredible amount [sic] of activities, clubs, and organizations to get involved with at Tufts." Club sports include rugby, tae kwon do, Ultimate Frisbee, baseball, and fencing, while intramural teams play Wiffle ball, floor hockey, and dodgeball.

Teams with strong records in recent years include men's cross-country, men's lacrosse, and sailing. The Gantcher Family Sports and Convocation Center, opened in 1999, houses an indoor track and four indoor tennis courts. The jogging college president has helped bolster athletics, however, as has a new $2.3 million boathouse built for the men's and women's crew teams.

YELLOW LIGHT

Tufts is a challenging place for conservative students. A student sums up the political atmosphere at Tufts by saying, "We're a northeastern liberal campus. That's no secret." Another says, "I can see how it would be difficult to be conservative here, because most people are liberal. If you're actively conservative people will actively dislike you and will try to engage you in an antagonistic dialogue." Another student says, "For the average student who just wants to have his own opinion without being assailed for it—I feel bad for that kid."

However, Tufts has avoided the more egregious free speech violations typical on college campuses. According to Inside Higher Ed, a Korean immigrant studying international relations made headlines in 2009 when he tacked up a parody of a campaign poster for a student Union Senate seat. The original poster featured a Korean-American candidate with the slogan "Small Person, Big Ideas," while the parody featured read "Squinty Eyes, Big Vision" and "Please vote me! I work rearry hard!" While several groups expressed their outrage and offense, Tufts took a hands-off approach and let student groups deal with the issue among themselves. For his part, the creator of the tasteless parody claimed that opening a dialogue about racial issues is exactly what he intended (along with, of course, offering a laugh): "I thought it would be funny to satire the oppressive environment of political correctness at Tufts," he said. "I think it's unhealthy that people feel afraid to express their views."

Tufts was surprised to find itself at the top of The Daily Beast's 2010 report on the nation's most dangerous campuses. The report calculated one murder, thirty-six forcible rapes, 100 robberies, 119 aggravated assaults, 174 burglaries, forty-nine car thefts, and an arson in a three-year period. These statistics were disputed by Tufts, which claims that most of those crimes were committed off campus on properties adjacent to campus. The school's own 2009 report noted two motor vehicle thefts, one robbery, seven forcible sex offenses, and forty-five burglaries in that year. Safety phones are located all over campus, a police force is present, and the grounds are well-lit, but students would do well to be aware of the dangers of the surrounding areas.

Tufts tuition is a hefty $40,664, which, combined with room and board, adds up to $51,932. "It's way too expensive," says one student. "There's good financial aid here, though, if you can demonstrate a need." Tufts meets the full demonstrated need of all admitted aid candidates. Financial aid has been the subject of a $1.2 billion campaign set to conclude in 2011, with $380 million going to support need-blind admissions. Forty-one percent of students receive need-based aid averaging about $25,000. For students who plan to work in nonprofit organizations or in the public sector, Tufts offers to pay off loans, since these jobs usually tend to pay less than do the more popular professional choices for Tufts grads. Still, the typical Tufts student who borrows graduates with a hefty $28,000 in debt.

Wellesley College

Wellesley, Massachusetts • www.wellesley.edu

More than a hen party

Wellesley College was founded in 1875 as a private, all-female institution by Henry and Pauline Fowle Durant. Since then, it has earned a glowing academic reputation. Today, it is considered by many to be the crown jewel of the "Seven Sisters," the most prestigious and selective women's colleges in United States. The college's endowment is more than $1.6 billion, although it has struggled recently to maintain that figure. Its prime location in Wellesley, Massachusetts—just thirteen miles west of Boston—gives Wellesley women access to all of the city's academic, political, and social resources, even as they live on 500 idyllic acres. "Student come fairly ambivalent about the single-sex aspect of the college, and simply fall in love with the beauty of the campus," says one faculty member. "It works its magic on them." Most of the campus was designed by Frederick Law Olmsted Jr., the creator of New York City's Central Park.

Wellesley has a distinguished alumnae network that is nonpareil among American colleges, and access to seemingly unlimited funding sources, both internal and external. Among the many programs for students is the Washington Public Service Summer Internship Program for juniors, which offers ten-week internships "including a living expense stipend and housing in local university dormitories."

In the past, Wellesley prided itself on the well-rounded liberal arts education it provided its students. While Wellesley's curriculum is still grounded in the liberal arts, much of that material is viewed through the jaundiced lens of multiculturalism—a political ideology intrinsically hostile to the very civilization that created and sustains the liberal arts.

Academic Life: Serious classroom environment

In lieu of a core curriculum, the school imposes some distribution requirements, of which one student says, "They can be as serious or as easy as you make them. But I like the idea that everyone has to be at least familiar with all fields of study." However, Wellesley is no longer a liberal arts school in the true sense. "There were too many classes at Wellesley where I did readings, went to lectures, wrote the papers, and in the end still knew nothing about the topic I couldn't have discovered on Wikipedia," an otherwise contented alumna says. Students are also required to take at least one course with a multicultural focus, i.e.,

VITAL STATISTICS

Religious affiliation: *none*
Total enrollment: *2,324*
Total undergraduates: *2,324*
SAT/ACT midranges: CR:
  640–740, M: *640–730*;
  ACT: *29–32*
Applicants: *4,156*
Applicants accepted: *35%*
Applicants accepted who
  enrolled: *40%*
Tuition and fees: *$39,420*
Room and board: *$12,284*
Freshman retention rate:
  94%
Graduation rate: *83% (4 yrs.),*
  90% (6 yrs.)
Courses with fewer than 20
  students: *68%*
Student-faculty ratio: *8:1*
Courses taught by graduate
  students: *none*
Most popular majors: *social
  sciences, foreign lan-
  guages and literatures,
  visual and performing arts*
Students living on campus:
  92%
Guaranteed housing for 4
  years? *yes*
Students in sororities: *none*

a course that focuses on (*deep breath*): "African, Asian, Caribbean, Latin American, Native American, or Pacific Island peoples, cultures or societies; and/or a minority American culture, such as those defined by race, religion, ethnicity, sexual orientation, or physical ability; and/or the processes of racism, social or ethnic discrimination, or cross-cultural interaction." (*Sigh.*)

Every new student is initially advised by a Class Dean—an administrator assigned to their entire class—and a faculty advisor. After selecting a major, the student can change advisors or keep the one she has. Fortunately, advisors at Wellesley really are *advisors,* professors who actually guide students through college and aren't just there to make sure students satisfy course requirements. The First-Year Mentoring Program pairs fifteen freshmen with a junior or senior who lives in the same dormitory complex and leads weekly meetings. There are also a number of peer tutoring resources available for students who need academic help. Since Wellesley does not have graduate students, professors—not teaching assistants—conduct all courses.

"The best aspect of Wellesley is the serious classroom environment," says one Wellesley woman. "Students come for the academic experience. They have high expectations for themselves and their learning and come prepared to work. Classes are very engaged; we have a good time and learn a lot."

There are many solid and popular courses offered (but not required) such as "History of Education," "Psychology of Creativity," "Introduction to Astronomy," and "Modern Poetry," "History of Modern Philosophy," and "Freedom and Dissent in American History."

But students also point to classes, professors, and entire departments where the rainbow of opinion has been squeezed by political uniformity into a few narrow shades of purple and pink. They nod at the usual suspects, such as peace and justice studies and women's studies, but also at certain courses in German and Spanish—complaining for instance that one professor in a foreign language course was "outspoken on socialist views and did not deal well with conservative students." Other students note that Africana studies, religious studies, and even chemistry held some minefields for women with more traditional views, and they complain of an economics course taught from a dogmatically Marxist perspective.

In the English department, majors are required to take one class each in critical interpretation, Shakespeare, pre-1800 lit, and pre-1900 lit. Their remaining six classes must be at intermediate or advanced levels, and they can take no more than two creative writing electives. While the major requirements could certainly be stronger, Wellesley offers excellent classes like "Milton," "Renaissance Literature," "Southern Literature," and "Colonial and Post-Colonial Literature," alongside race- and gender-obsessed courses that should be avoided.

History majors must complete a class in the history of Africa, Latin America, or Asia, and one class in the history of the U.S., Europe, or Russia. Of their seven electives, one must come from premodern history, and the department urges (but does not require) students to concentrate on a field, time, nation or theme, like "the history of women," or "the ancient world." Course offerings are impressive, from the traditional "Roots of the Western Tradition," and "The Rise of the West? Europe 1789–2003," to the innovative: "Alexander the Great: Psychopath or Philosopher King," "Strategy and Diplomacy of the Great Powers," "Heresy and Popular Religion in the Middle Ages," or "Bread and Salt: Introduction to Russian Civilization."

> ### SUGGESTED CORE
>
> 1. Classical Civilizations 202/204, Crisis, Drama, Classical Athens/Latin Literature
> 2. Philosophy 201, Ancient Greek Philosophy
> 3. Religion 104/105, Study of the Hebrew Bible-Old Testament/New Testament
> 4. Religion 216, Christian Thought 100–1600
> 5. Political Science 241, Modern Political Theory
> 6. English 112, Introduction to Shakespeare
> 7. History 203, Out of Many: American History to 1877
> 8. Philosophy 230, Nineteenth-Century Philosophy

More substantial are the requirements for a major in political science. Students are recommended to take an introductory course and one intermediate- or advanced-level class each in American politics and law, comparative politics, international relations, and political theory, as well as an additional advanced-level course in two of the fields. Finally, students complete three electives, such as "The First Amendment," "Political Economy of Development and Underdevelopment," "Gender and Conflict Resolution in South Asia," "International Environmental Law," "Race and Political Theory," and "Power and Politics."

The school has many virtues. Says one undergrad, "I like the small classes, and how everyone gets along. The professors are considerate to us." Inside the classroom, students say they generally feel comfortable sharing their own ideas and opinions, regardless of whether their thoughts align with those of their professors. "I knew my professors were generally very liberal, but I never felt looked down upon for my views," says one conservative student. "Wellesley's near-worship of tolerance has, for the most part, also been afforded to conservative students both in and out of the classroom," a student says. "When I quoted the Bible in an English class to emphasize a literary point about Dante, it was praised and not ostracized. After disagreeing strongly with a professor in my final essay about *Roe v. Wade,* where I preferred using 'baby' and she preferred 'fetus,' she gave the paper an A, writing that I was to be applauded for maintaining my conservative beliefs on a campus like Wellesley."

Another student disagrees, saying, "It is virtually impossible for a free marketplace of ideas to exist at the college, especially within the administration." She adds, "There is definite pressure to conform to political correctness here at every level. Certainly the faculty is asked to join the party line. Students should know this about Wellesley before deciding to come here."

Despite a number of opinionated departments, the alumnae, overall, are supportive of their picturesque alma mater, as are many current students. "I do enjoy Wellesley; I've received a good education from fantastic professors," says one. Teachers recommended by current and former students include Marion R. Just and Edward A. Stettner (emeritus) in political science; Thomas Cushman and Jonathan B. Imber in sociology; Karl "Chip" Case (emeritus) in economics; Kathleen Brogan and Larry Rosenwald in English; Andrew C. Webb in biology; Mary Kate McGowan, Nicolas de Warren, and Catherine Wearing in philosophy; Tracy Gleason, Beth Hennessey, and Paul Wink in psychology; Stephen Marini in religion; Miranda Marvin (emerita) and John Rhodes (emeritus) in art; Jerold S. Auerbach (emeritus) and Guy Rogers in history; and Ray Starr in classics.

Students are very vocal about their favorite instructors and make their opinions available to fellow students in an online server called "FirstClass," where such matters are discussed in forums not accessible to faculty. "The only rules on that forum are that they must be respectful of the professor and cannot comment about whether they are an easy or hard grader," says a student.

The average class size ranges from seventeen to twenty students, and the student-faculty ratio is an outstanding 8 to 1. Some introductory courses enroll more than a hundred students, but these classes divide into small discussion groups. However, as one student complains of humanities and social sciences seminars, "Discussion-based classes often turn into self-help groups, with each student . . . offering a personal example or story that might touch the theme of the reading but doesn't fully relate." Nonetheless, students say "there is no such thing as an easy A" at Wellesley, and anything lacking in class time is made up for with copious amounts of homework.

Due to the small student body, there are also opportunities for honor students to engage in independent research projects with faculty. Students agree that Wellesley is very good in supplying its students with the support systems they need. Rarely do students fall through the cracks; there is constant interaction between students and faculty both in and out of the classroom.

Wellesley is also proud of its science program. In the Science Center students have access to state-of-the-art instrumentation, including a confocal microscope, two NMR spectrometers, microcalorimeters, and a high-power pulsed tunable laser. The adjacent Whitin Observatory boasts sophisticated telescopes. The greenhouses and botanical gardens are used for study and are open to the public.

Wellesley students can register for courses at MIT, so science-minded students should have no problem finding classes they need. There are a number of exchange programs in which students may cross-register at MIT, as well as at Brandeis University, Babson, and Olin College of Engineering. In their sophomore year, students can apply to the five-year BA/BS program at MIT; in their junior year, they can approach Brandeis for a BA/MA in international economics and finance. Through the Twelve College Exchange Program, students may opt to study for up to two semesters at one of the participating schools, such as Amherst, Bowdoin, Dartmouth, Vassar, Smith, and Mount Holyoke.

There are many study-abroad opportunities of which several hundred students take advantage each year. The college administers programs in Aix-en-Provence, France, and

New England

Vienna. Wellesley is also a member of consortia that offer programs and exchanges in many different colleges and universities abroad.

Wellesley offers classes in Chinese, Hebrew, Japanese, Hindi, Korean, French, German, Italian, Spanish, Russian, Arabic, Ancient Greek, and Latin.

ACADEMIC REQUIREMENTS

Beyond their majors, students must complete the following requirements:

- One course in the fundamentals of prose composition. Options include "The Maternal in Film," "Great Debates in Education," "Love Manuals: Medieval and Modern," "Human Genetics and Ethics," and "*Hamlet*: Poem Unlimited."
- A quantitative reasoning requirement. Students must first pass a basic math course or an exam, then take one course that emphasizes statistical analysis or data interpretation, such as "Our Place in Space" or "Introduction to Probability and Statistical Methods." Most of these courses also have laboratory components.
- Coursework to prove foreign language competency through the intermediate level.
- One course with a multicultural focus. Students work with their advisors to find a class that "demonstrates awareness of a non-Western culture or of social dynamics involving minority groups within a Western culture." Numerous classes suffice, from "Race and Political Theory" to "Soviet and Russian Film" or "Modern Korea: 1800 to Present."
- Eight classes in physical education; the school offers a number of options, like hip-hop dance, table tennis, archery, or ballet.

Students must also take eighteen courses outside their major to complete distribution requirements:

- Three classes in language and literature and visual arts, music, theater, film, and video. Courses that meet the requirement range from "Dante" to "Blackness in the American Literary Imagination," from "Disneyland and American Culture" to "Contemporary American Queer Cinema."
- One course in social and behavioral analysis. Options include classes like "The Politics of Crime," "Adolescence," or "Resistance and Dissent in North Africa and the Middle East."
- Two classes in epistemology and cognition, such as "Language and Culture," "Psychology," or "History of Sexuality: Queer Theory."
- Two classes in religion, ethics, and moral philosophy. Courses such as "Children of Abraham," "New World Afro-Atlantic Religions," "Ancient Greek Philosophy," or "Religious Themes in American Fiction" suffice.
- Two classes in historical studies, ranging from "Athens and Rome: A Tale of Two Cities" to "Greed in America."
- Three classes in natural and physical science and mathematical modeling and problem solving, one of which must include a laboratory component. A large variety of classes qualify, like "Forensic Anthropology," "Number Theory," "Fundamentals of Chemistry," and "Hydrogeology—Water and Pollutants with Laboratory."

Student Life: Too much to do

Wellesley College is located in an affluent Boston suburb. Besides the on-campus Lake Waban, which offers outdoor recreation for the students, the most beautiful spot on campus is arguably the Academic Quad, defined by large, red-brick buildings. Other facilities like the Davis Museum and Cultural Center and the renovated Margaret Clapp Library also make significant contributions to the physical environment of this small school. This library contains more than 1.5 million books, and Wellesley belongs to the Boston Library Consortium.

Wellesley recently raised $472.3 million in a five-year capital campaign which, among many other things, provided the new Wang Campus Center—"Great food!" exclaims a student—and a parking facility; a new center for the humanities; new programs in neuroscience and environmental studies; a five-fold increase in the number of paid student internships; $90.9 million for student scholarships and financial aid for study abroad; extensive restorations of the campus landscape; and numerous new endowed professorships. Despite the school's considerable wealth, budget challenges have still affected it, and after losing 21 percent of its endowment ($344 million) in 2009, Wellesley was forced to cut 10 percent of jobs. Nearly fifty administrative and union workers were laid off and fifty staff members took early-retirement offers.

Wellesley's proximity to Boston means that there are plenty of opportunities for students to socialize with students from the area's numerous other schools—both on and off campus grounds. The college funds two forms of transportation: the Exchange Bus and the Senate Bus. Commuter rail runs within easy walking distance of campus.

Wellesley maintains an Office of Religious and Spiritual Life for students—although it's not picky about which spirits are invoked. The school chapel is beautiful, though much of what made it peculiarly "Christian" has been removed. It is now a "multifaith space" rather than a church. The college website pledges to "support the celebration" of Baha'ism, Buddhism, Christianity, Hinduism, Jainism, Humanism, Judaism, Islam, black and Native American traditions, Paganism, Sikhism, Unitarian Universalism, and Zoroastrianism. The larger faiths have associated chaplaincies or student groups.

However, students cannot be sure that all these chaplains or programs will present their respective faith traditions in unadulterated form. For example, the Catholic chaplaincy sponsors Dignity (a gay-advocacy organization officially condemned by the Church) and invites abortion-friendly speakers to campus. Religiously orthodox students should take the hint and attend services off campus—for instance, at one of the more conservative congregations in Boston or Cambridge.

At least the school's tolerance has begun to include conservative students; heretofore Wellesley has been at best a challenging environment for those with more traditional views. Despite a stubbornly leftist faculty, conservative students do report a growing curiosity and appreciation in their peers for other points of view. "I find that my classmates are becoming less ideological . . . and more curious about what is true," one student says. A professor concurs: "Now, any person could find a niche in Wellesley; it is becoming a much more open place than it was. People are now taking great pains to allow for differences of opinion." Another student assures incoming freshmen, "Wellesley is slowly but surely changing for the better." There is a chapter of College Republicans, a pro-life group, and a range of Christian organizations on campus, which are "small, but active."

Wellesley students seem to like organizing clubs, and there are nearly 200 of all stripes to choose from, though they vary greatly in activity level. Political and government groups tend to be very active (says one student, "Wellesley women can get 'up in arms' about *any-thing*!"), as are cultural organizations and singing, dance, and theater groups.

Academic clubs include the Biological Chemistry and Biology Club, Society of Physics Students, Economic Student Association, and Psychology Club. For fine arts fans, a Film Society, Flaire Art Club, and Orchestra are sponsored, and for those who prefer to perform, the school hosts a choir, Freestyle dance troupe, the Fiddleheads violin players, Wellesley Belly Dancing Society, Gospel singing group, Toastmasters, Dead Serious improv comedy troupe, Wellesley College Dancers, and the Shakespeare Society, among others.

Students interested in service will find opportunities like Campus Girl Scouts, Sexual Health Educators, and Habitat for Humanity, as well as the Best Buddies program, which pairs students up with mentally handicapped buddies. A number of cultural and ethnic clubs are available, from the Hellenic Society, Spectrum GLBTQA association (which hosts the school's annual Dyke Ball), or Hui O'Hawaii to the Wellesley Arab Women, Canadian Club, or Wellesley Asian Alliance. Literary and media outlets include *Counterpoint* journal, the *Legenda* yearbook, the Science Fiction & Fantasy Society, Wellesley College Television and WZLY radio.

Besides these activities, the college provides social and extracurricular options for week-nights and weekends. One persistent but compelling feature of extracurricular life at Welles-ley is the society houses and student centers. These buildings are not residences, but have dining facilities and social spaces where groups sponsor lectures and gatherings. Shakespeare House is for students interested in Elizabethan drama, while the Harambee house provides a gathering space for "students of African descent." Others focus on art and music, literature. Students may join society houses as early as the second semester of their freshman year.

Fourteen varsity sports are offered, as well as instructional programs in fitness, athlet-ics, and dance. Wellesley Blue athletes compete in the NCAA Division III and are affiliated with several other athletic associations, like the New England Women's and Men's Athletic Conference. The school offers club sports like soccer, equestrian, skiing, and water polo, and intramural kickball, mini-marathon, badminton, and dodgeball teams, among others.

The Keohane Sports Center houses volleyball, squash, and racquetball courts, dance studios, and the eight-lane Chandler Pool with a separate diving area, as well as indoor tennis and basketball courts, a 200-meter track, and an indoor golf practice area. Yoga and dance studios, a multipurpose gym, weight training and cardio rooms, and a sports medi-cine facility are also part of the extensive facility. Lake Waban and Nehoiden Golf Course join outdoor tennis courts and playing fields in offering Wellesley ladies plenty of recre-ational opportunities. Sports teams have recently been revamped—the current slogan: "Go Blue or Go Home!"—with a subsequent surge of school spirit in athletics. But Wellesley is still not known as a "sports" school, a fact about which some athletes complain.

Wellesley is almost entirely a residential college, with 92 percent of students (and all freshmen) living in fourteen dorms ranging in size from 38 to 300 students. A small-com-

YELLOW LIGHT

While Wellesley has been open to a diversity of ideas—even conservative ones—a group of students stirred up controversy in 2010 over the "Mr. Campus Freshman" contest on Wellesley's section of HerCampus.com. Students were meant to nominate their male friends from other schools, but their classmates complained that the contest was offensive to transgender and transsexual students at Wellesley who might have wanted a shot at the title themselves. HerCampus.com relented, and seven women from Wellesley participated in the competition, according to the *Boston Globe*.

It seems that remaining a conservative at Wellesley can make your professors sad. A history professor spoke of an "exceptionally bright" student in his class that he felt he had not well-served because, at the end of the class, "she was still conservative." The head researcher for the Wellesley Center for Women claimed in a speech that conservative women should be pitied because they've been used by men to work against their own interests. She was quoted as saying of Wellesley conservatives: "And to think these women are highly educated!" One person who attended the speech recalls that the speaker went on to "lament the failure of higher education to weed out or change traditional women."

munity atmosphere is preserved through the residence halls, where first-year students share both dorms (if not rooms) and meals with members of other classes. Specialty housing includes the Lake House independent living cooperative for upperclassmen, with a huge kitchen and no residential staff, the Instead feminist cooperative, and Casa Cervantes and La Maison Francaise language halls. Other language halls are located within larger dorms, and a Multifaith Living and Learning Community and Sustainability Co-Op are also available.

Wellesley women maintain an extensive social life with men from the many colleges around Boston, and men are welcome visitors on campus. "The official rule for guests is that they may stay over for three nights a week, but this is never enforced," one student says. "However, Wellesley women are vigilant about men in the dorms and will stop to ask [one] who he's with." The alcohol policy of the college is that a student must be of age and drinking in a private space, e.g., *not* a hall or living room. Students are pleased with a "Good Samaritan Policy" that prohibits disciplinary action against any individual who seeks medical attention for alcohol-related illness. "This keeps everyone extremely safe," says one source.

In 2009, the school reported seven cases of burglary, a motor vehicle theft, and one anonymous report of a sexual assault on campus. The college's police force promotes campus safety by providing blue-light emergency phones all over campus and an escort service and shuttle van for students out late at night, although the school makes it clear that the van is for safety and not transportation to and from social events.

Wellesley is a pricey pleasure, with tuition for 2010–11 at $39,420 and room and board at $12,284. However, 62 percent of undergraduates receive financial aid and Wellesley meets 100 percent of demonstrated financial need. The average Wellesley student carries a modest $13,324 in student-loan debt.

Wesleyan University

Middletown, Connecticut • www.wesleyan.edu

Do not enter

Wesleyan University was founded in 1831 by the Methodist Church to educate ministers. Since then, Wesleyan has assiduously abandoned most of its traditions. The school severed its ties with Methodism way back in 1910, and now refers to the school's namesake, John Wesley, founder of Methodism, merely as "the greatest Englishman of his time" or a "daring humanitarian." "Daring" is a word much in vogue at Wesleyan; the school sometimes seems to believe it has a corner on audacity.

Wesleyan is rich in physical and intellectual resources. Classes are usually small, professors care about their students, and the school is one of the top ten liberal arts colleges in terms of sending students on to complete PhDs. But there is little intellectual or political diversity in the classroom or elsewhere. And reading about current practices at Wesleyan makes one want to take a shower (with the door closed—see below).

Academic Life: Less than the sum of the parts

Wesleyan does not have any core requirements, and the set of "general education expectations" it "strongly encourages" are weak, allowing many students to graduate without any exposure to several major disciplines. Says one faculty member, "The students tend to be quite curious and, at times, adventurous. The relatively loose curriculum can create many opportunities to pursue one's bliss. However, the same curriculum can fail to force students to reintegrate their diverse studies or confront the larger debates that have been central to the Western tradition. Seniors routinely mourn the fact that all of their courses, when taken as a whole, failed to achieve sufficient coherence. The whole was far less than the sum of the parts."

One undergrad isn't troubled: "I suppose students (if they really tried) could graduate through 'puff' courses, but people come to Wesleyan to learn. Taking easy courses at a school like Wesleyan seems like a waste of money." The problem, of course, is that what some eighteen-year-olds see as foundational really isn't. For instance, "The Biology of Sex" is an approved general education requirement course in science. According to the course description, "By examining the biology of sex in detail, we will also debate the age-old topics such as whether sexual reproduction is sexist." The primary textbook used in this

VITAL STATISTICS

Religious affiliation: *none*
Total enrollment: *3,148*
Total undergraduates: *2,787*
SAT/ACT midranges: CR:
  640–750, M: *650–750*;
  ACT: *29–33*
Applicants: *10,068*
Applicants accepted: *22%*
Applicants accepted who
  enrolled: *32%*
Tuition and fees: *$42,384*
Room and board: *$11,592*
Freshman retention rate:
  95%
Graduation rate: *88% (4 yrs.)*,
  93% (6 yrs.)
Courses with fewer than 20
  students: *67%*
Student-faculty ratio: *9:1*
Courses taught by graduate
  students: *none*
Most popular majors: *psychology, English, economics*
Students living on campus:
  98%
Guaranteed housing for 4
  years? *yes*
Students in fraternities: *4%*
  in sororities: *1%*

foundational biology course is *Dr. Tatiana's Sex Advice to All Creation*. And there's more where that came from. Much more.

A professor complains: "The university has created a host of interdisciplinary programs that are weak and overly politicized: the African American Studies Program, the American Studies Program, the Science in Society Program, and Feminist, Gender, and Sexuality Studies are particularly weak and often indistinguishable with respect to their offerings." In fact, Wesleyan offers a vast array of controversial and academically questionable courses. Most of these classes even fulfill the distribution guidelines—for example, the aforementioned "The Biology of Sex," "Key Issues in Black Feminism," "Queer Literature and Studies," and "The Making of American Jewish Identities: Blood, Bris, Bagels, and Beyond."

Wesleyan's system is exacerbated by its emphasis on research. According to a professor: "While there is a strong teaching culture at Wesleyan, teaching is less important than research at tenure and promotion time and this fact shapes the decisions faculty members make regarding the use of their time. After tenure, some professors scale back dramatically on their research and could doubtless teach more. However, these are generally the very professors who should not be teaching anymore, either because they are no longer interested in scholarship or view the classroom as a context for political (re) education." The administration fails to deliver for different reasons: "Heavy university investments in fashionable studies have led to a systematic underfunding of core departments."

In the First-Year Initiative Program (FYI), freshmen take special classes that are designed to improve their writing and rhetorical skills. Taught in small seminars, usually fewer than twenty students, FYIs are "entirely optional," although "students are advised to consider taking at least one of these courses during their first year," according to the catalog. There is no English composition requirement; instead, the school asserts that writing skills are emphasized and developed throughout the curriculum.

Students receive faculty advisors upon entering the university and department-specific advisors after declaring their majors. Because the school does not impose any requirements, students will lose out immeasurably if they do not receive adequate support when designing their "individualized programs." The success of the system is said to hinge mostly on students being active and involved. As one student says, "The quality of advising

New England

is heavily dependent on the advisors. Some students love and praise their advisors" while others find their advisors useless.

Wesleyan University's student body consists of almost 2,800 full-time undergrads, as well as about 360 graduate students. "The English, government, and economics departments routinely attract the largest enrollments and for good reason: they tend to be the best departments, in each case characterized by strong research and quality teaching. The history and philosophy departments are also quite strong," says a professor. "The English department at Wesleyan—like at many institutions—seems to have a strong leftist bias and conservative students bemoan the heavy political content of many of the courses." English majors concentrate in one of five areas: American; British; race and ethnicity; creative writing; or theory and literary forms. Study of Shakespeare is not required, and course offerings include "Toni Morrison" and "Black Power and the Modern Narrative of Slavery."

History majors at Wesleyan are not required to take any broad survey courses in history, or indeed any class on the United States or Europe. The department only calls for six courses within an area of concentration—Africa, Asia, and Latin America; Europe; gender and history; intellectual history; religion and history; or the United States—and two courses outside of the concentration. Students must also complete three seminars and a final research project.

"The social science departments—with the notable exception of sociology—offer a less politicized curriculum regardless of the political orientations of the individual professors. There is a strong department norm—shared with economics—against ideological proselytizing," says a professor. Government majors choose from one of four concentrations: American politics and public policy; comparative politics; international politics; or political theory.

The College of Social Science is held up by some on campus as the school's venue for a "classical" education—if you can credibly use that word for courses that mostly assign authors who only date back to the nineteenth century. "The College of Letters tends toward a more politicized curriculum as exhibited by the fact that it was the home of the much celebrated course on pornography in which students were encouraged to make their own porn flick as a final project," says a teacher.

Some of the more worthwhile departments include medieval studies, architectural history, classics, molecular biology and biochemistry, biology, and physics. Wesleyan also has a strong literary tradition, reflected in the presence of its own university press and a series of prestigious summer workshops for writers.

SUGGESTED CORE

1. Classical Civilization 278, Greek and Roman Epic or English 251, Epic Tradition
2. Philosophy 201, Philosophical Classics I: Ancient Western Philosophy
3. Religion 201/212, Old Testament: Hebrew Bible/Introduction to the New Testament
4. Philosophy 261, Christianity and Philosophy (closest match)
5. Government 338, Modern Political Theory
6. English 205, Shakespeare
7. History 237, Colonial America
8. History 216, European Intellectual History since the Renaissance

New England

169

Politics is omnipresent at Wesleyan, inside and outside the classroom. "Most of the humanities, most of the interdisciplinary programs, and some of the social sciences are highly politicized and uniformly on the post-Communist left. Conservative and religious students would likely find them to be inhospitable unless they were willing to go 'under cover,'" says a faculty member. "I have found it to be a rather isolating environment for anyone who has conservative or libertarian inclinations."

"Interestingly, although the majority of students are on the left, they tend to be far more willing to consider alternative arguments than the professors, many of whom are strident and dogmatic in their political positions and show little toleration for conservative or religious students," says a student. "It would not be a stretch to describe the average student as a career-minded New Yorker interested in building a decent résumé." One professor notes that there is growing tolerance on campus for conservative (or at least libertarian) viewpoints. "I have found that even students who have cut their teeth on the classic Wesleyan curriculum (an odd amalgam of Toni Morrison, Noam Chomsky, and Michel Foucault) are open to consider the arguments made by the likes of Russell Kirk, Friedrich Hayek, and Murray Rothbard," says the teacher.

Wesleyan can justly boast of its strong student-faculty relationships. The student-faculty ratio is a strong 9 to 1. Students enjoy ample opportunities to interact with their peers and professors in and out of class, and graduate teaching assistants do not teach undergraduates. Standout faculty members include Andrew Szegedy-Maszak in classics; Martha Crenshaw, Marc Allen Eisner, and John E. Finn in government; Ron Schatz in history; John Bonin in economics; and Will Eggers and Richard Slotkin (emeritus) in English. Peter Rutland, who teaches Russian and Eastern European studies in the government department, is a notable scholar of Soviet economics.

Almost half of all Wesleyan undergraduates study abroad for at least a semester. The university runs programs on every inhabited continent. At home, Wesleyan's foreign language department offers American Sign Language, Arabic, Catalan, Chinese, Japanese, Korean, Swahili, Ancient Greek, Latin, French, German, Italian, Spanish, Portuguese, Russian, Hebrew, and Hindi, and also contains two state of the art language labs for student use.

Student Life: *Goat Boy and the Potato Chip Ritual*

Middletown, Connecticut, is aptly named, sitting in the middle of the state on the banks of the Connecticut River. Wesleyan's 360-acre campus lies in the center of this mid-sized, blue-collar town. Main Street, with its restaurants and shops, is within easy walking distance, but otherwise the town doesn't offer much to students. Wesleyan's architectural style varies widely. The school's oldest buildings are brownstones constructed in the middle part of the nineteenth century. Today, the campus is a mix of old and new. The Van Vleck Observatory was designed by Henry Bacon, architect of the Lincoln Memorial. The Olin Memorial Library's design was influenced by Bacon, and was originally built as a Greek revival, symmetrical building. In the 1980s, it was remodeled and expanded to add a modern flavor. Recently renovated to the tune of $22 million were the Patricelli '92 Theater and the neighboring Wesleyan Memorial Chapel, which features a 3,000-pipe organ and

New England

stained-glass windows depicting biblical scenes—and serves as a teaching and assembly space. In fall 2009, the Allbritton Center opened to house the Feminist, Gender and Sexuality Studies Program, among others.

Wesleyan is definitely a residential school, with 98 percent of the undergraduate student body living on campus. The nature of residential life probably contributes most to the "progressive" character of the Wesleyan experience. While the current university policy assigns first-year students roommates of the same sex, upperclassmen can choose coed dorm rooms and coed bathrooms. It is not unusual for students in these coed bathrooms to shower with the doors open. A housing official says, "The hall makes the decision [whether to have coed bathrooms] at the beginning of the school year, after they get to know one another." A recent graduate recommends Clark Hall for freshmen. It is a recently renovated residence that offers doubles, provides kitchen amenities, and is well situated in the middle of campus.

The Wesleyan Student Assembly is constantly pressing the administration to implement gender-neutral housing for all students. A WSA resolution states that since "gender and biological sex are separate and distinct concepts" and "the historical rationale for same-sex roommate assignments is based upon antiquated heterosexist assumptions and obsolete concerns," incoming freshmen should not be excluded from the right "to define their own gender and make housing decisions, irrespective of that definition." Mercifully, there are still a handful of single-sex residences for those who request them, and substance-free options are also available. Housing is guaranteed for four years; upperclassmen who wish to live off campus have to petition for permission.

Male students may opt to live in a limited selection of Greek housing; there are no houses for sororities. When former president Douglas Bennett declared that some fraternities should be coed, this provoked long overdue resistance from students as well as alumni. As an alumnus wrote in the student newspaper, the *Wesleyan Argus*, "Since Wesleyan endorses single-gender dorm floors, gender-based and ethnic and race-based houses, clubs, studies, publications, sororities, gender-based sports, race-based and sexual orientation-based alumni groups/networking, and partnerships with Smith College (which discrimi-

---

ACADEMIC REQUIREMENTS

Wesleyan has no core curriculum or distribution requirements, maintaining instead a set of general education "expectations." By the end of their second year students are "strongly encouraged" to take the following:

- Two classes in humanities and the arts. Choices range from "Survey of African American Theater" to "Protestantism: From the Reformation to the Religious Right."
- Two classes in the social and behavioral sciences. These include courses such as "Feminist Theories" and "The Psychology of Gender."
- Two classes in the natural sciences and mathematics. Course offerings include "Descriptive Astronomy" and the aforementioned "The Biology of Sex."

New England

nates against men), then it has no legitimacy to hypocritically force fraternities to go coed." Amen.

One conservative student complained of heavy social pressure from activist groups to adopt the most radical linguistic experiments in support of sexual diversity, citing a university-wide memo sent out by a student organization, the Wesleyan Trans/Gender Group, insisting that students replace he/she/him/her with "ze (subjective) and hir (objective and possessive). For example, 'I was talking to my friend Kris earlier. Ze told me that hir paper was due tomorrow, and it was stressing hir out.' Some students prefer to be referred to with gender neutral pronouns, and many students prefer to use gender neutral pronouns in papers instead of the universal he." Got that?

As you might guess, Wesleyan has gone to enormous lengths to promote multiculturalism and ethnic (not intellectual) diversity on campus. The university offers several academic programs to encourage minority students to pursue graduate degrees. The admissions department vigorously recruits minority students, sponsors a Students of Color Weekend, and on another weekend, flies in ethnic students from outside the Northeast to visit Wesleyan. In a newsletter for students of color, Wesleyan promotes minority scholarships, career opportunities, and political events. The Queer Resource Center serves an active and noisy homosexual student population. In its library, students can check out videos like *Goat Boy and the Potato Chip Ritual, Dress Up for Daddy, Female Misbehavior, Party: A Safer Sex Videotape for Black Gay Men, Stop the Church,* and *Two in Twenty: A Lesbian Soap Opera.* Along with pornography, the Queer Resource Center library serves up "free condoms, lube, and dental dam instructions."

Among the other student organizations at Wesleyan are the Black Women's Collective, the Wesleyan Christian Fellowship, Step One ("a confidential resource for students questioning their sexuality"), several *a cappella* groups, Wesleyan Film Series, Clinic Escorts (which chivalrously provides escorts for women heading to abortion clinics), Scrabble Club, Wesleyan Democrats, Woodrow Wilson Debate Team, and Wheatgrass Co-op. Second Stage is a student-run group overseeing Wesleyan's student theater. The company produces dance and theater shows that are entirely designed, directed, teched, and performed by Wesleyan students. The Center for the Arts, which focuses on contemporary and world arts, is a vibrant element of campus life at Wesleyan with its concert, dance, theater, and family series; exhibitions; and special events. The complex of studios, classrooms, galleries, performance spaces, and departments provides ample opportunities for students to engage in the arts.

There are religious resources on campus for those students interested in them. There are resident Muslim, Jewish, Catholic, and Protestant chaplains on campus, as well as groups associated with Buddhism, Unitarian Universalism, Christian Scientists, Quakers, Hindus, and Baha'is. In addition to religious-themed program houses, the university also sponsors several faith-based student groups—the majority of which are Jewish, to serve approximately 30 percent of Wesleyan's student body.

Wesleyan's professors and administrators are not alone in their embrace of the radical academic left. Students themselves are no slouches when it comes to leftist activism. Among the more politically oriented student organizations are the Environmental Organizer's Network, Ethnic Studies Committee, Trans/Gender Group, Wesleyan Satanist Advocates, the black student group *Ujamaa*, Wesleyan Feminist Network (which sponsored the auctioning of sexual favors for a fundraiser), Students for a Sensible Drug Policy, Amnesty International, a pair of ACLU groups, Students for a Free Palestine, Students for Democratic Action, and the Wesleyan Animal Rights Network.

Underage drinking is pervasive at Wesleyan. Drinking is permitted openly, often accompanied by liberal drug use, during the annual outdoor music festivals; Duke Day, Buttstock, and the Spring Fling.

Wesleyan sports teams compete in the NCAA Division III New England Small College Athletic Conference (NESCAC). Committed primarily to academics, the conference does not permit member schools to recruit off campus, to hold out-of-season practices, or to grant athletic scholarships. Among the men's and women's twenty-eight available intercollegiate sports, interested students should find ample opportunities to compete. Wesleyan varsity teams once competed as the "Methodists," but today, Wesleyan athletes are known as "Cardinals." The Freeman Athletic Center features ice skating, swimming, track, and basketball facilities; a fitness and strength-training center; and an exercise room. The center includes a gymnasium with seating for 1,000, a 7,500-square-foot fitness center, and eight squash courts.

> ## RED LIGHT
>
> We're tempted to replace our "Red Light" here with a brightly painted "Do Not Enter" sign. The items cited are merely the tip of a very dark iceberg.
>
> In an effort to cater to diverse student tastes, Wesleyan currently offers a number of special interest houses. The Womanist House is for students "who are committed to the issues of Wesleyan women, regardless of race, class, sexual orientation, or cultural background," while the Open House is "a safe space for lesbian, gay, bisexual, transgender, transsexual, queer, questioning, flexual, asexual, genderf**k, polyamourous, bondage/disciple, dominance/submission, sadism/masochism (LGBTTQQFAGPBDSM) communities and for people of sexually or gender dissident communities." Yep, they use all the letters.
>
> Then there is the student-run "C**t Club." The club is about "celebrating vaginas," and came under attack from community members when it sold a button reading "Vagina Friendly" to a first-grader attending a student activity fair. This sort of crassness may not be as shocking to Wesleyan students as it is to outside observers. One's sensibilities can grow dull over time.

One Wesleyan tradition remains, although in altered form. The Douglas Cannon dates back at least to the Civil War. After the war, freshmen would try to fire the gun as sophomores struggled to stop them. This "cannon scrap" is no longer practiced—the gun has wisely been rendered inoperable—but students again began stealing the cannon in 1957. Since then, students have cunningly stowed the gun away in dorm rooms, presented it to Russian UN representatives as a "symbol of peace, brotherhood, and friendship," given it to President Nixon in protest of the Vietnam War, and even baked it into a sesquicentennial birthday cake.

Community safety is maintained by a public safety patrol. While not a university police force, the patrol gives out free whistles to use in case of emergency and patrols the campus by foot, bicycle, and automobile. The school offers a shuttle service that stops at

New England

designated pick-up/drop-off points at night, and students walking around campus late at night can call for an escort. The campus is equipped throughout with emergency response phones. These safety precautions do not seem to be working. In 2009, the university reported a murder, thirty-five burglaries, three forcible sex offenses, two aggravated assaults, and two stolen cars.

Going to Wesleyan is a costly excursion into parts unknown; in 2010–11 tuition was $42,384, with room and board for underclassmen $11,592. The school currently offers need-blind admission and commits to meeting 100 percent of a student's demonstrated financial need; however, the school has a mixed record of being able to meet this commitment, since its endowment is about half the size of peer schools. Only 48 percent of the undergraduates who applied for financial aid for the 2009–10 academic year received a need-based award. The average Wesleyan student graduates with $29,174 in student-loan debt.

Williams College

Williamstown, Massachusetts • www.williams.edu

If every college were thus located

Founded in 1793, Williams College is a richly endowed liberal arts school in the gorgeous Berkshires of western Massachusetts—about which Henry David Thoreau wrote, "It would be no small advantage if every college were thus located at the base of a mountain." He calculated that the scenery was worth at least the equivalent of one endowed professorship. Whether it's the vista or the prospect of demanding, intimate classes, top-notch applicants have been drawn to Williams since the beginning. Williams students are rather a privileged bunch: less than 60 percent are graduates of public high schools. However, in recent years the school has increased the number of students receiving financial aid, now up to 52 percent. In fall 2010, Adam F. Falk, former dean at Johns Hopkins's School of Arts and Sciences, was inaugurated as seventeenth president of Williams. There's no reason to think he will radically alter the character of the school, which one might nicely sum up as a high-minded, genteel liberalism secure enough to be tolerant of intellectual dissent.

Academic Life: Diversity and tutorials

Past generations of Williams scholars faced a curriculum that covered the most important texts of Western civilization. Sadly, this no longer prevails; in fact, students face only vague distribution requirements, which can be fulfilled by quirky or politicized courses if they do not choose carefully.

Williams students can easily graduate without having studied the basic texts of Western civilization. Williams did recently add requirements for one course in quantitative or formal reasoning and two courses designated as writing-intensive. These mandates add some backbone to a curriculum that might otherwise allow a student to earn a degree without ever having to answer a question with a right and wrong answer. Some students say they appreciate the flexibility in the relaxed curriculum. "It allows the student to take courses in areas that interest him or her while exposing the student to different departments," a history major says.

Not every undergrad likes the system or the attitudes it enables. One says that too many of his fellow students "tend to be focused on career paths that lead to high-paying jobs rather than opportunities to discuss events that occurred in the past. They only want to know enough about Thucydides to quote him in an argument on current events." Another agrees: "The study of Western civilization is given no special place in the curriculum. Sure, the courses in history, literature, and philosophy are often there—or at least seem to be—but it is entirely possible to leave here without reading any really great books or learning any history beyond that of race and gender."

While the requirements for particular departments at Williams are by no means trivial, they are sometimes too loose-fitting to be useful. For instance, English majors need simply take two courses set before 1700; in other words, Shakespeare is optional. They must also take two courses set between 1700 and 1900, one course set after 1900, an analytical writing "Gateway" course and a class on literary criticism. The department *urges* students to choose corresponding classes in the humanities "with a view to supporting and broadening their studies in literature" and strongly recommends that students study classical and modern languages, along with foreign literature, but falls short of actually demanding either.

Likewise, the history major simply requires that students take courses from three different geographical or temporal areas. They may choose from Africa, Asia, Europe and Russia, Latin America and the Caribbean, the Middle East, or the U.S. and Canada, or premodern history. The seminar "Approaching the Past" is required, and students much take at least three courses "linked by common themes, geography, or time period" in order to develop a concentration within their major. Since the concentration is self-determined, anything from "Military History" or "Women in Asia" to "Colonial Cultures" could satisfy—and a student could major in history at Williams with "Latinas in the Global Economy" as his only American history course.

Political science majors have the option of choosing a "traditional subfields" or "individual concentrations" approach to the subject. The more traditional route requires an introductory course and capstone class, plus two electives in American politics, international relations, political theory, or comparative politics. Additionally, these students must take two classes in other subfields. Those who opt to determine their own concentrations simply take five classes on a theme, as well as two classes in another area. Previously approved concentrations include "Justice in Theory and Practice," "Democracy," "Politics of Disempowered People," "Environmental Politics and Policy," or "Global Icons."

An article in the *Williams Record*, the student newspaper, indicates that there is some student frustration with the obsession with diversity and the effect it has on the curriculum. The author notes that many traditional courses have been eliminated to make room for more politically correct material, resulting in choices that have become homogenized. He bemoans the proliferation of "classes about minorities" over "classes about stuff deemed important for the last hundred years." Or the past 2,500 years, for that matter.

Though there is no Western civilization requirement, entering students must take at least one Exploring Diversity (ED) course. Categories include "Comparative Study of Cultures and Societies," "Empathetic Understanding," "Power and Privilege," "Critical Theorization," and "Cultural Immersion." The courses must "promote a self-conscious and critical engagement with diversity." Thankfully, a number of worthy courses do fill the requirement, so students can skip "Feminist Bioethics" in favor of "Traditional Chinese Poetry" or "cultural immersion" in a study-abroad program.

Students select from a list of thirty-six majors with economics, English, political science, psychology, art, and biology the most popular—while departments like classics, computer science, women's and gender studies, and foreign language studies each produce fewer than ten majors per year. The student-faculty ratio is an excellent 7 to 1.

> **SUGGESTED CORE**
> 1. Classics 101, The Trojan War
> 2. Philosophy 201, History of Ancient Greek Philosophy
> 3. Religion 201/211, The Hebrew Bible/The New Testament
> 4. Religion 214, The Christianization of Europe
> 5. Political Science 232, Modern Political Thought
> 6. English 201A/201B, Shakespeare: Illusion and Reality/ Shakespeare on the Edge
> 7. History 252, North America and the United States, 1492-1865
> 8. History 227/337, A Century of Revolution: Europe, 1789 – 1917/Origins of European Social Thought and the Social Sciences

Williams puts a great deal of emphasis on tutorials; it has recently increased the number it offers and opened them to underclassmen. A tutorial typically enrolls ten students grouped into five pairs, which meet for an hour each week in the presence of the professor, who observes as one student presents a short paper and his partner critiques it. One faculty member told the *Chronicle of Higher Education* that his tutorials were "without a doubt, the single best teaching experience I ever had." More than half of graduating seniors have taken at least one of the school's sixty tutorials.

Students who seek attention from professors will readily receive it. "The key is finding and working with the best professors," says one student. "They're out there, and you can usually build a strong major around one or two of them." Another student says, "Professors are definitely accessible to students. Every professor provides plenty of office hours, and many give you their home phone numbers to call them any time. . . . Many professors I've had enjoy meeting outside the classroom for coffee or a meal."

The best departments at Williams are in the sciences—especially biology, chemistry, physics, geology, computer science, mathematics, and neuroscience. The Chinese and Japanese departments are strong, and the art history program is said to be extraordinary. Students can take advantage of the Williams College Museum of Art and the nearby Clark Institute of Art. In political science, the international relations program is described as "excellent." Highly praised professors include Eugene Johnson, Michael Lewis, and Sheafe

Satterthwaite in art; Stephen Fix in English; Charles Dew and James Wood in history; Joseph Cruz in philosophy; James McAllister and Darel Paul in political science; and Robert Jackall and Jim Nolan in sociology.

Advising at Williams appears to be moderately strong. Freshmen are advised by members of the general faculty. Students are assigned departmental faculty advisors after they declare a major; this normally occurs after their sophomore year. Individual departments determine their own advising policies.

Williams maintains an honor code that administrators and students take very seriously. Students broadly adhere to it and faculty report that they feel safe in leaving exams unproctored and even allowing students to "self-schedule" tests as take-homes.

Williams operates on a two-semester schedule, with a four-week Winter Study Program between semesters. The distinctive 4-1-4 schedule gives professors the opportunity to test-teach new classes or materials, or to concentrate on a smaller subject that can be covered in less than a semester. During January, students take a single course pass/fail. Topics run the gamut from teaching practica, independent study, senior thesis work, and courses like "Ephquilts: An Introduction to Traditional Quiltmaking," and "Get Focused and Step It Up—Climate Change Activism."

Study abroad at Williams is encouraged during the junior year. Students may elect to spend an entire academic year or a semester literally anywhere in the world; the college lists hundreds of approved programs, but Williams students may submit a request to study at any foreign university. Additionally, the college's Wilmers, World, and Lawrence Fellowships fund international travel. Another excellent opportunity is the Williams-Oxford program at Oxford University's Exeter College.

Despite the school's commitment to "Exploring Diversity" and providing study-abroad opportunities, Williams imposes no foreign language requirement. It offers foreign language majors in German, Russian, French, Spanish, Chinese, Japanese, and Ancient Greek and Latin. It also provides instruction in Italian and self-study courses with native speakers of Hebrew, Hindi, Korean, and Swahili. The school recently added Arabic to the list of tongues offered, and Arabic Studies as a major.

Student Life: Amherst *delenda est*

The college is remote and bucolic, some 145 miles from Boston and 165 miles from New York City. The campus itself adds much to the landscape, with the older buildings designed in traditional academic style. Each member of every graduating class since 1862 has planted a sprig of ivy next to some building or wall.

Almost all students live on campus due to the college's eight-semester residency requirement, and more than 90 percent of upperclassmen have single rooms. "The living space has recently been divided into four 'neighborhoods' that are meant to be self-governed. Students are expected to remain in the same community for all four years," reports the school housing office. Williams has no frats, sororities, or special-interest housing. Housing is guaranteed for all four years, and first-year students are housed together in "living groups" of twenty-two, with two Junior Advisors per living group.

New England

Upperclassmen can live in mansions confiscated from campus fraternities in 1962. The six freshman dorms were all built before 1930. The Gothic Morgan Hall (1882) comes complete with gargoyles. The dorms are coed. A Web description of Williams and Sage halls says the bathrooms are "*usually* single sex and are shared by [four to six] people." Such conditions at Williams inspired conservative alumna Wendy Shalit's heartfelt manifesto *A Return to Modesty*, which Shalit published when she was only twenty-three.

Much of students' out-of-class activity takes place on campus, with many involved in sports, student organizations, and social events. The campus proper is 450 acres, but the college also owns the 2,200-acre Hopkins Memorial Forest and maintains a top-notch golf course on campus. The athletic program is one of the strongest in the nation in the NCAA Division III; the school almost always wins the division's Sears Directors' Cup, a national award based on the aggregate success of a school's teams. The school mascot is a purple cow and teams are called the Ephs after college founder Ephraim Williams. About 40 percent of students participate in intercollegiate athletics, 34 percent in varsity athletics. However, because athletes are academically strong, students report that cliques do not tend to develop along team lines, and student-athletes are as much students as they are sportsmen.

The Ephs compete in purple and gold in nearly every major sport, from basketball and baseball to crew, volleyball, skiing, field hockey, or swimming and diving. Club sports

---

ACADEMIC REQUIREMENTS

Williams students need three courses—pretty much anything from any related department—in each of three areas:

- Languages and the arts. Choices range from "The Ancient Novel," to any of Williams' foreign language options, to "The Human Image: Photographing People and Their Stories."
- Social studies, including everything from "British Colonial America and the United States to 1877" to "Wise Lady or Witchy Woman? The History of Witches."
- Science and mathematics, with options ranging from "Marine Ecology" to "Perspectives on Sex."

Students are also required to take the following:

- Two courses that are designated as writing intensive. Current choices include "Art, Life, Death: Studies in the Italian Renaissance," "Writing about Bodies," and "Two American Public Intellectuals: Noam Chomsky and Edward Said."
- One class that emphasizes quantitative and formal reasoning. Choices range from "Artificial Intelligence: Image and Reality" to "Principles of Macroeconomics."
- One Exploring Diversity course. Choices include "Nordic Lights: Literary and Cultural Diversity in Modern Scandinavia" and "African Rhythm, African Sensibility." The requirement can also be met by completing a foreign study-abroad program.
- A swimming course, provided the student cannot pass the school's first-year swim test, as well as four physical education classes (or participation in intercollegiate sports during two semesters).

New England

GREEN LIGHT

Williams is one of the few liberal arts colleges that hasn't completely given itself over to political correctness and leftist posturing. With reasonable student conduct policies, an outstanding faculty, a relatively decent set of requirements, and a strong athletic program, the school retains the respect of academic circles and the world at large. In October 2010, MSNBC broadcasted an election special with Williams students, three Williams professors received separate grants worth $691,000 total, and the school hosted a four-day global economic forum with policy-makers (and a Nobel Laureate) from around the world. All that, in just thirty days.

For a college not much bigger than a typical high school, Williams certainly earns its sterling reputation. As far as politics go in the classroom, most faculty members at Williams are said to be fair-minded liberals. "I have yet to take a class where I thought the professor's ideology influenced the course or my evaluation in it," a student says. "If anything, the course I took that had the strongest ideological tilt (a very slight one) was from a conservative professor in a course on American imperialism. . . . I even had [a different] professor regularly ask me if I thought the course was leaning to the left, as he knew I was a conservative."

include rugby, sailing, equestrian, water polo, gymnastics, cycling, figure skating, cricket, fencing, and several martial arts.

In 1821, a Williams president nearly depopulated the college by leaving to found Amherst College—taking with him most of its faculty and students. Since then, the schools have been bitter rivals, and Williams generally stomps Amherst in their annual football game. Williams played Amherst in 1859 in the world's first intercollegiate baseball game.

"The Mountains," written at Williams in 1859, was the first school song in the nation. Mountain Day is still held each year; students head to the top of Mount Greylock, where a festive lunch is served. In other traditional activities, the graduating class drops a perfectly functional watch eighty feet from the tower of the college chapel. If it takes that licking and keeps on ticking, class members will enjoy good luck for the rest of their lives.

Newer "traditions" include the raucous Coming Out Days in October, with opportunities for a Queer Bash, a Sex Jam, and viewing gay pornography. Spring ushers in "V-Week," which features the inevitable production of *The Vagina Monologues*. While the default position at the school is distinctly blue-state liberal (students receive a free subscription to the *New York Times*), student discourse on matters political typically remains civil and high-minded. Students who dissent from the left-liberal line may find the atmosphere a bit stifling. However, one undergrad says that Williams "has not proven to be the liberal hippie bastion that I was told it would be, though it has its share of leftist activism." He went on to opine that "attending a school like Williams known for both its academic rigor and liberal political leanings will better serve conservative students than seeking out a college with like-minded students." Conservative students should seek out fellow travelers, of course—for instance by joining the college's pro-life organization.

All told, the college sponsors over 150 student groups. Student offerings vary widely: the Astronomy Club, Williams Gaming Alliance, Clarinet Choir, and Students for Sensible Drug Policy exist happily alongside the Williams Outing Club.

The Williams Literary Circle gives budding writers a chance to critique one another's work, while Springstreakers gives budding exhibitionists the opportunity to honor and catalog one another's "achievements." Other groups include the numerous *a cappella* choirs, the Public Health Alliance, Queer Student Union, Tap Ensemble, Photography Club, Gospel Choir, Habitat for Humanity, Voice for Choice, and Zambezi Marimba Band.

Those interested in media may consider writing for the ad-supported *Williams Record*, which circulates 3,000 copies of its broadsheet paper weekly. Smaller journals include the *Williams Telos* (a Christian journal), the *Literary Review*, and the *Mad Cow* humor magazine. Any student of Williams College—or adult member in the surrounding community—may host a program on 91.9 WCFM. For over forty years, the station has hosted an all-night trivia contest for students, professors, and alumni.

The college has a multicultural center that hosts a number of speakers and events per year. It offers a preorientation program intended to create a "network of support" for incoming minority students through a variety of social events and forums. The college reports its "U.S. minority enrollment" as 32 percent (a recent jump from 23 percent). Spirituality persists amidst the uplifting natural vistas of Williams, which hosts active religious communities in a variety of Christian student groups, including a Catholic Newman Center, along with Jewish and Islamic organizations—as well as a spirituality group and a secularist community.

Williams is a safe campus, with burglary being the most commonly reported offense, with eighteen incidents in 2009. Two forcible sex offenses were also reported that year, along with an aggravated assault, five arsons, one incidence of intimidation/harassment and two incidences of vandalism.

Williams is one of the costliest schools in the country, with tuition, room, and board weighing in at more than $49,640 for the 2010–11 academic year. However, because it is also rich, it can afford to be generous. Though Williams's endowment has dropped by half a billion dollars over recent years, the school still has one of the highest endowment-to-student ratios in the world. Admissions are need blind, and the college promises to meet 100 percent of demonstrated need for every student. Because of budget problems, the school has had to rescind its once-innovative no-loan admission policy for needy students. Still, about 52 percent of the students receive some aid in amounts that average $39,540, and the average Williams student graduates with a student-loan debt of just $8,359—which may reflect the fact that many students come from wealthy backgrounds and don't need to borrow.

Yale University

New Haven, Connecticut • www.yale.edu

Stained glass . . . and gargoyles

Based in a battered but recovering New England city, Yale University is the second oldest university in the U.S. Its campus, as one student boasts, is "a Gothic wonderland with a dash of Georgian stateliness." Students arriving at Yale will find not only crenelated buildings, but a vibrant intellectual life, the best political clubs in the nation, a vast array of artistic opportunities, and a high-minded respect for ideas. Yale, however, is not for the faint of heart. Those with conservative or religious convictions will find themselves in the minority and will certainly be challenged and sharpened by debate with some of the best and brightest liberal opponents. They will also study under the leading scholars in the world.

Academic Life: Direct your studies

While Yale's commitment to undergraduate education is stronger than that of many other schools, it nevertheless leaves students completely free to define their own education—before they know enough to do so. Its distributional requirements force each student to take a smattering of courses in a variety of disciplines, but nothing like the foundational classes contained in a traditional core curriculum. Mature, responsible students may select challenging classes and avoid politically-charged classes—or they can overspecialize, load up their transcripts with technical courses, and emerge with yawning gaps in knowledge.

The distributional requirements call for two course credits in: arts and humanities, sciences, social sciences, foreign language skills, quantitative reasoning, and writing. Each entering freshman is assigned a faculty member or administrator to serve as a first-year advisor. Once the student has declared a major, he selects a faculty advisor within that department. The stated goal of the advising office is to "to give students an understanding of what constitutes a liberal arts education at Yale." But the burden of choice rests almost entirely on the student himself. The freshman advisors are more for the sake of aiding with the "class shopping" period, to help the student discover what it is *they* want.

For Yalies who do seek an education in Western civilization, the college offers a marvelous resource: the Directed Studies program, which several conservative students agree is "the shining star of Yale academic programs." After admittance to Yale, interested students must apply (again!) for this program; only 125 students each year are admitted, about 10 percent of the average freshman class. Students in the program spend their entire freshman year taking three two-semester courses studying literature, philosophy, and historical and political thought through the close reading of primary sources in the Western tradition. According to one student, "They stick to the canon quite well, so it's worth doing just for the sake of what you read." This includes Homer, Sophocles, Virgil, Dante, Petrarch, Cervantes, Shakespeare, Goethe, and Tolstoy in literature; a survey of thinkers from Plato through Aquinas and then from Descartes through Nietzsche in philosophy; and sources like Herodotus, Plato, Livy, Aquinas, Machiavelli, Burke, and Hamilton in the history and politics course. Directed Studies immediately immerses undergrads in "small classes with brilliant professors," says one student. A professor adds that "kids in these classes are studying with a good proportion of the elite in their freshmen classes."

Given the weakness of the distributional requirements, much of the structure of a Yale education comes within a major. Students and faculty list the following programs as particularly strong: art history, biology, biochemistry, economics, genetics, mathematics, music, neuroscience, psychology, physiology, and religious studies. History and humanities are the two departments most praised by students. One said, "I know of no departments that are terribly weak, though the sciences in general are often perceived as weaker simply because they don't quite measure up to Harvard or MIT, whereas our humanities and social science departments do." History has "top notch" professors, according to students, among them being Joanne Freeman, John Lewis Gaddis, Donald Kagan, Paul Kennedy, and Jay Winter.

Other highly praised teachers include Gregory Ganssle, John Hare, and Karsten Harries in philosophy; Ian Shapiro and Steven Smith in political science, Miroslav Volf, Carlos M. N. Eire, Bentley Layton, and Harry Stout in religious studies; Matthew Giancarlo, David Quint, and Ruth Bernard Yeazell in English language and literature; Charles Hill in international studies; Dante scholar Giuseppe Mazzotta in Italian; Eric Denardo in operations research; Maria Rosa Menocal in Spanish and humanities; Paul Bloom, Kelly Brownell, and Laurie Santos in psychology; Vladimir Alexandrov in Slavic languages and literature; Brian Scholl in cognitive science; Sidney Altman in molecular, cellular, and developmental biology; and Stephen Stearns in ecology and evolutionary biology.

VITAL STATISTICS

Religious affiliation: *none*
Total enrollment: *11,593*
Total undergraduates: *5,275*
SAT/ACT midranges: CR: *700–800*, M: *700–780*; ACT: *30–34*
Applicants: *26,003*
Applicants accepted: *8%*
Applicants accepted who enrolled: *67%*
Tuition and fees: *$38,300*
Room and board: *$11,500*
Freshman retention rate: *99%*
Graduation rate: *90% (4 yrs.), 98% (6 yrs.)*
Courses with fewer than 20 students: *75%*
Student-faculty ratio: *6:1*
Courses taught by graduate students: *not provided*
Most popular majors: *economics, political science, history*
Students living on campus: *88%*
Guaranteed housing for 4 years? *yes*
Students in fraternities or sororities: *not provided*

SUGGESTED CORE

1. Classical Civilizations 254, Introduction to Greek Literature
2. Classical Civilizations 125, Introduction: Ancient Philosophy
3. Religious Studies 145/152, Introduction to the Old Testament (Hebrew Bible)/ New Testament History and Literature
4. History 226, Jesus to Muhammad: Ancient Christianity to the Rise of Islam or Religious Studies 161, History of Catholicism: The First Millennium
5. Political Science 114, Introduction to Political Philosophy
6. English 200/201, Shakespeare: Comedies and Romances/Histories and Tragedies or Humanities 219, Shakespeare: *King Lear, Macbeth, The Winter's Tale, The Tempest*
7. History 124J, Colonial American History
8. Humanities 293, Roots of Modernity or Religious Studies 164, History, Hope, and the Self: Modern Christian Thought

Yale's English Department has for many years been tainted by deconstruction. However, the department has among the most substantial and worthwhile requirements of any college in the country. Yale English majors must take fourteen courses in the discipline, including an introductory survey course on English poetry (or four separate classes on the major British poets) and either a survey course on tragedy or a drama course covering roughly the same material. In addition, majors must take at least three courses in literature before 1800, one in literature before 1900, and one course in American writing, and complete a senior essay. If a careful student is able to filter out the the ideological emphasis on race, class, and gender, he may receive a thorough literary education.

By contrast, the history department's requirements are less thorough. History majors need only take twelve courses, and while they must take at least two classes in U.S. or Canadian history and two more in European history, there is no reason to think that a graduate with a degree in history will have learned about the founding of the American republic, the Constitution, the Middle Ages, or ancient Greece and Rome. The department does require that students take three classes in "preindustrial" history, but this could be fulfilled with non-Western courses, or the study of Byzantine or early Russian history. Moreover, a major could skip the central path of U.S. history entirely by choosing classes focused on Canada, the slave trade or American medical regimens.

Yale's political science department has consistently proved popular among undergraduates. It permits students to meet requirements with many courses from other disciplines or through combined majors (the most common is political science/economics). Dividing the field into five distinct areas—American government, comparative government, international relations, analytical political theory, and political philosophy—the department asks students to take two classes in each of at least three of these fields, write a senior seminar essay and complete eleven courses in the major. But a major could easily graduate having never read *The Prince* or the *Federalist Papers*. Nevertheless, Yale has a reputation for being a "political science school."

Yale students are very positive about their professors. Not only are they serious scholars, deeply involved in research, they are warm mentors and devoted teachers. "Professors are generally extremely accessible, and office hours are very helpful, especially when it comes time to write papers," says one student. He also adds, "One of my friends was even given the keys to the apartment of one of his professors when he was leaving the country, so he could study a rare book." Another undergraduate notes that "professors often eat with students at 'Take Your Professor to Dinner Night,' sponsored by the residential colleges." Yet another student says, "You won't have trouble talking to your professors—even the ones in the big lecture classes will meet up with you if you're up to asking them."

"The focus is on undergraduate teaching at Yale—unlike at Harvard," one professor says. There are few if any genuinely mediocre professors at Yale, but some are better at teaching than others, while a few have trouble keeping their personal politics out of the classroom. Hence, students reading Yale's "Blue Book" should seek out the professors and programs recommended by this guide, trusted faculty advisors, and sensible peers.

There are many graduate student teachers at Yale, called Teaching Fellows or TFs. While they are not yet famous scholars, these younger academics are typically of very high quality. Students report that they enjoy the energy TFs bring to the small sections that supplement lecture courses with professors. "In my experience, the TFs are fantastic," said one undergrad. However, Teaching Fellows—especially those in the social sciences—are more likely than the faculty to infuse their pedagogy with radical politics.

Class sizes are small at Yale, and the student-faculty ratio is an outstanding 6 to 1. Grade inflation, a national problem, is found in some courses.

Yale professors, secure in the most coveted academic positions available, are famously magnanimous. This guide's lead editor recalls that as a callow 17-year-old freshman some twenty-five years ago—on his very first day of class, first semester—he interrupted the lecture of world-famous scripture scholar Bentley Layton to question him for off-handedly challenging the perpetual virginity of Mary. Professor Layton generously conceded the point, apologized, and thanked the student for his intervention.

Like most colleges, Yale has greatly expanded its study-abroad programs recently, so much so that nearly 1,400 students studied overseas for some or all of last year. Yale In London and a partnership with Peking University in Beijing are special programs offered by the Center for International Experience. Yale offers study-abroad programs in dozens of countries across the six inhabited continents.

Yale offers course instruction in over fifty foreign languages, with some study overseas. Languages on campus include such obscure dialects as Ancient Egyptian, Coptic, Hittite, Nahuatl, Pali, Sumerian, and Syriac. Major programs of study are offered in classics, East Asian languages and literature, French, German (and various Scandinavian tongues), Italian, Near Eastern languages and civilizations, Slavic languages and literature, Spanish, and Portuguese.

Student Life: Sex week and Gregorian chant

Student life at Yale College centers on the residential college system, a hallmark of Yale since 1932. The system was designed in imitation of the much more extensive college system at Oxford and Cambridge. In June 2008, Yale University decided to boost its undergraduate enrollment by 15 percent by adding two additional colleges, for a total of fourteen residential colleges. These new residential colleges—to be constructed, we are happy to report, in a traditional collegiate Gothic style—should open by 2013. To finance the expansion, the university is undertaking a $3.5 billion fundraising campaign. As of the end of September, 2010, Yale had just exceeded the $3 billion mark. This residential project is part of a greater "Yale Tomorrow" campaign, with an emphasis on strengthening undergraduate education.

Every college, headed by a residential master and dean, has developed its own personality over the decades. Graduates are almost as loyal to their college as to their school. As one student says: "Each college is like a microcosm of campus with its own dining hall, courtyard, administrative apparatus, and other amenities." All freshmen and sophomores must live on campus, and most undergraduates choose to live in their colleges throughout their four years at Yale; 88 percent of undergrads live on campus. Most of the colleges are quite beautiful, varying in style from meticulously "aged" Gothic replicas of Oxford colleges, to red-brick Georgian, and starkly modern residences that recall surrealist landscapes by Giorgio di Chirico. Students cannot choose their residence hall, although it is possible to transfer. After freshman year, students can pick their suitemates, but only from within their college. Unfortunately, Yale just began a pilot program, starting with the class of 2011, to allow coed suites for seniors.

Privacy is not always to be expected, although seniors, juniors and even many sophomores get single rooms. All individual suite bathrooms are single-sex, as are most freshman bathrooms. In many residential colleges, floors are coed, and as one student acknowledges, "The make-up of the floor determines whether or not the bathroom is single-sex." Students wishing to avoid floors with coed bathrooms can generally do so, but this will substantially limit their choice of rooms.

The residential colleges create tighter circles within an otherwise daunting 11,500-student university. A professor notes that the level of civility in the colleges is higher than in

ACADEMIC REQUIREMENTS

In the absence of a core curriculum, Yale imposes rather lax distributional requirements. In addition to his major and a total of thirty-six courses, each student must complete the following:

- Two courses in the natural sciences, ranging from "Organic Chemistry" I, to "Search For Extraterrestrial Life."
- Two courses in quantitative reasoning, which can include courses in economics, computer science, natural sciences, engineering, mathematics, or statistics. Options include "Geometry of Nature" and more formidable, math-heavy classes like "Probability Theory."
- Two writing seminars or writing-intensive literature courses.
- Two courses in humanities and arts. This includes a wide array of interesting and scholarly courses, but also classes like "U.S. Lesbian and Gay History" and "Intro to Photography" I.
- Two courses in social sciences. Options range from courses such as "Language, Culture & Identity" to "Sex and Gender in Society."
- Coursework or tests to demonstrate intermediate proficiency in a foreign language.

New England

most school dorms. The residential colleges provide some shelter from the stresses of college existence by allowing students the luxury of "a long dinner or relaxing in a common room." The menu offerings are diverse, plentiful, and usually good. Each of the twelve residential colleges offers healthy, "sustainable" food grown organically by local farmers.

Fraternities and sororities do capture the attention of many students. There are several Greek houses off campus and they are known for having some raucous parties. With party themes like "CEOs and Corporate Hoes" and the alleged sexual targeting of freshmen women, some fraternities are accused of creating a climate of incivility on campus. The Yale Women's Center is calling for the administration to change sexual harassment and assault policies and to establish an "official institutional relationship" between the university and Yale's fraternities. (Some fraternities are currently unregistered). There is a general, campus-wide "hookup culture," and according to one survery, a high percentage of students are sexually active. Institutional concern and attention was accelerated by a scandal in 2010 concerning a Yale fraternity whose members marched around campus chanting jokes about rape and necrophilia.

Students report a significant prevalence of frat-house drinking, but say no one is pressured to drink if he wishes to abstain. As for drugs, "there is a very small (almost nonexistent) group of drug users who largely keep to themselves," a student says. One college dean says, "Generally the demands of the courses are such that you can't do a lot of drinking and smoking weed. Most people realize that the demands are too great, after a brief period of experimentation." Yale's campus culture does offer many intellectually rewarding ways for students to use their time. In particular, Yale has perhaps the most vigorous undergraduate political scene in the nation. "Even though maybe three-fourths of the kids vote Democrat, there are actually a lot of active conservative groups on campus. They're not in the closet," a professor says. Campus conservative groups focus more on high-minded discussion more than activism, and members often forge lifelong friendships.

As a microcosm of America's degenerating social elite, the school makes room for every kind of postmodern madness known to man—as if to offer some Dionysian release to students whose heads are otherwise in the clouds. The college's annual Sex Week has evolved from academic discussions of sexuality to a more hands-on approach to the "interaction of sex and culture and manifestations of sex in America," reports the conservative *Yale Herald*. Using student fees and school facilities, in past years this event has provided as keynote speakers sex therapists, sexologists, and porn stars. While most of its events take place off campus, some occur in the university's central quadrangle, the Old Campus. The unsavory quality of the affair may also be indicated by its principal sponsor—a company selling sex aids whose logos and "toys" are prominently displayed.

There are many campus ministries. "Some of the larger and more active student groups are the evangelical Yale Christian Fellowship and Yale Students for Christ. Jewish students, too, have a remarkable variety of more or less Orthodox options through the Slifka Center for Jewish Life at Yale, Yale Friends of Israel, and such," says a student. More traditional Catholic students tend to attend St. Mary's on Hillhouse Avenue, where liturgies feature an exquisite Gregorian chant and polyphonic choir, rather than St. Thomas More chapel on campus. A weekly Latin Mass is offered at Sacred Heart Church in New Haven.

New England

The Yale Political Union (PU) is the nation's oldest and most respected student debating society. It is the largest undergraduate organization at Yale and several conservative students pointed to the PU as one of Yale's best assets—a place for "free and vigorous debate," said one student. The PU is divided into seven parties: the Liberal Party, Party of the Left, Independent Party, Federalist Party, Conservative Party, Tory Party, and Party of the Right, each with its own members and character. The conservative groups are best known for their private debates, conducted in business dress, on topics like "Resolved: Humility is a Weakness." Every year there are three major PU debates which award cash prizes to winners. Even if not interested in actually debating, many students come to hear guest speakers. Guest speakers have included Justice Antonin Scalia, Gov. Howard Dean, Al Sharpton, Dick Morris, Kenneth Starr, Nadine Strossen, Gov. Bill Richardson, and Ralph Reed, to name just a few.

Several students volunteered that the most appealing aspect of campus life is the abundance and variety of extracurricular groups. Among them are the Whiffenpoofs (a musical group); the Yale Entrepreneurial Society; the Yale Bach Society; and the Pundits, Yale's senior prank society. This merry band recently found themselves under investigation by the Yale Police Department when their 2011 annual "Naked Party" resulted in allegations of hazing and a possible sexual assault. The *Yale Daily News* reported that several attendees were hospitalized for alcohol overdoses, and the criminal investigations stem from their testimony to police of "forced, heavy drinking at the party" and "witnessing a member of the Pundits forcing attendees to kiss each other. . ." among many other less-printable depravities.

Campus publications include the conservative *Yale Free Press*; the *Yale Record* (a humor monthly); and the notoriously liberal *Yale Daily News*. Many Yale students also volunteer in the New Haven community, and many in the public schools.

Yale fields intercollegiate teams in all the major sports. Like other Ivy League schools, it requires that its athletes maintain high academic standards and does not award athletic scholarships. This often results in hilariously lopsided contests against more athletically inclined schools, with Yalies cheering on their hopeless Bulldogs with chants such as, "It's all right, it's okay/you'll be working for us someday," although Yale has done better in the last few years in football. The cheerfully obscene Yale Precision Marching Band provides some consolation and entertainment at the games. Each year the Harvard-Yale game (simply referred to as "The Game" by students) draws quite an enthusiastic crowd. Among the many intramural sports, which are organized by residential college, are golf, soccer, football, tennis, basketball, swimming, squash, softball, and billiards. Fifty percent of students participate in one or more intramural sports.

Yale is encrusted with cultural institutions, including the Center for British Art, the University Art Gallery, the Peabody Museum of Natural History, and a huge library system. Centered in the Sterling Memorial Library, Yale's collection of more than 12.5 million volumes is second in size only to Harvard's and is one of the greatest collections in the world. Designed to look like a cathedral, Sterling boasts catalogs in side chapels, phone booths in the shape of confessionals, and a vast image of "Lady Learning" over its main circulation desk—which looks so much like a high altar that annually (the legend goes) some Catholic freshman get confused and genuflect.

Traditional haunts for Yalies include "toasting sessions" at Mory's; Yorkside Pizzeria, home of impecunious grad students marking blue books; and J. Press, originator of the Ivy League look now popular among non-grungy young people everywhere. New York City, the shore, and the New England countryside are all within easy reach by train or car.

New Haven was once regarded by Yalies as "notoriously seedy," with crime kept at bay by the moats, wrought-iron gates, and turreted walls of the college. But thanks in large part to Yale's largesse, the town is recovering nicely. Within walking distance of campus students will find trendy shops, chic restaurants, and interesting nightspots. Boarded-up row houses a few blocks from campus are gradually being bought up, renovated, and rented to wealthy students. Crime is still a concern, however, and new students should learn their way around before straying too far. While it was not a street crime, in 2009, Yale grad student Annie Le was killed by a Yale employee seemingly spurred by psychotic jealousy. In 2009, the school reported that murder, along with seven forcible sex offenses, three robberies, seventy-four burglaries, two arsons, and twelve auto thefts. Most students say they feel safe but offer the proverbial warning that one should not go too far at night into the neighborhood behind fraternity row and the northern tier of the campus. To combat the problem of crime and keep students safe, Yale has an extensive campus security system. It offers a walking service from most points on campus and an around the clock shuttle to or from Yale to many destinations in New Haven.

YELLOW LIGHT

Despite Yale's many virtues, at the institution's heart there is a moral hollowness—which sometimes seems to extend up to its head. The squishiness was demonstrated in March 2010 when the dean's office announced that it was "inviting students to submit anonymous essays about their campus sexual experiences for a new online collection called 'sex@Yale,'" according to the *Chronicle of Higher Education*. In 2008, activists at the school commemorated Roe v. Wade, organizing medical students to perform mock abortions and demonstrating abortion techniques. Yale Medical School requires all Ob/Gyn residents to undergo training in performing abortions.

Despite the leftist orientation of most of the campus, Yale is a mostly tolerant place. While conservative students may be regarded as slightly gauche, professors generally treat them fairly. One student recalled that the only pressure he felt was about his social and religious conservatism, and that "there have been a couple of times in class or in discussions with friends that I have hidden the fact that I oppose gay marriage and abortion." Most intolerance faced by conservatives on campus seems to originate with students, who are quick to ostracize outspoken traditionalists. But nobody who overcame all the barriers to getting into a place like Yale is likely to quail in the face of a little old-fashioned shunning.

A Yale education does not come cheap. The tuition for 2010–11 was $38,300, plus $11,500 for room and board. Admissions are need blind, and the school guarantees to meet the full demonstrated financial need of admitted undergraduates. All financial aid is need-based, and some 50 percent of undergraduates receive it. Like several other Ivies, Yale does not expect any financial contribution from families with annual incomes of less than $60,000. The average recent graduate emerged with a modest $12,297 in student-loan debt.

NEW YORK

◆ Hamilton College

◆ University of Rochester

◆ Colgate University

◆ Cornell University

◆ Bard College

◆ Vassar College

◆ United States Military Academy

PENNSYLVANIA

Rutgers University ◆

◆ Lafayette College

◆ Grove City College

◆ Bucknell University

◆ Lehigh University

◆ Pennsylvania State University

◆ Princeton University

◆ Carnegie Mellon University

N. J.

NEW YORK CITY AREA
Barnard College
Brooklyn College (CUNY)
Columbia University
Cooper Union

Fordham University
The King's College
New York University
Sarah Lawrence College

PHILADELPHIA AREA
Bryn Mawr College
Haverford College
Swarthmore College
University of Pennsylvania
Villanova University

MARYLAND

◆ Johns Hopkins University

◆ St. John's College

◆ United States Naval Academy

WASHINGTON, DC
Catholic University of America
Georgetown University
George Washington University

Mid-Atlantic

Bard College • Barnard College • Brooklyn College (CUNY) •
Bryn Mawr College • Bucknell University •
Carnegie Mellon University • Catholic University of America •
Colgate University • Columbia University • Cooper Union •
Cornell University • Fordham University • Georgetown University •
George Washington University • Grove City College •
Hamilton College • Haverford College •
Johns Hopkins University • The King's College • Lafayette College •
Lehigh University • New York University •
University of Pennsylvania • Pennsylvania State University •
Princeton University • University of Rochester • Rutgers University •
St. John's College • Sarah Lawrence College • Swarthmore College •
United States Military Academy • United States Naval Academy •
Vassar College • Villanova University

Bard College

Annandale-on-Hudson, New York • www.bard.edu

Self-conscious "progress"

Founded in 1860 as St. Stephen's College by John Bard and the New York City leadership of the Episcopal Church, Bard College began as a men's college with a strong classical curriculum, and was affiliated for decades with Columbia University.

The college has changed radically over the years, most notably in the 1930s and '40s—when it became a coeducational haven for European intellectual émigrés in flight from fascism, and transformed itself into a self-consciously "progressive" institution. The school changed its name to Bard, then severed its formal ties with Columbia and the Episcopals. Today it very much embodies the values of the liberal, secular intellectual. As a professor put it: "A lot of the people here could be characters in a Saul Bellow novel."

Academic Life: Instant admission, painstaking study

Bard's undergraduate academic system is based partly on the Oxford and Cambridge tutorial method, with an emphasis on seminars, the process of "moderation," and the senior project.

To graduate with a bachelor of arts degree, students must complete Bard's distribution requirements (which do not form a core curriculum); finish a two-part first-year seminar; earn promotion to the Upper College; complete the requirements of a major; accumulate 124 semester hours of academic credit (40 of which must be outside their major); and complete a senior project.

The school initiated the "instant admissions" system in the late 1970s. Each fall up to 200 applicants sign up to visit the college, submitting applications in advance. On their visits, they discuss readings with professors, meet with the admissions staff—and, before they return home, find out whether they have earned a spot at Bard.

First-year students arrive on campus three weeks before the fall term in order to participate in orientation and the workshop on Language and Thinking (L&T). A recent L&T syllabus featured Charles Darwin's *On Natural Selection* and Kafka's *Metamorphosis.* First-years (as freshmen are called at Bard) enroll in the "First-Year Seminar," a two-semester course that introduces students to "worldwide intellectual, artistic, and cultural traditions and to methods of studying those traditions." The seminar is designed to train students in

VITAL STATISTICS

Religious affiliation: *none*
Total enrollment: *2,235*
Total undergraduates: *1,939*
SAT midranges: CR: *680–740*;
  M: *650–680*
Applicants: *4,828*
Applicants accepted: *33%*
Accepted applicants who
  enrolled: *36%*
Tuition and fees: *$41,670*
Room and board: *$11,810*
Freshman retention rate:
  82%
Graduation rate: *76% (4 yrs.)*
  79% (6 yrs.)
Courses with fewer than 20
  students: *72%*
Student-faculty ratio: *8:1*
Courses taught by graduate
  students: *none*
Most popular majors: *fine
  arts, languages and litera-
  ture, sciences*
Students living on campus:
  77%
Guaranteed housing for 4
  years? *no*
Students in fraternities or
  sororities: *none*

close reading, critical thinking, and analytical writing. The most recent curriculum including Genesis, Plato's *Symposium, The Aeneid, Othello,* Karl Marx's *Economic and Philosophic Manuscripts of* 1844, and Dante's *Inferno,* in addition to works by Freud, Rousseau, Nietzsche, Pascal, Virginia Woolf, and Mary Shelley. Also part of the First-Year curriculum is a "Citizen Science" three-week program in January, covering particular topics not usually covered in traditional science curricula. The 2011 topic is "infectious diseases."

Freshmen get guidance from assigned academic advisors, with whom they must meet several times each semester. Later, each student chooses a faculty member to serve as an advisor for the rest of his education. If their interests change, students may switch advisors.

As a transition from the Lower College to the Upper College, second-semester sophomores undertake a "Moderation," during which a board of three faculty members review the student's work, making critiques and suggestions for the transition to the Upper College, where the students undertake their major. The requirements for Moderation differ by program.

Seniors must undertake a "senior project" to graduate, which is a creative project "growing out of the student's cumulative academic experiences." A good deal of effort in junior and senior year goes into preparing for the senior project.

Bard has retained a commitment to academic rigor, and with only 1,939 undergraduates it has kept itself small. Professors teach all courses, and students report that "they keep office hours, and you won't have professors you can't speak to." Class sizes average around fourteen in the Lower College and eight in the Upper College.

Students at Bard major in a "program" or course of study. Most programs are straightforward; many are downright traditional, such as classical, medieval, and Victorian studies; biology; and sociology. But Bard's interdivisional programs are more inventive, and include Africana, Irish/Celtic, and Latin American/Iberian studies, among many, many others. Bard seems to be trying to keep some sort of balance in its academic offerings between respecting tradition and embracing the experimental.

The requirements of the literature concentration are disappointing. There is no mandate that majors read Shakespeare, medieval literature, or indeed anything written before 1700. One course in the comparative literature sequence is required, as well as various electives. Comparative literature classes all involve close readings of important texts in classes which focus on medieval, Renaissance, Victorian, American, and other such literature sections. Many of the upper-level classes are arcane, focusing on postmodern or feminist literature and critical theory. However, many other literature courses are of self-evident substance. One such class, "Nineteenth Century Novel," includes readings like *Crime and Punishment*, *The Red and the Black*, *War and Peace*, *Cousin Bette*, *Madame Bovary*, and *Buddenbrooks*.

The demands for the history concentration are similarly non-specific, consisting of "between six to eight history courses covering at least three world regions and one period prior to 1800." Before moderating, students must take at least four history courses from different regions and time periods, including a global survey. So students could easily skip ancient history, America's founding, and the Civil War, in favor of courses on the "history of gender and sexuality."

The politics department has four major areas of study: political theory, American politics, comparative politics, and international relations; students must take four courses in at least two of the four areas. Political science majors must complete "Introduction to Political Thinking," a political theory course in which students "think with Plato and also with complementary texts from Sophocles, Nietzsche, Thoreau, and Marx, they reflect upon key political concepts such as justice, democracy, and 'the individual.'" Also required is "Introduction to Comparative Government," which includes coverage of Plato's *Republic* and concepts such as federalism. American Government courses are not required. Throughout the major there is also an emphasis on global politics, environmentalism, and gender issues.

The senior project is what the college considers the "capstone" of a Bard education. Students begin preparing during their junior year, consulting with advisors, doing coursework, and participating in tutorials. Depending on the major, the senior project can be a research paper; a close textual analysis; a report of findings from field work; a photographic essay; a series of original experiments; an analysis of published research findings; a contribution to theory; an exhibition of original artwork; a film; or a musical or dance composition or performance. If students do not pass, they do not graduate, no matter how many credits they have.

An impressively high proportion of Bard's professors are famous and award-winning intellectuals and writers. The novelists Chinua Achebe, Mona Simpson and Francine Prose, the journalists Ian Buruma and Luc Sante, the choreographer Bill T. Jones, the violinists Ani and Ida Kavafian, and the soprano Dawn Upshaw are on the faculty. Well-known short story writer Bradford Morrow leads a literature class, famed biblical scholar Bruce Chilton

SUGGESTED CORE

1. Classics 125, *The Odyssey* of Homer or Literature 204A, Comparative Literature I: Ancient Quarrels—Literature and Critique in Classical Antiquity
2. Philosophy/Classics 261, Plato or Philosophy 362, Plato's Writing: Dialog and Dialectic
3. Religion 110, The Bible as Literature
4. No suitable course.
5. Political Studies 115, Introduction to Political Thinking (closest match)
6. Literature 2503, Studies in Shakespeare
7. History 119, United States History to 1865
8. Philosophy 213, Nineteenth-Century Continental Philosophy

teaches religious studies, and the school features an assortment of acclaimed refugees from the New York arts world, including composer Joan Tower and avant-garde theater director and former Public Theater head JoAnne Akalaitis.

Students praise the teaching skills of Thomas Bartscherer in classics, Jonathan Cristol in international studies, Michael Ives in English, Susan Merriam in art history, Gregory Moynahan in history and Susan Rogers in literature. A rare conservative on the faculty is Rabbi Jacob Neusner, an outspokenly pro-life scholar of religion. Bard professors are reputedly accessible to students. The student-faculty ratio is an impressive 8 to 1.

Most of the academic divisions offer an impressive selection of subjects and courses. Foreign languages, cultures, and literatures features the usual offerings, and then some: Ancient Greek, Latin, Sanskrit, Hebrew, Russian, Arabic, and Chinese. The Division of Languages and Literature is loaded with the kind of intensive, traditional courses that other left-leaning liberal arts colleges are phasing out, such as classes on medieval, Victorian, and Romantic literature.

Particularly strong programs include political science and international affairs, literature, film, music, theater, and biology. Economics students enjoy the resources of the

ACADEMIC REQUIREMENTS

Bard's academic breadth requirements are respectable, given the quality of most of its courses. Students must complete:

- The First-Year Seminar. This two-semester course includes a selection of the Great Books, and a wide array of other worthy ones.
- The Language and Thinking Program, a three-week writing intensive course for freshmen before the start of the ordinary semester.
- One laboratory class in the physical or life sciences.
- A course in mathematics, computing, statistics, or logic; students must also pass a "quantitative test" as a prerequisite.
- A history class. Options range from "Making of Europe to 1815" to "The American West in Film, Fiction and History."
- A course focused on language acquisition or study of literature in a non-English language. Classes are available in Chinese, French, Latin, Russian, and several other tongues.
- Literature in English. Choices are many, including "Poe" and "The Victorians: British History and Literature 1830–1901."
- A studio course in visual or performing arts, or creative writing. Some of the many options include "Cybergraphics," "Video Installation," and " Flamenco: Beginner."
- A class in the analysis of nonverbal art. Choices include " Introduction to Visual Culture" and "Manet to Matisse."
- A "Rethinking Difference" course. These focus on "globalization, nationalism, and social justice, as well as differences of race, religion, ethnicity, class, gender, and/or sexuality."

Jerome Levy Economics Institute; one student says he took a course with the founder of Oppenheimer Funds through this program. The political science department encourages and helps students find internships.

Alas, the drama and dance departments have a reputation for being rigidly avant-garde. Interdivisional programs and multidisciplinary studies tend to be the weakest and most politicized. Two of these are gender studies and multiethnic studies. Those concentrating in American studies can choose traditional history and literature courses—or the trendier classes available in the social sciences.

The college has a center in New York City where international affairs students can do a term of study. Another program assigns science students for a term of research with the graduate students and professors of Rockefeller University. Foreign-exchange programs are connected to the famed Smolny College in St. Petersburg and the Central European University in Budapest. Students can also study abroad in their junior year at approved programs in Berlin and Karlsruhe in Germany; Cape Town and Johannesburg in South Africa; and in Hong Kong and India. Reflecting the college's focus on current issues, it also is connected to the Rift Valley Institute, offering a course of study that exposes students sent abroad to current problems in Sudan. Students who wish to study under the aegis of the Palestinian Authority can do so (see Red Light).

Student Life: Catskill collegiate

Bard College lies in Annandale-on-Hudson, a small town of 2,400 residents an hour south of Albany. The college accommodates its 2,200 students on more than 500 acres along the Hudson River. Students can see the Catskill Mountains from their dorm rooms, and the area provides plenty of opportunities for outdoor activities. There is a waterfall in the woods and a pond where students can swim. Breathtaking trails through the woods surrounding Bard are marked for hiking, and canoeing and kayaking on the tributaries to the Hudson offer opportunities for outdoor adventure. It is a location of exceptional beauty.

The campus comprises nearly seventy-five buildings of different architectural styles, including the original stone structures and a number of mansions on the river. The college tries to spice up its student life by offering free trips each hour to local towns—and, each weekend, shuttles to New York City. But there's usually a lot happening on campus. A glance at two weeks in the student activities calendar reveals dozens of choices open to all students: a poetry reading; films; ballroom and Latin dancing classes; a series of open drawing workshops; concerts of new music by Bard Conservatory students; a math table; Chinese, French, German and Russian tables; and a series of lectures by internationally known scholars on the development of Christianity and Judaism.

The university has a special focus on classical music; college President Leon Botstein is a well-known orchestra conductor, and the school includes a conservatory. The Colorado String Quartet resides at the school, and its music program brings in other critically acclaimed chamber, orchestral, Early Music, and jazz musicians regularly. The popular and praised Bard Music Festival is held in August on campus. In addition, about a dozen student organizations perform or bring bands or theater productions to the campus. They per-

Mid-Atlantic

form in the 110,000-square-foot Richard B. Fisher Center for the Performing Arts designed by Frank Gehry, which houses two theaters and four rehearsal studios.

While performing arts are a major occupation of most Bard students, studies are not neglected. The well-used Stevenson Library contains 275,000 books and 1,400 periodicals and newspapers; further, it is part of a greater network of libraries, giving students access to millions of books and other resources.

The wackier side of student life is epitomized in the spectacle that occurred on the opening night of the Fisher Center, when students rode their bicycles through the lobby—naked. Students say alcohol rules have become stricter on campus since the "Drag Race," a drag queen ball, which was shut down due to numerous cases of alcohol poisoning. However, students can still walk through the center of campus with an open can of beer. Because of the liberal drinking policies, the party life is active; however, there is no Greek life to speak of on campus.

Bard's larger residences have kitchens and laundry facilities. The more than forty dorms range from eighteenth-century houses to ugly prefab buildings. Bard often accepts more students than it can hold, which creates housing difficulties and overflowing dorm rooms. Resident directors manage the dorms, and peer counselors manage the halls. Students praise peer counselors for being well-trained, accessible, and "nonjudgmental." All residence halls are coed except for two women-only dormitories. A housing officer says that the college also countenances a number of coed bathrooms, "mostly out of necessity," since men and women live next door to each other. A guest policy which mandates that visitors check in with security is loosely enforced. And, if parents and students request it, students can live with members of the opposite sex. Off-campus housing is available, and 23 percent of students take advantage of apartments in the nearby towns of Red Hook and Tivoli, especially.

The old stone Episcopalian church on the Bard campus is one of the treasures of the campus. There are five college chaplains: Episcopal *and* Anglican, Catholic, Muslim, and Jewish. The school features Jewish and Muslim student organizations; a Christian Students Fellowship; a Buddhist Meditation Group; and a Catholic community. Episcopal vespers ("evensong") are observed on Sundays in the Chapel of the Holy Innocents. A Christian evangelical group is somewhat active on campus, as are the Buddhists. In another Bard quirk, Jewish and Muslim students share a sacred space and a kitchen. This fits the mission of the school's chaplaincy, which promises to "help students of different faiths learn about each other."

When students aren't hitting the books—which they do a lot—they are participating in the ninety student organizations and clubs on campus. Arts and music clubs include the Jigsaw Puzzlers, the Bard Animal Rights Collective, and the Contra Dance Club, among many others. There is a College Democrat Club, but no College Republican Club; however, the school does offer a Libertarian Club. As a whole, however, the students at Bard are not very politically active. Service and community-based clubs include the well-known Bard Prison Initiative, in which students volunteer to teach inmates; Bard Cycling Club; Boxing, Croquet, Fencing, Jousting and Quidditch Clubs; the Migrant Labor Project; a Mah Jongg club; The Dimestore, whose sole purpose is to distribute free condoms and sexual lubricants, and the WXBC radio station. Ethnically and culturally based groups include the Asian Student Organization, the Queer-Straight Alliance, and other organizations for various ethnic groups. Other organizations celebrate beer brewing, cooking, digital media, martial arts and white-water rafting.

Some groups are better than others. The *Bard Free Press* thought it appropriate to review a series of porn films. About the same time, a "sexual lifestyles" magazine sprang up, called the *Moderator*.

Students or professors to the right of center are vastly outnumbered. According to one undergrad, "This is a very liberal school." Yet the few conservative faculty members on campus have fiercely and publicly disagreed with what they deem to be Bard president Leon Botstein's liberal orientation. And student publications (the *Bard Free Press* and the *Bard Observer*, both left-leaning) feel free to criticize the college's administration, often intelligently. Students do say that professors try their best not to politicize their lessons, utilizing the different viewpoints present in a classroom for honest intellectual exchange.

Sports play a smallish role at Bard, according to one student; however, the college does sponsor eight men's and seven women's NCAA Division III teams, as well as intramural and club sports. The "Raptors" volleyball and tennis matches are well attended, and, especially when it's Bard vs. Vassar, the rivalry is vigorously tongue-in-cheek. The Stevenson Gymnasium complex contains a six-lane, twenty-five-yard swimming pool; a fitness center; squash courts; locker rooms with saunas; an aerobics studio; an athletic training room; and a main gymnasium that houses basketball, volleyball, and badminton courts. Next to the building are six lighted tennis courts, athletic fields, and miles of groomed cross-country running and Nordic skiing trails.

Among the most beloved aspects of Bard life is, oddly enough, its commencement. Following graduation each May, an all-night fes-

RED LIGHT

The political climate at Bard may be gauged by the invited speech given on campus last year by the Maoist political theorist Noam Chomsky and the university's decision, backed by leftist billionaire George Soros, to create an affiliated study program with the Palestinian Authority's Al-Quds University. So, while Bard is making progress in becoming a place which is more tolerant of ideological variety, the right-leaning student who's considering Bard should expect to feel out of place nonetheless. The Princeton Review included Bard in its list of the top ten most liberal colleges.

That's using the word "liberal" generously. A recent controversy has erupted over Bard hosting a chapter of the International Solidarity Movement, a radical anti-Israeli organization. According to the pro-Israel group Stand With Us: "ISM is not just another student organization that spreads anti-Israel misinformation and propaganda. It irresponsibly and callously endangers students.

"Since its founding in 2001, ISM has recruited naive, idealistic young people ("internationals") to go to the West Bank and Gaza and intentionally violate Israeli law and military security zones and to serve as human shields for terrorists."

Bard president Leo Botstein dismissed concerns with the group as "unsubstantiated, exaggerated, and often vitriolic accusations." He claimed that the Bard group affiliated with ISM had violated no laws, and in a bizarre non-sequitur warned that its critics should moderate their own rhetoric in light of the (completely unrelated) shooting of Rep. Gabrielle Giffords in Arizona in January 2011.

tivity begins during which fireworks are shot up into the night sky, illuminating the opposing banks of the Hudson River and the lush green fields around the campus.

Bard's campus, isolated as it is, is quite safe, and students seem to feel secure. The Bard Department of Safety and Security patrols the campus, but they don't often find much action. Still, to make students feel more comfortable, new illumination and security talk-boxes have been added all over campus. A professor says, "The top security alert is bicycle theft." Occasional acts of vandalism are perpetrated on the campus by locals who don't attend Bard. Five forcible sex offenses and eleven burglaries were reported in 2009.

Bard is a pricey adventure. Tuition for 2010–11 is $41,670 and room and board $11,810. However, Bard admissions are need blind, and about 71 percent of the freshmen receive some aid. Some 60 percent of such students had their needs fully met. An average 2008 graduate who borrowed owed $20,201 in student loans.

Barnard College

New York, New York • www.barnard.edu

Columbia's little sister

Barnard College was instituted in 1889, when thirty-six students and six faculty members met in a brownstone on Madison Avenue in New York City. Columbia University's president, Frederick A. P. Barnard, wanted to offer women a broad liberal arts education, which Columbia at the time offered only to men. Today, Barnard College is recognized as one of the top liberal arts colleges in the country.

Columbia, located just across the street, has been coed for nearly three decades, but Barnard remains single-sex and financially independent from Columbia. Barnard students may take from Columbia University as many or as few courses as they desire. Only Columbia's "core" courses are off-limits, which is a shame since they're the best thing offered at either school.

One Barnard student says, "Most semesters, the majority of my classes are across the street. I study in Butler [Columbia's history and humanities library] every day, and most of my friends are Columbia students. . . . Columbia is a really good resource and is one of the major reasons I don't go crazy at Barnard." One of the things that might be goading this student toward madness is the suffocating atmosphere of radical feminism that pervades this women's college, from the classrooms to the student organizations to the upper ranks of its administration. Barnard president Debora Spar opined in a January 4, 2009, *Washington Post* op-ed that the worldwide financial meltdown could have been averted had women, rather than "rich, white, middle-aged guys," been at the helm. Since the head of the college feels comfortable engaging in such a trite, unprincipled *ad hominem*, one can only wish that courses in logic were part of Barnard's degree requirements.

Academic Life: Crossing the street

Each incoming Barnard student takes a first-year seminar, in which she learns writing and speaking skills in a small-group environment. Every student must prepare a semester- or year-long project or thesis within her major. Across the curriculum, and especially in the humanities, instructors emphasize good writing and communication skills. Seminars are limited to sixteen students and emphasize reading and writing. Those considering serious studies in math or the sciences at Barnard should be forewarned that most of their classes

VITAL STATISTICS

Religious affiliation: *none*
Total enrollment: *2,417*
Total undergraduates: *2,417*
SAT/ACT midranges: CR:
   630–730, M: *620–710*;
   ACT: *28–32*
Applicants: *4,174*
Applicants accepted: *31%*
Accepted applicants who
   enrolled: *45%*
Tuition and fees: *$40,546*
Room and board: *$12,950*
Freshman retention rate:
   94%
Graduation rate: *83% (4 yrs.)*
   91% (6 yrs.)
Courses with fewer than 20
   students: *70%*
Student-faculty ratio: *9:1*
Courses taught by graduate
   students: *none*
Most popular majors:
   *English, history, political
   science*
Students living on campus:
   90%
Guaranteed housing for 4
   years? *yes*
Students in sororities: *none*

will take place at Columbia, as Barnard offers very few courses in these subjects.

Barnard students can easily sign up for most of Columbia's classes, while Columbia students are less successful in gaining entry to Barnard's intimate seminars, although students report that there are "Columbia boys" in almost all Barnard classes. New York City also offers many opportunities for research, internships, and transfer credit from area colleges and universities. For instance, students can major in music by taking courses from Barnard as well as Juilliard or the Manhattan School of Music.

The Barnard advising system is by all accounts superb. Each student is assigned a professor from the department of her proposed major as an advisor. Most of these professors have volunteered for the job; they have both an interest in student success and a high level of expertise in their fields. Moreover, they are often helpful with last-minute advice on papers. All students must visit their advisors at least once a semester for approval of the advisee's course load.

Barnard's student-faculty ratio is 9 to 1, which helps students see a lot of their professors. Barnard students should count on half their classes being seminars (with five to fifteen students) and half lectures (most with fifty or fewer students). Some of the best professors, according to students, are Rajiv Sethi and Sharon Harrison in economics; Anne Lake Prescott in English; Joel Kaye, Herb Sloan and Robert McCaughey in history; Alan Gabbey in philosophy; and Kimberly Zisk Marten and Richard Pious in political science. Novelist Mary Gordon, whose books are often on college syllabi, usually offers an auditorium-sized lecture course on the modern English novel, as well as an intimate round-table creative writing seminar. Students agree that her teaching is superb. Other faculty members are not as well known, but perhaps deserve to be. Alan Segal, professor of religion and Jewish studies, is an expert on Judaism in the time of Jesus, and served on the advisory council for work on the three-hour film *The Gospel of John*. Graduate students do not lead classes at Barnard.

Barnard's strongest departments include English, political science, and psychology. Besides its respected English faculty, the school "excels in teaching writing" reports an insider. At the same time, the Barnard English major cannot help but learn a good deal about our literary past; in addition to her "Critical Writing" class, she must take two courses in pre-nineteenth-century literature as well as "The English Colloquium," a two-semester introduction to literature of the Renaissance and the Enlightenment. (Students may substitute appropriate courses—for instance, one on Shakespeare.) English majors also must choose three other advanced electives and two senior seminars. Allowing for heavy doses of feminism, many of the courses seem solid and interesting.

The Barnard history major is strongly geared towards developing a senior research paper. While this paper is only to be thirty-five to fifty pages, it is written as part of a two-term project. Overall, history majors must complete eleven classes in the major, including eight in a specific concentration area (e.g., medieval history), which is both preparatory to and counted along with the student's work on her two-semester research project. She must also take three introductory history classes. Two of these must be in her subject area of concentration. Most of the introductory history courses are substantive. Some typical classes, for instance, are "The Ancient Greeks" and "The Romans." However, a Barnard history major might well graduate without ever learning anything about the United States—to say nothing of the facts of the country's founding or the writing of the Constitution.

The political science major calls for fewer classes, but it's likely to provide more thorough preparation. A student in the major must complete nine courses, including introductory classes in at least three of the four areas of the field (U.S. government, international relations, comparative government and political theory). She also must take two colloquia (which include twenty-five to thirty page research papers) and a one-term senior research seminar. Still, it is possible to complete the major without learning the basics of U.S. government.

Weaker departments, students report, include economics, which one student says was "famous for being Marxist," while another said that her economics courses were a "joke at Barnard, but great at Columbia. At Barnard I never attended and got good grades." Said a professor: "Teaching is taken very seriously, but the small size of some of the departments may be an issue. Here's an example: the political science department's 'Plato to NATO' course is taught by a Gandhi scholar—although, to be fair, he is respectful of Western thinkers."

For all its virtues, Barnard is not an environment in which conservatives feel comfortable. A professor who has taught at several other highly competitive schools says that he was somewhat shocked by the climate at Barnard: "There's a casualness and thoughtlessness and partisanship to the political correctness that's more extreme. At a place like Harvard people know that you may not agree with them about every one of the liberal shibboleths. At Barnard they simply don't understand that." Symptomatic of this is the women's studies department, where "debate" takes place within very specific parameters: great thinkers

SUGGESTED CORE

1. Classical Literature W4300y, Classical Tradition
2. Philosophy V2101, History of Philosophy I: Pre-Socratics through Augustine
3. Religion V3501/V3120, Introduction to the Hebrew Bible/Introduction to the New Testament
4. Religion V2105, Christianity or Religion V3140, Early Christianity
5. Political Science V1013, Political Theory
6. English BC3163/3164, Shakespeare I or II
7. History BC1401, Survey of American Civilization to the Civil War
8. Philosophy V2301, History of Philosophy III: Nineteenth and Twentieth-Century Philosophy

who display hints of sexism or "antifeminism" are laughed at as buffoons. As one student observes, "It's just assumed that you should be a radical feminist." Another politicized major is human rights studies, an interdisciplinary program. This is often pursued as part of a combined major with political science, as is women's studies.

One student opines, "Undeniably, this school has major problems with political correctness and blatant bias toward liberal—even Communist—positions. I tried majoring in political science and then in history, but grew frustrated with these 100 percent-leftist departments. The English courses I've taken were just as bad: Marxist, feminist, race-con-

---

ACADEMIC REQUIREMENTS

Unlike its brother school Columbia, Barnard has no core curriculum. However, it maintains respectable requirements:

- One first-year English course. In fall 2010, students could choose one of four clusters: "Legacy of the Mediterranean," "The Americas," "Women and Culture," and "Global Literature: Travelling the Indian Subcontinent." Some students test out of this requirement with AP scores.
- One first-year seminar. Students may choose from three interdisciplinary clusters: "Reacting to the Past," "Reinventing Literary History," and "Special Topics." A few special topics offered in 2011 included "Crisis of Authority," "Ethnicity and Social Transformation," "Culture, Ethics and Economics," "Animals in Text and Society," and "Love."
- Two courses in laboratory science, both in the same discipline. Classes are offered in biology, chemistry, environmental science, astronomy, physics, and psychology.
- Four semesters in a foreign language.
- One Reason and Value course, such as "What Is Philosophy, Anyway?" or "Gender and War."
- One Social Analysis class, which offers a wide variety of options—most of them politicized, like "Gendered Controversies: Women's Bodies and Global Conflicts" and "Filthy Lucre: A History of Money."
- One Historical Studies course, which include options like "Introduction to Art History" and "The Sex of Science: Gender and Knowledge in Modern European History."
- One Cultures in Comparison class, including offerings like "The Horror Story: Between Jews and Others," "Negritude," and "Family and Sexuality in the Greek and Roman Worlds."
- One Quantitative and Deductive Reasoning class chosen from myriad disciplines, such as biology, astronomy, chemistry, computer science, economics, urban studies, political science, psychology, physics, and many others. Course offerings include "Biometry," "Environmental Data Analysis," "Surfaces and Knots," and "Social Statistics."
- One literature course, which can include anything from "Shakespeare in Performance" to "Litany for Survival: Lesbian Texts."
- One "Visual and Performing Arts" class chosen from the field of architecture, art history, studio art, graphic design, dance, music, film, or theater. Options range from "The Music of J. S. Bach" to "Feminist Theater in America."

scious—you name it. We actually read *The Communist Manifesto* in 'First-Year English.' When I tried to defend capitalism in class, the professor called me into her office for a private meeting. 'Surely, you have to admit that capitalism is a brutal system,' she insisted. I refused, and we argued at length. I ended up with a low grade in the class."

Barnard provides instruction in French, German, Spanish, Russian, Italian, Latin, and Ancient Greek, but other languages must be studied at Columbia. Barnard offers study-abroad programs in fifty-three countries, as well as off-campus study programs in the U.S. Barnard's programs partner with some famous schools like Oxford and Heidelberg universities, but also with colleges in less obvious places like Morocco, Niger and Nepal.

Student Life: They say the neon lights are bright

Most of Barnard's pedestrian-friendly campus is clustered between Broadway and Clare-mont Avenues. Space, of course, is tight, and Barnard has no room to expand. Architectural styles vary from building to building, but the main structures are Milbank Hall (which houses several administrative offices and academic departments), and Barnard Hall, holding classrooms, a gym, and a swimming pool. Most students consider the Barnard campus quite appealing, with its elegant Federal structures, several of which were designed by the legendary Beaux-Arts architects McKim, Mead & White. The Quad, a group of four residence halls with a courtyard in the center, is where most first-year students live. Students need only cross Broadway to get to Columbia. A series of underground tunnels connect buildings and halls around the Barnard campus, rendering umbrellas and snow boots almost unnecessary.

Barnard's social scene is enormously enriched by the surrounding city. Not surprisingly, students say that living in Manhattan is one of the greatest advantages of attending the school. The Upper West Side has a number of lively bars, from the beer-reeking frat hangout, The West End, to the more mellow 1020. Students report that these bars strictly enforce alcohol laws, and the drinking scene, compared to other colleges, is mild. With some exceptions, there isn't much partying on the Barnard campus—because, when it comes down to it, nothing compares to the city scene. Smoking is prohibited not just in university buildings, but even outdoors on the campus—except for two specially designated exterior smoker pens.

The college sponsors annual student events, including spring and winter festivals and Founder's Day. There is a plethora of diverse (and bizarre) student clubs and organizations on campus, including the AAA (Asian American Alliance), BOSS (Black Organization of Soul Sisters), Bach Society, Caribbean Students Organization, Psychology Club, Dance Dance Revolution Club, a television station, Barnard Flute Choir, Arab Student Association, Network of Pre-Medical Students of Color, Athena Pre-Law Society, and Q—a group that "promotes the visibility of lesbian, gay, bisexual, transgender, intersex, queer, questioning, two spirit, genderqueer, pansexual, omnisexual, and allied women at Barnard and Columbia." Trust us, they're already pretty visible.

The mix of religious adherents on campus helps enliven the school: There is, for example, a thriving Orthodox Jewish community on campus, and the cafeteria offers kosher food. It also offers special dining hours during Ramadan. Such diversity can make for some fascinating (and occasionally heated) theological conversations, students say. Students of faith can find numerous synagogues and churches (including the stunning Episcopal Cathedral of St. John the Divine) within easy walking distance. The Catholic community at Barnard and Columbia, hosted at the nearby church of Our Lady of Lourdes, is said to be especially vibrant.

Barnard and Columbia students spend many of their free nights and weekends downtown in Soho or the West Village, hanging out with students from New York's other schools. On weekends, students will often set off for raging nightclubs in fishnet stockings and platform shoes, but they also frequent coffeehouses to study or read for pleasure. Partly because of students' freedom to explore the city and hobnob with students from other area schools, Barnard lacks the close-knit atmosphere that other all-women colleges like Bryn Mawr and Mount Holyoke boast. In fact, Barnard's "all-women" status makes little practical difference. One student says that 90 percent of her classes are coed, as are her extracurricular activities—and so are some of the dorms (at Columbia, where Barnard students are allowed to live). "I wouldn't say the fact that Barnard is a women's school has too much effect on my social life, although I do wish that there were more guys around sometimes," she says. "Girls can be catty!"

The Barnard student body is comprised of 2,417 undergraduates from forty countries and nearly every state, with approximately 32 percent coming from New York State. Barnard has fewer international students than do most schools because it has little financial aid to offer them, but an admissions counselor says Barnard has a huge immigrant population.

Recently Barnard joined a group of eight American universities which announced their intention to expand study-abroad programs in Israel. To its credit, Barnard made this decision even as Columbia's Middle East and Asian Languages and culture program (MEALAC) has come under the influence of rabid anti-Zionist and anti-American Arabists.

Barnard embodies a well-known paradox: The more tolerant a student body claims to be, the less tolerant it will become. The Barnard community is very accepting of students, whatever their race, economic class, sexuality, or even sex (some Barnard students have chosen to define themselves as "men," despite their biology). But don't try sporting that pro-life button if you want to make many friends. Lesbianism is amply celebrated, and gay students tend to be more outspoken than their straight classmates.

The dorms themselves are neither luxurious nor uncomfortable, considering how tight space is in Manhattan. About 90 percent of Barnard students live in eleven Barnard residence halls and four Columbia residence halls, where some live in coed dorms with Columbia students. A housing official says that these are suite-style residences where men and women could potentially share bathrooms. The college also owns a few apartments in brownstones located in the immediate area. First-year students are housed together in freshman-only dormitories or floors. Barnard guarantees housing for all four years—no small feat in Manhattan.

Although sports are not terribly popular among Barnard students, there are several options available for those who are interested. Students at Barnard and Columbia play together in fifteen NCAA Division I-level and Ivy League varsity teams, and also team up in more than thirty club sports. Barnard offers intramural teams in basketball, badminton, lacrosse, soccer, equestrian, tennis, and volleyball, and students can also play on coed intramural teams at Columbia.

Barnard is intent on preventing crime. The gates to the Barnard campus—and almost every building within it—are closely guarded, and security is "tight" without being oppressive. There are guard posts on every block, with officers keeping watch twenty-four hours a day. A Columbia University van shuttles students between the campuses at all hours of the night and pledges to arrive within ten minutes of a call. In order to enter a campus dormitory, students and visitors must present valid Barnard College/Columbia ID to a patrolman—at any hour. A guest must show proper identification after receiving a resident's permission to be admitted. Barnard has updated and doubled the number of emergency call boxes campus-wide, installing a "blue light" system that is highly visible and incorporates new technology that will speed up the response time to any emergency. In 2009, Barnard reported four forcible sexual offenses and eleven burglaries on campus. It's worth noting that New York is now the safest large city in America, and has been rated in surveys as the friendliest.

Barnard is as pricey as any of the Seven Sisters, with 2010–11 tuition at $40,546. Room and board were listed at $12,950. However, its financial aid is generous; admissions are need blind, and the school guarantees to meet a student's full financial need. Some 44 percent of students are currently receiving need-based financial aid, and the average indebtedness of a recent graduate is $14,706.

RED LIGHT

Barnard's radicalism is so pervasive that most students have, according to one professor, "no awareness that what they're being taught is varieties of leftism. It's just different aspects of the truth, since there is no alternative ever contemplated. Perhaps the best illustration of this is casual (as well as administration-backed) references in class and conversation to 'activism' as another unquestioned good. Naturally, said activism does not include working for the Republican Party or the Heritage Foundation! If the only perspectives one offers are variants of leftism, then the choice is simple: Become 'active' in a leftist cause of one sort or another, or else 'apathetically' confine your leftist ideas to the classroom and don't do anything to put them into action."

The most active contingency of Barnard student life appears to be the gay community. "Barnard's and Columbia's campuses offer tons of ways to get involved in queer activism and social life," declares Barnard's website. Indeed. There are at least nine very outspoken homosexual organizations on campus. Queer Awareness Month (QuAM) sponsors a monthy "Casual Crossdressing" where undergrads attend class and mince about campus in drag. On December 3, 2010, Queer Alliance hosted The Vagina Ball in Barnard Hall wherein many students dressed up as various parts of female genitalia.

Brooklyn College (CUNY)

Brooklyn, New York • www.brooklyn.cuny.edu

Public excellence

Founded in 1930, Brooklyn College is one of eleven senior colleges of the City University of New York (CUNY). It gained a reputation for excellence early, and kept it until in the late 1960s open admissions and campus radicalism undermined its standards. A reform policy begun under Mayor Rudolph Giuliani succeeded in further raising admission standards and getting many of the city's better students to apply for admission. In 2005, a Brooklyn College undergraduate received a Rhodes scholarship, and in 2009–10, two Masters students received Fulbright fellowships. The school is advancing on several fronts. Thanks to its solid core curriculum and renewed commitment to excellence, Brooklyn College offers one of the best liberal arts educations available at any public college in America.

Academic Life: Loyal to the core

Brooklyn College is still one of the more academically traditional—and top-ranked—public academies. This can be seen in Brooklyn's Core Studies program, described by the school as "eleven core courses across three groups—Arts and Literatures, Philosophical and Social Inquiry, and Scientific Inquiry—organized into lower- and upper-tiers. The lower-tier courses are foundational; the upper-tier aims to be integrative, innovative, and to allow students to pursue more in-depth study." Distinctively, Brooklyn requires these courses of all candidates for a baccalaureate degree. This curriculum has been a national model for general education programs. One senior academic considers the core as "reflecting a sense of our traditional strengths and values . . . it is intellectually rigorous, sharply focused, and at the forefront of higher education."

While it makes serious demands of them—sometimes taking up the better part of their first two years—students seem to appreciate the core program. One undergraduate praised the program for "teaching you about modern history, philosophy, music, science—giving the whole thing context." Contrast this to most elite colleges, which are dominated by the anti-Western ideology of multiculturalism, and Brooklyn College really shines by contrast.

The core curriculum involves three courses in the arts and literatures section: "Classical Cultures," "Introduction to Art," and "Music: Its Language, History, and Culture." In the philosophical and social inquiry section the classes include: "Knowledge, Reality, and Values,"

"Shaping of the Modern World," and "People, Power and Politics." In the scientific inquiry section there are several options: "Thinking Mathematically" or "Computing: Nature, Power, and Limits"; "Biology for Today's World" or "Science in Modern Life: Chemistry"; and "Physics: The Simple Laws That Govern the Universe" or "Geology: The Science of Our World." After completing sixty credits, a student must take two additional "upper tier" courses in each of the three sections. Further requirements are two English composition classes, one foreign language and one speech course. Most of these classes place an emphasis on classical culture and the thinking that have formed Western civilization.

The college also offers a number of elite opportunities through its honors initiatives. The Scholars Program offers "an interdisciplinary liberal arts program, honors-level Core Studies courses, interdisciplinary seminars, and guided research on a senior thesis," as well as special scholarships and study and research abroad stipends. Its focus is on liberal arts. The Macaulay Honors College provides students with excellent academic facilities (and a new laptop) along with tuition scholarships and a wide variety of research, internship, academic and professional opportunities. Admission to such programs is very selective.

The 13,000 students at Brooklyn College can choose from over 125 academic programs. Advising works by appointment, but walk-in advising is also available. For the most part, advisors help students schedule their semester and, in small part, advise them in their degrees programs. When a student picks a major, he receives advising from professors in that department.

The English department offers comparative literature, English literature, creative writing, a high school teacher program, journalism, and linguistics majors. The English literature major consists of 2 courses in literature overview classes, fifteen credits in the fields of study, and a selection of seven areas of English literature, including medieval, Renaissance, eighteenth century, nineteenth century and Romanticism, American Literature, modernism, and postmodernism and contemporary discourses. At least two courses must be in medieval, Renaissance, or eighteenth century literature. A further six courses must be in electives, one of which must be a seminar. The electives may also be in an "allied discipline," following various cultural studies, art studies, American studies, and so forth. The Renaissance section has many Shakespeare classes and the other classes sport a good array of poetry and prose authors.

VITAL STATISTICS

Religious affiliation: *none*
Total enrollment: *17,094*
Total undergraduates: *13,069*
SAT midranges: CR: *470–580*, M: *510–610*
Applicants: *17,497*
Applicants accepted: *28%*
Accepted applicants who enrolled: *20%*
Tuition and fees: *in state, $5,054; out of state, $12,904*
Room and board: *$10,361*
Freshman retention rate: *78%*
Graduation rate: *17% (4 yrs.), 45% (6 yrs.)*
Courses with fewer than 20 students: *40%*
Student-faculty ratio: *15:1*
Courses taught by graduate students: *not provided*
Most popular majors: *business/marketing, education, psychology*
Students living on campus: *none*
Guaranteed housing for four years? *no*
Students in fraternities: *3%* in sororities: *3%*

1. Core Curriculum 1110, Classical Cultures
2. Philosophy 3111, Ancient Philosophy
3. English 3183, The Bible as Literature
4. History 3033, Christianity and the Church in Medieval Europe or Philosophy 3113, Medieval Philosophy
5. Political Science 3402, Modern Political Thought
6. English 3122/3123, Shakespeare I/II
7. History 3401, America to 1877
8. Philosophy 3122, Nineteenth-Century Philosophy

The history department, while offering a general BA, also features specialized options for aspiring teachers, both high school and primary. The major consists of thirty-three credits in all—an introductory class, and twenty-four credits in lower division courses, broken up into five sections: ancient, medieval, and early modern European history; modern European history; Transnational and comparative history; U.S. history; African, Asian, Caribbean, Latin American, and Middle Eastern history. The major requires at least one class in each of those areas. Further, it requires two classes in upper-division courses, one of which must be a colloquium. The picking seems slim for solid early American history classes, and there are plenty of classes with an eye toward feminist and environmental issues.

The political science department offers a standard BA as well as a focus on junior high and high school social studies teaching. The two fundamental classes for the the major are "Intro to Politics" and "Intro to American Government." Also required are the classes "Analytic Approaches to Political Problems" and "Research Strategies in Public Policy," as well as a senior capstone class. A further five classes count toward the major with a choice of areas: American and urban politics, international politics, comparative politics, political theory and methodology. Political science majors should graduate with some grounding in American politics.

Worthy faculty grace many of the departments. Says a student, "A lot of the best teachers are in English. There are also a bunch of terrific teachers in economics and in some of the business subjects like marketing and accounting . . . some of the teachers are definite characters." Strong classes are offered in the classics and English departments. Classics is very small, but the professors are dedicated, and they, not graduate students, teach most of the classes. A student tells us, "In my experience, all have been very accessible and helpful. The same goes for the English department. Most of its offerings are on the great texts of Western civilization, and there are relatively few courses that are designed for 'multiculturalist' indoctrination. This also applies very much to the history department," he says. Business and education are very popular majors, as are health sciences and psychology.

Some prominent faculty members include Pulitzer prize-winning historian Edwin Burrows, journalists Paul Moses and Eric Alterman, pianist Ursula Oppens, and the film director Agnieszka Holland. Among those who taught here in the past were the poet Allen Ginsberg, the psychologist Abraham Maslow, and the philosopher Hannah Arendt. Current professors that students particularly recommend include Caroline Arnold in political science, Jennifer Basil in biology, Edwin Burrows in history, and Thomas Carlisle and Mark Patkowski in English.

As big as Brooklyn College is, it has a decent student-faculty ratio of 15 to 1, but many of the famous professors either teach in large lecture classes or only to grad students. One undergrad says: "I have yet to get a big name professor." A significant portion of classes are taught by graduate students.

The school has three academic divisions: the College of Liberal Arts and Sciences, the School of General Studies, and the Division of Graduate Studies. Brooklyn College offers more than 120 undergraduate and graduate degree programs, advanced certificates, and programs in the humanities, sciences, performing arts, social sciences, education, and pre-professional and professional studies. Doctoral-level programs are available through the City University of New York Graduate Center in midtown Manhattan, with a number of courses offered on the Brooklyn College campus. The school also offers a combined MD

ACADEMIC REQUIREMENTS

The required courses in Brooklyn College's admirable core curriculum are:

- "Classical Cultures." This includes readings from Homer, Plato, Sophocles and Virgil, among others. Classes may also dip into non-Western cultures.
- "Introduction to Art." Exploration of major works of art and architecture from around the world.
- "Music: Its Language, History, and Culture." Introduction to music through the study of works representing different times, places, and peoples. Regrettably, half or more of the length of this class is now focused on American and non-Western music.
- "People, Power, and Politics," which looks for "insight into American society in broad terms, as well as in terms of such specific issues as social class, race, gender, community, equality, and opportunity."
- "The Shaping of the Modern World," which covers "European and American civilization since 1700 in its global context." This is a class offering a solid history of modern times from the Enlightenment through the rise of totalitarianism to the present.
- "Knowledge, Reality and Values." This is a philosophy course dealing with ethics and epistemology. Readings are wide-ranging and include Plato, Kant, and Pascal.
- "Biology for Today's World" or "Science in Modern Life: Chemistry."
- "Thinking Mathematically" or "Computing: Nature, Power and Limits."
- "Physics: The Simple Laws That Govern the Universe" or "Geology: The Science of Our World."
- Two upper tier courses from three areas: Exploring Literature, including classes such as "Literature and Film" and "Literature, Ethnicity, and Immigration"; Exploring Global Connections, with classes ranging from "The Jewish Diaspora" to "Islamic Perspectives on Modernity, Politics, and Culture"; and Exploring Science, with options like "Exploring Robotics," "Studies in Forensic Science," and "Climate Change—Torn Between Myth and Fact."

In addition, students must complete two terms of English composition, demonstrate a proficiency in spoken English and in a foreign language to the level of a third term course.

Mid-Atlantic

and BA program in conjunction with SUNY-Downstate Medical Center. Those interested in careers in medicine may wish to investigate this joint degree program. This program may especially appeal as SUNY-Downstate is an unusually affordable medical school for New York State residents.

The college boasts prominent alumni in every field. More than 300 Brooklyn graduates are presidents, vice-presidents, or chairmen of the boards of major corporations. Each year, the college's graduates receive more than 350 acceptances to law schools and medical schools, including Harvard, Yale, Stanford and the University of Pennsylvania.

The colleges of CUNY also offer many study-abroad programs in dozens of countries all around the world, in both semesters as well as during the summer. Countries include Ghana, Italy, Spain, Germany, Senegal, Ireland, Denmark, Argentina, and Israel. Many programs have particular academic focuses, such as "Mexico—Cooking, Art, Culture" and "Modern India: The Birth of a Modern Nation" and "China: Reaching to the Past."

Brooklyn offers a good range of modern and classical languages; a student may receive a BA in modern language and literature with an eye toward teaching. Languages offered include Latin and Ancient Greek, Russian, Spanish, Italian, and French; minors are possible in Chinese, German, modern Greek, Arabic, Haitian Creole, Japanese, and Portuguese.

Student Life: Crossing Brooklyn Bridge

The college's setting puts students within a subway ride of unparalleled cultural opportunities in Manhattan. But Brooklyn itself also boasts its own first-class orchestras; museums to rival the Metropolitan (and in some collections surpass it); a magnificent public library and park; the city and country's best visiting theater and dance productions at its Brooklyn Academy of Music Center, as well as bohemian arts enclaves and enough ethnic restaurants to challenge the most jaded palate.

In recent years much of the old East Village art and literature scene has relocated to the former Hasidic ghettos of Williamsburg and Greenpoint, and sections like DUMBO and Brooklyn Heights are among the city's most expensive and privileged. Boerum Hill is a key point in the city's fine dining scene, and Park Slope is commonly said to be New York's most beautiful neighborhood. The Midwood area around Brooklyn College, if less historic than Park Slope, is also famed for the beauty of its many Victorian bungalows, and the campus reminds many of Harvard's, with its Georgian architecture and well-kept quadrangles.

As the college describes its neighborhood, "the Brooklyn College Campus merges the surrounding areas of Victorian Flatbush, Hasidic Midwood, and West Indian Flatbush." Made up of fourteen buildings on a twenty-six-acre tree-lined campus on the site of a former golf course and circus grounds, Brooklyn College has no dormitories. The college welcomed its first building in forty years in September of 2009, a 145,000-square-foot building, doubling as a student center and a state-of-the-art athletics facility. Of the students at Brooklyn College, a fairly large portion are working adults. One student says "a lot of the students wind up graduating in five, six years, and it's not like they're going to show up at college dances or wear Brooklyn College sweatshirts. There isn't that much school spirit or even dating among students." On the positive side, campus politics and social pressures play a much smaller role in the typical student's career.

Since 1995, the school has received more than $500 million for capital expenditures, and in 2002, it embarked on a major capital improvement program called, grandly, the "Master Plan." Part of the plan called for all of Brooklyn's historic buildings to undergo complete refurbishing. In 2003, the school completed an extensive renovation and expansion of the Brooklyn College Library, which now boasts the most technologically advanced computer networking system in the CUNY system. The new West Quad provides a second large green space on the quadrangle, as well as a new building for student services and a sports complex, under one roof.

Many significant cultural events take place at Brooklyn College's Center for the Performing Arts, attracting large audiences from Manhattan. And planning has begun for a new $50 million Center for the Performing Arts, which will serve the Conservatory of Music, the department of theater, and the school's dance degree program and other related disciplines. These schools are well known, but they have their idiosyncrasies. The theater program is run by Mac Wellman, one of the country's most notoriously inscrutable leftist dramatists, and it has drawn in his acolytes. So, even if most students were on campus in the evenings, they might not want to see all the plays being staged.

Brooklyn College competes as the Bulldogs in NCAA Division III with men's and women's teams in basketball, cross-country, tennis, swimming and volleyball. The school also has a coed cheerleading squad, and it offers coed intramural three-on-three basketball and tennis.

Although Brooklyn College is a commuter school, there are about 260 undergraduate clubs and organizations. Among these are some twenty sororities and fraternities; groups for Black, Hispanic, Chinese, Korean, Jewish, Haitian, Panamanian, Greek, Irish, Italian

---

GREEN LIGHT

Brooklyn College's total student population comprises some 17,094 undergraduate and graduate students. Its ethnic, religious and racial composition reflects New York City's diversity, with students from more than a hundred nations. The school is more than 28 percent black, with many students born in all the parts of the Caribbean. It is also more than 13 percent Asian. Many students on campus are religious. The campus is especially accommodating to Jewish students at its Tanger Hillel Center. Yet there are numerous campus organizations devoted to Muslim and Christian believers. There is little radical activism—or activism period—on campus.

A senior reports that "religious students aren't freaks here. They're more apt to be the majority—and most of the faculty know and respect that." The tendentious and strident voices in the faculty can typically be found, however, and a recent decision on the part of the college brought some controversy. An alum claimed that he "disinherited his Alma Mater" when he heard that the college required all incoming freshmen and transfer students to read the book *How Does It Feel to be a Problem? Being Young and Arab in America*, which profiles the experience of seven young Arabs in the aftermath of 9/11 and authored by a radical pro-Palestinian professor.

As a whole, however, Brooklyn College is a sound and solid place to get a good education in the liberal arts and related studies, or to receive a strong liberal arts core in addition to a solid degree in the sciences or other such specialization.

and Palestinian students; for Roman Catholic, Adventist, Evangelical, Muslim, Buddhist, and Orthodox Jewish students; for future lawyers, black accountants,Hispanic journalists, and women scientists; for paintball-playing, slow food and so forth. Students at Brooklyn College do not seem to be too politically active as there are no political groups on campus, but there is a Brooklyn College Intercollegiate Studies Institute Group, sponsored by the publisher of this guide.

As there are no dorms, students all live in apartments—or commute from home by subway. The student who does not live at home might have to pay a great deal of money to live in a reasonably safe neighborhood, and often must cope with long commutes on public transportation.

Campus crime has been on a steady decline over the past several years. In 2009, the school reported seven robberies, one instance of aggravated assault, one instance of motor vehicle theft, and eight burglaries. However, the train line to the school passes through one or two dicey neighborhoods. The college itself is sufficiently policed and well maintained. The campus is gated, and a strict ID system is used to be keep possible intruders out.

Given its quality, Brooklyn College is an amazing educational bargain, with in-state tuition averaging at $5,054 per year, and out-of-state tuition at $12,904. The school estimates annual room and board to be around $10,361. Some 83 percent of students receive financial aid, and the average student- loan debt of a recent graduate was around $16,600.

Bryn Mawr College

Bryn Mawr, Pennsylvania • www.brynmawr.edu

The smart sister on the high hill

Bryn Mawr College was founded in 1885 by Dr. Joseph Taylor, a Quaker physician who wanted to establish a college dedicated to the liberal education of lady Friends. Bryn Mawr was the first women's school to offer graduate programs, and remains the only one to offer a wide range of advanced degrees. But while most of its individual courses and majors are strong, the college's curriculum is frail and sickly, and leftist political opinions permeate course offerings, content, and classroom discussion. If a conservative student is unwilling to live in such a hostile climate, she should look elsewhere.

Academic Life: The thin, permeable line

Bryn Mawr has far fewer general education requirements than other liberal arts colleges, even in this age of curricular drift. With enough AP coursework, students can avoid several required courses. Indeed, Bryn Mawr's distribution requirements do not demand a true breadth of study. One faculty member says, "It would be worse if we didn't have such serious girls, but, undeniably, the program of study is pretty vague."

Bryn Mawr does prescribe a full slate of rigorous courses for almost all its majors and boasts a distinguished faculty. The typical student is earnest about her studies; many opt to spend weekends in the library. "Everyone here really works," one student says. "I have a friend on the debate team. When she told me what the attitude of students at the schools she competed with—like Harvard and Yale—were towards attending class, I thought she was kidding." Another student adds, "It's not just the premeds who work in the lab courses. People think it's important. Why else come?" It may be indicative that mathematics is the fourth most popular undergraduate major, well ahead of history and economics.

Bryn Mawr students can choose from a full list of traditional majors, and it is encouraging that trendy departments (such as peace and conflict, feminism and gender, and Africana studies) are offered as only minors or concentrations. Students who feel constricted by the small college's offerings can create an independent major. Past independent majors have included American studies, linguistics, creative writing, and theater.

One of the main features of Bryn Mawr academic life is the strength of the relationships that develop between faculty members and students. Such relationships grow natu-

VITAL STATISTICS

Religious affiliation: *none*
Total enrollment: *1,771*
Total undergraduates: *1,307*
SAT/ACT midranges: CR:
  600–700, M: *580–680*;
  ACT: *26–30*
Applicants: *2,276*
Applicants accepted: *49%*
Accepted applicants who
  enrolled: *33%*
Tuition and fees: *$39,360*
Room and board: *$12,420*
Freshman retention rate:
  93%
Graduation rate: *74% (4 yrs.),
  80% (6 yrs.)*
Courses with fewer than 20
  students: *72%*
Student-faculty ratio: *8:1*
Courses taught by graduate
  students: *none*
Most popular majors: *English, psychology, biology*
Students living on campus:
  95%
Guaranteed housing for
  four years? *yes*
Students in sororities: *none*

rally, thanks to the school's small size and enviable student-faculty ratio of 8 to 1. Class sizes range from around thirty (for introductory courses) to just three (for senior-level topical seminars). Many students say that professors treat them as younger colleagues. Students visit their professors regularly, often discussing subjects unrelated to class. Faculty members view teaching—not publishing or research—as their main responsibility. "If you go meet with a professor at their office," one student reports, "there's almost always this good, inviting energy. They don't try to make you sweat for recommendation letters." Another student says, "There's a lot of personal attention—not only from the faculty but from the deans and from your advisor."

There are graduate students at Bryn Mawr who teach no courses but sometimes lead laboratory sections. Upon entry to Bryn Mawr, students are assigned a college dean as an advisor. After the student declares a major, she chooses a faculty advisor from her department.

Some of the many excellent professors at Bryn Mawr include Catherine Conybeare and Radcliffe Edmonds in classics; Robert Dostal and Christine Koggel in philosophy; Peter Briggs in English; Jeremy Elkins and Stephen Salkever in political science; and Nathan Wright in sociology.

Although Bryn Mawr is known as a liberal arts school, the college has also had great success in the sciences. "My bio professors all really cared about whether we understood what we were doing in lab, and all the math professors I have had you could understand," reports one science major. Professors from outside the department concur that "Bryn Mawr has consistently excellent science programs." Of all women awarded PhDs in physics, more began their educations at Bryn Mawr than at any other liberal arts school. (Traditionally, Bryn Mawr has sent a higher proportion of its women to complete doctorates than almost any other college in the country.) At Bryn Mawr, students in the sciences work closely with professors on research projects, gaining valuable experience and strengthening academic relationships with faculty members. Moreover, the science departments offer an escape from the feminist ideology that saturates the humanities departments as well as most aspects of campus life.

A veteran professor particularly recommends the classics, political science and philosophy departments. Another popular major is English, though many of the course titles suggest more of a trendy emphasis on women authors than a concern for teaching the most important figures in literature. There are whole courses for undergrads devoted to Virginia

Woolf and Toni Morrison, but none on Dickens, Twain, Hardy, or Shaw. Classes like "Topics in Film Studies: Queer Cinema" and "Gender & Technology" dominate the department's course catalog.

The philosophy department, though small, consists of professors who are "strong scholars and are attentive to students," according to one faculty member. The philosophy and political science departments offer strong introductory courses that "teach the intellectual history of the West"—more so than the history department, students note. The poli sci major must take "Introduction to American Politics" and "Introduction to Political Philosophy: Ancient and Early Modern," while the history major is not even offered–much less required to take—a basic Western civilization class. The art history department is strong, emphasizing the classical tradition, and giving students opportunities to study abroad.

Standard, leftist views are reinforced in courses such as the sociology offering "Social Inequality," which will provide an "[i]ntroduction to the major sociological theories of gender, racial-ethnic and class inequality . . . including the role of the upper class(es), inequality between and within families, in the work place and in the educational system," reports the catalog. Weirder perhaps is a course called "The Sociology of AIDS," which attempts to explain the "social construction of AIDS."

> ### SUGGESTED CORE
>
> 1. Classical Studies 270, Classical Heroes and Heroines
> 2. Philosophy 101, Happiness and Reality in Ancient Thought
> 3. Religion 118/122, Hebrew Bible: Literary Text and Historical Context/Introduction to the New Testament (both at Haverford)
> 4. Religion 124, Introduction to Christian Thought (closest match)
> 5. Political Science 231, Introduction to Political Philosophy: Modern
> 6. English 225, Shakespeare
> 7. History 201, American History: Settlement to Civil War
> 8. Philosophy 204, Readings in German Intellectual History

Many of the college's humanities course offerings are dedicated to the exploration of feminist issues or the politics of victimhood. Not so unusual, for instance, is the anthropology department's "African Childhoods" which provides a "gendered perspective on selected topics in the experiences of children and youth in Africa concerning indigenous cultural practices such as initiation ceremonies and sexual orientation." Students report that in such courses and in others, professors often make little attempt to conceal their political opinions—and that they are not above proselytizing. Office doors have political cartoons and leftist bumper stickers, making visits awkward for conservative students.

Bryn Mawr admissions policies put a high priority on having a racially diverse student body; about 25 percent of recent classes have come from minority groups. Once students are admitted, a panoply of ethnic-based programming awaits them. "Voices of Color," an orientation event held each April, is a "multicultural experience" during which admitted students learn that—surprise!—Bryn Mawr is a diverse and welcoming place for racial minorities. As if to make that point, students of African or Hispanic descent are given the chance to live . . . in separate residence halls.

In its mission statement, the Office of Institutional Diversity pledges to pursue "a policy of affirmative action in recruitment and employment." It oversees several campus organizations, including the Association of International Students, the Asian Students Association, Bryn Mawr Caribbean and African Students Organization, Half and Half (a group for students of mixed race), Sisterhood (a black women's group), and others. These organizations help the college to forward the notion that "community doesn't mean uniformity." (Except, perhaps, when it comes to political ideas.) Almost 10 percent of Bryn Mawr's undergraduates are international students, and 16 percent of its full time faculty are "professors of color."

Bryn Mawr offers several opportunities for students interested in supplementing a liberal arts education with other experiences. The community-based learning program called Praxis provides "real world" career preparation. Organized around the college's strong tradition of civic engagement, Praxis integrates intensive academic study with rigorous, relevant fieldwork.

The college's honor code and self-governance system are crucial to the school's identity; the college website says Bryn Mawr was the first college in the United States to "give students responsibility not only for enforcing rules of behavior upon themselves, but also for deciding what those rules should be." Faculty and peers trust that Bryn Mawr students are committed to honesty, and as a result students can schedule their own final exams and may take tests home.

The relationship between Bryn Mawr and its Philadelphia Main Line neighbor, Haverford College, is essential to academic life at both schools. Bryn Mawr students are free to take courses at either college, and can even major in a discipline at Haverford not offered at Bryn Mawr. If a desired course is not offered at either campus, a student can enroll at

---

ACADEMIC REQUIREMENTS

In the absence of a core curriculum, Bryn Mawr imposes certain requirements for the AB (bachelor's) degree, on top of those for each major:

- One first year seminar. Topics in 2011 included "Shakespeare's Hamlet and Ours" and "Anxious Masculinity."
- One mathematics ("quantitative skills") course, or sufficient test scores or AP credit. Courses include straightforward choices such as "Experimental Methods and Statistics" and "Introduction to Computing."
- Two intermediate or advanced classes in a foreign language. Students may test out.
- Two courses in social science, ranging from "Human Ecology" to "Sports and Society."
- Two classes in natural science or mathematics, one of which must include a lab. Options include "Introduction to Computer Science" and "How the Earth Works."
- Two courses from the humanities, one of which may be in the performing arts. Classes offered range from "Greek History" to "Fundamentals of Costume Design."
- Eight half-semesters of physical education and a swimming test. All freshmen must complete an online alcohol education program during the summer as well as a seven-week wellness course in the fall.

Swarthmore College or the University of Pennsylvania. A limited number of courses at nearby Villanova University are also available to Bryn Mawr students. Bryn Mawr's proximity and close connection to these colleges allow students to seek greater depth in their studies and to encounter views that may not be discussed at their own college. Through these close ties to other colleges, Bryn Mawr students can take courses in the same discipline from several different professors instead of just one or two. The Bryn Mawr, Haverford, and Swarthmore libraries allow loans between colleges, and together this collection amounts to more than one million titles. Frequent shuttle vans run among the campuses, and students who request a book typically receive it the next day.

An impressive one-third of Bryn Mawr students spend at least a semester abroad at some point, and students speak highly of the school's programs in more than a dozen foreign countries on several continents. At home, Bryn Mawr offers foreign language classes in Chinese, Japanese, Ancient Greek, Latin, French, German, Hebrew, Spanish, Italian, and Russian.

Student Life: Athena, clean bathrooms, and Wicca

Located about eleven miles west of Philadelphia, the college sits in the village of Bryn Mawr—which is Welsh for "high hill." Its magnificent 135-acre suburban campus was designed by Frederick Law Olmsted and Calvert Vaux, the creators of New York City's Central Park. When it was built in 1885, Bryn Mawr introduced the "collegiate Gothic" architectural style to the United States—complete with gray stone buildings, lush green lawns, and tree-lined terraces. Thomas Great Hall, a large room with high ceilings and dark wood, is a popular place to study. The room is also home to a statue of the goddess Athena, to whom Bryn Mawr women offer cigarettes, beer, ornaments, and notes asking her for help on exams.

Ninety-five percent of Bryn Mawr students live on campus, and happily so, as the school offers many comfortable dorms. Each room has its own charm—some have fireplaces, window seats, and high ceilings—and every residence hall includes common space for studying, socializing, and holding dorm events. First-year students live together in their own halls, but upperclassmen are housed close by. The Campus Center is a popular hangout between classes and in the evening, offering a late night cafe, post office, the Career Development Center, and offices for other student services.

Bryn Mawr women enjoy athletics—actually competing, not merely watching. The college viewbook spotlights serious athletes who manage to balance a rigorous academic schedule with sports training. A charter member of the Centennial Conference and the only women's college in the conference, Bryn Mawr sponsors a variety of varsity intercollegiate sports: badminton, basketball, cross-country, crew, field hockey, lacrosse, soccer, swimming, tennis, track and field, and volleyball. The college also sponsors varsity club rugby, and students at Bryn Mawr and Haverford have formed bi-college equestrian and Ultimate Frisbee clubs.

In addition to athletic programs, Bryn Mawr has a number of academic, artistic, outreach, and special interest groups. One of the most vocal groups on campus is the Rainbow

Alliance, a homosexual group whose membership has been mercifully declining steadily since the 1998–99 school year, when—as one student claims—almost half the student body belonged to it. The school hosts College Democrats and a fledgling chapter of College Republicans, but the most popular political causes on campus concern feminism and the environment. The school's political activists often participate in Philadelphia's many protests and rallies.

One of the maxims of radical feminism asserts that "the personal is the political." A corollary seems to be that the private is often made public—even when the result is embarrassingly vulgar. Many of the events on campus deal with body image and ways in which women can purportedly become more comfortable with their own. For instance, a decades-old tradition of dancing around the May Pole in white dresses now has its intentionally non-phallic feminist counterpart: a dance around the May Hole. (Do you feel empowered yet?)

Speaking of heathen rites, in addition to the ordinary run of religious organizations—Catholic, Protestant, Jewish, Muslim, and Quaker—Bryn Mawr features Athena's Circle, "a student Pagan group" for "Wiccans, Greco-Roman and Egyptian reconstructionists, Goddess-worshippers, Buddhists, and other magical people" who "worship during full moons, dark moons, solstices, equinoxes, and the other Wiccan Sabbats." Some followers of more mainstream Western creeds reportedly feel awkward on campus. Rev. John Ames, Catholic chaplain, told the Bryn Mawr alumnae bulletin that "some Catholic Bryn Mawr students have conveyed that speaking and living with religious moral convictions can be difficult." One student was a little blunter. The bulletin cited Kristin Henry '01, who "compared 'coming out' as a person of faith at Bryn Mawr with coming out as a homo- or bisexual."

Students who show up at Bryn Mawr not understanding the mores of its student body may be in for a surprise. "It took me a while to realize that other women were pursuing me," a student acknowledges. "When I did get it, it was a bit of a shock. I mean I've never felt harassed. But it definitely happens."

Bryn Mawr's community cherishes a number of traditions. One is Parade Night, when freshmen officially walk under the arches of Bryn Mawr College while sophomores pummel them with water balloons, juniors welcome them, and seniors sit back with an air of cool nonchalance. On Lantern Night, students receive lanterns to welcome them to their new academic class. Tradition has it that the first one to have her lantern go out will be the first to be married; the last student holding a lit lantern will be the first to receive her PhD. Walking on the Senior Steps before a student is a senior will jinx her from graduating. Bryn Mawr, with its own inside jokes and decades-old traditions, is a college that recognizes its differences from other schools and wears them with flair.

Bryn Mawr is an all-women's school, but many students don't even notice the difference—with men on campus for classes, frequent buses to and from Haverford and Swarthmore, and countless opportunities to interact with the opposite sex. (Bryn Mawr students can even live in coed dormitories at Haverford). One student says that while she sees men all the time in classes at Haverford, and she and many of her friends have boyfriends at area colleges, Bryn Mawr is an escape from testosterone. "In some ways you do feel more comfortable. There's less sense of competition and that you have to dress or act a certain way," she says.

On weekends, Bryn Mawr students sometimes take the Main Line train into Philadelphia to visit museums, night clubs, frat parties at the University of Pennsylvania, sporting events, and performances. Many students participate in volunteer work in the city. But plenty of entertainment options are available at home in Bryn Mawr and at Haverford. Students often stay on campus for speakers or other events, parties at Haverford, or casual socializing in the dorms. A weekend spent in the library is quite common, and sometimes even expected. As one student puts it, "They tell us about all the woman PhDs we've produced, and they want us to know we're expected to carry on the tradition."

The college and its surrounding affluent suburb experience little crime. During 2009, ten burglaries and two forcible sex offenses were reported on campus. To guarantee student safety, the college patrols the campus twenty-four hours a day.

Bryn Mawr offers a rare and privileged environment, and exacts a concomitant price: Tuition in 2010–11 was $39,360 and room and board $12,420. In an unhappy development, the school no longer offers need-blind admission. Fifty-seven percent of all undergraduates receive need-based financial aid, and the average student-loan debt of a recent graduate was $20,156.

RED LIGHT

At Bryn Mawr, the line between academic and political life is thin and permeable, even in many classrooms. Faculty members and students alike generally assume that contemporary feminism is an unqualified good and that no one at Bryn Mawr would question such a view. For example, one student complains that "feminist views are generally considered a given."

However, in recent years Bryn Mawr has seen the creation of a Campus Republicans group, a pro-life club, and a publication called *Unpopular Opinions*, which prints them. But such views are rare on campus and not always welcomed. At the other end of the spectrum is the popular literary magazine titled *Virgin Mawrtyr*, a self-described "literary erotica magazine devoted entirely to exploring issues of sex, sexuality, gender, feminism, and the body."

Bucknell University

Lewisburg, Pennsylvania • www.bucknell.edu

Best of both?

Bucknell University was founded by Baptists in 1846 as the University at Lewisburg. It later cut its Baptist ties and was renamed for William Bucknell, a Philadelphia benefactor who helped get the university off the ground. Bucknell bills itself as both a professional university and a liberal arts college that offers the best of both.

In June 2010 the university appointed a new president, John C. Bravman. A material sciences expert and award-winning teacher at Stanford, he has proven skillful at raising funds. His political views—he's one of the few major college presidents who is also a sometime donor to the Republican National Committee—may also serve as a useful counterweight to Bucknell's strident liberalism.

If the school he now oversees has been infected by a strain of obsessive political correctness, it also boasts strong academic programs, faculty members who enjoy teaching, and plenty of opportunities for students to get involved in research or study abroad. Bucknell students can earn a solid liberal arts education, but they'll have to be intent on attaining one, since the curriculum is riddled with loopholes, and it's up to the student to avoid them.

Academic Life: Plenty of monkeys

The university's two colleges—Arts and Sciences, and Engineering—enroll 3,500 undergraduates. About 80 percent study in Arts and Sciences, which offers forty-seven majors and sixty-five minors. (Many Bucknell students combine majors and minors.) The College of Engineering is much smaller, enrolling about 600 students, and offers a more research-based curriculum in computer science and the engineering fields.

The college ranks in the top twenty in the country in the number of alumni who go on to receive doctoral degrees. The College of Engineering is ranked as the eighth best undergraduate engineering program among schools without PhD programs.

Bucknell has no core curriculum, requiring instead that students in the College of Arts and Sciences complete the Common Learning Agenda (CLA), which specifies four types of requirements: Intellectual Skills, including a foundational seminar and lab sciences; Broadened Perspectives for the 21st Century, including ideologically charged classes on diversity in the U.S., environmental, and global topics; Disciplinary Perspectives, which involves courses on the arts and humanities, natural science and mathematics, and social sciences; and Disciplinary Depth, which completes the requirements of a particular major. The student is mostly free to experiment with specialized or trendy courses, instead of mastering common core of knowledge and skills. Bucknell honors programs are consigned to the different departments, involving independent study under an advisor, completion of a honors thesis or creative project, and an oral examination. However, there is no college-wide Honors program and no Great Books program.

The university's advising program is only what students make of it. For an Arts and Sciences student, the instructor in the required "foundations seminar" will be his academic advisor for the first two years, after which he may choose another. However, other faculty members are there to help, and the university has instituted a policy requiring the signature of a student's faculty advisor before the student can register for classes. After the first two years, advisors come by department and major.

Some of Bucknell's most risible classes are, not surprisingly, to be found in the women's and gender studies department. Dubious course offerings also are pervasive in the international studies major, for instance "The Political Economy of Race." Bucknell also offers a minor in the grim-sounding discipline "peace studies."

The College of Engineering at Bucknell is reputedly strong, as well as its theater, dance, and music programs. Also well-regarded are its environmental, ecology, and evolution studies programs.

Although the English department has some of the school's best-liked and most-respected professors, it has no clear plan of study. Students may choose one of three concentrations: literary studies, creative writing, and film/media studies. Literary studies involves taking nine classes, two of which are introductory classes for English literature and literary theory, two classes on medieval or early modern British literature (pre-1660), and a course in Enlightenment or nineteenth century literature. Unfortunately, a course in race and ethnic studies is also required. One could well graduate with an English degree without ever reading Shakespeare, Donne, Milton, or Tennyson. The department also offers dollops of toxic fluff, such as "Critical Approaches to Hip Hop Culture" and "Gender in Film."

History majors choose two of seven elective clusters, out of American, European, non-Western, intellectual, political and economic or social history, and history of science and medicine. At least eight courses are needed, and no more than six classes can be in a

VITAL STATISTICS

Religious affiliation: *none*
Total enrollment: *3,673*
Total undergraduates: *3,543*
SAT/ACT midranges: CR: *600–680*, M: *630–720*; ACT: *27–31*
Applicants: *7,572*
Applicants accepted: *30%*
Accepted applicants who enrolled: *12%*
Tuition and fees: *$42,342*
Room and board: *$9,938*
Freshman retention rate: *94%*
Graduation rate: *88% (4 yrs.), 90% (6 yrs.)*
Courses with fewer than 20 students: *55%*
Student-faculty ratio: *10:1*
Courses taught by graduate students: *none*
Most popular majors: *accounting, biology, business administration*
Students living on campus: *87%*
Guaranteed housing for four years? *yes*
Students in fraternities: *39%* in sororities: *40%*

Mid-Atlantic

single field. In spite of an abundance of respected teachers, there is no guarantee that a graduate majoring in the subject will have learned about such basic material as the American founding or the Renaissance, and there are plenty of politicized-sounding courses. But a sound and motivated student who chooses well can still get a solid formation.

Political science majors take classes in American government, classical and modern political theory, comparative politics and international relations. Many electives seem inflected with trendy campus politics; however, the major requirements seem solid.

Professors are lauded for their accessibility outside of class. Bucknell works hard to retain close interpersonal contact between students and professors. The administration has increased the size of the faculty in the last few years, and reduced teaching loads from six courses to five per year. Professors, not graduate students, teach all courses. The student-faculty ratio is 10 to 1.

For freshmen, Bucknell's residential colleges combine classroom and co-curricular activities. Students enrolled in a choice of seven theme-based houses live together, attend a course together, and participate in an hour-long discussion each week. Some houses go on field trips to further explore a theme, typically a topic in the arts, environment, global issues, humanities, social justice, or society and technology. Around a third of first-year students enroll in this living-learning program each year, which encourages intellectual discussion outside the classroom—but also contributes to politicization of the campus. The Social Justice and the Global colleges are the most partisan at the university. For instance, in the Social Justice College: "Recent courses studied poverty, inequality in education and health care, immigration, and gay and lesbian civil rights." Students say that most professors present such issues from a monochromatically leftist viewpoint. According to one student, "My professors—like a lot of professors—told us that we could say anything we wanted in class, if we were being respectful. But it turned out that we were supposed to regurgitate the liberal ideology we were being fed."

On a brighter note, Bucknell has plenty of monkeys. One of Bucknell's unique features is the psychology department's primate laboratory. Created in the 1960s and dubbed the "Monkey House" by students, it houses colonies of *Hamadryas* baboons, macaques, squirrel monkeys, and capuchin monkeys. Undergraduate and graduate students observe the animals for research and some courses include regular field trips to the center.

The university's best departments are said to be engineering, computer science, economics, physics, mathematics, English, chemistry, animal behavior, ecology, and accounting. Professors students name as the school's best teachers include Elizabeth Armstrong in East Asian studies; Morgan Benowitz-Fredericks and Kate Toner in biology; Katie Hays in English; Ned Ladd in astronomy; Robert A. Stockland Jr. and Eric Tillman in chemistry; John Enyeart in history; Scott Meinke and Michael James in political science; Richard Fleming and Peter Groff in philosophy; Mary Beth Gray in geology; Christopher S. Magee and Geoff Schneider in economics; and William R. Gruver in management.

As for weak areas, one faculty member says, "We offer a bunch of education classes. I think these people are mostly earnest, but the classes have no place at a serious school. Then there's peace studies. I'd rather not say what I think of that." One student reports ideological bias in a "Pre-Modern Europe" history class, noting that the professor "focused so much on how women and minorities were oppressed that I feel we didn't cover enough of the big events."

Last year, more than 300 students at Bucknell studied abroad at some sixty international educational sites on every inhabited continent. Some 40 percent of Bucknell students participate in a study-abroad program.

Beginning with the incoming class of 2014, there is no foreign language requirement at Bucknell. However, prerequisites for admission to Bucknell includes two years of foreign language in high school. The school does offer classes in Arabic, Chinese, French, German, Ancient Greek, Latin, Hebrew, Japanese, Russian, Spanish, and American Sign Language.

Student Life: It's Greek to them

Lewisburg, Pennsylvania, offers students a pleasing balance between peaceful beauty and university culture. The town's main drag, Market Street, is a quaint, tree-lined avenue

---

ACADEMIC REQUIREMENTS

Bucknell maintains no core curriculum, but it does impose certain requirements. Liberal arts majors (as opposed to engineering students) must complete the Common Learning Agenda. On top of the demands of a major, these include:

- A Foundation Seminar on any of a wide variety of topics. The focus is on writing skills.
- A laboratory science class, such as biology or chemistry.
- One course in the Natural and Fabricated Worlds, ranging from "Ancient Technology" to "Elvish Writing."
- A Human Diversity class, ranging from "Economies and Societies: Beyond Money" to "Gender and Sexuality in South Asia."
- Two courses in the arts and humanities or arts practice, ranging all the way from "Roman Civilization," and "Modern Dance Technique" to "Shakespeare and Outer Space."
- Two social science courses, with choices like "Consumption & Material Culture" and "Gender Issues in Education."
- A senior capstone experience, which can be a seminar, interdisciplinary course, thesis, independent study, or service learning project.

Mid-Atlantic

replete with more than forty boutiques, restaurants, and bars. The art deco Campus Theatre was purchased in 2001 by a Bucknell English professor, and its single screen now serves film festivals. The school is aggressively working to strengthen its role in the Lewisburg community, and through economic development efforts is seeking ways to link downtown Lewisburg with the campus. But for Bucknell's urbane student body, the town is smaller than it appears, and town-gown relations are strained. Lewisburg residents are said to regard Bucknell students as "spoiled brats" who crowd the bars and siphon off cheap housing, while Bucknell students—many of whom graduated from elite northeastern private schools—complain about the town's provincialism.

Bucknell University is located on a hill overlooking the Susquehanna River. The 450-acre secluded campus, with its wide expanses of green grass and rolling land, has the feel of a country club. This is the region that the Wyeths painted, and it is one of the most beautiful areas in the United States. Nature enthusiasts interested in field trips should investigate Chillisquaque Creek Natural Area, a sixty-six-acre ecological habitat owned by the university, located eleven miles east of campus

There are more than one hundred campus buildings and long-term plans for a new management facility, art building, museum, and more engineering labs are on the table. The university recently finished outlines for a $41 million building plan, including more dorms with space for 350 beds.

Bucknell guarantees on-campus housing for all undergraduates. Some 87 percent of the student body lives in the school's residence halls, apartments, special interest, theme, or fraternity houses. Though men can live in fraternity houses, sorority members are housed in Hunt Hall, an all-women dormitory. Most other residence halls are coed by room, meaning that men often live right next door to women. There are no coed rooms or bathrooms, except in apartments and special interest houses.

Recent theme housing has included the CHOICE substance-free and scholars residential programs. The CHOICE program is in high demand and now fills two residential halls on campus. The Residence Hall Association coordinates social activities for students living in campus buildings and is their representative voice. Students enjoy a wide array of events and activities, including a Semi-Formal dance every year.

Student life at Bucknell is dominated by the Greek system. More than half of Bucknell upperclass students are members of one of the twelve fraternities or eight sororities. The university has begun instituting standards for Greek admission, including higher GPAs, more educational programming, required community service hours, and an external review process. It is still reportedly easy to get into a fraternity or sorority, however. Says one professor, "Our students are not overwhelmingly intellectually curious. Most Bucknell students are more interested, frankly, in their Greek organizations, or their athletic teams, or their social lives, or all of the above, than in books and ideas."

Students have more than 150 student-run clubs to choose from—at least 65 of which are academically oriented. Arts groups include poetry slams, comedy improv, and theater. There are four undergraduate *a capella* groups. The *Bucknellian* is Bucknell's weekly student newspaper (the school, blessedly, does not have a journalism department). The Calvin and Hobbes group provides the campus with substance-free activities, while KRAID, a video game club, invites students to skip parties and instead socialize as first person shooters. The school hosts a student fashion magazine, and clubs devoted to art acquisition and purchase, equestrians, cars, juggling, Bollywood dance and fantasy writing, among many others. Bucknell has both College Republican and Democratic clubs. The campus offers ROTC, appropriately named the "Bison Battalion."

Social venues on campus without alcohol are the nightclub Uptown and the Seventh Street Cafe, which is a popular place to relax. The cafe is open every day and schedules music on the weekends.

Bucknell hosts a wide variety of activities, with annual events including the Chrysalis Ball, which kicks off the Bison basketball season. The Bucknell Forum brings a wide variety of speakers to campus. ACE, the student-run programming group, brings in comedians, hypnotists, magicians, or other entertainment on the weekends.

A full-time Protestant chaplain, Catholic priest, and Jewish rabbi provide weekly religious services at Rooke Chapel. Also offered are weekly Episcopal and Orthodox services, weekly Buddhist meditation, and daily Muslim prayers. There are quite a few Christian devotional and outreach groups on campus.

The school's traditional political apathy—which once earned the campus the nickname "Bucknell Bubble"—seems to have given way to a suffocating climate of liberal guilt, one fostered by the school. In 2010 the campus hosted a talk by a gay Army recruit; a lecture on intolerance from Judy Shepard, mother of gay-bashing victim Mathew Shepard; and a screening of an antinuclear film—all of these in a two week stretch.

Each February, the Office of Lesbian, Gay, Bisexual, and Transgender Awareness promotes "National Freedom to Marry Week." The university-funded office has provided T-shirts and buttons and sent out an e-mail to all students asking them to take a specific political stance in support of gay marriage. The left-leaning Bucknell Caucus for Economic Justice includes several professors from the economics department and concentrates on issues like the living wage. It collectively publishes the *Catalyst* with PULSE (Partnership for Unveiling Labor and Sweatshop Exploitation).

The Bucknell University Conservatives Club (BUCC), which calls for free speech and intellectual and political diversity, has been tirelessly active at Bucknell. The left is feeling the pain: "It seems like a lot of the liberal students groups' activities solely consist of complaining about the conservatives' club," says one student." The BUCC presents its ideas through its popular magazine, the *Counterweight.*

At Bucknell, where baseball legend Christy Mathewson is among the school's alums, athletics is a priority. In addition to twenty-two clubs and twenty-five intramural sports, Bucknell supports twelve teams for men and fourteen teams for women in its Division I athletic program. The Bucknell Bisons compete in the Patriot League in twenty-three sports. Bucknell's student-athlete graduation rate is among the highest nationwide, according to the NCAA.

The Christy Mathewson Memorial Stadium is home to the football and lacrosse teams and has an all-weather track. The Kenneth Langone Athletics and Recreation Center boasts a fitness center, 3,600-seat basketball arena, strength training center, tennis and racquetball courts, and an Olympic-size swimming pool. Bucknell's eighteen-hole golf course is home

RED LIGHT

A controversy erupted in 2009 when the university prevented conservative students on three separate occasions from engaging in satire. Forbidden topics included the Obama administration's stimulus plan and affirmative action. Students were not allowed to engage in a "diversity bake sale" meant to satirize unequal admissions policies for students of different races. The Foundation for Individual Rights in Education (FIRE) reported the Bucknell conservative students stood at "Bucknell's student center and passed out fake dollar bills with President Obama's face on the front and the sentence 'Obama's stimulus plan makes your money as worthless as monopoly money' on the back. One hour into this symbolic protest, Bucknell administrator Judith L. Mickanis approached the students and told them that they were 'busted,' that they were 'soliciting' without prior approval, and that their activity was equivalent to handing out Bibles." Closing ranks and stonewalling, university administrators refused to allow FIRE to purchase an ad in a student newspaper criticizing these abuses of free speech. We hope that the new administration's behavior is less Orwellian, but that remains to be seen.

to the men's and women's golf teams and open to all students.

The bacchanalian parties hosted by fraternities and sororities have attracted persistent attention from the liability-conscious administration. In an effort to stem the tide of reckless drinking (alcohol poisoning, acts of violence, and DUI) by students, an emergency alcohol policy has been implemented. The policy, based on a disciplinary point system, banned hard liquor. It provides the severest sanctions—including a semester leave—for minors and legal-age students who violate liquor laws or regulations. The university also initiated a mandatory alcohol education program for incoming freshmen—"Alcohol 101"—taught by professors and staff. Students say that this has increased the "coolness" factor for drinking but reduced the amount of dangerous and extreme insobriety. "There's not as much of the students puking on the lawns as at some schools, but obviously drinking hasn't stopped," says one graduating senior.

The university's Department of Public Safety operates an escort service, patrols the campus on bicycles, maintains call boxes all over campus, and hosts regular crime prevention workshops for students. In 2009, Bucknell reported four forcible sexual assaults, nine aggravated assaults, thirteen burglaries, 154 acts of larceny, and two hate crimes.

Bucknell is a pricey adventure. Tuition for 2010–11 was $42,342, with an average cost of $9,938 for room and board, for a grand total of $52,280. Some 62 percent of students get need-based financial aid. The average student-loan debt of a recent graduate is around $20,000.

Carnegie Mellon University

Pittsburgh, Pennsylvania • www.cmu.edu

Nerves of steel

Located in the Oakland neighborhood of Pittsburgh, the Carnegie Institute of Technology was founded by industrialist and philanthropist Andrew Carnegie in 1900 as a "first-class technical school" for the sons of local steel mill workers. In 1967 the school merged with the Mellon Institute of Industrial Research to become Carnegie Mellon University, and today is widely renowned for its academic excellence and international leadership in technological advances and research work.

CMU is also well regarded as a global research facility and a widely recognized leader in computer science, robotics, and engineering. Providing a liberal education has never been Carnegie Mellon's primary purpose, but it excels at its specialties—for instance in the fields of engineering and technology. With almost 11,500 students and 4,000 faculty and staff, CMU is large, even crowded, but the college is rising to the challenge. In October 2008, CMU launched "Inspire Innovation," a five-year, $1 billion comprehensive fundraising campaign—and as of December 1, 2010, the school had already raised $676.7 million toward its goal.

The vast majority of CMU students are very serious about their work and put in long hours outside of class. Add to this the fact that the typical CMU student is a career-focused, practical type, and one starts to understand why there is comparatively little interest in social and political issues on campus.

Academic Life: How do you get to Carnegie Hall?

Carnegie Mellon is comprised of seven schools and colleges: The engineering school in the Carnegie Institute of Technology (CIT), the College of Fine Arts (CFA), the College of Humanities and Social Sciences (H&SS), and the Mellon College of Science (MCS) enroll undergraduates, while the David A. Tepper School of Business, the School of Computer Science, and the H. John Heinz III College (which encompasses the School of Public Policy and Management, and the School of Information Systems and Management) are for graduate students.

CMU's statement promises to use knowledge and technical ability to "solve problems and benefit society." With this ethos, engineering students in the Carnegie Institute of

Technology boast that they learn not just by traditional classroom and textbook study, but also by doing the "fun stuff," including interactive research opportunities—wiring robots, designing Ferris wheels, and building steam engines. True to the pragmatism of its founder, CMU introduces students to "industrial experiences" by teaching them about customer needs, competitive markets, and manufacturing. One professor believes that a unique "mixture of creativity, practical problem solving, and innovation" is what makes a Carnegie Mellon education distinctive. For example, CMU engineering students are continually refining the video simulation *HazMat HotZone*, which trains emergency responders (such as the New York City Fire Department) how to react under catastrophic circumstances. In the past, CMU robots developed for Three Mile Island's nuclear meltdown were used at Russia's disaster at Chernobyl.

Students also have the option of combining their scientific know-how with philosophical insights by participating in the liberal arts programs of the College of Humanities and Social Sciences—or by working simultaneously for the bachelor of science *and* arts (BSA).

Since Carnegie Mellon is internationally recognized as a premier institution for the study of chemical and electrical engineering, it's surprising to find that the drama and music departments also have outstanding reputations. For instance, Carnegie Mellon is the only U.S. college to offer a bagpiping degree, and Alasdair Gillies, the instructor, is considered "one of the greatest bagpipers alive." While CMU promotes an unusual blend of science and performing arts, the liberal arts disciplines seem to get lost in the shuffle, almost being usurped by the very practically-minded pursuits of CMU academics.

The College of Humanities and Social Sciences contains a limited number of traditional departments (many of which are quite small): economics, English, history, modern languages, philosophy, psychology, social and decision sciences, and statistics. Most of them have two tracks: a more traditional "disciplinary" major (economics or philosophy, for instance) and a more specialized "professional" major (usually a compound name, like logic and computation, psychology and biological sciences, or policy and management).

While there is no core curriculum, undergraduates in all schools are required to take a certain number of general education classes in composition, the arts, history, math, humanities, and social sciences. In the College of Humanities and Social Sciences, students are presented, as one professor says, "with a broad range of course offerings." What is more, "faculty in this department are constantly publishing and doing new research." But placing the highest priority on new, innovative research in the sciences doesn't translate so well in the history department, resulting in classes like "Family and Gender in Russian History" and "Photography, the First 100 Years: 1839–1939," instead of fundamental Western civilization or basic American history classes. This tendency is painfully evident in the history major requirements. In addition to an introductory research class and the multicultural campus-wide general education requirement "Global Histories," there are only three required courses for history majors: "The Development of American Culture," which is more of a sociology class; one "regional" course, with options like "Mayan America"; and one non-U.S. class, such as "Modern China." History majors may fulfill their remaining requirements with classes like "Food, Culture, and Power: A History of Eating" and "Extreme Ethnicity."

Like the history department, one student describes the program in philosophy as anemic, perhaps because it was designed to serve as a second major. He says, "This is both a strength and a weakness: For those who are interested in other fields, but would like to also study philosophy, this major is one of the easier ones to complete. For those who want to make philosophy their primary field of study, they run into the problems of limited class selection, biased toward logic and computational philosophy, in a small, relatively new department." There is not a political science department per se, but rather a subdivision of the Social and Decision Sciences department called "Policy and Management." To graduate with this degree, students must take four clusters of courses: "The Analytical Methods," "The Research Methods," "The Organizational Context," and "The Management, Decision Making, and Technology." This is in no way a traditional poli sci degree; in fact, majors are not required to take classes in either the U.S. Constitution or American political theory.

Few students attend Carnegie Mellon to major in English, and with good reason. The English department is more politicized than most, stressing the importance of diversity and multiculturalism "by teaching the overlooked works of women and writers of color alongside well-known authors; by teaching comparative texts that highlight differences across literature and culture alongside the texts of the Western canon; by teaching film, television, and other storytelling media alongside conventional texts," according to its website. A Shakespeare course is not required, but is offered as an elective alongside classes like "Post-Race Culture."

Students at CMU who crave a traditional liberal arts education would do well to apply to the Humanities Scholar Program. Most Scholars participants agree to live in the same dorm in a "cluster," fostering community and discussion. They attend a seminar class

---

SUGGESTED CORE

1. English 221, Studies in Classical Literature: Books You Should Have Read By Now
2. Philosophy 250, Ancient Philosophy
3. No suitable course.
4. History 350, Early Christianity
5. Philosophy 135/235, Introduction to Political Philosophy/Political Philosophy
6. English 245/247, Shakespeare: Histories and Tragedies/Comedies and Romances
7. History 247, The Civil War Era, 1848–1877 (closest match)
8. Philosophy 253, Continental Philosophy

together each semester for the first two years. In the third year, students prepare a research proposal as prologue to their fourth year capstone project. Students report that the program teachers are enthusiastic. One participant lauds the "higher degree of academic dedication, which is assisted by the small-group dynamic that is cultivated."

Incoming freshmen in the humanities/social science college are assigned to one of just four academic advisors at the Academic Advisory Center. Once a student declares a major, he is offered a faculty advisor from his department—but meetings with advisors are optional. Since many students do not declare majors until the middle of the sophomore year, four advisors for the entire college is wholly inadequate, students complain.

As its impersonal advising and the varying requirements of its colleges suggest, Carnegie Mellon is not the best option for students seeking to use their college years as a period of soul-searching. CMU is a better choice for students who know with a high level of certainty what they want to study, especially if they seek a career in science or the fine arts. Carnegie Mellon does not allow students to experiment or dabble much in different disciplines before choosing majors. Transfer between colleges can be difficult, and changing majors may delay graduation.

ACADEMIC REQUIREMENTS

While they face no core curriculum, students in the College of Humanities and Social Sciences at CMU must complete a respectable set of distribution requirements:

- One freshman seminar. Many of the choices center on ethnic or sexual politics. Topics in 2011 range from "Performance and Gender" to "Barack Obama and the History of Race in America."
- "Computing Skills Workshop."
- "Interpretation and Argument."
- "Global Histories," with subtopics such as "Latin America and Global Environmental Change" and "The Civil Rights Movement and the World."
- "Statistical Reasoning and Practice."
- Two courses in writing and language. Class options include "The Rhetoric of Fiction," "Language, Power, and the Law," and foreign language classes.
- Two courses in humanities. Options range from "Studies in Classical Literature: Books You Should Have Read By Now" to "Introduction to Gender Studies" and "Environmental Rhetoric."
- Two courses in a different set of social sciences and humanities. Options here include "Principles of Economics" and "Religion in American Society."
- Three courses in math and science, with at least one in each. Class choices include "Differential and Integral Calculus" and "Physics for Future Presidents."
- Two courses in fine arts, where choices range from "Calligraphy" to "Survey of Western Music History."

In addition to these requirements and those given by his major, a liberal arts student must take two more courses from any of the above categories.

Professors at CMU are said to teach nearly all classes and students express satisfaction with the quality of teaching. One student says that he felt constantly challenged, by professors who for the most part were enthusiastic. As at any university where faculty members have many research responsibilities on top of their teaching duties, there are occasional complaints that certain faculty members are inaccessible. But most students indicate that professors are, on the whole, genuinely interested in getting to know their students. As one professor notes, "Research is emphasized, but we are putting progressive emphasis on teaching." Among the best professors at CMU are Kiron Skinner in political science; Bob Dammon in finance; Bruce Armitage and Garry Warnock in chemistry; Alex John London in philosophy; and Bob Dalton (emeritus) and Finn E. Kydland, a Nobel Prize-winner, in economics.

Students of all disciplines participate in the university's strong study-abroad program. Carnegie Mellon sponsors several university-wide exchange programs in Chile, Mexico, Switzerland, Singapore, Japan, Hong Kong, and Israel; has branch campuses in Qatar and Australia; and a partnership with CyLab in Seoul, Korea. Individual departments also offer exchanges overseas. The university offers a host of international job, internship, and volunteer opportunities for interested students. All CMU students are allowed to take classes at the neighboring University of Pittsburgh and Duquesne University. One student notes that in order to take courses in Greek or Latin, for instance, he needed to study at one of these other schools. Although it is weak in classics, CMU features a nationally respected modern language department. Students can take a major or minor in Chinese, Hispanic studies, French and Francophone studies, German, Russian, Japanese, European studies, or linguistics.

Student Life: Finding time

Pittsburgh is often a surprise to first-time visitors—who might still think of it as a smoggy steel town. That hasn't been true for almost forty years, as the U.S. steel industry has, sadly, moved to foreign shores. The economic downturn which hit Pittsburgh in the 1970s ironically helped save the city, preventing the kind of "urban renewal" that vandalized so many other American cities. The result is a place which is often listed by Rand McNally among the nation's most livable.

Pittsburgh offers students a wealth of activities at very reasonable prices—such as the unique Andy Warhol Museum (he grew up in town), and Carnegie Museum's famous dinosaurs are a short walk down the street from CMU. Other cultural venues, such as the stellar Pittsburgh Symphony Orchestra and the Pittsburgh Ballet and Opera, are a ten-minute drive downtown. For outdoor activities, there is sprawling Schenley Park and the manicured Frick Park. An hour outside of the city, one can take off for whitewater rafting in the Laurel Highland Mountains or visit two Frank Lloyd Wright homes: Fallingwater and Kentuck Knob. In addition to CMU's $36 million Purnell Center for the Arts, which houses two theaters, a dance studio, and the Regina Gouger Miller Art Gallery, students can also escape to the top floor of Hunt Library, where the Hunt Botanical Center surprises visitors with extensive exhibitions of botanical art and illustration. Housing is generally quite

Mid-Atlantic

affordable and many students opt to live off campus and do their shopping in the trendy Shady Side area or in residential Squirrel Hill. Sports fans will note that Pittsburgh hosts three major franchises: the Penguins (hockey), Pirates (baseball), and Steelers (football).

To a large extent, the character of student life at Carnegie Mellon derives from the school's demanding curriculum and particular strengths. Asked to name one of Carnegie Mellon's traditions, one professor responded, "Working hard . . . I wouldn't characterize this as a party school by any means."

The school has a reputation for having a student body of "nerds" and "geeks"—which is not entirely fair, but does indicate how academically serious students are, sometimes to the detriment of social life. There certainly isn't much of a fan base for the school's athletics teams. The student body is rather indifferent to intercollegiate athletics, and often ignore CMU athletics in order to cheer for the Steelers. Some students complain that there is virtually no school spirit at CMU. The Tartans (a nickname that honors the school's Scottish founder) field seventeen varsity athletic teams and are members in the NCAA Division III University Athletic Association. However, the relatively new athletic and physical education complex is a big hit among students and faculty. CMU boasts "state of the art facilities," including an indoor pool, gyms, weight room, stadium, and tennis courts.

First-year students are required to buy a meal plan. Student housing both on and off campus is available to all students over the age of seventeen. On-campus housing is located just a few minutes walk from academic buildings, while the Oakland Community Apartments is about a five or ten minute walk, and is served by the college's shuttle service. Almost all freshmen—currently 99 percent—live on campus in college-affiliated housing, typically in standard double or triple rooms. Most dormitories are coed, but the university also offers some single-sex dorms as well as plenty of smoke-free buildings and floors, not to mention New House, a new "green" dormitory designed to conserve energy. There are no coed bathrooms or dorm rooms in the residence halls. There are ample fraternities (eighteen) and sororities (eight) that offer housing throughout the chic Pittsburgh neighborhoods of Oakland, Shadyside, and Squirrel Hill.

Some 64 percent of the undergraduate student body live on campus. Most students and professors carp about the abominable quality of campus food. So health buffs and foodies spend Saturday mornings shopping in the Strip District downtown. The city's inadequate downtown subway and poor bus system make the campus shuttle or a car the preferred mode of transport for most students. Public parking is reasonably cheap throughout Pittsburgh.

Students continue to complain about the school's imbalance of men to women, particularly in the engineering and science schools. The university hovers at about 58 percent male, while the engineering school is almost 75 percent male. On the other hand, this makes CMU a refreshing exception to the trend at most colleges in America, where women have begun to outnumber men (in many places) by a ratio of 60 to 40 percent.

The Spring Carnival is the most important annual tradition at CMU, a time when students turn their creativity to crafting elaborate housefront themes for the fraternities that stand across the street from the university. As you might expect at a college that places so much emphasis on the sciences, part of the fun is oriented around technology, with autonomous "mobot" (short for 'mini robot') races. Aerodynamic carts or "buggys," raced at thirty miles per hour, is another activity unique to Carnegie Mellon.

During the rest of the year, students frequent fraternity and sorority parties. A healthy Greek system exists at CMU; approximately 15 percent of male undergraduate students enter one of the eighteen fraternities, while approximately 10 percent of female undergrads are members of the school's eight sororities. Undergrads can also join a vast number of student organizations—including political groups from all across the spectrum. The College Republicans and Respect Life are especially popular among conservative students. Many of the 240 student organizations center on ethnicity, such as Multicultural Alliance, Muslim Student Association, and Young African Leaders Alliance. There is also a designated branch of the Student Life department dedicated exclusively to sexual orientation issues for the campus homosexual group, ALLIES. Other clubs and organizations include orchestra, mock trial, photography, astronomy, ballroom dance, prelaw, poker, Big Brothers/Big Sisters, and Habitat for Humanity.

GREEN LIGHT

Carnegie Mellon's rather grinding workload and preprofessional atmosphere dampen most campus activism, and the school is known for relative tolerance of various political viewpoints. Most CMU people we consulted agreed that theirs is a largely apolitical campus; people are just too busy in the lab or studio to go marching for a cause. One student says, "CMU is very proud of its diversity. This means that there are religious beliefs and political leanings of all kinds, but they're uniformly downplayed as personal choices and opinions."

However, occasional troubling incidents take place on campus—not that most people seem to notice. For instance, AB Films, a division of CMU's Activities board, has been known to show pornographic films. CMU's official response was that while it is not "consistent with our values as a university community, it is not prohibited by university policy."

On a more traditional note, the school offers many religiously oriented clubs, including organizations for Baptist, Methodist, Mormon, Episcopal, Jewish, Lutheran, Orthodox, and Catholic students, as well as Christians On Campus, Intervarsity Christian Fellowship, and the Asian Christian Fellowship. Pittsburgh is known as the city of a thousand churches; there are many churches of any denomination and faith around CMU's campus. The Heinz Memorial Chapel, also located next to the campus and modeled after Sainte-Chapelle in Paris, is open for nondenominational services, tours, and events throughout the year. The imposing St. Boniface Church, a short drive from campus, offers Latin Mass on Sundays with a chant choir. Catholic undergrads should seek out the excellent study group FOCUS.

The crime rate in Pittsburgh is low, a fact which is reflected on campus: thirty-four burglaries were reported in 2009, along with four forcible sex offenses and one stolen car.

Carnegie Mellon may have been founded by a philanthropist, but it isn't free. Tuition was $41,940 in 2010–11, with room and board $10,750. Forty-nine percent of undergraduates receive need-based financial aid, and graduate with an average debt of $29,546.

Catholic University of America

Washington, D.C. • www.cua.edu

Coup d'état?

Founded by the bishops of the United States and chartered by Pope Leo XIII in 1887, the Catholic University of America is this country's only pontifically sponsored school. The archbishop of Washington, D.C., serves ex officio as the university's chancellor. Catholic parishes across the country take up collections for the school each year. In recent decades, under the leadership of former longtime president Rev. David O'Connell, CUA became a solid destination for students seeking a traditional Catholic education. O'Connell recommitted the school to its Catholic identity and the ideals of liberal arts education—as evidenced by the hiring of professors who shared these ideals. In an interview with the *Chronicle of Higher Education*, O'Connell once asked rhetorically: "Why would you want to have someone teaching at a Catholic college or university who is not supporting the Catholic identity and mission? That doesn't make a lot of sense."

But now Rev. O'Connell is gone, promoted to coadjutor bishop of Trenton. His replacement, installed in January 2011, is John H. Garvey, former dean of Boston College Law School—whose track record at that school is deeply troubling. In a 2002 "Letter from the Dean," Garvey explained his own educational philosophy:

> On several occasions I have heard people express concern that the Catholic identity of Boston College and the Law School will require a certain orthodoxy, or suppress unorthodox opinions, among its faculty and students. No school that regulates ideas can justly call itself a university. Indeed, it is precisely because we are committed to the search for truth in an atmosphere of academic freedom that the Law School can render a useful service to the Church and the cause of justice. It is natural that we should have a particular interest in the intersection of law and religion. (Though this is not our only focus.) But when people address that subject here they do not speak for (or against) the church hierarchy. They follow where their inquiries lead them.

In 2009, Garvey signed a statement on behalf of the school affirming its "commitment to making our institution a welcome and safe place for all students, including LGBT (Lesbian, Gay, Bisexual, Transgendered) students." The statement was issued as a rebuke to BC law pro-

Mid-Atlantic

236

fessor Scott Fitzgibbon, who appeared in a TV commercial defending traditional marriage. According to Catholic-Culture.org, Garvey "made a point of telling reporters that Fitzgibbon was only speaking for himself, and BC Law was happy to have faculty members who would argue strenuously in support of homosexual marriage."

In 2007, the Cardinal Newman Society harshly criticized Garvey for choosing as commencement speaker congressman Edward J. Markey, a self-styled Catholic with a 100 percent "perfect" pro-choice voting record, according to the National Abortion Rights Action League. In a statement, Garvey gushed: "congressman Ed Markey is one of the most distinguished graduates of Boston College Law School, whose career of public service reflects the very best values and traditions of the School. I don't believe Boston College has ever had a better friend in the United States Congress than Ed Markey."

It is safe to assume that President Garvey will now make such "friends" for Catholic U. What his leadership will mean for the nation's flagship Catholic educational institution will depend on the extent of the permissive will of God.

Academic Life: Intellectual genealogy

Catholic University was founded as a graduate research institution; it wasn't until 1904 that undergraduates arrived on campus. However, in the past decade undergraduates have swiftly and steadily crept up on the traditionally graduate-dominated campus, now accounting for a little over half of the total CUA student body. A former teaching assistant notes that "Too many faculty still behave as if CUA were an exclusively graduate institution and tolerate undergraduate teaching as a necessary burden." What is more, he says, "graduate teaching assistants are pervasive, even in the honors program."

CUA offers seventy-two bachelor's degree programs in six schools: arts and sciences; architecture and planning; engineering; music; philosophy; and nursing, which is ranked as one of the best in the country. Although CUA is not a Great Books school, these texts are taught, if a student knows where to look. One outstanding option is the honors program, which a professor calls "a fine opportunity to gain a genuine liberal arts education, especially with its director, Dr. Michael Mack." At a Freshman Convocation, Mack told students, "During college, make a hobby of intellectual genealogy. Trace your ideas back to their origins. Discover the traditions that you are part of."

VITAL STATISTICS

Religious affiliation: *Roman Catholic*
Total enrollment: *6,868*
Total undergraduates: *3,466*
SAT/ACT midranges: CR: *510–610*, M: *500–600*; ACT: *21–26*
Applicants: *5,044*
Applicants accepted: *86%*
Accepted applicants who enrolled: *19%*
Tuition and fees: *$34,205*
Room and board: *$12,742*
Freshman retention rate: *81%*
Graduation rate: *65% (4 yrs.)*, *72% (6 yrs.)*
Courses with fewer than 20 students: *57%*
Student-faculty ratio: *10:1*
Courses taught by graduate students: *not provided*
Most popular majors: *architecture, political science, nursing*
Students living on campus: *70%*
Guaranteed housing for four years? *no*
Students in fraternities: *1%* in sororities: *1%*

SUGGESTED CORE

1. Comparative Literature 207, Masterpieces of Western Literature
2. Philosophy 201, The Classical Mind: The Origin and Growth of Western Philosophy
3. Theology and Religious Studies 200/210, Introduction to the Old/Introduction to the New Testament
4. Theology and Religious Studies 220, Church Through the Ages: Paul to Luther
5. Politics 360, Modern Political Thought
6. English 461/462, Plays of Shakespeare I/II
7. History 257, American History Survey I
8. History 341, Modern European Intellectual History II

The honors program offers five different study sequences, some of which seem more traditional than others: "An Aristotelian *Studium*," "The Christian Tradition," "Critical Exploration of Social Reality," "The Environment, Energy, and Policy," and "Tradition and Renewal in Contemporary Catholicism." According to students, other strong departments include politics, philosophy, history, and English.

Catholic University does not have a true core curriculum, but it imposes a stronger set of distribution requirements than most. One student boasts, "My curriculum in politics and philosophy (double major) and minor in theology is *nothing but* studying the Great Books from those subjects. Especially for philosophy, *everything* is teaching directly from the sources themselves." However, another student claims that some of the distribution requirements are actually weaker than they appear. The religion requirement, for instance, can be met "without ever having to do anything more substantial than a few 'reflection' papers—the sort of thing that begins with the words 'I feel.'"

Religion majors can concentrate in biblical studies, Roman Catholic studies, religious development and religious education, or religion and culture. For each of these concentrations, the curriculum is carefully structured and serious. Students can earn an arts and sciences degree in the discipline or an undergraduate certificate in pastoral ministry. The quality and fidelity of classes vary with the professors, sources say. They recommend students ask around before choosing classes, to find out which are rigorous and orthodox. One former instructor commented that "It is sad to admit, but most heterodoxy was to be found in the school of religious studies." A graduate instructor commented, "The seminarians enrolled in my Latin class regretted that CUA's pontifical status required that they study Latin. Their preference was—if any foreign language—German so that they would have greater access to 'progressive' theologians."

Politics is considered one of the strongest departments for undergraduates and is particularly solid in political theory. This is augmented by CUA's location, of course, as one student comments: "The opportunities provided by being in D.C. are amazing for politics majors." However, one student warns of only "limited offerings for undergraduates in the formation of the Republic, the meaning of the Constitution and the Framers." The offerings may be limited, but poli sci majors are at least required to take introductory classes in the U.S. Constitution and American political theory. Students say the best faculty members in the department are Phil Henderson, John Kromkowski, James O'Leary, Claes Ryn, and David Walsh. One professor claims the "politics department is quite strong for those who care about a real liberal-arts-oriented education, rather than the trendy behavioral studies that have polluted political science almost everywhere else." Another professor laments that the world politics concentration is weak. An exclusive and exciting option that is available for political science students at CUA is the study-abroad program wherein a student may intern for a semester or summer at the British Parliament at Westminster, the Irish Parliament in Dublin, or the EU Parliament in Brussels, an opportunity a student calls "a politics major's dream."

The academic pride and flagship school of CUA is its School of Philosophy, which is highly regarded nationwide for its programs in classical and medieval thought. Professors V. Bradley Lewis, Kurt Pritzl, Timothy Noone, Matthias Vorwerk, Tobias Hoffman, David Thayer and Kevin White are named as some of the best in the school, along with Robert Sokolowski, who specializes in phenomenology, and John F. Wippel, an expert on Aquinas and metaphysics. Regis Armstrong on Franciscan theology; Joseph Capizzi in moral theology and ethics; and William Loewe in Christology.

Other notable professors in the university include Michael Mack (famous on campus for his Shakespeare class), Ernest Suarez, Christopher Wheatley, Rosemary Winslow, and Stephen Wright in English; Virgil Nemoianu in comparative literature and philosophy; Dr. Mario Ortiz in Spanish; Dr. Sarah Ferrario in classics; and Katherine L. Jansen and Jerry Z. Muller in history.

Harold Bloom, the renowned literary scholar and critic, has listed Catholic University's English department as one of the few in the country to have maintained exceptionally high standards of teaching and scholarship. The requirements for an English major are excellent, including "History of English Literature" I and II, "Intensive Readings in Lyric, Drama, and Narrative," "Chaucer and His Age," and "Plays of Shakespeare." As one student testifies, "Teaching and scholarship are important. The more liberal literary ideologies are almost nonexistent in the classroom."

The history department, on the other hand, is weaker, offering an overabundance of "diversity" and multicultural classes. The major requirements reflect this trend as well, although students must take two foundational world civilization courses in order to graduate with a history degree.

Most students say that the CUA faculty is committed to teaching as its first priority. Four out of five professors teach at the undergraduate level and the student-faculty ratio hovers around a strong ten to one. Graduate students regularly teach introductory courses, especially in the social sciences and foreign language courses. The university says it closely monitors them for quality control, and one student thought so highly of his TA that he re-enrolled in another introductory class taught by the same graduate student. Further, the university requires teaching assistants to take a pedagogy class before teaching their first course, which one former TA describes as, "Excellent. I was very, very closely monitored." One professor notes, "For a research-oriented university, our teaching loads are high. The number of professors who nonetheless work hard at their teaching is noticeable." A student confirms this, saying "teachers have always been accessible enough for me."

Class sizes—once you get past the introductory courses—are usually small, with the average class size at seventeen. Small groups encourage discussion and faculty-student interaction. Class participation is often part of a student's grade, especially in seminars.

Mid-Atlantic

Every freshman has two advisors, an academic and a first year advisor. The academic advisor is in the major department, so students are encouraged to make an early, tentative choice of major.

Science majors sometimes complain that the chemistry and biology departments lack adequate, modern facilities—a problem which the school has acknowledged and is trying to remedy. Students and faculty alike say that music and drama are especially strong programs at Catholic, and that modern languages is the weakest.

CUA is a member of the Consortium of Universities of the Washington Metropolitan Area, which allows students to take courses at eleven other area schools, including Georgetown, American, George Washington, and Howard.

CUA offers many study-abroad opportunities through its CUAbroad department. The flagship programs in Rome and Oxford are the most popular, but many students decide to study at the school's seventeen other affiliate programs in Argentina, Australia, Chile, China, Ecuador, France, Germany, Greece, India, Ireland, Japan, Mexico, Morocco, New Zealand, Poland, South Africa, and Spain.

At home students are offered foreign language classes in French, German, Italian, Spanish, Ancient Greek, Latin, Hebrew, and Arabic.

Student Life: In the city, but not of it

Catholic University lives at the center of a wide variety of related institutions, which has gained its environs the local nickname of "Little Rome," which one alum recalls as "part slum, part haven for hyper-orthodox grad students." The university stands alongside the massive Shrine of the Immaculate Conception, the Dominican House, the Washington Theological College, and the U.S. Council of Catholic Bishops. CUA students—largely East Coast, Catholic, parochial-schooled, and middle- to upper-middle class—tend to take their college careers seriously. Nevertheless, they find time to take part in the life of the nation's capital. CUA is a mere three Metro stops from the city's rail hub, Union Station.

Students are required to live on campus for the first two years of school unless they commute from home, have proven financial hardship, or are twenty-one years old. Many contacts reported that the university has had trouble supplying sufficient space to provide housing for those who wish to live on campus, especially past their sophomore year—but the addition of the seven-story, environmentally friendly Opus Hall has largely solved this problem. Most dorms are coed, but men are usually separated from women by floors or wings. There are no coed bathrooms or dorm rooms in the residence halls. The university also offers a couple of all-female dorms. In the "wellness" dorm, students pledge to go without alcohol. Students are not allowed to have overnight guests of the opposite sex; such guests may not stay past midnight on weeknights and 2:00 AM on weekends. However, there is apparent student dissatisfaction with the visitation policies, according to campus newspaper, the *Tower*, which asserts: "Nobody abides by its intent or letter, including resident assistants. Enforcing this rule would have a catastrophic effect on both the academic and social lives of students." According to one student, with the exception of orientation lectures on the dangers associated with alcohol, drug use, and promiscuity, "moral formation seems to be left to the student rather than entrusted to the school." One graduate remembers the undergraduate dorms as "having the reputation of controlled brothels, with the RAs undermining [former] president O'Connell's efforts at creating an environment of sanctity and scholarship." Aside from the rowdy dorm atmosphere, CUA's campus offers little in the way of a night life. Students into the party scene typically leave campus to frequent the bars and dance clubs in D.C. and surrounding cities.

The university has over a hundred registered clubs, organizations, and professional societies, as well as one fraternity and one sorority. A new campus group, the Society for a Virtuous Culture, is affiliated with Intercollegiate Studies Institute (the publisher of this guide). CUA also hosts many "multicultural" student organizations for African, Chinese, Filipino, and Islamic students; a chapter of the National Society of Black Engineers; an umbrella organization called Minority Voices; Amnesty International; and two international affairs organizations. A gay and lesbian organization, with the support of a priest

---

ACADEMIC REQUIREMENTS

While it doesn't offer a core curriculum, Catholic University offers stronger distribution requirements than many schools. For the School of Arts and Sciences, students must complete the following:

- An introductory English composition course.
- Four courses in philosophy, including two introductory courses and two others, such as "Philosophy of Natural Right and Natural Law" and "Metaphysics."
- Four courses in theology and religious studies. Hundreds of courses fulfill this requirement—many of them sound and useful classes in the Bible, Church history and Catholic doctrine, such as "History of Catholic Moral Theology" and "Biomedical Ethics," although one could take "Ways of Peace in World Religions."
- Four courses in social/behavioral sciences, from some 200 mostly worthy choices, such as introductions to psychology or sociology, "The Classical Mind," and "Critical Issues in Cyberspace Media."
- Four courses in mathematics or natural sciences, such as anthropology, biology, chemistry, computer science, environmental studies, math, and physics; however, one of the courses must be math. Choices include "Euclidean and Non-Euclidean Geometry" and "Calculus" I, along with the less demanding "In Search of Extraterrestrial Life."
- Three courses in humanities, out of hundreds such as "The Crusades," "The Renaissance 1300–1530," "Women and Gender in the Middle Ages," or even "History of British Cinema."
- Two courses in literature. Again, a long list of courses qualify—most of them solid subjects like "Milton" or "Major Victorian Poets."Other choices include "Modern Irish Drama," and "Film Narrative: Hitchcock."
- Two courses in a foreign language at the intermediate level. Students may be exempted by presenting sufficient standardized test scores in a language.
- Either a comprehensive exam or comparable project during senior year.

YELLOW LIGHT

In recent years, Catholic University has had a markedly more traditional atmosphere than most Catholic-founded colleges. One professor says: "There's little to no PC stuff around here." (Not yet.) A student agrees that in the classroom "CUA is great at encouraging debate. Dissent is usually encouraged. There is perhaps some condescension towards conservative students, but not usually anything beyond that." One alumnus said, "Many of my teachers were moderate liberals—obviously so. Occasionally we were required to do absurd things like avoid using B.C. and A.D., and instead use B.C.E. and C.E., but for the most part, even the politically correct faculty were demanding scholars and interested in genuine discussion and serious reading."

Says one student of the political atmosphere on campus, "generally everyone knows this is a conservative campus, even though some pockets of strong liberals endure. The College Republicans dominate student life in the political sense and in numbers, the College Democrats are always at a loss to compete with Republican efforts and the general attitude on campus."

Several students reported that the College Republicans chapter is very active, often bringing speakers from the national stage to campus to address the student body. Until recently, a student says, "the College Democrats [were] always hard pressed to get their speakers approved by the administration, because they [could] not bring pro-choice persons to campus except under very tight circumstances." Given that President Garvey actively sought out pro-choice commencement speakers at his last post, expect CUA's morally sane policy to be overturned—just as it was at Notre Dame.

who'd formerly been in charge of campus ministry, was narrowly defunded and defeated by orthodox students. On the whole the student body tends to be more conservative than the faculty and staff, a graduate notes. Both College Democrats and College Republicans have chapters on campus.

Students are very active in campus ministry at CUA. Organizations like Habitat for Humanity, the House, Knights of Columbus, and Students for Life bring students together for spiritual and charitable purposes, emphasizing the university's Catholic tradition. One student says, that the school's Campus Ministry "offers a ton of activities and advice for all students to have a proper moral formation and religious formation. Not only are there daily student liturgies on campus, but there are always organized and impromptu programs to unite faith and reason: Theology on Tap; scripture studies; 'Renew' prayer groups, et cetera."

While the immense National Shrine of the Immaculate Conception stands adjacent to campus, students also have access to Saint Vincent's Chapel and Caldwell Chapel for on-campus prayer. Caldwell Chapel—which is open twenty-four hours a day, seven days a week—underwent some renovations and, says one student, is "beautiful." The Latin Mass is occasionally offered in one of the smaller crypt chapels.

CUA competes in the NCAA Division III with twenty-one varsity sports teams called the Cardinals. The university also offers eleven club and fourteen intramural sports, ranging from coed indoor soccer to racquetball and badminton.

The Pryzbyla Center houses all of the student organizations; two cafeterias; student lounge areas; and the Office of University Center, Student Programs and Events, which manages the facility. Catholic bought forty-nine acres from the Armed Forces Retirement Home, increasing the size of the university's campus by more than 30 percent and making CUA the largest university in D.C. by land area, although there are no current plans to develop the property.

There are many campus improvement projects underway and many that were recently completed. Opus Hall opened in spring 2009 on the north side of campus, and three more dorms are under construction to eventually replace the old ones on the south side. Large student parking areas on the north and south ends of campus were added, as well as the expansion of the DuFour Athletic Center's facilities. Another upgrade worth mentioning at CUA concerns the food. With the Anytime Dining meal plan students can eat full meals or snack all day, until midnight on weekdays and until 2:00 AM on weekends. Meal choices range from vegetarian/vegan, sushi, and freshly baked bread, to restaurant quality platters. While students warn that the cafeteria food is still nothing to write home about, the addition of popular favorites Starbucks and Quizno's has made the on-campus situation more palatable.

A Metro stop at one corner of the campus provides easy access to the rest of the Washington area. One student gives a taste of the plethora of diversions awaiting CUA students: "From volunteer-ushering at Ford's Theater to enjoying class trips to the National Gallery, from ice skating in the Sculpture Garden to walking the monuments at moonlight, D.C. has been an education and an adventure in itself."

While enjoyable and fascinating, Washington D.C. is not the safest place in the world; though crime rates have fallen in recent years, students should be cautious when they leave the confines of the school—or make the decision to live off campus. There are lighted emergency phone boxes all over campus, and security personnel patrol the university grounds twenty-four hours a day. Escort services provided by Public Safety and the Saferides program take students home from late-night study sessions and parties. The campus crime statistics are impressive given that Washington, D.C. is statistically the most violent city in the country. In 2009 the school reported two forcible sex offenses, one robbery, one aggravated assault, twenty-two burglaries, and three car thefts.

Catholic University's tuition in 2010–11 was $34,205, with room and board totaling $12,742. The school does not practice need-blind admission or guarantee to meet a student's full financial need. Fifty-eight percent of undergraduates receive need-based financial aid, and the school refuses to release the average indebtedness of its recent graduates.

Colgate University

Hamilton, New York • www.colgate.edu

A glowing student body

Founded in 1819 by the Baptist Education Society, and taking its name from the famous soap-making family that first lent its support in 1823, Colgate University has long been a small, quality-oriented liberal arts college focusing on undergraduate education. With a very good student-faculty ratio, no teaching assistants, professors who care about student learning, and a faculty full of experienced scholars, at Colgate "the students are the faculty's main priorities, and advising them is a close second," says a student. Visit the campus today, a remote but beautiful location (designed with input from Frederick Law Olmstead), and you may notice the wholesome glow of the students. According to one professor, "Colgate is still a place committed to a well-rounded kid who is smart, socially adept, and politically moderate. Kids have genuine intellectualism, but the school produces CEOs, not PhDs."

The outgoing administration of president Rebecca Chopp (she took power in 2002), however, made it a priority to transform the sleepy university into a leftist moralist training academy. Chopp's background and primary research interests were in feminism and theology; she was once director of the Institute of Women's Studies at Emory University. Fittingly, perhaps, she adopted the role of moral matriarch, seemingly intent upon infusing the school and its students with a new, postmodern creed.

But according to one insider, Chopp's ambitions have mostly fallen flat. Furthermore, a new president with a different outlook has taken the helm. Jeffrey Herbst has served as chairman of the Princeton political science department and, most recently, Provost at Miami University in Ohio. One insider is "cautiously optimistic" about his upcoming ascendancy: "His inauguration in fall 2010 will bring to an end the seven year reign of Rebecca Chopp. . . . Her efforts clashed with Colgate traditions, and largely failed. The new era of Herbst is likely to be more positive in favoring academic achievement, classical liberal arts, international studies, and entrepreneurship. This will be a welcome change to many who admired Colgate's traditional liberal arts education and practical students, yet who also hope for a more intellectually intense campus climate."

Unlike many northeastern schools, Colgate has not yet become a haven for the young, alienated, radical neurasthenic. It may be a measure of Chopp's failure that *Men's Fitness* magazine ranked Colgate the second fittest college in America.

Academic Life: The mental obstacle course

Nonetheless, the changes Chopp made to Colgate were such that the university is now a kind of intellectual obstacle course. The prize—a genuine liberal arts education—is attainable, but it requires jumping hurdles. One of America's most prolific critics of the politically correct university, Alan Kors, sent his son to Colgate and, according to the lad's faculty mentor, he "came out with a fine education."

However, the school leaves such an outcome largely to chance. According to the American Council of Trustees and Alumni (ACTA), Colgate's core curriculum leaves major gaps in the education it requires of undergraduates. In particular, there is a dearth of history instruction covering the years A.D. 700–1700, while the formative period of Christendom is virtually skipped. One professor familiar with the university's introductory Western civilization course says that after a stint on ancient Greece and Rome, "There's nothing on Hellenism, medieval Christendom, the Reformation, the Renaissance—and then we get to the modern period."

Furthermore, politics can intrude into the classroom. One student recalls a core class that was "supposed to be about Homer and the Bible. But the professor wanted to talk about the Iraq War. . . . There are plenty of liberal professors with agendas." The student adds that in the second semester core "Challenge of Modernity" class, "We read a lot of Virginia Woolf and W. E. B. DuBois. It seemed at times like they were trying to turn it into an anti-old-white-males class." But another student says that with the exception of one notorious professor, Colgate doesn't have the "horror stories that trickle out of other schools concerning the stifling of debate." This does not, however, mean that the orientation of the curriculum is functioning as it should. Too often first-year courses at Colgate take a narrowly twenty-first-century perspective and challenge the student to consider such hot-button issues as global warming, stem cell research and AIDS before he has studied such foundational subjects as religion, philosophy, or Western history. According to one faculty veteran, the core is awful. "It's staffed by the faculty's husbands and wives who are insufficiently employed and by departments lacking enrollment."

But the deft student can sidestep these dead-ends. The first-rate Professor Barry Shain's popular introduction to political science has a huge waiting list and explicitly tries to fill in what other core offerings lack.

VITAL STATISTICS

Religious affiliation: *none*
Total enrollment: *2,837*
Total undergraduates: *2,825*
SAT/ACT midranges: CR: *630–710*, M: *640–730*; ACT: *29–32*
Applicants: *7,816*
Applicants accepted: *32%*
Applicants accepted who enrolled: *30%*
Tuition and fees: *$41,585*
Room and board: *$10,190*
Freshman retention rate: *95%*
Graduation rate: *85% (4 yrs.)*, *90% (6 yrs.)*
Courses with fewer than 20 students: *61%*
Student-faculty ratio: *10:1*
Courses taught by graduate students: *none*
Most popular majors: *social sciences, foreign languages and literature, history*
Students living on campus: *91%*
Guaranteed housing for 4 years? *yes*
Students in fraternities: *32%* in sororities: *29%*

Freshmen participate in a first-year seminar, which, according to the catalog, "emphasizes all aspects of the learning process including the exploration of individual needs and strengths, interactions with classmates, and the multiplicity of resources beyond the classroom." Students must also complete a two-semester track recently updated for the class of 2014 and composed of "Legacies of the Ancient World" and "Challenges of Modernity." These revised offerings, according to the course descriptions, "will no longer emphasize a distinction between Western and non-Western cultures." Rather, they "will consider how important movements and ideas within the ancient Mediterranean world and in Western Europe and the United States in modern times are in dialogue and conflict with other traditions." A third core course will focus on "Communities and Identities within cultures anywhere in the world" and a fourth "interdisciplinary course will continue to explore scientific perspectives on the world." All in all, "the new program will require students to complete six courses from six different departments or programs distributed across the curriculum."

As one professor describes it, Chopp's academic legacy may "corrupt" students "but not in the way you'd think." They are not brainwashed by flaky offerings from the left. Instead, "they become cynical. Education becomes instrumental."

Until recently, ideological bias seemed mostly localized in the usual places—departments such as women's, Africana, and Latin American studies. However, the political virus is said to be infecting some traditional departments such as philosophy and religion. For example, students can fulfill one of their scant humanities requirements with "Philosophy and Feminisms," in which they study feminist, "womanist," and *mujerista* interpretations of politics. The course focuses on the "interconnections among oppressions," the (allegedly unique) political characteristics of violence against women, and the "barriers separating women and embodiment." Another option is "Sex, Love, and God: Religion and Queer Studies," the title of which pretty much speaks for itself. One could take care of a social science requirement with "The Law and Politics of Abortion in the United States," taught from a decidedly pro-abortion perspective.

However, such courses can be avoided by the savvy student. "With care, you can skip the crackpots and get a great education, but you have to show initiative in selecting your courses," a faculty member observes.

Colgate's advising system does seem to do a fine job of guiding students, especially if they are lucky enough to receive help from a professor like the above mentor. Even before entering Colgate, students can ask for help from "prematriculation advisors," who help students choose their courses for the first semester. As freshmen, students turn to their first-year

Mid-Atlantic

seminar instructors for guidance. These professors serve as advisors until students choose their majors, at which time they select a faculty advisor from their major departments.

Unlike most colleges and universities, Colgate expects its students to take only four courses per semester. They may take five courses with special permission, but are not allowed to enroll in more than that. The idea is to give students the chance to focus more closely on the courses they do take. Besides satisfying general education requirements, students must also choose a major, where they will generally receive more structure. For instance, the English department requires its majors to take a broad range of courses. Unfortunately, the English curriculum has been watered down in recent years and no longer includes a survey course that exposes students to such canonical authors as Chaucer, Shakespeare, and Milton. History majors do not have to take American history before 1900. In this area, too, Colgate appears to be blindly following trends set by other, more prestigious schools.

There does seem to be a genuine commitment to teaching at Colgate. According to a professor, "Colgate is a place where teaching and research are equally balanced. And teaching is an important consideration in deciding on which professors get tenure." Another professor notes, "At Colgate there are no TAs. You have to grade all the papers." Indeed, graduate students do not teach courses at Colgate. Faculty members hold regular office hours, and most students take advantage of these. Colgate, says one student, offers "incredible accessibility to professors. . . . Only a handful of classes have more than forty students. The largest (Psych 151) is limited to 150."

Colgate boasts some excellent departments, especially political science and economics. Some courses in political science are so beloved that the department often has hundreds of students on the waiting list to enroll in them. By contrast, according to one undergrad, some areas to skip are "peace and conflict studies, women's studies, and Africana and Latin American studies. Those are the three academic departments most looked down upon by students and faculty alike as being 'soft.' Courses there are generally to be avoided." Another student says that "English, religion, and women's studies are way too liberal and don't prepare students for reality."

A professor familiar with the mess that the religion department has become says, "You can take a course in African religion or Native American religion, but not in American working class Protestantism." There is nothing on Calvin, for instance. And Catholicism is taught from a feminist perspective. Students warn that some professors in this department are "known for being closed-minded . . . and hostile to critical thinking. Students' opinions are worthless if they are in conflict with that of the professors."

If it's any consolation, the political science department is so strong, one professor can boast, "We probably teach more theology [here] than they do in the religion department. It's a top-flight department with four or five conservatives, and even those on the left are very decent." (It does not, however, require that political science majors study American constitutional theory.)

One teacher points to the "very good" philosophy and classics departments and the school's strong programs in the natural sciences. He adds, "For students interested in hard science, Colgate might be a better choice than they think. There's more attention to undergrads than they'd find at a research institution and more chance to work with faculty on experiments." The university recently completed the new Robert H.N. Ho Science Center, a $30 million building that houses the environmental studies, geography, geology, physics, and astronomy departments and programs. "Colgate is the only undergraduate college in America with a study semester at the National Institutes of Health, offering undergraduates six-month, intensive research experiences in NIH labs," the school reports. One student recommends, "If you're interested in natural sciences, economics, political science, or international relations, then Colgate is for you."

Students name the following faculty members as among the best at Colgate: Tim Byrnes, Fred Chernoff, Michael Johnston, Robert Kraynak, Nina Moore, and seminal conservative scholar Barry Alan Shain in political science; Stanley Brubaker in law and political science; Douglas MacDonald in international relations; Kay Johnston in education; Susan Cerasano, Margaret Maurer, and Jane Pinchin in English; Karen Harpp, Amy Leventer, and Paul Pinet in geology; Takao Kato, Jay Mandle, and Robert Turner in economics; David Dudrick in philosophy; Ray Douglas in history; Doug Johnson in psychology; Grace Ts'ao in accounting; and Thomas Balonek in physics and astronomy.

Students interested in study abroad may wish to consider the school's popular Geneva Study program, which includes a Eurail pass and offers the chance to see Europe from the home base of a gorgeous and centrally located city. Colgate offers study abroad on every continent except Africa, along with some interesting programs for specialists. "The London Economics Study Group, which Colgate has been running since 1962, studies the economy and economics of Britain and the European Community," the school reports. Closer to home, undergraduates can get "an insider's look at Washington, D.C., political life through

ACADEMIC REQUIREMENTS

- A two-semester cultural survey, "Legacies of the Ancient World" and "Challenges of Modernity."
- A single course from the category Communities and Identities. Current offerings include "North American Indians" and "Russia at the Crossroads of East and West."
- Another course from the category Scientific Perspectives on the World. Choices include "Genes and Human Fate" and "Sport and the Scientific Method."

Students must also take two courses from each of the following three academic disciplines:

- Human Thought and Expression: "Chaucer's *Canterbury Tales*" will count. So will "The Female Protagonist."
- Natural sciences and mathematics. Choices range from "Neurophysiology" to "Astronomy in Culture"
- Social Relations, Institutions, and Agents. Options include "Biogeography" and "Economy."

Also, students must take at least one course with the Global Engagements designation, helping them, as the Colgate website describes it, "analyze the conditions and effects of cross cultural interaction." The choices here are too numerous to mention.

the Washington Study Group. Begun in 1935, it is the oldest of Colgate's study groups and was the first program of its kind established in D.C."

Colgate offers foreign language majors in French, Spanish, German, Latin, Ancient Greek, Chinese, and Japanese.

Student Life: From *Animal House* to *Animal Farm*

Hamilton is a small town located about a half-hour southeast of Syracuse and a half-hour southwest of Utica. Since these cities provide relatively few cultural opportunities, most students stay on campus on weekends. With only 3,784 full-time residents, Hamilton's population almost doubles during the academic year. The Colgate community enjoys a comfortable relationship with the town; many residents attend university events, and students support local businesses. Students can easily walk to shops or restaurants or to the village green at the center of town, where the university hosts a college-town picnic at the start of each new year. One of the most popular attractions in Hamilton is the Palace Theater, which now serves as a dance club. Colgate's 515-acre campus includes Taylor Lake, a favorite spot for watching local wildlife.

Colgate is largely a residential school, with 91 percent of students living in university-owned housing. The university guarantees housing for all four years. Students can choose single-sex or coed dormitory floors; no single-sex dorms are available. There are no coed dorm rooms for freshmen and sophomores, and all bathrooms are single-sex. There is no intervisitation policy. Colgate offers a number of theme houses for first-year students and upperclassmen. Some of the choices include Curtis Hall for environmentally conscious students interested in the Outdoor Connections program, and the Harlem Renaissance Center. Others include the Asia Interest House, the Creative Arts House, and *La Casa Pan-Latina Americana*.

Seniors wishing to live off campus must obtain written approval from the director of residential life. This isn't usually hard to get, but the number of students (all seniors) allowed to live off campus is capped at 250; if more apply, the college holds a lottery to determine who lives where. Colgate obviously recognizes the benefits of having a primarily residential school and works to make sure the campus remains one.

Colgate's new Residential Education program is dramatically changing the student housing experience. Former President Chopp made this opportunity to reach a "captive audience" the cornerstone of her reform program. Students are placed in housing specified by year and are required to participate in scheduled programs intended to produce a student body that is "forward thinking" and "progressive." In 2008, Chopp appointed a new vice president and dean of diversity, Keenan Grenell, who "established diversity initiatives" for students such as the "Breaking Bread" program and the "Skin Deep" workshop. All replaced the forcibly suppressed Greek system on campus (see our Yellow Light). Even without a Greek system on campus, Colgate students still know how to party, perhaps too well; in 2010 Colgate placed number nine in The Princeton Review's category "Most Beer Drinkers on Campus."

Devout students will find religious houses on campus. There is a Jewish Union, a Christian Fellowship, a Muslim group, and a Newman Center. More traditional Catho-

YELLOW LIGHT

In July 2003, under the direction of former president Chopp, the school decreed that all Greek houses be sold to the school, and that any student who belonged to an unrecognized fraternity could face suspension or expulsion. Colgate now prohibits groups of more than eight students from living together without its approval. By changing school rules to require that students live in on-campus housing, President Chopp forced the fraternity and sorority houses just off campus to sell their buildings to the university and come under the school's direct control. Only the school's Delta Kappa Epsilon chapter fought the move, but its lawsuit was dismissed by the New York State Supreme Court.

Now that the changes have been in place for eight years, according to one professor, the frat houses are now "creatures of the university. Before, the frat boys competed to show off their masculine stupidity. Now they compete to do service projects for various charities. The administration's goal was androgynization. But the boys are still mostly boys and girls still mostly girls."

Chopp's attempts to remake Colgate into a soft, postmodern place have been even less successful in other areas: somehow conservative professors were able to prevail upon her to help establish two right-leaning institutes on campus, the "Center for Freedom and Western Civilization," directed by Robert Kraynak, and the "Philosophy, Politics, and Economics Institute (PPE), directed by Stanley Brubaker. The latter is a forum for public policy debate on campus. Their existence bodes well for the future of free expression at Colgate and helps promote genuine intellectual diversity at the school.

lics may enjoy attending St. Mary's parish in Hamilton.

For students interested in debate, the school resurrected a team that had been on ice for several years. Activists hungry for extra-curricular leftism may choose from an array of student organizations. Colgate's political organizations include grandly named groups like Advocates (queer/straight alliance), Sisters of the Round Table, and Students for Social Justice. Those who find these causes too general may choose from organizations such as Students for Environmental Awareness, Rainbow Alliance (the campus "lesbian, gay, bisexual, transgender, and questioning" group), African American Student Alliance, Colgate Democrats, or even College Republicans (there is no conservative student paper).

There's also the Colgate University Geological Society; Debate Society; Philosophy Club; Physics Club; Badminton; Equestrian; Juggling; Ski Racing; Spring Party Weekend Taskforce; Ballet Club; Kuumba Dance Troupe; Sojourners Gospel Choir; We Funk; Caribbean Students Association; Russian Culture Club; Students for a Free Tibet; CUTV; the *Maroon News*; and the Hindu Student Association.

Some political groups receive considerable support from the university. When a group called the Feminist Majority Leadership Alliance needed help organizing and funding a pro-choice event, the student group turned to the university's Women's Studies Center. The day's festivities included the promotion of abortion on demand and "educational" activities focusing on issues like "domestic violence, sweatshops, abortion, [and] welfare." Tuition dollars at work. . . .

The Colgate Activities Board sponsors plenty of apolitical activities, including concerts, comedy shows, and free movies. The university also hosts five student singing groups that perform regularly on campus. Colgate has won considerable attention for a five-year program financed by the Brennan Family Foundation of Ohio, which asks a group of undergraduates interested in philanthropy to select and guide a $10,000 charitable donation each year.

Among the school's most cherished and beautiful traditions are the Torchlight Ceremonies. As part of freshman orientation, students walk uphill to the Academic Quad, and when they graduate they walk downhill to the lake, each time holding torches that symbolize the light of learning.

In the area surrounding the university, outdoor activities abound. The Outdoor Education program is hugely popular with students, allowing them to rent backpacks, tents, and other outdoor equipment, and conducting a Wilderness Adventure Program for freshmen.

More than 70 percent of Colgate's student body participates in the university's intramurals program, which holds over fifty tournaments in twenty-three sports each semester. In addition to these activities, Colgate maintains its own boathouse, shooting range, bowling alley, and climbing wall. The university offers its students thirty-one club sports, in which 16 percent of the student body participates. For more serious athletes, the university's twenty-five varsity teams compete in the Patriot League (NCAA Division I) against schools like Army, Navy, and American University. Colgate is the smallest school in the country to compete in the NCAA's Division I-A.

Plans promoted by the alumni to bring back a Reserve Officer Training Course (ROTC) have borne fruit, with on-campus instruction beginning in 2009. ROTC students meet at the Huntington gym, the outdoor track, and Sanford Field House. Additional program commitments are required and full tuition scholarships are available to Colgate students who participate in ROTC, according to the school's website.

The Colgate campus is equipped with emergency call boxes, and each dorm is secured with a keypad lock. A security force patrols the campus around the clock and a volunteer foot patrol monitors the area at night. The university has also organized a walking escort service to help students home after dark. Colgate's administration says that the theft of CDs is by far the most common offense. Says one student, "Crime is no concern here. We're in the middle of cornfields." In 2009, the school reported four forcible sex offenses, four burglaries and two robberies.

Colgate's 2010–11 tuition was a hefty $41,585 with room and board averaging $10,190. Admissions are not need blind, but the school does meet the full financial need of those who get in. The school admits students, and offers aid, on a first-come, first-served basis. After the money runs out, Colgate stops admitting students who require financial assistance. About 35 percent of Colgate undergraduates receive some form of need-based aid, and the average student-loan debt of a recent graduate was $19,202.

Columbia University

New York, New York • www.columbia.edu

God save the King's College

Columbia University in New York City was founded in 1754 as King's College, and after the American Revolution was refounded as Columbia University in 1784. The school became a national center of humane letters, which it has remained ever since, and was the first American college to grant medical degrees. Columbia also has passed along Western civilization and American history by means of the traditional liberal arts education it provides, as enshrined in its worthy (and sadly, almost unique) core curriculum.

A few years ago, five students staged a hunger strike criticizing, among other things, the "Major Cultures" requirement of Columbia's core, which they said "marginalized . . . issues of racialization, colonialism, sexuality and gender." Instead of telling them to eat cake, university officials rewarded their tantrum—spending some $50 million to morph the "Major Cultures" requirement into something called "Global Core," and expanding the school's Office of Multicultural Affairs.

Will Columbia president Lee Bollinger save the remainder of this curriculum—Columbia's single greatest strength—in the face of a strongly, if not quite monolithically, leftist student body and faculty? So far, "Major Cultures" is the only significant casualty. Bollinger's willingness to resist nutritional blackmail will determine whether Columbia retains its distinctive excellence or casts it aside, leaving a grand McKim, Mead and White-designed campus shorn of its special mission, and its soul.

Academic Life: Uptown cosmopolitan

With some of the most respected scholars in the country on its faculty, Columbia's elite reputation is well deserved. This reputation is further justified by the university's requirement that all undergraduates take a number of courses focused on the Western canon; this core dominates the course load for freshmen and sophomores and is popular among many students of different political stripes—who knew what they were getting into before they enrolled. "[The core courses] will stay with me for the rest of my life. . . . No one can graduate from Columbia without being well-rounded," said one undergrad. Indeed, Columbia is the *only* Ivy League college from which it is impossible to graduate without having read Homer, Shakespeare, and the Bible or having listened to Bach, Beethoven, and Mozart.

Columbia also has a number of very strong departments, mostly in the humanities and liberal arts, and history in particular. Among the department's famous faculty are Eric Foner, former president of the American Historical Association; Alan Brinkley, a popular historian; and Kenneth Jackson, former head of the New York Historical Society. Most courses offered are solid and free from the overt historical revisionism of political correctness. Unfortunately, history majors are not required to take American history courses before or after 1865, although they are offered.

English majors must complete ten departmental courses with three of these covering periods before 1800. These required classes must include (we are pleased to note) one covering Shakespeare, plus another in British literature, one in American literature, one in English-language writing from outside the U.S. and U.K., one in drama, one in poetry, and one in prose or narrative. The requirements seem very flexible, but the English major coupled with the core classes guarantee a solid study of the Western canon of literature.

The political science major requirements are a little more vague. Majors must take two of three intro classes: "Intro to American Gov and Politics," "Intro to Comparative Politics," and "Intro to International Politics." Students must also take three classes in any of four subjects: American politics, comparative politics, international relations, or political theory, plus four other classes in other distinct subfields. The emphasis seems to be shifting toward contemporary workings of the American system rather than the founding or Constitution—with plenty of trendy choices concerning race, gender, environment, and the media in politics.

The controversial Middle Eastern and Asian languages and cultures (commonly known as "MEALAC") department bears the stamp of the late leftist scholar Edward Said—a member of the Palestine Liberation Organization who supported armed violence against Israel. His intellectually dishonest "classic" *Orientalism* helped corrupt the entire discipline of Middle Eastern studies, turning many departments (like Columbia's) into apologists for Islam and anti-Western extremism. Jewish students have made repeated complaints that faculty in this department are biased toward Arab perspectives, and that this had led to classroom incidents of anti-Semitism. On the positive side, the MEALAC faculty also includes Turkish Nobel Prize-winning novelist and memoirist Orhan Pamuk.

VITAL STATISTICS

Religious affiliation: *none*
Total enrollment: *27,606*
Total undergraduates: *7,934*
SAT/ACT midranges: CR:
 680–770, M: *680–780;*
 ACT: *29–34*
Applicants: *21,748*
Applicants accepted: *8%*
Applicants accepted who
 enrolled: *61%*
Tuition and fees: *$41,160*
Room and board: *$12,160*
Freshman retention rate:
 99%
Graduation rate: *87% (4 yrs.),*
 96% (6 yrs.)
Courses with fewer than 20
 students: *79%*
Student-faculty ratio: *6:1*
Courses taught by graduate
 students: *not provided*
Most popular majors: *social
 sciences, engineering,
 history*
Students living on campus:
 94%
Guaranteed housing for 4
 years? *yes*
Students in fraternities: *7%*
 in sororities: *4%*

SUGGESTED CORE

Required core curriculum courses (such as Humanities C1001–C1002: Masterpieces of Western Literature and Philosophy and Contemporary Civilization 1101–1102) may be supplemented with the following:

- Religion V2105, Christianity
- English W3335/W3336, Shakespeare I/II
- History W1401, Survey of American Civilization to the Civil War

Besides the previously mentioned faculty, excellent teachers at Columbia include Carol N. Gluck and Simon Schama in history; Elaine Combs-Schilling in anthropology; Andrew Delbanco, Frances Negron-Muntaner, Michael Rosenthal, and James Shapiro in English; Richard Betts and Robert Leiberman in political science; Stephen Murray in art history; James E. G. Zetzel in classics; Jeremy Dauber in Germanic languages and literature; Daniel Helfand in astronomy; and Alessandra Casella in economics. One of the most rewarding courses, students report, is Kenneth T. Jackson's "History of the City of New York," which culminates in an exhilarating all-night bike ride, on which the professor leads the whole class through the city. Students seeking out the best professors can—and should—make use of the Columbia Underground Listing of Professor Ability (www.culpa.info) for its professor ratings by students.

Columbia makes a wide—if not overwhelming—variety of courses available. But a common complaint among students is that the advising system is at best inadequate. Advising systems vary by department, and most do not assign students to specific faculty mentors. Several departments require students to meet with faculty members periodically, but these meetings usually are formalities during which students have professors sign off on plans of study developed wholly by the students. In any event, Columbia's mediocre advising system has long been a part of the university's tradition. While the core classes are celebrated for their small class sizes and personalized attention, students have to actively seek out advisors. One student makes a special point about this: "If you don't like your instructor or they're low-rated on CULPA, the smart thing may be to make a change in your schedule so you get someone else. But getting a change in your schedule can be time-consuming with all the bureaucracy."

Usually, the more famous the professor, the less likely it is that he will grade any of a student's work over the course of a semester. Classes with well-known professors are lecture courses of up to 400 students, so while the university touts the fame of many of its professors, students may have trouble getting to know them. While all professors have office hours twice a week, unless students take the initiative faculty members will rarely learn their names. Grade inflation varies by department. "As a rule of thumb," one senior says, "in hard science classes grades are deflated, in social sciences they are left alone, in the humanities they are inflated, and in the arts they are all As." The student-faculty ratio is a stunning 6 to 1. Though professors conduct almost all classes, graduate students do teach—particularly the small "recitation" sections of fifteen to twenty students that usually accompany large lecture courses, where assistants are responsible for the grading. Their quality is said to vary, sometimes dramatically. This is an issue especially for sections of foreign languages and, as at so many universities, math.

ACADEMIC REQUIREMENTS

Admirably, amid the general collapse of curricula across the country, Columbia has maintained a serious, rewarding core, along with several other requirements. The Columbia core consists of the following:

- "Masterpieces of Western Literature and Philosophy" (two semesters). In small-group seminars, students read original works such as *The Iliad, Homeric Hymns, The Odyssey*, Herodotus' *Histories*, *The Oresteia, Oedipus Rex, Medea*, Thucydides' *History of the Peloponnesian War*, Plato's *Symposium*, *Lysistrata*, the Bible, *The Aeneid*, Ovid's *Metamorphoses*, St. Augustine's *Confessions*, Dante's *Inferno, The Decameron*, Montaigne's *Essays*, *King Lear, Don Quixote, Pride and Prejudice, Crime and Punishment*, and *To the Lighthouse*.
- "Contemporary Civilization" (two semesters), a small-group discussion course. Students read works by Plato and Aristotle, selections from the Bible (Old and New Testaments), Epicurus, Epictetus, Augustine, The Qur'an, Aquinas, Al-Ghazali, Machiavelli, Descartes, Galileo, Hobbes, Locke, Kant, Rousseau, Smith, Hume, The Declaration of Independence, the U.S. Constitution, the *Federalist Papers,* The Declaration of the Rights of Man and the Citizen, Robespierre, Burke, Wollstonecraft, Tocqueville, Hegel, J. S. Mill, Marx, Darwin, Nietzsche, DuBois, Freud, and Virginia Woolf.
- "University Writing," an English composition course. Each section has no more than twelve students.
- "Art Humanities," in which students study the Parthenon, Notre Dame, the Cathedral of Amiens, Frank Lloyd Wright's houses, Michelangelo's and Bernini's sculptures, and paintings by Raphael, Brueghel, Rembrandt, Goya, Monet, Le Corbusier, Picasso, Pollock, and Warhol.
- "Music Humanities," teaches students to appreciate and understand music in the Western world, from Josquin des Prez to Bach, Verdi to Stravinsky.
- "Global Core," formerly the "Major Cultures" requirement, the only element of the Columbia core that deviates from the curriculum's focus on Western civilization. This newly revamped requirement is a bone the administration cravenly threw the "diversity" contingent in response to hunger strikes and sit-ins. Topics covered include "Political History of Sexuality in the Caribbean" and "Gender and Genre in African Literature."
- "Frontiers of Science." This weekly science class involves lectures by leading Columbia scientists and seminar sections with researchers (all with PhDs) that include lab experiments. A recent topic was "The Human Species: Its Place In Nature."

Other general education requirements are:

- Four semesters of a foreign language or demonstrated proficiency to the intermediate level.
- Two additional science courses in any natural science department. Columbia offers two-term sequences designed for nonscience majors in astronomy, biology, engineering, computer science, ecology, earth and environmental sciences, psychology mathematics, and physics—including one called (with refreshing candor) "Physics for Poets."
- One physical education class. Students must also pass a swimming test or take beginning swimming.

Much more criticized is the school's luxuriant bureaucracy. Columbia's administration is famously bad at dealing with ordinary student foul-ups with respect to forms, registration, and paperwork. One student we spoke with told us that "getting an error on your Financial Aid Form corrected is difficult. There can be lines at the beginning of the fall semester for everything." Prospective students, aware that in 2010 Columbia had just shy of 8,000 undergraduates, may mistakenly assume that Columbia is smaller and more intimate than schools like Brown and Yale, when in fact it has more than 26,000 students, and dealing with bureaucracy is part of the Columbia experience. Columbia University, after all, also encompasses Barnard College (covered elsewhere in this book), the School of General Studies (an undergraduate night school), the country's largest "post-bac" program for would-be medical students, and dozens of graduate and professional schools.

A more serious threat to consistent quality at the university may lie in its president's obsession with race-based admission policies. As an outspoken proponent of affirmative action, President Bollinger's name actually "graces" the Supreme Court decision upholding racial preferences in education, since he was the litigant defending admissions quotas at the University of Michigan.

The university offers many highly regarded junior-year abroad programs, including a special program with Oxford and Cambridge and a popular study program in Berlin. The programs in Japan and China have greatly increased in popularity in the past couple of years. The college offers study-abroad programs to around forty countries, including New Zealand, France, Ghana, India, Italy, Argentina, the U.K., South Africa, Australia, Brazil, and the Russian Federation.

The school offers foreign language majors in classics, East Asian studies (Chinese and Japanese), French, German, Italian, Middle Eastern languages and literature (Arabic, Hebrew, Hindi), Portuguese, Russian, Slavic studies and Yiddish studies. In addition, Columbia offers classes in Armenian, Bengali, Czech, Dutch, Farsi, Finnish, Hebrew, Hausa, Hindi and Urdu, Korean, Polish, Punjabi, Romanian, Sanskrit, Swahili, Tamil, Tibetan, Turkish (Modern and Ottoman), Ukrainian, Serbian/Croatian/Bosnian, Swedish, Vietnamese, Wolof, and Zulu.

Student Life: Annexing the neighborhood

The university is developing a seventeen-acre site in Manhattanville, connecting West Harlem to the new Hudson River waterfront park, slated for completion in 2015. The development plans for a "new kind of urban academic environment" has created controversy over the displacement of current residents and abuses of eminent domain. Housing in New York City is notoriously expensive and hard to find, so it's not surprising that 94 percent of the Columbia student body lives on campus. All freshmen are required to live on campus, and Columbia guarantees housing to its undergraduates for all four years.

Dormitories are coed, but the university sets aside a few floors solely for men or women. Women students can also live at Barnard, which offers all-women residence halls. Columbia does have a few coed bathrooms, but students can easily avoid them. Special-interest housing allows groups of students to live together in one of several townhouses.

Quiet hours and noise regulations govern almost every dormitory. Sensitive students may have trouble getting these policies enforced, but most students on campus do not view noise as a major problem. Although it is up to the discretion of the residence advisor, most floors offer some sort of "condom box," making contraception widely available to students. Likewise, some floors have signs that provide information on the "morning-after pill" and other "health" services. Some dorms, like other areas of New York, have had trouble with bedbugs and cockroaches. Apparently the dorm lottery is very hit or miss.

A row of fraternity houses lines the two blocks just south of the university's increasingly chic Morningside Heights neighborhood, and the university does have a frat scene, although the school's frats are a bit more cosmopolitan than houses at many other schools. (Consider that when Beat Generation novelist Jack Kerouac attended Columbia, he joined the campus's chapter of Alpha Sigma Phi.) Students generally say that there is not much Greek life at Columbia, and that it is very self-contained.

Students have plenty of opportunities to engage in off campus activities—it is New York, after all. Within the immediate vicinity are a huge number of coffeehouses, bars, bookstores, and restaurants, while all Manhattan's resources and attractions are within easy reach. A Columbia University ID card will give students free admission to almost any museum in the city, and students may enjoy movies not likely to be screened elsewhere in the country in local art house theaters. Discounted tickets for some theaters are even sold at Undergraduate Class Centers, so students can avoid paying the full $12 ticket price common throughout Manhattan. There is also a wide variety of cheap or free things to do on campus that comes with the price of tuition.

As part of orientation week, the university sponsors a number of tours to familiarize students with the city. One graduating senior says simply, "Don't miss the first-week tours. As someone from the Midwest who didn't know the city at all, I can really say that it really made my first year in New York more comprehensible—and you meet a lot of your classmates at the same time." Other activities during freshman orientation are more controversial. Informational sessions on the dangers of date rape are mandatory for all students. Selected freshmen also attend receptions segregated by race or interest, including the Black Students Reception and the Gay, Lesbian, and Transgender Students Reception. Reportedly, the purpose of all these talks is to indoctrinate students in the ubiquity of oppression. However, "they went over like a lead balloon" with freshmen, said one student.

The school has about 500 official student organizations, including the Artist Society, Brazilian Jiu-Jitsu, Chess Club, Club Sports, Columbia University Poker Club, Dance Marathon, Earth Coalition, Figure Skating, Gospel Choir, Haitian Students Association, Japan Club, Law School Student Senate, Multicultural Greek Council, Nightline (Peer Counseling), Sailing, Saving Mothers, and U.S. Military Veterans of Columbia University.

The politically active population on campus comprises only a minority of students, but it is an outspoken group with strong allies in student government and the faculty. There are around forty politically active groups at the college, supposedly more than any other in the nation. Groups include the College Democrats, College Libertarians, the Columbia Political Union, and the College Republicans. For all the problems the school has had with truculent leftists, there are more conservatives at Columbia than one might think.

Mid-Atlantic

YELLOW LIGHT

At Columbia, a tolerant and open-minded brand of liberalism is more or less regnant among the faculty. Most Columbia professors remain traditionalists when it comes to how and what they teach and how they approach their scholarship. The propagandistic African American studies, Middle East languages and cultures, and women's and gender studies departments are the exceptions. But keep in mind that these are small departments in a huge school.

Columbia was on the cutting edge when it came to gay rights, advocating the homosexual lifestyle even before Woodstock. The first support network for gay students was founded at Columbia in 1967 as Columbia's Student Homophile League, better known today as the Queer Alliance. Other popular activist groups include a local chapter of the International Socialist Organization, Columbia Atheists and Agnostics, Students for Choice, Students Against Imperialism, Students for Economic and Environmental Justice, and the distinctive Conversio Virium: "Columbia University's Student BDSM Discussion Organization." The International Socialist Group is a particularly hard to avoid and unpleasant bunch, which aggressively pursues students on "College Walk demanding the U.S. let Iran get nuclear weapons, or alternately, physically attacking students at College Republican events," comments one undergrad. The Columbia University Conservative Forum (C4) exists as a kind of support group for lonely right-wing students, sometimes hosting speakers from the Intercollegiate Studies Institute, the publishers of this guide.

The Columbia College Republicans currently boasts a membership of over 500. Columbia has not had an ROTC program since 1969.

Devout students will find chaplains representing most common (and many uncommon) faiths. The friendly, active, and orthodox Catholic chaplaincy sponsors the highbrow Augustine Club, which features doctrinal discussions and lectures. The school also hosts a Hillel, a chapter of Campus Crusade for Christ, an Orthodox Christian Fellowship, a Muslim Students Association, a Ba'hai and a Buddhist organization, among many others. Episcopalian students—and fans of exquisite architecture—should check out the nearby Cathedral of St. John the Divine, the largest (and perhaps the laxest) Gothic church in the world.

But don't look for spiritual guidance in the religion department. When asked whether he believed in God, chairman of the religion department and co-director of the Institute for Culture and Religious Life, Mark C. Taylor said, "Not in the traditional sense. God, or, in different terms, the divine, is the infinite creative process that is embodied in life itself. As such, the divine is the arising and passing that does not itself arise and pass away. This process is actualized in an infinite web of relations that is an emergent self-organizing network of networks extending from the natural and social to the technological and cultural dimensions of life." So at least we're clear about that.

Perhaps the only lifestyle that has not been embraced by the campus community is the athletic one. The Columbia Lions, who compete—if that is the word—in the Ivy League, are known for their record losing streaks. The urban setting of the campus does not lend itself well to intramural or varsity sports teams, and while a state-of-the-art gym is only a couple of blocks from most dormitories, the football field and other sports arenas are located some distance from campus. Defenders of the school's athletics like to point out that Lou Gehrig attended Columbia. But he did not graduate.

A great Columbia tradition is the annual Varsity Show, which has attracted some of the most storied names in American entertainment. Among the undergrads who helped write and compose the show in past years were Richard Rodgers, Lorenz Hart, Oscar Hammerstein, and Herman Wouk. Rodgers even transferred to Columbia from Juilliard expressly so he could write the show's music.

Many prospective students and their parents still worry about New York's crime rate, though it is now the safest large city in America. Says one student, "People think we're living in Harlem. It's quite safe. I feel I'm in more danger visiting friends at other schools. I went to visit a friend at Oberlin. *That* was scary." Columbia has its own security squad and the New York Police Department contributes its resources. In 2009, the school reported fourteen forcible sex offenses—more than twice the previous year—four robberies, three aggravated assaults, and forty-nine burglaries on campus.

Columbia students pay for their privileges: Tuition in 2010–11 was $41,160 and room and board was $12,160. However, admissions are need blind and the university promises to meet the full need of any student who gets in—and does so generously. Columbia, like most of its peers, recently announced broad changes to its financial aid policies in that all need-based loans became grants. Students from families with annual incomes below $60,000 do not have to pay any tuition or room and board, and families making between $60,000 and $100,000 per year "see a significant reduction" in parental contribution toward tuition. About 50 percent of students receive need-based financial aid, and the average student-loan debt of a recent graduating class was $18,420.

Cooper Union

New York, New York • www.cooper.edu

Free as air and water

The Cooper Union for the Advancement of Science and Art was founded in 1859 by entrepreneur and philanthropist Peter Cooper as a "unique educational and charitable institution" for "the advancement of science and art" in New York City. Cooper famously stated that education should be as "free as air and water" to deserving poor students "of good character." Located in a historic brownstone building in Greenwich Village, Cooper as an institution has historically had a high profile in American public life. The Great Hall was the site of Lincoln's "right makes might" speech, among other famous speeches advancing causes considered "progressive" from the Civil War period through World War I, including the women's suffrage movement and the foundation of the American Red Cross. Speakers at its podium have included several U.S. presidents and presidential candidates (most recently President Obama), Mark Twain, Henry Ward Beecher, William Jennings Bryan, W. H. Auden, and Orson Welles.

The first fact that leaps out about this venerable New York institution is that Cooper Union is free: the select few who gain admission receive full-tuition scholarships (presently valued at $140,000). This makes the school very attractive and allows it to be extremely selective—its acceptance rate is less than 10 percent (less within some disciplines), lower than many Ivy League colleges. But it's not exactly a "free ride." Cooper Union's work regimen is more demanding (some say "grueling") than almost any other in the country.

Cooper has an intense and demanding focus on its specialty disciplines, but it still shows a surprising degree of commitment to its efforts to provide a substantive liberal arts education. A highly motivated student committed to pursuing one of the fields in which it specializes should place Cooper Union at the top of his list of schools to consider.

Academic Life: The union of all the liberal arts

Cooper Union consists of the Irwin S. Chanin School of Architecture, the School of Art, and the Albert Nerken School of Engineering. Education in each of the three schools is generally described as stellar, although art students we spoke to seemed less impressed with the school than did the architecture and engineering students.

Professors have a reputation for being very engaged. They are seen often on school grounds during the weekends, and it's not unheard of for them to respond to e-mail or even phone inquiries on weekends. Professors work hard to be innovative, and they try to incorporate into the coursework the bustling and thrilling environment of New York City. Class size is generally capped at around thirty (classes never hold more than thirty-nine students), often yielding a family atmosphere. Frequent collaborative projects and generous studio workspaces tend to forge close friendships and lasting relationships among classmates.

The engineering school offers a five-years master's program and bachelor's degrees in chemical, civil, electrical, and mechanical engineering, as well as interdisciplinary engineering. Interdisciplinary areas of study include environmental and energy resources engineering, systems and computer engineering, bioengineering, and ocean and aerospace engineering. Students are required to declare a field of study before entering the program, although they may change majors within engineering with faculty approval (and a 3.0 GPA).

The architecture bachelor's program (which boasts a five-to-one student-faculty ratio) takes at least five years to complete—and frequently longer. The architectural school styles itself a liberal arts institution of sorts:

> The philosophical foundation of the school is committed to the complex symbiotic relationships of education, research, theory, practice, and a broad spectrum of creative endeavors relevant to significant architectural development. . . . Fundamental to the school is the maintenance of a long-established creative environment where freedom of thought and intuitive exploration are given a place to flourish, where the intangible chemistry of personal and public interactions stimulate an intensity of purpose and dedication, where the gifted mind and spirit can seek the means of expression and the mastery of form, and where a sense of the vast and joyous realm of creation can reveal an unending path for gratifying human endeavor.

Indeed, the student body includes quite a few Renaissance men and women; you're likely to find them using their free time studying esoteric Asian martial arts or discussing philosophy over chess.

The art school offers a generalist curriculum that covers all of the fine arts and promotes an integrated perspective. The school's literature states that "students are taught to

VITAL STATISTICS

Religious affiliation: *none*
Total enrollment: *1,000*
Total undergraduates: *50*
SAT/ACT midranges: CR: *620–710*, M: *640–780*; ACT: *27–31*
Applicants: *3,055*
Applicants accepted: *9%*
Applicants accepted who enrolled: *73%*
Tuition and fees: *tuition is free, but there is a mandatory fee of $1,650 per year*
Room and board: *$14,000*
Freshman retention rate: *93%*
Graduation rate: *64% (4 yrs.), 85% (6 yrs.)*
Courses with fewer than 20 students: *68%*
Student-faculty ratio: *9:1*
Courses taught by graduate students: *none*
Most popular majors: *engineering, fine arts, architecture*
Students living on campus: *16%*
Guaranteed housing for 4 years? *no*
Students in fraternities: *10%* in sororities: *5%*

become socially aware, creative practitioners, and historically grounded, perceptive, and critical analysts of the world of contemporary communications, art, and the culture at large." More than two-thirds of a student's class time is spent in studio courses. The art school's facilities include painting studios, sculpture and print-making shops, photography studios and darkrooms, and film and video facilities.

Instead of departments such as English or political science, Cooper has a single "faculty of humanities and social sciences." The department requires a set of core liberal arts classes for each student regardless of school, a program that was enacted in the late 1990s. The core humanities courses in the first year are devoted to language and literature; in the second year, the core covers history and political science in the "making of the modern world." Freedom to pursue humanities electives is generally limited to the third and fourth years. Although classes required for one's major are guaranteed, lines for enrollment in choice electives can start in the wee hours of the morning.

All the bachelor's programs in the engineering school and architecture school require a minimum of eight classes in the humanities and social sciences (including the four classes in the core program). Art students must complete nine liberal arts classes plus three art history courses.

If you compare the books assigned in the four required Cooper humanities classes with those typically assigned in classes at Harvard and Yale, you might find that some courses at Cooper are more substantive. Introductory courses include works by Plato, Aristotle, and Descartes, along with such texts as Aristophanes' plays, *Jane Eyre*, or the writings of John Stuart Mill. There is additional reading of classics and short stories in the second year. One student reports studying a full array of selections from Enlightenment and modern Western philosophers. A freshman says he has already read Hesiod, *The Odyssey, The Aeneid, Medea, Inferno*, and Shakespeare. Even so, one Cooper faculty member we spoke with said that these classes show "a serious decline [of late]. . . . The Western Humanities classes are genuinely respectful, but they're not taught with the seriousness that they once were."

That said, it isn't only the "core" classes that look to meaningful texts. In the sophomore year's survey of the roots of geopolitical modernity students work their way through the actual writings of Marx, Lenin, Mussolini, and Hitler. The most recent catalogue includes a class on morals featuring Hume, Descartes, and Kant, and a class on poetry covering Virgil, Horace, Lessing, and Keats. Fred Siegel's class on American Radicalism includes not only leftists such as C. Wright Mills and Herbert Marcuse but also thinkers like Dorothy Day, Lewis Mumford, and the founders of the neoconservative movement.

With an impressive commitment to respected texts, Cooper Union struggles constantly to balance a thorough humanities education with the heavy demands of students' technical fields of study. One engineering student complains, "We do interesting stuff in the humanities classes, but, with all we have to do in engineering, I sometimes wonder if we have the time to think through all the stuff we're given."

Consequently, the administration now seems to be evaluating just how much students can handle. Still, the school struggles mightily to make humanities courses more engaging, to keep the interest of students tempted to complain that they didn't come to Cooper to study the Great Books. As a professor comments, "Teaching is taken seriously at Cooper, and it's a serious factor in tenure decisions—and the teaching load is about right." The school's administration wins praise for being "pretty bureaucracy free."

Distinguished humanities professors include the widely published political writer Fred Siegel and the film critic James Hoberman. In art history, classicist Mary Stieber is highly respected and popular. Peter Buckley's and Brian Swann's classes in English literature are also recommended. (The humanities faculty, while excellent, is small—like the school itself.)

Despite Cooper's relative seriousness about Western thought in its core curriculum, New Left critical theory and ideology do have some sway at the school. There is a class offered in "Gender Studies" and a course titled "Women and Men: Power and Politics." But even these left-leaning courses seem to have some intellectual depth: a class on environmental literature includes the writing of Wordsworth and Thoreau; the "Literature, Gender, the Body" course (although incorporating "feminist, gender and queer theory") examines the works of Bronte, Hemingway, Wilde, and Woolf. A class on "Love in Western Art and Literature," despite "specific attention to the body, gender, and identity," begins with Plato's *Symposium*, and surveys Shakespeare, Keats, Shelley, Austen, and Derrida.

Other electives currently offered include worthy classes such as "American Foreign Policy," "Russian Art, Architecture and Literature," "The 'Genius' of the Baroque," "Leonardo, Scientist and Engineer," "History of the Book," and "Macroeconomics."

Student Life: Cooped up

A graduate of Cooper's engineering school says that students here "are known for having very little social life due to the demanding curriculum, which is designed to give the students a master's level of coursework in their field by graduation." This graduate says that most social activities at Cooper "center around the standard nerd celebrations: science fiction, video gaming, study groups, and the like." Students admit that their reputation of eccentricity is not entirely unfair. Indeed, they tend to revel in it (still, any jokes about pocket protectors might make you unpopular). The current predominance of hipsters and yuppies in the once-Bohemian East Village has made bars and markets a bit pricey. However, for those who can get away from the study carrels, the environs of the school are almost unparalleled for live music, quirky bookstores, and countless reasonably priced restaurants of every possible variety. Within a ten-minute walk you can find affordable Afghan food, Tibetan clothes, live jazz and blues, herbal medicines, Ukrainian crafts, or Belgian beer served to the tune of Gregorian chant at a student hangout called Burp Castle.

Although Cooper is right in the heart of New York and all its attractions, some students say they hardly notice because of the heavy workload. Some insist that only about a fourth of students have a really active social life. On the bright side, this means that drugs are fairly unpopular on campus. It's said that those who do drugs don't last long, and one can hardly imagine how they could, given the rigorous study demands. Put simply, as a professor says, "Students work very hard."

The driven nature of most Cooper Union students is evidenced by the types of clubs they develop. From Anastylosis club, which appears to be devoted, somehow, to "printed matter as a democratic multiple," to the Web Design Team, Engineers for a Sustainable World, or Students Promoting the Idea of Neurodiversity, student activities at Cooper differ greatly from the typical university's offerings. However, even engineers have a lighter side: students can also join the Ice Cream Club, Pro Musica, New York City Experience, Gospel

---

ACADEMIC REQUIREMENTS

Although it is mainly a studio arts and technical school, Cooper Union gives its students an abbreviated core curriculum and solid distribution requirements that put most liberal arts schools to shame. In addition to the demanding requirements of their major, art students must take the following:

- "Literary Forms and Expressions," a literature course concentrating on poetry and drama.
- "Texts and Contexts: Old Worlds and New," a study of texts and topics from 1500 to 1800.
- "The Making of Modern Society."
- "The Modern Context: Figures and Topics."
- One science elective.
- Four courses of electives chosen from among courses in art history, foreign languages, history of architecture, humanities, social sciences, and sciences.

On top of their heavy load of science and mathematics courses, architecture students must take:

- "Literary Forms and Expressions."
- "Texts and Contexts: Old Worlds and New."
- "The Making of Modern Society."
- "The Modern Context: Figures and Topics."
- At least nine classes in general studies, chosen from electives in humanities and social sciences, visual arts, mathematics and sciences, and languages.

In addition to their demanding math and science curriculum, engineering students must take:

- "Literary Forms and Expressions."
- "Texts and Contexts: Old Worlds and New."
- "The Making of Modern Society."
- "The Modern Context: Figures and Topics."
- Four courses in general studies selected from art history, foreign language, humanities, or social sciences.

Band, 16–86: The Experimental Performance Club, Cooper Dramatic Society, or one of the school's two fraternities or single sorority.

A number of professional and honor societies are available, from the American Chemical Society to the Societies of Hispanic, Black, or Women Engineers. Sports clubs include an outdoors club, several dancing clubs, martial arts, running, triathlon, roller hockey, and yes, knitting.

Ethnic cultural groups hold popular events: Hillel, the Jewish student association, is quite active, and the South Asia society is also popular, especially its Diwali (Indian New Year) celebration. Surprisingly, there is a large Campus Crusade for Christ organization at Cooper. Beyond this group, the environment is quite secular. However, New York is replete with busy houses of worship. A devout student will find synagogues and Protestant churches of every denomination within walking distance; the nearby New York University is said to have a very active and worthwhile Catholic chaplaincy. A magnificent Ukrainian Catholic cathedral stands right across the street from Cooper's main building, offering reverent liturgies in an exotic tongue.

> **GREEN LIGHT**
>
> What political activism exists at Cooper Union tends to lean left. The campus newspaper has featured pieces fiercely denouncing the war in Iraq as a corporate enrichment conspiracy, and the university's main hall is directly across the street from the offices of far-left alternative newspaper the *Village Voice*. A fringe Left element can sometimes assert itself, but not much more than in most contemporary urban college settings.
>
> However, students at Cooper tend to be weighed down with the rigor and volume of their studies, and what free time they have, they devote to recreational activities. Weighty conversation and divisive debates might send this group of driven young adults over the edge. Partisan groups have arisen but not taken root at Cooper Union, and while most conservative students gravitate toward the engineering school, no one interviewed reported feeling any sense of oppressive political correctness, among faculty or fellow students.

Dorm housing is apartment-style with three-, four-, and five-person apartments, but only freshmen are guaranteed dorm space. The administration frequently worries about how to mitigate the stress of transition to second year by making more housing available, but there simply isn't space. Currently almost all sophomores from out of town are cast out to fend for themselves in New York's very pricey and sparse rental market. Students also complain that Cooper's facilities are old and dirty, and sometimes regret the lack of amenities such as a gym. Nevertheless, there are both intercollegiate and intramural sports, with five intercollegiate men's and women's teams (basketball, tennis, cross-country, soccer, and volleyball), and many intramural coed teams and clubs. Cooper's teams are fairly good given the lack of both facilities and funding for sports—the tagline on the athletics web page is "No gym, no courts, no fields, no pool, no horses, no time . . . no excuses." For the noncompetitive, a quite cheap, surprisingly good New York City gym, the Asser Levy Recreation Center, is a long walk or short bus ride away at 14th Street and Avenue D, featuring weight machines, exercise classes, and a well-kept pool.

Believe it or not, New York City is one of the safest metropolises in the country, and Cooper Union has an impressive campus security record: from 2005–2010, two burglaries and four instances of vandalism were reported to campus security. Most disciplinary problems involve liquor law violations (between two and thirty-two per year). Of course, since most students live off campus, Cooper Union undergrads face the typical dangers that attend urban existence.

The school is an amazing educational bargain for those who can get it. In accordance with the wishes of its founder—a son of the working class who wished to share his self-made wealth—the school offers a free tuition scholarship to anyone admitted. First-year housing on campus costs approximately $14,000, while local rents thereafter can be pricey, and students are responsible for fees, books, general living expenses, and health insurance. The school does offer financial aid to help students with that expense, and the typical Cooper Union graduate completes school with less than $7,000 in debt.

Cornell University

Ithaca, New York • www.cornell.edu

Hybrid vigor

In 1865 Quaker philanthropist Ezra Cornell wrote, "I would found an institution where any person can find instruction in any study." This he did by endowing several colleges as integral parts of New York's land-grant university, which was then named for him. Today, Cornell is a unique and successful public-private partnership in American higher education. Students from New York majoring in technical subjects can receive an Ivy League education at a state university price, although for students of the liberal arts, and for all out-of-state students, tuition is close to the market rate for elite colleges.

Cornell places heavy emphasis on research; the university stands in the top fifteen institutions nationwide in research spending (over half a billion dollars a year), with 55 percent of that from federal grants and contracts. Its endowment is around $4 billion, and twenty-eight Rhodes scholars and more than forty Nobel Prize winners have spent time as students or faculty at this school in remote upstate New York.

Liberal arts and social science students are a distinct minority on campus. Other undergraduates outnumber Arts and Sciences students two to one—and in Arts and Sciences, the hard sciences have pride of place. Three decades of student protest and administrative capitulation weakened the morale of the undergraduate liberal arts—inspiring the revulsion of neoconservative Allan Bloom, who left Cornell for the University of Chicago. There he meditated on his Cornell experience and wrote *The Closing of the American Mind*.

But with science trumping the humanities and the applied sciences ruling all, campus politics have had less importance for Cornell than they would at most places. With so many good classes, professors, and programs, the university offers the chance for a stellar undergraduate experience. However, if you are a political or social conservative in the liberal arts, sources on campus suggest you prepare either to practice discretion or face conflict with intolerant fellow students.

Academic Life: Seven colleges, no waiting

Undergraduate Cornell is divided into seven colleges: the College of Agriculture and Life Sciences; the College of Architecture, Art, and Planning; the College of Engineering; the School of Hotel Administration; the College of Human Ecology; the School of Industrial and

VITAL STATISTICS

Religious affiliation: *none*
Total enrollment: *20,633*
Total undergraduates: *13,931*
SAT/ACT midranges: CR:
  630–730, M: *660–770*;
  ACT: *29–33*
Applicants: *34,371*
Applicants accepted: *22%*
Applicants accepted who
  enrolled: *78%*
Tuition and fees: *$39,666*
Room and board: *$12,650*
Freshman retention rate:
  96%
Graduation rate: *85% (4 yrs.),
  92% (6 yrs.)*
Courses with fewer than 20
  students: *56%*
Student-faculty ratio: *9:1*
Courses taught by graduate
  students: *not provided*
Most popular majors: *engi-
  neering, business/market-
  ing, agriculture*
Students living on campus:
  56%
Guaranteed housing for 4
  years? *no*
Students in fraternities: *32%*
  in sororities: *23%*

Labor Relations; and the College of Arts and Sciences. There are also six graduate and professional schools. In a rare kind of partnership, three of the colleges—Agriculture and Life Sciences, Industrial and Labor Relations, and Human Ecology—are sponsored by the state of New York. The rest are private colleges whose funds come from Cornell. The College of Arts and Sciences is the subject of this profile, although several of the others are well regarded—especially Engineering, Architecture, and Hotel Administration. If a student's interests lean toward life science or human ecology, he can qualify for the economical land-grant tuition rate.

Within the College of Arts and Sciences, one will find thirty-nine departments in the humanities, the arts, basic sciences, and social sciences, offering forty-two majors and serving 4,100 undergraduates (out of some 13,931 students on campus). One will, however, not find a core curriculum. Students must fulfill a set of distribution requirements, but no courses are required by name—a fact of which the university boasts, but which led one faculty member to call Cornell's requirements "meaningless and arbitrary."

There is one worthy vestige of the old curricular ideal that students share a base of knowledge: The entire freshman class reads a common book before arriving on campus—just one, and not always one of the Great Books. The class of 2014 will read Philip K. Dick's *Do Androids Dream of Electric Sheep?* and discuss the work in small groups at orientation, in freshman writing seminars, and at other events. Depending on the book, screenings of film adaptations (in this case, *Blade Runner*) or a speech by the author may be included in the reading project.

The two required freshman writing seminars, with just fifteen to twenty students per section, draw the most praise. The university offers a hundred choices, "so whatever your interest, you'll find a cool class," says a student. "You will become a better writer by default. You'll be writing papers on a regular basis." Classes range from the bizarre ("Cigarette Cultures") to the traditional ("Greek Myth"), thoughtful ("Philosophical Problems: Relativism"), and ridiculous ("Lesbians, Transmen, and Bears, Oh My! Masculinities in the Margins").

Since the distribution courses and electives (which include four physical and biological science classes and five courses from four different humanities disciplines) can come from any undergraduate college, there are literally a thousand options at a student's disposal. The trick is whether a student can put together a coherent program of study that addresses fundamental intellectual skills and areas of knowledge—much less one that provides a grasp of Western civilization. The university itself has not taken on this responsibility, and given the insularity of its technologists and the trendy leftism of its humanists, that may be just as well.

There are indeed thousands of solid courses at Cornell, and a remarkably small number of frivolous ones. What is more, many of the latter do not fulfill requirements. The school's faculty is top-notch and devoted to teaching. "Many of the faculty are widely renowned in their fields, have published the authoritative works, are heads of international institutions, and have done groundbreaking research. And these are the people teaching the intro courses to freshmen," a student says. "The best professors are the ones teaching the freshmen," says another. That may be because many faculty members who teach upper-level courses are more involved in research and publishing than they are in teaching. It is publications, not teaching skills, according to a full professor, that are given almost exclusive consideration in decisions regarding tenure.

Fortunately, it is very rare for a graduate teaching assistant to be the sole instructor of a class, and students say that the TAs who deliver the occasional lecture and supervise section discussions are first-rate. Those sectional meetings can be important in survey courses that enroll up to 500 students. Cornell has one course, "Psychology 101," which, according to the school's website, is the world's largest lecture at 1,600 students and two TAs, with dozens of tutors to lead smaller groups.

With such an amazing proliferation of course choices, students clearly need guidance. Students select their own faculty academic advisors from their major departments. However, warns one undergrad, advisors vary in quality. "They can be great or completely ignorant, depending on the person. Do not trust your advisor with your academic career. Seek multiple sources of advice and information." The university has a Peer Advisor Program that pairs upperclassmen with new students. Advice includes "anything from campus resources to social life to dining options," according to the campus paper, the *Daily Sun*. The university also has a strong and well-advertised Career Office for both academic and career counseling.

Students say that some courses are hard to get into—such as the infamous and wildly popular wine appreciation course offered by the School of Hotel Management, which is infamous not for its subject matter but because it is the toughest, most frequently failed course at Cornell, according to a student. However, with persistence even the most popular courses usually become available at some point.

SUGGESTED CORE

1. Classics 2601/2612, The Greek Experience/The Roman Experience (closest matches)
2. Philosophy 2200, Ancient Philosophy
3. Religious Studies 2724/2629, Introduction to the Hebrew Bible/New Testament Seminar
4. Religious Studies 3150, Medieval Philosophy
5. Government 2605, Social and Political Philosophy or German Studies 4150, Marx, Freud, Nietzsche
6. English 2270/3270, Shakespeare
7. History 1530, Introduction to American History
8. History 3340, Nineteenth-Century European Culture and Intellectual History or Philosophy 2220, Modern Philosophy

Many departments have outstanding teachers, and most Cornell faculty members are committed to undergraduate instruction and are available during office hours. The students whom we interviewed praised the following teachers: Isaac Kramnick, Theodore J. Lowi, and Elizabeth Sanders in government; John Najemy and Richard Polenberg in history; Gail Fine in philosophy and Patricia Carden in Russian literature. A hotel school student also mentions Bill Carroll in microeconomics, noting that "Not only does Professor Carroll present his curriculum in a clear and concise way, but he makes sure the students have fun learning, going as far to hand out $20 bills to students in class during the lecture on Game Theory." Mark McCarthy's "Micro-Computing" was "voted by seniors the most practical course" while the law class taught by David Sherwyn (academic director of the Center for Hospitality Research) is said to be "a ton of fun" with his stories of his days as a trial lawyer. He causes his students "never look at a situation without thinking of the legal repercussions ever again."

Cornell has some academically weak and polemical departments, including Africana studies and feminist, gender, and sexuality studies. Unfortunately, even the economics department is somewhat politicized. "There used to be a greater mix of political views," one longtime professor told the *Cornell American,* a conservative campus journal. "There was more interest in political debate. . . . Debate was more fun, and you got more out of it."

One worthy initiative at Cornell we can't resist mentioning: the Small Farms Program, designed to help New York family farmers stay in business. It publishes a journal, *Small Farms Quarterly,* which should interest agrarian-minded students. Also of note is the Cornell Lab of Ornithology. While the lab does not award academic degrees, it is dedicated to research, education, conservation, and "citizen science" focused on birds throughout North America and the world. The lab hosts about 55,000 visitors per year and includes an audio collection of over 165,000 animal sounds—the largest such collection in the world.

Cornell students can study abroad literally anywhere in the world, so long as their advisor and college approves it. Students have recently traveled to places as diverse as South Africa, Senegal, Israel, China, and Argentina, and students are not limited to academic institutions: programs may include field study, research, service work, an internship, or some combination thereof. About 500 students travel to forty different countries each year, mostly as juniors, to study or work for a semester or two.

For those who prefer to stay on American soil, over sixty foreign languages are taught, from the traditional French and Italian to Cantonese, Czech, or Nepali. Cornell offers six Southeast Asian languages and intensive summer programs in languages like Arabic, Swahili, American Sign Language, or Greek. The school's FALCON program provides full-time language study in Chinese or Japanese, giving students three years' worth of instruction in a single year. Language courses often go hand-in-hand with majors in departments like China and Asia-Pacific studies, Near Eastern Studies, Russian Literature, and of course, French, German, Italian, or Spanish.

Student Life: Home to Ithaca

The winter weather is lousy—let's admit that up front. But students and visitors alike speak highly of the natural beauty of Ithaca, New York, and surrounding Tompkins County. The

Finger Lakes area is full of parks, waterfalls, and woods, while "Ithaca itself is a thriving small city with great opportunities, nightlife, and restaurants," a student says. "You name it, it's available." A city website claims that the area's number of restaurants per capita is nearly as great as New York City's.

The Cornell campus features a mix of traditional buildings, such as the McGraw Tower with the Cornell Chimes, and modern ones—including an art museum designed by I. M. Pei and a spectacular Center for the Theatre Arts. The lovely Sage Chapel and numerous Gothic and Victorian buildings add architectural beauty to a campus marked

ACADEMIC REQUIREMENTS

In lieu of a core curriculum, the Cornell University College of Arts and Sciences imposes certain (mostly distribution) requirements. Students must pass five courses in the humanities and social sciences, representing at least four different categories, with no more than three in the same department. The categories are:

- Cultural analysis, with classes like "Discovering Hip Hop," and "Studies in Contemporary World Fiction."
- Historical analysis, with choices including "History of Economic Analysis," and "Marriage and Sexuality in Medieval Europe."
- Knowledge, cognition, and moral reasoning. Options include "Critical Reason, The Basics: Kant, Hegel, Marx, Adorno," and "Global Thinking."
- Literature and the arts. Many courses will do, from Shakespeare seminars to "A Survey of Jazz."
- Social and behavioral analysis. Choices include "Ethnicity and Identity Politics: An Anthropological Perspective," and "Law, Science, and Public Values."

Students must also complete:

- Two first-year writing seminars.
- One foreign language course above the introductory level, or at least eleven credits in one language (usually "an introductory sequence" of classes).
- Two science classes chosen from a list including "Evolution of Human Behavior," "Physics of Musical Sound," "Why the Sky Is Blue: Aspects of the Physical World."
- One course in applied mathematics from a list including "Statistics and Research Design," "Introduction to Computer Programming," and "Game Theory."
- One further course in mathematics or science.
- One Arts and Sciences course on an area or a people other than those of the United States, Canada, or Europe, such as "Introduction to Biblical History and Archaeology" or "African Cinema."
- One course on an historical period before the twentieth century, such as "Roman Social History," or "Introduction to Western Civilization."
- Four to five electives not used to fulfill other requirements and not in the major field.
- A swimming test and two single-credit, nonacademic courses in physical education.

Mid-Atlantic

by buildings thrown up when the student body doubled in size after the G.I. Bill. A 3,600-acre preserve and botanical garden, Cornell Plantations, adds natural beauty, and Cayuga Lake is visible from the campus, which is bordered by waterfalls. A new physical sciences building is under construction. The $140 million project houses eighty research and teaching labs, a 120-seat auditorium, and some of the world's most noise-free, vibration-proof labs. Plans also began in 2010 to build William H. Gates Hall to house the Departments of Computer Science and Information Science. The 100,000-square-foot building is expected to be completed in 2014.

At a university of Cornell's size, students can find plenty to fill up time outside of the classroom. Students and their primary interests run the gamut, as one would expect. "You can't label the students," one says. "I knew brains, stoners, athletes, artists, well-rounded and balanced students, drug addicts, alcoholics—they were all in the mix. On the whole, however, most students practiced the 'work hard, play hard' motto at Cornell. During the week, they studied, and then on the weekend they partied."

Cornell's Big Red athletes compete on thirty-four sports teams—sixteen for each sex—at the NCAA Division I level with an unofficial bear mascot. Students who are not varsity material can play sports through the largest intramural program in the Ivy League, with more than thirty leagues and tournaments to choose from.

Student organizations skew to social or cultural themes; more than two dozen chaplaincies on campus support Jewish, Protestant, Catholic, Muslim, Buddhist, and Hindu students. Religious services include Chabad, Humanist and Unitarian Universalist, African-American Worship, Quakers, Mormons, Chinese and Korean Christian Churches, Campus Crusade, Navigators, and InterVarsity Christian Fellowship, along with mainline and evangelical Protestant services and Catholic Masses.

With about 33 registered student organizations (and 240 organizations in all), Cornell students have ample opportunities to get involved. Political groups include College Democrats and Republicans, as well as Asian Pacific Americans for Action, the *Cornell Progressive Paper*, the Islamic Alliance for Justice, Amnesty International, La Asociacion Latina, Students Acting for Gender Equality, or International Students for Social Equality.

Arts and sciences and cultural clubs include a Chinese Music Ensemble, Afghan Women's Advocacy Group, Celtic Club, Akido Club, Society of Women Engineers, HealthNutS, Karaoke Club, Film Club, French Society, the Melodramatics Theatre Company, Origami Club, Q (the LGBTQ and Ally Magazine), Association for Students of Color, Sustainability Hub, Japanese Animation Society, On Tap Dance Troupe, and Quiz Bowl Club.

Fifty-four different organizations offer recreational activities from Marching Band to Track and Field to Israeli Dance or the Whistling Shrimp Improv Comedy Troupe. Numerous organizations exist for honors societies and areas of study—engineering, hotel, law, vet school, and so on—and a number of departments and organizations offer publications and journals. Best known is the *Daily Sun*, whose staff has included E. B. White, Dick Schaap, Kurt Vonnegut Jr., and Frank Gannett. The *Sun* became the first collegiate member of the Associated Press in 1912.

Campus activities are varied at Cornell, but one of the most popular is Slope Day. Slope Day is a massive party held on a campus hill called Libe Slope on the last day of classes. Another beloved tradition is the offering of free hockey tickets to freshmen; upperclassmen brag about camping out overnight for hockey tickets.

A good way to experience the natural surroundings of the college is through Cornell Outdoor Education, a group that sponsors backpacking and kayaking trips and maintains "the largest indoor natural rock climbing wall in North America," according to its Web page. With over 25 percent of the student body pledged, the Greek system is "the center of the social scene on campus," says the *Daily Sun*. According to a student, however, "there is a huge underground drug culture that pervades the Greek system."

The student body is a mixture of different types, but "the majority is rich white kids from Long Island and New York and the rest of the Northeast. . . . Most people are very competitive, ambitious, driven, and have connections from their parents. Most are well off and many went to private school before Cornell," says a student. University statistics show that about 40 percent of undergrads hail from New York state, while some 8 percent are foreign students.

The university guarantees housing only for students' first two years (all freshmen live on campus). Undergraduates choose their housing from dormitories, program houses, cooperative programs, and fraternities and sororities. Most "freshmen stay in North Campus [housing], which has brand-new dorms and the best food in the nation," a student says. Freshmen can choose program houses, so long as they are on North Campus. The *Daily Sun* reports that students housed in some of the older dorms are petitioning for renovation, citing poor heating, unsanitary bathrooms, and bedbugs among the list of complaints.

Ethnic options include the black activist Ujamaa Residential College, Latino Living Center, Multicultural Living Learning Unit, or Akwe:kon American Indian hall; other less politicized sites include the Risley Residential College for the Creative and Performing

YELLOW LIGHT

Although students and faculty do seem to lean left, as is commonplace in a university setting, a healthy conservative movement continues to flourish at Cornell. Perhaps because of this, the left at Cornell tends to display the hysterical stridency of a besieged minority.

The long-embattled *Cornell Review* (the conservative student newspaper founded by, among others, Ann Coulter '84) is a frequent source of conflict. In repeated incidents, papers have been stolen, dumped, or burned. In recent years, the paper has come under fire for publishing an article criticizing self-segregation in racially-themed houses and a piece satirizing radical Muslims in the U.K. (the latter was written by an American Muslim). Calling the articles "offensive, ignorant, and . . . full of hate," the Student Assembly proposed a resolution to disaffiliate the paper with the university. Ironically, the purported goal of the Student Assembly is to promote the university's commitment to "a more diverse and inclusive campus."

In 2008, the Cornell Coalition for Life (CCFL) was forced to remove a pro-life display featuring photographs of a developing fetus. The group had received prior permission to put up the light-hearted posters, and was later allowed to replace the signs, but staff members first attempted to hide the signs. The university maintains that the posters were only removed pending verification that the display was authorized.

Arts—a lovely old building with its own small stage, gallery, rehearsal space, art studios, and a darkroom and video editing facility—Ecology House, Just About Music house, Holland International Living Center, or Language House Program. Residence halls are usually coed, but the university has a few single-sex dorms, even for those not in fraternities. There are no coed bathrooms or dorm rooms in residence halls, although dormitories do not have restricted visiting hours. "We're not a Christian school and this isn't the 1950s," a student says. "General rules of respect and order are enforced by the Resident Advisor, but it depends on the RA. Some might not care about drinking or drugs in the dorm, some might."

The university received a score of 4.5 (out of 5) on Campus Pride's "LGBT-Friendly Campus Climate Index" which rates schools on their policies regarding lesbian, gay, bisexual and transgender issues. Cornell has also made efforts to become more environmentally friendly and was one of 200 university systems to sign the President's Climate Commitment, pledging to reduce greenhouse-gas emission and develop a plan to become climate-neutral.

Those who live at Cornell consider the campus quite safe. In 2009, eighteen burglaries, four forcible sex offenses, and one aggravated assault were reported. The university's Blue Light program has 86 outdoor phones (and 275 indoor phones) for emergency purposes. Escorts are available to accompany students or visitors around campus.

Cornell's tuition system is unique. For a narrow range of students—those hailing from New York State, who wish to study in the Colleges of Agriculture and Life Sciences, Human Ecology, or Industrial and Labor Relations—tuition was only $23,526. For all others, tuition was a more standard $39,666. Standard (double) room and traditional board run $12,650 for everyone, with books, supplies, and expenses estimated at $2,360 for most students, with artists and architects needing more. Admission is need blind, and the school promises to meet the full need of admitted students; it provides need-based aid to some 46 percent of students. However, Cornell has the smallest endowment and largest student body of all the Ivies. In 2009, the university announced a plan to eliminate parental contributions for students from families earning under $60,000 per year, and capping annual loans at $7,500 annually for students from families with incomes above $120,000. Still, the student-loan debt of a recent graduate is $21,549.

Fordham University

Bronx, New York • www.fordham.edu

Jesuits at their best

Founded as St. John's College in 1841 by Bishop (later Archbishop) "Dagger" John Hughes, who built St. Patrick's Cathedral, Fordham was the first Catholic college in the region. Since then, it has gained a distinguished academic reputation—first, as the college of choice for graduates of New York's parochial schools, and now as a top institution of American Catholic education.

Fordham University has an idyllic campus in the Bronx, another in the Westchester suburbs, and a third at Lincoln Center. A shuttle bus regularly runs from one campus to another, and students are free to choose classes from any of the three campuses. The school now serves about 14,500 students (just over half are undergraduates) offering nearly fifty majors. More than most Jesuit colleges, it has stayed connected to its liberal arts mission and Catholic identity—making it a worthy option for ambitious, hard-working students. Fordham's academic culture is one of mutual respect. Even though many at Fordham regard ethnic and sexual "diversity" as a value in itself, liberal tolerance also extends to philosophical differences and grants traditionalists a place at the table.

Academic Life: Dig for the treasures

Fordham's curriculum displays both breadth and rigor. Students describe the core classes as thorough and demanding. One undergraduate says, "I think Fordham has a great liberal arts education. . . . It is one of our strengths." Another says that the core "was the best part" of college life at Fordham. However, one student warns that because some course offerings have thematic titles, "teachers can teach almost anything," neglecting essential primary texts in some instances. A note of caution: Fordham's core is under revision as this guide goes to press. We hope it stays strong.

Fordham's honors program is highly competitive; each year only about twenty-five students at Rose Hill and sixteen at Lincoln Center get in. Participation fulfills the university's core requirements—and goes significantly beyond them. Students are required to take eighteen specific courses: during their first semester, they must take an "Ancient Literature" class which examines "the Greek, Roman, and biblical texts which have played a central role in the definition of the Western tradition," and similar classes in ancient phi-

VITAL STATISTICS

Religious affiliation: *Roman Catholic*
Total enrollment: *14,544*
Total undergraduates: *7,950*
SAT/ACT midranges: CR: *570–670*, M: *570–670*; ACT: *26–30*
Applicants: *24,557*
Applicants accepted: *50%*
Applicants accepted who enrolled: *15%*
Tuition and fees: *$37,545*
Room and board: *$14,491*
Freshman retention rate: *90%*
Graduation rate: *75% (4 yrs.), 79% (6 yrs.)*
Courses with fewer than 20 students: *50%*
Student-faculty ratio: *13:1*
Courses taught by graduate students: *not provided*
Most popular majors: *business administration, communications, psychology*
Students living on campus: *52%*
Guaranteed housing for 4 years? *no*
Students in fraternities or sororities: *none*

losophy, ancient history, in classical art, as well as honors mathematics. During their second semester, students take classes in medieval literature and art, philosophy, and history; in their sophomore year, students move on to similar courses in the early modern, then the contemporary period. Juniors take a religion and an ethics class, while seniors write an honors thesis research project in their major field. This program is the single best option at Fordham.

One professor observes that the history, English, theology, and philosophy programs require introductory courses "that center directly on Western intellectual and cultural life." Of all the departments, philosophy garners the most praise for its emphasis on the great traditions of Christian thought. A good number of Jesuits teach here, infusing courses with their classical formation from extensive studies for the priesthood. Philosophy professors most often praised include Michael Baur, Christopher Cullen, S.J., and Joseph Koterski, S.J. The department is home to the American Catholic Philosophy Association, the Society for Medieval Logic and Metaphysics, and the Fordham Philosophical Society. According to one philosophy graduate student, "My conservative political views put me in the minority. But for the most part I've found that others are respectful and willing to have rational discussions."

Right-leaning students are less positive about the political science department. One major says that she keeps a low profile as a conservative. Another undergraduate says that the stated views of his political science professors actually caused him to switch his major to history. On the other hand, poli sci can boast several highly recommended teachers; one of them is William Baumgarth (who also teaches classics). Baumgarth is the editor of the book *Aquinas: On Law, Morality, and Politics.* Students must take "Introduction to Politics" as well an intermediate or advanced class from three of the four subfields: American politics, political theory, international politics, or comparative politics. Additionally, Fordham requires an upper-level seminar and five intermediate or advanced electives.

History majors must take "Understanding Historical Change" (an upper-level seminar), four upper-level electives, and one advanced course each from medieval, European, American, and African/Asian/Latin American/Middle East history. "Historical Change" classes cover ancient Greece or Rome, medieval history, and early modern Europe, among others. While a history student could graduate from Fordham without any significant encounter with American history, Fordham is particularly strong in ancient and European history, and offers an impressive breadth of innovative and fascinating courses. One conservative student in the department states that although he has not found philosophical allies there, his views are respected. The department teaches history as an academic subject, not as a pretext for activism. Highly recommended professors in history include Paul Cimbala, Richard Gyug, and Michael Latham.

Fordham's English department offers both a solid curriculum and reasonable electives. Majors must take three courses from selections that cover English literature up to 1800, including ample offerings in Chaucer, Shakespeare, Milton, and other greats. Among more contemporary courses one finds electives like "American Catholic Women Writers."

The Fordham theology department is a mixed bag. One student notes that the required theology courses are often taught as world religion classes. Among other core requirements, all students must take two theology classes, the first in "faith and critical reason," and the second a course in "sacred texts and traditions" such as the Jewish scriptures, the Christian New Testament, the Qur'an, and *The Divine Comedy.*

Four theology professors are also on staff at the medieval studies center, a first-rate option for intellectually curious students. Comprised of faculty from many departments, it offers undergraduate BA, graduate MA, and PhD programs.

> **SUGGESTED CORE**
>
> The school's required core curriculum, previously excellent, was under revision at this writing and could not be assessed. If the new core does not suffice, the following courses are recommended:
>
> 1. Classical Civilization 2000, Texts and Contexts: Myth in Greco-Roman Literature (closest match)
> 2. Philosophy 3501, Ancient Philosophy
> 3. Theology 3100/3200, Introduction to the Old Testament/Introduction to the New Testament
> 4. Theology 3330, Medieval Theology Texts
> 5. Political Science 2403, Modern Political Thought
> 6. English 3206, Shakespeare
> 7. History 3775, The Early Republic
> 8. History 4575, Seminar: History and Theory

Fordham's Catholic identity is still moderately strong, students feel. As one undergraduate says, "The school is a very Catholic place if you want it to be." One student, who entered the philosophy department in order to strengthen his faith and "go deeper into the thought of St. Thomas Aquinas," reports that his aspirations were "well supported" at Fordham. Another philosophy student says that "there are tremendous Catholic intellectuals at Fordham and an undergraduate can get an excellent Catholic education if he or she takes the right professors." He says that the priests he has met at Fordham are scholars "making something of philosophical ideas rather than cataloguing them."

The university as a whole, however, does not always live up to this ideal. One student says: "I don't think that the university makes enough of an effort to give a defensible account of the Faith. I rarely find a Fordham undergrad who can give me an intelligent explanation for why the Church holds its moral positions." One Jesuit faculty member, proud of the job Fordham does in liberal arts education, concedes that it could go further in giving such an "account of the Faith."

Fordham is neither as overtly secularized as rival Jesuit colleges Holy Cross or Georgetown, nor as deeply committed to Catholic restoration as, say, Ave Maria University. But given all the resources and opportunities that the campus affords, one graduate student asserts that the "proactive undergraduate *can* get a good grounding in the Catholic tradition" at Fordham.

Thanks to the wide connections of the Jesuit order with missionaries around the world, Fordham offers extensive opportunities for study and travel abroad. Fordham maintains Global Outreach programs in the English-speaking World, and in Africa, Asia, Europe, and Latin America. Fordham also maintains an MBA program in Beijing with Peking University and has a new affiliation with Heythrop College in London. The Fordham University London Center provides semester-long study-abroad programs in theater and business. Fordham offers an impressive list of programs in fifteen African countries (Ghana, Morocco, and South Africa, to name a few) and twenty-two European lands (from Wales to Hungary and Sweden to Italy). Students can also elect to study in the Far East (with nine offerings, including Thailand, India, and Mongolia) or one of seven countries in the Middle East (Israel, Tunisia, and Turkey, for example). Australia, Fiji, Indonesia, New Zealand, and Samoa all have approved programs, as do sixteen Latin American nations, like Peru, Costa Rica, and the Dominican Republic.

One of Fordham's most distinctive options is the International Honors Program, which takes students around the world following a theme. Recent programs included "Cities in the Twenty-First Century," which began in New York and traveled on either to China, India, and Argentina or to Brazil, South Africa, and Vietnam.

Foreign language options on campus include Ancient Greek, Latin, Spanish, Russian, Portuguese, Chinese, Japanese, Italian, German, French, and Arabic.

Student Life: Roses in the Bronx

Fordham's eighty-five-acre Bronx campus offers a gracious retreat from New York City's hectic pace. Its Gothic stone architecture, towering shade trees and expansive central lawn all contribute to the atmosphere of an oasis. The Campus Ministry office advertises pastoral events, retreats, Mass schedules, and a weekly Bible study group that has a small but committed core of twenty to thirty attendees. The campus chapel, which seats 500, is always full for the Sunday evening Mass. "I think our religious community is vibrant and growing every day," a student says. Another observes that "both the numerous Masses and the more numerous service opportunities provided by the campus ministry are very well attended." Students are known for their ongoing work with various projects sponsored by the Jesuit Volunteer Corps.

Fordham is hardly shy about assisting campus Catholics who wish to nourish their lives with regular Mass attendance, faith-based social activity, and opportunities for service and leadership.

There is a full-time Protestant chaplain on the staff of the Campus Ministry, as well as priests and lay members. Connections to local Protestant, Eastern Orthodox, Jewish, Islamic, Buddhist, and Hindu congregations can all be made through the office. Students in search of more traditional Catholic worship should investigate the Latin Mass at Our Lady of Mount Carmel Church in the Bronx.

An active chapter of Respect for Life pursues a program both to raise consciousness about the sanctity of human life and alternatives to abortion. Together with the Jesuit seminarians of Ciszek Hall, the Respect for Life group networks with other New York clergy and laity to distribute information on adoption and pregnancy shelters near abortion clinics in the area.

Fordham does have a party culture. Students "are serious about having a good time, but are also here for academics," says a student, while another counters that "the student body is overly focused on partying."

ACADEMIC REQUIREMENTS

Fordham's admirable core curriculum is currently under revision. As of press time, students must complete:

- A required composition/rhetoric class and a critical reading class, plus an elective chosen from one of the following topics (reading lists may change from year to year): "Literature and Society," "Poetry and Poetics," "History and the Novel," "Tragedy and Comedy," "Traditions of Story-Telling," and "Chaucer, Shakespeare, and Milton."
- "Philosophy of Human Nature" and "Philosophical Ethics."
- Two courses in theology. Options range from "Old Testament" to "Sacred Books of the East."
- Two courses in history: "The West from the Enlightenment to the Present" and an elective covering modern American, ancient, medieval, Latin American, Asian, African, or Middle Eastern history.
- Either "Finite Mathematics" or "Structures of Computer Science."
- Two courses in natural science with lab components, such as "Introductory Biology" I and II or "Mind, Brain, and Behavior."
- Two social science classes, chosen from a wide range of disciplines, such as anthropology, communications, economics, political science, psychology, or sociology.
- One fine arts course.
- Language courses sufficient to demonstrate "advanced" mastery of a foreign language (a lower standard of fluency is required of BS candidates).
- One "Senior Seminar in Values and Moral Choices," chosen from a changing variety of courses offered mostly by the theology and philosophy departments.

Students at Fordham College's main Rose Hill campus must also complete:

- A freshman seminar, which functions as "a community-building intro to college work."
- One course designated as "Global Studies," which covers "the significant variations in customs, institutions and world views that have shaped peoples and their lives." Options here include "Chinese Philosophy" and "Medieval Traveler."
- One course in "American Pluralism," dealing with "diversity" issues.

GREEN LIGHT

Fordham is admirably eager to protect the rights of its students to assemble, publish, and speak. The student handbook clearly states, "Each member of the University has a right to freely express his or her positions and to work for their acceptance whether he/she assents to or dissents from existing situations in the University or society." Many of the prohibitions Fordham enforces seem reasonable and in keeping with the "dignity of the human person": no ads for alcohol, tobacco, reproductive services, sexual services, or hate groups are permitted in student publications. Restrictions on speech are mainly common-sense laws of behavior: "grossly obscene or grossly offensive" speech is restricted and sexual harassment is defined more objectively than is typical as "pervasive, offensive or abusive . . . interfering with an individual's work or educational performance."

While culture-war conflicts play out at Fordham (for example, students petitioning the university to rescind an honor granted to a pro-abortion justice and struggles over whether the PRIDE Alliance student group should be permitted to continue meeting) the university's recent decision to extend same-sex benefits to faculty partners has disappointed a great number of Catholics. This decision, which mirrors the policies of Jesuit colleges nationwide, is incompatible with irreformable Catholic doctrine.

Despite the fault lines that run through the school and mark it as distinctly a modern Jesuit (rather than a traditional Catholic) college, it seems a place where students of faith, with conservative views about society, can gain a first-rate education in an atmosphere of free debate and intellectual rigor.

The curfew for visits from members of the opposite sex is a surprisingly late 3:30 AM. Most dorms are coed, with single sex floors or wings (and hence single-sex bathrooms). Upperclassmen may live in university-owned apartments off campus, such as those in the Little Italy neighborhood nearby.

Some residential halls provide programs to weave together the campus community, such as Bagel Brunch, Chick Flick Monday, faculty-led discussions, or weekly Meditation and Prayer. One hall, the Queen's Court, holds a regular community dinner and evening meetings. Participants take turns practicing public speaking and debate. One Jesuit faculty resident notes that the students who shine in such sessions typically emerge as leaders in other campus activities and later in their chosen careers. Debates often extend beyond the sessions and continue later over pizza, producing truly challenging discussions and lifelong friendships.

Student athletes will find a strong program featuring a wide range of varsity sports: baseball, men's and women's basketball, football, golf, rowing, men's and women's soccer, softball, squash, men's and women's swimming, men's and women's tennis, men's and women's cross-country, men's and women's indoor (and outdoor) track and field, volleyball, water polo, and cheerleading. Football is the school's most prominent sport; Fordham was Vince Lombardi's alma mater.

Fordham offers a number of club sports as well, from crew, hockey, and sailing to Ultimate Frisbee, rugby, and tae kwon do. Intramural leagues include flag football, soccer, basketball, dodgeball, volleyball, and softball.

The Campus Activities Board offers social and cultural activities for Fordham students. The CAB brings speakers, musicians, and comedy acts to campus. Peer educators promote student health through education about alcohol abuse and drugs. Three student government associations regulate the student body and advise the administration, oversee policy and programming for Rose Hill students, and govern the residence halls.

Other student activities range widely, from a campus chapter of Amnesty International to a Young Republicans club, including an extensive array of ethnic and culturally based and preprofessional organizations. There are over one hundred student organizations, including Respect for Life, Pershing Rifles, Mock Trial, Hellenic Society, Ignatian Society, PRIDE Alliance (for gay students), and numerous academic, political, performance, and music organizations.

Students staff an award-winning, NPR-affiliated radio station, WFUV, and the Fordham Nightly News program, and two undergraduate papers (one published at Rose Hill, the other at Lincoln Center), the *Ram* and the *Fordham Observer*. Other student publications include literary magazines the *Ampersand*, the *Vagabond*, and the *Kosmos*, while *the paper* is Rose Hill's alternative newspaper. Students also publish a law review, business journal, bilingual newspaper (the *Dimelo*), and produce The Liberty Forum, a conservative media outlet consisting of a magazine, blog, and TV show.

Crime is not a major issue on Fordham's Rose Hill campus. In 2009, the school reported one forcible sex offense, thirty-five burglaries, and three aggravated assaults. The school's security department provides twenty-four-hour protection at each campus, and works closely with local police departments. A late-night shuttle bus runs to and from the Rose Hill campus, and security phones dot the environs of the school.

Fordham's price tag is on the high end for private colleges, with 2010–11 tuition running $37,545. Room and board average at $14,491. According to the most recent data, 88 percent of undergraduates received institutional aid or scholarships averaging around $11,000. About three-quarters of students received grants or loans. The average cumulative indebtedness for degree recipients in 2009 was $37,184.

Georgetown University

Washington, D.C. • www.georgetown.edu

Ignatius wept

Georgetown University is one of the most prestigious American universities, certainly the best-known school founded by Catholics. In its clamber to the top, Georgetown has had to shed many attributes as excess baggage—including most of the characteristics of a Catholic school. The religion on which the school was founded in that ill-starred year, 1789, now lives on there as a kind of ghost that is rumored to haunt the premises. Whether that spirit may someday once again take flesh—or more likely, be exorcised by some helpful Jesuit—is the question facing the leaders of the college.

Today the university has a national and even international flavor, with approximately 7,553 full-time undergraduates (and another 9,318 graduate students) from across the country and around the world. It is still, formally, a Jesuit, Catholic institution. Its website states that in 2011 there were fifty-nine members of the Jesuit community active in the school, with thirty-nine of those holding positions as professors or administrators.

But the university has proved schizophrenic in its treatment of Catholic morality: Georgetown properly denied a pro-choice student group official recognition. On the other hand, Georgetown is so proud of its former professor the pro-abortion congressman Rev. Robert Drinan that the school has an endowed chair in its law school in Drinan's name. While the medical school's hospital does not perform abortions, it is reported to have done research with embryonic stem cells. According to a September 2010 feature in the left-leaning *Georgetown Voice*, when Hoya professor Joseph Palacios, an openly gay priest, cofounded an organization favoring the legalization of gay marriage, the Cardinal Newman Society criticized Palacios. The rector of Georgetown's Jesuit community was swift in his response—an attack on the Cardinal Newman Society. Likewise, when American bishops condemned Notre Dame University for conferring an honorary degree on President Obama in 2009, Georgetown responded by hosting the president on its campus—covering up Catholic images at his request. Georgetown University here showed once again its unseemly eagerness to render unto Caesar the things that are God's.

Academic Life: Philosophy yes, theology no

Georgetown University has seven academic divisions: three graduate and professional schools (law, medicine, and arts and sciences) and four undergraduate schools (Georgetown College, the liberal arts and sciences division; the Edmund A. Walsh School of Foreign Service; the McDonough School of Business; and the School of Nursing and Health Studies). There is also a School of Continuing Studies for summer students and adults. Within Georgetown College, there are over thirty major programs—ranging from philosophy and classics to an interdisciplinary major in women and gender studies—and forty minor programs.

Georgetown College is the largest undergraduate division. To satisfy the college's general education requirements, students must take at least two courses each in the humanities and writing, history, philosophy, theology, science and mathematics, and the social sciences, and must also demonstrate "mastery of a foreign language through the intermediate level," according to the undergraduate bulletin.

The College has no core curriculum or Great Books program, and although serious courses are offered in most of Georgetown College's distribution areas, there are notable deficiencies in some of the freshman courses. A professor notes, for example, that the "Introductory American Government" course "has been cut to one semester and few faculty have the comprehensive knowledge of the system to do a good job." Similarly, "history has no one to teach a comprehensive course in Western Civ." On the other hand, says one teacher, "With guidance a student can get a good traditional liberal arts education, but guidance is essential." For instance, students can fulfill their philosophy requirement through "Aquinas on the Mind"—or "Philosophy of *Star Trek*." There is some talk about adding a class on diversity as part of the general education requirements, but this most likely won't happen until after the university completes its reaccreditation process.

Both history and government are among the most outstanding departments (and popular majors) at the university, according to both faculty and students. "We get a lot of the best people in these fields because they want to be in D.C.," says a faculty member. "Obviously, you have to choose carefully, but there are some superb instructors."

Government majors take ten courses overall in the department, including four introductory courses such as "International Relations," "U.S. Political Systems," "Elements of

VITAL STATISTICS

Religious affiliation: *Roman Catholic*
Total enrollment: *16,871*
Total undergraduates: *7,553*
SAT/ACT midranges: CR: *640–740*, M: *650–750*; ACT: *26–32*
Applicants: *18,616*
Applicants accepted: *20%*
Applicants accepted who enrolled: *42%*
Tuition and fees: *$39,768*
Room and board: *$12,240*
Freshman retention rate: *96%*
Graduation rate: *85% (4 yrs.), 93% (6 yrs.)*
Courses with fewer than 20 students: *61%*
Student-faculty ratio: *10:1*
Courses taught by graduate students: *not provided*
Most popular majors: *international relations, finance, political science*
Students living on campus: *70%*
Guaranteed housing for 4 years? *no*
Students in fraternities or sororities: *none*

The Liberal Arts Seminars 001 through 006 in the Interdisciplinary Studies Program is an eighteen-credit series of courses which suffice for a somewhat abbreviated core.

Political Theory," and "Comparative Political Systems." The department is notable both for the quality of its faculty in general and for the surprising number of conservative scholars: George Carey, Patrick Deneen, and James Schall, S.J., qualify as among the best in both categories. Anthony Arend and Michael Bailey are some of the other star government faculty.

Students who wish to major in history are given a wide array of classes from which to choose to fulfill the eleven-class requirement. Three classes must cover any part of Africa, the Middle East, Latin America, or Asia, and three classes must cover Russia, Europe, or North America. In history, Roger Chickering, David Collins, S.J., and Jo Ann Moran-Cruz are among the better teachers.

The most outstanding resource that Georgetown students should explore is the Tocqueville Forum on the Roots of American Democracy, whose purpose is to highlight "the two main roots of American democracy, Western political philosophy and the biblical and Christian religious tradition." Its founding director, Professor Patrick Deneen, is a leading scholar in classical political theory and a popular cultural commentator. The forum offers lectures and conferences featuring first-rate authorities ranging from Andrew Bacevich to Patrick Fagan, and also serves as a meeting place for many of the most thoughtful students on campus.

Conversely, students should be wary of the school's Saudi-funded courses on Islam and the Middle East, which tend to sugarcoat the aggressiveness and intolerance of Islam, and paint Christians, Americans, and Israelis as perennial villains.

The university has had a long record of bringing in "star" faculty who are out of office but who have previously served in high-ranking government posts. The latest to follow this path, which was most famously trod in the past by Henry Kissinger, is former Clinton secretary of state Madeleine Albright. However, Albright's class in international relations gets mostly low marks, with students accusing her of having fallen into her "anec-dotage."

Philosophy is another highly respected department with praise liberally offered for its classes in bioethics. Well-regarded philosophy faculty include Mark Murphy and Alfonso Gomez-Lobo. There are rigorous requirements for philosophy majors, including mandatory four-credit courses in "Ancient and Medieval Philosophy" and "History of Modern Philosophy," plus at least one four-credit "Text Seminar" (involving intensive study of selected parts of a key text, for example John Locke's "Essay Concerning Human Understanding") and one course in logic by the end of the student's junior year.

In the English department, majors take a combination of courses with at least one Gateway Course, which features intensive writing. Beyond the gen ed requirements and the Gateway courses, students need to take only take seven additional upper-level English classes. As with much of the education at Georgetown, students *can* select a good curriculum that includes courses on masters such as Shakespeare, but such classes are not required. Students instead may pick options such as "Transnational Modernism." The department's philosophical tenor can be seen from its interdisciplinary programs such as "Women and

Gender Studies," "Programs on Peace and Justice," and the "Lannan Center for Poetics and Social Practice." English professor Paul Betz (emeritus), an expert on Wordsworth, gets plaudits from students; undergrads call him "exceptional," "inspiring," and "modest, a fine guy and a good teacher."

Scandalously, one of the weakest departments at Georgetown, as reported by students and faculty alike, is theology, which "is not exactly doctrinal—or logical," says one student. The student adds, "It's not just that they're not clearly Catholic. You really haven't a clue if they're even Christian." This department recently began offering a PhD in "religious pluralism." Nor can any student escape exposure to this department, given the general education requirement that students take two courses in theology—one of which must be either "Introduction to Biblical Literature" or "The Problem of God." These courses vary greatly "depending on which prof you get," reports a student. Two theology teachers are noted by students and professors alike as standouts in the department: Rev. Thomas King and Rev. Steven Fields. King is "beloved" by devout students and is said to be very funny as well.

As is the case with most top-tier universities, Georgetown has come to place a high premium on research at the expense of teaching. Instructional quality varies widely, since tenure decisions rarely place emphasis on teaching skill. On the positive side, faculty report that they're not overworked: Despite its immense size and the presence of quite a few huge lecture classes, the school is well-staffed. Including adjuncts, the school has approximately 1,400 faculty members, and the student-to-faculty ratio is a strong 10 to 1. Hence, even most intro classes are generally taught by regular faculty. Most grading is done by TAs, and current students will oftentimes give tips on which TAs to avoid.

Like many other prestigious college and universities, Georgetown attracts a fair share of students who are more interested in credentials and career prospects than in the life of the mind. (President Clinton is an alumnus.) "An impressive number of the kids come here for our name, and are thinking about law school from the day they arrive," says one professor. Another professor notes that some students are "superior, but most could be a lot more curious."

Many students participate in study-abroad programs. Georgetown offers opportunities to study in Argentina, Australia, Austria, Brazil, Chile, China, Dominican Republic, Ecuador, Egypt, England, France, Germany, Hungary, Ireland, Israel, Italy, Ivory Coast, Japan, Mexico, the Netherlands, Poland, Russia, Scotland, Senegal, Spain, Switzerland, and Taiwan.

Foreign language courses are plentiful and rigorous at Georgetown. Majors are offered in Arabic, Chinese, classics (both Ancient Greek and Latin), French, German, Italian, Japanese, Portuguese, Russian, and Spanish. Minors are offered in most of those languages and in modern Greek and Hebrew. Courses in Turkish, Polish, Korean, Ukrainian, and Persian are also offered. Perhaps more importantly, an unusual number of the school's best-regarded faculty teach these classes. The Spanish department in particular receives positive response from students.

Student Life: Top of the world

Georgetown University is located on a hilltop standing above the Potomac River in the historic Georgetown neighborhood in Washington, D.C., proper. A graceful blend of neo-

Gothic and Georgian architecture predominates on campus, though some modernist buildings—including the main Lauinger Library—are eyesores. Thirteen U.S. presidents have spoken from the steps of the oldest building on campus, Old North Hall. The Royden B. Davis, S.J., Performing Arts Center provides "a site for interdisciplinary performance exchange for the extended Georgetown community" and features a 300-seat theater. Work is under way on new sports facilities and a business school.

Approximately 70 percent of undergraduates live in campus residential halls or in nearby university-owned apartments and townhouses. All freshmen and sophomores are required to live on campus. Life in the Georgetown neighborhood, with its attractive architecture and many restaurants (many offering half-priced food and drinks on certain days to Hoyas) and shops, is one of the attractions of campus life. Housing for underclassmen tends not to be a problem. Residence halls are all coed, with some female-only floors. (The undergraduate student body is 55 percent female.)

Georgetown's main campus is about two miles from the White House and four miles from the Capitol. On a moderately clear day, the Washington Monument is visible from higher elevations on campus and the nearby Key Bridge. There is no Washington, D.C., Metro stop within the immediate Georgetown vicinity, but university shuttles provide

---

ACADEMIC REQUIREMENTS

Students enrolled in Georgetown College must meet the following general education requirements:

- Two courses in the humanities and writing, of which one course must qualify as an Intensive Writing Seminar; courses that meet this criterion include "Virtuous Hero: Medieval Poetry" and "Russian Realism." The other course must be "an introduction to a humanities discipline other than philosophy, theology, and history, taught in English, with a writing component." Courses that qualify include "Writing About Performing Arts" and "East Asia: Texts and Contexts."
- Two courses in history, such as "Intro Early History," and Intro Late History." Students may test out.
- One course in general philosophy (such as "Intro to Philosophy" or "I and the Other") and one course in ethics (such as "Intro to Ethics" or "Political and Social Thought").
- Two courses in theology, one of which must be either "The Problem of God" or "Introduction to Biblical Literature." Any intermediate-level theology class, such as "Womanist Theology" or "Intro to Catholic Theology," can satisfy the second requirement.
- Two courses in mathematics or science, such as "Ecology and the Environment" and "Computer Graphics" or "The Quantum World Around Us" and "Mathematics in Society."
- All students majoring in subjects other than biology, biochemistry, chemistry, or physics (BS) must take two courses in either anthropology, government, economics, linguistics, psychology, or sociology.
- Students must demonstrate proficiency through the intermediate level in a foreign language.

students with access to the Rosslyn stop, otherwise a twenty-minute walk away, and the Dupont Circle stop. For nightlife, students frequent Georgetown itself, the fashionable Dupont Circle neighborhood, and above all the Adams Morgan district, which is replete with music bars, cafes, and delightful ethnic restaurants—including several fine Ethiopian bistros and Brazilian coffee houses. Popular campus bars include the Tombs, Third Edition, Chadwick's, and the Rhino Bar and Pumphouse. Most bars are said to be either a long walk or a short cab trip from campus—which given D.C.'s still-high crime rate is a real drawback.

Masses are held daily at Dahlgren Chapel of the Sacred Heart, although more conservative students travel to Old St. Mary's church in Chinatown or St. Matthew's Cathedral. St. William's Chapel in Copley Hall is the site of Protestant services. Protestants compose about a fifth of Georgetown's student body; Catholics account for approximately half. The university also has Jewish and Muslim chaplains and student organizations. Jewish students are said to represent about 6 percent of the total undergraduate student body, while Muslims comprise around 2 percent.

Georgetown University does not recognize or allow on campus any fraternities or sororities other than service organizations. Indeed, according to the student affairs policy, the university has a ban on "secret societies: groups that do not disclose their purpose, membership or activities, or whose purpose, membership or activities are discriminatory." As a vestige of its character as a religious school, all student groups fall under the Office of Campus Ministry. Because of the absence of frats, the most popular on-campus nightlife events are dorm parties. As the *Georgetown Voice* reports: "Upperclassmen throw everything from 'Guido Bros and Jersey Hos'

YELLOW LIGHT

Except for the indifferentism and heterodoxy that predominates in the theology department and the detours into servile multiculturalism that dominate Islamic studies (the department is funded by a hard-line Islamist Saudi prince), sociology, and women's studies, classrooms at Georgetown are mostly free of overt politicization. "In general this is not a problem, to my knowledge," notes one longtime professor, who also says, "On the whole, I don't detect any disparagement of Western civilization, or our system of government or society in general." Political debate on campus "is free but not vigorous—there is a standard liberal slant," notes a professor, who continues, "My feeling is that this comes more from the students themselves than is imposed from above."

Conservatives on campus tend more toward philosophical discussions than activism, as the (liberal) *Georgetown Voice* reported in September 2010, noting that "even though conservatism at Georgetown has increased its campus presence within the past year—official recognition was granted last year for two new conservative groups, Hoyas for Liberty and Georgetown University Republican Women—conservatives at Georgetown, and the disparate clubs and organizations that represent them, have not adopted the populist energy, tone, and activist tendencies of the Tea Party movement. . . . Unlike some of the more progressive groups at Georgetown, whose members are seemingly unabashed in their willingness to demonstrate and hold rallies . . . conservative students at Georgetown tend to avoid direct action in favor of dialogue and discussion."

ragers to post–basketball game bashes. There's also a spirit of inclusiveness you don't get at Greek schools."

For all the lure of Washington, D.C., there is no shortage of activities on the Georgetown campus to keep students engaged. There are 144 official student organizations, including health and fitness clubs, ethnocultural groups (including an Armenian Students Association and Irish-American Society), performing arts groups, religious and political organizations (such as a Catholic Daughters of the Americas group and Students Against the Death Penalty), professional and academic organizations, and many more. One of the most respected student groups is the Philodemic Society, founded in 1830, which organizes weekly debates. Student publications include the major, twice-weekly campus paper, the *Georgetown Hoya*; the monthly *Georgetown Independent*; a liberal publication, the *Georgetown Voice*; the libertarian *Federalist*; and the conservative *Georgetown Academy*.

The university's sports teams are called "the Hoyas" and participate in the NCAA's Division I. Georgetown competes in the Big East Conference in most NCAA sports. Intercollegiate men's and women's sports include basketball, track and field, lacrosse, cross-country, crew, golf, sailing, soccer, tennis, and swimming. There are also women's volleyball and field hockey teams and men's football and baseball. Head coach John Thompson III, son of the legendary Georgetown coach John Thompson Jr., has brought the men's basketball team back to national prominence, reaching the NCAA Final Four in just his third season at the helm. Georgetown has produced a number of NBA players, including Patrick Ewing, Dikembe Mutombo, Alonzo Mourning, Allen Iverson, and Greg Monroe.

Serious crime is not unknown in the Georgetown neighborhood, but for the most part it is well policed and the campus is safe. The city's dangerous slums are physically remote from Georgetown's tony surroundings. In 2009, university police reported nine forcible sex offenses, three aggravated assaults, and twenty-seven burglaries. The Department of Public Safety has become very conscientious about reporting crimes and students may sign up to receive e-mail alerts of crimes in particular neighborhoods.

Annual tuition at Georgetown as of 2010–11 was $39,768, with room and board an additional $12,240. Georgetown University practices need-blind admissions and guarantees to meet demonstrated student need. Approximately 45 percent of students receive some form of scholarship or need-based financial aid. (To its credit, the school support offers Air Force, Army, and Navy ROTC programs.) However, as the school is not as well endowed as many comparably prestigious but smaller schools (its endowment is under $1 billion), its aid packages may be inferior to those of rival schools'. The average student-loan debt of a recent graduate was $25,085.

George Washington University

Washington, D.C. • www.gwu.edu

Politics in practice, if not in theory

Located in the capital's historic Foggy Bottom district (home to the U.S. State Department) and within walking distance of the White House, George Washington University is surrounded by the trappings of political power. And its students feel the attraction: opportunities abound to intern or otherwise work for various departments of the federal government, the national media, and other institutions in the orbit of the Beltway. The university also draws upon the talents of innumerable foreign-policy experts, Washington press correspondents, and other denizens of the Beltway as lecturers and adjunct faculty.

The university's history dates to 1821, when Congress chartered Columbian College, which would be renamed the George Washington University in 1904. Today it has over 25,000 graduate and undergraduate students in nine schools, the largest of which is the Columbian College of Arts and Sciences.

Steven Knapp, university president since 2007, is a scholar of eighteenth- and nineteenth-century English literature, and his administration has helped keep GWU a solid place where a good liberal arts education is available (particularly for students who seek it out, for instance in the school's worthy honors program) in a relatively apolitical environment.

Academic Life: Doing, not thinking

Beside Columbian College, GWU includes the School of Medicine and Health Sciences, the Law School, the School of Engineering and Applied Science, the Graduate School of Education and Human Development, the School of Business, the School of Public Health and Health Services, the College of Professional Studies, and the Elliott School of International Affairs. Unsurprisingly, given the university's location, political science and international affairs are the most popular and prestigious majors at George Washington. "Most poli sci professors at GW are adjuncts," says one student, noting the preponderance of public-policy experts drawn from outside the school.

There is no core curriculum for the university's 10,558 undergraduates, and course requirements vary from school to school. One knowledgeable professor says that the school's requirements are "in theory, not bad. However, in reality, the students find ways

VITAL STATISTICS

Religious affiliation: *none*
Total enrollment: *25,061*
Total undergraduates: *10,558*
SAT/ACT midranges: CR: *600–690*, M: *600–690*; ACT: *27–30*
Applicants: *19,842*
Applicants accepted: *37%*
Applicants accepted who enrolled: *36%*
Tuition and fees: *$41,242*
Room and board: *$12,680*
Freshman retention rate: *91%*
Graduation rate: *76% (4 yrs.), 81% (6 yrs.)*
Courses with fewer than 20 students: *56%*
Student-faculty ratio: *13:1*
Courses taught by graduate students: *2%*
Most popular majors: *social sciences, business/marketing, psychology*
Students living on campus: *67%*
Guaranteed housing for 4 years? *no*
Students in fraternities: *23%* in sororities: *23%*

to overweight their programs with 'social sciences,' and downplay anything smacking of literature and traditional history."

Some students concur: "GW isn't a university that really awakens people to intellectual life. Students come here for practical experience—internships on the Hill, work on campaigns—not so much for deeper, intellectual stimulation," one says.

Not all GW students are pure pragmatists, of course. Says a teacher: "I have encountered a large minority of truly curious students. Every semester I find at least one student who is a real seeker after truth. I've been able to pass on a number to excellent PhD programs."

English majors take ten courses with five of them covering works written from the seventh century through the nineteenth century. However, most professors specialize in psychoanalytical, feminist, queer, or sociopolitical theories and approach a variety of genres with these views in mind. One professor described his recent work as focusing on "'violent male bodies' in sixteenth-century prose, Shakespeare and modern film." Recently, the department has reinstated a requirement to complete a course in minority literature or post-colonialism. A GWU graduate majoring in English student will certainly be better versed in minority literature than in Shakespeare, the study of whose work is an option but not a requirement. English majors may dual major in Creative Writing with several professors who are well-published poets.

Political science at GWU is among the top departments in the country. Majors must take ten courses, with requirements including courses on American government, international politics, law and organizations, research methods, and political thought—plus six courses in social sciences and at least two in economics or history. While not required, there are several opportunities for important internships on Capitol Hill, in the White House and with embassies, among others. Qualified students may complete a BA/MA program in only five years.

The history department appears to have thin requirements for coursework, but it provides many internship and research opportunities. Three required courses cover vast time periods (like "European History in its World Context 1715 to the present"), and students may test out of these with AP courses or SAT subject tests. Beyond the introductory courses, students must take only one pre-1750 course and then two courses that cover each geographical area: United States, Europe, and a third group that includes the rest of the world.

Mid-Atlantic

However, research opportunities are unparalleled, with partnerships at the Folgers Research Library, First Federal Congress Project, National Security Archives and others. Reactivated in 2008, the Phi Alpha Theta national history society is very active and offers students another opportunity to connect with other historians, which easily translates into academic and career opportunities.

The university offers several outstanding departments and individual faculty members. "The language teaching in Japanese is superb," says one professor; there is "none better in the whole country, under the leadership of Professor Shoko Hamano." Professor of Chinese Jonathan Chaves, a noted authority on Chinese and Japanese poetry, is another exemplary faculty member in the well-regarded East Asian languages and literatures department. The Slavic and Germanic program has a similarly high reputation. In the sciences, a professor notes, "physics is strong; it brings in a good deal of grant funding for research, and appears entirely unpoliticized."

In history, one notable professor is department chairman Tyler Anbinder, who has staunchly fought grade inflation. One student also hails Anbinder as "the only professor who has ever really criticized my writing thoroughly and made me a better writer." The department also boasts Robert Emmet Kennedy, whose course readings in European intellectual history one student characterizes as, "Phenomenal. In addition to Hegel, Comte, Marx, Nietzsche, Freud, and Darwin, Professor Kennedy balances the reading by requiring students to read Bonald and de Maistre at the beginning and then C. S. Lewis and Solzhenitsyn at the end."

The honors program is a particularly rich option that allows students to take classes with limited enrollment (fewer than twenty students) and interact with professors both inside and outside the classroom in social and academic settings. Best is the Proseminar, which provides "a firm grounding in the Western tradition," according to a student, though he warns that many later courses in honors "offer typical modern multicultural" fare. Other honors offerings include "classes on just war theory (taught by an Eastern Orthodox priest) as well as an English course on C. S. Lewis and J. R. R. Tolkien."

A professor gives high marks to the university's special "Dean's Seminars," which are "limited to first-semester freshmen and capped at [twenty] students, to provide new students with an opportunity to study with senior faculty."

Adjunct faculty, of which George Washington has a higher proportion than most other universities, are "a benefit when the professors are State Department officials teaching about foreign policy or an Associated Press editor teaching a journalism course," says a student. However, "too frequently these adjunct professors are underpaid and uncommitted."

Full-time faculty members show a devotion to students. "Professors are very acces-

---

SUGGESTED CORE

1. Classical Studies 2107: Greek and Roman Drama
2. Philosophy 111, History of Ancient Philosophy
3. Religion 9/10, Bible: Hebrew Scriptures/Bible: New Testament
4. Religion 143/144, Christianity in the Ancient World/ Medieval Faith and Symbolism
5. Political Science 106, Major Issues of Western Political Thought
6. English 128, Shakespeare
7. History 71, Introduction to American History
8. History 124, European Intellectual History

sible and helpful," says one student. "I must say this school places admirable emphasis on teaching," a professor remarks, contrasting George Washington to schools where most of the energy is spent on publishing.

Ideological politics hold little sway in the classroom. Most professors "have a generally leftist tilt," reports one faculty member, "though conservative voices are more likely to gain a decent hearing and that is one of our strengths." While English and the social sciences have experienced some politicization—as evidenced by courses with titles like "Working-Class Texts and Class-Conscious Performance" and "Homeless Chic? Poverty, Privilege, and Identity in Contemporary American Democracy"—a student notes that "professors usually leave their politics at the door."

Exceptions are not unheard of. One student relates that she was consistently graded down by a teaching assistant for expressing the "wrong" political views. Students also report episodes in which adjunct faculty made left-wing political events mandatory class activities.

George Washington University offers abundant study-abroad opportunities to fit almost every student need and circumstance, which is why over 1,400 students a take take advantage of them annually. GWU offers many locations for international experiences, including schools in Albania, Ecuador, Argentina, Costa Rica, Chile, Czech Republic, Thailand, Taiwan, Australia, Belgium, Botswana, Cyprus, South Africa, Spain, Denmark, Austria, Romania, Ghana, Morocco, Kenya, Senegal, Madagascar, Mali, Vietnam, Mongolia, Singapore, Nepal, Netherlands, Slovakia, Tunisia, Brazil, China, India, Italy, Ireland, Turkey, Greece, Portugal, Israel, England, Poland, and France. Some locations require foreign language study, in languages such as Arabic, Chinese, French, German, Ancient Greek, Hebrew, Italian, Japanese, Korean, Latin, Russian, and Spanish. However, for the student wishing to learn a language without harming his GPA, a student run organization offers free classes in over twenty languages in any given semester.

Student Life: The little campus that couldn't

George Washington University's main campus occupies more than a hundred buildings—including thirty-five residence halls—on a forty-three-acre parcel of land in the Foggy Bottom neighborhood of northwest Washington, D.C. Many of the dormitories were once apartment buildings or hotels. This means that the GW complex feels like no campus at all. "Our campus is the city really," a student says. "We have office buildings next to academic buildings." However, the school has made efforts to address this problem by creating a vast number of choices for student housing, including "House Life," which allows a student to remain with its same housemates throughout their four years of school.

Says one student, "The joy of GW isn't as much the school as it is the location. . . . There are just so many opportunities that you wouldn't have anywhere else. I can see the White House from the front porch of my sorority house." The nearby Foggy Bottom/GWU Metro stop on the Orange and Blue lines of the capital's Metro rail service provides students with ready access to the rest of the city and nearby Virginia and Maryland suburbs.

Many of the school's traditions are, like its buildings and campus life, blended into or dependent upon the wider Washington scene. The school's commencement ceremonies take place on the National Mall, for example.

One part of the campus stands apart from the surrounding community and the rest of GW—albeit for all the wrong reasons. Thurston Hall, which houses nearly half of the university's freshman population, "has a bad reputation for sexual promiscuity," in one professor's words. A student puts it more bluntly: "It's nasty. That place is a cesspool of disease!"

All GW dormitories but one (an all-female dorm) are coed. Dorm units—all suites, except for the women-only dorm—are single sex, as are the bathrooms. (At least in theory.) Dorms are said to range from the quiet to the raucous. One student wrote of them in an online forum: "Dorms are noisy, and often smell (of various things I won't mention). You'll hear/see plenty of drunk people stumbling in at all hours. You'll probably want to go to the library to study."

While much of the social life of GW students (who are known as Colonials) is assimilated into Washington, D.C., the university does boast a variety of student organizations—almost 380, ranging from ethnic clubs to sporting and fitness organizations (Aikido GWU, GW Club Baseball) and academic and professional groups (the Society of Physics Students, the Spanish Club). Campus media and publications include the WRGW radio station, a twice-weekly student newspaper, the *GW Hatchet*—as well as a "conservative and libertarian" paper, the *GW Patriot*—and a handful of literary journals, such as the biannual *G.W.*

ACADEMIC REQUIREMENTS

In lieu of a real core curriculum, students enrolled in GW's Columbian College of Arts and Sciences must complete classes in seven categories:

- Three writing-intensive courses, including the mandatory "University Writing" freshman course and two courses designated as "Writing in the Discipline." Such courses include "Songs About Something Other Than Love: Music as Social Commentary" and "The Israeli-Palestinian Conflict"
- Two classes in mathematics, logic, or statistics. Examples include "Finite Math: Social and Management Sciences" and "Single Variable Calculus" I.
- Three courses, with laboratories, in the natural sciences in at least two groups. Courses meeting this requirement include "Our Place in Nature" and "Minerology."
- Two courses in the social and behavioral sciences, such as "Game Theory" or "Sex Industry."
- One course in the creative and performing arts, such as "Shakespearian Washington" or "Electronic and Computer Music."
- Four courses in the humanities. Courses that count toward this requirement include "War and Diplomacy in Antiquity" and "Freud, Shakespeare, and Dostoyevsky."
- Two courses in a language other than English or (unfortunately) "in aspects of foreign, non-English speaking cultures." Examples range from "Beginning Latin" to "German Women Writers of the Nineteenth and Twentieth Centuries."

GREEN LIGHT

With classrooms marked overall by fairness and the apolitical, balanced discussion of course materials by professors who leave their personal views unstated, most of the hostility faced by conservatives on campus comes from fellow students. One incident involved a member of the GWU College Democrats desecrating crosses used in a prolife display. The student involved was disciplined. The second incident occurred when the Young America's Foundation (YAF) was in the early weeks of planning a "Beware of Islamo-Fascism Week." Seven students posted bigoted, anti-Muslim posters pretending to advertise the YAF event, which led to YAF members being accused of intolerance. When the posters were revealed to be a hoax, the perpetrators were fined.

Overall, the campus seems to make room for a wide variety of views. A student notes that religious organizations particularly shine: They constitute "one of the most impressive and unexpected things about GW," he says.

Review and the online *Mortar and Pestle.* The university has twenty-two sports teams and is a member of the NCAA Atlantic 10 Conference. Many GW students—who are broadly described as "ambitious"—use their free time working at unpaid internships at D.C. think-tanks or on Capitol Hill, trying to launch careers in public policy.

The university has thirty-one national fraternities and sororities, in which almost a fourth of students participate. The groups engage in a wide range of community volunteer activities, and are said to be not particularly cliquish. Most Greek parties are fairly easy for nonmembers to attend. Given the sheer variety of night-time activities available in Washington, D.C., and the large number of students from other schools (Georgetown, Catholic U., American U.) who throng the city's nightspots, fraternity and sorority life doesn't dominate campus socializing. Still, students report that rushing one of the school's fraternities or sororities is a good way to find a network of friends.

Political groups on campus embrace both sides of the spectrum. Leftist groups include Allied in Pride (gay), the College Democrats, Feminist Majority Leadership Alliance, National Organization for Women, Progressive Student Union, Roosevelt Institute, and Students for Justice in Palestine. Rightist organizations include the College Republicans, Colonials for Life, Liberty Society, and Students for a Free Cuba. In 2011, The Princeton Review ranked GW fourth for "Politically Active Students."

There is a wide variety of religious ministries and clubs on campus, including the Agape Campus Christian Fellowship, Buddha Nature, the Canterbury Club (Episcopal), Catholic Daughters of the Americas, the Knights of Columbus, Taizé, Intervarsity Christian Fellowship, the Jewish Student Association, First Year Students at Hillel, the Muslim Students Association, the Newman Catholic Student Center, the Protestant Campus Ministry Association, Raaja Yoga, and the Sikh Students' Association.

Students say they feel safe on GW's main campus and the university's smaller, bucolic Mount Vernon campus (acquired in 1999). In 2009, the school reported twelve robberies, seven aggravated assaults, eight stolen cars, three incidents of arson, seven forcible sexual offenses, and 109 burglaries.

As of the 2010–11 academic year, annual tuition at George Washington University for new students was $41,242. (GW offers fixed tuition rates for each year's incoming students for up to five years of full-time undergraduate study.) Room and board was an additional $12,680. All freshmen and sophomores are required to live on campus and housing is guaranteed for four years. GW offers a number of grants, loans, and other forms of student financial support; one-third of GW students receive need-based financial aid. The university reports that in the average debt of recent graduates was $32,547.

Grove City College

Grove City, Pennsylvania • www.gcc.edu

Faith and freedom

Founded in 1876 as a Christian academy with ties to the Presbyterian Church that nonetheless would admit students "without regard to religious test or belief," Grove City College today remains a bastion of traditional, Christian liberal arts education.

Grove City is one of the most conservative colleges in the country—refusing to accept any federal funding, including federal student financial aid.

As one recent student says, Grove City College remains "a rare breed of Christian college that seems to be nearing extinction in America. It upholds a Christian worldview and champions Western civilization."

Former First Lady Laura Bush headlined the 2011 Commencement ceremony and kicked off Grove City Matters: A Campaign to Advance Grove City College, a $90 million capital campaign, the largest in Grove City's history.

Academic Life: Heritage

Grove City's humanities core curriculum is required of all students in both its School of Arts and Letters and its School of Science and Engineering. These six courses focus on "America's religious, political, and economic heritage of individual freedom and responsibility and their part in the development of Western civilization."

The humanities core receives mixed reviews from students. One calls it "one of the highlights. All the classes are critically respectful of our Western heritage and do a very good job." Others, however, report that "students can get through the humanities core by taking only the easy, not-very-thoughtful professors," and that "the classes only skim the surface and neglect the intense, face-to-face, soul-searching encounters of the Great Books." Furthermore, "the same intellectual standards historically associated with the liberals arts are not equally applied to engineering/science/education students." The sources used in the humanities core—in most cases, textbooks and selected excerpts, rather than the full texts of classic works—may also leave something to be desired.

Another factor is the motivation of students themselves. One recent alum reports, "I am definitely a better person for having taken the harder professors and have learned a great deal of respect not only for American institutions, but Western civilization as a whole."

He cites Professors Jason Edwards, Joshua Drake, and Gil Harp as excelling in the core program. Some professors suggest that too few students display genuine intellectual curiosity—and that too many teachers present a single perspective without examining alternatives. Academic advising is intense and hands-on at Grove City, involving professors along with career counselors and staff of the student life office. The school says that its advising program is "thoroughly Christian and evangelical in character."

Teaching, rather than research and publishing, is the emphasis of all of Grove City's departments. Students reap the benefits, and many note that professors are readily available for consultation outside of class. Faculty are generally devoted to the students and loyal to Grove City's mission. One student says, "Each professor has a unique viewpoint on life, but one thing they all share is a faith in Jesus Christ." Grove City College is overall quite politically conservative, a student says, "but there are definitely students who hold opposing points of view. The college brings in many guests and speakers who help foster an atmosphere of debate about different ideas."

Popular majors include engineering, business, and accounting—all of which, according to one professor, are highly regarded regionally and attract many potential employers for on-campus interviews. Mechanical, electrical, and computer engineering and biology/molecular biology are very popular as well. Among the best science professors are Eric Andersen in engineering, Michael Falcetta in chemistry, Christian Gribble and Dorian Yeager in computer science, and Dale McIntyre in math.

The English department is praised by students and professors alike. One major says: "My experiences with my English classes have challenged me to wrestle with fundamental questions of humanity, to develop a critical mind, and to uphold truth and virtue in my own life." Appropriately, a course in Shakespeare is required of majors (as it is not at many elite colleges). Notables in this department include Eric Potter, Janice Brown, and Collin Messer.

Political science has a strong conservative orientation, and attracts students by its reputation. One major says that the department has "a distinguished reputation and excellent track record for placing its graduates in jobs, especially at 'movement' conservative institutions in Washington." American constitutional theory is required of majors. Marvin Folkertsma, Paul Kengor, and Michael Coulter are known to be exceptional instructors.

VITAL STATISTICS

Religious affiliation: *Presbyterian*
Total enrollment: *2,530*
Total undergraduates: *2,530*
SAT/ACT midranges: CR: *560–690*, M: *570–680*; ACT: *25–30*
Applicants: *1,761*
Applicants accepted: *64%*
Applicants accepted who enrolled: *56%*
Tuition and fees: *$13,088*
Room and board: *$7,132*
Freshman retention rate: *93%*
Graduation rate: *80% (4 yrs.), 84% (6 yrs.)*
Courses with fewer than 20 students: *40%*
Student-faculty ratio: *16:1*
Courses taught by graduate students: *none*
Most popular majors: *business management/marketing, biological and life sciences, engineering*
Students living on campus: *93%*
Guaranteed housing for 4 years? *yes*
Students in fraternities: *15%* in sororities: *24%*

Students give high marks to the history department, especially professors Mark Graham, JonDavid Wyneken, Andrew Mitchell, Gil Harp, and chairman Gary Smith. Fittingly, majors must study American history before 1900. Options for concentrations include Latin American and modern Asian studies.

The economics department at Grove City also stands apart. For more than thirty-five years the department was led by Professor Hans Sennholz, a student of Ludwig von Mises—the leading exponent of the rigorously free-market "Austrian" school of economics. A strong Austrian influence is felt at Grove City to this day through professors Jeffrey Herbener (who extends hospitality to students through an "economics picnic" every summer) and Shawn Ritenour (described as "well-loved and very challenging"). However, one professor comments that economics teaching at Grove City is too "one-dimensional, and leaves economics majors ill-prepared for graduate studies in that field." Of course, one might take that as a critique of graduate economics departments.

In religion, a recent grad says, "the majority of the faculty is fantastic. The bent of the department is decidedly Reformed and evangelical. . . . The systematic theology courses that I took were presented from a broad Protestant perspective; though the professor himself is solidly Presbyterian, he gave evenhanded explanations of various positions. Ianin Duguid is an excellent teacher . . . T. David Gordon (a favorite with students for his liveliness) is a recognized scholar in Reformed circles and publishes some interesting books."

Possibly because of its religious orientation, the school's music department also excels, especially in organ (taught by Richard Konzen), and thanks to inspiring instruction by Paul Munson, Joshua Drake, and Beverly Carter, the required humanities music selection "is probably the only course where not one section is a dud."

The most popular majors at Grove City are within the field of education, and indeed Grove City is renowned as a teacher-training school. "Education is easily the largest department" says one professor in another field, "and based on placement after graduation is the best program in Pennsylvania and essentially the nation. If you graduate from Grove City's education department, you are going to get hired."

Even so, more than one student suggests that within Grove City the education department has "a reputation for being somewhat lackluster academically." A former education major characterizes the department as "weak," even though "education majors are unnecessarily overworked [with] tedious and banal projects and worksheets rather than intellectually challenging readings." An exception to this trend in the education department is Professor Jason Edwards, whose classes, according to one student, are "a shock to many freshmen. He challenges students to think deeply, and he's also a very thorough and hard paper grader." Beginning in fall 2010, one of his classes will be required of all freshman education majors. His reading lists include authors like Wendell Berry, Neil Postman, and C. S. Lewis. Another recommended professor is David Schaffer.

As for general science requirements, "These are good introductory courses that offer students an easy way to access the sciences even for those who are uninterested," a teacher says. Math, on the other hand, poses a greater hurdle since "some of the toughest professors teach the lower level math courses."

A good number of students study abroad. Particularly popular are the faculty-led trips, usually conducted during the first few weeks of January. In 2011, the school spon-

---

ACADEMIC REQUIREMENTS

All students are required to take the three-year humanities core, which consists of the following courses:

- "Civilization," which offers "an examination of foundational questions, worldviews, major movements, and decisive developments in the history of civilization" and "emphasizes the formation and spread of the principles and institutions of freedom."
- "Civilization and the Biblical Revelation."
- "'Civilization and the Speculative Mind' . . . an analysis and defense of the Christian worldview. Other major contemporary worldviews such as naturalism, existentialism, pragmatism, postmodernism, and humanism are also examined."
- "'Civilization and Literature' . . . a study of great works of literature that represent the major periods in the history of Western civilization."
- "'Civilization and the Arts' . . . an examination of outstanding works of visual art and music that represent the major periods in the history of Western civilization."
- "'Modern Civilization in International Perspective' . . . an exploration of the seminal ideas, major movements, decisive events, and key individuals in world civilization since the American and French revolutions."

Students must also complete a variety of distribution and other requirements, including:

- Either "Science, Faith, and Technology," or "Science and Religion."
- One course in the social sciences, selected from a list that includes "Foundations of Economics," "Foundations of History," and "Foundations of Psychological Science," plus a few others.
- Two courses in "Quantitative/Logical Reasoning."
- Two courses (along with labs) in "Natural Sciences."
- Two credit hours of physical education.
- "Second-year proficiency" in a modern foreign language. Students may test out of this requirement, and hard-science BS majors are exempt from it altogether.

Students who score below 500 on the Verbal/Critical Reading or Writing section or under 20 on the comparable section of the ACT must take English 102, "Effective Writing."

sored "Science and Religion in the Galapagos Islands"; "Modern Civilization and Engineering Management," taught in several cities across France, and "Revisiting the Reformation," which took students from England, through France and Switzerland, to Germany and Austria. On top of these academic jaunts, the college also sponsors mission trips every year. "These ICO or Inner City Outreach trips are a great way to spend a week across the country or across the world serving God and others. I have yet to meet a participant who has not come back a changed person," a student says.

Grove City is not strong in foreign languages: BA students and nonscience BS students need only demonstrate "second year" proficiency in "a modern, widely spoken foreign language." Serious language courses are in short supply, with only French and Spanish majors, and nonmajor courses offered in Hebrew, German, Chinese, Japanese, and Ancient Greek; Latin courses are offered intermittently. A recent graduate complains: "The classes are a joke and do not really prepare the students for a career in the language field."

Student Life: A Christian community

As Grove City's website points out, "Unlike many colleges and universities today, Grove City embraces a strong traditional and residential campus experience," with over 91 percent of students living on campus—all students except those who live with their parents or spouses, or are over 25 years old. There are ten residence halls—all of them single-sex. "Dorm life is great," says a recent alum. "I had a fantastic experience and have made friendships on my freshman hall that will continue forever. I was able to stick with my freshman hall for all four years of my college experience. The limitations are not bad at all and are easy to live with."

Alcohol is not allowed on campus, and there are limited hours for visitation between male and female students. Many students appreciate this, as it facilitates their rigorous study schedules. Full-time resident directors and student resident advisors supervise life in the dormitories. Students speak well of the RAs. "The RAs are very friendly; they enforce the rules, but will make exceptions when necessary. I had five fantastic RAs that made my college experience great." Says one upperclassman, "My two RAs were both true men of God who helped me and the guys on my hall to grow spiritually and socially." RA-organized activities ranging from basic auto mechanics and financial planning to Bible studies and ballroom dancing. Grove City provides all students with laptops and color printers as part of the tuition package, to facilitate schoolwork in the dorms. The college is currently in the process of renovating the campus dormitories one at a time, with Mary Ethel Pew Hall slated as next.

Outside the dorms, "the most impressive part of the campus is easily the architecture," says a student. "All the buildings follow a neo-Gothic pattern and match very well. They contribute greatly to the atmosphere."

Religion suffuses student life at Grove City, both formally and informally. Students are required to attend sixteen chapel events each semester—scanning their student ID cards at the chapel door to prove it. But students do not limit their religious activities to the formal requirements of the school. There are many other outlets for religious life, including over twenty Christian service organizations. Fraternities (15 percent of men are members) and sororities (19 percent of women belong) are Christian-based, and are more like small-group fellowships than traditional Greek organizations. Many students contribute to international and community service causes.

One group recently urged students to fill shoeboxes with toys, gifts, and Christian literature, for shipment to children around the world. The student organization, Streams of Justice, works to "increase awareness of social justice issues—Christian persecution, sex trafficking, poverty, and hunger—and provide opportunities to put that knowledge and faith into action," according to the student newspaper, the *Collegian*. Streams of Justice sponsors relevant speakers, and also recently sent "action packs" to persecuted Christians in Pakistan. Although the college retains its traditionally Protestant, Presbyterian flavor, a professor notes that "Catholics do not feel uncomfortable on the campus and the Newman Club is very active." The faculty includes teachers from many faith traditions.

Grove City offers a range of sports teams, fraternities and sororities, and over one-hundred other extracurricular organizations. These include: Amateur Radio Club, Classics Society, Clowns for Christ, Dead Theologians Society, Environmental Club, Fellowship of Christian Athletes, Law Society, Men of God, Ornithology Club, Outing Club, Philosophy Club, Physics Club, Ski and Snowboard Club, Society of Women Engineers, Speech & Debate Team, Student Musicians Organization, Warriors for Christ, and Women of Faith. The school also hosts College Republicans, College Democrats, and College Libertarians. The Republicans are by far the most popular political group, and it bears mentioning that Grove City College does not have a single pro-abortion, homosexual, or feminist organization on campus.

There are nineteen NCAA Division III sports at Grove City, which is a member of both the Presidents' Athletic Conference and the Eastern College Athletic Conference. Over half of Grove City's students participate in one or more of the college's thirty Intramural Sports and Club Sports programs—a statistic that prompted *Men's Fitness Magazine* to name the college the seventh fittest college in the nation. Other student activities range

---

GREEN LIGHT

The political climate on campus, is far from stifling for the traditionally-minded. One insider says: "Since Grove City is arguably the most conservative school in the nation, it is the liberals that may feel unwelcome. . . . The professors, however, do a very good job of keeping their politics out of the classroom. As with anything there are exceptions, especially in political science and sociology. Professors are quite religious and do come from a variety of religious backgrounds, including Catholic, Anglican, Lutheran, Presbyterian, and other Christian denominations, so any religious student should feel right at home. . . . In terms of debate, the college encourages it as much as can be on a relatively homogenous campus. There is always a platform for dissenting views and I have been in several classes where professors will encourage debate and accept any differing views."

Several students also pointed to the school's lack of racial diversity as a drawback: "The most disappointing thing about Grove City might be the lack of diversity in both race and thought among the student body," says one student.

from honor societies and department clubs to award-winning student dramatic productions and the college's 200-member marching band. The dance troupe, Orchesis, is very active and performs often on campus. The college also owns an AM and an FM radio station, which provide students with opportunities for broadcasting experience.

One of the few traditions at GCC happens on a predetermined night each week of finals. Hundreds of students congregate on the campus quad and release their tension and anxiety with a great "primal scream."

The town of Grove City (population ca. 8,000) is a peaceful place some seventy miles north of Pittsburgh. As a small manufacturing center, it is known for its General Electric factory that produces diesel locomotives. Serious crime is virtually unknown, both in the town and on campus; a recent graduate recalls, "I usually didn't lock my car and would often leave my laptop, books, and notes at a desk in the library for hours when I wasn't there." Because crime is so rare, students say they find the campus police more burdensome than helpful: "One assumes they have nothing better to do than issue unnecessary parking tickets" and generally make "minor annoyances" of themselves. "The bottom line," says one student, is "if you don't feel safe in Grove City, you probably won't feel safe anywhere."

Although it accepts no federal money, Grove City has been able to keep tuition and other costs far below the national average. In 2010–11, tuition was $13,088, and room and board $7,132. Grove City offers both need-based and merit-based scholarships and works with PNC Bank to provide students with private in lieu of federal loans. Some 43 percent of students receive need-based financial aid, and the average student-loan debt of a recent graduate was $24,895.

Hamilton College

Clinton, New York • www.hamilton.edu

Just say "no" to Western Civ

Founded in 1812 as an all-male college (which would merge with the nearby all-female Kirkland College to become coed in the 1970s.), Hamilton once had a rigorous curriculum that obliged its young men, already well schooled in Greek and Latin, to continue their studies in those ancient languages, as well as in mathematics, religion, history, philosophy, and the humanities.

Today, the college "urges" and "suggests" certain kinds of courses, but it does not require any in particular. One professor complains that Hamilton's curricular freedom makes it "likely that students will learn more about condoms than the Constitution." The school is said to be a haven for tenured radicals, where the Western heritage survives by sufferance and is kept alive by a cadre of excellent teachers who swim against the tide. The student who wants a real liberal education can still find one here—if he hunts down the best advice.

Academic Life: Gagging on the core

A decade ago, Hamilton College took its already watery set of distribution requirements and diluted them to a homeopathic dose. As one student says of the program that resulted (the Hamilton Plan), it "allows each student to have the freedom of choice and puts the burden of widening our minds on us." We think that for $41,280 a year students deserve a little more—for instance, proper guidance so they don't waste four of the most critical years of their lives. In the past few years, Hamilton has attempted this by emphasizing its advising program, which is now meant to ensure that "faculty members help students develop their own academic programs and understand the implications of their choices." How useful is their advice? It varies, students report. We suggest that fledgling Hamilton students seek out wise counsel from the professors recommended further down in this essay.

Nothing in the Hamilton Plan requires educational breadth. Students can conceivably graduate without ever taking a course in history, philosophy, English, or a foreign language. Another effect of Hamilton's curriculum is that many students choose to double major, and since each major imposes its own unique requirements, some students graduate having taken most of their courses in just two disciplines.

Mid-Atlantic

VITAL STATISTICS

Religious affiliation: *none*

Total enrollment: *1,861*

Total undergraduates: *1,861*

SAT/ACT midranges: CR: *650–740*, M: *650–730*; ACT: *27–31*

Applicants: *4,857*

Applicants accepted: *29%*

Applicants accepted who enrolled: *33%*

Tuition and fees: *$41,280*

Room and board: *$10,480*

Freshman retention rate: *88%*

Graduation rate: *82% (4 yrs.), 86% (6 yrs.)*

Courses with fewer than 20 students: *74%*

Student-faculty ratio: *9:1*

Courses taught by graduate students: *none*

Most popular majors: *social sciences, foreign languages and literature, physical sciences*

Students living on campus: *98%*

Guaranteed housing for 4 years? *yes*

Students in fraternities: *33%* in sororities: *17%*

The general education requirements for the class of 2014 have changed a little. Students must now take a course in quantitative and symbolic reasoning. This goal can be satisfied by taking a class in statistics, mathematics, or logic. The class of 2014 will be "encouraged" to also take four or more "proseminars." These oddly named sessions "offer intensive interaction among students, and between students and instructors, through emphasis on writing, speaking, and discussion and/or other approaches to inquiry and expression that demand such intensive interaction." Many departments have their own proseminar options. There is the "Anthropology of Japan," and then there is "Twentieth Century-Fiction." One of the more interesting sounding proseminars is entitled "The Voyage of Life." Its description promises, "This interdisciplinary course will examine questions of life and death from antiquity to the early modern period," sampling everything from the Gospel of St. Luke to Voltaire's *Candide*.

The class of 2014 must also take three or more writing-intensive courses. Some courses look better than others. "Cursing and Taboo Language," for instance, sounds a bit odd, although it's hard to know. "Seminar in Linguistic Semiotics" is more orthodox, if a bit esoteric.

Classes at Hamilton are small, with roughly one-third of all classes having ten or fewer students. About three-quarters have twenty or fewer; and the student-faculty ratio a strong nine to one. So students enjoy close interaction with their teachers. "[Professors] have always been more than accessible and always willing to listen when I needed time," a student says. One professor says that he has never had a student come in to question a grade. Instead "they come in to figure out what they could do better."

Hamilton places a strong emphasis on writing. Students can improve their skills by visiting the Writing Center, which is open until 11:00 PM five nights a week, where peer tutors help students choose essay topics or revise essays. Professors and students alike report that the Writing Center is very good at what it does.

English majors often study abroad in England, Ireland, and Australia. Students either concentrate in literature or creative writing, and must take ten courses in their concentration and two in language studies to earn an English degree. All majors take courses in literature from the sixteenth through the twentieth century, so they do encounter Shakespeare.

History is "regarded as perhaps the most demanding department on campus," according to one professor in the department. History majors will take ten courses and complete the senior program requirement consisting either of a research seminar or an independent senior thesis. Student must take one course on the U.S., one on Europe, and three on Africa, Asia, Latin America, the Middle East, or Russia—and at least one course in premodern history. So majors could possibly miss the American founding or Civil War.

The government department is also strong, offering concentrations in Basic Government, World Politics and Public Policy. One of the more traditional courses is a "Survey of Constitutional Law," which is recommended for all three concentrations. Government majors must take at least two classes in American political theory and a basic American government course.

The philosophy department is solid and surprisingly popular. One philosophy professor says that these "are excellent students, and many are quite involved in moral and social issues."

Some of the better teachers and scholars at Hamilton are Douglas Ambrose, Alfred Kelly, and Robert Paquette in history; Daniel Chambliss in sociology; Barbara Tewksbury in geology; James Bradfield and Derek Jones in economics; Bonnie Urciuoli in anthropology; and Philip Pearle (emeritus) in physics. Classics professor Barbara Gold was recently named the first female editor of the *American Journal of Philology*, and for the first time in its 120-year history, this prestigious publication is headquartered in a liberal arts college rather than a research university.

Hamilton offers majors in Africana studies, Asian studies, and women's studies, and a minor in Latin American studies. The American studies department offers plenty of grim-sounding courses like "Ethnic Autobiography." Hamilton's interdisciplinary studies departments, along with the Spanish department and comparative literature, are said to be the most politicized. One faculty member says that instructors in these departments are "more activists than scholars." A student echoes the sentiment, charging that many faculty members in these departments "use the classroom as a forum to preach political ideology and their personal beliefs."

When Hamilton dropped most of its general education requirements, it also eliminated its cultural diversity requirement, although courses with a "diversity" focus are still strongly encouraged. In fact, in most departments it would be hard to avoid them. In religious studies, for example, students could choose to take courses such as "From Different to Monstrous: Muslim (and Christian) Subversions and Coercions," "The Dao and the Buddha-Mind," or "Seminar on the Celluloid Savior." The department does also offer seminars on the New Testament, biblical parables, and one called "Jesus and the Gospels."

SUGGESTED CORE

1. Classics 250, Heroism, Ancient and Modern (closest match)
2. Philosophy 201, History of Ancient Western Philosophy
3. Religious Studies 111/257, Ancient Jewish Wisdom: Introduction to the Bible/ The New Testament
4. Religious Studies 412, Seminar in Early Christianity (closest match)
5. Government 377, Enlightenment and Counter-Enlightenment
6. English 225, Shakespeare
7. History 241, American Colonial History (closest match)
8. History 226, History of European Thought: 1830 to the Present

Mid-Atlantic

Diversity programming dominates academic and extracurricular life. The Office of Multicultural Affairs has its own dean. The college sponsors events such as Voices of Color Lecture Series, Celebrate Sexuality Week, and Womyn's Energy Week. Many academic departments and campus centers join forces to sponsor events such as these, and one faculty member says that many professors "actively deny the distinction between advocacy and scholarship."

One of the college's programs in this area is the Diversity and Social Justice (formerly the Kirkland) Project, which a student calls "an institutional fix of liberalism that does not even entertain any other ideology." In spring 2010, the project launched an events schedule that featured Kenji Yoshino, a professor at NYU law school, entitled: "The Hidden Assault on our Civil Rights." The lecture concerned his experience as a homosexual Asian-American. Many of the other events were geared towards gaining sympathy for illegal immigrants.

The Kirkland Project attained brief national notoriety in 2005 when it invited leftist radical Ward Churchill to speak at Hamilton. Conservative students, faculty, and alumni publicized his now notorious statement that the victims of the World Trade Center bombings were "little Eichmanns" who got what they deserved. The furor that resulted was briefly promising: The speech was canceled; Churchill went on to lose his job at the University of Colorado; the Kirkland Project was terminated (at least on paper); and a new and alumni-funded Alexander Hamilton Center for the Study of Western Civilization was announced. But tenured radicals have a way of wearing down their enemies.

College president Joan Stewart's attempt to shutter the disgraced Kirkland Project and open the proposed Hamilton Center for Western Civilization provoked a storm of faculty protest, which ground her down. In 2006, Stewart agreed to reopen the Kirkland program under a new name, and to reject the generous funding offered for the Hamilton Center by conservative alumni. The donor who had offered to back the Hamilton Center resigned from the school's board of trustees. Some places cannot be saved from themselves.

There are still many good opportunities at Hamilton. Through a number of strong cooperative programs, students can earn joint degrees in engineering, law, medicine, or other professional programs by taking courses at other colleges and universities in the area. Hamilton offers two well-known study-abroad programs—the Hamilton Junior Year in France and the Junior Year in Spain—but students can also transfer credit from other university programs in other foreign countries. At least 40 percent of each junior class studies abroad, studies at another school, or undertakes an internship.

Majors are offered in Chinese, classics, French, Japanese, Hispanic studies, East Asian languages and literatures, Russian studies and German studies, and courses in Arabic, Hebrew, and Italian.

Student Life: Dress for success

Hamilton graduates love what they remember about their alma mater, and this means dollars for the school. Hamilton is one of the top ten colleges in the nation for alumni support. The college also boasts a substantial endowment for a school of its size—it reached about $780 million before the stock market crash, the impact of which has not yet been announced by Hamilton. "The resources here are amazing," says one professor. "Hamilton is very, very well endowed." Other resources are just as important. As one student says, "The typical Hamilton student will use his or her connections made here with alums or others to get himself a good job after graduating."

Hamilton's campus has two parts: the older Hamilton section is known for its ivy-covered stone architecture, while what was once Kirkland College is more modern. Twenty-three residence halls house Hamilton's small student body. Hamilton has no single-sex dormitories, although it does offer single-sex housing by floor. Some halls have coed bathrooms, but only by unanimous consent. The college also offers coed apartments—with separate bedrooms, a housing official says. Smoke-free, substance-free, and noise-free areas are available for those who request them. Students take meals at either of the college's two large dining halls, at the school's diner, or at the campus pub.

A few years ago, the college trustees launched a kind of urban renewal on campus, attempting to bulldoze the school's Greek system. It seized the residence spaces from campus fraternities, reluctantly allowing them to continue as student organizations. Until 1978, when Hamilton merged with Kirkland College, about 90 percent of the student body belonged to a fraternity, according to the *Chronicle of Higher Education*. In order to convert the school from a residential fraternity campus, Hamilton has spent about $20 million to restructure the campus's residential life. A *Christian Science Monitor* article says that fraternities were banned in 1995 to produce a "civilizing effect," or in other words, "to equalize housing and improve what many perceived as a male-dominated social scene." Hamilton also wanted to "attract better academically qualified women." The university couldn't quash all Greek life, however; today, some 33 percent of men and 17 percent of women participate. Indeed, students say the Greek system is still the social focus on campus providing the majority of the party scene activities. A popular guide written by students urges newcomers to join up—and invest in an expensive wardrobe.

The student body is mostly white, wealthy, and preppy. Although the largest chunk of students come from the Northeast, Hamilton is attended by students from throughout

---

ACADEMIC REQUIREMENTS

The requirements of the grandly named "Hamilton Plan for Liberal Education" can fit comfortably on a bar napkin (try it!). On top of their majors, students are asked to take:

- Four small "proseminars." Recent options include "Female Parts: Gender Play on the Western Stage" and "British and American Drama."
- Three writing-intensive courses. Choices range from "Truth and Justice, the American Way" to "Writing About the Environment."
- At least one quantitative literacy course. Options include "Language and Sociolinguistics" and "Statistical Reasoning and Data Analysis."
- A senior capstone seminar or project.

RED LIGHT

One professor insists that the Hamilton community welcomes students of all political beliefs: "I think the political climate on campus is quite good. Liberals and conservatives don't shy away from disagreeing and seem to do so in intelligent (as opposed to knee-jerk) sort of ways." In comparing Hamilton to a similar school of similar size with a noticeable liberal climate, he says, "Hamilton seems to be more open to all sides."

Others assess the situation differently. Only one faculty member at Hamilton is generally seen as outspokenly conservative, though three could be found to work on the ill-fated Hamilton Center. Until recently there was no conservative student organization; a College Republicans club had a membership in the single digits and did "very little," according to a professor. Recently there have been some more signs of life on the right. A conservative newspaper started on campus, The *Right*, ceased publication, but has recently been replaced by *Dexter*, which promised to be "a vehicle for the expression of under-represented or stifled opinion."

There's surely a need for it. As one student says, "In terms of political/ideological diversity on campus, there is little to none. This campus ... has a faculty that is very liberal-minded and one-sided on all issues." Even though many students are moderate to conservative, says this student, they are afraid to speak up in class or in outside activities.

the United States and by a number of international students.

The small town of Clinton doesn't offer much by way of entertainment. Utica is a ten-minute drive away and offers a few more options. There are a few things to do on campus, however. In addition to its permanent collection, Emerson Gallery offers lectures, films, and workshops in the arts. The theater and dance department sponsors concerts and student performances regularly, and the music department is also quite strong.

One student says that "the administration puts the burden of social programming on students, but does not supply us with the proper amount of funding to fully entertain all options. Our location makes the need for social options even greater, yet the school is very tight with money to student organizations."

Hamilton does bring in a pretty wide range of lecturers. Recent speakers have included Colin Powell, Desmond Tutu, Ralph Reed, Oliver North, Jimmy Carter, Cornel West, Julian Bond, Jonah Goldberg, and Rudy Giuliani. However, when distinguished economist Walter Williams—author of this guide's introduction—came to campus to speak on the "Hypocrisy of Diversity: How Much Can Discrimination Explain?" faculty members called him a racist. (Williams is black.) Some even sent out an all-campus e-mail demanding that the college cancel the speech. The president had to hire extra security for Williams's talk.

Religious life at Hamilton is especially vigorous. The campus ministry is mainline Protestant, but not ashamed of being Christian, and features a proudly traditional service of lessons and carols at Christmas. There is also an evangelical Christian fellowship, a Newman community with noon Masses on Tuesdays and Thursdays, and an Orthodox Christian group. There is also a Hillel, an Islamic Association, and an interreligious meditation group. This is diversity in the good sense, and impressive for a small, upper-crust Protestant-founded college.

Student groups include the Asian Cultural Society, Black and Latino Student Union, Russian Club, Spanish Club, Classics Club, Emerson Literary Society, Fishing Club, Young Socialists, Bikram Yoga Club, Model European Union, Amnesty International, the *Daily Bull* (a newspaper), College Republicans, and (most encouragingly), the Christopher Dawson Society—devoted to the great conservative historian.

The Hamilton Continentals field twenty-eight NCAA Division III teams. Freshmen and sophomores can play on junior varsity teams. In a typical year, 35 to 40 percent of the Hamilton student body participates in varsity or JV sports. Hamilton sponsors more than a dozen club sports and about fifteen intramural activities each year; at least six in ten students participate in intramural sports.

A popular organization on campus is the discouragingly named Hamilton Action Volunteers Outreach Coalition (HAVOC), a group that organizes community service opportunities like tutoring in city schools, soup kitchens, and nursing home visits. A $10 membership fee in the Outing Club allows students to use camping and ski equipment. The club also sponsors hiking, rock climbing, and other outdoor activities throughout the school year. For relaxation, students have easy access to the Root Glen, a 7.5-acre wooded garden on campus.

The isolated location usually helps keep the campus and its environs safe; Hamilton's latest crime statistics (2009) report three forcible sex offenses and twenty-three burglaries, and one aggravated assault on campus.

For a place with such left-leaning sympathies, Hamilton is hardly welcoming to the proletariat. Tuition in 2010–11 was $41,280, and room and board cost $10,480. Admissions have just become need blind, but the school does not guarantee to meet student's full need. About half of students get need-based aid, and the average student-loan debt of recent graduates who borrowed is $19,466.

Haverford College

Haverford, Pennsylvania • www.haverford.edu

Fast friends

Haverford was founded by the Religious Society of Friends in 1833. Haverford is not "officially" Quaker, but you hear a lot about the Quaker mindset and principles at the college. This is felt most strongly in the school's honor code, the main point of which is to instill trust in one's professors, in one's classmates, and in oneself. One student says, "It really works! You are guaranteed to come out of here valuing honesty as the highest of virtues." Students make eye contact, leave their backpacks in the dining hall lobby while they eat and leave their mailboxes wide open. It's a placid and familial school—no small virtue these days.

Unfortunately, some other traditional educational values, such as a solid curriculum, have fallen by the wayside. Haverford's reputation for academic excellence is well deserved, but, since we're being honest, the school's penchant for progressive politics and overwhelming price tag make it a tough sell for some.

Academic Life: Intense friends

Haverford's distribution requirements impose no real constraints on students—seventy-two different courses in the English department alone satisfy the humanities requirement, while twenty-nine courses in political science could stand in for social sciences. As one professor put it, "A student seeking a 'traditional liberal education' can find that at Haverford. But he can also avoid it." One student says. "The best scholarship in almost every discipline is out there if you want to go and grab it. But if you don't, no one can really force you to."

The college attracts intellectually curious students, most of whom are eager to take a wide variety of courses. Unfortunately, their options include classes like "Sex, Gender, and Representation: An Introduction to Theories of Sexuality" and "Native American Music and Belief"—each of which fulfill basic humanities requirements. Even the natural sciences are dicey: one's sole science course could be "Disease and Discrimination," which "analyzes the nature of discrimination against individuals and groups with . . . diseases."

On the positive side, academic life at Haverford is not as politicized as at other schools. Haverford still offers many traditional courses, and is one of only three top-ten liberal arts colleges to offer comprehensive surveys in English, history, and political science, as well as a history course in Western civilization. The history department offers courses in all the discipline's fundamental areas, as do the philosophy, religion, and English departments.

Sadly, the requirements for important majors are fairly loose. A student majoring in English must complete at least seven courses, at least two of them in works from before 1800. But he need not study any Shakespeare. Study of the American founding is not required of history majors, and political science majors can graduate without covering the U.S. Constitution. Still, academic life at Haverford is intense, say professors. One points to "many students here who are adventurous and do take courses merely to learn and not simply to get a good grade." Students expect to work every night during the week and during the day on weekends. "People here really want to learn, and they study hard," a student reports. And classes are rigorous: "It is virtually impossible to have a perfect GPA here, no matter how hard you work." Every student must complete a senior thesis, a comprehensive exam, or a special project paper or series of classes.

Students struggling with their papers can find assistance at the college's Writing Center, where student advisors offer advice and editing every evening, Sunday though Thursday.

Haverford benefits from a close relationship with its sister school, Bryn Mawr College, and nearby Swarthmore. Haverford students can take courses at the other two schools and even choose to major in a discipline offered only there. More than 2,000 students are cross-registered between Haverford and Bryn Mawr, which is just one mile away. Haverford also offers a 3-2 engineering program in which students spend three years at Haverford and two at Caltech, emerging with degrees from both institutions. Haverford students can also take courses at and use the library of the University of Pennsylvania, but this (rather distant) option is used less frequently.

Haverford is strongest in the sciences, particularly biology and chemistry, and the school boasts that it is one of only two undergraduate colleges in the country (along with Pomona College) to guarantee research opportunities for students in the sciences, the humanities, and the social sciences.

Among the most highly praised professors at Haverford are Linda Gerstein in history; Kimberly Benston, C. Stephen Finley, and Laura McGrane in English; Mark Gould in sociology; Kathleen Wright in philosophy; and Richard J. Ball in economics.

Faculty-student relationships at Haverford are about as close as one sees anywhere—and no wonder, with a luxurious student-faculty ratio of 8 to 1. A professor says that one

VITAL STATISTICS

Religious affiliation: *none*
Total enrollment: *1,169*
Total undergraduates: *1,169*
SAT/ACT midranges: CR: *700–800*, M: *700–800*
Applicants: *3,311*
Applicants accepted: *27%*
Applicants accepted who enrolled: *37%*
Tuition and fees: *$40,260*
Room and board: *$12,346*
Freshman retention rate: *96%*
Graduation rate: *88% (4 yrs.), 94% (6 yrs.)*
Courses with fewer than 20 students: *80%*
Student-faculty ratio: *8:1*
Courses taught by graduate students: *none*
Most popular majors: *social sciences, physical sciences, biological and life sciences*
Students living on campus: *98%*
Guaranteed housing for 4 years? *yes*
Students in fraternities or sororities: *none*

1. Classics 212, The Classical Tradition in Western Literature
2. Philosophy 210/212/310, Plato/Aristotle/Topics in Ancient Greek and Roman Philosophy
3. Religion 118/122, Hebrew Bible: Literary Text and Historical Context/Introduction to the New Testament
4. Religion 206, History and Literature of Early Christianity
5. Political Science 231, Western Political Theory (Modern) (offered at Bryn Mawr)
6. English 225, Shakespeare: The Tragic and Beyond
7. Political Science 276, American Political Thought from Founding to Civil War (closest match)
8. Philosophy 323, Topics in Nineteenth-Century Philosophy

of the school's greatest strengths is its "dedicated teachers across the board, who spend a lot of time with students." Without a graduate program or the pressure to secure large grants, Haverford teachers can typically afford to invest more time and energy into teaching. However, one professor claims that "the administration's expectations of research have been rising." Students generally agree that professors are readily available for help, and not only during office hours: one student says his math professor "gave us her home phone number and told us to call her whenever we feel we are stuck on a problem for more than forty-five minutes—even if it is past midnight!" Each freshman is assigned both a faculty advisor and an upperclassman "peer advisor."

Haverford's honor code strengthens relationships between students and teachers. Students say they are amazed at the amount of trust faculty members place in them. "Cheating, plagiarism, and other dishonesty in the classroom are incredibly rare because students are not willing to break that trust," one says. Students can usually take exams home and complete them on their own time. One student reports that when he brought an exam home, his time ran out mid-sentence; he turned it in just like that. The honor code is student written and student run. Students who violate it are judged by peers on an honor council, and the most serious consequence of breaking the code is "separation," which is essentially a one-semester expulsion.

Aside from the plentiful academic options close to home, Haverford students can also benefit from educational partnerships further afield. The school's study-abroad program has been expanding of late, and 40–50 percent of students spend at least one semester abroad in foreign locales as diverse as Northern Ireland and South Africa. The big expansion has been due to grants from the Center for Peace and Global Citizenship (CPGC), which funds student internships in foreign places, as well as in inner cities in the U.S. Foreign languages offered at Haverford include Chinese, French, German, Italian, Japanese, Spanish, Ancient Greek, and Latin.

Student Life: Varsity cricket

One of the greatest of Quaker ideals and goals is peace, and peace is what you'll find in the architecture and grounds of Haverford College. The campus once consisted solely of one long stone building, Founders' Hall, where students studied, attended classes, ate, and slept. While Haverford has expanded considerably since then, the college wisely continues to build in a manner that is consistent with its past. Nearly every building is of gray stone, though architectural styles vary. Between the classrooms and dormitories lie lush expanses of green lawn and centuries-old trees originally landscaped by the English gardener William Carvill. The 216-acre campus includes more than 2,500 labeled trees, more than 400 species of trees and shrubs, and a 2.3 acre duck pond. A two-mile nature trail surrounds the school, offering a place for quiet contemplation.

In place of residential advisors, Haverford appoints CPs ("custom people") to show the first-year students the ropes and catechize them about the school's traditions. This arrangement dates back to the mid-1800s.

Quakerism encourages confronting problems through dialogue, and promotes reaching agreement by consensus. So things go at Haverford. When a dispute arises—something as minor as a hallmate playing music too loud or as major as whether the nation should go to war—students' first reaction is to face the other side and initiate a discussion.

The undergraduate population stands at around 1,169 students from forty-five states and thirty-eight countries, some 47 percent male and 53 percent female. Around 31 percent of Haverford students are members of a minority group (including international students), and the college is intent on admitting and retaining a more racially diverse student body.

ACADEMIC REQUIREMENTS

Haverford's rather laissez-faire curricular requirements include one semester of a writing-intensive seminar, chosen from any of the college's academic departments. Among the 2009–10 courses qualifying were "Introduction to Literary Analysis," "The Culture of War," and "Excursions in the Void: Existentialism, Nihilism, and Radical Doubt."

Students must also take three courses in each of the three divisions of the curriculum, choosing from at least two different departments in each division:

- Humanities. Choices range from "Introduction to Literature Analysis" to "Sex, Gender, Representation."
- Social sciences. Options include "Introduction to Western Civilization" and "Anthropology of Gender."
- Natural sciences. Choices include "Classical and Modern Physics" and "Perspectives in Biology: How Do I Know Who I Am?"

Students also face at least one course that meets the school's "quantitative requirement." Suitable courses focus on statistical reasoning, quantitative data, graphical relationships, or "using mathematics to obtain concrete numerical predictions about natural or social systems."

The school's foreign language requirement can be met by scoring high on an Advanced Placement; scoring 600 or higher on a language achievement test; taking one full year of language study; or studying a language in a summer program abroad or semester abroad.

Haverford also requires students to participate in six quarters (half-semesters) of the physical education program during their first two years at the college.

Mid-Atlantic

GREEN LIGHT

Haverford is by-and-large a liberal institution where you're not likely to run into many Quakers who are still orthodox Christians like their founder, George Fox. One professor seemed to hit the nail on the head by characterizing the college as "soft left." Students and faculty tend to be "quite liberal socially," he averred and for students, "capitalism arouses as much suspicion as communism." Politics on campus, while clearly left-leaning seem fairly thoughtful. Above all, one insider said, "Haverford's way" is one that is both "polite and suffused with tolerance." Conservatives are not likely to find themselves in the political majority at Haverford any time soon, but they can still seemingly count on being treated fairly.

But one student complains that while "Haverford is sufficiently diverse racially and ethnically, and students are accepting of other cultures . . . we're not really diverse socioeconomically—we're all privileged and upper class."

Haverford, along with Bryn Mawr and Swarthmore, sponsors a summer orientation program for incoming minority freshmen. Haverford's Minority Scholars Program offers a bonanza of support services for minority students. For its size, Haverford has a plethora of minority student groups, among them Alliance of Latin American Students, Asian Students Association, Queer Discussion Group, Caribbean Essence Organization, and Women in Action, which focuses on "dialogue and activism regarding feminist issues." However, the school still has a ways to go toward attaining ideological diversity.

The student body supports the usual academic organizations, like Debate Team, Model U.N., and the Haverford Journal. Far out special interest groups, such as the Cornhole Ring of Champions and Haverford Hookah club, stand in distinct contrast to their more sober counterparts, the Chess Club and Cigar Society, much as "innovative" spiritual groups like Athena's Circle darkly mimic more traditional counterparts like the Newman Catholic Campus Ministry.

The College Democrats seem to hold a comfortable hegemony over their competition, as the College Republicans club was formed in 2002 to "make sure all Republicans and conservatives on campus know that they are not as outnumbered as they believe they are."

Haverford students confess that their school is not exactly an athletic powerhouse in the NCAA Division III Centennial Conference, where it competes with Swarthmore, Bryn Mawr, Franklin and Marshall, and Johns Hopkins, among others. Academics come first, and classes are scheduled so that students have no conflicts with practice. "We're not spectacular, but we always have a lot of fun," says one student, who ran for the track and cross-country teams without any previous experience. "On every team, there is an incredible range of abilities." Around 40 percent of students are varsity athletes. There are twenty-one varsity squads (but no football team). Haverford fields the only varsity cricket team in the nation; their competition comes from adult cricket leagues and club teams at area universities. The college also has a physical education requirement, which consists of six half-semester courses during a student's first two years at Haverford. So students are a physically fit lot. "At four o'clock every day, the library clears out and everybody is outside doing something. Haverford students are incredibly active," says a senior. The $20 million

Douglas B. Gardner '83 Integrated Athletic Center and $1 million Johnson Track provide students with ample space to work off that freshman fifteen.

Haverford's multitude of options—traditional dormitories, single rooms in suite-style arrangements, on-campus apartments, and the dorms at Bryn Mawr—leaves students with virtually no reason to live off campus, and only about 2 percent do. At the beginning of each school year, students decide whether to make the bathrooms single-sex or coed, and for some reason, students usually choose the coed route.

As small as Haverford College is, there is still plenty to do. Regular buses to Bryn Mawr and Swarthmore colleges expand options even further. One student says that, in general, "Haverford students tend to think of 'Mawrtyrs' as weird—either gay or promiscuous. Swatties [Swarthmore students] are just weird and snobby." The party atmosphere is muted, with many students content to hang out with friends, play board games in Lunt Cafe, or attend the lectures and concerts held on campus every week. Fords Against Boredom (FAB) sponsors free social events like midnight bowling, trips to Phillies games, a weekly film series, and the ever-popular mud wrestling.

Philadelphia's Center City is only a ten-mile, cheap train ride away. The city offers numerous restaurants, nightclubs, and other attractions for the work-weary student. The Philadelphia Museum of Art is the largest of many cultural institutions visited by students, and historic sites dating from before the founding of the nation are within easy reach. Students can often score special rates for tickets to events at the Kimmel Center for the Performing Arts. The New Jersey and Delaware beaches are an easy drive, as are ski resorts in the Poconos. Closer to home, Haverford, Bryn Mawr, and other neighboring upscale towns along the Main Line offer a large assortment of restaurants and other centers of shopping and entertainment.

Crime at Haverford appears to be decreasing. In 2009, the school reported seven forcible sex offenses, twenty-two burglaries, one robbery, and one aggravated assault. Drug and alcohol offenses crop up occasionally, but not enough to think of Haverford as a party school, and blue-light emergency phones situated all over campus give students easy access to police.

A year at Haverford costs a stiff $40,260 in tuition, plus $12,346 for room and board. Some 48 percent of undergraduates receive financial aid, and the average student-loan debt upon graduation is $13,985.

Johns Hopkins University

Baltimore, Maryland • www.jhu.edu

Life in the lab

When Johns Hopkins University inaugurated Daniel Coit Gilman as president in 1876, Gilman asked, "What are we aiming at? The encouragement of research . . . and the advancement of individual scholars, who by their excellence will advance the sciences they pursue and the society where they dwell." Gilman's vision lives on at Johns Hopkins, the first research university of its kind and still one of the world's finest. Johns Hopkins was also the first university to offer an "undergraduate major" as opposed to the traditional liberal arts curriculum, establishing this model for most research universities in America. Unfortunately, Hopkins' specialized focus has come at a cost. The school's emphasis on research and faculty publication leaves undergraduate teaching in the lurch, especially when it comes to general education. In a study of civic literacy on fifty of the nation's campuses, Johns Hopkins ranked dead last; its seniors knew considerably less about American history and institutions than did its freshmen.

On the other hand, many faculty members do use their research to complement their teaching, especially in the sciences and engineering, and 85 percent of undergraduates supplement their coursework by participating in faculty research projects. Hopkins is for serious students who don't mind putting their social lives (and learning in the humanities) on hold for a few years, so that they can work with the best scholars in specialized fields. As one student says, "Prepare to spend four years studying, not making friends." And while the campus is largely apolitical, with students too busy grinding for grades to wave any placards, there are occasional partisan conflicts on campus in which the administration consistently sides with the left, earning Johns Hopkins one of the worst free speech ratings in the country.

Academic Life: Darwin and Hobbes

Hopkins has made it clear from the beginning that it is primarily a research university, not a liberal arts college. Even today the administration proudly informs students about the lack of a core curriculum: "Instead of a rigid core of compulsory courses, Hopkins requires only that you fulfill general distribution requirements in several academic areas (depending on your major), a writing requirement, and for some majors, a language requirement. Beyond that you're free to concentrate on what you love, or to explore more broadly." Few students, particularly in the sciences, come to Hopkins to explore a variety of disciplines, but they are still required to take thirty credits outside their major. For humanities and social science students, twelve of those credits must be in math, science, or engineering; math, science, or engineering students must take eighteen to twenty-one credits in the humanities or social sciences. Outside of their major, however, students basically have free rein in deciding what remaining courses to take, and many science departments save required electives entirely for the junior and senior years, when the student has a firm grasp on his own major and theoretically needs less time to struggle through technical assignments.

Each field also has its own course requirements, of course. An English major, for example, must take two introductory courses outside the English department, one year of a foreign language at the intermediate level, and ten courses in English. Worthy classes such as "American Literature to 1865" and "Shakespeare: Then and Now" are offered, but not required.

The history department, one of the largest in the liberal arts at Johns Hopkins, admits to being a little unorthodox in its requirements and in its teaching manner: "The kind of history taught in these classes depends largely on the interests of individual professors, but in general has very little to do with the kind of narrative history . . . with its emphasis on names and dates and asking students to remember 'what happened?' at a given place or time." American history courses before and after 1865 are offered, but none of these are required; in fact, history majors may skip them altogether and take instead courses like "History of Latin America," "History of Africa," and "History of East Asia."

The political science department, one of the first in the country, continues to be well-respected in the field, especially in the areas of political theory and international relations. All poli sci majors must take thirteen courses in their major, with at least one course each in American politics, comparative politics, political theory, and international relations. Poli sci students are required to study the American Constitution and other fundamental topics, we are pleased to note. The most popular branch of the poli sci department is international relations, perhaps in part because many of the classes are taught at the university's Paul H. Nitze School of Advanced International Studies in Washington, D.C. Many students choose to intern while in the nation's capital, but the internships do not count toward the major.

VITAL STATISTICS

Religious affiliation: *none*
Total enrollment: *6,680*
Total undergraduates: *4,954*
SAT/ACT midranges: CR: *630–740*, M: *660–770*; ACT: *29–33*
Applicants: *16,133*
Applicants accepted: *25%*
Applicants accepted who enrolled: *30%*
Tuition and fees: *$41,180*
Room and board: *$12,510*
Freshman retention rate: *97%*
Graduation rate: *83% (4 yrs.), 91% (6 yrs.)*
Courses with fewer than 20 students: *66%*
Student-faculty ratio: *10:1*
Courses taught by graduate students: *not provided*
Most popular majors: *biomedical and medical engineering, public health, international relations*
Students living on campus: *56%*
Guaranteed housing for 4 years? *no*
Students in fraternities: *23%* in sororities: *22%*

Besides the required two to four semesters of writing-intensive courses, students—especially those in the sciences—have little flexibility to pursue a broad liberal arts degree, as their semesters are filled with the requirements of their majors.

Most classrooms are free of extraneous politics. One finds, of course, the obligatory "gender"-fixated courses offered in several fields, but these are easily spotted and shunned. The only exceptions appear to be courses in the anthropology and sociology departments—disciplines that would prove quite uncomfortable for conservative students, according to our sources.

If Hopkins students aren't always well rounded or even particularly interested in ideas, they are at least set to become experts in their fields. Undergraduates are intelligent and ambitious, sometimes to the degree of being antisocial, cutthroat competitors. One student says that premedical students' approach is so Darwinian that they spend more hours than necessary on assignments simply trying to earn the best grade in the class. In a physics lab, one alumnus says, some of the most overachieving students spent hours collecting iron filings, not because they needed so many samples, but because they wanted to outdo their classmates. Another student says that professors lock organic chemistry labs to prevent students from sabotaging classmates' experiments. But if a student can survive such competition with his sanity intact, a Johns Hopkins diploma is surely valuable. Alumni graduate and professional school acceptance rates are well above the national average: 92 percent for medical school and 90 percent for law school, for example. Hopkins tries to alleviate some student stress by "covering" the students' first-semester letter grades with a mark of "satisfactory" or "unsatisfactory." There is also a January term that students can use as an extra-long vacation or to take an intensive interim course, thereby easing the strain in future semesters.

Students may learn some of their competitive habits from their professors, many of whom are top researchers vying for grants and awards. But persistent students should be able to find professors willing and eager to help with coursework and to offer advice. "Every professor has office hours and almost all of them are friendly and helpful when students talk to them," a student says. "I had one professor who announced his office hours every lecture and told us that there was no need to do poorly in his class. . . . All we had to do was come in and talk to him." Another student says, "Students must show some initiative . . . but once [the professors] come to know you, they are generally most helpful." Professors teach almost all classes, but teaching assistants play a slightly greater role in engineering courses than they do in the humanities.

The extent to which faculty members offer students guidance is said to vary. One student calls the freshman advising program "atrocious," since students can avoid personal relationships with professors by using the Office of Academic Advising. After the first year, each student is assigned a faculty advisor based on the student's academic interests, but another way to foster strong academic relationships with JHU faculty members is by taking advantage of one of the many research opportunities, especially in the sciences. For most research projects, students can even earn academic credit while preparing themselves for graduate school or a science-related career. The online registration procedures make it more difficult for students to choose the best courses, students tell us—and in some instances they have found themselves unable to take required courses in a timely manner and therefore graduate on time.

Students name the following as among the university's best undergraduate teachers in the liberal arts: Jeffrey Brooks, John Marshall, David Bell, and William Rowe in history; William Connolly, Daniel H. Deudney, Eliot Cohen, and Richard Flathman (emeritus) in political science; Michael Fried in art history; Laurence Ball in economics; and Tristan Davies in the writing seminars. The science and engineering departments have a wide range of good professors, students say.

Hopkins is best known for its hard-science departments. The biology program was the nation's first; biology, biomedical engineering, neuroscience, and public health are some of the university's best. But JHU also maintains other excellent departments. The Romance language departments are all highly regarded, as are German and art history. Students interested in a variety of disciplines can choose so-called "area majors," which are "multidisciplinary programs tailored to their own academic concerns," i.e., self-made majors that allow students enormous flexibility in their curricula. Past "area majors" have combined American history, literature, and philosophy; religion and philosophy; and science and philosophy. A similar option in the natural sciences allows students to create majors that bridge two or more academic disciplines—for example, biology and chemistry or physics and chemistry. In both area majors, students work closely with advisors to structure a four-year curriculum.

Art students at Johns Hopkins can take advantage of a pilot program available at fewer than forty campuses in the world: ARTstor, an online repository of over 500,000 images drawn from major university collections, which high-tech observers cited by the *Chronicle of Higher Education* think might someday replace the art history textbook—or at least the classroom projector.

Hopkins students had better enjoy the art at home, since few of them will see it in the flesh. Only 16 percent of undergraduates study abroad, although Johns Hopkins offers programs in dozens of foreign locations. At home Hopkins students may choose to study modern Greek, Latin, French, Italian, German, Spanish, Portuguese, Yiddish, Hebrew, Chinese, Arabic, Russian, Japanese, Kiswahili, Korean, Hindi, Urdu, Persian, Sanskrit, Sumerian, and Ancient Greek.

Mid-Atlantic

Student Life: Hunker in the bunker

What do America's future doctors and engineers do with their free time? They study. Johns Hopkins attracts some of the most academically focused students in the nation, and therefore the school lacks most of the community atmosphere and entertainment options one finds at other colleges. "Social life is what you make of it," a biology major says. "Many people go to the library and practically live there. I'm in a very hard major, but I still find time to enjoy at least part of my Friday and Saturday. Maybe go see a movie or go out to eat."

Johns Hopkins currently has ten residential halls, varying from single units to suites. The most recent housing development, Charles Commons, houses some 618 students, as well as a new central dining facility, a bookstore run by Barnes and Noble, and a café that serves Starbucks coffee. All dormitories are coed, but there are no coed bathrooms or dorm rooms. Many students say that they met most of their friends during their freshman year, when all live in dormitories on one residential quad, where students leave their doors open and hallmates often drop by to say hello. Most sophomores, however, live in university-owned apartments, and social life suffers accordingly. The more intense students emerge, blinking, from their dorm rooms only to attend class or visit the library.

The main Homewood campus is composed primarily of Georgian-style red-brick buildings with white marble columns, and a recent donation allowed the school to replace the campus's asphalt pathways with more harmonious brick ones. Gilman Hall is the oldest and most photographed building on campus. The seal of the college, in the foyer of the building, is so hallowed that it has curses tied to it: Prospective students who step on it will not be admitted, current students who step on it will not graduate, parents who step on it will not receive financial aid, and faculty who tread on the seal will not receive tenure. (Alumni who tread on the seal, we presume, will simply explode.) The Milton S. Eisenhower Library, an amazing resource, is built five stories underground so as not to be as tall as the revered Gilman Hall. Students say each floor becomes progressively quieter as you move downstairs; those studying on D level should expect annoyed stares at the slightest cough or crinkle of paper. "The Beach" is a green lawn behind the Eisenhower Library and bordering Charles Street, where students sunbathe and play soccer or Frisbee when the weather is pleasant. The Student Arts Center features a black-box theater, practice rooms, and arts and dance studios.

On June 6, 2010, the university broke ground on a state-of-the-art, high-tech library, named after longtime university supporters Bill and Wendy Brody. The Brody Learning

ACADEMIC REQUIREMENTS

Johns Hopkins has no university-wide curriculum. The only requirements that every undergraduate must satisfy are a series of writing-intensive courses and at least eight to ten classes outside of his major. Such writing-intensive options include "Readings in Fiction: Faulkner, Fitzgerald, and Hemingway" and "Writing About Science." For science, math, or engineering majors, roughly six of their outside courses must be in the humanities or social sciences. Class options include "Shakespeare: Then and Now," and "Feminist and Queer Theory."

Commons will connect to the main Eisenhower Library on several floors and will feature innovations such as movable walls, worldwide video-conference tools, digital collections, and HDTV. The building will also provide more than 500 new seats, add fifteen group study rooms; house the department of rare books and manuscripts, provide new laboratory and instruction space for the Department of Preservation and Conservation, and provide a new atrium and cafe for students and faculty. The university calls the new project the "library of the future"—allowing laptop-toting junior scientists ample space to converse and share research. The project is set for completion in July 2012.

Hopkins boasts more than 360 student organizations, many of which are preprofessional societies or academic interest groups; others revolve around ethnicity, community service, media, sports, hobbies, the arts, and religious faith. A number of chaplaincies and student ministries serve Hopkins students of various creeds. The campus Hillel chapter is housed in the Smokler Center for Jewish Life, a four-level, 19,000-square-foot building. The Newman Center at JHU seems particularly solid, sponsoring talks on the theology of Pope Benedict XVI and on the Catholic Catechism, and visits by members of faithful religious orders. Other active Christian groups include Catholic Community, Eastern Orthodox, Fellowship of Christian Athletes, and Agape Campus Christian Fellowship. The university estimates that a full 70 percent of students participate in at least one volunteer activity. Existing activist groups on campus, left and right, include the American Civil Liberties Union, Amnesty International, College Democrats, College Republicans, Voice for Life, Students for Environmental Action, and the NAACP.

Students who have attempted a bit of conservative activism have hit roadblocks

YELLOW LIGHT

With the student body largely focused on school work and making the grade, the average Hopkins student has little time for political activism. Students are typically either apolitical or apathetic. One student says that "while the campus has a slight leftist tendency because of the large number of students from Washington, D.C., and the northeastern states, politics just isn't a priority." One conservative student says there are "committed leftists here and there, but they are quite obvious and can easily be avoided."

The administration, on the other hand, has consistently earned Hopkins the worst possible free speech rating from the Foundation for Individual Rights in Education. Hopkins is one of only five schools on FIRE's Red Alert List, for having "acted with severe and ongoing disregard for the fundamental rights of their students and/ or faculty members." Hopkins's nebulous speech code prohibits any "rude, disrespectful behavior," speech deemed "tasteless," or any written or spoken word that "breaches civility." The penalty for speech offenders is swift and severe, including school suspension, diversity workshops, community service, and dozens of multicultural book reports. A student suffered all of these blows after posting a Halloween invitation on his Facebook page that the administration considered "tasteless."

Hopkins's 2010–11 student government president, Marc Perkins, recently wrote an open letter exhorting the administration to uphold the civil liberties of students by overturning its speech code, accurately describing it as "allow[ing] the university to punish students for merely expressing views that are controversial," which in turn "hurts the cause of academic freedom at our university and has a chilling effect upon all forms of free speech." So far, no response.

from the administration. The *Carrollton Record* was founded by members of JHU's Republican club about ten years ago. Shortly thereafter the Student Activities Council (SAC) decreed that publications must constitute their own student group and cannot fall under another group. Conservatives complained when the *Donkey*, a liberal student publication, was granted easy recognition as a student group and received school funds—which have consistently been denied the *Carrollton Record*. In fact, over the past five years, the paper has been unable either to obtain regular status as a student group, or to receive student activities funding. The SAC has repeatedly changed the criteria for recognition and unfairly withheld funding from the paper, students complain.

About one-fourth of Hopkins students are involved in its thirteen fraternities and eight sororities. One student says of the Greek system, "You can take it or leave it, and students can attend any of the campus fraternity parties." As for alcohol, one student says, "I think it's a lot less prevalent than in many other places, but it's here if you want it. There's a lot of stuff to do here, so there's no need to drink." But another humanities major says that since the school has no social life, "students drink themselves to oblivion at one of the many frat parties. Most students still try to have a life when there is really no possibility of having one, and for this reason they are by and large miserable."

Varsity athletics do not play a significant role in life at Hopkins and almost all varsity teams are Division III. One exception is lacrosse, the school's only Division I sport, and a national power. "Everybody goes to their games," says one student. "Lacrosse is huge." The admissions department says that 75 percent of the student body participates in sports—varsity, club, or intramural. The Ralph S. O'Connor Recreation Center is a frequent haunt for undergraduates.

Historic Baltimore, while suffering some urban blight, has its bright spots. The Baltimore Museum of Art is free for students and is only a short walk from campus, as is the Walters Art Museum. Johns Hopkins's own Peabody Conservatory of Music is a prime cultural venue. Charles Village, next to campus, has a number of pubs, restaurants, and shops, as does Fells Point, further away. The Inner Harbor, a touristy area with bookstores, shops, restaurants, historical attractions, and the National Aquarium, not to mention nearby stadiums for the Orioles and Ravens, is a popular escape. Washington, D.C., and its array of attractions is a five-dollar train ride away on the MARC, Maryland's commuter train system.

Hopkins's urban setting deters many students. However, the school has taken major steps in the last few years to ensure the safety of its students. Dorms use electronic surveillance, security guards, and a pass key system to restrict access. One student says that getting into dorms can be difficult for residents, never mind outsiders. As an added service, the university provides shuttles and escorts around campus, as well as a free taxi service for students who find themselves stranded off campus. On-campus crime statistics for 2008 include only two burglaries, demonstrating the success of the university's efforts.

Elite schools such as Johns Hopkins come at a premium price: Tuition for 2010–11 was $41,180, with room and board at $12,510. Forty-six percent of undergraduates received need-based financial aid, and the average student-loan debt of recent graduates amounted to $21,859.

The King's College

New York, New York • www.tkc.edu

The basement on top of the world

In 1775, young Alex Hamilton of New York's King's College held off a revolutionary mob with a lengthy speech, allowing Loyalist college president Miles Cooper to escape to a British warship. The college closed the next year, but reopened in 1784 as Columbia College (now university). In 1938, Percy Crawford, later a pioneer televangelist, opened the King's College in Belmar on the New Jersey shore. In 1955, it moved to affluent Briarcliff Manor in New York's Westchester County—where financial difficulties forced it to close in 1994. In 1999, the Campus Crusade for Christ reopened the King's College (TKC) in Manhattan, with the lofty mission of "preparing exceptional students for principled leadership."

In 2010, the school made a surprising choice for its new president, conservative pundit Dinesh D'Souza. Long a policy analyst, never an academic, D'Souza appalled many in the conservative movement with his 2007 book *The Enemy at Home: The Cultural Left and Its Responsibility for 9/11*, in which he blamed Islamic terrorism against the West not on theological extremism but on America's homegrown moral decadence—essentially attributing the 9/11 attacks to Islamic outrage at Britney Spears. Long a Catholic, D'Souza rebranded himself as a speaker and writer in Evangelical Christian circles. The prominence of his name is likely to help the school attract students and donors.

Academic Life: Art deco Oxbridge

In the past thirty years, academic traditionalists and religious conservatives have launched a number of small colleges to counter broad, destructive trends in higher education seemingly impervious to reform: the dismantling of core curricula, the shock-secularization of church-founded schools, and the advent of what Roger Kimball has called (in a book of the same name) "tenured radicals." A few such schools went bust, while others have become institutions with subcultures all their own, elaborate traditions, and distinctive interpretations of culture—where the children of their married graduates now take the same courses, sometimes from the same professors. Perhaps because they were founded as acts of secession from "mainstream" institutions that had become corrupt or decadent—or maybe because the real estate was cheaper—these small schools were often founded in rural areas, far from the nearest city of any size. This "splendid isolation" no doubt helped

VITAL STATISTICS

Religious affiliation: *Christian (nondenominational)*
Total enrollment: *302*
Total undergraduates: *302*
SAT/ACT midranges: CR: *590–690*, M: *530–610*; ACT: *25–28*
Applicants: *663*
Applicants accepted: *74%*
Applicants accepted who enrolled: *21%*
Tuition and fees: *$27,350*
Room and board: *$12,100*
Freshman retention rate: *68%*
Graduation rate: *50% (4 yrs.), 52% (6 yrs.)*
Courses with fewer than 20 students: *40%*
Student-faculty ratio: *14:1*
Courses taught by graduate students: *none*
Most popular majors: *economics, philosophy, political science*
Students living on campus: *90%*
Guaranteed housing for 4 years? *yes*
Students in fraternities or sororities: *none*

the colleges focus inward on their mission, but it also kept away certain types of students. Eighteen-year-olds who were excited by the prospect of living in the woods with a few dozen other undergrads and a small group of faculty were happy with these schools—but what about everyone else? Until now, no small, conservative, start-up college in the U.S. has been situated in a major city.

The King's College is located in New York. In Manhattan. In the Empire State Building. If this suggests that the founders intend to engage the culture—well, they do. The tiny school (only 302 students so far, and 17 permanent faculty) was founded to serve the following mission: "Through its commitment to the truths of Christianity and a biblical worldview, The King's College seeks to prepare students for careers in which they will help to shape and eventually to lead strategic public and private institutions: to improve government, commerce, law, the media, civil society, education, the arts, and the church."

In practice, this means taking a body of largely evangelical Christian students and introducing them to a level of academic engagement which many have never before encountered.

One key element in the King's College education is its solid core curriculum. A professor at TKC said of these courses:

Our introductory classes in Western civilization and American history and politics are deeply respectful of the heritage they present. Among the distinctive features of Western civilization we emphasize are the dignity of the individual; the capacity of Western civilization to reform itself (it alone abolished slavery), and its quest for scientific knowledge. We teach the American founding as one of the signal events in Western history, and pay particular attention to the rule of law, the separation of powers, freedom of religion and speech, and the protection of property rights. These are not courses on the West or the United States as perfected. The struggle to form a 'more perfect union' rightly implies the limitations of any human order.

As the school's former provost, Professor Peter Wood wrote in the *American Conservative*, "Because the curriculum is mostly a 'core,' with most of the students taking the same classes in the same sequence, they know each other's views, opinions, and intellectual styles as familiarly as the village elders might in a nineteenth-century New England town."

Beyond its wide-ranging core, The King's College limits its mission, offering just two degrees in four programs: a bachelor of science in business management; and a bachelor of arts in a program called Politics, Philosophy, and Economics (PPE)—the latter modeled on famous programs at several Oxford colleges that trained numerous generations of British cabinet ministers. The

> ### SUGGESTED CORE
>
> The Common Core, which consists of twenty required courses, suffices.

PPE degree offers concentrations in literature, theology, media, and education. Said one student of the PPE major, "Very few schools offer this unique degree, but I believe it to be valuable because it speaks to the three most influential areas of human interaction with God, money, and power." Another said that "the strongest aspect of this major is the philosophy portion, and in particular, political philosophy. You come away from this course being able to think very critically about issues and also (hopefully) being able to write well. The economics portion is somewhat weak in my opinion, but I know that the school is working to develop this end of the major."

According to a faculty member, "The emphasis in economics had been very free-market. It could have been described as all-Hayek all the time, but that's changing." In one economics class, a professor integrates his free-market approach with the school's biblical inspiration—for instance, by using the parable of the Prodigal Son to illustrate the U.S. trade deficit and profligate federal spending. The political science program bears a heavily philosophical stamp, in part because the school's chancellor, J. Stanley Oakes, and several of its faculty were trained by followers of Harry Jaffa, the constitutional theorist most influential among neoconservatives.

The King's College "is a magnet for a very ambitious sort of self-consciously Christian student who loves the intense focus of the curriculum and who thrives on the tight-knit, face-to-face community," wrote former Provost Wood. However, many of these students "aren't aware of the powerful intellectual tradition within evangelical Christianity," another professor says. "I have to remind them that C. S. Lewis was a literary scholar at Oxford—and that most of America's great universities were founded by devout Christians. That helps them understand that developing intellectually is part of the walk of faith." This is important because "the evangelical world in which these students were raised isn't known for pushing hard on intellectual rigor," Wood wrote. "Keeping true to the faith, reading the Bible every day, and treating others with heartfelt sincerity count a lot more in these communities than sharp elbows and a manic work style. And evangelicals tend to be forgiving when it comes to things like crisp writing, precise diction, and an agile grasp of political theory. . . . [However,] I expect them to develop an ethic of unrelenting excellence in their writing, speaking, and analysis. That's the only way they will succeed in the elite institutions that they aspire to join."

Students seem to appreciate being held to such a high standard. According to one, "In a recent student satisfaction survey conducted at King's, the aspect of the school most valued by students is academic rigor. King's students work hard for their grades, and most are, of necessity, 'awakened' intellectually." At The King's College, faculty foster such awakenings through small classes with an emphasis on the Great Books and great ideas, trips to the innumerable artistic and cultural treasures of one of the world's great cities, and work in local soup kitchens as part of theology class. Since the school's emphasis is on that "mere Christianity" shared by most broadly orthodox believers, it attracts as students and faculty both Catholics and Protestants—although the latter, unsurprisingly, predominate. Renowned Catholic philosopher Peter Kreeft has for several years come down each week from Boston College to teach philosophy classes, while other distinguished professors come in from points much farther south and west. However, the school is building its permanent faculty and will probably diminish its reliance on visiting professors.

By all accounts, members of the permanent faculty work closely with students outside of the classroom—and even visiting professors make sure to schedule extensive office hours. "King's professors are for the most part extremely accessible," a student says. Fur-

ACADEMIC REQUIREMENTS

At The King's College, students are exposed to a serious, integrated core curriculum like those that used to prevail at most elite American colleges. At TKC, students must take twenty core courses in a particular sequence:

First Year:

- "College Writing" I & II.
- "Western Civilization" I & II.
- "Introduction to the City."
- "Introduction to Economics."
- "Introduction to Old Testament Literature."
- "Pre-Calculus/Calculus."
- "Philosophical Apologetics."
- "Logic."

Second Year:

- "Introduction to Politics."
- "Introduction to New Testament Literature."
- "Microeconomics."
- "Introduction to American Thought and Practice" I.

Third Year:

- "American Thought and Practice" II & III.
- "Scientific Reasoning."
- "Biblical Interpretation."

Fourth Year

- "Foundations of Judeo-Christian Thought."
- "Persuasive Writing and Speaking."

thermore, "many professors are involved as faculty advisors in the House system. Through this channel and others, professors get very involved in students' lives. From frequent meals or coffees in between classes, to sharing home-cooked meals, to just walking about the city discussing the pressing issues that our country and world face, the professors go out of their way to extend the education experience beyond the classroom," reports the student.

Favorite teachers include Kreeft in philosophy; David Tubbs in politics; Ron Harris in business; Henry Beattler in media; and Robert Jackson in English. One undergrad singled out Steve Salyers in communications, praising him for the care he shows students: "He spends almost all of his time on campus, and frequently has students to his home for dinner or parties. He really extends the process of learning beyond the classroom." Theology teacher Robert Carle is said to be "incredibly knowledgeable, [with an] incredible grasp of material he teaches—whether it's civil rights, church history, writing, or comparative religions."

The school's own library is small and full of conservative and religious classics, and the texts used in classes. TKC stands, however, only one block from the Science, Business, and Industry division (and ten blocks from the main branch) of the New York Public Library—so nearly any text which a teacher or student could possibly need is easily accessible.

Some of the acknowledged weak points at TKC are areas which the school has not found time to address in all the flurry of starting up a college and crafting a focused program to serve its stated mission. The school teaches only two mathematics courses and no hard sciences or foreign languages. The college hopes to roll out a number of study-abroad options in the near future; presently, "International Ventures" allows students and faculty to study for up to three weeks in places like the Carribean, Albania, Bulgaria, Israel, Uganda, and Turkey. Students from King's have also done summer mission projects in Peru, Asia, and the Middle East, and have joined ministry teams led by TKC's organization, Campus Crusade for Christ. No doubt, for many of the students at TKC, living in polyglot, postmodern New York feels like they are already studying abroad.

Student Life: Jonah in Nineveh

If you visit The King's College, don't expect a panoramic view; the classrooms, library, and student lounge are in the basement, and all entering must pass through strict security checkpoints. One student reports that "it's really cool to flash your Empire State Building security pass and skip the lines." Administrative offices are on the fifteenth floor—still not much of a view. The facilities are clean and have a slightly corporate feel, although the students have made the lounge their own; it looks like a trendy coffee shop.

As one might expect of a Christian school that locates itself in what many believers might consider the heart of Mammon, The King's College takes a more laissez-faire approach towards student life than many religious colleges. The school is not "value-neutral," of course, and it maintains a reasonable set of rules for a Christian college. But rather than build up an elaborate structure for discipline, TKC has emulated American military academies and older religious schools in crafting an honor code, which students adopt and enforce themselves. "We see that as more suited to young adults living in a major city," said an administrator. "We want the students to take ownership of these values and internalize

GREEN LIGHT

The political atmosphere at King's College "is by no means monolithic," one teacher insists. As one student says, "People often joke that King's is a cookie-cutter school of right-wing Republicans from Middle America. The student body is actually quite diverse—King's has many international students and students from all over the country. Divergent opinions are well tolerated." Another agreed, saying, "debate is quite vigorous on campus, especially on issues such as . . . gay rights. A big campus-wide debate concerns to what degree religious morality should enter the American political arena. As TKC is a Christian college, religious students are quite welcome, and on the flip side, more-liberal, less-religious students are also very welcome. Non-Christians have come to King's and loved it. They said they didn't feel oppressed by religion in the classroom."

them—not look at a list of imposed, detailed rules which they're immediately tempted to try to circumvent. That's just (fallen) human nature," he observes. One student reports, "The school's location in New York City is a huge boon. King's students are not in a 'Christian bubble,' but in an extremely worldly city that is 'the center of the universe.' The school's location is strategic for cultivating leadership in the secular national institutions of government, business, media, education, etc."

There are no dorms per se, but blocks of apartments in three nearby buildings. All male students live in the Ludlow Residence, and female students reside in Harold Towers or The Vogue. The residences are divided into ten "Houses" with two faculty advisors and a five member core leadership team consisting of a president, a helmsman (responsible for new House members), a chamberlain (resident assistant), a scholar (responsible for cultivating intellectual life), and vicar (responsible for cultivating spiritual life). According to the college, "a House consists of twenty-five to thirty students who live, study, and work together. Each House is named after a great historic leader who left his/her mark on our world . . . and carries with it the values and traditions particular to that House." (Several houses are named for political figures, including Margaret Thatcher, Ronald Reagan, Winston Churchill, and Queen Elizabeth I.) As students are wont to do, they have already begun to come up with their own traditions, sources report, in the hope that they will eventually become venerable. The student Houses compete in debates, contests, sports, and projects for missionary outreach.

Said a student, "It's an interesting environment for college life, because we share those buildings with hundreds of other tenants. Our rooms are spread throughout the buildings, so we're not really clumped into one big party hall. Students spend a lot of time studying with each other in the various apartments. Because they all have kitchens, group meals are also a frequent part of 'dorm life.' Every apartment has four students (typically), and each apartment has its own bathroom." Said another student, "The residence director lives with his family in the girls' buildings. All visitors are announced by the buildings (they check in at the desks and are buzzed up). All overnight guests must be reported to a chamberlain. Guys cannot be in girls' rooms and vice versa past 1:00 AM." Of these arrangements, a student says, "housing rules are actually very limited. King's wants to treat its students as adults and let them make their own decisions. You can smoke or drink, if you are of age, but not in the apartments themselves—out of respect for your roommates (and New York laws). And there are 'privacy hours.' This is not so much a curfew but a way to make sure two or three roommates don't dominate the apartment over the others."

Infractions of rules are handled by student committees, in accord with the school's honor code. Said one student, "Dorms are dry, and most students don't drink. But if students do come back to the dorm really drunk, they're likely at most just to be questioned." There is no attempt to police the private lives of students or faculty off campus or on break. In other words, The King's College would never airbrush the smokes and drinks out of photographs of their beloved C. S. Lewis—as happened, sources report, at Wheaton College.

Current clubs and organizations at King's include Artisan's Guild, The King's Debate Society, SPARK (Students Promoting Awareness and Responsibility at Kings), King's Dancers, NeW (Network of enlightened Women), Tent (a bi-monthly worship service), BreadBreakers (a cooking club), and the school's paper, the *Empire State Tribune*.

King's introduced club sports to its athletic department in Fall 2010. Soccer, volleyball, basketball, running, and Ultimate Frisbee are available for competition on a regional and national level. Intramural sports offered are soccer, basketball, volleyball, flag football, and Ultimate Frisbee. Recreation sports for students with common interests include cycling, swimming, golf, tennis, snowboarding, and skiing.

Students seem enthusiastic about their location, and manage to get their work done despite the many distractions offered by a many-splendored city—which offers every possible variety of theater, popular and classical music, arts performance, and ethnic cuisine, along with dozens of museums and hundreds of historic buildings. Churches of every denomination are a short walk or a safe subway ride away. Best of all, said one student, "The King's College is in the Empire State Building—what could be cooler than that? It's impressive to watch the Macy's Thanksgiving Parade walk past your front door, and to walk to New York's largest building every day and think 'that's my school building.'" Conversely, said the same student, "Sometimes I go uptown to Columbia University to study or relax and think that it would be nice to have a campus."

Crime is not an issue inside the heavily patrolled Empire State Building or in the nearby dorms, and the Midtown area is one of the lowest-crime areas of New York—itself now one of America's safest major cities. The school's crime statistics do not yet appear in the Department of Education database.

As private colleges go, TKC's costs are midrange, with 2010–11 tuition at $27,350 and room and board at $10,500. No board plan is offered; students have kitchens, and there are literally hundreds of eateries within walking distance. Meals have been conservatively estimated at $1,600. The school works hard to help students financially; 100 percent of full-time undergraduates receive need-based financial aid, but the average debt of recent graduates is still $15,434.

Lafayette College

Easton, Pennsylvania • www.lafayette.edu

Happy medium

Lafayette College, in Pennsylvania's Lehigh Valley, offered its first classes in 1832. While its current curriculum is nothing extraordinary, interaction between Lafayette's faculty and students is frequent and highly valued. Professors kindle a love for learning in their students, and teaching rather than research is the top priority. The college's beautiful hilltop campus in Easton, Pennsylvania, makes Lafayette a pleasant place to spend four years.

Academic Life: On the marquee

For all its devotion to teaching, Lafayette has followed the nearly universal trend toward a lax curriculum. The school's graduation mandates give students enough leeway to ignore entire academic disciplines, should they choose to do so. As a history professor states, "We have a very weak set of requirements for our students." The school has few distributional requirements to speak of.

All students take a first-year seminar, followed by an English course, "College Writing," (AP credits can exempt them). Another seminar in "Values and Science/Technology" encourages students to think about ethical issues raised by technology. Along with these, Lafayette students must take courses in the Humanities and Social Sciences divisions, three total, at least one in each division. A mathematics course is required and two lab science classes. Every course in the catalog will satisfy at least one of the distribution requirements, but nothing forces or even encourages students to choose classes that contribute centrally to a broad liberal arts education. "To get the depth of knowledge envisioned for a liberal arts college, the burden falls on the student," says one. But a teacher asks, "How would they know?" One faculty member jokingly remarked to us, "Lafayette is pretty liberal about its liberal education." He added, "I'm not sure how much difference this makes for our engineering students, whom we prepare well, but it's a weakness for a lot of our humanities majors."

At Lafayette, professors are usually enthusiastic mentors. With no graduate students at the school, faculty members keep their focus on teaching. A professor who arrived after doing his graduate studies at a respected West Coast university told us, "The students are generally good. And they get real care in how and by whom they are taught." The student-faculty ratio is 11 to 1. "Lafayette, more than any other school I've ever seen, has professors who genuinely care if their students are learning the material," says a student. "I've never been turned away by a professor if I was seeking help. My professors' doors are always open." A history major says, "Professors are so accessible. Most of them even give you their home phone numbers and encourage you to call with questions. When I raise my hand in class, my professor knows my name."

Further, the faculty is becoming more impressive. One professor says that when the college hires teachers, it usually gets its first or second choice. "Per person, the faculty is extraordinary," the professor says. "As a whole, the faculty works very, very hard, partly because Lafayette is small enough that everyone would notice if you didn't."

But even teachers who are not up-and-coming "names" in their field are still very devoted to their students. For instance, Lafayette's math department is not of the top rank in terms of research, but it gets higher marks from students for teaching than many larger, more prestigious programs. Says one student, "I was kind of shocked to hear friends at other schools say that their math instructors were bad and didn't know English. Math isn't my major, and I took two extra classes in the subject because my professors were so good." Classes at Lafayette are small—seminars are capped at twenty-five students, while most other classes have fewer than twenty. The average class size is seventeen.

In the advising program, each freshman pairs with a faculty member; once the student declares a major, he can choose another advisor. The website states that the advisors have an eye toward postgraduate education. One student majoring in government and law says, "The advising program is what you make of it . . . I am a very self-sufficient person, so I only need my advisor to help pick courses and to keep me abreast of research/work opportunities in the department."

The deepest student-faculty relationships are fostered in the course of academic research and independent study. The EXCEL Scholars program allows students to gain valuable research experience while getting paid for it; around 160 students participate each year. According to one teacher, "Students in EXCEL get a good sense of what grad school is. If anything, they get more personal attention through EXCEL than they will in most Masters and PhD programs." Sources agree that Lafayette has one of the strongest undergraduate research programs in the country.

VITAL STATISTICS

Religious affiliation: *Presbyterian*
Total enrollment: *2,406*
Total undergraduates: *2,406*
SAT/ACT midranges: CR: *570–670*, M: *600–710*; ACT: *24–29*
Applicants: *5,760*
Applicants accepted: *42%*
Applicants accepted who enrolled: *26%*
Tuition and fees: *$38,810*
Room and board: *$11,959*
Freshman retention rate: *95%*
Graduation rate: *86% (4 yrs.)*, *89% (6 yrs.)*
Courses with fewer than 20 students: *57%*
Student-faculty ratio: *11:1*
Courses taught by graduate students: *none*
Most popular majors: *social sciences, engineering, English*
Students living on campus: *96%*
Guaranteed housing for 4 years? *yes*
Students in fraternities: *26%* in sororities: *45%*

SUGGESTED CORE

1. Comparative Literature 121, Greek Literature in English
2. Philosophy 214, First Philosophers
3. Religion 201/202, The Biblical Imagination: Torah, Prophets, Writings/Christian Scriptures
4. Religious Studies 214, Christianity: From Jesus to the Third Millennium (closest match)
5. Government and Law 244, Modern Political Theory
6. English 301, Shakespeare
7. History 230/234, Early American History, 1600-1840/Slavery, Civil War, and Reconstruction
8. History 253/254, European Thought, Society, and Culture

Lafayette was one of the first American colleges to offer an engineering program, and the department remains Lafayette's best known. Students say that its teaching is first-rate. Besides engineering, Lafayette's strengths lie in its economics and business departments, but there has also been recent improvement in the natural sciences, especially biology, chemistry, and physics. The college boasts forty-seven majors within four branches of study: humanities, social sciences, natural sciences, and engineering.

The English major requires nine classes beyond the basic college writing course: one in literary theory, and one in literary history, and seven electives, five of which must be advanced. There are good offerings in Shakespeare and pre-1800 literature, and throughout the American and British tradition; however, none of them are required. The English department also has a close relationship with theater, and there is the possibility for an English major with a drama/theater concentration, a film concentration, and a writing concentration.

The history major also entails at least ten courses, including a class on the history of the modern world (1450 and onwards), historical analysis, a research seminar, an advanced course, and a course on Europe, non-Western history, and America. Ancient and medieval history are not required, nor is American history before 1900. There are too few offerings in premodern history.

The government and law major requires students to choose intro courses in three out of four subject areas (U.S. government, international politics, comparative politics, and political theory), exposure to all four sub-fields, three upper-level classes, and either a senior seminar or an honors thesis. Majors cannot emerge without studying the American political system. One student says of the department, "It never fails to impress me. My political theory professor has a talent for encouraging a discussion-based environment."

For those who want them, multicultural courses and majors exist, ranging from Africana and women's studies to Jewish, Latin American and Caribbean, and East Asian studies.

Lafayette's recommended list of teachers is lengthy and spans all fields of study: Diane Ahl in art history; Ethan Berkove, Evan Fisher, Gary P. Gordon, Jeffrey Leibner, Elizabeth W. McMahon, John Meier, Clifford A. Reiter, Derek Smith and Lorenzo Traldi in mathematics; Paul D. Barclay, and Robert I. Weiner in history; Robert Cohn and Eric Ziolkowksi in religious studies; Paul Cefalu and Carolynn Van Dyke in English; Bruce Allen Murphy, and Helena Silverstein in government and law; Yvonne Gindt in chemistry; Edward N. Gamber in economics and business; John F. Greco and Ismail I. Jouny in electrical and computer engineering; Mark Crain in economics; Steven Kurtz in civil engineering; and Steven M. Nesbit in mechanical engineering.

Among the top thirty liberal arts colleges in the country, Lafayette has the fifth-highest rate of participation in study-abroad programs. Under the auspices of other colleges and universities, Lafayette students may take approved programs abroad in such locales as New Zealand (four programs), Uganda, Namibia, and Bali. These are in addition to courses of study in the U.K., France, Argentina, Spain, Germany, Australia, Japan, and other countries, nearly forty in all.

Each January and May the school offers an interim session. This takes place when most students are on break. During the interim session, the faculty travel with students to teach a wide assortment of on-site classes like "The Geologic Evolution of the Hawaiian Islands" and "Inside the People's Republic of China." These courses have proved very popular, and while they are not covered in the regular cost of tuition, many students sign up.

Lafayette's departments tend to have a sensible focus on straightforward subject matter. This is somewhat a function of necessity. Says a professor: "There are areas where we don't have teachers because of the school's size." This narrows the range of things like foreign language instruction. Lafayette offers majors in French, German, and Spanish. It also has classes in Hebrew, Latin, Ancient Greek, Japanese and Russian, and Chinese—but not in Portuguese, Arabic, Turkish, or Italian, among other languages.

ACADEMIC REQUIREMENTS

Lafayette has no core curriculum, maintaining instead a modest set of distribution requirements. All students must take:

- One First-Year Seminar. Students may choose among many options, ranging from "Masculinities: Maleness in Contemporary American Culture" to "Folktale in Society: From Beauty and the Beast to Big Foot."
- One freshman writing course, "College Writing."
- A Values and Science/Technology Seminar (VAST). Among the fifty or so courses that fulfill the requirement are: "Oil, Politics, and the Environment," "Mapping Urban Ecology," and "Telepathy: Advances in Brain-Machine Interface Technology."
- Three courses in humanities or social science. Humanities choices include "Literary History," "Post-Colonial Literature," and "Classical Mythology." Social sciences choices range from "Principles of Economics" to "Deviance."
- Two laboratory courses in biology, chemistry, geology, physics, or psychology.
- One course in mathematics, computer science, or logic.
- Two upper-level writing-intensive courses, chosen from a long list that includes everything from "British History" to "Feminist Philosophy."

Liberal arts students must also complete a "foreign culture cluster," either by studying abroad, reaching intermediate proficiency in a foreign language, or by taking three related courses on another (non-English-speaking) culture.

Mid-Atlantic

Student Life: Beer can Priapus

More Lafayette students come from across the Delaware River in New Jersey than from the college's home state of Pennsylvania. A solid majority of students hail from these and surrounding northeastern states, but they tend to stay on campus once they get there. Students say they usually head home only on official breaks, not weekends, since the college provides plenty of reasons for students to stick around.

On-campus housing is guaranteed for all undergraduate years and required for freshmen students not commuting from home. Most residences are arranged in traditional corridor halls, but there are suite-style and townhouse options as well. Dormitories are coed, except for two all-female residences and one all-male hall, and most bathrooms are shared by floor. RAs are said to do their jobs, and enforce the rules. Soles Hall, an all-women suite-style residence, has a fitness center in its basement for residents. Many students choose living units whose residents share an interest in a particular theme; in 2010–11, these included the Japanese Interest Floor, ACIF (African-Caribbean Interest Floor), CAFE (Cooking and Food Enthusiasts), HOLA (Heritage of Latin America), TreeHouse (environmentalist), and the Industrial Arts Floor. All dorms are smoke-free. Both the P. T. Farinon and Conway Houses are specifically designed for freshmen "who choose an academically focused residential environment."

The past two presidents of Lafayette worked to broaden the ethnic mix of students. "Diversity makes for a better learning environment on several levels," President Weiss said in a college publication, claiming "it is a fact of life that familiarity with other kinds of people makes you more successful in the world." Since 1970, the college has supported the Portlock Black Cultural Center, which hosts lectures on multicultural topics, and it has sponsored student groups like the Association of Black Collegians and the Brothers of Lafayette. In 2010, Lafayette hosted a number of black performers and speakers including rapper Kid Cudi and popular astronomer Neil deGrasse Tyson. Other cultural groups include the Arab Club, *Aya* (a black literary magazine), and the French club. Lafayette employs a director of intercultural development; runs a visitation weekend for black and Hispanic prospective students; and sponsors annual festivals that celebrate Hispanic heritage, international food, and the recently invented holiday of Kwanzaa. Despite these fervent administration efforts, Lafayette remains overwhelmingly white, and minority students are said to self-segregate.

Lafayette College offers dozens of social, political, and academic organizations. Greek life in Lafayette flourishes: more than one-third of Lafayette students are members of fraternities or sororities. However, students report that these groups are not exclusive. One student says, "A lot of the frats welcome other frats to their parties. The allegiance guys hold is first and foremost towards Lafayette, not their frat." Students cannot rush fraternities or sororities until their sophomore year, a rule that allows students to make friends with hallmates and classmates before settling into Greek organizations, should they choose to do so.

Other student activities include the *Lafayette* newspaper, musical groups, the Forensics Society, and student government. The college's Landis Community Outreach Center promotes volunteer activities like Habitat for Humanity; Prison Tutors; Alternative Spring Break; and visits to nursing homes, schools, and hospitals.

Lafayette also has religious groups for several different faiths. But one insider says, "Few students are interested in God. To talk about religion is seen by a lot of students as almost weird." Lafayette does have an active Newman Association for Catholic students, and regular Sunday Mass is held in the school's Colton Chapel. Protestant students typically join either with the Lafayette Christian Fellowship or the ecumenical Sojourners group, which has regular Bible study meetings. There are also a Muslim Student Association and Hillel Society just across from campus. However, there is no Kosher-meal or Halal-meal alternative at Lafayette. The university instead claims to offer "Kosher-style" meals on Jewish holidays.

Lafayette has nearly 250 student-run organizations and groups in total, a small sampling being: American Institute of Chemical Engineers, Lafayette Dancers, College Theater, Madrigal Singers, Philosophy Club, Muslim Student Association, Mock Trial Team, German Club, Quintessence—Student *a cappella* group, *Marooned* (an independent newspaper), Anime Club, Investment Club, History Club, and campus radio station WJRH (104.9).

> **GREEN LIGHT**
>
> Groups such as Students for Social Justice and QuEST (Questioning Established Sexual Taboos) are among the most outspoken on campus. QuEST also organizes National Coming Out Day activities on campus each year as well as other events and protests, but students say that these and similar events draw little interest. At the same time, the college hosts a small College Republicans chapter of about forty members who work on campaigns and bring speakers to campus. As a whole, however, the "the student population leans to the left/middle" says one student. "If there is a conservative, nonreligious group on campus, I haven't heard of it."
>
> Lafayette faculty tend to be liberal, but seem tolerant of disagreement. Sources say the faculty seems to be moving further to the left—even as the student body is trending more conservative. One student told us, "In general, professors respect students and their views—and vice versa. Most people are here to learn."

The city of Easton, best known nationally as the home of Crayola crayons, adds little to the school environment. Lafayette looks down on the town from what is known as College Hill. "Parts of Easton are economically depressed," says one student, "and for the most part we don't really do things in the town below." What students mostly seem to do is go to the town's liquor stores. One undergrad says that, "some of us were geeks in high school. Others were the jocks on school lacrosse teams. Whichever, we like campus parties."

Lafayette's sports program has never been central to the school, but as of 2005, Lafayette began to offer athletic scholarships. The Lafayette Leopards compete in the Patriot League in twenty varsity sports—a large number for a school of Lafayette's size. The college also offers a nice array of club sports and intramurals. Lafayette's archrival, "the oldest college rivalry in the country," is nearby Lehigh University. "We hate Lehigh," says a student. "That's our only real tradition at the school." In March 2010, this rivalry led to an embarrassing incident in which Lafayette students began chanting obscenities at Lehigh players during a college basketball game—earning a reprimand to the whole student body which the college president issued by e-mail.

Among Lafayette's club teams are crew, skiing, Ultimate Frisbee, volleyball, ice hockey, tae kwon do, and an equestrian club. Intramural sports are popular as well. The college's Kirby Sports Center, is an excellent facility for nonvarsity athletes, with a forty-foot indoor climbing wall, racquetball and squash courts, a gym, and a fitness center. Informal group exercise classes like cardio-kickboxing, spin cycling, and zumba keep students fit.

Lafayette's geographic isolation helps keep campus crime relatively infrequent. According to one student, crime is "not at all" a problem. "I always can walk around at night," he says, "and it's very well lit, and security is prevalent." In 2009, the school reported four forcible sex offenses, thirty burglaries, and one arson on campus. A recent Lafayette scandal involved the sexual harassment of five young women by an officer in the public safety office. Lafayette agreed to a settlement, giving each of the young women $200,000.

Lafayette is not one of the bargain options for parents; tuition in 2010–11 ran $38,810, with room and board at $11,959. Admission is need blind, but the school does not guarantee to meet a student's full financial need. Some 57 percent of students receive need-based aid. Average student indebtedness is $20,745 at graduation.

Lehigh University

Bethlehem, Pennsylvania • www.lehigh.edu

A can-do school

In 1865, Asa Packer, a Pennsylvania businessman who made his fortune in the Lehigh Valley Railroad Company, decided to give something back to the region that had enriched him by donating the then-princely sum of $500,000 to found Lehigh University. Although much of the curriculum focused on the engineering sciences, Packer envisioned Lehigh not just as a technical school, but as an institution where students could receive a liberal arts education as well as a grounding in the pure and applied sciences. Competition was stimulated through an entrance examination—for the first twenty years of Lehigh's existence, students who passed this difficult exam received free tuition. But eventually Packer's fortune dried up, and so did the scholarships.

Today, Lehigh no longer needs to offer this kind of incentive to attract competitive students to its mostly practical and preprofessional programs. The school maintains a small liberal arts contingent of modest powers and limited influence, but thankfully comprised of mostly solid and traditional departments.

Lehigh's thirteenth president, Alice Gast—former assistant provost at MIT—was installed following the familiar campus-wide call to increase "diversity" at Lehigh through the appointment of a female or minority president. After her appointment, the Council of Equity and Community (CEC) was formed to continue this trend. Although Lehigh is a traditionally conservative campus, there's no telling the impact such an institution of ideological activism will have on the university. If other colleges' tales can be trusted, no good can come of it.

Academic Life: Hands on

Lehigh has four undergraduate colleges: the P. C. Rossin College of Engineering, the prestigious program which has made the school's name; the College of Arts and Sciences; the College of Education; and the College of Business and Economics. This last school was ranked twenty-seventh in the U.S. for "Quality of Undergraduate Business Education" by *Bloomberg BusinessWeek* in 2010. Lehigh's business college imparts a solid foundation in the principles of running an enterprise, obliging students to fulfill a regimen of challenging prerequisites, in addition to major requirements. The school also offers an innovative

Mid-Atlantic

VITAL STATISTICS

Religious affiliation: *none*
Total enrollment: *7,051*
Total undergraduates: *4,781*
SAT midranges: CR: *590–630,*
  M: *630–710*
Applicants: *11,170*
Applicants accepted: *33%*
Applicants accepted who
  enrolled: *42%*
Tuition and fees: *$39,780*
Room and board: *$10,520*
Freshman retention rate:
  94%
Graduation rate: *76% (4 yrs.),*
  86% (6 yrs.)
Courses with fewer than 20
  students: *49%*
Student-faculty ratio: *10:1*
Courses taught by graduate
  students: *not provided*
Most popular majors:
  finance, accounting,
  mechanical engineering
Students living on campus:
  68%
Guaranteed housing for 4
  years? *no*
Students in fraternities: *39%*
  in sororities: *38%*

minor in entrepreneurship, which focuses on the challenges involved in managing start-up companies.

Lehigh's engineering school is also highly ranked. To finish its competitive program within four years, students are expected to declare their major as early as possible, normally by the end of freshman year. Like the business college, the engineering school sets out very specific guidelines for the chosen course of study; however, the majority of requirements differ according to the choice of specialization, sometimes at the expense of a broader education. Says one professor: "Although business and engineering students might excel in their own specializations, their grounding in liberal arts is oftentimes woefully small."

Lehigh's College of Arts and Sciences (CAS) is the smallest of the four undergraduate colleges. One professor claims that Lehigh seems to have "neglected the arts and sciences in its focus on maintaining and enhancing the reputations of the business and engineering schools." Many CAS programs lack graduate counterparts, and some undergraduate majors struggle to maintain academic focus. For instance, while one student mentions the many avenues of study available in the English department, another notes the predominance of American history courses at the expense of European and world history. Some areas are simply understaffed. A liberal arts professor complains of the chronic need for more language instructors, especially in the budding Asian studies department.

On the positive side, the relative lack of resources in the humanities has prevented the departments in those fields from succumbing to popular, ideologically infused academic trends. There are relatively few courses offered in grievance-based disciplines such as feminism, Marxism, or racial particularism. According to the school, "The English major emphasizes rigorous study of literary periods, genres, and authors. Majors take at least nine courses, four of which must be advanced (300-level) investigations of authors or literary periods." Requirements for majors include at least one class in British literature before 1660, another in British authors from 1660–1900, and one in American writers before 1900, which suggests that English majors emerging from Lehigh are likely to be better grounded in literary history than those at other schools where courses are trendier and requirements laxer.

The philosophy department's offerings, with one or two exceptions, seem conventional and foundational—indeed, one professor labels Lehigh's liberal arts offerings as "very, very traditional." The history department is solid as well, requiring all majors to take Western civilization survey classes in the history of Europe from ancient times to 1648, and from 1648 to the present; its electives seem mostly substantial.

On the other hand, the political science department leaves much to be desired, requiring neither a U.S. Constitution nor an American political philosophy course, and many of the electives seem ideological or trendy, such as "Politics of Women," "Gender and Third World Development" and the nonsensical-sounding "Politics of Authenticity."

Both students and professors say that several programs in the College of Arts and Sciences, particularly Earth and environmental science and the biological sciences, are burgeoning with new professors, new majors, and new curricula. The CAS also offers several distinctive honors options, including the Eckardt College Scholars Program—which fosters independent research through seminars and a senior honors project—and the Global Citizenship Program, a cross-college, multi-disciplinary certificate program which incorporates courses in international relations and modern languages to prepare students for foreign service and international business.

> ### SUGGESTED CORE
>
> 1. Classics 101, Greek Literature, or Classics 208, Homer, Virgil and the Ancient Epic
> 2. Philosophy 131, Ancient Philosophy
> 3. Religion Studies 111/114, Jewish Scriptures/Old Testament; Christian Origins: New Testament and the Beginnings of Christianity
> 4. Religion Studies 75, The Christian Tradition
> 5. Political Science 102, Modern Political Heritage
> 6. English 328, Shakespeare
> 7. History 41, United States to 1865
> 8. History 356, European Cultural History

Undergraduates majoring in the College of Arts and Sciences are assigned faculty members as their academic advisors. According to the school's website, "Faculty teach the courses and design the curricula, so who better to guide students in course selection and curriculum navigation?" Entering students are initially assigned a non-major advisor. On declaring a major, students are then assigned to a major advisor in their program who guides them through the remainder of their undergraduate career. In addition to appointed advisors, students may take advantage of Lehigh's excellent Career Services, Dean of Students staff, and Associate Deans of the Colleges personnel for additional guidance and support.

Some highly recommended professors at Lehigh include Rajan Menon in international relations; Connie Cook in Asian studies; Eric Salathe and Joseph Yukich in mathematics; Michael Baylor and C. Robert Phillips in history; Keith Schray in chemistry; David Amidon (emeritus) in urban studies; and J. Richard Aronson and Frank Gunter in economics.

Several innovative programs at Lehigh promise the kind of hands-on, practical learning that seems to embody the school's heritage. The university offers various "integrated learning" initiatives designed to combine "what you learn in the classroom . . . with the solution of real-world problems for real-world 'clients.'" One example is the Integrated Product, Process, and Project Development (IPD) program, which, according to its website, is "a set of courses that allows students from any college at Lehigh to work with students from other disciplines on a real-world industry sponsored project. Each project team has a faculty advisor and together with an industry mentor, the team follows a proven process that identifies a problem, formulates it into a business opportunity, encourages wild ideas to generate innovative solutions, provides the resources to fabricate, build and test the best solution for technical, social, economic and personal relevance and value. Undergraduates can spend two or three semesters on this project and this experience can be continued into a Master of Engineering in IPD."

Another integrated learning initiative is The Lehigh Earth Observatory (LEO), which is involved in a "range of projects includ[ing] water-quality monitoring on the Lehigh River, the development of a geographic information system for the Lehigh River watershed, operating a seismic station and a network of weather-monitoring stations, and collaborative work with the Nature Conservancy and the Wildlands Conservancy."

Many students take advantage of Lehigh's 200 study-abroad programs in over sixty countries such as Botswana, Madagascar, Rwanda, Uganda, Bolivia, Brazil, Chile, Ecuador, Nicaragua, China, Indonesia, India, Australia, New Zealand, Austria, Germany, Denmark, Egypt, and Israel, among many others. Unlike most schools, Lehigh has an Abroad Faculty Policy Board comprised of faculty members who approve which study-abroad programs qualify for Lehigh credit.

It is curious that Lehigh does not require undergraduates to study a foreign language, given that the university has a first-class Modern Languages and Literature department, in which students may major in French, German, and Spanish, or minor in Chinese, Japanese, and Russian. Latin, Ancient Greek, Hebrew, and Arabic are also offered.

Student Life: Rust Belt rehab

Located a little more than an hour's car ride from Philadelphia and New York, Lehigh is a going concern in a town whose main employer, Bethlehem Steel, declined through the 1990s and closed its gates permanently in 2003. The school's central Asa Packer Campus sits in the economically depressed south side of the city, now largely inhabited by recent immigrants, retired steelworkers, and students. The 1600-acre campus is described as "attractive," although it is surrounded by partly empty buildings that once belonged to the steel company—some of which are now being converted for reuse. There is life among the ruins, locals say, pointing to a "large row of quaint artsy shops and cafes" that have appeared on the south side to cater to students, along with bars and pizzerias.

Across the bridge lies the nicer, northern side of town, where the school maintains its Mountaintop Campus, home to its College of Education and many of its science departments. Abutting the campus of nearby Moravian College, this neighborhood features "big beautiful mansions, quaint shops and eateries, brick pavements, a cool old (pre–Revolutionary War) cemetery, a big public library, and mature trees," according to a student. Another school complex, the Murray H. Goodman Campus, lies in a more wooded area in the Saucon Valley.

Several campus buildings were recently renovated, including the Linderman Library, which houses many of the school's 1.3 million volumes, 18,000 print and electronic journal subscriptions, and over 100 scholarly databases. During the renovation, study rooms, skylights, and a student commons were added, in addition to laboratories and showrooms for the humanities' programs and collections. Showcased in the "new" library is Lehigh's impressive rare book collection that includes works by Charles Darwin and James John Audubon. Facelifts have been given to several other buildings on campus, including the Rathbone and Cort dining halls and a residential hall, Umoja House. Lehigh has also seen Lamberton Hall recast as the Hawk's Nest Diner, and the construction of the Campus Square dormitories for upperclassmen.

All students are required to live on campus for their freshman and sophomore years. Freshmen normally live in doubles in coed dorms (a substance-free housing option is available), while sophomores usually room in groups of three or four. Students can rush a fraternity or sorority house during their freshman year, but given the constant prevalence of alcohol—Lehigh is described as a "party school," and local residents regularly complain about the antics of tipsy undergraduates—serious students will want to opt for alternative housing. Juniors and seniors are given the choice of living off campus or continuing to stay in Lehigh's dorms. All bathrooms on campus are single sex.

Lehigh's Office of Student Activities supervises more than 150 academic, social, and religious clubs and organizations on campus. Students can immerse themselves in a variety of activities, from Best Buddies to STAR Tutoring, baseball to paintball, fencing to video gaming, honor societies to community service groups. Many religious and conservative groups, like the College Republicans, the Catholic Student Union, and the Fellowship of

---

ACADEMIC REQUIREMENTS

Lehigh imposes no core curriculum and only a weak series of distribution requirements outside those imposed by a student's major. All students in the College of Arts and Sciences must take:

- "Choices and Decisions," a one-credit course designed to help students adjust to their first semester.
- One first-year seminar. Recent class offerings include "Culture and Body Image" and "Looking at Venus and Mars: Or How Genders Position Themselves."
- "Composition and Literature" I & II.
- One math class. Courses in algebra, calculus, statistics, and computer science qualify.
- Two courses in natural science. There are dozens of qualifying classes in astronomy, biological sciences, chemistry, earth and environmental sciences, and physics. At least one class must include a lab.
- Two courses in social science, such as "Introduction to Psychology" or "Religion, Witchcraft, and Magic."
- Two to three courses in arts and humanities, with choices ranging from "Survey of Europe Since 1648" to "Anthropology of Fishing."
- One writing-intensive course, normally taken in the junior year. Recent class offerings included "World Literature" and "Cultural Fictions and Public Lying."

Mid-Atlantic

GREEN LIGHT

In the world of higher education, Lehigh's political atmosphere is perceived to be predominantly conservative—a reputation that one student believes can be attributed to the teaching staff. Lehigh professors, he says, tend to be "hard-working researchers who would rather work on a math problem than picket on the university lawn in defense of a liberal cause." With the exception of some in the political science and English departments, few professors let their own political opinions intrude upon classroom material.

This general freedom of political thought extends beyond the classroom as well. Many conservative students join the College Republicans; write for the *Lehigh Patriot*, the school's bipartisan political newspaper; and participate in one of the numerous religious groups on campus. But there are several very visible and vocal leftist activist groups on campus as well, particularly the Women's Center and the Progressive Student Union, who regularly agitate for liberal causes.

Christian Athletes, have grown and thrived on campus. The town of Bethlehem is home to dozens of lovely historic churches—some dating from the early nineteenth century—which once served the rich ethnic mix of European immigrants who toiled in the now silent steel mills. Students with an eye for traditional architecture or piety will enjoy exploring them, one source says.

Athletic students can participate in a variety of sports, including Lehigh's top-rated football and wrestling teams. The Lehigh Mountain Hawks compete with twenty-four teams in NCAA Division I, and over fifty intercollegiate sports are offered along with twelve intermural teams. The spectacular Taylor Gymnasium houses racquet sport courts, basketball courts, climbing walls, swimming pools, multi-purpose exercise studios, locker rooms, an athletic store, and the state-of-the-art Welch Fitness Center.

Lehigh's campus is quite safe during the daylight hours, although one student points out the subpar nighttime lighting on campus as a danger largely unaddressed by the campus administration. He wryly notes that it would be wise for the university to "put some of the money squirreled away for beautification projects to good use by installing more lighting fixtures around campus." However, Lehigh's many other safety precautions—a bus service during the day, the TRACS escort service during the night, and a twenty-four-hour campus police patrol—have created a safer university setting. In 2009, the school reported three robberies, nine burglaries, one forcible sex offense, and one stolen car. Since most students inhabit the still-depressed south side of Bethlehem, caution is nevertheless advised.

Lehigh's price tag for 2010–11 was $39,780, with room and board $10,520. Forty-five percent of Lehigh undergraduates received financial aid, and the average indebtedness of recent graduates was a hefty $31,123.

New York University

New York, New York • www.nyu.edu

It takes the Village

New York University was founded in 1831 and from its start offered courses in the practical sciences and arts, such as business, law, and medicine, as well as the liberal arts. The school continues to accentuate the practical, and many students participate in internships in the city as well as hands-on research at the school.

If going to a college nestled among dive bars and congested traffic bothers you, New York University is not your school. Located in the middle of Greenwich Village around Washington Square, NYU's setting is also its strongest drawing point. The neighborhood runs right alongside the West Village; once a low-rent bohemian enclave, this scenic section of nineteenth century townhouses is now the most expensive and fashionable neighborhood in the city.

The last two decades saw a huge rise in wealth among the many CEOs and corporate law partners who attended the school; their generous donations allowed NYU to acquire plenty of property and other resources. By going to NYU, students sacrifice many traditional college experiences—tailgating and football, for instance, and a bucolic, undisturbed central campus green. (Instead, they have Washington Square Park.) On the other hand, they gain four years spent in one of the world's great cities, among its future movers and shakers.

Academic Life: Morse for "core"

NYU has fourteen divisions, including schools of medicine, business, social work, dentistry, and law. The total undergraduate enrollment was 21,269 at last count—that's more than many major state universities. NYU is now among the top fifteen schools in the country in its number of National Merit scholarship winners.

NYU undergraduates interested in a liberal arts major enroll in the College of the Arts and Science or the Gallatin School of Individualized Study. For more than forty years, NYU has also had a separate conservatory for arts majors, the Tisch School, which attracts would-be actors, film and TV directors, playwrights, screenwriters, animators and composers.

Arts and Science students must meet the requirements of the Morse Academic Plan (MAP). One professor says the school's curriculum "is better than nothing, but it's half what it should be. The best classes are probably the required science classes. The Foundations of

VITAL STATISTICS

Religious affiliation: *none*
Total enrollment: *42,189*
Total undergraduates:
  21,269
SAT/ACT midranges: CR:
  620–720, M: *630–720*;
  ACT: *28–31*
Applicants: *37,245*
Applicants accepted: *32%*
Applicants accepted who
  enrolled: *39%*
Tuition and fees: *$40,082*
Room and board: *$13,507*
Freshman retention rate:
  100%
Graduation rate: *77% (4 yrs.),
  84% (6 yrs.)*
Courses with fewer than 20
  students: *55%*
Student-faculty ratio: *12:1*
Courses taught by graduate
  students: *not provided*
Most popular majors: *visual
  and performing arts,
  business/marketing, social
  sciences*
Students living on campus:
  52%
Guaranteed housing for 4
  years? *yes*
Students in fraternities: *1%*
  in sororities: *2%*

Contemporary Culture program, which is supposed to be our Core . . . is really more like a Chinese menu.'" Arts and Science undergraduates must take a class in Western civilization, called "Texts and Ideas," and the class descriptions boast a good array of primary sources, albeit with a special emphasis on the nineteenth century and thinkers like Marx, Darwin and Nietzsche. Some professors assigned to teach these classes have an agenda and will present the Bible as middle-class mythology, sources say. The other three classes in the Foundations of Contemporary Culture are on non-Western topics.

One professor says that "the program was developed when the school had a poorer average caliber of students than it does now, and they made up requirements that they knew these less bright students could consistently meet. Now, professors . . . inject some of their ritualistic political correctness into the thing."

One alternative offering smaller classes and a different curriculum is the Gallatin School of Individualized Study, home to about 1,200 undergraduate students. It offers many internships and private lessons in the arts. Most notably, the Gallatin School teaches many seminal, primary works of the Western tradition from the ancient and modern worlds. However, only self-motivated students should consider Gallatin; some students warn that undirected dilettantes have given the school a bad name—one additionally besmirched by radical faculty members. Gallatin's great strength is its interdisciplinary seminars, which cover great works by authors such as Dante, Shakespeare, Plato, Homer, Nietzsche, Freud, and Marx as well as modern works by Toni Morrison, Elie Wiesel, and others. Seminars span the subjects of the humanities, social sciences, and natural sciences. While NYU has a fairly weak advising system for its College of Arts and Sciences, the Gallatin Division places a great deal of emphasis on its advisors helping students develop their academic plans. Hundreds of faculty members serve as Gallatin advisors.

Outside Gallatin, advisors are available for students who ask for help, but as is typical of NYU, students have to take the initiative. One student reports that "my advisor was very nice, but she didn't seem to know which classes were worth taking. Often she would just shrug."

While NYU is a giant school, classes are not necessarily large—at least in the humanities. The average class size is under thirty. In the sciences, one student says, most courses are "huge lectures with professors," and graduate teaching assistants actually do more of the teaching. Some students say that the professors can be surprisingly accessible. One says, "I had profs who gave out their home numbers and others who changed their office hours in response to e-mail requests." But there are certainly NYU students who found the faculty less than welcoming. "If you're in a big class with a big name professor, they're never going to know who you are," says one recent grad. This seems to be a particular difficulty with the sciences. "Most of my classes have had at least more than 100 students, with a few having as many as 250 or 300. The professor is unlikely to recognize you. . . . Graduate students teach far too many classes, even upper-level courses." Furthermore, "teaching is definitely second to research," reports one professor. Graduate TAs also teach lower-level foreign languages and the mandatory freshman writing course, as well as many of the weekly discussion sessions for the larger introductory courses.

Philosophy majors must complete a strict core that ensures students will graduate with a broad knowledge of the discipline, including logic, ancient philosophy, modern philosophy, ethics or political philosophy, metaphysics or epistemology, the philosophy of mind or language, and upper-level seminars. There are very few "philosophy of feminism," "eco-ethics," or other such courses at NYU.

The English, Spanish Judaic studies, Middle Eastern studies, Italian, and math departments are said to be strong. History is less highly regarded, and it houses a number of tenured radicals (as do the anthropology, sociology, and women's and black studies departments). History course offerings include few ancient or medieval options, a wide selection in modern and contemporary history, and too many "gender issues" classes. One student says "There are decent professors. But it's like everything here. You've got to ask around and find out who's good." The history major consists of nine classes, six of them upper level, with two courses in each of three geographical areas (U.S., European, and non-Western) and one advanced seminar. Students need only take one course set before 1800, and could easily miss any study of the American founding or Civil War.

The math department attracts many of the school's best students. A good number of these students are from the city's population of Russian immigrants, and the department has become a significant feeder of foreign-born actuaries seeking out lucrative positions in the city's large insurance industry.

The program in undergraduate English requires four core courses—British literature (two terms), American literature, and a class in literary interpretation—plus one course in critical theories and methods, one in British lit before 1800, then three English electives, and an advanced seminar. Courses in Shakespeare aren't technically required, but they are offered each year, and his work would be hard to miss.

SUGGESTED CORE

1. Classics V27.0146, Greek and Roman Epic
2. Philosophy V83.0020, History of Ancient Philosophy
3. Hebrew and Judaic Studies V78.0023, The Bible as Literature and Religion V90.0302, Introduction to the New Testament
4. Medieval and Renaissance Studies V65.0060, Philosophy in the Middle Ages
5. Politics V53.0110, Topics in Modern Political Thought: 1500 to the Present
6. English V41.0410/0411, Shakespeare I/II
7. History V57.0009, The United States to 1865
8. Conversations of the West V55.0404, Antiquity and the Nineteenth Century

Politics majors take two seminars in economic principles, one in international relations, one in statistical methodology and a senior thesis, among ten total classes, two of which are core courses. Further, one course must be taken from three of five subject areas: analytical politics, political theory, American government and politics, comparative politics, and international politics. Political theory throughout is weighted heavily toward the modern and contemporary. It is possible for a politics major to get through without taking a serious course covering the U.S. Constitution—and there are many ideologically charged options worth avoiding.

Given its location, it is no surprise that NYU is widely recognized for its film and television, theater, and business schools. The list of the school's alumni—and its dropouts—includes Neil Simon, Woody Allen, Debra Messing, Alec Baldwin, Billy Crystal, Martin Scorsese, M. Night Shyamalan, Billy Crudup, Philip Seymour Hoffman, Ang Lee—and even Adam Sandler. One student there says that the Tisch school "is competitive. But it's in a mostly healthy way. They give you equipment and let you work. If you want to be in TV and film it's a great place to go and get experience." One way that students get internships and part-time jobs is by attending events at which alums turn up on campus. Students also pound on the doors of nearby employers in finance, entertainment, advertising, and fashion.

Those studying television can attend a Midtown taping of an NBC program. Theater students can apprentice themselves in off-Broadway theaters down the street. Many business students work on Wall Street, earning course credit and work experience. One student notes, "NYU has, with its location, direct access to major employers. NYU operates a brilliant career center that hosts fairs, recruiting receptions, et cetera, as well as providing walk-ins with advisors specialized in career development."

Some of the best teachers at NYU, according to students, are Simon Bowmaker in economics; Chris Chan-Roberson in film; Nicola Cipani and Chiara Marchelli in Italian; Padraig O'Cearuill in Irish (language); Nils Froment in French; Paul Glimcher in neuroscience; Evelyn Birge Vitz in French; Michael Tyrell in English; Marilyn Horowitz in creative writing; Michael Peachin and Roger S. Bagnall in classics; David Engel in Hebrew and Judaic studies; Jorge Castaneda and Shinasi Rama in politics; and Anne Lounsbery in Russian and Slavic studies.

NYU's weakest departments are in the sciences, music technology and in fields like sociology, women's studies, and African studies. The journalism department is said to have become more politicized over the past few years, and the education department has been positively radicalized.

Students should ask for advice on classes from older students whom they respect. However, most sources told us that classroom politics at NYU are more often implicit, and therefore tolerable. "Most professors, at least all I encountered, were liberal but reasonable. There is a sort of assumption that everyone is liberal, so no one asks," says one student. Another, majoring in chemistry, said her experience was that "politics generally didn't intrude into the classroom." Students at the school are said to be more politically "apathetic" than activist.

NYU encourages students to study abroad for at least a semester. According to the Institute of International Education, NYU has more students studying abroad than any other school in the country. Destinations include Germany, Argentina, Italy, England, France, Spain, the Czech Republic, Ghana, and China.

NYU offers more than twenty-five foreign languages, ranging from Ancient Greek and Latin, to Irish, Swahili, Turkish, and Japanese. Through an agreement with Columbia University, NYU students can take other languages there, including Aramaic, Egyptian, and Cantonese.

Student Life: Bright lights, big city

As one student puts it, NYU students consider themselves Manhattanites who just happen to be taking classes. Students never lack for things to do, although they might lack the money to do them. Several museums, such as the Metropolitan Museum of Art, are always "pay what you wish." Soho's trendy galleries—free to enter—are a short walk away, as are the best art house movie theaters in America; hundreds of inexpensive, excellent ethnic restaurants; dozens of new and used bookstores; several premium jazz, blues, and folk venues; charming old-world cafés; and landmark houses of worship, including both a Ukrainian and a Russian Orthodox cathedral. There are dozens of churches of every denomination, and historic synagogues within walking distance. The school maintains vibrant chaplain-

---

ACADEMIC REQUIREMENTS

NYU does not have a traditional core curriculum, but its distribution requirements known as the "Morse Academic Plan" for the students of the College of Arts and Sciences go some way towards making sure students receive a broad exposure to the humanities. Students must take:

- "Writing the Essay."
- Courses or tests to prove proficiency in a foreign language through the intermediate level.
- Two natural science courses, such as "Quarks to Cosmos" or "Brain and Behavior."
- One mathematics class, such as "Math Patterns in Nature" or "Elementary Statistics." Students may test out.
- Foundations of Contemporary Culture, a series of four coordinated courses in the humanities and social sciences:

  Texts and Ideas: Options include both "Justice and Injustice in Biblical Narrative and Western Thought" and "Freedom and Oppression."

  Cultures and Contexts: Choices range from "African Diaspora" to "Multinational Britain."

  Societies and the Social Sciences: Choices range much too widely from "U.S. History since 1865" to "Power, Resistance, Identity: American Social Movements."

  Expressive Culture: Options range from "Painting and Sculpture in New York Field Study" to "Sounds" (an intro music class).

cies and religious clubs, including Campus Crusade for Christ and the Bronfman Center for Jewish Student Life, along with Lutheran, Episcopalian, and an Islamic ministry. The Catholic Student Center is said to be especially active and faithful.

NYU sits squarely in one of the most interesting parts of America's most cosmopolitan city. Perhaps consequently, fraternities and sororities are not a big part of student life—only 1 percent of men join NYU's seventeen fraternities, and only 2 percent of women join the eleven sororities on campus.

The school sports over 350 student groups and organizations, including the College Libertarians, Gentleman of Character, Actuarial Society, Amateur Astronomers Association, Objectivist Club, Fine Arts Society, Break Dance Club, Gallatin Photography Club, Habitat for Humanity and several other community service groups, Women in Computing, Polish Club, Organization of Black Women, and Toastmasters at NYU.

The undergraduate population draws from around the world, with students coming from 140 countries. Still, about a quarter of the student body are from New York, New Jersey or Connecticut. Some 50 percent are white and 20 percent Asian, and more than three-fifths of students are female.

Students are often devoted to the school. Located half-way between the skyscrapers of Wall Street and Midtown, students really do seem to get caught up in the sense of adventure which the location imparts. One student shares, "Many times while walking around Manhattan, I'll experience a strange sense of pride coming across a random NYU building in an unlikely place (always designated by a purple flag outside). It's something hard to describe . . . But NYU just seems exciting because it's growing."

NYU students tend to be ambitious and focused on their future careers. Over the past decade there have been repeated incidents in which students committed suicide in the most public way possible, leaping down the cavernous atrium of NYU's Bobst Library. In response, the school beefed up counseling services—and glassed in the upper-level balconies.

Tight housing, like high pressure, comes with the downtown territory. While students in Columbia University apartments uptown tend to get their own private rooms, such luxuries are scarce at NYU. Still, students get a bed, sometimes a kitchen and a living room. The university has five traditional dormitories—one of which is exclusively for freshmen—plus a number of row houses, apartments, and suite-style residence halls. The university recently purchased a twenty story building on 23rd Street and Third Avenue (a mile from the main campus) to house 876 undergraduates. Another new dorm on 12th Street between Third and Fourth Avenue just opened up 700 beds for freshmen. There is room for 12,500 students in the twenty dorms on campus. More than half of undergrads live on campus, and 90 percent of freshmen. Each dorm is coed, but "all student rooms have their own bathrooms, which is a huge plus," one student says.

Over the next twenty years, NYU is planning to expand its campus onto Governor's Island—formerly the headquarters of the First Army, later a Coast Guard base—and into downtown Brooklyn, hoping to add six million square feet by 2031. This would expand the campus by 40 percent.

NYU is not finished growing. It just built a liberal arts campus in Abu Dhabi, the first comprehensive liberal arts campus established abroad by a major U.S. research university. The new $28 billion project was funded entirely by the United Arab Emirates. Buildings designed by notable architects like Frank Gehry and Zaha Hadid, will include branches of the Louvre and the Guggenheim museums, a maritime museum, the New York Film Academy, an exhibitions pavilion, and possibly a Lincoln-Center-run performing arts center.

NYU is also merging with Brooklyn's distinguished Polytechnic University, making it the engineering schools' sole shareholder. In 2012, it will open a satellite campus in Washington, D.C.

Athletic facilities exist at NYU, and sports teams as well, although no one seems to care about them, except when there is the occasional high-profile victory. One student says, "I don't know anyone who's ever been to a NYU athletic event," before amending her opinion to allow that she knows one male student "who'd been to a women's basketball game . . . once." Even so, NYU does field ten men's teams and nine women's varsity teams—but no varsity football team. Intramural sports include bowling, volleyball, basketball, tennis, football, softball, and something called Quikball.

Many NYU students are in preprofessional programs, and their ambition leads

YELLOW LIGHT

No question about it, NYU is a left-leaning campus, at least in the arts, humanities, and social sciences. The school does boast a strong, active College Republicans chapter that claims to be "the most publicized and influential group of students on any American campus," with appearances on ABC, CBS, NBC, MSNBC, CNN, FOX News, BBC, and other networks, as well as articles in the *New York Times*, the *New York Post*, the *New York Daily News*, the *Chicago Sun-Times*, and *Rolling Stone*. "[C]hallenging the political bias imposed upon us in the classroom . . . we spread a powerful message of independence and social responsibility absent from much of NYU and the perceptions of our peers," the CRs boast. The group brings in speakers such as Ann Coulter and hosts an annual debate with the College Democrats. There is also a (somewhat beleaguered) group called Students for Life. But it's fair to say that most NYU students are too career-oriented to care very much. As at other big universities, a sound-minded student can leave with a good education, if he is good at digging and fishing.

them to work extraordinarily hard. Students also tend to be ferociously independent. Says one student, "With such a large student body, NYU tends in general to be pretty stark in terms of personal attention. Many things are relegated to bureaucratic process and the ubiquitous 'NYU ID number.'" The college can be impersonal, and sometimes overwhelming.

Crime can occasionally be a problem, as at any urban university, but New York City is now the safest large city in the country, and Greenwich Village is among its safest neighborhoods. One student told us that he does not worry about coming home at "any hour," and NYU crime statistics bear his attitude out. In 2009, with more than 40,000 students, the school reported seven forcible sexual assaults, seven robberies, three aggravated assaults, and ninety-seven burglaries.

NYU costs as much as any of the Ivies, with a 2010–11 tuition of $40,082 and room and board at $13,507. Some 54 percent of students receive some aid, but the university is not notably open-handed, and does not practice need-blind admissions. The average student-loan debt of a recent graduate who borrowed was a heavy $34,850.

University of Pennsylvania

Philadelphia, Pennsylvania • www.upenn.edu

All about the Benjamins

The University of Pennsylvania was founded by Benjamin Franklin more than 250 years ago to teach both the practical and theoretical arts, and as the university's website notes, "Franklin's practical outlook has remained a driving force in the university's development." Some insiders worry that pragmatism has largely trumped liberal education at Penn. As one professor puts it, "Three of the four undergraduate divisions, Wharton, Engineering, and Nursing, don't pretend to cultivate the life of the mind but rather aim primarily to prepare one for a career."

Under the leadership of President Amy Gutmann Penn has nearly doubled its research funding, and tripled both its annual fundraising and the size of its endowment. While the campus leans far to the left, that doesn't seem to affect classroom behavior as badly as it does at many schools. A good number of faculty express independent views, and the school has been responsive to defenders of political free speech. Still, the weakness of the school's curriculum, the preprofessional spirit that prevails, and the tragicomic episodes of political correctness that have taken place on campus are troubling.

Academic Life: Penn is mightier than the word

Like most elite schools, the University of Pennsylvania has traded a core curriculum for distribution requirements. "The trend has been away from a 'traditional' education," an insider says. Students at the School for Arts and Sciences must now take a course in U.S. "cultural diversity." Diversity courses "focus on race, ethnicity, gender, sexuality, class, and religion," and almost all choices are heavily politicized. Says a campus source: "The university instituted the 'diversity' requirement—in my cynical opinion—to boost enrollments in otherwise unsuccessful 'oppression studies' courses. One has to seek out the more traditional courses as fewer and fewer are actually required."

Advising, according to students, is somewhat anonymous; one calls it "a joke," saying that professors are unfamiliar with course requirements and, in general, unhelpful. Before declaring a major, underclassmen are assigned pre-major advisors (not necessarily faculty members), but after that they are given faculty advisors within their departments—not that this seems to solve the problem. Reports a professor: "Penn is a big university. Some students work very hard and do very well. They become known to the faculty and have plenty of access. But others just drift along." Drifting along is entirely possible, students report, saying that no one would really notice unless a student started failing courses.

Happily, most Penn students have enough intellectual ambition to choose foundational courses on their own. Says a professor, "The students are certainly very engaged and curious. The stronger departments tend to attract the best students." However, he warns, "In order not to lose students, some departments have started to lower grading standards. I have heard that in some classes, TAs cannot give grades below B-." The School of Arts and Sciences (SAS) (called on campus "the College") typically attracts 60 percent of some 10,000 undergraduates. Other students are divided among the School of Engineering and Applied Science, the School of Nursing, and the Wharton School for business students. Undergraduates can take classes in any of the four schools. Penn also has twelve graduate and professional schools that annually enroll another 10,000 students.

The serious-minded student will find ample opportunities at Penn. Says one graduate, "From personal experience, I would recommend students to try to do a senior thesis. It teaches good research skills and puts one in contact with good faculty members. There is also an honors program that allows students to do advanced level seminars—it is called Benjamin Franklin Scholars. These seminars tend to attract the best students and the most talented professors. The classes are very rigorous." Other recommended departments include chemistry, politics, philosophy and economics (PPE), religious studies, and economics. An insider adds, "Based purely on reputation, I think the business school (Wharton) and the joint degree program in Business and International Relations are among the strongest."

Penn has its share of high-profile professors, including seven MacArthur Award recipients, six National Medal of Science recipients, five Nobel Prize winners and five Pulitzer Prize winners. Stars in their field, as at many other elite colleges, these faculty members are encouraged to value research and publishing over teaching. As one professor says, "The only thing more important then getting published is getting famous. Still, the quality of teaching continues to be high despite the lack of incentives." Another insider reports, "Overall, there's a good balance. Students get enough contact with the faculty." One student suggests that "humanities students, by and large, should have no problem getting to know their pro-

VITAL STATISTICS

Religious affiliation: *none*
Total enrollment: *19,311*
Total undergraduates: *9,768*
SAT/ACT midranges: CR: *660–750*, M: *690–780*; ACT: *30–34*
Applicants: *22,808*
Applicants accepted: *18%*
Applicants accepted who enrolled: *61%*
Tuition and fees: *$40,514*
Room and board: *$11,430*
Freshman retention rate: *98%*
Graduation rate: *88% (4 yrs.)*, *95% (6 yrs.)*
Courses with fewer than 20 students: *72%*
Student-faculty ratio: *6:1*
Courses taught by graduate students: *not provided*
Most popular majors: *business/marketing, social sciences, engineering*
Students living on campus: *62%*
Guaranteed housing for 4 years? *no*
Students in fraternities: *30%* in sororities: *27%*

SUGGESTED CORE

1. Classical Studies 360, The Epic Tradition
2. Philosophy 003, History of Ancient Philosophy
3. Religious Studies 015, The Bible as Literature
4. Religious Studies 433/434, Christian Thought From 200–1000/Christian Thought From 1000–1800
5. Political Science 181, Modern Political Thought
6. English 101, Shakespeare
7. History 020, History of the United States to 1865
8. History 343, Nineteenth Century European Intellectual History

fessors. It's the science and other preprofessional classes that are too large for that."

While students seem to agree that all Penn departments lean at least a little to the left, there are several in which more traditional professors and respect for honest intellectual discourse are present. One source says that "history and classical studies are the strongest programs in the humanities. They have some excellent professors and most faculty members teach at least three courses a year."

All history majors must take a course each in four out of five geographic areas and two courses in history before 1800. This means it would be easy to skip the founding years of U.S. history. Still, says one history major, "The history department at Penn has one of the strongest intellectual history programs. The professors who teach medieval and early modern intellectual history are world class scholars and great pedagogues . . . it is easy to find good teachers." On the negative side: "Like many departments, history has a fair number of professors who are ideologically driven. They care less about teaching history and more about teaching their political views. In history, it has also become popular to attack the notions of objectivity and of objective truth—a tactic that allows some faculty members to justify their own tendentious and ideologically-driven teaching," the student says.

Another student warns, "Based on my personal experience I have found the sociology and the anthropology departments to be very tendentious. The departments are very ideologically driven and have set agendas. The English department has many professors with similar problems."

In English, majors pick among a wide variety of courses, many of them burdened with leftist ideology, focused on the unholy trinity of "race, class, and gender." However, the department does require a substantial core for majors, one class in literature before 1660; one in literature from 1640–1830; and one in nineteenth century writing. Majors could still graduate without having studied Shakespeare, though few probably choose to. The department also requires one diversity class in "difference and diasporas."

Political science is the most popular major in the SAS. Majors are not obliged to take courses in political philosophy—though these are certainly offered, and we highly recommend them. Majors must also take at least one course in each of three subfields: American Politics, Comparative Politics, International Relations, and Political Theory.

The list of recommended faculty must begin with Alan Charles Kors, a professor of history who cofounded the admirable Foundation for Individual Rights in Education. Other worthies include Robert A. Kraft in religious studies; Martin Seligman in psychology; John J. DiIulio Jr., and Stephen Gale in political science; Michael Gamer, Al Filreis and

Anne Hall in English; Thomas Childers, Walter McDougall, Ann Moyer, Edward Peters, Jonathan Steinberg, Roger Chartier, and Arthur Waldron in history; Gary Hatfield in philosophy; Philippe Met in French; and Rita Copeland and Jeremy McInerney in classics. In 2006–7, Penn added forty new professors to its standing faculty of arts and sciences. According to one undergrad, "The new professors tend to get rave reviews from students."

"Recent hiring decisions have been very good," says one professor. "I think we have perhaps the finest junior faculty in the country." Another teacher says, "Conservative opinion is represented, though as anywhere else, the dominant worldview is a rather archaic and romantic liberalism." However, the level of political "intrusion" into the classroom depends on the particular faculty member. Admits one Penn insider, "Obviously, the various minority studies and gender studies departments tend to be hostile to religious and conservative students. There is some debate on campus, but liberal and left-wing opinions tend to be more prevalent and more accepted. The student newspaper used to have a token conservative voice, but they do not even bother to pretend any more."

Many students point to its dual-degree programs and the school's interdisciplinary majors as the best part of Penn. The school's many study-abroad opportunities also earn praise, and it has one of the highest percentages in the U.S. of students who spend semesters in other countries. The university offers study-abroad programs in almost fifty countries, and every year, about 1,700 students travel internationally to study, research, train, or volunteer. Destinations include Russia, Egypt, Ghana, Chile, Denmark, Japan, France, and Australia, and just about everywhere in between. Short-term, semester, and year-long programs are available. Penn ranks first among the Ivies for the number of students studying abroad.

Penn offers a wide variety of languages, including Latin, Ancient Greek, Dutch, Mandarin, Sanskrit, Cantonese, Italian, Russian, Hindi, modern Greek, Swahili, Sumerian, Old Egyptian, Judeo-Spanish, and German.

Student Life: Throwing toast to the team

Located in the center of the Washington–New York corridor, Philadelphia itself has plenty to offer, and many quirks that make it unfailingly interesting. Besides world-class museums, historical sites, and concert facilities, the city offers plenty of unhealthy, delicious cheesesteak and hoagie shops, snowcone stands, sports teams whose fortunes are passionately followed and bemoaned (especially the Eagles), and myriad bars and restaurants, if a student can afford them. Getting downtown is "not hard to do at all, and there's tons to do and see down there," says one student. Students from Penn are said to take full advantage of the city.

The 279-acre Penn campus includes attractions such as Houston Hall, the nation's first student union; the University of Pennsylvania Museum; Van Pelt Library, which, along with the university's other libraries, boasts over 5.84 million volumes; and Franklin Field, both the oldest collegiate football field still in use and the country's first double-decked college stadium.

Penn's beautiful campus intermingles old Victorian buildings with many new, modern structures. Recent additions include new athletic flooring, a mixed-use apartment building, the Roberts Proton Therapy Center, a vegetation-covered roof terrace, and the Annenberg Public Policy center. In 2010, the school's Music Building was renovated and expanded, providing soundproof classrooms, offices, and practice rooms. Ground was broken on Penn Park, which will turn fourteen acres of waterfront parking lots into parks, courts, and playing fields with elevated walkways. Penn Park will connect to the universi-

ACADEMIC REQUIREMENTS

The School of Arts and Sciences (SAS) at the University of Pennsylvania has the strongest distributional mandates at the school. Students must take one class in each of the following Sector Requirements:

- Society. Numerous courses will fulfill the requirement, from "American Capitalism" to "Religious Violence and Cults."
- History and Tradition. Approved options include "Ancient Greece" and "Comparative Medicine," as well as "Science, Magic, and Religion."
- Arts and Letters. Choices range from "Study of an Author: Shakespeare" to "Topics in Brazilian Cinema."
- Humanities and Social Sciences. Options range from "Introduction to Philosophy" to "Scandalous Arts in Ancient and Modern Societies."
- The Living World. Choices range from "Introduction to Brain and Behavior" to "Human Reproduction and Sexual Differences."
- The Physical World. Choices include both "General Chemistry" and "Global Climate Change."
- Natural Science and Mathematics. Options include "Philosophy of Biology" and "Eye, Mind and Image."

Students must also take the co-requirement "Foundational Approaches" classes, which often correspond with and overlap their sector requirements. These include:

- A writing seminar (not necessarily from the English department offerings).
- Competency in a foreign language. Students test into the appropriate courses or may demonstrate competency by completing high school at an institution where the primary language is not English, or by AP, A-level, or SAT II scores.
- A course in Quantitative Data Analysis. Options include "Statistics for the Biologist," "The Family," "Global Climate Change," and "Judgment and Decisions."
- A course in Formal Reasoning and Analysis. Classes are limited and generally do not overlap sector requirements. Options include "Ideas in Mathematics," "Calculus," and "Introduction to Cognitive Science."
- Cross-Cultural Analysis. Students may choose from options like "Beginning Sitar," "Comparative Medicine," the "History of Ancient Greece," or "Russian Humor."
- Cultural Diversity in the U.S. Options range from sound courses such as "Law and Society," to a long list of choices like "American Jewish Experience," "Discrimination: Sexual and Racial Conflict," and "Perspectives on Urban Poverty."

ty's current playing fields and eventually offer twenty-four acres of recreational land. Other planned projects include a special collections center in the library and pavilion attached to the fitness center. Locust Walk, once a city street but now closed to cars, is perhaps the most beautiful (and most congested) part of campus.

Over 60 percent of Penn's undergraduates live on campus, and those who don't usually stay nearby. Freshmen who send in their housing applications on time are guaranteed campus housing, and nearly all of them live in university housing. Most students live on campus for two or three years, then move to one of the rental houses around campus—which, students say, seem to be owned and managed by a near-monopoly called Campus Apartments. As a result, one student says, "It is very hard to find safe, affordable housing in University City." Some students live across the Schuylkill River in Center City, the heart of Philadelphia, but rentals there are pricey, too.

Those 6,000 undergraduate students who stay on campus can choose from eleven houses and two high rise towers. Between 2001 and 2009, UPenn spent $328 million renovating four of its houses: Rodin, Harrison, Harnwell, and W.E.B. DuBois, which are now "quite nice," according to one student. Off-campus properties owned by the university include Domus, an eight-story apartment complex and The Hub, a ten-story, mixed-use apartment and retail building. The $70 million, fourteen-story Radian Apartments were completed in 2008 and provide more off-campus housing to students. In the dorms, "gender neutral" housing is now available, allowing roommates of both sexes. Although residents are given the final vote on whether to allow them, coed bathrooms are found in many dormitories.

The real color of Penn is green: "While I have met people from all over the world, of all different nationalities, most people were relatively well off," one student says. "So I guess from a socioeconomic perspective, I wouldn't say the student body was that diverse." Other students agree. And while the school does offer substantial financial aid, particularly to low-income students, the simple cost of tuition, fees, and housing at Penn may frighten middle-class and poor students from applying.

Students who do apply are generally driven; they unanimously affirm that Penn is challenging and that their peers definitely have a competitive streak. They compete not just for the best grades in class, but also in the number of extracurricular activities in which they are engaged, their "how much work I have to do" conversations, and in their social lives. A recent psychology and counseling services survey found that stress is the top health concern among students at Penn.

For recreational activities, Penn has more than 200 student groups, about half of them academically oriented. Because of Penn's venerable age, it hosts a number of organizations and groups that are among the oldest of their kind in the country. The Philomathean Society, for example, is Penn's student literary society established in 1813. It sponsors informal Friday afternoon teas with professors, lectures, dramatic performances, and an annual recitation (though one student warns that this group is notoriously leftist). Another lively group is the 115-year-old all-male comedy group known as the "Mask and Wig Club." The International Affairs Association, founded in the 1960s, promotes awareness of international issues, including two Model United Nations Conferences. The association publishes

YELLOW LIGHT

Nearly every department at Penn has a few politicized courses, but students can sidestep these pretty easily if they wish, says an undergrad: "Most professors avoid politics." However, there are certain departments that contain more politically charged classes—such as English, psychology, sociology, and political science. Says one teacher, "It depends on who the professor is. Many are indeed very critical of both Western and American institutions. Most criticisms are respectful, but others border on the vitriolic. Capitalism receives particularly sharp attacks from most faculty members, in my experience." "On the whole," sums up another professor, "Penn seems rather hostile to the right-of-center."

Penn's president, Amy Gutmann, has taken very public stances in favor of euthanasia, and in 2007, she established the Institute of Regenerative Medicine at UPenn for the promotion of stem cell research, which entails the destruction of embryonic human beings. Penn is known for relative freedom of expression, perhaps thanks to the presence of Professor Alan Charles Kors, who cofounded the Foundation for Individual Rights in Education (FIRE) in response to political correctness he encountered at Penn. Kors has remained a devoted champion of student liberty at UPenn, and the university has generally responded well to FIRE's criticism, even changing certain policies which could infringe on student rights.

Although UPenn's guidelines aren't perfect, the university continues to stress its commitment to intellectual freedom, reaffirming that "the content of student speech or expression is not by itself a basis for disciplinary action."

six issues of "The Ambassador" newsletter every year as part of its program.

Penn is noted for its arts scene, which includes award-winning *a cappella* groups ranging from the traditional Counterparts to groups like Penn Masala, a Hindi singing group. Penn's arts scene highlights some of its more modern student organizations, such as the iNtuitions Experimental Theatre group and the socially concerned Front Row Theatre Company. The student government's Social Planning and Events group sponsors speakers, crafts fairs, a jazz music series, arts programs, concerts, dance parties, and other special events. Spring Fling is the largest college party and music festival on the East Coast.

Cultural groups include everything from Jewish Heritage Program to Canadians at Penn, Black Student League, and the Penn Vegetarian Society. UPenn has a number of environmental groups as well as several political groups like Amnesty International, College Democrats and Republicans, and Penn for Life.

A popular news publication on campus is the *Daily Pennsylvanian*, which receives prestigious national awards on a regular basis. Conservative students should also look into the well-written alternative campus paper, the *Pennsylvania Independent*. Other less-popular publications include the *F-word* feminist magazine, and the *WALK* fashion magazine, as well as numerous academic journals.

Athletically, Penn has a set of respectable teams. The sports teams are called the Quakers, and their colors are red and blue. UPenn participates in the NCAA's Division I (Division I-FCS for football) and in the Ivy League conference. Penn students take pride in cheering for the basketball team and throwing toast on the field at football games. (Get it? A "toast" to the team.) In recent decades, both teams have often been league champions, though only—it must be said—of the Ivy

League. The Penn Quakers play basketball at the Palestra, Philadelphia's historic arena, and the football team plays on campus at Franklin Field. The rowing and rugby teams are storied institutions at Penn as well. For recreation and practice, the David S. Pottruck Health and Fitness Center provides 19,000-square feet of fitness space and an Olympic-sized pool—it's definitely the most popular building on campus, comments one student.

Many students are involved in the school's intramural and club sports programs. Intramurals are offered in four divisions: competitive, recreational, "open," and Greek. Intramurals offered are flag football, tennis, golf, volleyball, basketball, soccer, softball, and squash. UPenn's wide variety of club sports include aikido, figure skating, cycling, synchronized swimming, roller hockey, and cricket.

Penn has a large Jewish student population, and cultural activities sponsored by Penn Hillel and other Jewish organizations are frequent. Other faiths are represented by the campus Newman (Catholic) Center and various Protestant, nondenominational Christian, Islamic, and Hindu groups. Reverend Charles L. Howard, the school's chaplain, is assisted by an associate chaplain and a campus minister for Muslims. Philadelphia is home to hundreds of historic synagogues and churches. Catholics might be interested in visiting the downtown shrine of St. John Neumann, the first American saint—whose body remains mysteriously incorrupt under the altar of a local Philadelphia parish.

At Penn, "there is a lot of room to express your opinion," says one student. Another agrees that, in general, the atmosphere of Penn is "one of vigorous debate," where both sides are usually given a chance to be heard. Another student characterizes the environment as "very centrist, perhaps slightly rightward leaning." However, some conservative students report that they felt silenced in classes during the most recent presidential election season when their professors made their own political affiliations known.

The Greek system dominates campus events: frat parties are the favorite activity for those too young to hit the bars. Drinking on campus is much more prevalent than drug use. Says one student, "Penn definitely lives up to its reputation as the 'Party Ivy.' . . . Penn is not very serious about stopping underage kids from drinking. All of my RAs have said something to the effect of, 'if you're going to drink, just don't cause any trouble on the hall.'"

Crime is a serious problem in West Philadelphia: in 2009, there were 305 homicides in "Killadelphia." Therefore, the school makes fighting crime a priority. The university paper has an online daily "Crime Log" with an interactive map. UPenn has taken other measures to protect its students, installing more than 400 surveillance cameras on or near campus, which are monitored by Penn Police, and "there's a University Police officer on every corner." Blue light safety phones have also been placed at major intersections, and students can call campus security for rides home after dark. The university utilizes the Penn Alert Emergency notification System to let students know when crimes occur. Despite these efforts, according to the university's annual crime report, in 2009, there were nine forcible sex offenses, twelve robberies, three aggravated assaults, twenty-two burglaries, one stolen car, and one arson on campus. Partly because of petty crimes, town-gown relations are somewhat strained. Students are frequently accused of vandalism and general rowdiness. Some students in off-campus housing report good relationships with their neighbors, but others report complaints about late-night partying and littering.

With tuition mounting to $40,514 in 2010–11 and room and board costs of $11,430, Penn is pricey. However, the university recently unveiled sweeping new financial aid policies and in 2009, abolished loans for families who qualify for need-based aid. Penn has committed $130 million to grant aid in 2010–11. About 40 percent of students receive need-based aid. Considering the cost of the school, the average debt of a graduating class is a relatively low $17,787.

Pennsylvania State University

University Park, Pennsylvania • www.psu.edu

State related

Pennsylvania State University became Pennsylvania's official land-grant college in 1863. Its goal was to incorporate scientific principles into farming, which stood as a dramatic departure from the traditional curriculum steeped in mathematics, rhetoric, and classical languages. Evidence of its agricultural past stands in the form of the University Creamery, which serves up all manner of cheese, yogurt, butter, and ice cream—a popular source of campus desserts.

Although it remains a "state-related" university rather than an entirely public one, the university receives about $350 million of state money each year, so it may as well be public. The University Park campus, Penn State's administrative and research hub, is located at the center of the state in a town called State College, and is the largest of the twenty-four Penn State campuses around the state. But the University Park campus is more popularly known by its location, Happy Valley.

Penn State is a strong research institution with a wide range of programs for its over 84,000 undergraduates (over half of them at University Park). In 2010, the university's endowment was valued at $1.22 billion, which serves the school well, as the twenty-four Penn State campuses spend to the tune of $3.5 billion annually, and employ overall about 40,000 faculty and staff.

As at most large schools, students do best who come in knowing what they want to study—with a map for the maze they will surely encounter. Unlike students at some other massive state universities, Penn State students aren't constantly up in arms about political issues, and the campus politics are usually kept to a dull roar. The university's storied football team, led by the legendary Joe Paterno, seems to inspire the most conversations on campus. Overall, with a large and diverse campus and no major cities nearby, Penn State successfully provides a big-school atmosphere in a small-town environment.

Academic Life: Not for agoraphobics

Penn State offers over 160 majors through the thirteen colleges at University Park. The largest colleges for undergraduates are those of engineering, liberal arts, and business. Only two colleges enroll fewer than 1,000, and so, whatever course of study they choose, stu-

VITAL STATISTICS

Religious affiliation: *none*
Total enrollment: *44,832*
Total undergraduates:
  38,630
SAT/ACT midranges: CR:
  530–630, M: *570–670*;
  ACT: *27–32*
Applicants: *39,089*
Applicants accepted: *52%*
Applicants accepted who
  enrolled: *31%*
Tuition and fees: in state,
  $15,250; out of state,
  $27,114
Room and board: *$9,030*
Freshman retention rate:
  93%
Graduation rate: *60% (4 yrs.)*,
  86% (6 yrs.)
Courses with fewer than 20
  students: *32%*
Student-faculty ratio: *17:1*
Courses taught by graduate
  students: *not provided*
Most popular majors:
  *engineering, economics,
  business/marketing*
Students living on campus:
  37%
Guaranteed housing for 4
  years? *no*
Students in fraternities: *13%*
  in sororities: *11%*

dents should expect to join a crowd. One student warns that the class sizes can be overwhelming; she reports that two of her introductory-level business classes had more than 400 students. Another student complains that some professors are not receptive to student requests for assistance: "The professor comes to teach the class and then leaves. There is little interaction." However, other students report that, aside from limited office hours, teachers are accessible, and one can make "excellent connections with professors" by being sufficiently assertive. The advising program especially is seen as outstanding for a large university—provided that students take advantage of it.

The choices for study at Penn State are vast, but the general education requirements are scant. The university admits that "successful, satisfying lives require a wide range of skills and knowledge," but in practice does little to ensure that its students will acquire them. The college categorizes many of the core requirements as "knowledge domains," and they have embarrassingly self-evident explanations such as "developing the skill to communicate by means of the written word is extremely important." It isn't hard to find a course that meets one of these requirements; dozens will do. More than 200 courses satisfy the humanities requirement, ranging from "The Life and Thought of Malcolm X" to "The Culture of Stalinism and Nazism" to "Shakespeare." In selecting the core courses, students should get advice from other students and the professors listed below, and use common sense. If a course sounds politicized or fluffy, it probably is.

One way to improve one's general education is to enter the Schreyer Honors College. Freshmen apply for admission to this college, which includes special honors sections that satisfy the general requirements, and independent study and research. Another worthy option is the Penn State Washington D.C., Program, which offers internships in the nation's capital at places such as the Nature Conservancy, CNN, NBC, and Pennsylvania congressman Jason Altmire's office. An interdisciplinary program called Classics and Ancient Mediterranean studies (CAMS) is solid and emphasizes primary texts.

One history professor says naming good departments at Penn State is like telling somebody about the weather in the United States: "You can't generalize. It's warm in Arizona, and cold in Maine. Penn State is huge, and even within each department there is tremendous variety." This diversity is best exemplified in the English department, where

Mid-Atlantic

British and American literature is purely optional, as majors "may choose from courses in all the major historical periods and genres of British and United States literature; in the work of individual authors (Shakespeare, Milton, and others); in three genres of creative writing; and in topics of rhetoric, African-American literature and culture, visual culture and media, ethnic studies, gender and sexuality studies, literature and science, and literary and cultural theory."

The history department is solid and has much to recommend it, reports an alumnus; all majors are required to take two Western civilization courses and two American heritage classes. The political science department is a bit weak, as majors are not required to take any courses on the American Constitution or American political philosophy. The business, agriculture, and engineering programs at University Park are well regarded both on campus and nationally, and Penn State's geography department is also among the best at the university, offering a balanced combination of hard science and social science courses.

The William Randolph Hearst Foundation gives high ratings to several journalism programs at the school. The education department is rated highly by several students enrolled in it. A professor on the Penn State faculty highly recommended by students was Philip Jenkins (author of *The Next Christendom*) in history and religious studies. Other recommended faculty include Sean Brennan, Kostadin Ivanov, Thomas Litzinger, Matt Mench, Timothy Simpson, and H. Joseph Sommer III in engineering; Herman Bierens and Neil Wallace in economics; James P. Lantolf in Spanish; Rosa A. Eberly and J. Michael Hogan in communications; Ann E. Killebrew and Gerald (Gary) Knoppers in religious studies; and Paul Amato in sociology.

The philosophy department is considered very good and offers a wide array of courses. Except for a course in basic logic, which is required, the course requirements vary depending on a student's concentration. But they all have strong breadth requirements. Of course, there are courses like "Philosophy and Feminism," alongside others such as "Business Ethics" and "Ethics of Science and Engineering." A well-regarded teacher in the department is John P. Christman.

Penn State is often described as a liberal oasis in a conservative region. According to a student, "politics intrude directly into the classroom" on a regular basis. Outside of the sciences, courses vary widely in terms of how infused they are with ideology. One PSU student says, "Obviously, classes are ideologically polarized, if not politicized. In (one) political theory class, we read extremist feminist authors, John Rawls, and Foucault, and this

SUGGESTED CORE

1. Classics and Ancient Mediterranean Studies 001, Greek and Roman Literature
2. Philosophy 200, Ancient Philosophy
3. Religious or Classics and Ancient Mediterranean Studies 110/120, Hebrew Bible: Old Testament/New Testament
4. Religious or Classics and Ancient Mediterranean Studies 124, Early and Medieval Christianity
5. Political Science 432, Modern and Contemporary Political Theories
6. English 129 or 444, Shakespeare
7. History 020, American Civilization to 1877
8. History 422, Modernity and Its Critics: European Thought Since 1870

is considered a good cross-section of contemporary theory." Another student says, "Some professors do not blatantly push their ideals on you, but their politics are usually obvious, and speaking from the right in a political conversation can be uncomfortable, if not terrifying. It is possible to voice other perspectives, but be prepared for at least a gentle rebuttal and possibly something more disconcerting."

Students who want to perform research at Penn State have many opportunities, even as undergraduates. The university is consistently among the top recipients in the nation of research funding. Some tenants of the university's Innovation Park research complex also take Penn State interns.

The library system at Penn State is strong; according to the Association of Research Libraries, it is ranked twelfth among public research libraries in the U.S. It includes some 5.4 million volumes, over 46,000 journal titles, and more than 536 electronic databases housed in two central buildings and six branches. It contains some 450,000 maps, 7 million microforms, and 171,402 films and videos.

With just 3,159 full-time faculty members at University Park serving 38,630 undergraduates and 6,202 graduate students, students can expect to find teaching assistants leading the discussion sections of large courses—although professors do teach most classes, and generally teach well, students say. Even those professors wrapped up in their research tend to pay attention to their undergraduate teaching, students report. One faculty member says that some students, especially in the humanities, genuinely enjoy learning and visit professors during office hours—not just to contest a bad grade, but to talk about ideas in the discipline. As for teaching assistants, the university offers courses and publications to prepare TAs for their duties, and these courses include instruction on how to evaluate student homework, participation, and exams. One student even reports that office visits to graduate teaching assistants are more helpful than visiting professors themselves. "It's a big school," says a student, "and, like all big schools, it is what you make it. You can either become a number in the system, or take advantage of its benefits."

Penn State president Graham B. Spanier is a sociologist and family therapist who has held his post since 1995. He has been the force behind many recent initiatives at Penn State, including the Schreyer Honors College, the Penn State World Campus, the College of Information Sciences and Technology, programs in forensic science, and "Security and Risk Analysis." Prior to his presidency, Spanier worked in a variety of professional and academic positions, but seems to especially enjoy interacting with students. He has made appearances with the marching band, glee club, and musical theater, and also occasionally serves as the school mascot during football games. Spanier is also, literally, a magician; he has opened for Penn and Teller and is the faculty advisor for the Penn State Performing Magicians. Spanier even ran with the bulls in Pamplona one year.

The student body is mostly white; only 17 percent of students are racial minorities, and only a quarter of students come from outside Pennsylvania. (However, all fifty states are represented in the student body, as are some 116 foreign countries.) Nevertheless, Penn State founded an Africana Studies Research Center, added new faculty to staff the African American studies department, and created new scholarships for students studying in these fields—all at considerable cost to the university. In addition, the university now offers a pre-freshman seminar "designed to acquaint incoming students with issues related to racism and diversity." Penn State's "Framework to Foster Diversity 2010–2015" details the school's "strides toward building a truly diverse, inclusive, and equitable institution and in establishing an infrastructure to facilitate effective diversity planning, implementation, and reporting processes." Penn State claims that "fostering diversity must be recognized as being at the heart of our institutional viability and vitality, a core value of the academic mission, and a priority of the institution." Not surprisingly, students point to the African and African American studies programs as among the most politicized on campus, alongside women's studies.

Most of the conservative students we consulted report that they feel unable to voice their opinions in class, and one describes being forced to read materials that clearly had a political agenda unrelated to the stated subject of the class. Another says: "It takes a strong

ACADEMIC REQUIREMENTS

Distribution demands at Penn State are modest. In addition to various requirements of one's major and college, a BA student must take:

- One first-year seminar introducing college-level work. Options include "First-Year Seminar in American Studies," "First-Year Seminar in African and African American Studies," and "Introduction to Health Aspects of Human Sexuality."
- Three courses in writing or speech. Class options include "Rhetoric and Composition" and "Contextual Integration of Communication Skills for the Technical Workplace."
- Two to three courses in mathematics, statistics, computer science, or logic. Choices include "College Algebra" and "Introduction to Spreadsheets and Databases."
- One course in health and physical education. Courses offered include "Introduction to Biobehavioral Health" or participation classes such as cycling, skiing, swimming, indoor rock climbing, snowboarding, ballroom dance, badminton, golf, fencing, ice skating, and dozens of others.
- Three courses in the natural sciences. Course choices include "Introductory Biological Anthropology" and "Plant Stress: It's Not Easy Being Green."
- Two courses in the arts, such as "Introduction to Art" and "Sexuality and Modern Visual Culture."
- Two courses in the humanities, with options ranging from "Shakespeare" to "Latina and Latino Border Theories."
- Two courses in the social and behavioral sciences, such as "Principles of Economics" and "Black and White Sexuality."
- One writing-intensive course within the student's major or college. Possible choices include "Understanding Literature" and "Anthropology of Gender."
- Two courses in Cultures and Diversity: one in "United States Culture," one in "International Culture." Course offerings include "Racism and Sexism" and "Society and Culture in Modern Israel."
- Courses or tests to demonstrate an intermediate proficiency in a foreign language.

person to not be swept onto the (liberal) bandwagon, because this faculty, with perhaps a few exceptions, is composed of fantastic intellectuals. That being said, there are many ways in which a conservative can find common ground without giving way to their rhetoric." She continues, "There are numerous opportunities, and many great professors to work with if you can work around the politics."

If a Penn State student really wants to experience diversity, he's better off doing it in a foreign country and culture. The university offers a wide variety of opportunities to study abroad, on six continents in dozens of countries such as Mexico, India, Italy, England, Denmark, Ecuador, Costa Rica, Kenya, Ireland, France, Egypt, Israel, Scotland, Turkey, Hungary, Czechoslovakia, Spain, China, Russia, Japan, Greece, and Tanzania. One particularly appealing three-credit physical education course is called "Hiking in the Alps." Students attend lectures and walk their way through the Mont Blanc region, which spans France, Switzerland, and Italy.

The school offers classes in Arabic, Chinese, French, German, Ancient Greek, Hebrew, Italian, Japanese, Korean, Latin, Polish, Portuguese, Russian, Serbo-Croatian, Spanish, Swahili, and Ukrainian.

Student Life: They don't call it Happy Valley for nothing

Happy Valley is isolated and surrounded by mountains—scenic, but not exactly cosmopolitan. Students lament the lack of movie theaters, but say there are good restaurants and bars, and that the school offers a decent program of on-campus events and concerts. The university requires freshmen to live on campus, but only about 20 percent choose to stay after that; Penn State only has room for a little over 13,000 of its almost 45,000 students. There are four university apartment complexes and the residence halls are clustered in five groups. Most are coed by floor (each floor is single sex), though one student reports that several dorms have coed floors as well. Students must use their ID cards to open outer building doors. Students say housing is in high demand, and more is being built, mainly for upperclassmen and graduate students. Off-campus students live in nearby apartments in the town of State College.

Penn State offers nineteen special living options (SLOs) where students "live and learn with classmates who share their interests . . . [and] have the opportunity to participate in field trips, group dinners, and other social and educational activities." In 2011, a few special living option houses included Arts and Architecture, Business and Society, Forensic Science, International Languages, Tri-Service ROTC, Health Education and Awareness, and Women in Science and Engineering.

With a large percentage of the student body in the Greek system, residential fraternities and sororities play a large role in solving the school's housing problem—and in social life on campus—which may be one reason why Penn State has earned the dubious distinction as a party school. "Many students take advantage of little aside from the bars and fraternity or sorority parties," reports one student. "Drinking is a serious problem."

However, not every student takes to the bottle. One student points out that the mammoth university boasts over 800 clubs and organizations, including activities in salsa, tango, and swing dancing, four stage and three movie theaters, and numerous musical recitals and concerts (from classical and jazz to rock), bass fishing, dodgeball, billiards, figure skating, and roller hockey. One activity most students remember to mention is the Penn State Dance Marathon, the largest student-run philanthropy in the world. Participants dance for forty-eight hours to raise money for children's cancer care and research, raising almost $8 million in 2010.

One popular destination on campus is the Palmer Museum of Art, which houses a diverse and compelling collection and plays host to a number of interesting lectures, foreign films, and special events—recent events included The Pennsylvania Quintet, a talk on modern art, and a choral music performance by the school's Chamber Singers. The strength of the permanent collection is American art, from eighteenth- and nineteenth-century portraiture and landscape painting to modern abstract and contemporary art.

The *Collegian* newspaper has been run by students for 117 years. It has a very left-leaning editorial page, which one student characterizes as "sometimes vicious." Nevertheless, students maintain that many of their peers are "fairly conservative," and campus speakers appear to be fairly balanced in their views. Conservative groups on campus include the Young Americans for Freedom, Students for Life, the libertarian Young Americans for Liberty, and the Conservative Coalition.

The school's fifteen varsity teams are known as the Nittany Lions. The word Nittany, derived from an Indian word meaning "single mountain," is the name of a peak near campus. The Nittany Lions compete in NCAA Division I in baseball, basketball, football, soccer, cross-country, fencing, golf, gymnastics, lacrosse, softball, swimming, tennis, track, volleyball, and wrestling. The thirty-

YELLOW LIGHT

While campus conservatives tend to get along comfortably enough, thanks to the tenor of the student body, the administration and faculty at Penn State lean heavily to the left, and make policies that reflect this fact. In a disturbing development, in December 2010, the faculty Senate "revised the school's academic freedom policy and submitted a new version to the president for approval," according to academic critic Mark Bauerlain. The new version of the policy deletes the following sentences contained in the old: "No faculty member may claim as a right the privilege of discussing in the classroom controversial topics outside his/her own field of study. The faculty member is normally bound not to take advantage of his/her position by introducing into the classroom provocative discussions of irrelevant subjects not within the field of his/her study."

Writes Bauerlain, "Apparently, the Committee regards the 'privilege' noted here as a feature of academic freedom; likewise for license to introduce 'provocative discussions of irrelevant subjects.'"

Further, Penn State's "Principles" speech code is one of the worst in the country. It is an intentionally arbitrary code that has the potential to be applied in a discriminatory way, creating a chilling effect on student speech.

Nor are students exactly zealous about defending such liberties as the freedom of association. The Young Americans for Freedom had their charter revoked by the student supreme court (and upheld by the administration) because of a reference to "God-given free will." YAF went to The Foundation for Individual Rights in Education for aid, and according to FIRE, "The day after Penn State President Graham Spanier received a letter from FIRE, he overturned Penn State's decision."

seven intercollegiate sports are very popular, as are the plethora of intramural sports offered at Penn, such as archery, bowling, boxing, cricket, racquetball, and squash. But football is king at Penn State. Coach Joe Paterno (for whom the University Creamery named their Peachy Paterno ice cream) could run for any office in the state and win. Before the 106,000 fans at Beaver Stadium, his teams have won more Division I games than those led by any other coach in NCAA history. He and his wife have donated $4 million to the university, and one of the main library buildings is named for him.

Penn State's campus is a relatively safe place. The Penn State University Police is a full-time police agency granted the same powers as the municipal police by city law, employing close to 250 police officers, security officers, police interns, and student officers who provide round-the-clock service. In 2009 the university reported eight forcible sexual assaults, forty-nine burglaries, two robberies, six aggravated assaults, two stolen cars, and fourteen arsons. This is actually not bad for a school larger than many towns.

Tuition in 2010–11 for Pennsylvania residents was $15,250, and $27,114 for out of state students. Room-and-board rates vary by dorm and meal plan, but average at $9,030. Forty-nine percent of full-time undergraduates receive financial aid of some kind, and the average student graduates with loan debt of $28,680.

Princeton University

Princeton, New Jersey • www.princeton.edu

The undergrad's Ivy

Founded in 1746 as the College of New Jersey—it didn't move for 10 years, or change its name for another 150—Princeton University is the fourth college founded in the U.S. It has historically been a competitive, elite institution—and now, often tying with Harvard, it's almost always rated the first or second best school in America.

Princeton prides itself as being the "undergraduate's Ivy." One professor describes it as being "as close to the intellectual ideal for undergraduates as one can find in a top research university." With its small graduate program, lack of professional schools, and student faculty ratio of 6 to 1, Princeton sends its big name professors out to teach. One student says that professors are "very accessible and helpful, overall." According to a student, "Princeton encourages students to pick smaller majors where they can get more attention from profs."

The growing student body is somewhat economically diverse, thanks to Princeton's excellent financial aid packages and the abolition of early admissions. The extra students should have plenty of room, as the school has expanded its campus recently. Princeton has extended its residential college system, opening the Whitman College, a 250,000-square-foot complex in the Gothic style, in 2007. That's right—Princeton is building new Gothic dorms. Additionally, 2010 saw the completion of the 265,000-square-foot Frick Chemistry Laboratory, and the university is planning work on the Firestone Library and Lenz Tennis Center, along with many other projects.

Out of all the Ivies, Princeton is the one most friendly to conservatives and people of faith. It's also near or at the top when it comes to academic excellence. Anyone who can get in should thank his lucky stars and attend.

Academic Life: No pain, no gain

Like most universities nowadays, Princeton lacks a core curriculum, although its students typically get a well-rounded education. The school requires undergrads to take a range of courses, covering seven distinct areas, including science and technology (with laboratory), historical analysis, literature and the arts, and "ethical thought and moral values." Students must also achieve second-year competence in a foreign language.

VITAL STATISTICS

Religious affiliation: *none*
Total enrollment: *7,802*
Total undergraduates: *5,220*
SAT/ACT midranges: CR:
  690–790, M: *710–790;*
  ACT: *31–35*
Applicants: *26,247*
Applicants accepted: *9%*
Applicants accepted who
  enrolled: *57%*
Tuition and fees: *$36,640*
Room and board: *$11,940*
Freshman retention rate:
  98%
Graduation rate: *90% (4 yrs.),*
  96% (6 yrs.)
Courses with fewer than 20
  students: *71%*
Student-faculty ratio: *6:1*
Courses taught by graduate
  students: *not provided*
Most popular majors: *social*
  sciences, engineering, bio-
  logical and life sciences
Students living on campus:
  97%
Guaranteed housing for 4
  years? *yes*
Students in fraternities or
  sororities: *none*

For those who want to get a serious education in the foundations of Western thought and civilization, we recommend the highly rated Humanities sequence—a year-long set of four courses that focus on Western literature, philosophy, religion, and history. While this is essentially a Great Books course, it is interdisciplinary, with reading complemented by museum visits, film, and discussion. A sophomore calls Humanities "one of the defining experiences of my intellectual life." This much-praised sequence, as a student remarks, is meant only "for the highly motivated who are seriously interested in developing a thorough grounding in the great literature and philosophy of the West." Another comments that "one of the best aspects for me came from the amazing students."

The Writing Seminars required for freshmen are relatively new to Princeton. The university offers over a hundred each year to compensate for the unfortunate fact that few high schools—even good high schools—teach analytical writing and reasoning skills.

Seminars are the smallest classes at Princeton, with no more than twelve students in each, but lecture classes aren't massive. Students meet twice a week for eighty minutes, which may not sound like much—but, as with other courses, these are supplemented by "precepts," small group discussion sessions. Although these are often led by graduate students, professors will take them where possible—even in some of the larger classes. One student notes that although English is generally considered "one of those majors where it's easy to get lost in the shuffle," lectures in the department "are small enough so that the professor takes all of the precepts . . . I've been incredibly impressed with how easy it is to develop truly meaningful relationships with some of the top professors in the country." Students have plenty of access to their professors, if they want. One undergrad says, "I find that most students don't use office hours, but that professors are consistently urging students to seek them out. I find it's always very easy to make appointments—and that professors are extremely accommodating."

Princeton's freshman academic advising system is one of the school's weak points. It has been known to leave freshmen floundering in classes that are over their heads, or misdirect them so that they have trouble finishing the requirements for their majors. Fortunately, this teething problem is usually resolved after freshman year, when "knowledgeable departmental advisors take over," as one student explains.

Students choose a major at the end of their sophomore year. In their third year, they write in-depth "junior papers," which often serve as the basis for a senior thesis—a requirement at Princeton. These independent research projects are both challenging and rewarding for students. "I think the combination of the junior papers and the senior thesis means that Princeton undergraduates do more serious, independent work than students almost anywhere, and they provide extensive opportunities for working one-on-one with faculty," says one professor. Scientists perform original research while creative writing students craft novels. Public policy students design new public and private programs: For instance, 1989 graduate Wendy Kopp's senior thesis became the basis for the volunteer program Teach for America.

Academics at Princeton are rigorous. Almost all Princeton students got straight As in high school, but that won't happen at the university. Grade deflation policies are in place to ensure honest evaluations. Graduate schools and employers have mostly been clued in about Princeton's admirable policy, so lower GPAs at graduation haven't hurt alums.

One special Princeton tradition is the honor code. Exams are unproctored, and students must sign their tests: "I pledge my honor that I have not violated the honor code during this examination." They also sign papers with a note saying the writing represents their own work in accordance with university regulations. Students must accept the honor code to attend Princeton. Violations are tried by tribunal and punishments include suspension and expulsion.

Literary types should apply for seminars in the creative writing department, where bestselling writers Joyce Carol Oates and Paul Muldoon critique student papers. A student says that English is "one of the strongest programs in the country [with] an incredibly dedicated group of professors who are passionately interested in getting to know students one-on-one" As to faculty, the same student recommends "flamboyant Victorian Lit professor" Jeff Nunokawa and "brilliant Spenser/sixteenth-century lit professor" Jeff Dolven. Departmental requirements are solid; majors take "British Literature from the 14th to the 18th Centuries" and an introductory genre course; two courses in pre-1800 British literature (only one can cover Shakespeare); a pre-1865 American literature class; a post-1800 literature course; a class in "Anglophone or U.S. minority literatures"; a class in theory and criticism; as well as a junior seminar. Students may opt to concentrate on tracks like comparative literature, creative writing, or British literature.

The history department is renowned for its strong faculty, with Harold James, Stephen Kotkin, Anthony Grafton, and lecturer Paul Miles singled out for special praise. A retired army colonel, Miles is a popular lecturer, with "impeccable manners and a lecture style that students find most illuminating and informative," says one professor. His balanced, respectful, and non-dogmatic approach to American civic and military history has made his course, "The United States and World Affairs," one of the most popular at the university. Majors must complete two prerequisite classes, and a course each in European, U.S.,

---

SUGGESTED CORE

Humanities 216-217-218-219, a four-course sequence on the history of Western culture, may be supplemented with the following:

- Religion 230, Hebrew Bible and Ancient Israel
- Religion 251, The New Testament and Christian Origins
- History 373, The New Nation

non-Western, and premodern history, as well as a junior seminar and four history electives. Students are required to determine a concentration (like the Near East, women and gender, or war, revolution and the state) and pass a comprehensive exam.

Classics is another strong department, where teacher Harriet Flower is highly recommended. One faculty member says, "The best humanistic education continues to be in the classics, but the liberal arts, engineering, and the natural sciences are very strong as well."

In the politics department, Robert George is described as "a great mentor, highly involved despite having one of the busiest schedules of anyone at Princeton." In fact, George was singled out repeatedly by students and faculty alike for his contribution to academic life. George is the director of Princeton's James Madison Program in American Ideals and Institutions—described by one student as "a must-join for conservatives." Its focus is "civic education," i.e., the study of American politics, the ideals of the American founding, the Constitution, the Declaration of Independence, democracy, and religion. Most importantly, the program brings dozens of speakers to Princeton every year to discuss issues of public policy and constitutional interpretation. Many of these guest speakers are religious, libertarian, socially conservative, neoconservative, or Jacksonian nationalist in outlook.

Politics majors must take two prerequisite classes, and one in systematic analysis like "Mathematical Models in the Study of Politics" or "Social Statistics." Students decide to concentrate in American politics, comparative politics, international relations, or political theory, and will write a senior thesis and complete a senior examination in the subject. Three classes in the primary field, two in another field, and one in a third are required as well.

The math and physics departments are well respected at Princeton, and science generally has a good name here. Computer science teacher Brian Kernighan, one student says, "is particularly great to work with." The math department, says another, "is the top in the country. One of the greatest professors is Nicholas Katz, followed by Robert Gunnig."

The German department came in for much praise, with one professor saying that "the German program is one of the country's best, led by a senior lecturer who specializes in secondary-language acquisition." One student singled out the teaching of Jamie Rankin, who is also known for "cooking an eleven-course reproduction of the last dinner on the *Titanic* for freshmen." (We hope they aren't served this just before finals.)

Many students take Econ 101 and 102, and almost all the professors for these courses are excellent, from libertarian Elizabeth Bogan to boisterous left-winger Uwe Reinhardt.

Course offerings in religious studies are extensive and are taught by a battery of distinguished professors ranging from dynamic leftist (and hip-hop artist) Cornel West to the popular traditionalist Eric Gregory.

Princeton offers a number of study-abroad programs, from summers, years, or semesters to research work, post-graduate programs, volunteer work, and international internships. Particular programs around the world are affiliated with Princeton, like the University of Queensland in Brisbane, Australia, a program in British Literature at the University College in London, a science program in Paris, and an architecture exchange program with the University of Hong Kong, among others. Despite Princeton's extensive offerings, just about 14 percent of students study abroad.

Languages offered on campus include Arabic, Chinese, French, German, modern or Ancient Greek, Hebrew, Hindi, Italian, Japanese, Korean, Latin, Persian, Russian, Spanish, Swahili, and Turkish.

Student Life: Parnassus in New Jersey

The Princeton campus is considered beautiful and harmonious, with most buildings constructed in some form of the "collegiate gothic" style which Princeton helped make famous. As a onetime president of Princeton, Woodrow Wilson wrote of the decision "By the very simple device of building our new buildings in the Tudor Gothic style we seem to have added to Princeton the age of Oxford and Cambridge; we have added a thousand years to the history of Princeton by merely putting those lines in our buildings which point every man's imagination to the historic traditions of learning in the English-speaking race." Even the school's newest buildings are being constructed in a compatible style—a refreshing exception to the still-widespread trend of beautiful colleges marring their landscape with aggressively modern, even Brutalist, structures.

And the campus is always abuzz: In addition to endless afternoons (and mornings and evenings) of free lectures, seminars, performances, and services, Princeton boasts over 200 student-run organizations—and according to one student, proposals for new organizations come in weekly. Students read a bevy of publications, including the *Daily Princetonian*, a humor magazine called the *Tiger*, *Business Today* (the U.S.'s largest student publication with a circulation of 200,000), the artsy *Nassau Weekly* and others. There is also a campus radio station, WPRB.

Six different theaters and an improv comedy group on campus provide Princeton's student population with ample room for self-expression. The French Theater Workshop *L'Avant-Scène* offers "an original combination of linguistic and dramatic training," founded on the principles of "*cours d'interprétation*" of the French conservatories. Princeton's Black Arts Company (BAC), aims to foster an understanding of "the human experience in the African Diaspora through dance." There are also the Princeton University Players, Theater Intime, and the rambunctious Triangle Club, famous for its all-male drag kickline. For those who prefer something more traditional, there is the Princeton Shakespeare Company. Even those not studying theater have a chance at acting. As one student says, "A school has to be pretty amazing to have an open-audition, Shakespearean theatrical troupe that puts on four to five theatrical productions a year—and that gets quite excellent and appreciative audiences."

Musicians and singers can join the University Glee Club, the Chapel Choir, the Lux Choir (which specializes in Anglican sacred music), the Princeton University Orchestra, Jazz Ensemble, Band (one of fewer than a dozen "scramble" bands in the U.S.), or Opera Theater, among others. There are also numerous *a cappella* groups, chamber music ensembles and dance groups.

These are exciting times for the arts at Princeton. Insurance magnate Peter B. Lewis presented the college with $101 million to expand resources for the arts. This funded the Society of Fellows in the Arts, envisioned as "a centerpiece of arts education at Princeton." At least six Fellows will be appointed each year, "writers, actors, directors, choreographers, musicians, painters, video and installation artists, and curators" who are innovative in their approach and in the early stages of their careers.

A number of students also join community service organizations, entrepreneurial clubs, multicultural groups—and ROTC, which offers merit-based scholarships that pay full tuition and fees. Founded by Princetonians James Madison and Aaron Burr, the American Whig-Cliosophic Society (Whig-Clio) is the oldest college political, literary, and debating club in the United States.

Princeton students have long had a reputation for heavy reading, but one student added that "they are very athletically inclined; they also like to exercise hard." Over 25

ACADEMIC REQUIREMENTS

Princeton has no core curriculum, but it imposes decent distribution requirements. AB (Bachelor of Arts) students must complete:

- A freshman writing seminar; subjects range widely from "The Anatomy of Gender" or "American Revolutions" to "Walmart Nation."
- Sufficient courses in a foreign language to show intermediate proficiency.
- One course in epistemology and cognition, with choices ranging from "The Psychology of Decision Making and Judgment" to "Plato: *Republic.*"
- One class in ethical thought and moral values, with such options as "Race and Medicine," "Sex and Ethics," and "Purity and Sacrifice in Ancient Israel."
- One course in historical analysis; choices range from "Saints and Sinners: Women and the Church" or "History of American Capitalism" to "Germany Since 1806."
- Two courses in literature and the arts; choices here are extremely wide, embracing everything from "Leo Tolstoy, War and Peace" and "Contemporary Korean Language and Culture" to "Beethoven" or "Black Women and Spiritual Narrative."
- One course in quantitative reasoning, such as "Imagining Other Worlds," "Algebra," or "Topics in Modern Astronomy."
- Two classes in science and technology, with lab; options include "Experimental Physics," "Natural History of Mammals," and "Art and Science of Motorcycle Design."
- Two classes in social analysis, such as "Introduction to Microeconomics," "The Bible in Modern Political Thought," or "Genes, Health, and Society."

For BSE (engineering) students, the school requires:

- A freshman writing seminar.
- Four mathematics courses.
- Two physics classes.
- One chemistry course.
- One computer science class.
- Seven courses in the humanities, including one course in four of the six areas mentioned above: epistemology and cognition, ethical thought and moral values, foreign language, historical analysis, literature and the arts, and social analysis.

percent of the student population plays varsity and junior varsity sports. The Princeton Tigers compete in orange and black on thirty-six varsity teams and are particularly strong in lacrosse and rowing. The school also hosts a vast array of club sports, ranging from Aikido to equestrian and ballroom dance to ice hockey. Intramural sports include sand volleyball, flag football, soccer, and of course, Pickleball and Rock, Paper, Scissors. State of the art gym facilities and organizations like Outdoor Action promise other opportunities for fitness through kayaking, rock climbing, and backpacking trips.

In recent years Princeton has earned a reputation for being one of the more faith-friendly elite universities in the U.S. There are several prayer groups and religious groups on campus, which, as one professor notes, "often draw sizable numbers of the religiously devout to their regular meetings." Religious organizations range from the Baha'i Club and Athletes in Action to the Orthodox Christian Fellowship or Muslim Students' Association. There is also the Anscombe Society, named for the British analytic philosopher and Catholic convert GEM Anscombe. The society puts on a number of lectures throughout the year, and has occasional "Pro-life, Pro-family" receptions and coffee evenings. Connected to the official campus ministry are a number of clergy of various denominations. These include David Buschman (Baptist), Keith Brewer (Methodist), and Fr. Tom Mullelly, the Catholic chaplain who heads the very active Aquinas Institute on campus. The institute sponsors a number of lectures throughout the year, and offers pilgrimages to places like Rome and Assisi—as well as rather more lighthearted weekend beach retreats. A Mormon church located less than a mile from campus and the "young, dynamic" Rabbi Eitan Webb attracts the more traditionally-minded Jewish students to Chabad.

Conservative groups on campus include the *Tory*, a moderate/conservative journal, the College Republicans, College Libertarians, Princeton Pro-Life, the aforementioned Anscombe Society, and the "Clio" side in the regularly scheduled Whig/Clio philosophical and policy debates. Rightist students also tend to network through events of the James Madison Program.

Nearly all Princeton undergrads live on campus, as do 70 percent of its graduate students. Several housing options are available to Princeton undergrads, including "close-knit residential college communities" (each with its own dining hall) and individual dormitories. All bathrooms are single-sex, and although the majority of halls are coed, students can request single-sex housing.

Nightlife is described as spotty, with a narrow range of bars in walking distance in a strip called The Street. Most other parties are sponsored by eating clubs, and are populated by upperclass members, and those underclassmen whom they choose to admit. "The eating clubs are one of the biggest and best traditions that Princeton has to offer," says a student. Membership in these clubs is one of the more expensive dining options for students (and the clubs have been criticized for promoting elitism), but joining comes with many benefits, and both juniors and seniors can receive some financial aid based on the cost of a club's meal plan. There are ten eating clubs, all of which are coed and open to both juniors and seniors. They are held in houses along Prospect Avenue and primarily serve as dining halls and social centers. Each is equipped with a study space, library, and Internet access, and provides students a comfortable place to study or relax. Additionally, eating clubs may offer field trips,

GREEN LIGHT

The faculty at Princeton is overwhelmingly left-of-center, but politics rarely enters the classroom to any significant degree, and different viewpoints are welcomed. As one student says, "As long as I do top-notch work, professors (even very liberal ones) respect it. I've never had a professor penalize me for voicing a different opinion; if anything, professors mark students down if they feel the student is merely parroting back what he has been told."

Princeton is one of few U.S. universities with a solid, intellectual conservative presence (the James Madison Institute) and its effect is noteworthy. Conservative and religious students will find a welcoming environment, far more open to conservative viewpoints than most secular schools. One student says that, at Princeton, students have "the very best arguments for conservative social and political ideals and beliefs, but also (from peers and professors) some of the sharpest liberal critics of those views. . . . The country's future conservative leaders are coming from Princeton."

movie nights, and campus concerts. Clubs will often invite professors to join them for dinner. About 75 percent of Princeton students enter a club, either through the elaborate audition process called "bicker" or by signing in with a club that accepts all comers. Upperclassmen are also given two free meals in the dining hall every week, "so that there's always some place where you can eat meals with upperclass friends," says one student.

Princeton has plenty of other dining options available, including several campus cafés, with a few closing as late as 2:00 AM, as well as plenty of local restaurants. The Center for Jewish life provides kosher food, and kosher or halal cuisine may be requested at the residential colleges. Three student co-ops (one vegetarian, one international cuisine, and one general cuisine) attract a few dozen members each. The Aquinas Institute also sponsors "fellowship dinners" on Tuesday and Thursday nights.

The surrounding borough of Princeton is beautiful if pricey, but town-gown interactions are few. Students report that they are not concerned about crime. Nevertheless, in 2009 the school reported nine forcible sex offenses, forty-five burglaries, two motor vehicle thefts, and three arsons on campus. Princeton provides emergency blue light phones around campus and on-demand escorts from 11:00 PM to 3:00 AM.

Like most top-tier universities, Princeton isn't cheap. In 2010–11 tuition was $36,640, with room and board costs at $11,940. But Princeton boasts of offering "the strongest need-based financial aid program in the country," and encourages applications from outside the elite. Admissions are entirely need blind. Princeton has eliminated loans from its financial aid packages, and awards grants and scholarships instead—with the average financial aid grant covering 90 percent of tuition. Princeton students almost never graduate with debt; less than a quarter take out loans averaging $5,225. One reason the school can afford to be generous is that alumni are unusually giving, since most look back fondly on their time at "Ol' Nassau."

University of Rochester

Rochester, New York • www.rochester.edu

Lore in a cold climate

Founded in 1850 by Baptists, this school expanded from a college to a university in 1897, when it offered its first master's degrees. It attracted the benefactions of George Eastman, founder of Eastman Kodak, who endowed the Eastman School of Music and Rochester's schools of medicine and of dentistry. In the 1950s, Rochester opened schools of engineering, business administration, and education. In 1986, Rochester's business school was named for donor William E. Simon, entrepreneur and former U.S. Secretary of the Treasury.

Over Rochester's more than 150 years, it has gained a reputation as an intellectually serious, academically rigorous school. Students drawn to Rochester aren't typically party animals. "If you come here, you're already on a path to deeper learning," one student says. However, you might not end up practicing what you professed; one well-known alumna, *New York Times* critic Janet Maslin, majored in mathematics.

The campus's most beautiful building is the main library, Rush Rhees—a stunning open-stacks structure featuring coffered ceilings and marble floors. Another treasure is the university's 3,094-seat Eastman Theatre. This opulent mix of gilt and crimson is one of the grandest and most beautiful concert halls in North America. The university's music school trained opera singer Renee Fleming and jazz trumpeter Chuck Mangione and was the long-time home of neo-romantic composer Howard Hanson. Intellectually or artistically ambitious students have long looked to Rochester to provide a solid foundation for their careers.

Academic Life: Getting in tune

Rochester is medium-sized. With approximately 5,000 undergraduates and 4,000 graduate and professional students—plus almost 1,000 students at the Eastman campus downtown—it's small enough that students have a real sense of familiarity as they walk about, if not so small that students are apt to be pigeonholed. Says one psychology major: "It's a nice small school, but it doesn't feel small." Says another student, "You run into people everywhere that you know, but there are lots of people to meet."

For all the intellectual earnestness of the school, its curriculum is surprisingly lax. The school doesn't impose language, physical education, or math requirements. The humanities rules are loose enough that exposure to Shakespeare, the U.S. Constitution, and the Bible

Mid-Atlantic

VITAL STATISTICS

Religious affiliation: *none*
Total enrollment: *9,867*
Total undergraduates: *5,398*
SAT/ACT midranges: CR:
  590–690, M: *640–720*;
  ACT: *28–33*
Applicants: *12,111*
Applicants accepted: *39%*
Applicants accepted who
  enrolled: *23%*
Tuition and fees: *$40,282*
Room and board: *$11,640*
Freshman retention rate:
  96%
Graduation rate: *70% (4 yrs.),
  80% (6 yrs.)*
Courses with fewer than 20
  students: *61%*
Student-faculty ratio: *9:1*
Courses taught by graduate
  students: *not provided*
Most popular majors:
  *economics, biological sci-
  ences, psychology*
Students living on campus:
  83%
Guaranteed housing for 4
  years? *no*
Students in fraternities: *23%*
  in sororities: *23%*

is optional. Indeed, the school boasts about this à la carte approach on its website, claiming, "Students do best when they love what they learn and are deeply invested in their studies."

In the Rochester curriculum there are no required subjects. Rather, students pursue a major in one of three divisions of learning (humanities, social science, and natural science) and take at least a cluster in each of the other two areas. The choice of subject matter and level of concentration (major, minor, or cluster) in each division is theirs. Students say they appreciate this freedom and flexibility, but to us it sounds like just another example of consumerism gone wild.

Freshmen and sophomores who are serious about a liberal arts education owe it to themselves to take classes in the school's Quest program, which is akin to an honors division. Quest students select a program in the humanities, social sciences, or science and engineering. In each program, classes are offered for small groups focused on the study of primary documents. Topics covered in Quest courses recently included *The Divine Comedy,* religion and society in modern Europe, cultural anthropology, and calculus.

As one might expect of a school that offers a major in optics—which includes courses like "Colorimetry, Optoelectronics and Interference and Diffraction"— there is less ideological piffle offered in the Rochester catalog than at many other prestigious schools. Obviously, it's possible to find courses of questionable value in departments like African and African American studies, and women's studies. Beyond that, students complain that certain English professors, for instance, introduce extraneous political material into the classroom. One teacher, who specializes in popular culture and baseball, was in the habit of making "derogatory comments about small towns—when he wasn't going off on twenty- to thirty-minute digressions about [former President] Bush," a student complains.

The history department (former home of celebrated scholars Christopher Lasch, Eugene Genovese, and Elizabeth Fox-Genovese—all now sadly deceased) requires that students take classes in at least three geographical regions, at least two courses from the period before 1800, at least one seminar, and at least five classes in a student's chosen focus area, such as American, African and African American, or intellectual history, as well as an upper-level writing course.

Admirably, English majors must take at least two of the following introductory classes: "Classical and Scriptural Backgrounds," "British Literature" I, "British Literature" II, and "American Literature." Majors must also complete a third survey class from the preceding list, or at least one of the following: "Great Books," "Maximum English," "Introduction to Shakespeare," "Introduction to African-American Literature," "Introduction to the Art of Film," or a seminar from the Quest program. They also need to complete at least two upper-level courses in British or American literature before 1800, two in British or American literature after 1800, and one research or honors seminar.

Majors in political science must take classes in at least four of the following: techniques of analysis, American politics, comparative politics or international relations, and political philosophy or theory.

Philosophy students also face a serious course of study, with required classes including "Philosophy of Religion," "Augustine, Anselm and Aquinas," and "History of Ancient Philosophy." They must also take at least three advanced classes—one in ethics, one writing-intensive seminar, and one class in any of the following subjects: logic, traditional philosophical disciplines, or the philosophy of science.

SUGGESTED CORE

1. English 112, Classical and Scriptural Background
2. Philosophy 201, History of Ancient Philosophy
3. Religion 101/102, Introduction to the Hebrew Bible/Introduction to the New Testament
4. Philosophy 268, Augustine, Anselm, and Aquinas
5. Philosophy 223, Social and Political Philosophy
6. English 111, Introduction to Shakespeare
7. History 145/146, Early America 1600–1800/Democratic America 1800–1865
8. History 233, Nineteenth-Century European Thought

Because of the presence of the Eastman School, Rochester offers a level of musical instruction and appreciation that may be unsurpassed among liberal arts colleges (as opposed to conservatories or music schools). Every student of "intermediate" ability is offered free tutoring in his musical area, whether or not he is a student in the Eastman School. Moreover, as one undergrad dryly observes, "they have a loose definition of 'intermediate.'" Hence, an economics major with past training in the flute can get further instruction in the instrument from a top music professor. Both the Eastman School and the River Campus have fine student ensembles and orchestras offering regular free concerts. The Eastman School ensembles feature promising future professionals, but there are also many ensembles apart from Eastman, along with quite a few undergrad singing groups. What's more, the Rochester Philharmonic offers some of its $60 seats for $5 to Rochester students.

Partly because the school is in a city long known for technology that still is headquarters for eyewear manufacturer Bausch and Lomb, UR has a highly regarded engineering school. Students and faculty also praise the school's programs in biomedical engineering, economics, psychology, English, history, business, and music.

One professor students consistently recommend is Robert Westbrook in American history. "He recommended books to me and takes time with students—plus he's balanced [politically]," says one undergrad. Others include Thomas Hahn, John Michael, and Curtis Smith in English; Allen Orr in evolutionary biology; Steven Landsburg in economics;

Gerald Gamm in political science; Jason Titus in music; and Michael Jarvis in history. In psychology, students praise Harry Reis and Richard Ryan.

Students say that the professors are generally accessible. "Everyone has office hours," a student says, "and they're easy to e-mail. You have to seek them out, but they will get to know you."

Because of the school's modest size, undergraduates can volunteer for lab jobs at the school Medical Center. Instead of "just cleaning Petri dishes and getting coffee," says one student now interning there, "it's figuring out the data, being an integral part of the study. . . . It's easy to say, 'I'd like to be a research assistant' and work on great research." The Medical Center is close to the campus dorms, lying just across a cemetery from the nest of buildings at the heart of the River Campus.

One generous initiative on Rochester's part is its "Take Five" program. Take Five scholars are permitted to stay for a ninth semester or even an entire fifth year without paying additional tuition, if they have distinguished themselves as undergraduates and can show a sound reason why they wish to undertake additional research. Rochester also offers a five-year business program (which combines an undergraduate and business degree) and an eight-year combined bachelor's degree and medical degree program.

Studying abroad is "easy to do," says one junior, and the university offers an assortment of overseas programs, including courses of instruction in such out-of-the-way places as Ghana, Senegal, and Peru—in addition to programs in more common destinations, like Belgium, Austria, Hungary, Italy, England, Israel, Japan, India, and China.

Although it does not have a foreign language requirement, Rochester offers instruction and majors in Classics, Chinese, Japanese, French, German, Italian, Russian, and Spanish. Students may also study Polish, Arabic, Latin, Hebrew, Ancient Greek, or American Sign Language.

Student Life: Tunnel vision

Most of the University of Rochester is located at its River Campus alongside the city's Corn Hill section, an elegant but sprawling neighborhood of old clapboard homes and handsome bungalows. Corn Hill is a short bus ride away from the city's downtown area—too far for most students to walk (even when it isn't snowing). Surrounding the River Campus's buildings are a great many parked cars—enough initially to make one feel as though the university might be a commuter school. There is a free bus (the number 72) taking students to the downtown, where the Eastman School of Music sits near the frequently vacant shop windows and the half-empty shopping mall in Rochester's faltering central business district. River Campus, where most students live and study, extends over eighty-five green, well-kept acres set apart from the Corn Hill section, divided from most of the town by the Genesee River.

This main campus is a mix of Georgian architecture and more modern structures that were mostly, sensibly, designed in matching cherry-red and charcoal brick, all illuminated by wrought-iron street lamps. In late fall and with the coming of spring, the campus can be quite lovely. But during the winter months students are apt to hunker down indoors—and travel from class to class through the school's extensive system of underground tunnels.

Mid-Atlantic

While this might sound a little like wartime Stalingrad, it beats facing the frost: the mean low temperature in January and February in Rochester is seventeen degrees. Moreover, because of nearby Lake Ontario, the city gets an average of ninety inches of snowfall each year. A sardonic student guide says: "In Rochester snow starts falling around Halloween and doesn't really stop until Easter. . . . Hope you packed your parka!"

Students say that there's plenty to do besides making snow angels and avoiding hypothermia. Including fraternities and sororities, there are some 220 registered undergraduate student organizations. There are a variety of groups for interests ranging from archery and debating to anime and bellydancing. Although there are many solid religious organizations for Christians, Jews and Muslims, there are also a Pagan student community and council for gender and women's studies. The university also has active campus Democratic and Republican clubs.

Dorms at Rochester are generally grouped by their entryway. Some entryways are designated as single-sex entryways, others as coed. Suites can be coed, and for students who choose this option, the bathrooms are coed as well. Within the dorms, the school also offers "special interest" floors for students keen on particular subjects like computers or film. Rochester also has a large, well-maintained, and free gym where students can keep in shape during the long, cold indoor months.

Rochester's best-known annual events are connected to the seasons—and constrained by the weather. In the fall, students take part in the Pumpkin Launch, a special Halloween celebration of imaginative engineering. Termed a "nerdy good time" by its organizers, it showcases Rochester students' enthusiastic and unashamed intellectualism. Engineering undergrads hold a contest to see who can best improvise a cheap trebuchet for firing the season's pumpkins the furthest distance. In the school's Wilson Quad, you may see a machine uniting a hibachi with a bicycle pump, and round orange objects flying like cannonballs into the sky.

Around Christmas time Rochester students take part in the Boar's Head Dinner, a seventy-two-year tradition that gets professors and administrators dressed up as medieval figures while musical groups serenade students who sit down to a grand, old-fashioned Yuletide feast. Christmas carols are followed by a "Reading of the Boar," a recited history

ACADEMIC REQUIREMENTS

Rochester imposes no core curriculum and only modest distribution requirements. They are as follows:

- One English composition class, "Reading and Writing in the College"—though students may test out.
- One or more writing-intensive courses in a student's major.
- Two "clusters" of three related classes in areas unrelated to their major. The school offers nearly 250 such clusters in subjects ranging from American Sign Language to computer art.

Mid-Atlantic

GREEN LIGHT

Rochester does not seem intent on enforcing any particular ideology. In general, says one avowed campus conservative, "politics don't intrude." "Apathy," says one conservative undergrad, "is a bigger problem than political correctness." Another says, "You have to do something extraordinary to attract attention where politics is concerned." Most professors remain nonpolitical in the classroom, and most traditional majors impose solid and serious requirements.

In October 2010, UR College Republicans sponsored a Second Amendment Appreciation Day on campus—suggesting that the group is both active and unafraid.

of the dinner. Then jugglers perform and student awards are given out.

Come long-awaited springtime, everyone on campus turns out for Dandelion Day, which features carnival rides, beer tents, and open houses at Greek organizations. Besides these seasonal feasts, Wilson Day is another tradition found on campus, on which day every year the incoming students spend the day doing acts of service for the local community, whether it be landscaping, putting on picnics or providing meals for the homeless.

While River Campus students can go over the short bridge fording the Genesee toward Alexander Street (or "A Street," as it's called) for the area's bars and clubs, they can also busy themselves on campus, thanks to the great variety of student activities. And that's probably a good thing, too; Rochester is in economic decline, and consequently isn't the safest city. As if to compensate, the university continues the expansion and improvement of its campus. A new science building is currently in progress, and the Eastman theater is also under renovation.

The River Campus is cut off from the rest of Rochester by the river on one side and the cemetery on the other, which insulates the campus from city-based crime. The Eastman School, however, located near the center of the city, is described by one nervous undergrad as "a question." To keep music students safer, the school offers free transportation to and from downtown and free rides anywhere in town at night through the school's security office. The crime rate at the university is still rather high, although things have gotten a little safer recently. In 2009, the school reported eight sex offenses, three robberies, four aggravated assaults, nineteen burglaries, and seven motor vehicle thefts on campus.

Because the school is richly endowed (impressively, despite the global financial crises, UR's endowment has only dropped from $1.8 to $1.5 billion in recent years) financial aid is widely available and 100 percent of demonstrated financial need was met last year, with the average aid package $31,690. In 2010–11, the school's tuition was $40,282 and room and board was $11,640. The average student graduated owing about $25,000.

Rutgers University

New Brunswick, New Jersey • www.rutgers.edu

The only game in town

Rutgers, now the State University of New Jersey, was founded as Queen's College in 1766, and it is the most prominent public college in the state. While there are many top-notch professors offering rigorous courses at Rutgers, the university admits 60 percent of its applicants, allows them to fulfill overly broad general education "requirements" with a crazy-quilt of classes, and makes an effort to retain any student who does his work. Professors do attempt to get to know their students personally, keep their office hours faithfully, are glad to help when asked, and are unhappy that more do not seek them out. There is some disappointment, however, that Rutgers isn't more selective, so that the quality of the student body might come up to that of the faculty; too many of New Jersey's best enroll elsewhere.

Still, Rutgers is a "pretty good place for people who don't have capital but have real intellectual ability," says one professor. Striving to be intellectually like the Ivies and athletically like the Big Ten while having to scramble for funds to keep the party going as the state trough runs dry, Rutgers has many challenges ahead. President Richard McCormick, an American historian inaugurated in 2002, has spoken of making Rutgers a top-tier research institution, improving its reputation, and increasing its economic impact on the state of New Jersey. Recent accomplishments he touts are the trans-Atlantic journey of the Rutgers underwater glider; the performance of the Rutgers Sinfonia and Symphony Orchestra at the Superbowl; a new high in fundraising for the Rutgers Foundation; and a record number of students earning Fulbrights. At the same time, Rutgers bears the weight of serving as the main state university for New Jersey; in spite of its population and wealth, New Jersey lacks a strong network of public four-year colleges and this puts an enormous burden on Rutgers.

And New Jersey is increasingly reluctant to pay the tab. According to news reports, Rutgers faces an "'extreme financial crisis,' brought on by state budget cuts." Staring at a deficit of nearly $97 million, the university is in what it calls "a very, very difficult situation, one that is unprecedented." In June 2010 the university canceled raises and froze pay across the board to avoid layoffs and course reductions. Ironically, in fall 2009 the school finished a $4.9 million football facility and a $7.5 million high-tech visitors center across from the football stadium. These came on the heels of a recently finished $100 million expansion to the stadium itself. Controversy over Rutgers's spending priorities shows no sign of abating.

VITAL STATISTICS

Religious affiliation: *none*
Total enrollment: *37,364*
Total undergraduates:
29,095
SAT midranges: CR: *530–630*,
M: *560–680*
Applicants: *28,624*
Applicants accepted: *61%*
Applicants accepted who
enrolled: *33%*
Tuition and fees: *in state,
$12,559; out of state,
$24,316*
Room and board: *$10,906*
Freshman retention rate:
92%
Graduation rate: *52% (4 yrs.),
77% (6 yrs.)*
Courses with fewer than 20
students: *41%*
Student-faculty ratio: *14:1*
Courses taught by graduate
students: *10%*
Most popular majors: *social
sciences, psychology,
biology*
Students living on campus:
50%
Guaranteed housing for 4
years? *no*
Students in fraternities: *6%*
in sororities: *5%*

Academic Life: I got my facts learned

Rutgers University serves nearly 55,000 students in three cities. The New Brunswick campus is the largest and oldest, and also the strongest and most selective. The New Brunswick branch is divided into nine schools for undergraduates, and recently combined its four liberal arts colleges into the School of Arts and Sciences.

Sadly, the liberal arts program at the School of Arts and Sciences is undermined by the school's lax distribution requirements. Rutgers lists more than 4,000 courses in its catalog; most fulfill one of the general academic requirements, and many are overspecialized or politicized. Hence, a Rutgers diploma means something different for each graduate.

The honors program is more thorough, requiring two semesters of honors colloquia and four designated honors courses, intermediate proficiency in a foreign language, and a six-credit capstone research project.

Advising is available but is not required—to the point where one student tells us: "I am not too sure about advising," one student says. "I would suspect that would be more in a graduate or higher-level undergraduate setting." Once a student has declared his major, he may visit a professor in his own department for advice—or not, as he likes. This policy is . . . inadvisable, as one professor observes: "A lot of students are alienated, overwhelmed, and confused."

Rutgers has recently instituted programs for motivated freshmen. One is the Burns Family Seminar, an offering of sixty to seventy one-credit pass/fail classes in which top professors from all areas of study in the university introduce themselves and their fields to students. The other is the First-year Interest Group Seminars program in which upperclass mentors give one-credit seminars to freshmen.

At Rutgers there is "a bias towards research over teaching," says a professor. Another says, "In tenure decisions, the ratio of emphasis on teaching to research is at least 30 to 70 percent, although very bad teaching can knock someone out. I also think that professors do far too little teaching, a problem at most research-oriented universities."

Graduate students do a lot of the teaching at Rutgers. An administrator admits that TAs teach courses "frequently"; however, professors lead most lecture courses, and although introductory classes can be as large as 300 students, upper-level classes are much smaller. One political science student says, "In upper-division courses in my major, most classes are small enough that the professor will know your name." All faculty members hold office hours, and "the professors there are helpful if there is a need," says one student.

A recent graduate recommends Rutgers's Camden campus over New Brunswick: "There are no TAs at Camden. This allows students to get to know professors. I was fortunate to get to know almost every professor in my department very well. Regardless of the department, campus, or school, the professors are always willing to spend time with students. I've spoken with students from other large state schools, and they were rather envious."

Rutgers's philosophy department is one of the top-ranked in the world. Rutgers offers an undergraduate medieval studies major, a commendable course of study if rounded out by a complementary minor like classics, philosophy, or English. One professor adds that math and physics also are highly regarded. He says that "Rutgers is pretty good about trying to build strength in traditional liberal arts disciplines."

The English department boasts some good faculty and an excellent array of courses in all periods. But an English professor laments that his department has gone postmodern: "[Trendiness] is a national disease, but Rutgers has it worse than most places. The tragedy is that Rutgers used to be one of the top 'literary' departments in the nation." He laments the dominance of "identity politics, junior faculty who couldn't make sense of a Donne poem to save their lives, gender blather, 'gay studies,' et cetera. It is a grim time." English majors are required to take a course in African American, "ethnic-American," or "global Anglophone" literature but not in Shakespeare.

There are some excellent offerings in history, but many of the faculty are leftist. Students can fulfill the American history requirement by taking such specialized courses as "Sport in History," or "Gay and Lesbian History in the United States." History majors must take introductory European or American history classes, but otherwise are free to choose with a minimum of oversight from the department, which requires at least two courses in each of three areas: 1) European, 2) American, and 3) African, Asian, Latin American, or Native American history, and one pre-1500 course.

Political science majors face anemic requirements, which include an introduction to "theoretical approaches in politics;" either "American Government" or "Law and Politics;" either international relations or comparative politics; and at least one 300/400 level course in each of three areas (theory, American, and international). Dubious electives like "Politics of Reproduction" and "Whiteness and U.S. Politics" fill up the department's offerings.

SUGGESTED CORE

1. Classics 50:090:238, World Masterpieces I
2. Classics 50:730:305, Advanced Topics in Ancient Philosophy
3. Religion 50:840:110, Introduction to the Bible
4. Philosophy 50:730:211, History of Philosophy I (closest match)
5. Political Science 01:790:371/01:790:372, Western Tradition: Plato to Machiavelli/ Western Tradition: Hobbes to Mill
6. English 50:350:331/50:350:332, Shakespeare I/II
7. History 50:512:201, Development of the United States I
8. History 01:510:427, Intellectual History of Modern Europe or Philosophy 50:730:307, Nineteenth Century Philosophy

Mid-Atlantic

A professor confirms that faculty and students are largely liberal, but he also says that, given the "gap they are trying to cover between literate and illiterate people, there is an evangelical aspect to teaching at Rutgers that transcends politics." A student says that teachers lean "very much to the left, and unfortunately it often does influence the content of the courses. Just last semester, I took a twentieth-century history course where the professor was extremely liberal and taught almost every lecture as if conservatives were the problem with society." But another says, "While professors may have had liberal views, I never found it to be a detriment to my education. I've never been punished for offering conservative view points; in fact, professors appreciate the diversity of opinion in the classroom. Professors' views aren't 'preached,' or the focus of the lecture, and they really don't change the classroom atmosphere."

Classics, art history, and archeology are said to be strong departments. The biological sciences, especially microbiology, are world-class. Disciplines that typically have a radical slant at other colleges, such as sociology and anthropology, are more soberly academic at Rutgers. Highly praised professors include David Mechanic in sociology; T. J. Jackson Lears, Paul Clemens, Allen Howard, Andrew Shankman, and Michael Adas in history; Bert Levine, John Weingart, Alan Rosenthal, G. Alan Tarr, and Wojtek Wolfe in political science and William Fitzgerald, William Galperin and William Dowling in English. This latter professor, who for years has been fighting what he sees as Rutgers's steep decline, runs an iconoclastic website called "WCD at Home," which prospective students should check out.

One professor laments that the "student body generally is not as good as the faculty." Another says, "Rutgers is like any other pretty good state university. Some students are genuinely interested in learning, some only care about grades and/or post-graduation jobs." With business the most popular major, followed by social sciences and psychology, there seem to be plenty of careerists. However, a recent alumnus says, "The intellectual life on campus can be described as both challenging and vibrant, if you choose it to be so. . . . Our diverse student body forces you into situations to defend your ideas. For this I am eternally grateful."

Despite its severe financial difficulties, "incredible bargains and opportunities abound at Rutgers, for people who know how to use them," says a faculty member. He mentions the Institute for Marine and Coastal Science, which is working to contain damage from the oil spill in the Gulf of Mexico; the Orestes Research Center, through which sophomores can apply for paid research internships with a professor from any discipline and which can lead to a senior thesis and even pay for research trips; archaeological digs; and the Institute for Healthcare Policy and Research.

Rutgers's study-abroad programs offer myriad opportunities in twenty-eight locations, from Barbados to South Africa. Rutgers teaches many languages on campus, including Akan, Arabic, Aramaic, Bengali, Hebrew, Hindi, Malayan, Persian, Sanskrit, Swahili, Turkish, Yoruba, Chinese, Greek (Ancient and modern), Latin, Japanese, Korean, Hungarian, Russian, Polish, French, German, Italian, Portuguese, Spanish, and Armenian.

Student Life: Ain't no sin to be glad you're alive

One Rutgers senior says, "New Brunswick is no New York City, but there's plenty to do here." Comedy clubs, ethnic restaurants, shops, theaters, and other activities are a five-minute walk from campus. The community surrounding the campus is filled with college students and "New Brunswick has a college town feel, most evident on football game days," notes an alumnus. The campus is sprawling, and auto congestion is acute. "Organizing the day is difficult for students," says one professor, who notes that many have off-campus jobs to make ends meet.

The social scene at Rutgers is . . . lively. "Unfortunately, alcohol does play a big role for a lot of people, especially in the Greek scene," a student says. "But many of us have a great social life without it." One sorority member says that "alcohol is there if you want it, but Rutgers is so large that there's no pressure to conform. There are so many different types of people, that if you don't like something you can find your own group of friends." Less than 10 percent of the student body goes Greek.

Rutgers University is not residential. No student is required to live on campus, and far less than half the student body chooses to. There are only beds to accommodate about one-third of the students. Most freshmen do live on campus, housed together in traditional hall-style dormitories or in Clothier, a huge building known as a party dorm. Every resi-

---

ACADEMIC REQUIREMENTS

Rutgers has nothing like a core curriculum, or even any requirement that students take courses grounded in Western civilization, but the distribution requirements faced by students in liberal arts are fairly extensive:

- Two writing courses (student may test out of one). Courses from "Buddhist Philosophy" to "Nineteenth Century British Fiction" may fulfill this requirement.
- Two classes in quantitative skills. (Students can test out of one.) Options for the intro course include "Topics in Mathematics for the Liberal Arts," and "Precalculus" II. Choices for the second course include "Introduction to Logic," "Computer Applications for Business," and Basic Statistics for Exercise Science."
- Two science courses in biology, chemistry, environmental science, geological sciences, meteorology, or physics.
- One class in social science. Options run the gamut from "The Construction of Contemporary Europe" to "Anthropology of Sexuality and Eroticism" and "Coaching Theory and Technique."
- One course in humanities. Again, the range of choices is staggeringly broad. Classes offered include "Gender and Power in Africa," "Introduction to Latin American Civilization and Culture," "Art History," and "Modern Greek."
- One class in "interdisciplinary studies" from any of over thirty departments. Options range from "Shaping a Life" to "South Asia and the Middle East."
- One additional course in social science, humanities, or interdisciplinary studies.
- One diversity class from a list of approved options such as "Cults, Magic, and Witchcraft" and "Minority Literature."
- One global awareness course, such as "World Cinema" I & II, "Law, Justice, and Rights in Bolivia," Backgrounds of Homoerotic Literature," or "Sedimentology."

dence has quiet hours, and most include twenty-four-hour study lounges where students can escape the often-chaotic dorm culture. All freshman dormitories are smoke-free, and each dorm has a residential advisor to enforce the rules. Although there are a few single-sex floors, men and women are often housed in rooms next to each other. There are no coed bathrooms or dorm rooms, however. And Residents of Douglass College (an all-female school absorbed by Rutgers) live in all-women dormitories, and students can also opt to live in one of many fraternity or sorority houses. There are a number of special houses available for students interested in foreign languages, areas of the arts, sexuality and gender, or academic subjects like history, political science, philosophy, religion and spirituality.

Areas of Rutgers University—especially Douglass College and the main academic quad of Rutgers College—are wonderfully charming, with ivy-covered collegiate architecture, but other buildings look more like prison facilities.

Rutgers funds a mind-numbing array of diversity programs, coalitions, task forces, and administrative offices and seems to revel in its standing as a lesbian, gay, bisexual, transgender-friendly place. "Rutgers Reaches Out to Meet the Needs of Transgender Students," gushes an article from the university's news site. The Office of Social Justice Education and LGBT Communities offers annual student programs like National Coming Out Week, World AIDS Day, "Gaypril," a month of LGBT awareness and activities, and provides career tips in a program called Out on the Job. The university also offers a "rainbow graduation" ceremony for graduating gay/lesbian students.

Rutgers also sponsors a group on campus through its Center for Applied Psychology called Answer. "Answer is a national organization dedicated to providing and promoting comprehensive sexuality education to young people and the adults who teach them," according to the website. Answer's twelve-person staff is headed by a former associate vice president of education and training at Planned Parenthood New York City. The organization publishes a magazine for teenagers called *Sex, Etc.* which has a teen editorial board.

Spending on and by Rutger's athletic program is lavish. Rutgers boasts hundreds of intramural teams and nearly fifty NCAA Division I and III varsity sports (each campus fields its own teams). High-ranking teams in recent years have included women's lacrosse, tennis, and basketball, and men's baseball, soccer, gymnastics, crew, and track. Rutgers's "Scarlet Knights," a Division I football team, have been called "resurgent" on the university's website.

There are also plenty of outlets for those who are neither diversity-obsessed nor jocks. Rutgers has hundreds of registered student organizations for everything from recreation to career advancement. For those interested in groups less charged with political or cultural significance, there are organizations like the Debate Union, Actuarial Club, the Equine Science Club, and many, many more. Religious students of all stripes will find groups of like-minded believers, Catholics, Protestants, Hindustanis, Orthodox, Jews, Muslims, Buddhists, pagans, even Pastafarians of the "Church of the Flying Spaghetti Monster."

While liberal groups far outnumber conservative ones, Rutgers for Life, College Republicans, and Young Americans for Liberty are active. One student says, "I am very much a conservative, and though it is a very liberal campus, I am comfortable being here. It's about making the right friends, taking the right classes, and knowing why you hold your views." A recent graduate adds, "The students—like almost every college in the northeast—lean to the left. But I consider myself fortunate to have the opportunity to study in a diverse classroom; I changed some opinions, clarified others, and formed new ones, largely because of the intellectual conversations I had with left-leaning students."

Some conservative students have rallied around campus alternative paper the *Centurion*—founded by firebrand journalist James O'Keefe, who went on to expose corruption in the "community organization" ACORN, and to face charges for a journalistic sting aimed at Louisiana Sen. Mary Landrieu. Others agree with a recent graduate who scoffs: "The *Centurion* is widely regarded by liberals *and* conservatives as outlandish and radical. I would say roughly 10 percent read it, and 5 percent believe it to be of any academic value."

Despite tough financial times, Rutgers continues to improve and expand its facilities. Currently underway is a three-year, $10.5 million classroom renovation project in response to student complaints that classrooms are "aesthetically unpleasing." In fall 2011 a $30 million dining facility for the Livingston campus opened, and by 2012 new housing complexes will add 500 beds to Busch and 1,500 to Livingston. Livingston also will get a new $85 million business school, construction on which is planned for 2011–2013.

Rutgers is not exactly an idyll of peace and order. The *Daily Targum*, Rutgers student newspaper, reported in May 2010 on the school's largest annual party:

> This year's Rutgersfest proved to be more of an ordeal than those of years past when a day of partying turned into a night of violence. We collected a rather impressive

pool of anecdotes about the night, all of which were negative. Fights broke out all around New Brunswick. People were driving on sidewalks. Wandering marauders jumped people in the College Avenue parking deck. At least one person had a gun pulled on them near the Grease Trucks. Then there's the physical evidence left

---

RED LIGHT

In fall 2009, the Rutgers *Centurion* offered the following commentary on the state of free speech at Rutgers: "Rutgers University likes to pretend that it doesn't have a speech code. . . . Unfortunately, President McCormick is either confused about what speech codes are, or is lying to us." The paper cited university rules stating the following:

"Clubs and organizations may not deny membership to anyone on the basis of race, creed, color, religion, naturally origin, ancestry, age, sex, disability, marital status, familial status, affectional or sexual orientation, or veteran status . . ." The *Centurion* also noted that students can be punished for the "use of words or phrases (written or oral) on the part of the perpetrator(s) which may be racist, sexist, heterosexist (homophobic), etc. in origin, but have been [sic] incorporated into his/her commonly used vocabulary."

Rutgers's institutional priorities and its commitment to diversity are called into question by a look at the 2010 commencement program, which was a veritable paean to the sexual revolution. Eleanor Smeal, "renowned feminist" and president of the Feminist Majority Foundation and former president of the National Organization for Women, was the featured speaker and received an honorary doctorate, as did Judy Blume, writer of smut for children, and Carl Djerassi, an inventor of "the pill." Proof of administrative tolerance and a commitment to diversity would indicate having Phyllis Schlafly next year.

over from the nightlong odyssey, including broken windshields, beer cans, liquor bottles, condoms, and undergarments.

In 2009, Rutgers reported thirteen forcible sex offenses, two robberies, seven aggravated assaults, fifty-two burglaries, and nine stolen cars on the New Brunswick campus. One campus resident says, "It's a good idea to always lock your door to your room, no matter if you know everybody in the building or not." The university maintains bike patrols, horse patrols, and van escorts. One crime at Rutgers in the news in early 2010 was a sorority hazing incident in which six members of the African American sorority Sigma Gamma Rho were arrested and charged with aggravated hazing for paddling pledges, sometimes until they bled. The university immediately suspended the Sigma Gamma Rho chapter.

If you're a New Jersey resident, Rutgers is a bargain. In-state tuition for 2010–11 was $12,559, while out-of-state students paid $24,316. Room and board were $10,906. Admission is need blind, but the school does not guarantee to meet every student's financial need. Some 56 percent of all undergraduates receive need-based financial aid. The average debt of a recent graduate was $19,760.

St. John's College

Annapolis, Maryland, and Santa Fe, New Mexico •
www.stjohnscollege.edu

Battle of the books

Founded as King William's School in 1696, then chartered in 1784 as St. John's College, St. John's was for most of its history an unremarkable regional school serving the men of Maryland. The college was about to close during the Great Depression, when pioneering educators Scott Buchanan and Stringfellow Barr approached its board of directors with a bold plan to save the school by making it distinctive. Barr was made president, Buchanan dean, and a radically new program was born. What was this revolutionary idea? To read old books—certain designated "Great Books"—and very little else.

The school quickly made an impression; by 1943, Barr announced to the world that six years of success "have convinced us that St. John's may serve as a model for the reorganization of liberal education in the United States." Supporter Mark van Doren of Columbia was telling his fellow professors of St. John's model: "Until it is accepted everywhere in America, we shall lack the right to say that liberal education exists among us." The divide between St. John's and most other colleges has only grown in subsequent decades, as it held firm to its self-hallowed canon, and they threw their curricula to the winds.

St. John's is one college on two campuses, which share the same program of study and many of the same characteristics. The teachers are called tutors and students and faculty all refer to each other by their last names—always preceded by "Mr." or "Miss." Classes are always taught by the tutors, never by graduate students. Grades are not routinely reported to students; many do not know their GPAs. Very few students are to be found playing on computers, watching television, listening to iPods, or texting on cell phones; they talk to *each other*. In that conversation, they help each other to live the life of the mind.

Academic life: From Plato to NATO

Reading and discussion are at the heart of academics at St. John's. A current student says: "I went to a large public research university for my undergraduate studies and found that although I had constant stress and work to complete, I did little in the way of genuine learning. Being at St. John's has given me that experience." Another student observes, "It is probably impossible to find another school in the U.S. with more reverence for Western civilization and the Great Books than St. John's. It's practically the campus religion." (That would

VITAL STATISTICS

Religious affiliation: *none*
Total enrollment: *1,050*
Total undergraduates: *883*
SAT/ACT midranges: CR:
  630–740, M: *570–680*;
  ACT: *27–31*
Applicants: *626*
Applicants accepted: *83%*
Applicants accepted who
  enrolled: *49%*
Tuition and fees: *$41,792*
Room and board: *$9,984*
Freshman retention rate:
  80%
Graduation rate: *55% (4 yrs.),*
  63% (6 yrs.)
Courses with fewer than 20
  students: *100%*
Student-faculty ratio: *8:1*
Courses taught by graduate
  students: *none*
Most popular majors: *not*
  applicable
Students living on campus:
  76%
Guaranteed housing for 4
  years? *no*
Students in fraternities or
  sororities: *none*

make it the only religion; despite its name, the school is deeply secular.)

Every course in the curriculum is required, and students at both campuses follow essentially the same program of study. Classes are small, about twenty or fewer students (the student to faculty ratio is 8 to 1) and are conducted using the Socratic method of discussion rather than lecture. The excitement of students is palpable. One says, "We study Ptolemy intensively, then in two years we study Einstein. . . . Sometimes we make connections across thousands of years, and the whole room has mutual understanding of all questions discussed for each. This is not restricted to math but is true in every subject."

The keystone of the program is the twice-weekly Seminar. Students break into groups of twenty or so, and enter discussions led by pairs of tutors. Some students note that seminars are dictated by the students, who are deemed equal to tutors—so the meetings can vary in quality. Works are studied chronologically, from the origins of civilization to the present. As one student says, "We are here to engage books in their own right, not to blindly accept what each subsequent author posits." These seminars give an overview of the greatest works of the Western world and discuss subjects such as philosophy, theology, political science, literature, history, economics, and psychology. The effectiveness of the Seminar depends, of course, to a great degree on the quality of the tutor. Several students reported an insistence on lock-step thought in the supposedly free-flowing seminars. "Question all you like, but don't declare a particular opinion," warned one.

Beside the Seminar, students participate in labs and take language, math, and music tutorials. The language tutorial takes place all four years and covers Attic Greek in the first two years and French in the latter two. One junior says that her favorite classes have been ones in which the entire period was spent in discussion of one phrase or sentence, quibbling over students' choices of various words in their translations. The math tutorials require students to work through proofs themselves, and music instructs them to sing and compose so that they understand how music functions.

St. John's students don't do quite *all* their learning through seminars. Every Friday night the school sponsors a rather substantive talk, known simply enough as the Friday Night Lecture. Students are expected to analyze the lectures carefully, as they are followed by a (usually) lively question-and-answer period, which can go on for hours. Sometimes the lecture is given by a tutor, often by a visiting scholar or expert; at others a concert or performance will be offered instead.

An especially refreshing aspect of the school is the de-emphasis on grades. At St. John's students are awarded conventional letter grades mostly so that they may later apply to graduate school or transfer if they wish. But the main feedback they get takes place in "Don Rags," in which tutors discuss each student's progress, strengths and weaknesses—in his presence. When the discussion is finished, he is allowed to reply. In the junior year, the Rags may be replaced by conferences where the student speaks first, giving a self-evaluation, and then the tutors share their remarks. Grades are not discussed.

> **SUGGESTED CORE**
>
> The school's prescribed curriculum suffices.

Preceptorials are offered in the middle of a student's junior and senior years, taking the place of seminar for about seven weeks. These are as close as students get to electives, and the choices differ every year. Students will often approach a tutor and ask to have certain subjects or authors treated; the topics are always based on a serious intellectual interest expressed on either the part of students or tutors.

To cap off the program, seniors write a substantive essay under the guidance of a faculty advisor. For a month-long period in the final semester, seniors' classes are suspended and they work on the essay. On the night essays are due, the dean "stops time" for an hour before midnight so tardy students can hand in their essays. Besides the essay, which must be accepted by the faculty, the student must give an hour-long oral defense of the essay, which is open to the public.

There are no majors at St. John's, but according to the school, a student who has successfully graduated can be viewed as having the equivalent of a double major in philosophy and the history of math and science, along with a double minor in classical studies and comparative literature.

Although the curriculum is set, this doesn't mean students only read and discuss the texts assigned. "Johnnies" (as students are called) have inquisitive natures and a broad interest in accumulating knowledge; they're the kind of kids who edit Wikipedia. Anywhere you go at St. John's, you will find students and tutors talking about anything and everything. Students often put together "guerrilla seminars," which are just a group of students (and very likely tutors) who get together in their free time to discuss topics of interest. These informal discussions are vital to the life of St. John's. The college also offers a "take a tutor to lunch" program, at the school's expense; students are well-advised to take the college up on this, since most tutors do not hold posted office hours.

One undergrad says: "Tutors are very accessible and generally helpful. All a student needs to do is to schedule an appointment with a tutor—no need to worry about long lines during 'office hours.' The shortest meeting I've ever had with a tutor, one on one, was twenty minutes, and the longest was three hours of intense intellectual discussion. Probably nowhere else in the U.S. can a student get that much individual attention and mentoring from tenured instructors."

Students choose who they take to lunch, but not who to study under. So the faculty we recommend for lunch are as follows. At Annapolis: the much-loved veteran Eva Brann, who received the National Endowment for the Humanities Medal in 2005; Dylan Casey, Paul

Ludwig, Robert Williamson, Jon Lenkowski, Carl Page, Michael Grenke, Walter Sterling, Stewart Umphrey, Peter Kalkavage, Jim Beall, and Henry Higuera. At Santa Fe: Jorge Aigla, Grant Franks, Peter Pesic, J. Walter Sterling, and Edward Cary Stickney. As one undergrad observes, "Just as students are required to take all classes, faculty are expected to teach across the curriculum, and have to learn Ancient Greek and astronomy and Baudelaire no less than the students. This is all part of the culture of St. John's." That said, in order to be effective, the Great Books program requires that each tutor be excellent—whereas, in a more conventional college, less talented instructors need not damage the quality of classes as much. At St. John's, a poor tutor (and there are some) can be a real handicap for his students.

About 75 percent of graduates go on to some sort of post-baccalaureate study. A surprisingly large number go on to work in medicine and the sciences. Many enter law, teaching, and the arts. Successful alumni include film directors (Lee David Zlotoff, *The Spitfire Grill*; Jeremy Leven, *The Legend of Bagger Vance*), journalists and editors (Lydia Berggren

---

ACADEMIC REQUIREMENTS

St. John's has an outstanding required curriculum based on the great books of the Western world. All students must complete:

- "Freshman Seminar," a "Greek year" that begins with Homer and ends with Aristotle.
- "Sophomore Seminar," which begins with the Bible and early Roman writers and continues through the medieval and Renaissance eras, right into the early Enlightenment.
- "Junior Seminar," which continues in the Enlightenment and covers works primarily from the seventeenth and eighteenth centuries.
- "Senior Seminar," which brings the student into the modern age and covers many early American political writings as well as modern philosophy and great modern literature.
- Greek mathematics, geometry, and astronomy.
- Astronomy, conic sections, transition to modern mathematics.
- Calculus, mathematical theory.
- Non-Euclidean geometry, relativity, topics in modern mathematics.
- Biology lab.
- Chemistry lab.
- Physics lab.
- Biology, genetics, and physics lab.
- Two years of Attic Greek (no Latin!) and two years of French.
- Philosophical logic and English poetry.
- Classical French prose and drama.
- French poetry, other poetry and prose.
- One year of music theory.
- One preceptorial.
- Three annual essays.
- An algebra test.
- Senior essay, with oral defense.

of the *New York Times*; Nancy Miller of Bloomsbury U.S.A. Publishing; Timothy Carney, columnist, the *Washington Examiner*; Ray Cave, retired editorial director of *Time*), broadcasters (Lisa Simeone, hostess, NPR's *World of Opera*; Seth Cropsey, former director of the International Broadcasting Bureau), and luminaries in many other fields.

Because of the unique program which builds upon itself over four years, transfer students must start as freshmen. Similarly, while students can transfer between the Annapolis and Santa Fe campuses, there is no study abroad. All Saint John's students spend a full four years (or more) studying at one of the Saint John's campuses. The only languages taught on campus are Ancient Greek and French.

Student Life: A school of two cities

St. John's decided to grow, while maintaining an intimate sense of community, by establishing a faraway second campus in New Mexico. Each campus has around 450 students. A certain friendly rivalry exists between the campuses. One Annapolis student says, "Santa Fe is for the weed-smoking hippies to hang out in the mountains." A Santa Fe student counters, "Annapolis is full of limousine liberals."

One of the great traditions of the Annapolis campus is croquet. Every year St. John's plays the Naval Academy in a heated match. It is said that when discussing their respective schools, a "Johnnie" was challenged by a "Middie" at any sport proposed. The "Johnnie" decided on croquet. The event has become an unofficial homecoming for alumni and the entire Johnnie community sits around eating strawberries and cream and sipping champagne. Later in the evening, there is a well-attended waltz party.

The Santa Fe campus has its own attributes, including a very well-regarded search-and-rescue team that works with state police. Students also enjoy river rafting, hiking, skiing, and many other outdoor activities. In recent years western Johnnies have been trying to put together a parallel event to Annapolis' croquet; some students hope that an Ultimate Frisbee match would work, but they have as yet been unable to find a worthy opponent.

The Santa Fe campus has townhouse-style buildings that students say can be a bit uncomfortable; however, the city of Santa Fe offers many more options than Annapolis, and many students move off campus in their sophomore year. A new residence center is soon to be built with a $5 million donation by an alumnus couple, and named for them. The Winiarski building will provide housing for many students as well as common rooms, seminar rooms, and faculty offices.

The unofficial mascot of St. John's is the platypus, which seems entirely fitting. Both campuses boast coffee shops that are the hubs of student activity outside of class and both offer many opportunities for extracurricular pursuits. There are student newspapers, drama clubs, film societies, religious organizations, political clubs, and parties. The school sponsors many dances throughout the year for students through the Waltz Committee. Swing and contemporary dance are also popular. Each campus has an extensive intramural program but no intercollegiate one.

Politics plays only a small role at St. John's. As one student writes, "Most students on campus are of the liberal mindset, but this certainly does not get in the way of friend-

GREEN LIGHT

The prevailing political attitude at St. John's is liberal, but the school is not highly politicized. Students with more conservative views, morally or politically, are readily accepted in the classroom and in the campus community. A student at the Annapolis campus writes:

"One of my favorite things about this college and the people who attend it is their acceptance of and respect for people of all walks of life. There is an unwritten rule of respect on this campus that everyone is expected—and wants—to follow. It is what makes our small community such a rich atmosphere for learning and growing, as well as a safe and friendly place to voice opinions and have serious discussions about the important things in life. The majority of St. John students have been raised by or are familiar with Judeo-Christian beliefs, but for whatever reasons do not currently choose to live by them. There are, however, a fair number of practicing Jews and Christians on campus who have formed student-run clubs and organize trips to temples and churches to worship together. Although they are a minority on campus, they enjoy their time here just as much as anyone else and have no trouble making friends."

ships or classes. I have not found there to be much political discussion on campus . . . but there are plenty of people to discuss politics with if one is interested in doing so. There is a St. John's Republicans group as well as a St. John's Democrats group on campus, both student-run and organized. Again, the opinions of others are accepted and/or tolerated by everyone—so long as those opinions do not harm anyone."

The school requires all freshmen to live on campus. In Annapolis there are eight dorms, the oldest of which was built in 1837 and the newest in 2006. Upperclassmen aren't guaranteed student housing, and in years past, many moved off campus as soon as they could. Maryland rents are keeping more of them on campus these days. According to one student, "Dorm life is in many ways similar to that at other schools. Students can be loud at odd hours, and sometimes there are disagreements among the students. On the whole, students are respectful of one another, and interested in maintaining a happy and fun community. RAs have all been impressive, in my experience. There are a few single-sex floors, but most dorms are mixed, with single-sex bathrooms." There are no restrictions on intervisitation, the bathrooms offer condoms, and one undergrad reports feeling uncomfortable at St. John's because of the expectation that casual sex was routine. Pressure at St. John's may be intense, and there have been a few suicides in the past two decades.

St. John's appears to have something of a problem with drug use. Students say that the Santa Fe campus reeks of weed. More serious are reports of harder drugs on the Annapolis campus in past years. Ten students were expelled in spring 2008 for illegal drug use (cocaine, insiders suggest), which led drug dealers onto campus. Most students only tipple, but enough drink to excess on a regular basis to raise concerns. Sober students can choose a substance-free dorm, but enforcement is said to be spotty.

St. John's is a secular institution, and religious life must be pursued off campus. The beautiful and historic old St. Mary's Church in Annapolis is the best local option for Catholics—although for traditional liturgies they'll have to go to Washington or Baltimore. Episcopalians will enjoy St. Anne's colonial-era ambience; but if they want traditional Anglicanism, they should visit St. Charles the Martyr. There is also a Greek Orthodox parish in town, and several Evangelical congregations and synagogues. New Age Santa Fe boasts several of America's most historic mission churches, and offers a wide variety of religious experiences.

Both campuses are rather safe. In 2009, the Annapolis campus reported four burglaries, eighteen thefts and fourteen acts of vandalism; the Santa Fe campus reported six burglaries. As anywhere else, students are encouraged to be cautious, especially at night. Both campuses offer security escorts to students who need to travel around campus at night.

St. John's is pricey, with tuition for 2010–11 at $41,792 and room and board some $9,984. Admissions are need blind and about 69 percent of students receive aid. All aid is need-based, although it may differ by campus. The average student-loan debt of a recent St. John's graduate is $23,638.

Sarah Lawrence College

Bronxville, New York • www.slc.edu

Boutique

Mark Twain once said, "It ain't what you don't know that gets you into trouble. It's what you know for sure that just ain't so." Most of what people think they know about Sarah Lawrence isn't true. It isn't a women's college; it has been coed since 1968. It was never one of the prestigious "Seven Sisters," though this is commonly believed. Nor is it a venerable institution; the college was founded in 1928. And while its post office address is that of the handsome and pricey Westchester suburb of Bronxville, its 44-acre campus sits entirely in the depressed industrial city of Yonkers, albeit in its fanciest section.

So what makes Sarah Lawrence so unusual, beyond the fact that it is currently the most expensive college in the United States? The answer lies in a unique method of organizing the curriculum and in the close relationship between teachers and students, one which seeks to imitate the teacher-student relationships for which Oxford and Cambridge are famous. Whether this method provides a thorough education depends entirely on the seriousness of the student.

The university's current President, Karen Lawrence, is no relation to the school's founder. Selected in 2007, she has shown a great inclusiveness, making an effort to invite every member of the freshman class over for a large Sunday dinner party she has each week.

Sarah Lawrence is not a comfortable place for politically conservative or religious students. Nor is it a school for the typical premed or prelaw student, and serious engineering and hard science majors might wish to look elsewhere. But it does offer something distinctive, and the abundance of famous graduates the school has produced provides some strong testament in its favor.

Academic Life: The Sarah Lawrence system

Sarah Lawrence's teaching system does not assure students—or prospective employers—that its graduates will have any specific base of knowledge upon graduation. There is no core curriculum, and no Great Books program available. There are also no majors and no letter grades. (Indeed, applicants need not take the SATs or ACTs.) Instead, students may if they wish declare what the university calls a "specialization" in a subject. The only requirements for graduating seniors are that they have completed 120 credit hours, have met some very minimal distribution requirements, taken a foreign language, and passed a non-credit physical education requirement which does not include a swim test. Lab science is not required. At the end, all students graduate with the same degree: a Bachelors of Arts in liberal studies.

Students typically take just three courses per term, instead of the four or five they would take at most colleges and universities. However, more than 80 percent of the classes offered are 85-minute, twice weekly seminars. Along with these, professors are obliged to meet separately with each student in their seminars at least once a week for forty-five minutes of one-on-one meeting and discussion. During this encounter, students work with the faculty member to develop a notion of what they will produce from the class, their so-called "conference work." This is a Sarah Lawrence term for what might be a pair of papers, a performance (in a dance or theater class, for example), or a forty to sixty page paper that might be comparable to a senior thesis at another school. The faculty member teaching the class is called its "don." As one student puts it, "This is an incredibly supportive place. You really talk with your professors. It's all about letting people develop their own style." This high level of attention is made possible by a student-faculty ratio of 9 to 1, and an average class size of thirteen.

To further facilitate the principle of openness, classes are usually in rooms with circular tables, and students are encouraged to express their opinions on an equal basis with the instructor. (Of course, if the student's views are on a par with the professor's, one must wonder why there is a professor, or why the school does not permit graduate students to teach classes.)

This system does inspire student enthusiasm about the faculty, and the school's proximity to New York City and its higher than normal pay for adjunct professors has allowed it to attract many famous instructors. In past decades, the likes of choreographer Martha Graham and novelist E. L. Doctorow have taught at the school.

Sarah Lawrence does not have majors, but it does have academic departments, although some of these may only have one or two full-time faculty. Among the school's forty-one disciplines are such politicized choices as Africana studies, ethnic and diasporic studies and Lesbian, gay, bisexual and transgender studies. Classes offered include "Queer Theory," "The Invention of Homosexuality," "Thinking Gender" and "Asian American Text and Image: Harold and Kumar Go Back in Time."

The departments which today seem to generate the most student enthusiasm are dance, theater, and literature—each of which displays the school's preoccupation with remain-

VITAL STATISTICS

Religious affiliation: *none*
Total enrollment: *4,080*
Total undergraduates: *1,383*
SAT/ACT midranges: *not applicable*
Applicants: *2,801*
Applicants accepted: *44%*
Applicants accepted who enrolled: *31%*
Tuition and fees: *$43,546*
Room and board: *$13,370*
Freshman retention rate: *86%*
Graduation rate: *70% (4 yrs.), 79% (6 yrs.)*
Courses with fewer than 20 students: *94%*
Student-faculty ratio: *9:1*
Courses taught by graduate students: *none*
Most popular majors: *not applicable*
Students living on campus: *85%*
Guaranteed housing for 4 years? *yes*
Students in fraternities or sororities: *none*

ing "cutting edge." The dance program has just one class focused on classical ballet among its more than two dozen offerings; theater is definitely oriented towards avant-garde productions; and the literature department leans heavily on eclectic courses such as "Contemporary African Literatures: Bodies & Questions of Power" and "Giles Deleuze and the Composition of Living" (while still offering a number of solid, traditional choices).

Certainly, Sarah Lawrence has produced an astonishing number of famous graduates in the arts, especially for such a small school. Among the famous actresses who have attended the school are Jane Alexander, Jill Clayburgh, Carrie Fisher, Robin Givens, Lauren Holly, Tea Leoni, Julianna Margulies, Holly Robinson Peete, Kyra Sedgwick, and Joanne Woodward. The school also graduated such famous directors as Brian De Palma, J.J. Abrams (Creator of *Lost*), and Joan Micklin Silver. Among the school's other illustrious grads are former White House Chief of Staff Rahm Emmanuel, singer-songwriters Carly Simon and Lesley Gore, "The View" hostess Barbara Walters, playwright David Lindsay-Abaire, novelists Allen Gurganus (*Oldest Living Confederate Widow Tells All*), A. M. Homes (*The Safety of Objects*), Anne Patchett (*Bel Canto*) and Alice Walker (*The Color Purple*), choreographer Meredith Monk and fashion designer Vera Wang. Beatle wives Linda McCartney and Yoko Ono were known for having their differences; one thing they had in common was that each attended Sarah Lawrence.

Among the current faculty members whom students and faculty most highly recommend are Fred Smoler in history and literature, outspokenly conservative Jefferson Adams in history, Mike Siff in computer science, Scott Calvin in physics, Lee Edwards in art history and Melissa Frazier in literature.

A colleague describes Smoler, who teaches a class on modern warfare, as "witty, fast, bright, and popular." Siff, who offers a class on cryptography that can be taken both by serious math geeks and nonmajors, is said to be "energetic and able to teach to multiple levels." A current student says that Edwards is "simply amazing—and she takes her students to the opera." This student calls Frazier, who teaches a class on the Russian novel, "someone who will push you and from whom you'll learn as much as you will from anyone you'll ever study with."

Along with its emphasis on individualized instruction, Sarah Lawrence strongly encourages its students to take term- or year-abroad programs, and it reports that more than 50 percent of its students will receive some of their instruction overseas. To this end, it offers study-abroad programs in Italy (Florence and Catania), Oxford, and Paris, as well as an acting program in London. Then there is one more: Granted the left-wing tilt of the school, it is perhaps unsurprising that Sarah Lawrence is one of the few American colleges to offer study abroad in Cuba. Through a program arranged with the University of Havana, the school sends some dozen or so students per term to study there. Sarah Lawrence offers language instruction in French, German, Ancient Greek, Latin, Italian, Japanese, Russian, and Spanish.

Student Life: You can't take the A train

Although the Sarah Lawrence campus is within the political boundaries of Yonkers, it is just a five- to ten-minute stroll from Bronxville's main street and, perhaps more significantly, the Bronxville train station. The station provides a quick means to get into New York City. Frequent Metro-North trains, which run from early morning until after midnight, take students from Bronxville to New York's Grand Central Terminal in about half an hour. This means students can get into midtown New York from campus as quickly as folks in many parts of Brooklyn and Queens. The price for the train ride is currently $6.50 one way.

Sarah Lawrence offers a regular shuttle to the Bronxville train station. Additionally, there is van service running four times daily, seven days a week providing regular, speedy, free travel to and pick up from New York's Upper East Side. (The van makes its stops in front of the Metropolitan Museum.) The city therefore serves as a lure for students, and on the weekends many students can be found in the city hanging out in raffishly chic downtown dive bars.

ACADEMIC REQUIREMENTS

Sarah Lawrence has no core curriculum and only anemic distribution requirements. According to the school, "During their four years, students take course work in at least three of . . . four academic areas." These are:

- Natural sciences and mathematics. Options range from "The Biology of Living and Dying" to "Physics for Future Presidents."
- Humanities. Choices include everything from "Ancient Philosophy and Law" to "Movement for the Urban Village: Dances of the African Diaspora."
- History and the social sciences. Everything counts from "American Elections and Political Institutions in the 21st Century" to "Standing On My Sisters' Shoulders: Women in the Black Freedom Struggle."
- Creative and performing arts. Choices range from "Acting Shakespeare" to "Little World Games: An Introduction to Game Development."

Students are also required to take two full-year lecture courses or the equivalent prior to their senior year.

Of the 120 credits required for the BA 60 can be in the creative and performing arts, up to 80 in history and the social sciences, up to 80 in the humanities, and up to 80 in the natural sciences and mathematics. No more than 50 credits may be earned in one discipline, and freshmen must select their courses from three different disciplines.

Mid-Atlantic

These parties of students headed into Gotham are often groups of girls or groups in which there is just one male. After all, reflecting Sarah Lawrence's founding as a finishing school for upper-crust young women, the school remains overwhelmingly female. The Class of 2014 will be approximately 70 percent female, and that's a more evenly balanced sex ratio than most Sarah Lawrence classes have had. And though the school is small—it still has incoming classes of fewer than 350—it has been growing. Consequently, the dorm rooms, which were once a selling point, are no longer so spacious.

Freshman dorms are either coed by floor or all-female, and girls may request to be on a female floor. However, upperclass students are typically in coed dorms with coed bathrooms, and they may even request to be in a coed suite. Many seniors and some juniors can get single rooms.

The student body is not very racially diverse. Only 5 percent of students are black, and just 4 percent are Hispanic. As one might expect, most of the students come from the two coasts; 52 percent are from New York, California, Massachusetts, Pennsylvania, and Connecticut.

Students living in New York City or Westchester County should be aware that Sarah Lawrence permits its students to attend as commuters, even during freshman year.

There are no sororities or fraternities at Sarah Lawrence. However, students may ask to live as upperclassmen in the school's "sustainable living" house, which features composting. The school's 190,000 volume library has racks of bikes which students may check out with their books. Similarly, the campus book store offers rentals of textbooks in place of sales. Wireless Internet access covers the entire campus.

Sarah Lawrence is not a member of the NCAA; its athletics teams compete with other schools in a small-school grouping called the Hudson Valley Athletic Conference, which includes colleges like Concordia and Marist. Sarah Lawrence has men's and women's teams in swimming, softball, tennis, basketball, equestrian, and crew, plus some intramural sports like squash.

The Sarah Lawrence campus, though small and architecturally eclectic, is an attractive mix of handsome private homes, which have been converted to classrooms and dorms, and college buildings in styles ranging from Tudor to elegant modern.

Most important in terms of the daily life of the college are the Charles R. De Carlo Performing Arts Center and the Siegel Center, a late-night student hangout, which as it once served alcohol, is called The Pub. The Pub is open late and students congregate there to watch TV and trade ideas. The Arts Center has a range of theater and rehearsal spaces, and it offers a constant roster of events extending from modern dance performances and ballet to presentations of classic plays. Every week at Sarah Lawrence, Concert Tuesdays features at least one music event that night, whether classical, jazz, or modern. Indie bands sometimes turn up and perform in another campus space called the Blue Room. This was one of the spots where cabaret singer Regina Spektor first made her name.

At least half of the school's undergraduate organizations fall into three categories: groups concerned with white, male, heterosexual oppression (e.g., the Alliance for White Anti-Racist Action, the Asian Pacific Islander Coalition for Action & Diversity and Queer People of Color), arts groups (Student Filmmaker's Coalition) and singing groups (Vocal Minority).

Along with these clubs are an odd mix of other clubs devoted to subjects like chess and bicycling. However, there are also some unexpected politically incorrect factions, including a group devoted to carnivorous eating, and the Christian Union. That said, this is Sarah Lawrence; hence, the campus has a Voices For Palestine club, but no College Republicans. A Princeton Review annual survey judged Sarah Lawrence the least religious college in America. Even so, Sarah Lawrence does have both a Hillel Group and a Muslim Student Association, and each has weekly meetings. Catholic students at Sarah Lawrence should seek out a local parish, such as Yonkers' St. Eugene Parish, where a weekly Latin Mass is offered.

One increasingly popular (if recently established) school tradition is the fall and spring formal dance called the Deb Ball. Used to being relaxed in dress and manner, many students are said to enjoy the chance to outdo each other by furnishing themselves with tailcoats and taffeta dresses.

Both the Sarah Lawrence campus and the wealthy enclave surrounding it are well-tended. Flower-gardens and neatly trimmed hedges intersperse with well-kept front lawns with rhododendron bushes. On the main streets of Bronxville there are the sorts of storefronts one might see in the Hamptons: real estate offices, French bistros, pricey dress shops, a furrier. It's pretty, quiet and reasonably safe. In 2009, the school reported eight burglaries, one stolen car, and two arsons on campus.

Sarah Lawrence is the most expensive college in America. Tuition for 2010–11 ran $43,546, and room and board cost $13,370. Students living in a private apartment complex next to campus can get out of the meal plan and for a little less money they are guaranteed air-conditioning. They will not, however, enjoy the pretty moldings and dormer windows of the dorms. About 61 percent of students receive financial aid, and the school says that it aims to provide aid packages competitive with those provided by schools like Middlebury and Haverford. The average school grants for a financial aid student run to just under $30,000 for four years. The average student in 2009 graduated with a relatively modest debt of $17,246.

YELLOW LIGHT

We did not turn up horror stories of classroom bias or college restrictions on free speech. Nevertheless, if you're looking for a place where students and teachers stand at all points of the political spectrum, and all feel free to express their opinions, Sarah Lawrence might not be the place. We couldn't put it any better than Sarah Lawrence's official college magazine, which writes:

"There's an easy way to pick a fight at Sarah Lawrence College: proclaim yourself a Republican. In 2007, over 85 percent of first-year students identified as either liberal or very liberal, while barely 1 percent called themselves conservative.

"By all impressions the ratio among teachers is similarly lopsided, and at the big table in the faculty dining room—where colleagues gather for lunch, conversation, and debate—you'd have to listen long and hard to hear a conservative opinion. Sarah Lawrence is overwhelmingly pro-choice and pro-gay marriage, antiwar and anti-enhanced interrogation techniques. It may be true that, as former dean of the College Barbara Kaplan wrote . . . Sarah Lawrence emphasizes 'individuals finding and defining roles and values that are appropriate to themselves—and often bucking convention,' but this self-definition takes place within a liberal framework that is itself seldom bucked."

Swarthmore College

Swarthmore, Pennsylvania • www.swarthmore.edu

Quaker roots and cash

Founded during the Civil War by Quakers as a coeducational institution, Swarthmore College has been nonsectarian since 1908. Approximately 1,500 students study on 399 acres of picturesque land in a residential suburb thirty minutes from Philadelphia. Despite a huge endowment and high academic reputation, Swarthmore is less than the sum of its parts. The school's curriculum has deteriorated into a Chinese menu of choices, some sound, but many politicized and shallow. Swarthmore has traveled even further down the path of radical chic than most other East Coast liberal arts schools—and that's a long journey, indeed.

Academic Life: A trip to Sam's Club

Swarthmore has its virtues. The students certainly pull their weight. "We have some genius types here, but more than that we have a lot of very hard-working people," says one student. The school is self-conscious about the fact that its classes are rigorous and high grades comparatively more difficult to obtain. "Anywhere else, it would have been an A," reads one popular T-shirt. Graduate schools are said to adjust for the rigor of Swarthmore's grading when evaluating applicants. One student describes the general atmosphere as "the revenge of the nerds." Another says that the best thing about Swarthmore is the quality of the intellectual environment: "You're surrounded by . . . brilliant people."

However bright and industrious they are, we doubt that 20-year-olds are qualified to design their own curricula. But that's what Swarthmore expects of them; its distribution requirements exert only marginal influence on students' choices. As one says: "The requirements are designed not to encourage some sort of grounding in the basics, but a diversity of perspectives. . . . This is good, but not enough." One professor says that "there is so much choice among introductory courses and departments that . . . one can't count on common background in respect to anything. We don't teach enough survey Western civilization" courses.

Of the modern languages and English departments, one professor says, "It's a classic case of third-rate minds studying second-rate minds." The English department, says one student, seems to cater to the "political interests" of the student body. Swarthmore English majors must take at least nine "units of credit" in the department, including three in literature written before 1830—not necessarily including any Shakespeare, or any specific time periods within that range—and three in literature written after 1830, along with a senior colloquium. Courses in multicultural, feminist, or queer theory are not required, although the department abounds in them, and many of the eligible courses are taught through such ideological filters.

One student calls the history department "infamously partisan" and another conservative student agrees that the department shows a "strong leaning" to leftist viewpoints. A history major must complete nine units in the department, including at least one course addressing the period prior to 1750 and at least one covering Africa, Asia, Latin America, and the Near East, and a senior research seminar. There is no requirement that the student study the history of the United States or of the Western world.

Swatties majoring in political science must take at least eight units in the department and complete a senior comprehensive exercise. Courses must include at least each one in either ancient or modern political theory, American politics (not necessarily addressing Constitutional theory or American political philosophy), and comparative and international politics.

The sociology and anthropology major may not be quite as politically charged as the English major, but it is widely acknowledged to be one of the easiest. Students do not regard mathematics as particularly well taught.

Like most schools, Swarthmore has departments devoted to various races and a single sex, but these are not particularly extensive; the majority of their faculty and courses are drawn from other departments. One student warns that "religious students may feel a bit unwelcome in the philosophy department, which is typically very secular. Indeed, the religion department too has a few bizarre views on Christianity, but is generally open to debate/discussion."

There are some very good departments at Swarthmore. Engineering, economics, political science, biology, and physics all receive high marks from faculty and students, and there are pockets of strength in psychology and philosophy. Some highly recommended professors include the stellar conservative scholar James R. Kurth (emeritus) Benjamin Berger, and Kenneth Sharpe in political science; Barry Schwartz in psychology; Richard Eldridge, Hugh Lacey (emeritus), Hans Oberdiek, and Richard Schuldenfrei (emeritus) in philosophy; John Boccio in physics; Rosaria Munson and William Turpin in classics; Larry Westphal in economics; Amy Cheng Vollmer in biology; and painter Randall Exon in studio art.

VITAL STATISTICS

Religious affiliation: *none*
Total enrollment: *1,524*
Total undergraduates: *1,524*
SAT/ACT midranges: CR: *670–760*, M: *670–770*; ACT: *30–33*
Applicants: *5,575*
Applicants accepted: *17%*
Applicants accepted who enrolled: *41%*
Tuition and fees: *$39,260*
Room and board: *$11,900*
Freshman retention rate: *99%*
Graduation rate: *86% (4 yrs.), 93% (6 yrs.)*
Courses with fewer than 20 students: *78%*
Student-faculty ratio: *8:1*
Courses taught by graduate students: *none*
Most popular majors: *economics, biology, political science*
Students living on campus: *95%*
Guaranteed housing for 4 years? *yes*
Students in fraternities: *12%* in sororities: *none*

SUGGESTED CORE

1. Classics 011, First Year Seminar: Persuasion and Power in Ancient Greece
2. Philosophy 102, Ancient Philosophy
3. Religion 003/004, The Bible: In the Beginning. . . / New Testament and Early Christianity
4. Religion 014B, Christian Life and Thought in the Middle Ages
5. Political Science 12 or 101, Modern Political Theory
6. English Literature 20 or 101, Shakespeare
7. History 005A, The United States to 1877
8. History 003A, Modern Europe, 1789 to 1918: The Age of Revolution and Counterrevolution

Thanks to Swarthmore's stellar 8 to 1 student-faculty ratio, the easy accessibility of teachers is "one of the best things about the school," says one student. When they enter, students are assigned faculty advisors, who must sign off on their course selections every semester. Upon choosing majors, students get faculty advisors within their departments. In general, students report, the best advice on what courses to take (and to avoid) comes from other students, not their faculty advisors.

Swarthmore also provides a selective honors program, whose seminars have no more than ten students per section. At the end of their senior year, honors students are tested by outside examiners and often complete a written thesis. One professor cautions, however, that honors "has been reduced in scope and significance over the years, mostly because many of our best students found it too restrictive. . . . [I]n its current form, it is not very special in most departments. In a few, however, it is still extraordinary."

At Swarthmore the political atmosphere in class can be "oppressive and hostile" for those who don't conform, says one student. Another says that he purposely avoids English courses because of the "tacit assumption that everyone is a liberal. . . . Professors don't really encourage debate about that." A third student says, "There's definitely some tension from some of the more radical elements on campus, who feel that it's a place for liberals." But, he says, "most Swatties are open to new, different ideas."

A professor confirms the overwhelming impression that the Swarthmore faculty and administration is "self-consciously . . . self-confidently, and self-assertively left-liberal." The general feeling, says this professor, is that "non-leftists have something wrong with them." According to another teacher, "Being professional means being biased." However, in class "one can occasionally evoke a minority of articulate conservative voices." Students report that they usually feel as if they must censor themselves in the classroom; there is pressure "not to offend," and conservative students "are not terribly keen on admitting it." One student admits that "the real issue is simply one of numbers: There are far more liberal students and professors than conservative ones."

The left is given pride of place at Swarthmore. On the college's website, one student is praised for taking a yearlong college sabbatical to work on a campaign to defeat the proposed constitutional amendment defining marriage as between one man and one woman. This student says, "I felt this was the most important issue facing our country."

Swarthmore's agenda goes well beyond education—and extends into leftist activism. The college has employed its status as a shareholder to pressure any company in which it holds even a $2,000 investment—squeezing such companies as Lockheed Martin, Dover, and Masco corporations to add the category of sexual orientation to their nondiscrimination policies, for instance.

About 40 percent of Swarthmore students study abroad, often in their junior years. Study in virtually any corner of the world is possible through a wide range of programs. The less adventurous can spend time at various high-ranking colleges throughout the United States through exchange programs. Swarthmore also belongs to the Tri-College Consortium with Haverford and Bryn Mawr Colleges. Students may take courses at these schools, participate in their social activities, and use their libraries. A free shuttle bus provides transportation.

Foreign language offerings are broad for a small school, including Ancient Greek, Latin, Arabic, Chinese, French, German, Japanese, Russian, and Spanish.

Student Life: Organization kids

Swatties are ambitious achievers who have been "checking the boxes since they were kids," one professor says—young men and women who are "academic" in that they can study and discuss others' ideas smoothly and sometimes brilliantly, but not "intellectual," in that they do not tend to develop their own ideas. However, this professor continues, Swarthmore students "are even better than they were ten, twenty years ago. There really are an amazing number of insightful, proficient, innovative students. I learn from my undergraduates."

The serenity and simplicity of the 399-acre Swarthmore College campus is perhaps the chief legacy of the school's Quaker roots. The leafy, beflowered grounds, graced with the nationally-recognized Scott Arboretum, are dominated by the college's first building, Parrish Hall, which looks down on the wide, long lawn sloping down to the small Swarthmore train station and the "ville" of Swarthmore. On fine days, the lawn's white Adirondack chairs are filled with reading or resting students. Others play Frisbee or football. Nearby is a large rose garden. Carefully landscaped lawns, gardens, and stone walls punctuate the rest of the campus.

The town of Swarthmore is tiny (population under 7,000), safe, and wealthy. The business district, such as it is, includes a pizzeria, a couple of restaurants, a decent used bookstore, a pharmacy, and a few specialty shops. It is also dry—like Swarthmore's teetotaling founders. For students, the town of Swarthmore provides only a few basics. But with the train stopping just a couple of hundred yards from the dorms, Philadelphia's Center City and points in between are just a few minutes away. Other bars, restaurants, and stores can be found in the neighboring towns of Springfield and Media. The neighborhoods surrounding the campus are lined with large, unpretentious homes and make for rewarding walks. But in their free time, most students tend to stay on campus. The college generously funds student parties—although it insists that college money not be spent on alcohol.

Students are only required to live on campus for their first two semesters, but in fact 95 percent stay in college housing throughout their years at Swarthmore. Dorms range in size from 8 to 200 occupants. Juniors and seniors generally have singles. All students subscribe to the college meal plan. In 2000, the college changed its policy to allow coed rooming for upperclassmen. Swarthmore's bulletin is at pains to note that although 15 percent of its "residence hall areas" are restricted for single-sex living, single-sex housing is "not guaranteed." Visitation restrictions are voted on by students and can include twenty-four-hour visitation.

There are two fraternities which rent lodges on campus and provide a social outlet for the relatively few Swattie men (about 12 percent) who join. However, the frats do not offer residential or dining facilities and are not a major force in campus life. There are no sororities.

The political climate at Swarthmore is conventionally leftist. For instance, the school newspaper refers to the college's Republicans as being "in the closet." When the College Republicans proposed a Veterans' Day memorial service, leftists protested. "People here are soldier-hating, fascist liberals," says one embittered student. Swarthmore's alternative, conservative student newspaper, *Common Sense,* suspended publication some years ago for lack of editorial staff.

Student groups abound, ranging from Queer Peer Counselors, Feminist Majority, War News Radio, Swat STAND (addressing violence in Sudan) and Voicies for Choice, to a knitting club known as the Knit-Wits, a number of *a cappella* groups, a folk dancing club, Apple Pie (a philosophy discussion club,) a drama club and several comedy troupes. A College Republicans chapter had been meeting on campus but has been inactive in the past

ACADEMIC REQUIREMENTS

No specific courses are prescribed for Swarthmore students. However, students must take three courses in each of Swarthmore's three divisions:

- Humanities: Far too many classes qualify, from "Classical Mythology," "Ancient Philosophy," "Chaucer and Shakespeare," and "Anime: Gender and Culture," to "Queer Media."
- Natural sciences and engineering: Options include "Elementary Single-Variable Calculus," "Organic Chemistry," "Microbiology," "Chemistry in Context: Applying Chemistry to Society," "Introduction to Computer Science" and "Environmental Courses for Non-majors." One lab is required.
- Social sciences: Choices range widely from "Modern Political Theory," "The United States to 1877" "Modern Europe, 1789 to 1918," "Politics of Punishment," and "Comparative Perspectives on the Body," to "Race, Ethnicity and Gender in Economics."

Each of these requirements must be fulfilled by courses from at least two different departments within each division. Three of the above classes must be "writing-intensive." Students also must complete:

- Twenty credits outside their major area.
- A two-semester program in physical education. Credit is also given for participation in intercollegiate athletics or dance courses. All students must pass a survival swimming test or take up to one quarter of swimming instruction.
- Coursework, high school work, or test scores to show intermediate fluency in a foreign language.

year. Swarthmore Students Supporting Life is said to be fervent during those semesters when it has any members. (The Protestant campus chaplain was, however, unable to even recall the name of the group in a recent interview.) Students also produce a number of publications, including *Ourstory*, which, according to its editors, is "Swarthmore's biannual, all-campus diversity literary and art publication."

A number of religious groups meet on campus, including both a more secular (Ruach) and a more conservative religious (Chabad) Jewish group meeting under the umbrella of Hillel, and two Protestant groups, a "progressive" one and a chapter of InterVarsity Christian Fellowship which hosts regular Bible studies, prayer meetings, and other activities. Catholic Mass is offered on campus on Sundays and Wednesdays under the auspices of the Newman Club, which does not seem to be particularly active. Swarthmore shares a Catholic chaplain with Haverford and Bryn Mawr. Some students have been interested in "making Quaker values less implicit and more explicit" at Swat; a fledgling Young Friends group began meeting this year. Several people reported that there has been an upsurge of interest in religion and that the administration has become "more open to spirituality on campus."

The Lang Center for Civic and Social Responsibility reflects the school's Quaker roots in the many opportunities it offers students to work to better the world, both locally, (through tutoring and mentoring low-income school children in nearby Chester or helping adults with tax preparation there) and internationally, by raising money to help students in Ecuador attend high school and traveling there during the summer months to tutor young Ecuadorians.

The Swarthmore Garnet Tide teams, whose mascot is Phineas the Phoenix, compete in twenty intercollegiate sports in NCAA

YELLOW LIGHT

A left-liberal worldview is taken as a given at Swarthmore. Rebecca Chopp, a scholar of "progressive religious movements" was named the first female president of Swarthmore in 2009. In her commencement address to the Class of 2010, Ms. Chopp described worldwide disasters that occurred during the graduates' college years, but reassured her listeners that "the news has not been entirely bleak during your tenure with us—far from it. Two years ago we witnessed—and many actively participated in—the election of our country's first African-American president, who has since appointed the first Latina justice of the Supreme Court. And this past year brought the passage of a health insurance reform bill that was a hundred years in the making."

All forms of sexual activity are broadly accepted as worthy of being celebrated. The College sponsors an annual symposium on "a current topic for the lesbian, gay, bisexual, transgender, and queer community." Students do say that those with a more traditional religious approach to non-marital sexuality are accepted and not pressured. They must, however, have strong stomachs.

Conservative students seem to agree with other Swatties that "[t]his is a . . . nurturing environment where people care intensely about each other." Students occasionally express concerns about being penalized academically for their conservative views, but seem to agree that in most cases they are given a fair hearing. One student says that "The campus is very tolerant, but it is expected that people are willing to get along with those who disagree."

Division III. Intramural and club sports are said to be fairly popular, especially Ultimate Frisbee. One professor speculates that the demise of football some years back was driven by the school's affirmative-action policies, which ate up so many admissions slots. Other Swatties suggest that losing the team was a way of ridding the school of an undesirable symbol of traditional masculinity. Many Swarthmore types "definitely do not like the traditional jock," says one student.

Crime at Swarthmore and in the adjacent neighborhoods is not quite as low as one might guess. The school reported one forcible rape and three other forcible sexual incidents, fourteen burglaries, four car thefts, and one robbery in 2009. Still, in general, students feel quite comfortable walking the campus and adjoining neighborhoods at night.

Swarthmore isn't cheap, but aid is generous. In 2010–11, tuition was set at $39,260 and room and board $11,900. About 50 percent of undergraduates receive need-based scholarships, and starting in 2008–2009, grants replaced all student loans which were previously offered in aid packages. This means that all students on aid should now be able to leave school without a burden of debt.

United States Military Academy

West Point, New York • www.usma.edu

Duty, honor, country

There are few institutions, educational or otherwise, that can claim a heritage as long and as proud as that of the United States Military Academy at West Point. Over the last two centuries, those who have passed through the "Long Gray Line" have gone on to become presidents, ambassadors, generals, engineers, scientists, and intellectuals. In 1802, Congress enacted the legislation founding the United States Military Academy. Under the command of Colonel Sylvanus Thayer (1817–33) it was transformed into a rigorous center for civil and military engineering based on France's *École Polytechnique*. Much of the expansion of the young Republic was facilitated by West Point graduates, who designed the necessary roads, bridges, canals, ports, and railroads. During the Civil War, both sides were commanded by generals who had attended the academy. In every significant conflict the United States has been engaged in, from the Mexican War to the Persian Gulf wars, products of West Point have led the way.

In 2009 Brigadier General William E. Rapp was selected as the seventy-second commandant of cadets, and in 2010 Brigadier General Tim Trainor was made dean of West Point's Academic Board.

West Point's core curriculum is a very solid introduction to the liberal arts and the APL major permits an in-depth study of the ideas fundamental to the Western tradition. For the student who desires to combine a liberal arts education with military service, West Point is an excellent choice.

Academic Life: *Mens sana in corpore sano*

The formation of West Point cadets aims at creating *mens sana in corpore sano* (a sound mind in a sound body), an army officer capable of leadership, and a morally upright person who may be trusted in command. All of this takes place within a strict system of military discipline. Each cadet takes an oath "to defend the Constitution of the United States from all enemies, foreign and domestic"—that is, to be prepared to fight in this country's wars, near and far. (There can be no "conscientious objection" after the oath is administered.) The goal is "to educate, train, and inspire the Corps of Cadets so that each graduate is a commissioned leader of character committed to the values of duty, honor, country." These

VITAL STATISTICS

Religious affiliation: *none*
Total enrollment: *4,621*
Total undergraduates: *4,621*
SAT/ACT midranges: CR:
    550–650, M: *580–670;*
    ACT: *26–30*
Applicants: *11,107*
Applicants accepted: *14%*
Applicants accepted who
    enrolled: *77%*
Tuition and fees: *free*
Room and board: *free*
Freshman retention rate:
    91%
Graduation rate: *80% (4 yrs.),*
    82% (6 yrs.)
Courses with fewer than 20
    students: *96%*
Student-faculty ratio: *7:1*
Courses taught by graduate
    students: *none*
Most popular majors: *engi-*
    neering, social sciences,
    foreign languages
Students living on campus:
    100%
Guaranteed housing for 4
    years? *yes*
Students in fraternities or
    sororities: *none*

values are meant to animate "a career as an officer in the United States Army; and a lifetime of selfless service to the nation."

Admission is highly competitive, and candidates must receive a nomination from a member of Congress or from the Department of the Army. Each year the academy admits approximately 1,200 young men and (thanks to activist judges) women. Upon graduation, cadets receive a Bachelor of Science degree and a commission as a second lieutenant in the U.S. Army; they must also commit to at least five years of active duty and three years in a Reserve Component. The academy graduates more than 900 new officers annually.

Perhaps because of its intensity, the "West Point Experience" has proved adept at creating bonds of friendship and solidarity. After leaving both the Point and after serving in the Army, the fidelity of alumni both to the institution and to each other is strong. A West Point education can provide unique opportunities for leadership in the civil and commercial spheres, in addition to the military.

Academics at the Point are demanding. To begin with, there is a genuine core curriculum of twenty-six to thirty courses depending on the major. The core curriculum "provides a foundation in mathematics, basic sciences, engineering sciences, information technology, humanities, behavioral sciences, and social sciences," according to the school. Combined as it is with physical education and military science, this core constitutes the military academy's "professional major." Although based upon the needs of the Army, it is further intended to establish the foundation for a field of study or an optional major, of which West Point offers forty. The academy further requires the cadet to complete ten relevant electives, adding up to forty academic courses in total. Academic advising during the first two years (called "Fourth and Third Class") is done through "company academic counselors." In his third year (or "Second Class") the cadet is assigned a counselor in his major.

The United States Corps of Cadets, to which each cadet belongs, comprises thirty-two cadet companies grouped into battalions, regiments, and finally the corps as a whole. This structure is overseen by the Brigade Tactical Department, led by the brigade tactical officer (BTO), an active duty colonel. Other, lower-ranking officers and non-commissioned officers (NCOs) are assigned as tactical officers (TACs) to each of the cadet formations. They supervise each cadet's development—academic, military, physical, and moral-ethical. TACs function as commanders of each unit alongside the cadet officers and they act as mentors, counselors, leaders, motivators, trainers, evaluators, commanders, role models, teachers, and administrators. Each one is available for counseling purposes to the cadets daily from reveille to taps, and is involved with all cadet activities. In addition, the Center for Personal Development, a counseling and assessment center staffed by army officers trained as professional counselors/psychologists, provides individual and group counseling.

All teaching is done by the professors and the student-faculty ratio is 7 to 1, with classes usually numbering between 14 and 18 students. Some 75 percent of cadets do choose to complete a major in the general fields of engineering, math and science, or humanities and social sciences. There are currently twenty-two optional majors and twenty-five fields of study, covering virtually all the liberal arts (except classics), and all science and engineering disciplines found in equivalent highly selective civilian colleges. Each of these fields of study requires a cadet to pursue nine electives in courses specified by the academic discipline. Cadets who follow this path "follow a more structured elective sequence and complete a senior thesis or design project," the school reports.

> **SUGGESTED CORE**
>
> 1. English 351, World Literature (closest match)
> 2. English 388, Ancient Philosophy
> 3. No suitable course.
> 4. History 361, Medieval Europe (closest match)
> 5. Social Sciences 386, Political Thought and Ideas
> 6. English 394, Shakespeare
> 7. History 153, Advanced History of the United States
> 8. History 364, Modern Western Europe

Although engineering retains pride of place at West Point, the liberal arts are not neglected. The art, philosophy, and literature (APL) major, for example, offers courses from English, foreign languages, history, law, and social sciences. This major is the best choice for the would-be officer who craves a true humanistic education. It features very solid courses, such as the "Cultural Studies" class, which is mercifully not the politicized piffle it often amounts to elsewhere. Rather, the course considers "the thinking processes, investigative techniques, fruitful theories, and current methods of discourse relating to the study of art, philosophy, and literature, a rich nexus that contributes significantly to cultural identities." The course is team-taught, and focuses on "a group of cultural artifacts like the Acropolis, the *Republic*, and the *Iliad* or, perhaps, the work of Delacroix, Nietzsche, and Goethe." This fine course is part of the basic requirement for the APL major, together with an art history course ("Eastern Art," "Masterpieces before Giotto," "Special Topics in Art History," or "Giotto and Beyond") and an elective ("Criticism" or "Logical Reasoning"), as well as an information technology course, either "Theory and Practice of Military IT Systems" or "Advanced Military IT Systems," and a senior seminar.

Six electives, either in philosophy or literature, complete the major in APL: four literature or philosophy electives plus one departmental elective and a language elective. This major's literature track offers excellent courses, such as "British Literature I," "ranging from the Anglo-Saxon period through the eighteenth century"; "American Literature" II, "both traditional and nontraditional writings from the Civil War to the present"; "Shakespeare," "World Literature." In many colleges a course in World Literature is a sort of random survey; at West Point it teaches students "epics and tragedies of ancient Greece and Rome, Russian novels, works of medieval Islamic literature, haiku of Japan, Continental European novels of the nineteenth century, or postmodern fiction of South America." Cadets are asked to examine works selected for their intrinsic quality and significance without reference to any political agenda. If students choose instead the philosophy track, they'll face courses such as "Philosophy of Mind," where readings "come from classical sources, such as Descartes, as well as contemporary literature in philosophy, cognitive science, and artificial intelligence."

History majors take one out of the two above mentioned IT courses, "Colloquium in History," and one "integrative experience" course like "History of the Civil War in America" or "Race, Ethnicity, Nation." Eight electives complete the major, five from the "U.S. History" section ("Early National America," "Cold War America"), one foreign history (such as "Medieval Europe"), and two language courses.

Scholars of government may choose among three majors: international relations, comparative politics and American politics. The American politics major requires one of the two abovementioned IT courses, a course in "Political Analysis," "Comparative Politics," "Political Philosophy and Policy," and a course in either "Advanced American Politics, Policy, and Strategy" or "Public Policymaking Process." Three elective American politics courses, one elective in comparative politics and one in international relations, plus two foreign language courses complete the major.

The other side of academia at West Point is the Military Program, which begins on a cadet's very first day. Most military training takes place during the summer. New "plebes" (as first-year cadets are known) undergo cadet basic training—or "Beast Barracks"—in the summer preceding their first academic year. Cadet field training at nearby Camp Buckner takes place during the second year. The third and fourth summers are spent "serving in active Army units around the world; attending advanced training courses such as airborne, air assault, or northern warfare; or training the first- and second-year cadets as members of the leadership cadre." Military science instruction in the classroom is conducted during the school year. The distinct emphasis on military science means that all cadets graduate with a Bachelor of Science degree, even if they choose a more humanistic major.

The student can chose among the eight languages offered at West Point, which are Arabic, Chinese, French, German, Persian Parsi, Portuguese, Russian, and Spanish.

Student Life: God, country, and athletics

Despite the many official demands on a cadet's time, he does have plenty of options for the leisure time he gets. Golf, skiing, sailing, equestrian activities, and ice skating are all available, as are a cadet radio station, orienteering, rock climbing, and Big Brother-Big Sister. The Directorate of Cadet Activities operates the Eisenhower Hall Theatre, the Cadet Restaurant, Grant Hall dining and social facility, the Cadet Store, and the Cadet Bookstore, and cadets produce such publications as the *Howitzer* (a yearbook), the *West Point Calendar*, *Bugle Notes*, and the *West Point Planner*. Some outsiders may be surprised by the existence of the *Circle in the Spiral*, the literary/art journal of the Corps of Cadets, which features poems, artwork, and stories by cadets. Since the journal's origin in 1991, it has won praise from the Columbia Scholastic Press Association and the American Scholastic Press Association.

There are dances almost every week, as well as annual events like Ring Weekend, Yearling Winter Weekend, and Plebe-Parent Weekend. Festivities like 100th Night Weekend, 500th Night Weekend, Dining-In, and Hops help keep cadets from succumbing to the stress of academic and military life. Additionally, the Directorate of Cadet Activities sponsors 113 clubs, ranging from Amateur Radio, German Language, the Debate Team, the Nuclear Engineering Club, and the Korean-American Relations Seminar to the Inline Hockey Club, the Skuba Diving Club and the Hunting Club. There are no fraternities or sororities.

The academy requires a great deal physically: each semester, every cadet participates in an intercollegiate (NCAA I), club or intramural sport. Intramural sports range from basketball to handball, and flickerball. Likewise, the quite successful club teams include such sports

---

ACADEMIC REQUIREMENTS

Graduation from the Point (which brings with it a commission in the U.S. Army) has rather stringent requirements. All cadets must complete a core curriculum. This includes twenty-six to thirty courses (depending on the major) divided equally between arts and sciences, plus military science and physical education. All options for fulfilling these requirements are academically sound and serious. The courses required are:

- Three courses in English: "English Composition," "Advanced Composition," and "Literature."
- Four classes in history: two in general history such as "History of the U.S." I and II, or "Western Civilization," and two courses in military history, "History of the Military Art" and "Advanced History of the Military Art."
- Two courses in leadership, such as "Military Leadership" or "General Psychology."
- Two classes in computer science/information technology.
- One course in values and ethics, such as "Introduction to Philosophy," which examines among other topics the criteria for a just war.
- Two foreign language classes.
- Three courses in the social sciences, such as "American Politics," or "Economics: Principles and Problems."
- One course in Constitutional and military law.
- Four classes in mathematics, for example "Calculus" I and II or "Probability and Statistics."
- Two courses in chemistry.
- One course in geography.
- Two courses in physics.
- A "three-course engineering sequence in Civil, Computer, Electrical, Environmental, Mechanical, Nuclear or Systems Engineering" for cadets "pursuing most non-engineering specializations"
- Four courses in military science (plus military development/training). Courses offered include "Fundamentals of Army Operations," and "Platoon Operations."
- Seven semesters of physical education, such as "Fundamentals of Aquatics," "Fundamentals of Combatives (Women)," "Combatives II: Boxing (Men)," and "Fundamentals of Fitness."

GREEN LIGHT

As might be expected, life for cadets at West Point is extremely regimented. Of course, given the intensive academic, mental, and physical training undergone, this makes sense. But the academy, anxious to produce good leaders, is not content with mere regimentation. "Moral-ethical development" is important as well: the authorities aim to foster it through "formal instruction in the important values of the military profession, voluntary religious programs, interaction with staff and faculty role models, and a vigorous guest speaker program." But the most important moral element involved is the Cadet Honor Code, summed up in the line "A cadet will not lie, cheat, steal, or tolerate those who do." The Honor Code is supposed to govern cadet life—and to a great degree, it does.

However, one consideration for women (and their parents) thinking about applying to the Point is, to be blunt, sexual. Every few years or so there is a sex scandal at one of the service academies. Although no one can fault the patriotism and ability of the academy's female grads, the fact remains that placing young men and women at their sexual peak in intimate proximity and under heavy pressure is a recipe for erotic activity; the fact that such things are reduced to mere pastimes in many high schools does not help. Inevitably, a few commanding officers' careers are ended for such things happening on their watch.

as Judo, Boxing, and Equestrian. West Point is of course renowned for "Army Football"; the entire corps of cadets is required to attend—together with the school's mascot the "Mule"—and stand throughout each home game of the "Black Knights." Other intercollegiate sports include men's swimming and rifle and women's soccer and volleyball and many more.

The physical plant is quite lovely, and often stunning. When Charles Dickens visited the campus in 1841, he exclaimed "It could not stand on more appropriate ground, and any ground more beautiful could hardly be." Roughly fifty miles north of New York City and situated on the western bank of the Hudson River, the academy's grounds were declared a National Historic Landmark in 1960. The campus is the first American example of the distinctive nineteenth-century "military Gothic" style, found at military schools and colleges around the country. The campus is dominated by the Cadet Chapel, designed by that master of modern American Gothic, Bertram Grosvenor Goodhue. While the story that the tower of the witch's castle in the 1939 film *The Wizard of Oz* is modeled on West Point architecture is merely an urban legend, L. Frank Baum, author of the book on which the film is based, did attend the nearby Peekskill Military Academy, and is believed to have based the flying monkeys' uniform on that of the West Point cadets. In 2009 USMA opened its new library at Jefferson Hall with "state-of-the-art technology, classic-modern blend of architecture, and an amazing sky view of the campus." The Old Cadet Library and Bartlett Hall, built in 1913 and home to the chemistry and physics departments, are currently undergoing complete renovations.

West Point itself is part of Orange County in the state of New York and counts a population of nearly 8,000 (student population of USMA is 4,621). All cadets are housed in the campus' eight barracks. USMA Admissions informs that there are generally two or three cadets in a room. Women do room together, however, "with their assigned companies," on the same floor.

From the dawn of warfare, the need for religion to undergird the warrior's resolve has been acknowledged—at least until our own day. In 1972, federal courts ended mandatory chapel attendance at the federal service academies. Nevertheless, until and unless the civilian leadership banishes it entirely, religious life flourishes—on a purely voluntary basis—at West Point.

There are five chapels at West Point, each of which receives a great deal of use. Most notable architecturally, the Gothic Cadet Chapel was dedicated in 1910. The first pew features silver plates engraved with the signatures of such previous superintendents as Generals MacArthur, Taylor, and Westmoreland. This chapel features Protestant services every Sunday and hosts the Protestant Chapel Choir and the Protestant Chapel Sunday School. Its choir is famous and performs at a number of the academy's traditional ceremonies. The neoclassical Old Cadet Chapel was built in 1836. Originally located near the cadet barracks, it was removed stone by stone to its present location in 1910. Its interior contains many plaques, including one to Maj. Gen. Benedict Arnold, who commanded the fort at West Point before attempting to turn it over to the British. Located near the entrance of the cemetery, the Old Cadet Chapel hosts many funerals and memorials and has long been the home for Lutheran services. A third Protestant facility is the Georgian-style Community Post Chapel. Built in 1943, it is occupied now by a Gospel congregation.

Catholics attend the Chapel of the Most Holy Trinity, built in the Norman Gothic style in 1899, enlarged in 1959, and the oldest cadet chapel in continuous use. Amongst other features, it boasts twenty-two stained-glass windows showing soldier-saints and memorializing Catholic alumni killed in the service of their country. Masses are held on Saturday and Sunday, with music by the Cadet Catholic Choir and the Catholic Folk Group.

Opened in 1984, the Jewish Chapel contains an extensive Judaica collection, a library, and special exhibits. Sabbath services are held every Friday evening during the academic year, augmented by the Jewish Chapel Choir. The Eastern Orthodox community worships in St. Martin's chapel downstairs in the Cadet Chapel.

Cadets also develop their artistic capacities. The Eisenhower Hall Theatre is the East Coast's second-largest cultural arts theater, and it presents a host of world-class performances annually. Opera, dance, symphony orchestras, country, and rock concerts have all been performed here, and the place has been host to a wide variety of Broadway plays and important musicians, from *Les Misérables* and the Radio City Rockettes to Luciano Pavoratti, Johnny Cash, and the Twyla Tharp Dance Company.

The West Point Museum is the oldest and most diverse public collection of "militaria" in the Western hemisphere. Starting with captured British materials brought here after the British defeat at Saratoga in 1777, the museum collections have come to include trophies from each of this nation's wars, including such rarities as Mussolini's hat. The school does not report its crime statistics; however, apart from occasional sex scandals, there seems to be little criminal activity to speak of.

There is no tuition at West Point. Since all cadets are members of the Army, their education is free, and in addition they receive an annual salary of more than $6,500.

Mid-Atlantic

United States Naval Academy

Annapolis, Maryland • www.usna.edu

Naval raising

Founded in 1845 in response to a naval mutiny, as the Naval School at Annapolis, what is now the U.S. Naval Academy has expanded from its original ten acres and fifty midshipmen to 338 acres, and it now educates more than 4,000 men and women each year.

Since the Naval Academy educates its midshipmen to serve in the Navy and become naval officers, the liberal arts are not the primary focus. But this does not preclude providing midshipmen a good exposure to the liberal arts, not least because the academy puts a great emphasis on the moral and leadership education and formation of its future officers. (Two of the three most popular majors are political science and history.) But students at the academy will also face a solid core of science and engineering.

Academic Life: Seminars and seamen

Since 1933, the Naval Academy has awarded Bachelor of Science degree to graduates, some of whom will operate nuclear submarines and guided missile systems. The academy has also become a major source of new officers for the Marine Corps. As at West Point, jealously guarded Navy traditions continue to provide a sense of continuity, year after year.

Admission is highly competitive. To even be eligible, a student must be a single United States citizen; with no dependents; of good moral character; no younger than seventeen and no older than twenty-three; and not pregnant. In addition to scholastic, physical, and leadership requirements, applicants need a nomination from an official source, such as their congressman or senator. Male candidates should be able to run one and a half miles in 10 minutes and thirty secons, and complete forty push-ups in two minutes. Female candidates must complete the run in 12:40 and do eighteen push-ups.

Annapolis offers each of its midshipmen a core curriculum featuring engineering, science, mathematics, humanities, and social science courses in order to "provide a broad-based education that will qualify the midshipmen for practically any career field in the Navy or Marine Corps," according to the school. Quantitative courses include "Calculus" I and II, "Chemistry" I and II; humanities classes include "U.S. Government and Constitutional Development," "Preparing to Lead," "Rhetoric and Introduction to Literature" I and II, "Fundamentals of Naval Science," "American Naval Heritage," and "Introduction to Navigation."

Cadets also complete one of twenty-two majors. Of these, three—English, history, and political science—might be considered liberal arts. (Postgraduate degrees may also be started at Annapolis.) But even liberal arts majors receive a Bachelor of Science degree, owing to the technical content of the core curriculum. "Middies" pursuing history, English, political science, economics, mathematics, oceanography, and systems engineering majors are eligible for the honors program. Chosen for their "excellent academic and leadership performance," honors students complete a thesis or research project, which they will defend orally in front of a panel of faculty members. If successful, they graduate with honors.

An even more exclusive option is the Trident Scholar Program, through which midshipmen in the top 10 percent of their class in their junior year are invited to submit proposed research projects and programs of study for evaluation. The number of scholars selected has ranged from a low of three to a high of sixteen, with nine scholars in the class of 2011. Each scholar is given one or more faculty advisors who are well-acquainted with his field of study and serve as research mentors. Trident scholars, according to the academy, "may travel to nearby facilities such as the Naval Research Laboratory or the National Institute of Standards and Technology to use equipment not available at the Naval Academy."

Each company of new midshipmen is assigned two faculty advisors upon admission. After the summer advising is available on a need-basis. After the new "plebes" have selected majors, they get permanent advisors in those disciplines.

The student-faculty ratio at the Naval Academy is approximately eight to one. The faculty consists of officers and civilians in nearly equal numbers. "Officers rotate to the academy for two-to-three-year assignments, bringing fresh ideas and experiences from operational units and staffs of the Navy and Marine Corps" while civilian faculty—nearly all of whom have doctoral degrees—give "continuity to the educational program," the school reports. At the academy, the faculty's first priority is always teaching, rather than research. Students especially recommend two professors from the history department, Frederick Harrod and Marcus Jones. "They are just the best of the best," one senior reports. However, most faculty are said to be excellent.

English majors are required to take ten courses, including "Early Western Literature"; "Anglo-American Literature"; "Shakespeare"; two 300-level literary period courses, for

VITAL STATISTICS

Religious affiliation: *none*
Total enrollment: *4,552*
Total undergraduates: *4,552*
SAT/ACT midranges: CR: *570–700*, M: *600–700*; ACT: *25–30*
Applicants: *15,342*
Applicants accepted: *10%*
Applicants accepted who enrolled: *86%*
Tuition and fees: *free*
Room and board: *free*
Freshman retention rate: *98%*
Graduation rate: *89% (4 yrs.), 89% (6 yrs.)*
Courses with fewer than 20 students: *59%*
Student-faculty ratio: *9:1*
Courses taught by graduate students: *none*
Most popular majors: *political science, economics, mechanical engineering*
Students living on campus: *100%*
Guaranteed housing for 4 years? *yes*
Students in fraternities or sororities: *none*

SUGGESTED CORE

1. English 217, Early Western Literature
2. Philosophy 430, Political Philosophy (closest match)
3. English 222, The Bible and Literature
4. History 486, History of Christianity
5. Political Science 340, Modern Political Thought and Ideology
6. English 333, Shakespeare
7. History 346, Revolutionary America and the Early Republic
8. History 216, The West in the Modern World

example "Chaucer and His Age" or "The Renaissance Mind"; one 400-level seminar, for example "Literary Theory and Criticism" or "Studies in Literary Figures"; and four additional courses from department offerings. These requirements are better than those at most Ivy League colleges.

In addition to the three history courses in the core curriculum, each history major also takes "Perspectives on History" and a "Seminar in Advanced Historical Studies" plus eight electives from four of five distribution areas: American history, European history, regional history, naval and military history, and thematic history. Recent course offerings included "Imperial Rome," "The Age of Chivalry and Faith," "Germany and the Nazi Experience," "Art and Ideas in Modern Europe," "Civil War and Reconstruction," and "America in World Affairs." Again, this is an excellent academic program.

Political science majors must complete ten courses plus one capstone, with a final thesis supervised by a faculty member. Three courses are required: "American Government," "International Relations/Comparative Politics" and "Political Science Methods." Any graduate would emerge with an understanding of the political system he has volunteered to defend.

The average class size is eighteen, allowing professors to offer plenty of personal attention. The academy proudly points out that "all courses at the Naval Academy are taught and graded by faculty members, not by graduate assistants."

Given its mission to train officers, the academy also provides professional and leadership training. As plebes (freshmen), students are introduced to the life and customs of the naval service, where they learn to follow orders and obey commands. As midshipmen (sophomores, juniors, and seniors), they gradually take on positions of responsibility themselves. Students also acquire practical experience from assignments with Navy and Marine Corps units. In the classroom, such courses as "Leadership: Theory and Application," "Ethics and Moral Reasoning for the Naval Leader," and "Fundamentals of Seamanship" round out their education in this sphere.

The strongest memory that graduates of the Naval Academy take with them from Annapolis is Plebe Summer. This is the rigorous, sometimes traumatic, seven week period in which civilians are molded into plebes. "It's brutal, but it's also a bonding experience. Everyone goes through it and it just builds an understanding between your fellow plebes. It was the best summer of my life, but I'm glad I only had to do it once," reports a sophomore. On Induction Day, shortly after arrival, the new plebes are put into uniform and taught to salute; indeed, they will salute virtually everyone they encounter—officers and upperclassmen alike. The days start at dawn with an hour of exercise and finish long after sunset. "Plebing" builds a sense of identity with the academy and is the start of the sort of lifelong friendships that only hardship can bring. At Annapolis, Plebe Summer also means an introduction to seamanship, navigation, and combat arms. By the time the school year starts, the plebe is completely familiar with the academy's and the Navy's standards—particularly regarding such intangibles as honor.

As at West Point, the school maintains a strict honor system (here called the "Honor Concept"). Annapolis's Concept states, in part:

> Midshipmen are persons of integrity: They stand for that which is right. They tell the truth and ensure that the full truth is known. They do not lie. They embrace fairness in all actions. They ensure that work submitted as their own is their own, and that assistance received from any source is authorized and properly documented. They do not cheat. They respect the property of others and ensure that others are able to benefit from the use of their own property. They do not steal.

Offenses are dealt with by brigade honor committees made up of elected upper-class midshipmen.

All midshipmen majoring in English, history, and political science (as well as economics) are required to take four semesters of a foreign language. A major in Arabic and Chinese is offered as well as minors in Arabic, Chinese, French, German, Japanese, Spanish, and Russian.

Student Life: Such intangibles as honor

The city of Annapolis, the capital of the state of Maryland, is home to the Navy Academy. With a population of a little under 40,000, Annapolis is 26 miles south of Baltimore and about 29 miles east of Washington, D.C. Annapolis provides ample opportunity for leisure—for which the cadets have specific times allotted during the week. The academy permits plebes "town liberty" on Saturday afternoons and evenings and liberty within the Naval Academy complex on Saturday mornings and Sunday afternoons. Free time increases as students advance in the academy.

Two years prior, the academy completed the Wesley A. Brown Field House, a 140,000-square-foot multi-function athletic facility "that serves as the new indoor football practice facility and the home for the men's and women's track & field programs."

The academy is home to a number of student organizations, including several national scholastic honor societies. Community service societies include the Campus Girl Scouts, Joy Bright Hancock Group, National Eagle Scout Association, and the Midshipmen Action Group. Musical and theatrical groups include a Gospel Choir club, a Pipes and Drums club, a Trident Brass group, and the famous Masqueraders, who put on one production annually in the academy's Mahan Hall. Amongst the "Heritage" organizations are the French Club, the German Club, the Korean-American Midshipman Association, and the Midshipmen Black Studies Club. The academy's radio station and four publications, the *Labyrinth*, *Lucky Bag*, the *Log*, and the *Trident* offer opportunities for expression.

The old state military colleges, VMI and The Citadel, have already been forced through court action to stop the saying of grace before meals—a subversive practice which suggests allegiance to a higher power than the State. Yet at Annapolis, alone of all three academies, grace is still said before lunch. Thoughtfully, the ACLU has offered to assist any midshipman who might want to sue the academy to stop this. So far, no one has availed himself of this offer, and there's a good reason for that: Ultimately, military folk must be willing to die for their country, and without a connection to an even higher duty, this is simply too much to ask.

At Annapolis, the copper-green dome of the chapel symbolizes this awareness. It serves as the focal point of the Command Religious Program, which tries to "foster spiritual growth and promote the moral development of the midshipmen within the tenets of their particular faith or beliefs." The Chaplains Office conducts worship services and offers counseling. Services are held for members of the Catholic, Christian Science, Jewish, Muslim, Protestant, and Mormon faiths.

ACADEMIC REQUIREMENTS

USNA's rigorous core curriculum includes the following classes:

- "Calculus," I and II.
- "Chemistry," I and II.
- "Rhetoric and Introduction to Literature," I and II.
- "Preparing to Lead—Baseline Course for Leader Development."
- "American Naval Heritage."
- "Fundamentals of Naval Science."
- "US Government & Constitutional Development."
- "Introduction to Navigation."
- "Literature and Rhetoric."
- "U.S. Government & Constitutional Development."
- Two professional courses, one in navigation and the other in ethics and moral reasoning.
- One course each in naval warfare, naval engineering and weapons, naval electricity and electronics.
- A leadership course.
- A control systems lab relevant to warfare systems.
- A law course covering military justice and the law of war.
- A junior officer practicum aligned with service assignment.
- Another engineering course.

Midshipmen also face extensive physical education and training as well as a total of thirteen hours of infantry drill each year. Fourth Class (freshman) midshipmen take swimming, boxing and wrestling; Third Class students take swimming and "Martial Arts" I; Second Class students take swimming, personal conditioning/wellness and "Martial Arts" II; First Class midshipmen choose electives from among such sports and physical education areas as first aid, kayaking, introduction to climbing, and advanced climbing.

Eleven religious student organizations contribute to the religious element of a cadet's life. Among them are the Baptist Student Union, the Campus Crusade for Christ, Protestant, Catholic, Jewish, and Muslim Midshipman clubs, and the Officer Christian Fellowship.

The academy's athletic program is intensive, to say the least. Annapolis regards the midshipman's physical growth of comparable importance to his mental and moral development. A physical education curriculum and athletic participation are required of all students, either at the varsity, intramural, or club level. The academy's teams are well supported, both by their mascot Bill the Goat and by the loud crowd, as attested by anyone who has experienced an Army-Navy game. The eighteen men's, ten women's and four varsity teams play in the NCAA Division I. The academy offers twelve club and fifteen intramural sports. Club sports include cycling, triathlon, boxing and softball. Intramural offerings recently included amongst others soccer, wrestling, volleyball, and basketball.

A typical day at USNA is quite regimented, with reveille and watches. All students march to meals and do everything in uniform. Midshipmen live in Bancroft Hall, a

GREEN LIGHT

Even though it is primarily (like West Point) an engineering school, Annapolis offers a better grounding in the core subjects of the Western tradition and the American republic than do most civilian colleges, with no incidents reported to us of undue political content in the classroom. In keeping with the American military's nonpolitical tradition, there are no partisan or activist clubs at the academy.

As attractive as the Annapolis experience sounds, it is imperative to remember that it is first and foremost a naval academy. Its purpose is to train men and women to lead others in combat, whether on sea, on land, or in the air. Anyone with an ethical objection to combat—or moral scruples about which wars of choice the civilians leading the U.S. government might choose someday to launch—should not take the oath "to defend the Constitution of the United States against all enemies, foreign and domestic." Once taken, this oath becomes the cornerstone of the midshipman's, and later the officer's, personal code of honor.

massive dorm. The Brigade of Midshipmen is divided into companies. Each company has its own living area at Bancroft, called a "wardroom." Men and women are assigned to same-sex rooms but live on the same floor as the rest of their assigned company. Every bedroom (shared by two or more midshipmen) is wired for computers, Internet access, and phones. The companies are the focus of life at Annapolis, as each midshipman eats, sleeps, drills, and plays with the members of his own company, and competes against the other companies. This teaches the small-unit cohesion so integral to warfare and is the source of lifelong friendships. This is also where practical leadership begins—since, as he advances year by year, the midshipman will be expected to assume leadership positions at the company, battalion, and brigade level.

Almost everything a midshipman needs is available on the academy grounds: bookstore, uniform and tailor shop, cobbler shop, snack bar, barber/beauty shop, post office, and recreation rooms. There are also restaurants and an ice skating rink. Members of the brigade eat together at King Hall, where they enjoy such delectables as steak, spiced shrimp,

Mexican food, and home-baked pastries. Medical, psychological, and dental care is provided onsite, as well as legal and financial advice. In a word, other than applying himself to his studies and other obligations, the midshipman has little to worry about. The academy does not report its crime statistics to the government, as is required of civilian schools. However, it seems that the most common offenses have to do with sexual fraternization. For instance, there is a rule forbidding dating between plebes and midshipmen.

Although the various programs offered by the academy consume more time than the average college student is required to give, midshipmen do get Christmas and summer vacations (leave) plus shorter periods of time off (liberty).

Use of cars is restricted according to class seniority, although no midshipman may have a motorcycle in town. Drinking is forbidden to plebes at the academy. Needless to say, drug use is forbidden for everyone and results in expulsion from the academy. Random urinalysis is conducted.

Women now account for 20 to 25 percent of entering plebes and receive the same academic and professional training as the males. Thankfully, the academy has not tried to butcher the English language with "midshippersons." While the academy has been coeducational since 1976, many still question whether it is a good place for women to study, partly because of the sex scandals that have arisen in recent years. Others ask if a society that sends its young women out to fight its battles is really worth defending.

When accepted to the Naval Academy, the student joins the U.S. Navy. Not only is the education free of charge, but the midshipman earns a salary. Merit, not money, is required of entrants to the service academies.

Vassar College

Poughkeepsie, New York • www.vassar.edu

Vassar to Yale: Drop dead

Vassar College opened in 1865 to offer women an education equal to that available to men at Yale and Harvard. For more than a hundred years, Vassar reigned as a giant of women's education. When Yale proposed a merger with Vassar in 1967, the all-women's college turned down the offer. Two years later, Vassar caved and began admitting men. Though Vassar is now coed, it still retains the self-styled "progressive spirit" that animated its founding. It claims a mission based on "toleration and respect for diversity," a "commitment to social justice," and "a willingness to challenge the status quo." One liberal student characterizes Vassar as "liberal without doubt." Students and faculty at Vassar who are skeptical of "progressive" dogmas should keep a pretty low profile.

Academic Life: Our advice is . . . get advice

Vassar enjoys a reputation as one of the country's top liberal arts programs, but the college does little to ensure that students actually receive a true liberal arts education. Vassar's curriculum is quite unstructured, giving students virtually free rein to overspecialize or dabble aimlessly. A professor comments, "There's no core, really no distribution requirements, so it is up to the advisor to give good advice, and for the student ultimately to create his own program. But if you don't want to take a literature course, you don't have to."

Finding what is most useful at Vassar could be difficult, but advising at the school is said to be strong. Entering students are assigned pre-major faculty advisors. Once they declare majors, they are assigned to faculty members in their own departments. The dean of freshmen oversees the pre-major advising program and new student orientation. In 2010, the school established an online peer advising network, connecting freshmen to upperclassmen before they declare a major. Students must consult with their advisors before registering.

Requirements kick in when students start work within their majors. Students majoring in history, for instance, must take eleven courses in that discipline, including at least one in each of four areas: European history; American history; and two courses each in pre-1800 history (courses such as "Renaissance Europe," "From Tyranny to Terror: The Old Regime and the French Revolution," or "Colonial America"); and Asian, African, Middle Eastern, or Latin American studies. Finally, history majors complete a senior thesis. No

VITAL STATISTICS

Religious affiliation: *none*
Total enrollment: *2,453*
Total undergraduates: *2,452*
SAT/ACT midranges: CR:
    660–750, M: *640–720;*
    ACT: *29–32*
Applicants: *7,577*
Applicants accepted: *25%*
Applicants accepted who
    enrolled: *35%*
Tuition and fees: *$42,560*
Room and board: *$10,080*
Freshman retention rate:
    96%
Graduation rate: *88% (4 yrs.),*
    92% (6 yrs.)
Courses with fewer than 20
    students: *67%*
Student-faculty ratio: *8:1*
Courses taught by graduate
    students: *none*
Most popular majors:
    social science, visual and
    performing arts, foreign
    languages and literatures
Students living on campus:
    95%
Guaranteed housing for 4
    years? *yes*
Students in fraternities or
    sororities: *none*

study of the American founding or Civil War is required of majors.

According to a professor, political science is "a large department—about fourteen professors." The teaching is solid, and there are "courses on almost all areas of the world." Yet there is a "lack of ancient and medieval political theory courses. Generally (and as with many Vassar departments), the courses do not so much survey the field as focus on important aspects of the topic." Political science majors must take ten courses, including one in each of four major fields of study: American politics, comparative politics, political theory, and international relations. The political theory requirement is an uncommon one and a definite strength. Students need not necessarily study the U.S. Constitution, although most probably do.

The English major was recently bulked up—without really adding much beef. Students who enter Vassar now need twelve English classes to complete the major, at least four of which must be at the 300 level. In their senior year, English majors must complete a twenty-five-page paper in one of those 300-level courses. Students must also take two courses in literature written before 1800, and one additional course in literature written before 1900, as well as a course on race, gender, sexuality, or ethnicity. The department strongly suggests that students take "Approaches to Literary Studies" and English 101—though that introductory course may be as traditional as a study of early British literature or Western drama, or as trendy as a class on "chick lit." It is quite possible for an English major to graduate without taking a course in Shakespeare.

Classes at Vassar are small: just three Vassar classes enroll more than fifty students, and two-thirds have fewer than twenty. The student-faculty ratio is an excellent 8 to 1, and the average class size seventeen. One professor says, "You can't get tenure unless you're a good teacher. But you also need some scholarship—a few articles, a book, and evidence of scholarly commitment, and some service to the college." Adds an undergrad: "The professors offer lots of office hours, and they're very accessible. And they're also really good about getting back to you by e-mail if you want to get into a class. Generally they're very responsive."

Vassar's strongest programs include philosophy, biology, and art. English is considered "excellent in spots," and the programs in the Romance languages provide fine opportunities for study abroad. A student describes the history department as "small but with really great professors." The economics department offers a respectable range of courses, including introductory and advanced classes on Marxist economics along with a couple on neoclassical (free market) and game theory. A unique major at Vassar is Victorian studies, a program that combines history, literature, and sociology.

Students and faculty praise the following teachers: Nancy Bisaha, Robert K. Brigham, James Merrell, Leslie Offutt, and Michaela Pohl in history; Mark C. Amodio, Beth Darlington, H. Daniel Peck, and Everett K. Weedin in English; Nicholas Adams, Eve D'Ambra, Susan D. Kuretsky, Brian Lukacher, and Molly Nesbit in art history; Robert Brown in classics; Giovanna Borradori, Mitchell Miller, and Douglas Winblad in philosophy; Peter G. Stillman in political science; and Alexis Klimoff in Russian. Vassar's website also offers a student-run ranking of the faculty (for students' use only).

The required Freshman Writing Seminar is a small-group practicum designed to introduce students to the "Vassar experience" and to promote the effective expression of ideas in both written and oral work. A recent listing included an Africana Studies course entitled "The Fire This Time: Hip Hop and Critical Citizenship," and an English class on "The Symbolic Quest," which included readings from *Sir Gawain and the Green Knight* and *Paradise Lost*. The school's writing center recommends research books and looks over student draft papers.

The school's introductory courses are often interdisciplinary, and typically fascinating. Nearly every department offers a freshman course; a recent catalog lists about twenty, including the classics/philosophy/history class "Civilization in Question," which required readings from Homer, the Bible and (alas) Foucault; the history course "The Dark Ages: 400 to 900"; and "The Art of Reading and Writing" in English composition. Most students say these classes are an excellent place to learn the art of clear, concise expression. (Though they won't learn that from Foucault—a sex-obsessed culture critic who lauded Chairman Mao from a safe academic perch in France.)

By the end of their sophomore year, all students must complete a course in quantitative methods. Any math, laboratory science, or computer science course will do, as will select courses in anthropology, geography, and economics.

Outside of class academic opportunities are numerous, despite campus budget problems, and interested students should comb the catalog and discuss with faculty and other students the unique internship, research, and study-abroad possibilities that are available. There are also research opportunities in the sciences working under faculty. Vassar participates in the Twelve College Exchange Program, so students may spend a semester or a year at schools such as Amherst, Bowdoin, Dartmouth, Wheaton (the one in Massachusetts), or Williams.

SUGGESTED CORE

1. Classics 216b/217b, History of the Ancient Greeks/History of the Ancient Romans
2. Philosophy 101a, History of Western Philosophy I
3. Religion 225b, The Hebrew Bible; no suitable course for New Testament
4. Religion 227a, The Kingdom of God and the Empire of Rome
5. Political Science 270b, Modern Political Thought
6. English 240, 241, or 242, Shakespeare
7. History 275, Revolutionary America, 1750–1830
8. Philosophy 205, Nineteenth Century Philosophy

Dilettantes and ideologues have plenty of choices at Vassar—the women's studies program being a good example, offering courses like "Gender and Social Space," which teaches students to "understand gender itself as a spatial practice." Other options include "Feminist Perspectives on Environmentalism," "Transnational Queer: Genders, Sexualities, Identities," and "Latina Feminisms." The urban studies program takes a kitchen-sink approach. It claims to introduce students "to a temporal range and spatial variety of urban experience and phenomena" and to engage them "experientially in a facet of the urban experience." This might prove helpful to students who have never actually *visited* a city (Poughkeepsie doesn't count).

Much better to remedy that deficit through travel. Almost half of Vassar students study abroad at some point during their four years, and the college sponsors (or cosponsors with other colleges) study in Germany, Russia, France, Italy, Australia, China, Ecuador, Scotland, Spain, and England. Vassar students are also allowed to study abroad through another college or university. The education program sponsors a teaching internship at primary and secondary schools in Clifden, Ireland. Students majoring in international studies are actively encouraged to study in a foreign country. "Junior Year Abroad is huge," one senior reports.

Languages offered include Ancient Greek, Arabic, Chinese, French, German, Italian, Japanese, Latin, Russian, Spanish, and Hebrew.

Student Life: Shiny happy people

The Vassar campus is peaceful, and residential life is pleasant. Located in Poughkeepsie, New York, (population 75,000), seventy miles north of New York City, Vassar's Hudson River Valley surroundings look more like a Winslow Homer painting than a modern college campus. Throughout winter, the area's average temperature hovers in the twenties, but in more temperate months, students can take advantage of Vassar's 500-acre farm, complete with hiking and jogging trails. Other favorite outdoor attractions are Sunset Lake and the Falls, a local waterfall.

The school's mammoth College Center houses a snack bar, cafe, post office, bookshop, radio station—and the college pub and dance club, Matthew's Mug. Main Hall also has several administrative offices and student residences. The hallways in Main are notably wide and were intended to allow the college's first students to exercise indoors in their hoopskirts.

Four Gothic residence halls, housing about 150 students each, form a typical quad. The college has five other student residences off the main quadrangle, and approximately 20 percent of Vassar students (all upperclassmen) live in apartments or townhouses further from the center of campus. One residence hall is reserved for women only, but all other halls are coed and do not separate men and women by floor. Many bathrooms are coed, and students can share suites (though not individual rooms) with members of the opposite sex.

Sixty percent of Vassar's students are female. The school's admission department points out that women are 55 percent of all college students nationally, so Vassar is really not so unbalanced.

Each house at Vassar is self-governed, meaning that students make most of the decisions; there are no resident advisors in the buildings, so "student fellows" do most of the counseling and community programming that RAs oversee at other schools. Some floors in each dormitory are set aside as "wellness corridors" or substance-free areas. Students seeking a more "holistic" living experience can apply for the Dexter M. Ferry Cooperative House, where residents cook and clean for themselves. Smoking is prohibited in residence halls unless residents decide to designate a specific smoking location. Houses also maintain quiet hours between 11:00 PM and 10:00 AM.

About 98 percent of Vassar students live in college-owned housing. Housing is guaranteed (and required for full-time students) for all four years, but upperclassmen may have to live in double- or triple-occupancy rooms originally meant for one or two residents. Although Vassar did approve sex-neutral housing in 2008 to accommodate its vocal LGBTQ students, the university has not fully incorporated the policy, and suites or upperclassman apartments are the only way to live with members of the opposite sex.

The college's dining services rank among the nation's ten most vegetarian-friendly, according to PETA, and it recently expanded the vegan and gluten-free options. Vassar was founded by a wealthy brewer, and its students do drink—a lot. Drug use is also popular on campus: mostly marijuana, but students claim that anything is available, and that the administration often doesn't step in with budding alcoholics or addicts until it is too late. One regular Vassar event, the "HomoHop," was shut down by organizers a few years ago because of excessive intoxication. Raunchy Vassarites may still turn for consolation to the pages of *Squirm*, the student-run campus porn magazine, sponsored by an approved organization that recently hosted a movie night featuring two pornographic films.

Students with more refined tastes have access to a vast number of cultural events; Poughkeepsie is only two hours from New York City by train, and currently costs $30 or $40 round-trip. Although students often complain about the city, Poughkeepsie itself does have plenty of concert venues, dance clubs, and restaurants—the Culinary Institute of America is only minutes away, housed in a beautiful former Jesuit seminary. However, students caution, getting around without a car can be challenging.

More traditional students should contact the Moderate, Independent, and Conservative Alliance of Vassar, a puckish and independent-minded organization that has attracted university sanctions in past years for its publications.

Athletic Vassarites can participate in one or more of the school's twenty-five NCAA Division III varsity teams. The Brewers compete in the Upstate Collegiate Athletic Confer-

---

ACADEMIC REQUIREMENTS

Vassar's general education requirements are slim. Students must:

- Take one "Freshman Writing Seminar," a small-group seminar chosen from any department.
- Pass one quantitative (math or science) course by the end of the sophomore year.
- Demonstrate foreign language proficiency, either through coursework or test scores.
- Complete between ten and seventeen courses in their declared major.

Mid-Atlantic

ence against nine other small New York colleges in sports like basketball, fencing, rugby, soccer, volleyball, and swimming and diving. Intramurals allow students to chose competitive or recreational play in soccer (indoor and outdoor), volleyball, tennis, softball, and basketball, as well as tournaments in squash, flag football, golf, and badminton.

Club sports are big at the school, offering ballroom dancing, aikido, synchronized skating, polo, biking, FlyPeople dance troupe, Ultimate Frisbee, Quidditch, cross-country and downhill skiing, equestrian, and an outing club, which organizes backpacking, hiking, climbing, whitewater rafting, skiing, and skydiving trips.

Religious students will find a number of organizations on campus. The Catholic Community pledges to cultivate "religious life through faith, community, and social justice." In other words, skip it, and go to the Latin Mass at St. Joseph's parish in town. The Vassar Christian Fellowship promises that membership is "open to all Vassar students regardless of race, color, sex, ethnicity, nationality, political or sexual orientation, marital status, or handicap" (does that cover everybody?), and its main event is a twice-yearly book table offering publications and information on concerts and speakers. The Vassar Jewish Union offers fellowship to students of varying degrees of orthodoxy, "regardless of their backgrounds or form of Jewish expression," while the Vassar Pagan Circle "works to provide a space for all those who identify with or would like to learn more about Paganism." For those who cannot commit to many gods (or even One), the Unitarian Universalists offer a "liberal, non-creedal religious tradition that values the inherent worth and dignity of ALL people." Students who find that too constraining might prefer to join the Barefoot Monkeys, a club for jugglers.

Plenty of performance and production opportunities exist, from the Vastards, AirCappella, Measure 4 Measure, Night Owls, Devils or Matthew's Minstrels *a cappella* groups, to the Filmmakers group, Unbound experimental theater group, On Tap dance group, Wordsmiths spoken word poetry group, Shakespeare Troupe, a number of sketch comedy and improv groups, or the Woodshed Theatre Ensemble. Students can also participate in 91.3 WVKR, the college radio station, the *Miscellany News* student paper, or in the *Vassarion* yearbook.

Most of Vassar's other student organizations are politically-minded or focused on activism. Many are devoted to issues of sexuality (TransMission, which welcomes "transgender, genderqueer, and intersex people," ACT OUT, Queer Coalition, Intersextions dialogue group, and the aforementioned Squirm "sex-positive forum"). Other groups include UNICEF, PEACE, Vassar Greens, and the Vassar Green Party. Racial and ethnic groups include Poder Latino, the Feminist Majority Leadership Alliance, the Women of Color Alliance, Council of Black Seniors, African Students Union, Caribbean Students Union, or Black Students Union. Vassar has other issues-based groups, like the Animal Rescue Coalition and the Vassar Prison Initiative (which doesn't necessarily visit prisons—group members instead are "committed to raising awareness about issues related to the prison industrial complex").

In spite of the heavy radical-chic influence on campus, Vassar has a large number of prized campus traditions and ceremonies reflecting its legacy as the first accredited, stand-alone women's college in the country. The most popular customs are Primal Scream and

Founder's Day. The former marks the onset of exams, when students converge on a central quad at midnight before finals and scream at the top of their lungs. On Founder's Day, an all-day and night fair is held on a Saturday in the spring, complete with food, music, and fireworks.

To judge by crime statistics, Vassar is a very safe campus. A female undergrad says, "Crime might be a concern off campus, but not on. I wouldn't go out after midnight in Pousghkeepsie, but there's not much reason to really." A rare exception occurred just after midnight on November 15, 2008, when four students were robbed at gunpoint outside a central academic building. All residence halls are equipped with card-entry systems, and the student-organized Campus Patrol monitors the campus each night and runs an escort service for students walking across campus after dark. A student-run shuttle also takes students to and from many off-campus locations. Vassar does not have a police force, but the school does employ unarmed security officers. In 2009, the school reported three forcible sex offenses, one robbery, one vehicle theft (of a golf cart), and three burglaries on campus.

Tuition for the 2010–11 school year at Vassar was $42,560, plus $10,080 for room and board. Financial aid is readily available and admission is need blind. More than 55 percent of students receive financial aid, and the average first-year student received about $37,000 in 2009. Vassar awards more than $25 million in scholarships in addition to federal and state aid. The college has thus far resisted cutting financial aid in the midst of its current budget crisis, and the typical Vassar student graduates with a modest $19,000 in student-loan debt.

RED LIGHT

Vassar's reputation for radical, and sometimes bizarre, politics is as strong as its reputation for academic rigor. The college offers many explicitly politicized courses, the administration seems genuinely exhilarated at the prospects of promoting its own leftist agenda, and students are activists to the core. Professor Joshua Schreier raised eyebrows recently when the syllabus for his course, "The Roots of the Palestine-Israel Conflict" made clear his intention to take sides in the conflict. A major theme in class discussion, according to the syllabus, was "Why does Palestine, an area of the Ottoman Empire where the vast majority of people were Arabic-speaking Muslims only seventy years ago, currently host a 'Jewish' state whose national leadership claims to represent, first and foremost, only one of the ethnic/national communities living there?"

On the plus side, Vassar makes no pretense about its political leanings, and students can thank professors like Joshua Schreier for being upfront about what to expect—and helping them decide what to avoid, if they're so inclined.

From the "Kick Coke" campaign, which succeeded in having all Coca-Cola products removed from campus (after allegations that the company has repeatedly violated human rights and flouted labor and environmental regulations) to student reports that at times, their undergraduate "education" seemed more like liberal indoctrination, it's clear that conservative students considering Vassar should think twice. Maybe thrice.

Villanova University

Villanova, Pennsylvania • www.villanova.edu

Guiding spirit

Founded in 1842 by the Order of St. Augustine, Villanova University is named for St. Thomas of Villanova, a sixteenth-century Augustinian monk who was renowned as a "friendly and helpful" teacher. That attitude of service, together with a dedication to the spirituality and teaching of St. Augustine himself, imbues the Villanova faculty. Villanova University is still run by the Augustinians, though few of them teach. The school sits on a beautiful 254-acre campus on the affluent Main Line eighteen miles west of Philadelphia.

Villanova's liberal arts requirements and programs remain comparatively strong. The campus is relatively apolitical and there is a large and vibrant pro-life group on campus. Students seem genuinely to care for each other and for their neighbor. Compared to many of the nation's other Catholic universities, Villanova seems to be a solid intellectual and spiritual option for academically serious and community-minded students.

Academic Life: Getting more of Gus

When Villanova introduced its new "core" curriculum twenty years ago, "reading Catholic literature and discussing it seriously became the norm on campus," says one professor. Indeed, Villanova's curriculum is better than most. While it allows a bit too much flexibility to students, it does go some way toward providing them with foundational exposure to the best of the Western and Catholic intellectual traditions. One student says that Villanova "teaches students to be well-rounded people both inside and outside of the classroom," while another student characterizes the curriculum as "stretching." Students still need to make wise choices to avoid ideologically-driven courses, and one professor laments that there are few "intrusions" of Catholic faith into student life or the classroom. While the courses through which Villanova students are exposed to the classics and the Western heritage are "better than at most colleges," says one professor, they are still not of "the quality I'd advocate is needed to reverse the decline in undergraduate learning."

Villanova's thirty-second president, Rev. Peter M. Donohue, OSA, previously taught at the university and is very much in touch with student and faculty concerns. One professor reports that Donohue has a "vivid and personal style—and has fostered enormous loyalty among alums, students, faculty, and staff. His personal touch has energized the campus."

As former head of the theater department, holder of a doctorate in theater, and a Barrymore Award-winning director, President Donohue is both willing and able to help fill the fine arts void currently found at Villanova.

Of the student body, one student says, "I think we're getting noticeably more dynamic, interesting, and intellectual." A professor agrees: "The students get better every year. We're really starting to attract more intellectual, conservative, and genuine students." One student reports that her peers are "well-read before they get to college" as well as "determined and motivated."

The faculty is a mixed bag. While one professor worries, "There is a fair amount of focus by some faculty—especially new hires—on trendy, superficial subjects," others are more hopeful. One teacher points to several recently recruited professors who seek "to educate their students by opening their 'minds and hearts' to the whole truth." Says another, "We have an excellent faculty, and it's getting better every year. . . . Some of us are on the left in our personal politics, some on the right, but we're all serious about liberal education." He continues, "The [introductory freshman seminar] course we teach . . . reflects Villanova's ever-greater seriousness about its intellectual mission. In the first semester, students take 'Traditions in Conversation,' which is on the ancient, medieval, and Renaissance periods, and places Augustine's thought in dialogue with the other roots of the Western tradition." Other professors voiced similar optimism.

Students who want the best possible liberal arts education at Villanova should consider the humanities major, which is attracting some excellent professors and students. One professor calls this major "an integrated curriculum centered on the basic questions of human existence" which serves to promote "serious Catholic intellectual life at the university." According to the department's website, "The humanities major consists of four gateway courses, which are team-taught seminars that investigate basic questions about God, the human person, the world, and society both in relation to the wisdom of past and contemporary thinkers." This department is an exciting option for intellectually curious students.

One attractive program is the Matthew J. Ryan Center for the Studies of Free Institutions and the Public Good, which "promotes inquiry into the principles and processes of free government and seeks to advance understanding of the responsibilities of statesmen and citizens of constitutional democratic societies." (Intercollegiate Studies Institute, the

VITAL STATISTICS

Religious affiliation: *Roman Catholic*
Total enrollment: *10,172*
Total undergraduates: *7,201*
SAT/ACT midranges: CR: *580–680*, M: *620–710*; ACT: *28–31*
Applicants: *15,102*
Applicants accepted: *46%*
Applicants accepted who enrolled: *37%*
Tuition and fees: *$39,350*
Room and board: *$10,620*
Freshman retention rate: *94%*
Graduation rate: *82% (4 yrs.), 89% (6 yrs.)*
Courses with fewer than 20 students: *43%*
Student-faculty ratio: *11:1*
Courses taught by graduate students: *not provided*
Most popular majors: *business/marketing, engineering, social sciences*
Students living on campus: *70%*
Guaranteed housing for 4 years? *no*
Students in fraternities: *16%* in sororities: *31%*

publisher of this guide, is a cosponsor of this program.) The Ryan Center conducts small reading groups for faculty and students, and sponsors campus-wide events and seminars. A 2010 event topic was "Classical Political Philosophy and the American Founding Right" with a question and answer session with political philosopher Dr. Harry V. Jaffa.

Students with excellent SAT scores and high school class ranks may be invited to participate in the university's honors program, which comes highly recommended. To earn an honors degree, a student must take twelve honors-level courses, including a sophomore honors seminar, and complete a senior thesis. Students say honors advisors are better and get more involved in students' academic plans. There is no special honors curriculum or separate dormitory for honors students, but students in this program gain a sense of camaraderie by attending lectures, social events, and the occasional field trip to Philadelphia or New York City.

Villanova has the regular set of traditional majors, but students can also earn a concentration (eight courses) in seventeen different areas, including the ever-popular Irish studies program. In addition to Irish studies and the aforementioned humanities major, strong departments include astronomy and astrophysics (separate from the physics department) and the other hard sciences, the Center for Liberal Education, economics, political science, philosophy, and English. Weaker departments at Villanova reportedly are history, education, and communications.

English majors do not have to take a course in Shakespeare, although it is offered, as are many worthy classes in the history of literature such as "Chaucer," "Dryden, Swift and Pope," "American Short Story," and a solid course on the Catholic novel.

History majors must take two American and two European classes as well as one world history course. Western civilization is not required, unfortunately, nor is American history before or after 1865. (No wonder this is known as one of Villanova's weakest departments.)

The political science department is both popular and rigorous, requiring majors to take courses on the U.S. Constitution and American political theory, as well as comparative politics and international relations.

The Villanova School of Business is one of the university's best-known programs, and the College of Engineering has a strong advising program and several excellent professors, though one engineering student admits, "You'd be better off going to Penn State or a similarly big school with bigger labs and more money to throw around. That's really the only program that suffers from being too small, and that's just the nature of engineering."

Villanova enrolls about 3,000 graduate students, but generally only students in the Villanova doctoral program in philosophy are allowed to teach undergraduate courses. Professors are said to be intent on their students learning the material. "Many professors do care about their students and devote lots of time to them," reports a faculty member. A student agrees: "Professors are always readily available and unusually willing to help." Faculty are required to hold office hours each week, and many students say they take advantage of them—and not just right before exams (though some faculty say the students do not avail themselves of this opportunity as often as they could). Some faculty members give out their home phone numbers at the beginning of the semester and encourage students to call with questions. Villanova's largest classrooms, typically used for introductory biology and chemistry classes, hold approximately one hundred students. Faculty members are also dedicated to helping students make good choices in selecting their courses; students say the advising program is strong.

The best faculty members at Villanova include Richard Jacobs in education and human services; Andrew Bove, Peter Busch, Chris Daly, Greg Hoskins, and Catherine Wilson in the Center for Liberal Education; Jesse Couenhoven, Jeanne Heffernan Schindler, Anna Moreland, David Schindler Jr., Mark Shiffman, Thomas Smith, and Michael Tomko in humanities; David M. Barrett, Lowell Gustafson, Robert Maranto, Colleen Sheehan, A. Maria Toyoda, and Craig Wheeland in political science; Christopher Haas in history; Charlie Zech in economics; Earl Bader, Karen Graziano, James Kirschke, and Hugh Ormsby-Lennon in English; Tom Busch, John Doody, Daniel Regan, Michael Waddell, and Jim Wetzel in philosophy; Randy Weinstein in chemical engineering; Kevin Hughes in classical studies; Tony Godzieba, Martin Laird, Bernard Prusak, and Darlene Weaver in theology; Paul Lupinacci in statistics; John Santomas in math; and Sayed Omran in Arab and Islamic studies.

Villanova's Office of International Studies currently coordinates four year/semester programs in Ireland, England, Australia, and Italy. On campus, the university offers German, French, Italian, Spanish, Portuguese, Latin, Hebrew, Arabic, Chinese, Ancient Greek, Japanese, and Russian.

Student Life: Vanillanova

Villanova is only a short train ride into Philadelphia, but students tend to pass up Philadelphia's cultural events and nightlife to spend most of their weekends and evenings on campus. Thirty-one percent of women and 16 percent of men are members of Greek organizations, but because they do not have their own houses, Greeks are less exclusive and more service-oriented than at other schools. Students will find plenty of activities on campus to occupy their free time: publications, dances, some music and theater recitals, concerts, and free cultural and popular films in the student center. In addition, there are more than 250 student groups and organizations, as well as forty-four club and intramural sports.

Villanova lies along Route 30 (the Main Line), a couple of miles down the road from Bryn Mawr and Haverford colleges. The mostly Gothic-style campus has plenty of lush green lawns and was designated a national arboretum in 1993. The university has recently added a student fitness center, a large facility for the growing nursing school, and a parking garage for the law school. St. Thomas of Villanova Chapel is the dominant building on campus, but the Connelly Student Center is more frequently visited, with its dining areas, computer lounge, art gallery, ice cream shop, movie theater, and meeting space. Outside of Connelly is a black-and-white sculpture known by students as "The Oreo," where students often advertise events, gather for protests, or just hang out between classes. Cafes called "Holy Grounds" are conveniently located all over campus. Falvey Memorial Library holds over a million volumes, and students may also use the Haverford, Bryn Mawr, and University of Pennsylvania libraries through EZ-Borrow.

The university is primarily residential. Villanova guarantees housing on campus for the first three years; most seniors live in off-campus apartments. Villanova manages eighteen residence halls and eight apartment buildings. Students can choose to live in either single-sex or coed dorms, but even the coed dorms are segregated by floor, which means students never live next door to a member of the opposite sex. Villanova's luckiest juniors live in two-bedroom, one-and-a-half-bath apartments on campus. Many freshmen opt for the Villanova learning communities in which students live together in a dorm and share a core humanities seminar. As a result of this close interaction, one student says, "usually

ACADEMIC REQUIREMENTS

In lieu of a core curriculum, Villanova imposes a series of distribution requirements. On top of these, liberal arts students must take four courses each that are writing intensive or writing enriched. All students must complete:

- Two "Augustine and Villanova Culture" freshman seminars, "Traditions in Conversation" and "Modernity and its Discontents."
- One ethics class, such as "Ethical Traditions and Contemporary Life" or "Ethics and the Culture Wars."
- One course in fine arts. Class options include "History of Western Art: Renaissance to Contemporary" and "Black Theater."
- Two foreign language classes.
- Two courses in history, with choices ranging from "History of Western Civilization" to "American Women and Gender History."
- Two classes in literature, such as "Shakespeare" or "Race and Ethnicity: American Novel."
- Two courses in math. Choices include "Linear Algebra" and "Calculus for Liberal Arts."
- Two classes in philosophy, such as "Introduction to Philosophy" and "Eco-Feminism."
- Two courses in theology. Classes offered include "Understanding the Bible" and "Feminist Theology."
- Two classes in the natural sciences with labs. Offerings include "Microbiology" and "Planet Earth."
- Three social science courses, such as "Topics in Social Sciences" or "Social Inequality."
- Two diversity courses. Choices include "Gender and the World" and "Race and Ethnic Relations."

people get to know their hallmates a little faster." Recent themes included "Nature and the World" and "Mind, Body, Spirit."

One student characterizes the typical Villanova student as "an Irish or Italian upper-class Abercrombie clone from the suburbs." Another student says a common nickname for the school, whose student body is around 73 percent white, is "Vanillanova." This is rapidly changing. The administration embarked on an extremely aggressive diversity campaign a few years ago, resulting in the Caucasian population plummeting 12 percent in just six years. Minority recruitment and retainment initiatives abound. Villanova's Office of Multicultural Affairs coordinates student groups like the Black Cultural Society, the Hispanic Society, and the South Asian Multicultural Organized Students Association (SAMOSA). The office also handles the Minority Vita Bank, a database comprised entirely of minority job applicants that every university department is instructed to utilize when making hiring searches. The Villanova Intermediary Persons program pairs volunteers with incoming minority freshmen to serve as first friends on campus. In an example of "diversity gone wild," Villanova also provides gay, lesbian, bisexual, and transgendered clubs and support groups on campus.

Villanova maintains a Peace and Justice Center, which offers courses such as "Ecofeminism" alongside classes in real Catholic social teaching. The Center supports student groups such as Villanovans for the Ethical Treatment of Animals, Bread for the World, Villanovans for Life (a very active group on campus which regularly puts up pro-life displays), and Villanova Partnership with Catholic Relief Services. The Center for Liberal Education website maintains a library of work by Dorothy Day and Thomas Merton on how to integrate faith and economics, and Professor Charlie Zech has also contributed to such efforts to integrate Catholic thought with socioeconomic realities.

If there is one part of St. Augustine's teaching that is stressed more than any other at Villanova, it is his plea for true Christian charity. The school has a real "focus on service," reports a student proudly: "We have the largest Habitat for Humanity program in the nation and participation is huge in similar programs." The Campus Ministry office organizes volunteer opportunities such as weekly trips to soup kitchens, prison literacy programs, charity activities through fraternities and sororities, and mission and service trips. In 2010, service trip locations included Guatemala, El Salvador, Belize, Jamaica, Costa Rica, Peru, Santo Domingo, Ecuador, and several domestic locations including an Indian Reservation in New Mexico. The Pennsylvania State Special Olympics Fall Festival is the largest student-run activity of its kind in the world, and around half of the student body volunteers for the event. But students may find that Campus Ministry, while warm and welcoming, provides little of substance beyond a commitment to social justice. One student summarizes the tension that sometimes occurs between the oft-invoked, but ill-defined "Spirit of Saint Augustine" and the concrete teachings of the Church: "There is . . . a sense that campus ministry is striving to be inclusive and tolerant of any lifestyle or opinion that is adverse to the traditional doctrines within Christianity."

Some Villanova students embody the Villanovan spirit of service by offering it to their country. The Villanova NROTC program includes about 150 midshipmen and has produced more admirals and Marine Corps generals than any other school except for the

Mid-Atlantic

U.S. Naval Academy. The campus military center, John Barry Hall, is said to be the only federally funded building with a cross on it. Says one parent of an NROTC student, "The dedication and determination of the NROTC midshipmen is unparalleled." Lately, several NROTC students have chosen to minor in Arab and Islamic studies, another strong program at Villanova.

There are twenty-four NCAA Division I sports teams at Villanova and more than 500 student athletes. A large portion of the student body also participates in the school's more than forty intramural and intercollegiate sports. The Pavillion is the university's 6,500-seat multipurpose recreational facility and arena, and home to the wildly popular men's and women's Wildcat basketball teams. It is also used for concerts, trade shows, college and job fairs, Advanta International Tennis Championship games, NCAA Championship events, and the Villanova law school graduation.

The Sunday Masses for students are largely student-run and are often standing-room only. One student reports that at both the Masses and in campus ministry in general there is a tendency "to use inclusive language to the point that one can no longer distinguish Christianity from self-help manuals." More traditional students might wish to investigate one of the Latin Masses offered in nearby Philadelphia, for instance at the Our Lady of Consolation and Our Lady of Lourdes parishes.

Most students are Catholic, but all agree that religion "is never really in your face," as one student says. "We don't try to downplay Christianity," says another Catholic student, "but we are accepting of all faiths. . . . My best friend here is Buddhist." Popular organizations for non-Catholic students include Hillel and a Muslim student group. Despite the Catholic ethos of the university, one student cautions that "the average student does not take Catholic ideals completely to heart. Issues like sex before marriage, abortion, and general morality" are not necessarily approached according to Catholic teaching. "In that sense the average Villanova student is not too much different from the average public university student." Excessive drinking is the favorite weekend activity of students, according to one professor.

Mostly as a result of student complaints, the university loosened its visitation policy to allow students to allow visitors (including those of the opposite sex) until midnight on school nights and until 2:00 AM on Fridays and Saturdays. Upperclassman dorms can have these hours extended if all residents attend a session on "roommate rights and responsibilities," The student handbook talks the talk of Catholic modesty and chastity—however Villanova rarely enforces restrictions on intervisitation, students report. RAs are "pathetic," says one student, rarely taking note of violations or taking an active part in organizing activities or getting to know their hall-members.

The campus is secluded enough from the outside community that it suffers little crime. During 2009, Villanova reported three sexual offenses, one robbery, one aggravated assault, seven burglaries, and three cases of arson.

Villanova's tuition in 2010–11 was $39,350, and room and board $10,620. Admissions are need blind, but the school does not come close to meeting every student's full financial need. Only 51 percent of undergraduates receive need-based financial aid, and average indebtedness of recent graduates was a hefty $31,048.

Patrick Henry College
George Mason University
Christendom College
University of Virginia
University of Richmond
Washington and Lee University
College of William and Mary
Liberty University
Regent University
Centre College
Hampden-Sydney College

KENTUCKY

WEST VIRGINIA

VIRGINIA

Duke University
Wake Forest University
University of North Carolina

NORTH CAROLINA

Vanderbilt University
TENNESSEE
Davidson College
Belmont Abbey College

University of the South
Wofford College
Rhodes College
Furman University

ARKANSAS

Berry College
SOUTH CAROLINA

University of Mississippi
University of Georgia

ATLANTA
Emory University
Georgia Institute of Technology
Morehouse College

MISSISSIPPI
ALABAMA
Auburn University

LOUISIANA
GEORGIA

Louisiana State University
University of Florida

Tulane University

FLORIDA

Ave Maria University

South

Auburn University • Ave Maria University • Belmont Abbey College •
Berry College • Centre College • Christendom College •
Davidson College • Duke University • Emory University •
University of Florida • Furman University • George Mason University •
University of Georgia • Georgia Institute of Technology •
Hampden-Sydney College • Liberty University •
Louisiana State University • University of Mississippi •
Morehouse College • University of North Carolina •
• Patrick Henry College • Regent University • Rhodes College •
University of Richmond • University of the South •
Tulane University • Vanderbilt University • University of Virginia •
Wake Forest University • Washington and Lee University •
College of William and Mary • Wofford College

Auburn University

Auburn, Alabama • www.auburn.edu

Throwback

Founded as East Alabama Male College in 1859, Auburn University is in some ways a throwback to an earlier America: football is king, the Greeks rule the social scene, and political activism is next to nil. But the campus is changing: enrollment is at record levels, and the university is trying to get national recognition by drawing on its roots as a public, land-grant institution—even as state legislators cut funds.

Auburn administrators emphasize preprofessional departments such as forestry, fisheries, information technology, and poultry science. To save money, the university has chopped some programs and merged departments, particularly in the liberal arts, which leaves some professors questioning the university's commitment to providing a well-rounded education. Nonetheless, Auburn has a core curriculum that ensures that all students are at least exposed to more rarefied areas of inquiry than the migratory patterns of fish.

"Unlike most other universities, Auburn is conservative," says one instructor. Another adds, "It's just a very Christian, very professional atmosphere. It's dressier than a normal university campus. It just seems cut out of the past, in the good sense." According to a student, "The campus is gorgeous and the people are very southern. Everyone is very friendly."

Academic Life: Core all around

Auburn offers undergraduate degrees in more than 130 areas, including many highly specialized fields like forestry, aviation, and supply-chain management. While the university, thankfully, has retained a core curriculum, some professors say that the emphasis on the liberal arts has decreased.

The university is divided into ten colleges (Agriculture, Architecture, Business, Education, Engineering, Honors, Human Sciences, Liberal Arts, Sciences and Mathematics, and Veterinary Medicine) and three schools (Forestry and Wildlife Sciences, Nursing, and Pharmacy), plus the graduate school. All undergraduates must fulfill the requirements of Auburn's core curriculum. According to one student, the core "takes up your first two years of study, but it really ensures that all students, regardless of major, get a well-rounded education in liberal arts, math, and science."

VITAL STATISTICS

Religious affiliation: *none*
Total enrollment: *24,602*
Total undergraduates: *19,926*
SAT/ACT midranges: CR: *520–640*, M: *540–660*; ACT: *23–29*
Applicants: *14,862*
Applicants accepted: *80%*
Accepted applicants who enrolled: *33%*
Tuition and fees: *in state, $6,240; out of state, $18,720*
Room and board: *$8,972*
Freshman retention rate: *86%*
Graduation rate: *37% (4 yrs.), 67% (6 yrs.)*
Courses with fewer than 20 students: *27%*
Student-faculty ratio: *18:1*
Courses taught by graduate students: *15%*
Most popular majors: *business/marketing, engineering, education*
Students living on campus: *19%*
Guaranteed housing for four years? *no*
Students in fraternities: *21%* in sororities: *31%*

There is no common syllabus for the core courses, and topics can vary somewhat from section to section. The two required literature classes are broken down into "culturally diverse readings in world literature from the ancient period to 1600" and "culturally diverse readings in world literature from 1600 to present." The history classes are taught in an objective fashion: "The two history classes that I took were fair, and I have no gripes against what was taught," a student says. Another added, "It was just the facts."

There are several truly excellent departments at Auburn, but most are outside of the traditional liberal arts areas—preprofessional programs such as veterinary medicine, agriculture, forestry, architecture, and engineering are the strongest on campus.

The shining star at Auburn is its department of economics, which is based in the university's business college. The department boasts solid credentials and first-rate professors who understand the market economy. Majors must complete courses in macro- and microeconomics, math methods, international economics, econometrics, calculus, and statistics, as well as four electives, two foreign language classes, the university core, and a minor from outside economics. This department has on four occasions been included in the John Templeton Honor Roll for Free Enterprise Teaching. The nearby presence of the Ludwig von Mises Institute amplifies the appeal of Auburn to students with an interest in economics and libertarian politics.

The Mises Institute, one of the intellectual highlights at Auburn, is a nationally known educational and scholarly center. Named for the Austrian free-market economist, the institute defends capitalism, private property rights, and sound monetary policies. Students interested in free markets and free societies would be advised to look into the institute.

The history and philosophy departments are among the strongest at Auburn (as is the College of Engineering). Philosophy majors are directed to take two upper-level courses in each of the following: ethics and value theory, epistemology and metaphysics, and the history of philosophy. Majors must also take "Symbolic Logic" and complete four philosophy electives.

The history department does not provide much structure to its majors, requiring only "The Historian's Craft," two intermediate-, four upper-, and three advanced-level classes, each chosen from a short list. Students must also complete two foreign language courses, a class each in computers and public speaking, and a senior thesis project, as well as a number of liberal arts and history electives. Despite a lack of structure, by seeking advice from professors in the department, serious students can graduate with a thorough knowledge of the discipline.

The political science major follows a typical track, requiring the introductory class "American Government in a Multi-Cultural World," one class in political thought, and three courses chosen from comparative politics, international relations, public law and conflict resolution, and public administration. Students then opt to concentrate in an area like comparative politics or public administration.

English students are given some broad outlines for completing their major: they must take an introductory class, a literature course on "globalism, sustainability and diversity"—like "Survey of African-American Literature" or "Technology, Literacy, and Culture"—a linguistics or rhetoric class, and a critical theory class. Additionally, upper-level literature classes are required in British, American, genre-focused, and author/topic-focused literature. Students could emerge without having studied Shakespeare.

> **SUGGESTED CORE**
>
> 1. Foreign Language Greek 3510/Latin 3510, Greek/Roman Literature and Culture in Translation
> 2. Philosophy 3330, History of Ancient Philosophy
> 3. Religious Studies 1020/1030, Introduction to the Hebrew Scriptures/New Testament
> 4. Philosophy 3400, Medieval Philosophy
> 5. Political Science 3020, Introduction to Political Theory or Philosophy 3600, Political Philosophy
> 6. English 4610, Shakespeare
> 7. History 2010, Survey of United States History to 1877
> 8. History 5340, European Culture and Intellectual History

Business is a popular major, though some faculty decry its rampant preprofessionalism. For instance, interested students can attend sessions on what to wear to an interview or which utensils to use at dinner—a session that some on campus deride as "The Right Fork." Throughout the school, one professor notes a "definite pecuniary approach to education.... 'How much can I make?' 'Is it worth it?' These are the kinds of concerns that larger and larger proportions of students and parents openly express." Another student praises his education at the business school, saying that "the strongest point about the program was that professors were in touch with reality."

Professors to seek out at Auburn include Richard W. Ault and Roger W. Garrison in economics; Daniel D. Butler in business; Kelly Bryant in architecture; Joey Shaw in agriculture; King "Ed" Williams in journalism; Dennis Ray Duty and Mark Liles in biology; and James R. Barth in finance. Students report that "professors do not grade down conservative students," but some teachers do insist too strongly on their own views. "I was in a bioethics class, and of course there was the issue of when does human life begin. The teacher was blatant about her opinion and did not leave room for other opinions. My roommate was in a philosophical anatomy class where they did the same thing," a student complains.

The university's Honors College, which selects some two hundred freshmen from all of the colleges and schools each year, is one of the university's outstanding programs. Stu-

South

dents showing evidence of "leadership and service," with high school grade-point averages of at least 3.75 and strong standardized test scores, are invited into the program. During their first two years, these students take six of their core courses together. Honors classes are small and designed to promote in-depth discussions with fellow students and faculty. They can earn a senior honors certificate either by writing a thesis or by taking four "contract courses," which supplement regular courses with extra writing or field work. The program comes with perks: honors students can live in separate residence halls and receive priority at registration, among other privileges.

In recent years, Auburn has dedicated millions of dollars to new research initiatives in transportation, information technology, food safety, biological sciences, fisheries and allied aquaculture, poultry science, and forestry and wildlife sciences. In 2008, the university opened Phase I of the Shelby Center for Engineering Technology, a 156-acre research park. The high-tech quest doesn't sit well with many liberal arts faculty. "I would like to see us produce more well-rounded kinds of students," says a professor. "A student who wants a technical education in computers or business would survive here, but they would also survive at the DeVry Institute."

ACADEMIC REQUIREMENTS

Unlike most schools in this guide, Auburn retains many elements of a traditional core curriculum, which it combines with respectable distribution requirements. To graduate, students must fulfill the following:

- Two freshman writing classes.
- "World Literature" I and II, writing-intensive courses. The first course emphasizes ancient, medieval, and Renaissance literature; the second course considers literature from the seventeenth century to the present. Teachers are "encouraged to construct syllabi that contain a balanced representation of traditionally canonical works as well as works by women, by minority writers within Western culture, and by non-Western writers."
- One of three two-course history sequences—"World History," "Technology and Civilization," or "Human Odyssey," which focuses on "shifts in human perception resulting from discovery and invention."
- Two four-hour science classes, including a lab and a selected sequence in biology, chemistry, geology, or physics.
- A math course. Students are limited to finite mathematics, precalculus algebra or trigonometry, and calculus classes.
- A philosophy class. Students may choose among topics such as logic, ethics, health science ethics, or business ethics.
- One social science course in anthropology, geography, psychology, or sociology.
- Another social science class in microeconomics, political economy, or American government.
- A fine arts course in architecture, art history, music, or theater.

The same professor laments that academics on campus often must compete with other interests, complaining that football is "valued higher than academics, by the alumni, the administration, and everybody else. . . . Auburn is generally a party school, with athletics emphasized and academics downplayed and grade inflation like you wouldn't believe." According to one student, "You cannot go to Auburn if you do not like football." Grade inflation and an emphasis on sports over liberal learning remain Auburn's most troubling flaws.

Many students report little interaction with their professors. One science major informs us, "When I wanted to meet with my professors during office hours, I had problems finding them. However, e-mail always worked." Another student counters, "Professors here are very accessible. I have always been able to meet my professors outside of class. I have been taught by one graduate student, but there was also a professor who was helping to guide." Advising varies from college to college. Students in the College of Liberal Arts are invited to make appointments with nonfaculty advisors in the dean's office. Once a student has declared a major, he can meet with a faculty advisor within his department.

The university reports that graduate teaching assistants teach 15 percent of all undergraduate courses and most of the labs. Students can opt for professors by checking the class descriptions.

Many majors at Auburn require at least two semesters of foreign language study; the school offers Chinese, French, German, Ancient Greek, Italian, Japanese, Latin, Russian, and Spanish. Students looking for more intense language study can take advantage of one of Auburn's foreign language study-abroad programs in Vienna, Shanghai, Costa Rica, Italy, or Spain for summer study, and semester-long programs in Italy or Spain. A variety of other study-abroad options are available, like faculty-led programs, exchange programs, and programs through or direct enrollment in foreign schools.

Student Life: Sweet home . . . Auburn

Auburn is the sort of place that generations attend in succession, where football runs deep in the blood, and where you wouldn't be caught dead wearing a T-shirt that says ALABAMA. It was not unusual when Auburn sent out a press release a few years ago touting a South Carolina family that was graduating its sixteenth family member from Auburn. "We have two more darling granddaughters that I'm sure will go to school here at Auburn one day," the family's matriarch declared.

Football is the major focus of energy in the fall, culminating in the yearly showdown with Alabama, or perhaps a bowl game. The Auburn Tigers compete on nineteen Division I-A teams. The school is particularly strong in football, of course, as well as swimming and diving, women's basketball, and baseball. Auburn also offers club sports like cycling, sailing, water skiing, bass fishing, and lacrosse, as well as intramurals such as flag football, volleyball, and soccer.

Apart from athletics, fraternities and sororities dominate campus social life, and there have been some well-publicized incidents of hazing. Auburn now has a clearly defined hazing policy that includes prohibitions on everything from branding to "the use of demeaning names" to "having pledges perform personal chores or errands." About 21 percent of undergraduate men and 31 percent of undergraduate women belong to the Greek system, and many of the rest regularly attend weekend parties at Greek houses.

There are single-sex residence halls for women. In coed dorms, men and women are housed in separate wings or on alternating floors, and members of the opposite sex are not allowed to spend the night. Campus housing is in high demand. Only about 19 percent of students live on campus, but those who do seem to like it. One says: "Dorm life is great. Everyone loves living on the quad. The RAs are great people who try to connect with their residents."

Auburn offers hundreds of student clubs. There are around twenty-five religious organizations—mostly Protestant prayer groups and fellowships, but also a Catholic apostolate, a Jewish group, and a Mormon group. Media clubs include the award-winning *Auburn Plainsman* student newspaper, the *Southern Humanities Review*, the Eagle Eye TV News, and WEGL 91 FM. The politically minded student may join Democrat, Republican, or Libertarian groups, as well as the Young Americans for Liberty and Students for Life. There are also a number of service groups like Engineers Without Borders; Habitat for Humanity; Best Buddies, which aids the mentally handicapped; and the Kadettes, who support the Army ROTC.

Besides the Kadettes, several "hostess" groups provide support to Auburn men—the Tiger Splashers are swim- and dive-team spirit boosters, while the Diamond Dolls do the same for the baseball team, the Dunkin Darlings for the basketball team, and the Mariners act as Navy and Marine Corps ROTC hostesses.

Auburn is a lively place, and college traditions abound. Before every home football game, the school releases an eagle (its auxiliary mascot) in the football stadium, to screams of "War eagle!" After the game, fans walk from the stadium to Toomer's Corner, where Auburn campus begins, and toilet paper the trees. Campus "Hey Day" is a twice-yearly tradition that has everyone on campus wearing name tags and greeting each person they pass.

In 2010, the school made national news over reports that the pastor father of Cam Newton, its star quarterback, had solicited money for his son's "performance." Newton had previously been charged with burglary, larceny, and obstructing justice and was once considered for expulsion from the University of Florida for academic cheating. However, Newton was thoroughly defended by the school, led a winning season, and was awarded the Heisman Trophy in 2010. The message seemed to be that athletes function under one set of rules, while average students must obey another.

Auburn has some separate programs for minority students, which some say serve to keep races segregated. Some programs border on the patronizing—such as the Minority Engineering Program, which provides "academic support services to entering minority engineering students," as well as remedial tutoring and mentoring, according to university literature.

Auburn has an active Office of Diversity and Multicultural Affairs as well as a Diversity Leadership Council, which refers to diversity as "a core value at Auburn University." Black History Month in February is a big deal, with a series of lectures and concerts on themes of diversity, civil rights, and racism. Amid all this activism, one student says, Auburn "is a friendly campus. I have never thought of race as an issue."

Students and professors describe the town of Auburn—known as the Loveliest Village on the Plains—as a university town that reflects the school's atmosphere. Some students claim there's little to do in Auburn, but others say the town is perfectly suited for study, research, dining, and relaxation. The town offers many excellent restaurants and historical sites. Take, for example, the Auburn Chapel, where the first secessionist meeting in the Deep South took place in 1851. Ten minutes from Auburn is Chewacla State Park, which has a quiet lake and relaxing picnic spots. It's a local favorite for swimming and hiking.

The crime rate on campus is much lower than that for the surrounding community, which in turn is much lower than national rates. The 2009 crime statistics reported one aggravated assault, twenty-one burglaries, and three motor vehicle thefts on campus—among more than 24,000 students. In spring 2008, Auburn made national news when student Lauren Burk was kidnapped and shot a few miles north of campus. She died later at a hospital. Escorts are now provided to students from the library to a parking deck, and the hours of the on-demand campus security shuttle have been extended from 3:00 AM to 7:00 AM, when the campus's regular transit service begins. One student says, "I still feel pretty safe here. Most students do."

Auburn is quite reasonably priced—for a native. For 2010–11, in-state tuition was only $6,240, while out-of-state was $18,720. Room and board amounted to $8,972. Some 30 percent of students receive awards averaging half of their demonstrated need, and the average student debt at graduation is about $22,232 for those who do borrow money (but most do not).

GREEN LIGHT

There seems to be little political bias, left or right, in the classroom at Auburn—which is quite an achievement. "There are good teachers and bad teachers," says one professor. "It's still possible to get a really good education at Auburn if you pick and choose." Another professor says that older faculty members tend to be less concerned with political agendas than their younger peers. "They're hiring new, younger faculty members, and they bring the virus with them," he says. "But it's moving in the opposite way among students. The students are less politically correct, though they might be forced to mouth the words."

Politically, Auburn is best described as pleasant and noncontroversial. There are virtually no protests, no visible displays of angst, no significant groups of campus agitators. "There are very few leftists here," a conservative student says. "It's great, but sometimes it gets a little boring. There are no real wackos to fight with." The campus atmosphere is quite traditional. According to one student, "the typical student is preppy, courteous, and southern. It is a very friendly campus."

Ave Maria University

Ave Maria, Florida • www.avemaria.edu

Fresh, hot, and crusty

When Domino's pizza magnate and international Catholic philanthropist Thomas Monaghan announced in 2002 his bold plans to create a new Catholic university in Florida and develop a town around it, it generated surprise and curiosity. For thirty-five years, the church had witnessed the sometimes gradual, sometimes "shock" secularization of traditionally Catholic institutions. Given the success of other "start-up" religious colleges in reaction to this trend—Thomas Aquinas, Christendom, and Thomas More colleges, for example—many parents and students expressed strong interest in Monaghan's project. One thing that would set this new institution apart from such schools, which had been started on shoestring budgets, was Monaghan's strong commitment of financial support. This held forth great promise that the school could attract highly qualified faculty and offer campus facilities that other new Catholic colleges could not afford.

The university is in a blank spot on the map of Florida, around which Monaghan plans a profit-making development of an entire town called Ave Maria. The model for all this, some say, is the medieval European universities that sprouted their own communities. (Others invoke the building of Las Vegas.) But Ave Maria University did not begin in a vacuum. Instead, it is an outgrowth of the already successful Ave Maria College and Ave Maria Law School that Monaghan had founded in Ypsilanti, Michigan. Much of the resistance Monaghan has encountered in founding the university, which included widespread complaints by existing faculty and staff and several legal challenges, centered on his decision to close the Michigan schools and merge them into the new university.

The ongoing involvement of a businessman with no academic background or experience in the management of a university has posed problems for teachers and administrators, given the very different "cultures" that mark the world of entrepreneurship and that of academia. Some of the serious hitches to the foundation of the school—mentioned below—can be traced to the very different expectations that prevail in the business and academic worlds. However, faculty on the new Florida campus report that they are optimistic about the school and praise the "academic freedom" they enjoy, within the gladly accepted parameters of Catholic orthodoxy. Students sound enthusiastic about their classes and speak highly of their skilled teachers, whose course load is light enough that they can offer each student significant personal attention. It seems that after a rocky start,

Ave Maria University is on its way toward living up to its promise.

After several years on an interim campus in Florida, in the fall of 2007 Ave Maria University launched its first semester on the newly constructed campus with a student enrollment of 367. Within just three years, it had nearly doubled its undergraduate enrollment to 710 with another 150 graduate students.

In a promising development, Ave Maria announced in January 2010 that it had hired a new president with extensive academic experience—Jim Towey, former head of the White House Office for Faith-Based and Community Initiatives and president of Saint Vincent College in Latrobe, PA. According to the *National Catholic Register*, Towey also worked closely with Mother Teresa of Calcutta. Towey will also replace Monaghan as CEO of the university, giving him real control over its direction. Towey told the paper: "At Ave Maria, everything is new. What's exciting is that I've had calls from archbishops, cardinals, President Bush and Gov. Bush and many others who know about Ave Maria and are excited about its future. That's encouraging. My local bishop, Cardinal Donald Wuerl, twisted my arm a little bit when I was discerning to take the job. That, to me, is a good sign that so much of America's church leadership is excited about Ave Maria."

Academic Life: From the heart of the church

Although Ave Maria provides a core program steeped in the classical liberal arts, the university offers additional majors not found is some smaller, Great Books–based colleges. Traditional departments such as classics, philosophy, theology, history, literature, mathematics, and politics rub shoulders with disciplines such as biology, chemistry, and economics. In a departure from the typical focus of "alternative" Catholic colleges, Ave Maria also offers preprofessional studies, allowing students to earn certificates in business, prelaw and premedicine. The school also trains future organists and choir directors in its Department of Sacred Music. Summer programs offer intensive courses in language classes such as Ancient Greek and Latin.

The very solid-looking core curriculum, consisting of about sixteen classes, should appeal to anyone looking for a good, traditional grounding in the Western intellectual tradition. The core entails three theology, three philosophy, two Western civilization courses, two literary tradition, and elementary and intermediate Latin courses, with two classes in either

---

VITAL STATISTICS

Religious affiliation: *Roman Catholic*
Total enrollment: *860*
Total undergraduates: *710*
SAT/ACT midranges: CR: *510–640*, M: *480–600*; ACT: *21–26*
Applicants: *1,681*
Applicants accepted: *74%*
Accepted applicants who enrolled: *38%*
Tuition and fees: *$18,025*
Room and board: *$8,350*
Freshman retention rate: *68%*
Graduation rate: *56% (4 yrs.)*
Courses with fewer than 20 students: *27%*
Student-faculty ratio: *10:1*
Courses taught by graduate students: *not provided*
Most popular majors: *English, philosophy, theology*
Students living on campus: *95%*
Guaranteed housing for four years? *yes*
Students in fraternities or sororities: *none*

---

biology, chemistry, or physics, and an American studies class, a math class, and a noncredit liturgical music class.

The theology department is widely viewed by students as one of the university's strongest. Favorite teachers include Fr. Matthew Lamb, William Riordan, and Marc Guerra. Students praise them for their "enthusiasm" and "love for theology."

Ave Maria also offers a distinctive Pre-Theologate Program for men interested in the priesthood or the religious life. In addition to the regular theology requirements, this program offers courses in spiritual and pastoral formation from resident priests and spiritual directors, and mentoring intended to help candidates discern their vocations. A similar program exists for women considering the religious life. Students in the discernment programs live in separate dormitories but are free to mingle with the rest of the students.

Philosophy is cited as another solid major. Students cite the "excellent approach" taken by Maria Fedoryka. Courses in this department include classic subjects such as "Plato and Aristotle" and studies of St. Thomas Aquinas and John Henry Newman, but also "Recent Philosophy" and "Modern and Contemporary Philosophy."

The literature department, headed by Travis Curtright, is probably best known for including the prolific scholar and author Joseph Pearce, Ave Maria's Writer-in-Residence. The literary program includes courses such as "Early Modern Literature," "American Literature," and "Twentieth Century Literature"—a class that at Ave Maria includes, alongside James Joyce and T. S. Eliot, such unjustly neglected Catholic authors as Evelyn Waugh and G. K. Chesterton. Aside from the core courses, the literature major requires classes in medieval literature, Shakespeare, romanticism, American literature, the novel, early modern literature, twentieth century literature, and senior seminars.

Michael Sugrue, chairman of the history department, is highly praised by his colleagues for his teaching and his management of the department—which focuses on the story and civilization of the Christian West. Two core courses are required, as well as a historiography class, a seminar, and an American civilization class. Otherwise, six electives are necessary in a range of classes from ancient and medieval, European and American history. Solid classes include "Renaissance and Reformation and Absolutism" and "The Age of Revolution." The history program also offers a significant range of classes on American history, such as "The American Presidency" and "American Religious History."

The politics major requires "Intro to Political Thought," "Comparative Politics," "American Civilization," "International Relations," "American Government," "Catholic Political Thought," "Constitutional Law," a senior seminar, and two electives in various areas. Some recent electives were "American Foreign Policy" and "The Holocaust."

The newer Department of Sacred Music, headed by Dr. Susan Treacy, centers squarely on the traditions that grew up around the Roman Catholic liturgy and includes classes such as "Heritage of Sacred Music," "Choral Conducting," and "Gregorian Chant." Students and some faculty say that the department "needs more funding" and a "narrower focus."

The department of biology and chemistry places the school's theological mission at the forefront, stating on its website:

South

The study of science is born from the conviction of the fundamental intelligibility of the world. Science at Ave Maria University testifies to the Catholic Church's confidence in human reason and in its ability to know the truth about God's creation even apart from the illuminating power of grace. The natural sciences are not simply technological disciplines, but are truly liberal arts education in which we seek to know truth for its own sake. By enabling us to enter the simultaneous complexity and simplicity of physical reality, science instills within the students a deep sense of wonder at the natural universe.

Very promising. Recent graduates of this AMU department have been admitted to graduate programs at Michigan State and Boston universities and the University of Sussex, England.

Recommended teachers in other departments include biology and chemistry professor James Peliska, who is cited as a good mentor for premed students; "influential" math-

---

ACADEMIC REQUIREMENTS

The core required of all liberal arts students includes:

- Three courses in theology: "Sacred Scripture," "Sacred Doctrine," and "Living in Christ: Moral Theology," which includes Augustine's *Confessions* and selections from the *Summa* of St. Thomas Aquinas.
- Three classes in philosophy: "Ethics," with a heavy emphasis on Augustine and Aquinas as well as some modern alternatives, "Nature and Person," a look at the ancient and medieval understanding of the human being and the philosophy of nature, and "Philosophical Perspective: Metaphysics," especially Thomistic-Aristotelian metaphysics.
- Three courses in history: "Western Civilization" I, which gives a look at the Christian West from paganism to the Middle Ages; "Western Civilization" II, which tracks history "from the sixteenth century to the present covering the Protestant, Scientific, Industrial, and French Revolutions, the Napoleonic and Romantic era, the age of nationalism, and the often-troubled twentieth century"; and "American Civilization."
- Two semesters of literature: "Literary Tradition" I, the foundational epics of the West, looking at Homer, Virgil, and some of the Greek tragedies, and the class "Literary Tradition" II, which looks more at the Christian tradition in Dante, *Beowulf*, Shakespeare, and Milton.
- Four terms of Latin.
- One class in mathematics. Students may select from "Number Magnitude, Form," "Finite Mathematics," "Functions," and "Calculus" I & II.
- Two science classes. Students may select from among "Concepts in Biology" I & II, "General Biology" I & II, "General Chemistry" I & II, "College Physics" I & II, and "University Physics" I & II.
- Two noncredit practica in the fine arts, including a class in Gregorian Chant, followed by a course of the student's choice in chorus, instrumental music, studio art, dance, or theater.

South

ematics teacher Michael Marsalli; and economics chair Gabriel Martinez, who is praised for sharing with students an understanding of both the practical and the ethical aspects of business. This squares well with one of university founder Monaghan's aspirations: in addition to the school, he helped created Legatus, a national organization of Catholic businessmen devoted to charitable and ecclesial works.

Alongside these solid academic departments, there lingers turmoil that dates from the school's relocation and other policy decisions. The university's administrative staff suffers from high turnover, as members resign unexpectedly or are quietly released. Students report that administration members are keenly aware of their public perception in the academic community, which leads to an excessive concern (in one student's words) for "trying not to look 'fringe.'" Some higher-ups at the school are described by students as "paranoid" and "controlling," while lower-level staff members are reportedly "friendly and helpful" but "tight-lipped"—citing fears of dismissal.

The university drew criticism from students, donors, and parents after Fr. Joseph Fessio, the spiritual provost of the university, a longtime friend of Pope Benedict XVI, and the founder of Ignatius Press, was asked in March 2007 to resign and ordered to leave the campus because of disagreements with staff directives. Nearly the entire student body rebelled and gathered on campus to protest the decision and demand Fessio's reinstatement. Shortly afterward, the president, Nick Healy (who is unpopular among the students), announced that Fessio would be allowed back at the university as a "designated theologian in residence." Fessio then was dismissed again from Ave Maria before the start of the 2009–10 school year. He has not returned, nor plans to; he attributes the split to "irreconcilable administrative differences."

Teachers we contacted described themselves as contented and were reluctant to criticize university staff or the university—although several acknowledged unspecified "difficulties" within the administration. But one faculty member insisted, "Although the next few years will also have their own troubles, I think that the faculty and staff that we have now are optimistic and hard-working, the more so because we have hoped high and endured."

Despite these growing pains, the school keeps its promise about the type of education it offers. Its students enjoy the facilities of a university as well as the intimacy of a small liberal arts college with a highly qualified faculty. The student-faculty ratio is a strong 10 to 1, and the average class size is seventeen. Although a significant portion of the faculty is young, more than 90 percent of the full-time faculty possess a doctorate.

Students report an excellent relationship with faculty members. One undergrad cites "professors who are very concerned about their individual students and willing to dedicate a great deal of time and effort to helping them grasp the material." Another noted that his teachers reach beyond the classroom, to assist with students' spiritual and personal formation. "There is a great deal of nonacademic camaraderie between the students and the faculty, staff and their families."

First-year students are assigned an advisor from among the full-time faculty. Advisors "provide guidance with everything from course selection at registration, to choosing a major field, to career investigation." Then, if a student picks a major in which his advisor does not teach, he may get a different advisor within that field.

South

The university also offers a graduate program in theology, and two highly praised study-abroad programs—at Ave Maria's campus in Nicaragua and a program in Rome, Italy. The university has a Language Learning Center that provides computer-based study of Latin, Ancient Greek, Spanish, and French. It also supplies supplementary materials for Arabic, Chinese, French, German, Ancient-Greek, Italian, Latin, Russian, and Spanish programs. Both study-abroad programs are conducted in English.

Student Life: Tropical chastity

In 2007, students streamed into their new campus, which boasts a large three-story academic building, with new offices for the faculty, classrooms, a lecture hall, and state-of-the-art science labs. The school also boasts a shiny new student center containing a cafeteria, game rooms, a big (and aggressively ugly) chapel, a ballroom, and offices. The newly constructed Canizaro Library has the capacity to hold 400,000 volumes.

GREEN LIGHT

Ave Maria University combines a strong curriculum with a spirit of "joyful fidelity to the Magisterium of the Catholic Church." Unlike the vast majority of American Catholic colleges, Ave Maria follows the Vatican directive *Ex Corde Ecclesiae* and arranges for its theology faculty to obtain the *mandatum* from the local bishop, affirming their adherence to official church teaching. The college faculty publicly offers a Profession of Faith and an Oath of Fidelity to the Church at the beginning of every academic year.

Whatever its growing pains, Ave Maria provides a wholesome and hopeful environment for deeply committed Catholics to obtain a liberal arts education among like-minded people. Non-Catholics or dissenting Catholics would likely find the environment somewhat stifling—especially given the school's geographical isolation.

The campus has five single-sex dorms—two for women, three for men—with a total capacity of about 1,000 students. More than half of this became available in September 2009 with the opening of the school's "mega dorm." Intervisitation in common areas of the dorms is permitted from 9:00 AM to 1:00 AM. Sundays through Thursdays, and 9:00 AM to 2:00 AM on weekends. One student reports she is satisfied with the limitations, reporting that "it allows interaction with members of a different sex, while creating a healthy atmosphere that encourages chastity." Another student reports, "The RAs are very nice and very approachable, and there is a great dorm life. Everyone knows each other and talks." Some 95 percent of undergraduate students live on campus, and the dorms are reputedly excellent. Off-campus living is possible but pricey.

Some students report that it's "difficult to find things to do" on the weekends, noting that Naples, Florida, is a 45-minute drive. The town offers shopping, dining, and entertainment, as well as many golf courses and white beaches. Some students travel to the Everglades National Park for recreational activity.

Student organizations on campus include yearbook, tennis, and drama clubs; the Knights of Columbus; and various faith outreach groups, including the Chastity Team (not affiliated with the NCAA). There are no College Democrats or Republicans, and the closest thing to political organizations on campus are the Students for Life and the Thomas More

South

Debate Society. New athletic facilities support two soccer fields, a baseball diamond, basketball courts, and tennis courts. An ice skating club exists as well.

Other activities on campus include dances throughout the year, concerts, and intramural sports. The university supports club sports in women's basketball, soccer, volleyball, and cross-country, while men's club sports include basketball, soccer, and golf.

Liturgical opportunities include daily Divine Office (lauds, vespers, and compline), and daily Mass. Masses including Latin rub shoulders with charismatic and healing liturgies. Priests are available for confession, spiritual direction, and counseling. Student traditions include a community-wide Rosary walk every evening.

Security patrols the campus at all times, and students report it to be "very safe." In 2009, the only crimes reported on campus were two sexual assaults.

Tuition for 2010–11 was $18,025, while housing and meals added up to $8,350. Eighty-seven percent of students receive need-based financial aid.

Belmont Abbey College

Belmont, North Carolina • www.belmontabbeycollege.edu

The rule

Founded in 1876 by the Order of St. Benedict, Belmont Abbey is one of a small band of Catholic colleges that still adheres closely to its mission and identity. Its current president, Dr. William Thierfelder, a former Olympic runner and two-time All-American NCAA coach, has led a renaissance at Belmont Abbey that is reflected in an enrollment that doubled, an increase in academic assistance and sports programs, as well as a $14 million endowment and a new chapel. A faculty member says that under Thierfelder, "The school is becoming more liberal-arts minded." The monastic community continues to serve as the bulwark of the college. Benedictines sponsor the school, serve on its board of trustees, and teach. Its Catholic identity is further enhanced by the college's conformity with Pope John Paul II's 1990 decree *Ex Corde Ecclesiae*, which requires that theology faculty affirm their fidelity to church teaching and gain approval of local bishops. Belmont is one of the few American Catholic colleges to obey this Vatican mandate.

Academic Life: Monks and motorsports

Belmont's core curriculum is rooted in philosophy, theology, and the classical liberal arts, bracketed by a First-Year Symposium and a Great Books capstone course. Together, these guarantee that students have a broad exposure to Western civilization and Catholic thought.

At Belmont, teaching is of paramount importance, and it comprises "a principal factor in tenure decisions," one professor says. Many faculty have received honors for the quality of their instruction, including National Endowment for the Humanities and Fulbright fellowships. All professors carry a four-course load. As a result, a teacher wrote, "There does not appear to be much time for research." Another professor mourns that "our teachers are very busy preparing classes, grading papers, and attending meetings. These are the pressures which diminish the vigor of debate and (unfortunately) make philosophic and political discussion sometimes difficult to find time for."

One student says: "Teachers in accounting are remarkable for their hard work and clear articulation of concepts. Teachers in the theology department are exemplars of Christian virtue and take a keen and involved interest in all aspects of student life. Members

VITAL STATISTICS

Religious affiliation: *Roman Catholic*

Total enrollment: *1,638*

Total undergraduates: *1,638*

SAT/ACT midranges: CR: *440–580,* M: *450–570*; ACT: *20–28*

Applicants: *1,763*

Applicants accepted: *75%*

Accepted applicants who enrolled: *31%*

Tuition and fees: *$25,930*

Room and board: *$10,094*

Freshman retention rate: *59%*

Graduation rate: *43% (4 yrs.), 49% (6 yrs.)*

Courses with fewer than 20 students: *96%*

Student-faculty ratio: *16:1*

Courses taught by graduate students: *none*

Most popular majors: *business/management, education, accounting*

Students living on campus: *40%*

Guaranteed housing for four years? *yes*

Students in fraternities: *40%* in sororities: *30%*

of the business, psychology, and biology departments are indefatigable. . . . Students under their care and instruction have made remarkable progress as behavioral psychologists and natural scientists. There is a palpable collegiality."

The senior faculty members of the English department are known for their strong commitment to teaching. A sophomore notes, "So far, I have found only positive things through my faculty interactions. The courses are pretty basic: American Lit, Southern Lit, English Lit, Romantics, Shakespeare, Chaucer, et cetera." Requirements for majors are solid, calling for twelve literature courses, including "Literature of the English Renaissance," "Restoration and Eighteenth-Century British Literature," "Shakespeare," and "Literary Criticism." In addition, the major requires foreign language study and upper-level classes in history, philosophy, and theology.

One professor says that the political science department is "particularly strong due to the broad educational grounding of its members . . . steeped in the study of primary texts. The department places special importance upon the study of the American founding and critical moments in American political history: to the Declaration of Independence, the American Constitution, the *Federalist Papers*, Lincoln's speeches, and Progressive writings." Trendy classes do not get in the way. "Novelty is not big on this campus," says a professor. "There are no feminist, ethnic, or gay and lesbian studies here." Political science majors must complete introductory classes in political science and economics, as well as upper-level classes in comparative government, constitutional law, classical and modern political philosophy, international relations, and five upper-level electives.

Biology is a department noted for its family atmosphere, its excellent teaching, its rigorous courses, and an annual camping trip.

The philosophy department stresses breadth of knowledge and depth of analysis. Students study logic, ethics, metaphysics, and epistemology. With relatively few majors, advanced courses are taught on a cyclical basis—so a student might have to wait a few semesters for a course. Theology majors become well-acquainted with the Catholic tradition, sources say.

Admirably, the history department requires majors to take two survey courses each in "World Civilization" and "United States History," plus six more intermediate-level courses and two seminars, as well as two foreign language classes and upper-level classes in English, philosophy, and theology.

South

The school has taken advantage of its location near NASCAR's headquarters to create a Motorsports Management Program—the first of its kind. It is swiftly growing in size and prestige. A participant writes, "The board of directors is basically a 'who's who' of motorsports. The contacts that can be made in the industry are unlike anything else. Also, the internships that are required are incredible opportunities."

The Honors Institute at the Abbey provides students with up to $20,000 in scholarships annually and allows them to work with faculty on independent study projects and to engage in cultural activities outside the classroom. A student must maintain a minimum GPA of 3.4 in order to remain in the program. One of these fourteen honors students exclaims, "The Honors Institute here at Belmont is wonderful! It is not for the fainthearted, however! We concentrate on Plato, Aristophanes, Aquinas, Aristotle, Augustine, Bacon, Hobbes, Machiavelli. At no or minimal cost, we attend arts events throughout the semester, such as operas, ballets, and concerts." Honors professors receive high reviews from colleagues and students alike. Says one faculty member, "I have been impressed with the care and professionalism that Dr. Gene Thuot brings to the Honors Program he directs." Another highly praised honors professor is Michael Hood.

Teachers praised by students include Elizabeth Baker, Sheila Reilly, and Robert Tompkins in biology; Simon Donoghue in theater; Michael Hood and Mary Ellen Weir in English; Jane Russell, O.S.F., and David Williams in theology; Stephen Brosnan in mathematics and physics; and Angela Blackwood in accounting.

First-Year Symposium instructors serve as primary academic advisors for students. After a student declares a major, a professor from within the department will become his advisor. Each semester, the student must meet with him to discuss his choice of coursework. Students find the Academic Resource Center very useful. The center offers tutoring by faculty in core subjects such as math, biology, and English composition.

Despite a student-faculty ratio of 16 to 1, only 4 percent of classes contain more than thirty students, and the school maintains an average class size of seventeen. Strong relationships are fostered between professors and their charges. A professor says that John Henry Newman's motto, "heart speaks to heart," could describe faculty-student relationships at the Abbey.

An administrator notes, "Our study-abroad program has become more extensive over the past three years and is in the course of further expansion." Currently, it offers lan-

SUGGESTED CORE

1. English 201, World Literature (closest match)
2. Honors 288, History of Ideas I (Classical and Christian Perspectives)
3. Theology 105, Introduction to Scripture
4. Honors 240, Classics of Christian Theology & Spirituality or Government and Political Philosophy 402, Medieval Political Philosophy
5. Political Science 402, Modern Political Philosophy or Honors 289, History of Ideas II (Modern Perspectives)
6. English 410/411: Shakespeare: Tragedies/Comedies
7. History 203: U.S. History, 1492–1877
8. Honors 289, History of Ideas II (Modern Perspectives) or Government and Political Philosophy 404, Late Modern Political Philosophy

South

457

guage, business, history, and science programs in a number of locations, including Germany, India, Europe, Guatemala, and Peru. While the language studies program offers no majors, introductory and intermediate courses are taught in Spanish, French, Italian, and Latin. The school provides language-intensive studies overseas, as well as an International Leadership Semester in Rome and the School of Field Studies.

Student Life: Snowball fights with monks

Students overwhelmingly report that Belmont Abbey is a welcoming place, in part thanks to the hospitality of its ubiquitous monks. One student remarks, "Something that I've found very neat is the way the monks are so involved with the school. They are regularly walking around campus, eating with us in the cafeteria, or sitting in on a few of our classes." Says another, "The Benedictine commitment to hospitality affects everyone, even if you aren't Catholic. It's all about meeting each person as if he were Christ. Everyone here is trying to treat people that way, living so that 'in all things, God may be glorified.' And that means, for instance, trying to keep the bathrooms clean!"

A teacher says, "The student is encouraged to come here and learn how to be a good person in every way, to seek excellence in virtue . . . and to make the most of what they have been given. The emphasis at Belmont is on a balance of all the elements that make up the human person."

The quaint town of Belmont (pop. 15,000) is ten miles west and across the Catawba River from Charlotte, the largest city in the Carolinas and the "melting pot" of the South. The town's streets are lined with mansions surrounded by lilac, magnolia, and dogwood trees. Stowe Park, in the downtown area, is the site of special events like concerts and movies. Belmont is located two hours from the Great Smoky Mountains and four hours from the North Carolina Coast.

The Abbey's 650-acre wooded campus is home to the Belmont Abbey Monastery, the Saint Joseph Adoration Chapel, the Lourdes Grotto, and the Abbey Basilica. Most of the Gothic Revival buildings were designed and built by the monks themselves in the nineteenth century. The monks host thousands of visitors each year who come for tours and retreats.

For many of the students, the two dozen or so monks on campus are confessors, counselors, mentors, and friends who make the college a "real home away from home," as a student reports. A senior wrote in the *Crusader* student newspaper, "I love the fact that we get to learn from, take classes with, go on retreats with, eat with, watch basketball games with, laugh at, get into snowball fights with, cheer for, and mourn with the monks."

A resident remarks, "It's a beautiful campus, with brick Gothic architecture, lush landscaping, yet you can see Charlotte on the horizon." Says another insider, "There's lots to like here. It's a unique, warm, and friendly place, full of very nice people; there's a real atmosphere of peace, harmony, and spiritual goodness. The location is superb and physically beautiful; it's right off the highway and close to shopping centers and cultural events, but also has lovely architecture, tall old trees, and the charm of a little town."

The U.S. National Whitewater Center and Olympic Training Center sits across the

South

Catawba River from the school. This public park offers the facilities and amenities of an outdoor recreational center with a custom-made white-water river.

Almost 90 percent of freshmen—but fewer than half of upperclassmen—live on campus. Housing includes three residence halls and a four-building apartment complex where men and women live on separate floors. Overnight guests in student housing can stay only with students of the same sex. Visitation hours stop at midnight, and at 2:00 AM on weekends. A student comments, "The resident assistants are very helpful and do a very good

ACADEMIC REQUIREMENTS

Belmont Abbey's core is designed to familiarize students with the history, philosophy, and fundamental beliefs of Western civilization, as well as with the life and Rule of St. Benedict. All students must complete:

- "First-Year Symposium."
- "Writing on Contemporary Issues" and "Argumentative Prose."
- Philosophy 101: "Logic."
- Either "Mathematics for Liberal Arts," "Algebra for Sciences/Finance," "Trigonometry and Pre-Calculus," or any intermediate-level math, statistics, or calculus course.
- "Christian Thought: Early and Medieval" and "Christian Thought: Reformation and Modern."
- Either "Introduction to Philosophy: Ancient and Medieval" or "Introduction to Philosophy: Modern and Contemporary."
- Philosophy 250: "Ethics."
- Either "World Civilization" I & II or "American History" I & II.
- Either "World Literature" or "American Literature."
- English 202: "English Literature."
- One course in fine arts. Options include "Introduction to Stage Craft," "Introduction to Art in Western Civilization," and "Creative Writing," among others.
- Either "Natural World," "Cell Biology," or "Organismal Diversity."
- Either "General Chemistry," "General Physics" I, or "Physical World."
- Political Science 201: "American Government."
- Either "Introductory Economics" I, "Introductory Psychology," or "Principles of Sociology."
- At least one course designated as writing intensive.
- Any course that meets the "Global Perspective" criteria (including intermediate history or English courses or introductory art classes), an intermediate-level modern language, or five weeks or more of study abroad.
- "Great Books Capstone."
- Work demonstrating basic computer competency—either by passing a competency exam, taking a basic computer course, or a technology-intensive class in their major.

Students who wish to receive a "Community Service" designation on their transcript must complete ten hours of approved community service per semester (formerly a requirement for all students at the college).

GREEN LIGHT

There is a widespread atmosphere of acceptance and inclusion on campus. Administrators relate, "Students will find that we Catholics at Belmont are peculiarly open to discussion; if we are all seeking truth together, there should be no problem wherever we're going." That commitment to open inquiry is substantial: Belmont Abbey continues to impress those looking for a faithful Catholic environment. Recently, the school eliminated health care coverage for procedures and devices that violate church teachings—such as abortion, contraception, and sterilization. Despite being threatened with lawsuits, the college has maintained its stance, insisting that obedience to church teachings is precisely what makes the college Catholic. Yet just 55 or 60 percent of students at the college identify as Catholics, and the school's ability to balance its Catholic commitments with an approach that welcomes non-Catholics is a testament to its strength.

One teacher says, "Belmont is a comfortable mix of everything from orthodox Catholics to open atheists. This has provided wonderful interreligious discussions inside and outside of the classroom." His colleague agrees: "There is no department where conservative or religious students would feel unwelcome. . . . While there are liberal-minded and conservative-minded professors here, they do not impose their personal ideologies in the classroom." Yet another faculty member relates, "I am not Catholic, and I have felt welcome in all circumstances on campus. And to my knowledge, students do not feel excluded because of their faith, or lack of it.

job." Extramarital sexual activity is forbidden by the school, and violators of the policy face punishments, which can include expulsion.

Some students choose to live in close proximity to other students in "households," faith-sharing groups in the residence halls, or apartment buildings. Some 30 percent of women and 40 percent of men belong to one of the four sororities and three fraternities.

The dormitories have come in for some criticism; one inmate recounts, "Although recently renovated, the dorms leave much to be desired. It's a beautiful campus with historic, pretty buildings, but unfortunately that means the dorms are also old." While a bit small, dorms are pleasantly community-centered: they are module-suite style, with a hallway, four rooms, and a bathroom, and are connected to a quad. This common area is "the place where students come together to play sports, strum guitars, or walk out on balconies."

Students are expected to follow school guidelines on conduct between men and women and appropriate attire. Neatness, cleanliness, and good taste are the guiding norms for dress on campus.

At Belmont Abbey, alcohol is not permitted in public areas of residence halls; however, twenty-one-year-old students are free to imbibe in their rooms. Kegs, bars, drinking games, and punch containing alcohol are prohibited on campus. Events serving alcohol with more than fifteen guests require at least one campus police officer. "Wet" events are limited to four hours.

The College Union Board sponsors social weekends, dances, comedians, musical performers, coffeehouse performances, lectures, and other special events. Additional groups include the Student Government Association, Senior Class Counsel, Military Science and Leadership Group, International Club, the *Agora* (a literary magazine), the

Crusader (student newspaper), chess club, Quilting Outreach Program, Democratic and Republican clubs, Elite Dance Team, Crusaders for Life, the Abbey Cheerleaders, and the Abbey Pep Band, to name a few. Students gather frequently at the Holy Grounds coffee shop for socializing.

A sophomore remarks, "There's a lot of fun community service events, plenty of intramural sports to choose from, Greek life, households . . . and if they don't have a particular group, they'll probably help you form it."

The monks gather in the Abbey Basilica to pray the canonical hours or celebrate Mass four times a day. The students are under the spiritual care of the monks, and adoration and confession are offered daily. Each year a group of faculty, staff, monks, and students attend the March for Life in Washington. The Felix Hintemeyer Catholic Leadership Award provides full scholarships for qualifying students.

Sports is a particular passion of the college president, who wants nothing less than a "fantastic reputation" for athletes of Belmont. Belmont Abbey College Crusaders participate in the NCAA Division II, Carolinas Virginia Athletic Conference (CVAC). Abbey Athletics consists of eighteen varsity teams and two men's junior varsity teams (baseball and basketball). The Crusaders compete at the varsity level in men's and women's lacrosse, basketball, cross-country, golf, soccer, baseball/softball, tennis, and track and field. Additionally, men may wrestle, while women can play volleyball.

Intramural sports programs include dodgeball, bowling, Ultimate Frisbee, ping-pong, Texas hold 'Em, Wiffle ball, billiards, and basketball. The renovated Wheeler Athletic Center has a new fitness center, an athletic training facility, and auxiliary gyms.

Students can call campus police for escorts twenty-four hours a day, year round. Incidents of crime are quite low; in 2009, the school reported a single arson as the only major crime on campus. Says one student, "I feel very safe here as a lone female walking around campus. The campus police are on duty all the time; it's a small campus, so they tend to know if you aren't supposed to be there. Of course, it's not good to leave your dorm rooms open, or an iPod in an open car. Still, the campus police are generally quick to deal with incidents."

Tuition in 2010–11 was $25,930 for entering students, with room and board ranging from $10,094 to $10,774. Some 64 percent of students at the college receive need-based financial aid. The average student-loan debt of a 2010 graduate was $21,000.

Berry College

Rome, Georgia • www.berry.edu

Nestled in the South

Founded as a boys school in a war-torn part of Georgia by Miss Martha McChesney Berry in 1902, Berry became a four-year college in 1930. A little more than an hour northeast of suburban Atlanta, Berry College is a charming school that has remained somewhat hidden over the years. Berry boasts a fine, committed faculty, and one that's less afflicted with postmodern pathologies than the staff at better-known colleges. Particularly impressive is the refreshing campus climate, where students are friendly and professors for the most part care about their students' educations.

Academic Life: Diamonds in the kudzu

Berry College's academic requirements cannot pass muster as a core; however, they are more rigorous than at most schools. General education requirements consist of a list of courses chosen from four broad academic areas: three courses in communications, three courses in behavioral and social sciences, five in the humanities, four in mathematics and the natural sciences, and two electives outside a student's major. In addition, students must take three (shorter) health and physical education courses. The most politicized classes, sources report, are the two required English composition courses (English 101 and 102) and the mandatory class, "Introduction to Speech." One faculty member says the English composition sequence is where "virtually all the professors favor students who adopt their views. Not surprisingly, these courses are the least popular at Berry." Fortunately, that's the worst curricular silliness you're likely find at Berry; there are so far no schoolwide requirements at Berry for gender, multicultural, or diversity studies.

The religion and philosophy department offers a "solid curriculum based on the study of the great books of the Western philosophical canon," says a professor. Says another, "There's a strange kind of academic freedom that comes from being neither a state school nor a denominational school—in combination with a relatively diverse but still very liberal faculty and basically conservative students. It's one of the few places where both sides of *Roe v. Wade* can be discussed in class." Majors take an introductory class, a course in critical thinking or symbolic logic, and one course each in ancient/medieval philosophy and modern philosophy. This curriculum provides a solid overview of the discipline and "successfully avoids the twin perils of an overly analytic approach that ignores the history of the subject and of trendy Continental postmodernism," the professor adds. The department is quite small, with just five associated faculty members—one student called it "claustrophobic"—but students and faculty value the rigorous courses and praise those who teach them. "The religion-in-life program is especially vital," says one professor, who reports that he finds "faith flourishing" there.

The history department at Berry is also small, with only four full-time faculty members, but it too wins accolades. As one professor tells us, "Courses that may not be so fashionable elsewhere (e.g., military history) are offered regularly." Another says the department "has almost no 'social history' and is strong in both American and medieval." Here majors are required to take strong survey courses in "World History to 1550," "World History since 1550," "American History to 1877," "American History since 1877," and "Historiography," plus three upper-level electives in both American and European and/or world history.

The English department is a mixed bag. It is said to be plagued with political correctness; there is a required multicultural literature class, and some determined professors use any and all teaching material to promote their private agendas, students report. However, the department offers many solid courses, and the requirements for a major are quite comprehensive and traditional. English majors must complete an introductory course and a course on the "Western Literary Tradition," as well as one class each in pre-1800 British and post-1800 British literature, American literature, multicultural literature, and a senior-level class ("Studies in Cinema," "Studies in Southern Literature," "Studies in Genre," for example). The department requires students to concentrate in literature, secondary education, or writing; the literature concentration does plump up the major's requirements, adding a course in Shakespeare, one more course each in British and American literature, and an additional senior-level class.

According to one faculty member, there are a number of excellent teachers in the government and international studies department. Students should seek out the courses that focus on "philosophy, the connections between religion and politics, [and] the American founding." Students majoring in government must complete a departmental curriculum that includes "American National Government" and "Ancient Political Philosophy" in addition to several other worthy courses.

VITAL STATISTICS

Religious affiliation: *none*
Total enrollment: *1,922*
Total undergraduates: *1,777*
SAT/ACT midranges: CR: *520–640*, M: *510–610*; ACT: *22–28*
Applicants: *2,412*
Applicants accepted: *67%*
Accepted applicants who enrolled: *35%*
Tuition and fees: *$24,620*
Room and board: *$7,979*
Freshman retention rate: *74%*
Graduation rate: *48% (4 yrs.), 59% (6 yrs.)*
Courses with fewer than 20 students: *65%*
Student-faculty ratio: *12:1*
Courses taught by graduate students: *none*
Most popular majors: *education, communications, animal science*
Students living on campus: *91%*
Guaranteed housing for four years? *yes*
Students in fraternities or sororities: *none*

In the sciences, the physics department is particularly strong, with faculty members who are active researchers as well as devoted teachers. "They approach physics as an integral part of the liberal arts," says a Berry professor. The college's first-rate program in animal science boasts a high student acceptance rate into veterinary school and is one of Berry's most popular majors. A professor in another department calls Berry's animal science program "the best in the country connected with a four-year college." All the natural sciences offer excellent facilities: the Berry College Science Center cost $25 million when it was built in 2001, and the science departments have nicknamed the Berry campus a "26,000-acre lab."

Weaker areas at Berry include the education program, which is the school's most popular major. It is "good at placing graduates in schools but has the same problems and deficiencies as education schools elsewhere," says a faculty member. Marketing and management in the business school contain "the highest concentration of deadwood at the college," says a teacher. Other disciplines in the business school, such as economics and accounting, get higher marks.

Another strong program is the communications department, which is both academically sound and politically diverse, a professor tells us. Berry also offers preprofessional classes in dentistry, law, medicine, pharmacy, and veterinary medicine; however, faculty members tell us that students majoring in the humanities tend to be much more intellectually curious than their preprofessional peers.

Overall, departments are small, and the pickings for courses sometimes tend to be slim. But with just 1,777 undergraduates, Berry College can offer a student-faculty ratio of 12 to 1. Faculty members are required to hold ten hours per week of office time in order to be available to students, but many are even more accessible than that. As a professor in the humanities school explains, "Faculty here tend to 'be around' and to give students lots of attention. The result is we have 'high maintenance' students—in the good sense, and there's a real academic culture here." At least one student agrees, "Trust me, it would be hard to find a more helpful and willing bunch of professors."

Highly praised professors include Peter Lawler and Eric Sands in government; Chaitram Singh and Kirsten Taylor in international relations; Jonathan Atkins and Larry Marvin in history; Bob Frank ("a legendary teacher") and Randy Richardson ("one of the country's best forensics coaches") in communications; Gary Roseman in economics; Thomas Carnes in accounting; and Michael Papazian in philosophy.

The most willing students can be found in the college's honors program, which requires an ongoing 3.5 grade point average. One faculty member says the honors pro-

South

gram is particularly strong at the freshman level, when students are required to complete two three-credit honors colloquia. The first is "Perennial Questions," which focuses on the Great Books and ideas of the West. "My students read Aristophanes, Sophocles, Plato, and the Bible," says a professor. The second colloquium is called "Democracy and Its Friendly Critics" and concentrates on the American founding and the writings of de Tocqueville. An honors student says this course made "a great use of literature to help us build our understanding of democratic society." Additionally, honors students take three seminars together (most of which fulfill general education requirements) and then, as juniors and seniors, two honors thesis courses that culminate in a traditional research paper or some other "performative effort." Seniors defend their theses during their last semester at Berry.

The honors program provides a unique exchange opportunity at the University of Glasgow, where students take "The Ideas and Influences of the Scottish Enlightenment" as well as two or three classes in their major or minor. Other study-abroad programs are offered around the world, from Egypt to New Zealand. Berry also helps students find international internships in a number of subject areas and service opportunities around the world.

When it comes to foreign languages, the school is very limited: Berry offers only Spanish, French, and German. Students majoring in foreign languages are strongly encouraged to study abroad in France, Germany, Spain, or Central or South America.

Student Life: Chicken people

The student body has grown lately at Berry College, as has the number of white-tailed deer. In fact, with a population estimated at around 2,500, they outnumber the humans at Berry. They certainly have plenty of space: Berry's is the largest contiguous campus in the country at more than 26,000 acres of mostly forest land, much of which the Georgia Department of Natural Resources oversees. In some specified areas, hunters are permitted in order to keep the deer population in check. The enormous campus is ideal for outdoorsy students, who take advantage of trails for hiking, mountain biking, and horseback riding. The school's Society of Outdoor Life and Exploration (SOLE) helps coordinate recreation opportunities on and off campus.

Many of the buildings on campus are stately stone structures modeled on those at Oxford. Berry recently finished two residential halls and the much-needed Stephen J. Cage Athletic and Recreation Center, which opened in January 2008. Two years later, Kilpatrick Commons, an outdoor facility with ponds, a footbridge, and a waterfall, was completed, offering students a lovely area near the student and Cage centers.

Berry has more than outdoor beauty and an abundance of deer. It also has "chicken people." That's the campus term for those fortunate students who have gotten scholarships from WinShape, the charitable foundation of the Chick-fil-A restaurants. At Berry, 125 students receive a $4,000 per year scholarship toward the cost of tuition. (Berry often supplements the scholarship with additional aid.) The grant requires attendance at weekly meetings, participation at regular leadership discussion groups and in community service, and the practice of a "Christian lifestyle." Although Chick-fil-A work experience is no longer required for recipients, it is preferred.

South

WinShape students live in separate dormitories on Berry's "mountain campus," which is three miles from the main Berry College campus; according to one student, they are sometimes seen as isolated and cliquish. WinShape students are usually strong evangelical Christians who are "required to abide by a more stringent code of conduct than the other students," says a professor. This code includes a pledge to refrain from alcohol and drugs. "The WinShape students make the student body overall more conservative than it would otherwise be," he adds. "And they provide a welcome form of diversity to the college, though many of my colleagues do not share this view." The WinShape Foundation also hosts church, corporate, and marriage-enrichment retreats, as well as summer camps, at its 300-person retreat center, which is located on the Berry College campus.

Berry College students must attend a minimum of twenty-four cultural events (three per semester) in order to qualify for graduation. Qualifying cultural events for a recent semester include a soup cookoff that raised money for Ugandan orphans, readings from contemporary fairy tale authors and poets, the college symphony's fall concert, a "What Is Culture?" photo exhibit, and numerous theatrical events and discussion groups. Students say that there is always something worth doing on campus—get-togethers, concerts, campus activities, and club meetings.

A number of academic and professional organizations add to the Berry curriculum. The school hosts a Model United Nations, Politics and Law Society, Forensic Union for debaters, Astronomical Society, and Block and Bridle club for animal science students. Campus media groups include the *Cabin Log* yearbook, *Campus Carrier* newspaper, *Ramifications* literary magazine, and Viking Fusion multimedia group, which maintains a news and entertainment website.

The college does sponsor a few multicultural organizations (a Black Student Alliance, Hispanic culture group, and international club) and several political organizations:

ACADEMIC REQUIREMENTS

- Three courses in communication, including a two-course English composition sequence and "Introduction to Speech," a public-speaking class.
- Three classes in behavioral and social sciences. Choices come from a short list of courses that includes "American National Government," "Principles of Economics," "Contemporary World Issues," and "Cultural Anthropology."
- Five courses in the humanities. Qualifying classes range much too widely (any intermediate-level literature course or introductory religion or philosophy course suffices) but mostly consist of solid choices such as "Masterpieces of World Literature," "World History Since 1550," and "Appreciation of Music."
- One mathematics course and two laboratory sciences chosen from different disciplines (biology, chemistry, geology, or physics/astronomy).
- One health course such as "First-Aid" or "Self-Defense for Women," and two additional activity courses, such as rock climbing, ballroom dancing, or tennis.
- Two courses outside the student's major.

South

Amnesty International, College Republicans and Young Democrats, EMPOWER women's group, and Students Against Violating the Earth all have a presence on campus. Performing arts groups include the College Theater Company, men's and women's singing ensembles, and a women's dance team.

In the summer of 2009, Berry College became a provisional member of the NCAA Division III, while the college now holds dual membership in both the NCAA and the NAIA. The Berry College Vikings and Lady Vikings play in blue and silver on seventeen different teams. Men and women compete in basketball, cross-country and track, golf, lacrosse, soccer, swimming and diving, and tennis, while men play baseball and women are offered equestrian sports and softball. Club sports hosted by the school include men's soccer, rowing crew, and Ultimate Frisbee. Intramural sports include dodgeball, soccer, beach volleyball, innertube water polo, and racquetball. The school's Society of Outdoor Life and Exploration program offers climbing, caving, and hiking excursions for free or at nominal cost, camping-equipment rental, trips to professional sporting events, hammocks for those who need a break between classes, and seasonal activities like a corn maze in the fall.

Berry promotes service activities through groups like Kiwanis, Habitat for Humanity, and Rotary club. Many Berry students choose to aid their communities through the Bonner Center for Community Engagement, which sponsors a school-mentoring program, a Toys for Tots drive, and an Alzheimer's walk. Volunteer work begins in September with the First-Year Service Day, when freshmen work on area projects such as cleaning up local streams and painting playground equipment. The well-endowed Bonner Scholars Program helps students pay for school; Bonner Scholars must contribute at least ten hours of community service per week and demonstrate financial need.

Although it is not a distinctly Christian school, Berry retains its initial commitment to "the furthering of Christian values." The school pledges "an interdenominational, ecumenical approach to Christian faith and values," and most religious opportunities at Berry are Christian. A Baptist Student Union, Canterbury Club Episcopal group, Fellowship of Christian Athletes, Presbyterian Student Fellowship, Wesley Foundation, and a Catholic Student Association (which does provide a weekly Mass) all meet regularly, as does the school's Jewish Study Group. Three picturesque chapels are maintained on campus, and Mount Berry Church meets weekly with college chaplain Dale McConkey serving as pastor.

Some students might find social life a little dull at Berry—no Greek life exists, and the entire campus is dry. Students are not forbidden to drink off campus, but opportunities are generally limited to of-age upperclassmen, who can frequent the few restaurants and bars in nearby Rome. Many students report that the college borders on being a "suitcase school," where people pack up and go home on weekends.

Though Berry College is a relatively small school, it still offers a wide variety of residential options, from traditional dormitory halls to a log-cabin cottage that houses seventeen women. Thomas Berry Hall (for women) includes two-, three-, four-, and six-bedroom suites, most of which have full kitchens. The newest, Audrey B. Morgan Residence Hall and Deerfield Hall, include scenic views and outdoor fireplaces. The school's sixteen townhouses, popular with upperclassmen, have a capacity for 187 students. Most residential halls are single sex, although one coed hall is available. Berry College is a residential school,

GREEN LIGHT

Berry College is relatively conservative and has a reputation for being a haven for committed and evangelical (but not stodgy) Christians. As one student says, "Berry College isn't Bob Jones or anything, but we're definitely right of center." He adds, "The majority of the professors are more liberal than their students, sure, but they're all sensitive to just how right-leaning the kids are, and they respect it. Overall, it's the liberal kids I'd be worried about." Both students and faculty say Berry is a friendly place, where students usually greet each other as they pass on campus.

In the fall of 2010, the college hosted a "Stuck with Virtue" conference series, which brought in experts from across the political spectrum—with a healthy cadre of religious conservatives—to discuss Descartes, Locke, and Darwin and to examine how the concept of virtue is innate to humanity. There promises to be more such worthy events in future years.

and students are required to live on campus; the only exceptions are seniors and students whose families live within 40 miles.

It's not surprising that crime is infrequent at this secluded school. In 2009, the campus saw just nine burglaries and one forcible sex offense. A Berry student made headlines in 2010 for "attempted aggravated child molestation,"

Tuition at Berry College ran at $24,620, plus an average room and board of $7,979. The good news is that Berry College has a healthy endowment of $667 million—comparable to the endowments (per student) of elite Bryn Mawr and Carleton colleges. Nearly every single Berry student receives some type of aid, averaging $10,700, and the average student-loan debt carried by a Berry graduate is around $21,000. Berry College's motto, "Not to be ministered unto, but to minister," has been translated into the college's extensive work program, which guarantees every student a paying job on campus, regardless of his financial situation. Some students gain valuable research experience working side by side with their professors, an opportunity "especially desirable for students planning on graduate study," says one faculty member.

Centre College

Danville, Kentucky • www.centre.edu

Smack dab in the middle

Centre College is in the center of Kentucky, and the academic spectrum. It is neither a trendy school overrun by contemporary ideologies, nor a deeply religious college informed by a particular denomination. (The school is officially Presbyterian.) Founded in 1819, Centre College has a long history of service to both Kentucky and the nation. Throughout its history it has educated vice-presidents, Supreme Court justices, senators, congressmen, governors, Fulbright scholars, and Rhodes scholars—in addition to local leaders in the fields of business, law, education, medicine, and science.

In recent years, Centre has fought to transcend its narrow reputation and become more well known as a liberal arts college serving any student eager for a humane education. Through its required courses in the humanities and the "fundamental questions," students are at least exposed to the best ideas in the Western tradition and the important issues of faith and doubt. One student says of her experience, "Centre College is a wonderfully nurturing environment that cultivates lifelong learners who are civically active."

Academic Life: Solid Centre

Although the school offers no traditional core curriculum, Centre students face a rather structured set of general education requirements. According to one professor, "These kids don't have to learn Latin and Greek, but most get a smattering of the basics."

Students are appointed general advisors—usually matched by interests—during their first and second years. After selecting a major or majors toward the end of the sophomore year, students then choose an advisor in a specific academic discipline.

Requirements for the majors, especially in the humanities, are solid. Students majoring in English must explore literature from various centuries—including one course in Shakespeare (a rare requirement for English majors across the country, we regret to report). History majors also must take courses from different periods and places. Requirements, refreshingly, do include "Development of the United States" I & II. Most classes sound solid, apart from some electives, such as "Museums, Knowledge, Power" and "Gender and Sexuality in Western Society." We're pleased to see that government majors are required to take "American Politics and Institutions."

VITAL STATISTICS

Religious affiliation: *Presbyterian*

Total enrollment: *1,216*

Total undergraduates: *1,216*

SAT/ACT midranges: CR: *550–670*, M: *570–670*; ACT: *26–30*

Applicants: *2,056*

Applicants accepted: *69%*

Accepted applicants who enrolled: *23%*

Tuition and room and board: *$39,000*

Freshman retention rate: *91%*

Graduation rate: *79% (4 yrs.), 81% (6 yrs.)*

Courses with fewer than 20 students: *58%*

Student-faculty ratio: *11:1*

Courses taught by graduate students: *none*

Most popular majors: *social sciences, history, psychology*

Students living on campus: *99%*

Guaranteed housing for four years? *yes*

Students in fraternities: *34%* in sororities: *37%*

The college is historically Presbyterian, but the religion department does not hew to a particular Christian creed. Students would do well to ask around before signing up for courses in this department. One undergrad states that "the religion department is the weakest because of the inconsistency among professors." One student reports that she decided not to major in religion at Centre when she "discovered the professor teaching my class didn't think the Bible had any value other than anthropology. He isn't the only one who thinks like that, and I wasn't able to grit my teeth and get through it the way some students do."

Centre has a strong reputation in the sciences. One professor informs us that "biochemistry and molecular biology has an excellent track record for medical school acceptance. Its curriculum is rigorous and oriented toward developing laboratory skills. Their senior seminar is the strongest capstone experience in the college. Most students are heavily involved in some form of undergraduate research." The chemistry program has also had success in preparing students for graduate study and obtaining top summer lab internships.

Centre is a small school, and most of the academic departments are modest in scale. The philosophy department lists just five faculty members, the history department nine, and the psychology department eight. A professor says, "All these programs are very small, so if there is any faculty turnover, things can change very quickly." By design, Centre's approach to education is interdisciplinary, and many classes are cross-listed with those in other departments. One student notes, "It lets you find out how interrelated learning truly is." If the courses offered are limited, most are rigorous. One student says, "There is no grade inflation. . . . Sometimes I wish I had gone to an easier school, but I know it's worth it."

The small size of the school allows professors and students to know each other and work together. One student says "it is very hard to fall through cracks here. Professors know and care about who you are and what you want to do."

The administration demonstrates its concern for students by offering "the Centre Commitment." The school guarantees that students who meet the college's academic and social expectations will be offered three things: an internship, an opportunity to study abroad, and graduation within four years—or else they'll get a free year's study at the school. According to Centre, "Not once . . . have we had to pay for an additional year."

Given the number of institutions that routinely graduate students in five or more years, this is a huge bonus.

There are no teaching assistants at Centre, and the school does not require its professors to "publish or perish." Their main objective is to teach. A student says that "one of Centre's strongest aspects is the accessibility of professors." Another adds, "Professors are extremely helpful. I can always go to them after hours for any help I have with the classwork."

One student says that the faculty's devotion to students makes Centre a "very transformative experience. . . . Before coming to Centre, I had no idea what my intellectual passions were. It was not until I had the opportunity to study abroad in London for three months that I realized my passion was rooted in international studies, learning about the world, and in particular, advocating human rights and humanitarianism around the world. Now I know the direction of my life will never be the same," she says.

Centre faculty do conduct research and get published, however, at a quite respectable rate. Still, one professor tells us that "teaching is the central theme and the

> **SUGGESTED CORE**
>
> 1. Humanities 110, Introduction to Humanities-I (closest match)
> 2. Philosophy 210, Ancient Philosophy
> 3. Religion 110, Biblical History and Ideas
> 4. Religion 120, History of Christian Thought
> 5. Government 300/301, Western Political Theory I/II
> 6. English 301/302, Shakespeare I/II
> 7. History 230, Development of the United States I
> 8. Philosophy 330, Nineteenth-Century Philosophy

major factor in tenure decisions." However, he does complain that, in his opinion, "the emphasis of the administration on teaching and the corresponding deemphasis on research causes many faculty members to abandon scholarly activity after they receive tenure."

Some of the best professors, students report, include Christine A. Shannon in math and computer science; Preston Miles in chemistry; Jane W. Joyce in classical studies; Stephen E. Asmus and Peggy Richey in biochemistry; Robert E. Martin in economics; Ken C. Keffer in French; Donna M. Plummer in education; Mark T. Lucas in English; Richard D. Axtell (also the college chaplain) in religion; Stephen R. Powell in art; Lori Hartmann-Mahmud in government; Dan Stroup in political science; and Michael Hamm and Clarence Wyatt in history.

A student reports: "Our study-abroad program is very strong. Between 80 and 90 percent of each graduating class has studied abroad at least once." The school maintains its own facilities and professors in these foreign programs, so that "classes are very rigorous and take advantage of the location," a student says. The college operates residential programs in London, England, France, and Mexico as well as exchange programs with universities in China, Northern Ireland, and Japan. One student reports: "When Centre students go abroad, they are definitely more than tourists. When I traveled to Costa Rica, we lived with a family that had only one lightbulb in the house, where we had to wake up every morning with the rooster and cook meals with the 'mom,' go out to the 'psalms' to pick oranges, and come in by 1:00 PM, every day, before the rains came, then sit on the porch with our 'dad' and pick the bad pieces of rice out of the pile." Since travel can be expensive, the school has an endowed fund to assist students with need-based aid to cover the extra cost.

Foreign languages taught at Centre include French, German, Greek (Ancient or New Testament), Hebrew (biblical), Japanese, Latin, Mandarin, and Spanish. Majors and minors are offered only in French, German, and Spanish.

Student Life: Dead Fred

Built almost entirely in red brick, the Centre campus has as its most venerable building Old Centre—a large and majestic edifice with Greek columns and portico, which once housed the students' sleeping, studying, eating, and recreation quarters. Today, along with thir-

---

ACADEMIC REQUIREMENTS

While it lacks a true core curriculum, Centre does require its students to complete a respectable series of general education requirements:

- A First-Year Studies seminar designed to introduce students to college-level work. Past topics have ranged from "The Holocaust" to "The Art of Walking" (a class on aesthetics), and "An American Obsession: The Lawn."
- Another First-Year Studies course taken in the winter term of the first year.
- "Introduction to Humanities" I and II or "Expository Writing and Humanities" I and II.
- "Development of the Modern World" or "Development of the United States."
- One social studies course, chosen from introductions to "Cultural Anthropology," "Physical Anthropology and Archaeology,""Sociology," "Economics," and "Politics."
- One life science course, such as "The Unity and Diversity of Life" or "Introduction to Psychology."
- One physical science course: "Chemistry and the Modern World," "General Chemistry," "Natural Science" I, "Environmental Geology," "Introduction to Physics," or "Introduction to Astronomy and Astrophysics."
- Humanities 110 & 120. Both classes are a "study of literature, philosophy, and the fine arts." The first focuses on classical Greek and Roman civilization, the second on the Renaissance, Baroque, and Neoclassical periods.
- Two courses in "Fundamental Questions." Students must choose either "Biblical History and Ideas" or "History of Christian Thought," plus another from the philosophy or religion department, such as "Philosophy of Art" or "Happiness and Justice: An Introduction to Ethical Thinking."
- Two science courses, chosen from courses in the biology, chemistry, physics, and the natural sciences departments.

Centre students must also prove competency in:

- Math, with an acceptable score on the SAT or ACT or a passing grade in a basic course.
- A foreign language, by passing an exam or an intermediate language course.
- Expository writing, by taking a writing course in the freshman year (already mentioned) and, if necessary, another writing-intensive general education course.

teen other Centre College buildings, it is listed in the National Register of Historic Places. According to a student, "There is a seal in front of Old Centre. If two students kiss on the seal at midnight, they will get married."

Except for one or two unpleasantly modern buildings from the 1960s, the campus is quaint. The renovations of old buildings and constructions of new ones have conformed well to the style of the campus as a whole. Most recently completed was Pearl Hall, a 146-bed residence hall, and the new Campus Center, which replaced the original Cowan Dining Commons.

Sixty-one percent of the student body hails from Kentucky, but most students still tend to stay on campus on the weekends instead of heading home. Some 99 percent of Centre students live on campus, and students have several options for living arrangements, including traditional dormitories, suite-style living, and apartments. Most dorms are single sex, although some upperclassman dorms are coed by floor. Visiting hours are strictly enforced, and visitors must use the public bathrooms. One student tells us, "About 10 percent of our student body applies every year to be a resident assistant. The application process is *very* rigorous." RAs are paid a minimal stipend, but competition for the positions is high. "Nobody's in it for the money," one RA says. "We genuinely want to help each other out."

The most coveted living spots are those right on the main quad, but the campus is small enough that everything is within walking distance. Some students also live in the Greek Park fraternity and sorority houses, but space is limited, and the houses are primarily used for social events. One student stressed that Centre students genuinely *want* to be on campus. "Everyone is so polite here," several students report.

One professor says, "The most distinctive feature of the life at Centre is civility. The faculty and the administration prize it. The culture encourages people to be polite and to prevent ideological, pedagogical, and intellectual differences from becoming personal. We certainly do have our disagreements and arguments here, but they rarely turn nasty. Faculty who join us from other institutions are amazed. Visitors who spend any time here at all almost always remark on it." The fraternities and sororities are also known for being friendly and welcoming.

Danville is a small town, and quite pretty, but there is not a lot to do there—so students tend to stick to campus and make their own fun. Just about every weekend sees frat parties, which are technically off campus, and all students are welcome. There is, of course, a certain amount of drinking at these events—however, students report that alcohol consumption is pretty moderate, even at frat parties. College officials exercise some control over drinking at parties, since all official events must first be registered with the school. Danville is a "moist" town—meaning there are no bars or liquor stores, although restaurants can serve alcohol. For students who want a more lively nightlife, Lexington is about forty-five minutes away, and Louisville is an hour.

Students do report some odd patterns of behavior on campus: for instance, men and women almost never sit together for meals. There is no rule against it; it is simply not done. At many traditional schools like Centre, students date steadily and tend to marry shortly after graduation, but this is not the case at Centre, where students report there is very little

YELLOW LIGHT

Classroom politics, students say, are generally kept to a minimum. One student says the campus has a fairly free exchange of ideas and remembers a few instances that the school has itself encouraged political debate. However, a faculty member says it is rare that political ideas are actually exchanged. "Part of that is an inherently southern civility," he says, "and part of it is a student body that is generally rather conservative." While there are quite a few conservative students on campus, the faculty tends to be quite liberal. This has its impact on student life. A few years ago, a group of students wished to form a pro-life group but were effectively blocked from doing so because not a single faculty member would agree to sponsor the group. Students reported that while there are pro-life faculty members, they were apparently afraid to sponsor the group for fear of reprisals from colleagues.

According to one teacher, "While I would characterize most of the faculty as being politically left of center, I have not heard of anyone pushing his or her personal agenda in the classroom. On the other hand, many of the reading and course assignments, particularly in the humanities and social sciences, appear to reflect the political views of the professors."

dating among students. Of course, there is no rule against such fraternizing (this isn't a military academy), but for some reason—perhaps the significant course workload—the dating life at Centre isn't much to write home about.

With more than a hundred student organizations on campus, undergrads can stay busy. Groups include Association of Women in Mathematics; Badminton Club; B-GLAD (Bisexuals, Gays, Lesbians & Allies for Dignity); Centre Cheerleading; Centre Classics Club; Centre Cycling Club; Centre Equestrian Club; Deutschklub; French Society; Optimist Club; Orthodox Christian Fellowship; Philosophy Club; Photography Club; Psychology Society; Society of Future Educators; Swing Club; and *Vantage Point*, a literary magazine.

Each year a wide variety of cultural events come to the college—of which students must annually attend at least twelve during their time at Centre. In the past, these "Convocations" have included a speech by Justice Sandra Day O'Connor, concerts by the Boston Pops, and performances by the likes of Mikhail Baryshnikov. According to one student, "These convocations teach me so many things that I would not learn in the classroom."

Centre is steeped in traditions. A favorite one centers on "Dead Fred," a portrait of Fred Vinson, a Centre alumnus and former Chief Justice of the United States. Chief Justice Vinson was a dedicated member of his fraternity, Phi Delta Theta, and frequently returned to the college to watch football games. In 1953, he passed away—and that, one would think, was that. However, his younger fraternity brothers decided that death was no reason to miss a football game, and so they started taking his portrait to home games with them. Dead Fred has occasionally traveled to away games, acted as an honorary judge when students attempted to break the world record for continuous reading in 2002, and filled a seat at the 2000 vice-presidential debates, which were hosted at Centre. (In fact, he may have won them.)

Centre students are very proud of their sporting history, and they still boast about their upset football win over the previously undefeated Harvard team in 1921. (Centre went on to capture the football national championship that year.) Even today there is an excellent turnout for home games in all sports. The school competes in nineteen inter-collegiate varsity sports, with 40 percent of the student population participating. There are also fifteen intramural sports, in which 80 percent of students participate. The school offers no athletic scholarships.

Centre's religious roots remain relevant. The department of religious affairs offers many opportunities for Bible study and fellowship throughout the year, with Wednesday night Centre Christian Fellowship meetings particularly well attended. According to one student, the college student body has a strong Catholic presence—although the Catholic student organization is not as active as other ministries. (For Catholic students seeking something a little more traditional, a daily and weekly Latin Mass is offered in nearby Lexington, at St. Peter's Church.)

Crime is infrequent at Centre. One student says, "I have never felt unsafe at Centre. It is probably one of the safest campuses I have been on, but as always, students should have common sense when walking alone, et cetera." Another student informs us that "the Department of Public Safety just began a program that allows all Centre students to receive a phone call and/or text (message) whenever a campuswide alert is issued. I was woken up at 1:30 AM with a phone call alerting me of the potential danger due to a hurricane warning during a huge storm, as well as when the danger had passed." In 2009, the school reported one forcible sex offense and six burglaries on campus.

Centre is a moderately priced school with tuition, room, and board all together costing $39,000 for the 2010–11 school year. The college does its best to meet students' financial needs, and 59 percent of students receive need-based financial assistance. The average indebtedness of a recent Centre graduate is $17,190.

Christendom College

Front Royal, Virginia • www.christendom.edu

Restoring all things in Christ

Christendom College was founded in 1977 by a group of academics who sought to preserve the tradition of a Catholic liberal arts education, which they saw endangered by the secularization of most colleges once closely affiliated with the church—even those run by religious orders. Historian Warren Carroll, a convert to Catholicism, led a group of energetic founders in an attempt to offer a broad-based, intellectually venturesome liberal education informed by the teachings of the Catholic Church, in the hope of forming faithful and well-educated laymen who could serve as "apostles to the modern world." Some thirty years later, the college is flourishing, having gained a reputation for academic excellence, doctrinal fidelity, and a wholesome atmosphere where students cheerfully embrace the traditions of Catholicism.

The college's very name harks back to medieval Christian Europe and a social order that was entirely Christianized. The college states that the purpose of Catholic education is to form students so that they may learn and live "by the truth revealed by Our Lord and Savior Jesus Christ, 'the Way, the Truth and the Life,' as preserved in the deposit of Faith and authentically interpreted in the Magisterium of the Roman Catholic Church, founded by Christ, of which the Pope is the visible head."

In other words, do not expect to find doctrinal confusion on this campus. Indeed, while most Catholic colleges in America ignore the official Vatican policy requiring teachers of Catholic theology to affirm their faithfulness to church teaching, at Christendom, the beginning of every academic year sees the entire faculty make a public profession of faith and swear a formal oath of fidelity. All classes are also opened with prayer. This does not mean that the school feels like a seminary, however; students report that the school maintains an atmosphere of healthy debate and academic interchange.

Academic Life: To form the whole person

Christendom asserts that its mission is to "form the whole person for a life spent in the pursuit of truth and wisdom." The college seeks to give a student "the solid moral principles, core knowledge and skills, and intellectual flexibility suited to a liberally educated person," reports one professor. Another tells us that "Christendom does a great job in the liberal arts. There are few places that are better. Students will get a pretty solid grounding in the clas-

South

476

sics, in a setting that puts them in their context (i.e., not a Great Books approach)."

The college confers a bachelor of arts degree, with majors available in classical and early Christian studies, English, history, philosophy, political science and economics, and theology. Christendom also offers master's programs in theological and catechetical studies through its Notre Dame Graduate School in Alexandria, Virginia.

Students and faculty alike report a high level of academic dedication among the students. One professor informs us that "the intellectual curiosity of the students is higher than at most schools. Because things relate to their faith, students want to know more than they normally would. That is a great thing." Another faculty member adds, "Learning here continues outside of the classroom. Discussions do not end in the classroom, but continue on through the course of a student's term. Our students are particularly desirous of knowledge."

Christendom College assigns each student upon matriculation a faculty academic advisor to assist him in registering for his courses each semester and to advise him in academic matters. Once a student is accepted into a major, the student's advisor becomes the major department chairman or his delegate, the school reports.

Philosophy has long been and remains the most popular major. Within that department, students praise John Cuddeback, J. Michael Brown, and Steven Snyder. The department's classes are infused by the methods of St. Thomas Aquinas but also examine at length the works of modern and contemporary philosophers. According to one student, "The philosophy department has an amazing variety of professors who make the subject matter understandable, ranging from ancient and medieval to modern thinkers. The material helps to form your intellect to know truth and to be able to defend your faith."

History is also another well-populated major at the college; the school's leading founder was a historian. The school calls the discipline an inquiry into "God's dealings with man and the spiritual drama of man's relations with God and with his fellows." This providential view of history shapes the school's entire curriculum. One professor tells us that "history is the strongest major. It has professors who are the most interested in scholarship, and they are the most published."

Literature courses study complete works rather than selections. The freshman at Christendom acquires writing and critical reading skills through the study of the *Iliad*, *Odyssey*,

VITAL STATISTICS

Religious affiliation: *Roman Catholic*
Total enrollment: *450*
Total undergraduates: *389*
SAT/ACT midranges: CR: *590–670*, M: *520–630*; ACT: *23–28*
Applicants: *350*
Applicants accepted: *80%*
Accepted applicants who enrolled: *44%*
Tuition and fees: *$19,118*
Room and board: *$7,506*
Freshman retention rate: *80%*
Graduation rate: *69% (4 yrs.), 70% (6 yrs.)*
Courses with fewer than 20 students: *59%*
Student-faculty ratio: *14:1*
Courses taught by graduate students: *none*
Most popular majors: *history, philosophy, political science*
Students living on campus: *99%*
Guaranteed housing for four years? *yes*
Students in fraternities or sororities: *none*

Aeneid, and Aristotle's *Poetics*. Works by Milton, Dante, and T. S. Eliot round out the literature core and support the program's goal of fostering an appreciation and understanding of the "rich patrimony of Western culture."

Christendom describes its highly regarded theology program as "the search for a synthesis of knowledge as well as in the dialogue between faith and reason." Classes such as "Ascetical and Mystical Theology," "Theology and the Public Order," and "Latin Readings in St. Thomas Aquinas" build on the school's impressive core requirements in Catholic theology. The college has bolstered this department with the recent full-time hiring of one teacher whom students consistently praise, Eric Jenislawski. However, with only two full-time professors (the remainder are part-time and adjuncts), this department could use more faculty to serve "the Queen of Sciences."

In political science and economics (a single major), Christendom students speak highly of Bracy Bersnak (a favorite), Bernard Way, and William Luckey, and describe adjunct professor Rafael Madan as "one of the most influential" teachers at the school. Graduates in this major frequently opt for a career in politics in nearby Washington, D.C., or continue on to law school. One political science professor tells us, "The motto of the college is to restore all things in Christ. We think about the practical implications of that more than any other department. Political science is where the rubber hits the road."

Christendom maintains an excellent classical and early Christian studies department. According to one professor, the department "has a number of exceptionally talented instructors in both Latin and Ancient Greek. Students have many opportunities to study a wide range of both pagan and Christian literature from antiquity through to the medieval period. Hebrew and Syriac occasionally supplement the course offerings. Several students have won national awards for their achievements in Latin and Ancient Greek."

All classes at Christendom are taught by professors rather than graduate students. Faculty members keep office hours and usually eat meals with students. Students report easy access to their professors: "The professors are extremely accessible. They make themselves available to students for anything. They all have an interest in the students' well-being and are very inviting to anyone who may need their assistance with academic or personal matters. Their office hours allow the students flexibility in visiting them, and they also are willing to meet at the student's convenience," says a teacher.

The college prizes good teachers. Student enthusiasm for an adjunct professor is a key reason why he might be hired full-time. Once retained, full-time professors are initially on a three-year probation. There is no tenure, but a professor has never been fired after passing probation. One professor informs us that "while some faculty routinely publish books and articles, and others attend conferences or give lectures abroad, these activities are voluntary. Some faculty prefer to focus on teaching alone. The classroom performance of the professors is routinely evaluated, and teaching ability is a major consideration in hiring and retaining them."

"Christendom faculty and students share a common love of learning and of the church," says one professor. However, a professor adds, "political correctness does not exist on campus." Many issues remain open to debate. "The main factions on campus consist of Republicans, agrarians, libertarians, paleoconservatives, and *ancien régime* traditionalists. Sometimes debates between these groups enter into the classroom, but this is usually interesting rather than intrusive." Students report that they gather with their friends often to discuss issues outside of class. One says, "Sometimes I am drawn into a heated discussion with fellow students at an off-campus party about things as simple as the meaning of community, music, or economics."

One of the highlights for a Christendom student is the junior semester in Rome. In addition to their philosophy and theology core classes, students explore art and architecture and Italian. The program has grown increasingly popular since 2005, when students were present during the funeral of Pope John Paul II and the election of Benedict XVI. "The semester in Rome was one of the greatest experiences of my life," says an enthusiastic student. "It was a spiritual, intellectual, cultural adventure." One of the Rome faculty members informs us that the strongest points of the program are "the proximity to the Vatican, the chance to live and study in a foreign country, and the opportunity to see where Christendom started." Another professor notes that there is room for improvement in the program: "Study abroad is very popular. I don't have the impression that it is the most academic thing. It is more holy tourism than a part of a liberal education. The emphasis should be

---

ACADEMIC REQUIREMENTS

As part of its dedication to the liberal arts, the college requires an "integrated core curriculum grounded in natural and revealed truth." The core makes up two-thirds of a student's course work. The following courses are required of all:

- Four semesters of a foreign language. French, Spanish, Italian, Latin, and Ancient Greek are offered. Two years of Latin and/or Ancient Greek are required of all students majoring in classical and early Christian studies, philosophy, or theology; all other students need four semesters of the language of their choice.
- Six semesters in philosophy. The philosophy core is arranged according to the classical Aristotelian order, comprising an introductory philosophy class, ethics, "Philosophy of Human Nature," metaphysics, medieval philosophy, and modern philosophy.
- Six semesters of theology. Students begin in the freshman year with "Fundamentals of Catholic Doctrine," which is a survey of Catholic teaching, and move into the Old and New Testaments in the sophomore year. In the junior year, this segment of the core culminates with courses in moral theology and Catholic apologetics.
- Eight courses covering Western civilization, both its history and literature. This sequence leads the student more or less historically through many great books of the West, beginning with scripture and Homer's *Iliad* and *Odyssey*, moving through Latin classics, medieval works of Chaucer and Dante, through Luther, Shakespeare, up through recent authors such as T. S. Eliot and Pope John Paul II.
- One math class and one science class, usually "Introduction to Mathematical Thought" and "Introduction to Scientific Thought."
- Two courses in social and political doctrine: "Principles of Political Theory" and "The Social Teachings of the Church."

South

more on broadening the students' mind through encountering another culture. It is sold to parents as, 'This will bind your child to the papacy.'"

Most alumni retain a strong sense of loyalty to the school, and their giving rate is one of the highest in the country. In the words of one student, "I know many people who have learned much from this school and have shaped their lives according to the amazing education offered here." Every fall at Homecoming, the college hosts a very well-attended alumni reunion (complete with babysitting).

The college is not without weaknesses. The combined math and science department is sparse, with very few offerings. Modern languages are also reported to be comparatively anemic; French and Spanish are generally offered only through the intermediate level, while there is rudimentary Italian sufficient for the semester abroad in Rome.

A professor informs us that Christendom is known for an overemphasis on the moral at the expense of the intellectual life. He wishes instead that "our distinct and irreplaceable contribution to the spiritual and moral lives of our students should be through the cultivation of their intellects. If we focus on their intellect, then we will tailor their moral and physical lives. If we primarily focus on the moral, then there is no one left for the intellectual. If *we* do not force people to cultivate their intellect, then no one will."

Graduates of Christendom have become successful leaders in fields as varied as education, journalism, law, computer technology, and film production—while others have pursued graduate studies at Catholic University, Notre Dame, St. Louis University, Harvard, and the University of Virginia.

Student Life: Everybody knows everybody

Christendom's campus outside Front Royal, Virginia, is a scenic property on the Shenandoah River. Students take full advantage of the river, which offers canoeing, fishing, and swimming. Front Royal is a gateway to Shenandoah National Park, the site of the famous Skyline Drive and numerous hiking opportunities through the Blue Ridge Mountains. What used to be a rural town is quickly growing as a commuter city for the Washington, D.C., area; housing developments and strip malls are metastasizing throughout the region. Front Royal is not a "college town," with bars and stores catering to students. A modest collection of area bars and restaurants and a local movie theater constitute the main entertainments in town; however, cultural opportunities abound in Washington, D.C., about seventy-five miles away.

Moderate consumption of alcohol and tobacco are socially acceptable to most students, while illegal drug use is shunned. A strict policy banning the storage and use of alcohol on campus sends many student parties to surrounding properties or off-campus houses. "We do have our parties," says one student flatly, "but we try to drink within the realms of moderation." Student drinking spots known as the Meadows and the Field have been made off-limits by campus authorities due to frequent noise and trash complaints from area citizens. Punishment for breaking the alcohol policy is suspension from the campus. Illegal drug use results in expulsion.

The campus also has a policy banning romantic displays of affection or "RDAs." The college handbook states that public displays of romance, such as kissing, holding hands, or fondling on campus, tend to "break up the campus community into couples and non-couples, making it embarrassing or awkward for others." Punishment for an infraction is a $5 fine, usually issued by resident assistants. "Most of the RAs know what it's like to date," says one student. "Unless it's a blatant disregard of the rules, they are not out to bust you." In tune with Catholic teaching, school rules strictly forbid the sort of recreational sexual activity found on many secular campuses—and the punishment for violations is significant, up to and including expulsion.

Students admit that the rules are "frustrating" at times. Upperclassmen and resident assistants try to demonstrate how to live cheerfully within the rules, inspiring younger students struggling with the campus restrictions to do the same. One student tells us, "There are RAs or proctors on every floor, and they are extremely fun and helpful in any circumstances. They are all great leaders and show an interest in each person under their care." Another student tells us that a few of the RAs look more to the letter than the spirit of the law and continually bust people for very minor infractions.

The recently completed St. John the Evangelist Library houses more than 60,000 volumes. In the upstairs of the library, there is a rare-books room with collectors' editions by authors such as Chesterton and Eliot. The library also provides students with additional classrooms, study areas, and a modern computer lab. The John Paul the Great Student Center was completed in 2005, offering additional space for student activities. The facility houses student mailboxes, a student lounge, and the St. Killian's Café. The café serves beer during organized events such as Life on Tap and Pub Night, which host a speaker or a student band for entertainment.

Church feast days are campuswide holidays at Christendom, and classes are canceled on Holy Days of Obligation. Most social events, such as the St. Joseph/San Francesco Italian Feast, the St. Patrick's Day Celebration, and the St. Cecilia's Night Talent Show, are tied to the liturgical life of the church. Christendom's "zeal for Catholic culture" is apparent in its annual Medievalfest and Oktoberfest celebrations. The list of student groups is fairly short; clubs on campus are the Student Ambassadors, Christendom Players, Shield of Roses, Legion of Mary, Chester-Belloc Debate Society, Schola Gregoriana, Choir, the *Rambler* (newspaper), Holy Rood Guild, Film Club, Outreach, Shogi Club, Students for Life, Contra-Dance Club, and Swing/Ballroom Dance Club.

An active Student Activities Council puts on a variety of events, including numerous swing dances (no hard rock or rap, thank you very much), Christendom Jeopardy, Texas Western Night, and Coffee House. Every year, to raise money, the student council auctions off dinners prepared and hosted by different professors. Students form groups and bid on dinners with the professors. The prices can be quite high—at least $200–$300 per meal ($45/head). For extremely popular professors, that price can double.

A strict dress code enforces "a professional appearance" for students in class. Whereas men have it simple—dress shoes, socks, pants, a collared shirt, and a tie—women can find it confusing at first to meet a lengthy code of "business attire" requirements together with a strict modesty code banning all skirts that fall above the knee and thin-strapped tank tops. These modesty codes also apply to students outside of class, although "normal" attire such as jeans and T-shirts are acceptable.

South

GREEN LIGHT

Shield of Roses, a group of Christendom students, travels every Saturday to Washington, D.C., to pray at abortion clinics. On January 22 each year, classes are canceled so that students may participate in the March for Life in D.C. The college charters buses for the event, and the entire student body, along with the professors, must take part. (We'd like this universal participation even better if it were voluntary.)

Although one need not be Catholic to go to the school, it certainly helps. Non-Catholics, unless they are on the path to conversion, would probably feel uncomfortable. The overwhelming majority of students are serious Catholics, which serves as one of the strongest bonds in the community life of the college. Graduates report forming strong friendships that carry well beyond college years (and more than a few marriages). However, with a small student body, it is also true that, as one student warns, "Everybody knows everybody. It's very dramatic sometimes when everybody knows what is going on in other people's lives."

Christendom offers an abundance of spiritual opportunities. A full 15 percent of alumni go on to serve as priests and religious. Three college chaplains offer Mass twice a day and provide numerous opportunities for confession. Students lead the Liturgy of the Hours during the morning and evening and sing compline, a nightly chant in Latin, on weekday evenings. A campus rosary is also said every night after dinner. None of the spiritual activities are mandatory, but they are attended by a high percentage of students. One student tells us that one of the best things about the college is "our great love for the Holy Father." Students speak admiringly of the spiritual direction offered at the school. Many students volunteer their time to join the Chapel Choir, which sings hymns for the campus Mass on Sunday and routinely travels to area parishes.

As a member of the United States Collegiate Athletic Association (USCAA), Christendom fields intercollegiate teams in men's and women's soccer, golf, and basketball, men's baseball and rugby, and women's volleyball and softball. The athletic department maintains facilities and equipment to support a variety of student interests, such as tennis, racquetball, handball, soccer, basketball, volleyball, baseball, softball, and weightlifting. Intramurals are popular among the students.

Dorms are single sex and verboten to the opposite sex. The men's and women's dorms are situated on opposite sides of the campus. There is a curfew for freshmen and sophomores—midnight on weeknights and 1:00 AM on the weekends. The RAs and proctors strictly enforce this with room checks. Most of the student dorms are doubles, although some larger rooms are split into triples. Some 95 percent of the students live on campus.

So little crime occurs on campus that Christendom does not compile statistics, although students report a few thefts and the occasional rowdy drunk. Security guards monitor the campus during the night.

Tuition for the 2010–11 is $19,118, and room and board are $7,506. Some 51 percent of students received need-based financial aid, and the average student-loan debt of a graduating student in 2009 was $24,000.

Davidson College

Davidson, North Carolina • www.davidson.edu

Full-court Presbyterian

Davidson College opened just north of Charlotte in 1837. After recovering from the Civil War, Davidson rebounded to become one of the South's top colleges for men. In 1976, Davidson went coed. It is now one of the most selective schools in the country, producing an impressive twenty-three Rhodes scholars. But the 1,700-student college has no plans to grow into a large university with graduate programs, because it recognizes that its small size has yielded its greatest virtues: close faculty-student relationships, a strong college community, and a genuine commitment to the liberal arts.

Davidson was founded by Presbyterians and is still affiliated with that tradition (U.S.A.), although in 2005 the board of trustees voted to allow for 20 percent of the board to be non-Christian. Students are no longer required to attend chapel, but one-fourth of them describe themselves as Presbyterian. The college's statement of purpose pledges to emphasize "those studies, disciplines, and activities that are mentally, spiritually, and physically liberating." The college has followed this mission through an honor code that sets the tone for student life, a liberal arts curriculum that requires students to take serious courses, a community that welcomes spirituality, and a social scene that encourages students to be physically active. As a result of the college's adherence to its mission, Davidson students are some of the most well-rounded in the nation.

Academic Life: On course

Rather than provide a core curriculum, Davidson gives its students a set of distribution requirements. Davidson's mandated course selections are better than most, and a high percentage of courses offered are solid ones. "Despite being a numbers guy," says a math major, "I have read Plato, Milton, Flaubert, Nietzsche, and Hayek, to name a few." One faculty member says, "May a student graduate without taking a course in Milton? Yes. May a student graduate without thinking clearly and writing critically about fundamental issues in art, science, mathematics, literature, philosophy, etc.? No."

Certainly not if they enroll in the Humanities program. Taught by faculty from several departments who lead discussion sections of sixteen students each, freshmen and sophomores take a sequence of four courses focusing on the development

VITAL STATISTICS

Religious affiliation: *Presbyterian*
Total enrollment: *1,720*
Total undergraduates: *1,720*
SAT/ACT midranges: CR: *630–730*, M: *630–710*; ACT: *28–32*
Applicants: *4,494*
Applicants accepted: *26%*
Accepted applicants who enrolled: *42%*
Tuition and fees: *$36,683*
Room and board: *$10,346*
Freshman retention rate: *97%*
Graduation rate: *92% (4 yrs.), 94% (6 yrs.)*
Courses with fewer than 20 students: *72%*
Student-faculty ratio: *11:1*
Courses taught by graduate students: *none*
Most popular majors: *social sciences, history, English*
Students living on campus: *93%*
Guaranteed housing for four years? *yes*
Students in fraternities: *34%* in sororities: *44%*

of Western civilization, including "The Ancient World," "Late Antiquity and the Modern World," "The Renaissance through the Eighteenth Century," and "The Nineteenth and Twentieth Centuries." This program is basically an abbreviated core curriculum. Since the humanities sequence covers material from philosophy, religion, history, and literature, students participating in this program satisfy four distribution requirements. An addition to the Western civilization core is the newer "Cultural Diversity" requirement, which is "aimed at having students appreciate a culture other than the dominant cultures of the United States or Europe."

Although Davidson is primarily a liberal arts college, its science and undergraduate research programs are strong, and the balance it strikes between the arts and sciences is impressive. One Davidson administrator says that some of the most scientifically minded students will also minor in religion or another humanities discipline, and vice versa. The strongest departments at the school are philosophy, history, mathematics, political science, chemistry, and biology. Another highlight is the religion department, whose faculty members teach courses in, among other things, "Theological Ethics," "The Rise of Christianity," "The Genesis Narrative," "Christian Latin Writers," and "Christianity and Nature." Happily, the fetishes of gender and ethnic studies are mostly absent at Davidson, and religion is approached as a genuine discipline worthy of serious study.

The psychology department has switched from offering BA to BS degrees, giving the department a more experimental orientation. Davidson offers premed, predentistry, prelaw, preministerial, and teacher education programs, as well as an engineering cooperative in which students take three to four years at Davidson and two years in the engineering school at either Columbia University or Washington University in St. Louis.

Within the curriculum, the most politicized areas of study are the interdisciplinary concentrations, such as ethnic studies, gender studies, international studies, and the rare southern studies. Davidson added its "cultural diversity" requirement only a few years ago, long after many peer (and more liberal) institutions. However, the eccentric courses one finds in other liberal arts college catalogs are missing from Davidson's—and the cultural diversity requirement can be satisfied by a number of good courses in the history or foreign language departments. Davidson College remains essentially southern and conservative.

South

"However, there's definitely a balance of liberals, which I believe is increasing as the college increases its geographic draw and grows in prestige every year," says one student.

Just about every department at Davidson is reputed to be tough. One religion major says that she spends four hours a day studying: "It might be possible to get by with classes that are easier than others, but I don't know how." Another student says that every course is difficult. "I've been surprised to hear about my peers struggling more in music theory, art history, and drama classes than in their freshman science requirements like chemistry."

English majors are required to complete a class in literary analysis, historical survey courses in British literature through the 1900s, American literature through the twentieth century, and either nineteenth and twentieth century British literature or world literature. Additionally, students must take classes with a writing emphasis and five electives, four of which must be upper level.

> ## SUGGESTED CORE
>
> For a somewhat abbreviated core, the Humanities Program suffices:
>
> 1. Humanities 150, Western Tradition: The Ancient World
> 2. Humanities 151, Western Tradition: Late Antiquity and the Medieval World
> 3. Humanities 250, Western Tradition: The Renaissance to the Eighteenth Century
> 4. Humanities 251, Western Tradition: The Modern World

History students must complete introductory classes in the followings areas: Pre-modern Europe, modern Europe, U.S. history, and non-Western history, as well as a sophomore-level elective, five or six advanced-level electives, and a senior seminar. One class must focus on a premodern period.

A little more structure is given to political science majors, who must take a class each in political theory and American, comparative, and international politics, as well as "Methods and Statistics in Political Science" and a senior-level seminar.

Faculty highly recommended by students include Annie Ingram, Randall M. Ingram, Paul Miller, and Randy Nelson in English; Hansford M. Epes and Burkhard Henke in German; Lance K. Stell in philosophy; Karl A. Plank and H. Gregory Snyder in religion; C. Shaw Smith Jr. in art history; Magdalena Maiz-Peña and Samuel Sánchez y Sánchez in Spanish; Benjamin G. Klein in mathematics; A. Malcolm Campbell in biology; Sally G. McMillen in history; Kristi S. Multhaup in psychology; and Mark Foley in economics. The political science department is blessed with some particularly good teachers, including Peter J. Ahrensdorf and Russell Crandall. Of Brian Shaw, in the same department, one student says, "If you take any of his courses, he will make you a better thinker and writer."

"Ironically, some of the most-loved professors at Davidson are also the most challenging. I think this characterizes the academic atmosphere here well," says a student. While there are a few weak professors at Davidson, there are very few weak departments.

Davidson students and faculty agree that the school's honor code permeates academic and campus life. A supplemental Code of Responsibility reminds students that Davidson is a "college of liberal arts committed to the Christian faith," which tries to "develop the maturity of character." Any member of the Davidson community can charge a student with a violation of this code. These standards give professors the freedom from proctoring exams, and give students the flexibility to take tests home and schedule their own finals.

South

A student on the Honor Council says that only three or four violations occur per year, and most of those incidents are reported by the offenders themselves. The library stacks at Davidson are open, and students check out books without electronic scanners or security beepers. Students leave laptops on their desktops when they go for a break and even leave their dorm rooms unlocked. One sophomore says that all of these examples demonstrate the college's underlying "atmosphere of trust."

Student-faculty relationships at Davidson are strong. One student reports that she and her classmates frequently pop into professors' offices to talk about class or various intellectual topics. "The time I have spent one-on-one with my professors is a highlight of my experience here," another student says. The admissions director says that intellectual curiosity is the one attribute that Davidson students have in common and that the admissions office purposely chooses students who are "ready to have intellectual relationships." All incoming students are assigned faculty advisors. Once a student has declared a major, he is assigned (or can choose) a faculty member in his major department to serve as an advisor.

About two-thirds of Davidson students study abroad at some point during their four years, choosing from among the school's semester- or year long programs in France, Germany, India, and Peru. Summer programs are offered at Cambridge and in Spain, Berlin, Ghana, Cyprus, Kenya, and Zambia. The classics program also offers a special spring-semester tour of various areas associated with classical antiquity: Egypt, Greece, Turkey, Italy, and England. One student mentions Davidson's Cambridge program as being particularly strong.

All students must study a foreign language; the school offers classes in Arabic, Chinese, French, German, Ancient Greek, Latin, Russian, and Spanish.

Student Life: Body and soul

Davidson's beautiful Georgian-style architecture and shaded campus are well suited to its southern location. New, modern facilities blend in with century-old buildings, as the school has not abandoned its original style. The Knobloch Center contains an amphitheater, post office, fitness center with climbing wall, an outdoor center, meeting rooms, game room, student organization offices, a cafe, a bookstore, and a large terrace that overlooks the football stadium. The Knobloch Center adjoins the 600-seat Duke Family Performance Hall. The Belk Visual Arts Center, which includes two public galleries, provides private studios for art majors. Dana Laboratories give students in the sciences opportunities to use state-of-the-art equipment rarely seen at schools this size.

The town of Davidson is not exactly hopping, but it has classic southern beauty, walkable streets, and charm. Fans of antique shops, art galleries, and needlepoint shops will love the place. Admirably, instead of abandoning the downtown for suburban sprawl, residents have striven to preserve the town; the Village Store has sold necessities on Davidson's Main Street since 1903.

Four churches are within walking distance, and the on-campus Lingle Chapel offers services each week from a variety of communions, including Catholic, Episcopal, Muslim, Unitarian Universalist, and Jewish—along with ecumenical worship services on Wednes-

South

days and Thursdays. A Presbyterian minister serves as college chaplain, while a Jewish rabbi and Catholic laywoman are adjunct chaplains. The college hosts a variety of holy day services, from Ash Wednesday to Passover to the Hindu Diwali festival. Nearby Charlotte, only twenty-five minutes south and consistently ranked one of the top cities in the U.S., offers bright lights and entertainment; the Blue Ridge Mountains are two hours west; and the Carolina beaches are three or four hours to the east.

Above all, Davidson attracts and helps to form well-rounded students: academically, socially, athletically, and even morally and spiritually. About 70 percent of female students belong to the school's distinctive eating clubs (and 44 percent to its sororities), while half of male students join one of its eight fraternities, but students are not pressured to participate. The clubs are not residential, so social life centers on the dormitories as much as it does around the small club headquarters. "The eating clubs are not sorority-ish and are

ACADEMIC REQUIREMENTS

Davidson's curricular mandates are serious and respectable. Student must complete requirements in the following five categories:

- Core curriculum. A ten-course set of requirements from six major disciplines that must be fulfilled before the start of the senior year. It includes literature (one course), fine arts (one course), history (one course), religion and philosophy (two courses, at least one of them in religion), natural sciences and math (three courses, at least one in math and one in a lab science), and social sciences (two courses).
- Composition. Qualifying courses may be selected from the English department or other departments, or students may substitute Davidson's first-year Humanities Program. Recent course offerings that qualified have included "Does the South Still Exist?," "Food as Symbol and Spectacle," "Literature and Medicine," "American Reformers and Utopians," and "True Crime."
- Foreign language. Students must reach a level of proficiency in a foreign language equivalent to a third-level course.
- Cultural diversity. This one-course requirement must be fulfilled for graduation, and courses may be selected from most departments—including foreign languages. Options include an anthropology course in "Religion, Society, and Culture" or "African Civilizations," foreign literature courses, and a wide selection of history, sociology, political science, and music classes.
- Physical education. An impressive total of four physical education courses, along with a swimming competency test, are required. PED 101 (also called Davidson 101) is required of all students in their first semester. More of a health-class-meets-student orientation, the course offers alcohol and drug education, "Diversity-Celebrating Differences," sex education, and introductions to the library, career services, and student counseling center. The other three PE classes—one lifetime credit, one water credit, and one team credit—are fulfilled later. Additionally, one team-sport credit is required. It may be fulfilled through varsity, club, or intramural sports.

South

not exclusive or cliquey," one member says. Patterson Court—the organizing body of the fraternities and eating houses—lies at the center of the Davidson social scene.

Like any school, Davidson has a party scene centered in fraternities, eating houses, and senior apartments, but avoiding it is possible. Most school rules concerning alcohol use tend to be practical: alcohol is not permitted in public areas, kegs are forbidden from campus, and parties must max out at forty people and end by 2:00 AM. Many students report preferring to take part in the school's ample extracurricular activities.

Some 96 percent of the student body (including 100 percent of the freshman class) lives on campus. Before arriving, freshmen fill out an exhaustive roommate-matching questionnaire and even take the Myers-Briggs personality test. Coordinators spend weeks trying to find the best fit for each student, and most roommates end up being good friends, if not also roommates as sophomores: more than 40 percent of Davidson freshmen choose the same roommate for their second year. All floors and bathrooms on campus are single sex. Davidson also offers an Eco-House, which focuses on fostering a cooperative, sustainable community. Students engage in cooking, cleaning, and hosting events (such as a campus educational program on green living). Additionally, each year, Duke Residence Hall offers three internationally themed living-learning communities. In 2009–10, six to ten students lived in the "State of the Middle Eastern Teenager" hall, the "World in Words" hall (which focused on the literature and art of the Middle East, Asia, South America, and Africa), or in the "Youth in the World: Connections Through Understanding" hall. Finally, the school offers the Martin Court Apartments, where most seniors opt to live. Apartment life offers them a nice transition from dorm life to the real world.

Pleasingly, Davidson offers a full laundry service at no additional charge to students. For those who prefer laundromats, Davidson offers free machines and a lounge with wireless Internet, computer stations, TV, and snacks for students who are waiting for the tumble dryers to finish. To further streamline the process, Davidson offers a website displaying which machines are in use and how long they have left in their cycles.

Davidson is the second-smallest NCAA Division I college in the country, and Wildcat athletes compete on twenty-one varsity teams. A fourth of the student body participates in varsity athletics, and—due in part to the school's physical fitness requirement that each student play one team sport—90 percent participate in intramural sports programs (the school offers softball, beach volleyball, basketball, soccer, and coed volleyball). All students are trained in first aid and CPR, the fitness centers are always full, and a number of students play pickup basketball games in the evening. Davidson students are not couch potatoes, and Davidson athletes maintain rigorous academic loads: men's and women's swimming and diving teams were designated All-Academic Teams for 2009–10, with team GPAs of at least 3.0. Men's basketball is well respected, and the school's unique two-man croquet team won the National Championship in 2007, 2008, and 2010.

The students at Davidson have developed an impressive array of clubs and organizations to supplement their scholastic and athletic accomplishments. Academic clubs include two premed groups, prevet, prelaw, and predental societies, mock trial and debate associations, American Chemical and bioethics societies, Greek/Latin and Russian societies, and an Investment Financial Association that manages $200,000 of the college's endowment.

Arts and cultural awareness organizations are mostly ethnic—the Black Student Coalition, Curry Club, African Students Association, Hillel, Muslim Students Association, and Organization of Latin American Students.

Several health and sexuality clubs exist, from rape crisis groups to eating disorder support groups. First aid training, fitness encouragement, and service to the homeless are offered by other health clubs.

Davidson has an abundance of media and print organizations. The *Davidsonian* is the student-published newspaper, while *SHOUT* provides "an alternative, entertaining source of news, off-the-wall stories, perspective/editorials, art and other pieces rooted in creativity." The school has three literary/arts magazines and several venues for film buffs. For those interested in radio, WALT 1610 hosts Battle of the Bands and Freestyle Rap Battles.

Davidson students focus on service as well. The Engage for Change initiative combines the efforts of several student organizations to focus on education, service, and advocacy for a yearly topic. Another group, United Community Action, is an umbrella organization that provides students service opportunities in a number of venues: Adopt a Grandparent, free medical clinics, Alternative Spring Break, Habitat for Humanity, elementary student tutoring, and the Salvation Army, to name a few.

Crime is not much of an issue at Davidson College, mostly due to the school's location. The year 2009 saw fourteen burglaries, two forcible sex offenses, one aggravated assault, and one car theft. The grounds are well lit, blue-light call boxes have been placed throughout the campus, and campus police patrol the grounds on bikes and provide safety escorts and vehicle assistance. Residential buildings are accessible only with student

GREEN LIGHT

Although campus Democrats and Republicans maintain equal membership and campus presence, coursework and athletics occupy enough time that political activism is not a great part of the college experience. One student says, "Davidson is a pretty open campus. I don't think conservative students feel targeted or prejudiced against in any way."

One area where the school has been criticized, however, is its schoolmarmish speech code, which bans innuendos, teasing, jokes, dismissive comments, or "comments or inquiries about dating" that could be construed as harassment. "Patronizing" terms (some might call them terms of endearment) such as "girl," "boy," "hunk," "doll," "honey," or "sweetie" are prohibited. Students are also forbidden sexually suggestive clothing and (amazingly) "offensive" facial expressions. Despite a virtual absence of crime or danger on campus, such policies reveal a hysterical undercurrent that infringes on free speech.

However, it is doubtful that the speech codes are strictly enforced, and on the whole, Davidson seems a remarkably worthy institution. As opposed to many schools, where activism is cherished, Davidson's graduation ceremonies remain focused on academic achievement. In fact, according to *USA Today*, Davidson no longer invites famous figures for its commencement ceremonies, and hasn't since the 1960s, when "it moved ceremonies outdoors. The first year turned so hot, and the speaker droned on for so long, that the college has since limited speechifying to brief remarks by the president." Instead, the ceremony focuses on the graduates. Sounds like a good plan to us.

ID cards. Campus social groups take turns running the "Vamanos Van," a transportation service that takes students from weekend parties back to campus in an effort to prevent drunk driving.

Tuition for the 2010–11 academic year was $36,683, and room and board amounted to $10,346. The financial aid staff say that they will meet 100 percent of a student's demonstrated financial need. While most financial aid is need based (and 40 percent of Davidson students receive need-based aid), Davidson sets aside over $1 million in various merit-based scholarships, which are awarded to approximately 10 percent of each entering class. In 2007, Davidson dropped all student loans and replaced them with grants and work-study positions. The average student-loan debt of a recent graduate is $20,858.

Duke University

Durham, North Carolina • www.duke.edu

Not named for David

In 1838, Methodist and Quaker families in rural North Carolina founded Union Institute, later known as Trinity College. This became part of the new Duke University when the James Duke family established a $40 million endowment from their tobacco business, but to this day, the largest division of the university is called the Trinity College of Arts and Sciences. A metal plaque in front of the Duke Chapel still maintains that "the aims of Duke University are to assert a faith in the eternal union of knowledge and religion set forth in the teaching and character of Jesus Christ, the Son of God. . . ." To readers of Tom Wolfe's scathing novel *I Am Charlotte Simmons*—based in part on life at Duke—these noble phrases will ring poignant. Links to orthodox Christianity became tenuous over the years and finally snapped when the Duke Chapel allowed homosexual "weddings" in 2000.

Duke is still picking up the pieces from the infamous lacrosse case of 2006, when an African American stripper falsely accused three Duke men's lacrosse players of rape, exposing the sometimes tense town-gown relations between Duke and the city of Durham. The defendants were declared innocent of all charges, district attorney Mike Nifong was disbarred for grossly mishandling the case, and observers criticized Duke president Richard Brodhead for prematurely siding with the accuser. One student reports that, "Post-lacrosse case, the overall sentiment is that students are much less happy with Brodhead and his cronies."

While Duke is a leader in many areas of scholarship and research, it slavishly follows the academic ideological trends of elite schools nationwide. If its campus isn't quite yet a piece of Cambridge, Massachusetts, or Berkeley, California, transplanted to North Carolina, it's not because the administration hasn't been trying.

Academic Life: Beautiful fragments

Duke has two undergraduate schools: the Pratt School of Engineering and the Trinity College of Arts and Sciences. Trinity undergraduates may choose one of two programs to attain a bachelor's degree. Program I is the more traditional and popular choice; its curriculum, revised in 2000, revolves around four interrelated sets of curricular requirements: Areas of Knowledge,

VITAL STATISTICS

Religious affiliation: *none*
Total enrollment: *14,350*
Total undergraduates: *6,578*
SAT/ACT midranges: CR:
   660–750, M: *680–780*;
   ACT: *30–34*
Applicants: *22,280*
Applicants accepted: *19%*
Accepted applicants who
   enrolled: *41%*
Tuition and fees: *$40,253*
Room and board: *$11,622*
Freshman retention rate:
   97%
Graduation rate: *88% (4 yrs.),*
   95% (6 yrs.)
Courses with fewer than 20
   students: *71%*
Student-faculty ratio: *8:1*
Courses taught by graduate
   students: *6%*
Most popular majors: *social
   sciences, engineering,
   psychology*
Students living on campus:
   83%
Guaranteed housing for
   four years? *yes*
Students in fraternities: *29%*
   in sororities: *42%*

Modes of Inquiry, Small Group Learning Experiences, and a student's major subject.

Trinity also offers Program II, which allows students to "examine and explore a topic, question, or theme as a core area of study which is not generally available as a course of study within Program I." Students in Program II are not held to the requirements of Program I, including the requirements for a major. Rather, a student submits, in consultation with an advisor, a written proposal to the appropriate academic department and to the Program II Committee, who approve or reject the undertaking.

Individual majors impose further requirements. Philosophy majors, for instance, take two survey courses, "History of Ancient Philosophy" and "History of Modern Philosophy," both solid introductions. English majors must take at least one course in "Literary and Cultural Study" of the medieval and early modern period, the eighteenth and nineteenth centuries, and the modern and contemporary period. English majors are no longer required to take a course on a major author—Chaucer, Milton, or Shakespeare—as they had been in the past, but very few graduate without having taken one.

Political science remains one of the school's stronger departments. Standout teachers include Ruth Grant and Thomas Spragens Jr. in political theory; Peter D. Feaver in international relations; J. Peter Euben in political philosophy and ethics; and department chairman Michael C. Munger, who is a political economist. Albert F. Eldridge (emeritus) and Michael Gillespie are also favorites. One faculty member tells us that the department is weakest in American political institutions. Still, political science majors must take at least one course in American politics. According to numerous students, the excellent instruction in the political science department is tainted by the great power wielded by graduate teaching assistants, many of whom reportedly have difficulties with the English language. Students speak highly of the Gerst Program in Political, Economic, and Humanistic Studies, which aims to foster student understanding in "the central importance of freedom for democratic government, moral responsibility, and economic and cultural life" and has freshmen in the program beginning with four courses that help introduce students to the tradition.

History majors are required to take just one introductory class and nine other courses, including classes in three of five geographic areas, a concentration of four classes in a theme like "emotions and the psychology of self" or military history, and a senior seminar. Rec-

South

ommended professors Elizabeth Fenn, Barry Gaspar, Bruce Kuniholm, and Timothy Tyson all teach in the history department.

Other good teachers at Duke, according to students, include David Aers, James W. Applewhite (emeritus), Ian Baucom, Buford Jones, Michael Valdez Moses, Thomas Pfau, Deborah Pope, and Victor H. Strandberg in English; Diskin Clay (emeritus) in classical studies; Robert Brandon, Michael Ferejohn, Martin Golding, Alexander Rosenberg, and David Wong in philosophy; Mark Goodacre, who "resists a lot of disturbing trends in recent religious scholarship and is one of the few bright spots of the religion department," according to a student; and Craufurd Goodwin in economics. Thomas Nechyba, also in economics and the department chair, is described as a "true conservative with very strong values . . . and a hard grader." The economics department is one of the university's most respected, according to students and faculty; one student warns prospective students to beware of introductory classes: "They're generally used only to remove any students unqualified for the later classes."

The exploded rape accusations made against members of the lacrosse team were the occasion for countless displays of ideological preening by faculty members, including a full-page ad published in the *Chronicle of Higher Education* and signed by some eighty-eight Duke professors (the "Group of 88"). These faculty members are still widely blamed for rushing to condemn innocent students. As one student tells us, faculty and administrators are still fixated on "race, gender, and class."

The good news is that, except for some obviously radical classes, "Duke does a reasonably good job of keeping politics out of the classroom," as one student puts it, and many students and faculty agree. For the most part, faculty members are fair, even if they are intensely left wing.

Duke's Department of Public Policy Studies is an extremely politicized enclave within the university; many professors there live within a "liberal cocoon," one student complains. The sociology program is also quite weak, and one faculty member reports that the department "has simply decided to sacrifice education in exchange for higher enrollments. The classes are rudimentary and political. The 'Markets and Management' program, housed in the department, is really a fraud and should be avoided by serious students."

Academic advising at Duke is comprehensive, but it also places a good deal of responsibility on students. Freshmen are assigned advisors based on their residence halls. Some students say that this causes problems, since computer science professors, for instance, have little guidance to offer students who want to major in philosophy. After declaring a major

---

SUGGESTED CORE

1. Classical Studies 105, Ancient and Medieval Epic
2. Philosophy 100, History of Ancient Philosophy
3. Religion 100/102, The Old Testament/Hebrew Bible, The New Testament
4. Religion 120, History of the Christian Church
5. Political Science 123, Introduction to Political Philosophy
6. English 143/144, Shakespeare before 1600, Shakespeare after 1600
7. History 91D, American History to 1876
8. Germanic Languages and Literature 183, Classics of Western Civilization: The German Tradition, 1750–1930 (closest match)

(usually in the sophomore year), a student takes a faculty advisor within that major. At that point, it is up to the student to take the initiative and gain all he can from the relationship. Unfortunately, most students visit advisors only once a semester, and that only to obtain a PIN necessary for online registration.

Students report that many professors are willing to have discussions and even meals outside office hours. With an impressive student-faculty ratio of 8 to 1, Duke students have a real opportunity to get to know their professors. Too few do, sources say. One undergrad reports that Duke students are "mostly there to get a ticket punched and attend some parties along the way." A professor agrees: "There are many people who are dedicated teachers. The students don't take enough advantage of this." Economics and public policy majors are known for being inordinately interested in padding their résumés, while premed students are notorious grade grubbers, an alumna says.

Professors teach most courses, but graduate teaching assistants sometimes teach introductory classes and often grade exams. "Writing 20," Duke's one required course, is usually taught by graduate students, who decide course content and class discussion. One student says that this class is a "complete waste of time," often politicized by the instructors. Introductory freshman classes are often large (100 to 175 students), but by the junior and senior years, when most students are working on their majors, class sizes dwindle to a more manageable twenty-five or fewer.

Serious first-year students should consider Duke's Focus Program, where they'll have an opportunity to spend their first semester immersed in true academic life, studying, living, and socializing with other students in their same "cluster." Many of the courses in the Focus Program are small-group seminars taught by distinguished professors. One faculty member says the Focus programs "are the best way to start college and equal to the best programs anywhere else in America." The university offers about a dozen topics; "Visions of Freedom" and "The Power of Ideas" are the best, says another professor.

Duke offers a long list of study-abroad programs, and 46 percent of Trinity students participate in a program, most commonly with a semester in Italy, the UK, Spain, or Australia. Programs are available around the world, from St. Petersburg to Ghana to Costa Rica. Marine biology courses are available along the North Carolina coast, as well as programs in New York (arts and media or financial markets) or Los Angeles.

Duke teaches language classes in Arabic, Ancient Greek, Polish, Romanian, German, Serbian, French, Russian, Chinese, Hebrew, Hindi, Pashto, Persian, Latin, Italian, Turkish, Japanese, Croatian, Korean, Portuguese, Balto-Finnic, Hungarian, and Spanish.

Student Life: Are you Charlotte Simmons?

Duke University is located in Durham, North Carolina, a town of about 230,000 people making the transition from tobacco to technology. Lately, the "Durham Renaissance" has spawned new bars and restaurants close to Duke's East Campus. Still, most students remain on campus, venturing into the surrounding bar and restaurant areas only if they are upperclassmen and have cars. On weekends, if social life gets desperate, these students sometimes head to nearby Chapel Hill and its lively Franklin Street. Durham does, however, have a lot to offer, with a temperate climate, Durham Bulls baseball games, October's four-day Troika independent music festival, free bluegrass concerts on the American Tobacco Campus lawn, and film festivals throughout the year.

Duke students (and Duke admissions counselors) desperately want Durham to become a college town. While it's better now than it was a few years ago, it will take more than a few new restaurants to make the city and the school get along. Racial and economic tensions still run high between black residents and students at NC Central University and Duke. The rape case only exacerbated the turmoil between Duke students—predominantly white and wealthy—and Durham residents, many of whom are black and poor.

Duke's campus is one of America's most beautiful, both in its architecture and in the lovely flora that surrounds the campus. The Sarah P. Duke Gardens consist of fifty-five landscaped, wooded acres in the heart of campus. Duke Forest covers 7,700 acres and serves as an outdoor laboratory, a favorite picnic spot, and a jogging area.

Duke's two main campuses, the Georgian East Campus and the Gothic West Campus, are joined by a bus system. East Campus—once the women's college—is where freshmen live. It has its own auditorium, gym, athletic fields, classrooms, art museum, and a few of the humanities departments. West Campus is the main site of the school and is home to most administration buildings and academic departments, upperclassmen dormitories and fraternities, athletic facilities, and other venues.

ACADEMIC REQUIREMENTS

While it has no core curriculum, in the better of its two liberal arts options, Trinity College Program I, Duke requires that students take:

- Two courses in arts, literature, or performance, from a list of hundreds, ranging from "Shakespeare before 1600" to "Sexualities in Film and Video."
- Two courses in civilizations (history, philosophy, or religion), from a list of hundreds, including "The History of Ancient Philosophy" and "The History of Emotions."
- Two courses in social sciences, again from a list of hundreds, including much that is solid and not a little that is silly.
- Two courses in natural sciences and mathematics, chosen from a worthy list.
- Two courses in quantitative studies.
- Two courses in cross-cultural inquiry ("Advanced German: Culture and Society" and "Roman History" both count, as well as the usual multicultural suspects); science, technology, and society, for which many science courses qualify; or ethical inquiry, which many humanities courses satisfy.
- Three courses in a foreign language or satisfactory performance on a test.
- The freshman "Writing 20" plus two writing-intensive courses from other disciplines, such as "Europe to the Eighteenth Century," "Advanced Composition: Spiritual Autobiography," and "The Rise of Modern Science," along with a great many others.
- A research-intensive course like "The Philosophy of Religion" or "Principles of Animal Morphology," among others of less obvious value.

South

Renovations of student housing were completed in 2009, modernizing over 800 student rooms.

Those room updates will be appreciated, for Duke requires all students to live on campus for their first three years at the school. After freshman year, housing is chosen by lottery; the most popular real estate is on West Campus, which houses many upperclassmen and where all sophomores are required to live, and residents enjoy more convenient access to classes and social activities. Smoking is not allowed in any residence halls. Most dormitories are coed but divide the sexes by halls; there are no coed bathrooms. Single-sex floors are available for both male and female students. The university guarantees housing for all four years, but it is expensive. As a result, half of seniors move off campus. Substance-free and theme housing are available. Duke currently offers a multicultural house (Prism); a house focusing on social activity, community service, and faculty engagement (Round Table); Ubuntu service house; Women's Housing Option (which isn't a female-only house, but more like a housing area for women's studies majors); and the languages house, which has French, Japanese, German, Spanish, and Chinese halls.

Two major campus events are Oktoberfest and Springfest, each of which brings bands and local vendors to the main quad. The Last Day of Classes bash brings a variety of musical artists to campus (the 2010 concert featured R&B, Irish rock, ska, and pop performers), entertaining students and giving them a chance to relax and blow off steam before finals begin.

Students say that alcohol use has been "driven underground" by the administration after a student died in 2000, having choked on his own vomit after a night of binge drinking. Fraternities and sororities at Duke must hire a university-approved bartender for all their parties. Alcohol is forbidden on the freshman campus, and the policy is usually strictly enforced. When underage students drink—and they still do—they usually drink on West Campus, where drinking-age laws are not enforced, and behind closed dorm-room doors. Many students smoke marijuana, the only illegal drug in wide use at the school.

Duke has a plethora of student groups of all types, and students are welcome to create another one if the university doesn't already offer it. The university has a strong ROTC program, with Army, Navy, and Air Force options. Other popular student organizations are the daily newspaper, the *Chronicle*; community service activities through the Circle K; the InterVarsity Christian Fellowship; musical groups; and various cultural organizations. Since the 1980s Duke has had the continuous presence of a conservative newspaper, group, or magazine on campus, although the name, genre, and focus have changed several times. The university currently plays host to the Duke Conservative Union.

Religious organizations include the Lutheran Campus Ministry, Wesley Fellowship, Campus Crusade, Manna Christian Fellowship, Westminster Presbyterian Fellowship, Hillel, Cambridge Christian Fellowship, Muslim Student Association, Navigators, Unitarian Universalist Community, and the aforementioned InterVarsity. The campus also includes a Jewish, Catholic, and Episcopal centers.

Greek life is a big deal at Duke—over 42 percent of women and 29 percent of men belong to one of the thirty-eight sororities and fraternities at Duke. Only fraternities have designated housing (they live in sections or floors of the dorms). The dedicated residential sections are comprised mostly of sophomores, but some juniors and seniors choose to live in fraternity housing as well. The comingling of Greek and non-Greek students tends to have a leveling effect on cliques. Although some exclusive fraternities exist, most pre-rush-season parties are open and spill out of the residential halls.

Duke has a Multicultural Center, this in addition to the existing Williams Center for Black Culture; the Women's Center; the International House; the Center for Lesbian, Gay, Bisexual, and Transgender Life; and the Office of Institutional Equity. According to some students, the student body has become segregated as a result of the administration's support for "diversity," and students of different races rarely mix after freshman year. Those students who choose to live in on-campus apartments, for instance, are usually black, while fraternities are mostly composed of upper-middle-class whites.

Although Duke has a reputation for leftism, the student body as a whole is largely apolitical. Studying, playing sports, getting drunk, and hooking up rank above political activism for most Dukies. Still, it's rare that a week at Duke passes without a task force report on racism, a panel on gender issues, a rally against sweatshops or the treatment of pickle-factory workers, or the like. As one conservative student says: "There are so many leftist causes on campus that, after a while, you stop noticing any of them."

In reality, "the only thing that brings everyone together is sports," says a student. In men's basketball (and increasingly women's), Duke is always a strong contender for the national championship. Men's basketball players are gods on campus—gods who happen to attend class with you, even if they aren't taking notes. Coach Mike "Coach K" Krzyzewski is a living legend. The tent city that bears

RED LIGHT

Just months after the lacrosse team suffered false rape accusations, as Duke administrators, faculty members, and some students decried the degrading sexism and racism apparently so prevalent on campus, the university went out of its way to bring some blatantly degrading and sexist acts to campus—and paid for it with student fees and tuition money. In February 2008, the "Sex Workers Art Show," a tour of strippers, former strippers, prostitutes, and more, performed in a Duke University auditorium. A campus newspaper, the *New Right Review*, reported that the 300 audience members "delighted more in the sex workers qua sex workers rather than actually sympathizing with the workers' lot in society." The show was sponsored primarily by the women's studies department and the student health center, among other groups, including the "educational" health group The Healthy Devil. Its other winning programs include "Outercourse: Intimacy without Intercourse" and the popular "Sex Jeopardy."

In 2010, the Women's Center cancelled the "Discussion with a Duke Mother" event because it was sponsored by Duke Students for Life and some students disagreed with the presence of a pro-life group in the Women's Center. Director Ada Gregory stated that "mistakes were certainly made" and affirmed the group after the decision was exposed. However, Gregory found herself in the midst of controversy again in 2010 by supporting Duke's new "sexual misconduct" policy. The policy "can render a student guilty of nonconsensual sex simply because he or she is considered 'powerful' on campus . . . Duke's new policy transforms students of both sexes into unwitting rapists simply because of the 'atmosphere.'"

his name, Krzyzewskiville, is created each year before major home games, especially the one with archrival University of North Carolina. "Duke, along with Stanford, has the best blend of athletics and academics in the country," effuses a student. Students also participate in intercollegiate club sports, competing against other area colleges and universities on thirty-seven teams. Options vary from triathlons to table tennis to ice skating. A wide variety of intramural sports like soccer, dodgeball, basketball, tennis, and flag football are available, and these are especially popular with freshmen, who often organize teams according to their residence halls. Pickup basketball games can always be found on both the East and West campuses.

Durham is prone to crime, though the university insists it is taking steps to reduce crime on campus even as it continues to rise. Crime statistics in 2009 included thirteen forcible sex offenses on campus, four robberies, eleven aggravated assaults, forty-seven burglaries, eleven car thefts, and one count of arson. However, students who follow basic safety guidelines should generally feel comfortable. The university helps prevent campus crime by 24-hour patrols, van services, emergency phones, and card entry to all dormitories. East Campus and especially the Central Campus apartments are considered to be the most dangerous areas due to their proximity to the city center.

Duke is a pricey adventure. Tuition for 2010–11 ran $40,253; room and board are around $11,622. However, admissions are need blind, and all accepted students are guaranteed sufficient aid. Some 44 percent of Duke students receive need-based aid, and the average award is around $36,576. The average Duke student graduates with $23,000 in student-loan debt—possibly due in part to the financial obligation of living on campus for three years.

Emory University

Atlanta, Georgia • www.emory.edu

For God and mammon

Money won't buy everything, but you can't blame Emory University for trying. Drawing on its substantial endowment ($4.5 billion as of 2009), Emory has made its students extremely comfortable. Faculty are plentiful and highly qualified, research opportunities and internships are available in nearly every discipline, and students can choose one of seventy majors. Money can buy a lot.

About 175 years removed from its humble beginnings as a small Methodist college in Oxford, Georgia, Emory has shed much of its character and southern charm. Since Emory's main campus moved to Atlanta in 1919, the school has seen a steady shift in priorities. The liberal arts now play second fiddle to career-driven disciplines, and classroom discussions between students and professors have become less important than research. Late-night philosophical debates are rare; conversations on how to make money in investment banking are not.

Academic Life: New South

Emory imposes no core curriculum and has relatively anemic distribution mandates. Emory's "requirements are quite minimal and the 'fields' are very broadly defined," one professor says. "I'm sure it's quite easy to avoid courses that should be fundamental to a true liberal arts education. The laxness may be a blessing in disguise, however, insofar as students may avoid being forced by the college to take unserious or trendy classes."

Students should seek out the Program in Democracy and Citizenship, developed by Professor Mark Bauerlein and currently directed by Professor Harvey Klehr. The innovative program provides courses for freshmen, extracurricular events, and seminars intended to introduce students to the founding texts, arguments, and principles behind American democracy, capitalism, and culture. Professor Bauerlein created the program to "remedy the vacuousness of undergraduate knowledge of American foundations," gathering funding from the university and outside sources to sponsor traditional courses in the liberal arts.

Happily for students, Emory has pumped a good deal of its own money into improving teaching. Classes are small, and almost all are taught by full-time faculty members—except most of the required freshman English courses, which are run by graduate students, mean-

VITAL STATISTICS

Religious affiliation: *none*
Total enrollment: *12,755*
Total undergraduates: *6,890*
SAT/ACT midranges: CR:
  640–740, M: *670–760*;
  ACT: *30–33*
Applicants: *17,446*
Applicants accepted: *27%*
Accepted applicants who
  enrolled: *28%*
Tuition and fees: *$39,158*
Room and board: *$11,198*
Freshman retention rate:
  95%
Graduation rate: *82% (4 yrs.),
  88% (6 yrs.)*
Courses with fewer than 20
  students: *68%*
Student-faculty ratio: *7:1*
Courses taught by graduate
  students: *10%*
Most popular majors: *social
  sciences, business/market-
  ing, psychology*
Students living on campus:
  66%
Guaranteed housing for
  four years? *no*
Students in fraternities: *28%*
  in sororities: *30%*

ing that where students arguably need the guidance of professors the most, Emory doesn't provide it. However, "professors are extremely open to helping students and getting to know them outside of class," says one student. Honors theses, independent study, and research projects allow students to interact with faculty members in more formal academic relationships. Professors are required to hold weekly office hours, of which students often make use.

"Emory students are generally characterized by professional ambition more than by intellectual curiosity, and there is much obsession with grades (as opposed to the work required to get them)," says a professor. A colleague agrees: "Only a handful in a given year love the discussion of ideas for their own sake."

Over half of Emory students go on to graduate or professional school, and their undergraduate careers are often focused on landing at such a destination. One professor says, "Academics are taken seriously by a great many students, and the liberal arts, while under pressure, remain very strong."

Advising begins freshman year in the mandatory Pre-major Advising Connections at Emory (PACE), where freshmen are "matched with faculty and peer advisors with closely related interests." First-year students must also attend at least ten sessions offered by the Office for Undergraduate Education and Campus Life on such issues as academic integrity, scholarships, and course registration. Once a student declares a major, which he must by the end of sophomore year, he is assigned to a professor within that department. Advisors are usually helpful if students need them, but it is the student's responsibility to seek one out. "Students must use their good judgment, or the guidance of a good teacher, rather than depend on Emory for guidance," says one professor.

Among Emory's strongest departments are political science, psychology, English, history, anthropology, and biology. "Every professor in the philosophy department is great," a student says. However, one alum cautions: "I would advise undergrads to choose courses wisely. Much of what is taught will be biased toward a view that philosophy and truth have little to do with one another."

The English major calls for one course in English literature before 1660 and one after 1660, one course in American literature, and one course having an interdisciplinary or theoretical emphasis, with offerings such as "Postcolonial Literature" or "Literature and

South

Religion." An English major can graduate without reading Shakespeare, although students may choose to do so as one of their English literature requirements or as an elective.

The history department takes a traditional approach and offers a General Studies in History track, or requires students to concentrate on the United States, Europe, or Latin America and the Non-Western World. Course offerings vary from the traditional ("History of Rome") to the trendy ("Gender and Sexuality in the Middle Ages"). History majors pursuing the General Studies track must take courses in American history before and after 1860; European history before and after 1750; and at least one non-Western world history class.

Political science is less structured, with a broad list of classes that fulfill major requirements (from "Political Philosophy of Aristotle" and "The American Founding" to "Women and the Law" and "American Radicalism"). All poli sci majors must take a class on the American political system; political methodology; one course each from the four fields of American politics, international politics, comparative politics, and political theory; and four electives.

> ## SUGGESTED CORE
>
> 1. Classics 101, Classical Literature
> 2. Philosophy 250, History of Western Philosophy 1
> 3. Religion 205/348, Biblical Literature/The New Testament in Its Context
> 4. Religion 311, Early and Medieval Christianity
> 5. Political Science 302, Modern Political Thought
> 6. English 311, Shakespeare
> 7. History 231, The Foundations of American Society to 1877
> 8. History 376, European Intellectual History: 1789–1880

Emory's undergraduate business college admits students who have completed at least sixty-four credit hours and offers a unique bachelor's in business administration. As a program that is entered only once one is a junior, the BBA allows students to develop a solid liberal arts footing before beginning business training. While the business school has a strong reputation, economic studies at Emory are said to be less prestigious. The university retains a rigorous premed program.

Emory has almost as many graduate and professional school students as it does undergraduates. The graduate school offers degrees in forty programs, in which students earn either masters' or doctoral degrees. The powerful professional schools (and the campus presence of the Centers for Disease Control) can't be ignored, says one professor, "with the massive medical school tail sometimes wagging the dog."

Among the best teachers at Emory are Patrick N. Allitt and James Melton in history; Juan del Aguila, Robert C. Bartlett, Merle Black, Harvey E. Klehr, Randall W. Strahan, and Carrie R. Wickham in political science; Mark Bauerlein and Ron Schuchard in English; Marshall P. Duke in psychology; Donald W. Livingston and Donald Phillip Verene in philosophy; Timothy Dowd, Cathryn Johnson, and Frank J. Lechner in sociology; Arri Eisen in biology; and Paul H. Rubin in economics.

Two out of every five Emory students take their junior year or at least one semester abroad. Destinations literally span the globe: from Australia to Ecuador, Scotland, Namibia, the Netherlands, Russia, and Japan, an Emory student can study just about anywhere. With Chinese, Latin, Persian, German, Japanese, Russian, Tibetan, Yiddish, French,

Italian, Arabic, Dutch, Hebrew, Hindi, Ancient Greek, Spanish, Korean, Portuguese, and Tibetan offered, students can choose from an amazing variety of language courses.

Student Life: The real thing

If building projects are a sign of progress, Emory must be doing very well indeed. The main and oldest part of campus is a quadrangle of pink and gray Georgia marble buildings separated by a long green lawn. On warm, sunny days, students have classes here, study, play Frisbee, and talk with friends. The visitor cannot help but be impressed by the expansive beauty of the campus. And although the school's location in urban Atlanta makes expansion rather difficult, Emory has found room in other areas. The university developed Clairmont Campus about a mile from the main campus, abutting the university's Lullwater Park; students have to take a shuttle bus to reach their classes. But that's a small annoyance for those upperclassmen lucky enough to live there. "It looks like a country club," says one student. "We have apartments, tennis courts, cafes. My parents think I'm getting spoiled." With full kitchens and furnished living rooms, the $3,400–$5,594 per semester accommodations are a sure sign of the wealth that comes to Emory.

The Cox Computer Center offers rows and rows of equipment; some workstations have two large monitors for every computer. "There's almost no reason for a student to bring a computer to campus," says one student. A recent addition to student conveniences is Wi-Fi coverage over nearly the entire campus, including dorm rooms.

Freshmen and sophomores are required to live on campus, and 66 percent of upperclassmen choose to live there as well, since life on campus is convenient, traffic in Atlanta is horrible, and off-campus apartments can get expensive. Emory's expanded and improved shuttle system now helps those living in the area, as well as on campus, get around more efficiently. Except for freshmen, who live together in traditional dormitories, Emory students usually enjoy suite-style residences or on-campus apartments close to most academic buildings. Students select their freshman roommates online, through a sort of personals service where they list their interests and expectations in a roommate. Emory offers three types of dormitories: single-sex by floor; "grouped coed" floors, with stairwells or lobbies separating the sexes; and mixed coed floors. All bathrooms are separated by sex. Emory offers one all-female hall and theme houses such as the Student Experiment in Ecological Design, language or service-oriented houses, and the Black Student Alliance. Groups of between five and twelve students may apply to create theme houses based on their interests.

Students have practically every dining option available to them on campus, including organic, fair-trade, and local choices (the school even hosts a farmer's market)—but only one kind of soft drink. At orientation, freshmen are sent on a treasure hunt where they are told to find a can of Pepsi. It's a trick assignment, because it can't be done. One of the first gifts to Emory (a.k.a. Coca-Cola University) came in 1914 from Asa Candler, the president of the Coca-Cola Company; his brother was president of the university at the time. In 1979, two brothers gave Emory more than $100 million dollars in Coca-Cola stock, and a large percentage of the endowment is still invested in the company. As a result, Emory's endow-

South

ment didn't suffer the 25 or 33 percent collapse seen at many other schools in the 2008 stock market crash.

Emory has no football team, and any attention paid to sports is usually directed toward the soccer and basketball teams or to intramurals, which are very popular. One professor says, "While 'school spirit' is not what it is at football factories, Emory does have a serious intercollegiate sports program that is among the best in Division III in the country. Sports plays the role it should in a serious academic institution." About 80 percent of the student body participates in intercollegiate, club, recreation, or intramural sports. The

ACADEMIC REQUIREMENTS

In lieu of a core curriculum, Emory offers some loose distribution requirements. Each student must take:

- One First-Year Seminar. Selections include "The Black Athlete in American Society," "Coffee and Chocolate," "Trojan War/Travels of Odysseus," and "Evolution: Concepts and Misconcepts."
- First-Year Writing Requirement, to be completed in the first two semesters. The three choices are "Introduction to Literary Studies," "Expository Writing," and "Writing About Literature."
- Three writing-intensive courses, from a plethora of choices in every undergraduate department, including "Anthropology of Emerging Disease," "The Archaeology of Jerusalem," "Animal Communication," "A Survey of Wind Literature," "Modern Catholicism," and "Studies in Shakespeare."
- One course of four credit hours in mathematics and quantitative reasoning. Choices include "Computer Science Fundamentals," "Empirical Methods in Economics," "Introduction to Logic," and "Applied Statistics for Psychology."
- Two four-credit courses in science, nature, and technology, plus one lab. Courses available include "From Botox to Behavior," "Thermal Physics," "Meteorology," "Evolution: Human Brain and Mind," and "Drugs and Behavior."
- Two courses in history, society, and cultures for a total of eight credit hours. There is a very wide range to choose from, including "Jimmy Carter's America," "Ancient Greek and Medieval Philosophy," "American Elections and Voting," "Introduction to Irish Studies," "The Black Freedom Struggle," and "The Old South."
- Four courses in humanities, arts, and performance for sixteen credit hours. These must include two courses in a single foreign language (AP credits can exempt students). Courses offered include "Understanding Architecture," "Major Texts: Ancient to Medieval," "Novel Buddhas," "Human Goodness," and "Black Music."
- One health education class called "Personal Health" for one credit hour. (Students can test out.)
- Three courses in physical education and dance for one credit hour each—one of which must be a "Principles of Physical Fitness" course. Classes in ballet, modern dance, movement improvisation, swimming, jogging, step aerobics, and tennis qualify.

YELLOW LIGHT

While the Emory administration and faculty lean further left than the student body, most faculty members seem content with their situation and report the freedom to teach as they see fit. Clearly, this can lead to glory or disaster, depending on how they see things. With a generous smattering of diehard progressive and traditional professors and a massive variety of course offerings, Emory is truly a place where any type—and any quality—of education may be attained.

Emory can be most accurately criticized for what is not allowed to be said. The Foundation for Individual Rights in Education (FIRE) has warned students that Emory's speech codes include forbidding all negative stereotyping and "acts of intolerance," including "all 'use of epithets or names in a derogatory manner,'" a rule of the sort that the U.S. Supreme Court has deemed unconstitutional. Ironically, the school also prohibits students from interfering "with the rights of others to free expression," although in restricting types of speech (and, in a separate incident, banning T-shirts with the names of non-school-approved clubs), it does just that.

Emory has left interpretation of what constitutes harassment, "demeaning depictions," intolerance, or derogatory speech in the hands of the Office of Resident Life and Student Conduct—and in some cases up to the accuser. Because of this, FIRE warns, legitimate works of satire or parody could fall on the wrong side of the university's speech codes.

What political activism exists on campus is often conservative, and political fervor pales in comparison to the rich offerings for service and educational enrichment.

school is replete with fine fitness facilities: the George W. Woodruff Physical Education Center boasts an Olympic-size swimming pool, basketball and racquetball courts, a climbing wall, an indoor track, and weight and exercise machines. When Atlanta hosted the Olympic Games in 1996, Emory served as a practice facility. Students may also participate in the Outdoor Emory Organization (OEO), which sponsors outdoor weekend trips including rafting, hang gliding, hiking, pumpkin picking, rock climbing, and other activities.

Few students explore Atlanta. The university itself has nearly everything a student could require. Still, Atlanta is just a commuter rail ride away. Students can purchase reduced-rate tickets on campus to art exhibits and cultural performances throughout the city. Then there's the Michael C. Carlos Museum, Emory's on-campus art facility, with a fine permanent collection and diverse visiting exhibits each year.

Nearly a third of students are members of Emory's twelve fraternities and thirteen sororities, and Greek organizations provide most of the activities for weekend social life. Sorority Village was completed in 2006, featuring ten townhouses facing the fraternity houses. Each sorority house accommodates between ten and twenty-four women and contains a community space, kitchen, and large chapter room. "Greek life is strong here, but it's not as intense as at most other schools," says one student. Parties and drinking are prevalent on campus. "Because the majority of students are affluent, they are able to buy a lot of alcohol and throw big parties," one student says. "But most students' primary goal is academics and grades—when those are satisfied, anything else goes."

The school offers an impressive variety of activities. Arts students will enjoy the Breakdance Club, Photography Club, Karma-

Bhangra Dance, No Strings *a cappella* choir, and Rathskellar improvisation group; student government offers six associations and councils; cultural clubs include the Asian Christian Fellowship, the Persian Club, Thai Connection, and Chinese Calligraphy; media clubs include magazines, journals, and papers like *Alloy*, the literary magazine; *Black Star*, "Emory's Microphone to the Black Community"; and the humor periodical the *Spoke*. There's also WRME radio and ETV, a television station that runs student films and sports shows. The school has a number of academic groups, from the Society of Physics Students to Entrepreneur Network, Model United Nations, Pre-Physical Therapy, and Astronomy Club.

Emory hosts four political organizations: College Republicans, CSAmerica, Students for a Free Tibet, and the Young Democrats. The College Republicans were founded by Newt Gingrich in 1962 and have recently hosted Mitt Romney, Bob Barr, David Horowitz (whose 2007 speech at the campus was cut short after repeated interruptions by non-university-affiliated protesters), and Jonah Goldberg. In 2009, the Republicans and Democrats held their first joint meeting since 2007, debating health care and affirmative action. CSAmerica (the Collegiate Society of America) "encourages non-partisan political exploration in a social setting" through debate, dialogue, guest speakers, and political movies.

Emory's Cannon Chapel is the site of an ecumenical worship service every Sunday morning and a Catholic Mass and reception on Sundays and most Wednesdays. The chapel is spare, with its sign—not its architecture—identifying it as a church. Inside it looks more like a lecture hall. Religious student organizations abound and include Baptist Student Union, Christian Fellowship, Episcopal Campus Ministry, Reformed University Fellowship, Wesley Fellowship, Greek Orthodox Campus Ministry, and Catholic Campus Ministry, and many others, including Latter-Day Saints and Metropolitan Christian Church. Jewish, Muslim, Hindu, Buddhist, and Baha'i communities all hold services on campus. Although Emory is in the Bible Belt, it does not have the feel of a religious school. However, one philosophy graduate student says that "there have been quite a few students who have renewed their spiritual life as a result of their interactions with professors."

Crime is a drawback for most other Atlanta schools, but Emory is located in the relatively safe Druid Hills neighborhood. Still, in 2009 the campus reported nine forcible sex offenses, seven burglaries, nineteen stolen cars, and one arson. There are emergency phones all over campus. One female student says, "I've never felt unsafe, so I've never had to use them, but it's nice to know they're there." The campus does offer a late-night driving service, but since it has only one car, students report having to wait 20 minutes for its arrival, leaving them vulnerable.

Emory's price is as upscale as the experience it provides; in 2010–11, tuition was $39,158, while room and board average $11,198. Admissions are need blind, and Emory promises to offer full aid to accepted students. Almost 40 percent of students receive need-based aid averaging nearly $30,000, and the average student-loan debt of a recent graduate is $23,181.

University of Florida

Gainesville, Florida • www.ufl.edu

Swamped

The University of Florida is a major public land-grant research university—the state's oldest and most comprehensive. Located in rural northern Florida, the city of Gainesville revolves around the campus and its student population. In the 1860s, the state-funded East Florida Seminary in Ocala was consolidated with the state's land-grant Florida Agricultural College in Lake City. In 1905, the college became a university and was moved to Gainesville, where the first classes were held in 1906. Today it is one of the five largest universities in the nation, with over 50,000 students. The large student population, the popularity of Gator football, and a pervasive party atmosphere have a way of distracting many students—and others—from the university's academic mission.

Academic Life: Aim low, sweet chariot

The University of Florida has no core curriculum. Instead, it offers general education requirements. These are aimed at helping the student attain "competency in goals and methods in the humanities, physical and biological sciences, mathematics, and social and behavioral sciences." These requirements don't aim high enough. An unwary student could fulfill them without learning very much about a number of critical topics. Although one *could* fulfill these requirements—even the international/diversity requirement—with substantial courses rooted in traditional academic disciplines, there are also dozens of politicized, trendy, and frivolous choices, such as "Ecofeminism," "Contemporary Lesbian/Gay Literature in the United States," "Sex Roles: A Cross-Cultural Perspective," and "Women, Race, and Imperialism." One professor warns that "students have a broad selection of courses, given the size of the university," which means that while a "student seeking a strong major that promotes critical thinking can blossom," there's nothing to prevent a student from "seeking an easy way through the credentialist system."

"The general education requirements, in my opinion, dilute the education received in this university," a business student says. "Students take the most vapid courses in the university to meet the requirements, such as 'Wildlife Issues' for a bio credit or 'Astronomy' for physical education credit."

Sometimes students fall into these vapid courses not because they want to bypass more serious options but because the courses they want are not available. One student says that since "there are few electives offered per semester . . . students have to settle for a class they didn't want to get into in order to graduate." This student bemoans the relative paucity of faculty in certain departments. "The extremely low tuition means that a number of courses are large lectures, but junior- and senior-level courses are kept relatively small," a professor says. Another professor is more blunt: UF, he says, "is a large university and, to my mind, only worth attending if you can gain admission to the Honors College."

But what about the Honors College? The honors program promotes itself as providing "the richness of a small-college experience with the vast resources of a major research university." The program offers smaller classes, special honors sections of large courses, exclusive dorms, program-dedicated advisors, and a unique social and academic community for elite students during their first two years on campus. Sadly, some of the special courses offered in this program strike us as offering more quirk than core: offerings include "21st Century Skills in *Starcraft*" (a computer game), "Origami," and "Goodscapes: The Science and Culture of a Meal." One professor, originally drawn to the school to teach what used to be an "integrated humanities program," is disillusioned. The honors track is now a "hodgepodge." "No longer a balanced overview of the Western humanities tradition," he says, the program has lost its rudder in a sea of fragmentary offerings. "Professors propose courses, usually their own special interest. At UF, the idea of a general, or liberal, education, unfortunately, is long past." In other words, even UF honors students should not blithely expect to gain a humanistic education along with that fantastic tan. They'll have to search out the worthy courses among the dross. The honors program does at least offer an alternative to massive classes and impersonal sections led by sometimes unintelligible TAs.

A quick glance at some key departments shows that they, too, have rather diffuse expectations. English majors, for instance, do not need to read Shakespeare; they must simply take ten courses in the subject, including several upper-level seminars, whose approaches range from "British Literatures" to "Feminisms, Genders and Sexualities." History majors do not need to know anything about America before 1900; only two courses are required

VITAL STATISTICS

Religious affiliation: *none*
Total enrollment: *50,691*
Total undergraduates: *33,628*
SAT/ACT midranges: CR: *560–670*, M: *580–690*; ACT: *26–31*
Applicants: *25,798*
Applicants accepted: *42%*
Accepted applicants who enrolled: *58%*
Tuition and fees: *in state, $5,020; out of state, $25,160*
Room and board: *$8,640*
Freshman retention rate: *96%*
Graduation rate: *58% (4 yrs.), 82% (6 yrs.)*
Courses with fewer than 20 students: *40%*
Student-faculty ratio: *20:1*
Courses taught by graduate students: *not provided*
Most popular majors: *business/marketing, social sciences, engineering*
Students living on campus: *23%*
Guaranteed housing for four years? *no*
Students in fraternities: *15%* in sororities: *15%*

SUGGESTED CORE

1. Classics 3340, Ancient Greek and Roman Epic
2. Philosophy 3100, Ancient Greek Philosophy
3. Religion 2210/2240, Hebrew Scriptures/New Testament
4. Religion 3500, History of Christianity
5. Political Science 4053, Great Political Thinkers: Machiavelli to Marx
6. English 4333, Shakespeare
7. History 2010, United States to 1877
8. History 3091, Intellectual History of Europe, Renaissance to Modern (closest match)

in U.S. history, and both could focus on the twentieth century. Nor need political science majors study the U.S. Constitution, although a course in required in the U.S. federal government. All students, however, must take at least some math and science.

There is, however, one undeniable advantage to the open-endedness of the UF curriculum: flexibility. "Students can enroll in classes offered by other departments with ease," points out an urban planning student. In his specialty, he "can choose from a number of specializations, certificates, and concurrent degree plans, ranging from transportation engineering to sustainable design to historic preservation. Joint engineering or law degrees are often pursued by students. Additionally, [my] college offers several study-abroad programs [Brazil, France]. I was particularly stretched [in a good way] during the summer semester I spent at UF. . . . I enrolled in landscape architecture, environmental science, and history courses outside my discipline. Of these, the environmental science course was the most rigorous and most alien to my previous experiences." The Department of Urban and Regional Planning, he adds, "is ranked in the top twenty-five in the nation."

Despite UF's size, a psychology major says, "Professors are very accessible, as far as I have seen. Most professors post office hours and all are required to have office hours at some point during the week." However, students "often do not take advantage of office hours," a professor counters. The trouble may lie in the sheer size of lecture classes. One student in the Honors College says that while all of her professors have been very friendly, "the larger classes are less 'personal' and therefore there is less contact with the instructor." Another student laments, "I think mentoring is very weak at UF. There are too few professors for the size of the student body." Fortuitously, the university landed federal stimulus funds to hire approximately one hundred professors over the 2009–10 school year and rebuild its faculty ranks, which were recently decimated because of budget cuts.

But this may do little to remedy another obvious problem: the high percentage of undergraduate courses led by teaching assistants rather than professors. A psychology major says, "The role of the TA depends on the professor. In some classes, the TA is there to answer all questions by the students, grade exams and quizzes, and hold review sessions." Another student says that the role of TAs varies depending on the subject matter. About 20 percent of her classes have been taught by TAs, and sometimes the "system seemed to work very well." However, a student in the business department says that "many students complain about how bad some TAs are with dissemination of information, heavy accents, and lack of communication." Nearly all upper-division courses are taught by professors.

University leadership is aware of the complaints by many students about the teaching at UF. President James Bernard Machen seems committed to reforming the school. Machen has worked to increase funding for teaching—instituting a $150 million, multiyear fund-raising Faculty Challenge Campaign, still under way, to be used for graduate studies, faculty research, salaries, and benefits. The fund-raising campaign is part of the larger goal to make the University of Florida a top-ten school by improving the faculty, raising academic standards, and (of course) making "diversity" a top priority at the university.

As an indicator of where UF's priorities really lie, however, consider that while $150 million is now being raised to improve the faculty, a *$1.5 billion* capital campaign is under way to improve the facilities, and these are almost entirely affiliated with various specialized programs and schools. In 2010, the 70,000-square-foot Hough Hall was completed in the Warrington College of Business Administration at a cost of $21.5 million. About the same time, the 163,000-square-foot UF Biomedical Sciences Building opened to great fanfare, at a cost of $90.5 million. As if that weren't enough, the nearby 500,000-square-foot Shands Cancer Center affiliated with the medical school opened in 2009, costing $388 million. In two years, $500 million was spent . . . on facilities.

Where does the undergraduate go to find his way in such a mega-institution? Advising is the responsibility of each college, and therefore the quality varies from college to college. The Academic Advising Center primarily serves students who need help choosing a major. In some departments and colleges, students must meet with an advisor before they can register for courses, while other departments and colleges have a faculty advisor on staff, available for students who seek assistance. One PhD student notes: "If students are entrepreneurial, other options for academic advisement and support exist off campus."

In the classroom, professors seem to allow students to express a variety of opinions without fear. And while the faculty leans left, a number of conservative professors can also be found. More important, an atmosphere of freedom seems to prevail. One such faculty member says, "Yes, most of the university is left-leaning. But it's not ideological in the sense that there is intolerance of opposing views. It's not so pervasive that it affects instruction in individual classrooms. As a scholar, I never felt any pressure to shape my views to some politically correct standard." One student reports that he and some of his compatriots have felt "unwelcome in the political science and philosophy departments, and in some programs in the College of Fine Arts." Some professors in these programs are said to be very vocal in the classroom about their extra-academic opinions, leaving conservative students feeling it would be imprudent to dissent.

Some of the best academic programs at UF include business, nursing, journalism, psychology, education, engineering, agriculture, and microbiology (in addition to urban planning, mentioned above). Solid professors include Stephen McKnight (emeritus) in history; Sanford V. Berg and David A. Denslow in economics; Thomas Auxter (emeritus) in philosophy; Richard Conley and David M. Hedge in political science; Mary E. Collins in soil and water sciences; Bonnie Moradi and Carolyn Tucker in psychology; William Marsiglio and Hernán Vera (emeritus) in sociology; and Dawn Jourdan, Richard Schneider, Christopher Silver, and Paul Zwick in urban planning.

The intellectual curiosity of the student body is said to flicker, with some bright spots. A faculty member says, "I see the spectrum—village idiots to intensely motivated students." A student in one of the more rigorous departments says, "To be honest, the people I knew

South

who attended UF got more out of the athletics (Gator football) than the academics. Another student says, "UF offers a lot of 'fluff' courses for students looking to meet requirements, such as sports and bartending classes." (At UF, admittedly, the latter could come in handy.)

UF offers numerous languages and many short-term, summer-, semester-, or year-long programs in over eighty countries. Students can major in Chinese, Japanese, French, German, Arabic, Hebrew, Portuguese, Russian, or Spanish.

Student Life: No lines for tanning

Gainesville is a college town. The mild winters and hot summers allow for outdoor activities year-round. Plus, our urban-planning insider points out that "the city of Gainesville has made a concerted effort to preserve the trees and landscape within its limits. Parks and preserves (especially Paynes Prairie and Lake Wauberg) proved excellent recreational experiences. Dining in Gainesville is varied and vibrant—ranging from an idiosyncratic pizza joint (Satchel's) to a first-class Mediterranean restaurant (Ti Amo)." There are beaches within a ninety-minute drive, and popular destinations such as Daytona Beach, Orlando, Tampa, and Jacksonville are only two hours away. About 97 percent of students are Florida residents. When there's no football game or other activity to keep them around campus, students tend to go home on the weekends. "There are only two disadvantages to Gainesville: the traffic on game days and the summer heat/humidity."

Football is the life of the party at UF. On Saturdays in the fall, the Gators attract some 90,000 fans into Ben Hill Griffin Stadium, otherwise known as the Swamp. UF has a very physically active student body, so it should come as no shock that this large southern university prides itself on being consistently ranked among the top five NCAA programs in the nation in overall athletics for both men's and women's sports. In recent years, the revived

---

ACADEMIC REQUIREMENTS

With no core curriculum in place, UF imposes loose general education requirements:

- One course in composition. Classes offered include "Survey of American Literature" and "Issues in American Literature and Culture."
- Two classes in math. Offerings include "Basic College Algebra" and "Math, Art and Computing."
- Three courses in the humanities. Options are many, including everything from "Introduction to Shakespeare" to "Feminism."
- Three classes in the social and behavioral sciences. Choices range from "Marriage and Family" to "Minorities in American Society."
- Three courses in the physical and biological sciences. Classes offered include "General Chemistry" and "Food Analysis."
- Two diversity classes, one of which must have an "international" focus. Course options include "Key Issues in African-American and Black Atlantic Thought" and "Transnational Feminism."

South

men's basketball program has become a focal point of school spirit as well, especially with its first National Championship victory. Parties tend to revolve around Gator football and basketball games. "Football games basically shut down the campus on Saturdays, and parties are ubiquitous," a student says.

Gator Growl, an annual pep rally held before the homecoming game, brings to campus nationally recognized comedians and musicians. A full weekend of parties takes off from there. "The Gator Growl pep rally is unrivaled in the whole of America," says a student. Another recalls visiting UF "during Gator Growl and instantly knowing I wanted to come here. The school you see with your parents is not always the school you see on the weekend." (Parents take note!) Fortunately, UF is big enough to accommodate students who do not want to concentrate all their extracurricular time on football watching or drinking. "Whatever you like doing, you will find it," a student says. "If you dig the Greeks, we have them; if you like clubs, we have enough to make your head spin; if you like museums and performing arts, we have them; if you like clubbing, we have it—although the quality and variety is debatable." Every Friday, the Student Government Association sponsors Gator Nights at the Reitz Student Union as an alternative for students looking for fun away from the party scene. Students can count on a movie followed by free midnight breakfast. According to event publicists, "The program offers FREE first run movies, bands, comedians, improve shows, arts and crafts, novelties, interactive games, cultural events, interactive lectures, dances, DJs, artists, video game tournaments, popcorn and soda."

Athletic students have many options. One reports: "In addition to on-campus gyms and recreational facilities and fields, UF even owns a private lake off campus where students can use rowboats and canoes, or have a picnic or play volleyball." Another student says that many enjoy "lazing about on the grass of the Plaza of the Americas in the heart of campus and watching the bats leave the bat house at dusk and fly out over Lake Alice for an insect meal."

While most freshmen live on campus, only about 23 percent of the student body does. All on-campus residences are coed. However, male and female students are not allowed to share a dorm room and do not share bathrooms. (Actually, Florida law prohibits male and female students from cohabitation in on-campus apartments unless they are married.) With minimal space available on campus, the university does not guarantee housing for all four years. But Gainesville itself offers plenty of options and a welcoming ambience for students, as the city revolves around student life. Students at UF tend to pay a good bit of attention to their physical appearance, and the Florida sunshine lets them flaunt it. One of the more modest female students says, "I feel a little uncomfortable walking through campus while all of the girls are dressed in practically nothing."

Only 15 percent of students join a fraternity or sorority, but there are more than 800 student clubs and organizations, as well as more than sixty intramural and club sports in which to participate, all of which help make this giant university seem a little cozier. Student groups include the Florida Karate Club, Florida Swing Dancing Club, Gator Bujutsu Club, Hindu Students Council, Mennonite Student Group, Skateboarding Club, Woman Raising Awareness in People, Gator Free Thought, Fellowship of Christian Athletes, Gator Outdoor Club, International Folk Dance Club, Pro-Life Alliance, Hip-Hop Collective, Navy-Marine Student Association, Model United Nations, Union de Estudiantes Puerto-

South

One student says, "The atmosphere on campus lies between [left and right]. For example, a transgender ordinance was passed by the city, and fierce debate arose on both sides of the issue. Students on both sides campaigned before the vote took place. In general, the campus is left leaning, so that could be considered the prevailing orthodoxy, but the education provided to students is not stultified by political correctness."

UF has an admirable record of defending free speech, regardless of its source or content. Speakers ranging from the Ku Klux Klan to the People for the Ethical Treatment of Animals are permitted on campus. The school's director of student activities explains that even extreme voices are allowed in order to facilitate the free exchange of ideas. The Foundation for Individual Rights in Education "Red Alerted" UF for its censure of free speech in January 2008, when the university tried to stop a student showing of the documentary *Obsession: Radical Islam's War Against the West*. (The group had been posting flyers for the event with the headline "Radical Islam Wants You Dead.") After a call from FIRE, however, the college reaffirmed the students' right to free speech and allowed the movie.

riquenos Activos, Recurso, Close-Knit Gators, Club Alligator Swim Team, Gator Collegiate Cattlewomen Association, and Tennis on Wheels. In addition, there is a remarkably vivid religious presence on campus. Besides the usual Turlington Plaza preachers, thousands of students, and even some faculty, join religious groups, including Baptist Collegiate Ministries, Campus Crusade for Christ, Catholic Student Fellowship, Islam on Campus, and Jewish Student Union.

Political expression on campus is surprisingly balanced. Students are not activists, but both conservative and liberal perspectives are regularly aired on a range of topics. Students typically voice their discontent not in the classroom but rather in the mainstream student newspaper, the *Florida Alligator*, or through gatherings in Turlington Plaza to plug various causes or movements. The *Florida Frontier*, a conservative newspaper, debuted in 2006.

The UF campus itself is an oft-overlooked benefit: although there is no architectural theme, one professor says, since it accommodates "one of the most complex universities in the country, with twenty-one schools, that makes it a very interesting and large campus. They did a very good job of integrating the newer buildings with the older and more historic ones. It's a very attractive campus."

Crime on campus is not terribly prevalent, given the large number of students, and recently crime has diminished. In 2009, the school reported one aggravated assault, thirty-three burglaries, and three forcible sex offenses on campus. The university provides a free pickup service for any students who feel uncomfortable walking, as well as emergency call stations around campus. One female student says that usually "an officer will be there within thirty seconds." For the most part, students consider themselves safe, but they report unease about the issue of "date-rape drugs" and some prefer not to walk alone at night. One incident, in which the campus police shot a student in the spring of 2010, is still being investigated.

The University of Florida is generally considered affordable, and for those students seeking aid, plenty of options are available. Tuition for 2010–11 for in-state students was

South

only $5,020 (out of state, $25,160), and room and board were estimated at around $8,640. Says one student, "The good thing about UF is that for many Florida residents with good test scores, [a state merit] scholarship pays full tuition and cost of books. I know many friends who are at UF specifically for this reason." Some 41 percent of students get need-based aid, and the average student-loan debt of a 2009 graduate was $15,932.

Furman University

Greenville, South Carolina • www.furman.edu

Lapsing Baptists?

Founded in 1826 by the South Carolina Baptist Convention, the school takes its name from the prominent preacher and southern independence activist Richard Furman. When Furman broke formal ties with the Baptist convention 166 years later, some alumni and professors feared that this move would mark the beginning of the school's secularization—sending it down the worldly path to prestige already trod by once-devout Duke, Vanderbilt, and Emory.

Indeed, over the past two decades, Furman has risen steadily in reputation; once an excellent regional university, Furman is now one of the top liberal arts schools in the nation. Happily, it still maintains many of the things that have made it venerable, such as a close faculty-student interaction and a fairly strong liberal arts curriculum. Students now hail from forty-six states and thirty-one foreign countries, but the college draws a little less than one-third of its students from the state of South Carolina and around 75 percent from the Southeast. Perhaps that is one reason Furman has retained a unique atmosphere and fairly traditional orientation. In fact, if the reports of students and professors here can be trusted, Furman is one of the friendliest schools included in this guide. But the question remains: does Furman's Baptist heritage define the school any longer? The answer, as one professor puts it, is "not much."

Academic Life: The slippery slope to sameness

Devotion, once heaped on religion, has been rerouted to academics, and in the search for prestige the school seems to be shedding much of what made it distinctive. Under the leadership of its president, David Shi, who has just departed after fifteen years in office, the school worked hard, as one senior puts it, "to lose uniqueness." Indeed, he says, the school has "bent over backwards not to hire professors that reflect traditional values." It is unclear how the school may change under its newly hired president, Rodney Smolla, who was previously dean of Washington and Lee University School of Law.

The university approved a change to Furman's general education curriculum that took effect for the 2008–9 academic year. The new curriculum, intended to "invigorate intellectual life," breaks out requirements into three main areas: First-Year Seminars (every freshman must take two), Core Requirements (eleven courses distributed in various areas), and the Global Awareness Requirement (two courses—one in world cultures and one in human and natural environment). Says one senior of the new core, "it has become less rigorous." Another insider is more blunt, calling the changed system "vacuous." "The new curriculum," he says, "has literally no required courses, only a wide range of courses eligible to fulfill the distribution requirements." No less dubious are the additions to Furman course offerings, in which, for instance, religion is now rebranded as Ultimate Questions. One professor laments, "Unfortunately, our popular and serious year long humanities sequence did not survive the curriculum change, but there is hope among the faculty that it will reincarnate when we get used to the new curriculum."

While Furman administrators may hope to increase the school's national visibility, they do still seem to realize that big grants and research projects are less important than undergraduate teaching. "Faculty get tenure by being great teachers first," says a Furman professor. "Scholarship is very important, but secondary." Another professor tells us, "Teaching is definitely number one at Furman. In my opinion, Furman has, if anything, been a little too emphatic about teaching to this point." He adds, "We're moving in a slightly more research-oriented direction, which will, I think, be to the good of everyone in the long run."

Here, however, not everyone agrees, and some worry that the school's special advantages are being watered down. Says one graduating senior, "New time constraints demand that outstanding teachers teach less, teach at a more superficial level, and substitute their teaching by simply assigning reading—a level of 'teaching' I could have gotten at any state school."

Furman is a university—and not a college—only because of its two small graduate programs: a master of science in chemistry, and a master of arts in education. Classes are taught entirely by faculty members, including the writing courses associated with various majors. Introductory classes usually have twenty-five to thirty students, while upper-level courses in the major often include only ten students per class.

Business and political science classes, however, two popular areas at Furman, are always larger than those in other departments. "The professors at Furman are excellent," says a junior psychology major. "They are very approachable. I really enjoy my classes." Strong

VITAL STATISTICS

Religious affiliation: *none*
Total enrollment: *2,964*
Total undergraduates: *2,754*
SAT/ACT midranges: CR: *580–690*, M: *600–680*; ACT: *25–30*
Applicants: *4,538*
Applicants accepted: *68%*
Accepted applicants who enrolled: *21%*
Tuition and fees: *$36,296*
Room and board: *$9,170*
Freshman retention rate: *92%*
Graduation rate: *81% (4 yrs.)*, *86% (6 yrs.)*
Courses with fewer than 20 students: *57%*
Student-faculty ratio: *11:1*
Courses taught by graduate students: *none*
Most popular majors: *social sciences, business/marketing, history*
Students living on campus: *96%*
Guaranteed housing for four years? *yes*
Students in fraternities: *40%* in sororities: *47%*

professor-student interaction remains serious enough to instill undergrads with genuine interest in coursework rather than just in making the grade. "Furman students are curious and motivated," says one professor.

Furman students have plenty of opportunity for extra help should they need it. The Center for Teaching and Learning, a writing lab and technology help center, is frequented by students. On-campus tutoring is free.

Along with a classroom approach to the liberal arts and sciences, Furman also promotes something that it calls "engaged learning," encouraging students to participate in internships in the Greenville area to supplement their classroom experiences. Students can often receive course credit for the internships. According to the *Chronicle of Higher Education*, Furman offers two courses, "Medical Sociology" and "Medical Ethics," that combine internships at local hospitals with intensive study of the philosophical and social implications of medical practice. Preprofessional courses in business administration, accounting, and music performance are also encouraged. On top of what's offered at the Career Services Center, Furman students find their job prospects strengthened by a strong alumni network.

The strongest departments at Furman are chemistry, psychology, and political science. The history department is also sound. The internship and study-abroad opportunities in political science are especially plentiful and worthwhile. Furman students can take advantage of the close interaction between professors and students and the department's association with the study-abroad program in the United Kingdom. The physics department graduates eight to twelve majors per year—not bad for a school of Furman's size; the department chair boasts that 100 percent of Furman physics majors who sought admission to graduate schools were admitted to a program of their choosing.

Some key departments, however, have followed the general slippery trend. English majors, for instance, can graduate without reading Shakespeare. History majors need not study American history prior to 1877. Political science majors, though, must take American constitutional theory in "Introduction to American Government."

Furman's language offerings are surprisingly wide. They encompass Chinese, French, German, Hindi, Italian, Japanese, and Spanish, with majors in French, German studies, and Spanish. There is also an Asian studies major and English for speakers of other languages and Latin American studies concentrations. Beginning courses in Hindi and Italian can be had as well.

Students say some of the best teachers at the school are John Barrington, T. Lloyd Benson, Timothy Fehler, and David S. Spear in history; Chris Blackwell in classics; Sandra K. Wheeler in chemistry; Erik A. Anderson and James C. Edwards in philosophy; William M.

Baker in physics; Stanley J. H. Crowe and Margaret Oakes in English; David H. Bost, David W. Morgan, and Alvin L. Prince in modern languages and literatures; Paul R. Rasmussen in psychology; Weston R. Dripps in earth and environmental science; and Silas N. Pearman III in health and exercise science. Within the political science department, students name Donald P. Aiesi, James L. Guth, Akan Malici, Brent F. Nelsen, Benjamin Storey, and Aristide F. Tessitore as particularly good teachers. Nelsen, one student says, has a "genuine concern for the students," and as chair he has "recently redesigned the major, making it even more challenging and rewarding."

In 2008, Tessitore and Storey launched the "Tocqueville Program for the Study of Value in Politics." They received a $40,000 grant from the conservative Bradley Institute, a foundation "devoted to strengthening American democratic capitalism and the institutions, principles, and values that sustain and nurture it" for their inaugural year. The first theme (which offered its first course in the spring semester of 2009) is biotechnology and politics. The course brought a slate of high-profile, center-right speakers like Francis Fukuyama, Leon Kass, and Virginia Postrel to campus, studying the original, classic texts that engage with the problem and then looking at the application of those ideas in modern times. Professor Storey, most recently, received a prestigious grant from the National Endowment for the Humanities, concerning "Enduring Questions." With it, he will start a new "First-Year Writing Seminar" at Furman, to begin in the spring of 2011. The course's proposed title: "Know Thyself: But How?" Requiring texts by Jane Austen, Shakespeare, and others, the class will probe questions of self-knowledge, morality, politics, philosophy, and theology.

The university's Riley Institute (named for Richard Riley of Clinton administration fame) also brings in high-profile speakers. It leans slightly left, but as one professor says, "It's fair and, in general, is a high-class operation with which ambitious students should get involved."

The Charles H. Townes Center for Science is a $62.5 million science complex that houses the departments of biology, chemistry, earth and environmental sciences, and physics. It opened in fall 2008. The Townes Center is part of a $400 million capital campaign, over three quarters raised as of February 2010. Along with the science center, the funds will also help support current operations ($60 million) and other capital initiatives ($33 million), and will add $275 million to the university's endowment.

Student Life: Everyone's home

Furman is located in Greenville, South Carolina, the sixth-largest city in the state. The city has many venues offering a wide array of cultural events, many available at a student discount. The Peace Center hosts ballets, symphonies, Broadway musicals, civic events, and circuses throughout the year, while the 16,000-seat Bi-Lo Center is the main venue for major sporting events and concerts. Greenville has two professional local theaters, Centre Stage and the Warehouse, located in the city's historic West End, a favorite hangout with college students. Downtown Greenville is the preferred area for shopping, dining, and nightlife. Students are often found playing Frisbee in Falls Park on the Reedy, located in the West End, with twenty acres of gardens, several waterfalls, and a pedestrian suspension bridge overlooking Reedy River.

Furman is a residential campus, and with several new halls the university now requires that students live on campus for all four years of college. Freshmen and sophomores usually dwell in traditional corridor-style halls or suites, while upperclassmen can use the school's on-campus apartments (North Village) as a transition into life after graduation. "There's really no reason that you'd even want to live off campus—there are so many different choices in housing," says a senior. Freshmen arrive on campus a week before classes start and compete on teams with dorm mates, building camaraderie and school spirit. A highlight of the week is a meet-and-greet party with the university president.

Before Furman's split with the Baptists, men lived on one side of campus and women lived on the other, but today most dormitories are single-sex by floor—men live on one floor, women on the next. Furman is still traditional enough that students are permitted in the rooms of members of the opposite sex only during visitation hours—10:00 AM to 2:00 AM daily—and must in theory be escorted by a resident. The rule used to be strictly enforced, but one dorm escort confides that it is now a joke. The suggestion to follow a couple upstairs and deliver a 2:00 AM knock-knock, he says, would make supervisors "laugh their heads off."

Because Furman moved to its present campus in 1957, no building is much more than fifty years old. Most of the buildings are of red brick, but while none are jarringly ugly, the beauty of the campus lies in surrounding nature, not the architecture. The grounds are well shaded with a great variety of arboreta—walkways are lined with magnolia, pine, and oak trees. The main focus of the campus is a thirty-acre man-made lake with dozens of ducks and geese. Running trails and picnic tables surround the lake, and the dining hall shows off excellent views of the water. On one small peninsula stands the Bell Tower, a replica of a structure that stood on Furman's former downtown campus. A college tradition calls for every student to be tossed into the lake on his birthday.

Furman's messy 1992 divorce from the South Carolina Baptist Convention has led some on campus to worry about the school's religious identity. At least one professor fears that "Furman is on the slippery slope to secularism. We are still very traditional, but the administration is not committed to maintaining a Christian identity." Although there is no religion requirement in the curriculum and Furman is nondenominational, it is not quite secular yet. The Charles E. Daniel Memorial Chapel, with its cross-topped steeple, looks like a small town's First Baptist Church, and it is one of the most prominent buildings on campus. It holds a university worship service each Sunday morning and a Catholic Mass each Sunday evening. Any historical tension between Catholics and Baptists has mostly evaporated.

The Baptist Collegiate Ministry is still the largest student group on campus, hosting a "Tuesday Night Together" Bible study each week and mission trips, retreats, and concerts throughout the year. One Catholic student says religious activities are there if you want to take part in them, but "you're certainly not going to feel persecuted if you don't." A student-led Religious Council oversees the university's various ministry groups, of which there are several: in addition to the Baptist Student Union, Young Life and the Catholic Campus Ministries are also active. The Mere Christianity Forum, an interdenominational student group, has as its mission to "model the unity of the church, embody ecumenical tradition, and reclaim and proclaim the Gospel." Politically, the group Conservative Stu-

South

dents for a Better Tomorrow has recently coalesced (to make up for seeming complacency in the College Republicans) and brought eighteen conservative speakers to campus last year alone—including eighty-seven-year-old polymath Phyllis Schlafly. Furman students fill life outside of the classroom with countless activities—from parties to academic clubs (try the popular and competitive Mock Trial) to community service work in the Greenville area. But students say they spend most of their free time socializing with friends in their rooms.

Among the many student groups on campus are the American Chemical Society, Art Students League, Student Chapter of the Association for Computing Machinery, Bartram Society, Order of Furman Theatre, Le Salon Francais, Phi Mu Alpha Sinfonia, Philosophy Club, Society of Physics Students, Cicero Society, Debating Society, Murrow Society in communications studies, Psychology Club, Spanish Club, Political Thought Club, Bowling Club, Archery Club, Indie Rock Club, Percussion Club, Boxing Club, Ski and Snowboard Club, and Furman Powerlifting.

ACADEMIC REQUIREMENTS

Furman has no core curriculum, but does impose some general education requirements on all students, who must complete two first-year seminars, which must include at least one writing seminar, plus core requirements that include:

- Two courses in the "empirical study of the natural world."
- Two classes in the "empirical study of human behavior and social relations." Options include "Introduction to American Government" and "Introduction to Criminology."
- One course using "historical analysis to study past human interactions." Dozens of courses can fulfill this requirement. Options include "Ancient Europe and the Mediterranean" and "Media History."
- One class in the "critical, analytical interpretation of texts," with choices ranging from "Greek Epic" to "Environmental Writing."
- One course in visual or performing arts, such as "History of Western Art" and "Art Education for Elementary School Teachers."
- One math or formal-reasoning class.
- One course in foreign language.
- One class in Ultimate Questions (chosen mostly from the philosophy and religion departments). Choices include "Augustine of Hippo: His Life and Thought" and "The Bible and Gender Politics."
- One course "emphasizing the importance of the body and mind." Options include "Wellness Concepts" and "Realizing Bodymind: Whole Person Development."

Students also take two courses meeting global-awareness requirements, including:

- A course addressing humans and the natural environment, such as "Ecology" and "Environmental Politics in China."
- A course focusing on world cultures, such as "Mayan Archaeology" and "Women, Gender, Islam."

YELLOW LIGHT

Among Furman's most beloved traditions were once its rites for freshman orientation. These included a midnight serenade in which girls threw candy down from balconies to shirtless boys singing songs like "Brown-Eyed Girl"; a President's Picnic, with a pile of boys' shoes whose anonymous owners were paired up for blind dates with the girls who picked them; and a My Tie event where, similarly, a girl donning a given boy's tie became his date for the dance. Alas, these traditions have been choked off by the administration, fearful, we are told, that such openly heterosexual practices may offend those of other sex orientations on campus (although no gay group openly objected to them).

Another incident shows, at least, that speech at Furman may still be openly, if cautiously, expressed: pro-lifers received permission to place 200 crosses on campus to commemorate the anniversary of *Roe vs. Wade*—only to have them snatched away in broad daylight (but between classes) by unseen political opponents. The theft was perceived as an attack on free speech, and student groups of all political stripes banded together to denounce it, yielding a net moral victory for both speech and life. If it's any clue as to the direction the school will take under its new president, Rodney A. Smolla, his field of expertise is free speech. Such is his dedication to the cause that he has, with a style of subtle reasoning that *Kirkus Reviews* calls "scholarly, yet accessible," sided with both Larry Flynt (of *Hustler* magazine) against Jerry Falwell and with corporations against those who would limit their influence on government through campaign donations. With those credentials, he may even continue to allow social conservatives the right to speak at Furman as well.

The Paladins compete in NCAA Division I athletics and are members of the Southern Conference. Furman school spirit seems to be strong: the football team, although only Division I-AA, draws up to 15,000 fans for each home game—a good turnout, considering that the student body totals just under 3,000. Soccer games are also well attended; the women's team holds the record for the longest winning streak in the Southern Conference. There are also club sports (including an equestrian team) and intramurals.

Greek organizations claim a large minority of the student body, but the university has tried to keep them from becoming too exclusive. Furman has a "delayed rush" system, which begins in January, so freshmen get to know their hallmates before they go Greek. Fraternity and sorority houses are off campus and almost entirely nonresidential. They are used mainly for meetings and social events. Furman is officially a dry school, but the administration does make concessions for charity events on the outskirts of campus. Drinking does play some role in campus life, usually behind closed dorm-room doors or at off-campus bars. One student claims that the North Village apartments enjoy the semi-official privilege of being "wet." Students operate a sort of designated-driver shuttle service to downtown Greenville that runs from 8:00 PM to 2:00 AM on Thursday, Friday, and Saturday nights.

Cultural events at Furman are not only plentiful but also required. Students must attend at least thirty-two Cultural Life Program (CLP) events during their four years on campus. One student estimates that the university offers around 200 each year, meaning that a student need attend only about 5 percent of them. But many students go more frequently.

A single week in November 2008 listed the following activities: a student debate between the College Republicans and College Democrats; a lecture on "Hurricanes, Hunger, and Haiti"; an "Evening of One-Act Operas"; a Cultural Rhythms dance production; a talk on the dangers and statistics surrounding student drinking; and *The Glass Menagerie* performed by Furman students. Most students say the CLP requirement not only encourages students to attend cultural events but also pushes the university to offer them.

Furman is sufficiently secluded from the city of Greenville that crime rarely filters through the campus gates. In 2009, the university reported three forcible sex offenses, two stolen cars, twelve burglaries, and two aggravated assaults. The most common incidents are alcohol violations—of which there were 154, but none of these resulted in arrests. Students say they generally feel safe. The school recently installed "Code Blue" telephones all over campus to help prevent crime. Furman Public Safety also operates a nighttime safety escort service and offers self-defense courses for women.

In terms of price, Furman stands in the midrange of private schools. Tuition in 2010–11 was $36,296, with room and board at $9,170. Tuition has risen by $10,000 since the 2005–6 school year and is likely to keep on climbing. However, the school's financial aid is fairly generous—admissions are need blind, and some 85 percent of students receive some financial aid. The average recent graduate owes $27,373 in student loans.

George Mason University

Fairfax, Virginia • www.gmu.edu

Freedom U.

George Mason University was named for a great but lesser-known patriot—the author of Virginia's Declaration of Rights (a prototype for the Declaration of Independence and U.S. Bill of Rights). The school was founded in 1957 as a branch of the University of Virginia and became independent in 1972. In keeping with President Alan Merten's focus on "technology across the curriculum," this public university has indeed thrived in the sciences and technical fields, especially in serving the graduate students who constitute almost 40 percent of the student body.

The school has amassed an impressive faculty, including some of the country's leading free-market economists, among them the venerable Nobel Prize–winner James M. Buchanan. For such a young university, it is quickly reaching a critical mass, attracting students who seek both a fairly traditional education and college environment, even as they mingle with an ethnic cross section of the Global Village.

Academic Life: Home rule

GMU has an impressive economics department, sufficient solid courses for students to obtain a sound liberal arts education, and some state-of-the-art facilities. All this is available to Virginia students at a relative bargain, despite recent increases in tuition. The university is governed by the surprisingly powerful and traditionally conservative GMU Board of Visitors, which has often been at odds with the school's faculty senate. Precisely because of limited input from faculty, GMU has retained a moderately strong general education program. One student says, "The general education program at George Mason is superb. It ensures that dedicated students will be exposed to a wide variety of disciplines, producing well-rounded, informed individuals with global perspective and proficiency in subjects outside the specialized fields."

Students who want more structure may opt for one of the university's alternative educational paths. One of these tracks, Mason Topics, directs freshmen through the general education requirements according to a particular theme. On-campus students stay together on "living/learning" floors in the residence halls. They attend films and lectures together and form study groups. Each group has its own theme, such as the Global Village, the American Experience, the Information Society, or the Classical Presence. Another path is the interdisciplinary New Century College. One who followed it says, "I encourage all students, especially conservatives, to avoid New Century College. It remains politicized and out of touch with reality." But others speak favorably of New Century, with one student saying, "Its discussion-based environment is definitely the most informative and enlightening. . . . It has caused me to stretch my learning beyond my major and to integrate the different areas of my learning into cohesive projects," such as crafting an academic website.

Upon arrival, students are appointed professional advisors, moving on to faculty members upon choosing their majors. The advising process is a mixed bag. "Professors tend to be very accessible and warm," says one student. But another complains, "I don't feel like my advisor cares about my success. . . . I am pretty sure that if he saw me walking on campus, he wouldn't even be able to tell you that I was one of his students." Professors, for their part, complain of students who don't take advantage of opportunities for interaction. One professor says, "I have office hours every week, and fewer than ten students come to see me during the semester."

Elite students may fulfill their general education requirements through the honors program (offered by invitation only), which offers smaller classes and greater access to top faculty. Students are given access to the best resources and faculty on campus, as well as their own lounge and computer lab, priority registration, and their own floor in university residences. Through an integrated curriculum of interdisciplinary courses, honors students "learn to probe the foundations of knowledge, develop new skills in addressing complex issues, and think independently, imaginatively, and ethically." Unfortunately, many of the recent honors courses seem infused by multiculturalism or other postmodern fads.

The faculty is especially impressive at GMU. One student claims, "Mason is effective at recruiting top talent, as evidenced by the experts representing us in fields such as economics, neuroscience, conflict resolution, and politics. They are attracted to GMU's spirit of creativity, exploration, and independence." But some of the over sixty majors offered by George Mason attract better scholars than others. The English department, for instance, has garnered criticism for, in the words of one student, "replacing courses that examine individual genius with those that examine culture (e.g., African American literature) in a

VITAL STATISTICS

Religious affiliation: *none*
Total enrollment: *19,702*
Total undergraduates: *13,067*
SAT/ACT midranges: CR: *510–620*, M: *520–630*; ACT: *23–27*
Applicants: *13,732*
Applicants accepted: *63%*
Accepted applicants who enrolled: *31%*
Tuition and fees: *in state, $8,684; out of state, $24,500*
Room and board: *$8,320*
Freshman retention rate: *85%*
Graduation rate: *39% (4 yrs.), 63% (6 yrs.)*
Courses with fewer than 20 students: *29%*
Student-faculty ratio: *16:1*
Courses taught by graduate students: *not provided*
Most popular majors: *business/marketing, social sciences, English*
Students living on campus: *26%*
Guaranteed housing for four years? *yes*
Students in fraternities: *7%* in sororities: *6%*

SUGGESTED CORE

1. Classics 340, Greek and Roman Epic
2. Philosophy 301, History of Western Philosophy: Ancient
3. Religion 371/381, Classic Jewish Texts/Beginnings of Christianity
4. Religion 316, Christian Thought and Practice
5. Government 324, Modern Western Political Theory
6. English 335/336, Shakespeare
7. History 121, Formation of the American Republic
8. History 101/102, Foundations of Western Civilization/Development of Western Civilization

sad, egalitarian effort." The course descriptions for English, and a faculty that includes a number of experts in gender studies, minority literature, and pop culture, support this assessment. Still, the department has left room for interesting courses in writing and rhetoric as well as solid literature courses. Novelist Alan Cheuse, who teaches creative writing, is among the most esteemed of the English department faculty.

Other top teachers at George Mason include Robert Ehrlich in physics; John Orens in history; Hugh Sockett in public and international affairs; and Charlie Jones and Steven Weinberger in linguistics.

Once students declare their majors, they face varying departmental requirements. Political science majors, fittingly, must take an American constitutional theory class. English majors must take a survey course on writing and literature and at least one class in literature before 1800; in literature before 1915; in popular, folkloric, or minority literature and culture; and an upper-level elective. Unfortunately, it is possible for English majors to avoid Shakespeare and British literature altogether. History majors must take two courses in United States history; two in European history; two in global, Latin American, African, Asian, or Middle Eastern history; a course titled "Introduction to the Historical Method"; a senior seminar in history; and four electives. As in English, students can avoid important areas of the discipline if they really want to.

Most of George Mason's politicized departments can be found in the social and behavioral sciences, from which students must take one course; this area includes sociology, psychology, anthropology, and women's studies. And in a different sense, politics is present in George Mason's economics department—which is staunchly free market. One of its faculty says proudly, "The economics department is clearly the best freedom-oriented department in the world. It also houses many of the leading econ bloggers." There are a number of big guns on staff. Led for years by chairman Donald Boudreaux, who just stepped down, the department includes leading theorists of the Chicago, Austrian, and Public Choice schools of free-market economics. The faculty, according to another professor, "deliberately ignores political correctness and the conventional economic wisdom." One student says, "The most impressive thing about our school is, hands down, the economics department." The resulting curriculum is described by one student as "diverse and challenging, but also fun." Besides Boudreaux and Nobel laureate James Buchanan (emeritus), other excellent professors in the department include James T. Bennett, Peter J. Boettke, Bryan D. Caplan, Tyler Cowen, Garrett Jones, Dan Klein, Peter Leeson, David Levy, Russell Roberts, Charles K. Rowley, Thomas Rustici, Alexander Tabarrok, Gordon Tullock (emeritus), Richard E. Wagner, and Walter Williams. Many of these are nationally known as cutting-edge scholars heavily invested in their research—an investment that actually transfers into the classroom: "The best aspect of emphasizing research at GMU is that it translates directly into teaching material for those teachers willing to take a personal approach to the material," says a graduate student.

GMU does sponsor many trips and study-abroad programs, including ongoing opportunities to visit Belize, Cambodia, Costa Rica, Ecuador, Egypt, England, Eastern Europe, Greece and Turkey, India, Ireland, Israel and Palestine, Italy, Kenya, Mexico, Nicaragua, South America, Switzerland, Syria, and Spain. As for foreign languages, students may minor in Chinese, classical studies, French, German, Japanese studies, Latin, Russian, or Spanish. Students may major in foreign languages, with a concentration in either French or Spanish.

Student Life: Achieving critical mass

Until recently, George Mason's campus architecture could perhaps best be described as "spontaneous." Fairfax, Virginia, is part of the blur of the sprawling Washington, D.C., metroplex, with little architectural charm or cultural scene. However, the campus lies only fifteen minutes by rail from downtown Washington, D.C., which offers all the nightlife, social opportunities, and historical interest any student could wish for.

Owing to a spate of recent construction, several more stylish, neotraditional buildings have popped up on campus, surrounding pleasingly landscaped walkways and plazas. A little more than thirty years have passed since the university declared its independence from the University of Virginia and built its own facilities, so it has taken some time to move beyond a transitional phase, marked by a commuter-school culture. But at last, the traditional college experience is taking root. Today, as a professor notes, "the school is now the largest residential college in Virginia." A transfer student from out of state says, "New residential buildings are popping up all over campus, and it is becoming a more friendly place for traditional full-time college students. . . . Also opening in this same area was a new dining hall and a twenty-four-hour Starbucks. Southside, the new dining hall, was a major upgrade from the old one that was located in the ugliest building on campus. In addition, two new fitness centers equipped with basketball courts, weight rooms, treadmills, and the like opened this past year to accommodate the increasing number of residential students. More campus housing is scheduled to open this fall, equipped with new dining options that include a New York-style pizzeria."

As the living environment blossoms, so does student life. "The Housing Office at GMU does an excellent job of promoting community for the students who live on campus," says one of these students. "There are events going on every day in residential areas. All the resident advisors are required to do at least three to four events a month for their floors alone. There are so many housing events going on that they often overlap—these events are specifically for resident students. I've personally seen residents on the same floor get very close with each other by attending the different programs on campus."

Still, three fourths of students live off campus. For them, a student says, "there are other Mason-wide events going on almost every single day. GMU is such a fun campus with so many things going on that one would have a hard time feeling like he/she does not

South

belong." Less than 10 percent of students belong to Greek organizations, which neverthe-less, according to students, form the hub of a burgeoning social life on campus. As one freshman wrote in an online forum, "If you are an out of state student you're going to want to make friends right off the bat. It really becomes like a ghost town around here on the weekends. If you're a guy, join a frat or else parties are going to be almost impossible for you to get into." Campus parties tend to center around pre- and post-game celebrations of the school's popular basketball team.

Much of student life organizes itself around a network of more than 200 organi-

---

ACADEMIC REQUIREMENTS

George Mason does not have a core curriculum. Instead, it has two tiers of distribution requirements: "Foundation Requirements," which provide for basic communication skills and information-technology literacy, and "Core Requirements," which give the student a limited exposure to the range of the liberal arts and sciences. The "Foundation Requirements" are:

- Two courses in "written communication," English 101 (or English 100 for foreign students) and English 302. At least one course in a student's major must be writing intensive.
- Either "Oral Presentations" or "Interpersonal and Group Interaction."
- One course in information technology. Classes include "Computer Ethics and Society" and "IT in the Global Economy."
- One class in quantitative reasoning, such as "Linear Mathematical Modeling" and "Introductory Statistics."

Students must also fulfill the "Core Requirements," taking eight courses in various disciplines:

- One class in literature. Qualifying choices include "The Legacy of Greece and Rome" and "Major Hispanic Writers."
- One course in the arts. Options range from "Early Christian and Byzantine Art" to "Dance Appreciation."
- Two classes in the natural sciences, including a lab. Choices include "Introduction to Modern Astronomy" and "The Ecosphere."
- Either "History of Western Civilization" or "Introduction to World History."
- One course in global understanding. Choices range from "Major World Religions" to "Comparative Mass Media."
- One class in the social and behavioral sciences. Options include "Human Evolution, Biology, and Culture" and "Human Dimensions in Conservation."
- One "synthesis" course in which students are supposed to "communicate effectively in both oral and written forms; connect issues in a given field to wider intellectual, community, or societal concerns; and apply critical thinking skills." Options include "Experiencing the Criminal Justice System" and "Free Speech and Ethics."

South

zations. Groups include the Mathematics Club; Psychology Student Diversity Affairs Committee; Caribbean Student Association; Circle for Japanese Interests; Kurdistan Student Organization; Polka Club; Aviation Club; Biological Sciences Society; Physics and Astronomy Club; Society for Bioengineers; Badminton Club; Belly Dance Club; Chess Club; George Mason Medieval Swordsmanship; George Mason Quidditch Team; George Mason Swing Dance Club; and Table Tennis Club. Economics-related organizations are highly rated, including an Adam Smith reading group, led by Professor Dan Klein, and the GMU Economics Society. Says a member of the latter, "I personally discovered all of my best friends in it."

Religious ministries range widely, including Muslim, Jewish, Catholic, and a wide variety of other Christian chaplaincies. Conservative-minded believers should investigate the Fellowship of Catholic University Students (FOCUS), Chi Alpha Christian Fellowship, Christians on Campus, or Campus Crusade for Christ.

Political groups include the (far-left) Students for a Democratic Society, Animal Rights Collective, Campus Rand Association, College Democrats, College Republicans, Mason Liberty (libertarian), Feminist Student Association, and the gay-oriented Pride Alliance.

The Princeton Review regularly places GMU at or near the top of its rankings of most diverse campuses. Students do see some benefit from this: "With the diversity level at Mason being so high, class discussions are much more informative," says one. "There will be Muslim students in your 'War and Terrorism' class, who will provide a unique perspective."

Some of the most visible groups are nonpolitical organizations directed at students from specific countries, such as the Indian Student Association, and almost every conceivable religion is represented on campus. However, not all celebration of ethno-religious diversity

GREEN LIGHT

Students report that outside of a few unduly politicized departments, professors strive for balanced teaching and an atmosphere of genuine tolerance. Another student says, "George Mason is one of the most diverse campuses in the world. There is a wide range of professors in all political spectrums and religious backgrounds. From my experience, the classroom has always been one of free and vigorous debate." Another student concurs: "George Mason, although being one of the most conservative schools in the country, still makes all students feel welcome and is still relatively liberal compared to the nation as a whole."

With numerous outlets for libertarian interests, including various institutes, think tanks, the economics department, and the mostly conservative board of visitors, one professor reports: "Openness to conservative ideas in areas such as law, economics, and public policy make George Mason an unusually good fit for students with rightward leanings and practical policy interests." A student concurs: "I have noticed more vocal conservative students and a comparatively open environment toward all political viewpoints." GMU houses the Institute for Humane Studies, which promotes the study of freedom in the conviction that greater understanding of human affairs and freedom would foster peace, prosperity, and social harmony. IHS offers scholarships, grants, internships, and seminars to students at GMU and across the country.

at GMU is spontaneous and student driven. In addition to the Office of Equity and Diversity Services, the school spends money on an Office of Diversity Programs and Services, a Multicultural Research and Resource Center, a Black Peer Counseling Program, and a Women's Studies Research and Resource Center—all of which engage in the same hodgepodge of counseling, workshops, sensitivity training, and lectures devoted to feminism, racism, sexism, classism, homophobia, and other varieties of contemporary groupthink.

Facilities on the 677-acre campus are impressive. The campus library is stocked with more than a million volumes, while more ambitious undergraduates and graduate students make use of the extensive interlibrary system, which involves many D.C.-area institutions. There are excellent online databases and a popular Ask a Librarian feature, which gets students immediate help with resources through online discussion. Part of the library is housed in the George W. Johnson Center, a gargantuan 320,000-square-foot complex with computer labs, student services, class space, and a four-story open atrium where students can gather between classes and take advantage of a food court, banks, the campus bookstore, and various other services. The nearby Center for the Arts includes a 2,000-seat concert hall, two smaller theaters, dance studios, and assorted music and fine arts studios, while the Johnson Center itself includes a 310-seat cinema.

The university has several athletic fields, and the Patriot Center seats 10,000 for indoor sports (and rock concerts), an impressive number given that only 250 athletes compete in the twenty men's and women's NCAA Division I sports programs. Mason's Patriots men's basketball team is the star athletic attraction, one of the top-ranked teams in the country; it made the Final Four in 2006, and in 2007–8 it went as champion of the CAA conference to the NCAA tournament. Other varsity teams include baseball, cross-country, golf, lacrosse, rowing, soccer, softball, swimming and diving, tennis, indoor and outdoor track and field, volleyball, and wrestling—but no football. Many intramural sports are also available. The twenty-six club sports encompass everything from underwater hockey to bowling.

Crime is not unknown on the George Mason campus. In 2009, the school reported five forcible sex offenses, one aggravated assault, four stolen cars, two arsons, and four burglaries. These security problems have led to an on-campus escort service and "lots of police." Despite that, one professor says, "Everyone here feels quite safe." Students agree. Says one young woman, "I never get worried walking around at night."

GMU's undergraduate tuition for the 2010–11 term was $8,684 for Virginia residents and $24,500 for out of state students. Room and board averaged at $8,320. Admissions are need blind, but the school does not guarantee to match each applicant's need. The average student-loan debt of a 2009 graduate was $19,528.

University of Georgia

Athens, Georgia • www.uga.edu

Eat a peach

The University of Georgia has come a long way in just three decades. The school was founded in 1785, but for much of its history it has been regarded as little more than a training ground for agriculture students. UGA is now on the rise, drawing better students and more prestigious faculty, largely as a result of the state of Georgia's Helping Outstanding Pupils Educationally (HOPE) scholarship program, through which in-state students can receive full-tuition scholarships, inducing many of the state's top students to stay in Georgia. HOPE students must maintain a B average to keep their scholarships.

UGA's curriculum has quite a bit going for it. Distribution requirements for undergrads are comparatively strong, while the honors program is both highly regarded and competitive. One professor praises the sought-after Foundation Fellows Program as a "super honors program that truly offers an Ivy League experience at bargain basement prices." One student reports that she chose UGA over Columbia University when she realized that she could receive a genuine classical education at a bargain price. Throw in a low-key political atmosphere, a fantastic college town, and a strong sense of school spirit, and UGA is clearly one of the better choices for students interested in a southern state university.

Academic Life: Keep HOPE alive

Georgia's curriculum centers on a set of distribution requirements that collectively provide students as broad an education as one could hope for at a large state school. While students at UGA have flexibility in choosing their courses, it's impossible for them to get away with taking courses in just one or two disciplines, and most of the courses that fulfill the College of Arts and Sciences requirements are surveys in fundamental areas like "Introduction to Economics," "Introduction to Western Literature," and "Introduction to Political Theory." Furthermore, a full one-third of the courses students take are general education courses. While core course descriptions seem solid, professors have the freedom to teach as much or as little foundational material as they choose—an inevitable side effect of replacing a core curriculum with distribution requirements. Unfortunately, students may choose between "English Composition" II and "Multicultural English Composition."

VITAL STATISTICS

Religious affiliation: *none*
Total enrollment: *34,885*
Total undergraduates:
  26,142
SAT/ACT midranges: CR:
  560–660, M: *570–670*;
  ACT: *25–29*
Applicants: *17,776*
Applicants accepted: *54%*
Accepted applicants who
  enrolled: *49%*
Tuition and fees: *in state,
  $7,530; out of state,
  $25,740*
Room and board: *$8,460*
Freshman retention rate:
  94%
Graduation rate: *51% (4 yrs.),
  81% (6 yrs.)*
Courses with fewer than 20
  students: *36%*
Student-faculty ratio: *18:1*
Courses taught by graduate
  students: *27%*
Most popular majors:
  *finance, biology, psych-
  ology*
Students living on campus:
  27%
Guaranteed housing for
  four years? *no*
Students in fraternities: *21%*
  in sororities: *24%*

Many students regard a few course requirements as being insubstantial and easy and of little educational interest. Among these are the "United States" and "Georgia History and Constitution" requirements, which students can easily test out of. Students in the College of Arts and Sciences must also fulfill a cultural diversity requirement by taking one course in African American, Native American, Hispanic American, or Asian American studies. Most of the courses that fulfill these requirements seem politicized, but courses like "Topics in Romance Languages" and "American Indian History to 1840" are less so. Students must also take a multicultural class—not to be confused with the separate diversity requirement—such as "Race and Ethnicity in America." UGA students must also fulfill an "environmental literacy" course requirement. According to a science professor, courses in this area are typically solid. "Ecology here is science rather than politics," the professor says. "Same with agriculture; if you want to talk about the world hunger problem, you go and find agriculture experts who can tell you exactly what's going on."

As the state's flagship public university, the University of Georgia has reaped the benefits of HOPE more than any other school. A study conducted by two UGA economists and funded by the National Science Foundation reported that since the institution of the HOPE scholarship in 1993, UGA admissions have become more selective, and the academic profile of UGA students has correspondingly improved. The university boasts twenty-two Rhodes scholars and was the only public university with two Rhodes scholars in 2008. Tracy Yang was named UGA's twenty-second Rhodes scholar in 2010. Some alumni remark that they would never get into the school were they to apply now.

One professor who has taught at the university for several years attests to the changes: "University of Georgia students are dramatically better than they were fifteen years ago. Large numbers of gifted students who would previously have fled to private universities in the Northeast are now flocking to the University of Georgia." In fact, the study mentioned above found that 76 percent of Georgia students with combined verbal/math SATs of 1500 or higher have stayed in state.

Perhaps as a result of the influx of these higher-caliber students, the school's honors program has blossomed. The strength of this program lies in the rigor of its courses. For nearly all introductory-level classes, there is a corresponding (and more demanding) hon-

South

ors course, with fewer students and some of the best professors at the school. One classics student claims that her major is "one of the university's best-kept secrets. . . . For the money you can't beat it—and it is qualitatively better than some Ivy League classics departments." This same student has found that although UGA overall is more geared toward careerism than the liberal arts, there is a "rich intellectual current" to be found at the school. Some of the students who have caught that wave even enroll in graduate courses, as honors upperclassmen are welcome to do. Yet another perk of being an honors student is the chance to live in the posh quarters of Meyers Hall—one of the nicest dorms on campus.

The administration would like to see the school ranked in the same tier as the so-called public Ivies. Before this happens, Georgia must raise the bar in certain areas. For one thing, only 81 percent of students graduate within six years, and a mere 51 percent within four.

Some faculty cite a lack of intellectual curiosity among students. "Making the grade is the chief objective of a significant portion of our undergraduates," says one professor. Some students retort that many professors seem uninterested in students' intellectual growth. One student says that the university is very good at "grooming young professionals" rather than scholars. There is also considerable variance in the difficulty of the school's majors. "Education is the most obvious" example of an easy department, says one professor. "If one can get by the university-wide requirements, As and Bs are a sure thing in the College of Education for the rest of one's four years. On the other hand, majors like math, chemistry, physics, and computer science are brutally tough." Agricultural programs and the sciences are particularly strong, partly because they receive more government funding.

Although UGA has become a rather large research university that enrolls some 26,000 undergraduates, most students say their professors are focused on teaching. One says, "I've never run into a situation where my professor has put his own research over his teaching responsibilities." Undergraduate instructors are required to post office hours, and some have an open-door policy. "For the most part, professors are very accessible to students and friendly, too," the student says. "That's what I found so surprising at such a large university: my professors know my name and are happy to talk to students." UGA uses graduate teaching assistants as most big universities do: professors teach large lecture courses twice a week, and TAs lead smaller discussion groups once a week. Upon entering UGA, each student is assigned a professional, nonfaculty advisor who helps him choose a major. Once he has selected a major, a student is assigned a faculty advisor within that department.

SUGGESTED CORE

1. Classical Culture 4220, Classical Epic Poetry
2. Philosophy 3000, Classics of Ancient Western Philosophy
3. Religion 4001/4080, Old Testament/Hebrew Bible Literature; New Testament Literature
4. Religion 4101, History of Christian Theology (Ancient to Medieval)
5. Political Science 4020, Political Philosophy: Hobbes to Nietzsche
6. English 4320, Shakespeare I: Selected Works
7. History 2111, American History to 1865
8. History 4373, Nineteenth-Century European Intellectual History

South

531

Most UGA professors stand well to the left of their students, but a recent study ordered by the Board of Regents showed that only 20 percent of students felt that they needed to agree with the professor to get a good grade, while only 13 percent felt that a professor had inappropriately pushed his opinion on his students. Still, a number of teachers are known for importing liberal politics into the classroom and making conservative students feel uncomfortable. Conservative child- and family-development majors are required to take a "Human Sexuality" course, for instance, where they are pressured to watch films they call "pornographic." However, for each one of these negative anecdotes, we heard several positive accounts of UGA professors.

Faculty members most often mentioned as dedicated to undergraduate teaching include Noel Fallows in Spanish; Charles S. Bullock in political science; James C. Cobb, John C. Inscoe, Stephen A. Mihm, and Kirk Willis in history; Thomas M. Lessl in speech communications; Ronald Blount in psychology; Allen C. Amason in management; Keith S. Delaplane in entomology; John Pickering in ecology; Daniel E. L. Promislow in genetics; and Dwight R. Lee and David B. Mustard in economics.

English majors must complete thirteen courses, including two in British and American literature before 1800. These mandates, on top of the school's relatively strong general education requirements, mean that majors will likely emerge well prepared—although they could, apparently, escape study of Shakespeare.

The history department asks of its majors, among other things, three introductory and seven advanced history courses, spread out across various geographical divisions. There seems to be little cohesiveness in the department; students can fulfill these requirements with courses like "History of American Medicine: 1865 to present," "Cuba in the Nineteenth and Twentieth Century," "United States Westward Expansion 1763–1850," or "Food and Power in American History." University-wide requirements do guarantee a basic understanding of U.S. history and the Constitution.

Political science majors must take eight courses in the department, including two in theory and method, (e.g., "Political Philosophy: Hobbes to Nietszche" or "Theories of Political Choice"), two courses in American studies (e.g., "Bureaucracy and the Law" or "Judicial Process and Behavior), and one course in global studies with such choices as "Middle Eastern Political Systems" and "International Political Economy."

The University of Georgia ranks among the top five American universities for students studying abroad, with over 30 percent undergraduate participation. UGA offers over a hundred faculty-led study-abroad programs in over fifty countries on every continent, including Antarctica. UGA owns a three-story Victorian mansion in the heart of Oxford, England, as well as two other residential properties in Cortona, Italy, and San Luis de Monteverde, Costa Rica. The school has classes in some thirty foreign languages, ranging from Latin to Zulu and Bengali.

Student Life: Love shack

One couldn't ask for a better college town than Athens, Georgia, with nearly a hundred bars and restaurants, a movie theater, shops, and a renowned music scene. In fact, Athens is the birthplace of such bands as REM, the B-52s, and Widespread Panic. Students can still catch good local bands at the historic Georgia Theatre, Wild Wing Cafe, and 40 Watt. The on-campus Performing Arts Center and downtown Classic Center both host top-notch artists such as the Atlanta Symphony Orchestra. Students can easily get cheap tickets to these events.

Athens's appeal probably contributes to UGA's rank (according to The Princeton Review) as the top party school in 2010; UGA has been ranked among the top twenty such schools for most of a decade. Local authorities claim to have increased their efforts to clamp down on underage drinking, and the administration admits embarrassment at this notoriety, but so far efforts have done little to change UGA's reputation.

While a large percentage of the student body hails from Georgia, the university does not typically clear out on the weekends. "It depends on if there's a home football game," a student from an Atlanta suburb says. "If there is, nobody leaves town." The bright lights of

---

ACADEMIC REQUIREMENTS

While it has no core curriculum, UGA maintains quite a strong set of general education requirements. Students must take the following:

- "English Composition" I and II and one math course, with choices such as "Precalculus" and "Differential Calculus with Theory."
- Two science courses, one in life sciences (such as "Landscape Architecture" or "Basic Concepts of Biology") and one in physical science (such as "Elementary Chemistry" or "Introduction to Water Resources"). One lab section is required.
- A quantitative reasoning class. Choices range from "Strategic Visual Thinking" to "Analytic Geometry and Calculus"
- A world languages and cultures course, which can include classes in Zulu, French, Italian or Urdu as well as "Introduction to Religions of the World."
- One humanities course in a department other than one's major, with choices ranging from "History of Popular Music" to "Roman Culture."
- Three social science courses; options range from "Applied Microeconomic Principles" to "Multicultural Perspectives on Women in a Diverse Society."
- Classes on the constitutions of Georgia and of the United States, preparatory to required tests. (Many students simply skip the classes and pass the test.)
- Each department also requires a level of oral communication and basic computer skills appropriate for the major. In addition, the College of Arts and Sciences maintains a few requirements of its own:
- Courses or tests to show competency in a foreign language to the third-semester level.
- One literature course.
- One biological sciences course.
- One physical sciences course.
- One history course.
- Two courses in social sciences other than history.

Atlanta are within a ninety-minute drive, and most students go there at least a few times a year. For outdoorsy students, the Appalachian Mountains are about two hours northeast, and the beautiful beach towns of Savannah and Charleston are both about a four-hour drive.

Talk to any Georgia student and within a couple of minutes your conversation is bound to shift to football. Most students' social lives in autumn revolve around home games. One student says, "The students go crazy during football season and tailgate all day Saturday." (Although it should be noted that university policy now rules that tailgating cannot begin before 7:00 AM, a late start for die-hard Dawgs.) The Georgia-Florida game is the most coveted ticket of the year. Football may be the center of campus life—indeed, the stadium is located at the very center of campus. Other varsity sports also have been gaining popularity lately, and intramural sports are popular and plentiful.

The university has put a lot of work into its campus in recent years, restoring historic buildings, building new dorms, and restructuring traffic flow in order to create a more "green" environment. A new residence hall on the East Campus boasts carpeted rooms, in-room thermostat controls, wireless and ethernet Internet access, a computer lab, tutoring rooms, and proximity to public transportation. This residence is intended to be the first certified LEED (Leadership in Energy and Environmental Design) building on campus with eco-friendly furnishings, use of gray water in toilets, and the use of only Forest Stewardship Council wood which guarantees the wood, to be from trees in a "well-managed forest."

Many of the student groups that receive the most support from the administration are quite liberal, including the Lambda Alliance, a homosexual group, and Safe Space, which promotes a similar agenda. The *Red and Black*, the university newspaper, is well known for its liberal tilt. Its views are contested by the campus conservative alternative publication, the *Georgia GuardDawg* (named for the university mascot, the bulldog). In the university as a whole, says one professor, "there are all perspectives, but overall, people are levelheaded. Tolerance of diverse views is prevalent."

Students living on campus participate in Diversity Awareness Week at Georgia—or DAWG Days—which is sponsored by the Residence Hall Association. According to the housing webpage, "Topics covered include race and ethnicity, religion, sexual orientation, body image and size-ism, and students with disabilities, to name a few." President Michael Adams has told the *Red and Black* that he stands squarely behind these efforts. The university revised its antidiscrimination policies to include sexual orientation and has rules against harassment and intolerance. Some claim that these rules are so vague that they could be used to hinder the free speech of conservatives.

Around one-third of the student body lives on campus, and the university guarantees housing only for freshmen. Many more students would prefer to live on campus but are denied the opportunity because of a housing crunch, which have been eased somewhat. An upperclassman says, "Dorm life was the best thing about my freshman year. . . . I loved it so much. It is a great way to meet friends and get involved on campus." Residences include huge freshman dormitories, suites in East Campus Village, and other on-campus facilities. The university offers no men-only dorms and several women-only residences—including Brumby Hall, a 950-student dorm that has limited visitation hours. UGA does not have any coed dorm rooms or coed bathrooms.

The university's "learning communities" are another housing option. In Rutherford Hall, students in the College of Arts and Sciences live down the hall from faculty members and attend special academic programs. Another residence hall maintains tutoring, advisors, study areas, and classrooms for the students who live there. Students studying French or Spanish can immerse themselves in these languages by living in dedicated houses. For academic work, the new multimillion-dollar Student Learning Facility features leather chairs, thousands of computers, and the newest classroom technology.

As important to students as sleep is food, and the UGA kitchen "is extremely popular among students and wins awards yearly," says one student. The UGA dining halls have monthly themed nights that offer unique dishes and decorations.

Rentals in Athens, including nearby houses, downtown lofts, and scattered apartment buildings, are rather pricey. Almost a fourth of the student body goes Greek, and Greek organizations play a significant role in campus social life for both members and independents. Weekend parties at the houses are popular and generally open to all students.

The campus crime rate is low, but the city of Athens has some dangerous areas. On campus, students coming home late at night can take advantage of the escort van service. The school offers an extensive and effective bus system for students. There are emergency phones all over campus. Almost all dormitories have a handprint scanner that identifies residents, and community desks in the dorms are staffed twenty-four hours a day.

In 2009, UGA's campus saw eighty-two burglaries, two aggravated assaults, three robberies, four stolen cars, two arsons, and four forcible sex offenses.

For students from Georgia, this school is an amazing value, with 2010–11 in-state tuition at only $7,530 (out of state students paid $25,740). Room and board averaged $8,460. Admissions are need blind, and 32 percent of students receive aid. However, the school does not guarantee to cover the full need of every student admitted. The average student-loan debt of a recent graduate is $14,766, the school reports.

GREEN LIGHT

With a membership of more than 2,000, UGA has the largest College Republicans chapter in the country, making it the largest student group on campus. It also prides itself on being the largest student-run political organization in the U.S. One leader of the club boasts that its members are highly mobilized, bringing conservative speakers and political candidates to campus several times a year. It also provides several internship opportunities during an election year.

Although UGA is described as "friendly" to all groups on campus, conservatives on campus charge favoritism in funding. The university has a ban on political funding but does contribute to the gay activist group Safe Space; the College Republicans receive no funding and have not been given any office space for their expanding and very active group.

Georgia Institute of Technology

Atlanta, Georgia • www.gatech.edu

Eyes on the prize

Some say a better name for the Georgia Institute of Technology would be the "North Avenue Trade School." At Georgia Tech, most students enter knowing which career they want to pursue; a degree is just the means of attaining it. The liberal arts sit on the university's back burner, and most engineering students just enroll in them to satisfy curriculum requirements. Even humanities course descriptions are saturated with the words *science* and *technology*. But academic life at Tech is rigorous and intense. "One thing I believe about Tech is that they really want you to *earn* your degree," an engineering student says. "My degree from Georgia Tech will be something of immense pride and satisfaction. I will know that I earned it on my own merits and not anyone else's."

Located in the heart of Atlanta, Georgia Tech provides students with the advantage of living in the South's unofficial capital, which provides a fantastic number of educational, professional, cultural, and recreational opportunities. A few Tech students even find time to enjoy them.

Academic Life: Rigorous careerism

Academic life, as one computer science major puts it, is exceptionally tough, "but it will be well worth the hundreds of all-nighters and stress levels of 'eleven' once I get my degree and am looked at by future employers as one who knows what the heck I am doing because I graduated from such a highly ranked school." The chance to land a good job, not love of learning, seems to be the primary motivation for most Georgia Tech students. "Purely intellectual curiosity is a luxury most can't afford," one professor says. "Tech's an academic boot camp, and like Marines, most are justifiably proud of surviving it." Another teacher says: "The nature of the institution selects and rewards extreme task focus. Grades are most students' concern, especially in a course not part of their major." With the entire student body out to make the grade and land the job, one student says there is a strong sense of "competing against the system, and a lot of empathy among students. . . . We're all in it together."

Georgia Tech students must go through quite an ordeal before they can embark on their careers. Most engineering students require six years to graduate, and sixth- and seventh-year seniors are not uncommon. The course require-ments for the engineering program are so rigorous that they discourage students from taking a wide variety of courses before settling on their majors. A few years ago, Georgia Tech increased the required percentage of hours in the engineering major. As one professor comments on this change, "While training might be better, it's argu-able whether people are as well or better educated." One student observes that recently, however, there has been "a shift and an appreciation of broad-based education, even in the colleges of engineering and science." More students than in the past are opting for a bachelor of sci-ence in the College of Liberal Arts rather than in the Col-lege of Engineering, and some students who choose to major in engineering will minor in history or literature.

"Georgia Tech is not like the typical college people see in the movies; most students show up here knowing what they want to do, and do only that," says a student. "Since engineering is the university's main focus, most people do not take a wide variety of classes." Another engineering student says, "You can't come to Tech and think it will be like high school, where a minimal amount of studying will get you an A. Do that your first semester at Tech and you will flunk out."

Georgia Tech began as and remains a technical institution, but it does require courses other than those in engineering and the sciences. Upon entering Georgia Tech, students can choose from among the university's six colleges: Engineering, Computing Sciences, Sciences, Architecture, Management, and the Ivan Allen College of Liberal Arts. Georgia Tech is most renowned for its engineering program, which is among the nation's most difficult. Georgia Tech's nationally recognized engineer-ing facilities include the Manufacturing Research Cen-ter, where both undergraduate and graduate students "examine manufacturing processes, applications, and technical solutions," according to its webpage. Undergraduates participate in cutting-edge research that directly supports Tech's academic programs in engineering.

Not all engineering students can compete at this level. "Most engineering majors who do poorly tend to switch to easier coursework that can be found in [the] management, industrial engineering, and English majors," says one student. The engineering disciplines, with the exception of industrial engineering, require high-level math and physics skills that professors expect students to master quickly and to use in classes.

VITAL STATISTICS

Religious affiliation: *none*
Total enrollment: *20,291*
Total undergraduates: *13,515*
SAT/ACT midranges: CR: *580–680*, M: *650–750*; ACT: *27–31*
Applicants: *11,432*
Applicants accepted: *59%*
Accepted applicants who enrolled: *40%*
Tuition and fees: *in state, $7,070; out of state, $25,280*
Room and board: *$8,746*
Freshman retention rate: *93%*
Graduation rate: *31% (4 yrs.), 79% (6 yrs.)*
Courses with fewer than 20 students: *38%*
Student-faculty ratio: *20:1*
Courses taught by graduate students: *4%*
Most popular majors: *engineering, business/marketing, architecture*
Students living on campus: *60%*
Guaranteed housing for four years? *no*
Students in fraternities: *23%* in sororities: *33%*

South

South

SUGGESTED CORE

1. History, Technology, and Society 3028, Ancient Greece: Gods, Heroes and Ruins (closest match)
2. Philosophy, Science, and Technology 3102, History of Ancient Philosophy
3. No suitable course.
4. History, Technology, and Society 3030, Medieval Europe (350–1400) (closest match)
5. Philosophy, Science, and Technology 2050, Philosophy and Political Theory
6. Literature, Communication, and Culture 3228, Shakespeare
7. History, Technology, and Society 2111, The United States to 1877
8. History, Technology, and Society 3032, European Intellectual History

The College of Computing Sciences is also highly regarded. It conducts interdisciplinary research and participates in instructional programs within other academic units on campus. Students gain hands-on experience while developing logical and analytical skills in their computer courses. Computer science majors are required to take twenty-three semester hours of free electives, but many use this flexibility to take courses within their major department rather than to broaden their knowledge in other areas.

The College of Sciences offers undergraduate and graduate degrees in mathematics and the natural sciences in a high-tech environment. The new Biotechnology Complex was designed to "maximize the interactions between faculty members and their students in both offices and laboratories," according to Tech's website. This addition to the campus highlights the institute's pride and joy—its research. Georgia Tech's position as a leading research institute was confirmed by its recent admission into the Association of American Universities, a collection of the top research universities in the country.

The Ivan Allen College of Liberal Arts, which dates only to 1990, does not offer Georgia Tech's most highly touted academic programs. Only 963 undergraduates (out of more than 13,000) are enrolled in it, amounting to less than 8 percent of freshmen admitted in each of the past four years. The most popular program is international relations. Even within the liberal arts college, students cannot avoid mathematics and the sciences. For instance, instead of a philosophy department, Georgia Tech has a department of Philosophy, Science, and Technology, replete with courses like "Environmental Ethics" and "Introduction to Cognitive Science." The only ancient philosophy course concludes with "the early development of science in the fourteenth and fifteenth centuries." And instead of history, Tech has a history, technology, and society major. It features such courses as "Engineering in History," "The Scientific Revolution," and "Technology and Science in the Industrial Age." Students may take a course in American history, covering the founding and the Civil War, but they are not required to do so.

The English department has just two courses, both in basic composition, which explore technological or political issues. Needless to say, there is no stand-alone English major. Instead of political science, students may major in public policy—where they must take one course that covers the U.S. Constitution. However, most of the program requirements emphasize science and math. "They are not presenting a real liberal arts education," says one professor. There are students who prize the chance to take some broadly informative classes in the liberal arts while still acquiring a technical specialty—and those are the Georgia Tech students who generally enroll in Ivan Allen. Most would say, however, that this does not qualify the college as "liberal arts." The school makes no secret of this, offering only the BS degree, not the BA.

Ivan Allen College's School of Literature, Communication, and Culture offers bachelor of science degrees in science, technology, and culture (STAC) and computational media, with postgraduate degrees in digital media and human-computer interaction. These programs seem to assume that the future of the humanities will be primarily electronic. This school has very few actual literature courses; the emphasis, again, is on science and technology.

Many students and professors inside and outside the Ivan Allen College agree that this college is somewhat politicized—as if its faculty misunderstood the meaning of the word *liberal* when it modifies *arts*. One professor says that Ivan Allen "is a home for liberal activists who confuse advocacy with scholarship. Science it is not." A student says that it is not uncommon, for instance, for students to be graded down by vocally leftist professors for their more conservative viewpoints.

An onerous speech code, unevenly enforced against right-leaning students, led two Georgia Tech undergrads to sue the school in federal court, where judges struck down the school's policies as unconstitutional in 2006. The court victory gave new energy to the College Republicans, who held a First Amendment forum on the four-year anniversary of the ruling. But Georgia Tech continues to resist true freedom of speech. Vocally (as opposed to silently), conservative students and even faculty report a feeling of "persecution" at the hands of the administration.

Tech's College of Architecture, one of the oldest and most highly respected schools of its kind in the country, offers majors in architecture, building construction, and industrial design; the school is a national leader in city and regional planning. The college's curriculum challenges students to create innovative projects in modern lab facilities, especially through the IMAGINE (Interactive Media Architecture Group in Education) lab, a highly advanced computer modeling system for what might be called investigations in theoretical architecture. The college was recently recognized internationally after winning first prize from the Dubai Forum on Sustainable Urban Development for its proposal to rehabilitate Dubai's central business district.

Many students believe the quality of Tech's faculty is its most valuable asset. Almost sixty faculty members have received Presidential, National Science Foundation (NSF) Young Investigator, or NSF Career awards. Professors teach most courses; only a few are conducted by graduate teaching assistants. More often, Tech uses TAs to teach laboratory sections, hold office hours, grade papers, and lead weekly discussion sections.

One student says, "Professors are excellent at what they do, extremely intelligent, and know the subject. They have won high-dollar contracts for the school from huge companies, have tenure at the school, and do major research for which they get recognition." Not surprisingly, then, many professors are interested in their research above all else. One student says that, while faculty members are ready to help if asked, "normally the chain of command is notes, books, Internet, TAs, newsgroups, professors. Professors are generally

South

539

seen as a last resort. Their line of reasoning is that, in the workforce, you can't just go to the boss and say, 'How do you do this?'"

Freshmen are assigned advisors and are required to visit them, but upperclassmen can use their advisors to whatever degree needed. "In my experience, they offer suggestions and help you figure out classes," one student says. "However, they are very willing to let you plan your academic career."

Students name as some of the best professors at the university George F. Riley in electrical and computer engineering; George L. Cain Jr. in mathematics; William Leahy in the College of Computing; Ahmet Erbil in physics; Steve Potter and Eberhard Voit in biomedical engineering; and Charles A. Eckert in chemical engineering. Among active and visible younger faculty are marine biologist-biochemist Julia Kubanek, aerospace engineer and NASA contact Robert Braun, and nanotechnology guru Z. L. Wang.

Georgia Tech offers no majors in foreign languages, but there are degree programs in applied languages and intercultural studies, global economics and modern languages, and international affairs and modern languages. Students can take courses in Arabic, Chinese, French, German, Japanese, Korean, Russian, and Spanish. There is also one Latin course available. Students may participate in a vast array of study-abroad programs in countries such as Argentina, Egypt, Singapore, and Greece. Some departments offer unique faculty-led programs like the Architecture Senior Year in Paris.

Student Life: No time for rambling

Coursework at Georgia Tech is tough. Students spend vast amounts of time in the library, in laboratories, and in front of their computers. With only a third of the student population graduating in four years, some students can't afford to "waste time" with extracurriculars.

ACADEMIC REQUIREMENTS

Georgia Tech has no liberal arts core but instead requires a solid base of technical classes and a few humanities courses as well. Students must take:

- Two English composition courses.
- One calculus class.
- One computer science course.
- Two introductory-level humanities courses. Choices range from "Medieval Literature and Culture" to "Introduction to Gender Studies."
- Four science/math/technology courses, including a second calculus course for all students who are not liberal arts majors.
- Four social science courses, one of which must satisfy the statewide United States/ Georgia history and constitution requirements—usually fulfilled by "The United States to 1877," "The United States Since 1877," or another survey course. Other choices include "Ancient Greece" and "Psychology of Advertising."

South

But one student says, "We aren't called 'Ramblin' Wreck' for nothing. We work hard and study lots, then play hard . . . in that order."

Atlanta and Georgia Tech have grown and prospered together for more than a century. The neighborhood in which Tech sits has seen periods of urban decay but is now on the upswing. Several Atlanta schools, including Tech, have seen their neighborhoods transformed, revitalized, and made safer. Pioneer investors are shaping a more vibrant place to work, live, learn, and play. The newly built Technology Square has lent a special character to the Midtown renaissance, creating an artery between the campus and Midtown by way of the Fifth Street Bridge. The square welcomes pedestrians with the open-front School of Management building and retail outlets, and a new school bookstore, as well as a Barnes & Noble, various retail stores, and restaurants.

Downtown Atlanta has plenty of attractions for Georgia Tech students anxious to get off campus and away from the books. The High Museum of Art is one of the best museums in the South. Underground Atlanta is a subterranean marketplace with shops, bars, and cafes. The Varsity, a legendary quick-paced hot dog and burger joint, serves students and locals alike; it was started by Frank Gordy, a Tech dropout, in 1928. Sports fans can enjoy Atlanta Falcons football at the Georgia Dome, as well as Atlanta Hawks basketball and Atlanta Thrashers ice hockey at Philips Arena. Atlanta Braves games at Turner Field are popular spring and summertime events.

One third of women at Georgia Tech join sororities, and almost a fourth of men pledge fraternities, making the Greek scene an important hub of what social life takes place on campus. Independents sometimes complain that the frats are cliquish and exclusive—keeping nonmembers out of parties, for instance. Those who don't join Greek life are said to make the most of nightspots in the Buckhead neighborhood, which offers a number of opportunities for 18-year-old students who are content to sip Diet Cokes. Given the workload at the school, it's not surprising that it doesn't rank as a party school.

Georgia Tech athletics are popular among students, area alumni, and Atlantans, who often claim a partial ownership of the school—or at least of Tech sports. The Yellow Jackets compete in the Atlantic Coast Conference (ACC), home to such powerhouses as Duke, Florida State, Maryland, and North Carolina. Tech struggles from time to time, but overall its sports programs are strong. In the past decade, Tech saw three of its alumni win Olympic gold medals, sent its basketball team to the Final Four, and won ACC titles in football, tennis, golf, baseball, and women's volleyball. All games are free for students. And despite the workload, Tech consistently ranks among the top twenty-five schools in the nation in graduating its student-athletes (although it helps that Tech athletes are disproportionately more likely to major in management than in engineering). The university also offers intramural sports, including soccer, sand volleyball, flag football, Ultimate Frisbee, bowling, and Wiffle ball.

Besides sports, Georgia Tech offers plenty of extracurricular activities. Student clubs include those devoted to recreation, leisure, publications, and artistic and cultural productions, as well as honor societies, volunteer groups, and organizations for political, religious, cultural, and diversity purposes. Some of the myriad student clubs are Quizbowl, Rocket Club, Hellenic Society, Future Educators Association, SCUBA Tech, Soccer Club, Ballroom Dance

South

RED LIGHT

Surprisingly, given the overall conservatism of most of its tech-savvy students, Georgia Tech has an unexpectedly politicized campus, complete with sit-ins, political rallies, and professors pushing political agendas. What is more, the school's administration is said to be strongly biased toward the left, offering funding to activist groups like the Women's Resource Center, the African American Student Union, and the pansexual Pride Alliance—while denying student funds to conservative groups such as the College Republicans.

The faculty are said to lean heavily leftward; a March 2010 report by the *Conservative Buzz* found that the school's faculty "gave 89 percent of their political donations to Democratic candidates and a mere 11 percent to Republicans in the 2006 to 2009 campaign cycles." The *Buzz* noted that this fit a previous pattern at the school: "In 2007, the school was chastised publicly by watchdog groups and by the press for soliciting volunteers (using taxpayers' money) for an Obama campaign rally on campus in violation of state code."

In the ugliest incident at Tech, an activist conservative student was repeatedly summoned by administrators and reprimanded for expressing her Christian opposition to various displays of sexual radicalism on campus. Intolerant students set up a website depicting her face covered with swastikas, while others sent her letters and e-mails threatening her with rape, disfigurement with acid, and death. As the student victim told Front-Page magazine: "It is ironic that the Georgia Tech administration would enforce unlawful speech policies that silence disagreement with its preferred political agenda, but remains absolutely silent in the face of threats on a student's safety."

Club, Fencing, Softball Club, Dance Marathon, Field Hockey Club, Forensic Science Club, and Mars Society (they want to settle the planet). Not surprisingly, Georgia Tech also has a number of academic and professional groups, like the Earthquake Engineering Research Institute, the Institute of Electrical and Electronics Engineering, and the *Tower*, a journal of undergraduate research.

Religious groups and ministries on campus include the Fellowship of Christian Students, Orthodox Christian Fellowship, Baptist Collegiate Ministries, Chi Alpha, Catholic Student Organization, Hillel, Latter-Day Saint Association, Muslim Student Association . . . and, for the unconvinced, Campus Freethinkers.

Political groups include the College Republicans, Environmental Alliance, (gay) Pride Alliance, Students for Life, Anti-Genocide Alliance, Student Movement for Real Change, Students in Free Enterprise, Students of Objectivism, and Women's Awareness Month. The *Conservative Buzz* is a campus alternative paper.

Sixty percent of Georgia Tech undergraduates choose to live on campus; the rest live in the surrounding area. "To tell you the truth, campus housing is pretty scarce, and many students, after their required freshman year, choose to live off campus or in Greek-life housing," one student says. First-year students have the option of participating in Freshman Experience (FE), which offers a set of traditional dormitories on the east side of campus. Most of the dorms are single sex, and all dorms have an official escort policy for members of the opposite sex. All FE dorms are supposed to be alcohol free, and all have upperclassmen as resident advisors on each hall, a required meal plan, and twenty-four-hour low-noise rules. Undergraduates who are not a part of FE have limited options for housing. Traditional-style halls typically are single sex with two-person rooms. Some suite-style buildings are available, as well as four apartment complexes originally built for the 1996 Olympics. Apartments are usually the most coveted living options on campus; since housing is decided by lottery and by class, seniors usually snag these prime spots.

Student safety is of great concern at Georgia Tech. In 2009, the school reported two aggravated assaults, two forcible sex offences, sixty burglaries, and twenty-nine stolen cars on campus. The university has increased nighttime lighting on campus during the past several years and now uses campuswide e-mail alerts to identify suspicious activities. The campus police also track repeat offenders and have instituted a K-9 unit with police dogs. Campus safety programs feature extensive crime awareness workshops at freshmen orientation. In a bizarre incident, in February 2010, a graduate student and a campus police officer were injured in an attack by a samurai sword–wielding Georgia Tech alumnus, who received his PhD in aerospace engineering in 2008, according to the *Athens Banner-Herald*. Students who seek a Georgia Tech education but would rather not live in Atlanta can attend the school's Savannah campus instead—enjoying all the attractions of a small, lovely old southern city by the sea.

As a state-assisted school, Georgia Tech is considerably less expensive than other universities with comparable reputations. In 2010–11, tuition for Georgia residents was only $7,070, while outsiders paid a more standard $25,280. The housing and meal plans averaged around $8,700. Almost three-quarters of the student body come from Georgia; all in-state students maintaining a B average are eligible for the state HOPE (Helping Outstanding Pupils Educationally) scholarship and the free tuition that comes with it. *Money* magazine consistently ranks Tech as one of the nation's best academic values. The average student-loan debt of a recent graduate was $21,239.

Hampden-Sydney College

Hampden-Sydney, Virginia • www.hsc.edu

The alpha male

Hampden-Sydney College in Hampden-Sydney, Virginia, is a small school that provides an excellent liberal arts education to its approximately 1,000 students. And all those students are men. Hampden-Sydney is one of only three remaining all-male institutions of higher education in America. What is more, its curriculum has never been neutered. *Insight* magazine named Hampden-Sydney as one of the fifteen finest schools that "still teach the fullness of the Western academic traditions."

Hampden-Sydney was founded during the American Revolution and is named for John Hampden, who earned the title "father of the people" for leading resistance to King Charles I's government. (But we can forgive him for that.) Algernon Sydney, the college's other namesake, was a republican philosopher and an inspiration to both John Locke and America's founding fathers. Patrick Henry, revolutionary and anti-Federalist hero, helped found the college and sent six of his sons to the school. He aimed to help Virginia create "useful knowledge amongst its citizens" by supporting the college. James Madison, father of the American Constitution, also helped to shape the college during its formative years. Steeped in the history of English and American political thought and classical liberalism, Hampden-Sydney has not abandoned its roots, and for this reason alone it is a unique and noteworthy institution.

Academic Life: Solid at the core

Hampden-Sydney provides a challenging curriculum that encourages breadth and depth, and its distribution requirements are so structured and thorough that they almost constitute a traditional core curriculum. The heart of the Hampden-Sydney program is its Western culture requirement: three specific courses focusing on the West's classical beginnings and its development through the present. The courses cover three eras: History up through A.D. 900, 900 to 1800, and 1800 to the present. The Western culture courses, taught by professors across departments, are anchored in five "common texts" per era (such as Augustine's *Confessions* or Darwin's *Origin of Species*) and five "common topics and events" per era (such as the Protestant Reformation and the world wars). The courses include broad sketches of politics, art, religion, philosophy, and the intellectual history of Western society,

South

and combine history with the reading of Great Books. "A professor may discuss the possibility that eternal truths or human nature exist, as well as taking the typical historicist approach so prevalent in the humanities and social sciences in most colleges," says one faculty member. Another professor who teaches one of these courses says, "In my Western Culture 101 class, students read the Bible, Homer's *Iliad*, Sophocles' *Oedipus Rex* and *Antigone*, Aristophanes' *Clouds*, Plato's *Apology*, Aristotle's *Politics*, Plutarch's lives of Alcibiades and Caesar, and Augustine's *Confessions*." Another teacher says, "The core courses are serious—though, as anywhere, there are perceived differences in difficulty, depending on the instructor. To some degree, the differences are mitigated by the assessment procedure, which establishes common standards and goals." After taking the three courses in Western civilization, students then need two American studies courses, chosen from a short list of courses in the history, English, government and foreign affairs, and religion departments.

Hampden-Sydney's curriculum and faculty members encourage intellectual curiosity. "This semester we had nearly fifty students take a course on Plato and Aristotle," a professor says. "We had to open a new section of the course to accommodate the demand. So many students seem to be searching for something more than just careers."

Just as rigorous as these general requirements are the demands of major departments—although, sadly, some of the requirements are changing slightly for the worse. The English major now requires a "literature of difference" course—basically a cultural diversity requirement that has students choosing from options like "Introduction to African-American Literature," "Women and Literature," and "Multi-Ethnic Literature." The good news is that the department still requires survey courses in both English and American literature, as well as a course in Shakespeare; that's more than you can say for most college English departments these days. The English department's offerings in ethnic literature, postcolonialism, and cinema are kept to a minimum. One English faculty member says, "Our department used to be more traditional than it is now. The trend is definitely in the direction of requiring less literature written before the twentieth century."

In the history department, majors need three courses in American history, one in European history, and two outside of these areas, plus a colloquium. The U.S. requirement can be satisfied by classes like "American Intellectual History," not the bizarre his-

VITAL STATISTICS

Religious affiliation: *Presbyterian*
Total enrollment: *1,058*
Total undergraduates: *1,058*
SAT/ACT midranges: CR: *500–600*, M: *500–610*; ACT: *21–26*
Applicants: *2,528*
Applicants accepted: *54%*
Accepted applicants who enrolled: *23%*
Tuition and fees: *$30,994*
Room and board: *$10,126*
Freshman retention rate: *79%*
Graduation rate: *64% (4 yrs.), 68% (6 yrs.)*
Courses with fewer than 20 students: *69%*
Student-faculty ratio: *11:1*
Courses taught by graduate students: *none*
Most popular majors: *social sciences, history, business/marketing*
Students living on campus: *95%*
Guaranteed housing for four years? *yes*
Students in fraternities: *34%*

South

tory courses you find at many other liberal arts schools. However, students will also have to take a course from a different major to satisfy the requirement, and this class might be "Multi-Ethnic American Literature."

Professors and students say that English, modern languages, and history are more politicized than most other departments. Still, says one professor, "there is less nuttiness here than at most places. In our English courses, for example, *texts* are read and taught, not the latest literary theories." The English department offers four or five courses that sound more politicized, such as "Postcolonial Literature," but they are not the norm. Judging from the course catalog, the history department offers nothing but serious classes. "At Hampden-Sydney, there are no trendy departments," says another professor. "Everyone takes books and ideas very seriously. There are individual faculty members who present the 'latest' ideas, but generally in a sober and thought-provoking way." One student says, "The faculty is liberal, but I know several conservative professors. I have never had a professor try to push his/her beliefs on me or politicize the class." Other students disagree and report that some of their more outspoken professors do vent their own views in the classroom.

One of the strongest departments on campus is government and foreign affairs. At Hampden-Sydney, this department studies contemporary political problems in light of the writings of great Western and American political thinkers. According to the website, the requirement for a government major is thirty-four semester hours in government. Majors take a course on American government, another on modern governments around the world, and "Classical Political Philosophy." Students can then choose between several courses: "Medieval Political Philosophy," "Early Modern Political Philosophy," and "Modern Political Philosophy." Finally, all majors will complete "Pre-Thesis Seminar" and 'Senior Seminar and Thesis" courses.

Classics, while small, has in the past been considered one of the college's best teaching departments. Many Hampden-Sydney students major in economics, and the department is reportedly strong. The science departments are also good; faculty single out chemistry as the strongest.

The faculty has a reputation for sensible research in traditional areas, with only a couple of professors recently undertaking scholarship in areas like popular culture, film, and women's studies. A senior faculty member says, "It would be hard to find a professor trying to indoctrinate in the classroom here."

Hampden-Sydney assigns each incoming student a faculty advisor and a peer advisor. In addition, to help new students adjust to college, Hampden-Sydney requires that its students take an advising seminar, which is taught by the faculty advisor and aided by the

South

peer advisor. Once a student selects his major, he is assigned a faculty advisor within his department. Students must visit their advisors each semester before registering for courses.

Since Hampden-Sydney does not have graduate students, faculty teach all courses. The college has a strong student-faculty ratio of 11 to 1, and 69 percent of Hampden-Sydney's classes are limited to fewer than twenty students. No classes enroll more than forty. "Our professors are in their offices most of the time when they aren't teaching, so it's not a problem finding them," a government major says. "Most of my professors give out their home telephone numbers on the first day of class, and I have called them at home many times. I think that is one of the best aspects of Hampden-Sydney." Some of the best teachers at the college include David Marion and James Pontuso in government and foreign affairs; Anthony Carilli, Saranna R. Thornton, and Kenneth Townsend in economics; James Arieti in classics; William Shear and Alexander Werth in biology; Victor Cabas Jr. and Susan Robbins in rhetoric; and Ralph Hattox and James Simms Jr. in history.

Hampden-Sydney students value the small classes and personal attention they receive at the school. As one student recalls, professors "won't let you hide in the back" of a small class and fall asleep. Most classes are structured as a combination of lecture and seminar.

The study-abroad program sends students to all parts of the world, from Argentina to China. One of the grandest is the Oxford Program, in which a small group of students study Tudor-Stuart history and literature at St. Anne's College. The college offers majors in French, German, and Spanish, and teaches courses in Latin and Ancient Greek.

Student Life: Live white males

Of course, the most distinctive thing about Hampden-Sydney is that there aren't any women in class. "Being all-male is nice during the week because you do not have to deal with dating or being distracted by a good-looking young woman," a student says. "You also have the chance to form a unique brotherhood with your fellow students." Another student who went to a coed high school says, "I get a better education in the all-male classroom. Class discussions are vastly improved because more students are willing to talk and share their opinions." School parties do attract women to campus each weekend, and many fraternities host dances and mixers with nearby sororities. A number of women's colleges that maintain a close social relationship with HSC are within driving distance. As a popular bumper sticker reads, "I pay tuition to Sweet Briar, but my daughter goes to Hampden-Sydney." Longwood University, a coed school known primarily for teacher education, is only a few miles away and helps enliven the social scene. On weekends, students sometimes visit the University of Virginia, Virginia Tech, and North Carolina State, all within a comfortable drive. One student says, "There is normally something to do, but some weekends are slow, and Farmville is not a town with a nightlife."

Hampden-Sydney's rural, isolated setting helps bind the campus community together. Ninety-five percent of students live on campus, which is the locus of most social activity. The school provides a free guest house for visiting women, conveniently located on Fraternity Circle. Because of the school's honor code (see below), visitors are allowed to come and

South

go as their hosts wish. The few students who choose to live off campus can opt for a college-owned cottage or (with permission) test their luck on the rental market. One of Hampden-Sydney's dormitories offers a substance-free floor.

The college is home to America's second-oldest collegiate debating club. Since 1789, the Union-Philanthropic Literary Society has served as an extracurricular intellectual forum for students. Its discussions also provide one of the few outlets for political controversy on campus. "Some faculty members grumbled when the boys debated whether feminism was killing free speech, but no one tried to stop the debate," says one professor. "We are pretty old-fashioned down here. We say mostly what we like, and we are pretty civil about the whole thing."

Student social life is heavily influenced by the Greek system, which includes eleven social fraternities, one professional fraternity for chemistry and related majors, and fourteen honors fraternities. Close to one-quarter of Hampden-Sydney men join these groups. But one nonmember says, "There is not a sharp division between Greeks and non-Greeks, as on some campuses." Aside from college-sponsored speeches and lectures, most social, musical, and cultural events revolve around the Greek houses; these events are usually open

ACADEMIC REQUIREMENTS

Hampden-Sydney has a genuine, if abbreviated, core curriculum, which students are encouraged to complete during their first two years. Requirements are as follows:

- Three "Western Culture" courses, which cover the history of the West from Plato through NATO.
- Two courses in American studies. Eligible courses include "American Literature," "The Age of the American Revolution 1763–1815," and "Religion in American Life."
- Three set courses in rhetoric and one course from classical studies, English literature, or classical and modern language literature. Students must also reach the intermediate level in a foreign language.
- Two introductory courses chosen from biology, chemistry, astronomy, and physics (including at least one with a lab component).
- One mathematics course and one additional math or science course outside the student's major.
- One introductory social science in economics, government and foreign affairs, psychology, or sociology.
- International studies, which consists either in studying abroad or taking one course in international history or culture. "History of East Asia," "The Government and Politics of Central Europe," and "Islam" all satisfy this requirement.
- One course from a short list of classes in religion or philosophy. "Philosophy of Religion" or "Judaism" fits the bill.
- One or two courses—depending on the class chosen—in fine arts, chosen from a list that includes "Introduction to Music Literature," "History of Western Art," and "Intermediate Photography," among others.

South

to the entire campus. Each spring, students participate in Greek Week, a campus-wide festival.

The Hampden-Sydney Tigers compete in eight varsity sports in the NCAA Division III Old Dominion Athletic Conference—and Title IX obviously isn't a problem. Students have organized a few more intercollegiate club teams, including lacrosse and soccer. And the school has a strong intramurals program in which 65 percent of the student body participates.

Hampden-Sydney's biggest social event is the annual football game against the school's archrival, Randolph-Macon College. Tailgating before football games is a perennially popular activity. With a $2.5 million donation, Hampden-Sydney completed a new football stadium in time for the 2007 football season.

There is a certain demographic homogeneity at Hampden-Sydney. Eighty-seven percent of students are white, and 64 percent come from Virginia. "The typical HSC student is a white male who wears polo shirts and khaki shorts," says one student, "but the school is comfortable for those who don't fit the profile."

The college offers a number of Christian groups for interested students, and one member says the school is a "good place to grow in your faith because of growing campus ministry groups like the Baptist Student Union, InterVarsity, Chi Alpha Fellowship, Wesleyan Fellowship, and the Fellowship of Christian Athletes." However, he says, "The strong party culture provides a testing ground for a person's beliefs." The ministries and religion professors, as well as local churches, provide spiritual support. The on-campus College Presbyterian Church serves as the school chapel, where religious groups of various denominations hold services. Most students are Protestant, but Jewish and Catholic student groups exist.

GREEN LIGHT

For the most part, politics—faculty or student—has a different flavor at Hampden-Sydney than at other liberal arts schools. Students do not protest or stage sit-ins, and only rarely do they organize for political causes. However, Hampden-Sydney men do tend to have strong political opinions. One senior says, "We don't protest here, but almost everyone has strong views."

Outside of the classroom, the college political atmosphere is sometimes rather sedate. The one relatively liberal group is the College Democrats, which generally sticks to campaigning for candidates and squaring off with Republicans for debates. The Republican Society is dedicated to the study of American politics and "the philosophy of the Republican Party." Students have also organized the Society for the Preservation of Southern Heritage, dedicated to "the Constitution of the United States, a strong family unit, religious faith, courage, honor, and integrity." Except for a few explicitly political speakers, most guest lecturers are academics. In 2010, Paul Cantor, professor of English at the University of Virginia, spoke on "*South Park* and Homeland Insecurity: The Imaginationland Trilogy," which drew out the "socio-political nuances" in the show. Another lecture concerned the response of enterprises such as Walmart to Hurricane Katrina.

The college's new Intercultural Affairs Office tries to promote tolerance on campus by "creating an environment that is sensitive to the diversity of a multicultural community" and by offering "academic, administrative, and social support" to minority students. But by and large, contemporary academia's obsession with the clichés of diversity has bypassed Hampden-Sydney.

Farmville, Virginia, the small town five miles from Hampden-Sydney, is known for its furniture stores and agriculture. Prospective students should expect to encounter the typical symbols of rural southern life, from tobacco fields to the equally pervasive Walmart Supercenter. The campus blends in well with the rural setting. Shady, tree-lined paths connect the red-brick buildings, which look like old Virginia courthouses. The campus is small enough that new buildings are calculated decisions; the newish library blends in well with the rest of the campus.

Hampden-Sydney's academic and social excellence is founded on one of its oldest traditions: the honor code. Because one of the main goals of life, the school believes, is to live a "moral existence," the honor code assumes that all students will "behave as gentlemen" and will not lie, cheat, or steal. The system is administered by a court of student leaders, and service on the court is considered an honor. One former student, Stephen Colbert of Comedy Central's *Colbert Report*, insists that he still takes the honor code so seriously that decades after Hampden-Sydney, he can recite its text from memory. At Convocation, a ceremony at which new students sign the honor code for the first time, Hampden-Sydney men wear coats and ties, a sign of the dignity the ceremony commands. Faculty members affirm that the honor system works. Exams are not proctored, and, one professor says, "in my personal experience of forty years, never need to be."

Students and administrators say the honor code and the college's rural location are largely responsible for keeping the campus as safe as it is. In 2009, the last year for which statistics were available, the school saw one sexual assault and two burglaries.

Tution for 2010–11 is $30,994, and room and board $10,126. Some 80 percent of the student body receives need-based financial aid, and the average debt of a graduating student is $23,822. Unfortunately, Hampden-Sydney does not have the financial means to cover 100 percent of students' financial needs: in 2010, just 80 percent was met, However, the college recently completed a successful $91 million campaign; among other things, it will help strengthen financial aid.

Liberty University

Lynchburg, Virginia • www.liberty.edu

Creed and credibility

Liberty University is located in Lynchburg, a sprawling hill town of roughly 70,000 that is also home to Lynchburg College, Randolph College, and Sweet Briar. Not far from the coal country of West Virginia, Lynchburg sits in a hardscrabble land renowned for bluegrass, moonshine, and American revivalism. Lynchburg was also the hometown of the late pioneering televangelist Rev. Jerry Falwell, who founded the school as Lynchburg Baptist College in 1971. In creating the college, which has since grown into one of the largest Christian schools in the world, Falwell hoped to revive the long American tradition of orthodox Protestant education—even as so many colleges founded by evangelical Christians have slipped inexorably toward secularism.

Liberty University's chancellor is Jerry Falwell Jr., the founder's son. Students describe him as welcoming. As one says, "he regularly interacts with the students at sporting events, dining events, concerts, and more. He even invites graduating seniors over to his place at the end of every year." Chancellor Falwell has further won the affection of students by keeping a promise to hold down tuition costs. His father had already helped make this possible by leaving the school in his will the proceeds of $34 million in life insurance policies. This bequest allowed the school to retire most of its debts in 2007.

Like many schools founded by religious conservatives in recent decades, Liberty struggles to balance excellence and orthodoxy, to win acceptance and prestige without compromising its mission. It's an attractive option for conservative Christians, especially those who wish to work in ministry, politics, or pro-family activism.

Academic Life: Biblically centered

Liberty offers a wide range of undergraduate majors, sixty in all. These range from kinesiology to choral music to accounting. Liberty also offers undergrads a series of separate schools in addition to its main arts and sciences program. Among these are schools of aeronautics, communications, education, engineering and computational sciences, government, and religion.

The school maintains a serious curriculum, albeit not what we'd call a traditional core. All Liberty undergrads must complete at least 120 hours of course work during their four

South

VITAL STATISTICS

Religious affiliation: *Baptist*
Total enrollment: *46,091*
Total undergraduates: *11,918*
SAT/ACT midranges: CR:
   485–620, M: *445–550*;
   ACT: *20–25*
Applicants: *5,003*
Applicants accepted: *88%*
Accepted applicants who
   enrolled: *78%*
Tuition and fees: *$17,904*
Room and board: *$6,296*
Freshman retention rate:
   75%
Graduation rate: *28% (4 yrs.),*
   48% (6 yrs.)
Courses with fewer than 20
   students: *66%*
Student-faculty ratio: *23:1*
Courses taught by graduate
   students: *not provided*
Most popular majors:
   *psychology, business/mar-
   keting, philosophy*
Students living on campus:
   60%
Guaranteed housing for
   four years? *yes*
Students in fraternities or
   sororities: *none*

years, and some majors require as many as 145. In addition to this, the school requires students to complete a set of General Education (GNED) requirements, take one class in creation science, demonstrate competence with computers, and perform community service. Within the GNED requirement are three sets of two-term ethics and theology classes: "Contemporary Issues," "Systematic Theology," and "Evangelism and Christian Living."

In "Contemporary Issues," students address the challenges posed to Christian living by a post-Christian culture. Students explore hot topics such as euthanasia, homosexuality, and premarital sex—and as one recent student says: "They will not say that you are a sinner because you have tattoos and piercing." In "Systematic Theology," students read both the Old and New Testaments and explore their meaning in the light of Protestant theological texts. In "Evangelism and Christian Living," students lead discussions on topics like the meaning of salvation and the challenges of faithful living.

A professor says "The 'core,' if you can call it that, varies slightly according to major, but on the whole is pretty good—much better than at many schools. All students, for example, take English composition, intro to literature, and a semester of survey (world, English, or American) history. It's not the University of Dallas, but it could be much worse." The school also imposes a foreign language requirement of two terms for science majors and four terms for liberal arts majors.

The faculty at Liberty are not tenured, and judgments about contract renewal are made principally on the basis of teaching, not research. A professor says, "The school advertises itself as a teaching institution, and I think that's pretty accurate, although many of us try to publish regularly." As one recent grad now working for the school administration says, "Teaching is very central. Most of the workload is, and is expected to be, in teaching." Tied to this, every professor is required to keep twelve office hours per week, and students say that they really do see a lot of their professors. However, thanks to the school's rapid growth, its student-faculty ratio is a now a crushingly high 23 to 1—which is more typical of large state universities. Liberty will need to hire more faculty soon if it wishes to maintain and improve instructional quality.

All professors at Liberty must go through a selection process designed to identify people of faith. But academic qualifications matter; the school reports that 69 percent of its professors and instructors have doctorates, and those who do not are expected to obtain their within seven years. Few classes are taught by grad student assistants. One recent English grad says that in four years, he'd "hardly had a single class taught by a grad student."

Among the departments that seem to most consistently garner praise are English, history, theater arts, and nursing. The education department is one of the least highly regarded, according to our sources.

The English major requires that students complete twelve courses in the discipline, ranging across different periods and genres, the history of the language and (admirably) a class on Shakespeare. One grad lauds the school's "emphasis on the classics of Western literature." Among the most respected English professors is Carolyn Towles, a teacher of freshman composition who "really keeps the students engaged," according to a former student.

Liberty offers BA and BS degrees in history. Both require that students take two survey classes in American history. In addition, students must take upper-level seminars in both early and modern European history. One student especially recommends David Snead "for being very exacting, but also very approachable and helpful, William Matheny for his wealth of knowledge, and Douglas Mann for his engaging lectures and class discussions."

Liberty's government department likewise offers students BA and BS degree programs. There are, in fact, half a dozen slightly different degrees available. However, all require students to take classes in American government, comparative government, political philosophy, and the U.S. Constitution. The Liberty School of Government is named for Sen. Jesse Helms, who championed conservative and pro-family causes over many decades.

Two Liberty professors frequently singled out by students and faculty for praise are Esther Alcindor and Don Fowler. Professor Alcindor is a native Bahamian who teaches math and is "so easy to learn from," a student says. Professor Fowler is a longtime teacher of the Old Testament "who has lines outside his door of students waiting to speak to him . . . a selfless and caring man who's a good teacher and a great person. He invites all his students over in the spring for a big cookout."

Liberty's majors, across a wide array of subjects, are sound and traditional in their requirements. Indeed, there are simply no classes infused with postmodern, leftist ideology, no grievance-driven majors such as women's studies, and no courses in politicized ethnic studies.

In the middle of the campus, Liberty affirms its core convictions concretely in the form of its Center for Creation Studies. The center is run by four full-time faculty members, three biologists and a geologist who teach classes in creation science, a designated area of study at Liberty. These professors also act as a resource for legal actions and legislation on behalf of the teaching of creation science, and the center offers exhibits questioning the

SUGGESTED CORE

1. English 410, Classical Epic
2. Philosophy 301, History of Philosophy I
3. Bible 205/210, Old Testament/New Testament Life and Literature
4. Church History 301, History of the Christian Church I (closest match)
5. Philosophy 302, History of Philosophy II (closest match)
6. English 322, Shakespeare
7. History—United States 221, Survey of American History I
8. Philosophy 303, History of Philosophy III (closest match)

South

tenets of evolutionary theory. Graduates of Liberty who wish to work in the hard sciences can expect harsh scrutiny over their views on evolution at almost any graduate institution or employer to which they apply.

Not every discipline at Liberty is of equal quality. The athletics training major includes many classes that seem designed to serve less-qualified athletes. Students on the most competitive sports teams receive one credit hour for their participation, and the school has a broad assortment of full credit "training" theory and practice classes. Perhaps this should be expected; at least fifteen players who went on to the National Football League first played for Liberty.

While Liberty offers a huge number of engineering classes, it does not have a physics major, offering only six classes in the subject—enough for premeds and engineers but not for those deeply interested in physics.

The speedy growth of the school has led to a wide distribution in the skills of its students. One current professor remarks: "Liberty does not have a strong admissions policy, so the abilities of the students (and hence their curiosity in intellectual matters) run the spectrum. I have students who could do well anywhere—I mean that. Then again, I have some who should still be in high school—early high school."

Aware of this problem, Liberty has established an honors program. A recent grad says that students accepted into it get "smaller classes, and they get to register for classes even before student athletes. Plus, they get a lot of the top teachers, have the privilege of writing an honors thesis, and get special scholarship assistance." The scholarship for honors students is $3,750 per year. Admission requires a combined verbal/math SAT of 1270 or an ACT of 29, and an unweighted high school GPA of 3.50.

Liberty offers fall- and spring-term study-abroad programs at other religious schools in Sydney, Australia; Brussels, Belgium; Dalian, China; Quito, Ecuador; Cheltenham, England; Strasbourg, France; Brikama, Gambia; Marburg, Germany; Athens, Greece; Pondicherry and Mangalore, India; Derry, Northern Ireland; Sapporo, Japan; Xalapa, Mexico; Dunedin, New Zealand; and Barcelona, Spain.

Striking, given the school's size and missionary aspirations, is its anemic foreign language program. The school does offer an assortment of classes in French, Spanish, and biblical Greek, and a smaller number in German and Hebrew. But there are no courses in Italian, Russian, Arabic, Latin, or Chinese. Nor are there on-campus language immersion houses.

Student Life: Can adultery lead to dancing?

Liberty's campus is not beautiful, resembling a recently constructed state university with its mass of bland-looking buildings and clean but cookie-cutter dorms and parking lots. But this is a perhaps inevitable result of the speed of its expansion. Liberty now has 11,918 undergraduates on campus. That number is up from 7,000 just three years ago, and including its online and graduate students, it now has a total enrollment of over 45,000, with students from 50 states and over 80 foreign countries. Some 7,100 of the school's dormitory beds for undergrads are on campus, while another 4,800 are off the main campus.

Liberty uses 48 million feet of building space. (This includes athletics facilities, dorms and offices, in addition to classrooms and all other space.) To enter the school's campus is

South

554

to approach a whirlwind. Should you arrive on a spring day within this mass of construction, you will see hugely muscled young Christian athletes on the fields practicing javelin and pole vault, and swarms of respectably dressed students walking about smiling, chattering, and carrying their books to the student center cafeteria and to class.

A Liberty admissions counselor notes that while the school does not require that students be Christian, Liberty is very much an old-fashioned Baptist school. This means rules of behavior are strict. Students are prohibited from drinking and smoking, watching R-rated movies, entering the bedroom of a student of the opposite sex—or signing an unauthorized petition. There are no school dances. The school has a midnight curfew on weekdays, and students must be in their rooms by 12:30 AM on the weekends. There are no coed dorms or bathrooms. Male students cannot have hair that covers their earlobes. Students may wear jeans but not T-shirts, and in business and government classes a coat and tie is required for men. The school also has an honor code, which it calls the Liberty Way, and students must sign their papers affirming that their work is their own.

Attendance at Sunday chapel service is not mandatory, but convocation is—on Mondays, Wednesdays, and Fridays from 10:00 AM to 11:00 AM at the school's Vine Center. A worship service is part of every convocation.

Observes a student: "Dorm life is strict and can be hard to follow. Curfews, thrice-weekly room checks for cleanliness. . . . Liberty can be amazing or extremely frustrating. It depends on your attitude and what you are expecting from it. To succeed and enjoy the college experience here, incoming students must know and be prepared for Liberty's religious and ethical outlook."

Liberty is developing a major sports program, which it sees as an advertisement for its mission and a symbol of its students' calling as Christian warriors. (The school's teams are called the Liberty Flames.) The school's Division IAA Williams Football Stadium started off as a 12,000-seat stadium when it opened in the fall of 1989. It's now a

ACADEMIC REQUIREMENTS

Liberty's general education mandates do not add up to a traditional core, but they are respectable and well matched to the school's mission. Students must complete:

- "Contemporary Issues," "Systematic Theology," and "Evangelism and Christian Living."
- Two classes in English composition, one in public speaking, one in math, and one in natural science.
- Two terms of a foreign language for science majors and four terms for liberal arts majors.
- One class in the social sciences and one in the humanities. All options seem sensible and sound.
- One class in creation science.
- Coursework or tests demonstrating minimal competence with computers.
- Designated hours of community service.

20,000-seat stadium, and in five years it will hold 30,000. Liberty competes in twenty Division IAA sports leagues, and the campus is 5,000 acres. The acreage provides the terrain for the school's highly successful cross-country squad, which includes a student who last year won the NCAA title. And it offers students more than sixty-five miles of trails to hike and walk, along with a 550-foot-long synthetic snow ski slope and locations where students can play paintball in the woods and race motocross. There are also spots for organized archery competitions and the LaHaye Ice Center for skating. The campus's sprawl means that students without cars are apt to use campus buses to get from their dorms up to the hilltop main campus for their classes.

The senior Rev. Jerry Falwell's record and life is one of which Liberty is immensely proud, and up on the hilltop, in De Moss Hall, which serves both as the main administration building and a place for classes, there is a small museum dedicated to celebrating Falwell's achievements.

Liberty provides its undergrads with a wide range of wholesome activities. There are dozens of undergraduate organizations and clubs. Naturally, many of these are oriented toward ministry and Christian service and outreach. But an indication of the variety may come from the existence of Liberty's kung fu club, a pro-Israel group, the Women in Aviation society, a black students' group, the Christian Motorcyclists' Association and the Optimist Club. The school takes particular pride in its debate team, which regularly is ranked very high by the American Debate Association.

Liberty likes to boast of the $2 million that the School of Marketing's business students raised in working with UNICEF for the aid of the displaced and orphaned around the world. The school also notes that its students contributed more than 586,000 hours of community service in Lynchburg during the last year.

Each school term begins with a large event called the Block Party. In addition, the school attracts many famous speakers, especially at year-end. Among those who have come in the last few years are John McCain, Chuck Norris, Ben Stein, and Glenn Beck. As the school expands, it is also becoming less politically monochromatic; there is now a Campus Democrats group to go along with the Campus Republicans.

Most students say that they feel safe on campus. This perception is mostly backed up by crime statistics—although things got worse in 2009 than they'd been in previous years. In 2009, the campus was the scene of one murder, five forcible sex offenses, one robbery, two aggravated assaults, ten burglaries, two stolen cars, and six arsons.

Tuition at Liberty for 2010–11 was $17,904. Room and board were $6,296. There are additional grants for in-state residents, and for honors students. Some 78 percent of students receive some need-based financial aid, and the average student-loan debt of a recent graduating student was $21,171.

Louisiana State University

Baton Rouge, Louisiana • www.lsu.edu

Southern exposure

Founded in 1853, Louisiana State was once known as the leading outpost of the southern literary revival, hosting Robert Penn Warren, Cleanth Brooks, and the journal they edited, the *Southern Review*. In political philosophy, too, LSU had a stream of distinguished professors, including Eric Voegelin, Willmoore Kendall, and Charles Hyneman. Among the notable men who spent time in graduate study at LSU during this era were Hubert Humphrey, Richard Weaver, and Robert Lowell. Walker Percy once taught there, and some retired faculty members can still be found who knew him personally. The *Southern Review* continues to flourish, as do several excellent academic departments. Nevertheless, the intellectual environment at LSU no longer seems so dazzling, and the Agrarians and New Critics who made its English department famous are now held up for scorn in English classes taught by tenured carpetbaggers.

While LSU strives for a national reputation, it must also fulfill the mandate of a great state university founded in the Populist era. Indeed, Huey Long himself assumed the Louisiana governorship a couple of years after the university moved to his capital city of Baton Rouge, and he lavished resources on it in his dream of ennobling the masses. The public money has never been quite enough to do everything that educators had wanted to do, and the school must take in a great many students ill-prepared by crumbling public schools.

Still, there are more good courses and faculty at LSU than at many other state schools, and it has found gold and growth in research, which brings upward of $75 million dollars to the university each year. Focused students can find excellent teachers, distinctive academic resources, and hearty fellowship. The atmosphere in most departments is friendly to patriotism and faith while tolerant of liberalism. The campus is one of the most beautiful in America, though the summer heat can be brutal.

Academic Life: Honors and others

LSU is foremost a research university, and many of the university's initiatives seem directed at preserving the school's prominence as such—so it's easy to forget that there are over 23,000 undergraduates hanging about the place, some of them even aspiring toward a liberal education. The entering class of 2010 was the second largest in the school's history, with 5,400 new students.

The financial situation at LSU is currently grim due to the state misappropriating federal stimulus dollars to fund higher education—and becoming addicted to funds that have finally dried up. Without these federal millions, the Louisiana legislature was forced to institute devastating budget cuts, and for the first time in history less than 50 percent of LSU's operational budget is coming from the state. Since January 2009, there have been three permanent cuts to LSU's state appropriations, amounting to more than $42 million. Even larger budget reductions are promised for fiscal year 2012, and Chancellor Mike Martin is not optimistic: "These cuts and the cuts we face in the future are damaging. They hurt severely. We will fundamentally and structurally [have] to change the university."

Fortunately, the draconian cuts have not (yet) targeted the single best resource for a true liberal arts education on campus: LSU's Honors College. This program, for which a separate application is required, promises "the benefits of a small liberal arts environment within a large research university." The Honors College describes itself as a "campus within a campus," complete with residence halls, a dining hall, an administration building (the French House, a 1930s-style chateau), and an oak-lined outdoor common area. Honors students can also attend weekly afternoon teas with honors faculty. Students complete a traditional major in one of the regular academic colleges, including fields outside the humanities.

The University College Center for Freshman Year is responsible for the academic advising of each student until he declares a major, at which time he transfers to an advisor in that department. Students meet with advisors in person, by e-mail, or via a "virtual academic counseling" chat session. While in the University College, students begin completing the university-wide general education requirements. One student cautions that survey courses such as these can result "in a disappointingly shallow education," and for that reason, serious scholars should seek out more challenging classes—for instance, by taking the honors sections when they are offered. "LSU is a large state university, so of course there are a thousand ways to graduate while avoiding the most serious matters of study," says one professor. "But there are also some very fine faculty in a number of fields, and the student who wants to look will find them quickly enough."

Despite its financial constraints, LSU still offers an impressive number of strong academic programs. Within the humanities, English, political science, history, philoso-

VITAL STATISTICS

Religious affiliation: *none*
Total enrollment: *28,643*
Total undergraduates: *23,012*
SAT/ACT midranges: CR: *520–630*, M: *540–650*; ACT: *23–28*
Applicants: *15,093*
Applicants accepted: *69%*
Accepted applicants who enrolled: *46%*
Tuition and fees: *in state, $5,764; out of state, $16,549*
Room and board: *$8,210*
Freshman retention rate: *84%*
Graduation rate: *28% (4 yrs.), 61% (6 yrs.)*
Courses with fewer than 20 students: *35%*
Student-faculty ratio: *20:1*
Courses taught by graduate students: *17%*
Most popular majors: *business, biology, psychology,*
Students living on campus: *25%*
Guaranteed housing for four years? *yes*
Students in fraternities: *13%* in sororities: *20%*

South

SUGGESTED CORE

1. Classical Studies 3020, Classical Epic in Translation
2. Philosophy 2033, History of Ancient and Medieval Philosophy
3. Religious Studies 1004/1005, Old Testament/New Testament
4. Philosophy 4928, Medieval Philosophy
5. Political Science 4082, History of Political Theory from Machiavelli to Nietzsche
6. English 2148, Shakespeare
7. History 2055, The United States to 1865
8. Philosophy 4936, Nineteenth-Century Philosophy

phy and religious studies, music, and theater are notable for their quality instruction. The English department's requirements for majors are suspect, though; majors are required to take classes such as "Critical Strategies," "Modern Criticism," and an ethnic or women's literature course such as "Literature and Ethnicity" or "Images of Women." Happily, students must also choose at least one course on Milton, Chaucer, or Shakespeare, and a two-course sequence in either British or American literature. The English department has moved sharply to the left in recent decades; conservative and religious students should be *very* careful what opinions they express to their Marxist or feminist professors, sources warn.

The LSU geography department is one of the finest in the country. The economics department is free-market oriented, although professors use econometric rather than theoretical approaches to the subject. The political science department is strong in political theory, thanks to the heritage of the great theoretician Eric Voegelin, a former LSU professor. Poli sci majors are required to take an all-encompassing "American Government" course, but the rest of the curriculum is up to them. Excellent classes are offered, including courses in the U.S. Constitution, American political philosophy, comparative politics, and international politics and law, but none are specifically required. Students interested in learning the history of ideas should seek out the faculty associated with the Eric Voegelin Institute and enroll in their courses, which are among the best theory classes offered anywhere in the United States.

The history department is solid as well. All majors are required to take twelve hours of basic introductory courses in American, European, and world history, as well as an additional twenty-one hours of electives chosen from an impressive selection of advanced classes in American, European, Asian, and Latin American history. The mass communications school, while growing in size and reputation, is "soft academically," in the words of one student. Some have called classes in journalism "the easiest [they] have ever taken." Students in the business school are not known for their intellectuality. "Business majors may hardly ever if at all walk into the library," says a student.

Of course, at such a big school, one is bound to find intellectual gems. Among the many fine professors on campus are Edward Henderson, Gregory Schufreider, Mary Sirridge, and John Whittaker (emeritus) in philosophy and religious studies; Kevin Cope, Brannon Costello, William Demastes, Michael Hegarty, John Lowe, John May (emeritus), Elsie Michie, Lisi Oliver, Malcolm Richardson, James Wilcox, and Michelle Zerba in English; Gaines M. Foster, James D. Hardy Jr., Stanley E. Hilton, Paul F. Paskoff, Karl Roider, and Victor L. Stater in history; and Cecil L. Eubanks, Mark Gasiorowski, Wayne Parent, Ellis Sandoz, and James Stoner in political science.

Professors are said to be remarkably accessible for a school this size. "The teachers are willing to personally help you and take time out for you," a student says. Another student was surprised to find that in most of her honors courses, "the instructor has known the name of every student in the class." Professors are required to hold regular office hours, and most are known to warmly welcome students who need help or want mentoring.

Outside honors, the advising system is weak. The otherwise excellent history department, for instance, has one undergraduate faculty advisor to handle the academic needs of all majors. One student says the advising program "operates like a factory, and an inefficient one at that."

The foreign languages and literatures department is excellent, offering degrees in Arabic, Chinese, classics, German, Hebrew, Italian, Japanese, Portuguese, Russian, Spanish, and Swahili. Students wanting to learn a language immersed in a different culture can take advantage of the more than 300 study-abroad programs offered through LSU, in dozens of countries on every inhabited continent.

Student Life: Fun on the bayou

LSU sits on more than 2,000 acres in Baton Rouge. LSU's stately Italian Renaissance–style buildings (modeled on those at Stanford, which Huey Long visited and decided to copy) and classic art deco theater have undergone a thorough restoration. The school opened an art museum in once-desolate downtown Baton Rouge, featuring "fourteen galleries totaling 13,000-square feet of state-of-the-art exhibition space with soaring sixteen-foot ceilings and beautiful lighting," according to the university, to house LSU's impressive collection of fine and decorative arts. The English department building, Allen Hall, is graced by lovely Depression-era murals from the Works Progress Administration.

The campus is bordered on the west by the Mississippi River, and two Indian mounds built before the Pyramids of Egypt stand at the northwest corner of the campus. Live oak trees and colonnaded passageways dot the campus. In fact, it's possible to make most of one's way across campus without getting wet during one of the city's frequent, daylong monsoons. For nightlife, students head to blues and jazz clubs for live music and "meat market" bars for dancing. Tigerland, a group of apartments and bars near campus, is a popular place to go on weekends, as are the Varsity, where bands play; Louie's, a greasy spoon close to campus; and the Chimes restaurant.

Students also hang out at the LSU Union, which includes a bookstore, theater, games area, and food stands; or at the Parade Grounds, a grassy area where students play intramurals, lie in the sun, study, and play Frisbee. Baton Rouge's downtown has seen a renaissance of arts and small businesses, especially after its population explosion following Hurricane Katrina in 2005. The Baton Rouge Zoo is large and well worth visiting—as is the lavish, WPA-inspired Louisiana state capitol.

Baton Rouge has become much more congested since Hurricane Katrina, which thrust tens of thousands onto the streets of a city not known for civic-mindedness, with roads laid out like a bowl of spilled spaghetti, whose public transit system compares quite poorly to that of cities in India. Nevertheless, it's a friendly town with enough cultural

South

attractions—most of them on campus—hosting a school with plenty of potential in one of the most delightful states in the Union.

Student life at LSU is vibrant—if not particularly healthful. Drinking makes up a significant part of social life on campus, as students throng local bars in defiance of the drinking laws—which Louisiana adopted only under enormous pressure from the federal government and does not enforce with any great enthusiasm. Neighboring New Orleans still features drive-through daiquiri shops, and Cajuns to the school's southeast and west tend to take "one for the road" quite literally, flouting bans on open containers. If you prefer eating to drinking, Baton Rouge is a wonderful town to learn the intricacies of Cajun and classic southern cooking; it also hosts a surprising variety of ethnic restaurants.

Among LSU's numerous student organizations are agricultural and equestrian clubs, the usual Greek houses, religious clubs, and ethnic groups. Some of the more unusual include the Wargaming and Roleplaying Society, the Hip-Hop Coalition, and the Poker Strategy Club. A service group called Ambassadors and student government are comparatively popular among students.

ACADEMIC REQUIREMENTS

In lieu of a core curriculum, LSU imposes distribution requirements on undergraduates of all colleges of the university:

- Two courses in English composition.
- Two classes in analytical reasoning (math or logic).
- One course in the arts.
- Three classes in humanities. These can include foreign languages, communications, and classical studies, such as "Swahili," "Introduction to Philosophy," and "Modern Europe."
- Three courses in natural sciences.
- Two classes in the social sciences, such as "Human Geography: Americas and Europe," "Introduction to Psychology," or "American Government."

In addition, each of the ten colleges of the university has requirements of its own. A student entering the College of Arts and Sciences and majoring in a humanities discipline must take, in addition to the mandated courses above:

- Freshman English.
- Two courses in literature.
- One humanities class outside English or foreign languages.
- Courses up to the fourth semester in a foreign language (or show equivalent test scores).
- One yearlong course in the biological or physical sciences (with lab), plus an additional science class.
- One math course.
- One additional course in analytical reasoning.
- Two courses in history.
- Three courses in the social sciences.

There are also many Christian groups. Conservative Catholic students avoid the bland campus Catholic chapel and take refuge at St. Agnes Church, which offers weekly Latin Masses. New Orleans's Holy Trinity Cathedral, the first Orthodox house of worship established in the New World, has a mission in Baton Rouge. The Baptist Student Union is one of the largest and most active religious centers on campus. Alternatively, the Full Circle Wellness Center serves as a clearinghouse for what they proudly describe as "New Age" organizations and activities. Nearby Jimmy Swaggart Bible College still dispatches young evangelists to preach against the immorality and immodesty at LSU.

The Greek system has a strong presence at LSU. Although only 13 percent of men join fraternities and 20 percent of women join sororities, "their influence is way bigger than those numbers represent. Greek students have a big profile on campus. They're the ones holding office in student government," one student says. Disciplinary actions are taken against the fraternities and sororities quite frequently for violations ranging from alcohol to assault to hazing. "Fraternities keep doing stupid things and getting into trouble here," says a student. "We've had a couple kicked off campus." Indeed, two fraternities were removed from campus and another was put on probation.

Tiger football games are the true center of LSU students' social lives. LSU won its third National Championship in 2007, bestirring its historically fervent football fans to achieve a noise level of 122 decibels, according to ESPN. As one student says, "There is nothing better than to go to an LSU football game and sit in the student section. Everyone around you is so pumped." Tiger Stadium is the sixth-largest college football stadium in the nation, and the third largest in the SEC, holding almost 92,500 fans. Tailgating is extraordinarily popular, as alumni and others fill vast parking lots with pickup trucks containing propane stoves to heat gumbo and barbecue. The city of Baton Rouge clogs with traffic and pretty much closes down on game days as Louisianans converge from all over the state to throng the massive Tiger Stadium. If you don't like football, leave town—well in advance, as many tailgaters arrive on Monday to camp out in the stadium parking lot in anticipation of Satuday's game. LSU's mascot, Mike the Tiger, is a real, live tiger who lives on campus. At past games, he has been paraded in his cage during half-time so he could roar into a microphone.

The LSU athletic program is one of the best in the nation, with strong gymnastics, swimming, baseball, and men's and women's track teams. LSU fields teams in twenty sports (nine men's, eleven women's) and is a member of the Southeastern Conference and NCAA, Division I. In 2008, the women's outdoor track team won the NCAA national championship, and in 2009 the men's baseball team won its sixth College World Series title. The women's and men's basketball teams also have many fans. In 2008, the men's team was an NCAA Final Four participant. Students take part in a number of intramural sports, including Ultimate Frisbee, Wallyball, and flag football. At the LSU Union, students can enroll in art instruction or courses in wine tasting and Cajun dancing.

No student is required to live on campus, though many choose to live either in the dorms or in residential colleges—which range from the quaint and traditional (with ceiling fans) to the huge and hideous (which are at least air-conditioned). Happily, students no longer live under the bleachers of Tiger Stadium, as they did well into the '90s. (Huey Long couldn't get legislators to fund a stadium expansion, so he built dorms adjacent to the

South

GREEN LIGHT

Just fourteen of the more than 300 clubs at LSU have political purposes. (By contrast, there are thirty religious clubs.) LSU's College Republicans is consistently one of the largest such chapters in the country, at well over 1,000 members.

"Louisiana is a culturally conservative state, and it shows in the student body. There are no hippies, no lovefests on the Parade Grounds," says one student. A professor says, "Generally speaking, I would describe LSU students as conservative and religious but grounded in common sense and decency rather than fanaticism." The most prominent churches on campus are the Catholic and the Baptist chapels.

original stands and put bleachers on the roofs. No, we're not making this up; this guide's lead editor used to live in Tiger stadium.)

Some residence halls are single sex, while others separate the sexes by floor or by room. Students may opt to live in one of several living-learning communities. The Information Technology Residential College is designed to provide students training in just that. Herget Residential College was created "to foster a sense of community and to create an environment that encourages and facilitates academic effort and achievement." Students take some classes together and meet regularly with residential college mentors. The residential Vision Louisiana is a four-year program for students who "want to affect the future of Louisiana" by applying material covered in courses toward solving problems facing the state.

In 2009, the school reported four sex offenses, seventeen aggravated assaults, twelve robberies, thirty-one burglaries, twelve car thefts, and three arsons on campus. The LSU Police Department provides awareness and safety training to students but they are still understaffed. Safety is a more serious problem at LSU than at other campuses of the same size (dangerous slums sit just off campus), and students are well advised to exercise more caution than they might elsewhere.

Like most state schools, LSU is quite a bargain for residents of the state, who, thanks to Huey Long's populist "homestead exemption," pay very low local taxes, which is one reason the school is underfunded. It's also pretty cheap for visiting Yankees: in 2010–11, the school charged $5,764 in-state and $16,549 out-of-state tuition. Room and board are $8,210. Some 35 percent of students receive need-based aid, and the average student-loan burden of a recent grad was $18,118.

University of Mississippi

Oxford, Mississippi • www.olemiss.edu

The new South

The University of Mississippi, affectionately known as Ole Miss, first opened its doors to eighty students in 1848, only to close them again when the Civil War broke out and the entire student body enlisted in the Confederate Army. Their company, the 11th Mississippi Infantry, suffered a 100 percent casualty rate in 1863. When the school reopened after the war, it was led by former Confederate general A. P. Stewart, who shepherded the university through Reconstruction.

Today Ole Miss has grown to over 19,500 students and is one of the top thirty public schools with the largest endowment per student. Ole Miss celebrated its twenty-fifth Rhodes scholar in 2008 and is the proud alma mater to numerous Truman, Goldwater, Fulbright, Marshall, Udall, and Gates Cambridge scholars as well.

Obviously, it is possible to get a top-notch education at Ole Miss—but it's by no means necessary. The school's wide distribution requirements will not guarantee any such thing. Remarks a professor dryly, "Students can indeed graduate with a narrow knowledge base, particularly by majoring in 'soft' disciplines, which rarely demand more than rote memorization." Fortunately, good professors are also attracted to the school's picturesque location and traditional sensibilities; consequently, there are a good many quality courses at Ole Miss—if students are conscientious enough to take them.

Academic Life: Available, not required

The University of Mississippi's curricular and distribution requirements are inconsequential. While the school encourages students to pursue traditional areas of study, it does not require them—and students can knock off their requirements with courses of wildly varying quality. For instance, the two-course social science requirement for an English major may be met by any choices from anthropology, economics, political science, Latin American studies, psychology, sociology, or psychology, or Journalism 101. And so it goes through most majors.

The University of Mississippi offers sixty-nine bachelor's degrees through the eight undergraduate colleges on the Oxford campus. Degree programs are varied, from classics or geological engineering to criminal justice, hospitality management, dental hygiene, and elementary education. Should these options not satisfy, the College of Liberal Arts offers a liberal studies degree that allows a student to combine any three minors.

One distinctive degree offered is a bachelor of arts in southern studies. Ole Miss is the home of the Center for the Study of Southern Culture, which for over thirty years has been the premier place to study the writings of William Faulkner (longtime resident of Oxford) and the works of other southern luminaries. Thanks to a grant from John Grisham (who received his JD at Ole Miss Law), each year the English department hosts a visiting southern writer. Courses offered through the center vary by semester but include such gems as "Southern Literature and the Oral Tradition," "An Economic History of the South since the Civil War," "The Fiction of Faulkner's Yoknapatawpha County," and seminars on various major southern authors.

The rigor of major requirements varies. The English department (strong particularly in nineteenth- and twentieth-century American literature, southern literature, and creative writing) requires of its students fourteen classes in English. Students must take two composition classes, two intermediate-level survey courses, two upper-level seminars ("Major Authors in American Literature," "Literary Criticism"), and one Shakespeare class, as well as seven upper-level electives. The department offers just a few trendy or politicized options, such as "Gay and Lesbian Literature and Theory."

The history department demands eleven classes that "show a reasonable balance between United States and non–United States" history courses. All majors must take a two-course sequence on the history of Europe, two senior seminars, and at least two upper-level courses on the history of non–Western nations. Again, most choices are solid, although students can skip "The Golden Age of Athens" in favor of "Race, Gender, and Courtship in African American History."

Political science majors are required to take eleven classes in the discipline, including introductory courses in American politics (which cover the "Constitutional principles of U.S. governmental framework," as well as political participation, processes, and institutions), comparative politics, international relations, and political science methods. They must also take seven advanced-level electives, most of them in traditional areas of study such as "German Politics," "Mock Trial," and "Political Economy of International Development."

Academic advising is mandatory, but—as with the distribution requirements—its quality varies by school. Students in the College of Liberal Arts and School of Business are assigned faculty advisors, but those in the School of Accountancy are guided by the dean's office. The university's website makes it clear that, whatever the method or college, "students have the primary responsibility for planning their individual programs and meeting graduation requirements." Says a student, "The process usually involves a lot of waiting, but that can be avoided if students take advantage of early advising, appointments, etc." A student in the College of Liberal Arts says, "I think the system works very well. . . . Having the same advisor for the entirety of one's undergraduate career is helpful."

Professors at Ole Miss are readily available to students. "In general, the faculty are eager to help when called upon," says a student. "Because Ole Miss is rather small, undergraduates here are much more likely than they are at other public universities to receive instruction from full-time members of the faculty rather than

> ### SUGGESTED CORE
>
> 1. Classics 309, Greek and Roman Epic
> 2. Philosophy 301, History of Philosophy I
> 3. Religion 310/312, The Old Testament and Early Judaism/The New Testament and Early Christianity
> 4. History 375, History of Medieval Christianity
> 5. Philosophy 331, Political Philosophy
> 6. English 385, Shakespeare
> 7. History 105, History of the United States to 1877
> 8. History 341: The Darwinian Revolution or 358: Europe in Age of Revolution, 1789–1890

graduate students," says a professor. "Teaching matters here," another reports. "It's not just about publications and research grants." Nevertheless, Ole Miss *does* make use of teaching assistants, who teach lower-level courses, particularly those that students take to fulfill distribution requirements—but that is due in part to the budget crisis facing the school. State support has dwindled to one-fourth of the university's funding, and tuition payments represent the university's largest source of recurring income. As a natural consequence of the decline in funding, the number of students admitted has increased over the past couple of years while the pace of hiring new faculty has not kept up. The freshman class in 2010 was the largest it has ever been, at 3,089—a 20 percent increase over the previous year's class. Overall, the school's population increased by almost 7 percent between 2009 and 2010. Such practices have left the school with a student-faculty ratio of 17 to 1. "More has to be done with less," says a professor, "and graduate programs are under threat."

Some schools and departments are known to be more exacting than others. The School of Pharmacy and the E. H. Patterson School of Accounting are rigorous, and the economics, English, and physics departments of the College of Liberal Arts are particularly strong. However, one professor says, "The marketing and management majors are widely perceived as easy . . . preparing students for entry-level jobs in the banking, insurance, and real estate industries but failing utterly to equip them with the intellectual tools necessary for a lifetime of learning."

Highly recommended professors at Ole Miss include Benjamin F. Fisher IV, Donald M. Kartiganer, and Colby H. Kullman in English; William F. Chappell, John R. Conlon,

South

and William F. Shughart II in economics; Robert B. Westmoreland in philosophy and religion; Alice H. Cooper and John W. Winkle III in political science; John Czarnetzky in law; and Judith Cassidy, Dale L. Flesher, and Tonya Kay Flesher in the School of Accountancy.

Students from the university's Honors College and the Croft Institute for International Studies are, according to one professor, "the cream of the crop." The minimum admission requirements to the Sally McDonnell Barksdale Honors College are a 28 ACT (or 1240 verbal/math SAT) and a 3.50 GPA in high school. Honors College students are required to take at least twenty-nine hours of honors credits and must keep a 3.5 grade point average. They take freshman and sophomore seminars, complete a research project undertaken with a faculty mentor, and write a senior thesis. The remaining credit hours come from specially designated honors courses in regular departments, which offer smaller enrollment and more discussion-based classes. Honors students must also attend two performances, conferences, exhibits, or guest lectures each semester and volunteer ten hours per semester in community service. The Honors College website says it "offers an education similar to that at prestigious private liberal-arts schools . . . but at a far lower cost." The thirty honors classes include solid topics such as "Survey of American Literature to the Civil War," "History of Europe Since 1648," "Inquiry into Life: Human Biology," and "Principles of Macroeconomics."

The Croft Institute for International Studies admits just forty-five students each year, who must complete the institute's curriculum in addition to that of the College of Liberal Arts. Students take four core courses, introducing them to international studies and surveying East Asia, Europe, and Latin America. Students have a chance to examine their chosen areas firsthand, as the Croft curriculum includes foreign language training and a required study abroad.

For those outside the prestigious Croft Institute, study-abroad options are still numerous. With over sixty nations to choose from, including Mongolia, Austria, and Botswana, Ole Miss provides its students with excellent short-term, semester-long, and year-long options (including a brief January trip on "Multi-Media Reporting" in the Bahamas or "Education, Health, and Child Welfare" in Belize).

Stateside, students may pursue a number of foreign languages. The school offers Ancient Greek and Latin as well as Spanish, Arabic, Chinese, Russian, Portuguese, French, German, Japanese, and Italian. Minors can be pursued in all these languages except Portuguese, and the Modern Languages department offers majors in Chinese, French, German, and Spanish.

Student Life: Football and cornhole

Ole Miss offers all the advantages of a relatively small, southern, traditional state school—and all the temptations, too. Oxford, Mississippi, is a charming community of 19,000, just seventy miles south of Memphis. It is also a university town—Ole Miss being Lafayette County's biggest employer—and subsequently boasts an abundance of restaurants, bars, and boutiques in the historic downtown area (known as the Square) surrounding the Lafayette County Courthouse. Campus life is peppered with traditions such as the school cheer and lingo like "the Grove" and "the Square." And if university-town Oxford ever feels

South

too small, Memphis is less than an hour's drive away. Square Books in Oxford boasts signed editions of Faulkner and other major writers and serves as a hangout for literary types on campus. Faulkner's old home, Rowan Oak, stands in town and is certainly worth a visit.

A student says, "By far, the most popular place to hang out in Oxford is the Square, which truly feels like a movie set. There are upwards of thirty bars and restaurants around the town square area, so many students opt to spend time there at night." So many students spend time there, in fact, that another student reports, "Lines to get into the most popular bars can begin around 7:00 PM on Thursday nights."

Ole Miss is something of a party school. One student calls barhopping an "art" in Oxford. Over a third of students at Ole Miss go Greek, and many students follow family lineages to the university in the hopes of affiliating themselves with the same fraternity or sorority. Says a professor, "Sorority and fraternity activities dominate the social calendar throughout the year, but football is the number one priority in the fall."

Rebel fans support their teams—especially football—vigorously and throw grand parties before, during, and after football season. During that season, "bars are always packed with celebrations," according to a student. "Football is the lifeblood of Ole Miss."

ACADEMIC REQUIREMENTS

The University of Mississippi is like most state schools in that it imposes only weak, unhelpful distribution requirements. On the other hand, given the school's traditional orientation, many of the course choices are better than they are at other colleges. All undergraduates in the College of Liberal Arts must take:

- Two courses in English composition.
- One class in mathematics.
- Two courses in physical science or biology, each with a lab component.
- Two classes in English literature, with the choices "World Literature" (to 1650 and since 1650), "American Literature" (to the Civil War and since the Civil War), or "British Literature" (to the eighteenth century and since the Romantic period).
- Two social sciences classes. Choices are nearly endless: "Judicial Process," "Science of Emotion," "Archaeology of Death and Burial," "Muslims in the West," "Southern Folklore," "Principles of Microeconomics," or "The Sociology of Food" suffice, as do introductory and survey classes in the various disciplines.
- Two history courses. Choices range too widely, from "History of Europe to 1648" to "History of African Americans in Sport."
- One humanities class. Options vary wildly, from "Greek and Roman Religions," to "Women, Gender, and Society."
- One fine arts elective. Options are mostly introductory and include art history ("History of Art: Ancient through Medieval"), music ("Fundamentals of Music Theory," "Introduction to World Music Cultures"), dance ("Dance Appreciation"), and theater ("Appreciation of the Theatre") classes.
- A foreign language through the intermediate level.

South

Another says, "Game-day attire is very strict: children either have cheerleading outfits or Ole Miss jerseys on, girls have heels and dresses . . . and the guys have suits and ties. If you don't follow these fashion rules, then you're obviously with the visiting team." Another student describes it as "cocktail party meets hard-core tailgating."

Other sports are not nearly as beloved as football. However, of its fourteen teams in men's and women's sports, Ole Miss has a strong tennis team and women's soccer team. Golf, basketball, baseball and softball, and track and field are offered to both men and women. (Women also have rifle and volleyball teams.) There is an active intramural program, offering more than 6,500 participants each year flag football, 3-on-3 basketball, laser tag, table tennis, and special events like bingo, cornhole, and Texas hold 'em tournaments.

Because student life is so enticing, "Ole Miss seems to have a large percentage of fifth-year seniors. Many students choose to spread classes out for a lighter course load each semester," says a student.

Enough freshmen have trouble making the transition to college that, in 2001, the university's administration implemented a program called Freshmen Absence-Based Intervention (FABI). Designed to "circumvent student absences and potential student failure," according to its website, FABI calls upon professors who teach lower-level courses to report to a secure website the names of freshmen with over three absences. The burden of the intervention falls upon the student's residence-hall advisor and academic advisor.

For the slightly more motivated, Ole Miss offers a variety of student organizations. Student government is popular on campus, as is the student programming board, which brings in musicians and comedians and hosts the annual beauty pageant—something that at other schools would likely be restricted to male transvestites. Otherwise, "few of the professional or special interest organizations seem to be popular or prestigious," says a student. The school boasts nearly 270 organizations, most of which fall along religious, professional, or Greek lines.

Religious groups include Baptist, Episcopal, Catholic, and Muslim associations, as well as evangelical groups like Campus Crusade, Fellowship of Christian Athletes, and Young Life. Professional groups include Air Force, Navy, and Army ROTC, the Black Law Student Association, Mississippi Philosophical Association, and the Society for the Advancement of Management. Ole Miss also offers a number of international groups (African Caribbean, Chinese, Indian, Korean, Malaysian, Taiwanese, Thai, and general international) as well as sports clubs like badminton, ballroom dancing, fencing, and Ultimate Frisbee.

Special interest groups include an active College Republicans group, a Mac User Group, gospel choir, model United Nations, Gay-Straight Alliance, College Democrats, Financier's Club, and the Feral University Rebel Rescuers, whose mission is "to humanely control and maintain the homeless cat population."

For a school that had to be integrated at gunpoint by federal marshals some forty years ago, Ole Miss is now quite comfortably multiracial—if still rather self-segregated. Some 15 percent of the student population is black, and 78 percent is white (only 3 percent are Asian, and 1 percent Hispanic). As one professor told the *Daily Mississippian*, self-segregation is "a problem that all campuses and all aspects of society face. . . . I haven't noticed it being much different there than here. In fact, I'd say there are more mixed groups here than elsewhere." Despite the occasional controversy over the display of the Confederate battle flag—once

South

a staple at football games—the school has avoided much of the interracial animus (and resulting heavy-handed "diversity" initiatives) that afflict other schools North and South.

Students who do not reside in one of the twenty-four fraternity and sorority houses can live in university housing. A quarter of students live on campus, and freshmen are required to, but a tenth of them have commuter status and are exempt from the policy. The halls have set visitation hours, but during the first week of classes in the fall, residents may vote to extend the hours. Although Ole Miss does not offer theme halls or substance-free housing, residence halls at Ole Miss are strictly single sex, which is nearly unheard of at a public university. Student apartments are, naturally, mixed. The university recently undertook a multimillion-dollar renovation of most of the residence halls, adding amenities like kitchen facilities, study floors, music practice rooms, and courtyards.

Ole Miss is a safe place. The university's 2009 campus crime statistics report twenty-seven burglaries, by far the most in recent years, and three stolen cars.

For a Mississippi resident, the school is a real bargain, with 2010–11 tuition at a mere $5,436. Mississippi has, so far, resisted the extreme tuition increases common to other universities. Even Yankees get off lightly: out-of-state students pay $13,890, which is a more substantial increase over earlier years. Room and board cost about $8,000. Admissions are need blind, but the school cannot afford to guarantee full financial aid to all. However, in 2010, the school announced that a new scholarship program would guarantee financial aid for Mississippi residents with family incomes of less than $30,000, providing support for tuition and room and board. Some 38 percent of students receive need-based financial aid. The average debt of recent graduates is a surprisingly high $22,866.

GREEN LIGHT

Like many other state schools, Ole Miss has decided to impose a speech code on its students. Vague enough to be broadly threatening, the school prohibits "hateful" communication on the Internet (presumably to protect its students from cyberbullying or keep them from organizing a neo-Nazi club, but potentially applicable to a student writing on his Facebook page, "I hate Mississippi State! Hope we crush them on Saturday!"). Racially and ethnically motivated correspondence is also banned, which could, ostensibly, prevent the Malaysian club from inviting students to a meeting. While the speech codes are intended to protect students from abuse, an administrator or professor could easily harass or punish a student or group for innocent behavior or speech that is protected by United States law.

Students probably don't have much to worry about, though. While "there certainly are places where leftist and statist ideologies find their ways into the curriculum, particularly in the English, history, and sociology departments," according to one professor, students do not complain to us of professors' political views unduly affecting course content.

Describing her peers, one student uses three words: "Conservative, conservative, conservative." Another student says, "Ole Miss is an extremely conservative southern school, and most of the students value that." While the student body tends toward the right, the student newspaper, the *Daily Mississippian*, has been traditionally dominated by liberal students, according to a professor: "Lip service is paid to 'diversity,' and the homosexual agenda is in full flower on the paper's editorial page."

Morehouse College

Atlanta, Georgia • www.morehouse.edu

Disciplined minds

Founded in 1867 to train freed slaves, Morehouse remains the only historically black, all-male college in the country, and it has always had a sense of high purpose. Morehouse has helped to educate some of the most distinguished black men in America, including NAACP chairman Julian Bond, Olympic gold medalist Edwin Moses, and former Atlanta mayor Maynard Jackson. It is one of the top feeder schools for the nation's most prestigious law, medical, and graduate school programs. Says current Morehouse president Robert Michael Franklin (also an alumnus): "The mission of Morehouse College is to develop men with disciplined minds who will lead lives of leadership and service."

Students at Morehouse frequently don coat and tie (obligatory for new students during Freshman Week) and obey both an Appropriate Attire and a class attendance requirement. Southern politeness reigns; a professor from another university says, "I don't think I've seen so pronounced a sense of respect and decorum in any school."

"The House," as the college is reverentially called, is as profoundly steeped in tradition as any American academic institution. A professor mentions the inspiring graduation ceremony, where "500 young black men . . . are led through the campus by African drummers, walking past the grave of Benjamin Mays in front of Graves Hall, the original building on campus." During Freshman Week, upperclassmen impart the legends of such alumni luminaries as Martin Luther King Jr. and subject freshmen to impromptu quizzes on the school's history and lore.

In keeping with its Baptist roots, Morehouse continues to use religious, sometimes even explicitly Christian language in its literature, though it is no longer a religiously affiliated college. The college's Student Conduct Office seeks to "assist students in developing a high degree of integrity and moral character by encouraging acceptance of personal responsibility for behavior." A professor says, "It is not uncommon for students or professors to refer to their faith. . . . I've encouraged students struggling with career decisions to pray about it, if they are believers." One Morehouse junior repeatedly spoke of his fellow students as "Morehouse brothers," as men whom he could go to for help and with whom he felt a real sense of community.

South

Academic Life: A culture of excellence

Morehouse's core curriculum is not what it once was; it has dropped the requirement that all students complete courses such as "Shakespeare," "History of the United States," and "Ancient and Medieval Philosophy." Still, Morehouse's requirements remain better than those at many other colleges. Students have little choice of classes in the core and must sample almost every department. Morehouse still requires intermediate proficiency in at least one foreign language, as well as classes in music, art, religion, and philosophy.

"There is no leeway allowed in completing the courses," a professor says. "Students are encouraged to finish the core before the junior year, so they are eligible for Phi Beta Kappa." Morehouse puts a premium on maintaining a certain sequence of courses; each major has a strongly suggested four-year plan worked out in advance and made available through the course catalog.

Morehouse has three academic divisions, Business Administration and Economics, Humanities and Social Sciences, and Science and Mathematics, and twenty-five majors. Most departments show solid offerings, rather than the trendy courses seen elsewhere. Freshmen are assigned advisors with whom they meet to determine their first- and second-semester schedules. Advisement is mandatory. A sizable and attentive tutoring network is also available to help students stay on track. "If there is one thing to be said about Morehouse," says a former student, "it's that I never felt like I was simply on my own…. I felt like they wanted me to succeed." Since Morehouse does not have graduate students, there are no teaching assistants on campus.

Morehouse's small community allows students to have close relationships with faculty, who often give out their home phone numbers. One student says, "They know you by name and notice if you miss class. Some will even call you and get you out of bed if you aren't there." Another adds, "I almost always felt like they cared." One faculty member says, "The school talks about teaching all the time, but when it comes to tenure they primarily consider research. I'd say 70 percent emphasis on research and 30 percent on teaching. . . . However, most Morehouse professors love to teach and [we] give that emphasis over research." The student-faculty ratio is a middling 15 to 1.

Much of Morehouse's academic reputation rests on a few select departments, especially political science, business administration, and biology. The 5 percent of students who

VITAL STATISTICS

Religious affiliation: *none*
Total enrollment: *2,689*
Total undergraduates: *2,689*
SAT/ACT midranges: CR: *460–570*, M: *470–580*; ACT: *19–25*
Applicants: *2,352*
Applicants accepted: *67%*
Accepted applicants who enrolled: *41%*
Tuition and fees: *$20,394*
Room and board: *$11,494*
Freshman retention rate: *81%*
Graduation rate: *39% (4 yrs.)*, *60% (6 yrs.)*
Courses with fewer than 20 students: *45%*
Student-faculty ratio: *15:1*
Courses taught by graduate students: *none*
Most popular majors: *business, political science, psychology*
Students living on campus: *60%*
Guaranteed housing for four years? *no*
Students in fraternities: *not provided*

1. English 250, World Literature
2. Philosophy 310, Ancient and Medieval Philosophy
3. Religion 210/211, Introduction to the Old Testament/ New Testament
4. Religion 400, Introduction to Theology (closest match)
5. Political Science 462, Modern Political Theory
6. English 377, Shakespeare
7. History 215, History of the United States to 1876
8. Philosophy 312, Nineteenth-Century Philosophy

are biology majors are often on a premed track, but there seems to be a shifting emphasis toward the PhD instead of the MD. Many of the top Morehouse premed students go on to enroll in the college's own medical school, and others gain admission to the nation's most prestigious schools. The college reports that 23 percent of its alumni go on to graduate school soon after commencement; of those, 21 percent choose law, 14 percent medicine, and 12 percent theology.

Some say the school's general science and mathematics requirements for all students are not demanding and give nonmajors an easy way out, and one professor bemoans the "dilution of science in the interest of expediency." But another faculty member maintains that the system provides "useful and applicable general scientific principles without overwhelming the student with minutiae." Professor Kiandra Johnson, in mathematics, comes highly recommended by students.

Business is far and away the most popular major, with 36 percent of students choosing it, and graduates of this program are heavily recruited by top financial, accounting and consulting firms. "Even in 2008," one former student recalls, "many juniors and seniors were offered major internships in Wall Street firms." A former student in the department describes the coursework as "extremely rigorous but certainly worthwhile." Noteworthy professors include Keith Hollingsworth, Carolyn Davis, Emmanuel Onifade, and Belinda White.

"Morehouse College is known for its very heated political debates," says a recent grad. "However, when politics is brought up in the classroom, it's to add to the topic at hand. The school as a whole isn't exactly easy for conservative-minded students, which is something the school needs to address. The number of these students is much bigger than one may assume; however, they're what you call 'closet conservatives,' afraid to share their views for fear of being attacked or outcast. If you're a liberal thinker, you'll fit right in."

Morehouse no longer has a religious affiliation, but the religion department continues to offer solid courses. Majors are required to take Old and New Testament and an introduction to Christian theology. Lawrence E. Carter and Aaron L. Parker are recommended professors.

The history department comes highly recommended. Majors take fourteen specific courses and six electives. The core includes two-semester courses in "Topics in World History," "History of the United States," "History of African Americans," and "History of Africa," as well as single-semester courses in "Ancient History," "History of Modern Europe," "Latin American/Caribbean Studies," "Revolution and Modernization," "Great Men and Women of America," and "Public Speaking," an English course. Students recommend professors Alton Hornsby Jr. and Daniel Klenbort.

English majors follow a sensible curriculum that requires a class in Shakespeare and one on Chaucer or Milton. "American Literature" I and II and "English Literature" I and

II also are required. The preponderance of electives is in African American and Caribbean literature, in keeping with Morehouse's mission. Francine Allen and Melvin Rahming are mentioned as excellent teachers and mentors.

Political science is applauded both for its theoretical and practical approach to teaching politics, and for its graduates, many of whom go on to excellent law schools. One recent alumnus says, "It also teaches applied politics, that is, how to use research, media and communications to foster effective policy." Requirements for the major are traditional and solid, including courses in political theory and the American system of government.

One source mentions both foreign language and philosophy as weak departments. "I do not think the college offers enough foreign languages to choose from, and those that are offered are weak." Some philosophy professors "force their views onto students. Instead of fostering new approaches and ways of thinking, the students are taught only a few distinct mindsets."

Morehouse has an honors program, admission to which is competitive. Students must maintain at least a 3.0 GPA for the first two years. Benefits include smaller classes, a variety of scholarly, social, and cultural activities, special class sections in many core classes, and an honors program club. Juniors and seniors complete special course-related assignments, make presentations, and participate in seminars and departmental research.

One unique Morehouse offering is Project SPACE (Strategic Preparedness Advancing Careers in Engineering/Sciences), a joint effort between NASA and Morehouse designed to motivate students to pursue careers in the sciences, especially engineering. The program has provided scholarships to more than 300 Morehouse students since 1989.

Another Morehouse institution is the monthly convocation Crown Forum, offering lectures on ethics, culture, leadership, and current events. "A lot of schools tout their traditions but don't do much else to reinforce them," a student says. "Crown Forum means you don't forget." Students must attend at least six such events annually for three years.

With the all-female Spelman College, Clark-Atlanta University, Morris Brown College, the Interdenominational Theological Center, and the Morehouse School of Medicine, Morehouse is a member of the Atlanta University Center. Students at each school can take courses at any of the others. This also brings women on campus—especially from sister school Spelman. Morehouse men have access to 250 international study programs through the college, although only 8 percent of students study abroad. Languages taught on campus are French, Spanish, German, Swahili, Japanese, and Russian.

Student Life: House of funk

Morehouse boasts a vibrant life outside the classroom, with a wide array of student organizations, mixers with neighboring schools (especially Spelman), athletic activities, two student-run publications (the *Torch*, Morehouse's yearbook, and the *Maroon Tiger*, the student newspaper), and five historically black fraternities. This is in addition to the world of opportunity available in the city of Atlanta itself, with its more than 200,000 college students, and world-class dining, sports, and cultural facilities. As one student says, "There's a party every night in Atlanta."

South

But not necessarily on the Morehouse campus. Though there is plenty of the socializing, the student culture encourages getting one's work done first. Students seem to realize, as one puts it, that "if you party a lot, you might not make it out of Morehouse." A graduate says, "Morehouse College has the typical collegiate scene, however, to my knowledge only a small population of the student body uses drugs. There isn't a big party scene on campus but there is one off campus."

Apart from sharing some classes with female students, Morehouse men have plenty of organized opportunities to mix with women from neighboring schools. Morehouse men are even assigned a "Spelman sister," a relationship that they usually maintain throughout their Morehouse careers.

Fraternities play what students call a "huge" role in campus life. Greek houses are tightly knit, and members can come across to nonmembers as arrogant and exclusive, students report. Members of elite fraternities are treated with deference (and probably some quiet resentment) on campus. Hazing, once a major problem at Morehouse, is carefully monitored by the administration.

Morehouse fields teams in football, basketball, track and field, tennis, cross-country, golf, and baseball at the varsity level and competes as an NCAA Division II school and in the Southern Intercollegiate Athletic Conference. The college also has intramural competi-

ACADEMIC REQUIREMENTS

Every Morehouse man must complete what the school terms its core curriculum, which is much more comprehensive than what's required at most colleges. Every student takes:

- English composition.
- "World Literature," which includes study of the Bible as literature.
- "World History: Topical Approaches," with one-third emphasis on the United States including the African American experience, one-third on Europe, and one-third on Africa.
- Two math classes of the following four: college algebra, finite mathematics, precalculus, and calculus.
- Two foreign language courses at the intermediate (200) level. French, Spanish, German, Japanese, Swahili, and Chinese are offered.
- "Introduction to Religion."
- Either "Introduction to Philosophy" or "Introduction to Philosophical Ethics."
- One music course from a choice of six, including: "Introduction to Church Music," "Masterpieces of Music," and "History of Jazz."
- Either "Survey of Visual Arts" or "Introduction to African American Art."
- "Biological Science."
- "Physical Science."
- Two courses from a list of courses in the social sciences, including "Comparative Politics," "Social Problems," and "Psychology of the African American Experience"
- Two courses in health and physical education.

tions in most of these, as well as soccer and swimming.

The Morehouse College House of Funk Marching Band is known for its halftime performances, which combine dance and marching with music from various genres, including rap, traditional marching band, and pop music. Spelman provides the Mahogany in Motion dancers and a Maroon Mystique color guard. The marching band has performed at Super Bowl XVIII and Atlanta Falcons games, and on the *Today Show*. The band was also featured in the film *Drumline*. Morehouse has an impressive all-male glee club, a jazz ensemble, and, with Spelman, a concert band that gives symphonic concerts in Atlanta.

Most Morehouse men are grounded in their religious faith, and the college has a variety of religious groups. There are two Christian organizations on campus: the King International Chapel Ministry and the MLK Chapel Assistants. The Atlanta University Center consortium offers a (Catholic) Newman Club, a Baha'i club, and a Muslim student organization. Morehouse is no longer a Christian school, however. Says a professor, "A large number of students do not attend church but consider themselves men of faith or spiritual."

Members of Morehouse's College Republicans are very much in the minority on campus, but they seem quite active and upbeat, sponsoring lecture series, team-building courses, and parties for watching events like the State of the Union Address. Other groups on campus include the Young Democrats, an NAACP chapter, and Students for Enlightened Environmental Decisions.

Some 60 percent of Morehouse students live on campus. The college does not guarantee housing for all four years, but the housing director says there is sufficient space for students who request it. Freshmen are required to live on campus unless they receive special

GREEN LIGHT

On the whole, there isn't much political controversy on campus. "Morehouse has some pretty radical students and professors and some pretty conservative ones," says one student, "but I think that because we're all black and all guys, there's just less focus on politics. . . . There's not much opportunity to play 'us' versus 'them.' We're all pretty much on the same page." But another student, for the very same reason, expresses concern that Morehouse "reinforces the patriarchal hegemony so often associated with and manifested by black men." Out of this concern have sprung organizations and demonstrations aimed at promoting "sensitivity."

There was some controversy on campus after the institution by President Franklin in October 2009 of the school's Appropriate Attire Policy, which prohibits caps, do-rags, and hoods indoors; sunglasses at class or formal programs; decorative orthodontic appliances; jeans at major programs requiring formal or business casual attire; bare feet; sagging pants; going shirtless; pajamas worn in public or in the college's common areas; clothing with lewd or offensive messages; and, what was surprisingly controversial, "women's garb." This led to media attacks by defenders of cross-dressing, and accusations of homophobia—all of which distracted from the policy's real purpose. According to a professor, the policy is designed "to combat the 'thug' culture prevalent among young black men." One student says he had "no problem with the dress code. On campus we have to dress like gentlemen who are trying to reach certain goals. Maybe other schools will follow our lead."

permission. They live separately from upperclassmen. Students can choose from themed residence halls, including environmental awareness, religion and philosophy ("Soul House"), leadership, and "diversity and cultural change." Dorm residents must agree to a substance-free policy, which bans smoking, alcohol, and drugs on campus. The housing office says the school has a "zero-tolerance" policy toward violations. Student's describe suites as pleasant and clean but subject to crime.

"Dorm life is decent, the RAs are great and very supportive of your overall development," says one former student. He continues, however, "I personally preferred to stay off campus because the crime in the area is far too bad." A current student says that there is "more security and less crime" now. While the most recent (2009) crime data for the campus itself are not so alarming—there were six robberies, one aggravated assault, one forcible sex offense, and twenty-one burglaries—a sampling of recent crimes just off campus may give a prospective student pause. In April 2010, for example, three Morehouse students were victims of a carjacking. Campus police do patrol the grounds and will escort students at any time to or from the library, the Atlanta University Center Complex, MARTA public transportation stops, or various other locations in the vicinity. The area surrounding Morehouse is fairly barren of nightspots or decent places to eat within walking distance, students report.

The expense of attending Morehouse has been a growing concern; as one student comments, "I'm going to graduate on time. Morehouse is expensive." A number of students we interviewed spoke of having dropped out at various times in order to raise money to attend the school, even though Morehouse has generous funding available. Tuition for 2010-11 was $20,394, room and board $11,494. Financial aid is limited and goes to those who demonstrate financial need. Nevertheless, the difficulties students have in attending seem only to increase the loyalty that Morehouse men feel toward their college. That's impressive, since the average recent graduate owes a daunting $32,125 in student loans.

University of North Carolina

Chapel Hill, North Carolina • www.unc.edu

First in its league

Founded in 1795, the University of North Carolina at Chapel Hill was the first state university founded in the fledgling United States. Its distinctive virtues include the facilities of a large and prestigious research university (in 2010, research grants and contracts at UNC totaled $803 million, mostly in the sciences), the charm of Chapel Hill's college-town atmosphere, a multitude of student organizations, a strong faculty, and many hundreds of courses. Indeed, a student at the University of North Carolina can certainly graduate with a sturdy foundation in the liberal arts—or waste much of his time. The key is selecting courses wisely.

Academic Life: Queer medieval photography

Although it insists on nothing like a core curriculum, UNC's distribution requirements do a better job than most. Unfortunately, the wide latitude of choice students are given in choosing courses—from "The Medieval Church" to "Queer Latina/o Literature and Photography"—that fulfill requirements means that someone could easily blunder through four years and miss the liberal arts completely. One student sums up the watered-down quality of the general education curriculum by observing, "U.S. history is not required, and cultural diversity is."

UNC has a highly regarded honors program, which offers separate, smaller sections of existing courses and select interdisciplinary seminars. Each year, some 200 applicants are selected for this program, which carries with it enhanced financial aid. Others can apply to transfer in. Students praise the program for its rigor in liberal arts; however, honors relies for most of its classes on existing undergraduate selections, some of which are trivial or politicized, so it's hardly an intellectual utopia. But students can grapple with the writings of Machiavelli, Descartes, and the American founders in the honors seminar "The Elements of Politics" or study "Verdi's Operas and Italian Romanticism" and "The Romans," which features readings from Petronius and Virgil. One student says that honors classes "don't seem to be any more rigorous than regular classes, just smaller and more intimate."

Some students report strong relationships with faculty members, who generally maintain open-door policies—while others can't name one who has had an impact on them. As

South

579

VITAL STATISTICS

Religious affiliation: *none*
Total enrollment: *28,916*
Total undergraduates: *17,891*
SAT/ACT midranges: CR:
  590–690, M: *620–710*;
  ACT: *26–31*
Applicants: *23,047*
Applicants accepted: *32%*
Accepted applicants who
  enrolled: *54%*
Tuition and fees: *in state,
  $4,816; out of state,
  $23,432*
Room and board: *$9,306*
Freshman retention rate:
  97%
Graduation rate: *76% (4 yrs.),
  87% (6 yrs.)*
Courses with fewer than 20
  students: *44%*
Student-faculty ratio: *14:1*
Courses taught by graduate
  students: *not provided*
Most popular majors: *biology, psychology, mass
  communication*
Students living on campus:
  46%
Guaranteed housing for
  four years? *no*
Students in fraternities: *7%*
  in sororities: *11%*

one student explained, "You must take the initiative to seek help from them." Upon enrollment, every student is paired with an academic advisor. He must meet with his advisor at the beginning of his freshman year and when he declares his major, but these meetings can be in a group. One undergrad says, "Academic advising here is exceptional." Others disagree. Advisors, say another student, "will give you fifteen minutes before registration, but that's it. And sometimes they can confuse you. . . . Advisors know nothing about course requirements."

Recommended departments at Chapel Hill include business, health care, and "any of the sciences," according to a student. The Kenan-Flagler School of Business has an excellent nationwide reputation. The Center for Entrepreneurial Studies has been named among the best in the country and provides students with internships and other opportunities.

The English department is mentioned by some for its attention to teaching and its relatively traditional curriculum. One grad student suggests sticking to the earlier periods taught in the department (medieval and Renaissance) to avoid politically charged courses. On the other hand, a professor strongly recommends the American literature courses. Southern specialist Fred Hobson is a first-rate scholar and a fair-minded, conscientious teacher, a former student reports. Requirements for the major look excellent: students must take introductory classes in Shakespeare, British literature from Chaucer to Pope, either British literature from Wordsworth to Eliot or a seminar in literary studies, one pre-1660 course, two 1660–1900 courses, and one post-1900 course.

The history major, however, has barely any breadth requirements: students must pick a concentration in ancient/medieval, gender and women, modern European, global, Third World/Non-Western, or United States, and also take one course in Third World/Nonwestern history. Beyond that, all bets are off.

Political science majors must take introductory courses in American government and international relations, a lower-level course in comparative politics, and a course in political theory; the rest are electives.

Insiders describe the classics department as "rigorous," and among the best in the country. The School of Journalism and Mass Communication is also highly lauded. In 2008, ABC News selected UNC as one of five schools in the nation to house a digital bureau staffed by students. The art history department's strength is in teaching, which is made easier by the university's impressive art collection. Disciplines that students are warmly advised to avoid include the African American, sexuality, and women's studies programs.

One professor observed that while discerning and motivated students can cobble together a good liberal arts education from the seventy-seven departments at UNC, they will have more difficulty finding a strong intellectual community. As a remedy, he recommended the interdisciplinary studies programs—which tend to be smaller than other departments and to provide students with a more cohesive liberal arts program. Particularly recommended are the American and the international studies programs.

Students and professors name the following as among the best teachers at the university: Jean S. DeSaix, William M. Kier, and Patricia J. Pukkila in biology; James W. Jorgenson in chemistry; Barbara Day in education; Michael Salemi in economics; Robert Cantwell in American studies; Michael McFee, Christopher M. Armitage, Reid Barbour, Darryl Gless, Larry Goldberg, Philip Gura, Trudier Harris (emeritus), Joy S. Kasson, Ted Leinbaugh, George Lensing Jr., James Seay, and Jessica Wolfe in English; William L. Barney, Peter A. Coclanis, W. Miles Fletcher, Jacquelyn D. Hall, John F. Kasson, Roger W. Lotchin, and Jay M. Smith in history; Michael Hoefges in journalism; Sue E. Goodman in mathematics; James Ketch in music; Laurie E. McNeil and Lawrence G. Rowan in physics and astronomy; Michael Lienesch, Kevin McGuire, Mark Crescenzi, Georg Vanberg, Terry Sullivan, and Thomas Oatley in political science; Bart Ehrman and Ruel W. Tyson Jr. in religious studies; Michael Shanahan in sociology; and Daniel Gitterman in public policy.

Almost half of all classes have twenty or fewer students, and 70 percent have fewer than thirty—despite a lukewarm student-faculty ratio of 14 to 1. Large classes are broken up into recitation sessions led by graduate teaching assistants. "Most of the introductory-level classes are taught by TAs, but once you move into the more major-specific courses, you usually get professors," says a student.

The extent to which politics affects classroom policies and discussion varies. One student comments, "In the classroom, professors are rarely overtly political in my experience, but they are successful in creating an environment conducive to liberal and progressive thought. Right-leaning students can be too intimidated to speak up in class. Including me, every once in a while." A professor says, "My impression is that it is easy for conservative students to feel comfortable here among their peers, though they may feel uncomfortable with some of the faculty's prejudices in certain courses." The student body is indeed more

SUGGESTED CORE

1. Classics 055, First-Year Seminar: Three Greek and Roman Epics or English and Comparative Literature 285, Classical Backgrounds in English Literature
2. Philosophy 210, Ancient Greek Philosophy
3. Religious Studies 103/104, Introduction to the Hebrew Bible/Old Testament Literature; Introduction to New Testament
4. Philosophy 215, Medieval Philosophy
5. Political Science 271, Modern Political Thought
6. English and Comparative Literature 225, Shakespeare
7. History 127, American History to 1865
8. History 466, Modern European Intellectual History

politically diverse than the faculty. UNC's board of governors has mandated that 82 percent of the students in each class be North Carolina residents. This means that many of the students coming from North Carolina's small, rural towns and counties bring traditional and conservative values with them.

UNC has study-abroad programs in locations ranging from Iceland to Togo, and offers courses in Arabic, Bulgarian, Cherokee, Chinese, Chichewa, Croatian, Czech, Dutch, French, German, Ancient Greek, Hebrew, Hindi-Urdu, Hungarian, Italian, Japanese, Korean, Latin, Lingala, Macedonian, Persian, Polish, Portuguese, Russian, Serbian, Spanish, Swahili, Tamil, Turkish, and Wolof.

Student Life: Preachers in the Pit

The city of Chapel Hill (population 51,519) is often hailed as a great college town with a vibrant culture, cheap eats, and hopping nightlife. Both Chapel Hill and the neighboring town of Carrboro are known for their lively music scene, drawing national acts and sponsoring local talent. The town of Chapel Hill boasts several notable musicians who made their start there, such as James Taylor and Ben Folds. The famous Franklin Street is at the heart of student social life in Chapel Hill. After a Tar Heel men's basketball victory, revelers are likely to flood Franklin Street and kindle victory bonfires. The biggest event in Chapel Hill is Halloween. Every year, tens of thousands of partiers flock to Franklin Street in costume for a promenade of the spirits (most of them distilled).

Durham and Raleigh—home to Duke and North Carolina State, respectively—are close, both under an hour's drive. The Blue Ridge Mountains are three hours to the west, while the beach is three hours east. Students, however, need not even leave campus to find something to do. There is plenty to see right on campus. The Coker Arboretum is a peaceful five-acre retreat at the heart of the campus. The Morehead Planetarium is also well worth a visit. It holds the distinction of being the training ground for almost every U.S. astronaut from 1959 to 1975, and today it offers classes, films, changing exhibits, and sky-watching sessions.

Students hang out at the Pit, a sunken cement and brick area in the center of campus, where one sees and hears all sorts of people, from pot-smoking hippies to boisterous preachers warning the stoners about the Antichrist. The area is flanked by a dining hall, the campus bookstore, a library, and the student union. Spray-painted signs advertise upcoming events and publicize student groups.

The university boasts about 650 clubs, teams, and student organizations, of almost every kind imaginable, including the American Constitution Society, the Arab student union, Cadence all-female *a capella,* economics and meditation clubs, underwater hockey, a gardening co-op, Comedy to Overcome Medical Anxiety, Christian Apologetics, a scuba club, a rifle and pistol club, the Kamikazi Dance Team, the Carolina Boxing Club, and two debating groups—the Dialectic and the Philanthropic societies.

The Young Democrats is one of the university's most active student groups, with over 700 members. The recently formed UNC chapter of Youth for Western Civilization is quite active, despite trouble finding an advisor and a president and accusations of racism from opponents. The College Republicans are quite active, and the Students for Life website boasts that it is "one of the most well respected and active student pro-life groups in the country." The College Libertarians report growing interest in libertarianism on campus.

ACADEMIC REQUIREMENTS

In lieu of a core, UNC imposes loose general education requirements. All students must complete:

- A two-course sequence in English composition and rhetoric.
- Classwork to attain a foreign language proficiency through the intermediate level.
- One course in quantitative reasoning. Options range from "Introduction to Statistics" to "Intuitive Calculus."
- A single credit-hour class in lifetime fitness; choices range from "Aerobics" to "Walking."
- Two courses in the physical and biological sciences, including at least one lab. Choices range from "Cognitive Neuroscience" to "Human Evolution and Adaptation."
- Three classes from at least two different departments in the social and behavioral sciences—one of which must be a history course. Options range from "Constitutional Democracy" to "Archaeology of Sex and Gender."
- One course in philosophy or moral reasoning. Classes include both "Classical Political Thought" and "Advanced Feminist Political Theory."
- One class in literature. Choices range from "Melville: Culture and Criticism" to "Introduction to Gay and Lesbian Culture and Literature."
- One course in visual or performing arts. Options range from "Art of Classical Greece" to "Queer Latina/o Literature, Performance, and Visual Art" and "Stage Makeup."
- One math-heavy class. Choices range from "Introduction to Probability" to "Research in Exercise and Sport Science."
- One writing-intensive course. Options extend from "Advanced Poetry Writing" to "Theater for Social Change: Latina/o Performance Traditions."
- One class highlighting experiential education; internships and study abroad count, as well as classes like "Field School in North American Archaeology" and "Environmental Justice."
- One course in U.S. diversity. Choices range from "Introduction to the Cultures and Histories of Native North America" to "Introduction to Gay/Lesbian Literature."
- One class dealing with the North-Atlantic world. (This is PC-speak for U.S. history, though Quebecois chronicles would also suffice.) Choices range (too) widely from "History of Western Civilization" to "Native Americans in Film."
- One course dealing with culture, society, or history outside the North-Atlantic. Nearly everything counts, from "Dostoevsky" to "Comparative Queer Politics."
- One class on the world before 1750. Choices range from "Archaeology of Egypt" to "Sex and Gender in Antiquity."
- One course dealing with global issues and the "transnational" and "transregional" forces that have shaped the world. Options range from "Introduction to European Government" to "The International Politics of Sexual and Reproductive Health."

South

The *Carolina Review*, a conservative journal, is published monthly and also has daily blog entries.

"There is always something going on," a student says. Another student reports, "There are almost always frat parties . . . and the bar scene is very popular." About 9 percent of students join one of the forty fraternities or twenty-three sororities. "Greek life is very popular but surprisingly academic. Most fraternities and sororities are highly involved in community service and professional organizations," a student says. A faculty member points out: "Greek students at UNC have a consistently higher GPA on average than non-Greek students." Another student says, however, that the Greek culture is a "fairly isolated sector that the rest of campus pays little attention to."

There are student organizations for Baha'is, Buddhists, Friends, Hindus, Jews, Latter-Day Saints, Muslims, and Zoroastrians, as well as numerous Christian denominations; but houses of worship on campus seem to be a mixed bag. One student found more to praise in the student-run religious clubs than the chapels themselves: "I attended the Newman Catholic Center every Sunday last year as a freshman; there were a lot of student-run programs there. I was happy to see that." But he adds that, in general, "The churches here are more about spirituality and the liberal ideas on social justice and tolerance than religion, God, and duty." Both professors and students note a strong evangelical Christian presence on the campus, with vibrant chapters of InterVarsity Christian Fellowship organizing student missions on and off campus. Students of other faiths should probably seek out more traditional houses of worship in town.

Collegiate sports—led by basketball, of course—are very important to life at UNC (at least when the teams are doing well). The college participates in the Atlantic Coast Conference and the NCAA I division. The men's basketball team won the national championship in 2009. Rameses the Ram is the Tarheels' live mascot, cheering on thirteen men's and fifteen women's varsity teams. At more than $37 million for ten years, North Carolina's contract with Nike is the largest of its kind. Students are heavily involved in sports, either by supporting the school's teams or by participating in club or intramural sports. Every October students cram into the 21,750-seat basketball arena for a little "midnight madness" to watch their beloved team scrimmage at the stroke of midnight when the practice season officially begins. There are forty intramural sports and fifty club teams, ranging from Aikido to squash.

In 2010, an NCAA investigation brought charges of corruption against the UNC football program. The coach resigned and twelve players were suspended on charges of accepting illegal gifts from sports agents and having their schoolwork done for them by tutors.

The college recently completed a $205 million Physical Science Complex with large laboratory facilities, and in 2010 opened the new Venable Hall, home to the chemistry and marine sciences departments. Campus also boasts an art museum and the Rams Head Center, which includes a food court, recreation center, and grocery store. The university is currently building a new water plant and Genome Science Library, Biomedical Research Imaging Building, dental sciences building, and additions to the gym and stadium.

Students speak highly of the more recent dorms, apartment communities, and family housing at UNC, but one student says, "the dorms are pretty bad," and while recent renova-

South

tions have made improvements, "a lot of these dorms still have asbestos and other carcinogens in the wall supposedly behind several layers of paint." In 2009, the New North Hall replaced one of the old dorms and houses students and faculty, who praise it highly. There is no distinction between upperclass and freshman housing, and so all undergrads apply for the same slots. UNC does not guarantee housing, but most students who want housing can get it, whether or not they're happy with what they're offered.

Only 46 percent of students live on campus, but those who live off campus tend to reside nearby in fraternity or sorority houses or in apartments. Starting in fall 2010, freshmen are required to live on campus. There is a variety of theme housing options, including Chinese and Spanish language houses, Unitas (a program that attempts to minimize stereotypes and prejudices by mixing up roommates of different ethnicities, religions . . . and sexual orientations), and the Academic Enhancement Program. There are also substance-free areas available in various dorms.

North Carolina is southern enough that it still offers both all-men and all-women dormitories, although coed halls are the norm; only six of the thirty-six halls are single sex. Visitation policies vary from hall to hall; some allow visitors (with roommate consent) until 1:00 AM, while others permit visitors throughout the night. Says a student, "Visitation policies probably exist, but I am unsure of what they are. Needless to say, they are rarely enforced." On paper, a guest's stay is limited to no more than seventy-two consecutive hours. Guests of the opposite sex may not use the suite/floor bathroom, but rather a public restroom available in the building. "Luckily, there are no coed bathrooms here," says one grateful student. A guest may stay or sleep only in his or her host's room—not on the couch of a common suite, for instance. Starting in 2010, responding to student demand, the college selected three dorms to allow 24-hour visitation by the opposite sex.

Incoming freshmen are required to attend CTOPs (Carolina Testing and Orientation Programs). Every incoming freshman is asked to read a book assigned by the university and participate in a two-hour seminar. The program has in the past been controversial, and some students have seen the program as more of an opportunity for the university to push

GREEN LIGHT

Both students and faculty report an indefinable "mood" of political correctness on the UNC campus, but it appears not to be repressive. Pro-life students catch some heat for their activism and are undersupported by student government compared with events like UNC's semiannual drag show. Still, the last survey of student opinion on the subject (in 2009) turned up 94 percent of respondents agreeing that teachers "maintain an atmosphere that promotes intellectual freedom and welcomes diverse perspectives." Despite protests, conservative groups on campus have been quite active in recent years, bringing notable speakers such as Phyllis Schlafly, Tom Tancredo, David Horowitz, Dinesh D'Souza, and Jonah Goldberg to campus in 2009 and 2010. Tancredo's speech was cut short after five minutes by protesters breaking a window in the room where the lecture was being given but the administration showed its commitment to fighting this intolerance by giving Youth for Western Civilization, the group that sponsored Tancredo's visit, $3,000 to fund another speaker.

South

liberal views than a chance to "enhance participation in the intellectual life of the campus." UNC requires all incoming freshmen to own laptops in order to facilitate a multimedia learning experience.

One UNC tradition is the honor code, a policy that is taken very seriously by students. All students pledge to adhere to the code, which prohibits lying, cheating, and stealing. "Cheating is the most common offense but is by no means taken lightly," says one student. The code, however, doesn't mention public nudity: one frivolous UNC tradition consists of streaking through the library at midnight on the first day of exams.

UNC in 2009 reported six forcible sex offenses, two robberies, ten burglaries, five aggravated assaults, and four stolen cars on campus. The university offers an escort service and a shuttle at night. Still, for most students, safety isn't a big concern: "I've always felt safe in each of the three different apartment buildings in which I have lived," one student reports. But high-profile crimes make an impression—such as the March 2008 murder of Eve Carson, UNC's student body president, a mile off campus. So the university launched Alert Carolina, a safety campaign to alert students to campus emergencies. A siren system has been set up on the campus to warn students of dangerous persons, chemical spills, or tornadoes. Students can register their cell phones to receive text message alerts from campus police, and emergency call boxes and lighted walking corridors are available across campus.

Chapel Hill is still a bargain for locals, who in 2010–11 paid in-state tuition of $4,816; the out-of-state rate is $23,432. Room and board were $9,306. These numbers represent a steady increase, which is expected to continue in future years. Admission to UNC–Chapel Hill is need blind, and the college pledges to meet 100 percent of financial need; 64 percent of students receive need-based aid. Low-income Carolina residents can graduate from UNC debt free if they work on campus ten to twelve hours weekly. The average debt burden of a recent grad was a moderate $14,262.

Patrick Henry College

Purcellville, Virginia • www.phc.edu

Clarity begins at home

Patrick Henry College is part of a David and Goliath story that started more than thirty years ago, with the rise of the homeschooling movement. Despite its long history—George Washington, like most of the founding fathers, was educated by his family—homeschooling had become quite rare by the 1970s. In many states and localities, homeschooling was actually illegal. The impromptu legal-defense groups that homeschoolers started to defend their parental rights grew into a powerful movement, which in 2000 gave birth to Patrick Henry College. Founded and still led by Michael Farris (of the Home School Legal Defense Association), PHC is a four-year undergraduate school offering a complete liberal arts education and preparation for careers in government, politics, media, and education for homeschooled young adults, as well as graduates of private and public schools. The college is dedicated to the difficult and delicate task of harmonizing three things that many today think are in tension with each other: a liberal arts education, worldly success, and an evangelical Christian lifestyle.

Academic Life: A home for schooling

The school now hosts 405 students, a healthy student body for a school that has existed for only ten years, and PHC grads have already made their mark in the world. PHC students are in high demand in congressional offices, government agencies, public policy foundations, and news media outlets as interns. Under the Bush administration, PHC students were a conspicuous presence in the White House (at one point, seven out of a hundred White House interns were PHC students).

That mission is anchored solidly in the school's academic program, which requires of students a strong liberal arts core curriculum and then complements the academic majors they choose with practical apprenticeship programs. The core curriculum introduces students to the principles of the Western intellectual tradition, while the majors give both theoretical and practical grounding in particular fields in politics, journalism, or the humanities. The apprenticeship program is especially valuable in helping students begin a professional career while still in college.

Once students complete the significant core curriculum, Patrick Henry College offers majors through two departments. The department of government confers bachelor's degrees

VITAL STATISTICS

Religious affiliation: *Christian (nondenominational)*
Total enrollment: *405*
Total undergraduates: *405*
SAT/ACT midranges: CR: *620–730*, M: *550–650*; ACT: *26–31*
Applicants: *243*
Applicants accepted: *72%*
Accepted applicants who enrolled: *57%*
Tuition and fees: *$22,758*
Room and board: *$8,010*
Freshman retention rate: *85%*
Graduation rate: *not provided*
Courses with fewer than 20 students: *not provided*
Student-faculty ratio: *10:1*
Courses taught by graduate students: *none*
Most popular majors: *social sciences, communications, literature*
Students living on campus: *81%*
Guaranteed housing for four years? *yes*
Students in fraternities or sororities: *none*

in journalism and government, while the department of classical liberal arts offers BAs in literature, history, and classical liberal arts. This relatively narrow range of disciplines is actually an advantage, since the school is able to concentrate its resources in a handful of programs.

Students are assigned an academic advisor based upon their anticipated major. Advisors assist students with major declarations, course planning, and academic concerns.

The most popular and well-developed major at PHC is government, which offers four different tracks: political theory, American politics and policy, international politics and policy, and strategic intelligence. The political theory track is headed by Mark Mitchell, probably the most well-liked teacher on campus. Its students get a thorough training in classical political philosophy, studying thinkers from Plato and Aristotle to de Tocqueville, Eric Voegelin, and E. F. Schumacher. Political theory classes often reach the level of a graduate school seminar, sources say. An offshoot of the theory program is the Alexis de Tocqueville Society, which publishes an excellent student journal featuring articles such as "Ancient Views of the Body in Homer, Plato, and St. Augustine."

The policy tracks (both American and international) focus on the empirical and practical details of governmental decision making. The policy programs seem to give students a solid introduction to political praxis. One professor says that students are hampered by Patrick Henry's lack of emphasis on statistics and economics—although a student disagrees, arguing that the "policy track is solid. You delve into statistics that fuel research." An offshoot of the policy tracks is Libertas, a student organization that lobbies in Congress. Policy majors, says one student, are concerned with "how to make biblical worldview and policy match. How do we prepare legislation that's biblical and attractive to society?"

The strategic intelligence track in the government department, the largest government track, is an exciting program that is distinctive to PHC. Students learn to become intelligence analysts and undergo training that will give them a security clearance by graduation. Strategic intelligence students focus on a specific country or region (e.g., Venezuela or the Caucasus) and study languages such as Spanish, Russian, and Arabic. One student says that graduates are "getting really great jobs. Government agencies and private contractors are snapping them up."

The government department also offers a journalism program directed by journalist Leslie Sillars, whom students describe as an "extremely good" teacher. Journalism majors have a choice between two curricula: a government track that prepares them specifically for political and government coverage, and a classical liberal arts track that is aimed at journalism covering cultural and religious issues and topics. Says one student: "Journalism is really good at placing its students." One recent graduate landed a writing position with Slate.com.

Within the classical liberal arts department are three majors. Of these, the literature major is the most well-established. Headed by Steve Hake, whom students describe as "dedicated," the major offers courses in both critical interpretation and creative writing. Says one professor, "what I see every day are writers, very creative ones. Writers outnumber critics three to one. . . . I believe that some of the literature that is read in the twenty-first century will be written by some of these students." Students majoring in literature study the great works of European and American literature. They take two semesters of English literature and one semester of American literature. As part of major electives, they must take classes in either fiction or nonfiction writing, study a genre, and focus on one main author. Additionally, they expand on areas of interest by developing directed research and writing projects in literary studies or creative writing.

The history major offers strong instruction in European, American, and contemporary world history. David Aikman, an award-winning journalist formerly with *Time* magazine, peppers his lectures on contemporary world history with anecdotes of his own eyewitness experiences in world events, from Israel to Tiananmen Square. All history majors are required to take core courses in U.S. history, the history of Western civilization, and the philosophy and methodology of history. There are also electives in the history of Russia, China, and the Middle East, and electives on thematic topics like Islam. In the senior year, two major projects cap a history major's curriculum: a year-long senior thesis based upon primary source research, and a faith and reason integration project.

Paradoxically, the weakest major in the classical liberal arts department is the one called classical liberal arts. For a long time, teachers report, it was unclear as to what this major was even about. It has recently been settled that the major exists primarily as an education department, preparing students for careers as teachers in the rising movement of classical elementary and secondary education. The recent hiring of Laura McCollum as professor of education and academic dean has breathed life into this major, and there are plans for its expansion.

All of PHC's departments are said to have dedicated faculty and practical apprenticeship programs, and the college is so small that students describe their professors as very accessible. None of the classes are taught by teaching assistants. "I have the home phone numbers of two of my professors," one student remarks. "Some of my best memories are lunches with teachers." Another student says, "Professors are really personable, not aloof. . . . It's just like talking to your neighbor. A professor will say, 'Here, let me pray for you.' They care about you as people." Some more exceptional teachers at PHC are Stephen Baskerville in government;

> ### SUGGESTED CORE
>
> The school's required core curriculum suffices.

Gene Veith in classical liberal arts; Robert Spinney in history; and Michael Kucks in physics. Says one student, "I'm not good at physics, but I didn't want to miss a class because Professor Kucks teaches it."

In addition to working closely with faculty, all of the majors offer hands-on opportunities for working in their respective professional fields. Journalism majors intern with print, radio, or newspaper media companies. Literature majors can find internships with presses or policy foundations, or can work with outside professional writers and academics, such as Catherine Pickstock, Patricia Wrede, and Peter Leithart. History majors can intern with historical archives, and classical liberal arts majors find internships with local Christian private schools.

The overarching framework for all of these majors and the core curriculum is the college's Protestant faith. Patrick Henry's evangelical commitments are summarized in its two-part Biblical Foundations Statement, a bare-bones assertion of Protestant orthodoxy. All trustees, officers, faculty, students, and staff members of PHC must "fully and enthusiastically subscribe" to this statement. The college takes a neutral position on intra-Protestant doctrinal differences, and the student body embraces members of all denominations, from Anglicans and Calvinists to Baptists and Pentecostals. A Roman Catholic or an Eastern Orthodox can be admitted or hired, since the Statement of Faith is not explicitly Protestant.

Faculty, but not students, must subscribe to the Statement of Biblical Worldview, a more detailed theological statement. It goes into somewhat more depth on doctrines such as biblical inerrancy and the Trinity and applies them to particular questions—such as biblical creation, the structure of family life, and the "biblical basis" for democratic government.

There are no science or math majors at PHC, so the courses in physics, biology, and Euclid's geometry are designed to be especially intelligible for students who do not have great aptitude for math or science. Patrick Henry College does stand out from other liberal arts schools through its position on creationism. PHC is not merely skeptical of evolutionary theory. The school's Statement of Biblical Worldview categorically rejects evolution in favor of special creation and declares that all classes must adhere to an understanding of Creation in six 24-hour days—something St. Augustine questioned in the fourth century. However, PHC confers no BAs in biology, much less in anthropology or geology; the school is concerned primarily with theology, culture, and politics. The one core curriculum class in introductory biology touches on creation, but even that course is concerned with the full spectrum of biological issues that intersect with politics, such as genetics and stem cells.

The absence of a philosophy or theology department may make the course offerings in those disciplines relatively weak compared with the rest of the curriculum, but such courses are well-integrated into the political theory track of the government major, and the core curriculum contains both philosophy and theology requirements. There are three biblical studies requirements, two courses in the "Theology of the Body," and one in the "Principles of Biblical Reasoning." Prominent Christian apologist John Warwick Montgomery spends each fall semester teaching core courses in apologetics.

With its emphasis on politics, Patrick Henry College stresses forensic reasoning and debate ability. A sign of this is the success of Patrick Henry students in debate. PHC's moot court team has repeatedly won the American Collegiate Moot Court Association national tournaments, and even in past years has bested Balliol College, Oxford. PHC's newest debate team participates in the National Forensic Association, and it has already claimed top-ten speaker awards and team rankings at every tournament.

All PHC graduates must demonstrate intermediate-level proficiency in a foreign language. Government majors on the strategic intelligence track must study a modern foreign language. Classical liberal arts, history, and literature majors must choose a classical language. Aside from taking one of the languages PHC offers (currently, Ancient Greek, Latin, and Russian), students frequently choose to complete their language requirement by going overseas, although Patrick Henry does not offer a formal study-abroad program.

Student Life: Getting "Bob-tised"

Patrick Henry students are generally serious about their studies, and the campus atmosphere is fairly quiet and sedate. Drinking parties and dormitory bacchanals are absent. Alcohol use is forbidden (on and off campus), and students must follow a "business casual" dress code during school hours, Monday through Friday. Chapel service, held three times a week, is mandatory, and while attendance is now enforced by the honor system, the services are still well attended. On the other two days of the week, PHC holds small-group devotions and faculty-led book studies. These, too, are mandatory. Scripture study groups proliferate

---

ACADEMIC REQUIREMENTS

Patrick Henry College's core curriculum totals seventy-five credit hours—more than half of a student's total four-year course load. Students must take:

- "Freedom's Foundations," a two-semester political philosophy course that examines the history of the idea of freedom from ancient and biblical times, through the Middle Ages and the Reformation, up to the American founding and contemporary political ideologies.
- "Theology of the Bible" I and II.
- "Principles of Biblical Reasoning."
- "Logic."
- "Rhetoric."
- "Economics for the Citizen."
- "History of the United States" I and II.
- "History of Western Civilization" I and II.
- "Western Literature" I and II.
- "Euclidean Geometry."
- "Research & Writing," an introductory writing course in writing a research paper.
- "Philosophy."
- "Biology."
- "Physics."
- Demonstrated intermediate proficiency in a foreign language.

GREEN LIGHT

Patrick Henry College is an extremely conservative school, politically and religiously. (There is said to be only one Democrat on campus.) Nevertheless, PHC has a great deal of intellectual diversity. One student calls it "a melting pot of conservatism." The idea that PHC is "cranking out Karl Roves is untrue," says another. Almost every conceivable variety of right-of-center thought and sentiment is present on campus. There are *National Review*– and *Weekly Standard*–style neoconservatives, traditional conservatives, libertarians, "small is beautiful" localists, and Constitution Party supporters. Patrick Henry College buzzes with debate at all levels of political discourse, from horserace-style punditry about particular campaigns to the airy heights of political philosophy. When a new freshman steps onto campus, it is certain he will be forced to reexamine his political beliefs or inclinations in this atmosphere that promotes debate and critical thought. Furthermore, although PHC offers students many opportunities to get involved in practical politics, it is not an activist factory. "The school is not a place to make activists, but it is a comfortable place for activists," says a student.

After extensive interviews with students and faculty, we can safely say that there are no free speech issues at Patrick Henry College—except for an occasional prudishness on the part of some students that makes it difficult to discuss some of the racier bits of Western history.

on campus, but PHC students insist that they do not live in a "Bible bubble," entirely cut off from the outside world. A considerable number go to music clubs in Washington, D.C. (a one-hour drive), while others attend classical music concerts at the Kennedy Center and other venues. On campus, students listen to most genres of music ("classical, indie, country, and even some hip-hop," according to one student) and watch mainstream movies—although there is a prohibition against ultraviolent, pornographic, or blasphemous films. For the most part, Patrick Henry students are moderate and temperate in their tastes and lifestyle and are neither ascetics nor hedonists.

As on all college campuses, romance is an important part of student life. Patrick Henry students are said to abide by the college prohibition on sex outside of marriage, but they do date. While at first it was somewhat paternalistic, the administration now takes a more relaxed approach to students' private lives. So long as they observe the school's ethical standards (e.g., no cheating, drinking, or fornication), students are treated as adults.

Almost every day there is an Ultimate Frisbee pickup game. There are active intercollegiate men's and women's soccer and basketball teams. In 2009, the Sentinels, the basketball team, qualified for the Shenandoah Valley Athletic Conference. There is also intramural volleyball, basketball, football, soccer, softball, tennis, and table tennis. Residential areas in dormitories are sex segregated, but dormitory lounges are coed, and students frequently socialize and watch movies in the lounges. There are no foreign language immersion houses.

EdenTroupe, the student drama club, produces a play every semester. One recent production was a musical version of *A Tale of Two Cities* composed by a student. There is one "social" or off-campus dance each semester, and the Alexis de Tocqueville Society sponsors a Valentine's Day dance.

South

There are only a handful of student organizations (only about sixteen are officially recognized), but they offer a diverse array of choices. The Titan Society explores the world of finance; the Student Media Network produces and distributes student publications; *Sans Frontières* promotes a better understanding of foreign cultures; the International Justice Mission Club raises awareness of global human slavery, trafficking, and exploitation; the *Patrick Henry Herald* is a weekly newspaper, and *Scratch* is a monthly literary publication. Other groups include the Student Chorale, Strings Ensemble, fencing club, yearbook committee, and mixed martial arts club. There are no fraternities or sororities.

In addition to the Libertas Society and the Alexis de Toqueville Society, a Model United Nations chapter forms delegations to travel to New York City, and a College Republicans chapter is active, giving hands-on opportunities for PHC students to campaign for candidates and causes.

There are a few impromptu mascots on campus. Ducky, a three-person moose costume made out of a giant cardboard box, often makes her appearance, and an inflatable alien named Walter is stolen from one dormitory to the other. Minor pranks are frequent occurrences. Male students who get engaged are given Bobtisms. This means they are dunked in the campus's Lake Bob, even in the middle of winter.

Altogether, there is a very cohesive spirit at PHC. One undergrad remarks: "It's a tight-knit community. Be prepared to know everybody, and have everybody knowing you." Another student says: "You're friends with everybody, but gossip can be a problem. Spiritual life on campus is very good. Almost every guy in my dorm wing is a very zealous (in the good sense) Christian and is genuinely striving to follow God's will in life. There's a lot of encouraging going on and a high percentage of enthusiastic Christians."

The close-knit religious community on campus exerts a powerful effect on students. One says that he learned at PHC that "a lot of people are hurting, dealing with their own sets of issues and headaches. Realizing that has given me a better understanding of people and more of a concern for their well-being." Originally, this student wanted to run for higher office, but now he feels called to seminary.

The college, located in a pleasant green Virginia countryside, already has enough campus architecture for offices, dorm rooms, and classrooms. The buildings are large and well designed, and they sport Federal-style facades. In 2009, the Barbara Hodel Center opened, a 106,000-square-foot, $31 million student center. The building features a full-size gymnasium, dining hall, bookstore and lounge, running track, two racquetball courts, a fitness space, classrooms, and faculty and staff offices. The school's campus is isolated and extremely safe. While the school does not report annual crime statistics, there have been very few incidents since it was founded.

Tuition at PHC was $22,758 in 2010–11, and room and board averaged at $8,010. The average student-loan debt of a recent graduating class was a manageable $6,858. The school reports that 31 percent of students receive need-based financial aid, while 90 percent receive merit-based aid.

Regent University

Virginia Beach, Virginia • www.regent.edu

Christian soldiers in the culture war

You might not have high hopes for a school that was founded by a TV preacher—that is, until you reflected on the humble origins of colleges such as Harvard, Yale, and Brown. Each of those schools was founded as a center for spreading American Protestant doctrine—then followed its region's drift into secularism.

That won't happen at Regent University, or so hopes its founder, head of the Christian Broadcasting Network Rev. Pat Robertson—who started the school in 1978 under the unlovely name Christian Broadcasting Network University. In 1990, the school was rechristened Regent University, reflecting the school's ambition to "represent . . . Christ, our Sovereign, in whatever sphere of life."

Robertson may have started Regent, but he doesn't run it. The head of the School of Government emphatically says that "Robertson has never called me and told me what to do." A serious, highly credentialed team leads the school, and Robertson is not involved in the school's day-to-day affairs. But Robertson has picked the team leading and building the university, and he lives on the school's campus. There is even a pasture for the horses he rides. This is his school, and it reflects his ambitions, sensibilities, and beliefs. And it has been growing and expanding now for thirty-two years.

Regent is just now undergoing a change in leadership with its selection of a new president, Dr. Carlos Campo. Campo is the school's first Hispanic head and an expert on the plays of Arthur Miller.

While Regent isn't officially Baptist, it is the creation of one rich, influential Baptist intent on creating a top-tier school for the devout outside the secular world of the Ivy League and the Northeast. The faculty is ecumenical, but all who teach at the school must sign a ten-point statement of faith. Included in this statement is the view that the Bible is infallible and that Jesus will return to the earth in "power and glory." Students are also asked to accept this view if they wish to attend.

Academic Life: Pre-evangelical education

Regent does not have a Great Books program, and its general education requirements don't add up to a traditional core curriculum (see our Suggested Core instead). Still, the essential works of the Western canon appear in the history and English curricula, and the school does require students to take a wide range of classes in both the arts and sciences, including an introductory philosophy class, a U.S. history survey, a class in English composition, and a lab science class.

While Regent shows due respect to academic standards, it is not a traditional liberal arts college oriented toward disinterested learning. Indeed, faculty are clear about the university's mission. A dean at the college (himself a distinguished academic) says that the school aims "to be a Christian university, which is conservative, with professional schools which can influence American culture." As Regent's Government school website notes, its "ultimate priority . . . is to serve the Lord by preparing students to impact the world."

This requires that the school's graduates gain the degrees and the training by which they can, for example, move into jobs on congressional staffs or obtain career-track positions with television news channels. Thus, until recently Regent has been focused on graduate and professional education. This is the means by which the school moves forward in its goal of insinuating its grads into the overwhelmingly liberal and secular centers of power and influence in Washington, New York, and elsewhere.

To this end, Regent was set up with seven distinct graduate programs: Law, Education, Divinity, Government, Psychology, Global Leadership, and Entrepreneurship and Communication. The degrees granted include both doctorates and MBAs. While Regent now has an undergraduate program, there are only about 1,000 full-time undergrads studying on campus, compared with 4,417 graduate and professional students (half of whom study either part-time or online). Moreover, some of the school's best-known professors teach only grad and professional classes. (This is a problem, of course, at many universities.)

VITAL STATISTICS

Religious affiliation: *Protestant (nondenominational)*
Total enrollment: *5,555*
Total undergraduates: *1,046*
SAT/ACT midranges: CR: *460–600*, M: *430–580*; ACT: *21–26*
Applicants: *1,100*
Applicants accepted: *85%*
Accepted applicants who enrolled: *10%*
Tuition and fees: *$15,308*
Room and board: *$8,600*
Freshman retention rate: *68%*
Graduation rate: *not provided*
Courses with fewer than 20 students: *61%*
Student-faculty ratio: *17:1*
Courses taught by graduate students: *not provided*
Most popular majors: *psychology, business/marketing, communications*
Students living on campus: *12%*
Guaranteed housing for four years? *no*
Students in fraternities or sororities: *none*

Many of Regent's tenured professors were recruited away from top secular colleges and universities, and as one professor says, "Teaching is central, and . . . research is secondary." On the other hand, roughly two-thirds of Regent's faculty is composed of adjuncts—not a healthy long-term policy for any college. The student-faculty ratio is a dispiriting 17 to 1.

As the undergraduate program is still developing, prospective students should be aware that the programs it provides, though thorough and intensive in their course offerings, are limited. Many, if not most, of its areas of study are expansions from existing graduate programs. The majors offered are currently animation, biblical and theological studies, business, Christian ministry, cinema-television, communications, criminal justice, elementary education/interdisciplinary studies, English, government, history, information systems, technology, leadership and management, mathematics, psychology, religious studies, and theater. There are no undergraduate majors in chemistry or biology, to note just two otherwise common programs that are absent. The school does offer an assortment of additional minors, and it also grants associate's degrees.

Regent students have the option of taking some classes at other schools in the Virginia Tidewater Consortium, a thirteen-school group that includes William and Mary, Hampton University, and Old Dominion. But most of these schools are a considerable drive from campus.

Perhaps best known outside Virginia Beach is Regent's Robertson School of Government. In the words of that school's dean: "We have strategic alliances with key politically conservative organizations that need leaders. They seek our graduates because they know that Regent provides an exceptional academic foundation designed to enhance leadership traits." Undergraduates can take classes with many of the "name" professors, and they can attend its events. The best known of its recent visiting faculty are former U.S. attorney general and U.S. senator John Ashcroft and former Israeli prime minister Ehud Barak.

The Robertson School is housed in Robertson Hall, along with Regent's schools of Law and Divinity. The building sits just to the left of the steps leading up to the university's main library, and it includes a large, elegant atrium full of the flags of many nations. Behind these are an assortment of neat, well-kept classrooms and offices. The classrooms have been rigged up for televised presentation for its online students. (Among these students are U.S. Army officers in Iraq who have earned MAs while serving abroad.)

Classes are usually held in Robertson Hall. Most notable among its classrooms is a 372-seat theater specially designed for Moot Court Competitions. The school takes pride in the fact that it has won national American Bar Association moot court tourneys in 1995, 2002, 2006, and 2007.

All Regent English majors are required to take a solid list of courses ranging from Shakespeare and Romantic and Victorian literature to African-American literature. The program is further subdivided into five separate programs with distinct upper-level classes for those who wish to work in fields like speechwriting or public relations.

The undergraduate history major is among the most complete and demanding of the school's majors. Students must take fifteen courses in the major, including nine specific requirements, such as two semesters in Western civilization and two terms in world history.

Regent's government majors face a solid, meat-and-potatoes curriculum of required courses like "Comparative Government," two terms of "U.S. Government," and classes in ancient and modern political philosophy.

South

Criminal justice and government majors make use of Regent's law faculty for their classes in subjects like constitutional law. As Regent's law school has gained a national reputation, this means that undergrads can benefit from the better teachers the law faculty attracts. One professor widely praised is Jim Davids, a past president of the Christian Legal Society.

One doctoral student ranks the divinity program among the school's best. Certainly divinity is among the largest programs. Former students say that intellectual curiosity is widespread among students, who are no more troubled by the school's insistence on the inerrancy of scripture than were the Fathers of the Church. The undergraduate biblical and theological studies and religious studies majors make use of the school's faculty, and a wide range of classes is offered on subjects involving doctrine, the Bible, comparative religion and religious history. Regent is less theologically monochrome than many of its liberal critics presume. Its faculty mostly reject the controversial theory of "dominionism," which asserts that the United States should be run by Christian leaders along biblical lines—although the first dean of the Regent Law School (and a longtime aide to Robertson), Herbert Titus, held that view.

Regent has also cosponsored conferences with mainline liberal church groups like the National Council of Churches.

While Regent's communications program has as its goal training and guiding students committed to Christian news and entertainment, its theater studies department ranges widely across the theatrical repertoire. Recent mainstage productions have included *Spinning into Butter,* Rebecca Gilman's study of racism in academia; the offbeat, Freudian Stephen Sondheim musical *Into the Woods*; and *A Midsummer Night's Dream* presented with costumes and sets influenced by Japanese anime. In the spring each year, the school brings its acting majors to New York City to be presented to well-connected theater agents. Other communications programs include animation, cinema, journalism, and digital media.

Regents undergrads are effusive about their favorite professors. One singles out Mary Manjikian in history—a Wellesley, Oxford, and Michigan grad who teaches classes on topics like foreign service, homeland security, and terrorism. Another student praises Bible studies and law Professor Joseph Kickasola, who "has an incredible mind and is a fascinating expert on Middle Eastern politics who understands Islam and its role in world affairs." Law professor Benjamin Madison "ties class material into 'real world' practice." Theater teacher Doug Miller is "phenomenal at teaching cinematography and lighting and great at mentoring"; Eric Harrell, theater chairman, is "encouraging and a great teacher, and one of the best practitioners of the Lessac technique [for training an actor's voice and body] in the country"; while Michael Hill-Kirkland is "a terrific teacher of stage and screen combat." Business professor Michael Zigarelli is "very thorough." Among the economics department's most respected professors is macro- and microeconomics teacher Doug Walker, who worked for thirty years at the United Nations. One recent student says that Walker "has a strong biblical worldview on economics and a passion to motivate students."

Regent offers both graduate and undergraduate programs in psychology and education. The education major offers an assortment of programs for teachers in specific elementary and secondary school "need" areas, like English as a second language and special education.

Through the Council for Christian Colleges and Universities, a number of travel-abroad and off-campus domestic study opportunities are available for Regent students, including programs in China, Australia, Latin America, Russia, Uganda, and Oxford, England. Only French and Spanish are taught on campus at Regent, and neither has its own department or major program of study.

Student Life: The suburb of God

Regent's facilities reflect founder Robertson's faith and his patrician background; Robertson's father was a United States senator from Virginia, and he is not only an ordained minister but a Yale Law School graduate. The campus of large, elegant structures designed in a Georgian style recalls the University of Virginia.

The most impressive structure is the 140,000-square-foot School of Communication and Performing Arts Center, which includes a lavish 712-seat theater good enough that it serves as an alternate space for the Virginia Symphony. The building also holds TV studios (which are not connected to the Christian Broadcasting Network) with a full control room, a green screen and an anchor set. In addition, the school is completing a soundstage, and it already has a finished 4,400-square-foot film stage, a giant costume shop and costume collection, set shops, film acting labs, a studio theater, a ninety-nine-seat screening room, animation labs, and postproduction audio and edit suites. The facilities are state of the art, and the school makes a deliberate effort to make them readily available to students so they get as much hands-on experience as possible.

While it might sit in Virginia Beach, the campus is miles from the shoreline. There are no sandy beaches, and there are no waves to be seen. Rather, campus is characterized by green, leafy quadrangles, fountains, and well-tended gardens, a horse pasture, and neigh-

---

ACADEMIC REQUIREMENTS

Regent does not maintain a traditional core curriculum but imposes some worthy requirements. Each undergraduate student must take:

- "The Making of the Christian Mind" and "The Making of a Christian Leader."
- One course in public speaking and English composition.
- One introductory class in philosophy.
- One course in research and writing.
- One class in mathematics.
- Either a biology or an earth science course, with a lab.
- One course on the Old Testament, one on the New Testament, and "Introduction to Christian History and Thought."
- Five classes in different areas of the arts and humanities, including at least one U.S. history survey.
- The computer class "Keys to Online Learning."

South

boring Christian Broadcasting Network studios, which are just a short stroll away. Nearby are many historic locations of Old Virginny; the school is within an hour's drive of Williamsburg, Hampton Roads, and Yorktown.

The school's graduate dorms, called Regent Village, are a short walk from the main campus. The undergraduate dorms, Regent Commons, are right by the main classroom buildings. All male and female dorms are separate, and male students are not permitted to spend the night in female rooms. The school offers "family" dorms for its married students, but undergraduate students who are married with children must live in the graduate facilities.

Regent University is not a place for students who want to wear swimwear to class between games of beer pong or frat parties. One professional-school student says of sexual promiscuity on campus: "It is about zero on the surface. The sanctity of marriage and family are taken seriously here." He goes on to note, "We have a University Chapel every Wednesday and Law School Chapel every Thursday. This is a great time to come together to worship and receive God's message with my peers and professors. . . . The most special thing about the place is the Christian ambience. The school really strives to be Christ-centered, and it shows in every person who sets foot on campus."

> **GREEN LIGHT**
>
> At Regent, students or professors to the left of center are very much in the minority; the school is much more theologically and politically conservative than, say, Wheaton College. However, as the school grants more teachers tenure, the range of expressed opinion should expand. As of now, students shouldn't go to Regent expecting spirited, welcoming debates with professors about taboo topics like the theory of evolution.
>
> In 2007, the school dismissed a student who Photoshopped a picture of Pat Robertson to make it appear, falsely, that he had made an obscene gesture in public. The student then sued the school for wrongful dismissal, but a court rejected his lawsuit.
>
> One of Regent's most serious controversies emerged in the same year, when eleven full-time psychology and counseling graduate faculty resigned, claiming that a dean and another administrator were abrasive, domineering, and possibly hostile to homosexuals. The dean issued an apology, and the issue seems to be resolved.

There are over forty registered clubs and organizations on campus, including English Club/Inklings, Federalist Society, Psychology Club, Student Veterans Association, Association of Black Psychologists, Regent Students for Life, Ballroom Club, and Animation Club. The most popular conservative political organization is the Republican Club which hosts a speaker series and gets involved in local and national elections. There is also a Regent Democrats and Independents club, but it is, not surprisingly, less popular and active. Religious organizations include the Newman Club and the Religion Club.

On-campus students are bound by an honor code, and they must promise not to use alcohol, tobacco, or illicit drugs while on the school's grounds. The school does not have intercollegiate athletic teams but offers intramural men's and women's soccer and volleyball squads, and on many a day students can be seen playing Ultimate Frisbee.

Probably the best known of the school's traditions is its annual Clash of the Titans debate. This is a left versus right political contest held in the school's main theater and

South

preceded by a formal dinner taking place above the library. The debate has drawn famous names every year since its inception. For example, a debate on the role of the Supreme Court pitted a team headed by Ann Coulter against Alan Dershowitz and the ACLU's Nadine Strossen. Another debate was between former vice-president Al Gore and former Senate majority leader Bob Dole, and subsequent debates have drawn Newt Gingrich, Oliver North, General Wesley Clark, Karl Rove, Jeb Bush, Mike Huckabee, Steve Forbes, and Alan Colmes.

The school attracts special attention, as well, for its annual Ronald Reagan Symposium, which is held each year on or around February 6, the former president's birthday. The list of those who have spoken at the event over the years is a Who's Who of the conservative establishment. Past speakers have included *Weekly Standard* editor-in-chief William Kristol and columnists Michael Barone and Michael Novak. The school's website unashamedly observes that "political connections also offer a big payoff to students."

Students give the school high marks with regard to safety. The campus is secluded, and as one student says, "Security is tight, and I know of no recent incidents." In 2009, the only crime reported on campus was a single aggravated assault.

Regent is quite reasonably priced. Tuition for 2010–11 ran to about $15,308 per year, and room and board $8,600 (this amount can vary, depending on the room and board plan chosen). However, the school's financial position is said to be shaky, and tuition hikes are in the offing, according to the *Chronicle of Higher Education*. Some half of students receive need-based financial aid, but the average graduate still emerges with a daunting $33,451 in student debt.

Rhodes College

Memphis, Tennessee • www.rhodes.edu

Continually Presbyterian

Rhodes College has been affiliated with the Presbyterian Church (U.S.A.) since 1855 and aspires "to graduate students who are passionate about learning, effecting change in their communities and the world, and exemplifying leadership and service with integrity. Our emphasis on service is rooted in our Presbyterian heritage." The college maintains a chaplain but does not require students to take any religion or theology classes.

Rhodes campus occupies a hundred wooded acres in Memphis and enrolls 1,685 students from forty-six states and fifteen foreign countries. Though the changes at Rhodes over the past hundred years generally have kept pace with those at its peer institutions, the college does retain a commitment to giving all its students an exposure to the Western tradition. Something beyond the buildings has proved lasting, and in these times, that's something to applaud.

Academic Life: "Search" and "Life"

Rhodes College's general education (or foundation) requirements are presented as a list of a dozen goals. As freshmen, all Rhodes students are required to choose one of the two core paths: "The Search for Values in the Light of Western History and Religion" or "Life: Then and Now."

In "Search," students read primary sources (in translation) from the history and literature of the Israelites, the Greeks, the Romans, and the early church. Says one faculty member, "A student cannot emerge from this course without extensive exposure to the Bible, classical literature, classical philosophy, various revolutions in theology, and the principal writings and currents in early modern and modern thought. Particularly with a devoted instructor, this can be a life-changing experience."

The second choice, "Life: Then and Now," is a three-semester sequence focused mostly on theology and biblical studies. During the first two semesters, students take Religious Studies 101 and 102, "The Bible: Texts and Contexts," meant as an introduction to the Bible and the methods of studying it. Faculty from religious studies teach these two courses. The college catalog reports, "The third Life course is selected from an array that includes advanced study of the Bible, theology and ethics, philosophy, and the his-

VITAL STATISTICS

Religious affiliation: *Presbyterian*

Total enrollment: *1,730*

Total undergraduates: *1,712*

SAT/ACT midranges: CR: *570–680*, M: *580–700*; ACT: *26–30*

Applicants: *5,039*

Applicants accepted: *42%*

Accepted applicants who enrolled: *20%*

Tuition and fees: *$34,270*

Room and board: *$8,480*

Freshman retention rate: *88%*

Graduation rate: *75% (4 yrs.), 85% (6 yrs.)*

Courses with fewer than 20 students: *75%*

Student-faculty ratio: *10:1*

Courses taught by graduate students: *none*

Most popular majors: *social sciences, biology, history*

Students living on campus: *76%*

Guaranteed housing for four years? *no*

Students in fraternities: *45%* in sororities: *53%*

tory of religions." Staples include "Archaeology and the Bible," "King David," "Sex and Gender in the New Testament," "Paul," "Contemporary Theology," "Holocaust," "Islam," and "Religious Traditions of Asia," "Religion in America," "Medieval Philosophy," and "Ethics."

As with most small liberal arts colleges, Rhodes values teaching, and its students are enthusiastic about the attention and care their professors offer them. "Rhodes has the best professors in the world," one student effuses. Small class sizes are also common, with many including as few as twelve students. "I have had a 'directed inquiry,' one-on-one class with a professor every semester at Rhodes. I hang out with professors after class quite frequently and often go out to meals or hang out at their homes," a student reports.

One faculty member who has served on the tenure and promotion committee reports that faculty personnel decisions are based 45 percent on teaching, 35 percent on research, and 20 percent on service. Greater emphasis has been placed on research in the past decade, and this has had the effect of taking time away from students in some cases. However, most insiders seem to believe that Rhodes has got the balance about right. "Good teaching informed by scholarship" is the school's ethic, a faculty member reports. "A good scholar who is a poor teacher won't last long at Rhodes."

Rhodes students often work side by side with their professors on research projects. In fact, one of the greatest benefits of a Rhodes College education is the opportunity to participate in important research even as an undergrad. This is one reason why the science departments are so strong. Physics, for instance, cultivates in its students the ability to research and analyze and sends many of its students to "top-notch graduate programs," a teacher reports.

Research opportunities abound in Memphis. The Rhodes Institute for Regional Studies provides a $3,000 stipend, as well as housing and research expenses for academic research on Memphis and the Mid-South region conducted in a thirteen-week period, the first six weeks of which consist of an "intensive regional studies seminar." The Rhodes Learning Corridor makes partnerships with nearby neighborhoods and public schools to create civic engagement and educational opportunities for students and to improve teaching and performance at public schools. A research program with the nearby St. Jude Children's Research Hospital is also offered for freshmen, sophomores, juniors, and all science majors. To showcase all these research projects, the college has presented its own "Undergraduate Research and Cre-

South

ative Activity Symposium," basically a collegewide talent show and research fair.

The college's political science department is very strong. Faculty range across the ideological spectrum and are known to be good teachers who rarely allow their own biases to show up in the classroom. Methodology is eschewed in favor of "careful thinking about politics" itself—its moral foundations, government institutions, processes, and policy matters. Courses on American politics, says one professor, are "focused on practical problems that any informed citizen should think about." Politics majors take forty-eight credits, including "U.S. Politics," "Research Methods," a course in political thought and philosophy, and "The U.S. in the Twentieth Century." Also required is introduction to international relations or comparative politics.

The history department offers a wide range of courses, from "Medieval Europe" and "East Asia in the Modern World" to "U.S. Constitutional History to 1865," with plenty of solid offerings in American history, and expanded offerings covering the Middle East and the Islamic world. History majors are not required to take American history, but must take "The Historian's Craft," a senior seminar, and one class in a period "prior to 1500 CE [sic]."

Religious studies majors complete a thirty-six-credit requirement that includes at least one course in the Bible, a course in either Judaism or African American religions, a course on methods and theories, and a course on theology and ethics.

Rhodes's English department has an excellent cast of teachers, in particular Tina Barr, Gordon Bigelow, Marshall Boswell, and Michael Leslie. English majors have a hefty forty-four credits to complete but no very specific requirements. All must take "Text and Context," "Critical Theory," and a senior seminar, for which current semester offerings are "Faulkner/Morrison," and "Studies in the Novel." Other requirements depend upon whether one is following the concentration in literature or in literature and creative writing. Departmental offerings range from the standard "Eighteenth Century British Fiction" to the specialized "Fifties American Cinema." Though students are not required to take Shakespeare, they can benefit from the "Shakespeare at Rhodes" program, which is funded by the Pearce Shakespeare endowment. The Department of Theater has produced fifteen Shakespeare plays in its three decades.

Other good teachers at the school include Tim Huebner and Robert Saxe in history; Michael Nelson, Dan Cullen, and Marcus Pohlmann in political science; Luther Ivory, Steven McKenzie, and Bernadette McNary-Zak in religious studies; Kathleen Anne Doyle in

---

SUGGESTED CORE

For courses 1–3, see also Humanities 101–102: The Search for Values in the Light of Western History and Religion.

1. Greek and Roman Studies 245, Texts and Contexts
2. Philosophy 201, Ancient Philosophy
3. Religious Studies 270/280, Introduction to the Hebrew Bible/Introduction to the New Testament
4. Religious Studies 214, Early Christian Literature (closest match)
5. Political Science 314, The Modern Search for Justice (closest match)
6. English 230, Shakespeare's Major Plays
7. History 231, North America in the Colonial and Revolutionary Eras
8. History 426, Modern European Intellectual History

Spanish; and Pat Shade in philosophy. Julia "Cookie" Ewing, chair of the theater department, is a "real gem," says one faculty member.

The college's arts program is also quite strong. The music department boasts a good teaching faculty and strong vocal and instrumental groups, says a professor. Rhodes has an art gallery, a theater, chorale, chorus, and other musical groups. Each year, the college sponsors a number of Center for Outreach in the Development of the Arts (CODA) scholars, providing students with an annual scholarship of $13,000 in exchange for ten volunteer hours a week.

Some 65 percent of students do leave the Rhodes campus to study abroad. The ever-popular Coral Reef Ecology program allows students to escape for Roatan Island, Honduras, during May and June. The college's Field Studies in Namibia program is led by a Rhodes biology professor. Other opportunities exist in Belgium, Spain, France, Peru, Scotland, Germany, Mexico, Russia, and China, among others. Students can also choose from any number of non-Rhodes study-abroad programs.

Rhodes offers language instruction in Chinese, French, German, Italian, Latin, Ancient Greek, Russian, and Spanish.

Student Life: Service in stone

One of the loveliest things about Rhodes is the school's splendid collegiate Gothic architecture. This is by far the most striking aspect of Rhodes on a first impression. Every building on campus is of gray-orange stone, with slate roofs and leaded windows; between the buildings lie lush green lawns perfect for studying outdoors, playing Ultimate Frisbee, and other activities.

Students can live in coed or single-sex dorms and are required to live on campus for their first two years. Three-quarters of the student body lives on campus in a given year, some in a substance-free theme area or a "learning community." Housing is not guaranteed, and though most students who want them obtain rooms on campus, there may be a waiting list.

One professor characterizes Rhodes's students as "quite curious" and "quite diverse." And the college does a good job of developing the well-rounded student, exposing young minds and souls to a broad slate of disciplines, international study, spiritual questions, the arts, hands-on research, social functions, and service to those less fortunate in the Memphis community and beyond. We'd wager that there aren't a lot of students who spend much time in their dorm rooms playing video games.

Students say they spend most of their free time on campus, but Memphis, Tennessee, offers plenty of restaurants, bars, shops, blues clubs, and other forms of entertainment. The center of all the hullabaloo, Beale Street, is a short drive from campus. Elvis's Graceland is nearby as well.

Memphis also has many areas that are economically depressed, a problem that Rhodes College addresses in different ways. The college—faculty, staff, and students—seems to be more aware of its surroundings than are many other wealthy liberal arts schools. Indeed, one professor says that one of the distinctive practices of Rhodes is "connecting to the larger

ACADEMIC REQUIREMENTS

In lieu of a core curriculum, Rhodes prescribes twelve goals of a liberal arts education. Students must take courses demonstrating the following skills:

- Foundations 1: "Critically examine questions of meaning and value." Students choose either the three-course sequence "The Search for Values in the Light of Western History and Religion" or the "Life: Then and Now" sequence, which is two courses on the Bible, plus a third course like "Early Modern Philosophy" or "Synoptic Gospels."
- Foundations 2: "Develop excellence in written communication." Students take one freshman writing seminar and two writing-intensive courses.
- One course aimed at Foundations 3: "Understand how historical forces have shaped human cultures," with choices from "U.S. in the Nineteenth Century" to "Gender and Warfare in America."
- One class fulfilling Foundations 4: "Read and interpret literary texts." Choices include "Shakespeare's Major Plays," "Dostoevsky," and "Sex, Violence, and Rock n Roll."
- One course drawn from Foundations 5: "Participate in the analysis of artistic expression or in the performance or production of art." "Art and Spirituality in the Middle Ages," and "The Cinema of Alfred Hitchcock and Francois Truffaut" both count.
- One class aimed at Foundations 6: "Gain facility with mathematical reasoning and expression." Most choices come from the computer science and math departments, such as "Logic" and "Statistical Methods in Psychology."
- One course fulfilling Foundations 7: "Explore and understand scientific approaches to the natural world." Options come from the natural sciences and physics departments and must include a lab. Choices include "Topics in Biology" and "Physics of Sound and Music."
- One class in Foundations 8: "Explore and understand the systematic analysis of human interaction and contemporary institutions." Choices can be from anthropology, economics, international relations, political science, and psychology and include "Introductory Sociology" and "United States Politics."
- One course from Foundations 9: "View the world from more than one cultural perspective." On the list are "Ancient and Medieval India," "Anthropology of Gender and Sexuality in Latin America" among others.
- One or more classes fulfilling Foundations 10: "Develop intermediate proficiency in a second language."
- One course from Foundations 11: "Participate in activities that broaden connections between the classroom and the world." This can be satisfied by various field studies, internships, and study-abroad courses, plus courses like "Philosophy of Education," "Pain, Suffering, and Death," and "Environmental Change."
- Classes to fulfill Foundations 12: "Participate in activities that encourage lifelong physical fitness." This can be fulfilled by three half semesters of no-credit PE courses chosen from a long list that includes golf, Middle Eastern dance, aikido, and life saving, or by participation in intercollegiate or club sports.

YELLOW LIGHT

One professor complained of significant liberal bias among the faculty and a multiculturalist ideology that pervades the college's management. The Rhodes website seems desperate to show its commitment to diversity of every kind, claiming: "Rhodes' Multicultural Life program collaborates with student groups to sponsor events celebrating diversity in culture, ethnicity, religion and sexuality." Among the students chosen to represent "the faces of Rhodes" on the website, we see, in addition to students doing Native American and African American research, the student coordinator of Planned Parenthood and V-Day (*Vagina Monologues*) activities on campus and a Muslim who studied Islamic identity in the Middle East.

However, our sources say that in most cases the administration's diversity fetish does not impinge much on students. Few classes are infused with politics, and no students are made to feel unwelcome or ineligible to express their views. A professor says that, the school's public lectures are "predominantly on the liberal left," although "the student body has enough moderates and conservatives in it to keep debate fairly lively." The same professor remarked that, as a conservative, he felt happier at Rhodes than at other institutions, and he believed that conservative students were also content.

Memphis community." *Newsweek* recently named Rhodes "the most service-minded school in America," and more than 80 percent of students are reported to engage in community service; they serve the community by tutoring students at local schools, offering food to the poor in downtown soup kitchens, and building houses with Habitat for Humanity. The Kinney Program organizes most of these opportunities, as well as some more questionable ones at area abortion facilities and at community gay-activist groups. So students who don't want to do more harm than good should choose their activities wisely.

Rhodes still acknowledges its ties to the (quite liberal) Presbyterian Church U.S.A., and maintains a chaplaincy. This historic connection serves to bring in plenty of Presbyterian students, although diverse denominations are represented in the student body. Religious organizations include the Community of Rhodes Episcopalians, Catholic Student Association, Fellowship of Christian Athletes, Interfaith Ministry, Jewish Student Organization (Hillel), and Muslim Student Association.

As at many southern schools, Rhodes faculty tend to be more liberal than their students. At matriculation, when Rhodes students must pledge to abide by its (admirable) honor code, they also promise to uphold the college's "Diversity Statement." The Office of Multicultural Affairs and the Multicultural Resource Center orchestrate diversity programs, which have included a "multicultural graduation" for students of color; lectures with titles such as "Rhodes Sexuality Rehaul" and "Diversity in the University—Singing the Unsung Minorities." (Were they talking about conservatives?) The Office of Multicultural Affairs works closely with such student bodies as the Black Student Association (BSA) and Gay-Straight Alliance (GSA). Wherever he is, John Calvin does not approve.

The school has both College Republican and College Democrat groups. But one student says, "Rhodes students don't necessarily talk about politics that much." There are plenty of other organizations to join as well, including philosophy, math, and chess clubs;

South

Lipstick on Your Collar, an *a cappella* group for women, and Woolsocks for men; Rhodes Radio; and Advocates for the Homeless.

Around half of students here are members of fraternities or sororities, but since the groups do not have their own residences, they are neither exclusive nor cliquish. A student says, "Few make Greek life their whole social focus." Students can live in coed or single-sex dorms and are required to live on campus for their first two years.

The Rhodes Lynxes compete in NCAA Division III in the Southern Collegiate Athletic Conference. The school offers nineteen varsity teams—nine for men, ten for women— as well as many club-level and intramural teams. Sports clubs cross the board, from men's and women's track, tennis, lacrosse, soccer, and swimming to fencing club and cheerleading. Participation in sports is high: 26 percent of students play varsity sports and 65 percent club and intramural sports.

Serious offenses—by students or unwelcome visitors—are rare at Rhodes, and the college is very safe. During 2009, the college reported only two burglaries and no other crimes on campus. A stone wall surrounds the campus, and campus police patrol the grounds regularly. The college offers a student-escort service around the clock, as well as plenty of crime-prevention workshops.

The Rhodes experience doesn't come cheap. Tuition for 2010–11 was $34,270, with room and board $8,480. The college website reports that 85 percent of students receive financial aid (45 percent get need-based aid). Rhodes fellowships are a novel approach to funding, one that fits well at a college that encourages its students to be involved in the greater local and world community. Simply put, eligible students are given financial support in exchange for taking up internships, specified research, or even community service, gaining not only a financial benefit but also real-world experience. The average student-loan debt of a recent graduating student was a middling $18,131.

University of Richmond

Richmond, Virginia • www.richmond.edu

Reconstructed

The University of Richmond is far from a southern regional school, as it draws students from nearly every state in the Union and some seventy foreign countries. The university has risen in prestige over the past decade; unfortunately, it has lost most of its southern charm in the process. Still, the University of Richmond has research opportunities that rival those at the very top elite schools in the country, a strong study-abroad program that really does bolster international education, a billion-dollar endowment (per student, one of the top twenty-five in the nation), and a catalog filled with serious courses from which students will actually benefit. For the most part, faculty members understand and seek to impart the university's liberal arts mission: "to prepare you for life—not just for a job."

Academic Life: Where are the leaders?

Richmond College was founded in 1830 by Virginia Baptists; it wasn't until 1992 that the two academic wings of the all-male Richmond College and the all-female Westhampton College merged to form the University of Richmond's School of Arts and Sciences. Along with this school, UR also includes the Williams School of Law (established 1870), the Graduate School of Arts and Sciences (1921), the Robins School of Business (1949), and the School of Continuing Studies for evening and commuting students (1962). The worthy Jepson School of Leadership Studies, the "first school of leadership studies in the U.S.," was formed in 1992. Around two-thirds of the undergraduate student population, or about 2,300 students, are enrolled in the School of Arts and Sciences, while around 650 students are enrolled in the business school. The leadership school is still quite small.

Richmond has weakened its once-impressive core requirements. Instead of the excellent survey classes once required, all freshmen must now take two first-year seminars. The courses are small in size, discussion-focused, and drawn from every department in the university. Class choice varies hugely, as does quality. Options include "Baseballs, Body Parts, and Rosa Parks," "Guns in America," "Myth and Cult in Ancient Greece," "Moral Philosophy: How Should We Live?" "Seeing Is Believing? Theories of Representation and Sacred Art in Early Modern Europe," and "The Search for Self," taught by the university's humanities librarian.

Richmond students must also take six more classes in historical studies, literary studies, natural science, social analysis, symbolic reasoning, and visual and performing arts. In nearly every category, students can choose either solid or frivolous courses. But there are quite enough legitimate options that even the least disciplined Richmond students still tend to stumble upon worthy material. "I think the curriculum does a good job of drawing students into exploring new disciplines," says one professor. "There are certain gateway classes—particularly ones in philosophy and history—that open up a whole new world to students and inspire them to take more classes within that department." A student tells us, "The curriculum makes you get out of your comfort zone a little bit, but you still get to choose classes that you like." Each student is assigned to a faculty advisor, who is supposed to guide the student to attain a broad liberal arts education. Once a student declares a major, he is assigned a new advisor within the major.

Classes are small here. With fewer than 3,500 undergraduates and an excellent student-faculty ratio of 8 to 1, Richmond is comfortable enough that faculty members put most of their effort into teaching. One humanities faculty member says, "Teaching is always above research here, and a significant number of the faculty just teach traditional liberal arts fare." Although there are a few teaching assistants, they serve only a supplemental role, usually helping out in science labs. Students we talked to laud the strong relationships they have with professors. One student says, "There's definitely a bell curve of those who do take advantage of office hours and those who don't really care. I'd say most students meet with their professors once or twice a semester." A professor says, "Intellectual engagement has definitely risen over the last ten years. But it really depends on what class you're teaching."

The freshmen seminars are intended to help strengthen writing and reasoning skills, and the student-staffed Writing Center helps undergrads with their papers. Because the university also emphasizes proficiency in oral communication, Richmond runs the distinctive Weinstein-Jecklin Speech Center. There, students can video their speeches and then review them, and even schedule practice sessions with faculty and trained peers. "It's a great resource," says one student, "and many classes actually require that students visit the Speech Center at least once during the semester."

The emphasis on both written and oral communication is all part of the university's goal to create leaders among its students. This also motivated the founding of the Jepson

VITAL STATISTICS

Religious affiliation: *none*
Total enrollment: *4,344*
Total undergraduates: *3,387*
SAT/ACT midranges: CR: *580–670*, M: *590–680*; ACT: *26–30*
Applicants: *7,886*
Applicants accepted: *39%*
Accepted applicants who enrolled: *30%*
Tuition and fees: *$41,610*
Room and board: *$8,810*
Freshman retention rate: *92%*
Graduation rate: *81% (4 yrs.)*, *86% (6 yrs.)*
Courses with fewer than 20 students: *60%*
Student-faculty ratio: *8:1*
Courses taught by graduate students: *not provided*
Most popular majors: *business/management, political science, accounting*
Students living on campus: *91%*
Guaranteed housing for four years? *no*
Students in fraternities: *20%* in sororities: *26%*

SUGGESTED CORE

1. Classical Studies 205, Greek and Roman Mythology: Epic
2. Philosophy 271, Ancient Greek Philosophy
3. Religion 201, The Bible as Literature
4. Religion 258/356, Medieval Religious Thought/Religious Thought of the Renaissance and Reformation
5. Political Science 312, Modern Political Theory
6. English 234, Shakespeare
7. History 120, The United States to 1877
8. History 240/241, Modern European Thought 1650 to 1850/Modern European Thought since 1850

School of Leadership Studies in 1992, the first program of its kind in the country. The school offers both majors and minors in leadership studies. Majors begin with "Leadership and the Humanities," which integrates readings in philosophy, political theory, religion, and social theory, with an emphasis on "assessing these texts in light of reasoned argument and on drawing their implications for leadership studies." They must also complete a second introductory class, "Leadership and the Social Sciences," which incorporates readings in anthropology, economics, political science, psychology, and sociology. Most classes in this new major seem solid and worthwhile; it's surprising to us that so few students choose it.

Although Richmond boasts top-notch science facilities that have improved significantly lately, research projects here go well beyond the science fields. Recent years have seen student research projects in nearly every academic department.

On the down side, at Richmond, many departments have lax major requirements. English majors, for example, must simply take two courses "before the early to mid-19th century" (though solid classes like "Shakespeare" and "Early American Literature" are offered) and two courses from after (selections encompass mostly cultural themes: "Literatures of South Asia," "Race and Ethnicity in American Literature"); two advanced classes; and two seminars. The only two required classes are "Literature in Context: Genre and Mode" and "Literature in Context: Texts in History."

History requirements are similarly fluid: a single "Introduction to Historical Thinking" class is required, along with a course in U.S. history, European history, and Asian/Latin American/Middle Eastern/African history. Students must also complete a research seminar and four electives. Two-thirds of the required classes must be at intermediate or advanced levels.

The political science major requires two of the following: introduction to comparative politics, international relations, or public policy, as well as a political theory class and a methods class (in public opinion, public policy, or cross-national research). Majors also must complete four upper-level electives. It is unclear whether majors must study the U.S. Constitution.

Beyond the trendy classes offered by the English department, most of Richmond's bizarre courses can be found in the women, gender, and sexuality studies program.

International studies is a popular and much-talked-about interdisciplinary major at Richmond, and students choosing this major focus on one of seven different areas of concentration, choosing from Africa, Asia, international economics, Latin America, modern Europe, the Middle East, and world politics and diplomacy. In 2010, the university com-

South

610

pleted its new facility for international education, the Carole Weinstein International Center. The 57,000-square-foot center now houses the Office of International Education, the modern languages and international studies departments, and high-tech classrooms that allow students and faculty to work with others at partner universities all over the world.

In addition to international studies, other strong departments at UR are business, classics, and the sciences (especially biology, chemistry, and physics). Some academic programs distinctive to Richmond include "medical humanities" and "law and the liberal arts." Students majoring in rhetoric and communication studies encounter fascinating courses like "Classical Rhetoric," "Speech Writing," and "Business and Professional Speech." The rhetorical tradition—once so strong throughout the West—today mostly survives south of the Mason-Dixon line.

Students single out the following faculty members as particularly strong: Linda M. Boland in biology; Benjamin Broening and Jennifer A. Cable in music; and Walter N. Stevenson in classical studies.

Richmond's study-abroad program is quite strong, with around 350 students traveling each year and fully two-thirds of undergraduates participating sometime during their college years. The school offers more than seventy-five programs spanning thirty nations around the globe, from Tanzania to Belgium to Mongolia and Australia. One popular summer program is the "24 plays in 24 days" summer trip to London, which offers two course credits and gives students the opportunity to see a panoply of Shakespeare plays and to visit eighteen museums. Other summer programs led by Richmond faculty venture to Argentina, Japan, Russia, and Spain.

Students must demonstrate intermediate proficiency in a foreign language. Options include Arabic, Chinese, French, German, Ancient Greek, Italian, Japanese, Spanish, Portuguese, Latin, and Russian.

Student Life: Don't mention the Baptists . . .

The university is no longer associated with the Virginia Baptists, who cut ties with the school. "Nobody really talks about the link with the Baptists. It's long gone," says a student member of a Christian organization. The largest non-Greek student organization is InterVarsity Christian Fellowship, with a roster of 150 students. One undergrad says the university has been generous with funding for this organization. However, another reports that faith is not talked about much on campus and that most students are not particularly religious. The office of the chaplaincy, which has an endowed chair, seems to focus more on social justice activities than on religious affairs—although it does offer a pizza and conversation series, encouraging students to ask deep questions like "Who would God vote for?" and "God and Hurricane Katrina: Does faith make sense in a suffering world?" Ominously, it also helps sponsor the Allies Institute, a weeklong diversity program workshop; such programs typically begin with issues of race and swiftly move into feminist, pro-choice, and pro-gay activism. Installed in 2009, Methodist Rev. Craig Kocher serves as university chaplain. He teaches a class on justice and civil society at the Jepson School and is particularly committed to interfaith dialogue and ecumenism.

South

Other religious options include Zen meditation on Tuesday evenings, Shabbat prayer on Friday evenings, a nondenominational Christian service on Sunday afternoons, Catholic Mass at 5:00 PM each Sunday, and Jum'a prayer on Fridays at noon. Lutheran, Episcopalian, Presbyterian, African Methodist Episcopal, and Hillel are some of the school's available ministries. Other students are involved with local churches, many of whom will pick students up from campus if necessary.

Some dormitories are coed, although the sexes are divided by suite or wing. Freshmen are still required to live in single-sex dorms, and most residence halls are single sex for upperclassmen. Around 91 percent of all students choose to live on campus all four years. The fourteen residence halls vary from traditional hall-style living to suites to apartments—where seniors tend to gravitate. UR offers a few theme programs: Ready for Moore leadership program and Women in Science for female students, and Spinning Your Web leadership program, RC Xtreme (for extreme sports enthusiasts), and Explore UR World multicultural program for male students.

In 2008, the *Chronicle of Higher Education* spotlighted Richmond's painstaking method of hand-matching roommates for its incoming students. After being admitted to Richmond, students are sent a fifteen-question survey about their habits and preferences and then an open-ended essay that gives students the freedom to explain their aspirations and personality quirks. The method seems to work, and many students choose to live with their freshman roommates during subsequent years.

The campus itself is set about six miles from downtown Richmond in a 350-acre wooded landscape. Stately red-brick buildings are hidden among the tall pine trees. A man-made lake separates what was once Richmond College and Westhampton College. Today most of the academic buildings lie on one side of the lake and most of the residential buildings on the other. To cross from one side to another, students can pass through the well-used Tyler Haynes Commons—home to many of the student-life offices, the almost fast-food Tyler's Grill, and also to The Cellar, an on-campus bar where students can enjoy comedy nights, movies, live music, grill-type food—and yes, wine and beer.

Drinking is a problem. According to the most recent drinking survey conducted by the Dean's Office, in the first two months of the school year, eighteen students had already been taken to the hospital for alcohol-related illnesses. Eighty-three percent of UR students drink, consuming on average 5.6 drinks per party. However, drinking arrests are declining on campus. The university has been under pressure to enact Good Samaritan policies that will allow a student to contact emergency services for an intoxicated friend without fear of retribution from the school.

Says a student, "There are basically two Richmonds. A party scene, drinking on frat row. Then there's the art shows, dinners, music. You can choose one or the other." Some 26 percent of women pledge sororities, and 20 percent of men join fraternities. While these houses embark on many worthy service projects, much of the drinking also happens at Greek events, to which independent students are also invited. No Greek houses are on campus; fraternities maintain special houses for parties and social events. Fraternities even run shuttles between campus housing and their lodges for parties and game-day festivities.

South

Richmond hosts nearly 300 other student clubs and organizations, from the academic—Ambassador Club, Classics Club, Debate Team, Model UN—to the cultural—African Students Alliance Sankofa, West Indian Lynk, Asian Student Union, and the Horo Bulgarian Dance Club. Service clubs include ESL Tutor Project, Relay for Life of UR, Habitat for Humanity, Camp Kesem, and Volunteer Action Council. A few performance groups (Ngoma African Dance Company, Off the Cuff and Sirens *a cappella*, University Band, Dance, and Jazz Ensembles, Wind Ensemble, and University Players) allow musicians and dancers to exhibit their skills.

Politically minded groups include the Young Democrats, VOX (Voices for Planned Parenthood), Spiders for Life, Amnesty International, SSTOP (Students Stopping the Trafficking of People), SASD (Student Alliance for Sexual Diversity), Global Health & Human Rights Club, and College Republicans. Although liberal organizations greatly outnumber conservative, students say the campus is divided between strong factions of both, but the student body as a whole is for the most part apathetic. As usual, the administration and faculty leans more to the left than the student body.

Many club sports are on offer at UR, from cheerleading and equestrian to crew, ice hockey, martial arts, rugby, swimming, and dance. The school's Weinstein Center for Recre-

ACADEMIC REQUIREMENTS

All students at University of Richmond face an abbreviated core curriculum and worthy distributional requirements:

- "First-Year Core Course" (two semesters).
- "Expository Writing."
- At least one foreign language course at the intermediate level (students may test out).
- One course in historical studies, chosen from options like "The Classical Tradition," "Witchcraft and Its Interpreters," "History of Judaism," and "Native American Religions."
- One class in literary studies. Options range widely from "Shakespeare" to "Queers in Religion" and "The Black Vernacular."
- One course in natural science. Choices include "Astrophysics," "Emerging Infectious Diseases," and "Chemistry Detectives: Solving Real-World Puzzles."
- One class in social analysis. Options include "Principles of Microeconomics," "Dining and Drinking in Classical Antiquity," "Sexual Violence and War," and "News, Media, and Society."
- One course in symbolic reasoning, such as "Elementary Symbolic Logic" or "Minds and Machines" (a computer science class).
- One class in visual and performing arts. Selections include "Greek Art and Archaeology," "Music Fundamentals," "Plautus," and "Introduction to Costume."
- A wellness requirement. First-semester freshmen must complete an alcohol education class and two health workshops on topics like nutrition, fitness, sex, and stress management. The classes are ninety minutes long, run once weekly for six weeks, and do not count for credit.

South

YELLOW LIGHT

The Foundation for Individual Rights in Education warns that the University of Richmond has a questionable commitment to free speech because of its broadly written policy concerning harassment, bias, and hate speech, which deems it illegal for a student to make "unwelcome or offensive comments about a person's clothing, body or personal life," including "terms of endearment" or comments that "may be considered offensive or hostile, even though some staff or students might not find them objectionable." Such guidelines lend themselves much too easily to abuse.

But Richmond will defend some forms of offensive speech. In 2009, Professor Bertram Ashe taught an English course called "Geeks and Social Misfits in Society," which included required reading of notorious cartoonist Robert Crumb. The artist was later invited to speak at the campus's Modlin Center for the Arts, and Professor Ashe's students were required to attend. The school's art museum hosted a display of Crumb's cartoons during the same semester. Crumb's work has been lambasted by various groups for being misogynistic (he has illustrated sexual abuse on several occasions) and racist, and many student groups were outraged at the school's toleration of the course, lecture, and exhibit. The university defended Ashe, stating that intellectual freedom demands that even controversial figures be allowed a place in academic discourse.

ation and Wellness offers a three-court gymnasium, indoor track, six-lane pool with low and high dive, cardio and weight room, racquetball courts, massage therapy room, and game room with pool and ping-pong tables, televisions, and video games. Group exercise classes are available at no charge to students and entail everything from Pilates and zumba to Body Pump weight conditioning.

The school also hosts an Outdoor Adventure program, which includes ropes courses, day hikes, white-water rafting, biking, and beach trips. For those interested in more competitive activity, the school offers intramural soccer, volleyball, football, basketball, handball, floor hockey, and softball, as well as mini-tournaments in racquetball, swimming, golf, and basketball.

The University of Richmond competes in NCAA Division I competition through the Atlantic 10 conference, offering eighteen varsity sports. Richmond gained its team name and unique mascot, the Spiders, in 1893— when its baseball players, with their long striped arms, reminded onlookers of those critters. Men's basketball and football are still the most popular sports and in 2008 the Spiders won the NCAA Football Championship Subdivision (I-AA) national championship in football. Men and women compete in basketball, cross-country, golf, soccer, tennis, and track and field. Men also play baseball and football, while women are offered field hockey, lacrosse, and swimming and diving.

The university is set apart from the city and abutted by a country club. In 2009, the university reported one forcible sex offense, two aggravated assaults, thirteen burglaries, and sixteen car thefts on campus. One student tells us, "My grandma tells me not to walk around campus at night, but I do, and I feel perfectly fine. I've never heard of any problems at all." However, fall 2010 saw an increase in crime (with eight cases of reported assault from September 3–19 alone).

For the 2010–11 academic year, students faced a hefty tuition of $41,610, with room and board costs of $8,810. However, the university is generous with scholarships. One in fifteen students receives a full-tuition merit scholarship, and two-thirds receive some type of financial aid. Students coming from low-income families are awarded aid packages funded by grants (not loans) that cover full tuition, room and board. The average student- loan debt for a UR graduate is about $20,000.

University of the South

Sewanee, Tennessee • www.sewanee.edu

Mind of the South

The University of the South, commonly called Sewanee, really is unique. Geographically isolated yet not too remote, the Domain (as the campus is called) is adorned with beautiful buildings and 13,000 acres of forest and fields. In 1941, poet William Alexander Percy wrote of his alma mater:

> It's a long way away, even from Chattanooga, in the middle of woods, on top of a bastion of mountains crenelated with blue coves. It is so beautiful that people who have been there always, one way or another, come back. For such as can detect apple green in an evening sky, it is Arcadia—not the one that never used to be, but the one that many people always live in; only this one can be shared.

Sewanee was established by the southern dioceses of the Episcopal Church just in time to be shuttered by the Civil War. It reconvened in 1868 with nine students and four professors. Oxford and Cambridge universities sent books to help stock the struggling school's library, and with time and dedication Sewanee became a seat of learning and maturation for generations of southern men. It became coed in 1969 and abolished mandatory Saturday classes in the 1980s.

Sewanee has thus far maintained an atmosphere of high respect for the life of the mind. Its students are intellectually curious and its faculty inviting and eager to teach. Students usually dress up for class and honor students wear black gowns for special or official occasions. The school is a warm, friendly community. If it can avoid shedding its traditions to placate the insatiable devotees of multiculturalism, Sewanee will remain in the best sense a university of the South.

Academic Life: Shakespeare and Chaucer by popular demand

A student who thirsts for knowledge and is ready to learn is naturally easier to teach, so that's the kind of student Sewanee tries to recruit. "The approach to education here is intellectual, not mechanical," says a professor in the sciences. "Some students think about the practical so little that they're scrambling for jobs the last semester they're here." Not that Sewanee alums have too much trouble in that department: 98 percent are either employed or in graduate school within a year of graduating.

As it stands, Sewanee establishes a solid educational foundation and stresses the importance of good writing skills. The school requires all students—even those majoring in the sciences—to take an introductory composition class and at least two courses designated as "writing intensive." The best way to satisfy Sewanee's distribution requirements is to take the Interdisciplinary Humanities track. The four chronologically arranged courses begin with "Tradition and Criticism in Western Culture—the Ancient World" and continues with courses in the medieval and early modern periods, then the "Modern World—Romantic to Postmodern." In these courses, students fulfill four distribution requirements while reading the Great Books and exploring the art, history, politics, and music of each period. One of Sewanee's twenty-five Rhodes scholars, Robin Rotman, says of this program: "Humanities has helped me understand what it means to be a human being, living here and now, based on the cultural landscape of the past."

Despite its small size (1,469 undergraduates plus a tiny seminary program that qualifies Sewanee as a university), Sewanee has educational opportunities across the curriculum, even in its smallest departments. The philosophy department has just four faculty members and three visiting professors, yet it offers a major and a minor.

The English department—the most popular major on campus—has been home over the years to many literary figures of national note, including William Alexander Percy, Andrew Lytle, Allen Tate, and Caroline Gordon. Home to the nation's oldest and most prestigious literary quarterly, the *Sewanee Review*, the English department is traditional in focus. Its requirements are excellent, including two Shakespeare courses and at least two courses in English literature before 1750. The library stores an extensive collection of original Faulkner papers, which are studied in relevant courses. The university's School of Letters offers a summer master's program in English and creative writing.

History majors are required to declare a focus on the history of the United States, Europe, Great Britain, or Africa/Asia/Latin America, and then take at least five courses in this concentration and four outside of it. The political science department is excellent as well, requiring all majors to take classes in American political philosophy, the U.S. Consti-

VITAL STATISTICS

Religious affiliation: *Episcopal*
Total enrollment: *1,543*
Total undergraduates: *1,469*
SAT/ACT midranges: CR: *570–690*, M: *580–570*; ACT: *26–30*
Applicants: *2,488*
Applicants accepted: *64%*
Accepted applicants who enrolled: *26%*
Tuition and fees: *$35,862*
Room and board: *$10,250*
Freshman retention rate: *89%*
Graduation rate: *75% (4 yrs.), 82% (6 yrs.)*
Courses with fewer than 20 students: *72%*
Student-faculty ratio: *10:1*
Courses taught by graduate students: *none*
Most popular majors: *English, social sciences, history*
Students living on campus: *96%*
Guaranteed housing for four years? *yes*
Students in fraternities: *70%* in sororities: *68%*

tution, political theory, comparative politics, and international politics.

The environmental studies program, which now offers four majors (environmental policy, ecology and biodiversity, natural resources and the environment, and environmental chemistry), is also said to be excellent; the university's immense land holdings are an asset to the program. The department is interdisciplinary; faculty members are on staff in other departments, such as anthropology, biology, forestry, and geology.

Sewanee describes its admissions as "quite selective," and one freshman says, "Among my friends there is a general feeling of being overworked. Sewanee prides itself on preventing grade inflation." In the past few years, however, some lowering of standards has been alleged. The school now offers a women's studies minor, and other majors are changing for the worse, too. "New faculty members are often allowed to teach courses that they create, and the coherence of many majors in the humanities has been lost or severely damaged," a professor says. "There is no sense among the younger faculty of what a major should consist of, and the older members of the faculty seem willing to let the young have their way. Sewanee is experiencing ten years late what other liberal arts colleges have experienced."

Most students still report positive experiences at the school. As one student tells us, "I have had great experiences in many areas of study. One of the best was the independent study that was created for seven students who wanted to study biblical Greek. It opened a whole other reading of the New Testament for everyone in that class."

The extent to which academic fetishes like "multiculturalism" and "diversity" are catching on at Sewanee is a subject of some dispute. One professor notes that these terms "are seldom heard and affect the curriculum in minor ways if at all. Most efforts to import cultural diversity actually originate with the students involved in a handful of extracurricular groups." But another faculty member disagrees, insisting that "the ideas behind the words are having an impact."

Yet both of these professors say that the quality of the school's curriculum has been preserved nonetheless. "Our liberal arts curriculum is still strongly oriented toward the cultural legacy of Europe and toward canonical texts in most disciplines," another professor insists. "This is a campus where the most popular major is English and where the two most popular classes in that major are Shakespeare and Chaucer." According to one student: "The strongest points of the English major are the emphasis on writing and scholarly knowledge over a wide base of literature. The weakest point would be the lack of direction provided to students about what to do with their knowledge after graduation."

Students report that they feel a sense of connection with faculty. In part, relationships with teachers grow as students assist with faculty research or take independent-study classes. But one professor says the close connection is a fruit of the small community: "We see students outside the classroom all the time. Interaction with students is not only common; it's expected." Another professor says that Sewanee has "enough serious students who are grateful for the leisure to study to make teaching here rewarding." Freshmen are assigned faculty advisors by dormitory, so small groups of hallmates normally share both faculty advisors and an upperclassman proctor. After the first year, students are welcome to choose a faculty advisor and to change advisors at any time. Students say their advisors are knowledgeable and willing to offer support and guidance. The student-faculty ratio is a strong 10 to 1, and the average class size is seventeen.

One undergrad emphasizes the closeness between students and faculty: "Student-professor relationships are one of the best things about Sewanee. . . . It's not unusual to meet a professor at the local coffee shop just for a talk, or to have dinner in his home with a couple of other students, or to run into him at the basketball game, or to babysit his kids. All classes are taught by professors, never graduate students. I definitely consider a couple of professors my mentors." Another undergrad agrees: "It is hard to single out just one professor because they have all been helpful in any way possible. They love the students—and that is why they are here."

Students recommend among teachers John Palisano in biology; Sewanee's 2009–10 Teacher of the Year, Bran Potter, in forestry and geology; Harold Goldberg, Charles Perry, Woody Register, and Susan Ridyard in history; James Peters in philosophy; Gayle McKeen in political science; Timothy Keith-Lucas in psychology; Gerald Smith in religion; and Thomas Carlson, Pamela Macfie, Wyatt Prunty, and Dale Richardson in English.

Sewanee teachers are said to be more politically liberal than students, but not across the board. While most faculty members are genuinely fair-minded, one instructor is known to penalize a grade if a student refuses to use neutered, feminist English. "I'm not sure that any Sewanee department is 'politicized' in that it is dominated by an intolerant leftist agenda," says a faculty member. But so much is in transition now at the school that it's hard to say where the school will stand when many of the senior faculty members retire; they tend to be more conservative than the new hires, our sources report. One faculty member says, "A great deal could change very quickly after that, and I might be giving very different answers. . . . But for now, Sewanee is a good and valuable place."

One student says, "My experience has been that Sewanee is truly a community. Instead of political correctness, there is concern for people; diversity is accepted because people are accepted as they are. The general attitude toward different opinions (political, religious, or otherwise) in the classroom is that any position is welcome as long as it is well thought out, and pretty much any germane discussion is welcome as long as it is respectful." Adds another, "Most of my classes stay away from politics. It enters in where necessary, such as in political science, economics, etc. However, there are some places where politics would not be expected, but are present, such as education courses and biology."

The university offers opportunities for study abroad through its own programs and through partnerships with other colleges and universities. Students enrolled in the European studies program choose one of two study options, "Ancient Greece and Rome: The

Foundations of Western Civilization" or "Western Europe in the Middle Ages and the Renaissance," and spend four weeks at Sewanee before heading overseas to York, Durham, and Oxford, followed by five weeks on the Continent.

Students in all majors are required to reach the intermediate, fourth-semester level in a foreign language. Sewanee offers majors in French, Spanish, German, Ancient Greek, Latin, and Russian, as well as study in Italian, Chinese, and Japanese.

Student Life: Masters of their domain

The campus at Sewanee is about as pleasant a place as you can find—unless you're a hopeless city slicker. Perched on a flat-topped mountain in the Cumberland Plateau of southern Tennessee, Sewanee is a good distance from any urban center: Chattanooga is fifty-five miles to the east, and Nashville is ninety-two miles in the other direction. Students don't seem fazed by the relative isolation: "There are a lot of options if you need to get 'off the Mountain' for a day or a weekend," says one. The 13,000 acres known as the University Domain contain the town of Sewanee, the college campus, and plenty of the great outdoors. Town-gown relations are nearly perfect—and the university manages the town. Students volunteer at the fire department, serve on emergency medical service teams, tutor children at nearby Sewanee Elementary School, and visit the elderly at the Sewanee Senior Citizens' Center.

The school provides so many extracurricular options that four years isn't enough to sample them all. "The *joie de vivre* is remarkably similar to what I remember" from a generation ago, says one alumnus. "So many events are scheduled during the weekends that we are not likely to become a suitcase college," a professor says. In fact, another professor says the residential-life office faces problems each Christmas and spring break in getting students out of their dorms. "And many of the students do anything they can think of to remain on campus during the summer," she says.

In their free time—besides studying—students participate in nearly a hundred special interest clubs like the university orchestra, community service organizations, and sports teams. For politically minded students, Sewanee is home to College Republicans, College Democrats, and College Libertarians, as well as a Model UN group. The school has three student-run publications: the *Cap and Gown*, the annual publication of the student body recounting the year's activities; the *Mountain Goat*, a literary magazine published once a semester; and the *Sewanee Purple*, a bimonthly student newspaper. There are dozens of community service organizations that administer to the homeless, the poor, the elderly, the disabled, and at-risk youth.

Greek life is very popular with 75 percent of students counting themselves as members. The twelve fraternity and nine sorority houses are on campus, and most parties are open to nonmembers. "There is a strong frat scene, and little else," says one student. "However, there is very little pressure on those who do not want to drink. Many people participate in the social scene and do not drink." Of course, for those who do, help is at hand: "BACCHUS is an organization that encourages responsible drinking behavior within the campus community by providing safe rides on campus," the school reports. "The Greek system is very large at Sewanee, but all the parties are 'open'; you don't have to belong to the fraternity or sorority to go to the party and to be welcomed," a student says.

Sewanee fields eleven men's and thirteen women's NCAA III varsity sports teams and hosts the men's and women's intercollegiate club sports of fencing, lightweight crew, martial arts, and rugby. Students also participate in the intramural sports of basketball, football, golf, racquetball, soccer, squash, softball, tennis, and volleyball.

For outdoor enthusiasts, the Domain is heaven. The Sewanee Outing Program, which organizes group activities and loans climbing, hiking, camping, and caving equipment, points out that the 8,000 acres of undeveloped land include "fifty climbing sites, thirteen lakes, twenty-seven caves, sixty-five miles of trails . . . and countless streams and waterfalls." In addition to the Outing Program, the school offers Canoe Club, Crew Club, Climbing Club, and Paintball Club, as well as a Cycling Team and Ultimate Frisbee.

Wide expansive lawns are ringed with huge trees and numerous flowers, and most buildings are of native sandstone. These include a new dining hall that looks a century old and harks back to the age of collegiate Gothic. An on-campus movie theater provides convenient entertainment every night except Thursday, and the Sewanee Performing Arts Series sponsors six major theater, music, or dance performances each year, and theater arts majors can elect to spend a semester of their junior year in New York City at the Michael Howard Studio. Sewanee also hosts several academic events every year, including the

---

ACADEMIC REQUIREMENTS

In lieu of a genuine core curriculum, the University of the South imposes a respectable set of distribution requirements. Effective with the incoming class of 2010, all students must take:

- "Literature and Composition."
- Courses or tests to prove proficiency in a foreign language through the intermediate level.
- One class in mathematics. Choices include "Topics in Mathematics" and "Linear Algebra."
- Two courses in natural sciences (at least one with a lab). Options include "General Physics" and "Comparative Sexual Behavior" (which thankfully does not include a lab).
- One introductory course in history, such as "Topics in Western Civilization" or "History of the United States."
- One course in social sciences. "World Politics" or "Global Gender Issues" would do.
- One course in philosophy or religion, such as "Ancient Philosophy from Homer to Augustine" or "Old Testament."
- One fine arts course in art, art history, theater, or music, ranging from "Greek and Roman Art" to "The Films of Alfred Hitchcock."
- Two courses designated as writing intensive. Class examples include "Origins and Development of the English Novel" and "Faulkner."
- Two courses in physical education. Students may participate in ballet, tennis, fencing, aerobics, zumba, jazz, swimming, biking, golf, badminton, squash, yoga, and Pilates, among many other activities.

GREEN LIGHT

"Sewanee's students are for the most part rich kids from traditional, conservative, southern families," says a faculty member. "That's just the nature of the place." Generally, students are "moderately right leaning," says a student. "There tends to be a strong majority of students who favor conservative social positions. . . . However, there is a large minority of center-left students as well." Many of the student political groups are issue based rather than partisan, although there are both College Republicans and College Democrats on campus. Both conservative and liberal students generally feel comfortable voicing their views. According to another undergrad, "School officials encourage debates, but they are not well attended, with the majority of students being conservative, and the debates more often focused around liberal-leaning topics."

Sewanee Writers' Conference (founded with money from the estate of Tennessee Williams) and the Medieval Colloquium, both of which draw nationally known scholars and writers to campus. Those with vocal talent may join the University Choir, which sings for the services in All Saints' Chapel.

Ninety-six percent of students reside on campus, with only a limited number of seniors allowed off campus. Students seem to love living at the school, perhaps because Sewanee offers plenty of housing options. The university offers more single-sex dormitories than it does coed living spaces. Most dorms are arranged in suites with a common bathroom for every one or two students. Some of the residence halls were converted from the campus's previous incarnations as a hospital, an inn, and a military academy. Emery Hall, once a morgue, is now a small women's dormitory. Unsurprisingly, it is haunted.

"The life of Sewanee revolves around the dorms," reports an undergrad. "All students gather in them, study in them, live, work, play in them. The student aides, called 'proctors' and 'assistant proctors,' are dedicated to their dorms and want them to be the best places to both play and work, and they strive to make sure that their dorm maintains a great reputation during their time as proctors. Visitation ends at midnight during the week and at 1:00 AM on the weekends. Depending on the specific dorm, this may or may not be strictly enforced. Many dorms are not single sex, but they divide the sexes by floor."

Sewanee welcomes many different religious activities and groups, and although the school is officially Episcopalian, other denominations and faiths are supported. Baptist Christian Ministries and the Sewanee Catholic Community are active student groups, as are Fellowship of Christian Athletes and the Presbyterian Campus Ministry. The university bulletin reports that about a third of Sewanee students are Episcopalian. Sewanee's campus has three chapels—St. Luke's Chapel, the Chapel of the Apostles, and All Saints' Chapel. There are two traditional Eucharist services every week and an "informal folk Mass" called Growing in Grace. The school also supports Bible studies, the Canterbury Group (Episcopal), a Centering Prayer group, and other activities. Sewanee even refers to its academic year with terms from the church calendar—the year is divided into the Advent and Easter semesters, not fall and spring. As the school is owned by the Episcopal Church, "there is a heavy influence of that denomination, and students are presumed to have a working knowledge of the Bible, especially when used in class to explain allusions, et cetera. There is no pressure placed on the students, however, and all students are encouraged to worship if and how they choose," observes one student.

Crime is remarkably low. In 2009, the school reported one forcible sex offense, one car theft, one arson, and twenty burglaries on campus. The Sewanee Police Department provides twenty-four-hour patrol protection to the campus, school property, parking lots, dormitories, fraternities, and sororities. Says one student, "Crime is of very little concern. If there is any criminal activity, the police send out an e-mail warning students, and then (normally) thefts cease quickly. Many doors remain unlocked."

Tuition in 2010–11 was $35,862, and room and board $10,250. However, admissions are need blind, and the school uses its endowment of $246 million to provide 100 percent of each student's demonstrated need. There are also generous merit-based scholarships available. Some 54 percent of students receive need-based financial aid, and the average student-loan debt of a recent grad is $18,717.

Tulane University

New Orleans, Louisiana • www.tulane.edu

Coming up for air

In the aftermath of Hurricane Katrina, Tulane University was faced with the challenge of rebuilding for the second time in its history. Founded in 1834 as the Medical College of Louisiana, it closed during the Union occupation of New Orleans. In 1884, it was reorganized as the private Tulane University of Louisiana and grew into one of the country's leading private research institutions. Today the Carnegie Foundation for the Advancement of Teaching places it in the top 2 percent of schools for research activity nationwide.

Following the devastation of Katrina, the school faced crushing difficulties: some 80 percent of the main campus was underwater, which caused over $160 million in property damage and $125 million in lost research assets. But the loyalty of students, faculty, administrators, and alumni pulled the university through: by January 2006, Tulane reported that nearly 94 percent of its students had returned. In January 2009, the school reported that applications to the school had more than doubled since Katrina, a trend that continues. President Scott Cowen says that current "applicants, both in terms of numbers . . . and quality, are nothing short of phenomenal."

Much of the credit for Tulane's rapid comeback goes to Cowen, who toughed out the disaster himself. A massive restructuring created a smaller but stronger university, with a respectable set of distribution requirements, mandatory public service, a residency requirement, and more opportunities for interdisciplinary studies.

Academic Life: Learning to serve

The Newcomb-Tulane College oversees the undergraduate schools of architecture, business, liberal arts, public health and tropical medicine, and science and engineering. In addition to the requirements of the individual schools, all students must complete the distribution requirements, which are worthy but fall far short of a real core curriculum.

Students seeking a broad liberal education would do well to apply to the school's honors program, where "everyone works hard—students and professors," according to a teacher. Honors students must complete four honors of graduate-level courses before their senior year and maintain a GPA of 3.6 or higher. Courses are taught by full-time faculty members and are generally limited to twenty students. A recurring honors course offering is

South

the two-semester "Community, Polity, and Citizenship," which includes readings from Homer, Plato, Virgil, the Qur'an, Dante, Teresa of Avila, and the Bible during the first semester, then Machiavelli, Rousseau, Dostoevsky, and Nietzsche (among others) in the second. Honors seniors complete a thesis or research project of around seventy pages.

Tulane InterDisciplinary Experience Seminars (TIDES) include some of the school's most distinguished faculty. Students choose from over eighty topics, ranging from "Law and Order," "New Orleans Cities of the Dead: Cemetery Architecture & Its Cultural Legacy," and "The Physics of Baseball" to "Chinese Cinema," "The Dead Sea Scrolls," and "Confronting Our Capacity for Evil." These courses offer only one credit hour and meet in small groups of about fifteen to twenty students.

Tulane recognizes that it has an important role in rebuilding the city, so it has added a public-service requirement to its curriculum and recently inaugurated the Center for Public Service to oversee its implementation. Even though Katrina is fading into history—the class of 2009 was the last class to experience the effects of the storm firsthand, "Memories of Katrina are going to be there to shape our thinking here at Tulane," a professor says. "We're tied to our city more closely as a result of Katrina." Another professor notes that the stronger emphasis on community service at Tulane is also attracting a new kind of student—one "who is academically talented and intellectually curious, but also possesses strong interests in public service and the community."

In order to graduate, students must maintain a portfolio of their public-service experiences, complete a service learning course, and participate in one approved program from the Center for Public Service. A wide range of courses include a service learning component: sociology students, for example, may assist the New Orleans city attorney's office in rehabilitating a neighborhood, while seniors in biomedical engineering may participate in a yearlong design project.

Tulane ranks among the country's top universities, noted for its programs in architecture, international development, philosophy, political economy, Latin American studies, and economics. "The political economy major is particularly distinctive," says a professor. Students report that the economics department is largely free market in orientation, a rare thing these days. Students in this field can participate in a summer internship program (with grants of $2,000) and a study-abroad program at the Institute for Economic

VITAL STATISTICS

Religious affiliation: *none*
Total enrollment: *11,464*
Total undergraduates: *7,160*
SAT/ACT midranges: CR: *620–700*, M: *620–700*; ACT: *28–31*
Applicants: *39,920*
Applicants accepted: *26%*
Accepted applicants who enrolled: *14%*
Tuition and fees: *$41,884*
Room and board: *$9,824*
Freshman retention rate: *91%*
Graduation rate: *60% (4 yrs.), 73% (6 yrs.)*
Courses with fewer than 20 students: *not provided*
Student-faculty ratio: *8:1*
Courses taught by graduate students: *not provided*
Most popular majors: *finance, psychology, English*
Students living on campus: *57%*
Guaranteed housing for four years? *no*
Students in fraternities: *25%* in sororities: *30%*

1. Classical Studies 4060, Classical Epic
2. Philosophy 2010, History of Ancient Philosophy
3. Classical Studies 2100/2200, Introduction to the Hebrew Bible/New Testament: An Historical Introduction
4. History 303, Early Medieval and Byzantine Civilization from Constantine to the Crusades (closest match)
5. Political Science 478, Modern Political Theory
6. English 4460/4470, Shakespeare I/II
7. History 1410, United States History: Colonization to 1865
8. Philosophy 310, Nineteenth-Century European Philosophy

and Political Studies in London and Cambridge. In this department, students particularly recommend Professor Mary Olson.

The political science department is "filled with young and enthusiastic teachers that make classes very enjoyable," a student says. The department regularly offers a course called "Political Thought in the West," which covers Western thinkers such as Plato, Aristotle, Locke, Berkeley, and others. However, the political science major requirements are weak: students must take one class each in American and comparative political processes and institutions, a course in international politics, and a political theory class, as well as six electives in political science. One could study the Constitution in "American Government" class or dabble in "Environmental Politics and Policy." One's theory course could be "Greek Foundations of Western Political Thought" or the tiresome "Feminist Political Theory." Political science students recommend teachers Brian Brox, Thomas Langston, and Gary Remer.

Much more rigorous is the political economy division, which "provides an integrated interdisciplinary education in which majors take core courses in the field of political economy and other courses from related disciplines, including economics, political science, history, and philosophy," a teacher reports. In this program, students recommend Martyn Thompson and Mark Vail.

The history department is also strong. A student says, "The history department boasts some of the best teachers at the school. . . . I also appreciate that the history department at Tulane takes a classic approach." According to one professor, there's almost a built-in preference for the Western tradition at Tulane. "The (history) curriculum as a whole has made a huge investment in the Western tradition. That's the way the liberal arts were structured in the 1950s and 1960s, and that's the way it pretty much remains today." Majors must take classes in three of the department's six geographic fields, which include the United States, ancient and medieval Europe, the Middle East/North Africa, modern Europe, Latin America, and Africa. They will complete four classes in one field, three in another, and two in a third, as well as one from any field (which expands to include Asia, the Mediterranean, and the Atlantic). Although a student could study history with classes like "History of Voodoo and Other African Derived Religions in the Americas," classes like "Imperial Spain," "The High Roman Empire," and "Dictators" are more common. Recommended professors include George L. Bernstein, James Boyden, Emily Clark, Kenneth Harl, Colin M. MacLachlan, Larry Powell, Samuel C. Ramer, and Randy Sparks.

The English major at Tulane offers little in the way of real requirements, only calling for ten courses that include the introductory "Literary Investigations" class, an introduction to British or American literature, a pre-1800 literature class, a course in American literature, and a senior capstone. Although the department does offer two Shakespeare classes (one per semester) and one in Chaucer, most of the courses are lighter fare. "Children's Lit," "American Ethnic Literature," a great number of creative writing classes, "Literary New Orleans," "Literature and Film: Freud and Hitchcock," "Women in Stand-up Comedy," and "Performance Studies" fill the roster of available English classes. Students recommend Michael Kuczynski, who teaches British literature (including Chaucer) and a bibliography class.

Tulane's student-faculty ratio is an impressive 8 to 1, and most teachers are said to be eager to assist students. One grad student says, "In my experience, the professors have been *extremely* accessible and helpful." Another student says, "Tulane is an undergraduate-oriented school. This means that most undergraduate classes are taught by full professors, not teaching assistants. I have made friendships and worked on a close basis with full professors." A professor says, "Tulane students are as competent and serious as the best students at the best places in the country. They have a real seriousness about studying." A student says, "Everybody could have gone to an Ivy or a more selective school, but they came to Tulane—not because of the money, just for the experience, the town, the life."

Some of Tulane's best teachers in other departments, students and faculty say, are Ronna Burger, and Eric Mack in philosophy; James McGuire in physics; and Harvey and Victoria Bricker in anthropology (both emeritus).

For those interested in study-abroad programs, Tulane offers semester-, summer-, and year-long programs. Study-abroad options span the globe, from Ghana to Singapore. Tulane provides a number of foreign language options. Majors are offered in French, German, Italian, Portuguese, Russian, and Spanish. Students may take classes in any of these languages, as well as Hebrew, Latin, and Ancient Greek.

Student Life: Love in the ruins

Most of Tulane's beautiful campus and the surrounding neighborhoods are functioning at pre-Katrina levels. In fact, in the wake of the disaster, the campus has seen major improvements, such as a $7.5 million renovation to Turchin Stadium and a rebuilt university center, the Lavin-Bernick Center for University Life. Tulane is located in a part of New Orleans that was built above sea level and hence was not as heavily damaged as other parts of the city. Just across St. Charles Avenue, which borders the campus, is the exquisite Audubon Park, which includes a public golf course, jogging and walking trails, and lagoons. Across Magazine Street at the opposite end of the park is Audubon Zoo, one of the nation's finest.

For those students who aren't scared off by the sight of muddy, abandoned neighborhoods—mostly in the notoriously impoverished Ninth Ward—New Orleans is still an exciting and fun-filled place, perhaps to a fault. Tulane was long notorious as a party school whose students somehow found time to do a little homework. Students still say alcohol plays a tremendous role in most of their social lives. The university has tried to steer students away from the hard stuff by banning alcohol on campus for underage students. One junior says that the prevalence of drinking has decreased some and mostly moved off campus, where alcohol is easy to obtain. Other students insist that drinking doesn't get in the way of class work. "Tulane has students that do nothing but party," says one student, "but also a lot of students who live in the library. Although the party-going students are better known because they are louder, students wishing to spend long nights in study will not go unaccompanied. I think this mix is healthy."

Although around a third of Tulane's students reportedly join one of twenty-four Greek organizations, most don't live with their fraternities or sororities. None of the sororities have official houses, and few fraternity brothers opt to live in their off-campus houses. While this doesn't stop the Greeks from throwing large parties, New Orleans itself tends to offer more alluring social options. After the school's Pi Kappa Alpha chapter was shut down in 2008 because of a hazing scandal, the university purchased the fraternity's house and has converted it into a campus police station in the middle of fraternity row, further dampening the liveliness of the Greek scene.

Beyond the party life, students can find hundreds of ways to become involved at Tulane. The school has an active student government, as well as numerous clubs and organizations. Academic clubs range from the Business and Law Society and Classics Club to the Women in Science group or Psychology Club. Multicultural organizations include a multicultural council, and black, Asian, Chinese, Vietnamese, and Indian groups. Interest organizations vary from the Anime and Manga Society, Juggling Club, and Disability Union to the Foreign Film Society and Cheese Club.

Tulane provides more political organizations than the typical university. College Democrats and Republicans are represented, as well as a Socialist Organization, pro-Israel club, pro-life club, an Environmental Action League, and chapters of Amnesty Interna-

---

ACADEMIC REQUIREMENTS

Tulane's "core curriculum" is really a set of distributional requirements, many of which may be fulfilled by fine courses:

- An introductory writing course.
- One to four courses in a foreign language.
- One class in "quantitative reasoning," which may be a statistics, logic, calculus, or "theory of information" class, among others.
- Two classes in science and mathematics, including astronomy, biology, chemistry, physics, environmental sciences, and psychology.
- Four courses in "cultural knowledge," comprising one class each from the humanities and fine arts and two from the social sciences. Students must choose at least one course from the European tradition and one course outside the European tradition.
- A public-service component.
- One Tulane Interdisciplinary Experience Seminar.
- A senior capstone experience, as set by one's major department.

tional and the ACLU. Performance groups are few, but students may join the Shockwave dance group, or the PULSE Street Drumline, THEM!, and Green Envy *a cappella* groups.

For students interested in service, opportunities range from Habitat for Humanity, Green club, Face AIDS, and Red Cross to the Rotary International club and Hunger and Homelessness Action Team. Tulane also provides the chance to get involved in media, including the *Hullabaloo* newspaper, a literary society, and WTUL 91.5 FM.

Tulane offers religious support to its students as well. The university plays host to a Muslim student association, as well as a Hillel group and a Chabad Jewish Student Center. Christian organizations include Campus Crusade, Chi Alpha, Fellowship of Christian Athletes, Impact (a black Christian group), and InterVarsity, as well as Baptist, Episcopal, Lutheran, Presbyterian, Catholic, and Methodist centers or groups. Beyond the campus, New Orleans has historic churches and synagogues all around the city, including the gorgeous downtown St. Patrick's parish—one of the few places on earth where the Latin Mass was continuously celebrated after Vatican II.

Tulane's athletic teams, ironically known as the Green Wave, suffered a tremendous setback because of Katrina. From sixteen varsity teams, the school was down to ten (men's baseball and football; men's and women's basketball and cross-country; and women's track and field, volleyball, tennis,

---

GREEN LIGHT

"A political environment at Tulane exists, but it must be sought out," says one student. "Tulane sponsors organizations of different political leanings; the Tulane College Democrats and the Tulane College Republicans are the largest. Most of their political meetings and events, however, are conducted in private. There are very few open protests or demonstrations. For this reason, some go so far as to say that Tulane is politically apathetic. I don't believe this to be true. I think a good political debate is readily available at Tulane, but there is very little in-your-face politics."

Says another student, "It is a real struggle to get anyone but a core few on either side of the aisle interested. Faculty struggle to get students to debate in class, and are often pleased when conservative and libertarian students express their views on a legal subject matter." Tulane itself "encourages debate" and even "went out of its way to ensure that the College Republicans' Ann Coulter event went off without a hitch," he says.

In 2009, the prominent liberal James Carville was hired as a political science professor. The Democratic strategist, who managed or advised both Clintons on their presidential campaigns, has been well-received by students.

---

and golf). However, the school has been strengthening its athletic offerings and currently hosts fourteen Division I programs, with plans to be back up to sixteen by the end of 2011. Although Tulane is committed to its sports, no team has achieved real success in recent years. Prospective students may enjoy the school's intramural or club sports programs. Intramural offerings are considerable, from basketball, tennis, biathlon, and racquetball to flag football, ping-pong, and soccer. Club sports include aikido, gymnastics, rugby, running, lacrosse, cricket, ballroom dancing, and boxing, among many others.

All freshmen and sophomores are required to live on campus—although students may apply for exemption if they are over twenty-one, married, or live locally with a parent or guardian. Students are assigned to a residential college to which they belong throughout their undergraduate years. These colleges help to provide a community and extracurricular activities. Tulane offers a number of on-campus housing options, including coed dorms (the sexes are separated by floor), suites, and apartments. Four theme houses are available: an honors house, a wellness community, a "leadership village," and the Wall Residential college, which hosts a faculty member (with family) along with undergraduates. The all-women Josephine-Louise Hall is a bastion of southern propriety, requiring visitors to register at the front desk from 8:00 PM to 8:00 AM and male visitors to be escorted at all times.

Per capita, post-Katrina New Orleans is among the most violent cities in the nation and has a murder rate nearly double that in the next most dangerous U.S. cities, like Detroit. Students should not avoid Tulane for fear of crime, but they should be extremely careful and remember that, in New Orleans, dangerous neighborhoods sit right next to safer ones. Tulane's own Department of Public Safety includes forty-four full-time commissioned officers, fifteen support staff members, and more than forty part-time student employees. In addition to patrolling the campus twenty-four hours a day, Tulane offers an escort and shuttle service, and blue-light emergency phones are all over campus. On-campus offenses in 2009 included three forcible sex offenses, one aggravated assault, thirty burglaries, 193 incidences of larceny and theft, two incidences of arson, and five stolen cars. Not bad for a school in New Orleans.

Tulane charges Ivy League–level tuition of $41,884, and $9,824 for room and board. For freshmen beginning at Tulane in 2011, loans will be eliminated for those with family incomes of less than $75,000. Some 40 percent of students receive need-based aid, and the average student-loan debt of a recent grad is a typical $23,655.

Vanderbilt University

Nashville, Tennessee • www.vanderbilt.edu

Putting on a Yankee hat

Originally endowed by a New York rail tycoon, Cornelius Vanderbilt, as a gesture of charity after the Civil War, Vanderbilt University garners praise and stands high in national rankings. Vanderbilt's influence on the region is pronounced, since it produces many leaders in business and academia and has a higher national profile than most southern schools. Vanderbilt can also claim some international importance: in October 2006, Muhammad Yunus, Vanderbilt PhD (class of 1971), became the first economist to win the Nobel Prize for Peace. In all, three alumni and four faculty members have been awarded various Nobels, and Vanderbilt has bragging rights as the alma mater of over two dozen Rhodes scholars and two vice presidents of the United States.

Unfortunately, the school has done much to shed its southern heritage and weaken the emphasis on Western civilization in its liberal arts curriculum. Worried faculty and students see the school remaking itself on the model of northeastern academies, thereby losing what made it distinctive.

Academic Life: Goodbye, Great Books

In the absence of a liberal arts core curriculum, students in Vanderbilt's College of Liberal Arts and Sciences must fulfill a set of broad distribution requirements. Vanderbilt calls these mandates the AXLE Curriculum—short for Achieving eXcellence in Liberal Education. (We are not making this up.) An admissions officer explains that the Vanderbilt curriculum aims to teach students "life skills"—that is, competency in areas like quantitative reasoning, "problem solving," and communication. Vanderbilt claims to recognize the value of a broad liberal arts education—noting that companies recruiting students look for job candidates with a variety of skills, not simply proficiency in one academic discipline. "Majors don't decide what you do," the admissions officer says. Through the distribution requirements, liberal arts students encounter a variety of subjects but, absent a real core curriculum, can fail to meaningfully engage with any of them.

For the writing requirement, students must demonstrate "basic competency in English composition" through SAT or test scores or by taking a basic class, English 100. Beyond that, students must take at least three writing-intensive courses. Qualifying classes are offered

VITAL STATISTICS

Religious affiliation: *none*
Total enrollment: *12,714*
Total undergraduates: *6,879*
SAT/ACT midranges: CR:
   670–760, M: *690–770*;
   ACT: *30–34*
Applicants: *21,811*
Applicants accepted: *81%*
Accepted applicants who
   enrolled: *41%*
Tuition and fees: *$38,952*
Room and board: *$13,058*
Freshman retention rate:
   97%
Graduation rate: *85% (4 yrs.),
   91% (6 yrs.)*
Courses with fewer than 20
   students: *64%*
Student-faculty ratio: *8:1*
Courses taught by graduate
   students: *5%*
Most popular majors: *social
   sciences, engineering,
   interdisciplinary studies*
Students living on campus:
   85%
Guaranteed housing for
   four years? *yes*
Students in fraternities: *35%*
   in sororities: *50%*

in virtually every humanities department. Students must also complete three classes in the humanities or arts and three classes in international cultures, which can range from foreign language classes to international music or literature courses. Additionally, Vanderbilt students take a class in the "history and culture of the United States," three mathematics and natural science classes (one of which requires a lab component), two social science classes, and a "perspectives" class that gives "significant attention to individual and cultural diversity, multicultural interactions, sexual orientation, gender, racial, ethical, religious, and 'Science and Society' issues."

A history major says that some students view distribution requirements as a chore, a hurdle to jump before reaching the real goal—one's major. But another student says, "If you graduate from Vanderbilt with a degree from Arts and Sciences (perhaps excluding women's studies) you will have a great deal of knowledge and be prepared to enter the workforce."

The AXLE requirements allow for so much flexibility that core areas of knowledge—American history, ancient philosophy, European intellectual history, and the like—can easily be avoided. Students could knock off their U.S. history and culture requirement with courses like "Women's Health and Sexuality" or "Rhetoric of the Mass Media." One economics major says, "My course load is quite rigorous by choice, but you could create an easy schedule for yourself with a little research."

Vanderbilt has eliminated its dedicated humanities department, along with courses it used to offer, such as "Great Books of the Western Tradition." What humanities courses remain have been absorbed by the religious studies department. The best alternative still at Vanderbilt covering the Western tradition appears to be the European studies major.

The school has also implemented a new history curriculum, which now offers such gems as "Sexuality and Gender in China." To major in history, students must take five classes in a concentration like Asian, global and transnational, comparative, or European history. They must also complete a history workshop or junior seminar, one or two capstone courses, and two to four electives. Students may also elect to concentrate in economics and history or English and history, which provide unique interdisciplinary paths. They could easily skip all study of the American founding or Western civilization.

The English student at Vanderbilt must choose to concentrate in literary studies, creative writing, or specialized critical studies. Literature majors must first take an introductory class in poetry, literary criticism, or literature and cultural analysis, followed by three classes in pre-1800 literature and one class in "ethnic or non-Western literature." Additionally, students must complete five electives. While the department offers a variety of classes, it fails to acknowledge any kind of literary canon—or require the study of Shakespeare.

One of Vanderbilt's best departments is philosophy, which emphasizes American thought, Continental philosophy, and the history of philosophy. Philosophy majors at Vanderbilt are required to take a course in logic, one in ethics, and at least six hours in the history of philosophy. John Lachs, a distinguished scholar of American philosophy, teaches an interdisciplinary course (together with a historian and an economist) covering the history of the idea of liberty.

In contrast, students view the political science department as having a few good scholars but still suffering from the lingering effects of a war between proponents of a heavily statistical approach and those who favor qualitative and theoretical methods. The political science major calls for two introductory courses, choosing from American government, comparative politics, international politics, and justice. Students must complete an intermediate-level class each in political theory, comparative politics, international politics, and American government and politics, as well as four electives.

Vanderbilt's women's studies department was recently absorbed into the department of sociology. But never fear: such courses as "Pornography and Prostitution in History" will still be offered, as will "Gender, Sexuality, and the Body" and other recondite topics viewed through the lens of toxic ideology.

The Margaret Cuninggim Women's Center, a university-funded organization with its own campus building, holds meetings for Vanderbilt feminists and presents lectures and conferences such as "Gender and Sexuality," sponsored by the Warren Center for the Humanities. Other featured co-curricular programs include studies and activism about sexual health, body image, domestic violence, and lectures like "Homoerotic Flows: Sexuality Studies in Transnational Perspective" and "The Incredible Shrinking Public: The Sexual Politics of Neoliberalism."

Vanderbilt's religious studies department offers a wide array of traditional-sounding courses such as "Themes in the New Testament" and "Christianity in the Reform Era." These come alongside "Ethics and Ecology" and "Marriage in the Ancient Near East and the Hebrew Bible," which ponders the "institution" of marriage (their quotes) to "shed light" on and "reveal its complexities."

Vanderbilt's best professors include the aforementioned John Lachs in philosophy; Michael Bess, David Carlton, and Joel F. Harrington in history; Camilla P. Benbow and

SUGGESTED CORE

1. Classics 240, The Trojan War in History, Art, and Literature (closest match)
2. Philosophy 210, Ancient Philosophy
3. Religious Studies 108/109, Themes in the Hebrew Bible/New Testament
4. Religion 140, Great Books of Literature and Religion
5. Political Science 203, History of Modern Political Philosophy
6. English 210, Shakespeare: Representative Selections
7. History 139/140, America to 1776/U.S. 1776–1877
8. Philosophy 228, Nineteenth-Century Philosophy

Leslie Smith in psychology; Roy Gottfried, Mark Jarman, and John Plummer in English; Robert W. Pitz and Greg Walker in mechanical engineering; Lori A. Troxel in civil and environmental engineering; Douglas Hardin in mathematics; Stephen Buckles and John Vrooman in economics; David Weintraub in physics and astronomy; Robert Innes in human and organizational development; Susan Kevra in the French and Italian department; and Michael Rose in music.

Vanderbilt still places a good deal of emphasis on close relationships between professors and students. Students are very likely to know at least one of their professors from their freshman seminars, which are limited to fifteen students and mostly taught by senior faculty members. "In my experience, the professors are quite approachable," says a student, "I've eaten dinner at the homes of some professors. They give advice if you ask for it, and nine times out of ten, the professors are quite understanding and helpful to students."

On the other hand, other students have complained that "some classes are so big, it's hard to get help when you need it." Overall, however, Vanderbilt has been able to keep classes small, with the student-faculty ratio an impressive 8 to 1. Professors, not graduate teaching assistants, teach 95 percent of undergraduate courses. Graduate students usually lead the weekly discussion sections attached to large lecture courses and grade most tests and papers.

The formal advising program is weak. Each entering freshman is assigned a faculty advisor, who is supposed to help him choose courses and, eventually, a major. Once the student has declared a major, he is assigned to a faculty member within that field. Unfortunately, many students do not meet with their advisors as often as they should—though they are now required to do so before they can register.

As for the courses themselves, a junior says, "My favorite aspect of Vandy is all the opportunities I have to be involved in the extras—like music and athletics—along with my classes. I can do well in my classes and still participate." Another agrees: "The course load here is not so rigorous that students can't find time for extracurriculars and socializing, but succeeding here does take work. The administration pressures departments to avoid the grade inflation that occurs at other schools." But one engineering student complains that "liberal arts majors don't have anywhere near the workload carried by engineers or premed students." (He shouldn't worry; they likely won't earn the same salaries someday, either.)

Vanderbilt encourages students to study abroad, providing month-, summer-, semester-, and year-long programs in twenty-six countries. Students may study in Hungary, the Dominican Republic, Russia, Chile, New Zealand, South Africa, Spain, and China, among others. Depending on the program they choose, students live in dorms, with families, or in apartments (but they may not arrange for their own housing). Just under a third of students choose to study abroad in eighty preapproved programs.

Embarrassingly, there is no foreign language requirement, but interested students can take courses in Ancient Greek, Latin, French, German, Russian, Spanish, Chinese, Catalan, Hebrew, Italian, Japanese, and Portuguese.

Student Life: A night at the Opry

Nashville is an entertainment paradise, at least for country music fans. With the Grand Ole Opry and music performances every evening, as well as a number of other attractions, one would think that many Vanderbilt students would find it hard to stay on campus. But one student says that with their many academic and extracurricular responsibilities, including school-sponsored events like comedy shows and music night at the Pub (an on-campus bar and restaurant), most students venture into the city only about twice a month, and some not at all. Once outside of Nashville, students must drive a ways to get anywhere. Memphis is three hours to the west, and the Great Smoky Mountains are four hours to the east.

The campus is home to many different styles of architecture, some of which do not blend well into a whole. Except for one large lush green lawn, the main campus is quite compact, and one student claims that for Arts and Sciences students, the longest walk from

---

ACADEMIC REQUIREMENTS

In lieu of a core curriculum, Vanderbilt imposes certain distribution requirements. Students in the College of Arts and Sciences must take the following:

- Three courses in humanities and the creative arts. Choices come from most liberal arts departments and are as varied as "The Greek Myths," "Seventeenth-Century Art," "Literature and Law," and "Women and Humor in the Age of TV."
- Three classes in international cultures. Students can study a foreign language or take classes like "The History and Mythology of Black Women," "Contemporary Latin America," or "The Qur'an and Its Interpreters."
- Just one course in the history and culture of the United States. Options range from "U.S. 1776–1877" all the way down to "Feminism and Film."
- Three classes in mathematics and natural sciences, including one lab. Options include "Dynamic Earth," "Biological Anthropology," "General Logic," "Integrative Neuroscience," and "Probability and Statistical Inference."
- Two courses in the social and behavioral sciences. The many options include "Political Parties," "Spanish Translation and Interpretation," "Prison Life," "Money and Banking," and "Principles of Marketing."
- Perspectives. Students must complete a class like "Global Public Health," "Communicating Gender," "History of Fashion," or "Death and Dying in America."

Additionally, students must take three writing courses: a First-Year Writing Seminar ("The Arab-Israeli Conflict," "Neither Jezebel, Mammy, nor Sapphire: African American Women," "Bogus Science"); a 100-level writing course ("Introduction to Philosophy," "Conquest of Mexico," "The Chemistry of Everyday Things," "Darwinian Theory of Evolution"); and either another 100-level course, a 200-level writing course ("Augustan Rome," "Representative American Writers," "Blacks and Money"), or a class in oral communications ("Argumentation and Debate," "Organizational and Managerial Communication").

South

a dorm to a classroom is about five minutes. And that walk will be under trees: the campus has been designated an arboretum since 1988.

Vanderbilt guarantees students housing for four years and requires all unmarried students to live on campus unless they live with their parents or guardians. Students live in any of thirty-four residence halls, which include singles, doubles, efficiency apartments, one- or two-bedroom apartments, suites for six, and lodges that hold ten students. A tour guide claims that in recent years there hasn't been enough interest among students in single-sex dorms for the university to create any new ones, but many of the newer residences have single-sex floors. There are no coed dorm rooms or bathrooms.

Dorm life at Vanderbilt is comfortable, as many students enjoy such amenities as music practice rooms, laundry facilities, study rooms, twenty-four-hour convenience stores, and common social areas. Freshmen live apart from upperclassmen. Vanderbilt has ambitious plans to transform student life through the creation of residential colleges (à la Oxford) that integrate the living and learning environments. This would cluster students and faculty together into relatively small housing groups, thus stressing a greater interaction among faculty and students outside the classroom.

Many students say that campus life revolves around the Greek system; there are sixteen sorority houses and twenty fraternity houses, and over a third of men and half of women join. Not long ago, an article in *Seventeen* portrayed Vanderbilt as having a student body composed of materialistic rich kids. In the article, one student says, "At Vanderbilt University, it's easy to feel like you just landed at a country club." Lately, as the university has tried to bring in a more diverse student body, some faculty leftists have attacked the Greek system as a bastion of elitism. One senior says that the typical Vanderbilt student is "wealthy, conservative, attractive, well-dressed, drives a BMW, and is Greek." (No wonder their teachers are appalled.)

Vandy men wear jackets and ties to football games, and most students are reasonably well dressed for classes. A student complains that "Vanderbilt is a very hierarchically based institution, and people who are not comfortable displaying their wealth and size-two figures should go someplace else."

The Bishop Joseph Johnson Black Cultural Center, named in 1984 for the first black student admitted to Vanderbilt (in 1953), pledges to serve as the "'home away from home' for African-descended students." The center sponsors programs for black students, including a Soul Food Friday social hour, a lecture series featuring black scholars, a tutoring/mentoring project, Black History Month events, and several black student organizations. The Black Graduates' Recognition Ceremony, held the day before the university commencement, "is designed to honor all black graduating students." Similar attempts are made to help Asian and other minority students feel at home through groups like the Korean Undergraduate Student Association, Turkish Student Association, and the Masala South Asian Cultural Exchange. Perhaps more might be done to accommodate "majority" students from less-affluent backgrounds.

Students currently have the opportunity to participate in off-campus service opportunities like Alternative Spring Break, which sends 400 Vanderbilt students on service trips across the nation and internationally each year. Other service groups include Best Buddies,

Global Health Council, UNICEF, and Habitat for Humanity.

For the politically-minded student, clubs like Dores for Israel, Amnesty International, and College Republicans are available. A variety of special interest groups like the Alternative Energy Club, Law and Business Society, Chess Club, Model United Nations, Toastmasters, Fashion for a Cause, and American Constitution Society all provide extracurricular outlets for students. Arts clubs include the Momentum Dance Group, Vanderbilt Off Broadway, Vanderbilt Concert Choir and Chamber Singers, and Rhythm and Roots.

A number of spiritual and religious groups further enrich student life. The university supports chaplains for Muslims, Catholics, the Reformed University Fellowship, Jews (Hillel and Chabad), United Methodists, Presbyterians, Episcopalians, and Baptists. All of these religions have associated student groups, as do various other Protestant organizations, as well as faiths like Baha'i and Latter-Day Saints.

As a member of the Southeastern Conference, the Vanderbilt Commodores compete against such football powerhouses as Florida, Auburn, and Georgia. The school maintains membership in the conference even while retaining strict educational requirements for its players—a policy that doesn't always translate into the most successful team. However, in 2008, Vandy enjoyed a winning season and played a bowl game—the Music City Bowl—for the first time in twenty-six years. The basketball team is competitive, and intercollegiate club sports and intramural sports are also popular with students. Club sports range from cycling and hockey to fencing, triathlon, and jujitsu.

Crime is becoming a concern. On-campus crime in 2009 included four forcible sex offenses, two robberies, 114 assaults, thirty-six burglaries, 601 instances of larceny or theft, four motor vehicle thefts, and eighty-five instances of vandalism. The campus is not com-

YELLOW LIGHT

The Vanderbilt administration wants high national rankings, and so recent years have seen the university attempt to conform more closely to the political expectations of the academic establishment. In the classroom, this has meant more courses with obvious political agendas; on the rest of the campus, it has meant increased funding for "diversity" programming, liberal speakers, and leftist campus groups. It is a bad sign that the humanities department was swallowed up, even if "women's studies" was put under the auspices of the sociology department. (The feminist courses are still taught—not so the humanities classes.)

True to the school's multiculturalist leanings, it supported Awadh Binhazim, chaplain to Muslim students, in a religious controversy. Binhazim raised hackles when, in a public forum in 2010, he affirmed the position of Islamic law that demands execution of homosexuals. Binhazim claimed, "I don't have a choice as a Muslim to accept or reject teachings." Vanderbilt stood behind its commitment to free speech and Binhazim's right to submit to his religion's teachings, saying that the "university is dedicated to the free exchange of ideas. It is the belief of the university community that free discussion of ideas can lead to resolution and reconciliation."

Critics wondered whether the school would be so supportive of equally (or less) controversial positions implied by Christian or Jewish scriptures.

pletely sealed off from the city, and it is believed that many of the burglaries were committed by town residents. Campus police offer several programs to curb campus crime. A walking-escort service offers security for students crossing campus at night, and a nighttime van service stops at the library, dormitories, and other major buildings. Dormitories can be accessed only with student ID cards.

Vanderbilt is expensive, with 2010–11 tuition at $38,952. Room and board added $13,058. Vanderbilt pledges to meet all demonstrated need with institutional grants, scholarships, and work-study projects (rather than loans), and 61 percent of students receive an average of $40,600 in need-based financial aid. Vanderbilt works to reduce the financial burden on students and families, and the typical student graduates with a relatively modest $14,514 in debt.

University of Virginia

Charlottesville, Virginia • www.virginia.edu

So long as reason is left free

Thomas Jefferson founded the school known as UVA (just "VuhGINyuh" in the South) in 1816 and designed the stately grounds himself. Its famous lawn buildings, including the red-brick, white-columned Rotunda that Jefferson modeled on Rome's Pantheon, are a national historic landmark and quintessentially neoclassical and collegiate.

Teresa Sullivan took office in August 2010 as UVA's first female president. In a meeting with members of the press, she spoke at length about the serious financial challenges the university faces. UVA receives only $8,400 per in-state undergraduate student from the state of Virginia (compare with $17,600 at the University of Michigan, for example), and the allocation is likely to decrease. Faculty and staff have had no pay increase for three years, a fact that caused Sullivan to worry publicly that the best will be difficult to retain.

Thanks in part to a $2.5 billion endowment, UVA has withstood funding decreases better than many institutions. And despite the ubiquitous diversity and sustainability concerns that seem to preoccupy every major institution of higher learning today, it is still true that at Mr. Jefferson's university, many top-notch professors busy themselves with the "enduring questions," and bright students take academics (or at least their grades) very seriously.

Academic Life: Whereas God hath created the mind free

The intellectual quest envisioned by Jefferson is best represented today at his university by the Echols Scholars program. Students in this honors program comprise almost 10 percent of undergraduates in the College of Arts and Sciences; elite incoming freshmen are invited to join. Echols Scholars live together in their first year, register early for classes, and are exempt from distribution requirements. Echols scholars are usually high-achieving, career-oriented students, and their natural affinity for learning coupled with regular advising generally prevents them from misusing this complete curricular freedom. Yet some report being bored: "I didn't have to take any required classes, so I was never 'stretched'" intellectually, says one recent graduate.

Another choice for ambitious students is the bachelor of arts with honors program. UVA, unlike other universities, does not award honors to graduating students based upon grade point average. Rather, students must apply to pursue a course of independent study for their third and fourth years of college, during which time they study under departmental tutors. Candidates are evaluated by visiting examiners from other colleges and universities and may receive degrees with "honors," "high honors," or "highest honors" as the only grades for two years of work, or else they may be recommended for an ordinary BA—or no degree at all. Students who wish to be considered for a degree with distinction must apply to the distinguished major program of their departments. A senior thesis is usually required, and admission to these programs is selective in most departments. Achievement of a 3.4 GPA and completion of the program requirements result in the award.

Still another option, for those students seeking a liberal arts education in a smaller setting, is the University of Virginia's College at Wise, whose course offerings and general education requirements are better than those on the university's main campus. Classes in the English department at Wise include "Western Literary Tradition," "Arthurian Literature," and "Shakespeare." Instead of a feminism course, there is one on Jane Austen.

For better or worse, UVA's students are legatees of Jefferson's suspicion of authority. The university does not have a core curriculum, and its distribution requirements are so vague that a student would have to work hard *not* to fulfill them by graduation. Even the twelve credits (three or four classes) of natural sciences and mathematics are difficult to miss, given that the departments under that rubric range from astronomy to economics to environmental sciences.

More structure is provided within the majors. The top-ranked English department, for example, requires its students to take two pre-1800 courses, a 400-level seminar, and a three-course sequence on the history of literature in English. An English professor says, "We're full of postcolonial theory, currently very fashionable, but we're also very strong in traditional areas such as Shakespeare and medieval literature." Another professor notes that "while the department is quite strong, it offers comparatively very little in the way of theory compared to Michigan or Duke." High praise indeed.

In religious studies, students must take three courses in a single religious tradition, two courses in another creed, one course in a third, and a senior-level majors' seminar.

South

With twenty-nine full-time faculty members and six joint members, the department is the largest of its kind among public universities in the United States. Its undergraduate program has been highly rated for years.

History majors must take one course in pre-1700 Europe; one in post-1700 Europe; one in U.S. History, which could be as specialized as "History of the Civil Rights Movement"; two courses in a choice of African, East Asian, Latin American, Middle Eastern, or Southeast Asian history; and a major seminar. Five courses remain to complete the major, but no more than six courses can be from any one field of study.

The thirty-credit government major requirements include one class in American politics; one in comparative politics; one in international relations; and one in political theory; in addition to twelve credits in related disciplines such as history, philosophy, and social science.

Well-regarded disciplines at UVA besides English and religious studies include history, art history, economics, and classics. However, one professor did warn us that "the humanities are overwhelmingly liberal" and "do not take seriously" the Great Books and ideas of the West. A student adds, "The problem is that, in the liberal arts, the syllabi largely determine the class conversation, and sometimes you can't help but 'talk liberal' when you're reading liberal rhetoric." Another adds, "Generally, I'd stay away from SWAG (Studies in Women and Gender), education, sociology, and African Studies."

The School of Commerce is solid; one recent Echols scholar calls it "probably the best department," and it was recently ranked second in the nation among undergraduate business schools by *Bloomberg BusinessWeek*. On the other hand, the mathematics department, an insider says, "is mediocre nationally. Majors will learn very well but won't be working with the nation's leading scholars."

Professors highly recommended by students include Steven Rhoads, John M. Owen, and Larry J. Sabato in politics; James Davison Hunter and W. Bradford Wilcox in sociology; Ed Burton and Kenneth G. Elzinga in economics; Paul Barolsky in art history; Jenny Clay and John Miller in classics; Charles Marsh, Vanessa Ochs, Robert Louis Wilken (emeritus), Vigen Guroian, and William M. Wilson in religious studies; Gordon Braden and Paul Cantor in English; Gary Gallagher, Michael F. Holt, and Jon Lendon in history; David Herman in Slavic languages and literatures; and Louis Nelson in architecture.

The UVA advising program is described by students as rather meager, Each student is appointed an academic advisor before he arrives on campus, whom he can replace after he chooses a major; all advisors are teaching faculty.

UVA students do tend to be serious. Attending review sessions is de rigueur, although often these efforts are put forth in the pursuit of grades rather than out of intellectual

---

SUGGESTED CORE

1. Comparative Literature 2010, History of European Literature I
2. Philosophy 2110, History of Philosophy: Ancient and Medieval
3. Religious Studies 1210/1220, Hebrew Bible—Old Testament/New Testament and Early Christianity
4. Religious Studies 2050, History of Christianity I
5. Politics 3020, Modern Political Theory
6. English 2550, Shakespeare
7. History 2001, American History to 1865
8. History 3802, Origins of Contemporary Thought

---

curiosity. Students at Virginia worry that a fifteen-hour course load makes them look like underachievers, and they haggle with professors over B-pluses. Grade inflation is consequently a problem. Bias is also an issue, as one student tells us: "I have heard of students in the politics departments having papers marked down for their conservative views." Still, "economics is taught from what may be a slightly right-of-center viewpoint," according to a recent graduate. One student reports that political biases "certainly do" affect course content in some departments. Students recommend a close reading of course syllabi and using the two-week trial period each semester to drop a class if necessary.

Students are highly career oriented. "Everyone's pretty keyed up here about grades. It's a pretty intensely success-centered environment," says one. Another notes, "There is a high percentage of 'go-getters' who are often arrogant." One professor says that UVA students are "more careerist" than those he taught at two other esteemed public universities. Another faculty member reports, "Most students do not seem to be interested in the material for its own sake." On the other hand, another professor states that many of his students "are more grounded than their peers at other universities. They tend not to get carried away."

Introductory courses are large. They are taught by professors, but the smaller discussion sections are usually taught by graduate teaching assistants. Once students reach the sophomore and junior levels, class sizes shrink significantly to twenty or thirty students. Even in large courses, professors endeavor to be friendly and accessible, particularly to students who exhibit an eagerness to learn. University Seminars (USEMs) are offered to freshmen as a way to connect students with faculty. These once-weekly courses are kept to about twenty students and are taught by esteemed professors. Unfortunately, they can be highly specialized and politically biased, since they are often used to introduce students to the professor's current research.

Reportedly, professors really are concerned about their students, but as one teacher says, "when only 10 to 15 percent of the students care about what they are learning, it is tough." Another student adds, "A lot of our professors do care, and in fact complain that not enough students visit their office hours. Professors almost always teach classes, with very rare exceptions."

UVA can arrange for students to study practically anywhere in the world through the International Studies Office. The school sponsors its own programs on six continents. Foreign language programs offered include classics, Asian and Middle Eastern, (ESL), French, German, Slavic, Spanish, Portuguese, and Italian.

Student Life: Tippling with the Wahoos

UVA is nestled amid the eastern foothills of Virginia's Blue Ridge Mountains in the city of Charlottesville. The university's prime location—within minutes of the mountains, three hours from the beach, and two hours from Washington, D.C.—means that students (especially those with cars) have no excuse for being bored. Though a small city, Charlottesville offers a surprising number of cultural events. The Virginia Film Festival and the Virginia Festival of the Book are both held there. The Downtown Mall is a brick pedestrian walkway lined with shops, restaurants, bookstores, coffeehouses, and a pavilion for concerts. Within walking distance of the university is the Corner, a similar though smaller shopping and eating district.

UVA offers over 600 active student organizations. Popular groups include Madison House, a center for various service projects; UGuides, students who give tours of UVA; singing groups; First-Year Players, a theater troupe; student government; Honor Council; and a wide variety of Christian and other religious groups. Catholic students attend the nearby parish of St. Thomas Aquinas—whose webpage, we note with alarm, features folks playing guitars in church. There is a group called Catholic Students Ministry associated with the church; do not confuse it with the group called "Catholics United," which is for LGBT Catholics.

The school boasts a number of "secret societies," most of which are philanthropic in nature. (If any are misanthropic, they aren't telling.) The school's official newspaper is the *Cavalier Daily*. Student-run publications are organized within the Consortium of University Publications (COUP). This group is financially and editorially independent of the school and includes publications of the left such as the *Yellow Journal* and the *Declaration*, and the conservative *Virginia Advocate*.

The Queer Student Union and Queer & Allied Activism are among UVA's several highly active gay groups on campus. One student informs us, "There are some conservatives on campus, but the racial groups and Queer Alliance groups are gaining enough power to silence many of them." Minority and ethnic organizations are abundant. According to

---

ACADEMIC REQUIREMENTS

In lieu of a core curriculum, UVA imposes some loose requirements of study. Students must take:

- One or two first-year writing courses (some students are exempt).
- One writing-intensive course in any subject.
- Four semesters of a foreign language. (Students may test out.)
- Two classes in social science. Many courses count, ranging from "Sociology of American Business" to "Sex, Gender, and Culture."
- Two courses in humanities. Choices range from "Computers, Minds, and Brains" to "Yoruba Religion."
- One class in history. Choices run from "The Roman Republic and Empire" to "Sexuality in the West."
- One course reflecting a "non-Western perspective." Options here include "Modern China" and "History of Modern India."
- Four classes in natural science and mathematics from at least two separate departments. Choices may be from astronomy, biology, chemistry, environmental science, mathematics, physics, statistics, and a few psychology and economics classes, and range from "Statistics" to "Topical Ecology and Conservation in Belize." One class may fulfill several requirements.

South

643

one student, "The far left learned that 'de-Westernization' of the curriculum doesn't get far, so it started peddling 'internationalization.' There is also massive institutional support for groups like the Muslim Student Association, whose members can be anti-American. Conservative students are not as fearful here as they are at campuses like Columbia, but being openly conservative is not the norm." The university has a handful of conservative or classically liberal organizations, including the Liberty Coalition, an umbrella group of libertarian-leaning clubs, and the College Republicans. One student suggests that, overall, UVA "is a school with an immense silent conservative faction . . . who are more engaged in Greek life, the Commerce school, etc."

UVA's persistent preservation of its single-sanction Code of Honor in the face of periodic challenges is another indication of a deference for tradition and perhaps even an innate conservatism, at least in the student body. The Honor Council is a student-run manifestation of the Code of Honor, established in 1840. If a student is convicted of lying, cheating, or stealing, the only possible penalty is expulsion from the university. Some students recently have had their degrees revoked after graduation. Most students take the Code seriously, and exams are often unproctored.

At UVA, there has been a great emphasis on "diversity," mostly focused on race. A Diversity Center is located in the Student Union, and the administration has pushed a "black ribbon of tolerance" ("like the red ribbon for AIDS," says a student) campaign. According to one student, "there is definitely pointless diversity for diversity's sake." While the administration seems concerned about race relations, most of the students do not. Students admit that self-segregation is an issue on campus; the lower, older part of campus is 90 percent white and is the location for most of the Greek activity. The upper campus is much more diverse, and since foreign students tend to gravitate to that location, the ethnic clustering has taken on a self-perpetuating quality.

First-years are required to live on campus in dorms. The dorms are generally grouped into "old" and "new," the former being closer to central campus, but the latter offering more amenities. Housing in the first-year dorms is sex segregated by floor or by suite. Upperclassmen residential assistants run first-year orientation, which is mostly a recounting of university regulations but does include a sensitivity-training program.

UVA has three residential colleges. Hereford is the largest and houses about 500 students, most of whom live in single rooms. These students take charge of the budget and have opportunities to bring in speakers or sponsor events. They choose it, according to the website, because of its "programming and events built around themes of sustainability and cultural diversity." The 200 residents of Brown College—who are said to be quirky—live closest to the central "grounds" (UVA lingo for campus) but have to share their rooms. The newest residential college, IRC, is organized along the lines of parliamentary government, with elected officials. All the colleges are modeled on the residential experience at Yale, Oxford, and Cambridge. They offer community meals and house faculty members alongside students.

Upperclassmen may move off campus, and many do. Some fourth-years apply for the honor of living on the lawn, that lovely stretch of terraced grass behind the Rotunda edged by colonnaded brick walkways and pavilion buildings designed by Jefferson as the original college campus. The single rooms, with their wood floors, wood-burning fireplaces, and central location, are highly sought after, but a good bathrobe is required: restrooms cannot be reached without going outside. This historic part of the university was declared a World Heritage site by UNESCO in 1987.

Sports, especially in the South, are considered a big part of the college experience, and this is true at UVA. The Cavaliers won NCAA championships in women's rowing and men's soccer last year and consistently field strong teams in tennis, lacrosse, field hockey, and women's basketball and soccer. Performance in the big-time sports of men's basketball and football has been less stellar in recent years. The university sponsors thirteen varsity sports for women and twelve for men. The university recently built a $128 million basketball venue, the John Paul Jones Arena, even as "our academic buildings fall down around our ears," according to one professor.

The campus has grown immensely in the past twenty years. Scheduled to be completed in 2011 is the 100,000-square-foot Rice Hall. Plans for the technology engineering building include a courtyard, cyberlounge, 150-seat auditorium, a Visualization Lab for Scientific Computing, a Computer Vision and Graphics Lab, facilities to support distance education, workrooms, study areas, conference rooms and flexible teaching and research labs. Also slated for occupancy in 2011 is the Physical and Life Sciences Building, which will create new laboratory space for the College and Graduate School of Arts & Sciences. Other new buildings planned include the Ruth Caplin Theater, a $13.5 million, 300-seat facility.

Even with so much else to do, a notable occupation of UVA students is celebrating, especially with libations. In the old days, UVA was famous up and down the East Coast as a party school, and though the administration has done much to change that, UVA students manage still to have a lot of authorized

GREEN LIGHT

"UVA is itself liberal, but it is located in the Bible Belt with a large Christian contingent," reports one professor. "It also has a tradition of civility. The broader political climate and the tradition of civility mean that the institution is fairly tolerant toward conservatives on the faculty and in the student body."

The school has become more tolerant of free speech. The Foundation for Individual Rights in Education (FIRE) recently gave UVA its "green light" rating for having cleaned up its speech codes. A FIRE press release says, "While more than two-thirds of the nation's colleges maintain policies that clearly and substantially restrict freedom of speech, UVA is now a proud exception, having fully reformed four speech codes."

The administration is another story. One of Teresa Sullivan's first university-wide events as president was a Day of Dialogue decreed in response to recent campus murders (see below). The event included faculty, students, and staff in "discussion groups," as well as a "public art project" for the university community. An art and architecture professor designed a work that she said "expresses movement from the darkness of mourning to the lightness of healing and change." As the school website reports, "It begins with the Rotunda's columns being veiled in black, diaphanous fabric in the days leading up to [the Day of Dialogue]. 'This represents the university community's shared experience of grief and loss,'" said the artist. "When the veils are rolled back, the gleaming white columns once again will reveal all that they symbolize about Thomas Jefferson's learning community."

Art saves lives.

and unauthorized fun. Students call themselves Wahoos, after the fish that supposedly can drink twice its weight. Though only 30 percent of the student body goes Greek, parties on Rubgy Road are the center of attention on weekend (and some weekday) nights. One professor tells us "that the hookup culture is alive and well at UVA. Very little 'dating' in its proper sense actually occurs." Except, surprisingly, at football games, where the men show up looking like Virginia gentlemen in coat and tie, and the women don dresses and pearls.

A professor tells us that Charlottesville is a place where graduates love to live after they graduate: "Maybe not immediately, because the city itself does not offer that many jobs, but alumni will often purchase a second home here or move to Charlottesville if they have the option to telecommute."

Charlottesville, a relatively small city, has experienced some high-profile crimes. One student informs us that "at least a few students get assaulted each year by people in the ghetto right next to school." There are blue-light emergency telephones spaced throughout the grounds, and cell phones programmed with 911 are available for student loan at the libraries. Another student adds, "Programs to help students get rides at night are a big help." In 2009, the school reported eight forcible sexual assaults, six aggravated assaults, eighty-three burglaries, nine automotive thefts, two arsons, and two robberies. In fall 2010, UVA was reporting increased police patrols in response to a number of criminal incidents against mostly female students near the Corner shopping district.

Recently, university officials have resorted to the Code of Honor for help in crime prevention. Two shocking murders in the space of one year stunned the campus. A female Virginia Tech student met her death on or near the UVA campus in October 2009 after departing the John Paul Jones arena. In 2010, fourth-year UVA lacrosse player Yeardley Love was found dead in her apartment. Love's boyfriend, a classmate and fellow lacrosse player whose past arrest on charges of assaulting a police officer was unreported and unknown to UVA officials, stands charged with her death. Claiming that knowledge of his record could have helped avert the tragedy, the university will now require students "on their honor," which means on pain of expulsion for lying, to report any past criminal record. Initial proposals to do background checks on all students were deemed too difficult and costly.

If you're from Virginia, UVA is a real bargain: 2010–11 in-state tuition was only $10,836. For out-of-state students, tuition was $33,782, with room and board $8,590. Admissions are need blind, and the school commits to covering the needs of any student who enrolls—and 100 percent of those determined to have financial need receive aid; this is, however, only a little over a third of the student body. The average student leaves the school with $15,571 in debt.

Wake Forest University

Winston-Salem, North Carolina • www.wfu.edu

Sleepers, wake!

Founded by Southern Baptists in 1834, Wake Forest was until fairly recently an explicitly Christian institution. Over the past decade or so, however, the school has gone chasing after a national reputation—and like many other religious universities, it has found it useful to back away slowly, hands in the air, from its founders' religion. As one student says, "Wake Forest's current connections to its Southern Baptist heritage are little more than lip service."

Wake Forest has followed other academic trends by replacing its once-strong distribution requirements with a weaker regimen. But the university still maintains a number of outstanding academic departments, and it draws a good number of intelligent and morally serious students. Wake Forest's faculty members understand that they are teachers first and researchers second; the school does a good job of balancing the two facets of the university.

Wake Forest's religious traditions haven't entirely disappeared. Its president, Nathan O. Hatch, a former provost of Notre Dame who was inaugurated in 2005, is a renowned scholar of American religious history, and he has spoken publicly about the importance of taking religion seriously in what he has termed the current "postsecular era." One professor notes that President Hatch has invited to campus several ministers and religion scholars for lectures and conferences, suggesting that the administration is sensitive to charges that the school is running from its heritage.

Academic Life: Waking the dead

Wake Forest's catalog informs students that they "have considerable flexibility in planning their courses of study." And they do. The university recently cut the number of required courses by a full semester, and many of the classes that can be used to satisfy its distribution requirements are introductory. One professor laments, "Students take the most popular courses and often repeat what they took in high school."

Furthermore, the rigor of some of the courses fulfilling these requirements is open to question. One student says many fluff classes are available, especially in the communications, sociology, and political science departments. "A liberal arts student can truly graduate knowing very little beyond a limited scope," he says. This is evident in the English department, where majors are not required to take a Shakespeare class and other required classes have been watered down. For instance, a student claims that "the basic American and British literature courses are becoming less substantive, in my opinion. A quick glance at their reading lists would reveal that these classes are not filled with the great authors but rather works of radical chic with perhaps a play of Shakespeare or some Hawthorne thrown in." One student warns, "The liberal arts are increasingly becoming subject to political correctness and are drifting from traditional texts and subjects."

Fortunately, while Wake Forest offers a broad spectrum of majors, most of the trendy interdisciplinary areas such as women's studies, ethnic studies, and urban studies are offered only as minors—and therefore do not have the power or popularity that they do at other universities.

The history department is solid, requiring majors to take classes in American, European, and world history; unfortunately, a basic Western civilization course is not offered, much less required.

Although some complain that the political science department tends to promote the views of the left, it is one of the university's strongest academic departments—and one of the largest at the school. As one professor says, "This is due in large part to the quality of the faculty, many of whom are widely published and well regarded in their fields and are also excellent teachers who work closely with students." Poli sci majors are required to take one course each in American politics, political theory, international politics, and comparative politics.

The business school program is reputedly very challenging, as are the hard sciences (chemistry, biology, and physics). Outside of the business school and the hard sciences, Wake's better departments include economics, mathematics, and the foreign language programs, including Chinese, Ancient Greek, Japanese, Latin, Italian, German, Russian, Spanish, and French. "Philosophy remains a bastion of good, solid academic tradition," a professor says. "They're unwilling to go along with faddish multiculturalism." A classical languages major says that his department is "one of the few liberal arts departments at Wake Forest that still avoids being politicized." Wake offers a distinctive minor in early Christian studies, in which students take courses on the New Testament, the age of Augustus, and the Greco-Roman world, and select relevant courses in the art, history, religion, and philosophy departments.

Wake Forest seems to regard its religious past as an embarrassment. Down the road at Duke University, a school founded by Methodists, national rankings rose as Duke gradually shed its denominational heritage—and it was not long before Wake Forest followed suit. The religion department includes courses such as "Religion, Culture, and Gender" and is said to take a dim view of traditional Christianity, Baptist or otherwise. "That department is highly politicized and heavily influenced by liberal theologies," a student says. "For instance, a student I know who wishes to become an Episcopal priest has majored in Greek and avoids most religion classes because of their content." A student reports that in his sociology class on deviant behavior, the "correct" answer on an examination identified religious objections to homosexuality as bigotry. Well, that settles things, doesn't it?

The school's honors program allows Wake's most academically talented upperclassmen to take small-group seminars together. Those who take at least four honors seminars can graduate with distinction. In the English department, the honors courses are mostly specialty courses in topics like Chaucer, Milton, Victorian poetry, and the literature of the South. Topics for honors seminars in other disciplines vary by semester.

> ## SUGGESTED CORE
>
> 1. Classics 255, Classical Epic: *Iliad, Odyssey, Aeneid*
> 2. Philosophy 232, Ancient Greek Philosophy
> 3. Religion 102, Introduction to the Bible
> 4. Philosophy 237, Medieval Philosophy or Religion 372, History of Christian Thought
> 5. Political Science 276, Modern Political Thought
> 6. English 323, Shakespeare
> 7. History 251, The United States before 1865
> 8. Philosophy 352, Hegel, Kierkegaard, Nietzsche (closest match)

Every Wake Forest freshman receives an Lenovo ThinkPad and color printer, the cost of which is absorbed by tuition and fees. The university upgrades the computers after two years, and students can keep them after they graduate. These technological trimmings have earned the school a distinction as one of the nation's "most wired" campuses, according to *Yahoo! Internet Life* magazine. But at least one professor labels these efforts a grand marketing ploy that only serves to distract students—and their tuition-paying parents—from focusing on the quality of the liberal arts education the school offers. In addition, the classroom experience is intensely high tech. According to the university website, most assignments and projects are handed in electronically, much communication takes place via some form of electronic device, and students are encouraged to utilize pocket PC mobile phones to access information. A student seeking a traditional "collegiate experience" immersed in books and spent near quaint writing-desk lamps in the library will be disappointed.

Wake Forest has abandoned the SAT and ACT requirement for admission, choosing instead to consider students' talents, extracurricular activities, writing ability, and character—and it now "strongly encourages" applicants to undergo a personal interview. While standardized testing may have its drawbacks, this new emphasis on personality, talents, high school activities, etc., certainly demonstrates a positive attitude toward new-style education: group projects, "expressionist" writing exercises, and an abandonment of the purpose of liberal arts education for tech-savvy skills.

The close relationships between faculty and students often touted by the Wake Forest administration appear genuine. The student-faculty ratio is a good 11 to 1. Admissions literature says that the school "maintains its high academic standards by assuring that undergraduate classes, lectures, and seminars are taught by faculty members, not teaching assistants." (Teaching assistants teach only the lab sections of science and language courses.) Wake Forest faculty members do generally value teaching over research, and one professor says, "It is difficult to come up with schools that are truly analogous to Wake Forest in their teaching/research balance, and this is one of the most attractive features of the school."

Signs indicate that the university is moving in more of a research direction: faculty teaching loads have been reduced, and publication requirements for tenure have increased. However, teaching continues to remain strong. Students say that their professors are accessible and that they almost always welcome students, even outside scheduled office hours. Freshmen are assigned faculty members as advisors, who serve largely to make sure that students are satisfying the necessary distribution requirements. A student says that he "typically asks upperclassmen for advice" when selecting classes for his major.

Some of the best professors at Wake include Charles M. Lewis in philosophy; Robert Utley in humanities; William Moss and Eric Wilson in English; Roberta Morosini and M. Stanley Whitley in Romance languages; J. Daniel Hammond and Robert M. Whaples in economics; Richard D. Carmichael and James J. Kuzmanovich in mathematics; Kevin Bowen, Stewart Carter, Brian Gorelick, and Dan Locklair in music; Helga Welsh in political science; James P. Barefield in history (emeritus); and James T. Powell in classical languages.

Wake Forest is one of the dwindling number of colleges that still has an honor code. Entering freshmen attend an honor assembly in which a professor delivers a sermon on being honest and forthright. Students then sign a book, agreeing to the code and acknowledging the consequences for violating it—possible expulsion.

Wake Forest puts a good deal of emphasis on international studies (though they are offered only as minors), including Asian, East Asian, German, Latin American, Russian, and East European studies. In addition, certificates are offered in Italian studies and Spanish studies. The school owns residential study centers in London, Venice, and Vienna and runs its own study-abroad programs in these cities as well as in Benin, Cuba, Ecuador, Mexico, France, Spain, China, Japan, and Russia. There is a residential language center for students who wish to speak Russian or German on a regular basis. About half of Wake Forest undergraduates study abroad during their college years, and the college's domestic Wake Washington program has won national recognition. Since its founding in 2006, Wake Washington has sponsored over seventy undergraduates to Washington D.C., as interns in government agencies, departments, nonprofits, and media outlets.

Student Life: If a beer falls in the forest . . .

Wake Forest is situated in the old tobacco town of Winston-Salem, North Carolina, a city of about 217,000 people. The school is only a short drive from downtown, but it is separated from the city by a wooded area. Almost all campus buildings are red brick. A tree-lined quad with the chapel on one end and the main administration building on the other anchor the campus. Magnolia Court, containing dozens of varieties of the trademark tree of the South, is especially beautiful in the spring. Reynolda Gardens, originally owned by tobacco

South

giant R. J. Reynolds, comprises 125 acres of woodlands, fields, and nature trails, in addition to four acres devoted to a formal garden and a greenhouse.

In spite of the headlong secularization of the university, one of the most popular groups on campus is the Baptist Student Union—a social and spiritual group that sponsors summer missions, prayer groups, local ministries, intramural sports teams, and other social events. The Campus Kitchens group meets three times a week to cook and then deliver food to the needy in Winston-Salem. Musically inclined students can choose from a large number of groups, most of them Christian in nature. The InterVarsity Christian Fellowship hosts prayer and discussion groups on campus, and the Wake Forest Baptist Church holds services in Wait Chapel every Sunday morning. The Wake Forest Catholic Community has daily and Sunday Masses in Davis Chapel; a local Latin Mass is offered at the parish of St. Benedict the Moor. There is also an Orthodox Christian Fellowship and a Hillel on campus.

Wake Forest has almost 200 registered clubs and organizations, including ballroom dancing, chess club, Ultimate Frisbee, a handbell choir, a comedy troupe, Habitat for Humanity, Volunteer Service Corps, and the Brian Piccollo Cancer Fund, in honor of the famous NFL player and Wake Forest alum who lost his life to embryonal cell carcinoma.

ACADEMIC REQUIREMENTS

Wake Forest does not have a traditional core curriculum, but its distribution requirements are more respectable than those at many other schools. All liberal arts students must complete the following:

- A first-year seminar. Topics for 2011 included "G. K. Chesterton and Ayn Rand" and "Debating Capitalism."
- One writing seminar originally titled "The Writing Seminar." (Students may test out.)
- One foreign language course beyond the intermediate level.
- Two physical education classes: "Lifestyle and Health" and "Exercise and Health."
- Two humanities courses in history, philosophy, or religion. Choices include "Basic Problems of Philosophy" and "World Civilizations to 1500."
- One class in British, American, or foreign literature in translation. Choices range from "Studies in British Literature" to "African and Caribbean Literature."
- One course in the arts, ranging from "The Gothic Cathedral" to "Music of World Cultures."
- Two classes in the social sciences. Choices include "Introductory Psychology" and "Introduction to Cultural Anthropology."
- Two courses in math or the natural sciences. Choices for nonmajors include "Biology and the Human Condition" and "Everyday Chemistry."
- One quantitative reasoning class. Options include "Elementary Probability and Statistics" and "Explorations in Mathematics."
- One multicultural or "cultural diversity" course. Examples include "Race, Gender, and Housing Disparities in the U.S." and "Gay and Lesbian Film and Culture."

South

GREEN LIGHT

Wake Forest has come a long way from its Baptist roots. To give just one example, while the North Carolina Baptist Convention deems homosexual behavior sinful, Wake Forest pays employee benefits to same-sex lovers of faculty and staff, and the school's Wait Chapel now solemnizes same-sex "commitment ceremonies." One of the most influential political groups on campus is the Gay-Straight Student Alliance, which passes out rainbow stickers to faculty members and encourages them (with great success) to display them on their office doors.

However, overall, the Wake Forest student body is notable for being apolitical. A true spirit of tolerance is expressed in the university newspaper—where, a student reports, "There are a good number of conservative columnists and they maintain a vigorous debate with their liberal counterparts, and in no sense would I say that there is any stifling of debate." The same student notes that conservative and religious students are in the majority at Wake Forest and that campus religious organizations are active.

Students have so far raised over a million dollars for cancer research at the Wake Forest University Comprehensive Cancer Center.

Politically inclined students can join the College Republicans, which hosts a speaker series and plans campus events, and Democracy Matters, an organization that gets involved in local and national elections.

Wake Forest's Office of Multicultural Affairs, a university-funded department, sponsors many activities for ethnic minority students, including new minority student orientation, the Martin Luther King Jr. Celebration, Black History Month, Asian Awareness week, Multicultural Summits, and minority tutoring and scholarships. The office also advises the Black Student Alliance—one of the more active political groups on campus. A guide for multicultural students says that fifteen years ago, nearly half of Wake Forest's black student body attended on athletic scholarships. Since then, the university has tried to dramatically increase its number of minority students and faculty. So far, however, minority enrollment has risen only slightly, from 13 percent in 2000 to 17 percent in 2010, according to university statistics. Only 7 percent are African American.

Living off campus is the exception, not the rule. While all of the residential halls are within close walking distance of the campus's center, the coveted rooms are on the Quad, central to Wake's academic and social life. Most of the dormitories have men and women divided by floor; the university did away with its all-women residence hall a few years ago. Theme houses allow students to live with friends with shared interests in the languages or the arts. There are no coed dorm rooms or shower areas on campus, although some theme houses do have coed bathrooms. Substance-free (no smoking or alcohol) dormitories for freshmen and upperclassmen offer an escape from one's more Dionysian peers.

And substance use, particularly of alcohol, *is* heavy at Wake Forest. In the past decade or so, the community has seen fraternity parties become much more widespread. Students say that every weekend is a party weekend. Binge drinking is a genuine problem, with students frequently sent to the emergency room for detox. A popular tradition at Wake Forest calls for seniors, at the last home football game, to drink a fifth of liquor (750 ml) within twenty-four hours. The university has attempted (with mixed success) to counter the tradition with a campaign pointing out the dangers of binge drinking.

South

Winston-Salem, though not exactly a cultural metropolis, has its attractions. The Winston-Salem Warthogs are a minor league baseball team affiliated with the Chicago White Sox. Excellent medical facilities and high-tech companies employ many of the city's residents. The real advantage of living in Winston-Salem, though, is its proximity to other cities. Students sometimes visit nearby Greensboro for concerts and sporting events; and the Research Triangle of Durham (home of Duke University), Chapel Hill (University of North Carolina), and Raleigh (North Carolina State University) is only a short drive to the east. For outdoor enthusiasts, Asheville and the Blue Ridge Mountains are two hours to the west.

Wake Forest offers plenty of things to do on campus in the evenings and on weekends, often attracting lecturers and cultural performances to its halls. One student says, "At least once at Wake, one should attend a performance of the Lilting Banshees, a satirical student comedy group." Wake Forest athletics are probably dearer to students than anything else. The Demon Deacons compete on eight men's and eight women's intercollegiate teams in NCAA Division I, and the men's basketball team is usually a contender in the powerful Atlantic Coast Conference. Students also have plenty of nonvarsity options, including thirty-nine intercollegiate club teams. Intramural teams include basketball, bowling, inline hockey, tennis, and many others.

Wake Forest has become more dangerous in recent years, although the university police maintain a strong presence on campus, and a free bus service offers rides around campus at night. In 2009, the college reported fifty-three burglaries, six forcible sex offenses, four car thefts, one robbery, and one arson on campus.

Wake Forest is Ivy priced, with a 2010–11 tuition of $39,970 and estimated room and board at $11,010. However, admission is need blind, and all students who enroll are guaranteed sufficient financial aid; 38 percent of Wake Forest students receive need-based aid. The average indebtedness of a recent graduating student was $24,561.

Washington and Lee University

Lexington, Virginia • www.wlu.edu

White columns and an honor code

Washington and Lee is the nation's ninth-oldest university. Now named for two great statesmen, the school was founded in 1749 as Augusta Academy. When the first U.S. president intervened to save the school from bankruptcy in 1796, it took his name in gratitude. After Appomattox, General Robert E. Lee took off his uniform to lead the school until his death in 1870. Lee's ethos profoundly reshaped the school, which soon added his name to Washington's. The greatest southern poet, Donald Davidson, celebrated Lee's tenure at the college environs in his poem "Lee in the Mountains," in which the general pledges faith with his people and, by the peaceful means of education, to help their descendants

> To flower among the hills to which we cleave,
> To fruit upon the mountains whither we flee,
> Never forsaking, never denying
> His children and His children's children forever
> Unto all generations of the faithful heart.

Since Lee's tenure as president, W&L has earned recognition as one of the South's outstanding liberal arts institutions. Over the years, the university has produced four Supreme Court justices, twenty-seven senators, thirty-one governors, and sixty-seven congressmen. The brick buildings with white columns, the school's honor code, and a mostly conservative student body all attest to the school's aristocratic, southern heritage.

However, in recent years administrators have shown their dissatisfaction with the school's reputation as a bastion of regional elites and have striven to recruit a more diverse student body and a more "progressive" faculty. An increasing emphasis on "diversity," some say, threatens to overwhelm what makes the school unique. New, ideologically infused programs, the politically correct tone of campus publications, and a trend toward hiring what one alumnus calls "radicals" as teachers could mean that W&L is changing inexorably—in the same way that many once-distinctive religious and regional schools have already done. Lovers of learning hope that the virtues long treasured at W&L survive the pressures of politics "[u]nto all generations of the faithful heart."

South

654

Academic Life: Connecting the disciplines

Washington and Lee's distribution requirements are better than most—largely because nearly all the courses that fulfill them are solid and serious. "I have gained a great deal of experience in diverse disciplines," says a student. Notes another: "Some of my favorite classes have been a result of general education requirements." These requirements take up more than one-third of the credits required for graduation. Indeed, as one professor remarks, "It is difficult to graduate from WLU and *not* get a liberal arts education."

Taking classes in diverse disciplines alone does not a liberal education make, however. Students can graduate from W&L having little or nothing to do with what has traditionally been called the canon or with a study of America's founding or political institutions. A student *could* graduate having taken classes on Chinese lit in translation, dance, women's studies, East Asian anthropology, environmental science, general geology, computer science, and Indian religions to fulfill his "foundation and distribution requirements." Most won't, of course, but nothing is stopping them.

Major requirements impose more curricular discipline. For instance, the English department requires its majors to take at least three courses in each of three areas: earlier British literature, later British literature (including world literature written in English), and American literature.

History majors must take thirty-six credits, fifteen of which must come from one of three areas of emphasis: European and Russian, American, and global. There is no required American history or Western civilization sequence.

Politics students, on the other hand, are required to take "American National Government"; they face a hefty forty-one-credit requirement. One student says that politics professors masterfully articulate the "complex current political and economic phenomena. . . . We not only learn about current political events but are challenged to think about what Machiavelli or Locke would have said about them." A faculty member adds, "Politics is truly first rate. We are perennially one of the top three or four majors, and we offer a wide range of courses."

Academic advising helps students navigate requirements. Freshmen are assigned to an advisor who can guide their course selection "in exploration of the liberal arts curriculum."

VITAL STATISTICS

Religious affiliation: *none*
Total enrollment: *2,153*
Total undergraduates: *1,759*
SAT/ACT midranges: CR: *660–740*, M: *660–730*; ACT: *29–32*
Applicants: *6,222*
Applicants accepted: *19%*
Accepted applicants who enrolled: *40%*
Tuition and fees: *$39,500*
Room and board: *$10,243*
Freshman retention rate: *94%*
Graduation rate: *88% (4 yrs.)*, *91% (6 yrs.)*
Courses with fewer than 20 students: *not provided*
Student-faculty ratio: *9:1*
Courses taught by graduate students: *not provided*
Most popular majors: *business/marketing, social sciences, foreign languages and literature*
Students living on campus: *60%*
Guaranteed housing for four years? *no*
Students in fraternities: *81%* in sororities: *79%*

1. Classics 203, Greek Literature from Homer to the Early Hellenistic Period and Classics 204, Augustan Era
2. Philosophy 141, Ancient Philosophy
3. Religion 101/102, The Hebrew Bible: Old Testament/Introduction to the New Testament
4. Religion 250, Early Christian Thought: Orthodoxy and Heresy
5. Politics 266, Modern Political Philosophy
6. English 252, Shakespeare
7. History 107, History of the United States to 1876
8. History 326, European Intellectual History, 1880 to 1960 (closest match)

After choosing a major, they are paired with someone from their field. Students may register for classes only after obtaining their registration password from their advisors.

Another option for freshmen seeking guidance is enrolling in a small first-year seminar. These classes, which are capped at fifteen, introduce the student "to a field of study by way of a special topic, issue, or problem of interest." Options include "Fictions of Vietnam in France and the U.S." and "Hardboiled L.A.: Film Noir and the City of the Angels."

Freshmen and sophomores with a GPA of 3.5 or better might apply for the University Scholars Program, W&L's honors track, which requires that participants take one reading course and at least one seminar in each of the three areas of humanities, natural sciences, and social sciences. The University Scholars Program also offers students access to special interdisciplinary courses such as "Shamanism, Spirit Possession, and the Occult," "Time Machines," and "Avoiding Armageddon: The Politics and Science of Non-proliferation." Each University Scholar must also complete a senior thesis. Various departments at W&L offer their own honors tracks, but competition to enter them is stiff.

Offering forty-one undergraduate majors, W&L is proud to be the only top-tier liberal arts college with a fully accredited business school and a fully accredited journalism program. The English, philosophy, history, business, accounting, economics, and premed programs are widely considered the best on campus, and are thus among the most popular.

The student-faculty ratio is an outstanding 9 to 1. All classes are taught by professors. (Language departments make use of native-speaking assistants who do lead some sessions, though faculty teach the class itself.) Teachers are said to be accessible to students. "The professors' influence extends beyond the classroom, however, and they often become akin to good friends," says one undergrad. Another student lauds his teachers for their hard work: "They manage to teach three classes, schedule several hours' worth of office hours (which attract lines of students), advise students on everything from classes to careers, and complete their own research projects. As a result, students often develop very close personal and professional relationships with professors." Teachers often ask students to help with research work, giving them training in areas that are often available only as graduate study in other universities.

"Professors teach all classes," one student says. "And when I say teach, I mean *teach*. They don't just get up in front of a class and dictate for an hour." Some 72 percent of classes have fewer than twenty students, and few report problems getting into the courses they want.

When it comes to the classroom, teachers tend to be more left-leaning than the student body. On the whole, however, conservative or religious students and their ideas are welcome. "Even the most liberal professors and left-leaning courses enthusiastically welcome disagreement and discussion from the conservatives," says a professor. A real diversity of thought within the classroom—too rare on today's college campuses—often gives rise to lively discussions. Says one liberal student, "One of my economics professors, who's clearly left-leaning, had us reading Milton Friedman the other day." A faculty member says, "The best antidote to political correctness is a faculty committed to learning, by which I mean a faculty who still want to learn and not just teach. This sense of wonder preserves fairness. I am happy to say that I have colleagues with just this disposition."

Remarks another, "The faculty are uniformly superior and conscientious. They are outstanding scholars and teachers. There may be examples of faculty at some institutions who choose not to teach and instead simply do research and writing. That is not the case here. The beauty of our faculty is that they represent and manifest the ideal combination: they are active scholars who use their research and writing to inform their teaching; they can produce knowledge as well as disseminate it."

Students list many praiseworthy professors, including Bill Connelly, Tyler Dickovick, Robin LeBlanc, Lucas Morel, Bob Strong, and Eduardo Velásquez in politics; Marc Conner, Edwin Craun, and Suzanne Keen in English; Miriam Carlisle and Kevin Crotty in classics; George Bent in art history; Timothy Diette and Art Goldsmith in economics; and Lad Sessions in philosophy. One undergrad praises all his professors for being "superb and fair." Remarks one contented professor, "You can judge the success of a school by how long its faculty stick around. Faculty at W&L are here to stay."

Washington and Lee's academic calendar is divided into three terms—also known as 12-12-4—consisting of twelve-week fall and winter terms, followed by a four-week required spring term. During the spring term, special-topics courses are offered for which many students study abroad or work internships. A popular program is the Washington Term, wherein sixteen to eighteen outstanding students from all majors combine a Washington internship with class readings and discussions. After the discussions, students hear from a series of prominent speakers, including on one occasion the vice president of the United States.

The New York Internship Program is also highly praised. A professor explains that "students compete for summer internships in finance, government, and journalism. Like the Washington term, students participate in an academic seminar and meet with scholars and practitioners who speak on a host of issues ranging from international politics to commerce, finance, and economics." Also popular is Spring Term Abroad, which in 2011 includes trips to Denmark, China, Brazil, Italy, Tanzania, the Caribbean, France, Argentina, Costa Rica, Spain, and London.

Washington and Lee students can enroll in longer study-abroad programs, most of which are sponsored by other institutions with which W&L has agreements. Languages offered at the university are Spanish, French, Italian, Portuguese, Chinese, Japanese, classics, German, and Russian. Some 10 percent of the students major in foreign languages and literature.

South

Student Life: Drinkers yes, slackers no

Many students find W&L's atmosphere intoxicating. "Washington and Lee is all about the little things that can't be measured by *U.S. News & World Report*," says one. "Teachers who really care. A campus that's beautiful. Friendly people with character and integrity. A killer social life. If studies took into account all the little things that really make schools what they are, Washington and Lee would be number one." The red-brick, white-columned campus is handsome. Its historic Colonnade is undergoing a major renovation. Work was recently completed on 128-year-old Newcomb Hall, which contains faculty offices, two administrative offices, two group-study rooms, two large classrooms, three seminar rooms, and one computer lab. The total Colonnade renovation, expected to cost $50 million and take five years, is part of the university's new campaign: Honor the Past. Build the Future. Also in the works are a new sorority house and a new Hillel House.

Washington and Lee lies in the heart of the Appalachian town of Lexington, Virginia (population 7,000), also home to the Virginia Military Institute. Beautiful parks and rugged mountain hikes are just minutes away.

ACADEMIC REQUIREMENTS

In lieu of a core curriculum, students complete the following requirements:

- One writing seminar for First Year. (Students can test out.)
- Foreign language up to sixteen credits or third-year level competency determined by test scores.
- One from a choice of five mathematics or computer science courses, including "Calculus" I and "Scientific Computing."
- One class in physical education, covering four skills and a swimming test.
- One class in the humanities, which can include anything from "American Indian Religions, Landscapes, and Identities" to "New Testament" and "Introduction to Women's and Gender Studies."
- One course in the arts, with choices including "Ancient and Classical Art" and "University Dance."
- One class in literature, such as "Medieval and Renaissance Studies" or "Chinese Literature in Translation."
- A fourth course selected from any of the previous three categories.
- One laboratory course in the natural sciences, such as "Biology 101" or "Stellar Evolution and Cosmology."
- One additional science, mathematics, or computer science course, such as "Psychoactive Drugs and Behavior," "Introduction to Statistics," or "Science of Cooking."
- Two designated courses in the social sciences from two of the following areas: economics, anthropology, politics, sociology, classics, religion, psychology, environmental science, history, and journalism. Choices include "Media Ownership and Control" and "Race and Ethnic Relations."

The small downtown offers a coffee shop and a few bars and restaurants—and not much else. As a longtime W&Ler relates, "W&L is located in a beautiful part of the world, the Shenandoah Valley. This is the best and worst of small-town, small-college life. For some, that is intimate. For others, that can be claustrophobic. Along with the smallness comes a domination of the social scene by the sororities and fraternities. Again, if that is what a student wants, she or he will thrive here. But if you need the trappings of a bigger city—ethnic foods, sports, museums—then this probably is not the place."

The relative isolation makes for an atmosphere in which students study hard and then relieve stress over a glass (or a six-pack) of beer. But not everyone parties every night. "For every student who drinks four nights a week, there is a student who doesn't," says one student, who considers himself a moderate tippler.

One student warns, "Prospective students should know that if they are not at all interested in the Greek system when they come here, they are in for a very long four years." About 81 percent of men and 79 percent of women belong to the sixteen fraternities and seven sororities on campus. Although Greek organizations do their share of community service activities, they are also a center of student inebriation. "Partying is a major social activity at W&L," one student says. A teacher admits, "We suffer our issues with Greek life and drinking as any university, but we do a pretty reasonable job of managing them." However, a professor says that "hazing is another worrying reality at W&L. There was an egregious case . . . that resulted in the suspension of a fraternity for a full year." A professor reports that in the past decade, the university has had half a dozen alcohol-related deaths—alarming for a school of this size.

Still, classrooms are competitive, and "the workload can be daunting," says a student. "Most people here intend to succeed and take classes seriously." Still another reports that "intellectual discussions can occur anywhere at any time . . . in places you wouldn't expect, such as locker rooms." A faculty member finds that "academic life is very impressive here. Our students are highly motivated, increasingly diverse, and more international. Our typical student is extremely active, engaged in many pursuits, and on a twenty-six-hour clock." A second professor agrees, "Our students are W&L's greatest strength. They are honorable, decent, ambitious, smart, and friendly. Many are intellectually serious."

Traditionally, the student body at W&L has been generally rather conservative—unsurprising, at a school where Robert E. Lee and his family are buried below the campus chapel. (Lee's horse, Traveller, is buried *outside* the chapel.) Lee's presence is still palpable at the university. One student considers him "the physical embodiment of what all W&L students aim to be: honorable, of integrity and character." The Lee Chapel is the site of most public events; one professor recalls, with a certain irony, that when filmmaker Spike Lee came to speak on campus, he stood in front of the tomb of General Lee, flanked left and right by Confederate battle flags. "He knew what he was getting into," the teacher says.

Generous scholarship offerings, a major outreach to attract international students, and the addition of "diversity" programs on campus have begun to chip away at the school's southern identity. We just hope that all this diversity doesn't homogenize the school, rendering it as sanitized and politically correct as certain other colleges formerly known as southern.

GREEN LIGHT

Conservative-leaning groups are the most active and vocal on campus. There is a small gay and lesbian group, but that is about the only active organization that could be called radical. "Students are able to express any views they may have," one says. "W&L is likely one of the most conservative college campuses in the country. Despite this, no one is ostracized for having differing ideas." One College Republican suggests that W&L is labeled as conservative merely because it has a more balanced political atmosphere.

Most students are involved in more than one of the 120 clubs and organizations on campus, including a student newspaper, a radio station, and a cable television station. Among musical groups are the Chamber Singers, a chorus, a jazz ensemble, and a symphony orchestra. Religious organizations include the (Episcopalian) Canterbury Club, Baptist Student Union, Catholic Campus Ministry, Generals' Christian Fellowship, Reformed University Fellowship, Orthodox Christian Fellowship, and a Hillel club. There is also a student-run Campus Kitchen at W&L that provides "hunger relief."

There are politically active groups across the spectrum, with College Democrats and College Republicans, and Students for Life and Students for Choice. The one gay group is the GLBT Equality Initiative. The feminist group Knowledge Empowering Women Leaders (KEWL) combines coursework in women's and gender studies with programs outside the classroom.

W&L is an NCAA Division III school—which means its athletic program cannot offer scholarships, and student play is restricted to fewer games. A high percentage of students play varsity sports—there are eleven for men and ten for women—or intramural sports such as men's and women's fencing, rugby, lacrosse, water polo, and squash.

Fittingly, "the honor code established by General Robert E. Lee remains a strong force in the W&L community. It is taken very, very seriously and is extremely effective," according to a student. Incoming students pledge to abide by this code, which is run by their peers. Offenses against honor include lying, cheating, stealing, and other breaches of trust. For students found guilty, there is only one punishment—expulsion. The honor system is a manifestation of General Lee's "one rule" at the university: that every student be a gentleman. The Speaking Tradition, for instance, dictates that when people pass each other, they say "hello," even if they are strangers. One undergrad says simply, "The Honor System works, and the speaking tradition really does promote a friendly atmosphere."

Students are required to live on campus for their first two years, beyond which the university does not guarantee housing. About 60 percent of the student body lives on campus. All residence halls are coed, but men and women are separated by floor, and there are no coed bathrooms or dorm rooms. On-campus housing includes fraternity and sorority houses, where many students live as sophomores.

The Chavis House is a black-oriented residence named for John Chavis, a "free black who completed his studies" in 1799, when the university was known as Liberty Hall. (W&L's *second* black student, it's sad to say, didn't arrive until 1966.) The International House has similar aims. The Outing Club House is used for presentations and speakers and as a launching pad for most of the group's trips. It also features an indoor climbing wall, a bike workshop, a library, and gear for all types of outdoor activities. There is also a substance-free housing option. Resident advisors live in freshman housing.

Crime on campus is rare, though the school did run several years of "sexual assault summits" to address sexual misconduct on campus and in off-campus housing. In 2009, the school reported fifteen burglaries, one case of aggravated assault, and two forcible sex offenses.

Tuition for 2010–11 was $39,500, with room and board $10,243. Students are encouraged to apply for both need-based aid and merit-based aid to best avail themselves of the over $28 million in financial aid and scholarships. The school meets all demonstrated need. The average recent graduate emerged owing $23,615.

College of William and Mary

Williamsburg, Virginia • www.wm.edu

Usurping excellence

The College of William and Mary is the second-oldest college in the United States, so it's no surprise that the school has some of the oldest and most remarkable traditions in the country. Chartered by British "monarchs" William III and Mary II in 1693, the college created the first Phi Beta Kappa chapter and America's first honor code. Among its illustrious alumni are Thomas Jefferson, James Monroe, and John Marshall. William and Mary has scores of reasons to be proud of its past, and unlike many other colleges, it is.

Commonly known as one of the eight "public Ivies" for giving a superior education at comparatively little cost, W&M reserves a majority of its slots for state residents. And no wonder. The school has the highest Fulbright acceptance rate of all top research universities (fifty W&M students and alumni have won Fulbrights since 2000), and its graduates get into medical school at twice the national average. The college's focus on undergraduate teaching, its strong sense of community, its highly selective admissions, and its historic, beautiful campus will continue to draw serious students from all over the world.

Academic Life: It worked for Jefferson

William and Mary revised its curriculum several years ago, to emphasize breadth of knowledge. Now equal thirds of a student's courses come from general education requirements, electives, and a student's concentration. One recent alumnus says that students "must learn something of both the humanities and the sciences—although various paperwork games can be played to avoid a few things. However, the education requirements are established so that not too much can be worked around."

W&M's academic departments generally provide solid, rigorous courses for the requirements, but they certainly do not constitute a core curriculum. A history major says that while the courses at W&M are "well taught," he also complains that he "consistently" has trouble registering for courses because preferred classes "are very scarce in most majors due to state budget cuts."

English majors take thirty-six credits with at least one course in British literature of the Middle Ages and Renaissance, one in British literature from 1675–1900, with classes in Augustan satire, Romantic and Victorian poetry, and the Victorian novel; one course

South

662

studying a single author; an American literature course; and a research seminar.

W&M is well known for its American history program; its doctoral program in Colonial history ranks among the top four in the country. One history major says that his early American history course was surely among the best offered in the country. A broad survey of courses shows a more sober list than that found at many universities. History majors must complete a course on Europe before or after 1715; two American history survey courses; one non-Western history; and a colloquium described as "intensive reading and writing on a carefully defined historical topic or period."

According to faculty and students, the college's strongest programs are biology, classical studies, economics, history, anthropology, geology, physics, religion, and the School of Business.

Government has some excellent professors, but it has become increasingly ideological in recent years. A government major says, "William and Mary is definitely more liberal than conservative." But this rarely gets in the way of learning. "The students tend to know that people have those leanings; it doesn't mean the teachers are wholly partisan in the classroom," a student says. Majors must take thirty-three credits, including introductory classes in American government, comparative politics, and international relations; one course on political theory; a course on research methods; and a 400-level seminar.

Departments where students say that professors' political leanings influence learning include sociology, religion, and economics. A student says that conservative students are not routinely targeted by faculty members. "There are obvious exceptions, but this is generally not a major issue." Regarding the political atmosphere among the student body, one undergraduate feels that "apathy is worse on campus than bizarre political stances."

Professors seem to care about their charges. One student says, "Professors are very accessible, and they teach almost all the classes I take," noting that some teachers take on more of a mentoring role for students. Another student says that faculty are proactive with their students. "All the professors are required to have office hours, of course," the student says, "but even beyond that, they're willing to talk with you outside of class and get to know you."

VITAL STATISTICS

Religious affiliation: *none*
Total enrollment: *7,874*
Total undergraduates: *5,836*
SAT/ACT midranges: CR: *620–730*, M: *620–720*; ACT: *27–32*
Applicants: *12,109*
Applicants accepted: *34%*
Accepted applicants who enrolled: *34%*
Tuition and fees: *in state, $12,188; out of state, $33,764*
Room and board: *$8,600*
Freshman retention rate: *95%*
Graduation rate: *83% (4 yrs.), 91% (6 yrs.)*
Courses with fewer than 20 students: *48%*
Student-faculty ratio: *12:1*
Courses taught by graduate students: *not provided*
Most popular majors: *social sciences, business, interdisciplinary studies*
Students living on campus: *75%*
Guaranteed housing for four years? *no*
Students in fraternities: *25%* in sororities: *29%*

The student-faculty ratio is 12 to 1, which is excellent for a public university (and better than many private colleges). An administrator says, "When you walk into a classroom, that person in the front is a professor. What a novel idea!" Students say that professors teach all their courses, while graduate teaching assistants lead weekly discussion sections for the largest lecture courses.

Incoming students get a pre-major faculty advisor, whom they must meet with three times in the first semester. Later on, students get faculty advisors from within their major departments. A student says, "We're able to get whatever we need from the process."

For all its emphasis on teaching, William and Mary does place pressure on faculty to publish, and the occasional beloved teacher doesn't get tenure because he has failed to produce articles. Still, a professor says that the college makes it clear that faculty focus should be on the students—in the classroom and the laboratory: "W&M doesn't have a 'Research First' policy."

Some of the best professors mentioned by students include Phil Kearns in computer science; George Greenia in modern languages and medieval and Renaissance studies; Clayton Clemens and George Grayson in government; Charles Johnson in mathematics; Sarah Stafford in economics; Hans C. von Baeyer and Robert E. Welsh (both emeritus) in physics; and John Conlee and Kim Wheatley in English.

William and Mary has a respectable foreign language offering and many opportunities for international study. At W&M, one can take Ancient Greek, Latin, Hebrew, Arabic, Chinese, French, German, Spanish, Italian, Japanese, and Russian. The college sponsors over thirty study-abroad programs in twenty-three countries and gives students access to hundreds more through other schools. Perhaps most interesting is a new joint-degree program beginning in 2011 with the University of St. Andrews in Scotland. Admitted students will spend two years at each school and earn a diploma bearing the insignia of both.

Student Life: Nerds who know how to relax

The 1,200-acre William and Mary campus is located just off the grounds of Colonial Williamsburg. Ignore the thousands of tourists and the town is a scene from eighteenth-century America, complete with rustic taverns, fife and drum parades, the governor's residence (which dates from the time when Williamsburg was the capital of Virginia), apothecary shops, and "interpreters" in historic garb. Some of W&M's 7,874 students (graduate and undergraduate) work in the town's shops and museums, and all students can visit the attractions for free.

The main part of the William and Mary campus—the part where guides naturally spend the bulk of the tour—is an extension of the Colonial style of the surrounding town.

The Wren Building is the nation's oldest academic building remaining in continuous use; in it, Thomas Jefferson, James Monroe, and John Tyler all studied, dined, and attended class. The centuries-old trees and brick buildings bring a charm to what the admissions department calls its "Ancient Campus." William and Mary has obviously expanded since its Colonial beginnings, and beyond the main part of the campus the architecture is less pleasing.

New buildings abound. These include the Alan B. Miller Hall, the 166,000-square-foot, $75 million new home for the business school; and the new School of Education building. Under way are the $54.3 million Integrated Sciences Center, as well as the College Triangle Retail Project, a mixed-use building that will house student apartments above and restaurants and shops below.

Three-quarters of the student body live on campus. William and Mary guarantees housing only for freshmen and seniors, and seniors often prefer to live off campus anyway. Students who want campus housing tend to get it. Freshmen live together in all-first-year dorms. Campus dormitories are coed by wing or floor, but Greek housing remains single-sex. One benefit of the school's honor code is that at the beginning of the year, students and their RAs make their own decisions about campus living spaces—voting on when quiet hours are, visitation rules, etc. The dormitories are generally nothing to write home about; the coveted lodges, cottage-style houses in a central campus location that each house seven people, are always the first to be chosen in the housing lottery. "The new Jamestown dorms and the renovated Bryan complex are now quite popular," remarks one student. The off-campus Ludwell apartments are growing in popularity as well, housing mostly juniors and seniors. Special-interest housing includes an international house and substance-free housing. Languages students inhabit Arabic, French, German, Spanish, Russian, Italian, Japanese, or Chinese theme houses.

The Department of Women's Studies is active on campus, and one of its pet projects is Mosaic House, a full wing of the Jamestown Dorm reserved for students who want to engage in an ongoing "intellectual exchange about culture, diversity, interracial community and alternative life styles." Sign us up!

W&M's Office of Diversity and Community Initiatives oversees programs such as the Celebration of Cultures and talks entitled "What's Your Gay Point Average?" In general, the most active political groups on campus are on the left, including the LAMBDA alliance, which holds a Gay, Lesbian, Bisexual, and Transgender Awareness Week. (Some more conservative Virginians are known to call the school William and Larry because of its supposedly high Gay Point Average.) There is a branch of the NAACP as well as a group called the African American Male Coalition, which "focuses on black empowerment."

Student publications include *jump!*, the *Dog Street Journal*, the *Winged Nation*, and the *Flat Hat*.

Conservative groups are in a distinct minority. These include the Students for Life and the popular College Republicans—but they are generally "quiet," says one student. Not so the *Virginia Informer*, which frequently battles with the administration and was named the 2009 best paper of the year by the Collegiate Network. Another student notes that the law-school-student-led John Locke Society on campus also garners respect among conservatives. (Ironic, considering the group's name.) "The JLS is a conservative and classical liberal philosophical group that seeks to inform the intellectual and political debate on the W&M campus," a student explains.

Fraternities at William and Mary are mostly residential. About a quarter of students participate. But students say Greek life has an even stronger presence on campus than this statistic indicates. Weekend frat parties are popular and are open to the entire student body. Greek organizations host fund-raisers for charity, says one student, "that often take the form of laid-back Saturday afternoon sports tournaments." Another student speaks of Greek life on campus, explaining that "ongoing incidents related to alcohol consumption or property destruction have led to several fraternities losing their housing or charters in the past few years." The school has increased its efforts to stem underage drinking. Yet, by banning alcohol at regular events, the college has inadvertently driven many students to resort to private binges. One student notes, however, that underage drinking is usually addressed immediately by authorities. "The campus police deal with a heavy hand," the student says. Currently it is a matter of policy that a fraternity must report to the administration whether it intends to have a "wet" or "dry" party; if the party is "wet," the revelers can expect a heavy police presence.

Religious activities are fairly popular on campus, with interdenominational groups remaining the largest. There are over thirty religious clubs, ranging from Quaker to Catholic, Hindu to Hillel. A student says, "A lot of the major religious denominations are about as close to campus as you can get without actually being on campus. Some students will drive a distance for services they might prefer elsewhere, but for the most part worship is easily accessible." Another says, "There is a really vibrant religious community within Williamsburg and William and Mary, especially if you are Christian; Catholicism is the largest represented religion here; Catholics are very active and do a lot in the college community." Some 75 percent of students are involved in community service projects.

Others among the hundreds of recognized groups on campus include the Christopher Wren Singers, a madrigal choir; the Collegiate Tea Drinker's Society; the Queen's Guards, a military science organization; a massage club; the Irish Dance and Culture Club; Quizbowl; and Rhythm and Taps tap-dancing club.

Since most students live on campus, much of social life is centered there. Alma Mater Productions (AMP) is one of the most active student organizations. Each week in the spring and fall, AMP organizes Fridays@5, featuring free bands that play outside at a pavilion. Other AMP events include student talent shows, movie screenings, comedians, and speakers. At the Yule Log Ceremony, held just before winter exams, the college president reads *How the Grinch Stole Christmas*, and students enjoy hot cider and Christmas cookies. Another tradition in which the college president participates is the "primal scream," which the entire school emits midway through final exam week. The Last Day of Classes Bash is an all-day event held in the Sunken Gardens. The school also encourages an ongoing tradition in which incoming freshmen serenade the college president outside his office window. There are also Coronation Day, a King and Queen Ball, and senior Candlelight Ceremony.

William and Mary loves these traditions and cherishes quirky legends. One of the best known revolves around the Crim Dell bridge: if a couple kisses there, they are destined to marry—unless one throws the other off. A bawdier tradition centering on the Crim Dell bridge is the W&M "triathlon," which includes a dive into the Crim Dell, streaking the Sunken Garden, and jumping the wall to the old governor's mansion in Colonial Williamsburg.

A student says that support for the athletic program is generally good. W&M athletes, the Tribe, have some of the highest graduation rates in NCAA Division I sports. Aside from the twenty-three varsity sports programs, W&M also has plenty of club and intramural teams, with a high percentage of the student body participating in sports.

According to one student, the typical William and Mary undergrad is "nerdy and dedicated to his studies but able to relax." Students report that because of their workload, they must be driven to have a social life. One student acknowledges that the curriculum's rigor has led to the perception that W&M students are bookworms. "There's a reputation at W&M, I guess, that on any given Saturday soon after classes begin, you'll find students

ACADEMIC REQUIREMENTS

While it's not a traditional core, the curriculum at William and Mary imposes substantial general education requirements that can be met by mostly solid introductory surveys. Students take:

- One course in mathematics and quantitative reasoning, such as "Elementary Probability and Statistics" and "Calculus."
- Writing 101, a writing-intensive freshman seminar. Students must also meet writing requirements within most majors.
- Two courses in the natural sciences (one physical sciences class and a biological sciences class, plus a supplemental lab), such as "Great Ideas in Physics" and "Insects and Society."
- Two courses in the social sciences. Choices range from "Principles of Microeconomics" to "Sexuality."
- Three classes in world cultures and history: one in the European tradition, such as "Christian Origins" or "Europe Since 1945; one outside the European tradition, such as "Introduction to Buddhism" or "Nation, Gender, and Race in South Asia"; and one in a cross-cultural topic such as "Introduction to Religion" or "The Crusades."
- One course in literature or the history of the arts. Choices here are much too broad; you could fulfill this requirement with anything from "Reading the Bible in Hebrew" to "History of American Vernacular Dance."
- Two credits in creative or performing arts. Options here range from "Intermediate Jazz" to "Group Instruction in Guitar."
- One course in "philosophical, religious, and social thought." Options include "Ethics," "The Holocaust," and "Philosophy of Feminism."

A student must also reach the fourth-semester level of proficiency in a foreign language, and demonstrate an understanding of computers through coursework or a test.

South

GREEN LIGHT

The classrooms seem mostly nonpoliticized at William and Mary—no mean feat. The administration is another story. The W&M Diversity webpage proclaims the college's 2009–10 accomplishments: election of a transgender homecoming queen; "leading" other Virginia public colleges to revisit the legality of their antidiscrimination policies (to protect sexual dissidents); a president-appointed senior-level position to oversee diversity and community initiatives; and the Lemon Initiative, a study of race and slavery in the college's history.

William and Mary students do react to threats to what they see as their "rights." The *Informer* reported on an administration proposal to ban "items used predominantly for drinking games (e.g., pong tables and beer bongs)" and came out strongly in defense of students' rights to possess and use these tools: "Do we wish to be the poor man who can only say, 'First they came for beer pong, and I did not speak up because I did not play. Then they came for beer bongs, and I said nothing because I did not own one. Finally, they came for my Solo cups, and no one was inebriated enough to speak out for my drink?' No, surely we do not. Now is the time for action. Restore Honor. Restore Sanity. Restore Beer Pong."

packing the libraries to study," the student admits. "That's a little exaggeration, but I think students generally try to keep up with their studies." He adds, "I would not say that W&M is a party school—we have more of a scholarly focus. But if people want to come here and have an active social life, there are plenty of opportunities."

William and Mary boasts a low crime rate, mostly because of its setting, but also because of the honor code and the prevailing atmosphere of trust. "I don't walk by myself at night at three in the morning on the weekend," a female student says, "but we're no better or worse than any campus. I've never felt unsafe." The college reported in 2009 five forcible sex offenses, one robbery, six aggravated assaults, one arson, and seventeen burglaries on campus. The campus police provide a nighttime escort service and a van that shuttles students to area bars and parties. There are emergency phones all across the campus. Though not reported in the crime statistics, there were three suicides at William and Mary in 2010.

For a school of its caliber, William and Mary is an excellent value for Virginians, who in 2010–11 paid only $12,188; out-of-state students paid $33,764. Room and board averaged $8,600. Some 29 percent of students get need-based aid. The college covers most Virginia residents' demonstrated financial shortfalls, and the average graduate of W&M owes a moderate $18,410 in student loans. Undergraduates can also take advantage of a financial-aid program called Gateway William and Mary. This program is a combination of institutional, state, and federal grants for students from low- and middle-income families who display academic promise.

Wofford College

Spartanburg, South Carolina • www.wofford.edu

So very normal

The wave of radical change that swept over American academia in the 1960s transformed most colleges in this guide to the point where older alumni often hardly recognize anything about their alma maters, apart from the buildings and (sometimes) the mascots. It's refreshing, if only for the sake of genuine diversity, to come across a college that didn't turn into a pumpkin one midnight in 1968.

Wofford College has maintained, to an astonishing degree, continuity with its own best traditions and those of its region. "Most of the people running Wofford are creatures of the culture," says one professor, "and they know better than to try to change the students in outrageous ways." A teacher says, "It's as close as you can get anywhere to an old-fashioned southern college experience." He means that in the best sense: Wofford was one of the first private colleges in its region to voluntarily integrate, and its student body has a healthy racial variety.

The college acknowledges and reflects its Methodist roots. The fall convocation each year begins with a prayer, and along with a diploma, each graduating senior receives a Bible signed by all of Wofford's faculty members. "It's one of the school's greatest traditions," says a student. For a socially conservative student looking for strong liberal arts courses, a solidly free-market economics education, and a close-knit community of good-natured students and committed teachers, Wofford is a strong choice.

Academic Life: Small is beautiful

Wofford does not have a rigorous core curriculum, and it's possible to graduate without a deep understanding of Western culture. But the school offers substantial requirements for its majors and many serious courses taught by accessible, interested professors. "I find that students are hungry for the classics," says one faculty member. "I've taught them recently, and students said they'd wished they read these earlier. They were blown away." Such enthusiasm can be contagious—and books read in that spirit will resonate quite differently in the mind and form the character more profoundly than the same works considered suspiciously as relics of an oppressive, alien past.

The required Humanities 101 is offered in several flavors. Past choices offered have ranged from "Chili Cheese 'n Grits: New South/Old South" to traditional Western civilization courses. Also required is English 102, "Seminar in Literature and Composition." Again, options extend too widely, from "F. Scott Fitzgerald and the Jazz Age" and "Aspects of the South in Fiction" to "Novels of Dispossession."

Other requirements include choosing from two sections of a potentially admirable course titled "History of Modern Western Civilization," either from the Renaissance to 1815, or from 1815 to the present. However, one faculty member complains about this requirement: "Notice where it starts—in the early modern period. Students can finish their education without knowing anything about the classical period or the Middle Ages. That's a real problem. The general education requirement leaves a lot of wiggle room. A student can get through without having read many major works."

Wofford offers twenty-five majors, eight preprofessional programs like prepharmacy, preministry, and education, fourteen minors, and twelve interdisciplinary programs. Students have the option of taking some classes at nearby Converse College, which means more choices for those who don't find their interests met at Wofford. The school's Sandor Teszler Library houses 360,000 volumes, but students can also avail themselves of the holdings of nearby Converse College and the University of South Carolina–Spartanburg through interlibrary loan.

Wofford's English department boasts several highly regarded professors, but one teacher says that it suffers from "the most noticeable grade inflation on campus." English majors take one survey of pre-1800 and another of post-1800 English literature, and another American literature survey. They also choose one course each from early (Chaucer, Spenser, Shakespeare) and middle (the Romantic or Victorian period) British literature; American lit; contemporary literature; and either "European Masterpieces" or "Early Women Writers" or literary criticism or linguistics classes. Students must also complete five advanced electives. All in all, a solid program. There is a creative writing concentration, and each year Wofford publishes and distributes 2,000 copies of the best student novel. Visiting authors have included Doris Betts, Bill Bryson, George Garrett, and Lee Smith.

History majors complete pre-1815 and post-1815 surveys of modern Western civilization; three courses in American history; a class in early and another in modern European history; a course in either the modern Middle East, modern East Asia, or colonial or modern Latin America; two senior-level reading courses in history; and another senior-level course taught by a prominent visiting professor (these rotate). Teachers are called competent and dedicated, though younger ones tend toward hyperspecialization.

Majors in government must complete "Foundations of American Politics" and "Foundations of World Politics" and two classes in each of the department's subfields: American government, international relations and comparative government, and political theory, as well as two electives. Those who concentrate in American politics spend a term in Washington, D.C., studying and interning. World politics students study abroad. Political thought students take extra theory courses.

The philosophy department is among the more liberal at Wofford, and some consider it unserious. But its major requirements seem solid enough: one course on metaphysics or on epistemology, a three-course history of philosophy sequence, logic, ethics, and a senior project.

Religion courses range from broad but worthy classes such as "Christian Ethics" and "Religions of Asia" to "History of Christian Theology."

One professor says: "The economics and government departments are uniformly conservative, and the government department in particular takes a philosophical, even classical approach to the study of politics. In

> **SUGGESTED CORE**
> 1. English 336, European Masterpieces: Antiquity to the Renaissance (closest match)
> 2. Philosophy 351, Western Philosophy in Antiquity and the Middle Ages
> 3. Religion 201/202, The Old Testament/The New Testament
> 4. Religion 203, The Christian Faith (closest match)
> 5. Government 392, Modern Political Thought
> 6. English 305/306, Shakespeare's Comedies and Histories/Shakespeare's Tragedies and Romances
> 7. History 201, History of the United States, 1607–1865
> 8. Philosophy 353, Nineteenth-Century European Philosophy

these departments, the questions and concerns animating traditional liberal education still thrive."

Some faculty in the biology and language departments, says a teacher, are "evangelical" neo-Darwinians and "crusaders for the biotech enterprise," including stem-cell research and cloning. Some are "rabid in their disdain for religious and philosophical critiques of modern scientific hegemony," and they are prone to "attract many of Wofford's better students away from liberal arts."

The economics department faculty are mostly principled advocates of the market economy. There is a gender studies program at Wofford, but it is not a major, and it seems pretty tame. African American studies seems straightforward and not politicized.

It is apparently unheard of at Wofford for students to be graded down for expressing their views.

Classes are compact—the largest classroom holds just sixty students—which means close faculty-student interaction. Promotion is based solely on teaching. "You know all your professors here, and they know you," says a student. Some of the best professors at Wofford include Robert C. Jeffrey in government; Frank M. Machovec, John McArthur, Timothy Terrell, and Richard Wallace in economics; Ellen Goldey in biology; and Charlie Bass in chemistry.

Every student is assigned a faculty advisor, and freshmen and sophomores need their approval to register for classes. Once a student declares a major, he gets an advisor within it. A peer-tutoring program pairs upperclassmen with students who request the extra help.

The Community of Scholars program lets students spend a summer conducting serious research alongside Wofford faculty members. Each year, nineteen students are accepted as research fellows; in 2010, they completed their fellowships with projects like "The Chinese One-Child Policy: An Inquiry into Human Rights" and "Cultural Expressions of Afro-Latinos in South America: A Documentary Film."

Wofford's study-abroad options are plentiful and popular. Wofford's new "The Road Less Traveled" initiative offers scholarships to students who choose to study in places like Cyprus, Taiwan, Jordan, and Senegal. All told, Wofford students can travel all over the world for study abroad—in 2010, the school had students abroad blogging about their adventures in Spain, Bolivia, New Delhi, Ireland, Copenhagen, and more. Students can also make trips during the winter "interim" semester over Christmas break.

Language majors are available only in Chinese, French, German, and Spanish. Students should beware: "The language departments are evangelical in their crusade for multiculturalism," according to a faculty member.

Student Life: Traditions a' plenty

As one sophomore says, "There really is a Wofford family. You know everyone." Knowing your classmates isn't much of a stretch when there are fewer than 1,500 students on campus. But those students are mostly courtly, polite, and well rounded—southern ladies and gentlemen, according to one professor. He says that they have mostly "modest ambitions. They want to go to professional schools, teach school, get married, and raise families. . . . They don't overvalue either academics or athletics but balance the two. However, they'll do hard work when asked, and they really appreciate the opportunity to learn."

For most Wofford students, social life *is* Greek life. More than half the students are members of a fraternity or sorority, and each chapter has its own house. "On an average weekend night, we have 600 to 700 people down here," says one student. Local bands and theme parties are frequent and popular. Mostly because of fraternities and sororities, Wofford is said to be rather cliquish—fraternity rush begins during the second week of school, with sorority rush starting a week later. But at least "there is a clique for everyone, and they're not segregated," says one student. "You have your core friends, and then everybody else you're friendly with." A fraternity member says, "Wofford is a pretty 'wet' campus, and public safety often looks the other way. . . . You have to be pretty stupid to get an alcohol violation."

On average, about 60 percent of Wofford freshmen come from South Carolina, and another 20 percent from North Carolina and Georgia. Less than 1 percent of the student body is composed of international students. They probably just haven't heard of Wofford over in Bangalore.

Some 94 percent of students live on campus, and most unmarried students are required to. Most residence halls are coed, but Wofford offers one all-female dorm (with access limited to residents only) as well as one all-male dorm. Students must be ten feet outside a building entrance to smoke, and no alcohol or related paraphernalia is permitted in dorm rooms where both residents are under twenty-one.

In 2006, Wofford opened the doors to its new "neighborhood village" housing, allowing upperclassmen to live in four-bedroom, 1,200-square-foot, on-campus apartments that look like quaint cottages, with white rocking chairs on their wide porches. Now that the project is complete, the entire senior class is housed in the Village, encouraging upperclassmen to live on campus and remain active in student life. Sounds like a fine plan to us.

Wofford enrolls only around 1,400 students, but the school competes at the NCAA Division I level as a member of the Southern Conference. The Wofford Terriers compete in gold and black and maintain a higher-than-average graduation rate for student athletes. And though small, Wofford has some of the best athletic facilities in the region, thanks to an athletic building donated by Carolina Panthers owner and Wofford alumnus Jerry Richardson. In return for the gift, the Panthers use Wofford as their summer training center each year—not a bad deal for Wofford. The college also opened a new baseball stadium in 2004. About 40 percent of Wofford students play on one of the school's seventeen varsity teams. The school offers men's and women's basketball, cross-country, golf, rifle, soccer, tennis, and track and field. Men play baseball and football as well, and women play volleyball.

ACADEMIC REQUIREMENTS

Without a true core curriculum, Wofford still tries to guarantee breadth of studies with decent distribution requirements. Students must take:

- Humanities 101.
- "Freshman English" (English 102) and one sophomore-level course such as "Introduction to the Study of Literature" or "Survey of American Literature."
- One course in art, music, or theater, such as "Survey of the History of Western Art" or "African Art."
- One two-year introductory foreign language sequence or one advanced course.
- One two-course sequence in biology, chemistry, geology, physics, or psychology; or an introduction to science, with one semester in a life science and one in a physical science; or an intensive physics course.
- History 101 or 102.
- An introduction to philosophy or a sophomore-level philosophy course such as "Bio-Medical Ethics."
- One course in religion. Available offerings range from "Religions of the World" to "Søren Kierkegaard."
- A course in "Cultures and Peoples," which will "focus on the study of cultures other than European and European-settler cultures, or the interaction between and comparison of European and non-Western cultures."
- One course in mathematics.
- Two semesters of freshman physical education.

South

GREEN LIGHT

The school's traditional policies seem to sit well with Wofford students, who are naturally more conservative than those who typically populate liberal arts colleges. Of course, Wofford students are southern—they don't want confrontation and are unlikely to organize rallies and protests. While faculty members often hold different views from their students, civility reigns. One professor says that there is no political confrontation between faculty and students; conflict is more likely to arise over the faculty's general disapproval of Greek life.

Wofford's low profile on the national scene may be its greatest asset, some supporters say. Students report that it keeps Wofford administrators from conforming too closely to the trends and politics of other universities. "The best part about Wofford is that they're just not interested in all of the foolishness you find at other schools," says one alumnus. "Students just won't have it." Wofford's donors likely wouldn't have it either. A major benefactor of the school and the region was the late textile king Roger Milliken, a philanthropist, trustee emeritus, and sometime backer of presidential candidate (and crucial conservative thinker) Patrick J. Buchanan. While President Dunlap is reputed to be mildly liberal, students and faculty say he knows better than to push ahead with a radical agenda.

At Saturday afternoon football games, men wear ties, women wear dresses, and alumni and local residents flock to the stadium. Intramurals are also popular and usually organized by fraternities. Teams include beach volleyball, tag, disc golf, racquetball, and billiards. Recreational activities are mostly fitness classes like self-defense and tango, but the school does have an outdoors club for hikers and bikers. In club sports, Wofford offers lacrosse, Ultimate Frisbee, bowling, and shooting.

Apart from Phi Beta Kappa and student government, the school hosts a number of academic and professional organizations. The Economics Society, Teacher Education Student Association, American Chemical Society, and Scabbard and Blade military science club all supplement Wofford's course offerings. The school publishes the *Bohemian* yearbook, the *Journal* literary magazine, and *Old Gold & Black* newspaper. Performing arts groups include a gospel choir, men's glee club, show choir, women's ensemble, and concert and pep band. Special interest groups provide political and social outlets like Amnesty International, Mock Trial Team, College Democrats and College Republicans, and the Association of Multicultural Students.

Formed in 2000, Wofford's Office of Multicultural Affairs is administered by the Office of the Dean, but is only mildly influential at the school. Its programs include a Human Diversity Week held each fall and events to celebrate Black History Month each February.

Wofford provides outlets for a number of religious organizations, all Christian apart from the Hillel Jewish Student Organization. Baptists, Episcopalians, Methodists, and Presbyterians are all represented, as well as Fellowship of Christian Athletes, the Souljahs for Christ, service groups, and a Catholic Newman Club. Student-led prayer services take place in the school's Mickel Chapel each Sunday night.

Lately, the college has pumped up its arts and concerts calendar, encouraging intellectual and cultural interests for students and Spartanburg-area residents. The World Film

South

Series, featuring independent foreign movies, is free for students. Musical performances are said to be well attended. Many Wofford students are active in community service work through the college's Twin Towers Project, Habitat for Humanity, mentorships, and soup kitchens.

Wofford's lovely campus was designated an arboretum in 2002 in recognition of its hundreds of species of trees. The college has built several stunning facilities in recent years, including the $15 million Milliken Science Center and the Franklin Olin Building, which houses high-tech computer and language labs. The college's first building was Old Main, which was restored in 2001 and is home to several academic departments and Leonard Auditorium.

Spartanburg is a southern town "out of the 1950s, where you can get anywhere in fifteen minutes," a professor says. The city is noticeably depressed economically, although some areas downtown are being restored with restaurants and bars. Still, students spend most of their time on campus or in the off-campus houses nearby. Every Wofford student must hit the Beacon, Spartanburg's legendary hamburger joint, at least a few times. Order your sandwich "a' plenty"—covered in onion rings and fries, dripping in grease—along with the customary sweet tea.

Wofford College is, for most students, within an easy drive from home—and many visit their parents on weekends. But the college is not a suitcase school. "Typically, there is always something going on during the weekend," a student says.

Despite the area's economic struggles, on the Wofford campus, crime is very infrequent, with just two aggravated assaults and two car thefts reported in 2009. Students should be careful when leaving the confines of the grounds because the areas directly bordering the campus are "sketchy," as one student says.

As private universities go, Wofford is an average price; tuition for 2010–11 was $31,710, while room and board was $8,870. Admissions are need blind; however, the school cannot afford to guarantee full financial aid to all students. Still, about 51 percent do receive some need-based aid. The debt of the average recent graduate was a moderate $13,560.

NORTH DAKOTA

MINNESOTA

SOUTH DAKOTA

◆ Macalester College
◆ Carleton College

WISCONSIN

MICHIGAN

◆ Calvin College

◆ University of Wisconsin–Madison

Hillsdale College ◆

◆ University of Michigan

NEBRASKA

IOWA

◆ Grinnell College

CHICAGO AREA
Northwestern University
University of Chicago
Wheaton College

◆ University of Notre Dame

Case Western Reserve University ◆

◆ Oberlin College

OHIO

◆ Creighton University

◆ University
of Iowa

◆ Kenyon College

INDIANA

◆ Franciscan University of Steub

◆ University of Illinois
at Urbana-Champaign

◆ Ohio State University

KANSAS

◆ University of Kansas

◆ Wabash College

ILLINOIS

MISSOURI

◆ Washington University
in St. Louis

◆ College of the Ozarks

OKLAHOMA

Midwest

Calvin College • Carleton College • Case Western Reserve University •
University of Chicago • Creighton University •
Franciscan University of Steubenville • Grinnell College •
Hillsdale College • University of Illinois at Urbana-Champaign •
University of Iowa • University of Kansas • Kenyon College •
Macalester College • University of Michigan •
Northwestern University • University of Notre Dame •
Oberlin College • Ohio State University • College of the Ozarks •
Wabash College • Washington University in St. Louis •
Wheaton College • University of Wisconsin–Madison

Calvin College

Grand Rapids, Michigan • www.calvin.edu

The Institutes of Christian education

Calvin College was founded as a seminary for the Christian Reformed Church in 1876 and has remained committed to offering a liberal education thoroughly steeped in Christian "faith, thought, and practice." The curriculum has expanded to include professional training in fields such as nursing, accounting, and engineering, but Calvin still claims to place the highest premium on the liberal arts.

Calvin remains strongly influenced by the Reformed tradition, which views "a world made good by God, distorted by sin, redeemed in Christ, and awaiting the fullness of God's reign." A professor points to "a deep and intentional integration of the mission of the college into every fact of its life." Students interested in a liberal arts education with a decisively Augustinian bent will be at home at Calvin College.

Academic Life: Developing a Christian mind

Calvin educates students in order to "recapture society, culture, and all creation for Jesus Christ." Despite this lofty goal, its required curriculum cannot be called a true core. Rather, it is a set of distribution requirements that can be fulfilled with any number of classes—or, in some cases, by testing out. With the exception of a few courses, such as the freshman seminar, "Developing a Christian Mind," there is no common canon. For example, to meet the global and historical studies requirement, students choose from any of fifty courses from various departments.

To its credit, the school strives for integration among different disciplines and attempts to sequence courses in such a way that they build upon each other. One professor tells us that "if the students take our core in the proper spirit, it can serve as tremendous basis for further study and reflection throughout life. But for some kids, that is a mighty big 'if.'" Another professor calls the curriculum, "very good by contemporary standards. It's not Yale in 1890, but it's quite good by modern standards." It is clear that Calvin is not a Great Books school. However, its curriculum does encourage students to learn from a broad pool of traditional canonical texts.

All faculty must be members in good standing with a Christian Reformed church or another denomination that shares "ecclesiastical fellowship" with it, and they must sign a

VITAL STATISTICS

Religious affiliation: *Christian Reformed*
Total enrollment: *4,092*
Total undergraduates: *4,015*
SAT/ACT midranges: CR: *520–670*, M: *550–660*; ACT: *23–29*
Applicants: *2,529*
Applicants accepted: *93%*
Accepted applicants who enrolled: *40%*
Tuition and fees: *$24,870*
Room and board: *$8,525*
Freshman retention rate: *86%*
Graduation rate: *55% (4 yrs.), 75% (6 yrs.)*
Courses with fewer than 20 students: *39%*
Student-faculty ratio: *11:1*
Courses taught by graduate students: *none*
Most popular majors: *business, engineering, nursing*
Students living on campus: *57%*
Guaranteed housing for four years? *yes*
Students in fraternities or sororities: *none*

pledge of belief and promise to educate their own children in Reformed (or other approved) schools. According to one professor, "the faculty requirements are rigorous (some might say too much so) in an attempt to be sure that all faculty are not only 'OK' with the mission but committed to it." Calvin College places teaching before research, but a professor must engage in scholarship. The provost says, "Faculty usually come to this school because they are committed to undergraduate students but also want to contribute at the front edge of their field." Another professor sums up the college's perspective: "The quickest way to lose your job is to be a cruddy teacher."

"Professors at Calvin are extremely accessible," says one student. "With smaller class sizes, professors get to know you by name and can develop a working relationship with you. They are very gracious and generous with office hours, and you can even just walk into their office, too. They are there to help." Calvin classes are taught largely by full-time faculty, and the advising system is thorough. Says one professor, "Faculty advising, not just teaching and scholarship, is evaluated by the college." That's a good thing, because navigating through the complex requirements and the many options can be tricky. One student says, "The advisor will serve as the student's mentor and will often develop lifelong relationships with his advisees." With a student to faculty ratio of 11 to 1, students can generally get the attention they require.

Calvin boasts a number of strong disciplines. Philosophy, described by one faculty member as the college's "flagship department," has produced four presidents of the American Philosophical Association and two Gifford Lecturers, while faculty from the department have gone on to endowed chairs at Yale, Notre Dame, and elsewhere.

The English department is also quite solid, but according to one professor, "It has suffered a bit from recent retirements." English majors take world, British, and American literature courses, and supplement these with classes such as "Chaucer," "Shakespeare," and "Milton." The department hosts the world-renowned Festival of Faith & Writing. Past keynote speakers have included John Updike, Maya Angelou, and Katherine Paterson.

Science students might be interested to hear that Calvin College was named one of the "Best Places to Work in Academia" in 2010 by the *Scientist*, a magazine for the life sciences. Some 1,600 academics around the world were polled, and Calvin came in at number eight among U.S. colleges.

The history department receives mixed reviews. One professor says, "Our history faculty as a whole do seem to demand quite a lot. However, they are, in my experience, the most leftist-agenda-driven department on campus. Students seeking a balanced approach to history rarely feel as though they are getting it there." Although history majors must take Western civilization and American history classes, a student says, "In my experiences in history courses, many Calvin profs are quite critical of the Western heritage and American institutions. It is debatable whether it is respectful criticism or disrespectful. I think that it can go either way." However its teachers interpret historical facts, Calvin College seems to transmit them effectively; in the Civic Literacy Survey conducted by Intercollegiate Studies Institute (the publisher of this guide), which surveys student learning of history, American civics, and economics at fifty leading American colleges and universities, Calvin ranked in the top ten twice in two years.

The political science department does not require courses in the U.S. Constitution or American political philosophy but rather includes in its requirements courses in international politics, comparative government, and statistics.

SUGGESTED CORE
1. Classics 211, Classical Literature
2. Philosophy 251, History of Philosophy I or Philosophy 312, Plato and Aristotle
3. Religion 121, Biblical Literature and Theology
4. Religion 243, History of Christian Theology I
5. Political Science 306, History of Modern Political Thought
6. English 346, Shakespeare
7. History 252, The American Republic, 1763–1877
8. Philosophy 335, Nineteenth Century Philosophy or Philosophy 340, Contemporary Continental Philosophy

While business is the most popular major at Calvin, the business department "tends to attract our least reflective students," says one professor. A student agrees, calling the department "far from intellectually rigorous." However, another student praises its "experienced faculty. Many Calvin business faculty have left their prestigious positions in the private sector to be professors at Calvin." Alumni from the accounting department have a good success rate on the CPA exam. According to one professor, "Accounting is an excellent program, with our graduates placing among the top ten undergraduate programs nationally when evaluated by proportion succeeding in CPA exams."

The classics department and its professors attract some of Calvin's best students, many of whom double major in classics and philosophy or religion. Other strong departments include biology, chemistry, music, nursing, physics, and engineering.

Students recommend Professors Rebecca Konyndyk DeYoung, Del Ratzsch, Kevin Corcoran, and Ken Bratt in classics; Lee Hardy and James K. A. Smith in philosophy; Stephen Matheson and Curt Blankespoor in biology; Ronald Blankespoor in chemistry; Bill Stevenson in political science; John Schneider in religion; Susan Felch, James VandenBosch, and Karen Saupe in English; James Bratt, William Van Vugt, and Bert de Vries in history; and John Tiemstra and Kurt Schaefer in economics.

Professors indicate that most students are serious about academics, and those students who want to be challenged will find ample opportunities. Students with weak academic records (the college has a very high acceptance rate) often become much more driven to learn after a semester or two at Calvin. However, not everyone becomes a top-notch student. Another professor reports, "There are students in baseball hats at the back of the room, just taking up space. One kid I know says he appreciates them only because they subsidize education for everyone else."

Those students who are interested in pursuing academic excellence should consider Calvin's honors program. Honors courses are offered in most departments, providing students with the opportunity for rigorous undergraduate research. A professor says that honors is "a very active program, and the participants in it regularly get a lot of enrichment that regular kids miss out on." Additionally, there are many opportunities for faculty-student research collaboration. A professor points to "dozens of summer research positions in the sciences funded by federal and private-foundation grants, and a smaller number in the other divisions of the college."

Other special programs include the award-winning January Series, three weeks of lectures featuring "the world's greatest authorities in their respective fields," offered free of charge to students and the community. The series enables students to hear a "wide variety" of viewpoints. The Student Activities Office sponsors more than fifty performing artists each year.

Calvin also offers extensive study-abroad programs, ranking sixth in the nation among baccalaureate institutions for the ratio of students studying abroad. About two-thirds of students spend time off campus during their tenure at Calvin, either during "January term" or semester-long stays in England, France, Hungary, China, Honduras, Spain, Mexico, or Ghana. One student informs us that "Calvin is nationally known for its study-abroad programs. Each semester, Calvin students are studying around the globe, on each continent, in many countries. Especially in January, during Calvin's 'Interim,' a large portion of the student body will study abroad for that month. Personally, through Calvin's programs, I have studied in Honduras for five months, Ecuador for one month, and China for one month. I hope to study in Europe next January." At home, Calvin offers classes in Spanish, French, Italian, Chinese, Korean, German, Japanese, Latin, Ancient Greek, and Dutch.

Student Life: Living our faith together

Grand Rapids is located on Michigan's west coast. The city boasts historic neighborhoods, shopping, the Gerald R. Ford Presidential Library and Museum, a downtown riverwalk, four professional sports teams, and salmon fishing in the Grand River.

The college celebrated fifty-five years on its Knollcrest campus in 2010, which it purchased from local businessman J. C. Miller. The college has since more than doubled the original 166-acre purchase, including the addition of a ninety-acre Ecosystem Preserve, "Calvin's Crossing," a 400-foot-long skywalk, and the Prince Conference Center, the last of which is surrounded by forest and wetland, providing a "stress-free environment for fellowship, learning, and exchanging ideas." The new Bunker Interpretive Center and extensive trail system draws nearly 5,000 visitors a year to the preserve. The thirty-six-acre Gainey Athletic Facility—which also serves students from Grand Rapids Christian Schools—includes a cross-country course; softball, soccer, and baseball fields; and tennis courts. The H. Henry Meeter Center for Calvin Studies, located in the Hekman Library, contains one of the world's largest collections of works by and about John Calvin and other Protestant reformers, and the 55,000-square-foot, three-story DeVos Communication Center contains multimedia classrooms, a distance education classroom, television and audio studios, a 150-seat theater, and a speech pathology and audiology clinic. In 2009, after spending two years and $50 million, the college opened the Spoelhof Fieldhouse Complex—the largest building project in the college's history. The 362,000-square-foot facility includes the Ven-

ACADEMIC REQUIREMENTS

Calvin does not offer a traditional core curriculum but rather distribution requirements with a mostly solid selection of courses. They are as follows:

- Two freshman orientation classes, "Developing a Christian Mind" and "First-Year Prelude."
- "Written Rhetoric" or "Enhanced Written Rhetoric."
- One class in information technology. Class choices include "Foundations of Information Technology" and "Introduction to Engineering Design and Graphical Communication."
- One course in "rhetoric in culture." Options range from "Visual Culture" to "Oral Rhetoric for Engineers."
- Three physical education classes.
- One course in a foreign language, from "Elementary Chinese" to "Intermediate Latin."
- "History of the West and the World" either I or II.
- "Fundamental Questions in Philosophy."
- Two courses in Biblical Foundations or Theological Foundations—one introductory and one advanced. Options range from "Biblical Literature & Theology" to "Christianity and the World's Religions."
- One class in social sciences, from "Persons in Political Community" to "Diversity & Inequality in the United States."
- One course in the societal structures of North America, with choices ranging from "Principles of Economics" to "Sociological Principles & Perspectives."
- One class in literature, with options such as "Classical Literature" and "Introduction to the Hispanic World."
- One course in world history, with choices ranging from "Early Christian and Byzantine Arts" to "Studies in Central European Culture–Hungary."
- One class in fine arts, with options such as "Principles of Theatre" and "Architectural History" I.
- One course in math—anything from "Elements of Modern Mathematics" to "Statistics and Research Design."
- One class in physical science, ranging from "Planets, Stars, and Galaxies" to "Arts for the Elementary Teacher."
- One course in biological science, such as "Biological Science" or "Cell Biology and Genetics."
- One multicultural course. Many students fulfill this requirement through off-campus volunteer programs.
- A "core capstone" course during the final year, typically a small seminar with a major research project undertaken in the student's major field of study.

ema Aquatic Center, with an Olympic-regulation pool and seating for 500; the 5,000-seat Van Noord Arena; the Huizenga Center with four tennis courts and 14,000-square feet of weight training rooms and a custom-made rock-climbing wall; and the Hoogenboom Health and Recreation Center with racquet ball courts, exercise laboratories, and a large gym used for volleyball, basketball, intramurals, and PE classes.

The Student Life Division at Calvin offers, in its own words, "a wide array of programs and services that are consistent with, and complement, the educational opportunities that abound at Calvin." In the words of one student, "Calvin students will never say there is nothing to do on campus. The dorms are always hosting a myriad of activities, and Calvin's student development department and student senate often hold huge events for students." There are sixty-five registered clubs and organizations on campus, including professional clubs for engineering, nursing, business, prelaw, predental, and premedical students; religious organizations such as Prison Fellowship, Bible Bonanza, Young Life, and Breakthrough Gospel Dance Team; minority and multicultural clubs such as the Black Knights; and quite a few sporting clubs. Musical students can join one of many choral ensembles, including the orchestra, a jazz ensemble, a handbell ensemble, or the Calvin Collegium Musicum, the last of which performs music from the medieval, Renaissance, and Baroque periods. As might be expected, there is a strong Christian emphasis in Calvin's musical life, which is seen as a celebration of God and community. In the words of the orchestra's mission statement: "We study and play music from many times and places rejoicing with God in His good creation." Arts organizations include a Christian Writer's Guild and a theater group. There are a number of campus publications, including a student newspaper, *Chimes,* and a literary journal, *Dialogue.* Students participate in several political groups such as the College Conservatives, the Calvin College Democrats, and the Social Justice Coalition. There are no fraternities or sororities, and Calvin is not a party school by anyone's standard, but that doesn't mean students don't know how to have fun. Offbeat annual events include Chaos Day, the Mud Bowl, Airband, the Cold Knight Plunge, Siblings Weekend, and a cardboard-canoe contest sponsored by the Engineering department. The college celebrates Calvin's birthday each year with cake, ice cream, and a two-minute speech by a faculty impersonator of the dour theologian.

Calvin participates in NCAA Division III athletics with eight men's and nine women's teams and also offers numerous intramural sports. A student says, "Many students are very athletic (partially because the private Christian schools from which Calvin draws a large number of students emphasize this strongly), and so intramurals and student-organized games play a large part in student life." Calvin's longtime feud with nearby Hope College was named one of the top ten rivalries in the country by ESPN. And players from both the men's and women's soccer teams have been awarded All-MIAA honors. Students can also participate in swimming and diving, basketball, tennis, golf, track and field, cross-country, and golf, among other sporting activities.

Calvin students are housed in one of seven residence halls or in the Knollcrest apartments for juniors and seniors. "Meditation rooms," for quiet prayer and reflection, are located in the lower level of all residence halls. Lounge/study areas for both male and female students are also found on the lower level of the women's dorms, while the men's dorms include recreational areas. One student tells us, "The seven dormitory complexes are extremely unified and are a fertile ground for strong friendships and relationships to be formed. Calvin's residence-life department works hard to make the dorms a place of community and solidarity. Resident directors and resident assistants go through a rigorous selection process to ensure that a healthy living envirroment for students is maintained." Freshmen and sophomores (except those who are 21 years of age, married, or part-time) are required to live on campus or at home with their parents. Calvin's residence-hall policy prohibits, among other things, alcohol, noise (outside of the hours of 4:30–6:00 PM), offensive language or posters, pornography, and premarital sex. In addition, Calvin students are expected to observe Sunday "by keeping the spirit and purpose of the day." Visitation hours are limited, and students are not allowed to have members of the opposite sex in their rooms unless the door is open. The student conduct code is twenty-seven pages long.

The college offers numerous opportunities for worship, including daily chapel services, Bible Bonanza (a student-led Bible study), the Calvin Institute of Christian Worship, and Theology Forum. "Campus worship is an important part of the life of the college and, in fact, another aspect of the college that ties it to tradition and history," says a professor. He continues, "Chapel attendance is not at all required, [but] it is an important source of reflection and formation on the campus." Grand Rapids also hosts numerous churches of various denominations that students can attend. These include Spanish- and Korean-speaking churches, as well as African Methodist Episcopal, Catholic, Episcopal, Evangelical Covenant, Pentecostal, Presbyterian, and Lutheran churches.

For a school that believes in the "total depravity" of man (cf. the Synod of Dort), Calvin is usually considered a tranquil college. "Calvin and its neighborhood seem very safe," says one student. "All criminal incidents on campus that I have seen have been minor, though some neighborhoods popular with off-campus students (such as Easttown) are less safe but still far from dangerous." Crimes reported on campus in 2009 included one forcible sex offense, one robbery, and twenty-two burglaries. Calvin allows safety personnel with a police background to carry handguns in an effort to increase security.

Costs at Calvin are below the national average for other four-year private colleges: for 2010–11, tuition was $24,870, and room and board $8,525. Roughly 65 percent of students receive need-based financial aid and graduate with an average debt of $28,500.

GREEN LIGHT

Calvin is relatively free of the political polarities, either left or right, that afflict most campuses. "We have fewer in the extremes than typical universities or colleges do," says one professor of his colleagues. "Overall, I would say the college is a moderate campus. In general, left-leaning faculty tend to be more vocal but do not constitute the majority," says another professor.

Indeed, Calvin is influenced more by shared belief and Christian commitment than by the latest educational innovations or political correctness. The religious identity of the students is overwhelmingly Christian, and faculty are expected to adhere to the college's standard and expression of the Reformed faith. The stringent faculty requirements give Calvin rare unity of thought and mission, ultimately helping to insulate the college from many of the theoretical and ideological fads that have swept through most campuses.

Carleton College

Northfield, Minnesota • www.carleton.edu

Introduction: Educating Carl

Founded as Northfield College in 1866 in the tradition of upper midwestern progressivism, Carleton's political environment is sometimes as extreme as its weather. A campus publication once jokingly referred to Carls [as Carleton students are known] as "northern commies." Conservatives or even moderates are clearly outnumbered—or "overwhelmed," according to one Carleton student. However, since intellectual debate is one of the few activities available during certain months in Northfield, students find the college more tolerant than many others. In fact, a spirit of open discussion seems to prevail. "Carleton is the sort of place where you could walk by your floor lounge at any time and hear a friendly argument or discussion of any political or social issue between students," says one student. A longtime professor says, "Political debate is welcomed and even encouraged in classes and on campus. It is true that conservatives are in the definite minority, but I have not seen disrespect of their ideas."

"Many people think of the typical Carl as being pretty 'granola,' but we're not all vegans walking around in our bare feet," says one dissident Carl. At Carleton, students will find an intense intellectual atmosphere and especially good training in the hard sciences. That, plus plenty of Minnesota friendliness, helps take students' minds off the weather.

Academic Life: Rule of three

Carleton operates on the trimester system. During each ten-week term, students take three courses at a time. The system has its benefits: with only three classes, students can focus more intensely on the topics at hand. But with such short terms, exams are always just around the corner. While some students may complain about the calendar's hurried pace, others prefer the system. One says, "Having only three classes a term and having trimesters instead of semesters is probably my favorite thing about Carleton." The first trimester ends right before Thanksgiving, and the second does not start until after New Year's Day, freeing students—at least those from out of state—from six weeks of frigid Minnesota winter.

Among colleges its size, Carleton stands out for having world-class programs in the natural sciences. The college is one of the top liberal arts colleges for preparing students (especially women) to pursue PhDs in the sciences. According to the *Chronicle of Higher*

Education, Carleton has sent more women on for graduate science degrees than either Dartmouth or Princeton—each of which graduates twice as many women. Its natural science departments' focus on individual lab and field work even gives Carleton a leg up on most large universities.

Carleton's distribution requirements are nothing to boast about. Students are given relatively free rein to choose, creating either an education based on the classics or recent academic and ideological trends. "Students have a choice of courses within these requirements, and I have no doubt that some students leave here with something less than a full exposure to the liberal arts," a faculty member says. "But in general, most students get a solid exposure to the liberal arts." Another professor says, "I think that Carleton has a wonderful balance of traditional and avant-garde thinking. It's more 'both/and' than 'either/or.' It's not simply that in one class students read Plato and in another, Alice Walker. Rather, in a Greek philosophy course, students might be invited to consider contemporary notions of identity, and in a course on West African writers, students might discuss nineteenth-century French notions of nationalism."

Once a student declares a major, his study gets more structured. English majors, for example, are required to take two introductory British literature courses (which cover Chaucer to the Victorians), an introduction to American literature, and literary theory; they then can choose one course in each of four major areas of English.

The history department requires its majors to take courses in at least three of seven historical fields: American; ancient and/or medieval; early modern and/or modern Europe; Asia; Africa; Latin America; Atlantic world. This means history majors can graduate without taking a Western civilization or American history class.

Most of Carleton's departments are "of very high quality and well-balanced overall," says a professor. Another professor agrees: "Ask anyone: Carleton is an extremely democratic, unpretentious place. We tend not to want to single professors out as good teachers because, quite honestly, almost all of my colleagues are not only good, but excellent, teachers."

The most acclaimed departments at Carleton are the hard sciences and political science. Political science majors receive a solid foundation with required courses in political philosophy, comparative politics, international and world politics, and American political and constitutional theory. Professor Al Montero is "liked by everyone," says a student, and "although his poli sci intro class is one of the most difficult intros, it is one of the most

VITAL STATISTICS

Religious affiliation: *none*
Total enrollment: *2,009*
Total undergraduates: *2,009*
SAT/ACT midranges: CR: *660–760*, M: *660–740*; ACT: *29–33*
Applicants: *4,784*
Applicants accepted: *30%*
Accepted applicants who enrolled: *36%*
Tuition and fees: *$41,304*
Room and board: *$10,806*
Freshman retention rate: *97%*
Graduation rate: *89% (4 yrs.), 92% (6 yrs.)*
Courses with fewer than 20 students: *61%*
Student-faculty ratio: *9:1*
Courses taught by graduate students: *none*
Most popular majors: *social sciences, physical sciences, biomedical sciences*
Students living on campus: *95%*
Guaranteed housing for four years? *yes*
Students in fraternities or sororities: *none*

SUGGESTED CORE

1. Classics 112, The Epic in Classical Antiquity
2. Philosophy 270, Ancient Greek Philosophy: Knowledge and Skepticism
3. Religion 161/162, Patriarchs, Priests, Prophets, and Poets (Hebrew Bible)/ Jesus, Paul, and Christian Origins (New Testament)
4. History 130, The Formation of Christian Thought
5. Political Science 251, Modern Political Philosophy
6. English 244, Shakespeare I
7. History 120, Rethinking the American Experience: American Social History: 1607–1865
8. History 140, Modern Europe 1789–1914

popular." Laurence Cooper, Steven Schier, and Kimberly Smith are also highly regarded poli sci professors.

Other recommended professors include Mark Krusemeyer in the math and music departments; Alison Kettering in art history; and Nathan Grawe and Michael Hemesath in economics. Harry Williams, a professor of history, receives high marks from students for outside-the-box courses on everything from early African American journalists to black conservatism. William North, professor of ancient and medieval history, is recommended for his engaging teaching style.

Classes at Carleton are small. Sixty percent of classes have fewer than twenty students, and only extremely popular or introductory classes are ever full. A large class at Carleton consists of forty students, and no class ever enrolls more than eighty. Professors teach all discussion sections and lab sections; Carleton has no graduate school and therefore no teaching assistants. "Teaching is absolutely central and primary at Carleton," says a professor. "Professional research and writing are vital to sharpen and maintain faculty as top-flight teachers. The two are interdependent, but teaching is ultimately primary." While at some schools, students barely meet their professors, at Carleton it is not uncommon for students to eat dinner at their houses and play on intramural teams with them. "The professors are extremely approachable," says a student. Another says, "The professors here are amazing and so generous with their time." At Carleton, office hours are used for professor-student discussion and for extra help with course material, not for "grade grubbing."

"Until you choose a major, you have some randomly assigned advisor," one student says. "Mine wasn't too helpful, so I just ended up talking to older students and professors and just figuring it out for myself. The departmental advisors are of course much more helpful." Each entering freshman is assigned a faculty advisor and a "student registration facilitator" to help students choose classes, but students decide how much to rely on them for advice. Since faculty are usually friendly and accessible, students do not have trouble finding wise counsel.

Students view life at Carleton as intellectually intense and challenging. "I have never and don't think I will ever encounter as rigorous an academic environment as at Carleton," says one recent graduate. Says a current student, "Instead of grade inflation, grade deflation is almost the norm here."

Around 70 percent of students go on to graduate school, most for PhDs instead of MBAs. Since most students are not headed immediately to Wall Street or the business sector, the competitive preprofessionalism rampant at other colleges is less prevalent at Carleton. "Unlike at many other schools, the average Carl competes with herself or himself and not other students," says one student. A faculty member calls the students' intellectual curiosity the "leaven" of the campus and the most striking characteristic of the student body. Another professor says, "Carleton students seem comparatively unconcerned with grades."

A high 71 percent of Carleton students study abroad at some point. Many choose Carleton's own international programs, which allow students to take sessions in Spain, England, China, Mexico, Australia, France, Russia, or Ireland, or join study-abroad programs sponsored by other schools. The off-campus programs that are led by Carleton faculty are organized by discipline, so students choosing to study in Cambridge will study economics, while those heading to the South Pacific will study studio art. Carleton is especially strong in international relations, languages, and cultures as evidenced by the high numbers of Carleton graduates in the diplomatic service. At home, Carleton offers foreign language classes in Russian, German, Italian, Spanish, Ancient Greek, Latin, French, Chinese, Japanese, Arabic, Hebrew, and Portuguese.

Student Life: On the ascetic education of man

Carleton is also known for being intimate, if not isolated: Northfield is forty-five minutes from Minneapolis, and the winters are long and hard. Carleton's eclectic campus reflects its multifarious character. The Goodsell Observatory, built in 1887, is on the National Register of Historic Places. The first college-owned, utility-grade wind turbine in the country is here. The Laurence McKinley Gould library houses a collection of more than a million books. (Students can also collect librarian "trading cards," which have photos of the librarians and stats like "question fielding averages" printed on the back.)

Carleton's scenic 880-acre arboretum draws not only Carleton students but also local residents and students from nearby St. Olaf College. The campus has its own Japanese gardens, a "bouldering" cave, and the nation's first on-campus nightclub. The center of campus, known as the Bald Spot, doubles as an Ultimate Frisbee field or a giant ice-skating rink, depending on the weather. Students can walk to the quaint Northfield business district just a few blocks away. Those yearning for the big city can take a forty-five minute shuttle bus to Minneapolis/St. Paul on weekends. There students can take advantage of Twin Cities attractions, bars, theaters, restaurants, and assorted professional sports teams. For the most part, though, students stay on campus, and prospective students should anticipate a small community where students see familiar faces everywhere.

Housing at Carleton demands a certain stoicism. "Some of the housing is quite old, but that only serves to give it character," one graduate says. "I liked the majority of my accommodations through four years." Ninety-five percent of the student body (and a full 100 percent of freshmen) dwells on campus, and students must apply for an exception to live off campus. There are a variety of "shared-interest living areas," such as the Women's Awareness House and the Freedom House. Greek houses are banned at Carleton. A housing crunch a few years ago inspired Carleton to build townhouses, which have become some of the choicer picks for students. Sophomores generally get the worst housing, since freshmen are coddled and upperclassmen are rewarded for seniority. "There is a wide range of quality when it comes to on-campus housing," one student says. "There are nice dorms and then there are glorified closets." Students with high picks in the housing lottery get the nicer dorms or apartments.

The college has no single-sex dorms, but it does have a few floors designated for women. Carleton offers coed bathrooms (they can be made single-sex by vote) and suites, though members of the opposite sex are not permitted to share rooms. The college also has several substance-free housing options, in which students pledge that they will not drink, smoke, or use drugs.

Choosing the right housing at Carleton is important, since students will spend a lot of time in their rooms. "Living in the dorm that first year is an experience every freshman should have," a student says. "A majority of friendships are forged during the first few weeks of school when students are staying up late in common areas talking and experiencing life away from home for the first time. As the year passes and it gets colder, more of the day is spent indoors." As Carleton's own promotional material admits, a Minnesota winter takes some adjustment.

ACADEMIC REQUIREMENTS

Carleton's rather weak distribution requirements are as follows:

- One first year seminar and writing class, "Argument and Inquiry Seminar."
- Another writing course. Class choices include "Introduction to Classical Studies" and "Introduction to Latino/a Studies."
- One writing portfolio, consisting of three to five papers from at least three different departments.
- Quantitative reasoning. Classes offered include "Tour of Mathematics" and "Newtonian Mechanics."
- One international studies course. Options include "Economics of the European Union" and "Central Asia in the Modern Age."
- One diversity class. Students may choose from classes such as "Ethnic Conflict" and "Introduction to LGBT/Queer Studies."
- One humanities course, such as "American Intellectual History" or "Feminist Ways of Knowing."
- One class in arts and literature, with choices ranging from "Shakespeare" I to "Ceramics of the Islamic World."
- One arts practice course, such as "Introduction to Sculpture" and "Tradition, Transgression, and Transnationalism in Japanese Dance Cultures."
- One science class with lab. Courses offered include "Cell Biology" and "Population Ecology."
- One formal or statistical reasoning course. Choices include "Introduction to Statistics" and "Probability."
- One class in social sciences, such as "Anthropology of Humor" or "Psychology of Gender."
- Four physical education classes. Options range from aikido to modern dance.
- Proficiency in a foreign language. Carleton strongly encourages students to study abroad to meet this requirement.

The school presents itself as a place where nonconformist personalities serve to warm the brutal Minnesota winters. For instance, the admissions webpage contains profiles of the school's zaniest students, such as two classmates who started the Carleton Stone Skipping Society, of all things, as a way to reconnect with the soothing childhood experience of tossing pebbles in water. Students seem generally happy, and alumni remember being happy at the school. Carleton College has consistently ranked number one among liberal arts colleges for its alumni-giving rate; in 2010, it was reported that over 65 percent of all Carleton alumni give back to the school. Carleton College announced in June 2009 that it had exceeded its $300 million goal of the Campaign for Carleton, a new fund-raising record. The school hopes to spend it in four ways: approximately $90 million on teaching and learning, $90 million on financial aid, $90 million on facilities, and $30 million on ongoing needs.

Carleton students enjoy the outdoors, especially in the fall and spring. Intramurals are popular, particularly Ultimate Frisbee. "Everyone, I mean everyone, plays Frisbee," says one student. Carleton's intercollegiate Ultimate Frisbee teams are excellent and have a large following. Few of Carleton's other intercollegiate teams, which compete in the NCAA Division III, can say the same. Carls go to football games more to see the Gender Neutral Cheerboys (Carleton's politically correct and oh-so-tongue-in-cheek pep squad) and the marching band, the Honking Knights, than to watch the games.

The most popular Carleton activities are participatory. Students put together their own plays, music groups, and dance groups, to which even novices are generally invited. There is a single conservative political group on campus, the Carleton Conservative Union, which sporatically publishes a paper, the *Observer*. The numerous liberal political groups include Carleton Democrats, Carleton ACLU, Carls for Choice, AHA! (AIDS/HIV Awareness), Carleton In and Out (LGBT group), SaGA (Sexuality and Gender Activism), and Collective for Women's Issues. Other student groups tend to center on special interests such as grassroots activism (e.g., the Wellstone House of Organization and Activism—named after the late Paul Wellstone, onetime Carleton professor and U.S. senator); ethnic identities (the Coalition of Women of Color); or the bizarre (such as the Reformed Druid Society or the Mustache Club). Students looking for more traditional activities can participate in the popular student-run radio station or contribute to the nationally distributed *Lens Magazine*, which humbly calls itself "the first ever interdisciplinary undergraduate magazine . . . similar in terms of content and style to the *New Yorker* and *New York Times Magazine*." The school also has an active and successful Model United Nations Program that has won numerous best-delegation awards at national competitions.

The school's isolation does limit students' social options. Drinking is often the preferred activity at dorm parties, and students who are of age tend to visit one of the two Northfield bars. Nearby St. Olaf College's students ("Oles") come to Carleton on weekends, since St. Olaf is dry. As for the illegal stuff, "Pot is not hidden," as one recent graduate attests. "While Carleton's administration is fairly lax on underage drinking, the trend is toward lower tolerance," says one student. "There are more substance-free floors than four years ago, and Carleton security is cracking down on large parties more than they used to," he adds.

While the administration can tolerate the occasional student bong, it is deeply concerned about a perceived lack of racial diversity. In the eyes of the school, the 22 percent of students

YELLOW LIGHT

The Carleton Conservative Union intermittently publishes an alternative paper, the *Observer*. The same group has sponsored a "conservative coming-out" cookout on behalf of the worldview that dares not speak its name. A student says, "I find that my peers are generally very interested in what I have to say, almost to the point of surprise at my existence as a conservative at Carleton." Sexual "diversity" is certainly valued at Carleton, which hosts at least five student organizations devoted to the cause and boasted in a press release that it had been named "one of the 100 best campuses for LGBT students and . . . [was] included in the *Advocate College Guide for LGBT Students*, the first comprehensive campus guide to highlight the 100 most LGBT-friendly campuses in the United States."

who are Asian, Hispanic, Native American, and African American are not enough. "As far as ethnic makeup, it is not as diverse as the college would like," one student says.

The Office of Intercultural Life offers programs that seek to "enhance diversity and cultivate a fully inclusive community, enriched by persons of different ethnicities, nationalities, genders, economic backgrounds, ages, abilities, sexual orientations, and spiritual values." The Office of the Chaplain, which is equally concerned with diversity, hosts a variety of worship services. Any given weekly chapel schedule may include Shabbat services, Catholic Mass, Eid al-Fitr services, Buddhist meditation and teaching, and a Native American spiritual service.

There are less serious traditions honored at Carleton. The college website names some of the main ones, from blowing bubbles at faculty members during opening convocation to playing broomball and going "traying" (using a dining-hall tray as a sled) on the snowy hills. The Primal Scream allows students a lung-venting session during exams. Then there's Schiller, an old bust of the German poet that a select few students get to keep during their time at Carleton. Schiller tends to show up at important events. Every time Schiller appears, all the students cheer—and some of them try to steal it.

There seems to be relatively little crime on campus. In 2009, the school reported four forcible sex offenses and twenty-one burglaries. Given the number of students, it still does seem true that slipping drunkenly on the ice may be the greatest danger on campus.

Tuition for the 2010–11 academic year was $41,304, and room and board $10,806. As at nearly every school, school costs at Carleton have steadily risen each year. Aid is available for those who demonstrate a need, but students must present evidence of attempts to get funding from outside sources in order to get university funding. Fifty-six percent of all students receive need-based financial aid, and the average graduate owes $18,601 in student loans.

Case Western Reserve University

Cleveland, Ohio • www.case.edu

A serious case

In 1967, Case Institute of Technology (founded in 1880) merged with Western Reserve University to form Case Western Reserve University—now the largest private school in Ohio, with a strong reputation as a tech-oriented engineering and science school. It is now working hard to broaden its base, including the liberal arts. One teacher says that, in general, Case students are more conservative than professors, while another faculty describes Case as a school with "a very tolerant mood regarding political leanings and regarding lifestyles." Case *is* liberal, but it is mostly known for an atmosphere of intellectual seriousness, with hard-working students in a relatively sober environment.

Academic Life: The men in the white lab coats

Case Western Reserve is broken into eight separate schools: the College of Arts and Sciences, the School of Dental Medicine, the Case School of Engineering, the School of Law, the Weatherhead School of Management, the School of Medicine, the Frances Payne Bolton School of Nursing, and the Mandel School of Applied Social Sciences.

One student says of the university, "Case is a very academic school, so I found myself in a very supportive atmosphere—as I take school seriously." One professor says her academic charges include "top students (some were accepted to schools like Brown or Harvard)" who are "not afraid to work." With almost 4,300 undergrads, Case as a whole boasts an excellent student-faculty ratio of 9 to 1, with 95 percent of classes taught by professors rather than grad students. Still, those teachers face significant pressure to publish, according to one professor, who quips, "Case Western Reserve University could also be known as Case Western *Research* University." Nevertheless, students, especially in the smaller programs, report that the professors at Case genuinely make time for them and are "extremely willing to meet" and to help them out. One student says the professors in his department have an open-door policy, and he has personally "found these hours to be the single most useful academic resource at Case." A professor says that in his department, "When faculty are on campus, their doors are literally open." This is important, since the advising system at Case is "still in need of improvement," according to another student.

VITAL STATISTICS

Religious affiliation: *none*
Total enrollment: *9,738*
Total undergraduates: *4,228*
SAT/ACT midranges: CR:
  590–700, M: *650–740*;
  ACT: *28–32*
Applicants: *7,998*
Applicants accepted: *70%*
Accepted applicants who
  enrolled: *17%*
Tuition and fees: *$37,648*
Room and board: *$11,400*
Freshman retention rate:
  91%
Graduation rate: *63% (4 yrs.),
  81% (6 yrs.)*
Courses with fewer than 20
  students: *61%*
Student-faculty ratio: *9:1*
Courses taught by graduate
  students: *5%*
Most popular majors: *biol-
  ogy, biomedical engineer-
  ing, psychology*
Students living on campus:
  78%
Guaranteed housing for
  four years? *yes*
Students in fraternities: *30%*
  in sororities: *31%*

Case is very science-oriented. The strongest department is said to be biomedical engineering (BME), the school's second most popular major, which consistently ranks in the top five in the U.S. and attracts many students. However, as one of them notes, "Most majors have a difficult time connecting with professors, as [that department's] student-faculty ratio is unusually high. I have a lot of friends studying BME, and they often find that professors just don't have the time to work with individual students." As a result, one professor notes that many students are drawn to Case to study biomedical engineering but find themselves exploring other areas after they arrive.

In an effort to encourage students to forge closer relationships with faculty, the university implemented the Seminar Approach to General Education and Scholarship (SAGES) program. Designed to replace the traditional core introductory classes, SAGES mandates that each undergraduate take at least five or six small, interdisciplinary seminars, led by faculty drawn from across the university (and outside it). The First Seminar, taken during the first semester, serves as an introduction to college work. It involves reading, discussion, and intensive writing—incorporating experiences with local cultural and arts institutions. Students choose among a wide variety of topics for this seminar, within broad categories: the life of the mind, the natural world, the social world, or the symbolic world. Next, students take two seminars before the end of their sophomore year, chosen from three broad categories: thinking about the natural world, thinking about the social world, and thinking about the symbolic world. In their junior year, students take a seminar chosen from within their major departments. Finally, in their senior year, students face a Capstone project, which includes one or two seminars culminating in a major paper and a public presentation.

In addition to the school's distribution requirements, the SAGES courses help ensure that no Case student will get too narrow an education. Nevertheless, they're hardly a replacement for a real core curriculum, according to one professor, who bemoans the "lack of depth" as well as breadth of study in the humanities at Case. Students differ about the SAGES initiative. The university website quotes one student, "I enjoyed my first-seminar course, being it was one of my only discussion-oriented classes. It gave me the opportunity to speak my mind, as opposed to listening to a lecture. Also, I enjoyed the fact that the first-seminar SAGES course gave me the opportunity to meet students in other fields of study."

Midwest

On the other hand, an upperclassman tells us that he is thankful that he didn't have to participate in SAGES. "It's a seminar approach to learning, but as far as I can tell, nobody learns much," he says.

Through the College of Arts and Sciences, students can choose a major or minor from almost sixty programs, design their own major, or choose an integrated bachelor's/master's degree program. Students differ about the strength of Case's liberal arts and humanities departments, which several described as flawed but in the process of improving. "I have had mostly good experiences with my humanities courses. It really depends a lot on who's teaching them," says an upperclassman. Another student argues that "many of the humanities introductory classes are weak and directly attack America and the West." The history department does not require its majors to take a basic Western civilization course, but does require a fundamental American history class. However, as a student notes, "the main text was that of Howard Zinn, a Marxist historian who sees all of American history as an oppression of minorities and women."

Strong undergraduate departments include psychology and anthropology, as well as the music and art programs—which benefit from partnerships with the Cleveland Institute of Music and Art, the Cleveland Museum, and the Cleveland Playhouse. One student praises the classics department as "strong, due to its commitment to students."

The English department at Case Western is mostly solid. Majors must take English literature before and after 1800, with a heavy emphasis on Chaucer, Milton, and Shakespeare. Additional requirements include a traditional American literature class focusing on classics in the field instead of trendy or multicultural texts, and several electives and seminars that are also traditional in subject and theme.

Departments such as political science and physics benefit from small class sizes, and students in those departments report enjoying individual attention in a highly interactive, collaborative, and stimulating environment. However, political science majors are not required to take basic American political philosophy or U.S. Constitution classes but rather a catch-all introductory course called "The American Political System," which, according to the department's website, "address[es] the questions 'Who rules?' and 'Who benefits?' in the American political system." This is not promising, as the class description is subjective enough to accommodate professors' political agendas.

Some professors at Case are open about their leftist views and make political statements in class, but overall, faculty and students agree that Case is "relatively tolerant" of conservative students. With a few unfortunate exceptions, even the most vocally liberal

SUGGESTED CORE

1. Classics 203/204, Gods and Heroes in Greek Literature/ Heroes and Hustlers in Latin Literature
2. Philosophy 301, Ancient Philosophy
3. Religion 209, Introduction to Biblical Literature
4. Religion 373, History of the Early Church: First Through Fourth Centuries
5. Political Science 351, Modern Political Thought
6. English 324/325, Shakespeare: Histories and Tragedies/Comedies and Romances
7. History 410, Seminar: Early American Historiography
8. Philosophy 355, Nineteenth and Early Twentieth-Century Philosophy

professors are described as "respectful" of other views. One conservative student says, "I personally have never been in a situation in which the fact that my positions conflict with a professor's (which they frequently do) has influenced my relationship with him or her."

Case graduates and professors are frequent recipients of academic awards, such as Fulbrights, which are awarded to Case faculty and students almost every year. Professors who stand out for dedication to their students are Dan Akerib, Robert Brown, and Kathleen Kash in physics; Chris Butler in mathematics; Susan Hinze in sociology; Laura Tartakoff in political science; Judith Oster in English; and Paul Iversen and Martin Helzle in classics.

Case considers itself to be a leader in experiential learning. Close to 75 percent of students participate in undergraduate research, as well as in major theater productions in Cleveland, clinical work as nursing students, and co-op programs between semesters at

ACADEMIC REQUIREMENTS

Students face no core curriculum at Case, but there are certain distribution and other requirements. Students in the College of Arts and Sciences must complete five to six SAGES (the Seminar Approach to General Education and Scholarship) classes:

- One First Seminar taken first semester freshman year. Choices in 2011 ranged from "Art, Music, and the Museum" to "Science and Race."
- Two University Seminars to be taken by end of sophomore year. Class options have included "Food, Farming, and Prosperity" and "Learning to See: Architecture and Aesthetics."
- One Department Seminar drawn from a student's major to be taken junior year.
- One Senior Capstone, consisting of one or two culminating seminars involving regular consultations with a faculty member, a final written report, and a final public presentation. A couple of 2011 capstone topics included "Biorobotics Team" and "The Poetics and Politics of Gender and Race in Latin America."

Students must also complete:

- One Writing Portfolio, due at the end of sophomore year, includes graded assignments from the First Seminar and University Seminars submitted for evaluation.
- Two semesters of physical education, completed in the freshman year.
- Two courses in arts and humanities, such as "Classical Civilization: Rome" or "Modern Dance Technique."
- Two classes in natural and mathematical sciences, with options like "Nutrition" and "Dynamics of Biological Systems."
- Two social science courses, such as "Principles of Macroeconomics" or "Sociology of Deviant Behavior."
- One course in quantitative reasoning, such as "Calculus for Science and Engineering" or "Quantitative Methods in Psychology."
- One class in global and cultural diversity, with options ranging from the fascinating ("Indian Philosophy") to the grim ("Multicultural Issues of Human Communication").

local engineering firms. In addition, the Preprofessional Scholars Program grants Case freshmen automatic admission to a Case professional school (dentistry, law, medicine, or social work).

We rather hope that this doesn't fall under the rubric of experiential learning, but Case Western Reserve's Medical History Center possesses the world's largest collection of birth-control devices, with over 1,100 artifacts. Acquired in 2005, the exhibit "does not tackle the abortion issue" and "presents contraception in an evenhanded, forthright manner," according to the *Chronicle of Higher Education.*

Case also takes pride in its programs for service learning. This emphasis begins with orientation, when all new students take part in a project of their choice to benefit residents of greater Cleveland. Various volunteer opportunities complement a student's academic interests. For instance, teams of engineering students have built a greenhouse, students in education tutor at area schools through the Project Step-Up program, and accounting majors have helped people in the community decipher their tax forms.

Many students choose to study abroad through Case programs in England, Ireland, Australia, Spain, France, Chile, Cuba, South Africa, China, or Israel. There are also dozens of other approved programs available through Case's study-abroad office, and students may study Arabic, Chinese, French, German, Hebrew, Italian, Japanese, Portuguese, Russian, and Spanish through Case's Department of Modern Languages and Literatures.

Student Life: Earnest midwesterners hitting the books

Case's 550-acre campus is located in the middle of the cultural center of Cleveland, its University Circle. Besides Case, University Circle includes Severance Hall, home of the world-renowned Cleveland Orchestra; the Cleveland Museum of Art, one of the top five art museums in the country; and Cleveland's acclaimed Children's Hospital. Together, Case Western Reserve and University Hospitals form the largest center for biomedical research in Ohio. The Cleveland Botanical Garden, the Cleveland Institute of Art, the Cleveland Institute of Music, the Cleveland Museum of Natural History, and the Western Reserve Historical Society also form part of the Circle—guaranteeing that no student will be lacking for cultural uplift.

Nevertheless, Case students work very hard and stay busy. One Case undergrad told us that "a negative point about Case is that the students do not have enough fun. Too many rarely even leave campus and are far more concerned about getting good grades than actually learning anything." Not all students object to the atmosphere, however. As one notes, "It's great to be at a school where everyone is as focused on academics as you are. I know that's why I chose to come here!"

There are opportunities to get away from the books. Beyond the cultural riches of University Circle lies nearby Little Italy, which is full of good restaurants and small shops. Local clubs and bars sponsor live bands that attract students. Campus clubs include musical groups, drama, dance, a film society, literary magazines, student government, the student newspaper the *Observer,* twenty-four fraternities and sororities (which comprise an entire third of the undergraduate population), religious groups (from the Fellowship of Chris-

Midwest

YELLOW LIGHT

In some ways, Case could be a good school for socially conservative students. "A lot of the student population is religious—and sex, drinking, and drugs are activities that only a minority engage in. Most Case students honestly spend their Friday and Saturday nights studying, or watching a movie with friends," says a student. Not that the school cramps anyone's style. Students report that coed suites are available to upperclassmen upon request, and guests of either sex may stay in dorms for up to three days.

The political atmosphere at Case is mixed, with a largely traditionalist, midwestern student body; liberal but mostly tolerant professors; and an administration which is very liberal and mostly intolerant. One student suggests that "most of the discomfort a conservative or religious student would feel comes directly from the administration….. For example, if a prospective student asks a tour guide for information about Christian fellowships on campus, the guide is only permitted to discuss the one 'official' group, which is highly liberal. This despite the fact that Chi Alpha, InterVarsity Christian Fellowship, Campus Crusade for Christ, Navigators and several local churches all maintain large, active groups."

The national gay magazine the *Advocate* has consistently ranked Case Western as one of the top one hundred LGBT-friendly universities, and homosexual acceptance skits are performed as part of freshman orientation meetings. Many of the school-sponsored speakers (for instance, the rapper Puff Daddy) and roundtable discussions are said to hew to a stolidly liberal line. However, Case has always had an active and robust College Republicans group on campus in spite of a hostile administration.

tian Athletes to the Muslim Student Association), academic groups (Society of Plastics Engineers, the Physics and Astronomy Club), international/ethnic groups (covering nations from Egypt to Thailand), service groups (Habitat for Humanity), and special interest groups (from the Magic Club to the Feminist Majority Leadership Alliance). Politically conservative students will want to seek out the College Republicans of Case, which hosts meetings, lectures, and opportunities for activism in the local political scene.

The university supports nineteen varsity sports, all part of the NCAA Division III conference. The Spartans football team played in the Division III playoffs for three consecutive years, 2007–9. Case also hosts intramural, club, and recreational activities throughout the year (from volleyball to juggling).

"Dorm life is comfortable and even homey," says one student. "The resident assistants plan a lot of activities and are often friends with the students." Residential living arrangements range from single rooms to apartment suites to Greek housing. Sixty-four percent of undergraduates live in the dorms, all of which are coed, but there are single-sex floors, rooms, and bathrooms available. Unless they live at home, students must dwell on campus for their first two years at Case. During their freshman year, students live in one of three residential colleges, each with its own identity: one has a strong arts component (the Cedar), another celebrates multiculturalism (the Juniper), a third focuses on service leadership (the Mistletoe).

Most upperclassmen live in the North Residential Village, which is located near the museums, Severance Hall, and other cultural attractions. Trees and newly constructed athletic fields surround the residence halls. The first phase of Case's plan to replace all residential housing on campus began with the Village at 115, a very expensively built, living-learning environment for upperclassmen outfitted with the latest technology and environmentally "green" amenities, such as motion detectors that turn on and off lights and an electronic information kiosk that posts daily statistics on energy, water, and electrical use. The data is broadcast on the Internet, allowing researchers worldwide to access the information—which is either really cool or kind of creepy. Every building has wireless networking and multimedia capabilities, including a networked laundry system that alerts students by e-mail when their laundry is done.

Transportation options for students include a campus shuttle system and Cleveland public transit. Students who wish to have a car must deal with permits and very limited parking. In this matter and others (for instance paying tuition, obtaining financial aid, and completing other paperwork), students complain that the Case administration puts them through a good deal of red tape.

Besides the Village at 115, there have been several other architectural additions to Case's campus in recent years. The Weatherhead School of Management opened its Lewis Building, designed by famous architect Frank Gehry—known for his innovative, sculptural architecture. (The school paid for the privilege; the building cost $60 million, instead of the $25 million Case had budgeted for it.) The Wood Building Research Tower and the Wolstein Building were built to support medical research, and the environmentally friendly November Research Greenhouse was opened at the university's 386-acre farm. This Greenhouse has proved an important resource not only for biology faculty and students but also for local educators and schoolchildren.

One venerable tradition at Case is the Hudson Relays, an annual relay marathon held every spring, pitting the undergraduate classes against each other racing around the campus and the surrounding community. Begun in 1910, the relays mark the 1882 move of Western Reserve University from Hudson to Cleveland. Any class that wins the relay for four years running is awarded a champagne and steak dinner with the university president. Halloween at the Farm is a newer tradition (dating from 2002) in which students, faculty, and their families enjoy games, a bonfire, a concert, and hayrides at a local farm. Since 1974, the CWRU Film Society has held the Science Fiction Film Marathon—amply catered, to sustain students through thirty-six hours of nonstop sci-fi movies.

Crime is a major concern in downtown Cleveland. Undergrads report that they try to walk off campus after dark only in groups. The school maintains its own police department to hold offenses at bay, with moderate success. In 2009, the school reported thirty burglaries, four motor vehicle thefts, one robbery, and eight forcible sex offenses on campus.

For the 2010–11 school year, tuition was $37,648, and basic room and board $11,400. Admission is need blind, and each year approximately 64 percent of undergraduate students receive assistance through need-based financial aid. One professor reports that some of his students turned down other top-notch universities for Case because of its generous scholarships. Nevertheless, the average student-loan indebtedness upon graduation is a daunting $39,239.

Midwest

University of Chicago

Chicago, Illinois • www.uchicago.edu

Old school

As one of the nation's leading institutions, the University of Chicago has been shaping the intellectual lives of undergraduates for more than a century. A private institution chartered in 1890 and funded by John D. Rockefeller, Chicago's 211-acre campus on the shores of Lake Michigan has been home to over eighty Nobel laureates, the largest number affiliated with any American university. Chicago scientists were the first to split the atom, to measure the speed of light, and to develop the field of sociology into a full academic discipline.

The college is the largest academic unit of the university, which encompasses ten graduate divisions and professional schools, including on-campus law, business, and medical schools.

As part of a research university, the college offers both breadth and depth of learning and provides students with an almost unparalleled academic experience. One student describes Chicago as "a scientific and economic powerhouse." Students have the valuable opportunity to work in some of the same classes as advanced graduate students, while their core classes ground them in the essentials of a liberal arts curriculum that remains, even after some alterations, perhaps the most rigorous and comprehensive in America.

The university is under constant political and ideological pressure to change that curriculum. As one graduate student noted, "the core of old, what made the university famous in the first place, has been slowly dissolving." However, despite some controversial alterations made to the Western civilization requirement, a freshman entering Chicago can still obtain one of the best liberal arts educations available anywhere in the world.

Academic Life: Midwestern monastic

Chicago is one of the only well-known schools in America whose core curriculum is worthy of the name. With the help of an academic advisor, students navigate through the core and begin taking classes in their chosen major. They need not declare a major until the beginning of their third year. Chicago grants the bachelor of arts or bachelor of science degree in forty-nine fields in the arts, humanities, natural sciences, social sciences, and in such interdisciplinary areas as biological chemistry, environmental studies, and cinema and media studies.

Midwest

Along with its tradition of academic excellence, Chicago has a well-deserved reputation as a deeply serious, intense, and rigorous school that demands a significant amount of its students' time and devotion. (Some might even call its discipline ascetical.) The school uses a system of quarters instead of semesters. This allows the school to offer three different sessions of classes per year—in fall, winter, and spring. This system lets Chicago cover great quantities of high-quality material in a relatively short period of time. Well-organized and prepared students will flourish in this environment, but of necessity the pace of the school year allows for only a smaller margin for error.

One of the most notable and controversial changes to the curriculum in recent years has been the elimination of the three-quarter "Western Civilization" sequence. As one professor says, "The recent shift from a three-quarter Western Civ that went from antiquity to the present to a choice between an ancient Mediterranean Civ. or a largely modern Euro Civ. had the unfortunate effect of leaving most students without antiquity."

Still, the school imposes a very serious curriculum, grounded in some of the great works of the West. For students in search of a comprehensive overview of our civilization, we highly recommend the humanities sequence "Human Being and Citizen." In this sequence, students read the most important works of the Western tradition, beginning with Homer and continuing into the twentieth century. Another excellent humanities sequence is "Greek Thought and Literature."

Faculty make themselves available on a regular basis and are typically very interested in helping and guiding students in their work. Faculty advisors "are very available to those who seek them out," a student says. One student tells us, "Nearly all of my classes have been taught by professors. They are, by and large, eminently approachable. All have scheduled office hours, and as far as I know all are open to meeting by appointment." However, another student tells us that "professor and student interactions are more formal. As a student, you are a dime a dozen, and everyone wants a professor's time." Professors teach between two-thirds and three-fourths of the classes—a good thing, since "when TAs grade, because they are inexperienced, they are not always the most judicious graders," a student complains.

The University of Chicago is famous for its faculty, and many of its best professors still teach undergraduate classes. These include Rachel Fulton, Constantin Fasolt, and Hanna Gray in history; Paul J. Sally Jr. in mathematics; James Redfield in classics; John

VITAL STATISTICS

Religious affiliation: *none*
Total enrollment: *15,626*
Total undergraduates: *5,034*
SAT/ACT midranges: CR: *690–780*, M: *680–780*; ACT: *28–33*
Applicants: *13,565*
Applicants accepted: *27%*
Accepted applicants who enrolled: *36%*
Tuition and fees: *$40,188*
Room and board: *$12,153*
Freshman retention rate: *98%*
Graduation rate: *86% (4 yrs.)*, *92% (6 yrs.)*
Courses with fewer than 20 students: *73%*
Student-faculty ratio: *11:1*
Courses taught by graduate students: *not provided*
Most popular majors: *economics, biological sciences, political science*
Students living on campus: *55%*
Guaranteed housing for four years? *yes*
Students in fraternities: *8%* in sororities: *4%*

There are a number of ways to fulfill a core at the University of Chicago, as the school offers several strong sequences. This is just one example:

1. Humanities 12000, 12100, 12200, Greek Thought and Literature
2. Philosophy 25000, History of Philosophy I: Ancient Philosophy
3. Religious Studies 11005 /12000, Jewish History and Society I: Introduction to the Hebrew Bible/ Introduction to the New Testament
4. Philosophy 26000, History of Philosophy II: Medieval and Early Modern Philosophy
5. Philosophy 21600, Introduction to Political Philosophy or Social Sciences 15100-15200-15300, Classics of Social and Political Thought
6. English 16500/16600, Shakespeare I: Histories and Comedies/II: Tragedies and Romances
7. History 18700, Early America to 1865
8. Philosophy 2700, History of Philosophy III: Kant and the Nineteenth Century (closest match)

Mearsheimer, Charles Lipson, and Nathan Tarcov in political science; Nobel-winner Gary Becker and James Heckman in economics; Jonathan Lear and Robert Pippin in philosophy; Herman Sinaiko in humanities; Ralph Lerner in social sciences and the Committee on Social Thought; Bertram Cohler, also of social sciences; Michael Fishbane in Jewish studies; Isaac Abella in physics; and Jean Bethke Elshtain, Jean-Luc Marion, and David Tracy in the Divinity School.

Subjects that students may choose for their concentrations (the Chicago term for a major) are grouped into five collegiate divisions: Biological Sciences, Humanities, New Collegiate, Physical Sciences, and Social Sciences. We particularly recommend that students who want an intensive liberal arts curriculum explore the New Collegiate concentration "Fundamentals: Issues and Texts." Students in this major (which is dubbed "Fundies") choose six classic texts to study in detail in light of one overarching question. For example, the question "What is justice?" might be pursued through selected works of Plato, Aristotle, Cicero, Dante, Rousseau, and Marx. One Fundies student testifies, "I spent time at Oxford later on and found myself to be so much better prepared than my peers, both British and American. I attribute this to the Chicago core and Fundamentals." Students concentrating in Fundamentals write a research paper in their junior year and in their senior year must take a comprehensive exam on each of the six texts that they have chosen.

Other concentration choices range from the most common, like history and economics, to more obscure ones like early Christian literature and cinema and media studies. If a student cannot find a major that suits him, the New Collegiate Division allows him to create his own through Tutorial Studies. However, it is difficult to find a professor who is willing to commit to being a tutor.

On the down side, it is surprising to learn that English majors at Chicago need not take a class in Shakespeare, history majors are not required to study America, and political science majors need not take a course in U.S. constitutional theory. However, the excellence of Chicago's core, and the intense rigor of its faculty, make it unlikely that students will emerge without having read the key texts in their disciplines.

Sharply politicized classrooms are essentially nonexistent at Chicago. As one student says, "Although the administration may be introducing diversity and trying to get rid of the

Midwest

702

Great Books program, when professors teach what they teach, they are pretty evenhanded. We tend to attract the kind of people who are interested in what books are saying. . . . I call myself a conservative, and I've never been bothered by the political atmosphere in the classroom."

Some departments are more ideological than others. According to one student, "Here, as elsewhere, there seem to be a lot of bad and politicized classes, but you are not required to take any, and I have not." The departments of English, social administration and public policy, Near Eastern languages and civilizations, and sociology get relatively poor marks in this regard. One professor says that the English department in particular is "full of methodologists and ideologues." One member of the economics department says it is less political than in the past and characterizes the faculty as "heterogeneous . . . devoted to a wider range of theoretical and empirical issues, including game theory, auction theory, long-term economic growth, et cetera." Conservative professors can be found in a number of other departments, as well, from political science to the Committee on Social Thought.

Academic life at Chicago can be challenging and also discomforting in its challenges to all long-held assumptions and beliefs, and those who have the greatest difficulty with

ACADEMIC REQUIREMENTS

Chicago is one of the only well-known schools in America whose core curriculum is worthy of the name. The core requirements at Chicago allow some options—almost all of them good. In addition to a concentration and some electives, students must complete a total of six courses chosen from three critical areas. Students choose to emphasize one of the three:

- Humanities. There are seven humanities sequences from which to choose, not all offered in any given quarter. They range from "Greek Thought and Literature" and the highly regarded "Human Being and Citizen" to more modern fare such as "Media Aesthetics: Images, Sound, Text."
- Civilizations studies. Sequences include such area studies as "History of European Civilization," "Jewish History and Society," and "America in World Civilization." Students may also complete this requirement by participating in one of nine study-abroad programs.
- The arts. Classes here include "Introduction to Art," "Drama: Embodiment and Transformation," and introductions to Western and world music.

Students also take:

- Six courses in natural sciences or mathematics, including two in biological sciences, two in physical sciences, and one in mathematical sciences.
- Three classes in social sciences. Sequences include "Power, Identity, and Resistance," "Self, Culture, and Society," "Democracy and Social Science," "Mind," and "Classics of Social and Political Thought."
- Three courses in physical education.

Students must also demonstrate competence, equivalent to one year of college-level study, in a foreign language.

such challenges are often "people used to religiously homogeneous schools or communities, or who assume that religious principles are somehow more sacred than political principles and thus immune from open debate." One student says, "As a Christian, I have encountered innumerable people that disagree with me, but this has not made me timid: it has only required me to defend my beliefs against skepticism, which can hardly be anything but healthy. . . . I have no desire to be surrounded by people who think precisely like me. People who come here need to be willing to defend all of their beliefs, regardless of their ideology."

The intensity and rigor of academic life have tended to give Chicago a reputation for social austerity that bears mentioning. While it may be the case that, as one Chicago student famously put it, "fun is not linear," it is also true that students who come to Chicago should be prepared to enjoy their immersion in the life of the mind and their academic work. As one student noted, "The College is excellent academically but probably not suited even to all bright young conservatives. The key to a good undergraduate experience seems to be the capacity to get the vast majority of one's personal satisfaction from academic work. The way we have fun is entirely unlike the way the average college student has fun. While others might play Frisbee or beer pong, we argue about the niceties of Kantian metaphysics. Students for whom this does not sound appealing will not enjoy themselves here. They will be at best slightly out of place, or at worst miserable; I have seen instances of both."

Chicago sponsors its own study-abroad programs. Destinations include Athens, Barcelona, Berlin, Bologna, Cairo, England, Ireland, Cape Town, Freiburg, Jerusalem, Kyoto, Oaxaca, Paris, Pisa, Rome, St. Petersburg, Toledo, and Vienna. The university's newest center abroad, Beijing, promises to link its intellectual community with Asia as the center in Paris does with Europe. Chicago offers more than fifty foreign languages. Related majors are classical studies; East Asian languages and civilizations; Germanic studies; Jewish studies; linguistics; Near Eastern languages and civilizations; Romance languages and literatures; Russian studies; Slavic languages and literatures; and South Asian languages and civilizations.

Student Life: Talking shop

The architecture of most of the university's academic buildings matches the seriousness of purpose of the school itself. The graceful Gothic buildings impress upon student and visitor alike the institution's grounding in scholarly traditions dating back to the High Middle Ages. One student complains, "They have a few new buildings that are really nice, but why does the school not have air conditioning in a lot of places? The University of Chicago has a lot of money, so why don't they fix things up? The place is pretty, but some of the buildings are dilapidated." Recently, the university has taken to erecting more modern buildings. The Joe and Rika Mansueto Library, designed by Helmut Jahn, opened in 2010, houses up to 3.5 million volumes. In spring 2012, Chicago will welcome the new Reva and David Logan Center for Creative and Performing Arts, which will serve as a catalyst for creativity at the university. With Starbucks, high-end condos, and new landscaping, the university's campus and once-blighted Hyde Park neighborhood have probably never looked so posh.

Social life at Chicago is more subdued and definitely more intellectual than at most schools. Students do throw parties, and alcohol does play a significant role in the private

Midwest

revels of many of the students. Both the alcohol and "hook-up" culture found on most campuses are more subdued here. "ScavHunt" is a yearly celebration of insanity featuring a list of items to be scavenged—ranging from the bizarre to the sickening. Last year's list of more than 300 items included a walk-in kaleidoscope, an armadillo, and a "hot-air balloon made to Montgolfier specifications."

Chicago undergraduates also attend graduate workshops and lectures in their spare time and talk philosophy in the campus's numerous coffee shops. Neighborhood dining options are limited to a few ethnic restaurants and pizzerias. Students without cars will have some difficulty reaching much of the rest of the city. Hyde Park has a unique and fairly charming atmosphere as a neighborhood that stands somewhat apart from the rest of Chicago, but it comes at the price of being removed from much of the city's public transportation. Students may avail themselves of all that the city has to offer, from the many world-class museums to shopping on the Magnificent Mile to famous blues joints such as Kingston Mines and beer-soaked White Sox games. There are several excellent independent and used bookstores on or near campus.

Recreational activities on campus can hardly compete with the lures of Chicago, one of America's great cities, but there are many university-sponsored activities, including 19 men's and women's varsity sports teams, 40 intramural sports, and 30 active club sports, out of almost 500 student organizations, including a large number of religious groups. The Catholic Campus Ministry, based at Calvert House just off the main quadrangle, offers Mass daily and opportunities to meet for Bible study, prayer, and social and charitable work. Any Catholic student, however, should be sure to visit the gorgeously restored church of St. John Cantius on Carpenter

GREEN LIGHT

Because of the intellectual curiosity of students, greater political diversity in the student body, and a tradition of critical thought and inquiry, the University of Chicago has, in the words of a student, "one of the least politicized campuses I've seen." The school avoids many of the more intrusive infusions of political correctness or multicultural dogmatism that may interfere with academic life at other schools; conversely, it can also serve to reduce opportunities for political involvement and activism, to the extent that students are not themselves especially concerned with politics. This generally reflects the intensely focused and rigorous nature of the Chicago experience, in which the life of the mind and the bustle of strictly academic activity tends to take precedence over any type of activism.

Right-leaning intellectuals should check out the Edmund Burke Society, based at the university's law school, for Oxford-style debates on both political and philosophical topics. Both College Republicans and College Democrats are active on campus. Conservative students should also check out the nonpartisan political quarterly *Midway Review*. There are at times various leftist protests on campus, but they are almost always ignored by people on campus or are sometimes answered by satirical counterprotests.

The university is establishing the Milton Friedman Institute to build upon its strengths in economics and to honor the contribution of the late Professor Milton Friedman, a Nobel Prize–winning libertarian economist who long taught at Chicago. This decision has outraged leftist faculty, some 170 of whom submitted a petition to the university president demanding that the institute's name be changed, according to the *Chronicle of Higher Education*.

Street, which offers Mass in Latin with Gregorian chant. InterVarsity Christian Fellowship and Campus Crusade for Christ both have chapters at the university. The Chabad Jewish Center provides kosher Shabbat and holiday meals to all Jewish students, regardless of affiliation or observance. The Orthodox Christian Fellowship holds weekly vespers services on campus. The Hyde Park Vineyard Church two blocks north of the campus holds regular evangelical worship services and organizes smaller "house groups" for prayer and study.

The university guarantees housing for four years for every student. These dorms range from the newest building, South Campus Residence Hall, with its apartment-style living and view of the downtown skyline, to the neo-Gothic Burton-Judson, connected contiguously around two grassy courtyards. Freshmen are required to live in on-campus housing; all ten dormitories on campus are coed, although single-sex floors are available. Many bathrooms are coed in older dorms. Residential students may eat at any of three dining commons or two à la carte locations. The ten undergraduate residence halls are divided into thirty-five "houses," which were created to break up the living system into more human-scale, community-oriented units. Resident masters are senior faculty or staff members who live in the larger residence halls. Smaller halls share a resident master or participate in a larger hall's programming. Resident masters organize a program of social and cultural events that may include guest lectures, dinners, residence-hall special events, and trips for opera, theater, and sporting events—usually for very low prices. One student told us that "I lived in a dorm for two years and found the resident assistants to be very nice; they made an effort to foster a real sense of community among the students."

In the past, members of the opposite sex were prohibited from rooming together. But when advocates for transgender students demanded gender-neutral housing, the school began debating its sane, long-standing policies. After a successful pilot program spring semester of 2009, the new, posthuman plan was approved and now applies to everyone except freshmen, who are still assigned same-sex roommates.

According to one student, "Crime is probably the one major drawback to this university." Another adds that the surrounding neighborhood is "consistently populated by too many socially undesirable individuals." The campus itself and its immediate environs are fairly safe and patrolled frequently by university police (the largest private police force in the city), who can be summoned from any of 300-plus emergency phones placed strategically around campus. In 2009, the school reported twenty-seven burglaries, two aggravated assaults, one robbery, and one forcible sex offense. This actually isn't too bad for a school situated in the South Side of Chicago, one of the most crime-ridden areas in the country. One student tells us, "If you want to be here, you will want it so badly that you will ignore the crime rate."

Chicago is as expensive as it is excellent, with 2010–11 tuition at $40,188 and room and board at $12,153. Admissions are need blind, and Chicago guarantees to meet the need of any student it accepts. Some 49 percent of students receive need-based aid. The average student-loan debt of a 2006 graduate was $18,500.

Creighton University

Omaha, Nebraska • www.creighton.edu

Faithful to a mission

Creighton University took its name from Edward Creighton, a pioneer of the telegraph industry whose widow, Mary Lucretia, endowed the university, which was founded by the Catholic bishop of Omaha and the Society of Jesus in 1878. As Creighton has evolved, it has become a rising star in the region. Especially dedicated to the sciences, it is among the top national universities in the number of graduates who go on to medical schools. In 2010, Creighton was included among the colleges and universities that produced the most Fulbright scholars in the nation.

Students at Creighton embark upon a comprehensive core curriculum that pays special attention to philosophy, language, and theology coursework that all Jesuit colleges used to require of all their undergraduates. Notably, Creighton is the only Jesuit university in the nation (and one of a tiny set of Catholic colleges in the nation) that reports that all its Catholic theology professors have obtained a *mandatum* from their local bishop—official church recognition that they intend to teach in communion with the church, with "commitment and responsibility to teach authentic Catholic doctrine." In fall 2010, the school announced its new president, Rev. Timothy R. Lannon, S.J., previously president of St. Joseph's University.

Academic Life: *Ratio Studiorum*

The college of arts and sciences undergraduates must complete the school's excellent core curriculum requirements, as well as courses that comprise a fair chunk of a student's credits (a minimum of forty-nine credit hours, including four approved writing intensive courses, plus twelve to fifteen hours in the skills area).

Creighton's commitment to a well-rounded education begins with the *Ratio Studiorum* program, which includes a freshman one-credit seminar, "Culture of Collegiate Life," that examines "the meaning and value of a liberal arts education; the university's Jesuit, Catholic history and key Ignatian values; and the vocational aspirations and challenges common to all freshmen." Faculty members who teach the course are the academic advisors to the students in their classes through the first year. After that, students get pre-major and peer advisors until they choose a major—when they receive a department advisor.

Midwest

VITAL STATISTICS

Religious affiliation: *Roman Catholic*
Total enrollment: *7,385*
Total undergraduates: *4,133*
SAT/ACT midranges: CR: *520–640*, M: *540–650*; ACT: *24–29*
Applicants: *4,752*
Applicants accepted: *82%*
Accepted applicants who enrolled: *27%*
Tuition and fees: *$29,226*
Room and board: *$9,164*
Freshman retention rate: *89%*
Graduation rate: *64% (4 yrs.), 75% (6 yrs.)*
Courses with fewer than 20 students: *45%*
Student-faculty ratio: *11:1*
Courses taught by graduate students: *not provided*
Most popular majors: *business/marketing, health professions, biological and life sciences*
Students living on campus: *60%*
Guaranteed housing for four years? *yes*
Students in fraternities: *28%* in sororities: *37%*

The Honors Program at Creighton has played a role in helping to create more intellectual energy among the students, says a professor. "It attracts a select group of highly talented students who are given a relatively high degree of freedom to pursue their intellectual interests," the school reports. The current curriculum was implemented in 2005.

Requirements for honors students include three foundation seminars that explore the development of the Christian intellectual tradition within the context of Western civilization and the pluralistic world. They are as follows: "Beginnings of the Christian Intellectual Tradition," "The Rise of the West," and "The Modern World." Also required are critical-thinking courses (sources and methods) chosen from a selection that includes "The Age of Augustus," "The Literature of Mysticism," "Animals, Persons and Ethics," and "Intelligence: Multiple Perspectives." During their senior year, honors students take a core curriculum or honors "Senior Perspectives" course and undertake an independent research project in the field of their major under the guidance of a faculty mentor. To remain in the program, students must maintain a GPA of at least 3.3 for all courses and a 3.0 for all honors courses.

Creighton offers more than fifty bachelor degree programs in three colleges serving undergraduates: the College of Arts and Sciences (the largest), the College of Business Administration, and the School of Nursing. In addition, Creighton has Schools of Dentistry, Medicine, Law, and Pharmacy and Health Professions; a graduate school offering master and doctorate degrees; and a University College that serves part-time and nontraditional students. Concentrations that dominate at Creighton are premedical, pharmacy, dental, law, and physical therapy.

"Owing to the health schools, Creighton's undergraduate students tend to be ruthlessly focused on preprofessional training," says a professor. "As a consequence, a culture of inquiry is relatively weak. However, faculty are leading the charge to demand higher pay in exchange for increased expectations and higher standards in both research and teaching. Many are engaging their students late into the evenings and on weekends."

Teaching is "job number one" at Creighton, and this is reflected in tenure decisions, says a professor. The average class size is twenty-five students. Professors are "very accessible in class, and outside of class it is not uncommon for professors to give out home phone numbers and cell phone numbers," a student reports. Many "serve as advisors to student groups and help facilitate events in their respective college/department." In a recent report, a junior stated, "At Creighton, students come first, and it is as simple as that."

Creighton students can choose from a full list of traditional majors, while trendy disciplines (such as women's and gender or African and black studies) are offered only as minors. In 2008, the university added three majors: French and francophone, German, and Spanish and Hispanic studies. The strongest departments at Creighton are biology, chemistry, physics, psychology and Classical and Near Eastern studies. Faculty members at Creighton recommended by students and colleagues include: William Harmless, S.J., Thomas Kelly, Michael Legaspi, Russell Reno, and Nicolae Roddy in theology; Terry Clark, Graham Ramsden, and James Wunsch in political science; Geoffrey Bakewell and Gregory Bucher in Classical and Near Eastern studies; Carole Seitz in fine and performing arts; Isabelle Cherney and Matthew Huss in psychology; Michael Cherney, Gintaras Duda, and Michael Nichols in physics; Mark Reedy and Mary Ann Vinton in biology; Robert Dornsife and Jennifer Ladino in English; Joan Eckerson in exercise science; Betsy Elliot-Meisel, Heather Fryer, and Tracy Leavelle in history; David Dobberpuhl and Mark Freitag in chemistry; Natalie Ross Adkins in marketing; Tim Bastian in economics; Jeff Hause and Amy Wendling in philosophy; John Wingender in finance; Laura Mizaur in accounting; and Erika Kirby in communications.

SUGGESTED CORE

1. Classical and Near Eastern Studies 321, Epic Literature
2. Philosophy 370, History of Classical Greek Philosophy
3. Theology 201/207, Reading the Old Testament/Reading the New Testament
4. Philosophy 372, History of Medieval Philosophy
5. Political Science 365, Classics of Political Thought
6. English 409, Shakespeare
7. History 311, United States History to 1877
8. History 415, Nineteenth Century Europe (closest match)

Major requirements in the theology department at Creighton tend to be foundational, including "Old Testament," "New Testament," and "History of the Christian Church." However, students are not required to take courses in Catholic doctrine or to become well acquainted with the Catholic tradition of theological reflection. An undergraduate student highly recommends the teaching of Nicolae Roddy. "Dr. Roddy teaches 'Introduction to the Old Testament,' a challenging course, but Dr. Roddy's emphasis on learning and discussion ensures you will learn more from his class than any other class you take at Creighton," the student says.

English is not a common major at Creighton (accounting for only 3 percent of Creighton graduates), but the department offers a wide array of specializations, ranging from Irish literature to creative writing. Courses tend to be admirably traditional surveys of literature, but because Creighton's English department is small, few courses are offered at once; semesters may pass before a Shakespeare course is available.

Even smaller than the English department, Creighton's history department maintains stricter requirements, which include two courses in United States history. The political science major requires a specific class in the American political system.

Beyond Creighton's impressive curriculum, the school benefits from its location in Omaha, which is a consistently well-reviewed city. "Creighton's proximity to downtown businesses (literally blocks away) provides countless internships for Creighton students at *Fortune* 500 companies," says a business student. Warren Buffet, Omaha's most well-known businessman, speaks regularly at Creighton. In the 1960s and 1970s, he gave a free lecture course at the university. (The fact that Buffet is an outspoken advocate of legal abortion and population control has not prevented the university from hosting him.)

The school estimates that about 250 students participate each year in its study-abroad programs in forty countries. Students in Creighton's affiliate program at the University of Glasgow (Scotland), which is open to honors students, and the University of Limerick (Ireland) are fully integrated into the student body and take courses (fall or spring semester) alongside Scottish and Irish students.

The Department of Classical and Near Eastern Studies offers a classical languages major with either an Ancient Greek or Latin language focus. The other languages offered are Russian, Chinese, Arabic, Spanish, Japanese, French, Italian, and German. Students must take at least two semesters of a foreign language (or one if they have previously studied the language).

Student Life: In the heartland

Creighton University is located in Omaha, Nebraska's largest city, situated on the west bank of the Missouri River. The city has been hard at work developing a showcase riverfront, gentrifying the downtown area, and building world-class facilities. Holland Performing Arts Center contains a 2005-built 2,000-seat state-of-the-art concert hall where the Omaha Symphony Orchestra and Opera Omaha perform, as well as a recital hall that seats nearly 500 and a semiclosed courtyard that seats 1,000. The Gene Leahy Mall is a ten-acre park against historic and modern architecture in the heart of downtown with a lagoon, gardens, waterfalls, and walking paths that connect to Heartland of America Park. Omaha also boasts the nationally renowned Henry Doorly Zoo. Major attractions for college students located near Creighton's 130-acre urban campus are the indie-rock venue Slowdown and Film Streams, a cinema art house. Old Market is also a prime hangout; red-brick roads run past open-air restaurants, art galleries, bookstores, bakeries, pubs, and boutiques.

Creighton's campus consists of 130 acres with over fifty buildings and is almost completely enclosed, with all parking (about 65 percent of students have cars) on the outskirts and around the campus itself. A student says the campus's parklike setting, which is intersected by a tree-lined mall, contains "luscious plants, trees, bushes, and flowers filling every spare circle and pathway on campus, providing a wonderful environment in the spring for a game of Frisbee or reading your favorite book in the shade of one of the many trees." Recent additions to the campus include the $50 million, 214,000-square-foot Harper Living-Learning Center (completed in 2008), featuring classrooms, administrative offices, a fitness center, an alumni sports cafe, an indoor/outdoor latte bar, an auditorium, meeting spaces, and a bookstore.

Unmarried freshmen and sophomores from outside the Omaha area are required to live on campus (students from Omaha may live off campus but only with a parent or guardian), each class in its own housing. Most residence halls, with the exception of one women's dorm for freshmen, are coed, with men and women separated by floors. Some of the freshmen dorms are equipped with kitchenettes on the floors. Housing options for sophomores are suite-style or apartment-style housing. Rooms are equipped with air conditioning and cable television, and each building has its own laundry room and computer lab (*PC* magazine ranks Creighton fifth in its listing of Most Wired Colleges). A front desk in each hall is staffed twenty-four hours a day. In addition to resident advisors and resident directors, Jesuit priests and affiliated laymen reside in the halls as chaplains. Creighton's visitation policy does not allow members of the opposite sex to remain in a room or in a residential area past the designated visiting hours. Hosting an overnight guest of the opposite sex is considered a serious violation of housing policy.

ACADEMIC REQUIREMENTS

College of Arts and Sciences students at Creighton must complete the following requirements:

- "Culture of Collegiate Life," a college skills and mission class.
- "Christianity in Context," a course that studies religion "as a universal human phenomenon and Christianity within that context."
- One scripture course chosen from a short list. Representative courses include "Reading the Old Testament" and "Paul and His Legacy."
- One Christian theology course chosen from fifteen selections, ranging from "Catholicism Creed and Question" to "Eucharist: Sacrament of Unity or Disunity."
- Either "Philosophical Foundations for Ethical Understanding" or "Theological Foundations for Ethical Understanding."
- "God and Persons: Philosophical Reflections" and "Critical and Historical Introduction to Philosophy."
- "The Modern Western World" and a non-Western history course.
- "World Literature" I and II.
- One international and global studies course from a long list, with choices ranging from "International Political Economy" to "Issues of the Native American Experience."
- Two natural science classes that must include one laboratory component, in areas such as atmospheric science, biology, chemistry, astronomy, computer, and physics.
- Two courses in social/behavioral sciences. Choices range from "Introductory Microeconomics" to "Introduction to Native American Studies."
- One senior interdisciplinary course that "focuses on a major area of human and social concern." Options range widely from "Politics and Ethics of Science and Technology" to "Film and the Fine Arts."
- Four certified writing courses.

The following "skills" course requirements may be met via tests and portfolios:

- "Applied Mathematics" or "Calculus" I.
- One rhetoric and composition course.
- One speech or a studio/performing arts course.
- One to two courses in a foreign language.

Theme housing on coed floors in the residence halls includes the Freshman Honors Scholars Community, Freshman Leadership Program, and Cortina, a sophomore residential community focused on service, faith, and justice. About a quarter of Creighton students are members of the school's eight sororities and five fraternities. The school does not maintain Greek houses, and the sororities and fraternities uphold their commitment to service and academic life, rather than becoming party houses for a campus elite. (Greek students at Creighton consistently maintain above-average GPAs and offer awards to high achievers.)

With nearly 200 student-run clubs to choose from, Creighton undergrads should have no trouble finding organizations that interest them, whether academic (Pre-Law Society, Pre-Pharmacy Club, Biology Club, Oratorical Society, Italian Club, Mock Trial Team), sports (martial arts, lacrosse, shooting, hockey, rowing), professional (mostly medical and student associations of various sorts), service (Red Cross, Knights of Columbus, Habitat for Humanity), social (Swing Choir, Dance Club, Campus Quilters, Pep Band), cultural (German-American Club, Spanish Club, Chinese and African Student associations) or religious (Rosary Club, Jays for Christ, Protestant and Muslim Student associations) in nature.

Students seem committed to the mission of the university: in 2010, the school raised $220,000 for Haiti earthquake victims and, owing to relationships with an institution in the Dominican Republic, was able to send thirty-eight health care professionals and thousands of pounds of supplies immediately following the quake. In 2009, pharmacy students worked 502 community-service hours to help screen at-risk populations for heart disease, and similar programs (like free oral-cancer screenings) are given by the various schools and programs.

Creighton also offers a number of opportunities to participate in student government (many of the colleges have senates or student unions). Political groups include College Republicans and Democrats, Amnesty International, Creighton Students for Life, NAACP, and the Peace and Justice Cooperative. Honors societies are numerous as well, from the Freshman Leadership Program to societies in various disciplines (German, classics, teaching, accounting, and so forth).

Creighton's student-run newspaper is the *Creightonian*; its literary journal is *Shadows*. Creighton offers students ROTC programs in two divisions of the military: the Army on campus, and the Air Force in cooperation with the University of Nebraska at Omaha.

Creighton hosts a wide variety of activities and events including, Fallapalooza and Spring Fling, two big concerts that are held every year. Recent bands include the Black Eyed Peas, Cake, and Ben Folds. One of the most popular student events on campus is the annual all-night video-gaming event GameFest. Hui O'Hawaii, a student group, holds an annual luau. The Inter Residence Hall Government sponsors Christmas at Creighton, the Price Is Right game show, and Lil' Jays Weekend, when students invite young siblings and family friends to stay with them on campus.

Nearly fifty Jesuits live at and serve the Creighton community. "As a Catholic, Jesuit institution, Creighton welcomes all students of faith and has vibrant and active Jewish and Protestant student groups," says a student. "The interdenominational Christian group Jays for Christ attracts a large membership and provides activities for students of faith." The most active Catholic student groups at Creighton are Students for Life, the Rosary Club,

Midwest

and the Knights of Columbus. Many Creighton students are originally from Nebraska, Iowa, or Missouri, and about 60 percent are Catholic. Besides vibrant Catholic groups on campus, however, there are a few left-leaning groups, such as the Gay-Straight Alliance, whose purpose it is to "eliminate biases against any sexual orientation."

Students volunteer at local charities each week, and many take part in one of the many spring/fall-break service trips to build houses in Appalachia, gut homes in the Gulf region, or work with teenage mothers from the inner-city, among a multitude of other options.

In 2008, the Creighton campus became tobacco-free. The school administration requires all new students to complete "AlcoholWise," an online alcohol-education course, before arriving on campus. Once on campus, students attended a ninety-minute, peer-to-peer alcohol-education session. The program has succeeded in reducing cases of freshmen with severe intoxication by 66 percent—and Creighton keeps a careful eye on alcohol use, thanks to a set of innovative policies. If a student is determined to be legally intoxicated, he is taken to the medical center, and his parents are notified. Creighton approaches alcohol abuse not as a normal rite of passage but as an indication of more serious problems, and treats it accordingly.

There are a number of activities available beyond partying, and the Creighton Bluejays provide ample opportunity for wholesome recreation. The university fields fourteen NCAA Division I varsity sports that compete in the Missouri Valley Athletic Conference. The Creighton men's basketball games are played at the 18,000-seat Qwest Center among Division I schools, Creighton has ranked in the top twenty nationally for attendance at basketball games for the past four years. The soccer teams play on cam-

GREEN LIGHT

One professor says of Creighton, "I should note that the Catholic Church's views on abortion make the campus inviting to conservatives, while the church's views on social justice do the same for liberals. So, all-in-all, one will find the university quite tolerant of any mainstream religious or political view." A student adds, "Creighton leans right politically and is probably the most conservative Jesuit institution in the country. The vast majority of Creighton students are apathetic politically, but the College Republicans have a membership that is three times that of the College Democrats." Students say that, overall, Creighton serves as a strong example of free speech. Antiwar and promilitary demonstrations can be seen operating simultaneously. However, the university will not condone the activities of a student group when it "demands special treatment, is using funding to promote a message that runs counter to the university's religious identity, or a university department seeks to convey a message or viewpoint in the name of the university that runs counter to the Catholic identity."

Creighton has had a balancing act to manage with its faculty and the Archdiocese of Omaha. Controversial events include the canceled speaking engagement of author Anne Lamott (who supports abortion and assisted suicide), and the local archdiocese "severed ties with Creighton University's Center for Marriage and Family after two university researchers said the Catholic Church should allow engaged couples to live together and have sex before marriage," according to the Catholic News Agency. Students should ask around before signing up for theology classes at Creighton.

pus in Morrison Stadium, a 5,000-seat facility completed in 2004. Creighton also supports eighteen club sports (from jujitsu to cycling to lacrosse) and twelve intramural sports, each with numerous teams. Every June, baseball fans descend on Omaha for the NCAA College World Series.

The Creighton campus is relatively safe, with two forcible sex offenses, one aggravated assault, and four burglaries in 2009. The Department of Public Safety patrols the campus on foot, on bicycles, and in vehicles twenty-four hours a day. Closed-circuit-television surveillance cameras and blue-light emergency phones have been installed on selected sites.

Annual tuition at Creighton is a relatively modest $29,226, although certain programs are more expensive. Room and board averages out at $9,164. Some 50 percent of students receive need-based financial aid. The average student-loan debt of a recent graduate is $32,888.

Franciscan University of Steubenville

Steubenville, Ohio • www.franciscan.edu

Enthusiasm

In 1946, Franciscan friars established the College of Steubenville especially for young veterans of World War II. After nearly failing in the late 1960s, the college found new life in 1974 under President Rev. Michael Scanlan, TOR, whose vision bolstered enrollment while simultaneously making the college the focus of the Catholic charismatic movement. In 1980, the college was rechristened the Franciscan University of Steubenville, and it has grown to include a 124-acre campus in Steubenville, Ohio (forty miles west of Pittsburgh), and a campus in Gaming, Austria.

Rev. Terence Henry is the current university president, but the influence of Scanlan—now Steubenville's chancellor—lives on. And this is all for the good, since during his tenure, Scanlan transformed the college into a solid, seriously Catholic institution—in a time of secularization at most other Catholic campuses. Steubenville stands out among Catholic schools as one of a handful that proclaim a traditional commitment to the unity of faith and human knowledge. When the late Pope John Paul II ordered that Catholic colleges and universities require theologians who teach to possess a *mandatum* (certificate of doctrinal orthodoxy) from the local bishop, fewer than one in ten American schools complied. But Steubenville obeyed enthusiastically. The greatest challenge Steubenville faces is to tighten its academic focus and raise its standards, winning more prestige and acceptance outside the small but vital subculture of fervently orthodox Catholics.

Academic Life: Mind, body, and spirit

Despite its dedication to reason as well as faith, Steubenville's requirements for the baccalaureate degree seem a little . . . irrational. Its optimistically labeled Core Program includes courses in communications, humanities, natural science, social science, and theology. These requirements can be realized in a dizzying (and puzzling) variety of ways: for instance, the fifteen credits needed to complete the "communications core" can include courses in creative writing, drama, mathematics (including statistics), and some music courses. It is therefore possible for students to avoid American history in favor of economics.

Although students are free to avoid them, rigorous academic courses do exist at Steubenville, and the honors program is the easiest place to find them. Honors students embark on close reading and vigorous seminar discussion of a curriculum of Great Books, including authors such as Homer, Plato, St. Augustine, St. Thomas Aquinas, St. Bonaventure, Chaucer, Shakespeare, Jefferson, Kant, and Marx. To enter and stay in the program, a student needs a high school GPA of B+ and verbal/math SATs of 1220 (or 27 on the ACT)—and must keep a 3.0 GPA. However, one student warns that the honors program "is like all other academics at FUS: it has the potential to be challenging and to provide a really great education, but if you don't want to do the work, you can do really well without it."

Students should meet with their academic advisors at the beginning of each semester to receive help planning their course schedules. Peer tutoring is also available to students who meet certain criteria. All classes seem to be taught by the professors themselves and not teaching assistants.

Students at Steubenville can major in a wide variety of fields—perhaps too wide, given the size of the school: accounting; anthropology; biology (BA and BS programs); business administration with concentrations in economics, finance, international, management, and marketing and multimedia; catechetics; chemistry; classics; communication arts with concentrations in radio/TV and journalism; computer science; computer information science; drama; economics; elementary education; English with concentrations in drama, British and American literature, Western and world literature, and writing; French; German; history; humanities and Catholic culture; legal studies; math; mental-health and human services; sacred music; nursing; philosophy; political science; psychology; social work; sociology; Spanish; and theology. In 2006, new concentrations in international business and in multimedia were added. The most popular majors are currently theology, catechetics, nursing, business, and education, followed closely by philosophy, English, psychology, and communication arts.

Of these degree programs, theology is the best known and strongest at FUS. There are more theology majors at Steubenville than at any other Catholic school in America. A number of well-known professors, such as the popular biblical expositor Professor Scott Hahn, teach in this department; students also recommend Professor Michael Sirilla. To major in theology, a number of required courses must be completed, including "Christian Moral Principles," the two-part "Principles of Biblical Study," "Sacraments," "Theology of the Church," and "Theology of Christ" in the junior year, with electives saved mostly for senior year. Noticeably absent from the major, as one student points out, is a requirement for philosophy classes (although there is one in the Humanities core in the first semester of freshman year): "This means, in my opinion, they don't learn how to understand theology, but just how to regurgitate

SUGGESTED CORE

The eight-course Honors Program offers an excellent core curriculum.

what they learn," he says. Nonetheless, inspired by the school's dogged loyalty to church teaching in an age of academic dissent, many graduates of this department go on to careers working for orthodox Catholic dioceses or to pursue priestly/religious vocations.

The philosophy department offers a strong preparation to majors. Recommended professors in this department include Jonathan Sanford, whom a student cites as "one of the finest professors of philosophy at this university. He has a firm command of the material and can effectively present difficult concepts to his students." Another student praises Mark Roberts as "a stellar professor of the sort who truly teaches the lost art of thinking."

Economics is another highly regarded department, where Donald Materniak is hailed for being "amazing in accounting, great at explaining, extremely knowledgeable, with the ability to tell a quick joke."

The nursing program is also commended and recently re-earned an eight-year accreditation from the NLNAC (National League for Nursing Accrediting Commission). The education major is said to have room for improvement, with one graduate complaining that there are too many requirements and not enough alternative teaching methods (such as Montessori) offered.

All English majors are required to take core literature classes, including one in Shakespeare and another in classical mythology. One excellent professor in this department is Ben Alexander, a specialist in southern literature.

History majors must study the civilizations of Greece and Rome, Judaism, Christianity, the American founding (as well as events leading up to it), the American Civil War, and twentieth-century history. Classes such as "History of the Far East" are also available but not required.

Political science majors are required to study classical political theory and American constitutional law—contrary to many elite colleges.

The student-faculty ratio at FUS is 15 to 1—better than at a vast state university, but nothing approaching the intimacy of a top liberal arts college. However, students who wish to befriend these busy teachers will find mentors with impressive credentials—especially if they are interested in apologetics or pro-life activism. Political science professor Stephen Krason is renowned as a conservative scholar of the U.S. founding and Constitution. Legal studies director Brian Scarnecchia authored a three-volume work outlining and advocating a conservative approach to family issues. Also of note is the first fully endowed academic chair at Steubenville, created in 2008. Held by Professor Patrick Lee, renowned philosopher and bioethicist, the John N. and Jamie D. McAleer Chair in Bioethics has already sponsored conferences and engaged in spirited debates on human life issues ranging from embryonic stem cell research to human sexuality and abortion.

Another attractive feature of FUS is its popular study-abroad program in Gaming, Austria. Students there live in a fourteenth-century Carthusian monastery. Long weekends make trips to many countries possible; students report hopping on the train to Italy, France, Germany, Poland, and Spain. This program is especially attractive because the school keeps down the costs: a year in Gaming costs the same as a year in Ohio.

Apart from the classics major (Ancient Greek and Latin), students have the choice of only three language majors: German, French, and Spanish. Steubenville offers its language students the opportunity to study abroad in Austria, Germany, France, or Latin America.

Student Life: Slacks on the beach

Steubenville sits in an isolated setting on a high plateau overlooking the Ohio River—think Rust Belt or *The Deer Hunter*, a film shot nearby. But this does not mean that students have trouble filling their free time. "College life in Steubenville is fun, so long as you go to Pittsburgh—forty-five minutes away," one student says. "Many students go camping here, too. There are ways to have a blast. And there are plenty of enthusiastic people to have fun with." Another says, "The campus is quite nice, and there are lots of things to do."

In fact, some students (particularly those in the Pre-Theologate Program who plan to study for the priesthood) find campus social life pervasive—even overwhelming. The close-knit community and shared values of the students foster easier communication and tighter bonds than one would find at a large state school. "People are so enthusiastic about being together—you could be doing something every night, if you let yourself," one student says.

In order to maintain the school's strong Catholic identity, during his term as president Scanlan introduced a system of "households," essentially "a mix between a fraternity and a faith-sharing group." A "household" is defined by the university as "a Christ-centered group of three or more students of the same gender, who strive for healthy, balanced, interpersonal relationships while supporting and challenging its members to develop spiritually, emotionally, academically, and physically." Each household has an advisor and a written pledge or "household covenant" that expresses the common commitment and identity of the household. While a few students warn of households that are more social than productive, or of others that exhibit a pharisaical attitude, most of those who spoke to us indicated that being in a household was one of the best parts of being at Steubenville, a source of great support and sometimes of lifelong friendships.

In addition to households, Steubenville boasts of many student groups. Academic groups such as the Computer Science Club are founded to help students participate in on- and off-campus activities and events, and prepare for a real career in this particular field. Other such groups include the Chiron Society (education majors), Christopher Dawson Society (humanities and Catholic culture majors), Gemelli Society (psychology, mental-health and human services, sociology, and social work majors), Graduate Student Counseling Association, Mathematics Club, Phi Alpha Honor Society (national honor society for social work students, faculty, and practitioners), Philosophy Club, Political Science Association (open to all students), St. Thomas Society (legal studies), Sigma Beta Mu (biology),

Students in Free Enterprise, and Spanish Club. A community outreach program, "Works of Mercy," ministers to the poor in the Ohio Valley/Pittsburgh area, and its counterpart, "Missions of Peace," sponsors approved domestic and international student-planned mission trips. Student organizations include the FUS Anime Club, the Annunciations (a musical group for women), Baronettes (a dance group for women), and the Chesterton Society. The *Troubadour* is the student newspaper.

A factor that distinguishes Steubenville is the student body's devotion to activism on behalf of traditional religious values. Public policy, civic participation, and conservative grassroots groups are popular among students. On the anniversary of *Roe v. Wade*, hundreds of Steubenville students begin two days of pro-life activities, concluding with a procession to the nearby Tomb of the Unborn Child, which contains the remains of seven aborted infants, to whom the university gave a decent burial.

Outreach programs are varied and numerous. Some students serve as part-time missionaries in climes as diverse as the Bronx and Brazil. During Spring Break, participants in "Sonlife" head to Florida, where they spend their week evangelizing students on the beach. Steubenville students witness through skits, praise, and worship on the beach, talking to people, and by the example they set in their modest attire and wholesome social interaction. If such an outreach strikes you as creepy, Steubenville is not the place for you.

Steubenville competes as a provisional NCAA Division III member school. Varsity athletics include men's and women's soccer, men's and women's basketball, men's and women's cross-country, men's and women's tennis, men's baseball and softball, men's rugby, and women's volleyball. Intramural sports include Ultimate Frisbee, flag football, volleyball, and basketball. Events and tournaments are held in racquetball, Wallyball, softball, weightlifting, and tennis.

The atmosphere of the campus has been spruced up by the advent of much-needed construction and renovation, including the recently built J. C. Williams Center, where students go to pick up mail, have a quick meal, converse with friends, and shop at the bookstore. A cafe, walk-up computer stations, plenty of couches and tables, five new meeting rooms, and a sweeping staircase make the center an appealing hangout. Concerts, academic gatherings, and even dances can now take place in the forty-five-foot-high atrium, which offers many views of the nearby Christ the King Chapel.

The chapel is the "spiritual hub" of the university, where more than 700 students typically attend daily Mass. Hundreds of students come to participate in various ministries and a number of activities geared toward the spiritual growth of the students, such as daily recitation of the rosary, Liturgy of the Hours, and several retreats. On the other hand, its exterior, according to some aesthetically minded students, resembles a partially opened can of cat food. Inside, the chapel does sport lovely stained-glass windows and a seven-foot San Damiano cross.

There is little room for the expanding student body; Sunday liturgies reportedly leave students relegated to sitting in the foyer and even outside the chapel. The cafeteria experiences similar problems, with students sometimes standing or sitting on the floor to eat.

On a brighter note, two residence halls, St. Louis (male) and St. Elizabeth (female), opened in 2007—although some students complained that this just increased the crowding problems in the chapel and cafeteria. These were the first new living spaces at FUS in more than ten years. The halls include Internet and phone access in each room, study lounges, and laundry facilities. A central area for socializing features a gas fireplace and a kitchenette with an adjacent dining room. Recent renovations also have been made to St. Thomas More Hall, home to 287 female students, including air conditioning, technology upgrades, expanded rooms, larger lobbies, and new entryways. Dorms are single sex, and there are specified hours for intervisitation in residence-hall lounges, common rooms, and kitchens.

Steubenville does offer assistance to students seeking off-campus living but is exclusive of all contracts made between tenant and landlord. Off-campus living is permitted only to students who meet certain criteria.

The university has three daily masses, as well as a weekly Latin Mass. Confessions are held four days a week, there is perpetual adoration during the academic year, solemn vespers on Sundays, praise and worship each Tuesday, and a monthly Festival of Praise. Chapel ministries also offers marriage and confirmation prep, as well as an RCIA program.

Crime is infrequent in Steubenville, though it has shown a slight increase recently. In 2009, the school reported one aggravated assault and ten burglaries on campus. The university provides a safety escort service to and from various campus locations after dark.

The school is reasonably priced for a private university, with a recent tuition cost of $19,900, and room and board totaling $6,900. However, a student and his family will

---

ACADEMIC REQUIREMENTS

Steubenville does boast many excellent courses; the problem is that students can easily avoid them, if only by accident. The categories in which courses appear are organized according to an esoteric logic impervious to us, with the result that drama is lumped in with mathematics, and philosophy with history and art. The wise student will choose carefully (see our suggested core for this school). All Steubenville's baccalaureate-degree students must complete the following:

- Five courses in "communications," with choices ranging from English composition, foreign languages, speech, drama, mathematics (including statistics), and computer science to music.
- Five classes in humanities, chosen from courses in art, history, literature, philosophy, theology, and music.
- One course each in history, literature, and philosophy, with choices such as "Art Appreciation" and "Philosophy of Religion."
- Two classes in natural science, such as "Concepts of Ecology" or "General Physics."
- Two courses in social science, including choices in American history, political science, economics, psychology, and sociology. "Civil War and Reconstruction" and "Principles of Economics" are options.
- Two courses in theology, such as "Francis and the Franciscan Tradition" or "Christian Moral Principles."

Midwest

be paying much of that cost themselves; both students and alumni loudly lament Steubenville's lack of adequate financial aid. Need-based and honor-based scholarship recipients alike often receive aid packages in the area of $2,000, while other colleges can offer them several thousand more. This is because Steubenville's endowment is well below that of most schools its size. The *Chronicle of Higher Education* notes that despite the low tuition and living costs—and although nearly 80 percent of the student body receives some form of financial aid—Steubenville students still have to take out more college loans than most of their peers at other institutions. There are many who could barely attend based on the financial-aid packages; several report they had friends who could not make it at all. As one alumna recalls, "Each semester, I didn't know if I would have to end my college career due to pending loan approvals. Steubenville gave me loans, but loans I will be paying back until I am thirty." Indeed, the average student-loan debt of a recent graduating class was an imposing $30,180.

In answer to this problem, the university has launched an ambitious capital campaign, with a goal of $25 million. As of July 2010, the university had raised an impressive $22 million. Topping the list of campaign needs are student scholarships, a new friary, and academic expansion.

GREEN LIGHT

Steubenville prides itself on hewing closely to a traditional reading of Catholic moral principles. This traditionalism tends toward political conservatism, too: Young America's Foundation placed Steubenville among its top conservative colleges. During Barack Obama's campaign for the presidency, one Steubenville board member, Nicholas Cafardi, publicly endorsed Obama—despite his support for legal (even partial-birth) abortion. This generated a scandal that led to Cafardi's resignation from the board. Well over 800 students, faculty, and staff members attended the annual March for Life in Washington, D.C., in January 2010. However, the university is a big place, and students with more liberal views will not feel unduly pressured—unless they publicly challenge irreformable tenets of Catholic doctrine, such as the sanctity of life and marriage. Activist Catholic dissenters, or those seeking a party atmosphere, should probably look elsewhere.

Grinnell College

Grinnell, Iowa • www.grinnell.edu

Social Gospel, lots of capital

Founded in 1846, Grinnell is named for Josiah Bushnell Grinnell, an abolitionist minister. It began as self-consciously progressive, becoming the first college west of the Mississippi to grant degrees to both black students and women. Since then, the school has progressed very far to the left. Today it has a reputation as a place where granola-crunchers and radicals of all varieties feel particularly comfortable. In February 2010, the college selected Dr. Raynard Kington as its president. A qualified academic, Kington is also openly gay and will certainly advance Grinnell's already gay-friendly policies.

Grinnell is laissez-faire about much more than private conduct. It imposes no curricular or distributional requirements beyond a first-year tutorial; no science, math, writing, or foreign language courses are required. Students with the motivation and preparation to structure their own studies *could* get an excellent liberal arts education at Grinnell. The faculty is strong, the students bright, the community close, the location bucolic—and the $1.4 *billion* endowment makes Grinnell one of the richest liberal arts college, per capita, in the nation.

Academic Life: Recommend it and they will come

Whatever curricular course they choose, Grinnell students are expected to study hard. A professor says, "This is the rub and the shock for some students—they get into a course and find that the freedom ends there and they have to do what they are told." One science major notes, "There are a few less serious classes, but not many. The most common such courses are in science for nonscience majors (such as physics for poets)." Another student says that "the course load here is extremely rigorous and requires excellent time-management skills; I personally have close to five hours of homework each night, which is about the average here."

The one required tutorial is designed to introduce students to professors and to college-level work. Most recently, students could pick among courses such as "Humanities I: The Ancient Greek World" or "The Grace of Sleep or the Ineptitude of All-Nighters." The tutorial usually culminates with a research project. The professor with whom a student takes the tutorial also serves as his advisor until the student declares a major, when he gets a new faculty advisor from his major department. One teacher says the tutorial "usually ensures that students enroll in a balanced liberal arts curriculum for the first three semesters."

Some majors have serious requirements, while others allow inordinate flexibility. English majors, for instance, must take eight courses in all, with no single required class. In order to satisfy their early literature requirements, English majors choose one course in pre-modern literature (from two offered), one in British or postcolonial literature, and one in American literature. English students also must show proficiency in a foreign language. What students read and study in these courses varies by professor. However, one syllabus for "Tradition of Literature" II, a course that covers English literature from the seventeenth through the nineteenth centuries, reveals that students study traditional fare: Wordsworth, Shelley, Austen, and Dickens.

Grinnell's department of political science was the first in the country. Majors take an introductory class, and others in American, comparative, and international politics. Some of the courses require a reading of the United States Constitution, but students could get by without being exposed to it.

In the Grinnell history major, students must take a minimum of thirty-two credits within the department. Eight of these credits must be upper division. The department recommends that students "complete a history curriculum that embraces geographic and chronological diversity." No courses in U.S. history before 1900 are required. The department also *recommends* that students reach proficiency in a foreign language and in quantitative analysis. The syllabus for the basic course in early American history in fall 2009 included a number of secondary and politicized-sounding sources but not the *Federalist Papers* or the works of John Locke.

By now the Grinnell strategy should be clear: recommend but don't require, even if the course is essential. The vast majority of students will follow the recommendations anyway. A professor says, "It is interesting that, with no requirements, math, science, and foreign language courses are filled to capacity." Still, one professor warns, "The college does not like to talk about the fair number [of students] who get by with a poorly rounded course of study and with the help of grade inflation."

A student says, "Academic advising here is excellent, as advisors give very sound advice to students on what courses to take and also help in the career preparation of students."

At Grinnell, classes average about seventeen students, and only 5 percent of classes have more than thirty. The student-faculty ratio is an excellent 9 to 1. Because Grinnell

---

VITAL STATISTICS

Religious affiliation: *none*
Total enrollment: *1,609*
Total undergraduates: *1,609*
SAT/ACT midranges: CR: *610–740*, M: *610–730*; ACT: *28–32*
Applicants: *2,845*
Applicants accepted: *43%*
Accepted applicants who enrolled: *34%*
Tuition and fees: *$37,482*
Room and board: *$8,880*
Freshman retention rate: *93%*
Graduation rate: *78% (4 yrs.), 84% (6 yrs.)*
Courses with fewer than 20 students: *68%*
Student-faculty ratio: *9:1*
Courses taught by graduate students: *none*
Most popular majors: *social sciences, biology, foreign languages*
Students living on campus: *87%*
Guaranteed housing for four years? *yes*
Students in fraternities or sororities: *none*

SUGGESTED CORE

1. Humanities 101-I, The Ancient Greek World
2. Humanities 102-II, Roman and Early Christian Culture
3. Religious Studies 211/214, The Hebrew Bible/The Christian Scriptures
4. Religious Studies 213, Christian Traditions (closest match)
5. Philosophy 264, Political Theory II
6. English 121, Introduction to Shakespeare
7. History 211/212, Colonial and Revolutionary America, 1450–1788/Democracy in America, 1789–1848
8. Philosophy 234: Nineteenth-Century Continental Philosophy

is exclusively an undergraduate institution, there are no graduate teaching assistants. This lets Grinnell provide students with small classes and close interaction between faculty. In fact, according to one administrator, there is almost a master-apprentice relationship between professors and students, especially in the junior and senior years, when it is not uncommon for students to publish papers and attend conferences with their teachers.

"Professors are very accessible," a senior says. "All of them have regular office hours, and if a student is unable to make them, almost all professors are willing to set up some other appointment." Another student says, "If one needs to meet a professor, it's usually done the same day. The professors here know everyone in their classes by name, usually by the second day of class." For most faculty members, teaching is a clear priority over research or publishing. A professor says, "Good teaching is supposed to be, and rarely is not, the sine qua non of succeeding on the Grinnell faculty. But peer-approved scholarship appropriate to one's field is also a requirement for tenure."

"The professors here are the reason to come to Grinnell," a student says. Students name the following as some of the best on campus: Michael Cavanagh in English; Donna Vinter, director of the highly recommended Grinnell-in-London program; Charles Duke in physics; Bruce Voyles in biology; Monessa Cummins in classics; Sarah Purcell in history; Robert Grey, Wayne Moyer, Ira Strauber, and Barbara Trish in political science; David Campbell in environmental studies; and David Harrison and Philippe Moisan in French.

The best departments—biology, history, political science, and English—are also among the most popular. The classics department offers a solid and rigorous curriculum, attracting some of the best students in the college—many of whom graduate with honors. The department offers a full program of Ancient Greek and Latin. A weekly Ancient Greek and Latin Reading Group, held in faculty homes, has been a campus tradition for over forty years. The most ideologically fraught areas of study—no surprise—are Grinnell's twelve interdisciplinary concentrations, including gender and women's studies and global development studies. One professor warns, "There are many courses, even outside these areas, that are politicized."

More religious or conservative students will sometimes feel uncomfortable in the Grinnell classroom. For example, some courses in the social sciences departments use Marxist-Leninist theory. (Why not try phrenology?) However, professors generally try to keep their politics outside of the classroom. One conservative student says that while most students and faculty are "pretty far left," most of his professors "have been very good about teaching material from a wide range of viewpoints, many of which they disagreed with. The professors I've had also have always made it clear when they are talking about something they personally believe as opposed to established facts." Another student says, "Professors have told me personally they enjoy classes where conservatives are present, as it makes for a better discussion. I have never heard of any professors discriminating against students on the basis of their political beliefs."

Free and open debate seems to be the rule. A student says, "I would say that yes, this is a very liberal campus, and there are not a lot of conservative viewpoints in the faculty or in the student body. However, I would not say that a conservative (there are plenty of religious students here, and they are all very well accepted) would be uncomfortable in any classes I've taken unless they do not like to argue or don't have good ideological reasoning behind their views." On the other hand, many conservatives may find it more agreeable to keep their opinions to themselves.

Many academic programs offer faculty-directed scholarly or creative work for upper-level students through the Mentored Advanced Project (MAP). The college provides extensive opportunities for research and internships that are well funded by the school's vast endowment. Internships are offered all over the world, in anything from bioethics to community-supported agriculture or sports management. Students studying French might spend a year in France living with local families, visiting museums, libraries, national monuments, and interning in Parisian schools. In fact, 55 to 60 percent of each year's graduating class participates in an off-campus study program in places as different as Washington, D.C., and Cairo, Egypt. Study of international issues receives great emphasis at Grinnell, with strong interdisciplinary concentrations and a new Center for International Studies. The Grinnell Corps provides one-year service fellowships to new graduates in places including China, Greece, and Lesotho. Grinnell offers majors in Chinese and Japanese, French, German, Spanish, and Russian, and classes in Ancient Greek and Latin.

Student Life: Small town, U.S.A . . . without the "gender binary"

Grinnell is an idyllic college town. Fourteen sites are listed on the National Register of Historic Places, and Grinnell has been named as one of the "100 Best Small Towns in America." As a small college in a small town, Grinnell is closely integrated into its local community. The college lies in the center of town between Park Street and East Street. A railroad runs right through campus. Students gather regularly at the town gazebo, located adjacent to campus, to engage in the protest du jour.

The college would like to strengthen its ties to the town even further. It hosts "Town and Gown" events several times each year to encourage students and employees to interact more with the Grinnell townsfolk. Students pay an activities fee along with tuition, which funds campus events such as Disco, the Titular Head Festival (a film fest), the Mary B. James (a cross-dressing party), Winter Waltz and Spring Waltz (campuswide formals), and performances by artists such as the Russian National Ballet and the Prague Chamber Orchestra. A student says, "Grinnell is in the middle of nowhere, and no one will try to hide that fact. That said, campus life here is fun because the school and student organizations have to put that much more work into making it fun. Plus, no one leaves on the weekends, so you always have the whole campus to get to know and enjoy."

Technically, all Grinnell students are required to live on campus. Each year, about 13 percent of the student body (mostly juniors and seniors) moves off campus. It's hard to see why: most of the college's dormitories house fewer than a hundred students, and students can request to live on either coed or single-sex floors (no dorms are single sex). Some residence halls have coed bathrooms but only by unanimous consent of that floor. Grinnell now offers coed rooms in close to half of the dormitories as part of its push to provide environments "where the gender binary is not perpetuated." Nonsmoking dorms are available, and since the fall of 2004, the college also has been offering a substance-free residence hall. The college provides five language houses for students looking to immerse themselves in the language and culture of a particular country, including Spain, France, Russia, Germany, and China. Most residential halls are locked at 10:00 PM and do not reopen until 6:00 AM, but students can always enter by way of electronic access cards. To ease overcrowding and improve older facilities, the college recently opened four new residence halls. Grinnell has no Greek system.

Grinnell is particularly keen on racial and cultural diversity. Around 17 percent of the student population are members of some minority, and Grinnell recently has been taking significant steps to increase minority faculty presence as well. The college is a member of the Consortium for a Strong Minority Presence, whose main goal is to help minority scholars land faculty positions at top-notch liberal arts schools. The Office of Multicultural Affairs lists six student organizations for self-described minorities, including the Asian and Asian American Association (AAA), Queer People of Color (QPOC), and Concerned Black Students (CBS).

The college reports 250 registered student clubs and organizations, from the Jugglers Union and the Ceramics group to the Quidditch club and Wild Turkeys Water Polo. The school hosts Grinnell College Campus Democrats and many other liberal organizations, but few Republican or conservative political groups. There are only twelve religious groups, including Catholic Student Association, Chalutzim, Fellowship of Christian Athletes, a Jesus Christ of Latter-Day Saints group, Muslim Prayer Group, Pagan Discussion, Unitarian and Universalist, and Grinellians Investigating Religion and Spirituality. There are also a number of other student movements dealing with racism, economic disparity, and cultural diversity. At one point, Grinnell had an ROTC office, but it was shut down in

ACADEMIC REQUIREMENTS

Apart from the mandates of their particular majors, all students must complete only a first-year tutorial. This seminar is limited to twelve students per section. Students can choose from a wide-ranging list of topics, such as "Our Town: The World at our Doorstep," "Icelandic Sagas," "Health Care Reform," "Black Men in Higher Education," "Don Quixote and the Modern World," "More than Ourselves: An Exploration of Self-Improvement," and "Weird Music."

the 1970s after students forcibly occupied the building in protest of the Kent State shootings. The Stonewall Resource Center (SRC) serves as a "confidential safe space to serve the campus's gay, lesbian, bisexual, and transgender community and allies." In fact, Grinnell's whole campus is a "safe space" for these students, whose groups (along with other student organizations) receive considerable support from the college. The Princeton Review ranks Grinnell College as one of the top 15 most queer-friendly schools in the United States. On its webpage, SRC links to pertinent student groups at Grinnell: Stonewall Coalition (an umbrella group), Coming Out Group (a support group for students "questioning their sexual identity"), Queer People of Color, BiFocal (for bisexual students), Lesbian Only Movie Night and Organized Procrastination (LMNOP), and the Queer Rainbow Super Team, which "plays games and has fun!" Another group, the Grinnell Monologues, provides the important service of "perform[ing] a collection of monologues about gender and genitalia."

For those in search of more traditional collegiate activities, Grinnell offers a panoply of athletic opportunities. The first intercollegiate football and baseball games west of the Mississippi were played in Grinnell, and the home teams won. Today, the Grinnell Pioneers and its NCAA Division III athletic

> ## RED LIGHT
>
> A student says, "I do feel that there is often too much political correctness on campus, where students sometimes must think twice before expressing a thought that could in any way be perceived as insensitive to one of the many thousands of groups that could be considered a minority." The real minorities on campus are the conservatives, and the school's progressive atmosphere will not change anytime soon, as the administration is proud of its position at the forefront of progressive schools.
>
> There is a small conservative community at Grinnell. The president of the College Republicans says, "We have nearly twenty people on our mailing list, which is kind of amazing given the very liberal leanings at this school." According to its website, the Grinnell College Republicans (whose mission is to "ensure the conservative voice is heard amidst the sea of liberal propaganda") recently became affiliated with the National College Republicans and "has been growing rapidly ever since." Another student says that at Grinnell, "liberals feel very comfortable. Conservatives probably feel very out of place. Sometimes liberalism here feels a little like anticonservatism rather than its own set of beliefs."

program field twenty varsity teams in the Midwest Athletic Conference, but there are no athletic scholarships at Grinnell. The college also has a well-developed intramural program and club sports for intercollegiate competition, the most popular of which are football, rugby, and Ultimate Frisbee.

There has been a recent flurry of building projects on campus. In addition to a new Athletic and Fitness Center, completed in 2010, Grinnell has also opened a new admissions building and a $43 million science center. Grinnell's oval-shaped campus is punctuated by varied architectural styles. Goodnow Hall, the college's turn-of-the-century library, is Romanesque Revival; the refurbished building now houses the school's anthropology department. Steiner Hall, a Tudor building, houses classrooms and faculty offices. Just north of Steiner Hall stands the neo-Gothic Herrick Chapel. The college now uses it for religious services and secular events alike. The campus also includes prominent modern buildings.

Grinnell is a pretty safe place—like most of Iowa. In 2009, the school reported three forcible sex offenses, thirty burglaries, one stolen car, and ten arsons on campus—marking a significant uptick in crime over the previous year. In 1998, the college created the safety and security department, but it relies on the local police force for serious cases.

Tuition for 2010–11 was $37,482, with an additional $8,880 for room and board. Grants and scholarships form the bulk of Grinnell's financial aid, which is awarded primarily on the basis of need and is not considered in admissions decisions. Some 63 percent of students get some need-based aid, and admissions are need blind. The average student-debt load of a recent graduate is about $18,578.

Hillsdale College

Hillsdale, Michigan • www.hillsdale.edu

Reading in the snow

Founded in 1844 by Free Will Baptists (though officially nonsectarian), Hillsdale College has a heritage of resisting the trends and prejudices of its day. It was the second American college founded to admit women and African Americans, and since then it has forged a tradition of freethinking in the teeth of current opinion. The college football team turned down its spot in the 1955 Tangerine Bowl when told that its black players would be excluded; conversely, in 1975, when the federal government sought to impose racial quotas in admissions and hiring, the administration refused to abandon its independent tradition and went to court, believing that merit, not race, should determine admittance.

Perhaps the school is best known for its Supreme Court appearance in 1984, when the Court decided that every college or university receiving federal aid must fulfill intrusive federal regulations. Hillsdale responded by refusing to accept any federal funding. Despite these sacrifices, the college has successfully raised money through private donors to provide financial aid, grants, and scholarships to students on the basis of both need and merit. In fact, Hillsdale has one of the lowest tuitions in the country for a liberal arts college.

Walk onto Hillsdale's campus on a spring afternoon and you will not see skyscrapers in the distance, thousands of students on a gigantic campus, or significant ethnic and cultural diversity, as such diversity is typically understood. Hillsdale's campus is very rural and very "conservative"—socially, religiously, academically, morally, economically, and politically. Left-leaning students or those without any religious sympathies might feel the atmosphere a bit stifling here—but then there are plenty of alternatives for them.

Academic Life: Rigor and Reagan

The commitment of Hillsdale College to a "traditional liberal arts education" is best seen in its unusually extensive core curriculum. The Western heritage forms the basis of every student's academic experience. Hillsdale offers twenty-six traditional majors in the humanities and natural sciences, seven interdisciplinary majors, ten preprofessional programs, and three business degrees—accounting, marketing management, and finance.

While in past years, Hillsdale's humanities departments by far outperformed the science and fine arts programs, the gap has been closing recently. Most students spend their first two years fulfilling core requirements and exploring the different departments before declaring a major. Indeed, many students who had planned on other majors report that, after taking the core curriculum courses at Hillsdale, they switched to a major in the humanities. Regardless of discipline, all Hillsdale students must take a significant number of classes in language, literature, history, arts, political science, and the Constitution. No matter which major one chooses, the effect of the core is evident. For example, as one teacher says, "Business majors take the same core as any other major, and thus come out able to think, speak, and write in a more coherent fashion than most business majors from other schools." Adds another faculty member, "The core is well thought out and well taught. The students know why they are here, and they are very much alive in the classroom. It is a joy to teach in such an environment." Hillsdale graduates prove how useful a traditional liberal arts education can be out in the real world; 98 percent of Hillsdale alumni gain employment or admittance to graduate school within six months of walking the stage, according to the college's website.

The vibrant honors program at Hillsdale offers a heightened academic experience to qualified students. The students take special honors sections of the core curriculum, a one-credit honors seminar each semester, and in their senior year they complete and defend an interdisciplinary thesis. As a student says, the purpose of these seminars is to encourage "conversations that cross department boundaries," challenging and stretching motivated students. The program offers students special social and volunteer activities, group trips to historical cities over breaks, and the very popular, partially subsidized guided trip abroad to a location of historical or religious significance each year. (Past trips have gone to Turkey and Spain.) A maximum of thirty students, mostly freshmen, are accepted to the program each year—although it is possible to opt into the program later on.

Hillsdale's Center for Constructive Alternatives sponsors one of the largest college lecture series in America. CCA seminars are held four times a year on wide-ranging topics, attracting guests, alumni, and donors from across the country. Students enrolled for credit must then write a paper on the lectures. Hillsdale students are required to enroll in two CCA programs during their four years on campus, for which they receive one credit hour apiece. "For a small school," says one student, "there are plenty of opportunities to be enriched."

The department of philosophy and religion has seen recent improvements. The school has bulked up its course offerings, and now, in addition to "Old Testament" and "History of Christian Thought," students can take a course in "Roman Catholic Theology" and "Introduction to Islam." One professor reports that, at Hillsdale, there is "a much greater exploration of the connections between philosophy and religion than happens in most departments." Highly praised teachers in this department include Donald Westblade, Peter Blum, Donald Turner, and Thomas Burke.

The English department is one of the strongest and most popular at Hillsdale, boasting excellent professors and fine courses, such as "Renaissance British Literature: 1550 to 1660," "Restoration and Romantic British Literature: 1660 to 1830," "Colonial and Early American Literature: 1620–1820," and "Naturalism and Modernism: 1890–Present," to name just a few. Some of the most beloved teachers include John Freeh, Daniel Sundahl, David Whalen, Justin Jackson, and Stephen Smith. According to a student, "Dr. Smith takes the time to thoroughly examine each piece of literature he presents in the classroom. The work is not easy, but deeply rewarding."

> **SUGGESTED CORE**
>
> 1. Classics 321/401, Roman Literature of the Republic/ Greek Literature in Translation
> 2. English 101–102, Freshman Rhetoric and Great Books I–II
> 3. Religion 211/212, Old/New Testament History and Literature
> 4. Religion 213, History of Christian Thought I
> 5. Political Science 212/213, Modern Political Philosophy I/II
> 6. English 401, Special Studies in British Literature: Shakespeare
> 7. History 105, The American Heritage
> 8. Philosophy 217, Nineteenth-Century Philosophy

Another popular major at Hillsdale is history. While the department is impressive in U.S. and European history, "the offerings with regard to Latin America, Africa, and Asia are scanty," a teacher says. According to the department's website, the history major must take nine courses beyond the two mandatory Western civilization freshman core courses, including three additional Western civilization classes and at least two American history courses. Recommended faculty include Mark Kalthoff, Paul Moreno, Thomas Conner, Paul Rahe, Richard Gamble, Bradley Birzer, and David Raney. Students in the history department are endearingly enthusiastic about their particular favorites. One recent alum says of Dr. Birzer, "He teaches his students what it means to be human through the material and by example, as well as the consequent duties and responsibilities we thus have to ourselves, our families, and each other."

While one professor says that "the strongest majors on campus are history and English," he also believes that "the professors from these disciplines are a central part of the freshman core. They tend to be popular with students and yet also academically demanding, and they help create the distinctive Hillsdale education."

While education may be one of the smallest programs at Hillsdale, the department has recently created a new minor in classical education, which focuses on the medieval "trivium" and equips graduates to teach in many private schools where state certification is not required. The minor includes a teaching apprenticeship as well.

The music program is getting stronger every year, thriving in its home, the Howard Music Hall and Performance Center. Students and professors alike seem to take great pride in the program. One student happily reported that the performing arts encourage "diverse participation across campus," and her sentiments were seconded by a professor, who boasted that "the Music Department has really taken off. We are getting conservatory-level students who want a liberal arts education, and the resulting quality of performance and program is genuinely impressive."

Political science is said to be "especially good in political theory and American government, but could use some bolstering in foreign affairs," according to one teacher. The political science major takes a very impressive series of courses: "The U.S. Constitution," "American Political Thought," "Regimes: Classical and Modern," "Modern Political Philosophy" I & II, and "Introduction to American Foreign Policy," in addition to five electives. Highly praised teachers here include Mickey Craig, Nathan Schlueter, Kevin Portteus, and Gary Wolfram. Hillsdale also offers the popular Washington-Hillsdale Internship Program (WHIP), in which students receive fifteen academic credits for a semester-long internship in a D.C. political office, policy center, or media outlet.

The school's Dow Journalism Program offers a similar option for budding journalists, the Quayle Journalism internship. Students of all majors can gain experience by writing for the *Collegian*, Hillsdale's award-winning college newspaper, the oldest in Michigan, or the *Hillsdale Forum*, which provides a platform for political and religious discussion.

Also recommended are Carmen Wyatt-Hayes in Spanish; Kirstin Kiledal in speech; Joseph Garnjobst and David Jones in classics; Christopher Van Orman, Mark Nussbaum, and Lee Ann Baron in chemistry; Barbara Bushey, Anthony Frudakis, Sam Knecht, and Tony Frudakis in art; and Kenneth Hayes in physics. In economics, Dr. Nikolai Wenzel is said to be "a good person and good teacher rolled into one. Supplementing real-life stories as examples of economic principals and polices, his classes always have a current touch, keeping students engaged."

Thanks to a student-faculty ratio of 10 to 1, teachers and students are said to form strong relationships. One undergraduate fondly remembers an early encounter with a Hillsdale professor: "My first day of classes as a freshman, one of my professors strolled into the classroom, passed out the syllabus, reviewed it, and then pointed to the phone number at the top of the page, he said, 'Now, I realize that many of you are far from home, really far. This is my home phone number. My wife can cook. Please, feel free anytime you are feeling the grind, or just don't feel like eating at school, to give my home a call, and a place will be set at the dinner table for you.'"

Professors at Hillsdale tend to treat teaching as a privilege rather than an impediment to personal research interests. One professor enthusiastically proclaims that "teaching is the place's *raison d'etre*. For tenure, successful teaching is a sine qua non. . . . Nearly everyone on the faculty writes extensively, but everyone understands that we are here for the students, not vice versa." Another professor concurs: "The teaching load is about right, 3/3 [three classes per semester], though if we were to go to a 3/2, it might improve the reputation of the college as it would generate more research."

Students eager to escape the midwestern cold can opt for one of Hillsdale's study-abroad programs, choosing among Oxford, England; Tours, France; Saarland or Würzburg, Germany; Seville, Spain; Córdoba, Argentina; St. Andrews, Scotland; or London, England. Hillsdale teaches a limited range of foreign languages: French, German, Spanish, Latin, and Ancient Greek.

Student Life: Buried in the dale

The rural, south-central Michigan town of Hillsdale (population 8,000) is sleepy and sits an hour from the nearest big city, Ann Arbor, and ninety minutes from Detroit. For many, this makes focusing on the books all the easier. Indeed, the 200-acre college campus is the hub of this small town. For others, accustomed to wider cultural vistas (or shopping malls, Starbucks, and sushi), it can be frustrating.

As a result of the isolated location, however, the Hillsdale community is very close-knit, students report; they spend their nights and weekends primarily on campus, making their own fun or attending school-run activities. Many such activities are sponsored

---

ACADEMIC REQUIREMENTS

Every Hillsdale student must complete the following rigorous core curriculum:

- Two successive semesters of "Rhetoric and the Great Books." Students study literature from the ancient world up through the twentieth century, reading authors such as Plato, Virgil, Dante, Shakespeare, Goethe, Dostoevsky, Twain, and T. S. Eliot.
- "Western Heritage to 1600" and "American Heritage." Many professors teach these history courses thematically, weaving together a complex narrative rather than just names and dates.
- One introductory course from a selection of fine arts: music, theater, or speech ("History of Art," "History and Literature of Music," or "Understanding Theater").
- One course survey in period literature (such as "Anglo-Saxon and Medieval British Literature: 600–1500" or "Naturalism and Modernism: 1890–present") or classical studies (Greek or Roman civilization or mythology).
- One course in philosophy/religion ("Intro to Philosophy" or "Intro to Western Religion").
- One mathematics course (students with either an ACT of 24 or higher or SAT math score of 570 or higher are exempt).
- One course in physical science and one in biology.
- Two semesters of physical activities classes.
- An introductory course on the U.S. Constitution.
- One class in economics, psychology, or sociology.
- Two credit hours earned by attending seminars at the Center for Constructive Alternatives.

Those pursuing the bachelor of arts degree must show intermediate proficiency in a foreign language, while those obtaining the bachelor of science degree need extra laboratory science and mathematics courses and at least a minor in the sciences.

Midwest

733

by Hillsdale's more than seventy registered student groups, such as the Christian Fellowship, Swing Club, Prodigy Ping Pong Club, College Pep Band, Puppetry Club, some seven Greek houses, and thirty honors societies. Other events are hosted by the Student Activities office—which has given a much-needed shot of adrenaline to campus social life, students report. The school also holds a Garden Party dance, featuring a live band and dance floor in the school's beautiful arboretum, and a homecoming celebration featuring food, music, a bonfire, and fireworks.

A faculty member observes, "Hillsdale is isolated, and the winter is cold. As a consequence, the college is an inward-looking community. The administration turns that to its advantage. The concerts, dances, and plays are really good and are really well attended; the number of speakers who pass through is astonishing. It is hard for me to do my teaching and my writing and to find the time to adequately exploit the place!"

While this is a decidedly nonsectarian school, two of the largest and most active student organizations are the Hillsdale Christian Fellowship and the Hillsdale Catholic Society. Each group hosts many social, volunteer, and religious activities for students.

One of the largest and busiest groups on campus is the College Republicans, which hosts debates and political speakers, participates in campaigns, and organizes trips to conventions around the state and in Washington, D.C. The Hillsdale CRs are very well known and respected in national political circles, and students report that membership in the group has helped them find internships and even jobs upon graduation. While there is a College Democrats group on campus, it is very small and does not enjoy the same level of support from students or faculty.

The next item on Hillsdale's to-build list is a new chapel/auditorium, an intramural sports building, and an archive wing for the library. There will also be renovations to several existing facilities, including updating the dormitories, the Knorr Center, the Dow Leadership Center, and expanding the Roche Sports Complex. Comments a young faculty member, "I get a sense from my colleagues that every year the place gets better—new and better buildings, better students, new and lively colleagues." Indeed, in just a few years, the campus would be almost unrecognizable to alumni were it not for stately Central Hall still standing on the top of the "hill" (despite its name, Hillsdale is really quite flat).

Athletics also offer a relatively popular diversion for Hillsdale students—both the NCAA Division II varsity athletics and the competitive club sports leagues. Baseball and softball, men's and women's basketball, volleyball, track and field teams, woman's swimming, and (of course) the football team are all popular parts of Hillsdale's student life. Because of the tight-knit nature of athletic teams and intensive hours of training together, there is some segregation between the athletes and the general student population.

There are seven Greek houses (four fraternities and three sororities), and they still serve as a hub of campus social activities. While frat parties and underage drinking are an occasional problem on campus, Hillsdale's Greek system is better known as a harmless and often exemplary system that provides fellowship and social, volunteer, and leadership opportunities to its members. Most houses have academic requirements for entrance.

While all the Greek houses offer a residency option for members, there are plenty of other housing choices. Most of Hillsdale's nearly 1,400 students live on campus or in nearby apartments. Juniors and seniors may apply for off-campus housing if they wish. There are eleven single-sex dorms scattered across Hillsdale's campus. The visitation policies have been extended recently, allowing more mixing between the sexes. Still, they are much more protective of privacy and modesty than the rules at most colleges, and students report that the visiting hours—as well as the alcohol and drug policies—are strictly enforced. Notes a female student, "Visitation is a drag, but you adapt to it quickly." Another says, "It's really nice to know that most mornings, I don't have to worry about men being in the dorm to see me coming from the showers in my bathrobe."

The only coed dorm on campus is the Suites, an upperclassman residence with selective admittance, in which men and women are in separate wings protected by security-key access and divided by a lobby. All bathrooms are single-sex. The Suites has looser visitation hours and rules than other dorms. It features four singles arranged around a common room and kitchen. "The Suites had really improved the housing options for those who want to stay on campus their junior and senior years,"

> ## GREEN LIGHT
>
> Part of Hillsdale's strong national following stems from its well-known stance against federal encroachment into higher education. It circulates its high-minded newsletter, *Imprimis*, to more than one million readers—some of whom send support to keep the college growing.
>
> Most students agree that the Hillsdale faculty encourage intelligent student comments and participation in class, regardless of a student's political viewpoint. One faculty member notes: "What is really most 'conservative' here is . . . the traditional nature of the academic program, the emphasis on substantive academic study, and extensive—not specialized—learning on the part of students, the importance education is understood to have in perpetuating a free republic . . . and the respect for the Western cultural and intellectual tradition." That said, an outspokenly leftist student would probably not feel comfortable at Hillsdale.

says one student. "While we've had to deal with some initial problems with the construction of the building (leaky pipes, malfunctioning doors, thermostats, and phone jacks), overall, I've loved living there."

Another attractive part of Hillsdale's dorm life is the house "parent" who resides in a small apartment on the main floor of each dorm. These house parents are ultimately in charge of all dorm life. Most of them, as well as most resident assistants (RAs), seem to have good relationships with students; together, the dorm leadership enforces administration policies and provides students with help when they need it. As one student says, "The RAs are very friendly and a great help to all students." Another reports, "Dorm life is a lot of fun. RAs are students, usually just a year or two older than residents, who tend to be very approachable and fun, and just happen to be in charge."

Crime is seldom a concern on campus. Hillsdale is said to be one of the safest college campuses in this guide—although we don't have the numbers. Since it does not accept federal funds, Hillsdale is not required to report crime statistics. Still, sources at the college say that crime on campus amounts to a handful of burglaries each year—although students say fistfights with "townies" are not unheard of, especially for off-campus students. "Walk your girlfriends home after dark, guys," advises one student. In fact, walking women home is generally expected as a part of the unspoken chivalric code that is still alive and well at Hillsdale. Many men will offer to escort women home even if they are not "involved." The school has installed lights around campus and emergency phones on street corners. Students can always call security, and one of the patrols will be happy to walk them home if it is late. As one undergrad says, "The average student taking the normal precautions has virtually nothing to fear." In fact, comments another student, most incidents on campus are student pranks.

Hillsdale's tuition for the 2010–11 academic year was $19,960, an increase of only $580 since 2008, with room and board costing $7,990. While the school cannot guarantee to meet the full financial need of applicants, there are need-based, athletic, fine arts, and need-blind academic awards available. Hillsdale College allocates over $14 million to financial aid, resulting in an average aid package of nearly $12,000 per student. Some 28 percent of students get need-based aid. Many students also take advantage of the many work-study opportunities on campus, whether working for the library, computer lab, cafeteria, admissions, or security. The average student-loan debt of a recent graduating class was a modest $14,000.

University of Illinois at Urbana-Champaign

Urbana-Champaign, Illinois • www.illinois.edu

Riding Leviathan

Located some 125 miles south of Chicago, UIUC has a reputation as one of the country's top public universities, attracting to its campus a bevy of bright students and highly regarded faculty and maintaining more than a few excellent academic departments. But undergrads at this state-sponsored behemoth will need to seek out that education among a vast array of opportunities to waste their time. "This is a research university," says one professor. "We are not a teaching college. People don't come here to get small classes and individual attention. They come for the sports, for the first-rate facilities, and to make contact with some of the best thinkers in their field." Whether many Illini actually exploit such opportunities is an open question.

Academic Life: Diversityland

UIUC has no core curriculum, though its meager set of distribution requirements has become more structured over the past decade. In addition to two-semester English composition and three-semester foreign language requirements, students must now take a total of ten other courses distributed among broad liberal arts and science categories.

It's easy to get lost in the system at this university, which offers plenty of good courses—and at least as many paths of least resistance. The curriculum is unstructured, and the catalog lists an enormous range of disciplines—over 150 of them. "Students are pretty much adrift to take whatever they want; there's no real cohesion or body of knowledge they are building," one professor says.

Freshmen may choose to begin their college experience by enrolling in the First-Year Discovery Program, which offers small classes (up to twenty students) in a variety of disciplines, letting new students get to know faculty members. This is not always possible in the massive "intro" courses so often required.

A College of Liberal Arts and Sciences (LAS) professor complains that even in more traditional disciplines, faculty members' interests tend to focus on new, trendy areas of research rather than on more traditional topics, so that it is not uncommon for students to be fooled by course titles. A course in the Old Testament, for instance, may turn out to consist of feminist complaints about Yahweh and patriarchy. The business school is more cau-

VITAL STATISTICS

Religious affiliation: *none*

Total enrollment: *43,862*

Total undergraduates: *31,540*

SAT/ACT midranges: CR: *530–660*, M: *680–770*; ACT: *26–31*

Applicants: *27,310*

Applicants accepted: *67%*

Accepted applicants who enrolled: *56%*

Tuition and fees: *in state, $10,386; out of state, $24,528*

Room and board: *$9,714*

Freshman retention rate: *94%*

Graduation rate: *65% (4 yrs.), 84% (6 yrs.)*

Courses with fewer than 20 students: *34%*

Student-faculty ratio: *16:1*

Courses taught by graduate students: *25%*

Most popular majors: *engineering, business/marketing, public administration*

Students living on campus: *50%*

Guaranteed housing for four years? *yes*

Students in fraternities: *21%* in sororities: *21%*

tious; one professor says that the school's courses "cover the fundamentals with an eye to the contemporary." Of course, at a school as big as UIUC, it is statistically almost inevitable that a number of serious, well-taught courses will still be offered. UIUC is particularly well known for the quality of its programs in engineering, the sciences, journalism, and business. The College of Agriculture is one of the oldest in the nation, and its programs are widely respected. Other departments with strong programs include economics, labor and industrial relations, geography, and history.

The classics department has a distinguished history, several world-class scholars, and five majors to choose from: classical archeology, classical civilization, classics, Ancient Greek, and Latin. The religious studies program sounds surprisingly mainstream for a state university. Religious studies majors are required to take eight courses: "Comparative Perspectives," "Hebrew Bible in English," "New Testament in English," "Philosophy of Religion," a course in Asian religions, one in Western religions, and a two-course sequence on Western civilization from the history or comparative literature departments.

The English Department offers two options for majors in English: literature and teaching. Students can also decide to be rhetoric majors with a focus in creative writing. Lit majors will take twelve credit hours of courses focusing on British and American literature. They will then have to take eighteen more hours of English electives. It will be up to them, ultimately, whether they opt for "Women in the Literary Imagination" over a course on Shakespeare.

The history department's website warns: "Whether you're interested in gender and sexuality, law and society, science and technology, race and diversity, money and power—we have a course for you." Beyond a gateway research-methods course, majors complete six credit hours of U.S. history, six of European history, six of non-Western history, and twelve electives. The highlight of the program comes in junior year, when students take a seminar course and "make history by researching and writing."

The political science major requires three courses in basic political theory, four electives at the 300 level, and six at any level. Students may choose (or skip) courses on the U.S. Constitution and the U.S. presidency.

With its unstructured curricular landscape dotted by various academic land mines (as well as gold mines), it is unfortunate that the university's advising program is anemic. "Teaching professionals," faculty hired by the university to teach introductory courses, serve as departmental advisors. One political science major says that the system is "in dire need of review." The university provides a kind of virtual online "advisor" in the form of an informative webpage, upon which many students rely instead of consulting a teacher. Students are not required to discuss an academic strategy with a human advisor or to hand in a major plan of study until the beginning of their junior year.

The Honors Program is available to students who maintain a 3.25 GPA. Students in the program can take special, smaller honors courses and can register early. The bad news is that a number of the honors seminars deal with the trendiest areas of academia. The English department, for instance, offers honors seminars such as "U.S. Imperialism and Pop Culture" and "Rewriting Shakespeare in the 21st Century."

UIUC has a weak student-faculty ratio of 16 to 1. In some years, almost a third of classes have been taught by graduate students, though currently it's 25 percent. This is far above the norm, even at state universities. "Many departments have a problem finding faculty to teach basic courses due to the lack of professors carrying a full-time load for whatever reason," a professor says. "The courses that suffer are introductory-level ones." A student says, "My big lecture courses were always taught by professors, but a majority of my classes and all of my accompanying discussion sections were taught by TAs."

Students express a certain ambivalence about UIUC professors—perhaps because they see so little of them. But when professors are good, they are said to be very, very good. The best include Kevin Waspi in finance; Thomas Rudolph in political science; Keith Hitchins in history; Robert McKim and Rajeshwari Pandharipande in religious studies; and James Dengate in classics. John Griswold in creative writing was the 2009 recipient of the UIUC Campus Award for Excellence in Undergraduate Teaching, and Jose J. Vazquez-Cognet in economics has won several awards for his teaching over the years.

One student says, "In my opinion, some professors often depend way too much on TAs. A lot of times, it is the TA who has office hours that you go to." Another student says, "All professors hold office hours and check their e-mail frequently, but there are a select few who advise you to talk with your TA before seeking advice from them." When in doubt, look up the school's annual "Incomplete List of Teachers Ranked as Excellent by Their Students." Just remember that some teachers may have earned popularity by easy grading.

Like many schools these days, U of I suffers from pervasive grade inflation. "It's notorious," says a professor. "One introductory-level teacher was known for giving half the class

SUGGESTED CORE

1. Classical Civilization 221, The Heroic Tradition
2. Philosophy 203, Ancient Philosophy
3. Religious Studies 101, Bible as Literature, or Religious Studies 201/202, Hebrew Bible in English/New Testament in English
4. Religious Studies 440, Early Christian Thought or Religious Studies 108, Religion and Society in the West I (closest matches)
5. Political Science 372, Modern Political Theory
6. English 218, Introduction to Shakespeare
7. History 170, U.S. History to 1877
8. History 361, European Thought and Society since 1789

A's and the other half A-pluses. It's a pact. Students don't harass the professor, and the professor gives them easy grades." Of course, not all professors are willing to compromise, and lazy students sometimes get burned.

Some professors are unhappy with their charges. "I have students who fall asleep or read the newspaper in my class," says one teacher. "A lot of them just don't show up." Another professor says of his students, "Most seem to be interested in graduating and instrumental learning that can aid their careers." A colleague says, "Some students do get very involved, but I would say those are the exception, not the rule." A student says, "If you're smart, that's cool. But a lot of people just try to get by. They don't want to put in the effort."

Professors and students agree that LAS faculty have a heavy leftward tilt. One professor describes this division of UIUC as "highly politically correct." A student agrees: "The College of Liberal Arts and Sciences is exactly what it says: liberal—way left." One professor we spoke to cautioned conservative students to think twice about the school if they were planning on an English major.

Nor do politics stop at the classroom door. At UIUC, one student says, political bias "usually comes through in the way that course material is presented." A few students report blatantly ideological attempts to punish students who disagree with instructors. "I wrote a paper for my Rhetoric 105 class in which I argued against gay marriage," a student says. "The teaching assistant gave me a D on the paper because 'you can't argue for that sort of position without appealing to hate and religious bigotry.' I had to go to the department chair to get the grade raised to a C, and that's all I could do."

Support services at UIUC have been politicized—as evidenced by entities like the Chancellor's Committee on Diversity, and the Center for Democracy in a Multiracial Society, a research-oriented project that is "organized around a commitment to the practice of democracy and equality within a changing multiracial society." One of the school's (scant) general education requirements is devoted to cultural studies, with options like "Sex and Gender in Classical Antiquity" and "Minority Images in American Film." Academic departments at UIUC are being pressured to "diversify" their course offerings and hire preferred minority candidates. When a British history professor retired recently, he was replaced by a professor who specializes in the history of an indigenous group on a Pacific island. The classics department reportedly had to argue doggedly to persuade the dean to hire someone who specializes in Roman history. The political science department was ordered to hire an expert in Asian American politics, which barely exists as an academic field. Because of the administration's multiculturalist obsession, "more serious areas get neglected," says a professor. Looking for the most politicized departments at UIUC? Try English, education, history, and women's studies.

Those interested in real diversity should get out of Illinois. Helpfully, the university boasts literally hundreds of study-abroad programs, from engineering in South Korea and ACES in Spain at UPNA in Pamplona (Agricultural, Consumer, and Environmental Sciences). A wide range of language courses are offered at the university, including French, German, Spanish, Italian, Portuguese, various East Asian tongues, and Arabic, with majors in linguistics and even translation studies.

Student Life: Beer in Champaign

The University of Illinois at Urbana-Champaign (city population: 120,271) sits on 1,454 acres in the heart of the state. Located within three hours of Chicago, Indianapolis, and St. Louis, the university has an unmistakably midwestern feel. The oldest part of the campus, the picturesque Quad, recalls a park. It is surrounded by imposing buildings that house most of the LAS departments. The neighborhood known as Campustown is dotted with shops, coffeehouses, bookstores, restaurants, and bars. The Krannert Center for the Performing Arts mounts theatrical and operatic productions every year, as well as numerous chamber and orchestral performances.

Few of the more than 40,000 students, however, take advantage of cultural attractions in the area. When they are in town at night, they're usually drinking. There are bars "within fifty paces of the Quad," says one student. Says another, "When you get here, your first priority is to get a fake ID." To get into the bars, one must be only nineteen years of age, even though the official drinking age is twenty-one. The university is usually ranked as one of the top twenty party schools in the nation, "but it's not for lack of other things to do," says a student.

No indeed; the university has almost 1,000 registered student organizations, among them the Golf Club, the Illini Bowling Club, the Philosophy Club, Knittingillni (a knit-

---

ACADEMIC REQUIREMENTS

The rather loose general education mandates for UIUC require the following courses:

- One or two courses (depending on each class's demands) in composition. These seem to be straightforward rhetoric/college writing classes.
- One topic-driven class in advanced composition. Options range from "Writing in the Disciplines" to "Humane Education with Companion Animals."
- One course in "Cultural Studies: Non-Western/U.S. Minority Culture(s)." Choices include "Race and Cultural Diversity" and "Muslims in America."
- One class in "Cultural Studies: Western/Comparative Culture(s)." Options extend from "Masterpieces of Western Culture" to "Sex and Gender in Popular Media."
- Coursework through the third semester in a foreign language.
- Two classes in humanities or the arts. Options range from "Shakespeare on Film" to "U.S. Gender History to 1877."
- Two natural science or technology courses. Choices include "General Chemistry" and "Stem Cell Basics and Applications."
- Two classes in the social/behavioral sciences. Students may study anything from "Microeconomic Principles" to "Sexualities."
- One course in Quantitative Reasoning I, such as economics, math, or symbolic logic.
- One class in Quantitative Reasoning II, such as introductory physics or "Measure and Evaluation in Kinesiology."

Midwest

YELLOW LIGHT

Adjunct professor Ken Howell, who won teaching awards in 2008 and 2009 for his courses on Catholic doctrine, was fired by the school in 2010 after sending an e-mail out to his students explaining Catholic beliefs in preparation for their exam. He wrote, "Natural Moral Law says that morality must be a response to REALITY. In other words, sexual acts are only appropriate for people who are complementary, not the same." Ann Mester, associate dean, justified the firing, claiming that Howell had violated the "university's standards of inclusivity." Professor Howell explained to the *News-Gazette* in Champaign: "My responsibility on teaching a class on Catholicism is to teach what the Catholic Church teaches. I have always made it very, very clear to my students they are never required to believe what I'm teaching and they'll never be judged on that." After a faculty committee reported that Howell had not been granted "due process," and he threatened legal action, the university rehired him.

Outside the classroom, students report a good deal of tolerance for different viewpoints. Says one student, "I have had no problem being an open conservative on campus." In addition to many liberal student organizations, including the left-leaning *Daily Illini* student newspaper, the campus does have a few conservative organizations. The *Orange and Blue Observer* is a rightist paper that takes a vigilant, if not belligerent, approach toward the growing liberalism of the university. The paper has promoted events such as "Will ObamaCare Kill You?"

ting club), the Swing Society, and the Ladies Loving Ladies Club. The Student Government Association is large and active, but it tends to throw its weight behind left-wing causes. Politically minded conservative students can find a home with the College Republicans; Illini for the Second Amendment; the Illini Conservative Union, which advocates "free markets, individual choice, and personal responsibility"; and Illini for Liberty, which works with the local Libertarian Party to give students access to state and nationwide libertarian events. Church organizations are particularly popular on campus. "There is a very large religious presence here at U of I," says a campus minister. "There is a substantial Catholic presence at the Newman Foundation but also a wide variety of Protestant organizations, such as Campus Crusade for Christ and InterVarsity Christian Fellowship."

After drinking, campus life centers primarily on athletics; especially men's basketball and football. UIUC also boasts a strong intramurals program, offering some twenty sports, including badminton, basketball, flag football, miniature golf, and Ultimate Frisbee.

And from our "I-can't-believe-it's-come-to-this" file, UIUC's pre–St. Patrick's Day bar fest was recently the occasion of controversy when the alcohol-related activities surrounding the festival were denounced by one professor as being anti-Irish, anti-Catholic, and racist. The university administration refused to act on his complaint—probably at the insistence of Irish American students.

The Illini Pride organization is a fan club that holds barbeques and other events to support the teams. The homecoming celebration has been taking place since 1910. It consists of a one-week festival complete with parade, pep rallies . . . and lots of drinking.

The Greek system is enormously popular on campus. Roughly a fifth of students belong to a chapter, making the UIUC system one of the largest in the country.

Freshmen are required to live in university residence halls, in a fraternity or sorority house, or in one of the five privately owned certified residence halls. More than three-quarters of entering students choose to live in a university residence hall, of which there are several kinds, including a sex-free hall, a substance-free hall, and men-only and women-only dorms. There are no coed dorm rooms or coed bathrooms at the university.

UIUC also offers theme housing to students. These residences are markedly less politicized than similar houses at other schools. Some are "living/learning communities," each focusing on a different theme, including "Global Crossroads," "Leadership Experience Through Academic Development and Service," "Unit One" (a group that offers art workshops, credit courses, and field trips), "Women in Math, Science, and Engineering," and "Weston Exploration," which offers workshops like "Career Development: Theory and Practice," "Public Speaking," and "The College Experience." The program also holds a number of discussion sections in the Weston Residence Hall, encouraging students to discuss academic subjects with hall mates inside and outside the classroom.

In 2009, the university reported five aggravated assaults, five forcible sex offenses, eight robberies, eighty-one burglaries, and five stolen cars on campus. Students can use the university's SafeRides escort service for protection, and emergency phones are located all over campus.

Tuition at UIUC keeps edging up. In 2010–11, costs reached $10,386 for in-state students, and $24,528 for out of state. Add to that about $9,714 in room and board. Financial aid is not as widely used here as at other schools—perhaps because it's relatively cheap. Admission is need blind, but this is not saying much. The financial aid office functions mostly as the administrative arm of government aid programs. Tuition does fluctuate and differs according to one's choice of academic division, but students have the option of "locking in" the tuition rate at which they entered. The average debt of a recent graduate is $19,378.

University of Iowa

Iowa City, Iowa • www.uiowa.edu

Children of the corn

"You really ought to give Iowa a try," goes the old song. And anyone who does try Iowa City's distinguished 173-year-old university will find himself in illustrious company. Flannery O'Connor was a student at its famous Writers' Workshop, founded by Paul Engel, and others who either taught or studied there include John Irving, Jorie Graham, Andre Dubus, Wallace Stegner, and Kurt Vonnegut Jr. Iowa has first-rate faculty and well-regarded programs in medicine, education, science, and the arts, in addition to the writing program. Twenty-two of Iowa's programs are ranked in the top ten among the nation's public universities, and the school is a top twenty university for research, education, and service grant dollars. Its five-million-volume library houses more books than there are Iowans. And the Hawkeyes won the Orange Bowl in 2009.

What Iowa lacks is a coherent core curriculum, big-name prestige, and a prevalent culture of intellectual curiosity among the students. The university is big, diffuse, and not very selective in its undergraduate admissions. Its pedestrian general education requirements are far more general than educational and certainly do not guarantee a well-rounded student. Its more than 20,000 undergraduates come largely from Iowa and nearby Illinois, and are accepted at a rate of 83 percent. While there are some very fine students among them—often attracted by the low tuition—one professor says that most undergrads "are moderately smart and industrious, but not markedly so. Iowa is so small a state that you don't have to be that smart to get in." Still, says another professor, Iowa is "a fairly intellectual place."

What is true of so many similar schools is true of the University of Iowa: ambitious, motivated students can find a decent educational path among the many available dead-ends and bridges to nowhere. But they'll need to use a map and ask directions.

Academic Life: Triage time

Times are tough at Iowa. Persistent budget cuts over many years have starved the school of professors in the liberal arts, which means larger class sizes and fewer courses. According to the university's strategic plan, The Iowa Promise, the top budget priority for the past five years has been "raising faculty salaries to be consistent with peers and restoring faculty lines lost in recent years due to budget reductions." The college did receive several million

Midwest

744

in stimulus money from the federal government in 2009 that was allocated to cover budget shortfalls and various other projects. One professor complains that the "faculty and staff numbers are flat, but the bureaucracy has grown threefold." The student-faculty ratio at University of Iowa has gone up in recent years and currently is an unimpressive 15 to 1.

In early 2010, a provost-level task force convened and recommended eliminating fourteen graduate programs in response to steep budget cuts prompted in part by a 10 percent decrease in state funding. Among those on the block are American studies, Asian civilizations, comparative literature, German, and linguistics. Further budget cuts are anticipated in 2011.

There are many, many students at Iowa competing for attention and resources that have been growing scarcer; even so, opportunities abound, and good guidance can be found if sought.

Students are assigned advisors—not teaching faculty but "advising professionals"—at freshman orientation. Students switch to teaching-faculty advisors upon choosing a major. A professor says, "Advising is considered a 'service,' which basically means faculty get no credit for doing it. As you can imagine, that means that a lot of faculty don't put any time into it." Nor do many students. As one professor says of his advisees, "I usually have a couple of students who will come in on a regular basis, but most don't bother."

UI's emphasis is emphatically on research in tenure and hiring decisions. A professor says, "The 'secret' is that teaching isn't rewarded at all. Yes, there might be some recognition and small cash awards, but you can be a dreadful teacher and still get huge raises if you publish a lot. If your research drops off, they threaten you with increased teaching load. In other words, teaching is considered a punishment." Says another, "Teaching is important, and it's one of your jobs as a faculty member, but it's hard to measure. So long as your students are not complaining, all is well. Research potential is what gets you hired, and what keeps you here."

Students often are intent on just doing what they can to get by, and only 42 percent of them manage to do it in four years. According to one professor, "The main reason students don't get out in four years is because they are just acting dumb: not studying enough and drinking too much." As one student says, "Classes here are manageable. They don't prevent you from having a social life."

VITAL STATISTICS

Religious affiliation: *none*
Total enrollment: *28,987*
Total undergraduates: *20,574*
SAT/ACT midranges: CR: *500–640*, M: *560–640*; ACT: *23–28*
Applicants: *15,060*
Applicants accepted: *83%*
Accepted applicants who enrolled: *32%*
Tuition and fees: *in state, $7,417; out of state, $23,713*
Room and board: *$8,331*
Freshman retention rate: *83%*
Graduation rate: *42% (4 yrs.), 69% (6 yrs.)*
Courses with fewer than 20 students: *50%*
Student-faculty ratio: *15:1*
Courses taught by graduate students: *not provided*
Most popular majors: *business/marketing, communications/journalism, social sciences*
Students living on campus: *29%*
Guaranteed housing for four years? *no*
Students in fraternities: *8%* in sororities: *12%*

Midwest

SUGGESTED CORE

1. Classics 20E:014, Hero/God/Mortal: Literature of Greece
2. Philosophy 026:111, Ancient Philosophy
3. Religious Studies 032:011/032:012, Introduction to the Hebrew Bible/New Testament
4. Philosophy 026:112, Medieval Philosophy
5. Political Science 030:132, Modern Political Theory
6. English 008:147, Shakespeare
7. History 16A:061, American History 1492-1877
8. History 016:003, Western Civilization III (closest match)

There are many planning and advising resources available to students, as well as special first-year classes designed to help them find their way. These include computer programs that map out a four-year graduation plan; first-year seminars on special topics capped at fifteen students; Courses in Common, a program through which freshman can enroll in up to three classes with the same twenty students; and the Pick One program, which encourages involvement in Iowa's hundreds of student organizations. But students must take the initiative, and not enough do.

The approved courses that fulfill Iowa's general requirements *can* provide a student with a core body of knowledge. They can equally be fulfilled with eccentric, overspecialized, trendy, or agenda-driven classes. The *Daily Iowan* confirms this in a recent article for new students entitled "Outside the Straight and Narrow in UI Courses." It recommends "being tested on the Beatles. Learning about love. Studying the art of bicycling. Sound too good to be true? Not at the UI, where some nontraditional courses give students the chance to explore new things—and have a good time." Time wasted, we would say.

Iowa's first-year seminars, designed to allow freshmen to work closely with faculty members, indicate how overly specialized some course offerings are. These courses are capped at fifteen students, and faculty members recommend them and enjoy teaching them. But professors are encouraged to design them around their current research. As a result, seminars offered in fall 2009 ranged from the worthy to the weird: "Stimulation of the Brain: Cochlear Implants and Other Neural Prostheses," "Exploring Mini Comics, Zines, and Artists' Books," "The Souls of Black Folk: Tracing the 'Color Line' from Du Bois to Obama," "Could you, would you, can you, please? Making Requests Around the World," "People and the Sky," and "Being Young in Africa." Some of the strongest programs at Iowa are traditionally found among the fine arts. The Writers' Workshop is ranked first in the nation. The studio arts and theater programs are also strong, especially printmaking. The university was the first to accept creative work in theater, writing, music, and art on an equal basis with academic research. The English, history, sociology, and political science departments earn high rankings but are uneven.

The English department has recently improved the requirements for its majors, who must take at least one course from each the following six areas: literary theory and interdisciplinary studies; medieval and early modern literature and culture; modern British literature and culture; American literature and culture; transnational literature and postcolonial studies; and nonfiction and creative writing. The major's requirements are serious and impressive, and they guarantee that English majors from Iowa will have a better grasp of literary history than the alumni of many elite colleges.

The history department's requirements are also serious: Students need two classes each in American, European, and non-Western history, along with one course studying a period before 1700. Upon declaring a major, they take a small "colloquium" class with other history majors in which "reading, writing, and arguing" are emphasized. Finally, they must submit a portfolio of three graded history papers before graduating.

Refreshingly, political science majors are required to take an introduction to American politics, along with four other introductory courses from a sensible list of eleven choices that includes political communication, political thought and political action, and Russia and Eurasia. The remaining credits are elective.

Recommended professors include Evan Fales in philosophy; Michael Dailey and Joe Frankel in biology; David E. Klemm and Jay Holstein in religious studies; Brooks Landon, Garrett Stewart, and Jonathan Wilcox in English; Mitchell Kelly in educational psychology; Chris Brochu in geoscience; Astrid Oesmann in German; Rex Honey in geography; and Lawrence Fritts in music.

As the first state university "to admit men and women on an equal basis," in 1855, the university started off progressive and slid further left with time. Its Gay, Lesbian, Bisexual, Transgender, and Allied Union was founded in 1970, making it one of the oldest such campus organizations in the United States. Interestingly, Iowa has come rather late to the game in making diversity an academic requirement, just recently adding a "Values, Society, and Diversity" component to its general education requirements.

Those seeking off-campus enrichment also will look to Iowa's study-abroad programs; one professor cannot say enough about the "Winterim" program in India. He also recommends anything in the International Writing Program, which brings the world to Iowa. This program lasts for twelve weeks in the fall and is headed by Chris Merrill. Iowa also offers study-abroad programs on six continents in countries that include Ghana, Morocco, Brazil, Egypt, Tanzania, China, Hong Kong, India, Japan, Russia, South Korea, Austria, Germany, Belgium, Hungary, England, Ireland, France, Italy, Spain, Iceland, Greece, Poland, Turkey, Australia, New Zealand, Fiji, Argentina, Canada, Mexico, Chile, Jamaica, Peru, St. Lucia, El Salvador, and Uruguay.

Iowa offers a good range of foreign language programs, including Chinese, Japanese, Korean, Russian, Ancient Greek, Latin, French, German, Spanish, Portuguese, Italian, Arabic, Swahili, and Zulu.

Student Life: Flatland, U.S.A.

Iowa City is a community of 67,000 with a metro population of over 100,000, located on the east side of the state on the Iowa River. The downtown area, within walking distance of the university, features a bricked pedestrian walkway lined with stores, restaurants, and coffee shops. Throughout the summer and in early fall, Iowa City hosts a free Friday night concert series, and the Jazz Festival in early July draws a large crowd. A few times a year, the city holds a Gallery Walk with receptions at fifteen downtown sites. Iowa City affords plenty of recreational areas, including a skate park, a walkway by the Iowa River, and a state park a few miles away where students can swim, sun, fish, rent canoes, hike, and bike. "If you are a political junkie, Iowa is one of the greatest places in the country to be once every four years—and the [caucus] season lasts for months," says one professor.

Still, Iowa City is almost four hours from the nearest major urban center. As one professor says, "Once you leave Iowa City, you are in the middle of the Corn Belt: a world of hamlets, country towns, and small cities no bigger than Cedar Rapids." Students remain ambivalent about the place. According to one, "When people get here, they can't wait to get out of here. When they leave, they can't wait to get back."

The campus's traditional architecture is Greek revival, and its more modern buildings vary in style. Iowa survived a flood in 2008—but parts of the university, including much of the arts campus, did not. Those programs have dispersed to other parts of the campus as the university undertakes rebuilding. Planned new construction is going forward as well. A new athletics facility will open in the fall next to the library. Recently completed are the University of Iowa Institute for Biomedical Discovery, the State Hygienic Laboratory, which is Iowa's environmental and public health laboratory, and a new Iowa Flood Center.

UI has more than 450 student organizations. The largest include Students Today Alumni Tomorrow Ambassadors, University of Iowa Student Government, and College Republicans. More quirky choices are the Dart Club, Iowa Bass Fishing, and the Society of Composers. Religious students of most faiths will find a group on campus.

ACADEMIC REQUIREMENTS

Students in the College of Liberal Arts, which enrolls the bulk of undergraduates, must fulfill the following requirements—many of them in their first semester or year:

- "Rhetoric."
- One course in historical perspectives. Among the courses fulfilling this requirement are "Western Civilization," "Issues in History: Gender in Historical Perspective," and "Theater and Society: Romantics and Rebels."
- One course in quantitative or formal reasoning. No class in mathematics is required, though math through algebra is needed for admission to the university. Students can also opt for a course in computer science or "Theory and Practice of Argument."
- One class in social sciences, chosen from a list that includes introductory classes in economics, psychology, and political science, as well as "Media and Consumers," "Introduction to Human Geography," and "Perspectives on Leisure and Play."
- Two courses in natural sciences, including one with a lab. Choices include courses on botany, earth history, astronomy, physics, and chemistry.
- One class in "Interpretation of Literature." All students (except English majors) must take this course. Options include "Texts and Contexts in France and the French-speaking World" or "Nature and Ecology in French Philosophy and Fiction."
- Fourth-semester competency in a foreign language.
- Three "diversity courses," one chosen from each of the following three areas: International and Global Issues, Literary, Visual, and Performing Arts, and Values, Society, and Diversity. The list of approved courses was not available as this book went to press.

Midwest

One professor notes that it *is* Iowa and that "most students coming in are Christians," but another adds, "There is substantial religious diversity at Iowa. A number of the Christian denominations have campus ministries. Muslims and Jews are visible on campus as well. The campus ministry groups tend to have student worship meetings on Wednesday or Thursday nights. They provide one of the most useful alternatives to the bar scene." The preoccupations of UI students tend less to the spiritual than to spirits. "We go to football games and we go to bars," a student says. The *Daily Iowan* reports that "70 percent of UI students engage in high-risk drinking—four or more drinks in one sitting for women, five or more for men—while nationally, 37 percent of students do, according to the National College Health Association." The university is increasing efforts to combat this problem and recently launched "Ensuring Student Success: Making and Supporting Good Choices," an "orientation program designed to educate students and their parents on making healthy decisions in college."

As one might expect at a Big Ten school, sports are important at Iowa. The front of a newsletter for St. Paul Lutheran Chapel and University Center once announced: "Take Note! On Saturday, Iowa plays Wisconsin in football!" before going on to church news. "Sports are advertised a lot, especially guys' football and basketball," says a student. The wrestling team is famous, having won twenty national team and thirty-one Big Ten titles. The UI offers twelve varsity teams for women and ten for men. The school mascot is Herby (short for Hercules) the Hawk. Around 10 percent of students go Greek. For the other 90 percent, there is a lively social scene. "There are tons of bars, and they are full Thursday, Friday, and Saturday nights," says one source. Students hang out at restaurant bars like the Summit, Java House, and Tobacco Bowl. "The worst part of UI is its bar scene," says a student. His lament is borne out by statistics, which show 398 student alcohol and drug crimes in 2009, as well as 462 charges of public intoxication. "Partying is pretty big here," a student admits. Students report that freshmen regularly get served at bars and that "bar crawls are pretty prevalent."

Just who can enter the bars has become an issue that has students organizing petitions and protesting. (Iowa City recently increased the legal age for entrance to bars from nineteen to twenty-one.) Socializing in bars near campus remains a big part of student nightlife. Professors wonder aloud whether keeping underage students out would actually decrease the incidence of drinking or just cause them to seek less public venues for it, where more trouble might ensue.

Even as students unite to foment change on the local level, political activity on campus is relatively quiet and normal. Approximately 64 percent of students hail from Iowa and 21 percent from adjoining states—primarily Illinois—and the political leanings of the student body reflect the centrist populism of the region of the country. On the right, there is an active College Republicans club, and on the left there is the Iowa International Socialist Organization. One student calls Iowa's open atmosphere its best asset. And another says, "I am a conservative and I enjoy this campus; it is a challenge and a wonderful platform for discussions." Students of different opinions tend to get along well, a professor says, adding: "It's the faculty that have gone off the deep end!" Students say that for the most part, classroom indoctrination or intolerance of unpopular ideas is rare. However, according to one professor, conservative students are not vocal about their politics in case their instructors lean left—as many of them do.

YELLOW LIGHT

The National Association of Scholars (NAS) is drawing attention to an ongoing lawsuit against the university. A professional staff member in the College of Law's Writing Resource Center alleges that she was denied a full-time position because of viewpoint discrimination. She has filed suit in federal court. NAS summarizes her case:

"Wagner believes that she was denied the appointment on political grounds.... [S]he is a Republican. She was also outspoken in her advocacy of some conservative positions. None of this seemed to matter in a variety of professional positions she held before applying for the Iowa opening.... At that point, however, her appointment was blocked and the position was instead granted to an individual who had never practiced law or published, and who professed to 'hate' Republicans and 'right wingers.'"

The Foundation for Individual Rights in Education flagged the university for a school website, which defines sexual harassment in a way that violates its students' First Amendment rights by broadly defining sexual harassment as something that "occurs when somebody says or does something sexually related that you don't want them to say or do, regardless of who it is." Since this standard is fundamentally subjective, offenses *could* range from bawdy jokes to discussions of Leviticus, Dante, or Chaucer.

This excess of zeal is perhaps somewhat intelligible in light of two very high-profile sexual harassment cases at Iowa in 2008, both of which ended in the death-by-suicide of the accused professors. One current faculty member says that this is more macabre coincidence than any evidence of a particularly pernicious or permissive atmosphere at the university.

Around 90 percent of freshmen live in the ten residence halls—although students are not required to. UI offers a number of "learning communities" designed to "provide a supportive and engaging environment where students are challenged intellectually and have the unique advantage of bonding with other students who have similar academic goals." Students are selected on a first-come, first-served basis. There are learning communities focusing on the health sciences, women in science and engineering, honors, international crossroads, leadership in business and entrepreneurship, performing arts, transfer students—and refreshingly, men in engineering. There is also a "quiet house" option. All halls are officially substance-free—and tobacco is considered a substance. All residence halls are coed, with men and women separated by floor or wing.

If you don't crawl inside a bottle or get hit by a flying one, Iowa City is pretty sedate. A female student reports, "I feel very safe here." The UI Department of Public Safety offers self-defense training and recently implemented a special department dedicated to the investigation and prevention of sex crimes. There are emergency phones located throughout campus and a student-run safety escort service. In 2009, the school reported nine forcible sex offenses (and one nonforcible), one aggravated assault, and twenty-three burglaries on campus.

As a state school, Iowa is a sweet deal for residents: in-state tuition for 2010–11 was $7,417 (for nonresidents $23,713), plus $8,331 for room and board. Admissions are need blind, and the school undertakes to cover student need with a combination of grants, work/study, and loans. Some 42 percent of students receive some need-based aid. The average student-loan debt of a 2010 graduate was $20,234.

University of Kansas

Lawrence, Kansas • www.ku.edu

No place like home

The University of Kansas sits on a high ridge in a flat state. Founded in 1864 as Kansas's main state university, KU has risen steadily in reputation to become one of the more highly regarded public schools in the nation. Indeed, KU can offer one of the better state-school educations available, largely because it maintains comparatively strong liberal arts requirements. But given the mammoth size of the school and its impersonal approach to teaching, it's not for everyone. "A student who is at high risk for getting lost in a large, bureaucratically inclined institution should stay away from this place," says a professor. But self-directed students who know what they want to study can probably find it here.

Academic Life: Lost in the crowd

The KU humanities department, founded by the great liberal educator John Senior, once offered a deep, truly integrated exploration of Western civilization. Aggressive multiculturalists eventually dismantled much of what was best about this program, which now seems devoted largely to the celebration of "diversity," although worthy courses can be found by the student who reads the catalog carefully.

A better option seems to be the university honors program. One student insists, "The honors program is the only way to go for students who care about educational quality." Honors students take courses that are more challenging and smaller, at twenty to twenty-five students, and most live together in special housing.

Sadly, honors classes and upper-level courses within their majors are about the only places students will have the opportunity to develop relationships with faculty. Introductory courses enroll as many as 900 students. As one student spins it, "There is a beauty to giant lecture halls in that if you want to remain anonymous, you certainly can." Graduate students teach 17 percent of courses.

First-year students are assigned professional advisors in the advising center. A student says, "From everything I've heard, these advisors are very impersonal and just want to make sure all the boxes are checked off on your degree plan. I had good experience with the honors advisors, though." Once a student has declared a major, he can visit with a faculty advisor within that department, but he shouldn't expect too much. "Unfortu-

VITAL STATISTICS

Religious affiliation: *none*
Total enrollment: *29,242*
Total undergraduates:
  21,066
ACT midrange: *22–27*
Applicants: *10,653*
Applicants accepted: *91%*
Accepted applicants who
  enrolled: *40%*
Tuition and fees: *in state,
  $7,874; out of state,
  $20,680*
Room and board: *$7,404*
Freshman retention rate:
  78%
Graduation rate: *32% (4 yrs.),
  61% (6 yrs.)*
Courses with fewer than 20
  students: *39%*
Student-faculty ratio: *20:1*
Courses taught by graduate
  students: *17%*
Most popular majors: *bio-
  logical sciences, engineer-
  ing, business/accounting*
Students living on campus:
  22%
Guaranteed housing for
  four years? *no*
Students in fraternities: *13%*
  in sororities: *18%*

nately, many teachers are not available outside of class," a journalism major says. "Sometimes the size of the school can hinder a student from getting the type of advice and help he needs. KU is not a personal place, and you do not get much individual attention here." Another student disagrees: "To meet with a professor, you simply have to show up during office hours; it's not much harder than going to McDonald's." A professor advises prospective students, "Pick your faculty mentors well and you'll get all the encouragement you need."

As at many research institutions, good teaching is not necessarily emphasized or required for advancement. However, according to a professor, "The Center for Teaching Excellence has established a strong, active, and actually useful presence on campus (encouraged and financially supported by the upper administration). Activity in that center is rewarded, and faculty generally give good reports on the help the center gives for pedagogical training." Just as the quality of instructors varies, so does the quality of students. "There is huge variation in the intellectual ability and curiosity of the KU student body," a professor says. "Our best students can compete with the best students anywhere, but our weakest are pretty weak."

Students majoring in English are required to take one survey of English literature before 1800, one of English literature after 1800, two American literature classes (one before and one after 1865), a Shakespeare course, and an introduction to literary criticism and theory.

History majors must take five courses in one of two categories (ancient, history of science, medieval, modern Western Europe, Russia/Eastern Europe, and United States) and (Africa, East Asia, Latin America, Native America) and three in the other. While it is impossible to avoid Western history entirely, it would be quite easy to exclude most of it.

Majors in political science must take introductory courses in U.S. politics, comparative politics, international politics, political theory, and political science methods of inquiry. The U.S. politics course does cover "basic American governmental institutions, political processes, and policy."

Some of the best departments, professors say, are those in the humanities, political science, journalism, aerospace engineering, preprofessional areas, and music. A proud music major boasts that "KU piano students routinely beat Juilliard and other high-power music school students in competitions. The same is true for organ and voice. . . . For ambitious performance students who can't afford the big name conservatories, this is a good

Midwest

choice." Journalism majors are also ready to tout their department: "KU has one of the top journalism departments in the country, and it really does live up to the reputation." Recommend professors include Robert Basow, Kerry Benson, Ted Fredrickson, David Guth, and Chuck Marsh.

Among highly regarded professors in other departments are Hannah Britton, Allan Cigler, Thomas Heilke, Burdett Loomis, and Sharon O'Brien in political science; David M. Katzman in American studies; Douglas A. Houston in business; Stephen Ilardi in psychology; Tom Lewin, Rita Napier, and Leslie Tuttle in history; and Antha Cotten-Spreckelmeyer in Western civilization.

During the Vietnam War era, the University of Kansas was wracked by massive student revolts. Some of that spirit still haunts the town. "The state of Kansas is very conservative overall," says a student. "However, Lawrence is very liberal—much like Bloomington, Indiana, or Austin, Texas."

One professor insists that "there are plenty of solid, fair-minded faculty on both sides and the middle of the left-right ideological spectrum." The Hall Center for the Humanities sponsors a series of lectures from diverse perspectives, and the Robert J. Dole Institute of Politics, named after one of KU's most prominent alumni, features speakers from across the political spectrum.

Students report that a number of courses—especially those in the social sciences—are politicized. "Certainly there are times when I am afraid to state certain conservative or Christian views," says a student. "However . . . the few times that I felt singled out because of my views, I still received very fair grades." It's no secret that big state schools lean left, and KU is no exception. One student put the case bluntly by saying that "the religious studies department is a good place to study religions, but not if you are in any way religious yourself." Enough said.

KU's study-abroad program is excellent, offering programs in various locations in Australia, China, Costa Rica, Denmark, Finland, France, Germany, Great Britain, Ireland, Italy, Japan, Korea, the Netherlands, Spain, Sweden, and Switzerland, among other locations. Sadly, not enough students take advantage of these options; only some 19 percent of graduating seniors have studied on foreign shores. It seems that many students are just as apprehensive as Dorothy about leaving the fair state of Kansas. One student says that "the university is putting more resources into making study abroad accessible."

Foreign language offerings are plentiful. Choices include all the most popular European tongues and myriad other options, from Cherokee, Croatian, and Haitian to Wolof and Yiddish.

SUGGESTED CORE

1. Humanities and Western Civilization 304, Masterpieces of World Literature I
2. Philosophy 384, Ancient Philosophy
3. Religious Studies 124 or 324, Understanding the Bible
4. Religious Studies 530, Christian Origins: From the Beginnings to Augustine (closest match)
5. Political Science 301, Introduction to Political Theory
6. English 332, Shakespeare
7. History 128, History of the United States through the Civil War
8. Philosophy 386, Modern Philosophy: Descartes to Kant (closest match)

Student Life: Basketball *über alles*

The state of Kansas might call to mind cornfields and tornadoes spinning over huge expanses of flat land, but the city of Lawrence is in one of the few hilly parts of the state, and the campus itself is on top of Mount Oread, making the starting time of that 8:00 AM math class only half the battle. KU's limestone campus makes the trek worthwhile. A student says, "The campus is absolutely gorgeous. Sometimes in the winter, my roommates and I drive along Jayhawk Boulevard and stare up at the lighted windows and say, 'How are we so lucky that we get to go to this place?'"

The university's master plan, completed in 2002, cost an impressive $155 million for capital construction and landscaping. Recently constructed buildings include the lavish Ambler Student Recreation Fitness Center. This 98,000-square-foot facility was expanded by a "$6.3 million addition of approximately 45,000-square feet" and "includes four gym courts, racquetball courts, a martial-arts studio; and an extended track elevated over all eight courts," the school boasts. KU also has completed a $10.3 million expansion and renovation of its music building, Murphy Hall, which now has "new rehearsal halls, faculty offices, and a computer laboratory, plus an expanded music and dance library." The recently finished Hall Center for the Humanities features "a 120-seat conference room, a seminar room, a serving kitchen, and offices for Hall Center staff and research fellows." More recent additions to the campus include the 110,000-square-foot School of Pharmacy, which was funded by $50 million in state bonds. The next two years should also see the completion of a $7 million Bioscience and Technology Business Center as well as the $19 million Measurements, Materials, and Sustainable Environment Center. Fewer than one-fifth of students, mostly freshmen, live on campus; however, since that fraction still adds up to about 5,000 students, you are unlikely to feel like an oddball if you join them. Except for two all-women residence halls, dormitories are coed, with separate wings for each sex. One student describes dorm life as crowded, impersonal, and loud: "Fire alarms in the middle of the night happen a lot (usually pranks)," he says. "It can be just overwhelming to live in a tiny room with no personal space and 800 other people on eight floors." However, another student reports, the dorm experience "was wonderful. I made a lot of good friends and didn't have to deal with any of those horror stories that you normally hear about."

KU requires that a male student be escorted by a female student when visiting the female wing of a hall (and vice versa). This sounds more impressive than it is. A male student says, "There are supposedly visitation policies in the dorms, but that doesn't really change anything—sleepover guests are the norm." He adds, "Students are sometimes shocked to move out of home and be surrounded by other students having casual sex and attacking anyone who has a problem with that." In the two women's residence halls, where the policies are better enforced, men must be out by 11:00 PM on weeknights, but they can stay overnight throughout the weekend. At least you may have to deal with your roommate's boyfriend sleeping in the bunk above you only two nights a week.

KU offers several options for students who wish to live with other students who have interests similar to their own. There are also quiet floors for upperclassmen and scholarship halls, where students share all cooking and housekeeping responsibilities.

About 13 percent of KU undergraduates are members of a fraternity or sorority, and most members live in the organizations' houses. Fraternities and sororities contribute to KU's reputation as a party school, and drinking plays an enormous role in campus social life. "There is very much a culture of alcohol here, and it can seem at times like the only thing to do here is get drunk," says one student. "If you're afraid that you might party too much, you may want to take that into consideration." Another student insists, "Students at KU can drink as much or as little as they wish. The alcohol is available and accessible to all ages. . . . However, it is not the focus of the university's activities." Lawrence itself provides plenty of other options for weekend and evening entertainment in the form of live music, shops, bars, and restaurants. Students rate it highly as a college town.

One of the best attributes of large state universities is that there are usually other students who share your interests—for instance, in one of the more than 600 student clubs. These range from preprofessional societies—like the Pre-Dental Club, the Public Interest

ACADEMIC REQUIREMENTS

The University of Kansas has no core curriculum, but it maintains a decent set of distribution requirements for students in its College of Liberal Arts and Sciences. BA students must take the following:

- Any three introductory English courses—two in composition and one in literature.
- One class in oral communication or logical argument.
- Two introductory courses in math, or one in math and one in biology.
- Two specific classes in humanities and Western civilization. These cover many of the classic works of the West, from the ancient world through the Middle Ages to the dawn of modernity.
- One course dealing with a non-Western culture. Approximately 150 options qualify here—a few of which seem politicized—with good choices such as "Imperial China" and "Introduction to Ancient Near Eastern and Greek History."
- Three classes in humanities—one in history, one in literature and the arts, and one in philosophy and religion. History choices range from "The United States through the Civil War" to "Introduction to Jazz." Art and literature options include "Greek Literature and Civilization" and "Introduction to World Dance." Philosophy and religion choices range from "Understanding the Bible" to "Living Religions of the East."
- Four courses in natural sciences and mathematics. Options include "Fundamentals of Microbiology" and "Insects in Your World."
- Three social science classes—one in "culture and society," one in "individual behavior," and one in "public affairs." There are more than a dozen choices in each category, ranging from "Principles of Human Geography" to "Women's Studies: An Interdisciplinary Introduction."
- One course in laboratory science. This includes a laboratory or a natural science lecture course with an associated laboratory that constitutes four to five hours.
- Courses or tests sufficient to demonstrate fourth-semester fluency in a foreign language.

Midwest

GREEN LIGHT

On campus, left-wing students are the most vocal. "I would say that liberal elements are much more comfortable on campus, and conservatives just don't speak out enough," says a student. Students differ about the degree to which political ideology affects other classroom instruction. A journalism and political science major says, "The political science courses I have taken remain unbiased." A student says, "I never felt uncomfortable because my views differed from the professor's." A recent graduate agrees, "I never felt that my grades would be threatened because I spoke up in class about my conservative beliefs and/or religious/spiritual disposition."

The College Republicans are very active, as are the College Democrats, but both groups usually stick to party politics rather than philosophical issues, often bringing state politicians to speak on campus. Political clubs can obtain financial support through the Center for Campus Life (using student fees), but a representative from the office says most of the funding goes to general expenses like office supplies and fliers for the political clubs. "Controversial funding for speakers or protests, for instance, would have a much harder time finding financial support," he says.

Law Society—to the Philosophy Club, which sponsors lectures and an essay contest, and the KU Federalist Society, which brings conservative legal scholars to campus. Conservative students will also want to check out the KU College Republicans, a vibrant group that is very active in local and national politics and has a great networking base for political internships and jobs. The KU Republicans are countered by quite a number of liberals groups—which accurately reflects the political climate at KU. In fact, the liberal groups and organizations tend to swing far to the left, especially the KU Young Democratic Socialists, the Young Democrats of KU, and the Student Coalition for Immigrant Rights.

Religious clubs, especially evangelical Christian ones, are also quite popular at KU, and no student should have trouble finding a group that shares his faith: discussion groups, Bible studies, and prayer sessions abound. Some local churches shuttle students to Sunday services. KU is one of the few state schools with a chapel on campus. Danforth Chapel is nondenominational; its webpage says that it is a place for "individual meditation and prayer" as well as weddings, memorial services, and student activities. "A variety of conservative and not-so-conservative Christian student communities thrive here," says one professor. The St. Lawrence Catholic Center is well respected, and one student goes so far as to claim that active involvement with the center "gives you an intellectual and spiritual experience comparable to a good Catholic university."

One of the few interests that nearly every Jayhawk student shares is sports—and basketball above any other. How could they not at this school, where James Naismith, inventor of the game, worked for nearly twenty years? "Basketball is the only university-supported religion on campus," a student says. The legendary Allen Field House seats more than 16,000 fans, has hosted thirty-seven NCAA tournament games, and is considered one of the best places in the country to watch college basketball. Kansas has been a perennial contender for the NCAA men's basketball championship for decades.

Despite the dominance of basketball at KU, the football team also garners significant attention. The Jayhawks' rivalry with the University of Missouri Tigers is the oldest in college football. Besides varsity athletics, KU offers twenty-five intercollegiate club teams and many intramural ones, usually organized around residence halls and Greek houses.

Crime is relatively infrequent for a school of KU's size. The most common campus crime is burglary, and students who lock their doors and watch their laptops rarely become victims. The SafeRide service escorts students from one end of campus to the other between 10:00 PM and 2:30 AM. In 2009, the school reported six forcible sex offenses, eight robberies, four aggravated assaults, two stolen cars, three arsons, and thirty-eight burglaries.

Even though it has risen steadily in recent years, tuition at KU is still a bargain by today's standards, especially if you come from Kansas. Tuition for 2010–11 for in-state students was $7,874; for out-of-state students, it was $20,680. Room and board was $7,404. The school claims that "nearly half" of students will see no increase in tuition in the next year. Only a fourth of students receive need-based financial aid, and the average student-loan debt of a recent graduating class was a moderate $16,842.

Kenyon College

Gambier, Ohio • www.kenyon.edu

Ask not for whom

Every quarter hour, bells clang loudly from the Church of the Holy Spirit, resonating throughout the quaint clapboard town of Gambier, in north-central Ohio. The church sits on the campus of Kenyon College, founded in 1824 as an Episcopal seminary. "There's nothing better in Gambier than walking around the town on a warm Friday afternoon listening to the bells," recalls a graduate. However, the bells are now rung for different reasons. Over the past half decade or so, the bell has been tolled to solemnly mark the execution of criminals in the United States. This transformation of a venerable tradition into a political statement says quite a bit about what has happened to Kenyon College. Although Kenyon's hallowed Peirce Hall features stained-glass depictions of some of Western civilization's greatest heroes, we fear that their work and lives are now viewed on campus through the jaundiced lens of fashionable ideologies. What is left of Bishop Chase's old school is a devotion to hands-on instruction of students at a high academic level. And that's saying quite a bit.

Academic Life: Ransoming Lowell

Kenyon College has no core curriculum but imposes instead some rather vague distribution requirements. More structure comes in one of the thirty-five majors—most in traditional disciplines, except for interdisciplinary departments like African American or women's and gender studies. A few students each year create their own interdisciplinary curricula and pursue "synoptic" majors.

One popular program that we highly recommend is the Integrated Program of Humane Studies (IPHS), which introduces students to classic (and other) texts of Western civilization in seminar-style tutorials. Over the course of a year, students study the Old Testament, then works of Plato, Virgil, Shakespeare, Aristotle, Nietzsche, Mann, Woolf, Kafka, Foucault, and others. After the first year, around a dozen students typically choose to concentrate in IPHS, taking courses such as "Dante's *Divine Comedy*" and "Modernism and Its Critics." Students attending Kenyon who seek a real liberal arts education should look no further than this department, which carries on the best of Kenyon's humanistic heritage.

Political science is highly respected among Kenyon faculty for the quality of its instruction and its commitment to exploring fundamental issues. The department provides an impressive year-long freshman seminar, "Modern Quest for Justice," an introductory class that includes readings from the Bible, Thucydides, Tocqueville, Rousseau, and the American founders. Political science majors are also required to take a course called "Liberal Democracy in America" and must choose another American politics course in addition to three courses in comparative politics and international relations. Students also take one upper-level seminar.

History majors face a rigorous program but not one that requires courses in U.S. history; students can choose European courses instead, and the study of non-Western history is strongly emphasized. Majors must complete a history senior exercise (see below) and write and defend a senior research paper. Honors students write an impressive 80-page independent study complete with maps, illustrations, bibliography, and footnotes.

Kenyon's English department, the school's largest, was made famous by southern poet and critic John Crowe Ransom, who founded the *Kenyon Review*—which is still going strong. Many luminaries have taught at Kenyon over the decades, including Robert Lowell, James Wright, E. L. Doctorow, and William Gass.

But the department has slipped since those glory days. Some students and professors now call it "overrated." Although solid courses like "Advanced Fiction Writing Workshop" and "Chaucer" still dominate the offerings, there is also now a marked emphasis on postcolonialist, postmodernist, and defiantly eccentric approaches to literature. Literary theory courses are required, but a course in Shakespeare, sadly, is not.

The college offers several science-related majors: biochemistry, biology, chemistry, molecular biology, neuroscience, physics, and environmental studies. The mathematics department is described as strong, with award-winning teachers. After completing courses taught only by professors (not graduate students), Kenyon's math and science students are said to find their way to good jobs after graduation.

Students and professors speak proudly of one Kenyon institution—the senior exercise, a departmental project or comprehensive exam that in most majors serves as the capstone of an undergraduate career. In the humanities and some social sciences, a student can satisfy the requirement by writing a chapter-length paper on a topic determined by his advisor. In other departments, such as economics and political science, majors take a comprehensive test. Any of these options serves as an excellent preparation for graduate

VITAL STATISTICS

Religious affiliation: *none*
Total enrollment: *1,633*
Total undergraduates: *1,633*
SAT/ACT midranges: CR: *630–670*, M: *610–700*; ACT: *28–32*
Applicants: *4,509*
Applicants accepted: *31%*
Accepted applicants who enrolled: *32%*
Tuition and fees: *$39,420*
Room and board: *$9,500*
Freshman retention rate: *94%*
Graduation rate: *85% (4 yrs.)*, *88% (6 yrs.)*
Courses with fewer than 20 students: *70%*
Student-faculty ratio: *10:1*
Courses taught by graduate students: *none*
Most popular majors: *social sciences, English, visual and performing arts*
Students living on campus: *100%*
Guaranteed housing for four years? *yes*
Students in fraternities: *26%* in sororities: *20%*

school, and the college boasts that more than 70 percent of alumni find themselves studying for advanced degrees within five years. In other words, Kenyon's professors do a great job of forming . . . future professors.

Perhaps the students are inspired to emulate the devoted faculty they meet at Kenyon. "Students are our main 'business' in that we take them, their intellectual growth, and our teaching and learning seriously—intensely so," one teacher remarks. The faculty expects students to be enthusiastic about their educations and to crave learning for its own sake. Professors nurture students' intellects with constant book recommendations, additional reading assignments, and vigorous teaching. "We don't get caught up in rankings, future financial earnings, or prestige in general," says one student. "We immerse ourselves in learning."

Upon entering the college, freshmen are paired with faculty advisors and upper-class counselors (UCC) in the same potential major, who help ease the transition to college. "Without my advisor and UCC, choosing courses would have been a little overwhelming," says a recent alumnus. "Once admitted, students are given extraordinary support," reports one parent of a Kenyon undergrad, noting that her daughter's advisor mentored only five students. No one gets lost in the shuffle. The college boasts a strong student-faculty ratio of 10 to 1, and most classes meet around large conference tables.

Kenyon professors enjoy close relationships with students; according to a survey, 93 percent of freshmen have dined at a professor's house. Most professors are highly accessible and doggedly encourage students to visit them during office hours. One student says, "If you're not going to office hours, you're missing out on a wealth of knowledge." Students often crowd the hallways outside professors' offices during finals week.

Kenyon students say they rarely encounter indoctrination in the classroom. Regardless of their beliefs, students usually feel comfortable enough to express varying viewpoints. "Politics stop at the classroom door," reports one undergrad. They don't necessarily stop at the door of a meeting room, however. Two professors report their distaste for what one calls the "unspoken agreements among many or most people that ensure the hiring of people who are politically acceptable." Another professor says that a "darker side to faculty relations in certain areas" is unavoidable. "A few of us are maintaining rational discourse as best we can," the teacher says. Professors with conservative sentiments are a distinct minority at Kenyon.

Science, mathematics, and music are at last coming into their own at Kenyon, with new facilities and a stronger emphasis on developing these disciplines. The natural sciences reside in a newly built quadrangle, and the music department inhabits the impressive Storer Hall. There is also a new fitness center, and the school's master plan foresees the construction of new fine arts facilities and additional student housing, plus the renovation of existing buildings.

Midwest

The list of excellent professors at Kenyon is long. It includes Fred E. Baumann, John M. Elliott, Kirk E. Emmert, Pamela K. Jensen, Joseph L. Klesner, David M. Rowe, and Stephen E. Van Holde in political science; Jennifer Clarvoe, Adele Davidson, William F. Klein, P. F. Kluge, Perry Lentz, Sergei Lobanov-Rostovsky, and David Lynn in English; David E. Harrington and James P. Keeler in economics; K. Read Baldwin and Gregory P. Spaid in art; E. Raymond Heithaus, Haruhiko Itagaki, and Joan L. Slonczewski in biology; Robert E. Bennett in classics; Wendy MacLeod and Harlene Marley in dance and drama; Matthew W. Maguire in history; Bradley Hartlaub and Judy Holdener in mathematics; Natalia Olshanskaya in modern languages and literatures; Benjamin Locke in music; Juan De Pascuale and Joel F. Richeimer in philosophy; Frank C. Peiris and Paula C. Turner in physics; Allan Fenigstein and Michael Levine in psychology; and Royal Rhodes in religious studies.

Kenyon boasts a strong study-abroad program, sending students to sites across Europe, China, Japan, Russia, Latin America, and Africa. The college offers Ancient Greek, Latin, and eight modern languages: Chinese, French, German, Italian, Japanese, Russian, Spanish, and Arabic.

Student Life: Ninety minutes from Cleveland

"There's obviously a lot to love about going to a school on a hill in the middle of Amish country, and there's obviously a lot to hate," says a recent alumnus. The college's 1,000-acre campus in Gambier, Ohio, is home to about 2,000 year-round residents—who are almost outnumbered by the students. Gambier is some forty-five minutes northeast of Columbus and ninety minutes from Cleveland. The village has undergone little change since its founding, adding only a bank, two small inns, a nationally renowned bookstore, two coffee shops, a college bar, and a post office. Only two village buildings are not owned or operated by the college. One of these, the Village Market, still allows residents to purchase groceries

---

ACADEMIC REQUIREMENTS

In the absence of a core curriculum, Kenyon's distribution guidelines call for students to take eighteen year-long courses outside their major, including:

- Two courses in the fine arts. Examples include "Music Theory" and "The Screen Writer."
- Two classes in humanities. "Sanskrit" and "Afro-Caribbean Spirituality" both qualify, among others.
- Two courses in natural science. Courses include the traditional hard sciences, as well as mathematics and psychology.
- Two courses in the social sciences. Courses range from "History of the Early Middle Ages" to "Socialism at the Movies."
- One introductory foreign language class (students may test out).
- One course demonstrating quantitative reasoning. Most science, mathematics, and economics courses count.

Midwest

on credit slips, greets customers by their first names, and serves as a welcome sanctuary from urban anonymity.

This region of Ohio has its attractions. The prehistoric Indian mounds of nearby Newark are truly impressive and according to the *New York Times* reveal astronomical alignments comparable to those of Stonehenge. Hueston Woods State Park by the Indiana border offers comfortable and inexpensive facilities for those seeking a getaway from campus. Suburban sprawl is beginning to encroach on the area around Gambier, however. Kenyon officials are worried that new developments popping up around Gambier will damage the college's rural image and threaten its splendid isolation.

Middle Path, a mile-long gravel walk, runs the length of the campus and is the thoroughfare connecting the college's main academic buildings. The path is anchored at the north end by Bexley Hall and at the south end by Old Kenyon, a historic dormitory.

Kenyon is strictly residential, and nearly all 1,633 students live in college housing and purchase the college board plan. A handful of seniors live off campus; most students enjoy the college apartments and dormitories. The housing market is tight in Gambier and Mount Vernon, a neighboring town of 16,135. There are resident halls for first-year students and for upper-class students. Students have the option of living on single-sex or coed floors; in suites, apartments, smoking or nonsmoking dorms; and substance-free housing. All residence-hall bathrooms are single sex, as are dorm rooms. Students can also apply for special-interest housing if, for instance, they want to live with the Black Student Union or an unrecognized sorority. Kenyon is building a village green with twenty townhouses, to house some 220 students. Some of these should be completed in 2012.

There are more than 120 student clubs and organizations at Kenyon, ranging from the Art Club to the Chasers, which organizes rock and pop performances. Kenyon has both College Democrats and Republicans, although neither group seems to be terribly active. There are six religious groups on campus, five Christian and one Jewish: Canterbury Kenyon (Episcopal), Koinonia Open Programming Board, Newman Community (Catholic), Saturday Night Fellowship, Young Life, and Hillel. All groups are primarily dedicated to prayer and service, not political activism.

More lively are the student papers. The *Kenyon Collegian* is published weekly and reports on a variety of subjects. The *Kenyon Observer*, the school's conservative, student-run journal, is the oldest political magazine on campus. Students who have worked for the *Observer* have gone on to take prestige positions at *National Review* and *Forbes*.

Gambier is a quiet college town. For those who find the silence unnerving, the school offers a free shuttle to Mount Vernon and a cheap Saturday shuttle to Columbus. One student says, "The biggest fear one could face in Gambier is boredom." Students generally work hard, but several professors remark that students' interest in writing well and reading more is quickly slipping. "Students do not read as much as they used to," one faculty member sighs.

Although only one bar in Gambier serves alcoholic beverages until the legal closing hour (2:00 AM), the college's dozen fraternities and sororities do their part in hosting the student parties and dances that form the backbone of Kenyon's social life. The college holds an annual winter ball—the Philander's Phling—which attracts scantily dressed, tipsy students every year. The college also hosts an annual raucous weekend in May called Summer Send-Off, usually featuring musical performances, barbecues, and games on the lawn. College officials are said to be quite strict about underage drinking. The college employs several security officers to help enforce liquor laws to secure the safety of students.

Kenyon is a member of the NCAA Division III North Coast Athletic Conference along with Oberlin, Ohio Wesleyan, Case Western Reserve, and archrival Denison University. Though the college offers twenty-two intercollegiate teams and several club and intramural teams, the school has a thin reputation for athletic prowess. Kenyon's swimming program is an exception: the men's team maintained the longest national championship streak in NCAA history—an impressive twenty-six years. Also impressive: the women's swimming team has won nineteen straight conference titles. Other notable intercollegiate teams include women's tennis, men's soccer, and men's lacrosse. A $60 million Center for Fitness, Recreation, and Athletics opened in fall 2005.

Students can call for walking or driving escorts when out late at night, and blue-light emergency phones are available all over campus. Crime at Kenyon is rare. In 2009, the college reported one aggravated assault, three cases of arson, two motor vehicle thefts, and thirty burglaries.

Kenyon is on the pricey side, with 2010–11 tuition at $39,420, and room and board $9,500. Admission is not need blind, but students who get in are guaranteed financial aid to meet their full need. Seventy percent of students received need-based aid in 2009–10, and the average student-loan debt of a recent graduating class was a modest $19,934.

YELLOW LIGHT

Though students report that they spend most of their time studying, the college offers more than 120 student organizations, ranging from the Stairwells, a folk group, to the Students for Creative Anachronism. The school's women's center often hosts conferences and exhibits, like the Sex Workers Art Show, a traveling burlesque show staged by, uh, sex workers.

In any given year, the college typically has no more than fifty politically vocal students, usually of a liberal bent, sources tell us. The school hosts the J Street U Kenyon Center for "mainstream American Jews and other supporters of Israel," and a group called ALSO (Allied Sexual Orientation) "dedicated to political activism regarding LGBT matters and heightening campus awareness of national queer issues." The Crozier Center for Women and the Snowden Multicultural Center also pursue liberal agendas. The women's center annually sponsors Take Back the Night, a march against violence against women that students say usually turns into an orgy of rhetorical male-bashing. It hosts both the inescapable *Vagina Monologues* and the Sex Workers Art Show. Activists United is an umbrella organization that sponsors lectures concerning free trade, sweatshops, and the death penalty. (Guess where they come down on these issues.) The Crozier Center also publishes the journal *56%*, which is both liberal and racy.

Campus conservatives have hosted lectures by Andrew Sullivan (a dubious selection), Bay Buchanan, Alan Keyes, and Ward Connerly in the past few years, typically through the fledgling College Republicans organization.

Macalester College

St. Paul, Minnesota • www.macalester.edu

Tower of Babel

Founded by Presbyterian minister Rev. Edward Duffield Neill in 1874, Macalester is considered one of the Midwest's leading colleges, with an emphasis on "internationalism, multiculturalism, and service to society." To make this point, the United Nations flag has flown alongside the American in the center of Macalester's campus since 1950. And indeed, the college has become a center of globalist education. Some 18 percent of Macalester students are from abroad, and the student body represents 93 different countries and 49 American states. Over half of students study abroad at some point during their education.

Macalester seems obsessively committed to multiculturalism—an anti-Western ideology that political philosopher Paul Gottfried argued (in his thought-provoking 2002 book *Multiculturalism and the Politics of Guilt*) aims at a "secular theocracy." The high priests of this new faith at Macalester would have to be its Department of Multicultural Life, whose mission is "to integrate and affirm the peoples, discourses, thoughts, and experiences of marginalized people in the fabric of Macalester community" and to "infuse multiculturalism into all aspects of campus life." Macalester's Lealtad-Suzuki Center organizes "student collectives" based around racial identities such as women of color, black women of the diaspora, men of color, white identity, and queers of color. Students get together to discuss their multiple identities as "sometimes dominant and sometimes subordinate when we look at power and privilege in today's global society." The center also offers a first-year program called "Pluralism and Unity" and sponsors the Allies Project, an organization committed to "creating a safe environment and community for all people regardless of sexual orientation, race, ethnicity, national origin, gender, religion, age, or ability." The Tapas Series serves both its namesake Spanish appetizers and programs on—guess what? Cultural diversity. One recent offering was called "What Is Multiculturalism Today?" There are dozens more such initiatives on campus, by which the religion of diversity is drummed into students' heads with a fervor we can only call catechetical.

Academic Life: Ministry of tribe

Given the school's globalist preoccupations, it doesn't surprise us that it has no core curriculum focused on the history and culture of the West but rather a set of scattered distribution requirements. One professor says, "Macalester's curriculum is still too unstructured. Curricular sprawl is the rule." Each student must take a special freshman course during his first semester on campus. These small classes focus primarily on writing, and just about every department offers one. Additionally, students must take two courses in the social sciences, two courses in the natural sciences and mathematics, and three courses in the humanities and fine arts. There are requirements in international diversity, U.S. multiculturalism, and a foreign language. And, if all this diversity isn't enough, the college has recently approved a multiculturalism requirement.

Students can fulfill their humanities and social science course requirements with classes entirely outside of the Western tradition and graduate without ever having taken courses in the civilization of Europe or the history of the United States.

Many academic courses complement Macalester's focus on the curious, the queer, and the foreign. The history department features "The Politics of Food in Latin America," an offering that blames malnutrition in Latin America on the U.S. Then there is "Feminist Sex Wars," a course offered by the women's, gender, and sexuality studies department in spring 2010, which covers "non-monogamies," pornography, bisexuality, and "transgenderism/transsexuality." Most ominously, "Global Governance" investigates the emergence of "global civil society" and "the implications of these changes for democracy, legitimacy, and social justice, etc." Macalester also offers many fine, traditional academic courses, even as it actively encourages students to study politically charged and narrow topics.

The English department boasts that it teaches from a "variety of perspectives, including feminist theory, environmental and ethical approaches, queer theory, poststructuralism, postcolonial theory, black feminist theory, and critical race theory." That really runs the gamut from A to . . . B. Majors will take courses in British and American literature, probably (but not necessarily) including the works of Shakespeare. They will also take courses like "British Youth Subcultures," which proposes a meandering list of texts from Alan Sillitoe's "The Loneliness of the Long Distance Runner" to Mark Ravenhill's *Shopping and F***ing*. The "senior capstone experience" of the major is an independent study in senior year. Honors students write a longer paper (forty to sixty pages) on works of literature.

For the history major, options include "African studies, American studies, Asian studies, environmental studies, humanities and media and cultural studies, international stud-

VITAL STATISTICS

Religious affiliation: *none*
Total enrollment: *1,996*
Total undergraduates: *1,996*
SAT/ACT midranges: CR: *660–740*, M: *630–710*; ACT: *29–32*
Applicants: *4,565*
Applicants accepted: *46%*
Accepted applicants who enrolled: *27%*
Tuition and fees: *$39,846*
Room and board: *$9,078*
Freshman retention rate: *94%*
Graduation rate: *82% (4 yrs.), 86% (6 yrs.)*
Courses with fewer than 20 students: *51%*
Student-faculty ratio: *11:1*
Courses taught by graduate students: *none*
Most popular majors: *economics, political science, English*
Students living on campus: *66%*
Guaranteed housing for four years? *no*
Students in fraternities or sororities: *none*

ies, Latin American studies, legal studies, urban studies, and women's, gender, and sexuality studies." Requirements, however, are quite vague. Students must take some thirteen courses in history. They need not, however, take a class on the founding period of the United States or the Civil War.

Political science majors have the worthy requirement of enlisting in some sort of "internship, service-learning course, action-research project, or similar experiential learning experience." One valuable-sounding course is "American Political Thought," which "explores the diversity and development of ideas in the U.S." Sadly, it is optional; majors can graduate without a serious study of the American political system.

"Mac students," says an upperclassman, "are extremely politically and socially active regarding issues both on and off campus."

Students are encouraged to be quite involved in the communities surrounding them. Macalester's Social Responsibility Committee runs a program for thirty-five freshmen called "Lives of Commitment." In this program, "students actively participate in weekly service work as part of a small group at one of seven nonprofit organizations that support immigrant and refugee and children's literacy." Forty upperclassmen participate in the "Leaders in Service Program." These students "educate the campus about social issues, nurture relationships with local nonprofit partners, and recruit volunteers."

In many traditional metrics of academic quality, Macalester fares well. Most classes are small, and Macalester can offer strong student-faculty relationships. There are no teaching assistants leading classes, and students report that faculty members are accessible and extremely helpful. A student says, "I am a double major in political science and religious studies. The strongest point of both departments is the faculty. The professors in both departments are full of knowledge, are passionate about their subject material, love to teach, and love to assist students with just about anything."

The honors program is open to seniors of "exceptional achievement." A current honors student says, "I would recommend the honors program if you are interested in conducting your own independent research culminating in a one hundred-page thesis."

Students begin Macalester with advisors who also serve as their instructors in their First Year Course. They later pick advisors from their major department. All are faculty members.

The best departments at Macalester are economics, political science, psychology, the sciences, and foreign languages. The classics department is also solid, focusing on traditional approaches to the discipline. Students recommend Brooke Lea and Jaine Strauss in psychology; Susan Fox in computer science; Rabbi Barry Cytron in religious studies; J. Andrew Overman in classics; Karen Warren (emerita) in philosophy; Vasant A. Sukhatme and Sarah E. West in economics; David Bressoud in math; and Sung Kyu Kim in physics.

Students complain that the religious studies department lacks courses on . . . well, Christianity. "There is only one professor who teaches Christian theology and she often-times likes to impart her feminist theology to her students," reports a student. "There are tons of world religion and Eastern religious tradition courses. . . . I have dealt with this problem by taking theology courses at the University of St. Thomas . . . and from George-town University." Courses that are offered range from "Introduction to Islamic Law" and "Folklore and Religion" to "Jesus, Dissent and Desire."

Not surprisingly, Macalester's study-abroad program is extensive. More than half of Macalester's students study abroad, with most of these away for a semester and some for an entire year, in any of more than forty countries.

The International Center and faculty members carefully advise students on choosing the best program for their course of study—whether it be a classroom program at King's College in London, a field-study program in China or Cypress, an intensive-language pro-gram in Russia, or an internship in Cameroon.

Macalester also offers a number of individualized study opportunities through the honors program, academic internships, and research collaborations. More than ninety stu-dents receive research grants to work with professors each summer. In the 2009–10 aca-demic year, 301 students from all disciplines were involved in internships in the Twin Cities and around the world.

Macalester offers strong language courses in Latin, Ancient Greek, Spanish, French, German, Japanese, Russian, Arabic, Chinese, and courses that focus on the language and culture of ancient Rome, Greece, and Israel.

Student Life: Kilts and kente

One of Macalester's most attractive features is its location—a charming, historic neighbor-hood of St. Paul, Minnesota. The college sits midway on St. Paul's tree-lined Grand Avenue, which stretches for some thirty blocks from the Mississippi River to downtown St. Paul. Stu-dents are within walking distance of eclectic shops, restaurants, movie theaters, big-box stores like Target, and no fewer than nine coffee shops. The Twin Cities of Minneapolis and St. Paul (joint population: 2.88 million) offer a wide range of cultural events, museums, lakes, and parks. Minnesotans are especially adept at finding ways to avoid cabin fever during the long, cold winters. The St. Paul Winter Carnival is the nation's oldest and largest winter festival, complete with an ice palace and a coronation of its own royalty, King Boreas and the Queen of the Snows. During the winter, students enjoy outdoor activities such as skiing, skating, and broomball—a hybrid of hockey and curling. Known for its Victorian homes, Summit Avenue attracts joggers and those who just want to stroll around this historic neighborhood.

Macalester's fifty-three-acre campus includes seven academic buildings, ten residence halls, five language houses, a health care facility, and a library and technology center—many linked together by underground tunnels. During the 1990s, virtually every building on campus was renovated, including the Olin-Rice Science Center and the Kagin Commons student services building. In 2008, the 175,000-square-foot, $45 million Leonard Center athletic and wellness complex was opened. It houses a swimming pool, gymnasium, fitness center, field house, activity studios, snack bar, hall of fame room, and other spaces for students to gather,

Students are required to live on campus for the first two years. Incoming freshmen are housed in one of three first-year buildings: Dupre, Doty, or Turck Hall. Most floors are coed, with single-sex bathrooms on each floor (Doty has alternating single-sex floors). Students can request to live in one of five language halls, or on smoke-free, substance-free, or noise-free floors. But not on sex-free floors: there are no restrictions on overnight visits from the opposite sex. Other options include Hebrew Hall, a Veggie Co-op, and a Cultural House, where students may live and grill their Tofurkey together. The Cultural House, which is run by the Department of Multicultural Life, boasts "newer style lofted beds." Off-campus housing can be difficult to secure, since Macalester's campus lies near two other small colleges in a prime real estate area, and housing is commensurately expensive. Still, because the school is short of dorms, juniors and seniors often have no other choice. Macalester does not have a Greek system.

ACADEMIC REQUIREMENTS

Macalester's rather lax distributional requirements run as follows. Each student must complete:

- One "First-Year" course, during the freshman year. These special sections of ordinary courses in various departments contain no more than sixteen students and are writing-intensive.
- Another writing-intensive class in any subject.
- Two courses in the social sciences. Options here range from "Foundations of U.S. Politics" to "Feminist/Queer Theories and Methodologies."
- Two classes in the natural sciences and mathematics.
- One, two, or three courses in quantitative reasoning, depending on the course.
- Three classes in the humanities and fine arts (including at least one in the humanities and one in the fine arts). Humanities options include "The Greek World" and "Postcolonial Theory." Art choices range from "History of Art" I to "Romanticism, Realism, and Impressionism."
- One course in "international diversity" and one in "domestic diversity." Courses to fulfill these requirements can be found in over a dozen departments.
- Coursework or test scores to demonstrate a fourth-semester proficiency in a foreign language.
- One course in U.S. multiculturalism. Several courses in the American studies department satisfy this requirement, including "African American Literature 1900–Present" and "Sociology of Race and Ethnicity."
- A senior capstone experience in a student's major.

The eighty-five student organizations listed on the college website reflect the ethnic, religious, and political diversity of Macalester's student body in groups such as the Black Liberation Affairs Committee, the Macalester Association for Sub-Continental Ethnic and Cultural Awareness, and Mac Soup—which is "devoted to creating a fun, wacky, original social environment based around cooking and eating wonderful food" and holds monthly social events. Students can join clubs like Mac Bike, Mac Salsa, Minnesota Nice, and Mac Clabber (for those interested in Scrabble). Recently, plans by the Cheeba Club (Creating a Harmless Environment to Enjoy Buds Appropriately) to host a marijuana festival were overruled by the administration. In 2007, Macalester was recognized as one of the one hundred best campuses for lesbian, gay, bisexual, and transgender (LGBT) students by the *Advocate College Guide for LGBT Students*, as the school boasted in a recent press release.

Conservatives at Macalester can resort to the MacGOP. Students interested in working for a newspaper can write for the *Mac Weekly*, an independent student newspaper established in 1914. There is also the active monthly newsletter of the Department of Multicultural Life

A controversy arose in 2009, when a conservative Macalester alumni group, Macalester Alumni of Moderation, was denied the right to hold a discussion on campus during a class reunion.

In one of its more harmless nods to internationalism, Macalester honors the Scottish heritage of one of its earliest benefactors, a businessman and philanthropist named Charles Macalester. In 1948, the Scottish Clan of MacAlister adopted the school as a member, and since then, Macalester has taken up everything Scottish—from the student pipe band to the school's nickname, the Scots.

Athletics have long been popular at Macalester, with many students participating in one way or another. The school fields twenty-one varsity teams, and the Scots compete in

RED LIGHT

In case you missed the point, Macalester hopes to produce students "willing to assume leadership in a multi-civilizational yet transnationalizing world." Those courses that do discuss the West are often fairly hostile. A student says, "I took an intro to world history course that ended up being taught from the perspective primarily of Central America and Africa. The reading material did not paint the West in the best light, and the professor was clearly and openly a Marxist. . . . At the same time, she was always respectful toward me when I would disagree with one of our readings, and I never felt uncomfortable discussing my views in the class setting."

"At a school as liberal and atheist/agnostically oriented as Macalester," says a student, "you may, if you are conservative or religious, find classes and discussions to sometimes be an uncomfortable environment. Mac is not for the fainthearted conservative or religious person. If you want your beliefs heard, you can certainly expect opposition and in extreme cases ridicule. Overall, though, most students and professors are accepting of others' different viewpoints or viewpoints contrary to that of the Macalester mainstream. Although they may vehemently disagree and debate against you, your views will often times be respected." Another conservative student says, "I think the best way to sum things up is that almost everyone will respect you if you are respectful in return and if you can back up what you say and believe."

the Minnesota Intercollegiate Athletic Conference (MIAC), a league of small colleges in the area. There is a healthy rivalry with neighboring Hamline and St. Thomas colleges. Macalester women's water polo teams are also among the teams with the highest national grades and in 2009–10 came out on top for the third year in a row with a GPA of 3.52.

There is a lively party scene, although students complain that on-campus parties are cramped and sweaty thanks to small rooms and few alternative venues. So those who are of age and have a set of wheels take refuge in St. Paul's lively bar scene. Off-campus parties are popular, though students complain of police intrusions and subsequent walks home through the icy Minnesota night. Given the heavy workload at Macalester, students don't party as hard as they do at neighboring schools like the University of Michigan—whose events Macalester students often attend.

In 2006, the Chaplain's Office in Weyerhaeuser Memorial Chapel was renamed the Center for Religious and Spiritual Life, a name that, according to the center's website, uses more "inclusive terms." The center exists to "recognize and affirm the diversity of religious and cultural experience at Macalester College," providing worship opportunities for Christians, Jews, and Muslims as well as lecture series, films, and meditation sessions. The chaplain is a Presbyterian minister, Rev. Lucy Forster-Smith. Staff members include a Macalester graduate who, according to the school website, "is intensely involved in the national movement for the full inclusion of gay, lesbian, bisexual and transgendered persons within religious communities." Catholic students may resort to Bob O'Donnell, CSP, assistant director for religious and spiritual life and Catholic chaplain. (More traditional Catholic students should certainly check out the local mecca for Gregorian chant, the exquisite Church of St. Agnes.) Religious clubs on campus include the Mac Baha'i Association, Fellowship of Christian Athletes, Mac Catholics, Mac Jewish Organization, Mac Protestants (a liberal group), the Macalester Christian Fellowship (a more evangelical group), Mac Unitarian Universalist, the Muslim Student Association, Macalester Association of Alternative Spiritualities (Wiccan), and Sitting@Mac (Zen Buddhist).

Macalester is a relatively safe campus, given its urban location. The college reported four forcible sex offenses and two burglaries on campus in 2009. A student says, "Although the campus is very safe itself (various security personnel can be seen strolling around at any time of day), I wouldn't venture too far off of it alone after the sun goes down."

Tuition for 2010–11 was $39,846, plus $9,078 for room and board. In 2005, the college switched from a need-blind to "need-aware" admissions policy. Some 67 percent of students receive need-based financial aid, and the average student-loan debt of a recent graduate was $15,698.

University of Michigan

Ann Arbor, Michigan • www.umich.edu

Acting affirmatively

The University of Michigan prides itself as "leaders and the best," or at least Michigan's 107,000 football fans like to think so on autumn Saturday mornings as they file into Michigan Stadium to watch the Wolverines (usually) pummel an opponent. Whether it is Michigan's focus on research or its unwavering devotion to racial variety, Michigan has arguably become the standard bearer for America's public research universities. More's the pity.

Michigan made headlines with its Supreme Court battle in defense of affirmative action. Its English department recently added a "New Traditions" requirement, which requires a course "focusing on the cultural traditions of women, minority ethnic groups, and people of color." The university is a popcorn popper of outrageous ideas, and conservatives face quite a struggle in countering them.

Michigan has many remarkable features. The university is huge, accommodating more than 40,000 students, 8 million library books, 500 buildings, and 17,000 trees representing more than 150 species. Then there is the massive budget (over $5 billion in fiscal year 2008–9, larger than that of several *states*), which allows the university to attract some of the nation's best scholars and most talented students. There are plenty of both at Michigan, and a good number of solid and serious classes. But they're hidden, along with many other needles, in one great big haystack.

Academic Life: Behemoth U.

Like most state universities, Michigan has abandoned the core curriculum that once required of every liberal arts student that he gain a broad exposure to Western civilization. Instead, Michigan students must pick from a broad buffet of distributional requirements, many of which can be fulfilled with politicized or overly specialized courses. But students who want a solid education can find one here.

Michigan's honors program is one of the most respected in the country. New students in the College of Literature, Science, and the Arts (LSA) generally join it by invitation only, although interested students with good transcripts may apply. Honors students face a first-rate curriculum: They must take either a humanities course on classical civilizations or the Great Books during their first two semesters, along with two special courses

VITAL STATISTICS

Religious affiliation: *none*
Total enrollment: *41,674*
Total undergraduates: *26,208*
SAT/ACT midranges: CR: *590–690*, M: *640–740*; ACT: *27–31*
Applicants: *30,005*
Applicants accepted: *50%*
Accepted applicants who enrolled: *41%*
Tuition and fees: *in state, $11,470; out of state, $35,974*
Room and board: *$8,924*
Freshman retention rate: *96%*
Graduation rate: *73% (4 yrs.), 89% (6 yrs.)*
Courses with fewer than 20 students: *46%*
Student-faculty ratio: *15:1*
Courses taught by graduate students: *not provided*
Most popular majors: *social sciences, engineering, psychology*
Students living on campus: *63%*
Guaranteed housing for four years? *no*
Students in fraternities: *15%* in sororities: *19%*

each semester. The honors Literature and Ideas offerings include "Shakespeare's Principal Plays," "Arts and Letters of China," and "Faust." Some students choose to live in special honors housing.

Sources praise Michigan's Great Books Program, which starts with a two-semester sequence exposing students to canonical works from ancient Greece through the Renaissance. The history course "Debates of the Founding Fathers" covers the "making of the American Constitution, both as an intellectual and as a political event." In "Great Books of Modern Literature," students read *Don Quixote*, *Faust*, *Crime and Punishment*, *Madame Bovary*, and *Huckleberry Finn*. Other worthy options include "Great Books in Physics" and "Great Books of Japan."

The University of Michigan employs some of the nation's finest scholars, including several Nobel Prize winners. Of course, it varies how accessible these celebrity instructors are to undergraduates. As one student says, teaching "always comes second, after getting published." This student charges that although professors dutifully hold office hours and teach the obligatory lecture courses, "in reality, they largely couldn't care less about the classes they're teaching." Another student says that the quality of instruction is uneven: "They know what they are talking about, but do not know how to present it to a class." Upper-level courses often fill up quickly. "You practically have to beg, borrow, and steal to get into any 400-level classes," says one student.

Lectures are generally given and received in the Teutonic style: professors read them and students take notes, sometimes in one of the world's largest lecture halls, "Chemistry 1800" for example, which seats 500 students. One junior reports that she has never actually spoken personally with a professor. During the weekly discussion sections, TAs gloss course readings and delve more deeply into areas in which students have questions. If a student needs individual attention, he has to fight for it.

Michigan is massive and can appear overwhelming, and its advising program does little to remedy that. Advising for LSA students starts with a professional or peer advisor. Once a student declares a major, he can visit an advisor within his department. Students do not have specific faculty advisors assigned to them, and many students never establish academic relationships with faculty members. Almost every department has its bright spots, but the most respected departments are history, political science, classical studies, anthropology,

Midwest

chemistry, physics, engineering, Judaic studies, Chinese, psychology, economics, business administration, mathematics, Near Eastern studies, neuroscience, art history, and the Medieval and Renaissance Collegium.

Students name the following as some of the best undergraduate teachers: Gary Solon (emeritus) in economics; Ejner Jensen, John Knott (emeritus), and Ralph G. Williams in English; H. D. Cameron, Ludwig Koenen, and Charles Witke (emeritus) in classical studies; Astrid Beck and Scott Spector in German; John Fine Jr., Diane Owen Hughes, Rudolf Mrázek, and William G. Rosenberg in history; Ronald Inglehart and Greg Markus in political science; and Christopher Peterson in psychology.

Michigan's philosophy department is strong. Majors are required to take courses in logic, the history of philosophy, value philosophy, mind and reality, plus three more advanced-level classes. Unfortunately, a course in ancient philosophy is not required. The classical studies department offers concentrations in archeology, civilization, Ancient Greek and Latin, and modern Greek.

Michigan imposes a one-course race and ethnicity (R&E) requirement that, says one student, is "basically a course on why the white man is evil." Students select from a list that includes "From Harems to Terrorists: Representing the Middle East in Hollywood Cinema,"

> ### SUGGESTED CORE
> 1. Great Books 191
> 2. Great Books 202 or Classical Civilizations 388, History of Ancient Philosophy
> 3. Near Eastern Studies 121/122, Introduction to the Tanakh/Old Testament; Introduction to the New Testament
> 4. No suitable course
> 5. Political Science 302, Development of Political Thought: Modern and Recent
> 6. English 367/368, Shakespeare's Plays: The Elizabethan Years/The Jacobean Years
> 7. History 260, The United States to 1860
> 8. History 416, Nineteenth-Century German and European Intellectual History

"Introduction to Latina/o Studies," and "Asians in American Film and Television." Ideology also appears in many humanities courses—for instance, as one young woman tells us, "when you go into a class on Jane Austen and get a lecture on lesbians." The English department in particular is notorious for forcing feminist and leftist ideology onto students.

One student says, "It is often difficult to be the only person in a class to take a conservative stance on an issue and have to defend it against thirty of your classmates. It is even more difficult to write a paper and get a good grade when you disagree with what the professor says. Sometimes you have to sell out on your political beliefs for a good grade."

The university also allows creative-expression courses to satisfy distribution requirements. An article in the *Michigan Review*—an independent, right-leaning campus paper—complains that such measures have meant that a "strong classical education has been tossed aside and replaced with a cheaper, dumbed-down, cute and fuzzy, touchy-feely version that churns out moronic alumni who are unable to argue effectively, write profoundly, or think critically." Not to put too fine a point on it. However, the Great Books and the honors program offer a serious, intellectually challenging education—better than many other state schools can promise.

The requirements for English majors at Michigan are middling: students must complete nine upper-level classes, including three courses on literature before 1830, one of which must focus on literature before 1600, as well as an American literature class and a "New Traditions" course that emphasizes the "cultural traditions of women, minority ethnic groups, and people of color." Students could well emerge without having studied Shakespeare.

Political science students choose a concentration within the major (two classes in introductory Political Theory, American Politics, Comparative Politics, or World Politics), then complete five courses in two of those fields selected. Thus they could well graduate without having studied the U.S. Constitution or political system.

In the history department, majors take an introductory survey sequence in regional history (two classes focused on medieval and modern Europe, ancient Greece and Rome, East Asia, South and Southeast Asia, Africa, or the United States). Following the introduction, students take another eight classes, including a writing-intensive colloquium, that include a course each in U.S. and European history, two courses in non-Western history, and one class on pre-1800 history. While they must study U.S. history, they need not cover the American founding or the Civil War.

While each department attempts to provide some structure to its students, it would be all too easy for an undergraduate to graduate with a major in which he has no substantial knowledge—and in which he has simply taken one class per semester. Students would be wise to carefully consider their options to ensure they are pursuing a well-rounded approach to their chosen field.

Study-abroad programs send students throughout the Middle East, Africa, Asia, Australia, the Americas, and Europe. Michigan provides summer-, term-, and year-long programs for exchange and study-abroad students, as well as field studies as extensions to on-campus courses. For those who are interested, Michigan provides short-term service projects in the U.S. and worldwide through the Global Intercultural Experience for Undergraduates. Finally, Michigan sponsors half-term language-intensive programs in which students live with host families and can complete their foreign language requirements.

Nearly forty foreign tongues are taught on campus, and Michigan (laudably) requires students to reach the fourth-term level of a second language in order to graduate. Options range from Ojibwa, German, Italian, and Serbo-Croatian to Yiddish, Dutch, and Urdu. Perhaps as a result of this university-wide commitment to foreign study, the university has yielded record numbers of Fulbright Scholars in recent years, including forty-three in 2010–11.

Student Life: Numbers games

Ann Arbor, one of the nation's great college towns, is just a short walk from the dorms. Both on and off campus, Michigan students have a vast number of musical and cultural performances from which to choose, as well as theater, film, and comedy acts. Students enjoy canoeing on the Huron River or jogging in the arboretum, playing Frisbee in the Diag (the central part of campus, named for its diagonal sidewalks), or studying outdoors. As one student says, Michigan is "a very relaxed place to go to school."

With a total enrollment of more than 40,000, the University of Michigan is practically a city unto itself, but students can make it seem a lot smaller by taking advantage of certain campus residential options. Just over a third of undergraduates—including nearly all freshmen—live on campus. The university guarantees housing for the first year only. Michigan's dormitories include high-rise apartment buildings, old-fashioned houses, and large halls housing more than 9,500 students. Most of the dormitories are coed, separating sexes by floor, but the university does have three all-female dormitories, like the Betsy Barbour house, for women who request them. The Martha Cook Building, a quieter residence with sit-down dinners and teas, is an all-women dormitory that maintains limited visitation hours for men. The Henderson House offers all-female housing in a co-op style. Admirably, the university does not maintain coed bathrooms or coed dorm rooms. Just over one-quarter of the university's residence halls, floors, and rooms are substance-free.

For those who choose to live off campus, the housing department provides information and advice on finding apartments. However, local rents are generally high; housing

---

ACADEMIC REQUIREMENTS

Michigan imposes no core curriculum, but liberal arts students in the College of Literature, Science, and the Arts must take the following:

- A first-year writing class, which can be fulfilled by a broad variety of choices like "Nietzsche: Philosopher and Psychologist" and "Seeding the Future: Children's Literature and the Arts of Citizenship."
- An upper-level writing course on topics like "Moral Principles and Problems," "The Paradoxes of Time Travel" or "Phenomenology and Existential Philosophy."
- A race and ethnicity course, which can be checked off with an introduction to Latina/o, Asian/Pacific American, or Arab-American studies, or a course like "Culture, Racism, and Human Nature."
- One or two courses in quantitative reasoning, such as calculus, "Experimental Economics" or "An Introduction to Cryptology."

Students also take ten classes outside their major field of concentration, spread across the following five categories and including at least one class in each:

- Natural sciences ("Nutrition and Evolution" "Physics of Music," "Psychology of Thinking," "Biotechnology and Human Values").
- Social sciences ("American Indian History," "The Archaeology of Michigan," "Media and Public Opinion," "Modern Europe").
- Humanities ("Israel before the Exile," "Russia Today," "American Values," "Faust," "Shakespeare and His World," "History of Music").
- Mathematical and symbolic analysis ("Data, Functions, and Graphs," "Explorations in Numbers Theory," "Logic and Language").
- Creative expression ("Printmaking for Non-Majors," "Harp," "Congolese Dance," "Gospel Chorale," "Screenwriting").

Students must also demonstrate proficiency in a foreign language at the fourth-term level, either through coursework or tests.

should be arranged more than six months in advance (unless you enjoy walking a mile to class). Most students choose to live in the "student ghetto" south of campus, but many other options exist. For instance, several faith- and service-based groups offer options for Michigan students who want to live in a more wholesome environment.

Although only about 17 percent of students join fraternities or sororities, some students say the Greek system dominates campus life, at least on the weekends. Especially during their first semester, students often attend house and fraternity parties, usually held in the organizations' off-campus houses. One student says that "beer cans litter Frat Row" and that on the weekends "drunk, skimpily clad individuals can often be seen walking the streets."

Life at Michigan isn't just about fraternities and beer: there is also athletics. Football games at "the Big House" (Michigan Stadium, college football's largest, and the world's fourth-largest, stadium—with a seating capacity of 107,501) are incredibly popular. Students can currently buy football season tickets for $207, including admission to games with Michigan's three greatest football rivals—Michigan State, Ohio State, and Notre Dame (when they play in Ann Arbor). The atmosphere at men's basketball games is considerably more subdued, with Michigan's Crisler Arena said to be the quietest in the Big Ten Conference. Hockey fans, on the other hand, are known for their out-of-control antics and lewd cheers. The university offers students an extensive intramurals program—twenty-six sports, like broomball, racquetball, table tennis, and running—and fields forty-seven teams for intercollegiate club sports competition, including water polo, rugby, rifle sports, and ninjitsu.

Michigan's sheer size can make students feel like just a number, but as one student says, "the best thing to do is check out a bunch of organizations and groups at the beginning of the year and try to get involved in anything. It is difficult to make friends in class, so if you can become active in a group, you can have a core set of friends and expand from there." Surely one of UM's 1,000-plus clubs will be of interest.

The school offers thirteen different categories of clubs, from architecture and medical clubs like the American Pre-Medical Club, Black Pre-Medical Association, and Medical Students for Choice. Engineering clubs include Michigan Entrepreneurs, Biomedical Engineering Society, the award-winning Solar Car Team, and the Society of Hispanic Professional Engineers. There are two chemistry clubs and a number of business and law clubs, like the E-commerce Club, Consulting Club, and Mock Trial. Michigan has a respectable list of honor societies and student government and assemblies.

Student athletic and recreational organizations provide an alternative to the school's already-impressive list of athletic teams. Students may choose from an Alpine Ski Team, Juggling Arts Club, Indoor Track team, and Ballroom Dance Club. Recreational groups like the Wolverine Soft video-game development group, Fantasy and Science Fiction club, Photography Club, Chess Club, and Debate Team cater to more subdued activity.

Service-oriented clubs like the Animal Rights Society, Habitat for Humanity, and Relay for Life exist alongside politically motivated clubs like Model United Nations, College Republicans, Amnesty International, Anti-War Action!, and the Environmental Justice Group. The *Michigan Daily*, the official student newspaper, strives mightily to maintain impeccable leftist credentials. Students for Choice sponsors a few big-name pro-abortion speakers each year.

Politically conservative students will want to get involved with the College Republicans, an extremely active group that sponsors close to a dozen speakers and events each year, in addition to organizing trips to state and national Republican Conventions. The club is exceptional at finding internship opportunities for its members and providing many leadership positions within the organization through its various committees. Another group, Independent Students for Liberty, bills itself as a "socially liberal and economically conservative" stripe of the Libertarian Party, but it is essentially just a moderate wing of the College Democrats.

In keeping with its commitment to multiculturalism, Michigan has a long list of minority and ethnic groups, from the International Student Organization, Polish and Italian clubs to Armenian, Filipino, Indian, Lebanese, Turkish, African, Punjabi, and Hong Kong Student associations.

For the religiously inclined, Michigan has a variety of organizations, mostly nondenominational or evangelical, including Campus Crusade, All Nations Campus Ministry, Intervarsity, Campus Chapel, Christians on Campus, Students in Christ, New Life Church, Christian Challenge, and Harvest Mission Community Church. Other groups consist of Adventist Students for Christ, an Episcopal Center, Hillel, Muslim Students' Association, University Lutheran Chapel, the Catholic St. Mary Student Parish, and the Hindu Students Council.

> **YELLOW LIGHT**
>
> Michigan has shaky credentials when it comes to freedom of speech. It evicted the conservative *Michigan Review* from its offices, has limited the time of year and manner in which fliers can be distributed or posted, and implemented a speech code that forbids students from knowingly exposing others to "offensive material." Speech-code violations can include teasing someone about his accent, criticizing traditional clothing, or engaging in a Yankee-vs.-Southerner debate with a friend. Nevertheless, sources say that Michigan has been reasonably accommodating to pro-life and conservative groups. Students report that there used to be real discrimination against conservatives in campus employment—and Army ROTC members report being graded down and harassed because of their enlistment—but the hostility has begun to abate, perhaps because of the change in the military's "don't ask, don't tell" policy.

Despite the best efforts of the school, crime at the University of Michigan is a cause for concern. In 2009, forty-five forcible sexual offenses, six robberies, twenty aggravated assaults, two counts of arson, forty-one burglaries, and seventeen motor vehicle thefts were reported on campus. However, one junior says, "I feel very safe on campus. In a college community, it is pretty easy to spot people who do not belong." Emergency phones are placed throughout campus, and policemen patrol the campus and surrounding streets on bikes.

As a school with an Ivy reputation, the University of Michigan is undeniably a bargain for in-state students, at only $11,470 in 2010–11. Out-of-state students paid $35,974. Room and board (for a standard double) cost $8,924. Admissions are not need blind, nor does the school guarantee to meet students' full need. According to university data, 46 percent of students receive some sort of aid—but that number includes students receiving athletic scholarships and work study. The average student graduates with a sizable $26,819 in loan debt.

Northwestern University

Evanston, Illinois • www.northwestern.edu

Growing ivy in Evanston

A little more than 150 years ago, Northwestern University was founded to serve students in the Northwest Territory—an area that became the states of Ohio, Indiana, Illinois, Michigan, Wisconsin, and Minnesota. Today Northwestern is a national university with an international scope. A seasoned professor credits Henry Bienen, Northwestern's former president, with developing the school into a kind of midwestern Ivy. Bienen retired in 2009 and was replaced by Morton Owen Schapiro, a professor of economics who previously served as president of Williams College. The administration continues to make admission more selective as the school boosts its profile as a research university.

Northwestern has no required core curriculum, and degree requirements are decided individually by each of Northwestern's eleven schools and colleges. Among the six undergraduate schools, over half of all students are enrolled in the Weinberg College of Arts and Sciences. On campus, religion and spirituality are considered "a personal thing," a student tells us, and while the campus political climate is decidedly left of center, it is mostly respectful of opposing views.

Academic Life: Freedonian studies

Besides its main undergraduate division, the Weinberg College of Arts and Sciences, Northwestern's Evanston's campus includes the Medill School of Journalism, the School of Communication, the School of Education and Social Policy, the McCormick School of Engineering and Applied Science, the School of Continuing Studies, and the Bienen School of Music, as well as a graduate school, the Kellogg School of Management, and the Garrett-Evangelical Theological Seminary. Northwestern's impressive law and medical schools are located in nearby Chicago, allowing some students and faculty to take advantage of both campuses.

Weinberg College of Arts and Sciences enrolls almost 52 percent of Northwestern's 8,637 undergraduates. In it, students find a wide variety of academic choices—including some twenty-nine departments, thirty-seven majors, ten adjunct majors, and fifty-four minors. All Weinberg freshmen are required to take two thematic writing seminars, which include no more than fifteen students. Students should be especially careful in choosing freshman seminars because their seminar instructors are also their pre-major advisors and the evaluators of their writing proficiency.

The school offers no core curriculum but does have a decent set of distribution requirements. Students choose two courses from each of the following areas: natural sciences; formal studies; social and behavioral sciences; historical studies; ethics and values; and literature and fine arts, in addition to demonstrated proficiency in a foreign language. Although the majority of course offerings appear to be solid, some do appeal to grudge-driven identity politics. Despite the lax curriculum, Northwestern students typically have the foresight to choose courses from a variety of disciplines. One professor says few students graduate from NU without taking a broad range of classes.

Some majors, such as American studies, integrate different fields of study within the major in order to gain a broader understanding. There are also "ad hoc" majors that are created by students (with the approval of a faculty curriculum review committee) whose interests don't fit neatly into a traditional major. Students can also take "professional linkage seminars," which are led by non-academic professionals with the goal of linking a liberal arts education to professional issues. Students can initiate their own courses under the supervision of a faculty member.

Northwestern is one of just a few universities using the quarter system (three quarters plus a summer session), which means students face exam periods no fewer than six times a year, counting midterms and finals. "I always feel like I'm studying for some final or another," one student says. Time management is one key to success here; the other is course selection.

Northwestern seems to strike a reasonable balance between its commitments to research and to teaching. One humanities professor says there is keen pressure to "publish or perish" and that faculty members are supposed to spend 45 percent of their time on research, 45 percent on teaching, and 10 percent on administrative projects. Professors in the sciences, where the pressure to publish is perhaps greatest, tend to have lighter teaching loads.

One benefit of the strong emphasis on research is that undergraduates can take part in it and get paid to do so. The university supports this through several funds. To reward those professors who are actively working with their students in their endeavors, the university offers an award for excellence in "mentoring undergraduate research." Despite the emphasis on research productivity, however, one student says his "professors seem gen-

VITAL STATISTICS

Religious affiliation: *none*
Total enrollment: *18,935*
Total undergraduates: *8,637*
SAT/ACT midranges: CR: *670–750*, M: *690–780*; ACT: *30–33*
Applicants: *25,013*
Applicants accepted: *26%*
Accepted applicants who enrolled: *32%*
Tuition and fees: *$40,247*
Room and board: *$12,240*
Freshman retention rate: *97%*
Graduation rate: *87% (4 yrs.), 95% (6 yrs.)*
Courses with fewer than 20 students: *73%*
Student-faculty ratio: *7:1*
Courses taught by graduate students: *2%*
Most popular majors: *engineering, economics, journalism*
Students living on campus: *65%*
Guaranteed housing for four years? *no*
Students in fraternities: *32%* in sororities: *38%*

SUGGESTED CORE

1. Classics 211, Classical Greece
2. Philosophy 210, History of Philosophy: Ancient Philosophy
3. Religion 220/221, Introduction to the Hebrew Bible/ New Testament
4. Religion 340-341, Foundations of Christian Thought I (Early or Traditional Christianity)
5. Political Science 201-2, History of Political Thought II
6. English 234, Introduction to Shakespeare
7. History 210-11, History of the United States (Precolonial to the Civil War)
8. Political Science 303, Modernity and Its Discontents

erally interested in students. I haven't had one yet that wasn't concerned with my academic soul." Some professors focus more on research than teaching, but one faculty member notes that since Northwestern boasts many superb instructors, "there is a teaching culture here by tradition and so it's pretty good."

The admissions office boasts that NU faculty members teach 98 percent of courses. However, in larger lecture courses, professors typically teach twice a week, with students breaking up into smaller discussion groups, taught by graduate teaching assistants, once a week. Professors are described as "available" to those who "take the initiative," although, as one student puts it, "they are not going to hold your hand." A professor describes his students as "very curious" and adds that they "respond to good teaching and make it very rewarding." Students looking for professor reviews can access the CTEC (Course and Teacher Evaluation Council), which collects and records student evaluations of faculty.

Students and faculty have identified the following as particularly strong teachers: Gary Saul Morson, Andrew Baruch Wachtel, and Irwin Weil (emeritus) in Slavic languages and literature; Joel Mokyr, T. H. Breen, and Edward Muir in history; Kenneth Seeskin and Charles Taylor in philosophy; Mary Kinzie in English; Robert A. Gundlach in linguistics and the Writing Program; Sandra L. Hindman (emeritus) in art history; Andrew Koppelman in political science and law; Martin Mueller and Robert Wallace in classics; and Robert Gordon, Mark Witte, and 2010 Nobel Prize winner Dale Mortensen in economics.

Northwestern's Medill journalism program is regarded as a leader in the field nationwide, with a long list of graduates who have won the Pulitzer Prize. The School of Communication's theater program boasts graduates such as actors Charlton Heston, Warren Beatty, Julia Louis-Dreyfus, and producer-director Garry Marshall. The McCormick School of Engineering and Applied Science is consistently strong, which is not surprising since its faculty includes twenty-six members of the National Academy of Sciences and twenty-one members of the National Academy of Engineering.

The presence of the Kellogg management school helps boost the undergraduate economics program, which is consistently ranked in the top five in the nation by *Bloomberg BusinessWeek*. Other strong departments, according to students and teachers, include Slavic languages and literature and English. Within the English department, students may choose to major in either literature or writing. English majors are not required to take a Shakespeare class, although such courses are offered, but they must take at least three courses of literature written before 1798 and three written after. Only one class must be in American literature.

The political science department is solid, requiring students to acquaint themselves with Plato, Aristotle, Machiavelli, Hobbes, Locke, Rousseau, Madison, Mill, and Marx, among others. An American political philosophy class is a required course, although one in the U.S. Constitution is not.

History is a popular department at Northwestern, although the major requirements are quite weak: students are not required to take basic Western civilization or American history classes unless those topics fall under the rubric of their concentration.

The comparative literary studies, international studies, Latino studies, gender studies, and race and ethnicity studies programs are predictably leftist in tone and course content, but the economics department features several noteworthy free-market economists. Of Weinberg College's twenty-nine departments, a few could fairly be described as "politically correct," students report, including Asian American studies, Latin American and Caribbean studies, Jewish studies, and African American studies. A professor in the social sciences calls the profusion of ethnic studies departments a "waste of university resources." One teacher who has sat on hiring committees says that ideology "has not undermined things viciously," but in his own department he has seen candidates eliminated for their political views. According to Campusreform.org (based on data from the liberal Huffington Post), "93% of Northwestern faculty and staff who contributed to presidential cam-

---

ACADEMIC REQUIREMENTS

Students in Northwestern's liberal arts college face a series of distribution requirements and other mandates. Students need to take two courses in each of six areas:

- Natural sciences. Choices include "Molecular and Biochemical Biology" and "Sound Patterns in Human Language."
- Formal studies (math, statistics, and linguistics). Options include "Finite Mathematics" and "Harmony."
- Social and behavioral sciences. Choices range from "Introduction to Microeconomics" to "Gender, Power, and Culture in America."
- Historical studies. Options run from "Early Western Civilization" to "Sexuality and Its Discontents."
- Ethics and values. Choices range from "The Bible as Literature" to "Language, Politics, and Identity."
- Literature and fine arts. Options include "Renaissance Art" and "Survey of African American Literature."

Up to six of the above twelve courses may be satisfied by high scores on AP exams. Students must complete:

- Two freshman writing seminars. Seminar topics in 2011 included "Utopian Literature" and "How to Become an Expert in Roughly Ten Weeks."
- Three foreign language classes or otherwise demonstrate proficiency to the intermediate level.

paigns in 2008 donated to Democratic candidates. In all, 313 people donated more than $303,400 to Democrats—and just 25 gave money to Republicans."

Beware Northwestern's courses on human sexuality. In 2011, the campus was sickened by the following turn of events, as reported by the *Weekly Standard*:

> A tenured professor, teaching a heavily attended undergraduate course on human sexuality, decided to bring in a woman, who, with the aid of what was euphemistically called "a sex toy" (uneuphemistically, it appears to have been an electric dildo), attempted to achieve a climax in the presence of the students. The professor alerted his students about this extraordinary show-and-tell session, and made clear that attendance was voluntary. The standard account has it that 120 or so of the 622 students enrolled in the course showed up. Questions about what they had witnessed, the professor punctiliously noted, would not be on the exam.

Northwestern is known for its many opportunities for study abroad, with its overseas programs receiving enthusiastic reviews from students. The Study-Abroad Office coordinates over a hundred programs on six continents. Students can study abroad for just a summer or up to a full year. Since 2008, Northwestern has operated a satellite campus in Qatar, which offers bachelors degrees in journalism and communications. At home, students may study Chinese, Hebrew, Japanese, Korean, Persian, Swahili, Turkish, Latin, Ancient Greek, French, Italian, German, Portuguese, Polish, and Arabic.

Student Life: North by Northwestern

Although Northwestern students spend the majority of their time studying, there are many attractions nearby to lure them outside the library. The university's attractive 240-acre campus is located in the Evanston suburb, a few blocks from Lake Michigan and just ten miles north of downtown Chicago. The School of Music features frequent performances on campus, and the school sometimes hosts musicians from Chicago's jazz venues.

Several building projects are currently under way or were recently completed at the Evanston Campus. In 2009, the university opened the Richard and Barbara Silverman Hall for Molecular Therapeutics and Diagnosis, and renovation of Harris Hall (constructed in 1915), home to the department of history and general university classrooms, began in the spring of 2009. A garden-level addition is underway to accommodate the heightened demand for history faculty offices and classrooms. With nearly five million volumes, the university's book collection ranks tenth in size among America's private universities.

One student says NU is "definitely not a party school." Students are said to be heavily career-oriented. More than a third of undergraduates are members of the thirty-nine recognized fraternities or sororities, but even these organizations are not especially focused on partying. Besides the Greek system, student life at NU offers a full range of over 400 student groups and organizations, including 64 Squares (a chess club), Boomshaka (percussion-dance performance), Lovers & Madmen (a theater group devoted to Shakespeare), the Outing Club, College Republicans, and College Democrats.

There are several Christian groups on campus: Campus Crusade, Catholic Undergrads, and InterVarsity, to name a few. NU is also home to the Zen Society, the Rainbow Alliance, Northwestern Students for Life, Hillel, For Members Only (a black student group), and a long list of other ethnic, cultural, and religious organizations.

The university also sponsors festivals like the annual Dillo Day, during which students drink prodigious quantities of alcohol while listening to big-name bands, and the Dance Marathon, in which 500 students dance for thirty hours to raise money for charity. One of Northwestern's traditions is to "paint the rock," a big boulder in the middle of campus that students and campus groups have been painting to promote causes or events since the 1940s.

One professor notes a "dramatic improvement in the quality of athletics" in recent years. The Northwestern men's and women's Wildcats play nineteen varsity sports, from football to fencing, in the Big Ten Conference. In 2009, a total of 184 athletes received Academic All-Big Ten honors. But Northwestern isn't known for its sports success or student enthusiasm; the stands only fill up when teams are winning. Still, NU students have achieved excellence in a few sports. The women's lacrosse team won five consecutive NCAA I national championships since 2005. The football team, in spite of holding the all-time record of Division I-A losses, went to the Outback Bowl in 2010. (The last bowl game Northwestern won was the 1949 Rose Bowl.)

Intramurals at Northwestern range from equestrian sports to aikido and Ultimate Frisbee, while club sports such as tennis, billiards, and dodgeball provide a break from classroom pressures. Northwestern's high-quality recreation centers allow students

YELLOW LIGHT

The political atmosphere on campus is mixed, with some departments known as more conservative and others leaning to the left. Insiders speak of Northwestern as "liberal" but "nonaggressive." While the majority of professors seem to be politically liberal, they were described as largely "fair." The faculty certainly spans the political spectrum to include former terrorist Bernardine Dohrn; Holocaust denier Arthur Butz; leftist columnist Garry Wills; Templeton Prize winner Charles Taylor; Barack Obama's political advisor David Axelrod; Nobel laureates chemist John Pople and economist Dale Mortensen; and the author of "don't ask, don't tell," military sociologist Charles Moskos. But for the most part, political issues don't enter the classroom unless they further an academic understanding of a subject.

Northwestern does have the usual cadre of politically active students. The weekly *Northwestern Chronicle* offers news and commentary from a somewhat conservative point of view. The main student newspaper, the *Daily Northwestern*, is more liberal. The College Republicans sponsor conservative speakers a few times each year—although, unlike the College Democrats, they rarely pack the house.

Sadly, according to the Foundation for Individual Rights in Education, Northwestern's policy on "Hate Crimes and Bias Incidents" is so broadly written that it could easily be used to suppress the free expression of conservative views (for instance, on social issues).

Northwestern's law school employs several prominent members of the Federalist Society, a group that one NU professor calls "a great font of conservative and libertarian scholarship."

to participate in swimming, racquetball, aerobics, and other sports. The Sailing Center maintains a fleet of boats and provides instruction in how to sail them on Lake Michigan.

Sixty-five percent of NU's approximately 8,600 undergraduates live in the fifteen university residence halls. Residents choose from a wide variety of living arrangements, from small houses to huge dormitories to residential colleges. Students also have the option of single-sex or coed residences and can take their meals at any of the dining halls, which are located in the residences. All bathrooms are single sex. The eleven residential colleges at NU are intellectual living communities organized around different interests, such as engineering, community service, and the arts. Activities and special programs relate to each residence's theme. Masters and fellows are professors who are actively involved in each college.

Northwestern has managed to keep campus crime down during the past few years. However, as one student says, "At night, most girls I know don't walk alone." The university continues to take precautions. For instance, the Northwestern police patrol twenty-four hours a day, there are blue emergency lights scattered across campus, and there's a free escort service if a student needs to be picked up anywhere in Evanston. In 2009, Northwestern reported five forcible sex offenses, one car theft, one aggravated assault, and seventy-six burglaries on campus.

Northwestern stands with other well-known schools in charging a hefty tuition—$40,247 in 2010–11, with $12,240 for room and board. Financial aid is based on need, and the school guarantees to meet the full financial needs of students. Forty-two percent of students receive need-based aid, and the average indebtedness of a recent NU grad was $20,802.

University of Notre Dame

South Bend, Indiana • www.nd.edu

Land o' lapsed

The University of Notre Dame has long been one of the most visible Roman Catholic universities in the United States—known as much for its football program as for academics. In decades past, students could rest assured of the Catholic identity of the school, but this began to be undermined in 1967, when a group of Catholic college and university officials, gathering at Notre Dame's retreat in Land O' Lakes, decided that a firm Catholic identity was a liability in an increasingly secular age. Following Notre Dame's lead, these educators seceded from church authority and committed themselves to following the trends dominating secular education. As a result, few Catholic colleges in the United States are, well, Catholic.

At Notre Dame, a healthy core of faithful Catholic students and many of the faculty have persisted in fighting for the school's religious identity and its tradition of liberal arts education. However, the leadership of the university, especially its governing board and president (Rev. John Jenkins), have largely supported the ongoing secularization of the school and its moves toward emphasizing research over teaching. Notes an insider, "People thought that Fr. Jenkins would tilt things back towards a traditional outlook, but he has allowed the *Vagina Monologues* and alienated conservatives on campus. He also inaugurated a campus-wide yearly 'forum' centered around some big, liberal hot-button issue such as health care, immigration, or global warming." Notre Dame is still in play, and for many it can offer a solid education in a comparatively wholesome atmosphere. For how much longer this will be true, we cannot say.

Academic Life: Under the golden dome

ND has long had a solid commitment to undergraduate education as opposed to graduate research. There are still professors at Notre Dame who hail from an era when research did not matter at all, and they still do not publish. But the newer hires are very interested in publishing and do so as often as they can, churning out prodigious amounts of scholarly work. Despite this, says an insider, "I've never heard any complaints about students being unable to get attention from their professors." For now, tenure and promotion decisions include a lot of attention to teaching evaluations. However, with the president's new empha-

VITAL STATISTICS

Religious affiliation: *Roman Catholic*
Total enrollment: *11,731*
Total undergraduates: *8,363*
SAT/ACT midranges: CR: *650–760*, M: *670–760*; ACT: *32–34*
Applicants: *14,357*
Applicants accepted: *29%*
Accepted applicants who enrolled: *49%*
Tuition and fees: *$39,920*
Room and board: *$10,870*
Freshman retention rate: *97%*
Graduation rate: *91% (4 yrs.), 96% (6 yrs.)*
Courses with fewer than 20 students: *55%*
Student-faculty ratio: *12:1*
Courses taught by graduate students: *not provided*
Most popular majors: *political science, finance, psychology*
Students living on campus: *80%*
Guaranteed housing for four years? *yes*
Students in fraternities or sororities: *none*

sis on research, this may be changing. In 2009, Notre Dame opened "Innovation Park," a research park next to campus designed to further commercial applications of university research. In 2010, Notre Dame announced an alliance with Madison Center, a local provider of behavioral health care services, to facilitate research. Also in 2010, the university topped $100 million in research awards. Recent fields of research at Notre Dame include development of adult stem cells and a model to track the Gulf oil spill.

"ND is very ambitious to be regarded as a 'top tier' research university," one teacher says. "There is a lot of money being put into these projects. I have heard of at least one case where a theology professor was a great teacher but was essentially forced out for not doing enough research." This professor glumly concludes, "While many say that the focus of the school is teaching of students, the jury is still out."

Education at Notre Dame begins with the First Year of Studies Program, which freshmen attend before they choose a major. This division of the university, which has its own faculty and dean, requires a total of twelve courses. Thanks to admirably small classes, students find getting into a first- or even second-choice seminar sometimes difficult. The composition courses are particularly demanding, culminating in a final writing portfolio. Students may fulfill requirements through a wide array of courses. First-year seminars are offered in fourteen departments in the College of Arts and Letters, with more than fifty different university seminar sections.

Despite the lack of a core curriculum, most students we talked to were optimistic about the chances of getting a solid education at Notre Dame. Says one insider, "Even a student who does not care about the liberal arts in any way probably would get a fair amount of a traditional education by choosing the required non-major philosophy, theology, et cetera, courses at random." A faculty member muses, "The professors can be hit or miss. The education you receive, regardless of the school, largely depends on the classes and professors that you choose to take." A student remarks that Notre Dame is "very large and intellectually diverse. While there are some Catholic theologians in the department who are famously heterodox, there are more and more orthodox professors." Another advises, "I think the key is to avoid certain professors rather than to avoid departments entirely." Most classes (except in foreign languages) are taught by faculty rather than by TAs—who instead help with grading and discussion sections.

There are many students, sighs a professor, who come to Notre Dame merely "motivated to be in business or watch football." In contrast to this, however, "There is a serious minority of students who are hungry for knowledge and to discuss ideas." It's also fortunate that "the professors . . . always seem to add more to the education than just the basic facts and consider the larger implications by getting students intellectually involved."

First-year students are assigned professional advisors (some with teaching experience, some without). Only eighteen full-time advisors serve a freshman class of around 2,000. Once students pick majors, some departments match faculty advisors with a small group of students, while others have one faculty member serve the entire department. In sophomore year, students enroll according to their majors in one of four colleges (Arts and Letters, Science, Engineering, or the Mendoza College of Business). Also available to the Notre Dame student is the School of Architecture, the Law School, the Graduate School, and six major research institutes.

In the College of Arts and Letters is Notre Dame's justly renowned Program of Liberal Studies (PLS). Known around campus as the great books major, PLS offers a three-year sequence of seminars and tutorials. Starting with the *Iliad* and ending with *The Brothers Karamazov,* the program's reading list in the Great Books Seminar is impressive and should attract any Notre Dame student serious about a liberal arts education; indeed, many choose it as part of a double major. The program's excellent faculty includes Walter J. Nicgorski, Phillip Reid Sloan (emeritus), and Mary Katherine Tillman (emeritus).

Outside the PLS program, students are largely free to flourish or founder, but there are several areas of excellence, even genius, to be found at Notre Dame. The philosophy department is particularly strong. Highly respected nationwide, it includes Alasdair MacIntyre (emeritus), Alvin Plantinga (emeritus), and William David Solomon. As an insider states, "We have everyone from conservative Thomists to raging feminists here."

Another strong department is architecture, whose graduate program is world famous for its embrace of neoclassical forms. Says a teacher, "All of the students study the masterworks first hand in Rome during their third year." It is said that this five-year program (with one year spent in Rome) turns out graduates "desirous of building meaningful and attractive buildings" and who are well trained in ecclesiastical architecture. Notable faculty in this department include neoclassicist Duncan Stroik, who has designed buildings for several of the schools listed in this guide.

SUGGESTED CORE

1. Classics 10100 01, Ancient Greece and Rome (closest match)
2. Philosophy 30301, Ancient and Medieval Philosophy
3. Theology 10001, Foundations of Theology: Biblical/Historical
4. Theology 40201, Christian Traditions I
5. Political Science 30620, Modern Political Thought
6. English 40226/40227, Shakespeare I/II
7. History 10600 or 20600, United States History to 1877
8. Philosophy 3030401 Nineteenth Century Philosophy (majors only) or Political Science 30621, Continental Political Thought

Notre Dame's "Program of Liberal Studies" would provide an excellent core for students willing to major in the program.

Political science is another outstanding department; its recommended faculty include Mary M. Keys, Daniel Philpott, Michael Zuckert, and Catherine Zuckert. Students are admirably required to take eight courses—either two introductory and six advanced or four introductory and four advanced—with at least one course each in American politics, international relations, comparative politics, and political theory, plus two writing seminars. One poli sci major observes that there are "great courses, such as Professor Kommers's 'Constitutional Law,' Professor Roos's class on Congress, and Professor Lindley's foreign policy course."

Engineering benefits from expansive and up-to-date facilities, including a new building for the department, and is said to be mostly composed of conservative students. Similarly, the business school gets "ridiculously" high rankings. Relates a veteran, "The students get hired right away." One student says, "The business school portion of the faculty has not only the strongest conservatives but also some of the most devout Catholics." Recommended in this department is Dean Woo, a "very solid individual, committed to the Catholic mission of the University." In 2009, the business school opened the new Center for the Study of Financial Regulation.

Undergraduate history classes at Notre Dame are said to be "very good. They usually make primary texts their focus and encourage the students to wrestle with their implications in discussion," notes a teaching assistant. Students recommend the class "The World of the Middle Ages," taught by Thomas Noble. Other "all-stars" of this department are Mark Noll, John van Engen, and Sabine MacCormack.

The history major requires ten courses: one introductory workshop; four area courses, one of which must be pre-1500, from four out of five categories: Africa, Asia, and the Middle East, ancient and medieval Europe, modern Europe, Latin America, and the United States; three courses in a chosen concentration (ranging from Middle Eastern history to intellectual history to women's history); one seminar in the chosen concentration; and one elective. A history major could theoretically avoid studying any American history; he could also take a different track and study America but avoid any courses on ancient or medieval Europe.

Students and alumni have long griped about the theology department, home to well-known dissidents from church teaching. But it seems, as one degree-seeker puts it, to be "undergoing a renaissance." Like the philosophy department, the theology department is big enough, a student says, "to include wackos and solid professors." Another agrees: "While each do have professors that might be considered embarrassments to their department, the overall quality of the courses and scholarship is definitely top-notch." Theology professors who were highly recommended include Michael J. Baxter, Brian E. Daley, David Fagerberg, John Cavadini, Eugene Ulrich, James VanderKam, Gary Anderson, Robin Darling Young, Blake Leyerle, Joseph Wawrykow, Ann Astell, Matthew Ashley, Cyril O'Regan, and Randall Zachman.

Other outstanding faculty members at Notre Dame include Thomas Werge in English; John McGreevy and James Turner in history; Charles K. Wilber (emeritus) in economics and policy; Adrian Reimers, John O'Callaghan, Peter Wicks, and Fred Freddoso in philosophy; Rev. Bill Miscamble in history; Bill Kirk in accountancy; and David Veselik in biology.

The English department has the reputation of being rather weak and "very divided along ideological lines." Complains an undergrad: "One English course I took on Hemingway was particularly bad. It essentially taught that the West and all men were evil." A new Catholic professor was said to have quit in disgust over the inanity in this department. English majors do face decent requirements, which were recently beefed up: one writing-intensive introduction; one research seminar; and one course in pre-1500 literature; one in 1500–1700; two in 1700–1900; and one after 1900; one course in British literature; one in American; one in either American ethnic-identity literature or English-language literature outside of the United States or Britain; one course in poetry and two in fiction, drama, film, or critical theory.

Devout or conservative students should be leery of sociology, film, and (surprise!) gender studies, sources say. Perhaps the greatest danger to Notre Dame's identity lies in the careerist emphasis that dominates many departments. One teacher warns of "white-collar vocational education" and the craving for prestige as "the engine of secularization. We hire faculty whom we see as qualified not because they add to the catholicity of the school, but because they help in our quest for momentary greatness."

A number of institutes, think tanks, and study centers enhance intellectual life at Notre Dame. Students should check out the programs offered by the Cushwa Center for the

---

ACADEMIC REQUIREMENTS

While Notre Dame has no core curriculum, it does maintain respectable mandates for breadth of study. All students must complete the following:

- One semester of a university seminar in any of fourteen disciplines, including philosophy, theology, anthropology, and film, television, and theater. Choices range from "Rembrandt and His Contemporaries" to "Pirates in History."
- First-Year Composition."
- Two semesters of mathematics, usually a calculus or statistics sequence.
- Two semesters of a natural science. Students can choose from laboratory classes or "topical" courses such as "Evolution and Society" or "Common Human Diseases."
- Two semesters of physical education or ROTC.
- Three additional electives.
- One course in history, such as "Western Civilization" I or "Sex, Sexuality and Gender in the United States to 1880."
- One class in social science, such as "U.S. History to 1877" or "Feminist Political Thought."
- Two courses each in philosophy and theology. Options range from "God's Grace and Human Action" and "Ethics of Thomas Aquinas" to "U.S. Latino Spirituality."
- One course in fine arts or literature, such as "Religious Imagination in American Literature" or "Sinatra," as well as any of a slew of practical courses in photography, drawing, painting, music, and dance.
- Courses or tests to show intermediate proficiency in a foreign language (for students in the College of Arts and Letters).

Midwest

Study of American Catholicism, the Erasmus Institute, the Center for Ethics and Culture, the Jacques Maritain Center, and the Medieval Institute. Each fall, the Center for Ethics and Culture holds an annual conference that is highly regarded by students.

Notre Dame has a variety of outstanding study-abroad programs, in locales on every inhabited continent. The school offers courses in Arabic, Ancient Greek, Latin, Chinese (Mandarin), Japanese, Korean, German, Russian, French, Italian, Portuguese, Spanish, Quechua, and Irish.

Student Life: Touchdown Jesus

The campus itself is lovely—especially during the fall—despite the uninspired architecture of many of the newer buildings. The golden dome of the Main Building glimmers on the north end of campus, right next to the Basilica of the Sacred Heart and the Grotto. Beyond the basilica and grotto lie two small lakes.

Notre Dame added two new residence halls in 2008 and 2009, and plans on building three or four more when funding becomes available; other projects awaiting funding include a new art museum, an expansion and renovation of the Joyce Center athletic arena, a social sciences building, an Executive Education Center, and a student activities center.

The city of South Bend (pop. 107,789) and its neighbor Mishawaka (pop. 46,557) boast a symphony orchestra, several museums, the Civic Theatre, the Potawatomi Zoo, an annual festival of contemporary Christian music, and a minor league baseball team. However, it is remarkable just how little either city caters to the Notre Dame student. Nowhere is there a strip of bars, pizza joints, restaurants, coffeehouses, and shops targeting students— certainly nothing like what one usually finds at other major midwestern universities. In 2009, the university opened Eddy Street Commons, a "college town" next to campus that includes housing, restaurants, shops, a bank, and a bookstore.

There are twenty-nine dorms, none of them coed, and a priest or a nun lives in most of them. Each hall has a chapel and its own intramural sports teams. Intervisitation is restricted to certain hours, but most dorms also have lounges where the sexes can mingle 24 hours a day. On the whole, dorm life seems pretty wholesome for a large university. Hard liquor is officially prohibited in the dorms, for example, but students differ over how widely this ban is observed. (Students observe in online forums that RAs regard a closed dorm-room door as sacrosanct.) Eighty percent of undergraduates live on campus, and students are encouraged to stay in the same residence hall for all four years. Notre Dame student government provides resources for finding affordable and safe off-campus living, as well as social resources.

The party scene is said to be somewhat subdued, thanks more to the heavy ND workload than any strict enforcement of policies by the school. Still, students host on- and off-campus parties, and there is a knot of bars near campus that cater to students of age—although students complain about the absence of clubs with live music or other entertainment.

Masses are held several times daily in ND's beautiful basilica, and they are well attended. Dorms have their own chapels, each offering weekly liturgies. The university's

Campus Ministry directs students to choirs, retreats, Eucharistic adoration, Bible studies, plus an orthodox introduction to Catholicism for non-Catholics. It helps Protestant, Orthodox, Buddhist, Muslim, and Jewish students find local resources and places of worship.

One student says that ND has a strong "Catholic circle . . . a network of several devoutly Catholic student groups. It includes Militia Immaculata, Children of Mary, Orestes Brownson Council, Notre Dame Right to Life, the Knights of Columbus Council (the nation's oldest chapter), the Irish Rover, and a few others. These are groups that, while separate, have many close connections and shared members that create a network for the most orthodox of Catholics to find a great home." The conservative student newspaper, the *Irish Rover*, wages an ongoing campaign to keep Notre Dame true to its liberal arts roots and Catholic identity. An active pro-life movement on campus generates multiple initiatives, including conferences and fund-raisers for mothers in need.

Says one student, "On campus you can generally pick your own fate: if you want to be a serious Catholic, go to Mass somewhere between weekly and daily, and study a lot of medieval philosophy, you can do that. On the other hand, if you want to take a bunch of women's studies classes and donate your pocket change to Planned Parenthood, you can do that too."

The administration, sources say, is actively moving the school closer to the secular model of elite eastern schools. Annually, amid protests from campus groups such as the Knights of Columbus, there is a campus production of *The Vagina Monologues*, a trendy, toxic play that celebrates, among other things, lesbian statutory rape. The school's assistant vice president for student affairs has helped form the Core Council for Gay, Les-

YELLOW LIGHT

In a decision that outraged Catholics nationwide, in 2009 Notre Dame invited fervently pro-choice President Barack Obama to give the commencement speech at graduation and receive an honorary degree. Protest arose not only from student groups and faculty, but also from pro-lifers and church officials around the country, including over sixty bishops—Notre Dame's local bishop among them. The philosopher Ralph McInerny, who was retiring after fifty-four years of teaching at Notre Dame, called the invitation "an unequivocal abandonment of any pretense at being a Catholic university."

Some graduating students skipped their own commencement, instead attending a prayer vigil on campus. Over eighty protesters from outside the college, including an elderly priest, were arrested and face criminal charges that President Jenkins has refused to drop.

In 2010, Notre Dame fired associate vice president for residence life Bill Kirk, a twenty-two-year employee who was the only senior administration member to take part in the protest rally against Obama's visit. Although the university cites "restructuring" as the reason for Kirk's termination, Professor David Solomon of the Center for Ethics and Culture interprets it as an attempt to punish dissent. He told *National Review* that he foresaw "a chilling effect on the participation of other administrators, unprotected by the safety net of tenure, in the great debates about public policy and moral principle into which Notre Dame will be inevitably drawn. . . . [A] number of other administrators have told me that in light of Bill Kirk's treatment, they will in the future keep their heads down rather than dissent from the policies of the central administration."

bian, Bisexual, and Questioning Students. A "StaND Against Hate Week" is held in October by the unofficial Gay-Straight Alliance, and the group sponsored a day on which some students and faculty wore T-shirts that read "Gay? Fine by me."

Other student groups include ROTC, several chorales (including a liturgical choir), Habitat for Humanity, an undergraduate investment club, Humor Artists (a comedy troupe), a nationally ranked parliamentary debate team, a Big Brothers/Big Sisters chapter, an anthropology club, Women in Politics, an equestrian club, a ballroom dance club, a chess club, a model United Nations, the Medieval Society of Our Lady of the Lake, the Proponents of Animal Welfare Services, and a chapter of the NAACP.

The College Republicans are active in grassroots campaigning. A small, informal libertarian group has hosted 2008 Libertarian presidential candidate Bob Barr on campus. The College Democrats, however, are reported to be "one of the strongest College Democrat chapters in the country."

The spiritual center of campus, some say, is not the basilica but the football stadium. As one of many students would say, "The ND football spirit is phenomenal. All of the students are guaranteed tickets to all of the home games, and the student section remains standing and on fire with spirit throughout the game." Athletics—as well as many other social activities—revolve around the sport, which the school started playing back in 1887. The school gets precious national exposure thanks to an exclusive contract with NBC to carry all its home football games.

Notre Dame competes in NCAA's Division I and captured the 2010 Big East Conference title in women's swimming and diving, women's rowing, women's soccer, women's tennis, and men's indoor and outdoor track and field. There are thirteen men's varsity teams and thirteen women's varsity teams, as well as thirty club teams and fifty-seven intramural teams. The school's mascot is the leprechaun.

Campus crime is pretty infrequent. In 2009, the school reported two forcible sex offenses, two aggravated assaults, four motor vehicle thefts, forty-nine burglaries, and one arson. Notre Dame Security Police patrol the campus, and there are emergency call stations as well as free walking escorts at night. Monitored security gates limit car access to campus, and residence halls are locked at all times.

Notre Dame may have started out as a school catering to blue-collar immigrant kids, but it isn't cheap today. Tuition for 2010–11 was $39,920, with room and board at $10,870; however, admissions are need blind, and the school pledges to meet accepted students' full need. Over 45 percent of undergraduates receive need-based aid, and the average debt of a recent graduate was between $17,000 and $21,000.

Oberlin College

Oberlin, Ohio • www.oberlin.edu

Boundless, desolate fields

In 1833, two Yankee ministers founded Oberlin to train "teachers and other Christian leaders for the boundless and most desolate fields of the West." Since then, Oberlin has been one of the most "progressive" liberal arts colleges in the country. In 1865, the college founded its world-renowned music conservatory. Oberlin has grown considerably in reputation and influence and has left its original Christian mission far behind. The college has "progressed" to a curriculum soaked in ethnic, class, and gender obsessions. Oberlin students are known both for their intellectual firepower and for their leftist social activism.

Academic Life: Lasting relationships

Oberlin College has no core curriculum, nor even a decent set of distribution requirements. With such a minimalist curriculum, students can—and sometimes do—avoid intellectually substantive courses and devote themselves instead to grievance-based disciplines such as women's and ethnic studies.

The Arts and Science division (there is also a music conservatory) offers forty-seven majors. Some of these provide little more structure than the basic college requirements. Others, though still fairly weak, have improved somewhat over the years. Oberlin English majors must take one course in English literature before 1700, one in literature between 1700 and 1900, and one in literature from 1900 to the present. They are also required to take one course designated as American, one as British, and one as "Diversity"—not a bad balance. Courses in poetry and drama are also recommended. English majors also have the option of selecting interdisciplinary "concentration majors."

History majors can also avoid basic courses, although in 2010 the requirements were expanded a bit: majors must now take two introductory survey courses covering two different geographical areas, one premodern course, and one from each of the three following areas: Europe and Russia; United States and North America; and Asia, Latin America, and Africa.

The politics department's only breadth requirement is to take intermediate courses in three of these four fields: American politics, comparative politics, international politics, and political theory; students could easily avoid foundational courses.

VITAL STATISTICS

Religious affiliation: *none*
Total enrollment: *2,939*
Total undergraduates: *2,905*
SAT/ACT midranges: CR:
  640–740, M: *630–720*;
  ACT: *28–32*
Applicants: *7,227*
Applicants accepted: *34%*
Accepted applicants who
  enrolled: *33%*
Tuition and fees: *$41,234*
Room and board: *$11,010*
Freshman retention rate:
  93%
Graduation rate: *73% (4 yrs.),
  86% (6 yrs.)*
Courses with fewer than 20
  students: *68%*
Student-faculty ratio: *11:1*
Courses taught by graduate
  students: *none*
Most popular majors: *music
  performance, biology,
  political science*
Students living on campus:
  91%
Guaranteed housing for
  four years? *no*
Students in fraternities or
  sororities: *none*

Oberlin's Conservatory of Music, with a student-faculty ratio of 8 to 1, is the college's finest academic offering. Enrolling about 600 students, the conservatory offers eight bachelor of music degrees in music theory, music history, performance, composition, jazz studies, and other areas. Oberlin also offers an undergraduate performance diploma and a graduate artist diploma, as well as four master's degrees—conducting and opera theater for Oberlin students only, but historical performance and teaching for students from other institutions. About 170 students are enrolled in the five-year double-degree program, which awards degrees in both arts and sciences and the conservatory.

The sciences are also very strong at Oberlin. One professor says, "I think natural science at Oberlin is a little-known jewel—it has a crucial function in maintaining [Oberlin's] academic caliber and does attract some of the best students." In fact, three Oberlin graduates have won Nobel prizes, all in the sciences. More students go on to pursue PhDs in engineering and the natural sciences from Oberlin than from any other four-year institution. The science department boasts the Adam Joseph Lewis Center for Environmental Studies, home to the "Living Machine," which treats and recycles the building's waste water for reuse in the toilets and landscape. The college's observatory and planetarium recently installed a new state-of-the-art telescope.

Other strong departments at the college include classics, philosophy, politics, and mathematics. Excellent professors include Paul Dawson in politics; Jeffrey Witmer in mathematics; David Benzing (emeritus), Yolanda Cruz, and Roger Laushman in biology; and Martin Ackermann (emeritus) in chemistry and biochemistry.

Unfortunately for students, a good deal of Oberlin's political activity occurs within the classroom, where teachers lean overwhelmingly to the left. One professor says segments of the Oberlin faculty are "ideological and aggressive." A student sees things differently: "I wouldn't say that politics intrude in the classroom; they just make for some interesting debate." A professor says, "The whole public atmosphere is pretty much confined to the left. In the rhetoric that is constantly used at this place, in questions of sexual orientation and racial divides, there is a real balkanization that has taken place in recent years." One member of the College Republicans reports suffering verbal abuse for her political stance, and another "one of our members got beat up last year before the election, and although there is nothing to prove it was politically motivated, a lot of us have our doubts." He goes on to say, however, that he recommends Oberlin to conservative students and finds the teachers "respectful."

All classes are taught by professors, since Oberlin has only a few graduate students. Upon entering, each Oberlin student is assigned an academic advisor to help choose courses, majors, and future careers. The First Year Seminar Program offers several colloquia each year for freshmen and sophomores, with enrollments limited to just fourteen students. "Many of those courses are excellent due to the small class size and their interesting subject focus," a student says.

Oberlin also offers funding, internships, and other resources for student entrepreneurs. Recent student ventures range from nonprofit organizations to teach Vietnamese youth hygiene and to help Oberlin residents facing foreclosure to a fair-trade Moroccan craft company and a video-game development company.

Oberlin has study-abroad programs in almost two dozen countries on every inhabited continent. The college offers courses in Arabic, French, Italian, Chinese, Ancient Greek, Latin, Japanese, Korean, German, Spanish, Italian, Hebrew, and Russian.

Student Life: *In loco dementis*

Oberlin, Ohio (pop. 8,195), is thirty-five miles southwest of Cleveland. Given the lack of cultural options in the surroundings, the college works hard to create entertainment on campus. Admissions literature points out that 1,000 activities are offered on campus in a given year, including over 500 concerts and recitals, 200 film screenings, 2 operas, and 40 theater and dance productions. The town of Oberlin offers a few perks of its own, including good bookstores (such as Mind Fair Books) and coffee shops like the Java Zone. The Apollo movie theater, taken over and renovated by Oberlin in 2009, is in an art deco building in the downtown area that features current films at low prices. Oberlin was a key stop on the Underground Railroad and also boasts the Frank Lloyd Wright House, which is managed by the college. The town is twenty minutes from Lake Erie.

The music conservatory boasts amazing facilities: 150 practice studios, some 200 Steinway grand pianos, 40 music studios, 5 concert halls, a music library, and electronic and computer musical instruments that are rare at most undergraduate institutions. In 2010, the college opened the Bertram and Judith Kohl Building, which houses the jazz studies, music history, and music theory departments. The conservatory also supports the Oberlin College Artist Recital Series, which offers performances by professors, students, and visiting artists

---

SUGGESTED CORE

1. Classics 101/102, Homer's *Iliad* and the Myths of Tragedy/*The Odyssey* and the Myths of Comedy
2. Philosophy 215, Ancient Philosophy
3. Religion 205/208, Hebrew Bible in Its Ancient Near Eastern Context/New Testament and Christian Origins
4. Religion 217/218, Christianity in the Early Medieval World: 100–1100/Christianity in the Late Medieval World: 1100–1600
5. Politics 232, European Political Theory: Hobbes to Marx
6. English 204, Shakespearean Comedy (closest match)
7. History 103, American History to 1877
8. Politics 234, European Political Theory: After Marx (closest match)

---

like the Cleveland Orchestra, Opera Atelier, and the Juilliard String Quartet. Says one student, "Because of the conservatory, there are a lot of musical performances, most of which are fun and showcase excellent talent." Extracurricular clubs cover a wide range of interests; they include an Anime Club, student radio (WOBC), and a Zionist club.

Besides campus performances, cooperative activities, studying, and heading into Cleveland, students "otherwise go to the Feve (the only bar) or to the Oberlin Inn for pitchers night," says one student. Every year, one of the most popular and controversial events is Safer Sex Night, run by the Sexual Information Center. At one Safer Sex Night, education videos were broadcast on monitors throughout the buildings, and students arrived at the event scantily clad—some in nothing more than a bumper sticker. Faculty members performed demonstrations on how to safely use condoms and other contraceptive devices. This school-sponsored event is much anticipated on campus by students who enjoy games like "Sexy Twister," "safer oral sex" demos, and demonstrations like "Sex Toys 101." The night encourages sexual release, both with or without a partner, and shows students how to do this "safely," although "safely" in this case includes various sadomasochistic activities. After publicity and safety problems, the college banned the sale of alcohol at Safer Sex Night, stopped showing pornographic films, and closed the "Tent of Consent," which two students could enter for two minutes and do whatever they liked—as long as they had discussed their intentions beforehand. In 2009, Oberlin made another feeble attempt to rescue the event from debauchery by requiring students to attend at least one educational event before going to the party.

A less controversial event, Fire It Up @ Philips, offers free food and numerous games such as laser tag, rock climbing, karaoke, and zumba. Another popular annual event on campus is the Drag Ball (a "king" and "queen" are crowned at the end of this celebration of confused sexuality, which seems to be a recurring theme at Oberlin), once dubbed the "Mardi Gras of the Midwest" by *Rolling Stone*. The very popular ball annually attracts over 1,000 students, faculty, and administrators, and Oberlin's website lists it under the heading of venerable college "traditions."

Oberlin's brand of political radicalism is aimed primarily at the liberation of desire. As FrontPage Magazine has written, "Oberlin embodies a far-left paradise of agitation, Marxist activism, and sexual licentiousness." Students eager to "make a difference in the world" seem to thrive here and organize around groups such as the Peace Activists League and the Oberlin Action Against Prisons.

There is a slow-growing contingent of students with more conservative viewpoints. In 2005, an alumnus stepped in to reorganize the long-defunct Oberlin College Republicans—much to the chagrin of the college. The CRs have hosted conservative speakers such as William Kristol and Karl Rove and boast on their website, "We have established ourselves as one of the most active student organizations on campus." A CR member says that the conservatives on campus realize all too well that they are a minority but are guardedly hopeful that students are ready for a change.

As an Oberlin College Republican says, "During my time here, I have perceived a growing sense of discontent with the traditional liberal bent at Oberlin. I hear more and more people, while generally liberal themselves, complain of closed-mindedness in the political sphere." The Oberlin pro-life group dissolved about fifteen years ago, and the libertarian group has been inactive for several years. Another student says that while Oberlin is predominantly liberal, she had never experienced any hostility toward the conservative minority.

Oberlin has no fraternities or sororities, instead offering cooperatives. The several on- and off-campus cooperatives house about one in five Oberlin students and offer dining services. Nine of these co-ops are for dining only, and four are residential. Each cooperative is based on a particular theme and identity, ranging from the Kosher House to the Third World Cooperative. Co-op members divide tasks such as cooking and cleaning and take their attachment to the co-op seriously.

Other housing options at Oberlin include traditional dormitories and theme houses. In order to foster community, Oberlin requires all students to live and eat in dorms or co-ops; but recently it has run out of room, so it's allowing certain seniors to live off campus. Off-campus housing appears quite affordable, and the small town of Oberlin seems fairly safe. There are eleven dorms, "village housing" in college-owned apartments and houses, and nine program houses, themed by language or culture. The college no longer has single-sex dormitories, but it does section off various areas of dorms to be all-women or all-men, by student vote. There are a few coed bathrooms on campus, also by student ballot. Stu-

---

ACADEMIC REQUIREMENTS

Oberlin has no core curriculum and fairly weak distribution requirements. On top of their major requirements, students cannot count more than eighty-four hours (about twenty-eight courses) within a single division (i.e., arts and humanities; social and behavioral sciences; natural sciences and mathematics) toward graduation. Therefore, at least twenty-eight hours (about nine courses) must be taken outside the division with the highest number of credits, and no more than fifty-six credits (about eighteen courses) can be taken in a single department. Students must also earn nine credit hours (about three courses) in each of three divisions:

- Humanities. Just about everything will count, from "Art of the Italian Renaissance" to "Sexuality in Ancient Greece and Rome."
- Social sciences. Options here range from "Social and Political Change in Eastern Europe" to "Dirty Wars and Democracy."
- Natural sciences. Choices are many, including "Meteorite Impacts in Space and Time" and "The Brain: An Introduction to Neuroscience."
- Students must also complete three courses in "cultural diversity," defined as cultures and languages other than their own; however, world history and foreign language courses fulfill this requirement, so "cultural diversity" does not necessarily mean ethnic/gender/class propaganda. Most courses at Oberlin probably would count toward this requirement. Curiously, the school does not require proficiency in a foreign language.

Students must also take at least three winter-term credits and show proficiency in writing and quantitative skills by completing courses or passing tests.

dents must choose among the following options: "females only," "males only," "everyone," "just me," "just females (/males)," "female (/male) bodied persons," and "female (/male) identifying persons," whatever these might mean. Even more "open" is the recent option to room with someone of the opposite sex. Or, we guess, of neither.

Oberlin's newest dormitory is Kahn Hall, opening in 2010, with an environmental sustainability theme. Students living there pledge to come without a car and conserve water and energy, among other measures.

Oberlin offers a good deal of flexibility in its meal plans, from an all-inclusive plan to a monastic seven-meals-a-week option. Students can choose from among three dining halls at Oberlin, all of which follow strict health guidelines. Other eats can be found at the Science Coffee Cart, and DeCafe, a mini-mart with sandwiches and smoothies.

Health concerns seem not to extend to the use of liquor and other drugs. Students say that many Oberlin students are drug users and heavy drinkers. An *Oberlin Review* article reported that students, speaking anonymously, found drug use to be widely popular. One student says it is "really, really easy" to obtain drugs at Oberlin.

Conservative religious students are a clear minority at Oberlin. One source says, "The number of students who don't associate with any religion at all is probably the largest group." One Catholic student notes that there are over a hundred Catholics on the mailing list, but only around thirty go to weekly Mass. The Jewish community boasts the most students attending services.

Perhaps it is telling that on the Oberlin website for student organizations, faith-based clubs are listed under the same category as identity organizations such as La Alianza Latina and the Lesbian, Gay, Bisexual, and Transgendered Union. Still, there is a Christian fellowship, a Hillel, and a Muslim students association, as well as a Queers and Allies of Faith group. Local houses of worship include a Lutheran church, several evangelical and Pentecostal denominations, a Friends meeting, a Unitarian Universalist fellowship, and a Catholic church (though students should probably drive to Cleveland's Immaculate Conception, St. Rocco, or St. Stephen parishes for Latin Mass on Sundays). Jewish religious services are held weekly either at the Hillel center or at Talcott Dining Hall. The campus is also home to weekly Catholic, Muslim, Protestant, and Friends services.

The 150 or so clubs are governed by the Student Senate, whose budget committee controls how much money student organizations receive from the annual fee levied against each student. Organizations range from chapters of the ACLU and Amnesty International, Students for a Free Palestine, Pagan Awareness Network, and Queer Jews and Allies to contradancing, Gilbert and Sullivan Players, Potter Co-op, Astronomy Club, Model UN Club, and Linux User's Group. Campus publications include the *Oberlin Review*, the weekly student newspaper; the *Grape*, a magazine focused on world affairs and opinion; *Scope,* a student publication dedicated to artistic endeavor; *Oberlin on Oberlin*, "an online publication chronicling student life and student concerns"; the *Plum Creek Review,* Oberlin's literary magazine; and *Nommo*, focusing on issues relevant to blacks at Oberlin.

The Allen Memorial Art Museum has an expansive collection and even maintains a 400-piece rental collection that allows students, faculty, staff, and Oberlin residents to rent signed prints by Warhol, Picasso, and Toulouse-Lautrec, as well as paintings and sculptures by other artists. The museum closed in 2010 for renovation and expansion.

Although John Heisman began his coaching career at Oberlin, the college hasn't seen the likes of him lately. Athletics are not a major draw on campus. But that may be changing; according to one professor, "Athletics are more of a priority with the college than they have been in the past." Oberlin is a member of the North Coast Athletic Conference, an NCAA Division III group, and offers twenty-two varsity sports and between ten and fifteen intramural sports, depending on the year. Students can also participate in any of twelve club sports, including rugby, fencing, and tumbling and circus performance. In 2009–10, Oberlin's Yeomen took third place in cross-country and All-NCAC second-team doubles and singles in tennis, and the Yeowomen were All-NCAC first-team singles and doubles and second-team singles.

Crime statistics in 2009 showed twenty-eight burglaries, four aggravated assaults, one car theft, and four forcible sex offenses on campus. Walking safety escorts are available, student shuttles run from 9:00 PM to 2:00 AM, and an emergency telephone service is in place to help students in need.

With 2010–11 tuition at $41,234 and room and board at $11,010, Oberlin makes for an expensive trip out to left field. Nor does the school practice need-blind admissions. However, students admitted will find their full financial need met. Seventy percent of the student body receives need-based financial aid from the college, and starting in 2009 the Oberlin Access Initiative is providing students eligible for Pell Grants with enough financial aid to avoid taking out any student loans. The average debt of a recent graduate was around $20,000.

RED LIGHT

Several students complained to us about the pervasive climate of political correctness on campus. Meanwhile, the social atmosphere will probably be enough to make traditionalist students feel extremely unwelcome. Safer Sex Night and the Drag Ball are not just student parties but institutionalized traditions that students passionately defend and prospectives always hear about (sometimes looking forward to them, sometimes fearing them). One student boasts: "[N]othing is unusual here, from nudity in the quad to puking contests in the name of 'art' to men wearing dresses around campus. We are the social conservative's nightmare."

One recent event, however, offers a glimmer of hope: in 2010 the American Democracy Seminar brought Oberlin students together with students from Israel and Palestine to live together and study American democracy and its effects on the Middle East. On an issue that would normally barely even be debated at most colleges that are this liberal, Oberlin seems to have managed to facilitate a civil and productive discussion. An Oberlin professor says of the seminar, "The Palestinians in particular are trying to promote studies of the United States in the Mideast. We would like this to become a model for teaching American democracy in [a] manner that recognizes American flaws but doesn't demonize the U.S." According to the *Oberlin Review*, the Palestinian professor who helped organize the seminar "lectures about 'the two faces of American studies' and the challenges of overcoming stereotypes, misconceptions, and anti-American sentiments."

Ohio State University

Columbus, Ohio • www.osu.edu

The "Big" in Big Ten

Ohio State is big; it sits on a 1,755-acre campus, one of the world's largest, and enrolls the nation's second-largest student body, behind only the University of Texas at Austin. Founded in 1870 as the Ohio Agricultural and Mechanical College, the university has always been torn between the practical and the liberal arts—and so it resolved the debate by deciding to offer just about every subject under the sun. Among members of the OSU liberal arts faculty, it is a common view that students looking for a serious humanities education would be better served elsewhere. Only "focused, savvy undergraduates" interested in going on for a graduate or professional degree, according to one professor, should choose Ohio State. Another professor says, "A discerning and determined student can gain a good liberal arts education here. The problem is that he or she shouldn't have to struggle against the system to do it."

Academic Life: 50,000 of your closest friends

OSU's general education mandates give the student plenty of wiggle room so that, although a student may have to arrange his schedule so as to incorporate a few requirements, he will surely be able to find a course to his liking—not exactly the goal of a liberal arts curriculum.

One worthwhile initiative is OSU's Honors Program. Honors students typically come from the top 10 percent of their classes and must have verbal/math SAT scores above 1340. Honors students are eligible for merit scholarships and may live in one of four special residence halls. They may also choose from among approximately 500 honors classes taught by elite faculty with smaller enrollments. The Scholars Program is a similar initiative, whose 300 participating students live in housing specific to their academic interests, take advanced classes, and enjoy personalized advising and mentoring opportunities. One professor says that both of these programs compare "favorably with a decent middle-of-the-road Ivy League education."

Outside these programs, the picture is less impressive. After fulfilling the school's (rather lax) general education requirements, students go on to complete a major. Students of history take an introduction to the historical method and a senior seminar designed to hone their research skills, as well as fifty hours in their major, including at least twenty in one geographical region and fifteen from two or more other regions; and at least ten credit hours each in history before and after 1750. (Classes at OSU are taught on the quarter system, and most classes are worth five credit hours.) These are respectable requirements, and many of the departmental course offerings are excellent, but there are also the usual clunkers, like "History of Modern Sexualities." You'll notice that American history is *not* one of the requirements for the major.

English majors are required to take at least sixty credit hours in English, with a minimum of thirty-five at the 400-level or above; three survey courses, two in British literature and one in American literature; three writing classes, including one in critical writing; at least two courses set before 1900; one after 1900; a course in an area of English study other than literature; and at least three elective courses at the 300- to 500-level in English. Given the required survey courses, students would not miss encounters with Shakespeare.

Political science majors take at least fifty credit hours, including thirty-five at the 400-level or above. Major programs must include a four-course focus in one of the department's four fields (American politics, comparative politics, international relations, and political theory) and at least one course in each of the other three. Chances are good that majors will have to study the U.S. Constitution or political system.

Ohio State administrators seem less devoted to liberal arts education than to political purification, if we judge by the sheer amount of institutional energy devoted to the school's Diversity Action Plan, intended as "a national model for diversity." Toward this end, OSU vigorously pursues various affirmative action policies and sponsors events like "The President and Provost's Diversity Lecture and Cultural Arts Series," which amounts to lectures on topics such as "Strategic Priorities, Strategic Funding," "How the Media Teach about Diversity," "Diversity and the American University Professoriate: National Imperative or Political Correctness?" and "Nine Ways of Looking at a Poor Woman."

Reports about classroom politicization are mixed. According to one political science professor, OSU has "a very open political climate. Liberal and conservative voices are heard. The campus community is very tolerant." She insists that in her department, teachers "pride themselves on being neutral and playing 'devil's advocate' when one political

VITAL STATISTICS

Religious affiliation: *none*

Total enrollment: *55,014*

Total undergraduates: *41,348*

SAT/ACT midranges: CR: *540–650*, M: *580–690*; ACT: *25–30*

Applicants: *18,256*

Applicants accepted: *76%*

Accepted applicants who enrolled: *49%*

Tuition and fees: *in state, $8,994; out of state, $23,178*

Room and board: *$10,164*

Freshman retention rate: *93%*

Graduation rate: *42% (4 yrs.), 73% (6 yrs.)*

Courses with fewer than 20 students: *32%*

Student-faculty ratio: *15:1*

Courses taught by graduate students: *not provided*

Most popular majors: *business/marketing, social sciences, family and consumer sciences*

Students living on campus: *24%*

Guaranteed housing for four years? *no*

Students in fraternities: *6%* in sororities: *7%*

SUGGESTED CORE

1. Classics 101/102, Ancient Greek Literature in Translation/Roman Literature in Translation
2. Philosophy 301, History of Ancient Philosophy
3. English 280, The English Bible
4. History 507, History of Medieval Christianity
5. Political Science 471/472, Early Modern Political Thought /Modern Political Thought
6. English 220, Introduction to Shakespeare
7. History 151, American Civilization to 1877
8. History 513.01, European Intellectual and Cultural History: The Age of Modernity in the Nineteenth Century

opinion is expressed." A conservative student agrees. "I have had left-leaning, moderate, and conservative professors. I can say that I have never felt uncomfortable in a class, though. As a conservative, I have always been given a chance to voice my opinion, and even encouraged to do so, even when the professor is obviously liberal." Despite these claims, one faculty member maintains that "some topics are relatively taboo." This professor says that at least one "activist Christian" was denied tenure for political reasons. One student complains that in a panel on the Iraq war, "not one of the faculty members on the panel supported the war in Iraq, defended current U.S. policy, or even offered to play devil's advocate. . . . OSU has a long way to go in terms of academic freedom."

The most politicized departments are said to be the usual suspects (African American, African, and women's studies) along with psychology and English. Says a professor regarding the English department, "Too often I hear from students that they've been ridiculed or even downgraded on their work for their beliefs (whether political or religious), or that they've simply kept their mouths shut or parroted what they knew was party line in order to get decent grades. . . . It's fairly widespread, and seems to be worst in classes taught by TAs. Many of our students refer to the 'American Experience' second writing course as 'Indoctrination 101.'" The professor adds that "there are many dedicated teachers in the English department, and as long as students stay away from taboo subjects or don't air their religious views, they find the department surprisingly warm . . . for such a large one."

Currently, OSU is best known for its Fisher College of Business and College of Engineering. The school offers more than 170 degree programs, covering everything from jazz studies to turf grass science.

While none of the departments "specialize in undergraduate education," as one professor reports, nearly all have some excellent teachers, including Janet Box-Steffensmeier in political science; Gene Mumy in economics; Rick Livingston in comparative studies; Edward Crenshaw in sociology; In Jae Myung in psychology; Phoebe S. Spinrad in English; and Harding Ganz in history.

Because OSU is such a large campus, it is very important for students to "get connected," says a professor. "It is a big place. To not get lost, one needs to connect with professors." Smart students will generally stand out at OSU. Says a professor, "Those who want to distinguish themselves from the horde at OSU can do so quite easily because most of their undergrad colleagues aren't coming to see their professors and are happy with a C." Once a student identifies the professor with whom he would like to study and "makes a reasoned pitch, works hard, and shows his talent," he will, according to the same professor, receive a "remarkable undergrad education working with some of the top scholars in his field."

Students in the Colleges of the Arts and Sciences are appointed two advisors—one of whom *may* be a faculty member. Despite this "dual-advising system," OSU stresses students' responsibility to navigate the academic labyrinth. With six-year graduation rates hovering around 70 percent during the past three years, and the four-year rate at a measly 42 percent, this system doesn't seem particularly effective.

The university offers a series of orientation events as part of the First-Year Experience Program (FYE), in which students, during their first quarter on campus, are invited to "attend special lectures, seminars, and gatherings." Upperclassmen meet with freshmen to discuss the new academic demands and social challenges; seminars by faculty members introduce research methods and principles; and eminent writers arrive with fanfare and read from their best-selling books, after which students are invited to discuss and debate the contents. The themes for 2010–11 events blended the practical and appropriate with a helping of the ideological: "Academic Engagement and Exploration," "Financial and Debt Management," "Leadership," "Drug and Alcohol Use," " Health and Wellness," and "Anxiety and Mental Health." We're a little more dubious about what they'll gain from seminars titled "Diversity" and "Sexual Health." There are also FYE course offerings, ranging from the solid to the ideological or strangely specialized.

Professors at OSU can be surprisingly approachable. One student in a class of a hundred says that "the professor went to great lengths to make himself accessible. He ran two separate homework-problem help sessions (in addition to one run by the TA), and he didn't end them until all questions were answered. . . . I have been impressed by the effort he expends in order to serve his students." Students should seek out professors like this—especially since many of their lower-level courses will be taught by graduate students.

One way to avoid OSU's massive lecture classes is to take survey courses at one of the school's regional campuses. According to a student at the Columbus campus, "Many freshman students (myself included) feel that their first year of study is wasteful. . . . If one can avoid coming to the main campus and save money in the process by attending a regional campus closer to home, it would be well worth it." A student at the Newark campus says that "it is much better to take history classes here because the class size is much smaller. Thus, more attention is given to individual students." Well-regarded professors at the Newark campus include David Paul and Rachel Paul in political science, and Mitch Lerner in history.

Ohio State offers a broad range of thirty-two languages, including Latin, Chinese, Spanish, and Zulu. There are over a hundred study-abroad programs in more than forty different countries, and close to 20 percent of undergraduates study abroad. There are no on-campus language-immersion houses.

Student Life: It's a riot

Ohio State's campus is located in Columbus, the state's capital. It is the largest city in Ohio and, believe it or not, the sixteenth largest in the nation. Naturally, there is plenty to do in the city on any weekend and most weeknights. Hockey fans can catch the NHL's Blue Jackets, while soccer supporters can get a dose of the Columbus Crew. The prosperous city hosts a substantial arts scene, including museums, a symphony, and a ballet. The city is student-friendly: for example, students can use their university ID cards to ride the local buses free.

In the fall, OSU students tend to be consumed with football. Ohio State has finished first among the Big Ten consistently. Even when the team has suffered a defeat or two, Ohio Stadium, otherwise known as the Horseshoe, is usually packed to its 101,568-seat capacity (and during a 2009 game against USC, 106,033 fans somehow squeezed in).

Students gather to party before, during, and after OSU sporting events, especially football games. Unfortunately, students and locals sometimes lose control of their emotions, and "parties" become "riots." After Ohio State defeated Texas in 2006, violence broke out on the OSU campus. Almost forty fires were set in student neighborhoods, seventeen people were arrested, five for arson, and two cars caught fired when a nearby trash bin was set ablaze.

These riots usually begin at big parties in off-campus residences where hosts retain little control over who attends. Ironically, these mammoth house parties are the direct result of, in one student's opinion, the university's actions. Over the past few years, the university, in collaboration with the city government, used the power of eminent domain to drive out several bars on High Street, ostensibly in the name of revitalization. As a result, the campus drinking scene has moved to less centralized and less watched areas. The closing of close-to-campus bars, says one student, has severely dampened campus nightlife and increased concerns about drunk driving.

OSU hosts an array of male and female Greek organizations, though the university doesn't report what percentage of students belong. Students say that these groups are more party- than service-oriented, and don't play a major role in campus life—apart from hosting events that are usually open to nonmembers as well.

Students at OSU can take advantage of the 550 clubs the university offers, none of which officially sponsor riots. This number includes at least three dozen honor societies and nearly forty religious organizations. The latter include Baha'i, Buddhist, Catholic, Coptic, Jewish, Muslim, and a very wide array of Protestant organizations, as well as a Women and Spirituality Club. "Most students at Ohio State are involved in at least one club or activity," a student says. "There is nearly a club for every ethnic group and language," such as the American Indian Council, Thai Student Association, Ukrainian Club, Unplugging Society: Women of Color Think Tank, and Latina/o Graduate and Professional Student Association. There are no on-campus foreign "houses" where students can be immersed in a foreign language. Ohio State also offers many opportunities in academics (the Biomedical Engineering and History of Art Undergraduate clubs), activism (the Homeless Initiative, Buckeyes for Haiti Solace, and the Pro Life Club), the performing arts (Film and Video Society and Ukulele Club), or special interest (Quidditch League or Medieval and Renaissance Performers Guild).

Ohio State's intercollegiate sports teams and players are called the Buckeyes, and their mascot is Brutus Buckeye, and they participate in the NCAA's Division I in all sports and the Big Ten Conference in most sports. Ohio State's numerous sports offerings include football, basketball, golf, baseball, tennis and ice hockey. There are also many sports clubs (such as water polo and cricket), and about fifteen intramural sports.

The College Republicans chapter has a sizable membership. The College Democrats are not as popular, although according to one student, that is only "because there are several smaller liberal clubs on campus representing specific liberal interests." The mainstream student paper, the *Lantern*, is an "unapologetic mouthpiece for the extreme left wing," says one student. The *OSU Sentinel*, which represented conservative views, has not published recently.

In campus politics as in academics, OSU is no Wisconsin or Michigan—and in this case, that's a good thing. Political fervor is simply absent at Ohio State. As one student says, "Ohio State is generally a conservative campus; students more so than professors. However, since conservatism is the norm; rarely do conservative groups gain a lot of attention."

Nonetheless, one student considers the influence of the gay and lesbian community at OSU pervasive: "Gays and lesbians are a centerpiece of Ohio State's emphasis on 'diversity.'" He points to the FYE seminar called "Guess the Straight Person," as well as to the placards frequently displayed on university buses. The buses carry messages from the Gay, Lesbian, Bisexual, and Transgender Student Services office advertising ways students can work to

ACADEMIC REQUIREMENTS

Ohio State University general education requirements vary according to the college. In Arts and Sciences, students take:

- At least two courses in "writing and related skills," including an introductory composition course. The other class may be selected from a long list, including "Political Science," "African-American and African Studies," and "Yiddish."
- Three quantitative and logical skills classes.
- Three courses in the natural sciences, including one two-course sequence, at least one course in the biological sciences, one course in the physical sciences, and one lab.
- Three classes in the social sciences from a list of about forty approved courses of varying quality. Examples range from "Political Science" to "African American and African Studies."
- Two courses in the arts and humanities. Classes range all over the map from classics to Japanese, from medieval and Renaissance painting to landscape architecture and a number of women's studies classes.
- Two additional classes from the natural science, social science, or arts and humanities category.
- Two historical studies courses from a long list including women's studies, philosophy, history, and art.
- Three courses that will satisfy the diversity requirement. One course must cover "social diversity in the United States," and two courses must concentrate on "international issues," including one with a non-Western focus. Students can choose from courses such as "Jewish Studies" and "Geography."
- One course from a list entitled Issues in the Contemporary World. Classes in this category include "Plant Pathology" and "City and Regional Planning."
- Students must also show proficiency in a foreign language or complete coursework through the fourth-semester level.

YELLOW LIGHT

Faculty and administrators at Ohio State University lean left. However, as a big state university, OSU offers a smorgasbord of ideas and opinions. Still, the Foundation for Individual Rights in Education (FIRE) recently gave OSU a speech code rating of Red, emphasizing the problems with the Office of University Housing's Diversity Statement. Since that classification, OSU has revised this statement, replacing unconstitutionally vague prohibitions ("Words, actions, and behaviors that inflict or threaten infliction of bodily or emotional harm, whether done intentionally or with reckless disregard, are not permitted") with more clear language.

A 2009 article in the *Sentinel* points out that Ohio State could afford to make some more progress, stating, "As students, it is important to examine these policies and understand them so as not to become entangled in consequences of seemingly harmless actions which, if not for these ambiguous, ill-conceived policies, would not cause anyone to raise an eyebrow."

In a sobering episode, three professors filed a complaint of discrimination and harassment against a librarian who recommended four conservative books for freshmen reading in his role on the First-Year Reading Experience Committee. (The professors said the books he suggested made them feel "unsafe.") The Alliance Defense Fund, which takes on First Amendment violations, sent OSU officials a letter reminding them of the librarian's constitutional rights, yet the university is pressing forward.

stop "homophobia." Among the choicer recommendations: "Do not assume everyone is male or female."

Beyond the gridiron, intramural sports are quite popular. The large campus has many areas for running, cycling, and enjoying nature in the warmer months, and the Recreational and Physical Activity Center opened in June 2005. On fine days, the Oval, a grassy area in the heart of the campus, offers a place for students to study, socialize, and get a breath of fresh air.

The vast majority of students—82 percent—are from Ohio. Only about a quarter live on campus, and relatively few join sororities or fraternities. There are three female-only residence halls, none exclusively for males. The coed dorms house women and men in a variety of ways, sometimes on different floors, sometimes on the same floor but in different wings, and sometimes on the same floor and same wing. All the bathrooms are single-sex, and all dorms are smoke-free. Housing options include the Living-Learning Program, which pairs students with other students who share similar "interests, lifestyle, or commitment to an academic program." Some of these forty programs include the Afrikan American Learning Community, Substance Free program, First-Year Business Focus Community, and Women in Engineering program.

Ohio State has an office of Off Campus Student Services, which is helpful for students who choose to live off campus. The OCSS helps locate off campus housing in the University District and Columbus areas, provides sublet services, legal referrals, a DVD-camcorder rental service, among virtually any other resource dealing with living off campus.

In March 2009, Ohio State's new $118 million Student Union opened. The building is 320,000-square feet and was built on the grounds of the 1950s-era union. It's a three-story building that is "multi-multi-purpose." It is a place for students to study, eat, and hang out. The Archie Griffin Ballroom, which can seat up to 1,200 people, is an ornate place for concerts, meetings, and events. Dining options include Woody's Tavern, transplanted from the old union, and Sloopy's Diner, with a 1960s vibe.

The occasional riot is not the only crime about which students at OSU ought to be concerned. The part of Columbus surrounding campus is notable for its high crime rate. In 2009, the school reported twenty sexual assaults, ten robberies, four aggravated assaults, 178 burglaries, thirteen stolen cars, and ten arsons on campus. Still, one new professor says, "I used to live within walking distance of the campus of U. T. Austin. . . . I planned to live within walking distance here, but it truly is not safe." The campus police department offers both vehicle and walking escorts to students who want them.

Ohio State is quite a bargain for students from the state. While regional campuses are cheaper, even the main campus in Columbus charged only $8,994 in 2010–11. Out-of-state students paid a much heftier $23,178. Room and board averaged at $10,164. The average student-loan debt of a recent graduate who borrowed was $18,426.

College of the Ozarks

Point Lookout, Missouri • www.cofo.edu

Hardwork U.

Students at College of the Ozarks roll up their sleeves for a college education. In exchange for tuition-free classes, they work on the school's cattle and pig farm, bake and sell fruit-cakes, and staff the radio station and lodge—among the more than eighty available types of jobs at the school. About 90 percent of students are from low-income backgrounds, and many are first-generation college students. "Other schools may talk about the American dream (though I suspect far too few actually do); we *are* the American dream," says one professor.

The mountain campus is like a town—with its own hospital, fire department, farm, greenhouses, grain mill, meat processing plant, gas station, museums, motel, bakery and restaurant, all manned by student workers.

Since its founding in 1906 by James Forsythe, a Presbyterian missionary, the institution has transformed itself from a high school into a two-year junior college and, in 1965, a four-year liberal arts college. Forsythe wanted the school to be "a self-sustaining 'family,'" according to the college. Students "without sufficient means" working for an education is a continuing tradition at C of O.

Dubbed Hardwork U by the *Wall Street Journal*, the school draws tourists who visit its historic sites, dine on country-style cooking, and shop for products bearing the label "Hardwork U." Hand-in-hand with a solid liberal arts education, students learn lessons about the dignity of labor, personal responsibility, and free enterprise at this impressive blue-collar academy.

Academic Life: Educating citizens

The College of the Ozarks imposes a serious core curriculum, which every student must complete, guaranteeing that each graduate has the basics of a true liberal arts education. All students must take two religion courses, "Biblical Survey," and "Biblical Theology and Ethics." These classes are an introduction to the key themes of the Bible and the process of biblical interpretation. For math and science, College of the Ozarks requires only one college mathematics class and a natural science class. Bachelor of arts students must take two semesters of a foreign language, while bachelor of science students choose either an additional laboratory science, mathematics, or computer science course.

An excellent way to enrich the solid educational experience at C of O is by taking courses in its optional Character Curriculum, a Great Books program. The Character Curriculum focuses on ideals of virtue from different eras, including "[g]reat authors from Homer to Sophocles, Virgil to Dante, Shakespeare to Milton," says the program description. Course selections include "Biblical Ideals of Character," "Medieval/Renaissance Ideals of Character," "Reformation/Modern Ideals of Character," and "American Ideals of Character." One student reports, "I enjoyed drinking deeply from literature in 'Medieval/Renaissance Ideals of Character,' where we read Dante's *Inferno* and *The Confessions* of St. Augustine. I highly recommend the character curriculum for those who seek an intense steeping in the classics, and in other areas as well."

Along with academics and work, the college emphasizes spiritual growth and patriotism. "We seek to challenge students as they prepare for life, and we strive to develop citizens of Christ-like character who are also well-educated and patriotic," says the school bulletin. The school is not shy about proclaiming its values—one needs only to drive through the "Gates of Opportunity" at the entry of the campus to encounter the core values of the school. The streets are named, charmingly, Academic Avenue, Vocational Way, Spiritual Street, Opportunity Avenue, and Cultural Street.

The college offers more than forty majors in seven divisions: business and communication, education and health, nursing and human services, technical and applied sciences, humanities, performing and professional arts, and mathematical and natural sciences. In addition to traditional liberal arts disciplines, the school offers majors tied to the businesses on campus, including agriculture, conservation and wildlife management, criminal justice, dietetics, family and consumer sciences, hotel and restaurant management, and nursing.

College of the Ozarks offers its students extensive advising opportunities. Upon enrollment, students are assigned an advisor who is well versed in program requirements for their field of study.

Department requirements for English majors are impressive. The department mandates twelve courses: "Foundations of Literary Studies," "Introduction to Grammar," two "Survey of British Literature" and two "Survey of American Literature" classes, "Western

VITAL STATISTICS

Religious affiliation: *Presbyterian*
Total enrollment: *1,500*
Total undergraduates: *1,500*
SAT/ACT midranges: *not applicable*; ACT: *19–25*
Applicants: *3,000*
Applicants accepted: *11%*
Accepted applicants who enrolled: *91%*
Tuition and fees: *free*
Room and board: *$5,300*
Freshman retention rate: *80%*
Graduation rate: *66% (4 yrs.), 60% (6 yrs.)*
Courses with fewer than 20 students: *63%*
Student-faculty ratio: *15:1*
Courses taught by graduate students: *none*
Most popular majors: *business, criminal justice, education*
Students living on campus: *83%*
Guaranteed housing for four years? *yes*
Students in fraternities or sororities: *none*

Literature" (Greek, Roman, and medieval), three English electives, a literary criticism seminar, and a creative writing class. An English major says that the strengths of the department are its "dedicated and passionate faculty members." He notes that while course selections may be limited, teachers are "more than willing to craft special problems or directed reading courses which make up for this lack." Many work assignments in the school's work program reinforce an academic program in English, including positions in the Lyon's Memorial Library, KZOC radio station, the *Outlook* student newspaper, tutoring services, and public relations and academic offices.

History majors at C of O are required to take two Western civilization survey courses, an American history class, and a historiography class. The department calls for seven advanced courses, with at least three in American history and two in modern European history, one course in non-Western (or developing world) history, and one elective. Students also complete a writing-intensive seminar focused on a period or topic in European, American, or developing-world history and an ungraded portfolio class. Students say that while some of the history classes are taught from a liberal perspective, professors treat the Western heritage and American institutions with reasonable respect and welcome opposing viewpoints.

Political science majors are required to take "American National Government" and "American State and Local Government," as well as five other advanced political science courses.

A philosophy and religion major has found that the department is more focused on religion than philosophy but adds that professors are "more than willing" to create programs based on student interest and to research new topics for study side-by-side with students. The full-time faculty members are "extremely student-oriented" and mentor students inside and outside the classroom, he says. Required courses for majors include "History of the Christian Church," "Old Testament" and "New Testament," "Prophets," "Teachings of Jesus," "History of Philosophy," "Logic and Language," and "Seminar in Theology."

The agricultural programs preserve the agrarian tradition of the school and the region, while the military science programs foster character development, patriotism, and physical fitness. The most popular majors are business administration and early childhood education.

Among C of O's strongest departments are English; philosophy and religion; education; business; military science; and agriculture. Mass communication is considered by students to be the weakest department. They say that it suffers from a lack of leadership and too few teachers. One student reports, "There is little opportunity for career development and very little funding. Also, the professors do not offer much in the way of career counseling."

Noteworthy faculty members include Eric Bolger and Mark Rapinchuk in philosophy and religion; Kevin Riley and Rex Mahlman in business; Colonel Gary Herchenroeder and Major James Schreffler in military science; Dana McMahon and Danita Frazier in education; Daniel Swearengen in agriculture; Roberta Kervin in biology; James Bell, Hayden Head, and Larry Isitt in English; Gary Hiebsch in speech communication, and C. David Dalton and David Ringer in history.

Students say that professors are actively involved in their lives and that most faculty participate in different organizations on campus. "I believe that the accessibility and the willingness to help of C of O professors is probably one of the institution's strongest traits. Every professor I had at C of O took a vested interest in me; each wanted me to succeed," says a graduate who now works at the college. One transfer student from a large state university says that before Thanksgiving, he went to dinner with his class at a professor's home. "Upon leaving [the professor's] house that evening, he inquired about my Thanksgiving plans. I informed him that I was driving to my parents' home for the holiday, at which time he proceeded to ask me if I had enough money for gas. I assured him that I did, three times." Finally, the student says, the professor took his word for it. "This is just one example of how most professors from College of the Ozarks treat their students," he says.

The faculty at C of O do not have publishing requirements, teaching assistants, or tenure. Teaching loads are heavy—normally five courses in one semester, four in the other.

The college encourages faculty to enhance their education through travel and will contribute funds to worthy proposals through the Citizens Abroad Program. History faculty and students have traveled to Europe to study the history of World War II or gone to visit Civil War battlefields and national parks, historic civil rights sites in the South, and presidential libraries.

The foreign language department offers a major or minor in Spanish. Students in education may also pursue a course of study leading to a teaching certificate in a foreign language. Students may take up to two semesters in Hebrew or New Testament Greek through the department of philosophy and religion.

Student Life: Two miles from Branson

The College of the Ozarks sits forty miles from the city of Springfield, Missouri, and two miles from Branson, Missouri—which is, we are reliably informed, a popular vacation site. The area is known for its lakes, live performance theaters, theme parks, and historic downtown. The school's 1,000-acre campus provides a peaceful setting in Point Lookout, including a lovely view of Lake Taneycomo. Students take painstaking care of the landscaping, which includes walking paths, a pond, and fountains.

A focal center on campus is the Keeter Center, built in 2004. It houses Dobyns restaurant, a gourmet bakery, a gift shop, meeting and conference space, lodging rooms, an auditorium, and classrooms. The center is a re-creation of a vast log cabin displayed by the state of Maine at the 1904 World's Fair in St. Louis, then sold to the school along with 207 acres of land. The log cabin became one of C of O's original school buildings but was lost to a fire in 1930.

The newly renovated neo-Gothic Williams Memorial Chapel was built by students in 1956 out of locally quarried limestone. The structure features a soaring eighty-foot vaulted ceiling and stained glass windows depicting a chronological history of the Bible. Other notable buildings on campus include the Fruitcake and Jelly Kitchen, which makes and sells the school's famous fruitcakes (more than 40,000 cakes are baked each year), and a variety of jellies and apple butter.

Edwards Mill, a replica of a nineteenth-century grist mill, is powered by a twelve-foot water wheel turned by runoff water from nearby Lake Honor. Student workers grind whole-grain meal and flour. Upstairs is a weaving studio, where students design and produce rugs, shawls, place mats, and other items on traditional looms. Downstairs, students hand-weave baskets.

Ralph Foster Museum is dedicated to the history of the Ozarks region. Called the Smithsonian Institution of the Ozarks, the museum houses thousands of objects—including an extensive collection of western and Native American artifacts. One of the less scholarly exhibits displays the original vehicle used in the television series *The Beverly Hillbillies*.

ACADEMIC REQUIREMENTS

C of O provides students with the foundations of a liberal arts education and a familiarity with the Western tradition through its general education requirements. Students must complete the following:

- One course in "The American Experience" (covering our history from precolonial times to the present), one on the U.S. government, and one on state or local government.
- One American, Western, or classical literature class.
- One two-course sequence in English composition.
- One Western civilization survey class.
- One course in exploration of visual arts, theater, or music.
- One class in visual art, drama, or philosophy.
- One course in social science (for example, "The American Economy," "Introduction to Psychology," or "Introduction to Sociology").
- One natural science course.
- One college mathematics class.
- One information management class.
- "Biblical Survey" and "Biblical Theology and Ethics."
- One two-course sequence on "Citizenship and Lifetime Wellness." These classes are often taught by military science faculty and address and promote patriotism, citizenship, "leadership skills and intelligent decisions regarding health and wellness," the school reports.
- One fitness-based activity class.
- One public-speaking class.

Each C of O student works fifteen hours during the week and two forty-hour work-weeks over the course of the academic year. To cover their room and board, students pay cash or work in a summer program. The management of the work-study program is handled by the dean of work education. Students are assigned workstations as they are available on the basis of interest, experience, and ability. Freshmen are usually placed in the cafeteria or the Keeter Center their first semester and then transfer to another job, says a student. Students have supervisors, and grades are given for each work assignment.

Attendance at chapel and convocations is mandatory. Students with fewer than ninety-one hours are required to attend Sunday chapel a minimum of seven times during each semester. "The Christian faith is stressed and no denominational emphasis is made. The college's idea is to receive students of different denominations and help them become more faithful members of their respective churches," says the student handbook. Students also will need to attend convocations until they have accrued ninety-one hours at the college. The convocations include the Gittinger Convocation Series, forums, artistic programs, general interest, and Christian-themed lectures and events. Recent speakers visiting the campus were more political, including former governor of Alaska Sarah Palin and former White House press secretary Tony Snow.

C of O's intention to enhance the development of character and good citizenship among its students is manifest in its rules and regulations concerning conduct between the sexes, appearance, and alcohol and drugs. There are no fraternities or sororities, and 83 percent of the student body lives on campus in one of the six single-sex residence halls, where visits between the sexes are limited to the lounge areas. In order to live off campus, the student must be either married, a military veteran, or living with a parent or guardian. The RAs are "very friendly and the housing directors have a vested interest in students' well-being," a student says. Another undergrad says, "My dorm is fairly quiet, which is nice, but there are always plenty of activities planned by the housing staff." Students follow a sensible, work-friendly dress code. Regarding alcohol and drugs, the school has adopted a "zero-tolerance policy." Students say that failure to comply leads to immediate expulsion.

The school accepts only 11 percent of applicants. Ninety percent of the students from each entering class must, by school policy, be from low-income backgrounds—while the other 10 percent consists of children of alumni, scholarship recipients, and international students. About 70 percent of students are drawn from the largely rural and mountainous Ozarks region encompassing southern Missouri, northern Arkansas, and small parts of Kansas, Oklahoma, and Illinois. The remaining students come to the school from forty-one states and fifteen countries.

A graduate says that from C of O, he has gained a very large community of friends who are like family. It is a place where "healthy relationships" are the norm and where people "put others ahead of themselves," he says. "The work program weeds out the less-than-serious students," he adds. He adds that the educational experience at C of O is "broad and deep" and understanding the reasons and purpose of work gave him an edge when working on Capitol Hill. The former student has returned to rural Missouri to run for state representative.

One of the most active student groups on campus is the Student Senate. It organizes activities including the fall's Welcome Week, which involves skating or bowling, movies,

GREEN LIGHT

Recently, College of the Ozarks has attracted recognition at a national level. In December 2009, Fox News aired a live interview with two College of the Ozarks students who discussed the work program. Soon after, Young America's Foundation ranked it in the top ten among the nation's conservative colleges and universities. Students agree that professors are open about their beliefs but don't try to discourage or stifle debate nor do they pretend to be final authorities. A professor says, "We are freer to discuss controversial issues than the faculty and students at those campuses which are supposedly more open-minded."

In April 2011, the school invited George W. Bush to speak to the student body at the Character and Leadership Convocation. The event was open to the public and sold out within hours of its announcement.

and a dance; monthly coffee houses; residence-hall open houses; campus debates; and the Spring Formal.

Other activities that students enjoy when they are taking a break from hard work include Homecoming Weekend and Lip Sync, an evening of faculty and student performances to favorite songs. The vignettes are held together by onstage hosts and original video spots including creative, comedic commercials. It plays to a standing-room-only crowd every spring.

Students in Free Enterprise takes on many projects each year and travels internationally to pioneer other S.I.F.E. clubs. In addition to academic clubs, some of the other student groups on campus include the Student Alumni Association, Baptist Student Union, Catholic Newman Association, Math-Physics Club, Horticulture Club, Hotel and Restaurant Society, International Student Club, InterVarsity Christian Fellowship, Jazz Band, Jones Theatre Company, Christian Psychology Club, Public Relations Club, Graphic Arts Club, Chorale, Wilderness Activities Club, College Democrats and College Republicans, and ROTC. There are no "diversity" or multicultural clubs, nor are there gay and lesbian, feminist, or pro-choice organizations.

Campus ministry programs include the Camp Koinonia retreat in the fall and the College of the Ozarks Lifestyle Leadership program, which pairs up students with faculty for one semester to work on various service projects in order to teach life and leadership skills.

In 1925, College of the Ozarks chose their mascot: a bobcat. The inspiration came from a stuffed bobcat perched upon a fireplace mantle at the college. College of the Ozarks Bobcats participate in the NAIA (National Association of Intercollegiate Athletics) and is a member of the Midlands Collegiate Athletic Conference. It sponsors men's teams in basketball and baseball and has teams for women in volleyball and basketball. The school frequently hosts the Men's NAIA National Basketball Championship.

A student-administered intramural sports program includes basketball, flag football, soccer, volleyball, softball, tennis, and Ultimate Frisbee. The college fieldhouse has three basketball courts, an Olympic-size swimming pool, weight room, racquetball courts, dance studio, and volleyball, badminton, and table tennis facilities. Outdoor areas include an all-weather track, softball and baseball fields, and tennis courts.

C of O is one of the quietest campuses in the country. Students say that they leave residence room doors unlocked. "The only crime of which I am aware is the occasional student who tries to hide alcohol in his or her dorm," says a student. Although criminal offenses are quite rare by all accounts—three burglaries and one stolen car—campus security provides twenty-four-hour foot and vehicle patrols of the campus. There are emergency telephones located throughout.

The college charges no full-time tuition and requires all students to work at an on-campus job. Room and board, however, averages at $5,300. The college discourages student borrowing and does not participate in federal educational loan programs. Some 90 percent of students receive need-based financial aid, and the average student-loan debt of a recent graduate is only $4,648.

Wabash College

Crawfordsville, Indiana • www.wabash.edu

A few good men

There's only one rule at Wabash: The student will "conduct himself at all times, both on and off the campus, as a gentleman and a responsible citizen." The rule tells you a lot—for instance that the school aims to form gentlemen, not ladies. Wabash, founded by Dartmouth men in 1832, is one of only a few all-male colleges left in America. The emphasis at Wabash remains on continuity and tradition; the college president rings in freshmen during orientation and rings out seniors at commencement using the same bell Mr. Caleb Mills, the school's first teacher, used some 180 years ago. The school seems poised to carry on its traditions and distinctive mission for decades to come.

Wabash is a good choice for young men in pursuit of the liberal arts. The college does take seriously the ideal of the liberal arts—the education and development of the person. Moreover, destructive political correctness, with a few exceptions, is absent from campus and classes alike, and conservative students will find an environment that both supports and challenges their ideas.

Academic Life: Half Great Books, half . . .

The Wabash curriculum is better than at many liberal arts colleges. The faculty has an unusually clear idea of what undergraduate education is all about. The smallness of the place discourages self-indulgent specialization, and the single-sex student body means that students can "say what they think, without worrying about trying to impress girls" or "adjusting their remarks to placate feminist or other current orthodoxies," according to a professor.

Wabash's common requirements include a freshman tutorial, a worthy freshman colloquium entitled "Enduring Questions", and a sophomore year of "Culture and Traditions" (C&T), which is traditionally presented as a two-semester Great Books course.

However, one student says that C&T often becomes "an ideological dumping ground," infused with multicultural ideology and content. While only about 6 percent of Wabash men are black, almost one fourth of the materials studied in C&T appear to reflect the agenda of the school's powerful (and alarmingly named) Malcolm X Institute. As one student says, "it would be nice if I could accurately describe C&T as a Great Books course, but this unfortunately is not the case. I guess right now it's half Great Books, half propaganda." On the bright side, he suggests, "there is a possibility that as C&T is reduced to one semester, it will be refocused on Great Books, so we [conservatives] will be hitting that pretty hard in the near future, I would imagine."

"The college leans toward a Great Books ethos without actually claiming it," says one professor. "There are some of the typical courses you will find elsewhere, on film, masculinity, race, and feminism, for example, but the college is actually fairly conservative in its attitude toward topical classes geared toward contemporary concerns." Says another, "Writing is of prime importance. This is true across the board." A recent graduate agrees: "What particularly impressed me about Wabash is the premium it places upon writing. In most classes, students regularly are assigned ten- to fifteen-page reports; tests are in essay format, almost never multiple choice." At Wabash, professors actually have the time to give that kind of work the attention it deserves—without giving up their own intellectual lives. Classes are small; 77 percent enroll less than twenty students; the largest class size is thirty-three.

The present Wabash curriculum dates from 1927, with some minor revisions from 1973 and 2004. At the beginning of 2011, Wabash announced its new Asian Studies and the Liberal Arts program, which operates in collaboration with DePauw University. As the college reports, this program is part of the college's current strategic plan and focus on "internationalizing its curriculum and providing interdisciplinary teaching and learning opportunities for students and faculty."

VITAL STATISTICS

Religious affiliation: *none*
Total enrollment: *917*
Total undergraduates: *917*
SAT/ACT midranges: CR: *520–630*, M: *540–660*; ACT: *21–27*
Applicants: *1,588*
Applicants accepted: *49%*
Accepted applicants who enrolled: *32%*
Tuition and fees: *$30,400*
Room and board: *$8,300*
Freshman retention rate: *87%*
Graduation rate: *62% (4 yrs.), 67% (6 yrs.)*
Courses with fewer than 20 students: *77%*
Student-faculty ratio: *10:1*
Courses taught by graduate students: *none*
Most popular majors: *English, history, psychology*
Students living on campus: *86%*
Guaranteed housing for four years? *yes*
Students in fraternities: *49%*

Whatever the imperfections of the school's common curriculum, the requirements for majors and even minors are mostly quite strong.

English majors take three survey courses, chosen from six: "Introduction to Medieval and Renaissance Literature"; "Introduction to Shakespeare"; "English Literature 1660–1800"; "Introduction to English Literature 1800–1900"; "Introduction to British Literature after 1900"; "Introduction to American Literature before 1900"; and "Introduction to American Literature after 1900." Majors also take "Studies in Critical Reading" and four additional courses, such as "Studies in Literary Genres: British Drama: Medieval and Tudor"; "Studies in Individual Authors: Jane Austen" and "Seminar in English Literature: Science Fiction Studies." Majors also take comprehensive exams—a rare and worthy requirement.

History majors take one course in world history either before or since 1500; another course in the philosophy and craft of history; a research seminar; and six more courses

SUGGESTED CORE

1. Freshman Tutorial 010-M, Homer's *Iliad* and the Meaning of Masculine Heroism
2. Philosophy 140, Philosophy of the Classical Period
3. Religion 141/162, Hebrew Bible/History and Literature of the New Testament
4. Religion 171, History of Christianity to the Reformation
5. Political Science 335, History of Political Thought: Hobbes to the Twentieth Century
6. English 216, Introduction to Shakespeare
7. History 241, America to 1877
8. History 231, Nineteenth-Century Europe (closest match)

(including two advanced courses) such as "Topics in American History," "America to 1877," "Topics in Latin American History," "Topics in Asian History," "Classical and Imperial China to 1911," "Topics in African History," and "Advanced Topics, Medieval and Early Modern Europe." This means that one could emerge having studied little or no American or European history. Students must also maintain a portfolio of papers, the evaluation of which is part of the senior comprehensive.

The major in political science requires four introductory surveys—of American politics, comparative politics, political theory, and international politics. He takes two advanced courses in one area of specialization chosen from the four areas above, for example, "History of Political Thought: American Political Thought," "Topics: International Relations: Militaries as Political Actors," "Economic and Political Development," or "Topics in Constitutional Law"; plus at least two additional political science courses and a senior seminar with a research paper. One conservative student, however, laments that "there is not a single Republican—let alone a conservative—on the staff of the political science department. In my comparative politics course, I start out the morning with a (on a good day) ten-minute harangue about Republicans, conservatives, or why Scandinavia is 'God's country.'" He adds, however, that "the department grades fairly despite their obvious biases."

The department best known nationally is religious studies, which is home to the Center for Teaching and Learning in Religion and hosts an annual summer institute for professors of religion from other colleges. The program is particularly strong on Christian scripture, history, and theology, and is unusually encouraging to traditional understandings of the faith. Ironically, Wabash can get away with this because it has no church affiliation—and hence remains immune to the secularizing trends that have gutted so many "mainline" denominations. One professor of religion told us how pleased he was at the number of "devout Roman Catholics" teaching in other departments and their contribution to the spiritual and intellectual ethos of the campus community. Readers of this guide will be pleased to note that Stephen Webb, whose writings grace the pages of *Touchstone*, *First Things*, and *National Review*, is one of the stars of the Wabash religion faculty. A student tells us that all the professors in this department are fair and approachable teachers. "Even the resident liberal theologian (once affiliated with the Jesus Seminar) grades fairly essays that critique his positions."

English, history, and the classics are also strong. One student says that the English faculty "knows how to engage students and elicit vibrant class discussions" and that the department is seen as "one of the more dynamic academic programs" on campus.

One resource that keeps Wabash focused on its mission is the Center of Inquiry in the Liberal Arts, an institute on campus whose mission is "to explore, test, and promote liberal arts education, and to ensure that its nature and value are widely understood in an increasingly competitive higher education market." The center conducts research on the aims, methods, and results of liberal arts education on the national scene.

Wabash tends to attract top-notch professors who are revered among students. A recent graduate says that, "They come to Wabash, many of them at least, because it's a place that espouses cutting-edge academic research as much as it does excellence in teaching and student mentorship. Students are encouraged to seek out their professors and to use them as resources in their academic and personal lives. . . . By my senior year, I had dined or had drinks with most of my professors. . . . Wabash professors, especially Warren Rosenberg and William Placher, mean the world to me. . . . I graduated with the feeling that I knew my professors not merely as scholars or intellectuals, but as people." Another student agrees, "Many of the faculty do spend a great deal of time with students and attend student activities such as athletic events, concerts, and lectures." With a strong student-faculty ratio of 10 to 1, this kind of thing can happen. At Wabash it does.

Wabash students particularly recommend teachers Jon Baer and David Blix in religion; David Krohne, John Munford, and David Polley in biology; and David Kubiak in classics.

Wabash College offers twenty-one majors, including joint programs in law and engineering with Columbia University, another joint program in engineering with Washington University, and the recently announced combined, BA/BS program in partnership with Purdue's engineering school. Three quarters of Wabash graduates find themselves in graduate and professional schools within five years. Of Wabash alumni, one in eight holds the title CEO, president, or chairman; it also has a 95 percent acceptance rate to law school and 81 percent acceptance into medical school.

Through the Great Lakes Colleges Association and other means, Wabash men are able to study abroad in such exotic locations as Japan or Fiji. Indeed, a quarter of Wabash men go abroad to one of more of 140 countries, and their student-aid packages travel with them. And if a student comes up with a meritorious research proposal that doesn't seem to fit in anywhere, Wabash will do its considerable best to find funding for it. Wabash also encourages internships and collaborative student-professor research projects throughout the academic year and during summer breaks. Some destinations include New York for the arts, Italy to Assissi and an introduction to St. Francis, and Belgium and Germany for the study of the European Union.

Foreign languages offered at Wabash include Latin and Ancient Greek, German, French, Spanish, and Russian.

Student Life: The Sphinx and the village

The Wabash campus occupies sixty acres of woodland, Georgian brick, and well-kept grounds in the town of Crawfordsville, Indiana. The library, fine arts center, athletics and recreation center, biology and chemistry building, modern language facility, fraternities, and dorms have all been newly built or renovated within the past decade. The Lilly Library holdings include more than 434,000 books, 5,530 serial subscriptions, and an extensive media collection. The Malcolm X Institute for Black Studies's $2 million headquarters was designed to reproduce "the symbolism and spatial arrangement found in a traditional African village." It is the only African village for miles around.

Crawfordsville is only forty-five miles from Indianapolis. The nearest coeds are an hour away, at DePauw, Butler, Purdue, and the University of Illinois; Indiana University is even farther. But women are for the weekends, and so is drinking, that last refuge of the dateless; one hears little of drug use. Without women, there is no need to dress to impress, and while there are students of considerable means, they don't stand out. Indeed, the student paper warns that the Wally who wants to get a job had better learn to dress up for it.

ACADEMIC REQUIREMENTS

Wabash imposes a modest curriculum on students. As of now, all students must take:

- One freshman tutorial. Recent choices included "Founding Brothers and Revolutionary Characters," "The Supreme Court," "The Blues Experience: Exploring Blues Music, Cultures, and Literature in the U.S. South and the Global South," and "Men and Masculinities."
- One freshman colloquium, "Enduring Questions," devoted to "fundamental questions of humanity from multiple perspectives."
- Two semesters of "Cultures and Traditions."
- Two courses in history, philosophy, or religion. Selections included "Introduction to Existentialism," "The World from 1945–Present," and "History of Christianity to the Reformation."
- One course in language studies from a selection of rhetoric, English, Spanish, and French.
- Three courses in literature and fine arts. Choices include "Introduction to Shakespeare," "Music in the Middle Ages, Renaissance, and Baroque Era (to 1750)," "Introduction to Film," and "History of Western Art."
- Three courses in behavioral sciences, from economics, political science, and psychology. Courses must be taken from at least two of these three departments. Choices include "Comparative Economic Systems," "Survey of International Politics," and "Cognitive Neuropsychology."
- Three courses (with two labs) in the natural sciences and mathematics, from biology, chemistry, computer science, mathematics, and physics. Courses must be taken from at least two of these departments.
- One course in quantitative skills from a selected list in computer science, mathematics, philosophy, economics, political science, and psychology.
- Coursework or test scores to demonstrate proficiency in a foreign language as well as English.
- A maximum of nine courses in the student's major.
- Five courses in the student's minor.
- A senior oral and written comprehensive examination.

College life centers on its nine fraternities and the elite Sphinx Club, dedicated to "promoting campus unity, spirit, and togetherness among all students of Wabash through traditional and philanthropic events." About 50 percent of the student body are fraternity men, all of whom, including pledges, live in frat houses. Fraternities seem to dominate campus life. Independents say that the school caters more to Greeks and often ignores the concerns of others.

Wabash has more than sixty Student Senate–recognized clubs and organizations, such as student government; departmental clubs; political clubs; speech, music, and theater groups; various literary publications, a weekly newspaper, and yearbook; student-run radio; special interest groups; and religious groups. Examples include a Cooking Club, a Fiction Writers Club, a Film Club, a Wilderness and Adventure Club, a World Music Club, the Progressive Students Movement, 'sHOUT (the official organization for gay, bisexual, questioning, and supportive students), and the aforementioned Sphinx Club. Furthermore, Wabash College boasts a number of music and theater groups, such as the Wabash Chamber Orchestra and the Acting Company. The *Phoenix* is published by Wabash's Conservative Union. Other student-run newspapers include Wabash's the *Bachelor*, "the voice of Wabash since 1908," and *Callimachus*, an arts journal.

One of the most impressive things about Wabash College, says one student, is "the quality of outside speakers that the college and clubs bring in to lecture. Though we are a college with fewer than 1,000 students in a small town in the middle of nowhere, the college consistently attracts big-name and high-quality speakers and performers." In fall 2010, Princeton Professor Robert George spoke at Wabash on natural law.

The political atmosphere at Wabash in general, says one student—and many agree—is "one of free and vigorous debate. While the professors are overwhelmingly leftists, the student body leans more to the center-right." College Republicans are active on campus, as is the Conservative Union.

Emblematic of the Wabash spirit is something called Chapel Sing, in which students compete to see who can sing the school song the loudest.

GREEN LIGHT

Conservative and religious students will find Wabash a warm and tolerant place, but this doesn't mean that the professoriate is on the whole sympathetic to conservative or libertarian ideas. It does mean that teachers are unusually tolerant and really do believe that disciplined study and open discussion advance the cause of truth—on which they do not believe they have a monopoly. "While Wabash attracts a conservative student population, the faculty, which like most academic institutions leans more to the left than to the right, is not overtly political inside the classroom," a student says. "Professors have reputations for political bias, but I think they reserve their activism mainly to academic publishing, public speaking, and one-to-one informal conversations with students."

Of course, not all Wallys (as Wabash students are affectionately called) play on the same team. 'sHOUT (short for "Wabash OUT") has official recognition and funding for meetings, lectures, and an "alternative"—that is to say, drag—party that attracts many from other colleges. Wabash was one of the first in the region to stage Tony Kushner's homo-Marxist drama *Angels in America*.

Wabash competes in NCAA's Division III, so there are no athletic scholarships, and sports practice is kept to two hours a day at most. Men who wouldn't get to play varsity elsewhere make the team here; indeed, nearly half do. Much enthusiasm goes into the traditional football rivalry with DePauw, with the freshman class keeping night watch against invading pranksters on the eve of the big Monon Bell game. Beside football, Wabash competes in ten other varsity sports—cross-country, soccer, golf, basketball, indoor track and field, outdoor track and field, wrestling, tennis, swimming, and baseball—as a member of the North Coast Athletic Conference. Twenty-two intramural sports (including canoeing, cycling, cross-country, golf, handball, horseshoes, indoor carnival, indoor track, pocket billiards, racquetball) and five club sports (rugby, crew, cricket, lacrosse, and volleyball) round off the active sports life at Wabash. More than three-quarters of Wabash students participate in at least one intramural sport.

Crime is not much of a problem at Wabash. The only crimes reported on campus in 2009 were seven burglaries.

Tuition in 2010–11 was $30,400, and room and board $8,300. Roughly 80 percent of students receive some need-based aid, and the average debt of a recent graduate was $28,383. The good news is that the college gives an unusually large number of generous merit scholarships to students. As one student says, "Personally, I could not have gone to Wabash if it weren't for the merit scholarships it provided me."

Washington University in St. Louis

St. Louis, Missouri • www.wustl.edu

Truth and consequences

Washington University was founded as Eliot Seminary in 1853 and from small beginnings has distinguished itself as among the top universities in the country, with an ability to attract some of the nation's best students and renowned faculty. Attaining elite status for Washington has apparently included adopting the ideological fashions that prevail in such institutions. Sources say that the student attending Washington University will face a rigorously multiculturalist ethos pervading both campus life and the classroom. Nevertheless, there is a lot of scholarly firepower at this university, which makes it a worthy option for the self-directed student. One professor says that "a great deal of academic freedom" and a "nonintrusive administration" means that faculty are free to be more flexible in how and what they teach, and thus can more easily respond to the needs of students. Faculty are not notable for spouting politics in the classroom. One professor told us that he tried to "keep it out as much as possible."

Professors say that Washington University students tend to be more professionally than intellectually oriented. As one professor says, "They do the work; they're smart; they're capable," but they are also often "very worried about grades," which tends to mean that they can be less inquisitive. Another professor characterizes Washington University students as "pretty serious kids" and notes that "the library is always pretty crowded." The fact that such a large percentage of freshmen intend to become doctors and that the business school is so popular suggests that most students enter Washington University having already chosen a career.

Academic Life: Harvard of the Midwest?

Students can get a traditional liberal arts education at Washington but only if they seek it out. The school's distributional requirements are not particularly strong, nor are its science mandates (only one course in quantitative analysis is mandated for the BA in arts and sciences). Those who want something close to a traditional core curriculum should explore "Text & Tradition" (T&T), one of seven optional First-Year Academic Programs. In this interdisciplinary program "students explore the classic texts and intellectual traditions upon which American and European culture has been built." Reading lists "are chosen with

VITAL STATISTICS

Religious affiliation: *none*
Total enrollment: *13,820*
Total undergraduates: *7,138*
SAT/ACT midranges: CR:
  680–750, M: *710–790*;
  ACT: *32–34*
Applicants: *24,939*
Applicants accepted: *21%*
Accepted applicants who
  enrolled: *31%*
Tuition and fees: *$39,400*
Room and board: *$12,941*
Freshman retention rate:
  97%
Graduation rate: *86% (4 yrs.),*
  94% (6 yrs.)
Courses with fewer than 20
  students: *72%*
Student-faculty ratio: *7:1*
Courses taught by graduate
  students: *not provided*
Most popular majors: *arts*
  and sciences, engineering,
  business/marketing
Students living on campus:
  79%
Guaranteed housing for
  four years? *yes*
Students in fraternities: *25%*
  in sororities: *25%*

care from the best of Western thought," says one student, but "the T&T faculty seem to have no conception of the physical limits on reading." The same student says that Text & Tradition is "no substitute for a true liberal arts education," but that it "is absolutely essential if you go to Washington University, because it might very well be the only engagement to be had in the Great Books style."

Another noteworthy freshman option is FOCUS, a yearlong seminar program that explores one major topic from the perspective of a variety of disciplines. Eight FOCUS groups are typically offered each year (ten in the academic year 2010). Recent topics included "Nationalism and Identity: The Making of Modern Europe," "Cuba: From Colonialism to Communism," and "Law and Society." These courses are limited to fourteen to sixteen students each. "We want to encourage students to think more deeply about issues and to get into discussion with the faculty and with their peers," says one professor.

A worthy major that builds on the Text & Tradition program is the Interdisciplinary Project in the Humanities (IPH). One member of faculty says that there is "a lot of intellectual energy in the department." The faculty has a "high level of scholarship" with "a lot of publications" among professors. And students, says the same professor, "can get a lot of individual attention from the very beginning." The IPH Major consists of an introductory core, which introduces students to "the American and European philosophical, religious, and literary traditions." The project's cultural calendar, called the Lyceum, allows students to attend a wide range of cultural events, including concerts, theater, operas, and exhibitions.

Washington University also offers more than 250 "cluster courses" in four distribution areas: natural sciences and mathematics; social sciences; textual and historical studies; and language and the arts. Clusters consist of several courses grouped together and focused on a particular subject or method of analysis, enabling students to get a much richer experience in their chosen area.

The university assigns advisors to freshmen, but they seldom become close to the students. One student says, "Students are best served by seeking out for themselves professors whom they would like to advise them," since advisor assignments are usually "random and sometimes wholly inappropriate." Premajor advisors are not necessarily faculty members, but after declaring a major, a student is assigned a faculty advisor within his discipline.

Professors, not grad students, lead most courses. As at all research universities, there

Midwest

exists at Washington a tension between teaching and research. Commitment to teaching varies from instructor to instructor. A student says, "Most departments make it a priority to allow professors time to teach. . . . I doubt you'll find it better anywhere else, unless you go to a school where professors do nothing but teach." One professor says, "Most of the (science and nonscience) faculty I know take their teaching very seriously and put a great deal of time into it. On the other hand, there is very strong pressure to get research grants."

Indeed, Washington University has a first-class seat on the federal gravy train. The school ranks high among private research universities in the amount of federal research grant money it hauls in. Some departments are expected to keep the cash coming. So, in the humanities, "professors are extremely accessible to students," but science professors remain much more aloof, an undergrad reports. A graduate student says that "older faculty teach far more than they publish, while newer faculty have considerable workloads in both teaching and publishing." This means that the otherwise impressive student-faculty ratio of 7 to 1 is misleading.

Students interested in the hard sciences and engineering can use the university's emphasis on research to their own advantage. Opportunities abound for student research. The school's world-renowned medical center attracts many premed students. One student claims that most entering freshmen intend to be doctors, but

> ### SUGGESTED CORE
>
> 1. English 241e, Masterpieces of European Literature I
> 2. Philosophy 347c, Ancient Philosophy
> 3. Religious Studies 300/307, Introduction to the Hebrew Bible–Old Testament/Introduction to the New Testament
> 4. Religious Studies 393, Medieval Christianity
> 5. Political Science 392, History of Political Thought II: Legitimacy, Equality, and the Social Contract, Political Science 393, History of Political Thought III: Liberty, Democracy, and Revolution
> 6. English 395, Shakespeare
> 7. History 365, The New Republic: The United States, 1776–1850
> 8. History 442, European Intellectual History: 1789–1890

after realizing how intense the program is, only a fraction of them actually finish as premeds. The premed program and the other sciences together constitute the "university's crown jewel," says another student. Engineering is also outstanding, with a recent graduate remarking, "For an engineering undergraduate, there are no truly 'weak' programs." Another well-respected program is philosophy-neuroscience-psychology (PNP), an interdisciplinary concentration that studies the mind and brain.

A professor says the classics department shows a "willingness to work individually with students." Classics students can take a semester to study in Athens, Rome, or Sicily, or take part in an archaeological project in the Mediterranean, such as the Athenian Agora and the Iklaina Archaeological Project at Pylos.

With Nobel laureate Douglass North (who actually teaches undergraduates), the economics department is also strong, as are the School of Fine Arts and the School of Architecture.

The School of Engineering and Applied Science attracts some of the nation's very best faculty and students. One engineering major says, "Professors [in engineering] tend to be *very* accessible." Many students say the business school is less rigorous than the rest of the university, although it has improved in recent years.

Some departments are weaker than others. The philosophy department, which places a heavy emphasis on interdisciplinary crossover with psychology, linguistics, and cognitive science, offers no medieval philosophy courses and only in recent years added ancient philosophy.

Professors most often mentioned as particularly strong teachers include Eric Brown and Claude Evans in philosophy; Lee Benham and Stephanie Lau in economics; Gerald N. Izenberg, David Konig, and Mark Gregory Pegg in history; Robert Lamberton, George M. Pepe, and Susan Rotroff in classics; and Richard M. Kurtz in psychology. Another student says that those who take one class with professor of Russian language Mikhail Palatnik will "stay in Russian for the rest of their time in school. He's just that good." Other outstanding faculty include Paul Stein in biology, Dewey Holten in chemistry, Gary Jensen in math, and Barna Szabo in mechanical engineering.

Students who major in English will most likely study Shakespeare, but it is not required. Besides a course in American literature and a course in a major author—e.g., Jane Austen or Chaucer—the major further requires two courses in literature before 1700 and two courses before 1900.

Faculty in the history department are said to be excellent. Courses range from the traditional ("Russian History to the 18th Century") to the trendy ("Beyond the Harem: Women, Gender, and Revolution"). Requirements for the major are thin and can be fulfilled without taking either American history or the history of Western civilization. Still, many solid courses are offered by worthy teachers.

One student says that the political science department isn't theoretical enough, focusing on "electoral minutiae, never political philosophy." Departmental requirements permit majors to avoid the study of the American Constitution or American political thought. Students must select courses from three out of five subfields: American politics, comparative politics, international relations, political methodology, and political theory.

Washington University offers a great number of study-abroad options. However, these options are limited and vary according to the department. Thus, English majors can study in the UK and Ireland—as can political science majors, who also have options in Switzerland, Nicaragua, Kenya, Jordan, Israel, India, Chile, and Croatia.

The school offers majors in Arabic, Chinese, French, German, Hebrew, Italian, Japanese, Persian, and Spanish, and courses in many other languages.

Student Life: Under the arch

The city of St. Louis offers a wonderful variety of cultural activities. Sports fans can catch a Cardinals, Rams, or Blues game. The St. Louis Symphony Orchestra is also very popular. But there is much to keep students near the college. Washington University's hilltop campus is located between the quaint upper-class St. Louis suburb of Clayton, Missouri, and the multiethnic, commercially vibrant neighborhood of University City, which throngs with restaurants (most of which include outside dining), used-book shops and record stores, and other establishments catering to hip (and not so hip) student tastes. Forest Park—which includes 1,300 acres of forests, lakes, and hills, plus the St. Louis Zoo, St. Louis Art Museum, and Missouri History Museum—is just across the way from the university.

Most of the university architecture is neo-Gothic, down to the last arch and gargoyle. Key buildings were designed by the famed architects Walter Cope and John Stewardson. Graham Chapel, one of the oldest buildings on campus, is also one of the most frequently photographed. In 2009, the university opened its $1.6 million "living-learning building." The building, one of the first of its kind and part of the Tyson Research Center, where students conduct environmental research, is a "net-zero-energy building," producing all of its own energy and no waste water. Also in 2009, the university added two new residence halls, Umrath and South 40.

There is considerable university interaction with the surrounding neighborhoods (with residents of University City sometimes complaining of "gentrification"), and many of

---

ACADEMIC REQUIREMENTS

Washington University's rather anemic curriculum requires students to take the following:

- One course in English composition in the freshman year.
- One class in quantitative analysis (i.e., formal mathematics, statistics, etc.). Courses that qualify include "Introduction to Statistics" and "Awesome Ideas in Physics."
- One class in social differentiation, with options like "Gender and Education" and "Europe in the Age of Reformation."
- One class that fosters "an understanding of cultural diversity." "Greek History: The Age of Alexander" and "Race and Ethnicity on American Television" qualify.
- One approved upper-level writing-intensive course. Recent examples include "Writing about Greek Literature" and "Topics in Composition: Exploring Cultural Identity in Writing."
- A "capstone experience" in the senior year, such as joining a faculty member in a research project or completing a special project in one's chosen major.

Students must also complete three classes in each of four distribution areas:

- Natural sciences and mathematics. Qualifying courses include "Calculus" III and "The Dinosaurs: 'Facts' and Fictions."
- Social sciences. "History of Law in American Life I: English and Colonial Foundations" and "Lesbian, Gay, Bisexual Identity Development" meet this requirement.
- Textual and historical studies. Such courses include "From Bondage to Freedom in a Revolutionary World" to "Contemporary Female Sexualities."
- Language and the arts. Recent offerings meeting this requirement include "The Language of Early Christianity" and "Stage Lighting."

In each of these areas, students must take at least two courses that form part of a "cluster" of related classes.

the nearly 6,000 undergraduate students volunteer in the city, building houses, feeding the poor, teaching English to immigrants, and tutoring disadvantaged children.

Washington University boasts 270 student organizations, and the Student Union's Student Group Directory lists seven categories of student organizations. Among the numerous educational groups one finds the Undergraduate Economics Association, Pre-Law Society, Pre-Dental Society, Pre-Med Society, the Society of Automotive Engineers and a Debate Team, as well as a Math Club and Washington University Accounting Association. Recreational and cultural clubs include among many more the Washington University Swing Dance Club, the Outing Club, the Culinary Arts Society, the Hawaii Club, the Italo Club, and many ethnic clubs, such as the Turkish Students Association. Other groups include the Alternative Lifestyle Association, the Food Fighters (composed of students with food allergies), and the Committee Organized for Rape Education. Artsy students will enjoy the Washington University Pops Orchestra, the Aristocats (a coed all-Disney *a cappella* group), and More Fools than Wise (a small chamber vocal ensemble).

The university is very politically engaged. Active groups include the College Democrats, College Republicans, and the College Libertarians. The school also has a Conservative Leadership Association that is "nonpartisan and nonsectarian, but all conservative." The official college paper is titled, unimaginatively, *Student Life*.

The Washington University Bears compete on NCAA Division III teams in every major sport. The university particularly excels in women's sports. In 2009, the women's volleyball team claimed the championship, and in March 2010 the women's basketball team won its fifth national championship. The men's basketball team won the title in 2009. Plenty of intramural sports are also available, including racquetball, billiards, swimming, bowling, cross-country, volleyball, flag football, and men's and women's arm wrestling.

Fraternities and sororities attract about one-quarter of the student body. Students say that Greek life dominates the weekend social lives of students, especially freshmen. "For the first two years, if you don't like frat parties, or fratlike dorm parties, then you probably have good friends but nowhere to go with them," says one student. However, Washington University students deny that it's a party school. One professor says, "The university has become much more conscious of drinking problems in recent years." In response, administrators have been imposing ever more regulations on alcohol at parties, particularly the massive, all-campus Walk In, Lay Down (WILD) outdoor party held each semester—which typically features a nationally known band and has been one of the campus's defining traditions since 1973. Even under the administration's watchful eye, WILD is a Rabelaisian affair.

Speaking of spirits, there is a surprisingly strong religious presence at Wash U., with several active Christian groups, including the Baptist Student Union, Association of Christian Truth Seekers, and One Voice Christian Fellowship—plus Jewish groups and a great many clubs for members of other religious faiths. The Catholic Student Center works hard at being popular—too hard, according to Catholic students we interviewed. A better choice is the local Oratory of St. Francis de Sales, which features the Latin Mass with Gregorian chant.

Almost two-thirds of the undergraduate population—including all freshmen—live on campus in one of the ten residential colleges in an area known as South Forty. Each of these residential colleges includes one to three buildings and gives students the feel of a smaller university community. The university guarantees housing only for freshmen, most of whom live in all-freshmen dormitories. All residential halls are coed. There are no coed bathrooms or dorm rooms. However, one student says that on his floor, "the line between sexes in the bathrooms was often blurry." The same student also says that students on his floor also "openly drank" and that dorms were not policed properly. However, substance-free ("sub-free") housing is available to freshmen. The residential-life office offers an apartment-referral service for students who choose to live off campus, and the university also owns apartments near campus that in some cases are closer to classroom buildings than are the dormitories.

Safety is a concern for many Washington University students, especially those living off campus. One student remarked that although the college is located in a "fairly ritzy suburb," and is mostly "clean, crime-free, and well-maintained," students should avoid certain areas at night—especially to the north and east of the college. The university police department provides free security escorts at any time, more than one hundred emergency phones, and frequent crime-prevention workshops. Campus crime statistics, however, list few incidents. In 2009, there were five forcible sex offenses, six motor vehicle thefts, and seven burglaries on campus.

GREEN LIGHT

As with many other colleges, the Washington University campus and student body leans to the left. November 2009 saw a campus group called Green Action lead a protest against two coal companies when the CEOs of both St. Louis–based firms joined Wash U.'s Board of Trustees. One student recalls when former attorney general Alberto Gonzales spoke, "Some students dressed up in orange jumpsuits [and] placed signs around campus to get students to protest." However, the vast majority of students are too focused on grades and career to sign up for the latest rally or protest, or even to discuss politics. Consequently, political ideology generally does not intrude into the classroom. The College Republicans and College Libertarians are both active on campus, though political groups are probably less obtrusive here than at many colleges.

The college showed its commitment to political correctness in 2010 when it canceled a traditional orientation event hosted by a large corporation after it came out that the company had donated $150,000 to a Minnesota political action committee supporting a candidate opposed to gay "marriage."

Undergraduate tuition for the 2010–11 academic year was $39,400, with room and board averaging $12,941. Admissions are not need blind, but about 42 percent of undergraduates receive need-based financial aid.

Wheaton College

Wheaton, Illinois • www.wheaton.edu

Socializing the Gospel

Wheaton, founded in 1860 by antislavery father and son Jonathan and Charles Blanchard, prides itself on being "the Harvard of the Evangelical world." For 150 years, Wheaton has positioned itself as the bulwark of intellectual Christianity, educating students not only with knowledge but wisdom as well. And while Wheaton still has a reputation as a conservative school, over the past several years there has been a decidedly leftward shift. For example, over 60 percent of Wheaton's faculty polled in the *Wheaton Record* claimed to have voted for the pro-choice Barack Obama. (To put that in perspective, imagine, in an another election, that 60 percent of the faculty at U. C. Berkeley had voted for Pat Buchanan.) In addition, Wheaton's once-solid core curriculum now includes two mandatory, politically driven "diversity" courses designed to promote "races, genders, ethnicities, religions, and cultures other than Anglo-American and white majority European," according to the school's website. Not surprisingly, "students come in very hard-line conservative," says one professor, and while "few leave as liberals, many [become] moderates." It appears to some that this 150-year-old bastion of orthodox Christianity is inching down the road of the Social Gospel, which has secularized so many Christian institutions (and entire denominations).

In 2010, Wheaton selected as its new president Philip Ryken, pastor of Tenth Presbyterian Church in Philadelphia. Ryken graduated from the college in 1988 and has served on its board of trustees since 2006; Oxford educated and long associated with the orthodox Calvinist wing of American evangelicalism, Ryken may serve as a center of gravity for more theologically traditional forces at the school.

Academic Life: Illinois roundheads

Although Wheaton's general education requirements have been diluted in recent years, one student declares, "I believe the general education requirements are wonderful. . . . We get to dabble in subjects we might not have even known we would be interested in without those requirements." A professor says, "The core requirements are not as tight as they were a quarter of a century ago, and students must take the initiative. Still, Wheaton has all the resources for grounding yourself as deeply as possible in the liberal arts, through the courses in biblical and theological studies, English, philosophy, art history, history of music, political philosophy, and foreign languages."

Wheaton students choose from among forty undergraduate majors in the arts, sciences, and humanities. One of Wheaton's biggest disciplines is biblical and theological studies. Very close to it in popularity and reputation is the psychology department. These are the only departments at Wheaton that also offer doctoral degrees.

Biblical and theological studies is the "crown jewel" of Wheaton. It is the largest department in terms of both faculty and students. Most professors are published, but the department's main professional standard is quality of teaching. Although each biblical studies professor specializes in one of the two Testaments, the department as a whole gives equal weight to both canons. Theologically, the department is doctrinally conservative, although in methodology it is moderate or left of center, and one can find a fairly wide range of views represented.

The English department is very strong in both scholarly reputation and teaching. All majors must take two courses each in British and American literature, both pre- and post-1800, and may opt to concentrate in writing or secondary-school education. The English writing concentration offers very close working relationships with professors. "The classes are a lot smaller," says one student, "and professors pour a lot of effort into your writing." The department's Wade Center houses papers of C. S. Lewis, J. R. R. Tolkien, Dorothy Sayers, and others, and is a major international research center. The English faculty are outstanding for their publishing records and for winning faculty teaching awards. Classroom discussions are especially intense and engaging. According to one professor, students often have a "Protestant angst" that leads them to explore texts with intensity. "Reading books and poems are deeply engaging activities, often involving the states of their souls or emotions."

The department offers a summer program, Wheaton in England, which leads students to London, Stonehenge, and other culturally important locations, as well as Stratford-on-Avon, John Milton's cottage, and various C. S. Lewis sites. The program includes such courses as "Literature and Place in Romanticism" and "Medieval Literature." Another opportunity is the Scholar's Semester in Oxford, sponsored by the Council for Christian Colleges and Universities. Opportunities at Oxford are not restricted to English and literature, however. This program also offers in-depth studies in classics, theology and religious studies, philosophy, and history.

VITAL STATISTICS

Religious affiliation: *Christian (nondenominational)*
Total enrollment: *2,910*
Total undergraduates: *2,460*
SAT/ACT midranges: CR: *600–710*, M: *600–700*; ACT: *27–31*
Applicants: *1,950*
Applicants accepted: *71%*
Accepted applicants who enrolled: *45%*
Tuition and fees: *$27,580*
Room and board: *$8,050*
Freshman retention rate: *96%*
Graduation rate: *76% (4 yrs.), 88% (6 yrs.)*
Courses with fewer than 20 students: *54%*
Student-faculty ratio: *12:1*
Courses taught by graduate students: *none*
Most popular majors: *social sciences, theology, liberal arts*
Students living on campus: *90%*
Guaranteed housing for four years? *yes*
Students in fraternities or sororities: *none*

SUGGESTED CORE

1. English 101, Classics of Western Literature and Classics 258, Tales of Troy
2. Philosophy 311, History of Philosophy: Ancient Greece through the Renaissance
3. Bible and Theology 211/213, Old Testament/ New Testament Literature and Interpretation
4. Bible and Theology 315, Christian Thought (closest match)
5. Political Science 347, Renaissance and Modern Political Thought
6. English 334, Shakespeare
7. History 351, American History to 1865
8. Philosophy 455, Nineteenth Century Continental Philosophy

The "rising star" at Wheaton is the department of political science and international relations. This department has been growing in prominence at Wheaton, thanks to the school's increasing focus on international issues (a significant number of students are children of overseas missionaries) and its majors' dominance of student government. Over the past few years, the department has become one of the most popular at Wheaton. All poli sci majors must take courses in American political philosophy and the United States Constitution in addition to mandatory internships with governmental and nongovernmental agencies.

The history department is said to be mediocre, not requiring a Western civilization course but offering several world history classes instead. American history before 1865 is offered but not required of majors, alongside "History of Women in the U.S." and "Women's Voices in U.S. History." Students must take at least one course each in American, European, world (Asian, African, or Latin American), and Christian history.

The sociology and anthropology department is politically left of center, but it's still one of the few sociology departments in the country that attempts to place academically rigorous research within a context of biblical ethics. The geology department is described as "small but good," and Wheaton's Conservatory of Music has a strong national reputation, offering six degrees in music. The business and economic program is also well established. Overall, the humanities tend to be stronger than the sciences at Wheaton, although the premed program has been successful in getting students into medical school. The philosophy department covers all areas of modern philosophy and is very popular with students. It just recently filled the vacancy in ancient/medieval philosophy created after the former specialist was fired for becoming a Roman Catholic—which the school said voided his contract.

Foreign language studies have grown in recent years. This department offers the traditional majors in French, German, Spanish, and "Ancient Language" (Greek), and classes in Latin, Hebrew, and Mandarin Chinese. Students can take Arabic at the nearby College of DuPage for transfer credit.

Physics is the weakest science department, and apart from music, the fine arts at Wheaton are small and underdeveloped. The theater is excellent but small, and students cannot major in drama, except as a concentration within communications.

In terms of upgrading the sciences and arts, Wheaton is in the middle of a large capital campaign called the Promise of Wheaton, having reached the 80 percent mark for funds raised as of September 2010. In 2009, the school completed the expansion of its art building by 70 percent to include a new 70-seat lecture hall, new workspaces, new art galleries for professors and students, and an outdoor sculpture garden. Additionally, Wheaton is building a brand new $80 million science center, with eight new teaching labs, research space for every faculty member, research labs that open up into teaching labs, new state-of- the-art equipment (electron microscope, DNA sequencer, anatomy lab with cadavers), and a planetarium/observatory. The library has also been renovated, with long-term plans of building an additional wing.

Wheaton has several study-abroad programs. Its largest is Human Needs and Global Resources (HNGR), a program that offers a certificate in fighting world hunger. Students enter a six-month internship with a nongovernmental organization undertaking development work in a Third World country, while also completing course work. The HNGR program is more than just about fighting global hunger. Students can pursue any internship/research project through HNGR that deals with Third World issues, ranging from prostitution in India, treatment of women in Uganda, environmental sustainability in Thailand, anthropological research in South America, to medical missions in India. There are also various "Wheaton-in" programs (e.g., Wheaton-in-Spain, Wheaton-in-France), generally led by foreign languages faculty. The school runs many overseas ministries that give Wheaton students a chance to travel. Moreover, as one student puts it, "The overseas ministries allow students to both travel *and* serve. Service/evangelism is the main focus of these ministries abroad."

Wheaton's faculty is well regarded by students for its quality and accessibility. "Across the board," says one student, "professors are interested in you, without exception. They spend extra time to be available in office hours, especially for giving help for papers. It's a real consistent ethic." Many students take advantage of Wheaton's "Dine with the Mind" program, which pays for on-campus lunches between professors and students. Wheaton has traditionally placed its biggest emphasis on teaching, although the school "has begun encouraging faculty to integrate research into teaching," says one professor. "And the school has been making an effort to free up professors' time to do research, especially with undergrads. But in making hiring and other decisions, the balance is overwhelmingly in favor of teaching."

Recommended professors include Roger Lundin, Brett Foster, Alan Jacobs, and Leland Ryken in English; Robert Lee Brabenec and Terry Perciante in mathematics; Leroy A. Huizenga, Michael W. Graves, Tim Larsen, George Kalantzis, John Walton, and Dan Treier in Bible/theology; William Struthers in psychology; Mark Amstutz, Sandra Joireman, and P. J. Hill in economics; Sarah Borden and Jay Wood in philosophy; L. Kristen Page in biology; E. John Walford in art; Brian Howell in anthropology; and Paul Robinson in HNGR.

Wheaton's student body is in one important sense homogenous. As one student puts it, "There are different denominations, but there is one faith there, the Christian faith. And the school is predominantly Protestant. There may be a few Catholic students here or there, but I haven't met any in my three and half years." There are no speech restrictions at Wheaton, but its doctrinal outlook does impose limits that have caused controversy. All professors must sign a statement of faith that the school regards as compatible with most Protestant tenets but incompatible with Roman Catholicism. A controversy arose when an English professor, Dr. Kent Gramm, resigned after the college demanded an explanation for his divorce, drawing national criticism for its actions and prompting calls for a reexamination of its strict lifestyle standards. Students and faculty overwhelmingly supported the administration's decision. Says one undergrad: "The professors sign on to this when they take a faculty position with the college. . . . Our professors are not just teaching us . . .

ACADEMIC REQUIREMENTS

Wheaton does not have a core curriculum but rather a series of worthy distribution requirements:

- Two courses on the Old Testament. One must be "Old Testament Literature and Interpretation," and the other can be selected from classes such as "Life of David" and "Old Testament in Its Cultural Environment."
- Two courses on the New Testament. One must be "New Testament Literature and Interpretation," and the other can be selected from classes such as "New Testament Archaeology" and "Jesus of Nazareth."
- Two theology courses, "Gospel, Church, and Culture" and "Christian Thought."
- One philosophy course, either "Introduction to Philosophy" or "Contemporary Moral Problems."
- One world history class, such as "World History: Ancient to Modern" or "Topics in World History."
- One math class, such as "Quantitative Skills" or "Applied Calculus."
- Two social science courses, such as "Introduction to Psychology" or "Biculturalism."
- Two diversity classes. Course options include "Cross-Cultural Ethics" and "Feminist Theology."
- One laboratory science course, such as "Principles of Biology" or "General Physics."
- One class in biology, environmental studies, or geology. Course offerings include "Contemporary Issues in Biology" and "Global Warming: Science."
- One course in astronomy, chemistry, or physics. Classes offered include "Stellar Astronomy" and "Drugs and Society."
- One course in English, French, German, or Spanish literature, such as "Classics of Western Literature" or "Survey of Spanish-American Literature."
- One writing class, "Composition and Research."
- Two introductory courses in fine arts, one each in art history and music. Classes offered include "Issues in Art" and "Intro to Music: Twentieth Century and World Music."
- One public speaking class. Course offerings include "Fundamentals of Oral Communication" and "Argumentation and Debate." Students can test out by giving a speech to the satisfaction of a communications professor.
- Two foreign language classes.
- One course in applied health science, "Wellness," plus one hour of physical education. Students may choose from activities like rock climbing, swimming, self-defense, modern dance, skiing, snowboarding, table tennis, volleyball, running, and kayaking.
- A senior capstone course in a student's major.

they mentor and disciple us. It is of the utmost importance that they are practicing what they 'preach' if you will."

Student Life: Clean and sober

The leafy suburb of Wheaton, Illinois, is only twenty-five miles from Chicago. The parklike campus is pleasant, with most buildings constructed of red brick and designed in a vaguely Georgian style.

On campus, the Conservatory of Music puts on a wide variety of performances, and Wheaton has plenty of other activities to occupy students' free time, including movies, lectures, and social events. "Wheaton is a very well-rounded campus," says one student. "I have participated in informal sports, great conversations, movies, campus concerts, trips to Chicago, and a discipleship/Bible study group."

According to the *Chronicle of Higher Education,* Wheaton ranks second only to Brigham Young University in campus sobriety. Students are required to pledge to refrain from tobacco, alcohol, and gambling during the academic year. "There's not much of a party scene," says one student, "but don't worry, you'll make great friends and have a good time." Many students go dancing at the University of Chicago on Friday nights or attend concerts and movies in the Windy City.

The centers of Wheaton freshman and sophomore community life, however, are the dorms. Most juniors and seniors live in campus-owned houses and apartments. For them, these are the centers of community life. Each dormitory is structured as a residential community and is designed to support all areas of a student's campus life. Dorms are either single sex or coed; however, even the coed buildings have sex-specific floors with strict intervisitation rules. Each dorm has an upperclassman as a resident assistant, who ensures compliance with rules and arranges for weekly recreational activities. Of the RAs, an undergrad observes, "The resident assistants for the freshman/sophomore and upperclassman dorms

---

YELLOW LIGHT

Although Wheaton is known as a staunchly conservative Christian school, there is a disturbing leftward trend on campus. All faculty members of the education department must endorse a document known as the "Conceptual Framework," which cites as its influential thinkers the Brazilian Marxist Paulo Freire and former Weather Underground terrorist Bill Ayers. Wheaton trustee and president emeritus Duane Litfin enthusiastically embraces these radicals as "people you can learn from because they're going to teach us Christians that maybe we have some blind spots here, that we've been oblivious to certain kinds of injustice." Blind spots indeed.

Not surprisingly, one student says, "Politics have intruded into the classroom, especially during the past presidential election. As a large majority of faculty supported Barack Obama for president, teachers would often make subtle to not-so-subtle comments on the reason why Barack Obama was a better candidate than John McCain. Many times these comments by professors would make conservative students uncomfortable listening to and refuting the professor. One anthropology professor even subtly hinted that Barack Obama was the only candidate with 'true Christian principles', while John McCain 'only thought about his Christian faith before the election' and Sarah Palin 'didn't look at her evangelical convictions past the abortion issue.' This comment made me very uncomfortable, and I had no desire to refute the professor."

are selected through a competitive application and interview process to ensure that they are serious about serving other students and aren't just looking for a free rooming budget." Each dorm and floor has its own traditions, activities, and rivalries, and sponsors Bible studies and fellowship groups.

Wheaton students can participate in over seventy clubs and organizations, including drama, model UN, musical theater, Christian Feminists Club, College Democrats, College Republicans, Earthkeepers, German Club, Orphan Helpers, Pre-Law Society, Men's Glee Club, Student Global Aids Campaign, Tikvaht Israel Club, Wheaton Film Society, Women's Chorale, and thirteen honor societies.

Sports are a unifying force on campus, as Wheaton's teams are very good, and most students show interest and enthusiasm. More than 50 percent of students participate in intramurals, including badminton, basketball, bowling, water polo, golf, nontackle football, tennis, Ultimate Frisbee, track, and soccer. A full 25 percent of Wheaton's student body takes part in varsity or club sports like baseball, basketball, soccer, tennis, swimming, water polo, cross-country, golf, and wrestling. In addition, Wheaton is a Division III school with highly ranked soccer, football, and swimming teams, and competitive baseball, cross-country, basketball, golf, tennis, track, volleyball, water polo, and wrestling teams as well.

Three times a week, all undergraduates are required to attend services in Edman Chapel, and they agree to attend church on Sunday off campus as part of their signature of the school's Covenant. Most are also involved in some kind of active mission work during school, assisted in their efforts by the Office of Christian Outreach.

Wheaton is an extremely safe college. In 2009, the only crimes reported on campus were two burglaries.

As private colleges go, Wheaton College is quite reasonable. Tuition for the 2010–11 academic year was $27,580, with room and board $8,050. Half of all undergraduates receive need-based financial aid, and the average student-loan debt of a recent graduating class was $21,549.

University of Wisconsin–Madison

Madison, Wisconsin • www.wisc.edu

The state of the *Onion*

Founded in 1848, the gargantuan University of Wisconsin–Madison is known as one of the best public universities in the country. The state views the university as a great cash and research magnet. A 2009 National Science Foundation survey revealed that UW–Madison had reached over $1 billion in research expenditures. A total of $952 million of that was focused on science and engineering research. UW–Madison has a long history of scientific innovation; the first stem cells were isolated on its campus, using primates in 1995 and later embryonic humans. (Maybe it's time for a required course in ethics.)

While the quality of UW students has improved as the university has become more selective over the past decade or so, a professor says, "A high percentage of students are intellectually curious, but there are also quite a few who just coast through because we are so large. It would be wrong to say that a majority of students demonstrate true intellectual curiosity. But a large percentage does." One teacher says he teaches a course that often touches upon the writings of Plato and Karl Marx—two authors most of his students have never read before. "This is just basic literacy, but my students don't have any reference," he says. "We've created a college environment that deemphasizes academics for socialization and being good citizens; very little here is related to disciplined learning."

Academic Life: Area student lacks curriculum

Instead of a core curriculum, UW–Madison hopes to encourage students to widen their knowledge through breadth requirements. But it might startle you to find out just how *lame* those mandates are. "The breadth requirements are very weak and have been that way ever since 1970," one professor says. Another observes, "A new core curriculum was introduced in the middle 1990s, but it was too weak to produce any significant change in what students are learning."

But even these vague requirements, which can be fulfilled by hundreds of choices, are seen as a burden by some Madison students. One teacher warns that any student "interested in a solid education . . . needs a strong sense of independence and determination to find the right classes and seek out the quality faculty members."

VITAL STATISTICS

Religious affiliation: *none*
Total enrollment: *42,099*
Total undergraduates: *30,343*
SAT/ACT midranges: CR: *550–670*, M: *620–720*; ACT: *26–30*
Applicants: *24,855*
Applicants accepted: *57%*
Accepted applicants who enrolled: *40%*
Tuition and fees: *in state, $8,313; out of state, $23,063*
Room and board: *$8,040*
Freshman retention rate: *94%*
Graduation rate: *50% (4 yrs.), 82% (6 yrs.)*
Courses with fewer than 20 students: *44%*
Student-faculty ratio: *17:1*
Courses taught by graduate students: *not provided*
Most popular majors: *social sciences, biological and life sciences, business/ marketing*
Students living on campus: *25%*
Guaranteed housing for four years? *no*
Students in fraternities: *9%* in sororities: *8%*

Certainly the most onerous requirement for UW–Madison students is the ethnic studies requirement. Classes that satisfy this requirement are, typically, blatantly politicized, such as "Race, Ethnicity, and Inequality in American Education," and "Women in Ethnic American Literature." Students complain the requirement is often used by professors as an opportunity to foist a multiculturalist (that is, anti-Christian, anti-Western) ethos upon impressionable freshmen. Students who'd rather escape such toxic politics should look into the short list of *worthy* courses that meet this requirement, like "American Folk and Vernacular Music," "The American West to 1850," and "Local Culture and Identity in the Upper Midwest."

One program that takes the business of learning seriously is the Integrated Liberal Studies (ILS) program, "an interdisciplinary liberal education core curriculum and ever-changing set of special topics courses about Western history, philosophy, politics, art, literature and culture." The courses offered are wide-ranging and most are excellent. A professor reports that many students in ILS double major in political science, history, philosophy, or sociology. The ILS program is affiliated with the Bradley Learning Community, which brings together 250 serious students to live as a group in a residence. Bradley offers students reserved spots in high-demand courses, seminars, and noncredit courses, and greater access to the university's top professors. During the first year, almost all Bradley students participate in the Bradley Roundtable, a seminar that aims to ease the transition from high school to college. Once a week, the entire Bradley community has dinner together and hears a lecture by a university faculty member, after which students break up into small groups for discussion.

Wisconsin's College of Letters and Science (L&S) is the largest division in the university, comprising thirty-nine departments and five professional schools. Over half of UW–Madison students are enrolled at L&S. The best departments in L&S, according to professors, include sociology, political science, economics, philosophy, Slavic, and German.

History offers a decent range of courses but does not require its majors to graduate with a solid grasp of major historical eras. For instance, history majors can fulfill their United States history requirement with courses like "Ethnicity in Twentieth-Century America" or "American Business History." One professor explains that the department has been steadily declining in quality for at least a decade. He diagnoses the problem as "narrow specializations that concentrate research of trivialities, rather than on matter of great consequence." However, a student does tell us that the department "has great resources."

The political science department is well-respected nationally, but its requirements for undergraduates are too lax. Ten poli-sci classes must be completed, with at least one each in political theory and methodology ("Introduction to Political Theory" or "Understanding Political Numbers"), American government ("Introduction to American Politics" or "Introduction to State Government"), comparative politics ("Latin-American Politics" or "Political Power in Contemporary China"), and international relations ("Principles of International Law" or "Conflict Resolution").

The English department has more traditional requirements. Students must complete ten intermediate- or advanced-level classes, including "British Literature before 1750," "British and Anglophone Literature from 1750 to the Present," or "American Literature"; a Shakespeare class; an additional pre-1800 non-Shakespeare course; and five electives. Although the electives may be trendy classes like "Children's Literature," "Chicana/o Literature," or "Gender and Language," the required classes are mostly solid literature surveys. The department offers a surprising number of respectable classes on the major literary figures of the Western canon.

SUGGESTED CORE
1. Comparative Literature 352, Epic
2. Philosophy 430, History of Ancient Philosophy
3. Religious Studies 151, The Bible in the English Tradition
4. Religious Studies 208, Foundation of Western Religious and Intellectual History
5. Political Science 502, The Development of Modern Western Political Thought
6. English 162, Shakespeare
7. History 101, American History to the Civil War Era, the Origin and Growth of the U.S.
8. History 513, European Cultural History, 1815–1870

The university's weakest departments are, predictably, women's studies, Afro-American studies, and the global culture programs. Unless you enjoy political sermons in the classroom, just avoid them.

In part because of its sheer size, Wisconsin ranks second only to Harvard in the number of professors who have won prestigious awards and grants. "Research is king at Wisconsin," says a professor, "but many departments also stress teaching, and the College of Letters and Science has made many efforts to inculcate a culture that encourages good teaching." Another professor agrees, saying, "Student evaluation of teaching is a major input into the annual merit-pay increase exercise."

Among many excellent teachers, students single out the following: Rebecca Koscik in the School of Medicine and Public Health; John Witte, Howard Schweber, Donald A. Downs, and Charles Franklin in political science; Jean Lee, Robert Frykenberg (emeritus), and William Cronon in history; and Mary Anderson in geology.

Incoming freshmen are assigned not to faculty members but to professional advisors. After choosing a major, each is assigned an advisor (usually a faculty member but sometimes a graduate student or staff member) within that major. Students tell us that their advisors are not so much interested in helping them plan their education as making sure they graduate on time. Despite their efforts, just half of students graduate in four years. Thankfully, an additional year or two seems to do the trick for most students, as the graduation rate leaps to a decent 82 percent six years on.

While the average class size is twenty-nine, at a school as large as Wisconsin, many introductory courses are the size of a high school graduating class. Large lectures are usually supplemented by discussion sessions that include up to thirty students and are led by graduate teaching assistants. However, through a program called First-Year Interest Groups (FIG), the university is trying to overcome the impersonality of the large introductory classes. First-Year Interest Groups connect students and faculty in small classes that focus on interdisciplinary learning. Each FIG consists of twenty freshmen who live in the same campus "residential neighborhood" and enroll in a cluster of three courses united by a central theme. Some recent themes are as diverse as "Truth and the Meaning of Life," "Classical Myth and Modern American Culture," and "The World of the Vikings."

Other residential learning communities include Women in Science and Engineering, the Multicultural Learning Community, and the Chadbourne Residential College for students "committed to interdisciplinary learning and civic engagement." The FIGs may provide students at UW–Madison with their best chance of studying in a seminar environment and working closely with a professor. Otherwise, most students do not get a chance to participate in small seminars with professors until they are juniors or seniors—if ever.

All professors interviewed for this essay lament the fact that grade inflation is a serious problem at Wisconsin. "What is needed is an institution-wide policy so one does not penalize one's own students by grading them tougher than others do," one professor says. "There should also be some sort of national policy, as we do not want to penalize UW students in relation to those at other schools."

The university has other strengths, including a popular study-abroad program (UW–Madison ranks tenth among U.S. colleges in the number of students who venture to foreign lands) and a variety of internship opportunities in the state legislature, criminal justice institutions, Washington, D.C., and more. Study-abroad options include most of South America and Europe, as well as many destinations in Asia, Africa, and Central America. There are more than 150 programs to choose from.

Among more than eighty options, students can study languages (living and dead) from across the globe. From Akan-Twi or Xhosa to Old Church Slavic, Old High German, or Ottoman Turkish, numerous obscure languages are taught at UW–Madison. Students may also study more conventional options like Thai, Hindi, biblical Hebrew, Ojibwe, Icelandic, and French.

Student Life: Beer me

The University of Wisconsin–Madison is pleasantly situated in a vibrant location that combines a fine urban area with two large glacial lakes, Mendota and Monona. Although some students complain about the long, harsh winters, most find the inclement weather offset by the myriad social opportunities. "Bascom Hill is a major pain in the winter," says a UW–Madison graduate. "Walking down that hill is a serious challenge, especially for the less-coordinated loaded down with books. At least it helped us stay in good shape." State Street is the main off-campus student gathering place. A multimillion-dollar, 380,000-square-foot arts center was recently built there, close to the university and the state capitol.

The historic Memorial Union sits on the edge of Lake Mendota. It features a hotel for visitors and the famous Rathskeller, a large hall containing fireplaces, large wooden tables, a cafeteria, and a small bar. The union also has a terrace on the lake where students can study, listen to concerts, or simply relax. The Memorial Union is also home to the UW Hoofers. The Hoofers comprise several different outdoor programs that allow students, for a nominal fee, to head out of Madison and explore Wisconsin or other parts of the country. Students can go sailing, backpacking, scuba diving, hang gliding, and rock climbing, or simply attend one of the Hoofers' many socials. A favorite student custom is sledding on cafeteria trays down the local hills after the first snowfall. "It is a great way to take a break," says a student.

Madison has been known for its student activism ever since the 1960s, and radical student groups still often dominate campus debate, but the vast majority of students are uninterested in politics. A professor says that conservative students have "made their pres-

---

ACADEMIC REQUIREMENTS

In the absence of a core curriculum, all students at the University of Wisconsin–Madison must complete a series of vague general education requirements:

- Two courses in communications (mostly written). Students can test out.
- Two natural science courses (or only one, if it includes a laboratory component).
- Two humanities/literature/arts courses, ranging from "Western Culture: Science, Technology, Philosophy" to "Relief Printmaking."
- One social studies course, such as "England to 1688" or "Gender and Work in Rural America."
- Two courses in quantitative reasoning—but students can test out. Courses that qualify range from algebra and formal logic to statistics.
- One course in ethnic studies. Options here include "Black Music in American Literary Culture" and "Introduction to Lesbian, Gay, Bisexual, and Transgender Studies."

Liberal arts students in the College of Letters and Science face the following additional requirements:

- Courses in a foreign language to the intermediate level.
- Three units of mathematics (AP credits from high school can be applied here) for students earning a BS.
- Four additional humanities courses, including two courses in any kind of literature. For the purposes of this requirement, courses like "Introduction to Ethnic and Multicultural Literature" and "Shakespeare" are deemed equivalent.
- Four courses in the social sciences.
- Four courses in the natural sciences.

Midwest

ence felt." However, a student tells us that the "general feeling is that conservatives shouldn't say what they think. Pressure is from the students, not the professors."

The university made headlines in 2010 for a last-minute cancellation of an antiwar discussion panel, claiming that student fees were being inappropriately used to fund the event and that the notorious Cindy Sheehan, who was scheduled to speak, would cause security issues. After complaints from student groups and media outlets, the university reversed its decision. But one professor says that the university still tries to restrict free speech rights with "climate" and "professional conduct codes." The campus has just hired a new Vice-Provost for Diversity and Climate. "This fellow promotes himself as the campus's Chief Diversity Officer (CDO)!" says a professor.

The most active campus groups on the left are the Wisconsin Public Interest Research Group, UW Greens, and MEChA (a Chicano racialist movement). On the right, the College Republicans are active, and one alumnus says the campus paper, the *Badger Herald,* has become more libertarian of late. Although the independent conservative paper, the *Mendota Beacon*, ceased publication, another, the *Daily Cardinal*, has taken its place. One conservative student told us he is happy to have the opportunity to confront different worldviews. "This is a very political campus, and you have the opportunity to become politically involved," the student says.

A professor says, "Conservative students are not afraid to speak up and challenge the liberal orthodoxy of the campus, and there are now four student newspapers that represent a diversity of intellectual opinion. There is a dedicated group of faculty—the Committee for Academic Freedom and Rights—who have been very active politically in favor of free speech and discourse and have won many free speech victories over the years. Students are active in politics and free speech, which adds real energy to the institution—especially because student voices are much more diverse intellectually than they were several years ago. Conservative students should definitely consider Wisconsin, as they will find a vibrant niche, and they will find it challenging to counter the conventional liberal wisdom of the campus." However, one graduate cautions incoming students: "UW–Madison is a place for someone grounded in his belief system. Make no mistake, someone will question who you are, what you believe, and why."

Not all at Wisconsin is protest and counterprotest, though. Two undergraduates in 1998 launched the *Onion*, a must-read weekly satirical paper with a new TV series on IFC. The *Onion* may well be the state university's (and even the state's) proudest achievement.

The sheer size of the university means that there is an organization for nearly any interest. Student groups range widely, from the Ballroom Dance Association and the Tolkien and Fantasy Society to the Molecular and Environmental Toxicology Student Association, plus many student publications. Any student can find a club to match his interests—from the Actuarial Club to the Model United Nations. Arts and media groups include *Curb* magazine, Dance Elite, Gospel Choir, Milk Enthusiasts, Redefined A Cappella, and WSUM 91.7 student radio.

For the spiritually minded, UW–Madison supports (and at times, refuses to support) a broad variety of religious organizations and clubs. From the Vedic Science of Yoga club to the Social Work Christian Fellowship, and the Muslim Students Association to Calvary Lutheran or Chabad Jewish associations, a number of religious outlets exist, including Atheists, Humanists and Agnostics and Dialogue International interfaith discussion group.

An amazing number of ethnic and cultural student organizations are present at the school, including a L'Equippe Francaise, Society for Creative Anachronism, Arabic Language and Culture Association, Breakdancing Club, Wisconsin Association of Black Men, Working Class Student Union, Korean Drumming and Dance, and a branch of the Slow Food movement, which advocates awareness and responsibility in growing, selling, and consuming food.

With 750 clubs and organizations in all, the temptation for new students, in fact, is to become overcommitted and spend an inordinate amount of time on extracurricular activities. "There is a wide variety of activities available for students during the week and on the weekends as an alternative to partying," one student says. Union South, the university's student center built in the late '60s, will soon be torn down and replaced by a more architecturally inviting building.

And then there are the myriad pleasures to be found inside a bottle. Wisconsin has a well-deserved reputation as something of a school for tipsy smart kids. It won dubious distinction as the twelfth-best party school according to The Princeton Review and the third-best according to *Playboy* in 2010. Wisconsin has the highest percentage of binge drinking of any state in the union, with over 26 percent of residents age twelve and older admitting to binge drinking in the last month. Over 60 percent of Wisconsin college students admit to binge drinking in the past month, which is bested only by Maryland (a staggering—literally!—80 percent).

Such accolades forced the administration to admit that there is a campuswide drinking problem. Under pressure from the

YELLOW LIGHT

Wisconsin likes to assert its commitment to free speech, but in practice the school administration has revealed a pattern of hostility to religious student groups, which has landed it in court. From banning an antiwar discussion panel to denying religious student groups the same funding offered to other student organizations, UW–Madison has found itself embroiled in controversy. Particularly targeted seems to be any group associated with the Catholic Church. The campus chapter of the Knights of Columbus was refused recognition by the school unless it admitted women and non-Catholics as members. In a truly Orwellian moment, former chancellor John Wiley claimed that the group must open membership to all students in order not to "violate the separation of church and state." The university had also derecognized InterVarsity Fellowship and a Lutheran group. It took the Wisconsin Board of Regents to enact a new policy forcing all institutions within its system to let religious student groups choose their members based on their beliefs.

Despite the resolution of the issue, a few years later, UW yanked student funding and campus recognition from the school's campus Catholic group when it was hosting events focused on evangelism, prayer, or religious instruction (like a retreat that included Mass and prayer). The judge in the case noted that among those activities sponsored by the group are spiritual counseling sessions and a leadership retreat and that the university has no right to selectively discriminate against religious groups—or the particular activities of religious groups it deems undesirable—in its funding.

school, local bars agreed to eliminate drink specials on Friday and Saturday nights. Despite the school's efforts, the prevalence of alcohol abuse at Madison has not abated in the past two decades—although, thankfully, fewer students are drinking and driving, and far fewer are smoking cigarettes, according to the school's PACE study.

As a member of the Big Ten, the university fields several high-profile athletic programs. The Wisconsin Badgers, with mascot Bucky Badger, are main rivalries with the University of Minnesota. The two teams compete for the trophy Paul Bunyan's Axe in their football games. Fans from the university and around the state are extremely loyal to the Badger football team (whose football stadium, the fourth-oldest in the nation, underwent extensive renovation that expanded seating capacity to 80,000). Basketball games are well attended, too (the school cultivates a rivalry against Michigan State), and hockey has always been popular. Men and women compete in basketball, cross-country, golf, rowing, soccer, swimming and diving, tennis, and track and field. Men also wrestle and, of course, play football, while women can compete in lightweight rowing, softball, and volleyball.

Students also have plenty of club sports to choose from, like karate, triathlon, archery, cycling, dance, water skiing, and table tennis. Those interested in a little more competition may join an intramural team. Students compete in sports like golf, volleyball, flag football, and dodgeball.

Only around a quarter of undergraduates live on campus, although nearly 90 percent stay there for their freshman year. The undergraduate residence halls are divided into smaller "houses" of fifty to eighty residents. Dorms are as diverse as the students who inhabit them. Some dorms, especially those abutting campus on University Avenue, are well known as party halls. Quieter spots are Chadbourne Residential College or the Lakeside Dorms on Lake Mendota. The school's formerly all-women dorm, Elizabeth Waters Hall, has now gone coed and is located on a hill overlooking the lake and is especially popular. UW–Madison also hosts an International Learning Community and a Multicultural Learning Community, and Cole Hall is now the school's GreenHouse, providing housing to environmentally concerned students. The university has no coed dorm rooms or bathrooms, and even in the dormitories, men and women are separated by floor or wing. One current student says, "I despised the dorms. Rooms were too small, food was terrible, it was too loud, and I felt like I was in jail. I got out ASAP."

For its size, UW–Madison is rather safe. In 2009, the school reported eleven forcible sex offenses, two non-forcible sex offenses, one robbery, eleven aggravated assaults, eighty-three burglaries, twelve motor vehicle thefts, and one arson.

The university has its own small police force, as well as SAFEwalk and SAFEride bus and cab escort services for students at night—for instance, if they're too blotto to find their way home. With more than one hundred blue-light emergency phones around campus, the school does what it can to protect students, and Madison's crime rate is lower in every area than the national average.

For a state school, UW–Madison is pricey. Tuition in 2010–11 ran $8,313 for in-state students and $23,063 for out-of-staters. Room and board was an additional $8,040. The university grants need-based financial aid to 62 percent of students. A typical UW–Madison student graduates with nearly $22,000 in student-loan debt.

University of Washington
Gonzaga University
WASHINGTON
New St. Andrews College
Reed College
Whitman College
MONTANA

OREGON
IDAHO
WYOMING

NEVADA
Brigham Young University
University of Colorado
University of California at Berkeley
Stanford University
UTAH
COLORADO
CALIFORNIA
Colorado College
United States Air Force Academy

Thomas Aquinas College
ARIZONA
St. John's College
LOS ANGELES AREA
California Institute of Technology
Claremont Colleges
Occidental College
Pepperdine University
University of California at Irvine
University of California at Los Angeles
University of Southern California
University of California at San Diego
NEW MEXICO

TEXAS
University of Dallas
Southern Methodist University
Baylor University
Texas A&M University
University of Texas
Rice University

West

Baylor University • Brigham Young University • University of California at Berkeley • University of California at Irvine • University of California at Los Angeles • University of California at San Diego • California Institute of Technology • Claremont Colleges • University of Colorado at Boulder • Colorado College • University of Dallas • Gonzaga University • New Saint Andrews College • Occidental College • Pepperdine University • Reed College • Rice University • University of Southern California • Southern Methodist University • Stanford University • University of Texas at Austin • Texas A&M University • Thomas Aquinas College • United States Air Force Academy • University of Washington • Whitman College

Baylor University

Waco, Texas • www.baylor.edu

The Protestant Notre Dame?

Baylor, the world's largest Baptist university, was founded more than 150 years ago by Baptist missionaries, but unlike many of America's most prestigious colleges and universities, Baylor has strengthened its commitment to the faith of its founders. Baylor's Baptist tradition informs its academic programs and the social life of its students in increasingly significant and academically rigorous ways. In fact, Baylor seeks to inculcate in its students an understanding of the harmony between faith and understanding and to show them that they need not choose between academic excellence and Christian devotion. While many schools have dumbed down their academic standards, Baylor has strengthened its own.

In 2002, Baylor adopted an ambitious ten-year plan, "Baylor 2012," demonstrating its commitment both to the life of the mind and to the life of faith. The plan, championed by the energetic then-president Robert B. Sloan Jr., pledged to seek new levels of national prominence and Christian academic excellence. Baylor's goal was to become, as many put it, a "Protestant Notre Dame." The 2012 plan was constituted by twelve imperatives, and each general imperative included a set of concrete steps to be taken toward each end. For example, the Imperative I, "Establish an environment where learning can flourish," included the concrete steps to "Reduce student-faculty ratio to 13 to 1" and "Create an Academic Success Center to improve retention and graduation rates by 10 percent." Imperative VIII, "Construct useful and aesthetically pleasing physical spaces," included injunctions to create a prayer garden, build parking garages on the periphery of the campus, and increase emphasis on landscaping and artwork. Baylor 2012 also included plans to hire high-profile Christian faculty, to increase commitments to research and teaching, to erect more and better academic facilities, to support athletic programs with integrity, and to add doctoral programs. The plan, which can be viewed at Baylor's website, is detailed, sweeping, and ambitious.

And as its completion year rolls around, most of its objectives seem to have been achieved. Some Baylor faculty and supporters, however, were resistant to 2012. They did not see the need for a change and worried about the debt required, and about the burden on faculty to both publish and teach. Some were resistant to the hiring of "foreigners" (non-Texans) and Roman Catholics. Moreover, the speed and vigor with which Sloan implemented the plan alienated even a few of its initial supporters. In 2005, Sloan was forced

West

out as president. Following his term, Baylor had two interim leaders, another president (who stirred up some lesser turmoil of his own among faculty and the board of regents) and another interim leader in 2008. Faculty say currently, however, that the tension has eased. One professor suggests that many in the Baylor family are just exhausted from the battles of the last several years and are less likely to cause trouble. The political situation has also improved since many of the faculty hired at the start of the 2012 plan have now been tenured. Happily, students report that they feel unaffected by the political drama, and progress on the vision of 2012 continues.

Baylor's new President, Kenneth Starr, is the controversial former federal prosecutor who investigated a number of the Clinton scandals and then served as Dean of Pepperdine's School of Law. As the liberal *Chronicle of Higher Education* has noted, however, at Pepperdine Starr won over even the most left-wing members of the faculty with his inclusive and welcoming style. The *Chronicle* also points out that Starr is "almost impossibly energetic. His work ethic is legendary." Moreover, Starr took charge at a good time. In March 2010, Baylor received an anonymous commitment of $200 million to fund a center for the study of aging. This was the university's largest gift in history.

Academic Life: Faith and knowledge

While it does not insist on a traditional core, Baylor has one of the most solid curricula of the schools in this guide. Its general education requirements dictate more than half of a student's coursework. Of course, a few students enroll in less-demanding classes such as the geology class "Earthquakes and other Natural Disasters" (a.k.a. "Shake and Bake") to boost their GPAs, but faculty advising is generally solid at Baylor, and students who select their courses wisely can get a great education.

Some students choose to satisfy their general studies requirements through the Baylor Interdisciplinary Core (BIC), under the auspices of the newly-formed Honors College (which also includes an honors program for students across the disciplines as well as the Great Texts major). The BIC is not a major, but rather replaces the general education requirements of the university (and includes forty-four total hours of course work). Students in the BIC undertake a coherent and integrated interdisciplinary course of study that emphasizes reading primary sources (such as the Bible, the *Analects*, and Plato's dialogues)

VITAL STATISTICS

Religious affiliation: *Baptist*
Total enrollment: *14,900*
Total undergraduates: *12,438*
SAT/ACT midranges: CR: *530–640*, M: *550–650*; ACT: *23–29*
Applicants: *31,440*
Applicants accepted: *50%*
Accepted applicants who enrolled: *23%*
Tuition and fees: *$29,724*
Room and board: *$10,146*
Freshman retention rate: *85%*
Graduation rate: *47% (4 yrs.)*, *70% (6 yrs.)*
Courses with fewer than 20 students: *67%*
Student-faculty ratio: *15:1*
Courses taught by graduate students: *none*
Most popular majors: *business/marketing, biology, communications/journalism*
Students living on campus: *39%*
Guaranteed housing for four years? *no*
Students in fraternities: *10%* in sororities: *18%*

SUGGESTED CORE

1. Classics 3301/3302, Roman Civilization/Greek Civilization
2. Philosophy 3310, History of Philosophy: Classical
3. Religion 4305/4315, Topics in Old Testament/New Testament Studies
4. Religion 4352/4353, History of Christian Theology I/II
5. Political Science 3373, Western Political Thought: Modern
6. English 4324, Shakespeare: Selected Plays
7. History 2365, History of the United States to 1877
8. History 4339, Cultural and Intellectual History of Modern Europe or Philosophy 3312, History of Philosophy: Modern European Philosophy

from Eastern and Western traditions in their proper historical order. The BIC curriculum is made up of five sequences of courses: World Cultures, World of Rhetoric, Social World, Natural World, and the Examined Life. The courses are team taught by professors from diverse disciplines, and some students complain that BIC professors are forced to teach material unfamiliar to them.

Like the BIC, the Scholars Program (UNSC) replaces the university general education requirements, but the UNSC is also a major and is less structured than the BIC. Students in the UNSC program are required to take only five courses: two introductory religion courses and a rigorous three-course sequence of Great Texts courses (ancient, medieval, and modern). Aside from those courses, students are free to select any courses to craft their own major; they might combine courses in music and biology, for example. Each student's selection of courses is unique, and the program succeeds because of its outstanding advisors who meet often with students, and require them to take well-rounded schedules. One liberal arts student reports being "required" by her advisor to take calculus. In addition to taking classes, UNSC students must also compose a reading list of significant texts in the Western canon and complete a one-hour exit interview on it with the director of the program and other professors. Finally, UNSC students are required to research, write, and defend a senior thesis. The program is rigorous, and students typically go on to graduate school, medical school, or law school. One student says, "I would recommend this program to all students with an ardent curiosity and strong work ethic who desire a truly well-rounded undergraduate education that will prepare them for any and all careers to follow."

The major fields of study are likewise intellectually serious. Baylor students select from a broad range of generally solid departments; there are more than 151 undergraduate degree programs as well as 76 master's programs and 30 doctoral programs. Students speak highly of classics, biology, philosophy, business, nursing, law, and music. The premed program and engineering school are highly regarded nationally, as is Baylor's entrepreneurship program.

English majors must take four intermediate courses in British and American literature (out of five solid choices), advanced courses in the history of British literature, one upper-level class in American literature, and two English electives (such as "Oxford Christians" or "The Contemporary Novel"). They cannot graduate without encountering Shakespeare.

History majors must take introductions to world history and the history of the United States, choose two additional American history courses, two courses in African, Asian, Latin American or Middle Eastern history, and two European history courses, plus one general history elective (such as "Cultural and Intellectual History of Modern Europe" or "History of Gender in Latin America").

Baylor's political science department has sound requirements. The department proudly notes on its website, "Political Science students at Baylor learn about American political history and institutions, study the development of our constitutional law from the founding era to the latest Supreme Court decision, master the techniques of rigorous political analysis, examine the causes and effects of political change around the world, and survey the writings of great philosophers (such as Plato, Aristotle, Hobbes, and Locke)."

Students report that faculty research—encouraged by the 2012 plan—is not detracting from teaching, and some faculty find ways to involve undergraduates in their research. The current student-faculty ratio is 15 to 1, and students maintain that professors find plenty of time to spend with each of their students. One reports, "I have never had a professor with whom I did not have some meaningful or helpful conversation outside of class." It is not uncommon for professors to have students over to their houses, and eight professors have even moved right into the campus dormitories with their families through Baylor's faculty-in-residence program. Professors teach almost all courses, although students say graduate teaching assistants sometimes run labs or weekly discussion sections.

Vision 2012 includes the goal "to develop a world-class faculty" made up of scholars who "embrace the Christian faith and are knowledgeable of the Christian intellectual tradition," and Baylor has been on a hiring spree since adopting 2012, giving preference to those scholars for whom faith and scholarship are integrally related. The quality of the faculty members is quite high, particularly within the Honors College. The growing list of fine professors at Baylor includes David Corey, David Nichols, and Mary Nichols in political science; Julie Sweet in history; Phillip Donnelly and Ralph Wood in English; Michael Beaty, Robert Baird, Francis Beckwith, C. Stephen Evans, James Marcum and Robert Roberts in philosophy; Michael Foley, Douglas Henry, Thomas Hibbs, David L. Jeffrey, Robert Miner, and Sarah-Jane Murray in the Honors College; Julia Dyson Hejduk, Jeff Fish and Alden Smith in classics; Robyn Driskell in sociology; Robin Wallace in music history and literature; Joseph McKinney in economics; Bennie Ward in physics; and John A. Dunbar in geology.

Baylor offers a great many study-abroad options spanning six continents, with programs in twenty-seven European countries, plus more than twenty programs outside Europe. Baylor does not, however, offer programs in any Middle Eastern country except Turkey. Besides Latin and Ancient Greek, Baylor offers courses in Arabic, Chinese, French, Italian, German, Japanese, Korean, Russian, Spanish, Portuguese and Swahili.

Student Life: As perceived by Texas Baptists

Baylor is located in Waco, Texas, midway between Dallas and Austin. This college city is smallish by Texas standards (approximately 126,000), and off-campus attractions are mostly limited to hanging out in the newly restored downtown Warehouse District's trendy shops, restaurants, and clubs. Other popular cultural attractions in Waco include strolling through the city along the scenic River Walk which follows along the Brazos River; visiting

West

the Dr. Pepper Museum and the Texas Rangers Hall of Fame Museum; golfing, canoeing, and hiking in Cameron Park, and visiting the celebrated Cameron Park Zoo. For a more robust night life, Baylor students usually strike out a hundred miles north (Dallas) to visit trendy nightclubs, or south (Austin) to listen to live music and bar hop.

In 2004, Baylor began requiring all incoming freshmen to live on campus. To make this possible, the university completed several large, attractive residential facilities and renovated several others; Baylor's goal is to have 50 percent of students in residence halls by 2012. Qualified students have the option of living in one of two popular residential colleges, the Honors College residences or Brooks Hall. A senior in the honors residence reports, "There is hardly a resident whom I do not know and who would not be willing to discuss big ideas, play music, or pick up a Frisbee with me. . . . Students who live here share an eagerness for study, and yet also know how to have fun and grow together as a community." Both residential colleges host regular dinners, lectures (with "world-class speakers," according to one student), teas, and activities to build a community among the students, faculty, and chaplains who live together there.

Men and women live in separate residence halls, except for in a few living areas for married students, and university policies limit intervisitation to certain hours: 1:00 PM to 10:00 PM Sunday through Thursday and 1:00 PM to midnight on Friday and Saturday. Students report that these policies are enforced and infractions are punished. Baylor prohibits

---

ACADEMIC REQUIREMENTS

Students in the College of Arts and Sciences at Baylor face a structured curriculum. All students must take the following:

- Four courses in English. This requirement includes a two-semester introduction to "Thinking, Writing, and Research," a course in British literature (introducing students to the works of Chaucer, Shakespeare, Milton, the Romantics, and the Victorians), and a course in either American or world literature.
- "Christian Scriptures" and "Christian Heritage." Fittingly, these courses are taught by Baptists.
- Four courses in "human performance." Courses are one credit hour, and appear to be glorified gym classes that include bowling and ballroom dancing.
- Four semesters of a modern foreign language or two semesters of Latin, Greek, or Hebrew.
- Two semesters of history, including one course in either world history or American history.
- "American Constitutional Government."
- Three social science courses to be selected from anthropology, economics, geography, political science, philosophy, psychology, or sociology.
- Three classes of lab science, including both chemistry and biology, and one elective.
- Two semesters of twice-weekly chapel. (Attendance is recorded and students receive a pass or fail grade at the end of the semester.)
- One math class.

alcohol in all residences and smoking in all university buildings. One student claims that "alcohol is present just as it is on any campus," but another suggests that drinking at Baylor is more moderate than that found at secular universities. Baylor policy requires school officials to inform parents when their children violate alcohol laws or rules.

Students may find some of these regulations intrusive, but Baylor expects that each student "will conduct himself or herself in accordance with Christian principles as commonly perceived by Texas Baptists." The school is serious about maintaining a Christian community, and students must attend two semesters of mandatory twice-weekly chapel services in order to graduate. On Mondays at chapel, the speaker could be anyone from a religious rapper to a Christian movie critic. Chapels on Wednesdays are worship services with varied music. An optional weekly 15-minute prayer service is held in a chapel in one of the honors dorms. Optional prayer services are also held in the Robbins chapel, a peaceful space with beautiful stained-glass windows attached to the Brooks Hall dormitory. These and several other prayer gardens and chapels around campus aim to stimulate impromptu meditation and prayer. Numerous Christian denominations flourish at Baylor, with Catholics the second largest group after Baptists.

> **GREEN LIGHT**
>
> Because of its strong religious tradition, outsiders sometimes perceive Baylor as oppressively conservative. However, while Baylor students may be more conservative than those found at other universities, the campus is actually quite nonpolitical. Like most colleges and universities, Baylor is home to College Democrats and College Republicans, but the groups are small for a school of nearly 12,500 undergraduates. The most vocal conservative group is the school's chapter of Young Conservatives of Texas. Given the strongly religious, Texan atmosphere, most conservative students feel more than comfortable at Baylor. In the words of one professor, "Baylor is a great place due to the sheer number of conservatives."

Many university traditions center on Baylor athletics. The Baylor Line, organized by freshmen, helps welcome the football team to the field by waving flags. The student body also names "yell leaders" who lead fans in organized cheers. And at every homecoming, fans remember the "Immortal Ten," basketball players who died in a 1927 train wreck. The green-and-gold-clad Baylor Bears play a huge role in student life, and affection is high for the Baylor mascots, three small black bears housed in a new visitor-friendly living environment at the center of campus. Competing in the powerful NCAA Division I, Big 12 Conference, Baylor has struggled of late in some of the more popular sports, especially football, but the school excels in less costly pursuits like golf and track and field. Baylor also possesses a good women's basketball team, led by the country's best known female college basketball player, 6'8" center Brittney Griner.

Most students spend their time outside class studying and engaging in apolitical extracurricular groups. There are 260 chartered student organizations, and more than 83 percent of Baylor students are involved in at least one student organization. About half of Baylor students participate in the university's popular intramurals program. Baylor's chapter of Habitat for Humanity, the first in the country, is extremely popular as are mis-

West

sion trips sponsored by Baptist Student Ministries. The campus is home to a strong Greek community, including fourteen fraternities and nine sororities (none of which are allowed to maintain residences).

Although violent crime is not common in Waco, the area around the Baylor campus has relatively high levels of reported property crimes. In fact, a study in February 2010 found that the area around the campus was among the top fifteen college neighborhoods in the country for property crime. However, the campus itself is impressively safe. In 2009, Baylor reported two aggravated assaults and fourteen burglaries, and no other crimes on campus. The Department of Public Safety patrols constantly, and emergency call boxes are placed throughout the campus.

Tuition at Baylor for the 2010–11 academic year was $29,724, and room and board approximately $10,146. The university offers an installment plan to help with the cost of tuition, and 54 percent of students receive need-based financial assistance. The average debt of Baylor graduates approached a whopping $40,000 a few years ago, and the school has since stopped providing this information to the public.

West

Brigham Young University

Provo, Utah • www.byu.edu

A sacred purpose

Brigham Young University is, no doubt, a distinctive university. Founded in 1875 as a small pioneer academy, the school is named for one of the best-known presidents of the Church of Jesus Christ of Latter-day Saints (LDS), whose members are known as Mormons. BYU is unafraid of criticism and unapologetic about what it is: a devoutly religious institution dedicated to a sacred purpose in a secular world.

The Mormon influence in academic affairs, along with the university's requirements in religion and its unbending honor code governing most aspects of student life, are certainly peculiar nowadays. However, there is debate within the academic community over whether BYU should be primarily a ministry of the church or should strive to offer a first-class education within an LDS setting. "BYU is not the place for everyone," says a faculty member. But those who share the institution's vision should find themselves happily at home.

Academic Life: We're on a mission from God

Academics—as everything else at BYU—are traditional with an LDS twist. "There are three formal components to the baccalaureate at Brigham Young University: religious education, general education, and education in a major," says the introduction to the undergraduate program.

Students face a challenging general education curriculum. There are the familiar area requirements in science, math, arts, social science, and writing. More unusual in today's academic climate is the mandated study of world civilization in two classes and American heritage in one. But religious education has pride of place—it is the seven-class religion requirement that accounts for about one-third of general education credits and seems to dominate the curriculum.

BYU's major requirements are about as stiff as the general education requirements. And that's a good thing. For example, an English professor says that a decade ago, majors could "pick and choose so much that students could avoid Shakespeare if they wanted to." Now they must complete a prescribed core which includes a course in Shakespeare as well as at least five classes in British and American literature. The department also has students take a course in "Rhetoric, Professional Communication and Theory" and another in "Diverse Traditions and

West

855

Methods." Finally, majors complete twelve elective course hours and a senior seminar involving detailed research and writing. Constituting a total of forty-eight credit hours, the English major at BYU is rigorous and comprehensive, ensuring that students are exposed to the fundamentals of the English language and the Anglo-American literary tradition, and the English department isn't even known as being particularly demanding.

The philosophy program, however, *is* so known. Students take five courses under the rubric "sources and methods," two "historical periods" courses, one "values and conduct" course, two "following knowledge and reality" courses, and twelve additional credit hours. Totaling some fourteen courses, the requirements for BYU philosophy majors are much more structured than those at most universities where students sometimes have complete flexibility in choosing their classes. Another rigorous major is comparative literature, which prescribes nine courses, requires the completion of an individualized reading list, a thorough knowledge of two language traditions relevant to the program of study (including an upper-level language course), and four electives. Science majors also have stringent requirements, with chemistry at fifty-seven credit hours, math at fifty-four, and physics at sixty.

Those students to whom this sounds like too much specialization may be interested in the university's College of Humanities—which offers an interdisciplinary major with work in an area of emphasis such as philosophy, art history, English, foreign literature, or classical studies. It also sponsors myriad clubs and centers, among them the Center for the Study of Christian Values in Literature.

Brigham Young's two-tiered advising system is intended to guide students through these academic requirements. Undeclared students can visit the undergraduate Advisement Center, where full-time, nonfaculty advisors or trained graduate students help students with academic problems. Students who have declared majors meet with advisors within their departments. If a student wishes to speak with a particular advisor, he is free to wait, but most of them just take the first available advisor. With this system, new students may have a hard time establishing personal relationships with professors, but the help is usually there if students need it.

Just what does it mean that the university and LDS Church exercise academic control? Not as much as you might think. "The vast array of courses use exactly the same textbooks that are used in other strong undergraduate institutions," says a professor. "The curriculum reflects the religious teaching of the church wherever it is relevant.... Both faculty and students in the secular courses feel free to bring LDS teachings and values into the discussion of literature, politics, or whatever, and that's why they feel more free here than they would elsewhere, where they would be discouraged from doing that." Says a student, "In math class you learn math; in science you learn science. However, teachers are free to use the gospel of Jesus Christ as they are teaching, such as beginning the class with prayer."

This presence of secularism does not mean that open dissent from the teachings of the LDS church is permitted. "Does a person have a right to voice one's beliefs? Certainly. Would he or she be allowed to openly espouse those beliefs and continue as a faculty member or student on the BYU campus? Almost certainly not," says a BYU professor. One faculty member explains that professors can discuss, for instance, abortion politics in class, but cannot openly advocate legal abortion. In the same way, he says, "Professors can't argue that the Book of Mormon is a bunch of foolishness. One of the main purposes of this university is to provide a comfortable place for Mormons to study."

SUGGESTED CORE
1. Classical Civilization 110, Introduction to Greek and Roman Literature
2. Philosophy 201, History of Philosophy I
3. Religious Studies 101/111, Old Testament Survey/New Testament Survey
4. Philosophy 330, Studies in Medieval Philosophy (closest match)
5. Political Science 202, Western Political Heritage II
6. English 232/382, Shakespeare
7. History 220, The United States Through 1877
8. History 312, History of Ideas or Political Science 408, Hermeneutics, Deconstruction, and Politics (closest match)

There are very few non-Mormon faculty members or students on campus. In 2010 less than 3 percent of the students identified themselves as "Gentiles." The university requires that its faculty members, if Mormon, be LDS members in good standing, which means tithing, attending church regularly, and being chaste, among other things. Non-Mormons must still abide by the school's honor code. "BYU is really far beyond what you'd expect of most religiously affiliated schools," one professor says.

BYU is an enormous university, enrolling over 30,000 full-time undergraduates. Nevertheless, it is possible to enroll in classes of a decent size. Approximately 59 percent of classes had fewer than 50 students, and nearly half of all classes had fewer than 20. While the school doesn't calculate what portion of courses are taught by graduate teaching assistants, one student reports that "in large general education classes, TAs have most of the personal interaction with students." One student points out that honors students enjoy the benefits of small classes all the time, even for general education classes.

Another student says, "At the largest private religious university in the country, you would be surprised to discover that most professors are at least somewhat regularly available to help their students." In one student's experience, "My professors are very anxious and willing to help. I have talked to four different professors about performing undergraduate research, and each was excited about the idea and ready to help me get started, in many cases even providing some funding." Another student says, "I have always received personal

West

help when I asked for it. Professors are busy and their open office hours short (generally two to three hours per week), but few enough students take advantage of one-on-one opportunities that those who seek them out get them."

One faculty member says BYU has an "unusually strong commitment to teaching," and it is generally agreed that publishing comes after pedagogy in faculty members' minds. One professor says, "I can honestly say that professors (including TAs) are eager to engage their students. There is a very strong emphasis on student-teacher interaction. For all of the research that goes on at BYU—and there is an astounding amount taking place in many, many areas—BYU is really a teaching university where the students feel the interest of their professors in academics." Students and professors praise Stephen E. Robinson in ancient scripture; Dilworth Parkinson and J. Scott Miller in Asian and Near Eastern languages; John F. Hall in classics; Larry H. Peer in comparative literature; Ralph Hancock in political philosophy; Terrance F. Olson in marriage, family, and human development; Paul E. Kerry in history; James Cannon in mathematics; and Erin D. Bigler and Hal Miller in psychology.

BYU undergrads, grads, and faculty work together on substantial research projects.

ACADEMIC REQUIREMENTS

Students at BYU face something close to the traditional core curriculum, with some distinctive additions. Each undergrad must take:

- Two courses in "The Book of Mormon" taken during freshman year.
- One New Testament class, such as "The Gospels" or "Acts Through Revalations."
- One class on the LDS "Book of Doctrine and Covenants."
- One class in American heritage, or the more in-depth combination of one American government or economics course with one early-American history course.
- One quantitative reasoning class in math, formal logic, or statistics. Students may test out.
- One advanced math and one foreign language course. Math choices include mathematical modeling, calculus, and higher-level logic and statistics courses.
- Two classes in world civilization, one before and one after 1500.
- The wellness course, "Fitness and Lifestyle Management," or a combination of alternative physical education courses.
- A "Global and Cultural Awareness" diversity course. Options include "Social/Cultural Anthropology" and "Multicultural America."
- An arts class. Choices include "Introduction to Dance," "History of Jazz," and "Northern Mesoamerican Art."
- A "letters" course. Options here include "Introduction to Greek and Roman Literature," "Literature of the Latter-day Saints," and "History and Philosophy of Science."
- One biological science class.
- One physical science course.
- One social science class.
- Three to four religion electives.

West

One professor says, "Students can request support funds for projects of their own design and which they will conduct under the individual direction of a faculty member. Or students can be hired as research assistants to assist faculty with their own research projects. For example, I am currently working with over a dozen students on mentored research projects. I think the commitment of the university to support these projects really helps students to have a much more personalized academic experience." Although BYU is not a major research institution and spends relatively little on research, the College of Technology and Engineering makes supercomputers available to students and faculty for research projects. The university also built a $1 million virtual-reality screening room that is used for industrial-design work and screening student animation projects.

Approximately 97 percent of male and 32 percent of female BYU undergraduates take a two-year hiatus from their studies to serve as Mormon missionaries. Most of these students become fluent in a foreign language while serving; still, BYU offers classes in over seventy languages, as well as offering majors in French, German, Italian, Japanese, Korean, Portuguese, Russian, and Spanish. For students who want to study abroad without the missionary obligation, BYU's David M. Kennedy Center for International Studies offers programs in places such as in countries on every inhabited continent.

Student Life: Latter-day saintly

Brigham Young University's campus is stunning. The snow-capped Wasatch Mountains tower over the school and town, and the skiing, camping, hunting, hiking, and rock climbing in the surrounding back country are among the best in the country. "The outdoor opportunities are what really set BYU apart as far as location goes," says a student. "Rock Canyon is only minutes from campus, Utah Lake is just across town, and world-class ski resorts are within an hour's drive. Salt Lake City is only forty-five minutes away for those who are more interested in shopping and nice restaurants." But Provo (population 118,581) can hold its own: its residents are closely tied to the university, and the communities share cultural, entertainment, and recreational resources.

"Cultural events are a big part of student life," says a student. "BYU has many talented performing groups, including choirs . . . big ballroom-dance programs, and the like." In fact, two-thirds of BYU's student performance groups tour internationally. The Utah Symphony Orchestra frequently performs on campus, and Provo is only thirty to forty minutes from Park City, new home of the world-famous Sundance Film Festival.

Nothing is more important to BYU's mission of building a community of faith than the social and moral life of its students. Not surprisingly then, the university has taken a great interest in student life and has plenty of guidelines and regulations in place to support students in their faith.

The honor code requires all students to live by the standards of the Church of Jesus Christ of Latter-day Saints. LDS students make an extra commitment to continue active participation in the Church during their time at BYU, and to tithe—which allows them a discounted tuition. The honor code requires students to avoid "sexual misconduct," which is defined as "premarital sex, cross-dressing, and homosexual conduct." And BYU is serious about the consequences: any of the above is grounds for suspension or expulsion. For instance, a female cast member from MTV's *The Real World* was expelled from the university for rooming with male members of the show during filming.

The BYU honor code even governs students' personal grooming habits, imposing a strict dress and modesty code. BYU sees such regulations as part of its commitment to creating a moral atmosphere distinctive among U.S. colleges.

Housing at BYU, like academics and politics, is built around the ideal of a "Gospel-centered community." BYU does not have any coed dorms, bathrooms, or halls. Visitors of the opposite sex are restricted to visiting hours, which usually end around midnight. Even students who live off campus are required to obey university regulations regarding visitors of the opposite sex. Although some students find the visitation rules too restrictive, the church and the university insist that they promote an environment conducive to academic success, not to mention chastity, and most BYU students agree.

Although BYU does not require any of its students to live on campus, university culture has developed so that most freshmen choose to do so and most upperclassmen do not. A staggering 81 percent of students live off campus. "This is, in part," says a student, "because nearly all of the young men leave on a two-year mission for the church after their freshman year, and when they come back they are ready for a change and live off campus." It is also true that off-campus housing costs about half the price of the dorms. Students who live off campus must choose university-approved housing, and approval is based on whether the housing in question allows the student to adhere to the standards of the honor code. The owners of the housing complexes inform tenants of the codes of conduct, warning or evicting those who transgress, and reporting them to the university.

As no one familiar with the teachings of the LDS Church will be surprised to learn, alcohol consumption is banned by the school's honor code; what might be surprising is that tobacco, tea, and coffee are banned as well. The only Greek-letter organizations on campus are academic in nature.

Even with all this, a student says, "It is my experience that most of the students do not complain about the honor code—rather, they enjoy the freedom that it brings and the atmosphere that it creates. . . . Because everyone is following the honor code there is an incredible amount of trust among BYU students, even if they have never met before . . . A student is given two to five days to take a test in the testing center. There is nothing to stop a student from telling his classmates what was on the test other than his word of honor, and BYU students are honorable." But, this student allows, "a few don't like some of the rules, but they abide by them anyway. After all, they chose to come to BYU."

There are hundreds of clubs available to students, but many students find an attractive social outlet in their respective "wards." For Mormons, a ward is the analogue of a Catholic or Anglican parish. BYU students are organized geographically into units of about 150 students each. Wards include non-LDS students in their activities as well as students from other nearby colleges, should other students live nearby. The wards are almost exclusively staffed by students themselves, and almost every student has an assignment connected to his ward, such as teaching Sunday school or organizing social activities. "The ward unit meets for church every Sunday, for a 'Family Home Evening' every Monday night, as well as for weekly or monthly activities," says a student. Groups of wards combine to form a "stake," and there are more activities organized by the stake.

For many BYU students, college is a place to meet future spouses, and the ward system facilitates this—married and single students are placed in different wards. "BYU is a good place for LDS kids who come from places where there aren't many Mormons to meet other LDS kids—most of them hoping to find one to marry," a student says. The university even publishes marriage statistics on its website: upon graduation, more than half of BYU students have already wed.

BYU's nineteen varsity sports excite fans. The Cougars formerly competed in the NCAA Division I in the Mountain West Conference, but BYU football started the 2011 college football season as an independent, and other sports left to compete in the West Coast Conference. The university's intramurals program includes about thirty activities each year, ranging from flag football to inner-tube water polo. "Intramurals are a big deal," a student says.

Most students are genuinely happy at BYU, believing the university serves its purpose well. Says one student, "Everyone here is willing to help you, whether it is watching your stuff for a second when you leave the room or helping you study a subject you don't

---

GREEN LIGHT

Not surprisingly, most academics at BYU trend conservative—if they display any politics at all. Says a professor, "The university's avowed stance is to stick to the fundamentals rather than to turn to a curriculum tricked out to serve either left- or right-wing interests." One student notes that students and professors have their political opinions, but do not put one another down for disagreeing. He says: "All in all I think that one of the best things about BYU; despite our political differences and academic arguments, there's generally a strong feeling of cooperation, of being on the same side."

Although the university may authorize a political protest, it is inflexible about religious dissent. A few years ago, a popular part-time philosophy professor tested this by contradicting LDS policy in the pages of the *Salt Lake Tribune*. While the LDS leadership had called on its American members to support a constitutional amendment banning gay "marriage," this faculty member wrote opposing this amendment, and identified himself in the editorial as a faithful member of the LDS Church. His contract was not renewed.

---

understand. There is an incredible spirit of cooperation . . . not competition." Another said, "I love BYU. Yes, its policies are very parental, but they also tend to reflect the generally accepted standards of church members worldwide, and that is the community BYU has been created to serve. The atmosphere at BYU is wonderful, happy, and very free to me."

Crime at Brigham Young is rarely a problem; however, Provo is reputed to have a growing drug problem and gang presence. In 2009, the campus saw eleven sex offenses and eleven burglaries. BYU operates a full-service police department to patrol the campus, as well as a Safewalk program providing escorts for students throughout the night.

Brigham Young is one of the most affordable schools in the U.S. In 2010–11, members of the LDS church—whose tithes underwrite the school—paid only $4,420 in tuition, while nonmembers paid a still modest $8,840. Room and board averaged at $7,120.

West

University of California at Berkeley

Berkeley, California • www.berkeley.edu

Barnum and Bailey, step aside!

Berkeley's reputation for student activism may have outlived the reality. Here, at the flagship campus of the University of California, student zeal since the 1960s has gradually veered from politics to preprofessionalism—leaving activism to a relatively small cadre of exhibitionists. And the school has largely upheld the formidable academic reputation earned since its 1868 founding in the wake of the Gold Rush. Reposing at the base of the Oakland foothills in the East Bay bohemian town of Berkeley, this sprawling and woodsy campus is home to 35,843 students, 29 percent of whom are engaged in graduate work. To be sure, students seeking warm professors, small classes, and a traditional liberal arts education may find Berkeley intimidating and still politically discomfiting. Those who bump up against the residues of 1960s politics must stay academically focused, be ready to confront bureaucratic obstacles and political proselytizing, and retain a sense of humor.

Academic Life: Virtuosos and clowns

As at many universities founded before the 1920s, Berkeley's first students enrolled in a strong core curriculum of Latin, Ancient Greek, natural history, mathematics, English, and history. The now-gargantuan state university (comprising fourteen colleges) no longer requires its students to take even a semblance of that curriculum. While the school imposes certain breadth requirements, they are malleable to the point of absurdity. "It's pretty easy to make your own schedule and avoid classes you don't want to take," one student says.

The College of Letters and Science (L&S) at Berkeley enrolls three quarters of the school's undergraduate population and half of its PhD candidates. It offers over eighty majors in sixty-one departments and employs more than half the faculty at Berkeley. Instead of a core, students in the college must complete vague distributional requirements. For instance, in arts and literature, students can take "Language and Power," opting out of more traditional courses on American or British literature. Hundreds of courses fulfill the requirements in other areas. One professor maintains that "our students still graduate with a fine education," and no doubt many of them do. Yet with such broad requirements and the large selection of classes available to fulfill them, the university does next to nothing to ensure it.

West

A writing-intensive course is required of most Berkeley students, but many choices which fulfill this mandate have predictable political agendas, such as classes from the African American studies, Asian American studies, and women's studies departments.

However, most students are not flocking to take the wackiest courses. One insider says, "Politically, more students tend to be liberal than conservative but most are politically apathetic. They're just here to get to their classes and get their degrees."

One professor says the economics, political science, history, and sociology departments are not politicized, and "in fact, they are among the best in the nation." The economics department promotes a variety of viewpoints with the goal of finding the greatest efficiencies in a mixed economic system. In political science, says one major, "I felt that for the most part, professors were very fair and objective in their presentation of the subject matter. One of the best lecturers in the department is Dan Schnur who was the communications director of the McCain 2000 campaign and has incredible insight into both national and California politics."

UC–Berkeley—or "Cal," as it is familiarly known—has a number of other strong humanities departments. For example, history majors now must take twelve classes, including four lower-division courses that are surveys of American history, European history, any other world region's history, and an elective. Given the full range of possible classes and requirements, history majors *could* manage to take all of their upper-level history classes on gender or race—or a worthier concentration such as "history of religion" or "history of law." The department is especially helpful for students who wish to pursue intellectual history, such as the history of science.

The English department also has a solid set of departmental core requirements, while offering a number of special concentrations. English majors must take three intensive survey courses in English literature, from Chaucer through Milton to the twentieth century, an upper-division course in English literature before 1800, one upper-division seminar, and a course on Shakespeare (a requirement absent from many top schools' English lists these days).

To major in political science, students must "complete a total of eight upper-division courses," including one upper- or lower-division course from each of the five subfields and two upper-division courses from one subfield. The subfields are: "American Politics,"

VITAL STATISTICS

Religious affiliation: *none*

Total enrollment: *35,843*

Total undergraduates: *25,530*

SAT/ACT midranges: CR: *590–710*; M: *640–760*; ACT: *27–32*

Applicants: *48,650*

Applicants accepted: *22%*

Accepted applicants who enrolled: *41%*

Tuition and fees: *in state, $9,402; out of state, $32,281*

Room and board: *$15,308*

Freshman retention rate: *97%*

Graduation rate: *66% (4 yrs.), 90% (6 yrs.)*

Courses with fewer than 20 students: *60%*

Student-faculty ratio: *15:1*

Courses taught by graduate students: *none*

Most popular majors: *social sciences, biological and life sciences, engineering*

Students living on campus: *35%*

Guaranteed housing for four years? *no*

Students in fraternities: *10%* in sororities: *10%*

SUGGESTED CORE

1. Classics 34, Epic Poetry: Homer and Vergil
2. Philosophy 25A, Ancient Philosophy
3. Religious Studies C119, The English Bible As Literature
4. History 156, Topics in Medieval History
5. Political Science 112B, History of Political Theory
6. English 117, Shakespeare
7. History 7A, The United States from Settlement to Civil War
8. History 163A, European Intellectual History from the Enlightenment to 1870

"Comparative Politics," "Empirical Theory and Quantitative Methods," "Political Theory," and "International Relations." Students must also take three of the five introductory courses and one history course. Options include "History of Ancient and Medieval Political Thought" and "Racial and Ethnic Politics in the New American Century."

Students say that among the best professors are A. James Gregor in political science; Ann Swidler in sociology; Richard M. Abrams, Richard A. Muller, and George Smoot (a Nobel laureate who still teaches undergraduates) in physics; Thomas A. Brady, and David Hollinger in history; Ronald S. Stroud in classics; David J. Vogel in business; and John R. Searle in philosophy. One student calls Searle her favorite professor: "He's a major influence on Artificial Intelligence/Cognitive Science and the closest thing to a conservative at Berkeley."

Students register for classes online, but "one cannot get all the classes one wants without going on a waiting list," says a recent business major. Another student points out that waiting lists occur "usually just because people haven't solidified their schedules yet. I have gotten into every class I've wanted to, eventually. It just takes perseverance." It is not unusual for students to stay five years just to complete their graduation requirements, lax as these may be.

Classes are large but are mostly taught by professors. Weekly discussion sections, on the other hand, are led by graduate students—a typical arrangement at large universities. According to students, professors are available for meetings outside class. "If you take advantage of office hours, professors and graduate student instructors (GSIs) are very accessible. I got closest with my GSIs (mostly because they actually graded my work) and they were more than happy to write recommendation letters on my behalf if I asked them."

The university does not assign teachers to advise students before they have declared their majors. Instead students consult the Office of Undergraduate Advising, staffed by professional advisors rather than faculty members. Once a student has declared a major, he can visit an advisor within it, but even here the student does not have a specific faculty member who is responsible for him or to whom he is accountable.

The gender and women's studies department includes the usual dismal offerings: "Geographies of Race and Gender," "Transnational Feminisms," "Identities across Difference," "Alternate Sexualities in a Transnational World," and "Cultural Representations of Sexualities: Queer Visual Culture." One student cheerfully describes the department as "abominable."

Berkeley offers majors in Chinese, French, German, Ancient Greek, Japanese, Latin, Scandinavian languages, Slavic languages, and Spanish. Minors include French, German, and Spanish and Portuguese.

West

Berkeley's Education Abroad Program offers semester-long, year-long, and summer trips to thirty-four different countries, giving students "a broad spectrum of opportunities . . . to gain first-hand experience living in other cultures while progressing toward their bachelor's degrees."

Berkeley sponsors an honors program, which according to one undergrad is "intense and basically only for those students who are highly motivated to do research." Professors will "individually mentor undergraduates as they write original theses over the school year."

Finally, Berkeley offers a "Cal in Sacramento Fellowship Program" through the Institute of Governmental Studies. Twenty to thirty students will go to Sacramento in the summer and intern in public policy, perhaps in the state assembly or senate offices, or at the local TV news station. One devotee says, "The biggest perk is that the program provides free housing for the summer. I highly recommend it for anyone interested in public policy or state politics."

Student Life: Conservatives push back

Given Berkeley's reputation for leftist activism, it may come as a surprise to hear that there is a thriving conservative subculture on campus. In fact, of the many student political groups left and right, Berkeley College Republicans is the single largest. The BCR president has not only been a prominent spokesman on campus for conservative and Republican causes but has also become a minor national media celebrity. At the beginning of the semester, BCR holds a "Conservative Coming Out Day." BCR has countered anti-military protests on campus and held a "People Eating Tasty Animals" barbecue, which was a huge success. "The BCR also frequently debates the Cal Berkeley Democrats," in what is "now known as 'The Great Debate.'" The main function of BCR, however, is that it provides a friendly social space for Cal students who dissent from leftist orthodoxy. The BCR is an umbrella group that encompasses conservatives and libertarians of every conceivable stripe. Says one member,

> The Berkeley College Republicans have a range of right-leaning students. Some are pretty moderate or have libertarian leanings, while others are very, very conservative. We also have a few paleoconservatives as well. This provides a great atmosphere for debates and humor as we have diverse points of view on issues such as abortion, legalization of marijuana, border control, President Bush, gay marriage, and support of Israel. The one thing we as members of BCR can all come together on, though, is that we are fiscal conservatives . . . and not very politically correct. We stick together in solidarity on those issues and have fun debating the rest amongst ourselves.

Other conservative-leaning groups on campus include Berkeley Students for Life and, "owing to a recent influx of libertarians on campus," Students for Liberty.

The student-run paper, the *Daily Californian*, covers news well, but compared to other university dailies sometimes lacks substance. Other publications available on campus include the *Socialist Worker* and the *California Patriot*, a monthly conservative magazine which has garnered national attention for its assessments of Berkeley's hard left.

And the Left at Berkeley continues to supply the rest of campus (along with conservatives) no end of entertainment. In 2009, when the administration, facing gigantic budget cuts from the state, announced a formidable tuition increase, this, according to one observer, is what ensued:

ACADEMIC REQUIREMENTS

The University of California at Berkeley imposes certain curricular requirements, which seem deceptively substantive. In fact, given the vast number of courses that would fulfill most of them, it would take a concerted effort not to meet them. All undergraduates must:

- Demonstrate writing and reading proficiency. This can easily be satisfied by sufficient standardized-test scores or high school courses.
- Show some knowledge of American history and institutions. Many students fulfill this requirement in high school; others complete an introductory course during their first year at Berkeley.
- Complete a requirement called "Berkeley Campus American Cultures," which is meant to "provide students with the intellectual tools to understand better their own identity and the cultural identity of others in their own terms," according to the university catalog. Students choose from courses like "Lives of Struggle: Minorities in a Majority Culture" and "The United States from Settlement to Civil War."

Students in the liberal arts college must take one course in each of seven areas:

- Arts and literature. "Shakespeare" would count; so would "The Avant-Garde Film."
- Biological science. Options range from "Biochemical Engineering" to "Ecosystems of California."
- Historical studies. Choices range from "Origins of Western Civilization: The Ancient Mediterranean World" to "A History of Race and Ethnicity in Western North America, 1598–Present."
- International studies. Options range from "Sociology of Natural Resources" to "Agroecology: A Brazilian Perspective."
- Philosophy and values. Choices here include "Man, God, and Society in Western Literature" and "Death, Dreams, and Visions in Tibetan Buddhism."
- Physical science. This can be met by introductory math, chemistry, or physics classes.
- Social and behavioral sciences. Choices range very widely, from "Archaeology" to "Introduction to Chicano History."

Liberal arts students are also required to:

- Show second-semester proficiency in a foreign language ("letter grade of C- or higher.").
- Take or test out of a course in quantitative reasoning (mathematics, statistics, or computer science).
- Complete two writing-intensive courses.

West

Students gathered around a police barricade for most of the day and night to watch [a] handful of students that locked themselves in [Wheeler Hall]. Of course, the administration, campus police, and county police did nothing to get rid of them and allowed the situation to get worse. Students 'in solidarity' with the occupiers fanned out to other surrounding buildings and disrupted classes for the entire day by pulling fire alarms. While we are politically apathetic largely, we know how to be counterproductive by protesting lack of funds by wasting our few funds on unnecessary fire-engine calls.

It should be noted that a few protestors really got out of hand. They later—perhaps for old-time's sake—threw firebombs at the president's residence, and some were arrested on felony charges.

On most days of the week, Berkeley College Republicans man a table at Sproul Plaza, where they hand out literature, answer questions, and sometimes endure dirty looks and spiteful comments. Nevertheless, conservatives and libertarians do enjoy free speech at Cal. There have been no recorded incidents of censorship in the past few years. One is free, if he can handle the social pressure, to articulate an independent political position both inside and outside of class. The social pressure simply forces conservative and libertarian students to become excellent debaters. "You're really forced to articulate and think out what you believe," says one student.

According to Berkeley's catalog, the Center for Student Leadership recognizes "more than 800 student organizations, including fraternities and sororities and a variety of organizations that focus on the arts, academics, culture, politics, professions, publications, religion, sports, service and social issues." Examples include Filmmakers for Social Change, Live & Local: Student Music Club, Mathematics and Aesthetics in Origami, Oriental Organization of Orientals, The Cheese and Bread Conspiracy, Asians On Stage By Any Means Necessary, Blacks in Public Policy, Cal Queer & Asian, Harry Potter Alliance Chapter at Berkeley, Sikh Students Association, Cal Berkeley Democrats, Guns in Public Policy, Tobacc-NO, Girls in Tech @ Berkeley, Molecular Cell Biology Graduate Student Organization, Surfing Club at Berkeley, Unicycle Basketball Club, and In Christ Alone. If you want to get away from the campus circus, Berkeley is a thriving college town with its share of pleasant restaurants, good bookstores, and interesting shops. In their free time, students especially enjoy sampling the local music shops and bookstores. Amoeba Music, one of the area's largest music stores, sells both new and used music. Quips one student, "There is a running gag in Berkeley that on every block by campus there is a frozen-yogurt shop." There are also popular smoke shops, used-clothing stores, and body-piercing parlors in town. Lunchtime is not complete without the ultra-cheap, ultra-tasty pizza slices from the "Cheese Board." But at the pinnacle of all local establishments (and across the street) is Chez Panisse, the mother-house of California Cuisine established by the legendary Alice Waters decades ago and still going strong. The reliable Bay Area Rapid Transit (BART) train system runs throughout the region, as does an extensive (but less punctual) bus system.

For those new to the Bay Area, an even more captivating escape beckons. Those "hills" rising up behind campus are really mountains, which lead into something nearly approach-

West

867

ing high wilderness at the almost 2000-foot summit. A dedicated hiker or bicyclist, with an afternoon free, can weave his way through hairpin residential streets and up into unexpected bucolic isolation, looking down on Oakland, San Francisco, and the Golden Gate Bridge as if from an orbiting satellite, then find a quiet spot under a shade tree and crack open a book. Thoreau never had it so good.

From there, you can also put out of mind the din of unending construction far below: new buildings on the Berkeley campus include Stanley Hall, the cornerstone facility of an emerging initiative in the health sciences, the Jean Gray Hargrove Music Library, and the "green-certified Crossroads student-dining commons."

Since Berkeley offers relatively low in-state tuition—though not as low as it was until the recent steep tuition increases—and reserves spots for California residents, a large proportion of students (89 percent) come from that state. This means that Berkeley has a more parochial student body than do some other prestigious public universities, such as the University of Michigan or the University of Virginia. Given that no immediate financial remedies for California's budget crisis seem to be forthcoming from the wizards of the State Assembly, and that the nation and the world are facing an enormous recession, budget thinkers at UC are looking at further alternatives, to include "hiring more lecturers and fewer ladder-rank faculty, offering fewer course selections and larger class sizes, reducing operating hours for libraries and student services, and paring back other academic and administrative programs."

UC–Berkeley is not primarily a residential campus; some 9,000 students, most of them freshmen, live in the university dorms. As at most large, urban universities, students usually move off campus into theme houses, Greek houses, or rental properties after their freshman year. Housing is offered on a space-available basis and late applicants are usually forced to live in non-university-owned residences. As a service to students, the university provides information on alternative housing options through the Cal Rentals program. Most residences are coed, but the university does have one all-female dorm and one all-male dorm. In some coed dormitories, men and women are separated by floor, but in many dorms, halls and even bathrooms are coed. There are no intervisitation restrictions to speak of. Theme houses are university-owned facilities in which students with common interests live together. For instance, a student can choose to live in the African American house; the gay, lesbian, bisexual, and transgender house; or the women in engineering and science house.

Most students purchase dining debit cards, deducting the cost of meals in university dining halls with each swipe. The campus has six dining halls, in addition to seven restaurants.

Because classes are rarely scheduled on Fridays, weekends at UC–Berkeley traditionally begin on Thursday evenings. Besides the dozens of bars and clubs in Berkeley, the school is also home to more than sixty Greek organizations, to which about 10 percent of undergraduates belong. According to several students, Greek life is traditionally robust throughout the school year. High spirits have been tempered somewhat in the wake of a 2005 decision to ban temporarily "alcohol consumption at all events held by campus fraternities and sororities," according to the *Chronicle of Higher Education*. The school's dean of students explained the ban by pointing to an "alarming increase in problems with alco-

West

hol abuse, hazing, fights, and badly managed parties." As of January 19, 2009, neighboring residents filed a class-action lawsuit "seeking to stop the antisocial, unruly, and illegal conduct and multiple additional problems caused by fraternities at UC–Berkeley." The move is considered the first lawsuit of its kind in the United States, and was sparked in part because of one fraternity fracas that led to a student death. The student circus, apparently, is not limited to politics.

Despite the school's long-fashionable radicalism, it has kept up a goodly number of traditions, in keeping with Berkeley's status as the oldest link in the UC chain. Among a very few of these are: the Spring Sing; the Stanford Axe; the "Pedro" call; the Freshmen–Sophomore Brawl; the Daffodil Festival; the Big Game Week (activities leading up to the Stanford game); and, of course, Oski the mascot. "My favorite tradition," says one student, "is the Bonfire Rally the night before the Big Game with Stanford. If we are currently in possession of the Stanford Axe, however, it is called the Axe Rally. The bonfire is often called the 'biggest bonfire west of the Mississippi' and it probably reaches a height of forty feet. The event is awesome and includes a speech from the head coach of the football team, a re-telling of how the Stanford Axe became the prize it is today, Cal fight songs from the Men's Octet and the Golden Overtones, and a candlelight vigil."

Religious life at UC–Berkeley is, to say the least, varied. In addition to various standard Christian, Jewish, Muslim, Buddhist, and Hindu groups, there are such unique organizations as Progressive Students of Faith; Network of Spiritual Progressives; and Students for a Nonreligious Ethos. Catholics of a more traditional bent may not be extremely comfortable with the university's Newman club, whose modernistic chapel and liturgies are guided by the Paulists. Then again, the club does host a rosary and a pro-life group, as well as monthly talks bridging science and faith. The Orthodox Christian Fellowship offers a gateway to the many ethnic parishes of that denomination in the Bay Area. For Episco-

---

YELLOW LIGHT

The Berkeley political circus is not as scary as it looks. Here is one student's experience: "In my first semester at Cal, my psychology professor wanted to assure us that we would be safe in any campus psych experiments, and so she stated that, for example, we wouldn't go to an abortion clinic because there might be protesters who would throw rocks. I'm still not sure why she brought this up, but after class I talked to her about it and expressed my astonishment at such slander. She ended up retracting her comments and apologizing in the next class. Keep in mind that this class was held in Wheeler Auditorium, the largest lecture hall, and probably contained 600–700 people. I've found other professors to behave similarly. They might make extremely liberal remarks, but when called out on it, they are reasonable enough to take it back. This occurred especially when I took the class 'Mind, Language, and Politics' from Professor George Lakoff. He would state that conservatives simply don't care, they use fear to convince others, et cetera. But he welcomed an opposing opinion in the discussion-based classroom and even wrote me a letter of recommendation."

Surprisingly, amid the plethora of leftist organizations, Berkeley maintains a thriving and successful ROTC program, and the CIA and Department of Defense recruit from Berkeley during campus career fairs.

palians, there is a standard Canterbury Group, which may not serve the needs of more conservative Anglicans. Such may find the Chapel of St. Joseph of Arimathea on Durant Street more to their liking.

Berkeley fields twenty-five varsity athletic teams in the PAC-10 Conference. The Golden Bears maintain a heated rivalry with Stanford. The school also has a number of intramural offerings, with twenty-eight club sports and excellent facilities to accommodate them.

Berkeley is consistently among the top five universities in arrests for alcohol, drugs, and weapons. Crime statistics for 2009 show fourteen motor vehicle thefts, thirteen robberies, fourteen assaults, five forcible sex offenses, forty-eight burglaries, and twelve cases of arson—all on campus. The university is so intermingled with the city of Berkeley that it is hard to separate the two or to insulate students from urban pathologies (or the city from pathological students). Crime is a problem on and off campus, although the university has tried to curb it with self-defense workshops, night escort services and shuttles, and round-the-clock patrols.

Berkeley is no longer quite the bargain it used to be, with 2010–11 tuition at $9,402 and expected to rise steeply. Adventurous souls from other states paid $32,281. Room and board were report,ed by the school as $15,308. Some 45 percent of students receive need-based financial aid, and the average loan burden of a recent grad is a modest $14,493.

University of California at Irvine

Irvine, California • www.uci.edu

Student processing

The University of California at Irvine opened in 1965. In less than half a century it has grown into a major public research university with approximately 22,000 undergraduates and 5,000 graduate students studying in fifteen schools. The tree-lined suburban campus ripples out in concentric "circles of learning" from gracious, wooded Aldrich Park, with facilities for undergraduate study near the center and those for graduate work in the outer rings.

Irvine is largely a commuter school (96 percent of its students are Californian) where even students who live on campus disappear on weekends. Lack of school spirit is a common complaint. With a few egregious exceptions (see below) Irvine students tend to be largely apolitical and just concerned with getting their degrees and getting on with their careers. Many on the stellar faculty, with some noteworthy exceptions, are absorbed in their research and barely connect to the undergraduates to whom they must deliver their lectures. Visitors often say that the campus has a "corporate," impersonal atmosphere. Professors refer to departments "processing" or "servicing" students. The financial problems plaguing the University of California system in recent years exacerbated this problem, as classes bulge and departments cannot hire needed faculty. However, the student assertive and organized enough to pull it together—especially if he can get into an honors program and onto a research team and live in honors housing—can forge an excellent education and work closely with world-class scholars and bright students. And while the faculty has the liberal bent endemic to American education, the quiet political and social atmosphere and the presence of many deeply religious students make Irvine a relatively comfortable place to spend their undergraduate years.

Academic Life: "Mailing it in"

Irvine requires that undergraduates devote about a third of their coursework to fulfilling an extensive set of general education requirements, yet it does not demand that they learn anything in particular. These requirements can be met on an ad-hoc basis or through structured programs. The First Year Integrated Program (FIP) offers freshman the chance to bond with each other while fulfilling a number of the general education requirements. Rather than using this as an opportunity to provide the common background in the West-

VITAL STATISTICS

Religious affiliation: *none*

Total enrollment: *27,142*

Total undergraduates: *22,226*

SAT/ACT midranges: CR: *520–640*; M: *570–680*; ACT: *not provided*

Applicants: *44,123*

Applicants accepted: *42%*

Accepted applicants who enrolled: *21%*

Tuition and fees: *in state, $11,927; out of state, $34,806*

Room and board: *$11,400*

Freshman retention rate: *94%*

Graduation rate: *57% (4 yrs.), 82% (6 yrs.)*

Courses with fewer than 20 students: *45%*

Student-faculty ratio: *19:1*

Courses taught by graduate students: *not provided*

Most popular majors: *social sciences, biology, engineering*

Students living on campus: *35%*

Guaranteed housing for four years? *no*

Students in fraternities: *8%* in sororities: *12%*

ern canon—which professors complain is lacking in the Irvine population—FIP offers a trendy, hip curriculum, with three trimesters spent studying any one of the following: "Persuasion and Social Change," "Computer Games as Art, Culture and Technology," "Environmental Studies," "Natural, Cultural and Social Conditions of Music," or "Consciousness." Freshmen should run away screaming from this program.

A much better choice is the Humanities Core. While material is presented thematically rather than as a chronological survey (the theme for 2010–11 was "The Human and Its Others: Divinity, Society, Nature"), the Core covers many seminal works and great thinkers. According to the program description, in 2010–11 required texts included "works by Homer, Plato, Epicurus, Epictetus, Euripides, Maimonides, Galileo, Goethe, Elizabeth Cady Stanton, Frederick Douglass, Franz Kafka, Werner Heisenberg, Benjamin Britten, and Maxine Hong Kingston in addition to selections from African folk tales, the Jewish Bible, the New Testament, the Koran, and the U.S. Declaration of Independence." The Humanities Core course is open, space permitting, to all freshmen who have passed the school's entry-level writing threshold. Students are grouped by writing skill levels; those in the Campuswide Honors Program have separate, enhanced sections. For eligible students, that honors program offers many other advantages as well, not least of all priority registration—a huge benefit at a school where it can be hard to get the into the classes you need to graduate in four years, especially for a double major—a guarantee of housing on campus for four years, and more interaction with professors. Irvine's first Rhodes scholar is a recent graduate of this program.

Some schools also have their own honors programs. The small (about twenty-two students per year) Humanities Honors Program allows top juniors and seniors to study in intense seminars and interact closely with professors; students write senior honors theses. Social Sciences offers a more rudimentary honors program. In addition, the Undergraduate Research Opportunity Program and the newer Multi-Disciplinary Design Program give students in all disciplines the opportunity to do original research with faculty mentors and potentially to publish their results. Students who take advantage of these programs can get an excellent education. Others choose to skate through and, at least in the humanities and social sciences, can take advantage of grade inflation to get a degree without learning much. As one student says, "What students get out of their education is largely up to them, and some students artfully choose their classes to minimize their challenges. . . . The freedom that students have to shape their own curriculum means that some students will stick with what is familiar."

Academic advising is provided by a mix of teaching faculty and full-time advisors, along with peer advisors. The schools vary as to whether an undergraduate needs to review his schedule with an advisor before registering for classes. Humanities does not require this but leaves eighteen-year-olds free to dig their own graves if they choose. A biology major says of his school's advisors that "the administrators/counselors are exceedingly unhelpful. By the time I was a fourth year, I entered the counselor's office expecting to debate my requests."

The atmosphere at Irvine tends to be, laments one professor, "technical" and "corporate," not one of excitement about learning for its inherent value but of getting the grade to get a job. Many students are the first in their families to attend college—and a high percentage are the children of recent immigrants. While they have excelled in school, they are often unfamiliar with the Western canon and with American institutions. (One professor notes that many have never been to a museum.) The school does them a disservice by not working harder to enrich their educations with required courses in the humanities.

> **SUGGESTED CORE**
>
> 1. History/Classics 36 or History/Classics 37, The Formation of Ancient Greek Society or The Formation of Ancient Roman Society (closest match)
> 2. Philosophy 10, History of Ancient Philosophy
> 3. Religious Studies 141, Recent Western Religious Traditions (closest match)
> 4. History 110 A/B/C, Europe in the Early/Central/Later Middle Ages (closest match)
> 5. Political Science 31A, Introduction to Political Theory
> 6. No suitable match
> 7. History 140 A/B, Early America: 1492-1740/ Revolutionary America: 1740-1790
> 8. History 127, European Cultural and Intellectual History

Irvine is largely a commuter school. One professor says that students are more focused on beating the traffic home than on staying around to have an intellectual conversation, and that many hold full- or part-time jobs that seem to be their top priorities. He decries the "skewed values" of many undergrads, citing the materialistic culture of Orange County; too many students are scrambling to make payments on fancy cars rather than focusing on their educations. An honors student, however, says, "There's a lot of discussion of ideas from those classes that gets carried back to the dorms."

An unimpressive student-faculty ratio of 19 to 1 means that students have to try hard to be more than a number. Even advanced seminars can have well over 20 students; lectures of 300 or more are common, and, in the social sciences, even discussion sections led by teaching assistants can have 100 students. While many teachers are deeply committed to working with undergraduates, tenure (and salary) decisions are based almost entirely on research, and the pressure to produce is intense. As years go by without relief from the University of California's budget crisis, some departments are down to what one professor calls a "skeleton crew." Some students complain that it can be hard to get into the courses they need in order to graduate. Many courses are taught by lecturers and adjuncts, if not by graduate students.

As at most schools, the faculty is generally liberal and professors can make their biases known. A conservative student says, "Within the bio program at Irvine, politics were rarely brought up in the classroom. However, the level of political bias in the few classes I took outside my major surprised me. Professors in the humanities program rarely hid their political affiliation . . . although I was never grossly graded down for opposing their viewpoints. Be warned that a conservative viewpoint will be opposed often." However, as the student body is less liberal than on a typical American campus, it is not likely that a conservative student in most departments will have tremendous problems.

Whatever the Irvine faculty's political bent, it teems with brilliant scholars. Some who are recommended as teachers of undergraduates include Victoria Silver, Brook Thomas, Amy Wilenz, and "Shakespeare goddess" Julia Lupton in English; James Herbert, Cecile Whiting, and Bert Winther-Tamaki in art history; Alice Fahs, Bob Moeller, David Igler, Vinayak Chaturvedi, Philip Minehan, and Emily Rosenberg in history; Linda Levine in psychology; Peter Bowler and Bradford Hawkins in ecology and evolutionary biology; Roxane Cohen Silver and Linda Levine in psychology and social behavior; Bill Maurer in anthropology; Thomas Eppel in management; James Porter and Andrew Zissos in classics; and John H. Smith in German and humanities core.

Students and faculty name English, history, sciences, cognitive psychology, political science, art history, engineering and anthropology as strong departments. The sciences, despite their stellar researchers, have not been very user-friendly to undergrads; the university is supposedly working to improve the undergraduate experience. The *Atlantic* places Irvine's Creative Writing MFA program in the top ten in the United States; faculty teach undergraduates as well. Philosophy split some years back, apparently in response to the prevailing postmodernism of the department in the humanities school, and a separate logic and philosophy of science department formed within the School of Social Sciences. This latter department is generally considered the far stronger of the two. Some named economics as a weak and sociology as overly politicized.

The English major is heavily structured, with a large number of required classes, including a chronological four-course series covering highlights of medieval through modern literature, as well as four courses addressing different literary genres, two on literary criticism, and a class on "multicultural topics." Majors must also have two years of a foreign language and study some non-English literature, in many cases in the original language.

The history department's focus is "global." A major need not take any courses relating to the United States and could probably graduate without ever studying the history of Europe either. Similarly, a major in political science need not address the American Constitution or any other specifically American political philosophy, except to whatever extent it may be covered in the required political analysis, micropolitics, and macropolitics surveys.

All students must take three courses in sciences and technology and three in quantitative, symbolic, and computational reasoning. While there are some fluff courses that meet these requirements, it would be hard to satisfy them all without doing some real work in math and science. Students must take at least one lab.

Students can participate in the University of California's vast Education Abroad program, with satellites in thirty-five countries on six continents. Students who do not find

Italy, Spain, Ghana, Australia, New Zealand, Chile, South Africa, Mexico, Russia, China, Korea, or any of the other countries offered to their liking can structure other options as well. A professor who has taught in it says that many students find it transformative to spend a quarter at "UCDC," the University of California's program in Washington, D.C.— as many Irvine students have never been to the East Coast and have little knowledge of American institutions.

Currently Irvine offers degree programs in Latin, Ancient Greek, Chinese, Japanese, Korean, German, French, Italian, Spanish and Portuguese. Non-degree (but credit-bearing) courses are also available in Arabic, Hebrew, Hindi, Persian, Russian, and Vietnamese. There are no language-immersion residence halls.

Student Life: "Zot! Zot!"

Irvine's tame-looking suburban campus includes an arboretum and is home to a surprising array of wildlife, including bobcats, coyotes, blue herons, mountain lions, and seemingly hundreds of rabbits. The modern architecture sports various modern and postmodern styles, including "California Brutalist," contributing to the "corporate" feel of the campus. The beaches around Irvine are said to be among the best in California; the home page of Irvine's website links to the daily surf report. The city of Irvine (pop. 212,793) was planned in the aftermath of the creation of the university. It is quiet, safe, wealthy, and more liberal than most of Orange County. Newport Beach, also upscale, may appeal a bit more to students seeking night life. Those willing to fight the freeway traffic can visit Los Angeles, which is forty miles away. The mediterranean climate is lovely, with an average temperature of fifty-six degrees in January, and seventy-one in August. The comfortable weather and flat terrain are perfect for bike riding. Students have access to "Zot Wheels," blue and gold loaner bikes, as well as shuttle buses, to get around the sprawling campus.

Irvine students call themselves Anteaters, after the much-beloved school mascot Peter the Anteater, whose ant-crunching sound, "Zot! Zot!" resounds through sporting events. A student tells us, "Irvine is 'dead' compared to the stereotypical party atmosphere. But if you meet the right people there are some great times to be had. People here are not only intellectually stimulating, but also outgoing, friendly, and fun. The Christian community in Irvine is pretty strong. . . . Irvine's location is great too because it is surrounded by delicious eateries as well as Newport Beach."

Shocktoberfest and several other events attract many freshman as well as some upperclassmen. Past performers include Gym Class Heroes, Swayze, Kevin Rudolph, and Cali Swag District. One student says that "[s]tudent involvement seems widespread and enthusiastic. Nearly everyone I've met here is involved in at least one club or other school-related activity." Theater and dance department offerings are said to be often of high quality.

While 83 percent of freshmen live on campus, only 35 percent of students do. Of the students on campus, a huge number go home on weekends, making dorm life relatively quiet. One student says that a culture of sexual promiscuity is "almost non-existent. Campus life is driven in many cases by deeply religious students." The residences are generally attractive and clean. There are all-female floors in the freshman dorms, single-sex suites that include their own bathrooms available to male and female students in all years, and single-sex (or one-person) apartments available to upperclassmen. There do not appear to be rules regarding intervisitation. "Gender-neutral housing" has also come to Irvine but does not appear to be widespread. Camino del Sol, one of several new residences owned and operated on the campus by a private firm, is a bit more expensive than other housing but gets rave reviews for being "resort-like." It includes, among other amenities, private bedrooms, a swimming pool, hot tub and cabana, and outdoor kitchen with televisions. More housing is coming, with a goal of accommodating almost half of the undergraduates on campus.

There are a number of "theme houses," notably the Campuswide Honors Housing and Humanities Housing. The Greek houses, located in the Arroyo Vista complex, offer single-sex housing to members. About 12 percent of undergraduate women and 8 percent of male undergrads belong to the twenty-three sororities and twenty fraternities, which are said to be more service-oriented and less given to degeneracy than their counterparts on many campuses. A number of the Greek houses are ethnic-based, including Asian, Latino, Jewish, and Armenian. Except for Campuswide Honors Students, undergraduates are generally only guaranteed two years of housing. Apartment prices in Irvine and

---

ACADEMIC REQUIREMENTS

Irvine undergraduates must complete:

- Two lower-division and one upper-division writing courses, such as "Critical Reading and Rhetoric," "Writing About Subcultures," or "Yeats."
- Three classes in science and technology. Options available include "Game Systems and Design" and "Classical Physics."
- Three courses in social and behavior sciences. Choices range from "Introduction to American Government" to "Introduction to Political Theory."
- Three classes in the arts and humanities. Options range from "The Roman Empire" to "Soviet Animation."
- Three courses in quantitative, symbolic, and computational reasoning, which may include "Introduction to Game Simulation and Analysis," "Introduction to Computer Science," "Critical Reasoning," or "Calculus."
- One foreign language class. Students may test out.
- One course in multicultural studies. Options include "Queer History Making" and "Muslim Identity in North America."
- One class in "international/global issues." Choices range from "Japan and Animal Rights" to "Greek Orators."
- One laboratory or performance course.

Students must also either test out of the University of California's proficiency requirements in writing and in United States history and institutions (a C in high school American history suffices), or take designated classes in those subjects.

Newport Beach are steep, though some students are able and willing to pay for the freedom of living off campus, often in attractive apartments bordering the school. Huntington Beach offers slightly less pricey accommodations but a longer drive.

The Interfaith Foundation Center houses campus ministries, including the University Catholic Community and the Anglican ministry (headed by a female priest). A new Jewish center provides refuge for the approximately 1,000 Jewish students on campus; Shabbat dinners reportedly attract about 200 students weekly. Catholic Mass is offered Sunday through Thursday during the school year. Filipino, Korean, and Vietnamese prayer groups appear to be well attended and fervent. Catholics should attend the Latin Mass at Saint John the Baptist parish ten minutes away in Costa Mesa. Faithful Anglicans should attend Saint Matthew's Anglican Catholic Church in Newport Beach.

Irvine has a number of openly pro-life students. In April 2010 Irvine Students for Life sponsored a week-long public display to address the issues of embryonic stem-cell research on campus—which led to a multi-hour informal public debate with the director of the stem-cell facility. Many religious clubs are active, including After God's Heart Bible study, Asian American Christian Fellowship, Baha'i Club, Buddhist Association, Campus Crusade for Christ, CFC Youth, Chabad, Coptic Orthodox Christian Club, Crossroads Campus Ministries, Hindu Yuva, Progressive Christian Students, Presbyterian Campus Fellowship, and United Methodist Student Fellowship.

Secular groups include College Bowl, preprofessional clubs, Mock Trial, many ethnic clubs, Live Nude People With Clothes On (a comedy troupe), Acrobatics Today, Anteater Band, a new chapter of Young Americans for Liberty, Campus Republicans and Democrats, Habitat for Humanity, Helping Hearts for the Homeless, the Muslim paper *Alkalima*, and

GREEN LIGHT

The Muslim Student Union (MSU) is reputedly one of the most aggressive in the nation. According to Mindingthe-Campus.com, "Anti-Semitic incidents are common at the University of California at Irvine, and the Muslim Student Union is the major perpetrator." Most recently, MSU members heckled Israeli Ambassador to the United States Michael Oren so badly that he was virtually unable to speak at a campus appearance in February 2010. The organization denied responsibility, but was suspended for a quarter and its members had to perform one hundred hours of community service after e-mails came to light showing that in fact the group had coordinated the disruption in advance. While suspended, the MSU allegedly continued its activities under the guise of a campus Muslim publication. One Jewish professor believes that much of the Jewish-Muslim controversy is stirred up by outsiders who come to campus, and that most of the time students co-exist peacefully. She says, "It pains me that some Jewish students end up not enrolling because of all the bad press."

With this glaring exception, Irvine is a relatively welcoming environment for religious and conservative students. Committed Christians are a significant force in extra-curricular activity on campus. Political correctness infects the humanities and social sciences but seems to be the domain of faculty more than of students. The campus is quiet, even apathetic. In large part, no agenda is imposed on anyone.

Incite Magazine (intended to arouse student activism). The conservative magazine on campus appears to be defunct but the Campus Republicans club attracts a number of active students.

Anteaters compete in the Big West Conference of the NCAA Division I, playing basketball, baseball, cross-country, track and field, volleyball, golf, soccer, tennis, and water polo. Men's volleyball, men's and women's water polo, and women's indoor track and field are in the Mountain Pacific Sports Federation. There is no football team. Students say that the teams often have a hard time drumming up much enthusiasm, though the men's volleyball and baseball teams have done well in recent years. A very active school spirit group, Completely Insane Anteaters (CIA) makes sporting events fun for those who do attend. In 2010, Anteaters beat the world record for largest game of dodgeball, with a game involving 1,745 players and 800 balls. Intramural sports include soccer, flag football, Ultimate Frisbee, floor hockey, racquetball, dodgeball, volleyball, and water polo, among others. The many club sports include archery, cricket, sailing, table tennis, volleyball, water polo, and wrestling.

The FBI has named Irvine the safest big city in the United States each year since 2004. Students and faculty agree that the campus and surrounding area are quite safe. In 2009, the university reported three forcible sexual offenses on campus, twenty-four burglaries (bicycles and laptops are sometimes stolen), five motor vehicle thefts, and three instances of arson. A tragic killing arose from a custody dispute when a graduate student allegedly shot his child's mother. Emergency phones are located throughout the campus.

In-state tuition was $11,927, and out of state a hefty $34,806. Room and board are variable but listed by the school as $11,400. About 53 percent of students receive need-based financial aid, with an average loan burden at graduation of $15,529.

University of California at Los Angeles

Los Angeles, California • www.ucla.edu

The multi cult

Most students who choose to attend the University of California at Los Angeles know what they're getting: sunny beaches, Hollywood glamour, and cheapish in-state tuition—along with huge classes and scant interaction with professors. UCLA's literature boasts that it is the "most multicultural" university in the country, which is slightly ironic since it began in 1880 as the "State Normal School" for Southern California. By calling itself "multicultural," the school is not boasting about its ethnically diverse student body, but rather its proliferation of ethnic studies programs, courses fixated on race, and segregated graduation ceremonies.

As things stand, UCLA is a highly polished, shattered mirror of postmodern American culture. The good news is that one of the mirror fragments—the heritage of Western thought—has recently been retrieved from the trash and polished up, becoming a focal point for a lively coterie of motivated students and faculty. It is treated mostly with the same tolerance and respect accorded the other cultural shards. In other words, conservative students at UCLA are now considered a minority deserving tolerance. Given the situation at many other schools, this is nothing to sneer at.

Academic Life: San Andreas faults

Upon application, UCLA students choose to pursue a degree in one of the university's five undergraduate programs: the College of Letters and Science; the School of Engineering and Applied Science; the School of Arts and Architecture; the School of Nursing; or the School of Theater, Film, and Television. With over 24,800 students (graduate and undergraduate), Letters and Science is by far the largest academic entity at UCLA, and indeed is the largest school of its type in the University of California system. UCLA is on a quarter calendar (except for the Law School), so students graduate having taken more courses than the typical college student. It is not always clear that this is a good thing.

As at most state schools, the quality of a UCLA education depends heavily on the motivation and choices of the student. Undergrads themselves seem keenly aware of this. "I didn't want to take a philosophy class," admits a recent grad, "so I took one on Egyptian religion." Those seeking to avoid science can enroll in classes on "earthquakes, air pollu-

West

VITAL STATISTICS

Religious affiliation: *none*
Total enrollment: *39,984*
Total undergraduates:
  26,687
SAT/ACT midranges: CR:
  570–680; M: *600–730*;
  ACT: *24–31*
Applicants: *55,708*
Applicants accepted: *22%*
Accepted applicants who
  enrolled: *37%*
Tuition and fees: *in state,
  $10,781; out of state,
  $32,802*
Room and board: *$13,781*
Freshman retention rate:
  97%
Graduation rate: *67% (4 yrs.),
  89% (6 yrs.)*
Courses with fewer than 20
  students: *54%*
Student-faculty ratio: *16:1*
Courses taught by graduate
  students: *not provided*
Most popular majors: *social
  sciences, biological and life
  sciences, psychology*
Students living on campus:
  36%
Guaranteed housing for
  four years? *no*
Students in fraternities: *13%*
  in sororities: *13%*

tion, dinosaurs, and astronomy." Still, one alum says that a course he took to meet the "cultural analysis" requirement for general education inadvertently introduced him to the subject that became his major, classics. Says another pleased student, "It's a great school because if you're not sure of your major, there's a lot of options." On the other hand, "academic counseling is especially weak. I've been to the office five or six times and never really found the person who could tell me what I needed to know."

On a very hopeful note, law professor Daniel Lowenstein directs the "Center for the Liberal Arts and Free Institutions." One of its purposes is to "provide assistance and guidance for undergraduates seeking an introduction to the achievements of Western civilization." It now offers courses including "Liberty and Government in Europe" and "Lincoln and United States Politics," which must be taken together. Taught by Lowenstein and Andre Sabl, the offerings encourage "critical reading and writing," says a student. Sabl, furthermore, "could not have been better at bringing about balance in student discussion." Another student praises the one-unit "Fiat Lux" courses, one of which, she says "ties Greek culture to American history." We highly recommend that all UCLA freshman explore the center's offerings.

Some of the better teachers at UCLA include Sebastian Edwards in economics; Michael J. Allen, Edward I. Condren (emeritus), and Debora K. Shuger in English; Martie Haselton in psychology; Daniel Lowenstein (emeritus) in law; Ruth Bloch, Patrick Geary, Carlo Ginzburg (emeritus), and Richard Rouse (emeritus) in history; and Tim Groseclose, Victor Wolfenstein, and Marc Trachtenberg in political science. Trachtenberg has the largest fan club: "He is incredible—very rational, very balanced, very accessible, infectiously excited about his subject, and a true academic," says one student. "He is one of the founders of the Historical Society, an organization set up to counter the postmodern orthodoxy of the American Historical Association," says another.

The biology, chemistry, and economics departments are among the university's strongest, and the philosophy department is one of the best in the nation. Philosophy majors take thirteen courses in the department, including three basic courses in Greek philosophy, medieval and early modern philosophy, and modern philosophy, plus seven other courses divided among the history of philosophy, logic and semantics, ethics and value theory,

West

and metaphysics and epistemology. Students say Brian Copenhaver, Pamela Hieronymi, and Gavin Lawrence are particularly good in this department.

UCLA's Department of Film, Television, and Digital Media is considered the best in the country. It is also the most competitive: each year 1,400 applicants vie for the 135 spots reserved for undergraduates. Once admitted into the junior/senior program students can take courses like "History of American Motion Picture," "Introduction to Animation," "Advanced Film and Television Producing Workshop for Producers, Writers, and Directors," "Cinematography," and "Film Editing." This program is considered the front door for a career in the motion picture industry.

UCLA offers 131 majors in its five undergraduate schools, and many students choose to double major or earn minors. For students interested in research as undergraduates, UCLA is an excellent choice. The Student Research Program offers ninety slots each quarter in a wide range of projects. In addition to the experience, such research "is a good way to create close, long-lasting relationships with professors," a student says. The Undergraduate Research Center also supports student research in the humanities and social sciences every year.

> ## SUGGESTED CORE
>
> 1. Classics 142, Ancient Epic
> 2. Philosophy 100A, History of Greek Philosophy
> 3. English 108A/108B, English Bible as Literature: Old Testament/New Testament
> 4. History 1B/Introduction to Western Civilization: Circa A.D. 843 to Circa 1715
> 5. Political Science 111B, Early Modern Political Theory from Hobbes to Bentham
> 6. English 90, Shakespeare
> 7. History 13A, History of the U.S. and Its Colonial Origins: Colonial Origins and First Nation Building Acts
> 8. History 122E, Cultural and Intellectual History of Modern Europe, Nineteenth Century

Alarmingly, some of the larger lecture classes at UCLA enroll more than 300 students. "In a class such as that, the one way to form a real relationship is to go to the professor's office hours and to make yourself known by participating and asking questions," a student says. "It is not impossible to make an impression on a professor in a class of that size—it just requires some effort." Typically, professors teach larger courses and have graduate teaching assistants lead weekly discussion sections. In the smaller departments such as philosophy and some of the foreign languages, students are more likely to know their instructors well.

The university's advising program varies from department to department. The College of Letters and Science offers a ASK Peer with "undergraduates trained to respond to student questions and concerns in several convenient settings," as the website puts it. "No appoints are required; just walk up and ASK." Once a student has declared a major, he can visit a faculty or staff advisor in that department. The classics department, for instance, has one faculty member and one staff member to answer the questions of all the students majoring in the subject. There are also extra advising resources for athletes, honors students, and first-generation college students. Still, students we contacted described the school's advising resources as quite ineffective.

With smaller class sizes and distinguished faculty members, the university's Honors Collegium sounds promising at first hearing. But (with some exceptions, like those noted above in the new Liberal Education center) most of the seminars offered in the program

West

focus on non-foundational topics, with titles such as "Comparative Genocide," "Marxist and Post-Marxist Approaches to Cultural Studies," and "Stories of Cultural Distance and Imposed Assimilation." While the program gives freshmen the chance to get to know their professors and fellow students well, the price of participation is often a willingness to endure the program's dreary, heavy-handed ideological agenda.

UCLA has many ethnic studies departments: Afro-American studies; American Indian studies; Asian American studies; Chicana and Chicano studies; European studies; Islamic studies; Latina/o American Studies; women's studies; and lesbian, gay, and transgender studies. Many of these departments are politicized, mediocre, or both. The women's studies department offers such gems as "Women Healers, Ritual, and Transformation" and "The Media and Aggression against Women." Many women's studies courses are cross-listed with the lesbian, gay, and transgender studies department, including "Chicana Lesbian Literature." In the ethnomusicology department, students earn credit for courses such as "The Cultural History of Rap."

Even the more traditional departments have been tainted. A classics professor proudly proclaims in the course catalog that "issues of politics, religion, race, ethnicity, gender, and sexuality provide an overall framework of analysis in almost all my courses." The departmental website trills that "we have the highest number and proportion of women faculty in any classics department of our size at a major research university."

The political science department is also replete with ethnic offerings and does not seem to demand of majors a course in American constitutional theory. The history department is less trendy, it seems, but lacks a requirement that majors study nineteenth-century American history. Of key departments, English seems to have the most stringent major requirements, including two courses in Shakespeare, not to mention courses in Chaucer and Milton, and it seems to demand coverage in many periods.

UCLA has adopted what many multi-cult activists at the school have dreamed of for years—a diversity requirement. According to the catalogue: "The diversity requirement is predicated on the notion that students in the arts must be trained to understand the local, national, and global realities in which they make, understand, and interpret art. Those realities include the multicultural, transnational, and global nature of contemporary society."

Ironically, conservatives at UCLA seem fairly content. The "Academia Nut" section of the *Bruin Standard* (a conservative student publication) has made a habit of reporting on classroom abuses of conservatives. Aware that their off-topic comments might make their way into the campus spotlight, more politicized professors have been exercising self-restraint, students say. A writer for the paper says, "There's a little more pressure on them to stick to the subject." One conservative student avows, "I've been pretty impressed with how open others are. I have several liberal friends who are very supportive of the fact that I'm in the Bruin Republicans."

The best part of UCLA's emphasis on multiculturalism can be seen in its admirable foreign language offerings, which include Chinese, Japanese, Korean, Indonesian, Tagalog, Thai, Vietnamese, Yiddish, French, Afrikaans, German, Dutch, Italian, Hausa, Swahili, Wolof, Zulu, Quechua, Arabic, Armenian, Bashkir, Hebrew, Persian, Turkish, Uzbek, Danish, Finnish, Norwegian, Swedish, Czech, Hungarian, Polish, Romanian, Russian,

Serbian/Croatian, Ukrainian, Spanish, Portuguese, Catalan, Classical Latin, Medieval Latin, Ancient Greek, Mycenaean Greek, Oscan, Umbrian, South Picene, Volscian, Paelignian, Venetic, Messapic, Etruscan, Hittite, Palaic, Luwian (both cuneiform and hieroglyphic), Lycian and Lydian, Classical Sanskrit, Vedic Sanskrit, Pali, Prakrits, Old English, Old Irish, Medieval Welsh, Gothic, Old High German, Old Saxon, Old Norse, Tocharian A and B, Akkadian, Egyptian, Coptic, Sumerian, Aramaic, Chagatay (Classical Uzbek), Ottoman, Middle Turkic (Karakhanid or Khorazmian), Mamluk-Kipchak, Old Anatolian, Ugaritic, Phoenician, Classical Armenian, and Old Church Slavonic.

Not surprisingly, UCLA's study-abroad program is strong, with 140 programs in thirty-four countries, ranging from Australia to Argentina, Canada to China, and Germany to Ghana. Students pay UCLA prices and earn UCLA credit while hitting the books in Paris or Rio.

Student Life: Off to see the wizard

Residential life at UCLA is mainly for freshmen. About 94 percent of all freshmen choose to live on campus, compared to only 36 percent of total undergraduates. The university guarantees housing for three years, provided students apply by the deadline. The university provides apartment and house-share listings and a roommate matching service, and maintains seven off-campus apartment buildings so students won't be left out in the warm. If a student does live on campus, he will find himself in one of four high-rise dormitories, in one of two buildings with residential suites, or (best of all) in one of two village-type apartment complexes. All on-campus dormitories are coed, but some have sex-segregated floors. Bathrooms are all single sex. There are no visitation restrictions.

The UCLA campus has all the amenities of a small town. The school has its own police department and power plant, twelve restaurants, three coffeehouses, several theaters, medical clinics, and plenty of athletic facilities. Writes one student. "I love the campus. West Coast weather with the East Coast Ivy League look. They plant flowers that smell nice. Little Chinese courtyards that you can rest and do homework in. Lots of little finds in buildings. They have strict rules about posting flyers, so that keeps things looking nice. There are no trash cans overflowing." Students aren't exactly trapped on campus. One student says that many of her friends do volunteer work and community service in Los Angeles on the weekends. Third Street Promenade, a popular attraction accessible by bus and car, has movie theaters, restaurants, and shops, and is close to the Pacific Ocean and Santa Monica Pier. Westwood itself, where UCLA is located, offers attractions and nightlife closer to home. One recent grad "loved" UCLA partly because of the "college-town feel" of Westwood, with its large old theaters like the Fox where big Hollywood premieres are held. Movie stars can sometimes be glimpsed flitting by.

On campus, dorms sponsor such events as ice-cream socials and other get-togethers, but these are mostly geared toward freshmen. Students say that alcohol is prevalent on and off campus, but that drug use is not very popular or conspicuous. UCLA Housing has a zero-tolerance policy for drugs, but students are often seen drinking alcohol at campus parties. Off-campus fraternities and sororities have been steadily growing in popularity, and Fraternity Row swarms with parties, especially on Thursday nights. Besides the Greek system (to which more than 10 percent of students belong), other popular student organizations include community-service groups; activist and political groups such as CALPIRG (an environmental group that sponsors river and beach cleanups); groups devoted to voter registration and inner-city tutoring; and various campus media outlets. UCLA helps fund several ethnically oriented magazines, including *Al-Talib* (a Muslim paper); *Ha'Am* (Jewish); *La Gente de Aztlan* (Hispanic and Native American); *Nommo* (African); *Pacific Ties* (Asian); and *Outwrite* (gay, lesbian, transsexual, and transgender).

UCLA attracts all sorts of speakers, lecturers, and performers. Recent speakers have included Bill Gates, Whoopi Goldberg, and Tom Hanks, as well as a host of political speakers—including a few conservatives. UCLA has excellent music and theater departments, and student-run productions are usually of very high quality (and cheap, too).

Maintaining muscle tone is as important to most UCLA students as is having a healthy tan. Athletics at UCLA are consequently very popular. In addition to twenty-two varsity teams (and a whopping 106 combined NCAA national titles, the most in the country), UCLA offers many opportunities for club and intramural sports. The catalog claims there are more than 1,800 teams and 8,000 participants each year. It has been three decades since the "Wizard of Westwood," John Wooden, held the reins of UCLA's men's basketball team, and led them to win ten titles. Since he retired, the team has managed to win only one—not good enough for the Bruins's fans. But coach Ben Howland took the team to consecutive Final Fours in 2006, 2007, and 2008, raising fans' hopes (and expectations) accordingly. Among fond UCLA traditions are football's Blue and Gold Week—complete with bonfire, concerts, and dancing; the midnight yell every night during finals week; and the "undie run" at midnight on Wednesday of finals week.

Campus activism usually centers on the issues of race and ethnicity. The American Indian Student Association (AISA), a small but militant group, stages an anti-Columbus Day celebration each year. Many AISA members refuse to enter the anthropology building because it houses Indian bones (along with less-sacred European and African bones). UCLA can often seem like a haven for malcontents, with protests each week, chalked messages such as "Free Palestine" and "Living Wage Now" all over campus, and leftist student groups holding meetings nearly every night of the week. Although only a relatively small contingent of students actually stages these events, they do enjoy some official sanction and prestige. Instrumental in this is the university's "Community Programs Office" (CPO). Established in 1970, the office operates under the philosophy that its endeavors "are a reflection of student empowerment. This, in essence, means that students are viewed as the engine that drives social change. . . . Some of the greatest social changes have occurred when students realize that by changing their attitudes they can change the world."

Conservative students can try to stop them by joining the Bruin Republicans, whose membership numbers in the hundreds on this very liberal campus, where Democrats outnumber Republicans fifteen to one in the faculty. The Bruin Republicans maintain an extremely lively schedule, with social events, and guerilla theater—such as the "Affirmative Action Bake Sale." The group also conducts outreach to local high school students and a wide variety of other activities.

West

Bruins seem divided "about 50/50 between libertarians and traditionalists," says one insider, "so debate within the group is vigorous. And since we don't even agree on the issue, we can't even face off against the Bruin Democrats on abortion." Debates with these Democrats, by the way, have recently been revived after a two-year hiatus, making the political scene on campus even spicier.

Other right-leaning groups at UCLA include "Bruins for Israel" (said to be "huge"), "Live Action" (a pro-life group with feisty president Lila Rose who appears on Fox News regularly), and "Logic" (a Randian objectivist collective).

Other student organizations include Agape Christian Fellowship, Awaken A Capella, Ballroom Dance Club, BlaQue, Brazilian Club at UCLA, Bruin Feminists for Equality,

---

ACADEMIC REQUIREMENTS

Like all institutions in the University of California system, UCLA requires its students to complete only two university-wide requirements (as opposed to the four required until very recently):

- "Entry-Level Writing" or "English as a Second Language."
- "American History and Institutions."

Students in the College of Letters and Science face a few more requirements. They must:

- Show proficiency in quantitative reasoning by taking a basic statistics, math, or computer science course.
- Take or test out of three quarters in a foreign language.
- Take three courses in "foundations of the arts and humanities," including one from each of the following three categories: literary and cultural analysis, philosophical and linguistic analysis, and visual- and performance-arts analysis and practice. There are hundreds of courses to choose from, including foundational studies in various disciplines and specialized classes such as "Introduction to American Folklore Studies" and "History of Electronic Dance Music."
- Take three courses in "foundations of society and culture"—one in historical analysis, another in social analysis, and a third from either subgroup. Again, options range from the sublime to the truculent, with courses such as "Social Organization of Black Communities" and "Introduction to Lesbian, Gay, Bisexual, and Transgender Studies."
- Take four courses in the "foundations of scientific inquiry," including two from life sciences and two from physical sciences, with a laboratory credit accompanying at least one course from each subgroup.
- Complete a diversity requirement by taking qualifying courses in any of three parts of the students' overall program: (1) general education courses, (2) courses in the major, or (3) upper-division elective courses.

Depending on his major, the UCLA student can exempt himself from two general education courses. For example, an English major is exempt from one general humanities course and the literature course requirement.

YELLOW LIGHT

It is sadly true that races and ethnicities at UCLA tend to segregate themselves, with the school's encouragement. UCLA even sponsors segregated graduation ceremonies. "Lavender Graduation" is a commencement ceremony for gay, lesbian, bisexual, and transgender students. "La Raza Graduation" is sponsored by MEChA, a Mexican racial-nationalist group with the motto "For the race, everything. Against the race, nothing." In its "Plan Espiritual de Aztlán" MEChA declares: "In the spirit of a new people that is conscious not only of its proud historical heritage but also of the brutal 'gringo' invasion of our territories, we, the Chicano inhabitants and civilizers of the northern land of Aztlán from whence came our forefathers, reclaiming the land of their birth and consecrating the determination of our people of the sun, declare that the call of our blood is our power, our responsibility, and our inevitable destiny." (In case you were wondering, this manifesto was not in fact translated directly from the German.)

However, as one conservative student puts it, "You can't judge the entire UCLA based on graduation ceremonies." Despite these retrograde spectacles, civil discussion of political differences has dramatically improved of late. Ann Coulter spoke here in the 2009–10 school year. Bruin Democrats urged students not to raise a fuss; better to avoid the speech altogether. Many came anyway, but instead of heckling Coulter they raised polite and intelligent questions. The gathering of 400–500 mostly conservative students, according the head of the Bruin Republicans, was "like a large dinner" and Coulter was "the toast of the crowd."

Bruin Hikers Anonymous, Chemistry in the Community, Chinese Folk Dance Troupe, Earth and Space Sciences Student Organization, Enigma (the science-fiction, fantasy, and gaming club), Figure Skating Club, Girl Leaders, Grace Stewards for Christ, Hiking Club, Hindu Students Association, Japanese Animation Club, Filipinos in Engineering, queer x girl, and Shakespeare at UCLA.

The chaplaincy at UCLA offers clerics of every major faith, although few of these clergy appear to hew to the traditional morals of their respective faiths. For instance, the University Catholic Chapel offers such attractions as "Cornerstone, the LGBT (Lesbian, Gay, Bisexual, Transgendered) group." This group declares that its goal is "to provide a healthy and fun way for members and allies to become conscious of the fact that it is indeed possible to be religious and gay without being ashamed." The campus's Wesley Foundation proclaims on its website, "We do not believe that homosexuality is sinful. . . . Lesbian, gay and bisexual persons, no less than heterosexual persons, have the capacity for experiencing sex that is truly sacramental. Far from being sinful, such sex is truly holy and good." And so on, through most denominations. In other words, devout students at UCLA would do well to find a conservative congregation somewhere outside the campus boundaries. Fortunately (especially for those with cars), there is a cornucopia of choices.

Crime on campus is becoming more of a concern, especially because of an increase in sex offenses. In 2009, the last year for which statistics were available, the school reported five robberies, 111 burglaries, fourteen stolen cars, eleven forcible sex offenses, and nine aggravated assaults on campus. In view of the surge of sex crimes, it is perhaps no coincidence that UCLA now offers self-defense classes to "increase physical and psychological preparedness and heighten awareness of the complex issues of rape, sexual assault, and relationship violence."

Despite recent state budget hemorrhages, UCLA remains a pretty good bargain for students from California. In 2010–11, in-state tuition was $10,781, compared to $32,802 for those from out of state. Room and board was $13,781. The UC system is not immune to the budget woes afflicting California's state government. Things to watch for may include sharp rises in tuition, cutbacks in library and other services, and fewer course selections.

The school offers a dizzying array of scholarships, work study programs, loans, and grants—and some 56 percent of students receive need-based aid. The average loan burden of a recent grad is $16,733.

University of California at San Diego

San Diego, California • www.ucsd.edu

The science of it

The University of California at San Diego, one of the newer campuses in the massive University of California system, is not renowned either for athletic prowess or ideological fervor. And unlike the nearby San Diego State, it certainly is not a party or surfer-dude school. Instead, it has gone quietly about its business of building excellent programs, particularly in the sciences. The school boasts a major supercomputer, advanced research facilities, and cutting-edge faculty, seven of whom are Nobel laureates. Unfortunately, UCSD has not lavished the same affection on its liberal arts classrooms as it has on its laboratories, and there are a few departments at the school that should simply be avoided. But science-minded students and students of select humanities should consider spending their four years in San Diego, with its balmy climate, coastal location, and bustling downtown.

Despite its flaws, UCSD can be a fine school for serious students who are willing to put in the time and effort and able to delay gratification to later stages in life. "Be as diligent as possible going through your coursework in order to get out of this place in four years or less," says one student, "because the primary purpose of a UCSD student is to step to the next level."

Academic Life: Six colleges in search of a plot

UCSD is divided into six colleges: Revelle, John Muir, Eleanor Roosevelt, Thurgood Marshall, Earl Warren, and Sixth College. Admission to UCSD is accompanied by an assignment to one of the colleges (applicants rank the colleges in order of their preference for the particular "educational philosophy" of each). In some respects, the colleges are like distinct schools, complete with their own quasi-campuses, architectural styles, residence and dining halls, and central courtyard or center. Yet the differences between them are not all that substantial. The general education requirements at all of the colleges are sufficient to expose UCSD students to a healthy range of academic disciplines—without approaching a true core curriculum. All majors at UCSD are open to all students regardless of which college they attend.

The one requirement common to all UCSD students is that they work hard. "This is not a place to go and party," says one student, who adds that UCSD has "a semi-professional feel to it, with a lot of people who have taken on a responsibility in their lives and act like it." Another student is blunter: "It's definitely a rat race. A lot of students mix up the qual-

West

ity of the education with how hard the class is." UCSD, like other California universities, schedules its academic year in quarters rather than semesters, making each term shorter and more intense than in the semester system.

Revelle College has a fairly rigorous general education program, and it is strong in the sciences. Despite its discouraging name, Eleanor Roosevelt College appears to be even more traditionally minded. It requires of freshmen a serious sequence in the history of the West, a course sequence that also delves into Asian and other civilizations. In contrast, John Muir College—home to the departments of critical gender studies, contemporary issues, film studies, and Environmental Studies—vies with Marshall and Warren for having the laxest general education requirements.

Sixth College, which opened in 2002, emphasizes the intersection of culture, art, and technology and requires each student to take a three-course interdisciplinary sequence in that area. It promises to be the most elaborately equipped of the colleges, featuring its own "chief technology officer" and a "digital playroom" that offers students high-end equipment on which to collaborate on high-tech projects. Hewlett-Packard donates pocket PCs for every student and residence advisor.

Except at Roosevelt, students at UCSD do not need to take many demanding courses in the area of Western civilization, and the areas they are required to study lack cohesion. This doesn't please those who want students to have a traditional education. Says one professor, "You ask [students] basic questions about history or the world and they're just ignorant. All my courses turn out to be general education courses because I can't assume [students have learned] anything."

With such a dizzying set of choices—involving so many colleges and curricula—academic advising should have a critical place on campus. But it doesn't. "The school does not do a good job at all of guiding students," one student complains. Amazingly, he says, all too often the choice of a student's college is "based on its name or picked out of a hat."

These weaknesses aside, UCSD does have a number of excellent programs, chief among them engineering and the natural sciences. "We really have an astounding department of biology," a professor says, "and we have pretty good departments in physics, chemistry, and computer science." Such disciplines are bound to thrive under the leadership of Chancellor Marye Anne Fox, a well-known chemist.

VITAL STATISTICS

Religious affiliation: *none*
Total enrollment: *27,520*
Total undergraduates: *22,518*
SAT/ACT midranges: CR: *540–660*; M: *600–710*; ACT: *24–30*
Applicants: *47,365*
Applicants accepted: *42%*
Accepted applicants who enrolled: *22%*
Tuition and fees: *in state, $11,330; out of state, $22,879*
Room and board: *$11,522*
Freshman retention rate: *94%*
Graduation rate: *53% (4 yrs.), 86% (6 yrs.)*
Courses with fewer than 20 students: *44%*
Student-faculty ratio: *19:1*
Courses taught by graduate students: *2%*
Most popular majors: *social sciences, biological and life sciences, engineering*
Students living on campus: *33%*
Guaranteed housing for four years? *no*
Students in fraternities: *10%* in sororities: *10%*

Relatively few disciplines in the liberal arts are quite so good. "The humanities departments are variable," the professor says. "There are some very good people here and there in history and philosophy. On the other hand, we can't always keep them." Perhaps most noteworthy is political science, well known for its emphasis on Latin American politics (it's too much to expect, however, a requirement in the U.S. Constitution), and the theater department, described by one person as "really quite outstanding." Other generally worthy programs include economics, psychology, and sociology. The history department is known for excelling in both Asian history and Latin American history (but lacks a majors requirement covering America before 1900). The literature department is surprisingly solid, requiring all majors concentrating in English literature to take British literature before and after 1860, and U.S. literature before and after 1860. Classes offered are excellent, including those devoted to Chaucer, Keats, Byron, and Shakespeare in the Elizabethan period, the Jacobean period, and in more contemporary stage, film, and television. Of course, there are the usual politicized classes like "Gender, Text, and Culture" and "Chicano Literature in English," but students can easily avoid these.

The ethnic studies department, steeped as it is in left-wing ideology, should be avoided. "It's very politicized," says a faculty member. One student who took an ethnic studies course recalls that when an unknown party criticized his professor in a letter to the administration, the professor responded by highlighting that letter in class. "She basically showed how this letter victimized everyone in the room and how it was oppressive," the student reports. Similarly, another vindictive faculty member is said to have approached College Republicans on campus, told them they ought to be expelled, and burst out, "You people are a disgrace to the university." The student explains, "The university doesn't care about diversity of thought, only diversity of ethnicity."

The UCSD professors praised by students we talked to were clustered in the political science department—although there are good teachers throughout the university. Undergrads singled out for acclaim Steve Erie, Peter Irons (emeritus), Gary Jacobson, Samuel Kernell, and Sanford Lakoff (emeritus), all in political science. Other professors cited are David Jordan in history and Matt Herbst in anthropology, both affiliated with Eleanor Roosevelt's program "The Making of the Modern World." One student says, "a lot of classes are very large, so you won't have a sense of connection with the professor. Classes are very rigorous in terms of material. There's a lot of lecturing but not necessarily much learning."

Students, generally, should expect large classes. "The general education classes were usually in auditoriums with about 200 to 300 students per class," says one student. "As for lower division classes for majors, there are 80 to 120, and for upper-division courses there are 40 to 80." Another student says that "my classes have ranged from 50 to 200 people." Again, political science is one of the more impersonal departments. There, says a major, even "upper-level classes are ridiculously large, with 30 to 300 people and up to four or five graduate [teaching assistants]." For all that, waiting lists for some classes are still "horrible." He suspects that this is because the university "puts way more funding in science."

UCSD is "definitely research, not teaching oriented," one professor says, although "there have been and are excellent teachers." Teaching assistants conduct a significant portion of the classes, especially at the introductory level. "A lot of people, I think, don't like that," says a student, who points out that language difficulties with TAs who are not native speakers of English can be very frustrating. "I'm trying to learn advanced calculus and I have a TA who just came here four years ago," he says. "It has happened more than once." Another student, though, gives credit to poli-sci grad students for being well trained and maintaining high academic standards: "Our grad students are very tough," he asserts.

However, students do have many research opportunities available to them, especially in the sciences. One highly regarded program is the Undergraduate Research Conference, in which outstanding undergraduate students have the opportunity to present a research paper to faculty. Students can also graduate with honors in a department by completing an honors thesis. "Every year, the faculty are very enthusiastic about the theses," a professor says. "There's no question that they represent a lot of work." The Scripps Undergraduate Research Fellowship, which focuses on marine and earth sciences, takes place during the summer at the Scripps Institution of Oceanography.

A number of scholarships are out there for promising undergraduates, and there are dozens of research centers on campus where cutting-edge research is routine. For instance, in 2007, a team began a project using the newest technology to create a grocery-shopping assistant for the blind. The *Chronicle of Higher Education* has reported that UCSD is one of the only schools in the U.S. to employ the most advanced Internet Protocol 6, which San Diego engineers use "to control a giant electron microscope in Osaka, Japan, and see live, ultrasharp images produced by the device."

For the linguistically inclined, UCSD offers over eighty different languages, but only four of these involve majors: Chinese Studies, Japanese Studies, Judaic Studies, and Latin American Studies. On a related note, UCSD also offers the University of California Education Abroad Program, which features over two hundred choices in thirty-five countries. There is also a UCSD "Global Seminar" program that comprise "five-week-long study-abroad experiences led by a UCSD professor." Recent seminars have been held in Athens, Paris, Cadiz, Istanbul, Madrid, and Rome.

Student Life: There's always Tijuana . . .

If the demands at UCSD are so staggering and the rewards so distant, why are the classes so crowded and the waiting lists so long? One reason is comparatively cheap tuition, despite the recent and ongoing hike necessitated by the California budget crisis. Another lure is the school's location, which one otherwise-cynical junior calls "so amazing . . . it was one of my top reasons for choosing UCSD." Students may have to study long and hard, but most do it outdoors with a gentle ocean breeze rustling through their hair. The beach is only a five- to ten-minute walk from campus.

West

UCSD has the advantage of being in San Diego, a beautiful, vibrant city that offers plenty of things to do and see year round—a fact that may not be immediately obvious to those who consider the city merely a glorified naval base. (But be careful to ask beachcombing rickshaw operators the fare before hopping in for a joyride. They're known to gouge unsuspecting passengers.)

ACADEMIC REQUIREMENTS

Aside from the general requirements for all UC students—a writing class and a course in "American History and Institutions"—the distribution mandates are different at each of the six colleges making up UCSD. They are, in brief, as follows:

Revelle College:

- A five-course sequence in an interdisciplinary humanities program with intensive writing instruction.
- One course in the fine arts.
- Three lower-division social science courses, two of which are in a social science and the other in American cultures.
- Three quarters of calculus.
- Five courses in the natural sciences (four quarters total of physics or chemistry and one quarter of biology).
- Fourth-quarter proficiency in a foreign language.
- Either a minor or a three-course "area of focus" in a different field from one's major.

Eleanor Roosevelt College:

- An admirable six-quarter core sequence, "Making of the Modern World," which moves from prehistory to the present.
- Two courses in fine arts, one of which must include non-Western content.
- Basic conversational and reading proficiency in a modern foreign language or advanced reading proficiency in a classical language.
- Two courses in math, computer programming, or formal logic.
- Two natural science courses.
- One upper-level writing-intensive course.
- Three courses focusing on one geographical region.

John Muir College:

- One additional writing course.
- One three-course social science sequence. Among the choices are an introductory economics sequence and a critical gender studies sequence.
- One mathematical or natural science sequence.
- Two sequences selected from two of the following areas: fine arts, humanities, or foreign languages.

Partly because of housing restrictions imposed by the municipality of La Jolla, UCSD has a fraternity-unfriendly policy. "They don't welcome Greeks and they don't have policies that make being a Greek easy," says one student. There are more than a dozen Greek organizations at UCSD, though many of them are "multicultural." Because of UCSD's zero-tolerance policy on alcohol, there aren't any "real parties in the dorms," reports a student, who goes on to say, "But, of course, there's always Tijuana." The Mexican border town is only about thirty minutes away, and has an unsavory reputation for corruption, vice, and violence.

ACADEMIC REQUIREMENTS

Thurgood Marshall College:

- Three writing-intensive "Dimensions of Culture" courses: "Diversity," "Justice," and "Imagination."
- Two humanities courses, one of them focused on "diversity."
- One fine arts course.
- One course each in biology, chemistry, and physics.
- Two courses in math and logic.
- Four courses outside the area of one's major.

Earl Warren College:

- One additional writing course.
- "Ethics and Society."
- Two classes in calculus, symbolic logic, computer programming, and/or statistics.
- Two six-course "programs" in different departments and in a department different from one's major.
- A "cultural diversity" class, met by selecting from a long list of courses that includes "Contemporary Moral Issues," "Intellectual History: from Contact to Civil War," and ethnic studies courses such as "Sexuality and Nation" and "Hip-Hop: The Politics of Culture."

Sixth College:

- A three-course sequence called "Culture, Art, and Technology."
- A computing course.
- Two courses in social sciences.
- Two courses in humanities.
- Two courses in natural sciences.
- One course in math/logic.
- One course in statistical methods.
- One course in ethnic or gender studies.
- One course in ethics.
- Two courses in music, theater, dance, or visual arts.
- One upper-division project with a two-unit course in "practicum communication."

West

In lieu of Mexican adventure, you can simply wait until the annual "Sun God Festival" held on campus each year the second Friday in May. During this neo-pagan debauch, a fan reports, students and professor alike let out all the steam bottled up over months of studious self-denial. Even the professors arrive at class drunk.

Life on campus ordinarily may not hold a candle to Tijuana in terms of risk and adventure, but there are still ways to occupy one's time outside of class. A number of student clubs and organizations thrive, from religious groups such as the InterVarsity Christian Fellowship to political groups of all stripes. One student counts thirty-three student publications, thirteen of which are active. Of these, the most notable are the university-subsidized *Guardian*, the *Left Coast Post*, the satiric journals *Koala* and *MQ*, and the conservative *California Review*.

Among the more social of the groups is the College Republicans, now enjoying something of a resurgence along with other conservative clubs, such as Young Americans for Liberty and Young Americans for Freedom. The last named tends to be more activist and outspoken, holding protests and hosting controversial speakers such as David Horowitz. By coincidence, UCSD recently saw in the same embroiled week Horowitz, Angela Davis, Norman Finkelstein, and Van Jones—the far-left green jobs czar whom President Obama was forced to fire—all speaking and raising sparks on campus. "Contrary to popular belief, which is that we are apathetic," boasts a member of the conservative avant-garde, "UCSD is the new place to call home for those who want to expose leftism."

There is an active Office of Religious Affairs at UCSD. Under its aegis operate the Newman Center Catholic Community at UCSD, the Foundation for Jewish Campus Life, the University Lutheran Community, the Wesley Foundation, the Unitarian Universalist Campus Ministry, and the Canterbury Episcopal Community. The general atmosphere of its programs is indicated by its website's proclamation that "promoting racial, religious, ethnic, and cultural tolerance and appreciation of diversity on campus is a major goal of the O.R.A." This might mean traditionally minded students would do well to seek out a local, off-campus congregation. Still, religious organizations are among the fastest growing on campus.

There are no major sporting events at UCSD of the type that thrive at UCLA or USC (San Diego's football team is relegated to club status). But there are a number of varsity-level squads at UCSD, including men's and women's teams in basketball, crew, cross-country, soccer, volleyball, and water polo. UCSD's NCAA Division II basketball team, the Tritons, tends to be the focus of student spectator interest.

Housing on campus is generally clustered around each college, and there is a variety of options for students who live on campus. The residence halls offer both single and double rooms, along with some suites for eight to ten students, and there are on-campus apartments as well (mostly for returning students). There are no visitation restrictions.

The university guarantees housing to students for two years, but space is exceedingly limited and those who want to live on campus should be aware that some rooms contain up to three students. To make matters worse, parking is atrocious for juniors and seniors who must drive in, with a search for a spot that can last literally for hours. The university is aware of this predicament and recently finished renovating several dorms. Rooms and suites are, according to the college's website, "gender specific, and most buildings are

West

coed." Revelle College recently completed a new four-story addition, relieving some of the previously cramped conditions for staff. Also, Muir College has just opened the Affis Verde apartments, housing 452 more graduate and professional students.

While violent crimes and sexual crimes are infrequent on campus, there have been problems with theft, especially involving automobiles. "Auto theft and auto break-ins have been a big issue," a student says. In 2009, the school reported four forcible sex offenses, one non-forcible sex offense, fifty burglaries, thirty-eight stolen cars, two robberies, one aggravated assault, three arsons, and one aggravated assault on campus. One student says that campus security makes students feel personally safe—although they might occasionally have to wonder, "Dude, where's my car?"

UCSD calls itself "the affordable choice compared to private universities," and indeed it is—particularly if you're a native. In 2010–11, tuition was $11,330 for California students, $22,879 for non-residents. Room and board ran $11,522. Some 55 percent of students get need-based aid, and the average debt of a recent grad is $16,317. Of course, the recent budget woes of the state of California are likely to cut as harshly into UCSD as they

> ## YELLOW LIGHT
>
> In the 2009–10 school year, a black rapper hosted a fraternity party known as the "Compton Cookout." Coinciding with Black History Month, the event drew party-goers, both black and white, dressed in "ghetto" attire. Then the student-run satirical newspaper, the *Koala*, entered the fray, going on the radio and embellishing upon the event with overtly racist language. Next, a Klan hood was found on a campus statue, followed by a noose in the library. After the Black Student Association raised an outcry and made various demands, the administration clamped down by silencing all student publications, but relented after five weeks when the Foundation for Individual Rights in Education interceded.
>
> In the same year, at a talk delivered by David Horowitz, a UCSD Muslim student openly declared that she agreed with a statement that all Jews should be rounded up and sent "back to Israel," there to meet their demise. In response to this clear and unambiguous declaration of genocidal aspirations, the administration did essentially nothing.

will into every other state institution. As far back as 2008–9, the state budget cut $48 million from the university system—before the national economic collapse of autumn 2008. The state also demanded some $100 million in savings from the colleges, but even that was not enough. Most recently, Governor Schwarzenegger slashed another $65.5 million from the state's higher-education budget, with more cuts likely to come. It's unclear yet how these cuts will make themselves felt at UCSD in the form of higher tuition, reduced programs, and general penury.

California Institute of Technology

Pasadena, California • www.caltech.edu

Math camp

Caltech was founded in 1891 as Throop University, with thirty-one students enrolled to study arts and crafts. In 1921 its leaders, astronomer George Hale, chemist Arthur Noyes, and physicist Robert Millikan, renamed the school the California Institute of Technology. Caltech now calls itself the "world's best playground for math, science, and engineering." It's also one of the top sites for combining learning, research, and accomplishment. So far, 31 Nobel Prizes have been awarded to faculty and alumni; 67 have won the National Medal of Science or Technology; and 110 have been elected to the National Academies. Where Caltech imposes a core curriculum it is in mathematics and the sciences, while offering a respectable number of liberal arts courses. The institution wastes little time on ideology, in or out of the classroom, favoring instead scientific objectivity.

Caltech recently received the last of a whopping $600 million gift (the largest private donation ever given to an institution of higher learning) from alumnus Gordon Moore (cofounder of Intel) and his wife Betty. Moore explained: "By putting all your money in one place, you get more bang for your buck." At Caltech, most of the bang and most of the bucks come from the work of the faculty. So that's where the university is spending much of Moore's money—hiring the top researchers in their disciplines.

For those whose interests are in hard sciences or technology, Caltech provides a thorough, balanced grounding in a variety of scientific disciplines, rather than encouraging early specialization. As one student says, "It would not be far wrong to consider the program a 'liberal sciences education.'" The school states on its website "The breadth and depth of the Caltech core curriculum are virtually unequaled in American higher education." As far as the sciences are concerned, this claim is true.

Academic Life: The liberal sciences

Caltech is not an ivory-tower laboratory where students are treated as a mere pretext for the institution's existence; instead, they are the future of the university—and a critical part of its present, especially in the collaborative, labor-intensive, and highly remunerative world of laboratory science.

While many, if not most, universities rely on undergraduate tuition as their cash cow

West

(at USC it pays for 60 percent of expenses), at Caltech tuition accounts for only 3 to 4 percent. Meanwhile, the *average* Caltech professor brings in $600,000 to $700,000 a year in grant money. This funding is the university's lifeblood.

The school explains its science "core" this way: "The boundaries between scientific disciplines get blurrier by the week, and the most creative scientists are the ones who have a good grasp of developments in all the major scientific fields—not just their own. The need for intellectual range and flexibility can only increase in the future. The way we see it, the Caltech core curriculum has redefined the term 'liberal arts education' for the twenty-first century." The result? A student in engineering says, "I know enough math and physics to totally switch into those areas."

These requirements are in addition to those of a student's major (called an "option" at Caltech—it's one of the few things they get to choose). Of the twenty-four options that lead to a BS degree, several are divided further into "areas of study" or "concentrations." Those who opt for engineering and applied science may concentrate in mechanical engineering, for example. Students choosing this discipline also face a "core" set of courses, including a required seminar; one out of three applied math courses; twelve specific mechanical engineering courses; and two semesters of labs, one of which is required by name. Mechanical engineers get to pick a grand total of two electives in their field.

Students get guidance from their faculty advisors—professors assigned to them when they choose an option. The Career Development Center provides useful professional placement advice, while the Ombuds Office explains and interprets university policies, provides a place for student or faculty complaints or concerns, and handles other problems that don't get taken care of elsewhere. However, a student says that "most students don't take advantage of these services, because they listen to the upperclassmen instead."

The university is arranged into seven divisions; it claims to have no departments within those divisions, treating each as an interdisciplinary group of scholars, nicely amplifying and exemplifying the intent of the core curriculum. Six of the divisions are scientific: biology; chemistry and chemical engineering; engineering and applied science; geological and planetary science; physics, mathematics, and astronomy; and the independent studies program, which allows students to design, with faculty advice, a customized course of study of topics not covered by the traditional options.

VITAL STATISTICS

Religious affiliation: *none*
Total enrollment: *2,130*
Total undergraduates: *951*
SAT/ACT midranges: CR: *690–770*, M: *770–800*; ACT: *33–35*
Applicants: *4,413*
Applicants accepted: *15%*
Accepted applicants who enrolled: *37%*
Tuition and fees: *$36,282*
Room and board: *$11,397*
Freshman retention rate: *98%*
Graduation rate: *73% (4 yrs.), 89% (6 yrs.)*
Courses with fewer than 20 students: *64%*
Student-faculty ratio: *3:1*
Courses taught by graduate students: *none*
Most popular majors: *engineering, physical science, math*
Students living on campus: *95%*
Guaranteed housing for four years? *yes*
Students in fraternities or sororities: *none*

West

SUGGESTED CORE

1. English 116, Milton and the Epic Tradition (closest match)
2. Humanities 3a, The Classical and Medieval Worlds
3. No suitable course.
4. Philosophy 103, Medieval Philosophy
5. Philosophy 151, Eighteenth-Century Philosophy: Locke to Kant or Philosophy 186, Political Philosophy
6. English 114, Shakespeare
7. Humanities/History 2, American History
8. Humanities 3c, Modern Europe

The seventh division is humanities and social science. While few go to Caltech to major in the traditional liberal arts—one recent alumnus says, "People who go to 'tech' to study anything outside the sciences are doing themselves a disservice"—those who do choose this division can expect an education uncluttered by specialization and political correctness. Students have six options to choose from: business economics and management; economics; history; history and philosophy of science; social science; and literature. In literature, for example, the course list is serious and impressive, with representative titles including "Drama from the Middle Ages to Moliére," "Chaucer," "Shakespeare," "Milton," "Twentieth-Century British Fiction," "Twain and His Contemporaries," and "Austen, Brontës, Woolf." (One *can* take a course in "American Radicalism," savoring the canny insights of John Reed.) Required history courses include "American History," "European Civilization," and, not surprisingly, "Introduction to the History of Science." Of course, the usual multicultural fare is available with courses such as "Race Matters: Transatlantic Perspectives" and "Ethnic Visions." Political science courses are particularly weak, and classes in the U.S. Constitution and American political philosophy are not even offered.

Free-speech restrictions are not a problem on the Caltech campus, inside class or out. "As a rule, I'd say all the professors make themselves available to their students and are open to new viewpoints," one faculty member says. "Given, of course, that the viewpoints are backed up with some sort of thought."

The real strength of Caltech lies, unsurprisingly, in technology—particularly in research. NASA's Jet Propulsion Lab is now run by Caltech, among many other top-flight research projects, including the agency's Infrared Processing and Analysis Center. The Beckman Institute conducts research in chemistry and biology, while the SIRTF Science Center supports NASA's infrared Spitzer Space Telescope. The university also hosts the Laboratory for Molecular Sciences and the Materials and Process Simulation Center. Caltech owns and operates the Palomar Observatory in San Diego County and sponsors (with NASA and the University of California) the W. M. Keck Observatory in Hawaii.

Students use these facilities as part of their classwork, in the production of their senior theses, and in the course of their campus jobs. Students also have plenty of opportunities to participate in research projects with their professors. (Research assistants have earned stipends as high as $5,000 in recent years.) "So many profs need help," says one student, that "each student has the opportunity to develop cutting-edge research during his undergraduate career." Summer Undergraduate Research Fellowships (SURF) fund about seventy-five research proposals each year. SURF projects are conducted by each student for some ten weeks while working with a professor or grad student. Each student then writes an article and presents his findings at the university's SURF Seminar Day in the fall.

Even apart from collaborating with them on research, students have no trouble getting attention from their instructors. Professors teach most classes, with teaching assistants leading discussion sessions. The ratio of undergrads to faculty is an astounding 3 to 1 (undergraduates, at just 45 percent of the student body, are in the minority at Caltech). The faculty is as distinguished a lot as one is likely to find anywhere, with four Nobel winners on staff. Students especially like the teaching styles of Niles Pierce in mathematics; Steven Frautschi (emeritus) in physics; Axel Scherer in electrical engineering; and Christopher Brennen (emeritus), Fred E. C. Culick (emeritus), Melany Hunt, and Richard Murray in mechanical engineering.

With such a faculty, it is no surprise that virtually every program at Caltech is excellent. One faculty member says that it is impossible to single out the best disciplines, since "we have so many Nobelists, National Medal winners, and so on in all the departments." This isn't gross immodesty, just a statement of fact. It is fair to say, however, that physics, engineering, chemistry, astronomy, and biology are very strong in every respect. Departments in the humanities and social sciences are not bad, but do not match the quality of the engineering and hard science departments.

Academic pursuits are governed by the university's honor system, which consists of one sentence: "No member of the Caltech community shall take unfair advantage of any other member of the Caltech community." Most exams are take-home and none are proctored, and collaboration is encouraged on most homework assignments. Students routinely get keys to research facilities and can use them day or night. Discussions of the honor system form part of freshman orientation. The rest of orientation consists of Frosh Camp, wherein the entire incoming class camps with some faculty and administrators in the San Jacinto Mountains for three days. This practice is a refreshing alternative to the diversity indoctrination and cultural sensitivity seminars that go on at many schools' orientations, although in recent years some gay undergrads have used the trip as an opportunity to "come out." Given the workload these students are about to face, that's probably the last conversation any of them will be having about sex for the next four years.

Caltech started a Research Science Institute in 2003, inviting thirty-five high school students to campus for classroom training and research. If those students go on to attend Caltech, at least they will know in advance how hard they'll have to work. Grades at Caltech are not inflated—if anything, they're deflated. "I think the average GPA is 3.2, and the students work *really* hard for that," says a senior. "For instance, most classes have one homework set a week, and that set could last ten hours or more. The *least* time I've spent on a homework set would have to be four to five hours, but usually I'm working a lot longer." Rumor has it that some grad schools automatically add up to 0.7 points to the GPAs of Caltech students when considering them for admission. And if grad schools aren't doing that, they should be.

The school sponsors six study-abroad programs—Cambridge Scholars Program, London Scholars Program, Edinburgh Scholars Program, Copenhagen Scholars Program, Ecole Polytechnique Scholars Program, and Melbourne Scholars Program. Students must

West

apply during their sophomore or junior year for acceptance during their junior or senior year. If students are looking for a study-abroad boondoggle as a break from Caltech's demanding curriculum, they will be sorely disappointed. A minimum of twelve classes are required in the Scholars programs, and all are designed by Caltech faculty to correspond with the same grueling at-home curriculum.

Caltech's foreign language offerings are slim, but solid, and include German, French, Japanese, Spanish, and Chinese.

Student Life: The sorcerers' apprentices

Caltech is only forty miles from Disneyland, but the school is less Magic Kingdom than math camp. Caltech is never going to be a party school. Nor, given the economic realities, will it ever be mistaken for a country club. Since Caltech runs mostly on the overhead expense deductions from faculty grant money, the incentive for improving student accom-

---

ACADEMIC REQUIREMENTS

Caltech demands of students that they master the core subjects and methods of the hard sciences. Students must take:

- Five math classes covering calculus, ordinary differential equations, and infinite series; linear algebra; vectors and analytic geometry; calculus of several variables; and probability.
- Five physics courses in classical mechanics, electromagnetism, waves, quantum mechanics, and statistical physics.
- Two chemistry classes: lecture courses in general and quantitative chemistry.
- One biology class: a topical course introducing a variety of tools and concepts of modern biology.
- One freshman "menu" course: a term of astronomy, geology, environmental engineering and science, energy science, or number theory.
- Two introductory lab courses: freshman chem lab, plus one other lab chosen from offerings in applied physics, biology, chemistry, engineering, or physics.
- Two science writing classes: students research, write, and revise a 3,000-word paper on a science or engineering topic, which is then published in an online journal established for that purpose. Students work with a faculty mentor on the content of the paper and receive editorial guidance from science writing instructors.
- Twelve humanities and social sciences courses: two in writing; two in introductory social sciences; two in advanced humanities; and two in advanced social sciences. The remaining four courses are electives. Class offerings include "British History," "The Medieval Church," "Human Evolution," and "Introduction to Classic Hollywood Film."
- Three physical education classes. Students may choose from skin diving, power walking, aerobic dance, baseball skills, fencing, yoga, golf, water polo, karate, squash, and table tennis, among many others.

West

modations is limited. A Caltech education is a challenging apprenticeship in the modern sorcery of the technological elite—and apprentices have never had it easy. There is a reward awaiting their persistence, however. Caltech alumni, grad students, and faculty are eligible for membership in an elite private club—the Athenaeum. Seated in a historic on-campus location, this institution has hosted many of the greatest minds of the twentieth century. Graduates will also be at the top of the pecking order when it comes to grad-school admissions or employment.

Multiculturalism and quotas apparently play little role in hiring decisions and a very small one in admissions; the Caltech full-time faculty is only 16 percent female and about 13 percent minority, and the student body is a mere 1 percent African American, but a whopping 40 percent Asian American. This failure to be sufficiently "progressive" has not gone unnoticed. A recent university report concluded, "In essence, to achieve its full potential, Caltech needs to hire more women faculty, be more proactive in nurturing its junior faculty, and make itself friendlier to the working family." Lots of luck with that.

Caltech is only eleven miles of Pasadena Freeway away from Los Angeles, so students have plenty of choices for out-of-class activities—if they can find time for them. Yes, the university website insists that it's a myth that "all Caltech students do is study; there's no time for a social life." There may indeed be some time for nonacademic activities, but there isn't much. Students who took advantage of all the things Los Angeles has to offer would soon find themselves flunking out of Caltech.

There is a religious presence at Caltech, including the Muslim Students Association, Hillel, and Mandarin Christian Fellowship. Catholic students are served by the Newman Club, and the Caltech Christian Federation assists Protestants. Lacking a chapel at Caltech, members of these communities conduct services in various on-campus facilities. For Episcopalians looking for something traditional, Our Savior in neighboring San Gabriel will be more to their liking than nearby All Saints. The latter was General George Patton's parish, and it features a stained-glass window in his honor that must be seen to be believed. Catholic students should look into St. Therese of Lisieux Parish in nearby Alhambra, which offers Sunday Latin Masses with Gregorian chant.

In leading the studious life, Caltech students find a supportive community. As one student says, "Teachers are absolutely more collaborative than competitive. . . . Caltech is a challenge, but we want everyone to make it through. Support is completely mutual." Indeed, a remarkable 98 percent of freshmen return the following year. The core curriculum puts every student in the same boat, and the residential system, which is governed by the campus life office, promotes a comfortable atmosphere. Students are required to live on campus for their first two years, usually in one of eight coed houses. Caltech does not provide any on-campus single-sex dorms, but according to a housing assistant the office makes an off-campus residence available for women each year. Some on-campus community houses do have coed bathrooms, and a housing official says there are a few coed dorm rooms on campus as well.

Each on-campus residence houses sixty-fixe to one hundred students of all different classes. House members dine together and often play intramural sports as a team; in addition, study groups often form from the houses. Freshmen try out the residential houses

GREEN LIGHT

Caltech does not have a reputation as a politicized campus. Despite this, Caltech students are not disengaged by any stretch of the imagination, and are far from passively subservient in their "apprenticeships." In recent years, students have repeatedly galvanized themselves to action on matters directly pertaining to their own needs and those of the university. This mostly has centered on nonpolitical, school-related issues with a direct impact on students.

The "Social Activism Speakers Series" brings primarily left-wing speakers to campus. The program says it is "organized by a committee of undergraduates, graduates, and staff as well as community members. We work closely with other groups on campus such as the Caltech Y and the Caltech Democratic Club. This kind of collaboration ensures that we bring important and relevant issues to the campus." Still, "social activism" is about the last thing on most students' minds, no matter what speakers are brought to campus.

during what is called "Rotation," which follows freshman orientation. They submit their preferences, and a student committee makes the final assignments. Campus housing is guaranteed for four years, and some students remain in the same house for their entire careers. Others can enter a lottery for off-campus, university-owned housing, next door to campus.

There is no "typical" Caltech student. "We have a lot of pranksters, clubbers, partiers, video gamers, and the occasional athlete," a student says. The student government group, Associated Students of the California Institute of Technology, publishes *little t* (the title comes from the proper way to write Caltech—"Cal Tech" is wrong), a guide for campus living. There are around a hundred registered student groups, most of them nonpolitical (many of them science-related), covering all types of interests, including performing arts, religion, and recreation. However, while the Caltech College Democrats appear to be flourishing, the College Republicans are defunct.

There is an extremely lively gay group at Caltech called "Prism." On their website they feature "Coming Out" stories. One recent entry preens: "The student support networks are eager to show that they are true GLBT 'allies.' Many straight faculty, staff, and fellow students are equally eager to show their support. While there may always be a few idiots or a few fossils who just aren't retiring soon enough, I've discovered that the Caltech community is generally very open-minded."

Some Caltech students—though apparently not many—can even play sports at the NCAA Division III level. Caltech has nine varsity teams for men and eight for women, and while we'd hate to jump to any stereotypical conclusions, it took 201 games and many years before the men's soccer team finally won—once, in 2009. Men's basketball boasts a 259-game losing streak, with the decisive win against Bard in 2007 the first victory since 1996. Lest you think we're being hard on the men, the women's basketball team's most successful season to date was 2006–07—when it won two games. The men's football team, on the other hand, has remained undefeated since 1993—when the program was eliminated.

The grandest tradition at Caltech is Ditch Day, a fixture since 1921. On this day seniors leave campus and undergraduates attempt to trash their rooms—filling them with sand, gluing furniture to the ceiling, even disassembling cars or cement mixers and reassembling them in the rooms. Seniors don't just let this happen, of course; they turn their rooms into high-tech fortresses to withstand the siege. Some rely on sheer muscle, like a bunch of cinderblocks, or "complex, imaginative puzzles carefully planned out months or even years in advance," according to the university. "The original objective has undergone a subtle shift, from keeping underclassmen out of rooms to challenging them to get in. Underclassmen have told us that, in their desperation to decipher an essential clue, they actually find themselves remembering material from a long-repressed course." The web page says it best: "It's a peculiarly [Caltech] kind of fun."

Apart from this officially sanctioned vandalism, Caltech's Pasadena campus is remarkably safe. One robbery, two burglaries, and one stolen car were the only reported crimes on campus in 2009.

Caltech is fairly pricey—though cheaper than comparable Ivies—with 2010–11 tuition at $36,282 and room and board at $11,397. The school practices need-blind admissions and guarantees to meet the full financial need of students who enroll. Some 55 percent of students receive need-based financial aid, and their average debt upon graduation is a stunningly low $8,218.

Claremont Colleges

Claremont McKenna • Harvey Mudd • Pitzer • Pomona • Scripps

Claremont, California • www.claremont.edu

The five Cs

The consortium known as "The Claremont Colleges" is a group of five undergraduate colleges and two graduate universities located within a square mile in Claremont, California. The first of these, Pomona College, was founded in 1887. In the late 1920s, Pomona president James Blaisdell decided to create a group of residential colleges based on the Oxford system. Scripps College was founded in 1926; followed by Claremont McKenna (CMC) in 1946; Harvey Mudd in 1955; and Pitzer College in 1963.

Each of the Claremont colleges is distinct, but draws upon the vast array of resources the group offers. The colleges share twelve campus buildings, athletic facilities and teams, a student newspaper, and plenty of social activities; therefore, a student can benefit from the strengths of the four other colleges, making the weaknesses at his own more bearable. Generally speaking, the Claremont colleges boast dedicated and accessible faculty members, first-class facilities, excellent academic programs, small classes, and an intimate intellectual and social community. The colleges' peaceful campuses are just forty miles from the bustle of Los Angeles.

Academic Life: Prepare to work

It is generally accepted that Pomona, CMC, and Harvey Mudd are the toughest of the Claremont colleges, while Scripps and Pitzer are the least selective of the schools. Students arriving at any of the colleges, however, need to be prepared to work. CMC's intellectually rigorous education draws enthusiastic reviews rather than groans and moans from its students, 94 percent of whom return following their freshman years. "It's a really solid education," says one student. "It's very focused and very leadership oriented. I compare notes with friends back east at Ivy League schools and wouldn't trade my education at all. I think I'm very well served." Another student says, "We have a lot of general education requirements, so that helps students get a breadth of knowledge."

Students meet with faculty advisors shortly after their arrival at any of Claremont's colleges, to plan their freshman coursework. This system seems to be fairly effective at guiding students through the many options open to them.

CMC requires, with few exceptions, each student to complete a senior thesis under

West

904

the direction of a faculty reader. This is, according to the catalog, "a major research paper or creative project of substantial length." This requirement, relatively rare in today's higher education, usually strikes CMC students as a privilege, not a burden. "I think it's wonderful because it really gives you the opportunity to take what you've learned over the past four years [and use it], and you have a reader whom you work with very closely," a student says.

There is little departmental sprawl at the Claremont colleges. Each college has its academic strong suits and relies on the other colleges to make up for its deficiencies. Claremont's government and economics departments are top-notch, and its international relations program is also highly regarded. "The government department is arguably the best in the country for providing a sound liberal arts education with a major in government," says one professor. Says another, "The economics and government faculties are outstanding. . . . Many faculty have had high-level Washington experience [as] presidential appointees, cabinet-secretary appointees, and extensive involvement in politics at the national and state levels." Yet another professor says, "The government department has a wide variety of approaches to the study of politics: political philosophy, political history, constitutional history and constitutional law, institutional history and analysis. This is not a department dominated by rational-choice modeling or multivariate regressions on minutiae." However, we note with alarm that government majors are not required to study the U.S. Constitution or governmental system.

Unfortunately, not all of CMC's departments live up to the exemplary standards of these programs. Students report that the history department is the most politicized. "The focus is more on modern history," says one, "The program isn't what it could be." However, where once courses in premodern history were lacking, the colleges now offer a fair range of classes such as "Governing Rome: The History of the Roman Empire," "The Ancient Mediterranean," and "Late Antiquity and the Early Middle Ages," It also offers courses like "Queering the Renaissance" and "Modern Feminisms in East Asia," and allows history majors to skip, if they wish, the formative periods of American history.

The CMC literature department's offerings range widely, from "Dante, Shakespeare, and Dostoyevsky," "The Bible," and "Homer and Virgil," to "Gay and Lesbian Writers," "Black Politics and Literary Imagination," and "Paranoia in Modern Literature and Cul-

---

VITAL STATISTICS (CMC)

Religious affiliation: *none*
Total enrollment: *1,550*
Total undergraduates: *1,550*
SAT/ACT midranges: CR: *710–780*, M: *690–770*; ACT: *31–34*
Applicants: *6,149*
Applicants accepted: *16%*
Accepted applicants who enrolled: *39%*
Tuition and fees: *$40,230*
Room and board: *$13,000*
Freshman retention rate: *97%*
Graduation rate: *89% (4 yrs.), 95% (6 yrs.)*
Courses with fewer than 20 students: *66%*
Student-faculty ratio: *7:1*
Courses taught by graduate students: *none*
Most popular majors: *social sciences, interdisciplinary studies, psychology*
Students living on campus: *98%*
Guaranteed housing for four years? *yes*
Students in fraternities: *5%* in sororities: *none*

SUGGESTED CORE

1. Literature 113, Homer and Virgil
2. Philosophy 187, Tutorial in Ancient Philosophy
3. Literature 61, The Bible
4. Religious Studies 37, History of World Christianity
5. Literature 110/62/64/66, Shakespeare/Shakespeare's Tragedies/Shakespeare's Histories and Romances/Shakespeare's Comedies
6. Government 80, Introduction to Political Philosophy
7. History 80, Forging a New Nation, America to 1865
8. History 132E, European Intellectual History or Philosophy 43, Continental Thought

ture." One student tells us that conservatives should "beware this department." While it does have "sharp professors," he says, they are on the whole outspoken leftists. At Pomona, the English department is particularly strong. Scripps has excellent art, art history, and music departments. Pitzer's sociology department is highly regarded, but incredibly politicized (to the left). Literature majors, alas, can emerge without taking a single course on Shakespeare.

Among the best faculty at CMC are Joseph M. Bessette, Mark Blitz, Charles R. Kesler, Chae-Jin (C. J.) Lee, Chris Nadon, James H. Nichols, John J. Pitney Jr., and Ralph A. Rossum in government; Eric Helland, Manfred Keil, and Marc Massoud in economics and accounting; Paul Hurley in philosophy; Robert Faggen, John Farrell, and Nicholas Warner in literature; and Newton Copp in biology. (Copp has an appointment by the Joint Science Program that also serves Pitzer and Scripps.) At Pitzer, look for Barry Sanders in the "History of Ideas" and Albert Wachtel in English. At Scripps, John Geerken in history and Michael Deane Lamkin in music are excellent. At Harvey Mudd, try Michael E. Orrison in mathematics and Stephen C. Adolph in biology.

Most classes—in all five schools—are small and inviting, allowing students to interact freely with their professors. While there are occasionally some larger class sizes (around thirty) for courses that everyone needs to graduate, 66 percent of all classes have less than twenty students. Faculty-student closeness is impressive. "I can basically drop by their offices anytime," says one student. "I've had dinner with a number of their families, in fact. It's very easy to get in touch with them, and they really care about the instruction of the students. . . . We're at a teaching college." This closeness is "not merely a 'feel good' asset—it has practical benefits for students," says a professor. Take the all-important letters of recommendation when it comes time to find a job or graduate school. "We can discuss the students in detail, rather than writing vague generalities," the professor says.

Teaching assistants, as a rule, do not teach. "The use of TAs is minimal, and they are only used when there is an extraordinary demand for a certain class," one student says. "In these cases, [the college] may add a section taught by a TA from the Claremont Graduate University in addition to the already scheduled sections."

In addition to solid courses, students will find at the Claremont colleges a multitude of learning opportunities offered by some eleven research institutes. The Henry Salvatori Center for the Study of Individual Freedom focuses on "the study of political philosophy and freedom as it relates to American Constitutionalism and the American Founding." The Rose Institute of State and Local Government allows students to get involved with the

West

political process, working on "projects focusing on such topics as redistricting, fiscal analysis, California demographics, survey research, and legal and regulatory analysis." Harvey Mudd offers its students plentiful opportunities to gain research experience as summer interns working alongside faculty members. The school's Corporate Partnership program allows students to apply for scholarships from corporations such as Boeing, Dow, Motorola, and General Motors. Through the school's Clinic Program, corporations commission students to work on research projects throughout the school year and to present their research upon completion.

Also important are the diverse off-campus study opportunities that the Claremont colleges offer their students. As a group, the Claremont colleges have a very high participation rate in study-abroad programs. Students can participate in a semester of foreign study around the globe—from Kenya and Vietnam to Ecuador and Great Britain, or closer to home in Canada and Mexico. Some students opt to study across the country in the nation's capital, Washington D.C. One student says, "CMC's Washington Program is great. Students have full-time internships and take a full-time course load (we take classes at night). The program throws us into the fire—we have to arrange our own housing, internships, and survive basically on our own. It's a very hard semester, but my time in Washington was one of the most rewarding experiences of my college career."

The modern languages curricula are based on intercollegiate, cooperative programs among the five Claremont Colleges. Claremont McKenna College offers Arabic, French, Korean, and Spanish; other modern languages offered at the Claremont colleges include Chinese at Pomona, Italian at Scripps, Japanese at Pomona, and Russian at Pomona College. Latin and Ancient Greek are offered through Scripps's classics department.

Student Life: The Bar Monkey

While the Claremont colleges share many resources, each has its own feel and typical student. One CMC student helpfully provides the following stereotypes: "Pomona: pretentious liberal intellectuals." (An alumnus adds that they tend to be "filled with guilt over their parents' success.") The student continues, "Pitzer: hippies and 'crazy liberals.'" Another student muses, "Scripps: lesbians/bisexuals; artsy types. CMC: more conservative, beer-drinking, ambitious students. Mudd: math and science nerds; study a great deal, and often have quirky habits such as unicycle riding."

Some 40 percent of the student body comes from the state of California, and students from the different schools interact frequently. One student says, "There is definitely a feeling of individuality with respect to each school, but since so much is shared—classes, sports, facilities—there is also a feeling of overall commonality among the five Claremont colleges."

Claremont McKenna is "one of the most politically balanced schools in the country, with a good variety of views and with healthy representation among both liberals and conservatives," says a faculty member. A student says, "CMC is a very open environment both politically and religiously. Dialogue on both sides of political issues is open and fair. . . . For the most part, liberals and conservatives are happy to agree to disagree and argue points

West

academically . . . political argument from both sides is embraced." A survey conducted by the *Claremont Independent*, a conservative student publication, found that around a third of CMC students identified themselves as conservatives. "We have to be one of the most evenly split colleges in the country," says one student. Further, another student notes, "Many professors are conservative, and nearly every professor I've had has either kept politics out of the classroom or been fair to both sides of an issue." CMC's political environment is healthy and open, and regardless of a student's political leanings, he will find his views taken seriously and thoughtfully. "We're a very politically conscious campus," says one student, "but dissenting from orthodoxy is not a problem." Another student says, "From whatever side you come from, you always have allies in the classroom."

"Pomona is very left-wing and ideological—almost to the point that conservative viewpoints are not tolerated," one student says. For the most part, Scripps College follows the trend of other small liberal arts schools for women. Many of its course offerings are presented from a feminist perspective, and Scripps students may find it hard to avoid them. Sometimes this slant backfires, however; the *Claremont Independent* quotes one rare Scripps traditionalist: "Being at Scripps made me more conservative. I had to defend myself, and it made me see the flaws of liberal arguments more. Scripps forced me to delineate my beliefs." Pitzer College seems to be even less balanced. One student calls Pitzer "hopelessly liberal." Owing to its engineering and hard-science bent, students say Harvey Mudd is mostly non-ideological, since students there are likely to spend more time working on projects and internships than they are attending protests and political rallies.

The Marian Miner Cook Athenaeum, the site of lunch and dinner meetings four times a week featuring lectures by prominent speakers, along with less-frequent concerts and performances, is one of the highlights of the Claremont colleges. Not only does it offer a decent meal, it allows students to visit with their professors and hear a number of incredible speakers. "Recommend everyone go to the Athenaeum," one student tells us. "It's a formal setting," says another student, "a coat-and-tie type of thing." A look at the list of speakers shows an impressive array range: James Baker, Newt Gingrich, Paul Bremer, and Justice Antonin Scalia, as well as former attorney general Janet Reno, *New York Times* columnist David Brooks, Alan Charles Kors (director of the Foundation for Individual Rights in Education), and the Los Angeles Chamber Orchestra Soloists.

Religious life at the Claremont Colleges is overseen by a joint Office of the Chaplains, based at McAlister Center, which maintains the Volunteer Service Center. Events and activities include Volunteer Study Break (recruiting evenings), canned food drives, the Oxfam Hunger Awareness Program, Community Service Awareness Week, Habitat for Humanity builds, tree planting, and alternative spring-break trips. Denominational activities are offered, an easy task given that the full-time chaplaincy staff includes a Catholic priest, a Protestant minister, and a rabbi. There are many congregations of various denominations in easy driving distance.

The town of Claremont is charitably described as "sedate," even boring, at least for college students. "There aren't your normal college-town things in Claremont," says one student. All five undergraduate colleges are located within a square mile, so while the architecture on the individual campuses does vary, you're bound to find plenty of palm trees,

West

lush green lawns, and California sunshine. The Village, Claremont's town center, contains a number of shops, restaurants, and bookstores, but this represents the sum total of entertainment within walking distance. Having a car is most certainly helpful; Los Angeles is about forty miles to the west, although getting there can take upwards of two and a half hours if traffic is heavy. Closer to home are the suburban cities of Pomona (beware of gangs and guns here) and Ontario, both only a few miles away. Students who want to visit the beach head for Los Angeles or Orange County.

The colleges share a number of facilities. Bridges Auditorium is the site of many concerts, lectures, and performances, which are usually open to all Claremont students. The four libraries—Honnold/Mudd for the humanities and social sciences; Denison Library (at Scripps) for the humanities, fine arts, and women's studies; and two science and engineering libraries at Harvey Mudd—also make resources available for all Claremont students. These include two million volumes and 6,000 periodicals. Scripps has an excellent music program and facilities, including three performance centers. Another shared resource is the dining facilities—students are welcome to take meals at any of the Claremont cafes or dining halls.

Despite the sleepy environs, "Everyone has fun to some degree because there's so much going on," a student says. There are dozens of student groups and plentiful athletic opportunities, and the close-knit atmosphere makes it easy to find and make friends. Students of the five colleges also share membership in other organizations, including a debate union; Hillel; a Lesbian, Gay, and Bisexual Students' Union; the traveling, competing Claremont Colleges Ballroom Dance Company; Amnesty International; Claremont Colleges Fencing Club; the *Claremont Independent*; CMS Pep Band; Cycling Club; Hawaiian Club; Claremont Cougars Men's Lacrosse Club; and the Society for the Preservation of Acoustic Music (SPAM).

ACADEMIC REQUIREMENTS

General education requirements—taken in addition to the demands of any major—differ among the five Claremont colleges. The most liberal arts oriented, Claremont McKenna College requires:

- Two courses in science, both with labs.
- One math class, either "Calculus" or "Discrete Mathematics."
- An intermediate course or the equivalent in a foreign language.
- "Literary Analysis and Composition" and "Questions of Civilization."
- Courses selected from two of the following fields, which may not include a student's major: foreign literature, advanced literature, philosophy, and religious studies.
- Courses in social sciences outside a student's major, chosen from three of these fields: economics, government, history, and psychology.
- Three semesters of physical education or two seasons of a sport.
- A senior thesis.

GREEN LIGHT

Students at the Claremont colleges can join clubs that are either exclusive to one campus or available to students from all five. These clubs range from the far left to the respectable right. As one student says, "We take advantage of what goes on at other campuses, because in a sense we're all one campus." Student groups include Civitas, a well-supported community service group; the Pro-Life Society; and InterVarsity Christian Fellowship, the largest student group on campus. There are chapters of College Republicans and College Democrats; a pep band; a fencing club; and the *Collage*, a weekly newspaper that serves students on all five campuses.

Political correctness certainly does have a foothold at the colleges; in 2009, Pomona College banned its own official song, "Hail, Pomona, Hail!," after a college panel concluded that the song had originally—back in 1910—been written for a black-faced minstrel show. "Having your official college song banned is a little like "having your baby shot in front of you," Carl Olson, a Pomona College alumnus, told the *Chronicle of Higher Education*.

The Claremont colleges boast an impressive athletics program. Claremont McKenna, Harvey Mudd, and Scripps make up CMS athletics (Claremont, Mudd, Scripps). Students from these three colleges compete on varsity teams together. The men are known as the Stags, the women as the Athenas. Their archrivals are the Pomona-Pitzer Sagehens. Both groups offer about twenty varsity sports as well as a number of intramural teams, which are normally organized by dorm. A few club sports—rugby, lacrosse, Frisbee, and volleyball—also offer intercollegiate competition.

Except for three fraternities at Pomona, there is no Greek system on the campuses, nor is there any push for one. This means that students are left to their own devices when it comes to partying—something of which Claremont students reportedly do a good deal. However, the campus has dried up a little of late. "People drink, but not nearly as much as when I was a freshman," a student says. "The climate has changed, and people don't drink nearly as much—the keggers used to start on about Wednesday." However, another student says that "student life tends to revolve around alcohol consumption." Another student claims, "Drinking is almost a tradition here." However, another student reports that he has "felt no pressure to drink."

A few years ago, science students at Harvey Mudd put their technical minds to use and created something called a Bar Monkey, basically an automated bartender seemingly cribbed from a frat-movie fantasy: students type in the drink they want and the Bar Monkey serves it up. When administrators found out about it, the creators were charged with selling alcohol illegally, but the Bar Monkey is now allowed on campus as long as it is not used in a public place. The basic idea seems to be that it is better to have a wet campus with controlled conditions than to have students wandering off and getting into trouble in bars. One student says, "Everybody is very laid back here, which is nice. The student council buys kegs for parties out of student fees."

Scripps, like many women's colleges here and abroad, has a number of interesting social traditions that still reflect the atmosphere of gentility in which such institutions first arose. Among these are the Wednesday Afternoon Teas, the Medieval Dinner near

West

Christmas time, the May Fête, and the quarterly Candlelight Dinners. Claremont McKenna enjoys its own traditions as well, including "ponding," in which students get thrown into the fountain on their birthdays.

Housing on campus is abundant and adequate. Most Claremont students live on campus—close to 97 percent of CMC, Mudd, Scripps, and Pomona students, and about 75 percent of Pitzer students. At CMC, all dorms are coed, but most floors and suites are separated by sex. Residence halls, only about two to three minutes away from each other at most, are mixed by class—freshmen often live next door to seniors. This leads to camaraderie both within residence halls and among them. "Dorm life is a blast," says one student. "It feels kind of like a family." There is also a central dining facility where students take their meals—"very good for college fare," says one student—and there are enforced quiet hours in dormitory housing. (All dorms at Pomona are also coed, but rooms are single sex.) There are no freshman-only floors at CMC. CMC also leases a limited number of apartments at a nearby apartment complex where a small number of students reside. Claremont Hall, completed in 2008, is the newest dormitory with space for 109 students. Across the five colleges, dorms are generally coed, but with separated wings, floors, or suites. There are, however, coed bathrooms to be found among the schools.

Crime is a moderate concern on campus. "I don't think people worry at all," says one student. "We're in a sleepy little town." Students say that they don't feel unsafe, but they also say the largest problem is theft, so students should use common sense in safeguarding their belongings. In 2009, campus crime statistics from the five colleges counted twenty-seven burglaries, one aggravated assault, and two forcible sexual offenses.

Claremont McKenna College charged tuition of $40,230 in 2010–11; room and board came to $13,000. Some 44 percent of students receive need-based aid, and the average debt of a recent grad was $9,779. The numbers at the other four colleges are roughly comparable.

University of Colorado at Boulder

Boulder, Colorado • www.colorado.edu

Red rock college

The University of Colorado at Boulder was founded in 1876 as the state's flagship school. With a grant of forty-five acres and $15,000, the school began with a single building, Old Main, and a daunting mission: to educate the citizens of a state that was still very much part of the Wild West. At the school's opening in 1877, students and faculty sang the university anthem "We Hail Thee! Great Fountain of Learning and Light." Some 130 years later, that "fountain of learning and light" comprises nine academic colleges and serves nearly 33,000 students on a stunning 600-acre campus in the heart of the Rocky Mountains.

The campus is spectacular, the faculty is generally respectable, and the curriculum is above average for a state school. The university is large and diverse enough that a student with a strong sense of self-discipline can prosper; if he wishes to pursue a traditional liberal education here he will find the means to do so, but little encouragement.

Academic Life: Skills acquisition

What the University of Colorado calls a core curriculum is merely a rather flexible set of requirements in those dry modern realms of "skills acquisition" and "content areas of study." The student who values a traditional education and finds himself at Boulder can, with diligence, find solid courses to satisfy each requirement, especially in math and science.

The "skills" the school hopes to impart include writing, quantitative reasoning, and a foreign language—in other words, mostly things students used to learn in high school. Indeed, the foreign language entrance requirement can be satisfied by taking three foreign language courses in high school, a third semester college-level class, or by examination. Sufficient quantitative reasoning and math skills can be demonstrated by passing one to two math courses or a proficiency test. One of the two written communication requirements can be satisfied by sufficient AP English scores, and a student may test out of the second.

Several of the seven-content area distribution requirements can be satisfied through politicized courses in gender and ethnicity—indeed, the sheer abundance of such courses at Boulder is depressing. The "human diversity" requirement, for instance, can be fulfilled by "Introduction to Lesbian, Gay, Bisexual, and Transgender Studies." The courses fulfilling the "United States context" requirement include thumb-suckers like "America through

Baseball" and "Women of Color and Activism." The "contemporary societies" requirement can be satisfied by courses like "Black Politics," and "Literature and Social Violence." However, there are many excellent classes one could take instead. Even the diversity requirement can be satisfied by a course in traditional Asian civilization, while solid economics classes count for credit in "contemporary societies."

Around half of Colorado's classes contain fewer than twenty students, and 87 percent enroll fewer than fifty. Introductory-level courses for underclassmen are the largest. The university claims that students won't have problem getting into required courses and will not be prevented from graduating because of limited course availability. To back up this claim, CU has implemented a "Graduation Guarantee," under which students entering with a minimum of academic preparation are guaranteed to get into all the courses they need within four years. If the college cannot meet that promise, additional courses are free.

The honors program at CU–Boulder is one of the strongest in the country, and since a central honors council decides whether a student should graduate with honors, the distinction actually means something. The top 10 percent of incoming freshmen are invited, but other students may request admission. A student in the program can choose honors-level courses in any department and can graduate with honors by maintaining a 3.3 GPA and writing a thesis as a senior. The honors program also offers a number of interdisciplinary courses. Classes are capped at fifteen students and range from "The Bible" and "Folklore" to "Introduction to Women's Literature" or "Science and the Ancient World." An honors dorm is available for a hundred freshman participants.

Several departments at CU stand out. The sciences are generally very good. The aeronautical engineering program is well respected, and NASA recruits many CU students. Boulder has received millions from NASA over the years—some $1.5 million in 2008 alone—and seventeen astronauts have graduated from CU. The physics department is singled out by students and faculty alike as especially strong. From 1989 through 2001, five faculty members won the Nobel Prize in physics or chemistry. These departments are havens for conservative students: "Engineering, physics, and theoretical mathematics are the only subjects [in] which one is not subject to blatant socialist indoctrination," says one student.

VITAL STATISTICS

Religious affiliation: *none*
Total enrollment: *32,751*
Total undergraduates: *27,069*
SAT/ACT midranges: CR: *530–630*, M: *550–650*; ACT: *24–29*
Applicants: *19,649*
Applicants accepted: *84%*
Accepted applicants who enrolled: *33%*
Tuition and fees: *in state, $8,511; out of state, $28,193*
Room and board: *$10,792*
Freshman retention rate: *83%*
Graduation rate: *41% (4 yrs.), 67% (6 yrs.)*
Courses with fewer than 20 students: *47%*
Student-faculty ratio: *18:1*
Courses taught by graduate students: *9%*
Most popular majors: *social sciences, business/marketing, biological and life sciences*
Students living on campus: *24%*
Guaranteed housing for four years? *no*
Students in fraternities: *9%* in sororities: *16%*

Conversely, members of the humanities faculty are unhappy with the disproportionate emphasis they believe CU puts on the sciences. "The scientists support the school with federal grants, so, basically, anything they want, they get," says one professor. Another reports, "There is very little commitment to Western humanities or liberal arts; they've been gutted." Humanities receive much less outside funding, and so are starved of funds by the university itself, according to professors. Given the political slant of some of these departments, that may be just as well. One student says, "Most classics courses do not require students to read Thucydides, Aristotle, or even Homer aside from excerpts here and there. Instead, they seem dedicated to love poems and the desecration of modern culture by elitists who believe that Roman women had more rights than a modern American woman."

No discussion of CU would be complete without some mention of the infamous Ward Churchill. The University of Colorado made national headlines in 2005 when Professor Churchill compared the victims of the 9/11 attacks to Nazi war criminal Adolf Eichmann. (Don't ask.) When the state's governor called for Churchill's removal, a group of students supporting him successfully disrupted an open meeting of the board of regents on the incident. By March, the university's president, Elizabeth Hoffman, had herself resigned. At last, after various dramas that included the university finding him guilty of research misconduct and his exposure as a *faux* Native American, Churchill was fired in 2007. He sued the university for wrongful termination and was awarded $1 in damages but the judge refused to order Churchill's reinstatement. The lawsuits, however, continue.

Following Hoffman's resignation, former U.S. senator Hank Brown was installed as president of the college. Although there was significant faculty apprehension about hiring a onetime Republican politician, Brown proved to be a successful leader. He began his term by banning the purchase of alcohol with public funds for campus events. Before retiring in early 2008, he regained a great deal of trust for the university, resolving a rape scandal and attracting a record $133 million in 2007. Brown was succeeded by the current president Bruce Benson, who combines an ongoing interest in education and in CU (his alma mater) with success in a wide variety of business endeavors and in state Republican politics.

Outside the sciences, academic quality varies. (Even within the sciences, geology is bemoaned as inadequately taught.) "There are a lot of people very committed to mainstream teaching in English and American history," says one professor. However, several teachers point to political science as a "radical" department. (It does, at least, require its majors to study the American political system, however.)

Two of the most popular disciplines, psychology and environmental studies, are not recommended by more traditionally oriented faculty. Another professor says that sociology, which was once heavily Marxist, is "starting to get better" as retiring professors are being replaced by better scholars. For undergraduate teaching, the foreign languages, especially French, Spanish, and Italian, are quite strong.

English is described as "weak and chaotic" by one professor, who admits that "if you're intelligent and resourceful you can make your way through. Just ask around to find good professors." One English professor says, "If we believed in truth in advertising, we would change the department's name to cultural studies." The requirements of the English department bear out this professor's lament. It's true that majors must take at least one British literature course set before 1660, but another must cover advanced theory, genre studies, or popular culture, and still another multicultural or gender studies.

The history department maintains a more traditional approach. Students may choose a broad "geographic distribution" track or a "historical period" approach. All are required to take a lower- and an upper-level course in "World Areas," European, and U.S. history. Some students remark that Colorado's advising system entails "a lot of bureaucracy." Students unsure of their majors are shuffled into an "open option" program and assigned an advisor from a pool. Once a student chooses a major, he is assigned to an advisor from his department.

Some of the best professors at the university include the approachable and learned conservative scholar E. Christian Kopff in the honors program; David Gross and Patricia Limerick in history; Paul W. Kroll in East Asian languages and civilizations; Jules Gordon Kaplan in economics; and Thomas R. Cech in chemistry (who shared the 1989 Nobel Prize in chemistry for research on RNA). In 2004, Nobel laureate Carl Weiman was named national Teacher of the Year by the Carnegie Foundation. Weiman—who moved his Nobel Prize press conference up fifteen minutes so as not to be late for his freshman physics class—donated the teaching prize money to the university fund for the improvement of science teaching. He has since been appointed as the White House's Associate Director of Science in the Office of Science and Technology Policy. UC offers a good array of study-abroad options. The 2010–11 school year featured the following faculty-led seminars: "Economy, Politics, and Society in the Middle East" (Kuwait City), "Engineering for Developing Communities" (Haifa, Israel), the Rome Humanities Summer Program, "Art in Spain" (Madrid & Barcelona), "Art in France" (Paris), "Film & the French Aesthetic" (Paris), "Film & the Italian Aesthetic" (Rome), "Entrepreneurship and Empowerment" and "Reconciliation and Diversity" (Cape Town, South Africa), "Self Awareness and Images of the Other" (Xi'an, China), "Contemporary Nordic Society & Culture: Iceland," "London Finance Seminar," "Venice: Cradle of European Jewish Culture," and the St. Petersburg Language and Culture Summer Program.

CU offers Spanish, Arabic, Norwegian, Indonesian, Chinese, Portuguese, Russian, Latin, Italian, Farsi, Japanese, Swedish, Ancient Greek, Korean, German, French, Hebrew, Hindi, and American Sign Language.

Student Life: Party on, dudes

From any campus dorm room, students at CU could have a view of the Rockies, the campus pond, or a mountain meadow. But most CU students flee university housing after their first year. Housing options on campus range from small houses to high rises. All dormitories are

West

coed, but in some cases, men and women are separated by floor. Coed bathrooms and dorm rooms are available only for married students, who are normally housed in university-owned apartments. There are nine residential academic programs, which allow students to take small courses with faculty members who live in the same buildings, Oxford-style. The programs offer courses, programs, or co-curricular activities in areas like international studies, leadership, the fine arts, communications, or environmental studies.

Although just over a tenth of CU–Boulder students are members of a sorority or fraternity, it was ranked the number-one party school in the nation by The Princeton Review for several years. The administration has attempted to get tough on drinking, firing lax RAs. However, one student claims that "nearly every student of age" can be found in the bars on any given night. "The university gained the reputation for being a party school for a reason; that is still the culture of the university," says a student. The most egregious event on campus is surely the "smoke-fest," which occurs every year as thousands of pot-smokers light up on Farrand Field. After law enforcement attempts sparked student outrage, in 2008 and again in 2009, over 10,000 people turned up for the event, without any action on the part of the police.

The university offers dozens of intramural sports, from basketball to broomball, but students looking for more stringent competition can try out for an intercollegiate club or

---

ACADEMIC REQUIREMENTS

CU Boulder has no core curriculum, but does maintain distribution requirements. Each student must complete the following:

- Foreign language through the intermediate level.
- One course in quantitative reasoning and mathematical skills (QRMS). Courses include "Physics for Future Presidents," and "Mathematics from the Visual Arts."
- One lower-division and one upper-division class in written communication. A typical upper-level course is "Multicultural Perspectives and Academic Discourse" or "Advanced Writing in Religious Studies."
- One class in "historical context," such as "Maritime People: Fishers and Seafarers," or "The Rise and Fall of Ancient Rome."
- One course in human diversity, such as "Exploring a Non-Western Culture," or "Chicano History."
- One class in "U.S. context," such as "Religion in the United States," or "Asian American Women."
- Two classes in literature and the arts, one of which must be upper-division. Examples range widely from "Masterpieces of British Literature" to "Fairy Tales of Russia."
- Four classes, including one two-course sequence, plus a lab or field experience, in natural science, such as "Black Holes" or "General Chemistry."
- One class covering contemporary societies, such as "Emerging Democracies of Central and East Europe," or "'That's Amore: Introduction to Italian Culture."
- One class in ideals and values, such as "Feminist Practical Ethics," or "Philosophy, Art, and the Sublime."

West

varsity team. The Buffaloes, represented by their mascot Ralphie, formerly competed in the Big Twelve conference in seventeen varsity sports. In 2010, the school announced that it would leave the Big Twelve to join the Pac 10 conference in 2012. The Buffaloes have won a number of national and conference championships, excelling particularly in skiing and cross-country (practicing at high altitudes gives them an advantage). The school competes in six men's and eight women's NCAA Division I sports and has a long history of football successes. The football program has been hit by a number of scandals, including undercharging student athletes for meals, rape accusations against at least six football players, and the revelation that the recruiters were luring high school players with drugs, paid escorts, strippers, and alcohol. The university is working to rebuild its football program, and recruits are now supervised by coaches or parents, forbidden to go to bars, clubs, and parties, and subject to an 11:00 PM curfew.

Boulder (population 100,000), the bohemian capital of the West, boasts that it is home to more than 128 "new religions." At the same time, says one Christian student, "CU is an excellent place for students to grow in their faith. There is a multitude of Christian groups, service groups, and other such activities. Come to CU ready to be challenged in your faith." Given that Boulder is a state school, it is somewhat unusual in that it has its own chapel in the Old Main building, built in 1876—although the only religious services that take place there tend to be funerals. For Catholics, two parishes in town, Sacred Heart of Mary and St. Martin de Porres, offer Masses; the Aquinas Institute for Catholic Thought provides fairly solid catechism and devotions. St. Aidan's ministers to Episcopalians. There are organizations catering to mainline Protestants, Latter-day Saints, Orthodox, Adventists, nondenominational evangelicals, and Jewish, Islamic, Buddhist, Pagan, Hindu, and Baha'i students, as well as ecumenical and inter-religious organizations. Beware of the group called Campus Crusade for Queers. After some digging, our reporter discovered that it is not, in fact, a chaplaincy.

Official student clubs and organizations tend to be ethnically, professionally, or politically based, rather than performance oriented (unofficial groups are often recreational). Hiking, alpine, and crew clubs do exist, along with the Coalition for Creative Music, OnStage performing arts group, and the Buffons *a cappella* singing group. Students are active in the Japanese, African, Afghan, Persian, Chinese, Indian, Mexican, or Ovate Native American student organizations. Language clubs offer practice in German or Russian, while the Toastmasters allows students to hone oration skills. Academic clubs include the Black Law Students Organization, Sports Marketing Club, Philosophy Club, CU Gold leadership development, Neuroscience Club, Model United Nations, Real Estate Club, Mock Trial group, and Society of Hispanic Professional Engineers.

For the politically minded, College Democrats and Republicans exist, along with the far-left 180 Degree Shift at the 11th Hour activism group and BASE activist journal project. Student-run radio KVCU 1190 provides news and sports, and music ranging from Bollywood to Honky Tonk.

When asked to characterize CU's students, one professor says that they "take on a live-and-let-live attitude . . . and have a very strong commitment to looking good and skiing." A student says, "The workload could be heavier. But students are not so tied down by their schoolwork that they can't afford to party midweek or cut class on a Tuesday to ski."

West

YELLOW LIGHT

This campus in the heart of the Rocky Mountains attracts an environmentally conscious and liberal student population—the school continually has among the greatest number of Peace Corps volunteers. Its reputation as a school for pot-heads and politically radical students is merited. One undergrad says the school has been called the "liberal lighthouse of the West." Another says, "Boulder is known for its new-age thinking. . . . There is a sizable population of hippies, and Greenpeace activists are everywhere." Protests are a common occurrence.

CU isn't quite sure what it wants to be—a bastion for the left, a football powerhouse, or a haven for pseudo-hippies. As a consequence, it can restrict the freedoms of both its liberal and its conservative students. From forbidding an affirmative-action political-protest bake sale hosted by the College Republicans to informing the leftist Students for True Academic Freedom that they would have to pay $2,000 in security fees to bring Ward Churchill and William Ayers to campus, the university seems always to be stepping on someone's toes.

Even in trying to remedy its reputation as a party school and leftist breeding ground, CU just can't seem to get it right. The the school has established a fund to endow a faculty chair for a professor of Conservative Thought and Policy. The move has mostly been criticized; as a former president of the College Democrats says, "We are not promoting intellectual diversity—we are tokenizing a point of view that should be presented in all classes on political thought." That's a far cry from the "Great Fountain of Learning and Light" CU set out to be.

The school's largely wooded campus has won worldwide acclaim for its natural and architectural beauty. CU claims to average more than 300 sunny days per year. *Sports Illustrated* recently ranked Boulder the fifth-best college town in America. Students looking for outdoor activities of any kind should have no trouble finding them. Hiking, mountain biking, and skiing are extremely popular. One student warns, "If you don't ski, bike, hike, or climb you don't belong here."

The city's cosmopolitan atmosphere is highly appealing. "It's about a five-minute walk to the mountains," a student says, exaggerating only slightly. "That's probably why a lot of people come here." Some of the top ski resorts in North America, including Vail and Aspen, are within a two-hour drive, along with abundant opportunities for whitewater rafting, snowboarding, backpacking, horseback riding, and climbing. The university is also home to the Fiske Planetarium, the CU Heritage Center, the CU Museum of Natural History, and the CU Art Galleries.

In 2009, campus police reported nine forcible sex offenses, two robberies, five aggravated assaults, sixty burglaries, one stolen car, and two cases of arson. The campus has plenty of emergency call boxes and round-the-clock police surveillance. A safety escort service not only helps students get around campus but also escorts students throughout the city of Boulder. All dormitory visitors must present a student ID card or be escorted by a resident.

Boulder is rather a bargain for Colorado residents, who in 2010–11 paid $8,511 in tuition (out-of-state students paid $28,193), and $10,792 for room and board. Admissions are need blind, although the school doesn't promise everyone full financial aid. Only 34 percent of students get need-based assistance, and the average debt of a recent grad is about $19,000.

Colorado College

Colorado Springs, Colorado • www.coloradocollege.edu

Spaghetti Western Civ

This college was founded in 1874 by adventurous spirits. The campus is comfortably nestled at the base of Pike's Peak—a big draw for the school. Both faculty and students enjoy its beautiful environment not only for weekend recreation activities, but also for hands-on experience in various courses such as geology and history. It is not surprising to find CC students studying geology in the Grand Canyon or anthropology in Anasazi ruins. They are also prone to reading the Great Books, since they're an intellectually curious and highly qualified group. While there is no genuine core curriculum, and a relatively loose set of distribution requirements, students are directed to take two courses that explore "The West in Time." Given the school's location, one might fear that this is simply a history of the U.S. frontier, but in fact it incorporates classes on the civilizations of Greece, Rome, Europe, and the U.S., along with some courses on more global issues. By all accounts, these classes are given and taken in a spirit of intellectual seriousness, a spirit reinforced by the school's rare "block system," which enables students to focus intensely on a single topic before passing on to another class.

The classroom and campus atmosphere at CC is described as liberal but generally open-minded and tolerant. Conservative and religious students will definitely feel themselves in the minority, but probably won't experience any direct mistreatment because of their views.

Academic Life: Quantity time

Colorado College has thirty-one academic departments and majors along with ten interdisciplinary majors and eight interdisciplinary programs. The college describes the purpose of a liberal education as not only educating students in some specialized branch of knowledge, but also making them aware of the interconnections among different branches of knowledge.

Colorado pursues this purpose in part through "general studies" and "interdisciplinary" courses. The former approach a broad theme or subject matter from the point of view of at least two disciplines; the latter take on subject matter that will not fit easily into any traditional department. Both types may be taught by one instructor or team-taught by several instructors from different departments or even different divisions.

West

Colorado College operates on an intensive block-plan curriculum, a format that divides the academic year into eight three-and-a-half week "blocks." Students take just one principal course at a time, and professors teach just one at a time. Some courses may last for one block, others for two or three blocks, depending on the nature of the material. Despite their brevity, courses cover as much of a subject as a conventional semester class, which means that work is concentrated and demanding. One block or unit of credit is equal to four semester hours (instead of three, as at most schools).

Students and faculty speak highly of the block system. Students report they find it much easier to learn when their only focus is one class at a time, while one faculty member says, "It tends to favor process over content. Students do well with it, but it's not for everybody." It appeals to "the nature of the students who come; they're quick learners. They like the total immersion of it. Total contact hours are actually greater under the block system." At the same time, it helps distractible students organize their time. Says another prof, "It helps to keep them from siphoning off too much time and energy into one class at the expense of the others." A student says, "The block plan is what you will hear about most of the time if you ask any CC student what they like most about our academic environment, and it's true. . . . It works best (in my opinion) for students in the humanities and social sciences. I am a classics-history-politics major with a Spanish minor, and I have had amazing experiences in all of these departments."

One clear advantage of the block system is the freedom it allows for scheduling classes on campus, and for fieldwork and travel. A student says, "I took a great history course, called 'The American City,' at the Newberry Library in Chicago with professor David Torres-Rouf and didn't need to worry about missing any other classes because we only take one class at a time." One possible disadvantage is that not all disciplines, especially scientific ones, can adapt as well. Geology, clearly, thrives since field trips are the stuff of the discipline and the Rocky Mountains offer endless, nearby exploration sites. But the physics department, as one prof says, "feels the system works against them [and has] had to reduce the number of classes needed for the major." Some subject matters are difficult to master in a few concentrated weeks. There are, similarly, students for whom the block plan poses a mental block, and they tend to transfer out.

All courses are given equal importance, and students can give full attention to each.

West

Classes are kept small; the average size is ten to fifteen students, and almost all classes are limited to twenty-five. Formal lectures are rare; seminar discussions and active laboratories are the norm. The concentrated format and small classes are carefully designed with one vital educational principle in mind: that the student be an active participant instead of a passive recipient. For example, an archaeology class may be held at a dig in southeastern Colorado for one block, followed by a second block for laboratory analysis; a biology class might have a week of classroom orientation, then go to the field for two weeks; an English class can spend one morning reading a Shakespeare play aloud and the next morning discussing it or getting together with an acting class to perform a few scenes.

Although students compile their own programs and no two schedules are likely to be identical, most students spend several hours a day in class, usually in the morning. Students should expect to spend several hours studying for every hour spent in class. However, the hours of study certainly do not come without reward. Each block ends at noon on the fourth Wednesday, giving students four-and-a-half day mini-vacations called "block breaks." Some students relax by staying on the campus; others participate in college-sponsored recreational activities such as bicycle trips to Aspen, raft expeditions down the Colorado River, or volcano climbs in Mexico.

The First-Year Experience seeks to excite freshmen about ideas; to focus on vital skills; to foster conversation inside and outside the classroom; and most importantly, to prepare students to think critically. The program includes a set of courses taken in the first two blocks by all freshmen; it also seeks to connect the academic and the social realms by involving these new students with upper-division student mentors. A second-year economics major explains that First-Year Experience was critical in helping her adapt to the demanding challenges of college learning and deciding her major, while the upper-division mentors eased her entry into the college's high-octane intellectual program.

The First Course consists of either a single two-block course or two related one-block courses that each freshman takes immediately upon arrival at the college. First Courses include substantial practice in critical reading and writing; research supported by workshops in the library; course-appropriate use of the Writing Center; library instruction; lab techniques; fieldwork; and information technology resources.

If the virtue of the block plan is its depth, its drawback might be said to be a lack of breadth, or at least, overall coherence. The structure of the college-wide curriculum seems somewhat weak. One professor describes the general requirements as a "distribution trying to appear as a core" or "a multiple choice sort of core." Some of the requirements for majors

SUGGESTED CORE

1. English 207: Masterpieces of Literature: Greeks to Modern
2. Philosophy 101: Greek Philosophy
3. Religion 111/112: Hebrew Bible/New Testament
4. History 312: Faith, Reason, and Medieval Society
5. Political Science 103: Western Political Traditions
6. English 225: Introduction to Shakespeare
7. History 364/365: American Colonies, 1492–1763/ The American Revolution and the Constitution, 1763–1789
8. History 288: Intellectual History of Modern Europe

are more structured. Even the self-designed majors must have faculty advisors to give over-sight, and the major must have "depth," with courses at the junior and senior levels that build on lower-level courses. Because of "strong major requirements," says the same profes-sor, to that degree "there is no danger of being too cross-disciplinary." Students are allowed to double major in two departments, or in a traditional department and interdisciplinary program, provided there are no more than three courses in common between the majors. A student can pursue a "thematic minor" of five units from two departments outside the major. There are dozens of these minors to choose from—a student may even design his own—but each is interdisciplinary in approach.

Colorado offers students plenty of close contact with faculty. The school boasts many informal get-togethers at professors's houses (such as those of the "Classics/English Reading Fraternity" where a play is discussed twice a month) and extracurricular symposia (such as the "Fearless Friday" math seminars, earning ratings of G, PG-13, and R depending on how challenging they are). From these events flow, as one professor puts it, "good collegiality among students who want it," not to mention "light-hearted faculty guidance."

Among key departments, it is telling that English majors must take Shakespeare and political science majors must study American politics and government. History majors, however, do not need to study America before 1900.

Instead of a standard freshman composition class, Colorado offers writing-intensive seminars in standard curricular subjects, among which students may choose, and a "Writ-ing Practicum" option that they may add to their other classes. This allows aspiring natu-ralists to write essays about Western wildlife, for instance. Student writing in other classes is monitored by professors, who refer those needing improvement to the Writing Center, where upperclassmen skilled with the quill serve as mentors. The center also offers stu-dents "one-on-one consultations at any stage of any writing project; continuing tutorials for students with serious writing issues, students working on major projects, or speakers of English as a second language." In addition, students can use the Writing Center for extra-curricular and nonacademic purposes, such as help with grad-school applications.

Despite a few weak and politicized areas such as feminist and gender studies and soci-ology, the resources for an excellent traditional liberal arts education abound at Colorado College. For its success, the school relies primarily upon the quality and motivation of the serious students it attracts and the guidance of individual devoted professors. According to one professor, students continue to show a strong interest in canonical western subjects and authors such as Shakespeare—while also dabbling in multicultural studies. Students speak highly of Marc Snyder in biology; Carol Neel, Susan A. Ashley, and Dennis Showalter in history; Larry Stimpert in economics; Fred Tinsley and David Brown in mathematics; Sam Williams (emeritus) in religion; John H. Riker in philosophy; Timothy Fuller, David Hendrickson, and Eve Noirot Grace in political science; Eric Popkin in sociology; and of the entire neuroscience department.

Regarding campus politics, one professor writes in the *CC Bulletin*: "I especially cher-ish my conservative students. It takes courage to defend conservative views on a tradition-ally liberal college campus. Yet, conservatives, while a minority in the classroom, are not as alone as one might think. Center-left views do tend to dominate class discussions, but only superficially. Most students enjoy engaging a full range of political perspectives. Indeed, the majority of my students, conservatives and liberals alike, use class discussions to begin the process of political formation, not to bring it to a close." We hope his views are representative of most teachers at CC.

The block system also helps students to travel abroad. One undergrad, for instance, raves about the course "The World of Odysseus," taught by Lisa Hughes and Barry Sarchett and offered during the summer in Greece, calling it "an amazing educational opportunity only found at CC!" Colorado College does strongly encourage its students to take advantage of foreign study, offering programs on several continents. Some students head to Japan to study economics, while others go to France or Italy for architecture, history, and art. Some travel to Russia to study literature and dance, and others study environmental science in Argentina. The list of countries goes on: Sweden, Mexico, Finland, Botswana, Costa Rica, India, Tanzania, Germany, Wales, and Brazil. Colorado College directly administers a number of the programs. Close to 60 percent of the student body studies abroad. Students may major in French, Italian, German, Russian, and Spanish. Chinese, Latin, Ancient Greek, Hebrew, and Japanese are also taught.

Student Life: Garden of the gods

With just over 2,000 students, Colorado College boasts a closely knit community. Seventy-six percent of students live on campus; indeed, all students except seniors are required to do so. Housing options include coed and single-sex residence halls. There are no visita-

---

ACADEMIC REQUIREMENTS

While Colorado College has no real core curriculum, it does maintain decent distribution requirements and a few worthy common classes. All students must complete the following:

- At least thirty-two units of credit (one per block).
- At least one full unit in each division: humanities, the social sciences, and the natural sciences.
- Two blocks of "The West Through Time," emphasizing the contributions of Western culture. Options range from "Concepts of Freedom from Ancient to Modern Times" to "Topics in Music: History of Rock."
- Three blocks of "Diverse Cultures and Critiques." Options include "States and Empires in the Ancient Andes" and "Topics in Ethnomusicology: Music, Sex, and Intoxication."
- Two blocks of "Scientific Inquiry," one of which must contain a significant lab or field component in which data from the natural world is collected and interpreted. Options include "Field Zoology" and "Topics in Southwest Studies."
- A foreign language requirement that may be fulfilled by completing two introductory-level classes; taking a proficiency test; studying abroad in a foreign tongue; or having studied a language for four years in high school.

tion policies or hours. Group bathrooms are single-sex except in the gender-neutral housing. Students can also organize living arrangements around particular cultural and civic interests. The campus offers breathtaking mountain views, features some charming Tudor, Gothic, and Romanesque Revival buildings. The trailhead for Pike's Peak sits about a five-mile bus or bike ride away.

Colorado College likes to think of itself as "situated in a metropolitan area"—that area being Colorado Springs, which has a metro population of nearly half a million and is only an hour from Denver. But the proximity of 14,110-foot Pike's Peak and the Garden of the Gods (the nation's most spectacular city park), and the presence of hundreds of miles of hiking and biking trails, point to the wilder nature of the school's environs.

Freshman Outdoor Orientation Trips (FOOT) introduce newcomers to the region and its opportunities for backpacking, hiking, biking, camping, mountain climbing, and windsurfing. Such outings are not only encouraged by the college's location and prevailing culture, but also by the very structure of the block plan with its four-day breaks between each class. Sometimes during blocks, with no simultaneous classes demanding attention, professors schedule extended field trips, taking full advantage of the college's mountainous Baca Campus and several woodland cabins.

Three fraternities and three sororities attract about 3 percent of males and 10 percent of females from the student body. Students govern themselves through the Colorado College Campus Association and the Student Honors Council, which since 1949 has administered an honor code that allows exams without proctors and holds hearings when there are allegations of plagiarism or cheating.

Student organizations include the Ballroom Dance Club, Biochemistry Club, Colorado College Learning Initiative in the Mountains; Club Baseball, Cool Science Education for Village Children in India, Fencing Club, Great Performers and Ideas, HIV Awareness Club, Colorado College Rugby Football Club; Queer-Straight Alliance, AppreCCiate, Salsa Club, Shotokan Karate Association, Student Musical Theatre Group, The Philosophy Circle, Weight-Lifting Club, Women's Rugby, Student Anthropological Society, Students Taking Action Now: Darfur.

There is a strong chapel program, and an associated chaplain was recently added to the already vigorous activity of the campus ministry program. Although CC is nondenominational, and mandatory religious services were discontinued in 1956, Shove Chapel has been called "The best example of Norman Romanesque architecture in the United States." In addition to the college's Catholic Community, which offers Sunday Mass, traditionally minded Catholics will find the Priestly Fraternity of St. Peter in Colorado Springs at Immaculate Conception Church, offering Latin Mass with Gregorian chant. Conservative Episcopalians will find themselves at home with the local sponsoring parish, Grace and St. Stephen's, and there are opportunities for Methodists, Mormons, and most other denominations. There is also a Chabad chapter on campus for Jewish students.

The city of Colorado Springs is one of the hubs of conservative Christian activism in the West, playing host to Focus on the Family, Young Life Church, and the U.S. Air Force Academy—itself a hotbed of evangelical Christianity. Students seeking opportunities for activism or simply like-minded people will find plenty of them—off campus.

West

Students interested in journalism can work for the *Catalyst*, the campus paper; students interested in leftist activism, on the other hand, can turn to the *CiPher*, which covers "matters affecting the college, Colorado Springs, this nation, and the world, and strives to be a venue for creative, critical perspectives." There is also the *Leviathan*, a student literary magazine, and an off-campus associated publication called the *Loafer*, a "journal of philosophy, politics, and art."

Athletics are also very popular at Colorado College. The school boasts one of the top ice hockey teams in the nation. A wide variety of competitive varsity sports are available for men and women, along with intramural sports.

The college also encourages students to take an active interest in civic responsibility, offering grants to organizations that come up with new ways to improve the surrounding community through outreach and services. One faculty member notes that "educating our students about the importance and integral role they have in society is a fundamental part of Colorado College's mission."

> ## GREEN LIGHT
>
> One student says Colorado College is a "liberal campus" where "conservatives can regularly expect to have their viewpoints challenged." Conversely, one professor says that "neither conventionally conservative nor liberal students have been particularly prominent, though both exist here." The deeper truth appears to be that Colorado College is one of the more apolitical college campuses in the country, and for all the right reasons: students and faculty are too immersed in a quest for higher things. Another interesting campus development highlights the same phenomenon: while many other college campuses have poured more money and perks into football programs designed to earn prestige and appease the student herd, Colorado College, facing close to a million dollar budget shortfall, decided to abolish its football team—this, despite having the oldest college football stadium west of the Mississippi.

Crime is not a big concern; however, an on-campus murder (of a campus radio announcer, not a student) in the spring of 2002 remains unsolved. In 2009, Colorado College reported nine forcible sex offenses, eleven burglaries, and one stolen car on campus. Residence halls are accessible only with a college ID. CC has a twenty-four-hour security patrol that runs a number of crime prevention workshops and an escort service for students walking around campus late at night.

Tuition in 2010–11 was $38,748, room and board $9,416. Forty-seven percent of students receive need-based aid or non-need based aid. Merit-based scholarships are available to students majoring in the natural sciences. Thirty-seven percent of students receive need-based financial aid, and the average student-loan debt of a recent graduate is a moderate $16,172.

University of Dallas

Irving, Texas • www.udallas.edu

Mind over matter

A small but growing number of regional colleges across America are gaining prestige by offering their students a true liberal arts education in a traditional religious environment. The University of Dallas is one such school, known for its exceptional focus on an authentic and rigorous core curriculum, dedicated faculty, and serious student body. Founded by the Sisters of St. Mary of Namur in 1956, the university has a strong reputation among serious Catholics for providing a rigorous intellectual preparation.

University President Thomas Keefe was given the helm in 2010 partly because of his previous strength as a fundraiser. Keefe has already faced his first major controversy on campus. Students, alumni and faculty vociferously opposed the school's decision to offer a major in pastoral theology through the School of Ministry (SOM)—a longtime haven for dissenters from Catholic doctrine. Despite the efforts of those students and their allies among the alumni and faculty, the school's trustees voted in March 2011 to allow undergraduates for the first time to enroll in this program—which previously had only offered graduate courses, and lingered in a kind of academic quarantine. Now UD undergrads for the first time will have the opportunity to study under professors who openly reject the Church's teachings on crucial moral questions. We expect that students who trouble to seek out an overwhelmingly orthodox Catholic college like UD will avoid the SOM's offerings like the plague. After all, if what you're seeking is deracinated, postmodern Catholic dissent, there are much more prestigious schools where you can find it.

Academic Life: Seeds from the core

Overall, the University of Dallas takes seriously its mission as a Catholic liberal arts university and has built a core curriculum that reflects its seriousness of purpose. Consequently it has attracted and nurtured a faculty and student body that embodies the mission of the university.

All students at Dallas must take its excellent two-year core. This gives undergraduates a common bedrock of texts, authors, and ideas from which to approach their majors—and their lives. "My friends who went to more prestigious universities didn't have to study nearly as much as I did," says one recent graduate. A professor adds: "The core curriculum

West

926

is the strength of the school, period. All departments live off its strengths, its commitment to truth, its way of exposing students to the best in the Western tradition, its commitment to that tradition."

Upon enrolling in the university, each entering freshman is assigned a faculty advisor who helps to guide the student through the ins and outs of the core curriculum. After the first year, a student may select a new advisor from among the faculty in the major department or the university at large.

Students and faculty alike consider English, politics, theology, and philosophy to be strong departments. English boasts, according to one teacher, "superb professors who have a deep commitment to reading texts as revealing truth about the human condition (rather than as fashionable postmodern meaningless play with signifiers, or Marxist embodiments of race, class, and gender), and who have a deep commitment to the students through their teaching."

Theater students also will encounter a solid program. As one professor reports: "Drama is an unusual strength here, because of the core: The drama students can see modern and contemporary drama in the light of their strong backgrounds in classical Greek drama and Shakespeare, and—unlike drama students almost anywhere else—have serious grounding in history, philosophy, and theology."

"Philosophy is strong, and theology is strong both in scholarship and in its commitment to intellectually exploring yet remaining faithfully Catholic," says one teacher we consulted. "Departments like these do not hide from controversy or difficult questions, but they all do believe that truth exists and that the human is designed to seek it, find it, and live it."

The newly created major in pastoral ministry, in contrast to the sound theology program, is rife with dissent from Catholic doctrine, according to a report by Patrick Fagan of the Family Research Council. One faculty member has urged bishops to "alleviate the injustices imposed upon the People of God" by "allow[ing] women to be ordained." Another teacher assigns a two-book syllabus, which includes a text by a euthanasia advocate who "denies the existence of intrinsically evil acts." Another teacher assigns, as the sole book in his course, a work by leading dissenter Fr. Richard McBrien, who wrote in 2009 that the centuries-old Catholic devotion of Eucharistic Adoration is "a doctrinal, theological, and spiritual step backward, not forward." The president of the orthodox Catholics United for the Faith stated

VITAL STATISTICS

Religious affiliation: *Roman Catholic*
Total enrollment: *2,977*
Total undergraduates: *1,299*
SAT/ACT midranges: CR: *550–680*, M: *520–650*; ACT: *24–29*
Applicants: *1,161*
Applicants accepted: *75%*
Accepted applicants who enrolled: *37%*
Tuition and fees: *$27,815*
Room and board: *$8,650*
Freshman retention rate: *85%*
Graduation rate: *62% (4 yrs.), 73% (6 yrs.)*
Courses with fewer than 20 students: *49%*
Student-faculty ratio: *13:1*
Courses taught by graduate students: *not provided*
Most popular majors: *English, biological sciences, business administration*
Students living on campus: *60%*
Guaranteed housing for four years? *no*
Students in fraternities or sororities: *none*

that McBrien's work serves the purpose of making students "doctrinally illiterate." Still another teacher, in his class on the Old Testament, offers "a lengthy analysis of Leviticus in which he claims that Israel's holy law only ever meant to condemn the completed act of sodomy and that 'other forms of male–male sexual encounter, encompassing the whole range of physical expressions of affection that do not entail penetration, are not envisaged in these laws.'"

One professor says that the economics department "has a strong commitment to the ideas of classical liberalism in the strain of Adam Smith, and of Austrian economics in the strain of Hayek. It's a small department, but they do good things."

The medical school acceptance rate for Dallas graduates is 80 percent, indicating both that the science departments are excellent and that spending two years on core classes does nothing to prohibit students from pursuing a plan of study outside of the liberal arts.

Dallas students may augment their introduction to the liberal arts by participating in the Rome program at Due Santi, the university's campus located about ten miles from the heart of the Eternal City. About 80 percent of Dallas students participate in the program, typically during their sophomore year.

In addition to the Bachelor of Arts degrees offered through the Constantin College of the Liberal Arts, the university also offers a BA in business through the College of Business. Established in 2002, it houses both the undergraduate program and the Graduate School of Management. Undergraduate students majoring in business are also required to take the university core requirements. Additionally, business majors take a slate of courses in business leadership—in ethics, social justice, human resources, and leadership and organizations—as well as traditional business offerings in marketing, accounting, finance, and business law.

There are also graduate programs offered at the school, some centered on the liberal arts, as well as the aforementioned School of Ministry and an MBA program. In addition to traditional majors, students may complete a preprofessional or dual-degree program (e.g., predentistry or a joint BA/MBA program). Additional concentrations (e.g., journalism or medieval and Renaissance studies) may also be pursued.

Despite a few bad apples, teaching at Dallas is strong, as both graduates and professors from peer institutions attest. Some of the best undergraduate teachers include John Alvis, Rev. Robert Maguire, Gregory Roper, David Davies, and Gerard Wegemer in English; Richard Dougherty and Thomas West in politics; Rev. James Lehrberger in philosophy; Susan Hanssen, Thomas W. Jodziewicz, and Frances Swietek in history; Alexandra Wilhelmsen in Spanish; William Doyle in economics; Richard Olenick in physics; and Frank Doe in biology. Professors generally take an active role in university social events and extracurricular programs. Students give them high praise: "The professors really live what they teach," says one student. "They write what they think, and they behave the way they preach."

Dallas faculty are also actively involved in their respective disciplines, publishing and attending professional meetings. The university expects junior faculty to publish in order to be awarded tenure, but even tenured faculty continue to publish. "There's peer pressure to keep going," says one professor. "Everyone wants to pull his weight." There is no evidence, however, that publishing demands detract from professors' work in the classroom. According to one professor, "Here, I think we have the balance almost right."

Although University of Dallas is committed to a traditional approach to education, the school has experienced intense financial struggles in the last decade. Although faculty salaries have risen 10 percent, the consumer index has risen 20 percent, and many professors struggle to make ends meet.

Class sizes remain moderate. Graduate students who hold a master's degree may teach undergraduate classes—and an increasing number of them do, sources tell us. About half the classes offered in the English, theology, politics, and philosophy departments are taught by graduate students, instructors, or adjunct or visiting teachers. Business, history, foreign languages, the arts, and education also rely heavily on non-PhDs, but the sciences and the humanities retain more professors.

Although the Rome program is Dallas' only official study abroad, the university offers summer and holiday ventures around Italy, like the Eternal Cities tour in June 2010. Students traveled to Assisi, Rome, and Magna Graecia. The school also offers study tours for adults, high school students, and families, like "Shakespeare's Baroque Rome," a ten-day program to study Shakespeare's late plays and Rome's baroque art, "Latin in Rome," which combines intensive Latin lessons with visits to archaeological and historical sites, or a twelve-day creative writing program in Rome. Foreign languages offered on campus include Ancient Greek, Latin, French, German, Italian, and Spanish.

Student Life: Reading, writing, and rectitude

Perhaps the least attractive thing about the University of Dallas is its location, in a relatively joyless patch of sprawl called Irving, adjoining the Dallas–Fort Worth monsterplex. The university's Dallas Year program tries to overcome the place's limits by organizing outings for freshmen to the opera, museum, concerts, and sporting events. There is a bus stop in front of the school that serves students who do not have cars. Irving also has development plans for the near future, which include a light rail station and a new shopping center within walking distance of the school. Most students do not feel trapped at the school and feel they have plenty to do on campus with the various clubs and activities, such as music in the quad every weekend. Still, it's a good idea to own a car.

Overall, students and faculty seem impressed with their experience of the school. One professor says that the students are "hard working, respectful, and bright. I certainly do not see our students as closed-minded or set in their ways and thinking. They are, I think, truly open and unafraid. Many of them are devout Catholics, and that does provide a standard for their judgments. They are open to anything compatible with authentic Catholicism."

The fundamental agreement among Dallas students on core beliefs is an important contribution to the school's community atmosphere. "You are surrounded by kids who will enforce the school's ideas that there is truth, it can be known by man, and it is unchanging," a student says. As another student puts it, "There's always someone who has common ground with you, and it's easy to find them." However, some students have reported that it can be difficult to find a place between the conservative, homeschooled cliques and the rowdier, beer-drinking crowd.

West

The presence of the university has contributed to the development of a substantial Catholic community in the area. Students can and often do attend Mass at the beautiful Cistercian monastery nearby or the Dominican priory on campus. On campus, Mass is said twice daily at the university's ultra-modern Chapel of the Incarnation; many students attend, but there is little pressure, if any, for them to do so. It is possible to "get through UD and not learn anything about your faith," says one student. "But if you want to practice and grow in your faith there is opportunity to do so and you would never be ridiculed for it." Students seeking a more traditional liturgy should investigate the Latin Mass or Eastern Rite Catholic parishes just down the road in Irving.

ACADEMIC REQUIREMENTS

The University of Dallas has one of the most serious and enriching core curricula in the country. All students must complete the following:

- Three courses in philosophy: "Philosophy and the Ethical Life," "Philosophy of Man," and "Philosophy of Being." Here students tackle the foundational texts of Plato, Aristotle, Aquinas, Kant, Nietzsche, and Heidegger, among others.
- Four courses in English, composing the "Literary Tradition" sequence. The first course is a focused and intensive study of classic epic poetry. Students read *The Iliad*, *The Odyssey*, *The Aeneid*, *Beowulf,* and *Sir Gawain*. The second course studies the Christian epic poem: Dante, Milton, and a selection of lyric poets such as John Donne. Third is dramatic tragedy and comedy (featuring Aeschylus, Euripides, and five Shakespeare plays). The fourth is on the modern novel (including Melville, Dostoevsky, Austen, and Faulkner). Students may test out of some of these requirements.
- One elective each in math and the fine arts.
- Two electives in the sciences, one biological and one physical, with labs.
- Four set courses in civilization, two in Western and two in American. Students read primary texts, like Benjamin Franklin's *Autobiography*, Frederick Douglass's *Narrative*, and *The Education of Henry Adams*. For the Western sequence, they read, among many other texts, Thucydides' *History of the Peloponnesian War*, Boethius's *Consolation of Philosophy*, St. Thomas More's *Utopia*, John Calvin's *Institutes of the Christian Religion*, Edmund Burke's *Reflections on the Revolution in France*, Karl Marx and Friedrich Engels's *The Communist Manifesto*, and Pope Leo XIII's *Rerum Novarum*. Students may test out of some of these requirements.
- One set class in politics, with special attention to the Declaration of Independence, *The Federalist*, and *Democracy in America*.
- One set course in economics. This course has a free-market emphasis but is presented with attention to Catholic social teaching.
- Two set theology classes: an introduction to biblical scholarship, and "The Western Theological Tradition."
- Courses in a foreign language through the intermediate level.

As Catholic as UD is—about 70 percent of its undergraduates identify themselves as such—students and faculty report that non-Catholics generally feel comfortable at the school. There is little proselytizing by individuals, and none by the university itself. (Protestant worship services are available on campus.) Says one professor about non-Catholics, "those I have spoken with have expressed some surprise that no one ever approached them about becoming Catholic."

The University of Dallas takes a refreshing and productive view of the university's role in "entertaining" students. As the university handbook makes plain, the university attracts bright, imaginative, and forceful students, and the living quarters, recreational facilities, and social activities all conspire to create a proper environment for their moral and intellectual development: "The satisfaction of students is not here the aim of educational endeavor."

One teacher noted the intense student involvement in Charity Week, "a whole week of hilarious games, activities, etc. in the fall that raises tens of thousands of dollars for various charities—at the end of the week, for a fee of one dollar per student, professors get 'arrested' by their students and put in jail, and must buy their way out. Groundhog Day is the biggest party of the year. Both of these highlight what I like best about UD students—what I call 'playful seriousness and serious playfulness.' As a colleague said to me once, 'you almost never get that world-weary "whatever" from a UD student.'"

And students are involved at University of Dallas. With fifty student organizations to choose from and a very active student government, the school offers a broad variety of activities throughout the year. Those looking to strengthen their romance languages may choose French, Italian, classics, or Spanish

GREEN LIGHT

One teacher sums up the atmosphere at UD as follows: "This is a place founded on conservative and religious principles, and the practice of both is vigorous, thoughtful, and critical. We are not a 'safe little Catholic school to which to send your children,' if by that one means keeping them safe from challenging ideas. Yet all is done with a real eye to truth, respect, and decorum. Religious life is not predicated from above; in fact, students have several options and freely seek them out, and so the spiritual life of the campus often bubbles up from below, from the students themselves. Political correctness is an object of great scorn here."

In a deeply troubling move, UD responded in March 2011 to a request by the Bishop of Dallas (who faces a severe vocations shortage) and opened a program in pastoral ministry to undergrads, in the hopes of producing lay ministers who can aid priests in parishes. As noted above, the School of Ministry is home to several entrenched professors and administrators who dissent from irreformable Catholic teachings—on homosexuality, women "priests," birth control, and other issues. Students, alumni, and parents reacted strongly to the prospect of dissenting professors teaching impressionable undergraduates. "The UD School of Ministry possesses nowhere near the level of orthodoxy to form lay Catholics. It would de-form them with heresy," says one insider. Students would be wise to steer clear of the School of Ministry and its offerings, unless or until key faculty are replaced.

For the moment, however, students can still get an excellent Catholic education at UD, provided they avoid landmines like these.

clubs. Swing club and a dance team provide an outlet for the agile, while sailing, boxing, Quidditch, and Ultimate Frisbee organizations allow for athletic endeavors. The academically-minded might join the education, math, prehealth, chemistry, physics, robotics, or psychology clubs. The university also offers college Republicans and Democrats, as well as Crusaders for Life, the Preservation of Western Civilization club, Earth Service club, and Knights of Columbus. The *University News* provides a clear take on campus issues, as well as commentary on social, political, and religious matters.

Students do not generally attend UD for its sports programs, and the university retains its first commitment to education, saying, "The purpose of athletics at the University of Dallas is to provide an opportunity for students to compete in intercollegiate sports in an educationally sound environment." Still, the whole campus was in awe when the long-suffering UD basketball team made the 2004 NCAA Division III tournament for the first time in school history. Not too long ago, there was talk of starting a football team (this *is* Texas) but this idea aroused controversy by its likely expense, and was shelved. Nevertheless, the school offers thirteen NCAA Division III sports programs for those interested in playing for the Crusaders (their unofficial mascot is the Groundhogs), and in fall 2008 the University became an associate member of the North Eastern Athletic Conference. Some intramural sports are also offered, including flag football, soccer, basketball, volleyball, and softball, and they are popular. Rugby is a club sport with a good-sized student following. The school has completed a $2 million expansion of its fitness center.

All but the newest dorms are single sex, and even the new hall does not include coed floors or bathrooms. Visitation hours for members of the opposite sex are quite restricted, and students entertaining members of the opposite sex must keep the door propped open. About 60 percent of students live on campus; students are required to do so until they are twenty-one unless they are married, veterans, or living with their parents. In 2010, a new, four-story residence hall was opened to provide additional on-campus housing with private bathrooms and an underground garage for 298 sophomores and upperclassmen. Many students find off-campus housing across the street from campus; other apartments are relatively easy to find in nearby neighborhoods. While Dallas has become one of the more dangerous large cities in America, the campus is very safe. In 2009, the school reported two forcible sexual assaults and three burglaries on campus.

Undergraduate tuition in 2010–11 was $27,815, and room and board was $8,650. As at most universities, financial aid is offered in the form of loans, grants, scholarships, and work-study programs. Merit-based scholarships are available, and some 80 percent of the undergraduate population receive financial aid. The average debt of a recent grad is a moderate $23,184.

West

Gonzaga University

Spokane, Washington • www.gonzaga.edu

True to form

Founded by the Society of Jesus, Gonzaga University is no longer so tightly run by the Jesuits as it once was, but their legacy and their personal presence remain strong. A student says, "You don't always know because most of them wear regular clothes, but there are priests everywhere."

Like most other Jesuit territories in the U.S., the Jesuit Oregon Province is known for being rather theologically "progressive." But this tendency seems tempered at Gonzaga by a more conservative student body. Even the faculty, who tend leftward, seem to want to maintain the Catholic identity and traditional curriculum of the school. The long reign of academically traditionalist president Rev. Robert Spitzer, S.J. (who recently left) attracted many faithful Catholic students to Gonzaga, which helped revitalize its religious identity. Lay interim president Dr. Thane McCulloh shows no signs of wanting to change course. A recent alum says that "attending Gonzaga helped me to become my most authentic self—more of who I have always been."

Academic Life: Educating the whole person

Gonzaga's mission to "educate the whole person" revolves around its core curriculum. Whatever a student's major, it is enhanced by and integrated with courses in philosophy, theology, history, mathematics, literature, and the natural and social sciences, courses which give "a more well-rounded academic view," as one professor puts it. There is also a social justice requirement, but students who rightly shun a course in "Feminist Theologies" may instead take a philosophy class that discusses Plato and de Tocqueville. Although some students may complain about taking courses in logic and rhetoric, many admit later that these were among their most valuable.

The core program is underpinned by the faculty's emphasis on teaching over research. A longtime professor in Gonzaga's art and sciences division says, "Teaching is and always has been our main priority." While not all teachers are nationally recognized scholars, they gain respect from students by assigning them good texts and teaching them with passion.

The honors program at Gonzaga offers many amenities, such as use of a special building, Hopkins House. One student says, "The courses are of much higher quality due to the

VITAL STATISTICS

Religious affiliation: *Roman Catholic*
Total enrollment: *7,682*
Total undergraduates: *4,729*
SAT/ACT midranges: CR: *540–630*, M: *550–650*; ACT: *24–29*
Applicants: *5,026*
Applicants accepted: *78%*
Accepted applicants who enrolled: *33%*
Tuition and fees: *$30,440*
Room and board: *$8,300*
Freshman retention rate: *92%*
Graduation rate: *67% (4 yrs.)*, *81% (6 yrs.)*
Courses with fewer than 20 students: *45%*
Student-faculty ratio: *11:1*
Courses taught by graduate students: *none*
Most popular majors: *business/management, social sciences, communications*
Students living on campus: *57%*
Guaranteed housing for four years? *no*
Students in fraternities or sororities: *none*

seminar style and the quality of students discussing the topics." However, some conservative students complain that the emphasis in this program is "progressive."

Still, most teachers at Gonzaga seem to check their politics at the classroom door. Some students laud their professors as objective, while others complain that they seem "unwilling to take a stand on issues." (You can't win, can you?) As one alumnus reflects, "What I found so remarkable about the teachers is the absence of any personal self-importance." Professors seem committed primarily to students. Publishing and notoriety are less important at this school than being a good classroom teacher. Traditionally, Jesuits are trained to compare themselves not to other people but to their own ideal selves, and this virtue seems to carry over to the university's lay faculty and staff as well.

Gonzaga is experiencing a time of rapid growth and change. One teacher complains that this growth has led to the increased use of adjunct teachers, and retrenchment in the number of tenure-track positions at the university. This has undermined the "stability" of several departments and placed many teachers in the classroom who may be skilled instructors but "have no idea whatsoever of the Catholic intellectual tradition."

Moreover, these changes threaten Gonzaga's treasured spirit of community. "Alas," sighs a faculty member, "in recent years professors have become less accessible to students in person. The growth of online courses has encouraged the myth that communication is best done by e-mail." One online student concurs. "The online program was convenient, but I didn't really find professors available if I got stuck. "Gonzaga is serious about expanding its online courses," says a teacher. "The number of students enrolled in summer sessions is growing, but not the number of classrooms in use. Both administration and faculty show an interest in expanding online learning."

History, biology, communications, and philosophy are very popular majors, and many of Gonzaga's best teachers can be found in these disciplines. Highly recommended professors include Doug Kries, Bryan Clayton, Eric Schmidt, and Michael Tkacz in philosophy; Rev. Kenneth Krall in classical civilizations; Robert Carriker, Kevin O'Connor (awarded the 2010 Great Teacher prize), Rev. Michael Maher, S.J., and Eric Cunningham ("highly orthodox and immensely dedicated to his students") in history; Robert Prusch and Mia Bertagnolli in biology; Gary Uhlenkott in music; Todd Marshall in English; and Rev. Patrick Hartin in religious studies.

West

In communications, the theater program is strong, and has helped launch several students' careers in film and television.

Political science is going through a transition period after a rapid turnover of faculty, some under cloudy circumstances. (One professor changed sexes and then had the good grace to resign; another was facing a lawsuit). The department is "being forced to reinvent itself," says an insider, but "should recover in time." We are happy to note that majors must take a class in American constitutional theory.

The philosophy department is regarded as one of the best and most active in the school. Says one student: "I was surprised at how many different in-depth classes I could choose from." Faculty in this department are said to be divided politically and theologically, leaving plenty of room for students who cleave to the Catholic tradition. The philosophy department sponsors a group called the Socratic Club, in which students and professors meet to discuss a topic prepared by a professor or student.

> ## SUGGESTED CORE
>
> 1. Classics 320, *The Iliad* & *The Odyssey*
> 2. Philosophy 401, History of Ancient Philosophy
> 3. Religious Studies 105, Old and New Testament
> 4. Religious Studies 445, Church History to the Reformation
> 5. Political Science 331, Modern Political Thought
> 6. English 205/330, Studies in Shakespeare/Shakespeare
> 7. History 201, History of the U.S. I
> 8. Philosophy 412, Modern–Contemporary Philosophy

The religious studies department is said to contain a number of "progressive" theologians. One longtime teacher asserts that many members of the department "seem to sneer at the Magisterium." This is corroborated by other faculty and students, one of whom says, "Unfortunately, the worst class I have ever taken in my life was 'Catholicism,' and I have heard the same from everyone I know who has taken it." A student wishing to avoid classes like "Feminist Christian Doctrine" could find refuge in the Catholic studies concentration, where many of Gonzaga's best teachers are found.

The history major, reports a professor, is "strong in the area of writing. There are many opportunities to write, especially in upper-division classes. Student writing is seriously critiqued by professors who have published—a benefit of some of the department's recent hires." Unfortunately, study of American history before 1900 is not required of history majors. However, those who do take survey courses in Western civilization and U.S. history will find them strong, and fair-minded. Says a teacher, "They are overwhelmingly pro-Western and pro-America, but also not beat-the-drum uncritical."

English department requirements are fairly rigorous; majors must take upper-level courses in British literature both before and after 1660 and in American literature both before and after 1900. At the end of their studies, majors must also take a comprehensive exam. A course in Shakespeare is not required, but it would take some effort to avoid him.

The new Hogan Entrepreneurial Leadership Program at Gonzaga, a concentration of twenty to twenty-six credits, is open to any student majoring in business, engineering, education, or arts and sciences. The program involves a variety of co-curricular activities, including an annual business-plan competition among four area colleges, in which students invest real money and compete for more than $40,000 in prize money. To aid

West

those economics majors who wish to pursue graduate studies in the discipline, more math requirements were added to the major in 2007.

The engineering faculty are reputed to be solid, no-nonsense professors. Gonzaga's School of Engineering and Applied Science is highly rated nationally. Much of the credit for the strength of this program is due to its dean, Dennis Horn. The school is now housed in its gleaming, new "PACCAR Center for Applied Science," dubbed the university's first "green" building.

Gonzaga is widely known for its study-abroad program in Florence. Established in the 1960s, the program is described by one professor as "a jewel," albeit one that "needs polishing." Indeed, the word on campus is that many students treat the Florence program as a glorified drinking club. The new dean in charge of the Florence program is said to be aware of its reputation and determined to establish more academically rigorous classes while still allowing time for the travel and adventures that students crave. Gonzaga offers majors in French and Spanish, classical civilizations (including Latin and Ancient Greek), and minors in French, Spanish, German, and Italian. Courses in Chinese and Japanese are also available.

Student Life: Up and coming

As a general rule, students don't go to Gonzaga to be in Spokane. But if they knew more about it, they might. "Spokane is an underrated city," says an enthusiast. "It is growing quite rapidly and, while many students make jokes about Spokane and say there is nothing to do, those who are out for adventure will have no problem finding more gems than they bargained for. Spokane is full of hole-in-the-wall restaurants, cafes, and entertainment venues where the atmosphere and the people are easy to fall in love with. And Gonzaga Outdoors can hook you up with equipment and suggestions about beautiful hiking, backpacking, camping, rock climbing, and skiing and snowboarding places nearby. Another student says, "The city supports Gonzaga, and Gonzaga gives back to it as well." The city's economy (based on blue-collar work) and its surroundings (eastern Washington farmland) make Spokane a rather conservative and family-oriented community. A traditional student will not feel out of place here.

The Gonzaga campus is situated centrally in the city and adjacent to the picturesque Spokane River. A ten-minute walk along the scenic Centennial Trail leads students along the river to downtown shopping, festivals, numerous shops and cafes, a grocery store, and college hangouts like the Bulldog Bar and Starbucks. Movie theaters, shopping malls, parks, and more are within reasonable walking distance, and two major routes of the city's bus system run along Gonzaga's campus.

Gonzaga's presence and activities are a major part of Spokane's identity. In 2006, the newly refurbished Met theater downtown was renamed after alumnus and Spokane native Bing Crosby. During the basketball season, businesses and other organizations all over the city show their support.

Happily, Gonzaga students are well regarded by the local population. One storekeeper explains that he loves working in the area because "the students are so polite and friendly— a really nice addition to our community."

West

It helps that, according to one student, "one of Gonzaga's biggest focuses is social justice." Many student organizations are devoted to service projects that collaborate with townspeople. Basketball players tutor students with special needs under the Gonzaga University Special Recreation club (GUSR) while student members of the Public Relations Society of America have worked on neighborhood projects. In addition, "Gonzaga hosts several service trips including over three alternative spring-break trips and several summer programs to various locations in Africa.

Other student groups include the dancing club, Boundless; the Firm (a business club); the Right to Life club (very visible); Big Bing Theory; Black Student Union; Boxing Club; Bulldog Investment Group; Creative Gaming Club; Cycling Club; Dance Team; Dungeons and Dragons Confederation; Gonzaga Environmental Organization; Live Poets Society; Ski and Snowboard Club; and many others. There is also a vocal chapter of College Republicans. Good religious clubs, a student reports, include the Gonzaga Witness, the John Paul II Fellowship, and "a new gathering led by students along with Dr. Eric Cunningham called Catholic Conversations."

Gonzaga has been growing rapidly for the better part of a decade. Freshman enrollment has now leveled off at around 1,000 per year, and the campus (once taxed by the surging numbers) is finally ready to meet student needs. President Spitzer was a skilled fundraiser, and he improved greatly the physical size and the appearance of Gonzaga's campus. Increasing contributions from donors have allowed the school to make impressive improvements to its physical plant. Apart from the Foley Center, the school enjoys a brand-new baseball stadium and will soon offer new upper-division apartment housing. The $25 million McCarthey Athletic Center for basketball was opened in 2004, and a new performing arts center is planned.

Gonzaga offers many options for student housing, including sixteen residence halls, nine apartment complexes, and several theme houses. A number of comfy new dorms are luring more students to live on campus. One staff member notes that "there seems to be a

---

ACADEMIC REQUIREMENTS

In addition to specific degree requirements, undergraduate students must complete the following core curriculum:

- Thought and Expression, a set of three courses designed to be taken as a block in one of the semesters of an undergraduate's first year: "English Composition," "Critical Thinking," and "Speech Communication."
- Three courses in philosophy taken in sequence: "Philosophy of Human Nature," "Ethics," and one advanced elective.
- Three courses in religious studies taken in sequence: one in scriptural studies, one in Christian doctrine, and one in applied theology.
- One course in mathematics at the 100 level or above.
- One introductory course in English literature.

West

much greater student presence here now than even just five years ago." An undergraduate explains, "We hang out here a lot because everything is already here." Sodexho Marriott operates the cafeteria, which provides students an all-you-can-eat meal at each visit, as well as several cafes and snack bars around campus. "My mom came and visited and was really surprised by how good the food is," one student reports.

Single-sex and coed dorms ("dorm style" and "suite style"), on- and off-campus apartments (the new Kennedy complex is spectacular), and off-campus theme houses (eco, outdoorsy, cooking, rowing, hockey, honors, etc.) are all available. In dorms, visitation hours for the opposite sex, in theory, last from 9:00 AM to 2:00 AM. But enforcement is not a high priority and students are asked to "make their own decisions." Partying is quite common, and, as one alum recounts, "occasional huge house parties" take place off campus in which "freshman and sophomores are stuffed into a sweaty drunkfest like sardines until someone yells, 'The cops are coming' and everyone under twenty-one stumbles out of the house." Still, "after sophomore year, students get over the huge parties and find that they would rather spend a more laid back night with a small group of close friends playing beer pong or card games."

Students with literary, journalistic, and artistic interests can publish in various places, including the independent conservative Catholic newspaper the *Gonzaga Witness*; the school newspaper the *Bulletin*, which leans slightly to the left; the literary and arts magazine *Reflections*; and the small printed booklets that are circulated frequently around campus. For those more interested in other media, there is Gonzaga TV; a cable channel with live shows; and a campus radio station. It's not your average college radio station; this one plays classical music.

Gonzaga offers eight men's and eight women's sports in NCAA Division I. Men's sports include basketball, baseball, soccer, golf, tennis, cross-country, track and field, and rowing. Women's sports duplicate men's, with volleyball instead of baseball.

It is impossible to discuss Gonzaga without mentioning the basketball team, which has gone to the NCAA championships in each of the past ten years. Bulldog fever permeates the whole campus. "You can't get away from it," one student observes. And another says, "It's like the whole school is involved; everyone supports the team." Both men's and women's basketball games draw large crowds. A big part of the noise and cheering emanates from The Kennel, a student club whose main purpose is to cheer at games.

The Martin Center for Recreation and Athletics offers racquetball, basketball, and volleyball courts; an indoor running track; a swimming pool; weight room; light exercise room; dance studio; and a 4,000-seat pavilion. Students may choose from several recreation activities, such as cardio-kickboxing, fencing and even horseback riding. Gonzaga offers intramural volleyball, flag football, basketball, softball, soccer, racquetball, tennis, and Ultimate Frisbee. A variety of club sports also are offered, including rugby, ice hockey, lacrosse, martial arts, and snowboarding. *Men's Fitness* magazine recently ranked Gonzaga as one of the twenty-five most fit schools in the country.

Many students go to daily Mass in the newly refurbished student chapel in College Hall. "On Sunday," says a student, attendance is so heavy "there are often students standing in the back." New carpets and a general overhaul, including beautiful stained-glass depictions of saints, have rescued the space from its previous 1970s "decor-of-dull," as one alumna describes it. The response to the remodeling from students and faculty alike has been very positive, and more and more students are requesting to hold their weddings there. Major university Masses and academic convocations are conducted at the beautiful St. Aloysius church, a Spokane landmark dedicated in 1911. On Sundays, St. Aloysius has a healthy and visible student presence. Another new chapel was set up in the lower level of the recently built Kennedy apartment building.

The new leadership of the university's campus ministry has some students and faculty concerned. Until recently, the ministry was run by a doctrinally orthodox priest who left under pressure. One wary student says that in the wake of his departure, "I've gone to many retreats that campus ministry offers, but now I'm going to watch a little more closely and see what happens before I jump in." The school also hosts Protestant and ecumenical groups and a Protestant chaplain.

Most students feel quite safe on campus because security is always available to provide either an escort on the walk home from campus or a ride to one's apartment after dark. "When I lived off campus, if I ever felt unsafe, I would call Campus Security from campus and they would drive to right where I was and take me straight to my house," a student reports, "Most of my friends who have ever called Campus Security for anything say that they appeared at the scene before they were even off the phone." In 2009, the school reported three forcible sexual assaults, nineteen burglaries, and nine car thefts on campus.

Gonzaga is mid-priced for a private school, with 2010–11 tuition at $30,440, and room and board $8,300. Some 57 percent of students get need-based aid, and the average loan burden of a recent grad is $24,094.

New Saint Andrews College

Moscow, Idaho • www.nsa.edu

A Reformed education

Founded in 1994 as the outgrowth of a reading group at Christ Church, a Reformed congregation in Moscow, New Saint Andrews became an independent, self-sustaining institution in 2001. In 2007, the college launched its new graduate program with master's degrees in trinitarian theology and culture and classical Christian studies. It also offers a graduate certification in classical and Christian studies. The current president of the college is Dr. Roy Alden Atwood, who came to the position in 2000 after serving as dean of the college for several years. The college provides a classical education that is both intellectually rigorous and firmly grounded in the Christian tradition, immersing students in the Great Books and Calvinist theology. The college is situated within a historic town, a meeting place for farmers and tradesmen who might—like traditional liberal education itself—seem to belong to an older, almost vanished America.

Academic Life: Calvin in Moscow

New Saint Andrews holds that the liberal arts are formative of the whole person—not just the intellect. While the school is relatively young, the faculty and students see themselves within the continuum of an enduring tradition with its roots in the Middle Ages and the early Christian church.

Although students may choose from several electives during their third and fourth years, the vast majority of their classes come from the school's excellent core curriculum. Because New Saint Andrews offers only one major (with two- and four-year options) and its classes are interdisciplinary, the faculty work together without the distraction of departmental politics. As one professor explains, "Because we lack specialization, we work to strengthen our one degree."

Despite the fact that the curriculum is very structured, leaving room for few electives, the program still allows scope for individual interests. Professors report a high level of creativity and intellectual curiosity among students, which the school actively fosters. The weekly *Disputatio*, a public discussion of controversial topics attended by the entire faculty and student body, encourages questioning and debate.

During their senior year, students complete a forty-page senior thesis on an assigned question, determined by conversation between the student and his advisor, "that demands integration across the timeline and across disciplines," and must be defended before a faculty panel and a public audience. In addition, students frequently take advantage of directed studies in order to pursue interests not addressed directly by the set curriculum. One student informs us of his experience: "I think the irony of NSA's one classical liberal arts major is that it really does encourage a motivated student to pursue topics not generally addressed."

Students are not assigned advisors other than their thesis mentor in their junior and senior years, but the director of student affairs is available for counseling.

Classes at New Saint Andrews are rigorous in terms of both material and teaching style. The reading list for the bachelor's degree includes about a hundred texts that might be called Western "classics." Students cover the Western canon from the ancient Near East and classical Greece, through Augustine, Luther, St. Benedict, and Aquinas to Newton, Darwin, Nietzsche and Faulkner. The two-year course "Traditio Occidentalis" focuses most clearly on the literature, art, and philosophy of the Western world, but all the courses are concerned to some extent with these topics. One student reports, "These courses are critically respectful of Western civilization. They are careful not to make simplistic judgments either way, although the tenor is that the tradition is worth studying in depth."

Reading and writing requirements are heavy; New Saint Andrews also places a heavy emphasis on rhetoric—both prepared and impromptu. Beyond the expected discussion of readings, New Saint Andrews students often make declamations, oral presentations given before faculty and other students. Throughout their time at the school, students are also required to give weekly speeches. With the exception of some language tests, all students meet with their instructors for an oral exam at the end of each academic term.

New Saint Andrews remains small, accepting only about fifty applicants each year. The college has a self-imposed cap of 200 students, including graduate students. According to one student, "The best thing about the school is its size and community. You really do know your teachers well. The school is also tied to a local church and business community that you can't avoid being a part of, because, well, they don't have dorms. You live as part of Moscow, and are a good citizen, Christian, church member, and student. When you go to this school, you really do join a community, and not just an academic one." As the website states, "The community is our campus."

VITAL STATISTICS

Religious affiliation: *Reformed Christian*
Total enrollment: *181*
Total undergraduates: *163*
SAT/ACT midranges: CR: *560–700*, M: *480–590*; ACT: *23–28*
Applicants: *63*
Applicants accepted: *73%*
Accepted applicants who enrolled: *100%*
Tuition and fees: *$9,890*
Room and board: *$4,000*
Freshman retention rate: *92%*
Graduation rate: *52% (4 yrs.)*, *69% (6 yrs.)*
Courses with fewer than 20 students: *78%*
Student-faculty ratio: *11:1*
Courses taught by graduate students: *10%*
Most popular major: *liberal arts*
Students living on campus: *none*
Guaranteed housing for four years? *no*
Students in fraternities or sororities: *none*

Classes are taught in the tutorial style, and professors know their students. Students see this as a privilege and appreciate it: "New Saint Andrews teachers are so accessible they will actually go out of their way to meet with students." One student reports that after some personal setbacks, "I broke down crying in the hall. Mr. Josh Appel asked what the matter was, and if I wanted to talk about it. I sobbed that I probably should talk about it, and he asked, 'Well, would you want to come over for lunch with me and my wife, and discuss it then?'"

At New Saint Andrews the academic year is divided into four eight-week terms, each named after major doctrinal gatherings in Calvinist church history: the Jerusalem and Nicaea terms make up the fall semester, while the spring semester is divided into the Chalcedon and Westminster terms. A fifth term, the Dordrecht term, takes place during some summers when additional classes, such as the refresher courses in Latin, are offered.

All classes are grounded in a traditional Christian perspective of the world. One student informs us that, "you are not allowed to attend if you are not an orthodox Christian. . . . There is a lot of debate among students about how much we are supposed to approve of or reject the non-Christian aspects of the West (Greek philosophy, for example), and the faculty doesn't really push you either way too much, as long as you maintain Christian orthodoxy." One professor tells us that "the faculty are all dedicated to a very high-octane Reformed Christianity, which pervades everything we do and is really the motivation for the entire education."

The college also faces growing pains, and a shortage of professors. There are only sixteen part- and full-time faculty for undergraduates, and ten graduate faculty; and there is just one teacher in history. Other departments lament the shortage of professors as well. But these issues are simply dwarfed by the quality of what New Saint Andrews is doing, and the success which it has shown employing meager resources. The college is striving to provide an adequate faculty and keep costs low. It recently added professor David Erb in the music department. In 2010, professor Ben Merkle returned as Director of Student Affairs from his PhD studies at Oxford, and the college hired a new Director of Student Recruitment. All classes are taught by faculty except for a few Latin and Ancient Greek classes which are taught by one graduate student.

The college does not have an honors program, but it does have an optional study-abroad program in England during the summer. For two weeks, students visit numerous historical sites guided by a history professor. They cover an extensive range of English history and complete a paper on returning, receiving course credit.

Student Life: Vast, quiet fields of wheat

New Saint Andrews sits in downtown Moscow, Idaho (pop. 21,000), some ninety miles from Spokane, Washington. The area surrounding the town is agricultural, but the town offers a wide variety of cultural amenities. As the school's website boasts, "The local symphony performs just minutes from vast, quiet fields of wheat." The school's location on

West

the city's Friendship Square puts it near a weekly farmer's market and a small park that features open-air concerts and other outdoor activities. The college is also a short driving distance from sites for skiing, water sports, fishing and boating, and hiking and camping. One student adds, "Moscow has the neatest weather. Summer is breezy, balmy, blue sky. In the fall, everything turns orange. Crisp, with the smell of fireplaces. Bright orange flames against the sky. In winter it really snows; it's magical. Spring is really spring—crocuses and daffodils. It's the most beautiful place I've lived."

The college hosts an annual "Celebratio," a combination of festivities, academic events, and an open house for the school. The 2010 Celebratio ran for four days and included a writers' roundtable and C. S. Lewis seminar; dancing, soccer, and live music; college tours and the opportunity to sit in on classes; and a farmer's market, church picnic, men's theology breakfast, and science day camp.

ACADEMIC REQUIREMENTS

New Saint Andrews offers a two-year Associate of Arts and a four-year Bachelor of Arts degree in Liberal Arts and Culutre. For the Bachelor of Arts, students must complete the following very impressive core curriculum:

- "Lordship Colloquium," a yearlong, double-credit class "which introduces the world-view of historic, confessional Protestantism."
- "Principia Theologiae," likewise yearlong and double credit, which focuses on "biblical, historic, and systematic theology;" the Bible is the central text.
- "Classical Rhetoric Colloquium," a course in oratory, composition, and logic.
- "Natural History Colloquium" in biology.
- "Principia Mathematica," which studies Euclidean and non-Euclidean systems and their relation to astronomy, music, physics, and engineering, as well as the philosophical and theological issues raised by mathematics.
- "Classical Culture and History Colloquium," a systematic introduction to the Western heritage "from Near-Eastern antecedents up through modern times."
- "Traditio Occidentis Colloquia," a two-year sequence covering Greek, Roman, and medieval texts in the junior year, and modern texts in the senior year, focusing on "themes in Literature, Philosophy, Law and Politics, Art, and Architecture."
- Two years of Latin.
- Two years of Ancient Greek.
- "Music Colloquium," a class applying "Christian approaches to aesthetics," which focuses on choral singing.
- Three years of "Declamation," weekly classes where students practice rhetoric, public speaking, writing, debate, and argumentation.
- "Formal Logic," including symbolic logic and mathematical reasoning.
- "Persuasive Writing," which "applies the rigorous reasoning skills developed with symbolic logic to written argumentation and persuasive prose."
- A senior thesis of approximately forty pages.

GREEN LIGHT

Intellectual debate at New Saint Andrews is reported to be encouraged, respectful, and open. It is through open exchange that students form their beliefs. It is often the professors who try to stir up dissent in order to challenge the students. According to one teacher, "In my experience, the funny thing is, as a professor I think it's my job to create controversy. To get true learning to happen you have to spend time challenging their assumptions. I try to push students to examine things in a critical light." A student adds, "The atmosphere is certainly welcome to free and vigorous debate. NSA actively encourages it, beginning with the freshmen using mock debates in rhetoric class for the purpose of getting comfortable and feeling the liberty to openly, firmly, yet graciously speak your mind to others."

Another student reports: "Recently they had a microbiology professor from the nearby University of Idaho give a lecture. He asked the students how many had read Darwin's *Origin of Species*. All the students raised their hands. He was impressed, because at the University of Idaho they officially teach only evolution, but most students there have not read Darwin."

New Saint Andrews places a high value on integration, whether that integration is between the Christian and classical traditions, within interdisciplinary classes, or between the academic world and daily life. The school encourages students to take a lively part in the local community, and to mix both with the townsfolk and the students of nearby University of Idaho and Washington State University. To foster community engagement, to keep costs down, and "because dorms are notorious breeding grounds for immaturity, irresponsibility, and sexual sin," the college provides no student housing. Instead, students rent apartments or houses or arrange to board with families who reside near the school. The college provides students with a list of local families and professors who are willing to board students. Students speak highly of their experiences with host families: "Boarding—it's wonderful. It's really balanced. They don't act in place of parents. No curfew so long as you don't make noise. There is more stability." Some students, after becoming familiar with the school and the town, rent apartments with other students. Housing in Moscow is extremely affordable, with an average two-bedroom apartment at only $400.

The tiny school is entirely contained within a historic (late-nineteenth-century) building on the Skattaboe block of downtown Moscow. Facilities include a newly renovated student common room, the Augustine and Calvin classrooms, one seminar room, the college bookstore, administrative and faculty offices, two conference rooms, and the Tyndale library—which contains a small collection, supplemented by the libraries at the University of Idaho and Washington State University, where New Saint Andrews students have borrowing privileges.

The Code of Student Conduct reflects the Reformed Christian background of the school. Students are required to "pledge in writing their commitment to personal holiness, sound doctrine, cultural reformation, and academic integrity." This means, in practice, that everyone at the school belongs to some variety of Protestant church and tries to live by the tenets of traditional Christian morality. The college catalog gets pretty specific about the school's expectations: "Students should exercise their Christian liberties not as an occasion to indulge the flesh, but to serve others out of love through the wise and moderate exercise of their liberty (Gal. 5:13–14; 1 Peter 2:13–16). By God's grace and through the church's instruction and discipline, students should abstain from the works of the flesh, such as sexual immorality, idolatry, hatred, discord, jealousy, wrath, selfish ambition, drunkenness, or debauchery, and to flee all temptations to those sins (Gal. 5:19-21, 24, 26; Eph. 5:3-7)."

Furthermore, students are expected "to participate cautiously and critically in our predominantly pagan popular culture, and to avoid and to repudiate the culturally destructive (but often 'socially acceptable') glorification of sin found in contemporary films, music, video games, websites, and so forth."

Attendance at all seminars, recitations, and *Disputatios* is required, and modest, professional dress is expected at all classes and school activities. One student tells us that "all students who complete thirty credits in their first year must wear academic robes to events open to the public, including the *Disputatio*, with speakers such as city council candidates or prospective faculty members."

Student organizations vary from year to year and include Students for the Relief of the Oppressed, City League Basketball, writers' club, poetry club, Greek club, Latin club, and club rugby. There are no varsity sports, which the school believes to be a waste of money and a distraction from studies; but student-organized intramural sports are encouraged, including rugby, volleyball, softball, and basketball. The college also has a tradition of an end-of-the-year football game between the upperclassmen and the freshmen and faculty.

The entire city of Moscow (which includes the campus) reported in 2009 one murder, twelve rapes, one robbery, eleven assaults, seventy-nine burglaries, eighteen stolen cars and two arsons. The school is considered a very safe place.

New Saint Andrews maintains its freedom from federal micromanagement by refusing government aid—either for the school or for students. Nevertheless, the school strives to keep the cost of a private college education manageable; 2010–11 tuition was a modest $9,890. Room and board are estimated at $4,000. NSA also offers students the opportunity to lock in current tuition rates for up to five years.

Occidental College

Los Angeles, California • www.oxy.edu

Oxy-genesis

Occidental College (nicknamed "Oxy") was incorporated as a Presbyterian school in 1887. It grew quickly, and became an independent, secular school in 1910. Today, it is a fully developed college with ample resources and a national reputation—recently boosted by the fact that President Obama attended Occidental for two years and credits the college with awakening his political consciousness. Oxy combines the charm and human scale of a small college with the advantages of a great city. It is possible for students to receive an excellent liberal arts education by carefully picking the right courses; but it requires immersion in an almost exclusively liberal community that is largely intolerant.

Academic Life: Substance and Occident

Occidental offers thirty departmental majors and nine interdepartmental majors (such as cognitive science, American studies, diplomacy and world affairs, and biochemistry). In 2010, three new majors were added: Chinese studies, Japanese studies, and East Asian studies. Students at Occidental can choose a major (with or without a minor), a double major, or an "Independent Pattern of Studies," which is "an interdisciplinary study in areas where the college does not have a defined program."

Students must complete the school's optimistically named Core Program by the end of their junior year.

The Core Program begins with writing seminars and colloquia in "cultural studies" during the freshman year. Small groups of students meet with a single faculty member to explore a particular topic through lectures, reading, discussion and intensive writing. The quality of these seminars is hit-and-miss, depending upon individual professors. One student complains, "They're supposed to be interdisciplinary, but a lot of times, the professor is just there to boost his own program." The idiosyncratic objectives of professors also determine the content of these courses. Courses from the 2010–11 year ranged from "The Russian Experience" to "Gay Rights in the Era of Obama and Google."

Occidental's distribution requirements for the humanities and fine arts lack focus. A student must take three to five courses, chosen from approximately 340 courses in the humanities, social sciences, and fine arts—everything from "Race and its Discontents" and

West

"The Bible as Literature" to "Great Migrations: Immigration to the United States Since the Civil War" and "Early Christian and Medieval Art." The only guidance is geographical. Excepting courses in studio art, music, and theater, all courses fall into six cultural groups: Africa and the Middle East; Central, South and East Asia; Europe; Latin America; the United States; and "Intercultural." A student must take at least one course from three of these six groups, as well as one course in fine arts and one course "focused on the pre-1800s."

One can construct a solid Western liberal arts core curriculum from these choices, especially from the Europe, United States, and Intercultural group areas. Some course offerings in this vein are "Restoration and Eighteenth Century British Literature," "Introduction to Philosophy," "Judaism as a Religious Civilization," "Chaucer," "Constitutional Law," and three semesters of "European Political Thought," covering thinkers such as Plato, Augustine, Aquinas, Machiavelli, Hobbes, Marx, and Nietzsche. There are also a number of art history and music courses in the Core Program that will ground a student in the Western tradition of art.

Students are assigned faculty advisors in their first year, and an advisor in their field when they declare a major. They are also assigned to an Advising Center, which works closely with students, especially freshmen and sophomores, to help with basic problems like registration as well as to help students find faculty who can advise them on their specific interests. All classes are taught by faculty, not by teaching assistants.

There are also certain majors that make it easier to get a traditional liberal arts education. History, politics, philosophy, and religious studies majors can simultaneously satisfy Core Program and major requirements by taking courses in foundational texts and thinkers. This is especially true, however, of the English and Comparative Literary Studies (ECLS) department, which offers a number of courses in classical, medieval, Renaissance, and seventeenth and eighteenth-century literature. As one student reports: "I wanted to study the Western canon, and that's why I chose a major in ECLS."

Students unanimously praise professors' accessibility. "They're always available." "They're really good about office hours." "Whenever you have some question or something you want to pursue, they're ready to help." Every department goes out of its way to provide undergraduates with the opportunity to collaborate with professors, or to conduct their own independent research—sometimes on a graduate-school level. The high point of this

VITAL STATISTICS

Religious affiliation: *none*
Total enrollment: *1,989*
Total undergraduates: *1,972*
SAT/ACT midranges: CR: *600–700*, M: *600–680*; ACT: *28–32*
Applicants: *6,013*
Applicants accepted: *43%*
Accepted applicants who enrolled: *22%*
Tuition and fees: *$39,870*
Room and board: *$11,360*
Freshman retention rate: *91%*
Graduation rate: *77% (4 yrs.)*, *87% (6 yrs.)*
Courses with fewer than 20 students: *66%*
Student-faculty ratio: *10:1*
Courses taught by graduate students: *none*
Most popular majors: *psychology, economics, diplomacy and world affairs*
Students living on campus: *77%*
Guaranteed housing for four years? *yes*
Students in fraternities: *15%* in sororities: *15%*

SUGGESTED CORE

1. English 300, Survey of Ancient Greek Literature
2. Philosophy 205, Introduction to Ancient Thought
3. Religious Studies 130/175, Judaism as a Religious Civilization/The World of the New Testament, or English 309, The Bible as Literature and Philosophy
4. Religious Studies 190, History of Early Christianity (closest match)
5. Politics 252, European Political Thought: From Hobbes to Marx
6. English 320, Shakespeare
7. History 101, United States Culture and Society I
8. Philosophy 312, Nineteenth-Century German Philosophy (closest match)

is the Summer Undergraduate Research Program. Each summer, qualifying students receive full stipends to pursue summer-long research projects. Students also can take advantage of the Richter Scholars Program, which allows students to go anywhere in the world to study any subject they wish—even if it's not in their major (e.g., a chemistry student can do a project in music).

Student evaluations of teachers play a significant role in tenure decisions. According to one professor, "Oxy places greater value on teaching than research; however, they provide great research support for a liberal arts college.... I made the move to Occidental College because I think teaching is of the utmost importance, but I wanted to be at a place that also valued research and professional development."

Some of the professors mentioned as especially outstanding are Peter Dreier, Roger Boesche and Larry Caldwell in politics; Maryanne Horowitz and Wellington Chan in history; Jurgen Pelzer in German studies; Katie Mills in English/writing; Kory Schaff and Marcia Homiak in philosophy; Kerry Thompson in biology; Giorgio Secondi and Woody Studenmund in economics; and Martha Ronk and Damian Stocking in English; and Tamas Lengyel in mathematics.

Occidental is one of the very few liberal arts colleges that offers a program in diplomacy. Majors in diplomacy and world affairs (DWA) take courses in international relations and in economics, history, religious studies, and other departments. The Occidental at the United Nations Program offers students academic seminars while they intern with the U.N. Secretariat, the U.S. mission, or other affiliated institutions. Even on the Los Angeles campus, DWA majors study under former diplomats, such as Clinton administration official Derek Shearer.

The economics department also has a strong reputation and is politically the most moderate of the social science departments at Oxy. The faculty represents the full range of mainstream economic thinking, and it tends to emphasize the positive functions of markets. In general, the economics department stresses the practical application of economic theory, both in public policy and in business. Prospective CFOs can participate in the Blyth Fund, a program in which economics majors decide how to invest a portion of Occidental's funds. Occidental's location in Los Angeles also provides a number of corporate student internships.

Los Angeles appears in a very different light in the urban and environmental policy department—an interdisciplinary, left-leaning program working with organizations such as Occidental's own Migration Policy and Research Center, using Los Angeles as a political laboratory.

The history program provides a number of in-depth courses in American, European, Asian, African and Middle Eastern, and Latin American history. Majors are required

West

to take three classes from three of the above categories, as well as one course that covers the "premodern period." Up to three other course requirements may be filled by select classes from other disciplines. The department's faculty have won an impressive number of national awards and fellowships, such as the Guggenheim, Fulbright, and NEH awards. On the whole, history courses present balanced, diverse perspectives. One student writes, "They usually offer multiple ways to view the subjects in question." The American history courses, however, place a heavy emphasis on gender studies, and the American studies program emphasizes multicultural and racial issues. "It was all about race; I didn't think I was getting American history," says one student.

The politics department is even more polarized. The department covers a broad range of topics, with a heavy emphasis on political theory (including excellent seminars on thinkers such as Plato and Tocqueville) and on post-Communist societies. Requirements for the major include only one class in "American Politics and Public Policy," which also serves as the generic introduction to politics course. In some classes the political climate can be intimidating. "Many politics classes are pretty hard on conservative students," writes one student, who says that "far left bias helped dissuade me from majoring in politics. Some professors . . . are more balanced, but in general, because of the school's political atmosphere, the students in those classes turn any political argument into a shouting match with those right-of-center." On the other hand, the department has offered a course titled "Conservative and Libertarian Political Philosophy," and Professor Larry Caldwell, a distinguished expert on Soviet and Russian politics, serves as a faculty advisor for the Occidental College Libertarian Society.

One department at Oxy, however, is hostile territory for any non-leftist student: "critical theory and social justice," which actually replaced the anthropology department, shut down in 2005. CTSJ not only offers relatively "conventional" courses such as "Women of Color" and "Critical Theories of Sexuality," but also "The Phallus" ("Topics include . . . the lesbian phallus, the Jewish phallus, the Latino phallus") and "Stupidity" ("the double of intelligence rather than its opposite").

Occidental's administration seems obsessed with the secular religion of antiracism. Almost every humanities program has courses on race. (Ironically, a recent incoming freshmen class consisted of 42 percent nonwhite students, yet anxieties persist.) A 2010 discussion panel, "Integrating Oxy: Reevaluating our 'Commitment' to Diversity," led to an emotional discussion in which students lamented the "decline" of diversity at Oxy and claimed that minorities were admitted only as "puppets." One professor (not a conservative) comments, "Oxy is saturated with the ongoing discussions on diversity. There's a lack of proportion. Student body and faculty mirror diversity requirements, so why are we still talking about it?"

The religious studies major has no specific course requirements; it advertises a highly personalized course path to be determined in close collaboration with the advisor. The courses available, however, sound surprisingly balanced, comprehensive, and solid, ranging from "Sufism" and "History of Early Christianity" to "Religion and the United States Supreme Court" and "Contemporary Islam."

Oxy has an exceptionally good program in mathematics and the physical sciences. Los Angeles occupies some of the most interesting geological territory in the world, with a wide variety of landscapes formed by the proximity of so many tectonic faults. The geology department takes advantage of its site with field research in geological history. The physics department also offers excellent opportunities for scientific exploration. Physics students can do research projects as early as their freshman year, as independent studies or in close collaboration with faculty. In one memorable example, students worked closely with Professor Daniel Snowden-Ifft in designing a unique kind of dark matter detector, ingeniously constructed with materials largely bought at a hardware store. (In fact, he credits them primarily for coming up with the design).

Occidental also offers a number of programs in the fine arts. The music department is especially strong. It has an exceptionally dedicated faculty who teach all aspects of music, from music composition and theory to vocal and instrumental performance.

Occidental offers study-abroad programs in Morocco, Turkey, Jordan, Senegal, Ghana, Tanzania, South Africa, China, India, Japan, Taiwan, Hong Kong, Thailand, Australia, New Zealand, Russia, Greece, Italy, Hungary, Austria, France, Spain, Germany, the Netherlands, Czech Republic, England, Dominican Republic, Nicaragua, Brazil, Chile, and Argentina. Courses are offered in Arabic, Italian, Mandarin, Japanese, French, German, Russian, Spanish, Latin, and Ancient Greek, and student housing includes a Spanish-, French-, and German-themed Language and Culture Hall.

Student life: Intimate newness

One of the strongest impressions Occidental College makes on a visitor is the deep love and loyalty of Oxy students for their school. Occidental students are generally effusive in their praise. "I really love it here!" "This is such an awesome place—the campus, the classes, the people." Significantly, recent conservative and libertarian alumni generally praise Occidental. One newly minted alumnus writes: "I would tell any high school student to consider Oxy if they were looking at a small liberal arts college in a big city." "The campus is really gorgeous, the way the light plays," says one graduate. Another pointed to "many friendly, family-like friendships" with professors who "are accessible and willing to help. Most of them live close by or bike here. . . . They like to get into students' lives."

Given the age of the school and the vigor of school spirit, there are surprisingly very few traditions at Oxy. Everyone gets tossed in Gilman Fountain on his birthday. "O Week" (short for "orientation week") at the beginning of freshman year, consists of carnivals, movies, and dances. It is extremely easy to get around. One can cross the whole campus in less than fifteen minutes.

Occidental is an NCAA Division III school, meaning that there are no athletic scholarships. All athletes are students first. Nevertheless, interest in intramural and intercollegiate sports is high at Oxy, especially football. The Occidental-Pomona rivalry is one of the oldest in southern California. There are ten men's varsity teams and eleven women's varsity teams, and the mascot is Oswald the Tiger. Men's soccer is ranked first in the Southern California Intercollegiate Athletic Conference, and men's water polo and baseball and women's volleyball are ranked second. Women's water polo is ranked second in its NCAA division. There are also hundreds of intramural sports and seven club sports, such as rugby, lacrosse, Ultimate Frisbee, and crew. In 2010 the college added a new fitness center.

West

Some 77 percent of students live on campus, as they're required to for the first three years. About 15 percent live in sororities or fraternities—there are four of each, as well as one "coed fraternity." The surrounding Eagle Rock area provides many affordable, pleasant, and safe housing opportunities for single or group rentals. On-campus housing consists of thirteen student-run, coed residence halls (excepting Berkus House, which is all female), each with no more than 155 students; the exception is the newest hall, built in 2008, which houses 273. Most of the halls are single-sex by floor, wing, or suite. All dorms are described as fairly comfortable. "The dorm rooms are really huge," says a student. Nevertheless, the rooms allow for intimacy—a bit too much, some say: There are no visitation rules limiting overnight stays between the sexes.

The Residence Hall Association provides funds for residence hall weekly "spreads" or food parties, as well as seasonal events, dances and parties, and various incidentals, from replacement light bulbs to trips to the L.A. Philharmonic. "There are a lot of theme-based dances, a lot of things to do on campus," says a student, who notes that wild parties are rare. "A lot of parties are just students in rooms, doing some drinking." Some students complain that they have to go to student houses near USC or UCLA for "college life." Drugs do not seem to be more of a problem at Occidental than at other secular colleges. "Drugs aren't a big deal [here]," says one Oxy College Republican.

According to one student, "Oxy has a fairly strong religious community." The school hosts a (Catholic) Newman center, a Protestant fellowship, and several other Christian groups,

---

ACADEMIC REQUIREMENTS

Occidental has no core curriculum. In addition to the requirements in their major, all students must complete:

- Two seminars in cultural studies during freshman year. Choices range widely from the traditional ("Existentialism") to the politically charged ("U.S. Racial Politics and Collective Memories of Slavery").
- Tests with passing scores on two writing proficiency exams.
- Three courses in cultural studies covering three different groupings from the categories of Africa and the Middle East; South, Central, and East Asia; Europe; Latin America; the United States; and "Intercultural" courses. In theory, a student could avoid all study of the U.S. or Europe. Courses range from "Soviet Dissident Culture" and "Nineteenth-Century German Philosophy" to "Machos: Forms of Latin American Manliness" and "Queer Los Angeles."
- One course treating the pre–1800 era (choices are almost all straightforward, from "The Bible as Literature and Philosophy" to "Classical Chinese Thoughts and Sayings") and one treating fine arts (choices range from "Michelangelo" to "Topics in Digital Culture")—or participation in performance or other fine arts courses (e.g., Glee Club, orchestra, dance performance).
- Three courses in science and mathematics, with at least one lab science. Choices range from "Formal Logic" to "Evolutionary Psychology."
- Courses or tests to show first-year proficiency in a foreign language.

RED LIGHT

Politically, Oxy is extremely homogenous. Students repeatedly report that the few conservatives on campus are too afraid of confrontation to speak up in class and defend their views. In 2008, the school's Republican club disappeared, after gradually shrinking to only one member—a registered Democrat, who joined the club in order to promote political dialogue and diversity. The club's last member reports: "I'm sure there are plenty of people who would want to take centrist, or center-right, or conservative positions in classroom discussions, but simply can't because doing so exposes you to overwhelming criticism, both intellectually and personally." A conservative student says, "If someone brings up an alternate belief that is against the mindset of this campus, they're labeled very quickly as a villain and verbally attacked. "While some students and faculty members are devoted to widening political diversity on campus, they seem to be an ineffective minority.

A 2009 incident further illustrates the student body's hostility to political diversity. When Hillel members put up pro-Israel posters, according to a letter to the editor of the student newspaper, several of them were "verbally attacked and mocked" and the posters were defaced.

as well as a Hillel chapter, a Latter-Day Saints club, and Buddhist meditation and yoga groups.

Other student organizations include Women in Science, the Occidental Entrepeneurial Society, Future Business Leaders, Dance Team, Quidditch, Chinese Culture Club, Occidental Film Club, Women!, Queer-Straight Alliance, Circus and Acrobatics Club, Student Labor Action Coalition, Colleges Against Cancer, and the Occidental College Folk and Historical Dancers, as well as a glee club, orchestra, and jazz ensemble, several student newspapers, and a radio station.

The "Bengal Bus" provides several runs a week to Pasadena, Glendale, and Eagle Rock, and the new "Zip Car" may be reserved for off-campus trips as well, enabling students without cars to have full access to shopping and entertainment. Occidental is located in the hip Los Angeles suburb of Eagle Rock (pop. 34,466), but there are numerous trips to nearby attractions in L.A. and elsewhere sponsored by the residence halls and student organizations. Chinatown, Dodger Stadium, the Descanso Gardens and bird sanctuary, comedy club The Ice House, and several museums are less than fifteen minutes from campus; Disneyland, Universal Studios, and the beach are less than an hour.

Despite its urban location (Occidental's neighborhood is bordered by Glendale, Pasadena, and Highland Park), the school sees relatively little crime. In 2009 the school had four forcible sex assaults and four burglaries on campus. Occidental initiated a campus closure plan which dramatically reduced on-campus crime. Residence halls are locked twenty-four hours a day, and campus police are always on patrol. Safety escorts are provided, and in 2008 the college installed a campus-wide emergency siren alert as well as a system of alerting students by cell phone and e-mail. Students are also issued whistles to blow in case of emergency.

Occidental has nearly as much to offer as some of the Ivy schools—and its tuition reflects that fact. Students paid $39,870 in 2010–11, with room and board coming in at $11,360. Over 75 percent of students receive some sort of financial aid, over 70 percent of which is need-based—which must be fairly generous, since the average loan debt of a recent grad was a moderate $21,000.

West

Pepperdine University

Malibu, California • www.pepperdine.edu

Beach Boys for Jesus

Founded in 1937 by Christian entrepreneur George Pepperdine and affiliated with the United Churches of Christ, Pepperdine University remains remarkably true to the aspirations of its founder. Its brand of higher education is essentially aimed at cultivating a pragmatic—rather than intellectual—graduate who embraces Christian values, is conservative in disposition, and is poised for a life of leadership and purpose. Pepperdine brings together a relatively sound liberal arts curriculum, a religious orientation, and a warm, friendly atmosphere situated in one of most beautiful campuses of the United States.

Academic Life: Preprofessional, plus a core

Pepperdine's interdisciplinary curriculum with a small core is much better than most. Its three-course core sequence, "Western Heritage," takes students briskly from 30,000 BC up through the present. By adding a few courses, a student can construct a traditional liberal arts education, especially through the school's Great Books Colloquium. In it, students will find support from a serious and accomplished faculty, small classes, ample opportunities for close instruction, and an emphasis on teaching, rather than research. The colloquium has some of Pepperdine's "most engaging scholars," says one professor, and there are often fewer than ten students in each class, meaning students can develop a good working relationship with a professor. One professor says, "If a student wishes to get a solid liberal arts education at Pepperdine he or she must be involved in the Great Books program."

Every student is assigned an advisor from the Academic Advising Center and a first-year seminar advisor—or major advisor, if he has chosen one. The Career Center and Academic Advising Center provides additional assistance.

Pepperdine's small undergraduate population in Seaver College makes it fairly easy to get to know professors. "If you are a motivated student and you find professors with whom you hit it off," a professor says, "you can do a lot of one-on-one." Says a student, "The faculty members are extremely accessible. I really feel spoiled. All my teachers know my first name."

Professors are primarily teachers, not researchers. Graduate students do not teach classes. While research is valued, two out of the four standards used to determine tenure

VITAL STATISTICS

Religious affiliation: *Church of Christ*

Total enrollment: *7,733*

Total undergraduates: *3,439*

SAT/ACT midranges: CR: *550–660*, M: *560–680*; ACT: *26–30*

Applicants: *5,605*

Applicants accepted: *47%*

Accepted applicants who enrolled: *29%*

Tuition and fees: *$38,960*

Room and board: *$11,390*

Freshman retention rate: *90%*

Graduation rate: *73% (4 yrs.), 80% (6 yrs.)*

Courses with fewer than 20 students: *65%*

Student-faculty ratio: *14:1*

Courses taught by graduate students: *none*

Most popular majors: *business, communications, social sciences*

Students living on campus: *58%*

Guaranteed housing for four years? *no*

Students in fraternities: *18%* in sororities: *31%*

and promotion have to do with teaching. "Here at Pepperdine, teaching is the priority," a faculty member says. "Teaching is still the primary responsibility," another confirms.

Only a few courses—primarily in religion and the humanities—are taught in large lecture halls. Most courses at Seaver College are quite small.

Pepperdine University comprises Seaver College (for undergraduates); the School of Law; the George L. Graziadio School of Business and Management; the Graduate School of Education and Psychology; and the School of Public Policy, which opened in 1997. Pepperdine is well known for its programs in business administration and sports medicine, and it offers a sound economics program as well. Students may also pursue a BA through the Center for International Studies and Languages, with concentrations offered in Asian studies, international management, European studies, political studies, and Latin American studies. Less popular divisions at Seaver are natural science (a BA designed for students who intend to enter the dual-degree 3/2 engineering program), religion, and art.

Several faculty named philosophy as one of the weaker departments, with one suggesting that the discipline is almost ignored. Pepperdine largely regards philosophy as "integrated into other fields," as one professor put it. Required courses include "Introduction to Philosophy," "Logic," "Ancient Philosophy," "Modern Philosophy," "Ethics," and a "Major Philosophical Problems Seminar."

Speech restrictions and classroom politics are generally not an issue at Pepperdine. In September 2010, Pepperdine's College Libertarians sponsored a "free-speech wall" in honor of Free Speech Week at the university. The wall contained comments and statements by fellow students, which one undergraduate complains was filled with "racist and sexist" stuff—while another said that though she did not agree with certain comments, she would "still protect your right to say them." The paper wall was torn down by a lone protestor who disagreed.

The English department at Pepperdine offers three concentrations: writing, literature, and education, with different requirements. The literature focus prescribes ten courses: one introductory class; three in British lit (one of which must be pre-1800 and another post-1800); two American lit courses; a literary theory course; two electives (one designated as multicultural); and one senior seminar.

West

The major in history requires, among other things, "History of the American Peoples" "from precolonial times to the present" (two courses); "The American People and Politics"; an introduction to research; historiography; and a senior thesis. Students may concentrate on American, European, or global history.

Political science is divided into five subfields: methodology, political theory, American government and politics, international relations, and comparative government. All political science majors must take "The American People and Politics," one introductory course in four of the five fields, a research methods course, and a writing-intensive course.

Pepperdine does not demand much in math and the sciences. Only one course in mathematics (six choices) and one course in laboratory science (twelve choices, for example a biology lab course) are required of most students. Pepperdine's religion requirements are condensed into one three-course sequence titled "Christianity and Culture," in which students are introduced to the "world and literature of the Bible and considers its continuing cultural effects."

There are a number of truly outstanding professors at Pepperdine—although many, including Ted McAllister and James Q. Wilson in the School of Public Policy—generally do not teach undergraduate courses. Some of the best undergraduate faculty at Pepperdine include Ronald W. Batchelder in economics; Michael G. Ditmore in English; Paul Contino, Michael Gose, and Donald Marshall in Great Books; Don Thompson in mathematics; J. Christopher Soper in political science; and Ronald C. Highfield in religion.

Students can participate in one of Pepperdine's many international study programs. Seaver College offers six year-round residential programs in Florence, Heidelberg, Lausanne, London, Buenos Aires, Chiang Mai and Shanghai, along with summer programs in these countries as well as in Spain, East Africa, Russia, Fiji, Scotland and other locations.

Seaver College requires its students to take one language course in Chinese, French, German, Italian, Japan, Spanish, Ancient Greek, or Hebrew, and offers majors in French, German, Italian, and Spanish.

SUGGESTED CORE

1. Great Books Colloquium I
2. Philosophy 300, Ancient Philosophy
3. Religion 101/102, The History and Religion of Israel/The History and Religion of Early Christianity
4. Religion 531, Christian History and Theology I: Ancient and Medieval
5. Great Books Colloquium III
6. Great Books Colloquium II
7. History 520/521/522, Colonial America, 1492–1763/The American Revolution and the New Nation, 1763–1815/Jacksonian America and the Civil War, 1815–1877
8. Great Books Colloquium IV

Student Life: Riding the wave

Pepperdine has one of the most beautiful campuses in the nation. Located about thirty minutes from Los Angeles in Malibu, the school overlooks the beach. A student says, "the Malibu campus feel insular. Besides the ocean and beautiful beaches, there is not much activity in the vicinity. Malibu is a hideout for stars, and is prone to quietude and privacy."

West

Los Angeles is theoretically thirty minutes away (when there is no traffic—ha!) and is easily accessed via the Pacific Coast Highway. Of course, it provides all of the attractions and vices of a world-class city. Santa Barbara is two hours away. Santa Monica offers the Third Street Promenade, whose stores, shops, and restaurants are popular among students. In Malibu, there are many "destination" restaurants and stores frequented by college students.

The university, as one faculty member says, has no "town-gown relationship." For one thing, there's not much of a town; students have to drive most anywhere they want to go off campus. But Pepperdine offers many activities to keep students occupied—perhaps more than it should. "Sometimes there are too many social distractions, along with the beach, which keep students from studying," says one professor.

Pepperdine lists more than seventy registered student organizations in addition to a national Greek system of seven sororities and five fraternities. Examples include the Model U.N., Military Service Club, Dance Team, and Art History Society. Other clubs include the Black Student Association, Latino Student Association, and the Asian Student Association. Pepperdine operates TV-32 and KWVS FM 101.5. The Student Journalism Program produces a weekly printed newspaper, the *Graphic*; an online newspaper, the *Online Graphic*; and a biannual news magazine, *Currents*. Musicians join the University Concert Choir, the Flora Thornton Opera Program, the fall musical, the University Orchestra, Collegium Musicum, and the Instrumental Chamber Ensembles. The Young Democrats, College Libertarians and College Republicans are active on campus, though the student body leans Republican.

Housing at Pepperdine is limited, but freshmen and sophomores under twenty-one and not living with their parents must live on campus. Seaver College provides on-campus housing for approximately 1,900 unmarried students. The school imposes some rules—no alcohol, no firearms, no candles, no pets, no smoking in dorms, and no one from the opposite sex in your living area except during specified hours. As students share their accommodation with a roommate, they are also requested to keep guests to a minimum.

Pepperdine's religious commitment draws many of its students, and Pepperdine expects its students to pursue religious interests. Even so, one student says, "the relative conservatism of the student body is not evident in the way the girls dress. I have never seen such short skirts in my life." The college strongly encourages students to join a church, and it offers Seaver-wide worship assemblies, devotionals, small-group Bible studies, student-led ministries, monthly missions meetings, and an on-campus ministry (University Church of Christ). The University Church of Christ holds Bible study groups and conducts services on Sunday mornings. "Collide," a student-run devotional group, also meets every Wednesday. Besides these, there are a number of small groups that meet on campus. One professor says that there is a "healthy mix between the devout and the not-so-devout" among Pepperdine students. For Catholics, the rather liberal Our Lady of Malibu parish is close by.

Pepperdine's convocations, of which students must attend fourteen per term, "are usually religious, sometimes political, and [the latter] always liberal in nature," according to a student. "If there are conservative speakers, they never talk about politics, only religion."

Pepperdine University is a member of the West Coast Conference, the Mountain Pacific Sports Confederation, and Division I of the National Collegiate Athletic Association.

West

Pepperdine has a number of competitive athletic programs. The Waves are well known in water polo, tennis, and volleyball circles, and field teams; other varsity sports include golf, cross-country, basketball, baseball, track, soccer, swimming, and diving. There are also many club and intramural sports, and of course, team-watching is a popular activity. "The homecoming basketball game is huge—everyone from the school goes, packing the Firestone Fieldhouse, and the camaraderie is amazing," a student says. Among the intramural sports are volleyball, beach volleyball, soccer, and dodgeball. Pepperdine's club teams include an equestrian, a surfing and a triathlon club.

Pepperdine has twenty-two suite-style residence halls, which are designated either "Freshmen Only" or "Standard." The latter are open to all class levels, but usually house

---

ACADEMIC REQUIREMENTS

Pepperdine students face both core classes and certain gen ed requirements. All students must complete:

- "First-Year Seminar," in which students are introduced "to both the college experience and to academic inquiry."
- "English Composition."
- "Junior Writing Portfolio." Students submit graded papers, "accompanied by a detailed summary of each assignment," and "articulate and reflect on their writing process [and] strengths and weaknesses."
- "Speech and Rhetoric."
- A three-course sequence in Christianity and Culture, compiled from five class options. The most common combination is REL 101, a course on "the theological and religious dynamics of the Old Testament"; REL 102, "a study of the New Testament in its larger Jewish and Greco-Roman context"; and REL 301, a course in which "students study the ways in which Christianity shapes aspects of culture and ways in which these, in turn, influence Christian life and faith."
- A three-course sequence in "Western Heritage," from the prehistoric age to the present.
- A two-course sequence in the "American Experience."
- One math course, such as "The Nature of Mathematics" or "Introductory Statistics."
- One course that is designated as writing-intensive.
- A research methods/presentation skills class within their major.
- A foreign language course.
- A non-Western cultures course, such as "Traditional Chinese Thought and Society" or "Contemporary African Politics."
- One fine arts class, such as "Three-dimensional Drawing," "Greek and Roman Art," "Introduction to Music," or "Stage Make-Up."
- One course in literature, such as "Literary Study" or "British Literature."
- One laboratory science, such as "Introduction to Marine Biology" or "Physics" I.
- One class in human institutions and behavior, such as "Economic Principles," "Introduction to Psychology," or "Introduction to Sociology."

GREEN LIGHT

Pepperdine is a politically balanced university, and while there may be some slight variation in the atmosphere of some classes, from center-left to center-right, conservative as well as more liberal students should feel at home here. True to the vision of George Pepperdine, the school has integrated religion and religious themes into its curriculum and teaching, but this ethos comes naturally here. As one professor says, "The undergraduate and graduate faculty take faith seriously. Pepperdine has an active Christian worldview, which is both optimistic and highly affirming." Another teacher suggests that Pepperdine is "one of very few schools where the Christian emphasis has actually increased over the last twenty years." Perhaps the most serious challenge to the vision of Christian education at Pepperdine is the business ethos that prevails at the school, which diverts resources away from the teaching of subjects that appear to have few eventual vocational possibilities, such as philosophy.

only freshmen and sophomores. Each hall contains a double bathroom, a common living area, and four double bedrooms. The suites are clustered six to a hall surrounding a main lobby with a fireplace, television, and laundry room. The Rockwell Towers Residence Hall is reserved for 275 sophomores and upperclassmen; it has two wings for men and four for women, separated by the main entrance and lounge. The tower has double rooms, and each pair of doubles shares a bathroom.

The Lovernich Residential Complex houses nearly 300 students, all over the age of twenty-one. The complex is comprised of three blocks that overlook a landscaped courtyard. The blocks' apartments are made up of two bedrooms, one bathroom, a living area, and a kitchen, although two students share each bedroom. Apartments are designated for both men and women. However, an apartment housing male students may be located next to one housing female students (though they will not have access to each other's apartments). Each block also contains a common living area.

Located in Pepperdine's residential community is a twenty-four-hour recreational facility, the Howard A. White Center, where students may play table tennis, watch a big-screen television, or surf the Net at any hour. There are also various fitness centers and gyms (including the Firestone Fieldhouse, a 3,500-seat gymnasium, and weight and fitness center), a Tennis Pavilion, and an Olympic-size pool.

Located in the Tyler Campus Center, and with a panoramic view of the ocean, Wave's Café represents a "state-of-the-art platform dining concept," boasting "restaurant-quality food," four "entrée stations," and a salad bar. If students want a more casual experience, Oasis is right next door, and serves deli food, pizza, fruit, and cappuccino smoothies. There are also several cafes on campus, selling everything from mochas and cappuccinos to bread and other bakery items.

Pepperdine also hosts around 250 public-arts and musical events each year. The fine arts department has a number of performing ensembles—including a chamber music ensemble, jazz band, guitar ensemble, and wind instrument ensemble—and students may catch their performances at the college's intimate theaters. Equipped with a three-manual Rogers organ, and acoustically redesigned in 2004, Stauffer Chapel hosts a number of vocal

West

and instrumental chamber concerts. With its white-ash-wood pews, a vaulted coffered ceiling, and a magnificent stained-glass window depicting a swirling "tree of life," the chapel is visually, as well as musically, stunning. And, if that's too traditional for some, more avant-garde performances may be seen at the Helen E. Lindhurst Theatre.

Pepperdine is one of the safest campuses in the nation, and violent crime is almost non-existent. In 2009, the school reported only burglaries on campus, just twenty-two incidents.

It is not cheap to study in Malibu. Pepperdine's 2010–11 tuition was estimated at $38,960, and room and board at $11,390. Approximately 70–75 percent of Pepperdine students receive some form of financial assistance each year. Some 48 percent of students get need-based aid. The average loan debt of a 2009 grad was a stiff $28,299.

Reed College

Portland, Oregon • www.reed.edu

The fourth R

With a demanding curriculum and a number of rigorous courses, Reed College is for neither the academically lazy nor the intellectually timid. All its students benefit from a core freshman course in Western civilization, which—along with a senior thesis—bookends an intensely challenging journey into higher learning.

This tiny college in Portland, Oregon, was founded in 1908 by a bequest from pioneer Simeon Reed and his wife Amanda. The school has grown into a student body of 1,452 undergraduates, plus about three dozen part-time master's candidates. Notable Reedies run the gamut from Apple founder Steve Jobs and Wikipedia founder Larry Sanger to the musical comic Dr. Demento.

Reed continues to blend ancient and modern learning in a distinctive fashion. Incoming freshmen are still advised to read *The Iliad* over the summer, and some upperclassmen casually pepper their conversation with references to the ancient Greek term for "honor." This respect for classical antiquity has not only been preserved but has actually increased over time. The present custom of having a professor deliver a talk on *The Odyssey* during convocation only began in 1998. At the first Humanities 101 lecture of the year, classics professor Wally Englert leads the entire lecture hall in singing the opening lines of *The Iliad* in Ancient Greek (often with the help of older classics majors who show up in tunics for the occasion).

On the other hand, Reed has all the latest scientific resources that might warm the heart of Francis Bacon or Dr. Strangelove. Reed runs the only nuclear reactor in the country operated entirely by undergraduates (they receive certification in nuclear reactor operations). Science faculty routinely win government grants for advanced studies in biology and other disciplines. Learning for its own sake, an endangered species at other colleges, lives and flourishes in Reed's idyllic quiet.

Reed College's address is on Woodstock Boulevard, a name that aptly describes the student body's philosophical leanings. But Reed students are usually too busy with academics to engage in direct political action, seeing themselves as too high-minded for crass partisanship. Instead, students tend to gravitate together on the basis of issues in groups such as Amnesty International, and organizations focused on ecological issues are especially popular.

Academic Life: Reeding, writing, and mentorship

Reed freshmen are greeted with a week-long "New Reedie Orientation" program featuring field trips, a job fair, and an introduction to the academic departments. First-generation college students can take part in a Peer Mentoring Program retreat, where they pair up with upperclassmen for support during the coming year. Then the work begins. The two-semester core class, Humanities 110, began in 1943 as a way to combine the history and literature of ancient Greece and Rome. It now incorporates elements of philosophy, art history, and political science as it leads students from Homer and Aeschylus to Plato and Aristotle in the first semester, and from Seneca and Josephus to Athanasius and Augustine in the second. A professor sums up the school's traditional attitude toward the importance of this academic foundation: "We study the Greeks because they invented history and philosophy in the West."

Humanities 110 is team taught, and students are divided into sections with no more than sixteen in each group. In addition to the weekly three-hour seminars, the entire freshman class of "Reedies" meets three times a week for one-hour lectures, which are just as important for the teachers as for the students, as the professors are eager to impress their peers and rarely fail to deliver an illuminating and lively performance. At the end of the year, students put on a humanities play, which satirizes the course readings and syllabus.

During their first year, students write four major papers per semester just in Humanities 110, and their performance is evaluated regularly throughout the year. As sophomores, most students choose to continue their liberal arts education with a survey class on medieval Europe, modern Europe, or classical Chinese civilization.

By current standards, Reed has managed to preserve scholarly rigor. The departments of economics and history, frequent victims of politicization at other schools, include few classes that could be considered academically suspect. Economics majors are required to take a broad survey course called "Introduction to Economic Analysis," as well as "Microeconomic Theory," "Macroeconomic Theory," and a choice of either "Survey of Econometric Methods" or "Theory and Practice of Econometrics" (the latter focuses more on statistics than the former). The history department requires students to take a basic humanities course (like "Early Modern Europe") and six other history courses, including at least one

VITAL STATISTICS
Religious affiliation: *none*
Total enrollment: *1,481*
Total undergraduates: *1,452*
SAT/ACT midranges: CR: *660–760*, M: *620–710*; ACT: *29–33*
Applicants: *3,161*
Applicants accepted: *41%*
Accepted applicants who enrolled: *29%*
Tuition and fees: *$41,200*
Room and board: *$10,650*
Freshman retention rate: *88%*
Graduation rate: *59% (4 yrs.)*, *77% (6 yrs.)*
Courses with fewer than 20 students: *73%*
Student-faculty ratio: *10:1*
Courses taught by graduate students: *none*
Most popular majors: *biology, social sciences, physics*
Students living on campus: *64%*
Guaranteed housing for four years? *no*
Students in fraternities or sororities: *none*

West

SUGGESTED CORE

1. Humanities 110, Introduction to Western Humanities
2. Philosophy 301, Ancient Philosophy
3. Religion 152/164, Introduction to Judaism/Introduction to Christian Origins
4. Religion 165, An Introduction to Imperial Orthodoxy (closest match)
5. Political Science 230, Introduction to Political Philosophy
6. English 242/363, Introduction to Drama: Shakespeare/Studies in Shakespeare
7. History 361/362, Mapping Colonial America/Revolutionary America
8. Humanities 220, Modern European Humanities

in each of three areas: Europe, the United States, and regions or nations outside Europe, the United States, and Canada. Students must also take at least one history course before 1800 and one after 1800, but these can overlap with the geographical requirements.

The focus of the psychology department is straightforward, emphasizing scientific research. An unusually intense Chinese department emphasizes the history and literature of China through the ages in a format largely devoid of multiculturalist claptrap. The dance department concentrates on traditional Western forms of expression. The music department, which attracts many accomplished musicians to the school, provides an array of instruction and performance opportunities and waives many related costs for majors in their junior and senior years.

The English department is also solid, offering many courses on Shakespeare and other important authors and eras. Its areas of concentration include British culture, medieval literature, the Elizabethan era, poetry, and literary theory. However, English majors can graduate without taking a course on Shakespeare.

Political science majors are required to take classes in political behavior, political philosophy, comparative politics, international politics and economics, but not on the United States Constitution.

Reed is a secular school, but it has an active and popular religion department. The faculty offer courses on Christianity, Judaism, Islam, and Chinese religions. Perhaps because of Reed's emphasis on classics, the department offers solid courses on early and Byzantine Christianity, and religion students can study important but often neglected theologians such as Pseudo-Dionysius, St. Maximus the Confessor, and St. Gregory Palamas. Although Reed has a secular reputation, it provides a supportive environment for personal religious investigation. Donald Miller, a bestselling Christian author associated with the "Emergent Church" movement and an alumnus of Reed, describes Reed's culture as "pagan and intellectual," whose spirit of antidogmatic questioning will either break or refine one's faith.

The most politicized department at Reed is probably anthropology, which offers separate classes on the anthropologies of dreaming, colonialism, and fashion. Another class, "Sex and Gender," explores "the biological attributes by which a person is deemed 'male' or 'female.'" For some reason, this class occupies an entire semester—instead of, say, twenty minutes.

In all, the school offers twenty-three individual majors; eleven more majors are considered interdisciplinary, including mathematics-economics and chemistry-physics. A quarter of Reed students major in its strong science programs, particularly biology and physics. History, English, and psychology are the most popular liberal arts majors. Across the board, traditional disciplines dominate; very few Reedies graduate with a major that includes the word "studies" in its title. Then again, even the American studies interdisciplinary program is quite rigorous, requiring students to fulfill all the requirements of a traditional major in addition to classes specific to the concentration.

Most students who graduate from Reed eventually continue on to pursue further learning. Not surprisingly, about a third of Reed students eventually go into education as a profession, which is about as many Reedies as enter law and business combined. Within two years after graduation, 65 percent of Reedies have found their way to still-higher education.

Compared to other schools, Reed has experienced very little grade inflation. This attitude toward grading and evaluation stems from the very close mentoring relationships between professors and students. Reed gives the strongest institutional encouragement to professors to make teaching a priority. Says one veteran Reed professor of the school's teaching policy, "This is not mere lip service: from my experience of over thirty years here, I can say that effective teaching remains the central qualification for promotion and tenure."

Students say the intellectual relationships between faculty members and students are exceptionally close; even in the classroom, professors encourage independent and original thinking in their students. "Just because a lecturer said something about a work doesn't mean the students take it as gospel," claims a professor. The student senate even allocates money so that students can take faculty and staff members to lunch. Students say the best teachers at Reed include Peter Steinberger (dean of the faculty) in political science; Jay Dickson, Robert Knapp, and Lisa M. Steinman in English; Walter G. Englert, Nigel Nicholson and Ellen Greenstein Millender in classics; Robert H. Kaplan in biology; Enriqueta Canseco-Gonzalez in psychology; Mark Hinchliff in philosophy; David Griffiths (emeritus) in physics; and Kenneth Brashier and Michael Foat in religion.

Incoming freshmen are assigned faculty advisors within their expected fields of study. Students choose their own faculty advisors within their major departments once they have finalized their program selection, usually during the sophomore year. All students must pass a junior qualifying exam—the "junior qual"—in their majors before being promoted to senior status. These are very difficult, but most students over-study and pass them. History majors complete "a critical essay dealing with a given issue or problem within a particular historical field and period." For English majors, the exam has three parts "involving questions about a piece of fiction, a critical or theoretical essay, and a poem or poems (all of which are generally handed out to be read before taking the exam)," according to the department webpage.

At Reed, to paraphrase the bumper sticker, every degree is considered an honors degree. A senior thesis is required of all students. They typically run from 60 to 120 pages but have been as long as 250 pages. The completed works are archived by the school at its designated "thesis tower," and the thesis title of each student is listed in the program at graduation. "Most talk about it being the high point of their education at Reed," a professor says. "And it makes a PhD dissertation seem less daunting." The project culminates with a two-hour oral exam held before a group of professors from both inside and outside the field of the subject matter. The annual thesis parade, in which students file from the steps of the library to the registrar's office with champagne corks flying and their monographs in hand, is among Reedies' most beloved traditions. "It looks like a World Series victory," says a professor.

Ethics at Reed are guided by the school's all-encompassing Honor Principle, which holds the entire community responsible for "maintaining standards of honesty and mutual trust in their academic and social lives." Exams are not proctored, and students are free to take their tests with them. Says one student, "We are quite accustomed to taking final exams in our dorm rooms in our pajamas, and e-mailing our work to our professors by the approved deadline. And, yes, students do actually practice academic honesty, even when they're not being monitored or proctored. The academic integrity of students here is beyond anything I've ever seen." Upholding the tradition is considered a badge of honor among students. In addition, the student senate appoints a "J-board" each year of nine students who hear and resolve disputes.

Technology at Reed is state of the art, and the course material for most classes can be accessed online. Many of the school's classrooms boast Internet connections and high-tech projection screens. The library's Instructional Media Center has a language laboratory, a music listening room, and an array of electronic devices for student use.

Surprisingly, Reed does not have a foreign language requirement, but certain departments and majors do require proficiency in another language. Study-abroad programs are popular at Reed and are available in Australia, Argentina, China, Costa Rica, Ecuador, Egypt, Greece, France, Germany, Hungary, Italy, Israel, Morocco, Russia, England, Spain, Italy, and South Africa. Foreign languages offered are Chinese, French, German, Spanish, Russian, Ancient Greek, and Latin.

ACADEMIC REQUIREMENTS

Reed does not have a traditional core, but it does require all freshmen to take one admirable two-semester course on Western civilization (Humanities 110). Students must also complete:

- One full-year course or the equivalent in the same discipline, which may be selected from literature, philosophy, religion, and the arts. Options range from "Ancient Philosophy" to "The Black Radical Tradition."
- Two courses in either history, social sciences, or psychology. Choices include everything from "European Diplomatic History: 1848–1914" to "Clothing, Fashion, and Power."
- Two courses in the natural sciences. Courses here include "General Physics" and "Introduction to Biology."
- Two courses in mathematics, logic, foreign language, or linguistics. Class options include "Abstract Algebra" and "Language and Politics."

Students also must complete:

- Three semesters of physical education, an obligation that can be fulfilled by activities like bowling, badminton, juggling, or belly dancing.
- A junior qualifying examination.
- A senior thesis and oral examination.

West

Student Life: No time to relax

No doubt about it, Reed is a stressful place. Twelve percent of the incoming freshman class does not return, only 59 percent of students graduate in four years, and a stalwart 77 percent graduate in six years. "We do sometimes worry that we're asking students to do too much," says a professor. "It's demanding from the day the students get here."

Primed to help is Student Services, a multipurpose entity that provides students with everything from academic support to mental health treatment. In addition to one-on-one tutoring (students can get at least one hour a week, and often a second, free of charge), the school offers a math center and writing assistance. But the demands pay off. According to the *Chronicle of Higher Education*, Reed ranks among the top baccalaureate schools in the nation in producing Fulbright scholars.

Student organizations, of which there are almost ninety, include the Beer Nation (which says, "Even if you are below drinking age, support us, it will pay off"), and the apocalyptic club Chunk 666. Queer Alliance and Feminist Union are also present on campus, and their members are among the more politically active students.

Practically all students live on campus during their freshman year, while many move off campus after that. University housing, limited in comparison to most small liberal arts colleges, is awarded by lottery. Upperclassman advisors and recent graduates (not necessarily from Reed) reside in the dorms to offer support and guidance. Dormitory life has improved in recent years with the construction of three new residence halls. Reed also offers permanent language houses: French, Russian, Chinese, German, and Spanish. Most of the students who live there are majoring in the language, and each accomodation exchange students who are native speakers. There are also theme houses that vary each year. The 2011 themes include Arabic Culture, Mad Science, and Outhouse (those interested in conserving the environment). There are also women's dorms, apartments for single students, special housing for disabled students, cooperative housing, and wellness housing. There are no fraternities or sororities. Most dorms are coed with single-sex rooms, but coed restrooms. Each floor decides whether it will have "lights out hours," "quiet hours," or other details of community life, including visitation hours.

Reed does not participate in NCAA competition, but there are intercollegiate club sports in men's and women's rugby, coed soccer, men's basketball, coed squash, and Ultimate Frisbee. The most unusual student hobby at Reed involves working at its nuclear reactor. Other popular hangouts include the thoroughly equipped sports center and the campus theater, which welcomes participation from students in all majors. Also frequented is the Douglas F. Cooley Memorial Art Gallery, where studio art students can exhibit their work.

Reed is situated on what was once known as Crystal Springs Farm. The scenic 116 acres feature topography ranging from a wooded canyon to wetlands. Populated by swallows, shrews, salamanders, and a variety of fish, the canyon and its fauna have served as the objects of study for a number of senior thesis projects. There is even a section of the school website devoted to trees on campus, and the Canyon Clean-Up Day is another tradition cherished among Reedies.

West

GREEN LIGHT

Politics are present but not dominant on campus. One student says of her conservative and libertarian peers, "They're in the minority and will have an uphill battle in any political discussion, but they aren't ostracized or treated differently unless they happen to run into someone unbelievably closed-minded. But ideas matter more than political affiliation. I've seen a left-minded student who's belligerent and can't back up [his] political opinions challenged just as often and with as much conviction as a belligerent and flippant right-minded student would be." As for the instructors, "Most faculty don't talk politics with each other," the professor says. Other professors admit, however, that both the faculty and the student body lean decidedly toward the left. But, in general, political disputes are intellectualized at Reed, with students pouring their partisan energies into papers rather than rhetoric. This fundamental bias toward the books is illustrated by a favorite Reedie chant at sports competitions: "Hegel, Kant, Marx, Spinoza! Come on Reed, hit 'em in the nose-a!"

Off-campus student activity is organized by the Gray Fund, which sponsors a seemingly endless array of free field trips throughout the year, from skiing to whitewater rafting. When an event is oversubscribed, students and faculty are chosen by lottery to attend the event, but practically everybody ends up going on one excursion or another. The school has a ski lodge on Mt. Hood, which it encourages students to reserve; it also lends out skiing and camping equipment free of charge. Reed even helps subsidize tickets for many events in Portland. But despite the many extracurricular activities available, the books have first priority. Students can easily spend weeks without going off campus, buried in texts in their rooms or in the library. "Reed is not for everyone," says a professor. "It's a college for bright, motivated students who really want to work hard, but also want the rewards. Anything you ask them to do, they rise to the occasion and do it really well."

There have been reports of pervasive drug and alcohol use on campus, as well as some controversy regarding the school's lax policy toward the abuse of substances other than tobacco. (It takes a strong stand against smoking the legal stuff.) The annual spring Renaissance festival, known as Renn Fayre, is considered the high point in the campus calendar for illegal indulgences (most of which were unknown in the West during the relevant historical period; perhaps the students should stick to mead). As one student says of life at Reed, "You work extremely hard, and you play extremely hard."

A custom posing less of a legal problem at Reed centers on the Doyle Owl, Reed's unofficial mascot. The Owl is a three-foot-high, 300-pound concrete sculpture originally stationed atop the Doyle section of the Old Dorm Block. In 1913, the Owl was stolen as part of a dorm war. Nine students were taken "hostage," to be released in exchange for the owl, but they escaped. Since then, the Owl has been stolen and re-stolen numerous times. The unwritten rule, however, is that the dorm that has most recently stolen the Owl must exhibit it in a "showing," while trying to keep other dorms from re-stealing it. Some "showings" have involved the Owl being encased in ice, covered with Vaseline while hanging from a bridge, floating down a river, being set on fire with baking oil, being lifted off a roof by helicopter, and being thrown off the back of a speeding car. The Owl has been spotted in Disneyland, Seattle, and San Francisco, and (reportedly) in Paris and Jakarta.

Crime is not much of an issue on Reed's campus. In 2009, the school reported three forcible sex offenses, two burglaries (down from twenty-eight in 2008), two stolen cars, and one case of arson on campus. The college operates a bus service until 2:00 AM. The area of Portland surrounding the school is also relatively safe.

Reed tuition for 2010–11 is a whopping $41,200, and room and board are $10,650. Some 52 percent of students receive some need-based aid, and the average debt of a recent grad is $20,750.

Rice University

Houston, Texas • www.rice.edu

Against the grain

William Marsh Rice, a wealthy New Englander, used Princeton and Oxford as models when he founded the Rice Institute in 1912, which later became Rice University. It became a small school of the highest quality where students lived in residential colleges and faculty-student relations were warm and intense.

Although Rice is now much larger, those attributes still characterize the university. Teaching is still emphasized; with Rice's outstanding student-faculty ratio of just 5 to 1, no one need fall between the cracks. Socially, Rice University is very comfortable: its residential college system offers students the close-knit community atmosphere of a smaller school, alongside the resources of a larger one. And the lively (if sprawling) city of Houston surrounds the campus, offering cultural and sporting events and fantastic Tex-Mex food.

Rice is comparatively affordable, has an excellent academic reputation, a top-notch student body, and a $3.6 billion endowment. No wonder some consider it Texas's alternative to the Ivy League. It's a shame that a weak curriculum and troubling policies on free speech keep Rice from being a slam-dunk choice for traditionally-minded students.

Academic Life: No way of knowing

Rice's distribution requirements are pretty weak, mandating just four courses in each of three groups: Group I, which includes more than 200 courses in the departments of art, art history, English, philosophy, medieval studies, classics, theater, women's studies, foreign languages, and many others. Group II is a catch-all for the social sciences, and Group III covers "analytical thinking and quantitative analysis," covering the "various disciplines of science and engineering."

One professor defends this system as superior to its rigidly structured predecessor, in which students had no choice but to take politically charged subjects. The professor says, "Anybody has the right to take courses in queer theory, postmodern interpretations of everything, etc. But nobody is required to take them." Despite their academic liberty, even students recognize the weakness of Rice's curriculum. One comments, "Rice does not require any specific courses and a student could easily graduate without taking any history or English course." Still, "when our graduates write back from graduate school, they tell us it is easier—and professors at those universities . . . commend us for the preparation of our students," a professor says.

The degree to which departments promote traditional areas of study and free discussion varies. The sciences, engineering, and social sciences, according to one professor, appear to "have non-ideological faculties and tolerate believers of all stripes quite readily." The same professor says that "the humanities departments are definitely getting a lot more politicized." Another professor adds, "There are no strong departments in the humanities. They are uniformly postmodern." For example, the history department lost its two medievalists in 2000 and has not replaced them. Another professor called the atmosphere in the department "stiflingly present-minded."

Traditionally, at Rice, students had ample opportunities to develop relationships with their professors, who were said to be very accessible during office hours and outside of class. With a student-to-faculty ratio that bests any of the Ivies', Rice's median class size is fourteen students. "Professors are associated with a residential college and serve as advisors to entering students from those colleges until they declare a major," says one student. "These advisors, especially the older professors, are extremely accessible; they eat lunch in their residential colleges frequently." But as "old guard" professors retire, many of those who replace them exhibit a different ethos, insiders say. A faculty member says, "One problem with the younger faculty is that they have little patience, if any, for the claims of undergraduates."

Science professors who actually teach tend to be more involved in research than are humanities professors, but one student says that they at least "try to involve undergraduates" in their work. "There are many opportunities for engineering/science students to work in a professor's lab," says an undergrad. However, he pointed out, "Most full professors in science and engineering teach no more than one course per term."

According to students, some of the best teachers are J. Dennis Huston in English; Richard J. Stoll and Rick Wilson in political science; Baruch Brody, Tristram Engelhardt, and George Sher in philosophy; John S. Hutchinson, James Tour, and Kenton Whitmire in chemistry; Richard Baraniuk and Don Johnson in electrical engineering; Stephen Wong in bioengineering; Raquel Gaytan in languages; James Thompson and David Scott in statistics; well-known conservative scholar Ewa Thompson in German studies; and Steve Klineberg in sociology.

VITAL STATISTICS

Religious affiliation: *none*
Total enrollment: *5,556*
Total undergraduates: *3,279*
SAT/ACT midranges: CR: *640–750*, M: *680–780*; ACT: *26–30*
Applicants: *11,172*
Applicants accepted: *22%*
Accepted applicants who enrolled: *36%*
Tuition and fees: *$33,120*
Room and board: *$11,750*
Freshman retention rate: *90%*
Graduation rate: *75% (4 yrs.), 93% (6 yrs.)*
Courses with fewer than 20 students: *58%*
Student-faculty ratio: *5:1*
Courses taught by graduate students: *not provided*
Most popular majors: *engineering, natural sciences, social sciences*
Students living on campus: *75%*
Guaranteed housing for four years? *no*
Students in fraternities or sororities: *none*

SUGGESTED CORE

1. Classics 201: Homer and Virgil and Their Reception
2. Philosophy 201, History of Philosophy I
3. Religious Studies 122/365, The Bible and Its Interpreters/New Testament Writings
4. History 358, Early European Intellectual History From Augustine to Descartes, or Religious Studies 105, Introduction to Medieval Christian Thought
5. Philosophy 307, Social and Political Philosophy
6. English 321/322, Early Shakespeare/Late Shakespeare
7. History 117, America to 1848
8. History 370, European Intellectual History: Bacon to Hegel

Teaching assistants, who at Rice are undergraduates, help with review sessions; graduate students, sometimes called instructors, teach some introductory courses. The formal advising program "is a bit subpar, especially the general advising before declaring a major," says one student. Upon entering college, every student is assigned a faculty advisor based on his area of interest. Once he declares his major, he is assigned to the designated advisor for his major. Because there are usually just one or two official advisors assigned to a department, it's hard for students to get much time with them. "The advisor in your major department usually understands the issues of that department quite well, but typically just rubber stamps your decisions," a student says.

Rice's strict honor code is vigilantly enforced by students. Cheating on an exam, besides resulting in an automatic course failure, could lead to a three-semester suspension. For falsifying data on a lab report, a two-semester suspension is not unusual.

Rice advertises itself as a research school. It has traditionally been strongest in the sciences and engineering, and many students are in premed, a program that can be intense. One premed student says, "At Rice, most people are very serious about their work, but I've never felt threatened by any competitiveness among my peers. There's no competition in a cutthroat way, and many students study together, helping each other learn the material." Rice premed students typically have some of the highest MCAT scores in the country.

The School of Architecture is highly regarded. Students in the program must complete additional distribution requirements, foundation courses in architecture, and a "preprofessional sequence" in their junior and senior years. The Shepherd School of Music is excellent in music theory, history, and performance.

Rice's English department has its weaknesses. The requirements for majors are loose enough that a student may enter and exit without a thorough understanding of the literary canon.

Distribution requirements for the English major include three advanced-level classes in writing before 1900 (two of which must be from pre-1800 periods), only one of which may be a class on Shakespeare, as well as one class on "non-canonical traditions, such as courses in women, African American, Chicano/a, Asian American, ethnic, global, and diasporic writers."

History requirements are similarly simple: students must take ten courses distributed over premodern, European, United States, and Asian/Latin American/African history. Sadly, the requirement for U.S. history may be fulfilled by courses like "Caribbean Nation Building," or "U.S. Women's History."

West

Political science majors only have one required class: "Introduction to Statistics." A student could easily graduate without any substantial knowledge of the American political system or philosophy; in fact, Rice's dearth of political philosophy classes in general is troubling.

Rice offers a number of study-abroad opportunities, in semester- or year-long programs in India, Australia, Denmark, Hong Kong, France, Korea, Hungary, and England, among others, including programs at New York University and the American University in Cairo. The school teaches Ancient Greek, Latin, Arabic, Chinese, French, German, Hebrew, Hindi, Italian, Japanese, Korean, Portuguese, and Spanish. Foreign language majors are available in French, German, and Hispanic studies.

Student Life: Houston calling

Rice's residential college setup, modeled after the Oxford system, organizes nearly every aspect of social life at the school; some students choose Rice precisely for this reason. The eleven colleges mix students of various races and temperaments. Rice students self-segregate much less than at other schools—there are no ethnic awareness halls, for instance, nor political-issue or gender-issue dormitories. Students are integrated ethnically, politically, and culturally—whether they like it or not. As a result, the residential colleges lack distinctive character. Paradoxically, Rice students are very loyal to their individual colleges. "People will do almost anything for their college. Your college is your family," says one student. In the words of one student, "It creates a small community for each student and college activities are the center of social life. College spirit and intercollegiate rivalries add an element of fun to the Rice experience."

Unfortunately, Rice University's residential colleges do not have enough room for its 3,000-plus undergraduates, and a quarter of them have to live off campus, missing the benefits of the college system. Two new colleges, Duncan and McMurty, were established in 2009, adding 648 new beds for student housing. The colleges were built, in part, to accommodate Rice's goal of increasing its undergraduate enrollment by 30 percent between 2005 and 2015. Further building projects and housing innovations (including off-campus facilities) will be necessary to accommodate the enlarged student body.

A student's closest friends usually come from his own college. "With the residential college system as opposed to the Greek System, Rice students get to know a much more diverse group of people. Freshmen are living on the same halls with upperclassmen. Varsity athletes are living next to math nerds," a student reports. All dormitories are coeducational, but each college offers a few single-sex floors, and all bathrooms and shower areas are single-sex. Students in the newer colleges enjoy suite-style living, while those in the older buildings enjoy nicer architecture. A faculty master lives in a house next door to the residence halls of each college and serves as a live-in advisor.

Rice colleges have their own traditions. Baker, for instance, has something called the "Baker 13," which involves students running through campus wearing nothing but shaving cream; this occurs on the 13th and 31st of each month (or 26th if the month does not have a 31st). Weiss College goes "pumpkin caroling" every Halloween, Lovett College throws a

West

casino night each February, and Brown College's residents are bound to be dunked in the Fairy Fountain on their birthdays. Rice students say there is never a lack of events on campus to occupy what free time they have. "We work incredibly hard, but students know how to leave work behind and have a good time," says one student.

Cultural clubs include the Aegean Club, catering to Hellenic interests, the Asian Business Student Association, *Open* Magazine, which seeks to shed "light on the social, cultural, and health aspects of sex and sexuality," the Rice Karate club, and the Egyptian Queens club, whose "mission is to increase unity among minorities and women of color."

Service clubs give students the opportunity to get involved in the ESL tutoring program, the American Red Cross, One on One Mentoring with Houston school kids, or the Fairy Godmother Project, which helps high school students find prom clothes at low or no cost. Special interest clubs range broadly from the National Society of Black Engineers, Toxic Assets band, Community of Rice Entrepreneurs, Queers and Allies group, Low Keys Female *a cappella*, and the Chess Club, to the Legalese Pre-Law Club.

Churches of almost every denomination stand near campus, and many are accessible on foot. InterVarsity Christian Fellowship and Campus Crusade for Christ are the largest and most active religious groups on campus. One professor says that Rice "has active private support groups for Catholics and Evangelicals. Rice's anticlericalism is of long-standing vintage, but the conservative Christians have managed to obtain on-campus support." Conversely, in an opinion piece in the student newspaper, the *Rice Thresher*, an atheist complained, "As a non-Judeo-Christian at Rice, I appear to be in the minority."

Other traditions at Rice are represented by clubs like Canterbury (the Episcopal Stu-

---

ACADEMIC REQUIREMENTS

Rice has no core curriculum, no foreign language mandate, and weak distribution requirements. On top of the demands of each major, Rice requires students to take four courses each from each of three broad groups, in each case with classes from at least two different departments:

- Arts, values, and culture. Any of some 200 courses in the departments of art, art history, English, philosophy, medieval studies, theater, women's studies, and foreign languages will qualify. Options range from "Literature of British Enlightenment," to "Women in Greece and Rome."
- Human society. Disciplines include anthropology, economics, history, psychology, and sociology. Options range from "Conservative Studies" to "Psychology of Gender."
- Analytical thinking and quantitative analysis. Appropriate courses come from the math, computer science, physics, chemistry, and biology departments. Options include "Geometry" and "Oceanography."
- Two noncredit Lifetime Physical Activity Program classes.

In addition, students who do not pass an English composition exam given during orientation week must take English 103, "Introduction to Argumentative and Academic Writing."

---

dent Association), the Baptist Student Ministry, Progressive Christians at Rice, Interfaith Dialogue Association, Rumi Sufi Islamic club, a Mormon group, and Lutheran, Catholic, and Jewish chaplaincies. Political views are voiced in columns or letters to the *Rice Thresher* student paper, rather than in demonstrations. "The student body is largely apathetic," an undergrad says. An independent student magazine, the *Rice Standard*, gives voice to conservative views (among others) and space for literary contributions. Many students were enthusiastic about Ron Paul's campaign for the Republican nomination in 2008, in part because Rice sits in congressman Paul's district. Political clubs offer outlets for libertarians, a Rice branch of the ACLU, and a pro-Israeli group, as well as Young Democrats and the Rice Conservative Forum.

One thing more popular than politics at Rice is drinking. The university's biggest and most beloved tradition (since 1957) is the annual Beer-Bike contest. Preceded by a week of activities—picnics, a baseball game, a big dinner, and "beer debates"—students then get down to business with chugging and biking races. Everyone participates in the festivities, even the college president. "Rice is a wet campus with a relatively relaxed alcohol policy, so plenty of students drink," a student says. "There is a lot of drinking on campus, but there are also a lot of things to do for those who don't drink. I've never felt any pressure to drink," says another.

Cultural shows, dances, operas, and other musical performances (both student recitals and professional ones), political lectures, and the residential colleges' themed parties are favorite attractions. Through a program called Passport to Houston, students traditionally have access to many of Houston's attractions for free or significantly reduced rates. This includes the light rail and bus sys-

YELLOW LIGHT

Rice may boast a more conservative student body than most schools outside of Texas, but many of its major liberal arts departments are ideologically slanted. In the words of one professor, "I would not recommend Rice for humanities. . . . No department in the School of Humanities would be comfortable for a conservative student." While its hard sciences departments might not be infused by politics, some professors display a lack of humane ethical judgment: in 2006, Rice accepted a $2.5 million grant from the government of Qatar for a research project involving the destruction of human embryos in stem-cell research.

Rice's speech code includes a prohibition against sending unsolicited "material which explicitly or implicitly refers to sexual conduct" or that "contains profane language or panders to bigotry, sexism, or other forms of prohibited discrimination." While Rice has affirmed that it has no intention of punishing protected speech (i.e., a mass "e-mail from a conservative student organization advertising a speech by an opponent of illegal immigration"), the policy certainly allows it to do so. Opinions vary on what effect administrative policies or campus politics have on student expression. One professor says, "I think students are rather free to express their views on anything." However, another professor reports that "free speech by students is completely stifled. The previous president, Malcolm Gills, hired a senior administrator just to keep the student newspaper in line." One student adds, "We may have a fairly decent number of conservatives at Rice, but it's hard to know. Many of us are afraid to voice our opinions in class or in papers for fear of being shot down by the almost monolithically liberal faculty."

tems, the zoo, museums, the Houston Ballet, the Grand Opera, and major sporting events. Rice Village, with its restaurants and shopping, is a fifteen-minute walk from campus. Hermann Park, which features a public golf course and the Houston Zoo, is literally across the street. The Museum District, home to the Houston Museum of Fine Arts (the nation's sixth largest) is also within walking distance. Five miles away stands Houston's revitalized downtown, replete with theaters, concert halls, and the city's best nightlife. With Houston's city sprawl—and the beaches of Galveston just an hour away—many students recommend having a car. About half of upperclassmen do, and for a fee, students may park in the stadium lot.

Rice athletes have the highest student-athlete graduation rate in NCAA Division I, with men and women competing in basketball, cross-country, tennis, and track and field. Men's sports also include football, golf, and baseball, while women compete in soccer, swimming, and volleyball. The Rice Owls, whose colors are blue and gray, have found success with their baseball team, which finished well in the 2003, 2006, and 2007 College World Series. The women's teams have consistently competed in NCAA tournaments for soccer, basketball, track and field, and tennis.

The university's tongue-in-cheek Marching Owl Band (MOB) is known as a scramble band—they don't march; they scatter. Some members play non-traditional instruments for a marching band, like strings (including a cello), electric piano, or even the kazoo The school offers a broad variety of intramural sports, like coed indoor soccer, sand volleyball, and flag football, as well as swim meets, billiards, dodgeball, and inner-tube water polo. Students can also choose from two dozen intercollegiate club sports, including basketball, lacrosse, Ultimate Frisbee, break dancing, aikido, soccer, and equestrian.

Rice is a reasonably safe place; it has seen a recent drop in crime. In 2009, Rice reported two forcible sex offenses and thirty-three burglaries. However, bike thefts are common. Rice provides an escort service seven days a week, from 10:00 PM to 6:00 AM. Students may call for a safety escort or use one of the school's blue-light emergency phones to request one. "I've never felt at risk," says one student, "but you have to remember you're in Houston."

Rice University is mid-priced for a private school, with tuition in 2010–11 $33,120 and room and board $11,750. Admission is need blind, and the school does not impose loans on students with family incomes of less than $80,000. Some 70 percent of students receive some sort of financial aid, but a substantial amount still borrow money to pay for college, and the average student graduates with $18,633 in student loans.

University of Southern California

Los Angeles, California • www.usc.edu

Believing its own press

Founded in 1880, when Los Angeles was a provincial backwater of some 10,000 inhabitants, USC is now big, rich, and intensely preprofessional. USC has a number of truly world-class programs, and it more than adequately prepares its students in these programs to compete in the outside world. Classes are inviting, with twenty-six students on average, and despite its size, the school offers a true sense of close-knit community. But, as with all schools, certain parts of USC are stronger than others. In other words: caveat emptor.

Academic Life: Ready for my closeup

Many of USC's strong professional programs are known throughout the world, especially the School of Cinema-Television—which regularly produces top-flight screenwriters, editors, and directors—the Viterbi School of Engineering, the Thornton School of Music, and the Marshall School of Business. Sure enough, at USC the high achiever will find that the sky is the limit. However, the basement is also an option. As one student says, "You can just slide through one of the easier schools . . . and get no education."

Of the school's pallid distribution requirements, another student says, "I don't know anyone who didn't just consider them a thing that you have to do." In fact, he says, the prevailing attitude toward the requirements is "just get an A and get it over with." Even if students aren't serious about these courses, it seems that USC is; one professor notes that the school has grown stricter about which courses fulfill these mandates. What is more, some of them with offbeat titles are in fact good classes, poorly named—it's a marketing thing. "In many departments and among many faculty, there is an effort to *avoid* looking traditional or canonical," the professor says. "The titles look like conference titles." However, notes a grad student, "The composition program is highly advanced—a forerunner in the field, a model that many other universities base themselves on. This is incredibly important because learning to express yourself well is one of the best ways to get ahead in the workplace." Students must complete one class each in "Western Cultures and Traditions," "Global Cultures and Traditions," "Scientific Inquiry," "Science and Its Significance," "Arts and Letters," "Social Issues," and two writing classes: "Critical Reasoning" and the advanced "Writing 340."

West

975

In addition to the school's distribution requirements, students face a mandatory diversity requirement—one course selected from a list of many that don't offer much meaningful learning, even for those dedicated to learning about other cultures. For instance, American studies offers a course on "Race and Class in Los Angeles." Such a course should be of interest only to future diversity enforcement officers or civil rights ambulance chasers.

The Honors Core, or "Thematic Option," offered by the College of Letters, Arts, and Sciences, is the best way to complete the school's requirements. "I doubt that there is any Ivy League school that has as tough an academic challenge," says one honors student. According to USC, the honors curriculum "is arranged around four core courses which focus on the history of Western civilization through the close reading of primary literature and philosophical texts." It is heavy on reading and writing, and it focuses on all the right things. Unfortunately, the program only admits 200 students each year, and the typical enrollee has a high school GPA of 4.0 and a 2100 SAT score—which suggests that this program is slightly harder to get into than Harvard.

Another worthy initiative at USC is its Renaissance Scholars award, which is given to select students who combine study in two widely divergent fields—physics and theology, or computer science and poetry, for instance. These scholars compete for a $10,000 award upon graduation "for the purpose of post-baccalaureate study."

While USC students have a reputation of being more conservative than those at most other West Coast schools, there is no denying that both students and faculty with traditional views have experienced problems when it comes to expressing themselves in the classroom. "The politicization of speech in the classroom is clearly confined to certain humanities departments—English, comparative literature, and somewhat in political science and history," says a professor. Some students would add the religion department to that list. "One student says, "I would characterize the Western humanities courses as critically respectful of Western ideals and American institutions, but rarely agreeing with them. Often, I find that these classes acknowledge their presence, but resent them."

Yet another undergrad rues the lack of actual instruction in the Western canon and in American institutions. "The founding fathers would have never known what hit them here. I was the only one in class who had read *The Federalist* and the Constitution, and the

West

Declaration of Independence. . . . The emphasis here is on 'non-Western traditions.' This is fine, but, there is a decidedly strong bent against learning about the philosophical underpinnings of our laws and government. We need stronger work that honestly addresses our history and traditions and culture respectfully, instead of assigning pejorative terms to dismiss it."

As one professor notes, "things are uneven" at USC, and "a lot can depend on what faculty you get, and what departments and what courses." A student says, "USC, in a lot of ways, is really school-by-school." Another student reports, "Unfortunately there is no continuity in teaching ability. Many professors are primarily researchers who are obligated to teach a course every semester, often quite begrudgingly. Very few professors at USC will equip students to be citizens, to be financially wise, to be discerning, or to be good. This simply does not happen. There is no consensus about what constitutes knowledge or what constitutes a noble life."

Even so, an undergraduate *can* get a good education at USC. According to a student, "I found it transformative on quite a few levels. . . . I was taught to think for myself. I was taught to be critical, even if my colleagues in classes were not. (And many weren't. It was like they worked so hard to get here and all they wanted to do was party and do minimal work.)"

Finding the right professor can help students achieve a real education. Among the outstanding faculty at USC are Gene Bickers in physics and astronomy; Peggy Kamuf in French and comparative literature; Leo Braudy in English; Paul Knoll (emeritus) in history; Sharon Lloyd in philosophy; John Bowlt in Slavic languages and literature; Don Hall in the School of Cinema-Television; Howard Gillman and Janelle Wong in political science; and Juliet Musso in the School of Policy, Planning, and Development. One student says, "The best professor on the USC campus is Dallas Willard in the philosophy department. He has been at USC for over thirty years and is an excellent resource for guidance about what professors and courses to take. He goes out of his way to care for his students in every dimension."

The university also offers opportunities for undergraduates to get involved in both the hard and the social sciences. "The president and the provost have continually pushed faculty" to include undergraduates in research, a professor says. Among other programs, thematic-option students can participate in an annual undergraduate research conference. Undergraduate opportunities abound in the Summer Undergraduate Research Internship Program at the Southern California Earthquake Center.

SUGGESTED CORE

1. Classics 325, Ancient Epic
2. Philosophy 315, History of Western Philosophy: Ancient Period
3. Religion 111g/121g, The World of the Hebrew Bible/ The World of the New Testament
4. Religion 509, Early and Medieval Religious Thought in the West
5. Political Science 371, European Political Thought II or Philosophy 101g, Philosophical Foundations of Modern Western Culture
6. English 430, Shakespeare
7. History 351/478, The American Revolution/The U.S. 1789–1850, or History 200gm, The American Experience
8. History 420, European Intellectual and Cultural History: The Nineteenth Century, 1790–1870

West

USC's music program is excellent. There is a fine program in linguistics, and the Slavic department is well regarded. So is the history department. One professor says, "Learning history is something USC values highly, and the faculty has responded. The intellectual rigor and attention to analysis even in first- or second-year classes is impressive. It forces one to think."

To major in history, a student must complete three survey courses, as well as "Approaches to History," and six upper-division classes. Students must take one course each in Asia and Eurasia, Europe, and North and Latin America; one pre-1300 class, one 1300–1800 class, and one post-1800 class; and three of their courses in one area of concentration like "the Middle Ages," "visual and popular culture," or "history and international relations." Apparently, the history of the American founding and Civil War are not required.

English majors must take three of the following classes: pre- or post-1800 English literature, American literature, or a genre course like "Introduction to Poetry." Additionally, two pre-1800, one nineteenth-century, and one American literature class are required, along with three upper-level English classes. Thus they could miss Shakespeare, if they aren't careful.

For the political science major, two introductory courses (from "Theory and Practice of American Democracy," "Ideology and Political Conflict," "Comparative Politics," or "Law, Politics and Public Policy") are required. Students must then choose one class each from the fields of American politics, comparative politics, law and public policy, and political thought, as well as two upper-level electives and another elective. The U.S. Constitution and American political philosophy might well slip through the cracks.

USC's School of Cinema-Television is perhaps the best in the world. As one student says, "I'm twenty-one. Give me $40 million and I could make a feature film better than the one I saw last week in the theater. I realize how well prepared I am." At the very least, the program teaches self-confidence. And where else could you find something called the "Hugh M. Hefner Chair for the Study of American Film"?

Class sizes at USC are generally on the small side, typically including fewer than thirty students in upper-division courses. However, students are concerned about the quality of teaching. "Some professors I've had have made me question the tenure program," a student says. "At a university like USC, tenure is mostly based on research and not teaching. Sometimes, unfortunately, it shows." Another student says, "It is vital you not rely on your academic advisor when choosing courses or professors," because he or she is likely to steer advisees "towards the most popular or most professionally decorated teachers" regardless of teaching ability or course content.

But there is no dearth of excellent professors at USC, and while some courses are larger—especially the lower-level intros—many professors are quite reachable. "They're accessible," says a student. "You can send an e-mail to a professor and get an answer within an hour." Professors are expected to keep at least four office hours per week. "The administration tells us to be there for our students," a professor says.

The university also offers plenty of chances to study abroad. USC offers programs around the world, from Cape Town or Taiwan to Chile or Italy, and recommends overseas programs based on major.

West

978

Students are required to demonstrate competency in a nation's language before they study abroad, if classes in that language are offered by USC. Language options are classics, Arabic, Chinese, French, German, Hebrew, Hindi, Italian, Japanese, Korean, Portuguese, Russian, and Spanish. (The school explains that students begin learning other languages like Czech, Twi, or Greek "upon arrival in the host country.") Although USC offers solid language options, it has no language requirement.

Student Life: Have your people call my people

Student life at USC is a motley assortment of activities, undertaken smack-dab in the heart of Los Angeles, with all its diversions. "It *is* L.A., you know," a student says. "There are unlimited options." Another student says that those attending USC can try "anything and everything." One student complains, "There isn't too much of a night life around USC. So students with cars flee campus for Westwood, Hollywood, Santa Monica, Pasadena, and Huntington Beach." Most of these destinations are a short car trip away, and they offer everything that a college student could want—restaurants, shopping, bars, and, of course, the warm, sandy beaches of the Pacific Ocean. The university also sponsors movies and dorm events. However, "the campus itself is pretty uninviting for general hanging out," a student says. "It's easy to feel trapped at USC. The campus is essentially a two-square-block island dropped into a horrible area of downtown Los Angeles."

In 2010, the $150 million Ronald Tutor Campus center opened, providing "student offices and work space; collaborative project and group study areas; multi-purpose areas for events and gatherings; meeting and board rooms for student organizations; study lounges . . . technology resources; and game and entertainment areas." The center features the Seeds Marketplace deli, Traditions bar, the Moreton Fig upscale restaurant, California Pizza Kitchen, and a Coffee Bean & Tea Leaf coffee shop, among other dining options. The 193,000-square-foot building is centered around an outdoor plaza and offers ample social space for students.

USC sits near the center of U.S. popular culture—Hollywood—so students can expect to be exposed both on and off campus to the whole panoply of postmodern weirdness. On campus, there are around 700 student organizations catering to nearly every interest. Students recommend Troy Camp and Spirits in Action, two of USC's prominent philanthropic organizations. There are numerous ethnic clubs and various preprofessional societies, like the Asia-Pacific Students Entrepreneur Society, Women of Cinematic Arts, Integrative Medicine Club, Fashion Industry Association, the Association of Indian Students, or Black Voices. Over 300 academic groups include Chicanos for Progressive Education, USC Book Club, Theatre Students Association, and Christian Legal Society.

USC hosts a Russian club, ALIVE, Jewish Alliance for GLBTs and Straights, and Craft Crazy, among a few hundred others. Political groups include Beyond Coal Campaign, Christians United for Israel, UNICEF, and Women's Creative Collective for Change, as well as College Democrats and the American Constitution Society. USC is home to the College Democrats and USC Law Democrats, but not a single Republican or conservative club or organization is represented among the seventy-three registered political groups on campus.

West

979

The school is known for having an extremely active contingent of religious groups, from the USC Coptic Club, Hillel, Secular Alliance, or Seventh Day Adventist Chinese Student Community to the Sikh Student Association, Pagans and Wiccans at USC, Quakers at USC, or the Catholic Student Association. The campus hosts multiple "Places for Reflection and Worship," like the Little Chapel of Silence, The Fishbowl multi-faith chapel, the Chapel of the Cross ecumenical Christian space, Muslim Prayer Space, and the United University Church, "a progressive Christian Church in the Methodist and Presbyterian traditions." Currently, Hindu devotee and religion scholar Varun Soni acts as the dean of religious life.

Despite being broadly available, not all the chaplaincies on campus have a record of orthodoxy, so students might prefer to seek houses of worship off campus. There are plenty of options.

Athletics play a big role in campus life. USC's principal rival—hated crosstown foe UCLA—is always a welcome target for Trojan partisans. "Even if you are not a major sports fan, it's hard to avoid being pulled into Trojan pride and whipping out your victory sign when USC beats UCLA or Notre Dame," a student says. Things can get ugly: two football fans were stabbed as they tailgated before the USC-UCLA football game in December 2010. Police officers reported that the brawl involved some fifty to seventy-five people and included assaults on two officers who attempted to calm the situation.

For those who don't make one of the nine men's or eleven women's teams, the school boasts plenty of club and intramural sports like flag football, soccer, beach volleyball, climbing, boxing, archery, polo, and shinkendo, among others.

USC also has a well-entrenched Greek system, with sixty recognized Greek organiza-

---

ACADEMIC REQUIREMENTS

USC has no core curriculum. Besides a two-course writing sequence, all students must take one course from each of the following six broad categories:

- Western Cultures and Traditions. Options range from "Philosophical Foundations of Modern Western Culture" to "Diversity and the Classic Western Tradition."
- Global Cultures and Traditions. Choices here include "Introduction to Chinese Culture, Art and Literature" and "Early Native American Stories."
- Scientific Inquiry. Choices range from "General Chemistry" to "Crises of a Planet."
- Science and its Significance. Options include "Earthquakes" and "The Nature of Human Health and Disease."
- Arts and Letters. Students have the option of taking one of two survey courses on general themes relating to the liberal arts.
- Social Issues. Choices here are mostly tedious ("Gender Conflict in Cultural Contexts" or "Changing Family Forms") but some are solid: "Law, Politics and Public Policy" or "Religion and Ethical Issues."
- An approved "Diversity" course, of which the school offers many, ranging from "Medieval People: Early Europe and its Neighbors, 400–1500" to"Women's Spaces in History: 'Hussies,' 'Harems,' and 'Housewives.'"

West

tions on campus. Greek life is mostly confined to Fraternity Row along 28th Street, just north of campus. "The Row is generally open only to people in the Greek system," says a student. "They only very infrequently have open parties to which everyone is invited." Getting into fraternity parties is easy for pretty girls, students report, but nearly impossible for non-Greek men. Another student calls it "a world unto itself," but he also notes that it does carry weight around the college: "The Greek system is huge at USC."

Non-Greek housing at USC is primarily coeducational, although men and women are assigned to different wings or floors of certain buildings and bathrooms are single sex. Seven residence halls are primarily for freshmen, who make up the vast majority of the dorm population, although many of USC's school-run apartments are also set aside for first-year students. Students say rooms are sometimes hard to come by. "There are some nice dorms on campus, and none of them are infested or particularly dirty," a student says.

The Deans' Halls are some of many special-interest housing facilities on campus and are open to students who are the recipients of various university scholarships and those participating in honors programs. Other special-interest housing includes residential colleges that house faculty members as well, and floors like Somerville Place for black students, Latino floors, the Rainbow floor for GBLT students, as well as floors for students interest in art and architecture or music. On-campus houses for Jewish and Muslim students feature kosher and halal kitchens, respectively. "Diversity" at USC seems to involve less the mixing of cultures than their self-segregation, says one student: "Unfortunately the Koreans all hang out with other Koreans and the African Americans all hang out with other African Americans. There is no USC community—there are tiny communities that often fail to interact."

YELLOW LIGHT

"USC is a little more conservative than UCLA or the University of Washington or UC Berkeley," says one student. Another notes that the new Unruh Political Student Association "is meant to foster political discussions and events through this student-based group sponsored by the Unruh Institute of Politics. So far, they have encouraged events from both sides politically. "According to one student, because of the dynamic Christian religious groups on campus, "a lot of Christians on other campuses look to us and say 'That's what we want on our campus.'"

Such students might not envy USC's classroom atmosphere, however. One undergrad says, "If a student wishes to discuss religion, and he does not agree with the professor, that student will be made to look like a fool." Another student says, "I think you can see a humanistic, liberal secularism [in] everything on campus." Says one teaching assistant, "As a graduate student who teaches a class and takes English courses, I am by far in the minority in terms of political and religious views. My boss frequently goes on anti-fundamentalist/evangelical Christian rants in front of the entire department of eight assistant lecturers. No one objects, although the content is quite inflammatory. And the requirement for students to write essays for the 'Academic Community' is often just shorthand for kowtowing to left-leaning ideas."

The food is generally good, and it is available at numerous restaurants on campus and at one central dining facility. Freshmen in the dorms should expect to be forced onto the college's meal plan.

Students can't complete their USC experience without brushing up against traditions. They include kicking the light poles on the way to the Coliseum for a football game, the rivalry with UCLA, the annual Skull and Dagger prank, homecoming, the famous fight song, and taping up Tommy Trojan—the school's mascot—to save him from pranks at the hands of interloping UCLA students. "USC is nothing," says a student, "if it's not tradition-rich."

Students differ on the impact of crime on campus, though many point nervously to the dangerous surrounding neighborhood, known for homelessness and gang activity. In 2009, the school reported nine forcible sex offenses, one robbery, one aggravated assault, twenty-two burglaries, eight motor vehicle thefts, and two incidences of arson on campus. The north side of campus, where most students live, is generally safe; students say to avoid the south and west sides of campus, especially at night. "I feel very safe on campus, even at night, because we have a good Department of Public Safety here," a female student says. However, another considers "the area outside USC to be incredibly dangerous" and recommends that "all Metro buses are to be avoided, especially as a female." Says one student, "Let me be unequivocally clear: the surrounding area of the school is extremely dangerous. Muggings, hit-and-runs, and knifings are common in the blocks surrounding our area." The university does, however, send its armed public safety officers (who are police academy graduates) across campus and into surrounding neighborhoods, run a tram service, and provide students with "Campus Cruisers" to escort them around campus at night.

One thing many students have in common is money—a lot of it. 2010–11 tuition was $41,022 and room and board $11,580. However, admissions are need blind, and the school commits to meet the full need of any student who enrolls. One needy student says that USC "has one of the best financial-aid programs in the country." Some 60 percent of students get need-based aid, and the average loan debt of a recent grad is a manageable $16,663.

Southern Methodist University

Dallas, Texas • www.smu.edu

Oh Lord, won't you buy me . . . a presidential library

Southern Methodist University is known as one of the leading schools in the Southwest—and as a finishing school for children of the Texas business elite. There are probably more Mercedes-Benzes with Jesus fish parked here than anywhere in the world. (One professor notes wryly, "It's easier to find the Mercedes than the Jesus fish.") Yet the school also has been steadily developing its serious side—attracting and displaying serious scholars, not only in areas in which the school is traditionally competitive such as business and fine arts, but also in political science, history, psychology, and engineering. And after a contentious debate, the school agreed to house the $250 million George W. Bush Presidential Library on its campus when a faculty vote led by opponents of the library failed to win a majority. The library is patterned less on previous postpresidential archives than on the Hoover Institution at Stanford: the university website reports that "the George W. Bush Presidential Center . . . consists of the presidential library, containing documents and artifacts of the Bush Administration; a museum with permanent and traveling exhibits; and an independent public policy institute." This is already attracting and employing scholars and policy wonks at SMU and increasing the prestige of this already gold-plated university.

There are plenty of positive opportunities at hand at this prosperous, business-minded university. Whether the average freshman will know how to take advantage of them is another question. Says one teacher, "SMU combines many of the best features of liberal arts colleges and big research universities. It has the intellectual resources of a big school, with relatively small classes and a personal focus, a happy medium that offers the advantages of both."

The school's curricular requirements are no stronger than at most northeastern schools. Says one professor, "We don't have a very strong core. There's a lot of choice for students—as in 'one from Column A or B.' If you don't want a grounding in the classical Western tradition, you don't have to get it. You could fulfill your requirements through a hodgepodge of fluff, or entirely non-Western courses. Still, it's very possible to get that grounding, if you're motivated to get it." That is more than one can say for some other, more prestigious and expensive schools.

VITAL STATISTICS

Religious affiliation: *United Methodist*
Total enrollment: *10,891*
Total undergraduates: *6,228*
SAT/ACT midranges: CR: *560–660*, M: *580–680*; ACT: *25–30*
Applicants: *8,356*
Applicants accepted: *53%*
Accepted applicants who enrolled: *30%*
Tuition and fees: *$37,320*
Room and board: *$12,735*
Freshman retention rate: *88%*
Graduation rate: *62% (4 yrs.)*, *77% (6 yrs.)*
Courses with fewer than 20 students: *59%*
Student-faculty ratio: *11:1*
Courses taught by graduate students: *not provided*
Most popular majors: *business/finance, social sciences, communications*
Students living on campus: *33%*
Guaranteed housing for four years? *no*
Students in fraternities: *25%* in sororities: *32%*

Academic Life: That education business

Freshmen enter the university through Dedman College and are oriented through the General Education Curriculum, in which the liberal arts are divided into such groupings as "cultural formations" (interdisciplinary humanities and social sciences options, emphasizing writing) and "perspectives" (arts, literature, religious and philosophical thought, history, politics and economics, and behavioral sciences). Students majoring in the humanities, mathematics, the natural sciences, and the social or behavioral sciences remain in Dedman College. Others apply to the Cox School of Business, the School of Engineering, the Simmons School of Education and Development, or the Meadows School of the Arts.

A freshman looking for a liberal education will need to choose carefully in order to find a college education imparting substantive and foundational literacy in Western literature, history, and thought. There are hidden treasures available to budding humanists who seek them out. One graduate student says that his sense "is that, if so inclined, an undergraduate could successfully carve out a substantive 'classics' curriculum at SMU." However, among many students one finds a "disturbing utilitarian mentality, where people are looking to check off the boxes and move off to a preprofessional program. A little too much of a tendency to ask, 'What am I going to do with this?'" says a professor.

SMU is one of the tonier places to pursue a business or related degree in the region. It's the principal training ground for Dallas professionals, and the Cox School of Business offers the most popular majors—business and finance. According to a professor, the school "is considered one of the top twenty in the U.S. It's selective—you need a good GPA to declare a major there." One special opportunity for select business undergraduates is the BBA Leadership Institute, a seminar program taught by outside business leaders and professionals. Part of the Cox School, the program offers classes and seminars that address real-life business situations.

Despite its heavy business focus, the university seems to genuinely want to fulfill the mandate of its Master Plan of 1963, which stated that "professional studies must rise from the solid foundation of a basic liberal education." SMU promises to provide small classes, and in fact prides itself on this: most course sections have fifty students or fewer. The University Honors Program is even better, allowing about 600 students to take intimate seminars on

West

special topics with enrollment in each course capped at twenty students. Teaching assistants rarely preside over such classes.

Entering freshmen at SMU are required to take courses comprising a "wellness program," an attempted primer on methods for maintaining personal well-being and balance in undergraduate life. Most call the classes easy; the word "fluff" also comes up. SMU's Department of Wellness "challenges students to think critically about who they are" and seeks to enhance the social, physical, emotional, and spiritual well-being of students. There's something of an emphasis on an "I'm OK, you're OK" self-consoling approach to life issues in the program. One student says, "I think that the part about making good life choices is great, but the part that basically says that 'no one is ever wrong' really bothers me." The existence of, and early emphasis on, the wellness program is emblematic of a university administration that is known (and looked upon with gratitude) as being highly solicitous of the personal needs of individual students. The administration is said to actively seek the views of students on matters affecting campus life and is quite willing to spend money to address frequently voiced concerns.

Professors are considered easily accessible and often show an unusual degree of willingness to give one-on-one attention to freshmen. The university also provides what it calls an "academic safety net" for its students in the form of the Learning Enhancement Center, where students can take seminars on time and stress management, receive writing tutorials, or enroll in an elective that builds study skills.

The university has a solid academic reputation in the humanities that continues to improve. English and history are well regarded at SMU, and its theater and arts programs are nationally recognized. Psychology "has built itself into quite a good department," says a professor. "It used to be one of our weaker ones. The faculty made the major more challenging and did a lot of hiring of more productive research faculty." Anthropology offers excellent training in archaeological research, particularly in the Americas. "We have someone doing cutting-edge work in Mayan spots, and a campus facility and summer program in Taos, New Mexico," says a professor.

The history department shines in the study of the American Southwest, thanks to a special endowment from former governor Bill Clements. The department is mostly solid if you make it a point to avoid the ethnic studies and women's studies programs and their course offerings. History majors are required to take classes in American history before and after 1865, and are offered a fair amount of traditional Western civilization courses as well. Majors must also complete a rigorous junior seminar in research and writing.

SUGGESTED CORE

1. Religious Studies 3319/3326, Introduction to the Hebrew Bible/New Testament
2. English 2310-002, Imagination and Interpretations: The Epic Foundations of Western Literature
3. Philosophy 3351, History of Western Philosophy (Ancient)
4. Religious Studies 3349, Early Christianity or History 2321, Philosophical and Religious Thought in the Medieval West
5. Political Science 3361, Modern Political Thought
6. English 4333-001, Shakespeare
7. History 2311, Out of Many: U.S. History to 1877
8. History 3376, Social and Intellectual History of Europe

West

A student describes the university's English department as "professionally distinguished" and has high praise for some of its professors. There is an annual literary festival on campus, and the university also publishes *Southwest Review*, one of the four oldest continuously published literary quarterlies in the nation. English majors must study medieval, early modern, and modern literature, as well as poetry and literary criticism. Shakespeare is not specifically required, but he would be hard to miss. There are many other worthy classes available to fulfill the major requirements.

SMU offers some exceptional opportunities for political science majors. The department has a strong focus on American government and politics, and in political theory—"especially in Enlightenment and modern political thought," says a professor. All poli sci majors must complete courses on the U.S. Constitution and American political philosophy as well as classes in international politics and political theory. The department is bolstered by a prestigious political studies institute, the John Goodwin Tower Center for Political Studies (named for the former senator), which focuses on international relations and comparative politics. The center was established to support teaching and research programs in international studies and national security policy, and one could hardly think of a more relevant area of concentration in these tense and ideologically inflamed times. The center offers competitive internships in Washington, D.C., and a limited number of research fellowships for undergraduates. Fellows receive stipends of up to $700 per semester for a maximum of four consecutive semesters and develop research projects under faculty supervision for publication or presentation to professional organizations or faculty committees. The Tower Center has also worked with distinguished polling organizations such as Zogby in conducting research into the views of the American public on foreign nations and international politics.

The hard sciences are not as strong as the social sciences, a teacher tells us. "Those departments are mostly fairly weak, smaller than they should be. SMU has somewhat underinvested in those areas. I also hear negative reports on teaching in those departments—for instance, grad students not fluent in English," he says.

However, the university's Meadows School of the Arts is highly esteemed. Its facilities include the Bob Hope and Greer Garson theaters, funded by those performers. Also of note is the Meadows Museum which exhibits one of the finest collections of Spanish art outside Spain, according to the university website. The Meadows School has earned a prominent place nationally among American art schools and offers diverse programs—visual arts (art and art history), performing arts (dance, music, and theater), and communications (advertising, cinema-television, corporate communications and public affairs, and journalism), as well as an excellent program in arts administration.

Highly recommended SMU professors include John Lamoreaux in religious studies; Joseph Kobylka, Michael Lusztig, Dennis Simon, and J. Matthew Wilson in political science; Willard Spiegelman and Bonnie Wheeler in English; and Jeremy Adams, Edward Countryman, and Dan Orlovsky in history

For students looking to study abroad, SMU offers over two dozen year-long, semester, and summer abroad programs to places all over the globe, including Egypt, China, New Zealand, Ecuador, Australia, Vietnam, Brazil, Turkey, Peru, Ghana, India, South Africa, Sengal, and many others. Students who need a break from the upper-class environs of The

Park Cities without leaving the country can study during the summer at SMU's campus in beautiful Taos. Located in a former Civil War fort, SMU–Taos is "contained within the Carson National Forest and surrounded by the Sangre de Cristo Mountains," standing "at an elevation of almost 7,500 feet," according to the school. Classes are held from May through August in subjects such as "anthropology, art, communications, cultural formations, English, history, religion, wellness," and several of the sciences.

SMU offers majors in French, German, Spanish, and Italian area studies or simply in foreign languages. Minors are offered in Chinese, Japanese, Latin, Ancient Greek, and Russian.

Student Life: Greek envy

SMU is located in Highland Park and University Park (a.k.a. "The Park Cities"), an affluent section of Dallas with many dining, cultural, and nightlife attractions and conveniences.

ACADEMIC REQUIREMENTS

Southern Methodist does not have a traditional core curriculum, but maintains a respectable set of distribution requirements. Unfortunately, most of the seemingly substantive mandates can be met by taking bizarre or politicized classes. All students must take the following:

- Two English composition classes.
- One math course.
- One class in information technology, such as "Introduction to Computing Concepts" or "Mass Media and Technology."
- Two laboratory courses, at least one of which must be selected from biology, chemistry, geology, or physics.
- One fine arts class. Class options include "Basics of Photography" and "Music: The Art of Listening."
- One literature course. Course offerings range from "History of British Literature" to "Literature of Minorities."
- One course in religious/philosophical thought. Class choices include "Introduction to the New Testament" and "Introductory Logic."
- One history/art history class. Because these two disparate categories are thrown together, students can avoid taking anything weightier than the "History of Photography."
- One course in politics and economics. Course options include "Introduction to Comparative Politics" and "Exploring Economic Issues."
- One behavioral sciences class. Course options include "Introductory Psychology" and "Sociology of Gender."
- Two cultural formations classes. Options range from "Bioethics from a Christian Perspective" to "Lesbian and Gay Literature and Film: Minority Discourse and Social Power."
- One "diversity" course. Choices here include "The Holocaust" and "Female Trouble: Stories of Women."

West

Some consider the school a haven for rich kids more concerned with their choice of fraternities or sororities than with academics. In fact, the stereotypical SMU student is an affluent Texan or southern preppy. While the campus is overwhelmingly white, there has been an increase in Latino students in recent years coinciding with the administration's obsession with "diversity" on campus. At the same time, many students emphasize that the climate is basically upbeat, open, and friendly, with little snobbery publicly evident. Given the context of SMU's tradition of rather homogeneous social elitism, such "diversification" efforts are not quite as absurd as they are on most other campuses.

A third of all students live on campus where the facilities are excellent and "feature a variety of room types, bathroom styles, and community areas," according to the school's website. The ten residence halls, four apartment halls, and eight theme houses are all coed, non-smoking, and have high-quality, state-of-the-art accommodations, including carpeted rooms, local phone service with voicemail, Internet access, air conditioning, 24-hour security card access system, laundry rooms, microwaves, and vending machines. Single, double, and triple occupancy are available in the residence halls, and each hall has both a resident assistant and a Hall Director who are in charge of resident life and manage a support staff of students. All halls observe a minimum of ten quiet hours a day, typically beginning 10:00 PM on weeknights and midnight on the weekends, although hours may be adjusted by community vote. There are no visitation hours, but all guests must be escorted at all times by the hall residents whom they are visiting.

SMU also owns several unfurnished efficiency, one-bedroom and two-bedroom apartments adjacent to campus that are available for a monthly rental rate.

A third of all undergraduates are also in fraternities and sororities and most of their upperclassmen live in the Greek houses. Although students involved in Greek life frequently go out of their way to insist that the social atmosphere at SMU is open, friendly, and nonexclusive, there's no denying the heavy social dominance of the fraternities. Recent graduates have reported that some young women actually choose to transfer to other schools when they don't make their sorority of choice.

Social life revolves around the weekly fraternity parties. It's said that the weekend begins on Thursday night, to the degree that Friday has the greatest manifestation of class-skipping. Friday night is devoted to relentless revelry, Saturday to recovery, and Sunday to cleaning up and gearing up for the week ahead. Campus parties continue to draw seniors and juniors who have moved off campus.

Special-interest-club social activities are lively during the week, and theater and political groups are popular. Social and student government "leadership development" activities, such as the Leadership Consultant Council (LCC), Program Council, Student Foundation, and Student Senate are also unusually prestigious at SMU. The university is traditionally a launching pad for careers in politics—especially if you're a Republican. However, the local atmosphere is changing: in recent years, Democrats have swept most local offices in Dallas, a city that has been written up nationally as both increasingly liberal and "gay friendly."

The student newspaper, the *Daily Campus*, has a fairly healthy reputation for vigorous debate between contributors of various viewpoints. One provocative exchange involved a proponent of the "intelligent design" critique of Darwinian evolution, biologist Michael Behe, and

West

SMU professor John Wise. This exchange was notable for the newspaper's willingness to give Behe's views a serious hearing in the first place.

"SMU has a strong group of ethicists, including Robin Lovin at the Perkins School of Theology," says one student. "There is a core of religiously committed students, but overall the campus is pretty secular," says a professor. "There is no hostility to religion. Christian students won't encounter opposition, but SMU doesn't have a genuine Christian flavor. It's about as palpably religious as Georgetown. Religious programs are there, but students would have to seek them out." Still, a student observes that there seem to be "a large number of students involved in on-campus Christian ministries." Campus Crusade for Christ alone draws roughly a hundred students to its weekly meetings. There are many local churches and other houses of worship available in Dallas—and the more devout students should probably seek them out. The comparatively conservative St. Thomas Aquinas Catholic parish is a short drive away, as is Park Cities Presbyterian, a solid Protestant congregation.

SMU's fifteen sports teams, the Mustangs, compete in the NCAA's Division I, and the school's thirteen club sports and eighteen intramural teams are very popular with students. The state-of-the-art fitness and recreation center was recently completed and the athletic facilities are second to none, including the spectacular Gerald Ford football stadium.

There is ample police presence on campus, and female students say they feel quite safe; however, in 2009 the school reported seven forcible sex offenses, two aggravated assaults, three robberies, thirty-three burglaries, and nine stolen cars on campus. Contrary to common perception, Dallas is one of the more dangerous major cities in America, so students are advised to exercise caution.

With 2010–11 tuition at $37,320 and room and board at $12,735, SMU is fairly expensive. Only 36 percent of students receive need-based financial aid, and the average student-loan debt of a recent graduate was $20,146.

GREEN LIGHT

The SMU student body is moderately conservative. Many note that the professors are generally more liberal than either the "decidedly Republican" student body or the larger community, although the faculty is said to be less left-leaning than comparable universities. One professor calls his colleagues "more conservative than that of most major American research universities. There is ideological diversity, with conservatives and Republicans on the faculty. I've heard of very few incidents of political intimidation in class—most of them in rhetoric classes in the English department taught by instructors."

One student states that the campus "is located in an extremely conservative community and surrounded by a [relatively] conservative urban area. Occasionally I've observed some liberal groups who have placed fliers around campus. The school newspaper seems to be more to the left." Some students have noticed elements of political correctness they find irksome. The Office of New Student Programs requires its student leaders to take part in a diversity exercise that one student says "demeans every white, rich male who happens to be fortunate enough to be born with a mom and a dad in the home." Privileged treatment of "designated victim" groups can occur. One freshman reports that recently the school axed the debate team for not having enough members, while leaving intact the homosexual organization, which had fewer members.

Stanford University

Palo Alto, California • www.stanford.edu

Make yourself useful

Leland Stanford, founder of Stanford University, was a successful businessman and politician who also valued the liberal arts. "I have noticed," Stanford once said, "that technically educated boys do not make the most successful businessmen." Cultured citizens, Stanford argued, were also useful citizens. Leland Stanford's insight appears to have been lost on those who now look after his patrimony. Stanford University's reputation as a leader in both the sciences and the liberal arts began to fade in 1987, when it abandoned its Western civilization requirement—after a storm of student protest directed by Jesse Jackson, who led the infamous chant, "Hey hey, ho ho, Western Civ has got to go."

Today, instead of Western civilization, Stanford requires courses in world cultures, American "cultures," or gender studies. Perhaps as a result, Stanford students have found little to entice them to explore the liberal arts and have increasingly turned toward technical fields such as computer science and engineering. The growth of the high-tech sector and the transformation of Stanford's Silicon Valley home in Palo Alto from sleepy farmland to the center of the new economy has further solidified the university's position and reputation as a leader in the technical, rather than the liberal, arts.

There are bright spots: the Stanford philosophy department was rated number nine in the United States by the Philosophical Gourmet Report, and Stanford has used its technological prowess to pioneer making scholarly collections available free online. On the other hand, Stanford has become a factory of stem cell research that cannibalizes human embryos for parts. One of the leading critics of such research is Stanford's own William Hurlbut, a renowned pro-life neurobiologist.

Yet Stanford continues to attract the "best and the brightest." Its graduates are found on the United States Supreme Court (Justices Breyer and Kennedy, as well as the retired Sandra Day O'Connor, and the late William Rehnquist). Eighteen Stanford graduates, including Sally Ride, have served as astronauts. Stanford is second only to Harvard in the number of graduates serving in Congress.

However, students who want a broad, humane education at Stanford must piece it together at a school that can seem uninterested in the traditional humanities but excels in the technical fields. In other words, Stanford specializes in solving the question of "how" to achieve a goal. It has lost sight of the question, "why."

Academic Life: The decline of Western Civ

Students who are mature and savvy enough can find good liberal arts courses at Stanford. As one conservative student wrote, "Stanford definitely has its share of politicized courses with their multicultural dogma. But the courses which form a foundation in Western civilization, although not mandatory, are readily available for the taking." The best option is the Program in Structured Liberal Education (SLE), a "year-long, residential, rigorous writing and literature course that intensely covers the canon of Western civilization along with some material on Hinduism and Buddhism," says a past participant. SLE freshmen live together in three houses, allowing them to learn and discuss ideas outside the classroom. An alumnus warns "It's not exactly super friendly to conservative Christian viewpoints. But fortunately, a Catholic SLE alumnus started a program of 'SLE talks' explaining the Christian perspective on various issues SLE covers a few years back, and we've kept it alive."

Stanford boasts a stellar six-to-one student-faculty ratio. Students say that professors are accessible to undergraduates, despite the pressure to publish that many faculty members experience. "I've yet to have a professor, of any rank or stature, not return an e-mail," one student says. "In terms of access to professors, you really can't beat Stanford." Graduate teaching assistants rarely teach courses, but they do often lead discussion or laboratory sections for larger lecture classes.

Over the years, students and faculty have complained that grade inflation is a problem at Stanford. A student says that "a popular saying at Stanford is, 'You must work hard to get an A but you must do absolutely nothing to earn a C.'"

Each freshman is assigned a "pre-major" advisor with whom he must meet before he can register for classes. Advisors are also located in each freshman dorm. After choosing a major, each student is assigned (or chooses) a faculty advisor. One student warns that "quality varies dramatically, and the good advisors are in high demand. Professors really do act as mentors." Another adds that he has "access to a pool of conservative professors who are eager to help like-minded students and who aren't in high demand from the rest of the student body."

Stanford's humanities departments are riddled with politically correct programs, such as the Center for Comparative Studies in Race and Ethnicity, African and African

VITAL STATISTICS

Religious affiliation: *none*
Total enrollment: *19,535*
Total undergraduates: *6,940*
SAT/ACT midranges: CR: *670–760*, M: *690–790*; ACT: *31–34*
Applicants: *32,022*
Applicants accepted: *7%*
Accepted applicants who enrolled: *72%*
Tuition and fees: *$38,700*
Room and board: *$11,876*
Freshman retention rate: *98%*
Graduation rate: *78% (4 yrs.)*, *95% (6 yrs.)*
Courses with fewer than 20 students: *70%*
Student-faculty ratio: *6:1*
Courses taught by graduate students: *not provided*
Most popular majors: *biology, economics, international relations*
Students living on campus: *91%*
Guaranteed housing for four years? *yes*
Students in fraternities: *13%* in sororities: *13%*

SUGGESTED CORE

1. English 314, Epic and Empire
2. Philosophy 100, Greek Philosophy
3. English 180: The Bible as Literature
4. Philosophy 101A , Medieval Religious Philosophy (closest match)
5. Political Science 130B, History of Political Thought II: Early Modern Political Theory
6. English 373c, Shakespeare
7. History 150A/150B, Colonial and Revolutionary America/Nineteenth-Century America
8. Modern Thought and Literature 136A, European Thought and Culture in the Nineteenth Century

American studies, and feminist studies (which now includes "queer" studies). This last program has, as one student puts it, "a huge" presence on campus, sponsoring lectures, activist workshops, and essay contests.

On the bright side, Stanford's history department boasts three Pulitzer Prize winners: David Kennedy (emeritus), Carl Degler (emeritus), and Jack Rakove. According to one history student, " I would not say there was an overt bias against Western civilization, and it's fairly easy to avoid the 'politically correct' classes and still fill your requirements. So far, such classes have fairly obvious clues regarding their nature and have not been a problem. But there are a lot of them." Another student says, "Many of the political science classes are liberal and PC, but if you look you can find some classes that are taught by conservative professors," a student says.

A number of Stanford faculty members are tabbed by students as outstanding teachers, including Judith L. Goldstein in political science and public policy; Robert Sapolsky and William James Nelson in biology, Philip Zimbardo (emeritus) in psychology; David Kennedy (emeritus), and Norman Naimark in history; Jack Rakov in history, American studies and political science; Scott Hutchins in English; John C. Bravman (emeritus) in materials engineering; Jack Baker in Civil and Environmental Engineering; Kathleen M. Eisenhardt in management; Alyssa O'Brien and John Peterson in writing and rhetoric; Brad D. Osgood in electrical engineering; Douglas D. Osheroff (emeritus) in physics; George Springer (emeritus) in aeronautics and astronautics; Mark Lucianovic in mathematics; Eric Roberts and Mehran Sahami in computer science; Michael Bratman in philosophy; Roger Noll (emeritus), Michael Boskin, and Robert Hall in economics; and William Hurlbut in bioethics.

Political science, especially, is reputed to have excellent undergraduate teaching, with several professors having filled key administrative positions in Washington, D.C. Condoleeza Rice, former Secretary of State under President George W. Bush, is back at Stanford, based at the Hoover Institution and on the political science and graduate school of business faculties. She teaches a popular by-application-only undergraduate seminar, "Challenges and Dilemmas in American Foreign Policy."

Political science majors must declare a concentration in international relations, American politics, political theory, or comparative politics, and take six courses in that area, as well as at least three courses in a secondary concentration. All majors must also take a "methods" course and complete at least one advanced undergraduate political science seminar. One of the courses taken towards the major must entail "sustained research and writing." A major could easily miss any courses addressing the American Constitution and political system.

West

To major in English, a student must take "Poetry and Poetics," "Narrative and Narrative Theory," and "Critical Methods;" and "Literary History" courses I, II, and III—covering, respectively, British literature before 1750, British and American literature from the seventeenth through the nineteenth centuries, and literature/media from the nineteenth to the present—plus an additional literary history class and a senior seminar. Majors concentrate in English literature, English and creative writing, English and philosophy, or English with an interdisciplinary emphasis. Shakespeare makes an appearance in one of the survey courses.

History majors at Stanford must complete at least two courses in each of the following categories: premodern history; the Americas; Africa, Asia and the Middle East; and Europe. None of these courses need address the founding of the United States or the Civil War, or any precontemporary aspect of Western civilization or European history. Students must complete at least four courses in an area of concentration; these must include a colloquium or research seminar.

The strength of Stanford now resides in its science and engineering programs. Over the years, Stanford has been able to attract a core group of premier physicists and physical scientists, including several who have been awarded the Nobel Prize: Steven Chu (emeritus), Robert Laughlin, Douglas D. Osheroff (emeritus), and Burton Richter (emeritus). They develop and conduct research at the Stanford Linear Accelerator Center, a world-renowned center for physics that offers a number of educational programs to the public. Despite the school's stellar reputation in engineering and science, students majoring in other disciplines can graduate without a very rigorous experience in math or science, given the broad "general education" requirements.

Students can study classics, Arabic, Catalan, Chinese, French, German, Italian, Japanese, Korean, Portuguese, Slavic, Spanish, and Tibetan languages, as well as some other languages by special arrangement. Stanford students can study abroad in virtually any corner of the globe, and generous financial aid policies help make this possible for all students.

Student Life: Silicon implants

Stanford sits like a high-powered microchip in suburban Silicon Valley. Even with downtown San Francisco only forty-five minutes away, students find little reason to leave campus, for Stanford seems to have it all. The buildings are inspired by the California Mission style, with red-tiled roofs and sandstone walls. Student amenities abound, such as attractively renovated residence halls, and the university's own shopping center, with stores such as Macy's and Nordstrom's. Stanford is in the midst of a building boom. The university has recently completed state-of-the-science complexes for its engineering and medical divisions, its morally bankrupt stem cell program, and a new economic policy center. Among ongoing projects is an "arts district" being formed at the entrance to campus, to be anchored by the Bing Concert Hall.

Most students live on campus all four years, as Bay Area housing prices are exorbitant. Housing is guaranteed for four years. In general, students enjoy living on campus; as one student says, "Stanford's on-campus housing is wonderful." There are many different styles of living, from apartments to house-style units, dorms, and co-ops. Except for one all-female residence, dormitories are coed, with some single-sex floors, but fraternities and sororities provide single-sex options. One student states that bathrooms are usually single-sex. A pilot program begun largely to meet demands of "transgender" students has now resulted in permanent implementation of "gender-neutral housing" in a number of student residences, allowing students of opposite sexes to share a double room. There are no male/female visitation rules. Many of the dorms and houses are theme-oriented, including houses primarily for members of certain ethnic groups, as well as academic interest houses and dorms offering foreign language focus. Some have unofficial designations, such as the

ACADEMIC REQUIREMENTS

Stanford has no core curriculum. Instead, the university requires that students complete:

- "Introduction to the Humanities" ("IHUM"), a three-quarter introductory humanities sequence. A student wrote in the *Stanford Review*, "The program is so universally hated that I sometimes suspect that it was designed to give freshmen some shared misery over which to bond." Citing "monotonous lectures, pointless reading, [and] inscrutable grading," the student called the program "a failed 'forced compromise' between an attempt to present the Western canon and and a 'broad brush' approach to appealing to students' interests."
- Two writing-intensive courses in any discipline and one in the major department.
- One year of foreign language study.

Student must take one course in each of the following disciplines, with hundreds of course options qualifying:

- Engineering and applied sciences. Choices include "Introduction to Chemical Engineering" and "Fail Your Way to Success."
- Humanities, where options range from "Masterpieces of English Literature I: Chaucer, Shakespeare, Milton, and their Contemporaries," to "Stand Up Comedy and the 'Great American Joke' Since 1945."
- Math. Choices range from "Calculus" to "Mathematics of Sports."
- Natural sciences. Options include "Organic Chemistry Lab" and "Views of a Changing Sea: Literature and Science."
- Social sciences, where choices range all the way from "Introduction to American National Government and Politics" to "Poetics and Politics of Caribbean Women's Literature."
- Students also take two courses out of the following four categories: ethical reasoning, the global community, American cultures, and gender studies. Many of these classes "offer little more than leftist politics," according to a student. Options include "Introduction to Feminist Studies," and "The Daoist Body" as well as "Colonial and Revolutionary America" and "Introduction to Medieval Philosophy." One student recommends the popular course "Justice," taught by Professor Joshua Cohen.

West

"gay" or "lesbian" house. The *Stanford Review* has voiced criticism of the ethnic dorms, citing those who say "that the dorms encourage the formation of 'separatist enclaves.'" A student notes that "RAs are immensely helpful on all fronts. I, however, do lament the very lenient policy regarding alcohol in dorms."

About 13 percent of undergraduates belong to the sixteen fraternities and thirteen sororities (a new sorority was added in January 2011), which provide a significant source of social life as well as single-sex housing, albeit often in a party atmosphere. (Greek houses are periodically placed on suspension for alcohol violations.) Ten of the Greek organizations have residential houses on campus, while the rest are unhoused. The frats don't have a monopoly on the campus party scene, however; Stanford allows alcohol in some of its dorms and students say that nearly everyone drinks, although there is no evident peer pressure to do so, and that alcohol and drug use are no more prevalent than at comparable California schools.

Undergraduate students are not the only ones living on campus—56 percent of graduate students and 30 percent of faculty also reside on "the Farm," the nickname for Stanford's scenic 8,200-acre spread.

Stanford is what the student makes of it. As one undergrad says: "Between the entrenched *Stanford Review* and the Stanford Conservative Society, I'm fairly confident that conservatives and moderates can find a home away from the propaganda." The Conservative Society serves primarily as a forum for conservatives to gather socially rather than for in-depth discussion. A student does tell us, however, that "the Veritas Forum and some good, truth-probing multi-faith panels are also increasingly active on campus, "providing lively discussion and conservative and faith-based viewpoints on various topics.

Another place where conservatives might find solace is the Hoover Institution, a public policy research center housed on Stanford's campus. Hoover frequently sponsors lectures, has an active internship program, and is a resource for reasoned scholarship on issues of considerable public interest. Three current Hoover affiliates are Nobel laureates: economists Gary S. Becker, Michael Spence (emeritus), and Douglass North. The *Stanford Review* sponsors "Hoover luncheons" with Institution fellows, open to the entire campus.

Some conservatives report feeling that they need to hide their views from peers. One undergrad student tells us that she received hate mail after writing an article favoring California's Proposition 8, a successful legislative initiative to preserve traditional marriage. A writer for the *Stanford Review* says that it is "a popular target of casual mockery among most students."

While Memorial Church is certainly a masterpiece (its splendid mosaics are world famous), the services there may disappoint believers in anything in particular. According to the church's website, its Sunday morning service is entirely ecumenical, including male and female ministers and a rabbi.

The Catholic presence on campus is strong, with "a very solid core of students who are quite orthodox in their beliefs and practices. The preaching and teaching is typically quite faithful to Church teachings, and the entire ministry staff is wonderfully and admirably dedicated to the spiritual welfare of the community." However, more conservative Catholic students frequent Our Mother of Perpetual Help parish in nearby Santa Clara, which offers Latin Masses.

A number of conservative undergraduates tell us that while Stanford is predominantly liberal and secular, they are still relatively comfortable there. One traditional Christian undergraduate says, "I have not had personal experience with a particular department being consistently unwelcoming to conservative or religious students. It is much more common for a particular professor, TA, or even student to make their (usually liberal) political ideas known to the class. In general campus is lively and open to political debate, as there is a strong minority of conservatives here." The student says that "Students for Life holds a memorial on the anniversary of *Roe v. Wade* every year, placing white stakes, resembling grave markers, in the center of White Plaza. The club then stands at a table nearby in case anyone has questions or wants to talk. It has become a tradition for pro-choice students to then rally in White Plaza as well and play loud music and pass out free condoms."

Another student says, "I have not heard one complaint about people's viewpoints affecting their grades, even in departments commonly considered 'hostile' to conservative ideas.... [W]hile there is certainly a quite vocal contingent of students eager to quash all dissent with regards to gender and sexuality issues, I don't feel that most people are unwilling to engage in open debate and discussion on most issues."

There is a joint Episcopal and Lutheran ministry at Stanford, so more orthodox-minded Episcopalian/Anglican believers should seek out Christ the King Church in Campbell, a more traditional parish. Evangelical Christians have a number of active groups on campus and InterVarsity Christian Fellowship holds weekly Bible studies in all freshman dorms.

Stanford appears to offer a student club or society for nearly every interest. Hundreds of organizations, ranging from academic to preprofessional to athletic to religious to multicultural are available. Clubs include Chabad and Hillel for Jewish students, Student Organization, a number of publications including the *Stanford Daily* and the *Cardinal Principal*, humor magazines, and an undergraduate philosophy journal, career and preprofessional clubs, music, dance, and drama groups, Stanford Dragon Boat, a radio station, Women and Youth Supporting Each Other, Reformed University Fellowship, and the ReJOYce in Jesus Campus Fellowship. Beside the *Review* and the Conservative Society, there are other worthy groups such as Stanford Students for Life. The Haas Center for Public Service provides numerous opportunities for students.

Palo Alto offers students plenty of distractions, especially restaurants and shops, but it "just isn't a college town, and there isn't much there for Stanford students," says one student. Another student says Palo Alto is a pleasant enough place, but that it "is somewhat pricey. A better bet is Castro Street in Mountain View [five miles from campus].... The area is more middle class and less yuppie, the food is cheaper, and there aren't as many crazies around."

Cardinal athletics are an important part of student life at Stanford. Stanford is a Division I school, fielding teams in baseball, softball, men's and women's basketball, rowing, water polo and soccer, football, and many other sports. Since 1980, the Cardinal (not Cardinals; the name refers to the school color) have won almost ninety-nine NCAA team championships. Tiger Woods, Mike Mussina, and John Elway are three former Cardi-

West

nal athletes who have gone on to stardom. Stanford has won the National Association of Collegiate Directors of Athletics "Directors' Cup," based upon highest overall success in intercollegiate sports, for sixteen consecutive years. The university also has a number of intramural and club sports, plus several noncredit recreation programs in activities such as Afro-Caribbean dance, rock climbing, and golf. Stanford's mascot, "The Tree," is regularly featured on "worst mascot" lists.

Most students say they feel safe on campus. However, the numbers make us nervous. In 2009, the school reported ten forcible sexual assaults, 146 burglaries, fifteen stolen motor vehicles, two robberies, five aggravated assaults, and one arson on campus. Directly off campus, students say Palo Alto attracts many homeless people, who, one student notes, "may threaten to kill you." According to one student, the most common thefts are of bikes and there is some evidence that transients from the Palo Alto area occasionally break into the dorms and steal laptops. Students returning home late at night can call for an escort if they don't feel safe. While the campus is well-lit, surrounding streets are not.

Stanford offers a world-renowned education and charges a commensurate tuition, which in 2010–11 was $38,700, with $11,876 for room and board. Stanford does not ask any parental contribution towards tuition or room or board for families with incomes under $60,000. It is the school's policy to provide grant-only aid and not require students to take loans. Of students who did borrow, however, the average debt of a recent grad is $14,058.

University of Texas at Austin

Austin, Texas • www.utexas.edu

Wal-Mart U.

Founded in 1883 on just forty acres, with a single building, two departments, eight teachers, and a little more than 200 students, the University of Texas at Austin is now one of the largest public universities in America. The main campus, just a quarter mile from the Texas State Capitol, has grown to 424 acres with more than 21,000 faculty and staff, seventeen colleges and schools, and over 50,000 students.

If the typical large university is a mall, then as one student says, the University of Texas at Austin is "the Wal-Mart of higher education." With more than 350 undergraduate degree programs on offer, it's a one-stop shop where all political ideologies, oddball hobbies, and career interests are nurtured or, in some cases, pandered to. The good news is that a first-rate classic liberal arts education is available to enterprising students who seek it out. One graduate student reports, "Overall, the campus is a hotbed of political correctness, but if a student is smart and does research into which classes to take and what professors in those classes teach, he can still get a solid education. It just takes a little effort."

Perhaps the most salient political issue on the UT campus is race and its use in admissions. After a Supreme Court decision permitted it to reinstate the use of race in admissions, the university has been doing so aggressively since the entering class of 2005. Given that state law since 1997 has required UT to automatically admit all high school graduates in the top 10 percent of their classes who wish to enroll, these policies have combined to put an extraordinary strain on the university. Texas lawmakers make noise every year around election time promising to repeal or alter this crippling law, but the outrage subsides and the promises are forgotten after election day, only to be resurrected with the same furor when re-election campaigns resume.

To add insult to injury, current UT president William Powers Jr., instituted a "four-point strategic plan" to ensure that race is paramount in determining admissions and new hires. One UT student claims that "diversity of skin color, diversity of national origin, etc., are valued, but diversity of thought, in general, is not." The term "diversity" itself is frequently a code-word for outright hatred of Western culture and all its works; the religious pursuit of this unholy grail has ruined other universities. Texans, stay tuned.

Academic Life: Attention, shoppers!

In keeping with its home state's ethos, that "everything's bigger in Texas," UT has more than 170 fields of study and 120 majors, and the sheer quantity of choices on offer demands that students have some help in making wise ones. Yet academically, most UT students go it alone. "What we can't do at a place like UT is maintain any serious quality control," a professor says. "That someone has 'earned' a BA at a large state university means nothing." What universities like UT do instead, this professor says, is "magnify the dangers that are inherent in the modern elective system—they offer a smorgasbord of dislocated and quirky courses on a far larger scale. They also offer the raw materials for a classic liberal education, if you know how to find them and put them together."

The flip side of an abundance of choice is that there's a niche for everyone, a situation most students praise. Rapidly locating and scurrying into that niche is critical at such a massive school. While UT students are not unfriendly, the vast majority of faces will be unfamiliar as you're hoofing it across the sprawling campus from class to class. "I feel about as much camaraderie with my fellow students at UT as I do with someone off the street who wears the same brand of shoes I do," one student says.

At many colleges it is easy to be a science or engineering major and never encounter the great works of the West; at UT that is also possible for liberal arts majors. "Play your cards 'right' in UT's liberal arts college and watch yourself learn nothing toward a classical education," a student says. "All in all, you can get a liberal arts degree from UT and really have no education at all."

Happily, a group of distinguished faculty at UT rose to the occasion and developed a serious initiative which addresses the curriculum's civilization gap. Lorraine and Thomas Pangle, professors of government and directors of the Thomas Jefferson Center for the Study of Core Texts and Ideas, stepped forward as leaders for the revival of a Great Books canon. The program hopes to offer students throughout the university the opportunity of satisfying the core curriculum requirements with courses that include "major works of philosophy, religion, history, and literature; seminal writings in the sciences and social sciences; works of art; and major political documents and speeches, with special attention to the development of ethical, political, and religious ideas as reflected in works of enduring value." The Thomas Jefferson Center describes its Certificate Program in

VITAL STATISTICS

Religious affiliation: *none*
Total enrollment: *50,995*
Total undergraduates: *38,168*
SAT/ACT midranges: CR: *530–660*, M: *570–700*; ACT: *24–30*
Applicants: *31,362*
Applicants accepted: *46%*
Accepted applicants who enrolled: *51%*
Tuition and fees: *in state, $9,418; out of state, $31,218*
Room and board: *$10,112*
Freshman retention rate: *93%*
Graduation rate: *48% (4 yrs.), 81% (6 yrs.)*
Courses with fewer than 20 students: *36%*
Student-faculty ratio: *17:1*
Courses taught by graduate students: *not provided*
Most popular majors: *biology, business, psychology*
Students living on campus: *20%*
Guaranteed housing for four years? *no*
Students in fraternities: *10%* in sororities: *12%*

SUGGESTED CORE

1. Classical Civilization 322, Classical Literature in Translation
2. Philosophy 301K, Ancient Philosophy
3. Religious Studies 315N, Introduction to the New Testament or English 358J, The Bible as Literature
4. Philosophy 349, History of Medieval and Renaissance Philosophy
5. Government 351D, The Theoretical Foundations of Modern Politics
6. English 321, Shakespeare: Selected Plays
7. History 315K, United States, 1492–1865
8. History 332, European Intellectual History from the Enlightenment to Nietzsche

the Core Texts and Ideas as an "introduction to the liberal arts through the study of the great books . . . open to all UT undergraduates to complement any major with an integrated sequence of six courses that can also meet the UT general education requirements." Students interested in a less structured alternative to the Core Texts and Ideas program may take either a six-course concentration in Western civilization or a four-course minor in Core Texts and Ideas. The Jefferson Center also sponsors a book club, a lecture series, and an executive seminar series for local professionals and community leaders.

Other ways students can improve on UT's inadequate general distribution requirements are through programs that serve as challenging interdepartmental options for advanced students. For example, Plan II Honors, a major in itself, is a core-like sequence designed for students who show high proficiency in both language and mathematics. Plan II students are very bright, with average combined verbal and mathematics SAT scores of over 1400. Acceptance in the program is highly competitive; in 2010, the program received over 1,400 applicants for its 180 slots. Plan II seeks to foster a tight community through common coursework and small class sizes. Freshmen begin with a yearlong English literature course and a semester of logic. That is followed in the sophomore year by "Problems of Knowledge and Valuation," a two-semester philosophy session. Freshmen and juniors take seminars whose quality and relevance vary. Spring 2010 selections ranged from "Race and Medicine in American Life" to "Making the Self-Made Man."

Most Plan II seminars and sequences are heavy on writing, and in their fourth year students write—and probably rewrite—a thesis of 7,500 to 15,000 words. (Outside Plan II, only honors-track students write theses.) Virtually anything can be a "thesis," including artwork (accompanied by a paper), performances, and scientific studies. "Morale in Plan II is high, and rightly so, both for students and teachers," says a professor. "However, it does not have its own faculty and depends on the departments. Individual faculty members are usually eager to teach and offer courses in the program, but the departments are not always happy to see their best faculty drawn off to teach a course that has a maximum enrollment of fifteen."

Like Plan II students, if to a lesser degree, students who enroll in the College of Liberal Arts Freshman Honors Program benefit from smaller class sizes and honors sections of introductory courses during their first two years. In addition, these students receive helpful advice concerning their academic schedules and broader career goals. Liberal arts students with sixty hours of completed coursework and a UT GPA of at least 3.5 may apply to the Liberal Arts Honors Program (Upper Division), which provides special seminar-type classes and an honors diploma.

Other schools and departments offer special programs. The McCombs School of Business has the Business Foundations Program, directed toward students who are completing a nonbusiness major but desire more courses applicable to the "real world." The College of Natural Sciences offers the Dean's Scholars Program, which facilitates undergraduate research projects and interaction between students and faculty. The Turing Scholars Program in computer science does the same for young programmers.

Majors in the business school, including the professional program in accounting and the Business Honors Program, are considered some of the best in the country. Many other UT departments rank highly; philosophy is excellent, as are psychology, classics, and linguistics. In the natural sciences, physics, math, and chemistry are all solid, as is the computer science department.

Majors to which the least-prepared students gravitate are education and English. These are also two of UT's most left-leaning departments, students report. English majors are not required to take a Shakespeare class, but must choose a multicultural course from among such titles as "Gay and Lesbian Literature and Culture" and "Mexican American Literature and Culture." The communications department is very ideological, according to a student we consulted. He says it "mostly comprises far-left liberals determined to use the media to drive conservative ideas out of the public sphere altogether . . . That department made the English department look moderate by comparison."

The history department is politically charged and the requirements reflect this. Majors must take two U.S. history classes, but the choices range from "United States, 1492–1865" to "History of Mexican Americans in the U.S."

The government department does not require majors to study the American Constitution, and an American political theory requirement can be fulfilled with such classes as "Racial and Ethnic Politics." Religious studies is not a road to salvation, UT insiders report. "Students should be cautioned that most religious studies courses are hostile to religion," says a professor, "though a growing number of courses that treat religion with respect, unaffiliated with that program, are springing up."

Budding journalists at UT have access to a unique resource—the original notes made by reporters Woodward and Bernstein from their investigation of Watergate. The Harry Ransom Humanities Research Center holds these notes and recently received additional materials that had been withheld to protect the (now-exposed) identity of "Deep Throat," the reporters' principal source. Those interested in another presidency should visit the Lyndon Johnson Presidential Library, located on the other side of campus.

As might be expected of a school its size, the academic advising at UT is mediocre except in very small majors and special freshman programs. The average student is best off educating himself in detail on degree requirements and interests and acquainting himself with the inches-thick book of course offerings, and only then meeting with an advisor to double-check. "You get as much out of the advising process as you put in," one student says. "Advisors are just happy if you have your act together ahead of time so they can move down the list. However, advisors are generally knowledgeable, and when prompted can be quite helpful in helping you determine what courses and instructors best fit your needs. But they don't waste time providing this support if you don't ask for it." A professor says that advising is better in some of the less-populated departments, like classics and philosophy.

Some assistance may come from faculty and graduate teaching assistants, who hold regular office hours. Students commend faculty for generally being willing to reach out to anyone willing to show up. "I've never met a professor who wasn't more than happy to receive students for one-on-one tutelage," a student says. A professor notes, "There is an overall atmosphere and opportunity that should not be short-changed. I think the brighter students who already have some sense of their own interests and direction really have a good time here and get a good education."

Because UT is so large, it is difficult to characterize the general intellectual character of students. One professor says that students are "less curious than in the past," but another says that students "in the past year or two have begun showing more interest in academic studies than I've ever seen here." In this, as in everything else at UT, both curious and apathetic students can find a niche.

With a student faculty ratio of 17 to 1, UT relies heavily on graduate students to teach everything from massive lecture courses to small seminars. "Too much of the burden of teaching still rests with graduate students," says a professor. "Unfortunately, financial support for graduate students has not kept pace with support in a given field available elsewhere, and this means that UT is not competitive with universities of similar or higher rank. The quality of graduate students inevitably suffers."

UT can boast of many professors known for their excellent teaching and advising. Among them are J. Budziszewski, Roderick Hart, Thomas and Lorraine Pangle, David Prindle, Alan Sager, Devon and Dana Stauffer, David Leal, and Jeffrey Tulis in government; George Forgie, Brian Levack, William Louis, Tiffany Gill, and Guy Miller in history; David Hamermesh and Dale Stahl in economics; John Ruszkiewicz and Jeffrey Walker in rhetoric and composition; Randy Diehl, Phillip Gough (emeritus), Joseph Horn (emeritus), Robert Josephs, Peter Mac-Neilage, James Pennebaker, and Del Thiessen (emeritus) in psychology; in classics Karl Galinsky, Thomas Palaima, Stephen White and Robert Hankinson (also in philosophy); Jean-Pierre Cauvin in French; Michael Starbird in mathematics; Larry Carver, James Garrison, Ernest Kaulbach, Martin Kevorkian, and Wayne Rebhorn in English; Daniel Bonevac, Robert Kane, Robert Koons, A. P. Martinich, Alexander Mourelatos, Stephen White and Paul Woodruff in philosophy; Michael Harney, Stanislav Zimic, and Madeline Sutherland-Meier in Spanish; and John Butler, Christopher Ellison, Norval Glenn, Mark Regnerus, and Robert Woodberry in sociology; Samer Ali, Hina Azam, and Harold Liebowitz in Middle Eastern Studies.

The University of Texas offers degrees in a wide array of foreign languages, including classics, Spanish, Italian, French, German, modern Greek, Russian, Chinese, Japanese, Hindi/Urdu, Malayalam, Sanskrit, Czech, Hebrew, Portuguese, Turkish, and Persian. In addition, UT has one of the largest study-abroad programs in the world, offering more than 700 programs across the planet.

West

Student Life: Keeping it weird

Though they may agree on little else, nearly all of UT's over 50,000 students confess to one thing: Austin is the perfect college city. It's a place where offbeat people are known to congregate, and conventional people have a tendency to "go native." There's even an active community group called "Keep Austin Weird"—it seems that many longtime locals haven't exactly been delighted to see their bohemian city steered towards normalcy by Silicon Valley types and assorted other yuppies who have migrated to Austin's technology industry in recent years. But Austin is not Dallas or Houston, at least not yet. Formalities are rare: In Austin, "dressing up" still simply means wearing your Ropers instead of your flipflops. The city is renowned for unpretentious intellectuality in a region full of down-home pleasures such as the annual Wiener Dog Races in the nearby town of Buda, which attracts fanatical dachshund owners from around the country.

Just as the city of Austin's politics are unrepresentative of the state of Texas as a whole, so is its remarkable natural beauty, as seen in the nearby Texas Hill Country. To cool off

---

ACADEMIC REQUIREMENTS

The quality and content of UT's general education courses varies greatly according to department and section. The reading lists for these courses are posted well in advance, and can range from classics of Western civilization to ideological pamphlets. This undergraduate "core" consists of:

- A First-Year Signature course. Class offerings include "The American Experience as Told Through Autobiographies" and "Fundamentals of Ethical Leadership."
- One class in writing and rhetoric, either "Rhetoric and Writing" or "Rhetoric and Writing for Nonnative Speakers of English."
- One literature course, "Masterworks of Literature," either British, American or world, with an additional study hour each week.
- Two courses in American civics; one must be "American Government," and the other may be in either American or Texas government, such as "Issues and Policies in American Government" or "U.S.–Latin American Relations."
- Two American history courses, only one of which may be in Texas history. Selections include: "The United States, 1492–1865," "Texas, 1845–1914," "Black Power Movement," and "History of American Feminism."
- One social or behavioral science class. Courses available include "Introduction to Psychology" and "Blacks and Asians: Race and Social Movements."
- One math class. Available courses include "Foundations of Mathematics" and "Introduction to Statistics."
- Three science courses, two must be in the same field of study. Class offerings include "Introductory Biology" I and II , "General Physics" I and II, and "Animal Sexuality."
- One fine arts course. Options range from "Introduction to Visual Arts Studies" to "Contemporary Dance Techniques."

West

after a rigorous run or ride on one of the city's many hike-and-bike trails, students can paddle a canoe down Barton Creek or take a chilly dip in spring-fed Barton Springs Pool, both of which are situated within Zilker Park, a downtown beauty that spans 351 acres.

As the state capital, Austin provides many opportunities for students to release their political energies; the capitol building is within walking distance of campus. Hundreds of student organizations fit almost every need or interest; all that's necessary to start another group is three interested students. The all-male Longhorn Hellraisers (women can join the Hellraiser Honeys) paint their faces burnt orange and white, take off their shirts, and scream at football and basketball games.

UT's thirty-five fraternities and twenty-seven sororities are lively, though unable to exert control over the raucous campus social scene. Just two sorority houses (and not a single fraternity) are actually located on campus, and their off-campus location at a school of this size means the Greeks are not much of a social focal point at UT; in fact, they actually have a good reputation on campus for their involvement in the community. UT is known as a party school, but the partying usually takes place in the city of Austin, not on campus.

UT students can participate in almost 1,000 clubs and organizations. Language clubs, film series, and discussion groups abound. The most award-winning daily student newspaper in the nation, the *Daily Texan*, rivals many midsized city newspapers in its professionalism. Alternative publications come and go, but the largest college humor magazine in the nation, the "loud, lewd, and totally inappropriate" *Texas Travesty*, is always good for a laugh. UT has many religiously oriented student organizations. Christian students wishing to remain so should generally avoid the churches adjoining campus, sources tell us. Catholic students, for instance, should skip the Catholic Student Center, perhaps in favor of Mass at a local parish like Sacred Heart.

University clubs and organizations students might want to explore include the American Constitution Society, College Republicans at Texas, Libertarian Longhorns, Young Conservatives of Texas, Students Against Cruelty to Animals, Blanton Museum of Art Student Guild, Culinary Chops, Greeks in Business, Hook 'Em Arts, UT Concert Chorale, Austin Agape, Christian Legal Society, Fellowship of Christian Athletes, Campus Crusade for Christ, Courage, Young Life College Fellowship, Habitat for Humanity, Gigglepants Improv Comedy Troupe, Longhorn Cricket Club, Texas Triathletes, UT Dance Team, University of Texas Cycling, University French Club, Chess Club, Spirit of Shakespeare, and Willie Nelson Center Students.

Football is king in Texas, and in an age of mushy sentimentality it is refreshing to see the healthy, hearty hatred that persists between the Longhorns and the Texas A&M Aggies. UT participates in the NCAA I conference, where the Longhorn football team is consistently ranked in the top ten and the UT men's and women's basketball teams are usually among the nation's best as well. The men's baseball, cross-country, golf, swimming, tennis, and track teams also participate in the conference, as do the women's crew, cross-country, golf, soccer, softball, swimming, tennis, volleyball, and track. Intramural sports are quite popular, though some of the playing fields are unfortunately situated a couple miles north of campus. Teams include men's and women's basketball, golf, lightweight football, racquetball, soccer, softball, swimming, tennis, Ultimate Frisbee, volleyball, team handball, and outdoor track and field.

West

Residence-hall living is not the norm at UT. The university's fourteen residence halls have a combined capacity of just over 7,100, even with the mammoth Jester Hall, which holds just shy of 3,000 residents. The vast majority of students dwell off campus, many in private dormitories adjoining the campus, but most students live in the thousands of apartments surrounding the school; the farther from campus, the cheaper the rent. For those who do live on campus, single-sex dormitories are available for both men and women. There are no coed dorm rooms or bathrooms.

Freshman orientation on campus is available but not required. Much of the programming is suspect, so incoming students may want to give it a miss. One student recalls attending an orientation program on diversity. "We were told to accept everything and be open-minded to all. Those who did not would be considered intolerant, racist, and close-minded," she says.

Famous nationwide for its offbeat and often radical, if not large, protests, the West Mall steps beneath UT's famed clock tower are as active as ever. On the West Mall and in other university-designated "free-speech zones," students are allowed to hold sound-amplified events between 11:30 AM and 1:30 PM. The Young Conservatives of Texas have been tastefully rowdy in recent years, and socialists and Greens are always protesting something. The Campus and Community Involvement Office, while notorious for its bureaucracy, is the institutional backbone behind the thirty-seven political groups on campus.

In 2009, the school reported ten forcible sex offenses, three aggravated assaults, three robberies, forty-four burglaries, six stolen cars, and one arson. Students report feeling reasonably safe on and around campus, and given the size of the school, the incidence of serious crime on campus does not appear to be alarmingly high. There are, however, occasional incidents on Guadalupe Street (the "Drag"), which borders the west side of campus and tends to collect runaways, vagrants, and the weirdest of the weird. (Ever seen the cult movie *Slacker*? It's set at UT, provides a pretty accurate picture of this side of campus life, and makes the school seem oddly appealing.)

UT is attractive to Texas residents, with 2010–11 tuition at $9,418 (in state) or $31,218 (out of state), and room and board at $10,112. The school practices need-blind admissions, and while it can't fulfill all requirements, it claims to meet "the need of most students, and particularly those with higher needs," according to the financial-aid office. Around 50 percent of students get need-based aid, with 2010 graduates owing an average of $22,102.

> ## YELLOW LIGHT
>
> The Foundation for Individual Rights in Education recently gave UT a speech code rating of Red in part because the campus police arrested a man in August 2010 for asking inconvenient questions during a recent visit by Barack Obama. A student says of the political climate at UT, "Any outspoken conservative thought is generally regarded as unenlightened, racist, and narrow-minded. Intelligence is gauged by how few convictions students hold, how often they 'experience' other cultures, and how quickly they denounce traditional moral values." One professor agrees, "Lots of students drop my course when I tell them I am conservative and Republican. . . . I have over the years been called a Nazi, UT's Rush Limbaugh, and so on, although my evaluations are very good. . . . Students have told me about being penalized [in other courses] for their conservative writings or about having to write what the professor wants, not what they really think."

Texas A&M University

College Station, Texas • www.tamu.edu

Marching Orders

Texas A&M University at College Station has undergone rapid changes during the last fifty years—none greater than in 1963, when the school converted itself from an all-male military academy to a full-fledged coeducational university. But Texas A&M, which every year hosts a traditional candlelight "Aggie muster" ceremony, has retained much from its military-school past. The university still sponsors the Corps of Cadets, which, with 2,000 members, is the largest uniformed body of students outside the three main U.S. service academies. Although it is still in agriculture and mechanics that A&M excels, the university is actively attempting to improve its liberal arts programs.

The Texas A&M student body is primarily responsible for maintaining the deep traditions and sane conservatism of the campus. In a recent school-sponsored report describing the incoming freshmen, 25 percent of the new class consisted of first-generation college students. A student explains, "This is not a crowd that worships academia like the East and West coasts. These are people that place relationships with God, country, and family out in front." We wish that the liberal arts curriculum at the school did more to gently encourage a love for the genuine goods of academic life, in this wholesome environment mostly free of contemporary toxic trends. Instead, recent administrations have seemed intent on smuggling in the strange gods of multiculturalism and feminism. We hope that resistance among alumni, faculty, students, and state legislators frustrate these efforts.

Academic Life: Room to grow

Like other state universities in Texas, A&M requires undergraduates to complete a set of distribution requirements which, depending on the courses chosen to fulfill them, need not be particularly demanding.

Roughly 20 percent of the undergraduate population majors in some type of engineering, and the programs are among the finest on campus. Virtually every engineering program offered, from aerospace to petroleum, ranks among the top twenty in the nation, and several are among the top five. The Lowry Mays College and Graduate School of Business also receives high marks, with programs in accounting, management, and marketing ranked among the top twenty-five in the nation in popular surveys. The College of Archi-

West

tecture, with more than 1,500 students, is one of the largest in the United States.

The university's offerings in the College of Agriculture and Life Sciences are extensive, including fields like agricultural journalism, dairy science, and wildlife and fisheries sciences. The College of Veterinary Medicine is widely considered to be one of the most advanced in America. The school continually makes national headlines, most notably when the cloning program replicated several kinds of small animals. The school also offers some useful exchange programs, led by faculty, available to students wishing to study native habitats first hand.

The College of Liberal Arts enrolls about 15 percent of all undergraduates. The course offerings don't stand out as academic challenges, but at least they have not morphed into the ideological circus acts seen on many "progressive" campuses. Degree requirements are prescribed by each department and there may be some overlap with the college-wide distribution requirements. Students majoring in a liberal arts discipline must take extra courses required by the College of Liberal Arts, including two literature, two additional humanities, one additional social and behavior sciences, and two intermediate-level foreign language courses.

Classics is only available as one of the college's several minors, as are religious studies, women's studies, comparative cultures, and five others. The American politics component of the department of political science ranks among the top twenty in the country, and the economics department consistently appears in rankings of the top forty programs. According to its website, the political science department "offers courses in all facets of the discipline: American political institutions and political behavior; international relations; comparative politics; political theory and methodology; public policy and administration," and (in a recent kowtow to political correctness) race and ethnic politics. Poli sci majors must take classes in the U.S. Constitution and American political philosophy, and most of the department's course offerings are solid and traditional.

The English department offers three bachelor degree tracks: literature, rhetoric, and creative writing. All tracks are quite good, requiring solid courses, including Shakespeare and American literature as well as several writing components.

The history department is solid as well, requiring Western civilization and American history courses, and offering many worthwhile classes ranging from ancient to modern history.

VITAL STATISTICS

Religious affiliation: *none*
Total enrollment: *48,713*
Total undergraduates: *38,810*
SAT/ACT midranges: CR: *530–640*, M: *570–670*; ACT: *24–30*
Applicants: *22,757*
Applicants accepted: *67%*
Accepted applicants who enrolled: *32%*
Tuition and fees: *in state, $8,387; out of state, $23,717*
Room and board: *$8,008*
Freshman retention rate: *92%*
Graduation rate: *45% (4 yrs.), 80% (6 yrs.)*
Courses with fewer than 20 students: *22%*
Student-faculty ratio: *18:1*
Courses taught by graduate students: *15%*
Most popular majors: *business, agriculture, engineering*
Students living on campus: *24%*
Guaranteed housing for four years? *no*
Students in fraternities: *5%* in sororities: *12%*

SUGGESTED CORE

1. Classics 372, Greek and Roman Epic
2. Philosophy 410, Classical Philosophy
3. Religious Studies 211/213, Hebrew Scriptures/New Testament
4. History 220, History of Christianity: Origins to the Reformation
5. Political Science 350, Modern Political Thought
6. English 212, Shakespeare
7. History 105, History of the U.S.
8. Philosophy 414, Nineteenth-Century Philosophy

One of the university's former presidents, Ray Bowen, made several moves that some alumni thought were aimed at conforming A&M to the progressivism often characteristic of elite public universities. "Vision 2020," a long-range planning document authored by Bowen, included twelve recommendations designed to make Texas A&M one of the top ten public universities in the nation by the year 2020. One recommendation was to "diversify and globalize the A&M community," which could be accomplished partly with a "plan that will require students to take six hours of international or cultural diversity classes," one alumnus says. Conservatives contend that the plan was implemented merely to pacify critics who say that A&M students suffer from provincialism. "[The new requirement is] just one step in a larger plan to sacrifice the values that make A&M special" says a student, going on to make the most damning accusation one can make against an A&M president: "He wanted to make us just like the University of Texas."

Bowen's successor, former Secretary of Defense Robert Gates, followed in Bowen's footsteps in ways many students and alumni found disturbing. "He seemed to be pushing the same Vision 2020 that Bowen had," says a professor. Despite state budget cuts, Gates established a new vice president and associate provost for institutional diversity—the only VP-level provost who reports directly to the president. This provost was tasked with implementing "a campus-wide program to support diversity," including compulsory diversity training for members of the Student Government Association and the campus daily, the *Battalion*. "You have to understand that around here, diversity still means cultural diversity, not sexual diversity; regardless, it's a politically charged word," insisted a source on campus, noting that this is still a school at which the president introduces himself with a "howdy." Gates's successor, Elsa Morano, was the worst yet in pushing the "progressive" agenda, but mercifully she lasted just a little over a year. We hope that her replacement, current president Bowen Loftin, will focus on accentuating the university's traditional strengths instead of trying to turn A&M into a pale copy of the leftist research factories that so many state universities have become.

Texas A&M is a large state school so it isn't surprising that graduate teaching assistants teach some courses, but more commonly they lead weekly discussion sections for large lecture classes or laboratory sections for science courses. "Professors are accessible to students [during] office hours," says a student. However, an undergrad warns, "The advising program is not well advertised, so students need to be aware of the services on their own." Underclassmen who have not yet decided on a major can speak with professional advisors in the General Studies Program, the "keynotes" of which are, according to the program, "exploration and flexibility." More often, students visit their major advisors (either faculty members or professional advisors), who help the students choose courses, fulfill degree requirements, and prepare for graduation and careers.

Noteworthy professors include Robin Smith in philosophy; David Vaught in history; Dan Lineberger, Tracy Rutherford, and Jodi Sterle in agriculture and life sciences; Roel Lopez in wildlife and fishery sciences; and David Bergbreiter, James Pennington, Michael Rosynek, Eric Simanek, and Gyula Vigh in chemistry.

The school does offer an honors program. Honors students, who must maintain a 3.5 GPA, apply for the program within their area of study. They are not "lock[ed] into a four-year program separate from the regular curriculum," the university website boasts, but instead pick and choose from the 300-plus honors-level courses offered throughout the university. An honors student can also enroll in one of the honors study sequences: the Engineering Scholars Program, the Business Honors Program, or the College of Liberal Arts

ACADEMIC REQUIREMENTS

The self-described "core curriculum" is actually a decent set of distribution requirements that includes the following:

- Two courses in communication, including "Composition and Rhetoric," plus another from a list of ten approved courses in English, communication, or agricultural journalism.
- Two classes in mathematics. Almost all mathematics courses—and three philosophy courses—count toward this requirement.
- Two or three courses in the natural sciences, including a lab. This can be fulfilled through introductory courses in biology, botany, chemistry, geology, physics, zoology, anthropology, horticulture, entomology, or renewable natural resources.
- One course in the humanities—history, philosophy, literature, the arts, culture, or a language class—will qualify, as will hundreds of others, including some clunkers from women's studies and Hispanic studies.
- One class in visual and performing arts. More than eighty courses qualify, such as "Survey of World Architecture History," "Art History" I, and "Jazz Dance" III.
- One class in social and behavioral sciences, addressing anthropology, economics, political science, geography, psychology, sociology, or communication.
- Three classes in U.S. history and political science. Thanks to the Texas legislature, there is a four-course citizenship requirement, including the required political science courses "American National Government" and "State and Local Government," as well as a choice of two American history courses, usually satisfied by a survey called "History of the United States," but which can also be fulfilled by one course on Texas history and another on U.S. history.
- Two classes in international and cultural diversity. Good choices among the 200 possibilities include "The History of England" and "World Literature"—but only if a student thinks he can live without "Introduction to Gender and Society" or "Postcolonial Studies." Foreign languages also fulfill this requirement.
- One course in kinesiology (physical education).

West

Honors Plan. The liberal arts plan begins with a freshman honors seminar; past seminar offerings have included "Toleration in Theory and Practice" and "Rites of Passage across Cultures and within American Subcultures"—both infused by a pro-homosexual agenda, sources report. Then they take two sophomore courses, "Foundations of the Liberal Arts: Humanities" and "Foundations of the Liberal Arts: Social Sciences." This is where students will find politically correct courses that tend to sacrifice rigorous academic perspective, a teacher reports, commenting, "In keeping with the notion that there is a fundamental correlation between ignorance and conservatism, the first stages of rot appeared in the honors program. This is where you will find the queer studies and the feminism."

Texas A&M offers a wide array of study-abroad opportunities all over the globe, including Antarctica (!), Bangladesh, Bolivia, Cyprus, Croatia, Fiji, Iceland, Qatar, Samoa, and hundreds of others.

At home, students can study Latin, Ancient Greek, French, German, Russian, Spanish, Arabic, Chinese, Japanese, and several more foreign languages. A foreign language component is not a university core requirement for graduation, but quite a few departments insist on several semesters or demonstrated proficiency in order to earn degrees in certain majors.

Student Life: Shout it out

To many Aggies, College Station is the center of the world. Most Aggie alumni make at least one pilgrimage a year to visit campus and watch their beloved football team at Kyle Field. In fact, CBSSportsline.com declared, "There are simply no other fans who get into their team more than Aggies."

Texas A&M is a member of the Big 12 athletic conference, and as such, sports—especially football—are a high priority. In addition to the nineteen varsity teams, students have thirty-four club sports and dozens of intramural teams from which to choose—including, for sedentary nerds, a Playstation tournament. The athletic facilities are staggering: a soccer stadium, a softball complex, a golf course, a tennis center, a "coliseum" just for volleyball, two track stadiums (indoor and outdoor), the Freeman Arena (the 70,000-square-foot home of the equestrian team), Kyle Field (the enormous state-of-the-art football stadium), and several other large venues.

Instead of cheerleaders, the Aggies have "yell leaders." If the Aggies win, students throw the yell leaders into a campus fountain (a.k.a., the Fish Pond). And if A&M loses, students and alumni stay in the stands to practice school yells for the next game. Midnight yell practices, held the night before every home game, often attract as many as 30,000 people. Another remnant of Texas A&M's past is the tradition of kissing one's date after each touchdown, extra point, or field goal.

Most students at Texas A&M prefer to tailgate and drink beer before (and after, and between) football games, listen to country music, and just make it through their engineering classes. The city is full of terrific honky-tonks, dance halls, and restaurants. Favorites include the Dixie Chicken, which proudly proclaims "more beer sold per square foot than anywhere in the world." The owners of the Dixie Chicken have done so well they have a virtual monopoly on nightlife in College Station; they also own the Chicken Oil Company, Dry Bean Saloon,

West

Shadow Canyon Dance Hall and Saloon, and Alfred T. Hornback's. One local is quick to point out that while there are only a few coffeehouses, there is a vibrant music scene—including popular open-mike nights at bars frequented by local singer-songwriters and their fans. "This may not be Austin," he says, "but it is in fact an important center for Texas-style country music." Another Aggie favorite is Wings 'n More, which serves up some of the nation's best wings at varying degrees of heat.

Only some 8 percent of Texas A&M students are involved in Greek life. Instead, Texas A&M boasts the largest student-union program in the nation, with more than 700 university-recognized clubs and organizations. If you can't find one that interests you, then you aren't looking: the groups cover all interests, from Aggieland Mariachi and the Philosophy Club to a group dedicated to water polo. The list of student organizations includes dozens of religious groups, most of them Christian, including Aggie Promise Keepers, Resurrection Week, and Christian Business Leaders. One student says, "I'd have to say that a lot of A&M students turn to religion-based recreation, such as Bible study, praise and worship groups, and other religious social activities." St. Mary's Catholic Center on campus seems vibrant and orthodox, featuring traditional devotions, pro-life activities, and significant intellectual support; it's refreshing to be able to say that about such a campus ministry. There has been an explosion of Catholic devotion on campus, resulting in a wave of priestly and religious vocations from A&M, meriting national media attention. A 2011 A&M football game against rival UT-Austin featured dozens of nuns and priests in the stands on the A&M side, leading commentators to remark that UT didn't stand a chance. (It didn't.)

While there are many opportunities for political involvement at Texas A&M, student life more characteristically revolves around organizations that enhance the "Aggie spirit." For years thousands of students were proud to consider the building of a massive bonfire as their primary extracurricular activity—until a tragic accident in 1999 crushed twelve students

GREEN LIGHT

It won't surprise the reader that an A&M school in Texas is fairly traditional. One professor describes the average faculty member as "at least moderately conservative" and the average student as "pretty conservative." This same professor says, "Some, maybe even many, midlevel administrators are hostile to the views of the [typical] A&M student and consequently seek to transform the largely Christian, conservative student body into something more 'representative.' Consistent with this, faculty now undergo a mandatory diversity class in which orthodox Christian and conservative beliefs are treated essentially as the root of bigotry, and, by implication, inconsistent with the diversity thrust at A&M."

The administration is also at odds with the average A&M student. The school endorses a Gay Awareness Week and sponsors an annual performance of the ubiquitous *Vagina Monologues*. Various activist groups push for the nontraditional programming offered at most universities. Alternative radio exists for students interested in bucking the crew-cut crowd: KEOS-FM offers a mix of music and agitation courtesy of programs like Democracy Now, an activist organization funded by MoveOn.org. The administration's attempts at "diversity education" seem likely to encourage partisanship and divisive politics on campus, but these dragon's teeth have not yet borne fruit.

under the pile of wood and buried the tradition. Or so it seemed. Persistent students and alumni have organized an off-campus "student bonfire," which continues to attract over 1,000 participants each year. Every log is cut and stacked by a student, and the stack is designed and approved by an engineering firm, with safety as a priority. Traditions die hard here.

Many students also join the Corps of Cadets because of its prestige on campus. Almost all of Texas A&M's many traditions have their genesis in the school's military past, to the extent that the corps even serves a vital role at football games. For example, to be a member of the Fightin' Aggie Band, one must first be a member of the Corps of Cadets, as the band wears military uniforms and marches military style.

The food in the residence halls at Texas A&M leaves much to be desired, according to some students, but thankfully Aggies are not required to live in them; in fact, there are fewer than 8,000 on-campus housing spaces available for non-corps students. Twelve residence halls are single sex, and the coed dorms split men and women by floor. There are no coed bathrooms or bedrooms in the residence halls.

College Station is an extremely safe town, and the campus within is no different. In 2009, A&M reported twenty-five burglaries (mostly laptops, students say), one robbery, one aggravated assault, one car theft, and one arson on campus.

This school is quite a bargain for in-state students, with 2010–11 tuition at $8,387; the cost for out-of-state students recently rose to almost triple that, coming in at $23,717. Room and board cost $8,008, but only 24 percent of students find space on campus. Half of all undergraduates receive need-based financial aid, and the average indebtedness upon graduation is $21,182. The Aggie 'Assurance Program covers tuition costs for any full-time student who is a Texas resident with a family income of less than $60,000 and who maintains at least a 2.5 grade point average.

West

Thomas Aquinas College

Santa Paula, California • www.thomasaquinas.edu

Baptizing Socrates

In 1971, in response to the shock-secularization and academic decline of Catholic colleges in America, a small group of scholars in California envisaged something different—an education built on the Great Books of the Western world, viewed through the lens of the greatest thinker in Catholic history, St. Thomas Aquinas. They would eschew textbooks, lectures, secondary sources, the tenure system, and all the facets of the German university model that other Catholic schools had embraced to their peril. Thus began Thomas Aquinas College.

Its success, both by the founders' standards and by the world's, has been remarkable. The program to which they have adhered from the beginning is widely recognized as one of the most rigorous in the country. Over 40 percent of those who complete it go on to graduate study in virtually every field. Thomas Dillon, the college's second President, led the college for twenty-two years, and oversaw the completion of the neoclassical chapel, Our Lady of the Most Holy Trinity Chapel. Dillon died soon after the consecration of the chapel. His successor, Michael McClean, was Dillon's college classmate and a longtime colleague, and he is equally committed to the founding vision of the school.

Academic Life: No textbooks, lectures, or majors

At TAC, there are no majors, minors, electives, or concentrations. All students take the same four-year program, and earn the same bachelor's degree in liberal arts. The course of study features theology, philosophy, natural science, and mathematics. Students take Latin during their freshman and sophomore years, as well as a music during their junior year. "Seminar," an evening class for discussing literary, philosophical, historical, and political works, starts with Homer and Plato in the freshman year and concludes with works such as the Lincoln-Douglas debates and, in senior year, the writings of Edmund Husserl and Flannery O'Connor. In each of their four years students have regular recourse to the works of the school's namesake, St. Thomas Aquinas.

Thomas Aquinas College considers the Great Books authors themselves to be the real teachers. In a charming touch, the college lists the authors of the Great Books (such as Plato) as "permanent faculty." Textbooks are used rarely; instead, students are in "con-

VITAL STATISTICS

Religious affiliation: *Roman Catholic*
Total enrollment: *340*
Total undergraduates: *340*
SAT/ACT midranges: CR: *615–730*, M: *570–658*; ACT: *25–30*
Applicants: *189*
Applicants accepted: *79%*
Accepted applicants who enrolled: *69%*
Tuition and fees: *$22,400*
Room and board: *$7,400*
Freshman retention rate: *84%*
Graduation rate: *69% (4 yrs.), 73% (6 yrs.)*
Courses with fewer than 20 students: *100%*
Student-faculty ratio: *13:1*
Courses taught by graduate students: *none*
Most popular majors: *not applicable*
Students living on campus: *100%*
Guaranteed housing for four years? *yes*
Students in fraternities or sororities: *none*

versation" with Great Books authors. Permanent faculty members with one or even two PhDs take the title "tutor." Although TAC is a socially conservative institution, no college has a more egalitarian classroom protocol. Everyone in the classroom, whether college president or raw freshman, is addressed as "Mr." "Miss" or "Mrs." The tutor, who is officially the chief student, begins discussion with an opening question. Each class session is dedicated to understanding and evaluating a great text through the give-and-take of formal but friendly conversation. Discussions can be contentious, and there are always students who participate more than others. Some students admit that they don't always end up with a conclusion or final answer after a seminar class, but add that the content of the texts stay with them. "Seminar classes allow students to meditate on the texts and learn *how* to think rather than *what* to think," one tutor explains, "they teach students to concentrate and puzzle through the real value of the text on their own, making these perennial ideas and questions their own."

For TAC, the chief mark of a liberally educated person is his ability to engage in a fruitful conversation. For example, a graduate may know very little about sociology. If he meets a sociologist, however, he should be able to understand the sociologist's argument, determine if his conclusions follow from his premises, identify significant terms that need definition—and most importantly, find the principles that underlie the whole conversation. One alumnus says, "The intense study of mathematics truly stretched my mind. I thought in ways I never had before—in ways I hadn't known I could think—and it was amazing how much I felt I gained in sheer mental ability from the years of studying geometrical proofs." Students are expected to master the general theological and philosophical principles that govern various disciplines, from literary interpretation to chemistry to biblical studies.

Students read a wide range of authors—from the likes of Newton and Einstein, to Karl Marx, St. John of Damascus, Tocqueville, Cervantes, and Archimedes—who are central to understanding diverse areas of knowledge.

The courses are highly interdisciplinary. During a discussion of Newton's *Principia*, for example, students may cite examples or raise issues from Shakespeare, Aristotle, or Dante. This is possible not only because all students are taking the same courses according to the same schedule, but also because all tutors are expected to be able to teach all courses. A new faculty member might teach Euclid, Latin, and freshman Seminar, and the next year

West

teach philosophy, laboratory science, and sophomore Seminar.

Most importantly, students are initiated into the encyclopedic breadth of Aristotelian philosophy and Thomistic theology. Students take four years of philosophy, and, although they study the major dialogues of Plato, the emphasis is on Aristotle's works. Graduates of the college will have spent intensive study on all of Aristotle's most important philosophical works: the *Organon*, *Poetics*, *Rhetoric*, *Physics*, *Nicomachean Ethics*, *Politics*, and *Metaphysics*. The theology course is more varied, with freshman year dedicated solely to reading the whole biblical canon; sophomore year to saints Augustine, Athanasius, John of Damascus, and Anselm; and junior and senior years to Aquinas's *Summa Theologiae*. Still, the emphasis is on the essential principles of Thomas's theology, as well as his interpretation of Aristotle.

> ## SUGGESTED CORE
>
> The college's required curriculum suffices.

The keystone to Thomas Aquinas College's education is its corporate commitment to a rationally knowable objective reality. TAC believes that Truth, with an emphatically capital "T," is accessible through faith and reason. St. Thomas Aquinas is the chief model, guide, and teacher for using these faculties to grasp "the nature of things." TAC does not press its ideas onto students through lectures and textbooks, but genuinely tries to lead them through the Socratic method, placing the emphasis on their own reasoning powers as engaged with a text and other readers.

As one student puts it, "Seminar encourages you to think. You're not just expected to sit there and take notes. In it, we set our own pace—which is often faster than in a lecture course."

Students report excellent relationships with their tutors, a significant number of whom are returning students. Perennial favorites include John F. Nieto and Paul J. O'Reilly. "The tutors are very helpful," says one student, "not only with questions or problems arising from class, but also concerning graduate schools, career choices, your spiritual life, sports, and even dating."

Some disciplines, such as statistics and sociology, are not covered at all. Other fields are only treated in a cursory fashion; students read Adam Smith and Karl Marx, but they do not cover the basic principles of modern economics. Some sciences are only partially covered. Students read and discuss Gregor Mendel, but do not read about modern genetics. Students read Einstein on relativity, but no authors on quantum mechanics. In the humanities, history is treated in a hit-or-miss fashion. Students read some of the greatest historians of the classical world, such as Thucydides and Gibbon, influential philosophers of history, such as Vico and Hegel, and some foundational American political documents. There is comparatively little treatment of literature. "We just don't have time," says one student simply.

Thomas Aquinas graduates have a good record of being admitted to excellent graduate programs in many areas, some of which their undergraduate education does not touch at all. For example, a number of recent TAC alumni have been admitted into Notre Dame's prestigious graduate program in architecture. Others may use their degree to enter law

West

schools (including Duke, Stanford, and Harvard) or take additional classes to enter medical school.

Some cite the relative infrequency of writing assignments as a weakness of the program, particularly in considering it as a preparation for graduate school. "I wrote less as a student at Thomas Aquinas College than I did as a high school student," says an alumnus. Freshmen craft five short papers, one each in math, language, theology, philosophy, and the literature seminar. Sophomores write four longer papers, and juniors write two 1,500-word essays in theology and philosophy. Seniors do write a thesis (about sixty pages) on a question raised by the curriculum, working with an advisor over the course of the senior year and finally defending it in an oral examination conducted by three tutors.

The use of secondary sources in papers, excepting the thesis, is discouraged. "More of the thoughts in my college papers are originally my own than is typical for college writing assignments, I think," a student says.

Students report that faculty members are extremely accessible; most tutors live close to campus, and all dine in the same refectory with students. It is not uncommon for tutors to continue a class discussion over meat loaf or tacos with a group of students. Beyond office hours, students visit tutors in their homes for informal dinner-seminar symposia, and for holidays.

To strengthen teacher-student relationships the college holds "Don Rags," allowing each student to meet with his tutors to discuss the student's performance. The tutors review the student in question, and allow him or her to listen in, respond, and ask questions. "Don Rags principally allow teachers to improve class conversations," says one tutor. "They help a tutor to adjust, or give pointers on a student's class participation." Students report that despite some nervousness, they enjoy these rags and benefit from them.

TAC has no study-abroad program and teaches no modern languages—*sola Latina*. Every graduate must complete the full four-year program, so the college accepts no transfer credits.

Student Life: A very small town

Santa Paula is a small, rural, oil-and-citrus town in Santa Clara valley, located forty-five miles northwest of Los Angeles. The campus itself sits on a mountain pasture and former ranch at the base of Los Padres National Forest, and is surrounded by the Topa Topa range of the Los Padres Mountains. This natural setting, where students can see the stars they read about in Ptolemy and Copernicus, subtly endorses the school's emphasis on the primacy of natural order. The campus accommodates up to 360 students (TAC's maximum full enrollment) in California Mission-style buildings with red tiled roofs and white walls. Its central building is the new chapel, the fruit of ten years planning and building.

Students say that their time at Thomas Aquinas College is spent in a "close-knit community," noting that the shared classes and small size allow students to build well-rounded friendships bound together by numerous ties of solidarity and fellowship. According to one graduate, "You don't spend every meal drawing math diagrams on napkins, or every evening in the dorm talking about proofs for God's existence. But the seminar classes, the

West

ACADEMIC REQUIREMENTS

Thomas Aquinas College offers one of the strongest curricula in the U.S. The course of studies for all students is as follows:

Freshman Year

- "Seminar": Major Greek authors, including Homer, Socrates, Plato, and Thucydides.
- "Language": Latin, English composition.
- "Mathematics": Euclid's Elements.
- "Laboratory": classical, medieval, early modern scientific treatises, including Aristotle and Galen.
- "Philosophy": Dialogues of Plato, Aristotle's writings on logic and Aquinas' *Posterior Analytics*.
- "Theology": The Bible.

Sophomore Year

- "Seminar": Literature and philosophy from Virgil through Spenser, along with works from the likes of Boethius, Dante, and Chaucer.
- "Language": Latin (selections from Horace, Cicero, and Thomas Aquinas).
- "Mathematics": From Plato through Copernicus and Kepler.
- "Laboratory": From Aristotle to atomic theory.
- "Philosophy": Pre-Socratics and Aristotle's *Physics* and *On the Soul*.
- "Theology": Augustine, Athanasius, Guanilo, Anselm, and John Damacsene.

Junior Year

- "Seminar": Literature from Cervantes through Shakespeare to Milton and Racine; philosophy from Hobbes and Locke through Adam Smith and the *Federalist Papers* to Kant.
- "Music": classical and medieval music theory; Mozart's sonatas.
- "Mathematics": The development of algebra and calculus in the seventeenth century, with reference to Greek mathematics.
- "Laboratory": Descartes, Galileo, and Newton.
- "Philosophy": Aristotle's *Nicomachean Ethics* and *Politics*.
- "Theology": Thomas Aquinas, *Summa Theologiae*: "On Sacred Doctrine," "On God," "On Law."

Senior Year

- "Seminar": Literature and philosophy from Goethe, Tocqueville, and Flannery O'Connor, to Freud, Newman, and the documents of Vatican II.
- "Mathematics": Pascal, Taylor, Dedekind, Lobachevski.
- "Laboratory": Huygens and Newton on optics; Einstein; Gilbert, Ampere, and Maxwell on electricity and magnetism.
- "Philosophy": Aristotle's *Physics* and *Metaphysics*; Aquinas' *On Being and Essence*.
- "Theology": Thomas Aquinas, *Summa Theologiae*: "On the Trinity," "On the Sacraments," "On the Passion of Christ."

common curriculum, and the small community lead to significant personal discourse. Because of this, there are many opportunities for friendships with people who are, at least superficially, very different from you or from the kind of people you usually hang out with."

A student says, "It is nearly impossible to come here without meeting and becoming very good friends with amazing, interesting, and very charitable people. It is simply a life that is the envy of any other place I can imagine." This kind of community, of course, is not for everyone. Says one student, "everybody knows everything about everybody. There's a real small-town mentality."

If the classrooms are the center of TAC's academic life, the dormitories form the basis for its community life. There are six single-sex dormitories on campus. Ninety-eight percent of students live on campus. With rare exceptions, all unmarried students must live on campus, unless they are staying with their families. Each dorm room houses two students. Freshmen are paired with other roommates based on their responses to a questionnaire. Sophomores through seniors are encouraged to select their own roommates. The center of each dorm is a large, spacious lounge, equipped with a billiards table and other amenities.

Peace and order are maintained by student prefects, whom one student characterizes as "mostly people I could respect—not too uptight or rigid, just honest people with good judgment." Each male dormitory traditionally elects a "dorm tyrant" who is a ceremonial and social figurehead, like a rowdy constitutional monarch. The dorms play pranks on each other, and every school year opens with "dorm wars," with water balloons, wrestling, and competitive feats of strength.

Although students have computers and cell phones, dorms do not have Internet access or television sets. Full Internet access is available in the library and student mailroom. Smoking is also forbidden inside the dorms, so many students smoke and talk on balconies, porches, or just outdoors. These last areas are also sites for parties. Students also socialize in "the commons" (the large dining area) and at the campus coffee shop, which offers late night snacks. Some students also go to wholesale food distributors and sell soda pop, corn dogs, and other staples of college life from their rooms.

Dorm visits by members of the opposite sex are grave violations. A nightly curfew is in effect at 11:00 PM on week nights and 1:00 AM on weekends—except on first Fridays for twenty-four hour Eucharistic adoration and during final exam week. Students who break curfew without permission must perform community service.

The school insists on a professional dress code and modesty regulations. Inside classrooms, the chapel, and "the commons" during school hours, men must wear slacks and collared shirts, and women must wear skirts or dresses that reach the knee. Public displays of affection, such as holding hands or romantic embraces, are also forbidden. Students report that couples are still frequently seen on campus, and express their affection by acts of courtliness. Other students report "taking advantage" of the surrounding college grounds for privacy.

To its credit, Thomas Aquinas College abides by its own standards of integrity. For example, when the fast-food company headed by a board member advertised in one of Hugh Hefner's salacious publications, the school removed the board member, heedless of any potential loss of funding.

West

1018

Students regularly go on hikes and ski trips. Many students also have cars, and go off campus often for shopping, movies, bowling, etc. In fact, students highly recommend having a car during one's tenure at TAC. There are also various parties and barbecues on feasts such as St. Patrick's Day. Students report several dances each year that are usually wildly popular.

There are ample sporting opportunities at Thomas Aquinas College. TAC does not participate in intercollegiate sports, but the school does have a part-time athletics director and various intramural teams. Students also play in local county leagues. Sports on campus include flag football, soccer, and basketball (which are the most organized), as well as rugby, hockey, and tennis. Most sports are contingent on students having their own supplies. There are five or six flag football teams, with a final match at the end of the year. There is also an annual "Turkey Bowl" pitting upperclassmen against underclassmen. A group called Bushwhackers maintains trails in the nearby Los Padres National Forest.

Students also develop their artistic sides. *Demiurgus* features essays, caricatures, poetry, and humor by students and tutors, while the *Aquinas Review* is a vehicle for more formal writing. The Schola is an all-male choir that sings Gregorian chant; the St. Genesius Players is an on-campus Shakespearean troupe. Students also practice their creativity with Trivial and Quadrivial Pursuit, a "stump the student" contest. Informal groups meet over meals for the study of Ancient Greek, Hebrew, Latin, French, and German. Musically inclined students are encouraged to enter the college choir or join the cast of the musicals produced each year. A student orchestra practices and performs together during the year.

Thomas Aquinas College is a deeply devotional school. In this college of 340 students, there are three fulltime chaplains and three Masses per day, with confessions before and after. The Sunday Mass is in Latin, accompanied by Gregorian chant, polyphony, or classi-

GREEN LIGHT

The overall atmosphere at TAC is reminiscent of a rural small town. Innocence and order are maintained by a fairly strict set of rules—perhaps not as rigorous as those of some evangelical schools, but certainly stricter than most Catholic colleges. Drinking on campus is forbidden under pain of expulsion, even for those who are of age. The latter, however, may store liquor with prefects, and may drink off campus. They are also served wine and beer at some school functions. The use of drugs is also grounds for expulsion. Every few years, TAC expels a few students for such offenses. Still, students are generally supportive of off-campus drinking, so long as moderation is observed.

The atmosphere at TAC is not politically charged. Some students participate in attend conferences sponsored by groups such as the National Young Republicans, Young America's Foundation, and the Intercollegiate Studies Institute. The Tocqueville Society is a student-run club that exists primarily to consider political issues from a philosophic point of view. It coordinates lectures and hosts forums for students. In recent years, a number of students have attended the "Walk for Life," a large annual Pro-Life march in San Francisco. A college donor usually charters a bus or students drive their own cars for the six-hour drive to the event. TACers for Life also arranges weekly vigils outside an abortion clinic.

cal music. Just about all Catholics on campus (some 96 to 98 percent of the student body) attend one of these three Masses—and many take part in other devotions.

Two of the three men's dorms have a priest in residence, available for confession and spiritual direction. Women students can also arrange confessions and spiritual direction sessions, and some students go through an Ignatian retreat. Priests dine in "the commons" with students, and are very accessible. Some students go on to develop their own religious vocations. A large number of students and alumni have gone on to priestly, religious, or monastic life. TAC grads can be found in monasteries from France and Italy to Oklahoma.

Although Thomas Aquinas is a Catholic college, several non-Catholics also attend, as they are attracted to the rigorous liberal arts program and the class format. There are no mandatory chapel requirements, however, and students are perfectly free to follow their own religious or philosophical convictions.

The school is extremely safe; the only crime reported on campus between 2007 and 2010 was one burglary. The campus does have its own security.

In terms of cost, Thomas Aquinas stands in the middle rank of private colleges. Tuition in 2010–11 was $22,400, with room and board coming in at $7,400. A majority of students receive aid by working campus jobs in the school's work-study program. Some 81 percent of students receive need-based financial aid, and the average student-loan debt of a recent graduating class was $15,000.

United States Air Force Academy

Colorado Springs, Colorado • www.usafa.af.mil

Into the wild blue yonder

Starting small, with a few reconnaissance planes in World War I, the U.S. Air Force grew enormously during World War II and the subsequent Cold War, tripling in size to nearly one million personnel by 1954. As aeronautic technology and nuclear weapons gave rise to the need for more technically educated officers than other service academies could provide, the Pentagon saw the need for an Air Force academy—which was founded in 1954. The architecture of the place was "Space Age," as "a living embodiment of the modernity of flying," the school reports. Today, the faculty consists of around 540 military officers and civilian faculty. As one of its members notes, "All of our professors are dedicated to teaching and ensuring our cadets succeed academically. They are available at the cadets' request whenever extra instruction is need. We do not have tenure for our professors." Faculty research and publications are not emphasized by the USAFA, and cadets are granted substantial attention from their teachers as they work their way through the school's rigorous curriculum.

Academic Life: Active duty

The Air Force Academy is state of the art in every way—just what one would expect in a school so given over, by necessity, to the mathematical and the technical. There are laboratories, observatories, and a library containing more than 1,744,000 volumes. As one cadet notes, "All students fly, all gain valuable survival training and character building education, and many have other opportunities such as jumping out of airplanes, flying propeller aircraft, and more. In addition, you gain the best leadership training in a college environment. You are in a solid academic environment with small classes and attentive professors."

Academy students are called "cadets." As at West Point and Annapolis, cadets are organized into a self-run corps, the 4,620-strong Cadet Wing. Although the school's curriculum is heavy on science and math, it is possible to gain a solid liberal arts education here, and the academy offers thirty-two majors. However, as much time and thought are put into developing both the cadet's personal character and his leadership abilities as his academic skills. Character development is attained "through an emphasis on Air Force core values, the Cadet Honor Code, ethics instruction, human relations education, and

West

1021

moral/spiritual development." The curriculum, extra-curricular activities, and daily life all work in concert to create a well-rounded cadet. One staff member comments, "Development is the thread that binds all of our programs—academic, athletic, and military—together. Hence, character development is part and parcel of every job requirement."

Each cadet, after commencement, is commissioned as an officer in the Air Force for at least five years. Upon entrance to the academy, each cadet swears on his honor to "support and defend the Constitution of the United States against all enemies, foreign and domestic." There is no room for conscientious objectors.

Criteria for acceptance are rigorous. As the academy's website says, "A well-rounded program of academic, leadership, and athletic preparation is important. You must also carefully consider whether you possess the characteristics of dedication to duty, desire to serve others, ability to accept discipline, morality, and the enjoyment of challenge." A nomination to the academy is essential. This must come from an applicant's U.S. senator, congressman, or the vice president. As one school insider warns, "It's tough to get into the academy, and even tougher to stay here."

The Center for Character & Leadership Development (CCLD) includes the Honor Division, which guides a cadet committee in administering the cadet Honor Code ("We will not lie, steal, or cheat nor tolerate among us anyone who does"). Those found guilty of violations will generally be expelled or placed on a six-month-long, intensive honor probation program. The code is considered the "foundation" of cadet's "personal concept of professional ethics," and as such it is the "minimum standard of integrity." The CCLD holds four graduation requirement seminars per year, so that cadets gain greater insight into leadership and responsibility.

And, of course, the school calls for a highly technical core curriculum. Given that these are literally life-and-death topics for Air Force officers, the scientific courses are taught painstakingly and well. About 60 percent of a cadet's time in school is taken up by core courses, but all majors provide solid guidelines toward completing both academy and departmental requirements. Available majors include English, foreign-area studies, history, humanities, legal studies, political science, and social studies.

English majors at the USAFA are required to complete an impressive set of classes beyond the school's core curriculum. They substitute "Literary Criticism" and "Speech

West

Communication" for "Literature and Intermediate Composition" and "Advanced Writing & Speaking." Additionally, they must take a Shakespeare class, a pre-1780 and post-1780 British literature courses, and an introduction to American literature. They also complete a junior and senior English seminar, four semesters of foreign language, and six electives.

The history major calls for a similar structure: students take eleven history classes, including "Historiography and Methodology," "The Foundations of Modern America," and "The History of Modern America." They must also complete an AeroSpace History class and a course focusing on an area or time, like "History of Traditional East Asia," "Foundations of Middle Eastern History," or "Modern European History." Four of the five must be in American history or military history if a cadet wants an American history or military history designation on his diploma. Finally, a capstone course in American, military, or global history must be completed. Students are also required to take an elective from any area and complete four semesters of a foreign language.

Political science majors take an introductory course, a class in political theory, and the "Politics of National Security." They then select one course each from a short list in American government, international relations, and comparative politics. A capstone seminar completes the set curriculum, but cadets must also complete three political science electives, any social science or humanities class, and four semesters of foreign language study.

For the student looking for a broader liberal arts approach, the humanities major provides a creative option. Students pick a class each from English, fine arts, history, military and strategic studies, and take a course called "Great Philosophers." Additionally, they must complete four humanities electives and four semesters of foreign language. One staff member comments, "Our core curriculum is heavily weighted toward math and science. However, we do have a vibrant liberal arts program with numerous liberal arts majors available. At graduation, however, all of our cadets receive a bachelor of science degree, regardless of their major."

There are, of course, a great many strictly military courses at the USAFA, as well as airmanship and aviation training sessions, designed to prepare the cadet for his career in the Air Force. Some courses include soaring or gliding and free-fall parachuting. In addition, all manner of military training is conducted year round.

According to several cadets who wrote in various online forums, the academy's education exceeds anything they expected. One cadet lauds the academy's "small class sizes, highly qualified instructors, and limitless opportunities to talk personally with your instructors and receive tutoring and extra instruction. You will have professors with PhDs willing to remain for one or two hours after class with you personally to help you with your work. None of the educators there are getting paid to do research [but] only to teach, meaning that 100 percent of their effort is focused on students. Keep in mind, however, that the academy is . . . both physically and mentally demanding to the point that many students are not able to handle it." Another cadet agrees: "The education is excellent, the friends you

West

make there will remain friends for life, and you will test the limits of your mind and body. It will also probably be the hardest four years of your life, as it was for me."

Rather than traditional study-abroad programs, which would clash with the school's rigorous requirements, the USAFA provides cross-commissioning with other military academies—providing, say, an aspiring helicopter pilot a path to that coveted career in a less-competitive branch of the military.

Foreign language courses are also required of all cadets—two semesters for technical majors, four for nontechnical majors. Cadets are encouraged to pursue "strategic languages" such as Arabic, Chinese, and Russian, although French, German, Japanese, Portuguese, and Spanish are also offered.

Student Life: Careful about the branding

Arrival at the Air Force Academy means exchanging civilian gear for a uniform, having one's hair cut, taking the oath, learning the lingo, and making the transition to military life. This is not the environment for edgy fashions. Piercings need to be removed before admission (non-removable piercings are not allowed). The school warns, "Tattoos or brands must not be excessive. Nor may they contain inflammatory, obscene, racist, sexist or similar content."

Basic Cadet Training (BCT) starts six weeks before academics begin. Fresh arrivals at Colorado Springs are called "doolies" (from the Greek *duolos*, "slave"). Basic training—the academy's version of boot camp—is extremely challenging and meant to separate the wheat from the chaff. Often it results in lifelong friendships—and sometimes in a hasty departure.

In the first half of BCT, doolies are instructed in military customs and courtesies, the Honor Code, Air Force heritage, marching, and room inspection. The second portion of BCT takes place in Jack's Valley, a rugged, wooded area on the academy grounds. This training is particularly physical—among other things the cadet will learn small-unit tactics and proper use of firearms. He will also make his way through several rigorous training circuits: the assault course, obstacle course, and leadership reaction course. The BCT ends with the Acceptance Parade which marks the doolies' entrance into the Cadet Wing and the commencement of the school year.

Drawn from the first-class (senior year) cadets, the Cadet Wing commander oversees four cadet group commanders, who in turn monitor the commanders and their staffs of forty squadrons, each composed of about 110 cadets. Supervising these cadet officers are air officers—commanding and noncommissioned academy military trainers, who are located in each squadron and group.

Each year at the academy brings the cadets specific challenges. The fourth-class (freshman) cadet will end his first year "with an initial foundation of Air Force history, heritage, honor, discipline, drill, and followership skills." The third-class (sophomore) year includes learning survival, land navigation, and water-survival skills. The third summer involves practical training in Air Force military skills, as second-class cadet military training prepares the cadet to be a primary trainer of third- and fourth-class cadets. Life as an

West

ACADEMIC REQUIREMENTS

The Air Force Academy presents a challenging academic environment, offering no easy ways out. The school imposes a highly technical core curriculum, consisting of thirty-two core courses, three of which are "tailored." Here are the requirements:

- Fourth-Class (Freshman) Cadets:
- "Introduction to Behavioral Sciences."
- "Applications of Chemistry."
- "Introduction to Computing."
- "Introduction to Air Force Engineering."
- "Introductory Composition and Research."
- Two foreign language courses.
- "Modern World History."
- "Calculus" I.
- "Calculus" II or "Advanced Placed Calculus" II.
- "General Physics" I.
- Third-Class (Sophomore) Cadets:
- "Applications of Chemistry" II.
- "Introduction to Economics."
- "Fundamentals of Mechanics."
- "Literature and Intermediate Composition."
- "Law for Air Force Officers."
- "Military Theory and Strategy."
- "General Physics" II.
- "Politics, American Government and National Security."
- Second-Class (Junior) Cadets:
- "Fundamentals of Aeronautics."
- "Foundations for Leadership Development."
- "Introductory Biology with Laboratory."
- "Principles of Air Force Electronic Systems."
- "Introduction to Military History."
- "Introduction to Statistics, or Probability and Statistics for Engineers," or "Scientists/ Advanced Probability."
- "Ethics."
- Science and technology energy/systems option.
- First-Class (Senior) Cadets:
- "Introduction to Astronautics."
- "Language, Literature, and Leadership: Advanced Writing & Speaking."
- "Management and Command."
- "Joint and Coalition Operations."
- "Geopolitics."

(continued on page 1026)

Air Force Academy cadet is a year-round experience, including summers; cadets generally get only three weeks of leave in the summer. The balance of their time is spent in a variety of training or education programs, or as the trainers of incoming new cadets.

Every cadet takes two physical education courses each semester; it is mandatory for him to participate in either intercollegiate (club or varsity) or intramural sports as well. There are more than forty athletic teams available. Team sports are seen as a further part of the cadet's education, instilling in cadets "a sense of initiative, self-confidence, and the knowledge that they are part of something greater than themselves," says the school. Intercollegiate sports are strong, consistently competing in national championships—the school's boxing team has never ranked lower than second nationally. Most of the twenty-seven intercollegiate teams are members of the NCAA Division I Mountain West Conference. The USAFA Falcons compete in sports as varied as swimming, ice hockey, rifle, water polo, gymnastics, and wrestling, as well as football, basketball, soccer, and tennis. The academy maintains heated rivalries with West Point and the Naval Academy, and the schools compete in football for the Commander-in-Chief's Trophy.

To allow for all of the required academic, military, and athletic training, daily life is carefully regimented. There are four, fifty-three-minute periods each morning and three each afternoon. Cadets march to breakfast and lunch, and (save for those involved in intercollegiate sports) play on intramural teams two afternoons a week, after classes. On the other three afternoons there are squadron military activities or free time. Evenings after dinner are spent studying in one's room or at the library, as are those Saturday mornings not given over to parades and inspections. Saturday afternoons and Sundays are generally free.

During BCT, the doolie may not have visitors or phone calls. During the remainder of the fourth-class year, phone calls and visitors are permitted on at set times on weekends. Third-class cadets have limited opportunities to leave the campus. Such privileges increase each year, depending on one's academic and training performance. Only the top two classes

ACADEMIC REQUIREMENTS

Additionally, cadets must take a minimum of ten physical education courses. Physical education courses during each of the eight semesters, each consisting of an eight-lesson block of instruction, except for basic swimming, which is sixteen lessons. Cadets must take a physical development course as well as three "combatives" and two "aquatics" from the following:

- "Boxing" (males only) or "Self-defense," (females only).
- "Swimming" or "Basic swimming."
- "Water Survival," or "Basic Water Survival."
- "Basic Swimming" II.
- "Unarmed Combat" I.
- "Unarmed Combat" II.
- One course in racquetball, tennis, or golf.
- One class in volleyball, basketball, soccer, softball.
- One course in scuba, team or individual sport, independent exercise, or cadet instructor.

may own or drive cars at the academy. Along with summer leave, cadets receive two weeks of Christmas vacation and ten days during the spring.

Despite all this, there are plenty of activities for social and other leisure events. Arnold Hall, the academy's student union complex, features formal and informal social events, as well as a food court, dancing, television, games, movies, and live performances by popular entertainers. A military reception and ball are featured once a year.

Weekend skiing is popular among cadets (who are, after all, living in the Rockies) and ski equipment may be checked out from Cadet Recreation Supply in Vandenberg Hall. Nearby are the Cadet Recreation Lodge and the Lawrence Paul Pavilion, which are used for squadron parties and picnics. Farish Memorial Recreational Area offers picnics, ice skating, snow tubing, and hiking.

In addition, the school hosts competitive teams ranging from Judo to model engineering, and from combat conditioning to ultimate Frisbee. Pride of place among recreational clubs is the Cadet Ski Club, but Amateur Radio, a dramatic club called the Blue Bards, the pistol and rifle teams, equestrian and hunting clubs, an FM radio station, and rodeo are just a few of the many special-interest clubs. There are also choirs, drill teams, and professional organizations. All told, there are more than eighty competitive and recreational clubs cadets can join.

This would not be a military academy if it were not subject to meddling by judges. In 1972, U.S. courts ruled that chapel attendance could no longer be mandatory for cadets. Nevertheless, the cadet chapel remains the architectural crown of the campus. It has been described as being "at once old and new, physical and spiritual, solid and soaring, of the earth and of outer space." Featuring sev-

GREEN LIGHT

There seems to be little ideology of any kind infusing coursework at the academy. As one cadet states, "We have true academic freedom in our classrooms. Debate is highly encouraged, but so is respect for opposing views. There are no 'campus politics' here that intrude into the classroom." In keeping with the traditions of the American military, there are no political clubs at the academy, although civic involvement is encouraged through volunteer community service.

However, CNS News reports a distressing incident of political correctness in January 2011, when the USAFA chaplain's office retracted an invitation to former Marine officer and Family Research Council President Tony Perkins after he criticized President Obama's repeal of the "Don't Ask, Don't Tell" policy regarding homosexuals in the military. Republican congressman Trent Franks, a member of the House Armed Services Committee, was outraged at the USAF and blasted it from Capitol Hill: "It is absolutely political correctness, if in the name of inclusiveness we throw out someone who is a Christian or has a view that might a little bit different than Mr. Obama's, then we've dishonored the very service that fights to uphold and defend the Constitution." Dr. William Donahue, president of the Catholic League for Religious and Civil Rights, agreed and publicly condemned the USAF's action, saying, "The decision to silence Tony Perkins, an ordained minister and Marine veteran, represents political correctness at a dangerous level ... [w]hile the most immediate issue is the blacklisting of Perkins, the larger issue is the 'chilling effect' this decision will have on the free speech and religious liberty rights of all those who serve in the military."

enteen stunning spires, the chapel has several levels, each serving one of three faiths groups (Protestant, Catholic, and Jewish). Mormon cadets attend services in Colorado Springs. There are also special rooms in the cadet chapel for services and ceremonies of other religions such as Buddhism and Islam, and the school even accommodates those practicing paganism/earth-centered spirituality through an outdoor, hilltop stone circle. Catholic masses are held across the week, while Protestant services are also held on Sunday.

In 1976, at court insistence, women were admitted to all three academies. Now while there is no doubt of the patriotism or prowess of Air Force alumnae, there is a basic biological fact that the civilian leadership has chosen consistently to ignore: the tendency of people of opposite sexes kept in close quarters to . . . well, *fraternize*. Every few years a sex scandal emerges at one or another of the academies. In 2003, a stinging Pentagon Inspector General report chronicled extensive sexual misconduct at Colorado Springs, to which the academy responded by setting up Sexual Assault Response Coordinator that can be contacted 24 hours a day, and victim advocate services are available on an ongoing basis. Victim advocates "provide support, liaison services and victim care."

As members of the U.S. Air Force, cadets pay no tuition; in fact, they receive a small salary while attending. As one graduate noted, "USAFA is a tough place to be. However, when you get out, you have a responsible job with good pay, and limitless opportunities. I've gotten several interviews on the strength of only the interviewer's curiosity about my background." Another alum boasts, "I make more money than all of my friends and I have zero college debt to pay off."

West

University of Washington

Seattle, Washington • www.washington.edu

A niche in Red Square

Founded in 1861, the University of Washington is the largest university in the Northwest and the oldest on the West Coast. UW has all the usual advantages of state schools—including affordable in-state tuition and a national reputation—along with all the deficiencies of a large state research university—uneven teaching, a weak core curriculum, inadequate advising, and insufficient housing.

Also predictable are the UW students and faculty who are outspokenly political and politicized, and not just when participating in protests on Red Square, a central campus location where radicalism flourishes. (And yes, it actually is named Red Square.) However, in a school with almost 33,000 undergraduates, there is a niche for everyone, including conservative students desiring a solid liberal arts education.

Academic Life: Mass market

The behemoth known as the University of Washington includes seventeen schools and colleges, twelve of which offer degrees for undergraduates. The College of Arts and Sciences, the largest, houses thirty-nine departments, with 931 faculty members offering over 6,300 classes to almost 25,000 undergraduates annually. In a school this size, it is not surprising that a student can graduate from U-Dub—as the university is called—with exposure to only a very narrow field of knowledge and a transcript filled with unserious classes taught by mediocre instructors. Or he can get a solid education, if he knows where to find it.

The graduation requirements in the arts and sciences program are vague and unstructured. Hundreds of courses satisfy these requirements, and many courses suit more than one category at the same time. Consequently, the magic word *flexibility* appears frequently in university literature. For instance, to satisfy the fine arts requirement students can choose either "Intellectual History of Classical Greece" or "Lesbian Lives and Culture."

UW students face entirely too *much* flexibility. The course catalog is the size of an old-fashioned, big-city phone book. Ideally, an incoming freshman would seek advice from a faculty member on how to make the most of his time at the university, but some students graduate from UW without ever having received advice regarding courses, majors, or their careers after college. The university offers one-size-fits-all advising on selecting courses and

West

VITAL STATISTICS

Religious affiliation: *none*
Total enrollment: *45,943*
Total undergraduates: *32,718*
SAT/ACT midranges: CR: *530–650*, M: *570–680*; ACT: *24–30*
Applicants: *21,268*
Applicants accepted: *58%*
Accepted applicants who enrolled: *45%*
Tuition and fees: *in state, $8,701; out of state, $25,329*
Room and board: *$10,215*
Freshman retention rate: *93%*
Graduation rate: *54% (4 yrs.), 81% (6 yrs.)*
Courses with fewer than 20 students: *33%*
Student-faculty ratio: *12:1*
Courses taught by graduate students: *6%*
Most popular majors: *social sciences, biology, business and marketing*
Students living on campus: *23%*
Guaranteed housing for four years? *no*
Students in fraternities: *6%* in sororities: *5%*

majors. Students who have not declared majors can visit the Undergraduate Advising Center, where they make thirty-minute appointments with professional advisors, not faculty members. According to UW's website, "there are upwards of 7,000 new students starting each autumn quarter and only twelve pre-major advisors." Once students have declared a major, they are assigned departmental advisors, who, according to a specialist in the advising center, are either full-time professional advisors or, more likely, graduate students.

According to a recent graduate, to flourish at the University of Washington, "students must be independent, self-motivated, and ambitious. At UW, you can go to class, go back to your room and play video games for the rest of the day . . . or you can be involved intellectually, socially, and in extracurricular events. It's up to the student."

Because UW has such a large student body, many classes—especially at the introductory level—are huge. These are taught by professors, graduate teaching assistants, or both. In a typical intro-level course, the professor teaches the class two days a week, and students break up into smaller discussion groups led by TAs once a week. "TAs normally grade most papers and exams and generally have a lot more contact with students than the professors do," says one student. Foreign TAs without a working knowledge of English is a common complaint among students. Thankfully, as students begin to specialize in their majors, class sizes grow smaller and students have more opportunities to create relationships with faculty members.

In an effort to ease the transition from high school to an enormous state university, UW offers an option to freshman, the Freshman Interest Group (FIG) program, that includes optional housing and adds structure to the curriculum while providing a smaller academic community. FIG is advertised as a program that creates groups of twenty to twenty-five freshmen with similar academic interests to share courses for the first term of college. However, not all FIGs are based on shared academic interest. Others form around volunteer service or, predictably, the participants' shared ethnicity. There is also a Freshman Seminar Program that "offers first-year students access to small, discussion-oriented classes," according to the program's website. The seminar topics vary each year, as do their quality. The entering class of 2010 had several seminar options, including "Shaping Your Future Through Self-Knowledge and Skill Development" and "Sustainability: Globally, Locally, and Personally."

West

The College of Arts and Sciences has many strong departments. For instance, the philosophy department is solid, emphasizing the philosophy of science, an area in which it has several eminent scholars. Majors take a course in logic, one in modern philosophy, and one in ancient philosophy, ancient political philosophy, or the history of ancient ethics.

The history department is said to be more committed to teaching than are some other majors, but the requirements are too broad. History majors must take an "Introduction to History" class; one course each in European, American, and non-Western history; and two courses each in premodern and postmodern history.

Students claim there is not much political indoctrination in the classroom unless you are taking courses in one of the more politicized departments. Students say that in addition to the ethnic studies programs and the women's studies department, political science and international studies—particularly Middle East studies—are particularly left wing. A political science major says, "As a conservative Republican, I find myself in the decided minority." The political science major covers four broad fields: American politics, comparative politics, international relations, and political theory. In addition to these classes, poli sci majors must take a statistics class, and are strongly encouraged to pursue faculty-supervised independent study and an optional senior thesis. Economics and business are said to have less ideological faculties.

Every humanities department offers the usual trendy and trivial choices. An English professor says that his department is among the worst in this regard. In his department, students can, for example, take courses in "Introduction to Cultural Studies," "The Water Crisis in Literature and Cinema," "Women and the Literary Imagination," and "Gay and Lesbian Studies."

English major requirements are excellent, however, as students concentrating in language and literature must take at least one course in each of several historical periods: medieval to Shakespeare, seventeenth- and eighteenth-century English literature, nineteenth-century English literature, American literature to 1917, and twentieth-century British and American literature. Courses focusing on these periods are generally traditional and include studies of Chaucer, Shakespeare, and Milton, and one called "American Literature: The Colonial Period."

Happily, a cultural and ethnic diversity course requirement has been proposed and rejected several times over the years by UW faculty. An arts and sciences administrator says, "It's still in the works," and the director of the Task Force on Diversity in the Curriculum says she is attempting "to enhance the number of courses on race, ethnicity, gender, class,

---

SUGGESTED CORE

1. Classics 424, The Epic Tradition
2. Philosophy 320, Ancient Philosophy
3. Near Eastern Studies 240/ Religion 220, Introduction to the Hebrew Bible: Old Testament/ Introduction to the New Testament
4. Ancient and Medieval History 360, Medieval Christianity (closest match)
5. Political Science 310, The Western Tradition of Political Thought: Modern
6. English 225, Shakespeare
7. History of the Americas 301, Foundations of American Civilization
8. Modern European History 406, European Intellectual History: Nineteenth Century

West

etc. on campus" even without faculty backing for a diversity requirement. The task force evolved into a full-fledged Center for Curriculum Transformation Project, a university-funded program operating out of the Office of Minority Affairs and Diversity that seeks "curriculum change related to gender and cultural pluralism." The project leads workshops for faculty members on how to incorporate diversity issues into their courses. Topics in 2011 included "Race in the Classroom," "Diversity in the Classroom," and "Infusing Global Learning Goals into the Curriculum," and faculty seminars explored topics like "Creating Inclusive Classrooms" and "Colonizing Knowledges."

An alternative to the standard Arts and Sciences curriculum is the Interdisciplinary Honors Program, a four-year track during which students take at least one designated honors course per quarter, participate in two experiential learning projects, and keep an ongoing learning portfolio. The honors program was revamped in 2010 to include its own designated core courses that parallel UW's basic core curriculum. Eligible students may also choose to participate in Departmental Honors or College Honors—the latter a particularly ambitious program requiring the simultaneous completion of both the Interdisciplinary and Departmental Honors programs in at least one of their majors.

One student in the Interdisciplinary program says, "Honors professors as a breed tend to be a little stranger and some are decidedly better than others." Many of the courses are rigorous—especially the science courses, which are much better than the usual "science for non-science majors" fare. Another student describes the program as "very intense, with only the most serious students." According to its website the program offers many perks, including "personalized and comprehensive" academic advising; small classes; special seminars; aid in finding internships and research opportunities; special study-abroad programs; peer mentoring; a designated computer lab; designated residence hall floors; and several other benefits exclusive to the honors programs.

Recommended professors at UW include Jon Bridgman (emeritus), James Felak, and R. Tracy McKenzie in history; Gerald Baldasty in communication; Keith Leffler in economics; G. Alan Marlat in psychology; David Thouless in physics; Daniel Weld in computer science; and Jonathan Mercer in political science. One upperclassman advises students to check online course evaluations before registering for courses; from these, students can often find out how past students have rated faculty, and choose their classes accordingly.

The university is constantly updating or adding to its facilities. Most recently, Paccar Hall was completed in 2010 to accommodate business leaders, alumni, faculty and students of the Foster School of Business. The Molecular Engineering Building is in the midst of a two-phase, 160,000-square-foot project to house the molecular engineering research and teaching labs, which is slated for completion on November 12, 2011. On July 1, 2010, after a five-year fund-raising campaign, the Husky Student Union began a two-year renovation scheduled for completion in the fall of 2012.

UW's Office of International Programs and Exchanges provides guidance for students participating in the university's over 300 study-abroad programs, on all inhabited continents. At home, students may study American Sign Language, Chinese, French, German, Italian, Ancient Greek, Latin, Hebrew, Japanese, Korean, Russian, Spanish, Swahili, Ukrainian, Uygur, Danish, Finnish, Norwegian, Swedish, Arabic, Aramaic, Egyptian, Per-

West

sian, Turkish, Ugaritic, Tagalog, Bengali, Hindi, Indian, Indonesian, Sanskrit, Thai, Vietnamese, Portuguese, Estonian, Latvian, Lithuanian, Bulgarian, Czech, Polish, and Russian, among several others.

Student Life: Living in the Emerald City

As one professor notes, "The best thing about UW is the location. Seattle is a wonderful town, and the campus, though in a city, is safe, has lots of greenery, and its buildings are readily accessible." On the weekends, Seattle offers a number of options for students eager to escape campus, including theaters, bars, and art galleries. Downtown Seattle is easily accessible via the U-PASS bus system (a great deal for students), and the Canadian border is less than two hours away by car. Seattle also boasts a number of local bands, including many who carry on the city's venerable "grunge" style. Pike's Place Market, located on the pier in downtown Seattle, is a popular place to buy produce, fresh flowers, and crafts produced by local artists. UW has a large number of outdoor enthusiasts. Many students head out of town to go hiking, biking, skiing, and camping on weekends. The Cascade Range is only minutes away; Mount Rainier is only an hour-and-a-half drive. Students are quick to point out that, implausible as it sounds, both Boston and New York receive more rainfall each year than Seattle. Visitors to the Emerald City are often struck by its beauty as it shimmers in the sun after a morning shower.

The University of Washington is too large for stereotypes. With so many students, it is a truly diverse place, including a number of international students, fraternity and sorority members, arts aficionados, environmentalists, and athletes. There is certainly a niche for everyone, with over 500 registered clubs and organizations, including over sixty cam-

---

ACADEMIC REQUIREMENTS

- One English composition course. Offerings include "Introductory Composition" and "Interdisciplinary Writing in the Humanities."
- Two writing classes, such as "Introduction to Sylistics Through Composition" and "Environmental Response."
- One quantitative, symbolic, or formal reasoning course. Class offerings include "Algebra with Applications" and "Statistical Concepts and Methods for the Social Sciences."
- Four fine arts (visual, literary, and performing arts) classes. Students may choose from such courses as "Music for Dance" and "Survey of Western Art: Medieval and Renaissance."
- Four social science courses, such as "Introduction to Psychology" and "Indigenous Feminisms."
- Four natural science classes. Course selections include "Introductory Biology" and "General Physics."
- Three additional classes in fine arts, social sciences, or natural sciences.
- Three foreign language classes or demonstrated proficiency to the intermediate level.

West

pus ministries (the Muslim Student Association, Athletes in Action, Baha'i Student Association, Campus Crusade for Christ, Catholic Newman Center, and Hillel, among many others); a jazz band; a radio station; a television station; a symphony orchestra; musical theater; model U.N.; College Republicans and College Democrats; close to twenty honor societies; and over fifty minority and international groups, including the Arab Student Organization, Association of Black Social Worker Students, Latino Student Union, and the Mixed Club for students of mixed race. Sources say that the student body is overwhelmingly politically and socially liberal, especially when it comes to homosexual and minority entitlement issues.

But since the school is enormous and most UW students live off campus, some undergrads still find it difficult to attain a comfortable sense of community. As one student reported, "I can walk through the middle of campus and not necessarily see anyone I know." As a result, many students—roughly 3,600—opt to join one of UW's fifty fraternities or sororities. Although the Greek residences are private housing facilities, the administration has every fraternity and sorority sign a recognition agreement in which they submit to "certain well-defined rules" (in particular, a pledge to keep residences alcohol free). Any Greek group that does not abide by the agreement is not officially recognized by the university. In any case, Greek life has kept some students from becoming just a number. "If I had to do it over again, I would have joined a fraternity," says an upperclassman. "They provide a sense of community."

Housing on the UW campus is not guaranteed, even for freshmen. The student housing office attributes this policy to the high demand. In fact, housing is difficult to find off campus, too, because Seattle's cost of living has been rising steadily. The student housing office confesses that "UW is primarily not a residential campus"; only a fifth of undergraduates live in the university's fifteen residence halls and off-campus apartments. A volunteer student group helps students find off-campus housing by posting listings of area apartments. The university is attempting to address the housing shortage with a massive three-phase construction project scheduled through 2020. Phase I includes three six-story residence halls and two apartment complexes on West Campus; Phase II is the renovation of six existing halls; and Phase III includes additional as-yet-unspecified new construction to result in a grand total of 2,400 additional beds.

Married couples and same-sex domestic partners are allowed to live together in UW's family housing buildings. In the residence halls, the university offers single, double, and triple units, but no single-sex dorm option for undergrads, and students can choose men-only or women-only floors. In many of the residence halls, men and women live next door to one another. However, there are no coed dorm rooms or bathrooms.

Athletics are a fundamental element of student life at UW. The ten men's and thirteen women's varsity teams compete in NCAA Division I-A and the Pacific Ten Conference. Huskies football dominates the fall semester with the unique tradition of tailgating by boat, as UW's Husky Stadium is built on the shores of Lake Washington. In fall 2010, UW began a $260 million remodeling and renovation on the stadium—the most expensive in NCAA history. In 2009, the men's rowing team and the women's softball team won their national championships. The same year, the university's athletic department discontinued

West

the men's and women's swimming programs due to budget cuts.

UW also hosts thirty-two men's and women's intercollegiate teams and more than twenty-five intramural sports. The Intramural Activities Building houses top-quality athletic facilities, including a state-of-the-art fitness center, five gyms, squash courts, climbing walls, indoor track, swimming pool, racquetball/squash courts, multi-activities studios, saunas, indoor cycling studio, health food cafe, outdoor sports fields, thirteen tennis courts, and running and walking trails.

Besides sports, the university also hosts all manner of artistic and cultural performances in a 1,206-seat theater in the Meany Hall for the Performing Arts, and the School of Drama stages productions in three smaller theaters. The School of Music offers a wide range of events throughout the school year "from the intimacy of a small chamber music group to the power of the Studio Jazz ensemble, there is something for every student," says the department's website.

UW has a relatively safe campus, despite its large size and urban location. However, the area surrounding UW is not as safe; according to the *Seattle Times*, nearby University

---

YELLOW LIGHT

A campus journalist at UW once quipped that "15 percent of the student body is liberal, while 10 percent is conservative. Everybody else is pretty much waving in the wind—apathetic or indifferent. The institution, but not necessarily the campus as a whole, is obliging to liberal views." Part of "the institution" is the student government, a group of usually liberal students who nominate their own successors and are thus able to perpetuate their own power and views. And one student says that the official campus newspaper, the *Daily*, is an "unabashedly and poorly edited liberal mouthpiece."

Although it's true that the majority of students and faculty are politically and socially liberal, there is a growing conservative presence on the UW campus including the Young Americans for Liberty, a continuation of Students for Ron Paul, that has steadily grown in the past couple of years. Our sources also tell us that the conservative Greeks exert a disproportionate influence on campus as well.

Way is one of the most crime-ridden areas in Seattle, and burglaries on campus have been increasing over the last few years. The campus police, an accredited state police force, provides around the clock security and surveillance, and the school also offers several escort and shuttle services at night. In 2009, UW reported six robberies, six aggravated assaults, eighty-three burglaries, eight car thefts, and two arsons.

University of Washington is an amazing bargain for in-state residents with 2010–11 tuition at $8,701 (out-of-state is $25,329), and room and board $10,215. Thirty-seven percent of UW undergraduates receive some form of need-based financial aid and graduate with an average debt of $17,800.

Whitman College

Walla Walla, Washington • www.whitman.edu

Walden West

Whitman College was established in 1883 by Cushing Eells, in memory of Christian missionaries Marcus and Narcissa Whitman—but it was chartered as a secular, not a religious school. Whitman is known for being independent from sectarian and political control; however, a default liberalism certainly pervades the campus. One professor explains that although there is no "direct silencing of any particular groups," one can joke about the political right "without raising an eyebrow, but joking about the absurd hyperbole of liberal activists would require a detailed defense." While one student says, "It would be hard to be a conservative here," another reports: "I was blessed with an intellectually aggressive class that wanted to discuss, debate, out-and-out argue, and then go to lunch together afterwards."

Academic Life: Antiquity and modernity

Whitman's worthy General Studies Program requires all freshmen to take a two semester course, "First-Year Experience: Encounters" which is an "introduction to the liberal arts and the academic construction of knowledge" and is "[o]rganized around a variable theme." In 2010–11 that theme was "Encounters Ancient and Modern." Students meet in small-group seminars of no more than sixteen. A third (optional) general studies course entitled "Critical Voices" is less promising. The course warns that it "will call into question the dominance of traditional Western worldviews by critically examining the historical and ideological roles played by 'others.'"

A music major says that "as a liberal arts school, Whitman really forces you to stretch intellectually with all its general education requirements (two courses in each the humanities, social sciences, and the fine arts). While I wasn't thrilled at the prospect of taking a biology course, it was good to have a class that forced me to learn something about the environment and to think more concretely about the Earth."

The gen ed requirements at Whitman don't go far enough. One teacher explains that "it is possible to get a strong liberal arts education at Whitman, *if* the student chooses wisely from the potpourri of diverse offerings, and *if* the student gets solid direction from his/her advisor." For example, because there are so many options offered, English literature majors could possibly "avoid hundreds of years of English lit, traditional major authors, and important periods." Another teacher points out that only so much can be achieved in two semesters. It is possible to receive a grounding in a traditional liberal arts education by supplementing what the core lacks throughout one's next three years of study. However, students are not required to take these courses, making it possible to easily miss receiving a strong liberal arts education if they don't choose their courses very carefully.

Upon submitting an application, students are given a pre-major advisor, a faculty or staff member. After four semesters at Whitman, students choose a major and receive an advisor in that department.

Whitman offers forty-five majors and thirty-two minors. Students may also enter double majors (most commonly combining environmental studies with another program); or an individually planned program; past examples include political philosophy, peace and conflict studies, American studies, environmental studies, creative writing, or astrophysics.

Popular majors at Whitman include biology, BBMB (biochemistry, biophysics, and molecular biology, a program unique to Whitman), English, politics, psychology, sociology, environmental studies, and history. One teacher comments that biology, chemistry and geology are among the strongest departments, with "dedicated faculty members and good opportunities for undergraduate research." Both teachers and students told us that there isn't a single weak department at Whitman. However, there are some which "could use more professors or space," says a teacher.

English majors must take "Approaches to the Study of Literature," four "period courses in English and American Literature with at least two courses in English and one in American literature ("Studies in Renaissance Literature," "Studies in British Literature," or "The American Literary Emergence, 1620–1920." They also take one single-author course ("Chaucer," "Shakespeare," or "Milton"); one seminar in English and American literature ("Postcolonial Melancholy, Cosmopolitan Success" or "Historical Novels"); and two additional advanced courses ("Colonial and Anti-Colonial Literature" or "Humor in the Literary Short Story"). Admirably, all seniors must pass a written comprehensive and an oral examination. Shakespeare would be hard to miss, and he's almost certainly on the test.

History offers courses in seven geographical areas: ancient Mediterranean, East Asia, Europe, Islamic world, Africa, Latin America, and the United States. A major must take at least one course in each of three of these areas, at least one course treating a period before

VITAL STATISTICS

Religious affiliation: *none*
Total enrollment: *1,555*
Total undergraduates: *1,555*
SAT/ACT midranges: CR: *610–720*, M: *610–720*; ACT: *27–31*
Applicants: *3,164*
Applicants accepted: *47%*
Accepted applicants who enrolled: *28%*
Tuition and fees: *$38,450*
Room and board: *$9,720*
Freshman retention rate: *92%*
Graduation rate: *80% (4 yrs.), 85% (6 yrs.)*
Courses with fewer than 20 students: *63%*
Student-faculty ratio: *10:1*
Courses taught by graduate students: *none*
Most popular majors: *social sciences, biological and life sciences, visual and performing arts*
Students living on campus: *67%*
Guaranteed housing for four years? *no*
Students in fraternities: *39%* in sororities: *30%*

West

1. Classics 227, Greek and Roman Epic
2. Philosophy 201, Readings in Western Philosophical Tradition: Ancient
3. Religion 201/202, The Hebrew Bible/The New Testament and Early Christianity
4. History 202, European Intellectual History, 386–1300
5. Politics 122, Introduction to Modern European Political Theory
6. English 351/352, Shakespeare
7. History 105, Development of the United States (1607–1877)
8. History 277, Nineteenth Century Europe, 1815–1914 (closest match)

1500 AD, and "two related courses within one geographic area" ("Topics in Middle East History," "Alexander the Great and the Hellenistic Kingdoms"). Majors start with a course in "Historical Methodologies," another called "Topics in Comparative History," a "comparisons and encounters" elective ("The Roman Empire," "Modern European Imperialism," "The United States in the World"); and one seminar ("Seminar in Ancient Mediterranean History," "Seminar in European History"). It seems that students could emerge without taking classes in the American founding and Civil War.

The politics department's requirements are less concrete, with no common introductory requirements. The students choose seven courses, take one senior seminar and write a senior thesis. Course offerings recently included "Introduction to Ancient and Medieval Political Theory," "Introduction to Modern European Political Theory," "The Politics of Film: James Bond," "Political Ecology," and "American Political Theory."

Seniors must complete senior assessments with a passing grade in the major field they have chosen. The examination may be completely oral, or a combination of both written and oral. Some individual majors are also expected to complete an extensive project of a written or multimedia thesis, a presentation, or a recital.

Whitman provides many excellent teachers: Timothy Kaufman-Osborn (who recently assumed the office of provost and dean of the faculty of Whitman College), Paul Apostolidis, Phil Brick and Jeanne Morefield in politics; Nina Lerman and David Schmitz in history; Pete Crawford, John David Earnest, Lee Thompson, Susan Pickett and David Glenn in music; Bob Carson, Kevin Pogue, and Pat Spencer in geology; Delbert Hutchison and Paul Yancey in biology; Leroy Wade in chemistry; Dana Burgess in classics; Jonathan Walters and Walt Wyman in religion; Michelle Janning in sociology; and Jan Crouter in economics. "Teaching excellence is a top priority," says one teacher, although another laments that "research is becoming more important in decisions regarding tenure and promotion."

Students may participate in the college's urban-semester study and internships in Chicago, Philadelphia, and Washington, D.C. In addition, students have the opportunity to apply for many science research internships available through the college. Whitman also offers a Semester in the West program, where environmental majors study "public lands conservation in the interior American West." Topics range from grizzly bear and wolf reintroduction plans to environmental justice in New Mexico. Throughout the semester, students meet with activists, read what others have written about the West, and write extensively themselves.

Whitman also provides combined programs where students can receive an advanced degree and specialized training from another school that specializes in a given field. These

West

cooperative programs include engineering and computer science with Caltech, Duke, Columbia, the University of Washington, Washington University in St. Louis, and Duke; environmental and forestry degrees with Duke; law with the Columbia School of Law; and education with the University of Puget Sound. The University of Washington confers degrees in both oceanography and computer science. Engineering and computer science degrees are a 3+2 program, meaning that students spend their first three years at Whitman and the next two at a sister school. Law with Columbia University is a 3+3 program, while the education program with Puget Sound is a 4+1 program.

Whitman is also known for its undergraduate conference, established just a few years ago. Whitman helps fund student research and internships, and then approximately 175 students present the results of their research during this one-day conference. Presentations are given as recitals, expository papers, original scientific research, original plays in the college theater, or studio art exhibits. To help every student attend, Whitman cancels all classes for the day.

Whitman keeps a low student-faculty ratio of 10 to 1. "Professors are *incredibly* helpful and available—and you don't even have to be a student," exclaims one undergrad, recalling her visit as a prospective student. Faculty at Whitman are known to collaborate with students on research projects, join them on the intramural sports field, serve on committees with them and bring them home for dinner. It is generally agreed on campus that "teaching has always been the central responsibility at Whitman College."

Since Whitman is an undergraduate college, there are no graduate assistants teaching classes. However, "There are a significant number of adjuncts teaching regular courses at Whitman, especially in the first-year core," says a faculty member. Due to staffing issues, many of the private lessons in the music department are taught by adjuncts.

One teacher speaks highly of Whitman's study-abroad programs, which "are offered in many countries around the world (China, Japan, France, Scotland, and Australia to name a few). About half of all students spend some time studying abroad." Students may choose from thirty-eight programs and have the option of studying on five continents.

Foreign languages taught at Whitman include Chinese, Latin, Ancient Greek, French, German, Japanese, and Spanish.

Student Life: Nature and culture

Whitman College is located in the town of Walla Walla, in the southeastern corner of Washington State. Geographically, it is surrounded by mountains, with the Snake and Columbia Rivers nearby. Walla Walla is home to three colleges, college and civic theaters, and a summer play and lecture series, as well as the oldest continuously operating orchestra west of the Mississippi. The small town of about 30,000 is splendidly isolated, with the closest large city two and a half hours by car (Spokane), and Portland and Seattle both more than a four-hour drive away.

Whitman offers boundless opportunities to enjoy the great outdoors. Students will find many options for open-air activities in close proximity, including hiking in Rooks Park and in the Blue Mountains, skiing at Bluewood, skating at the Ice Chalet, fishing the South

West

Fork of the Walla Walla River, camping in the Umatilla National Forest, whitewater rafting in northeastern Oregon, and berry picking in the nearby mountains. Students say that everything in Walla Walla is bike-able—but many students have cars, which are helpful for escaping the immediate vicinity.

Whitman College provides some eighty student organizations, which include honor societies (Phi Beta Kappa, Sigma Delta Pi, the Order of Waiilaptu); religious organizations (Whitman Christian Fellowship; Hillel-Shalom; Unitarian Universalist Community; and Atheists, Humanists, and Agnostics); minority organizations (Club Latino, Club for the Recognition of Cultures and Minorities, Wakilisha Afrika, Vietnamese Cultural Club, and Black Student Union); and a wide variety of liberal organizations like Feminists Advocating Change and Empowerment, Voices for Planned Parenthood, Whitman Civil Liberties Union, Young Democrats, the inevitable homosexual advocacy groups, Coalition Against Homophobia and GLBTQ. There is but a single politically conservative organization on campus, the Campus Conservatives, which strives "to bring speakers to campus, educate our fellow students about conservatism, cultivate an atmosphere of healthy political discussion, and ensure that the campus gives fair voice to the conservative end of the political spectrum," according to the group's website. Other popular campus organizations include Outdoor Programs, Renaissance Faire, Whitman Science Club, and Speech and Debate. Students may also participate in choral groups, student film society, a radio station, and much more. One student reports, "The problem at Whitman is that there is too much to do. Any given night offers five different lectures, movies, presentations, parties, and dances."

ACADEMIC REQUIREMENTS

Whitman offers an abbreviated but worthwhile core curriculum, along with certain distributional requirements. All students must complete:

- Two semesters of "First-Year Experience: Encounters."
- Two courses of "Alternative Voices," a multiculturalist examination of non-Western cultures and minority groups in the West. Choices range from "German Film and the Frankfurt School" to "Queer Religiosities."
- Two courses in social sciences. Choices range from "Financial Markets and Investment" to "The Sociology and History of Rock 'n' Roll" and "Topics in African History."
- Two courses in humanities. Choices here range very widely from "Chaucer" to "American Protest Literature" and "Greek and Roman Intellectual History."
- Two classes in fine arts. Options include everything from "Visual Culture of Renaissance Europe, 1250–1500" to "Beginning Photography" and "Fundamentals of Public Address."
- Two courses in science (with one lab section).
- One quantitative (mathematics) course. Course examples include "Principles of Astronomy," "Chemistry in Art," and "Energy and the Environment."

Religious students who come to Whitman should "actively seek out a faith community on or off campus and become as active as possible," one professor says, noting that "only a minority of students are religiously active." Walla Walla provides places of worship for both Catholics and Protestants, as well as a small but active synagogue. Other interesting communities in Walla Walla include St. Silouan Orthodox Church, and Seventh-Day Adventists (neighboring Walla Walla University is affiliated with the Seventh-Day Adventist Church). While historic St. Patrick's church in Walla Walla is very beautiful, tradition-minded Catholics may choose to drive an hour to St. Joseph's Church in Kennewick, which hosts regular Latin liturgies.

Whitman proudly fields twenty-two varsity athletic teams for men and women, for example alpine and nordic skiing, cycling, rugby (men and women!) and three "coed" sports: water polo, tae kwon do, and triathalon. The school is affiliated with both the National Collegiate Athletic Association (NCAA-III) and the National Association of Intercollegiate Athletics (NAIA-II). Whitman's ski team competes in the U.S. Collegiate Ski Association. Of the club sports present, the "fighting missionaries'" cycling club team can boast four DII National Championships within the past six years. More than 70 percent of Whitman's student body chooses from a dozen intramural sports (20 percent in varsity sports). For non-competitive students, there is a plethora of physical education classes. Whitman also provides excellent outing programs that take advantage of the school's idyllic location.

About 67 percent of Whitman students live on campus; all students under twenty-one must live on campus for at least four semesters. The campus offers residence halls arranged in both traditional dormitory style

YELLOW LIGHT

In describing the political atmosphere of the school, one teacher explains that "Whitman College is clearly left-leaning, but not as oppressively so as most of the liberal arts colleges back East." Another professor says that although the faculty is overwhelmingly liberal, "We don't wear our politics on our sleeves."

Out of all the departments at Whitman, the politics department is known as farthest left. However, one conservative teacher defends the department, saying that "they intentionally aim to prevent their own politics from entering into the classroom, and several [professors] have said that they far prefer a thoughtful conservative student to a run-of-the-mill liberal student. In fact, because the pedagogical goal in these classes involves using classic texts of the Western tradition to challenge students' preconceptions, and because many students come with left-of-center preconceptions, even liberal politics professors end up articulating and defending important conservative perspectives."

There are danger signs. George S. Bridges, Whitman's president since 2005, focused much of his academic research on problems of racial and ethnic minorities in the juvenile justice system. Since at Whitman, he has centered his vision for the college on racial and ethnic diversity, and helped push what critics call discriminatory policies, such as the "Diversity Upgrades of Temporary Appointments" initiative, which a professor warns may politicize and racialize hiring. The teacher says, "Although the college maintains that it does not discriminate in hiring for the 'diversity' positions, the record shows that it is difficult or impossible for a white male to be offered a 'diversity' position, unless he shares the position with a nonwhite spouse."

West

1041

and in suites. All dorms are coed, except for one that houses freshman women and some sorority members. Members of the four fraternities live in separate houses and enjoy separate dining services. Douglas Hall houses a few single rooms and suites of eight students, and is an option for upperclassmen. A housing official says that each year a handful of students opt for coed dorm rooms (they must have parental approval). Almost all dorm rooms, however, are single sex. Except for those in the "interest houses," all residence hall bathrooms are single sex. Whitman's eleven interest houses include La Casa Hispana, La Maison Française, Tekisuijuku (Japanese House), Das Deutsche Haus, Asian Studies House, Outhouse (an environmental studies house), Fine Arts House, Community Service House, the MECCA (i.e., Multi-Ethnic Center for Cultural Affairs), Global Awareness House, and the Writing House. The Glover Alston Center, completed in 2010, serves as a "resource to facilitate Whitman's commitment to sustaining a diverse community," the college announced.

In a small town like Walla Walla, you wouldn't expect much crime—but there is a little, and some of it takes place on campus. In 2009, the school reported three forcible sex offenses, four burglaries, two robberies and one arson.

Whitman is not cheap. For the 2010–11 academic year, tuition alone cost $38,450, while room and board were $9,720. However, Whitman provides a very comprehensive and diversified financial aid program, including grants, scholarships, employment opportunities, and loans. Some 40 percent of students received need-based financial aid during the 2010–11 school year, and the average student-loan debt of a recent graduate is $14,285.

Asking the Right Questions

What You Need to Know to Choose the Right College

If you are like many readers of this college guide, you will soon be visiting various colleges and universities in an attempt to get a better feel for which institution is the best option for you—or for your son or daughter. In this section we offer some advice on how to make the most of these visits by doing some research of your own. Our hope is to alert you to some of the questions that you might wish to raise, and issues to which you will want to be sensitive, while visiting any campus, so that even if you are not visiting one of the institutions profiled here or on our companion website, CollegeGuide.org, you will be able to make a more informed choice.

The following questions—similar to those we asked in conducting our research for *Choosing the Right College*—are divided into the same areas of inquiry as the preceding essays: Academic Life, Student Life, and the Red, Green, or Yellow Light. The first two sections, Academic Life and Student Life, suggest questions to be asked of student tour guides, professors, and administrators. Each question is followed by a brief explanation of its importance.

A word of advice: Questioning on-campus representatives is a delicate matter that you should approach with savvy and tact. Don't assume that tour guides, in particular, will know the answers to some of the questions that follow. After all, they are often young students themselves and may have never thought about these issues. Therefore, you should be prepared to seek out professors and administrators, chaplains and coaches, who will be better able to address your concerns. And of course, it is important to be polite, to size up each encounter individually, and to base your assessment on the totality of your on-campus experience.

The final section, the Red, Green, or Yellow Light, is intended to inform you of some widespread and often controversial issues affecting campus life. Raising such matters can be difficult, particularly in a group setting. The questioner in this instance risks appearing confrontational or overbearing when pressing student guides who might be leading a group of parents and students. Other official campus representatives are unlikely to acknowledge the existence of campus controversy. Being aware of the problems adverted to in this section, however, will allow you to identify trouble spots on any campus with confidence and ease.

I. Academic Life: Key questions

Question: What percentage of classes is taught by teaching assistants (TAs)? Who is doing the grading?

Explanation: At many schools, particularly large state universities and research institutions, both public and private, professors are recruited and retained by reducing (or even eliminating) their teaching loads. Therefore, undergraduates may be taught by graduate students in their twenties working their way toward a PhD rather than by the famous professors lauded in university literature. Pay particular attention to freshman and sophomore classes, where the use of TAs is greatest. Where tenure is decided primarily on the quantity of publications rather than the quality of a candidate's teaching, professors have a disincentive to pursue pedagogical excellence. So ask a faculty member what is the balance at this school between teaching and research in tenure decisions. You'll get some raised eyebrows—and maybe some candid answers.

Question: Is there a true core curriculum made up of required courses across the liberal arts and sciences that all students must take, or do you instead rely on distribution requirements that allow students to pick and choose from among numerous courses within a given discipline?

Explanation: Most schools long ago abandoned their core curricula, which required each student to take a series of informative courses that ensured that everyone emerged broadly educated in the arts and sciences regardless of his academic major. Many colleges falsely state that they have a core curriculum when they don't. If your sources answer this question affirmatively, ask them how many choices exist within each disciplinary requirement. If the answer is more than one or two, there is no core curriculum worthy of the name.

Question: Must all students study Western history and literature?

Explanation: When the core was abandoned, most schools still required students to take history and literature survey courses that exposed them to the broad sweep of our civilization's accomplishments. Today, however, an increasing number of schools have made these courses optional. Therefore, many students graduate without ever studying the history of Western civilization or its finest texts and thinkers. Students may often study cultures or works of literature that are either best left to more specialized studies or that do not merit serious academic attention.

Question: Is a course on American history required for graduation?

Explanation: The study of U.S. history has disappeared from many schools' graduation requirements in much the same way Western history has been removed from the required curriculum. While the absence of such courses from the required list does not mean that they are not available, it does reveal an administration lacking a commitment to foster in its students an understanding of our nation's past.

Question: To what extent are students advised by faculty members? If faculty members are not advising students, who is carrying out this important task?

Explanation: Many colleges assign students advisors or employ professional advisors, thus fulfilling, on paper, an important obligation. Yet these advisors often know little about the particular courses in which a student may be interested, or else are professional "educrats" with little qualification for the job. Professors, on the other hand, are best qualified to advise students on which courses and professors to take, as well as to offer insight into academic majors, internships, and postgraduate study. Of course, even assigning professors sometimes fails to guarantee access to good information. As documented in the *Chronicle of Higher Education*, some faculty members are often difficult to track down and hold infrequent office hours. Who your advisor is will impact your life during and after college. Choose wisely.

Question: On average, how many years does it take to graduate? What percentage of freshmen graduate at all?

Explanation: Universities often fail to offer required courses in numbers sufficient to accommodate every student's needs. Courses fill up and leave students with no recourse but to spend additional semesters, and even a fifth or sixth year, fulfilling graduation requirements. Parents must pay more in tuition, while students postpone entry into the workplace and often assume additional debt. This administrative decision also increases the demand for teaching assistants, thus justifying universities' large doctoral programs while relieving professors of their obligation to teach. Everyone wins but the student (and parent).

II. Student Life: Information to gather

Question: Can a student be assured of securing a room in a single-sex dorm if desired? Are bathrooms coed? Are dorm rooms?

Explanation: Many colleges today offer only coed dorms. Some have single-sex floors within dorms, while others are single sex by room. Yet others have shared bathrooms—toilet areas and showers shared by both sexes. Increasingly, under pressure from "transgender" activists and cohabiting undergrads, some colleges are offering coed dorm rooms as well. Decide if this is the right environment for your son or daughter.

Question: Can a student be assured of living on campus each year if he so desires?

Explanation: Living on campus is a very important element of the college experience. It places students in closer proximity to one another and to campus events, and is therefore key to the development of a close-knit campus community. Dorm life also exposes students to others from varied backgrounds and with diverse interests. Off-campus housing can be expensive, neighborhoods can be dangerous, and students live with no supervision at all.

Question: Are there substance-free dorms?

Explanation: Responding to demands from both students and parents, some schools have established special dorms, or floors, whose residents agree to abstain from alcohol, drugs, and tobacco. These areas provide a welcome relief for students seeking a more civil lifestyle in residence halls.

Question: Is there any mandatory student orientation that exposes students to sexually explicit material or graphic explanations of sexual practices?

Explanation: Films that most parents would consider pornographic are often shown during orientation. Practices that violate family morals may be presented in positive terms or even advocated.

Question: How much crime is there both on and adjacent to campus?

Explanation: Some schools engage in statistical trickery in order to hide the true crime rate from parents, students, and donors. For example, schools often ignore crimes committed in areas immediately adjacent to campus—surely a distinction without a difference—in order to lower the apparent crime rate.

III. Red, Green, or Yellow Lights: What they mean

Issue: Speech codes operating under the guise of sexual harassment codes.

Explanation: In recent decades, many schools instituted speech codes that sought to intimidate into silence any students or professors who questioned the emerging politically correct orthodoxies. A public outcry ensued, colleges lost several important court challenges to the speech codes, and administrators publicly distanced themselves from speech codes in name if not always in practice. Today, the same degree of intimidation is sometimes achieved through so-called harassment (or sexual harassment) codes. While purporting to protect students, these codes can be used by schools to silence or punish those who disagree with politically correct mandates.

Issue: Ostracizing or punishing students for speaking their minds when they disagree with received academic opinion.

Explanation: Numerous examples exist of official harassment of students who voice dissenting opinions on matters ranging from the importance of feminist scholarship or the morality of affirmative action to questions of religious beliefs and sexual propriety. Expressions of traditional moral and social attitudes can sometimes find themselves censored as "hate speech." Defending your beliefs in the face of criticism is part of the college experience; facing official sanction for voicing them is unacceptable.

Issue: The politicization of the curriculum. For example, literature courses often ignore literary masterpieces in favor of comparatively trivial topics (like graphic novels or video games)—or worse yet, hijack the great works in the service of ideologies such as Marxism, feminism, or multiculturalism. These classes can turn into political indoctrination sessions, where dissenting students are either silent or subject to punitive grading.

Explanation: Remember that course titles can be misleading. For instance, a class titled "American Revolution" may present the causes of the Revolution, the search for constitutional order, or the founding generation in a relentlessly cynical light. Some professors will teach the entire period through the lenses of race, class, and gender, which allows them to condemn the founders for failing to live up to the ideals of our own time. This type of approach is increasingly common among historians.

Issue: The lack of intellectual diversity within academic departments. New faculty members are often expected to share the political opinions of their colleagues.

Explanation: Radical faculty have consolidated their hold on many departments by gaining control of the hiring process for new professors. By hiring only those who share their politically correct views, they reduce opposition to their own schemes while persecuting dissenting colleagues, ridiculing religion, offering highly politicized courses, or harassing students who speak out against them. This is one of the most disturbing trends in higher education.

In addition to this college guide, there are other sources you should mine. Recruitment literature, college websites, and the university bookstore are especially important. Visit the school's website and look at course offerings in the departments of English and history, two bellwethers of a school's curricular trends. Many schools post syllabi on their websites, and you can learn much from perusing these sources. Look for classes that cast their subjects in the language of victimology. Course descriptions or readings that employ the terminology of race, class, gender, and other trendy academic categories usually indicate a high degree of politicization—the substitution of politics for genuine learning. In the campus bookstore, visit the course readings section. You may gauge the quality of departments by the number of politicized works assigned. Note titles that condemn America and the West, deconstruct literature, or celebrate political action over rigorous study. A preponderance of such books reveals a department run by professors who would rather indoctrinate than educate. Ask around and see if the school has a conservative newspaper or pro-life group—and if you can, get contact information for these organizations. Ask their leaders what it's like for someone with such views to study at this college. Is this a fair and open-minded institution?

Get a Real Education from ISI

Choosing the Right College has been produced by the staff of the Intercollegiate Studies Institute (ISI). Founded in 1953, ISI is a nonprofit, nonpartisan educational organization whose mission is to "educate for liberty"—to inspire college students to discover and embrace the principles and virtues that make America free and prosperous.

Even after you've chosen the right college, you need to make sure you get the education you deserve.

Tens of thousands of students across America look to ISI to help navigate the college experience. The reason is simple: No other organization can provide the attentive guidance, top-flight programming, educational resources, and close relationships that ISI does.

Though it costs you nothing to join ISI, what you gain is invaluable.

Join ISI for FREE and Get:

- A Welcome Package containing a free e-book, audio downloads, a 40%-off coupon, and more
- A free digital subscription to the *Intercollegiate Review*, ISI's flagship journal on politics, economics, and culture
- Access to an influential network of student groups and faculty
- Contacts with professors who can help mentor career direction and post-graduate studies
- Invitations to ISI's extraordinary range of lectures, debates, and conferences
- Opportunities to start a student publication
- Books and publications to help you succeed in your coursework and in the battle of ideas
- An unmatched archive of video and audio lectures
- Leadership opportunities—on your campus and even across the country
- Great chances for internships and fellowships, with prizes up to $40,000
- Friends and connections that last a lifetime

join.isi.org